CHECKLIST OF CITES SPECIES

LISTA DE ESPECIES CITES

LISTE DES ESPECES CITES

A reference to the Appendices to the
Convention on International Trade in Endangered Species
of Wild Fauna and Flora

Una referencia a los Apéndices
de la Convención sobre el Comercio Internacional de Especies
Amenazadas de Fauna y Flora Silvestres

Référence aux annexes de la
Convention sur le commerce international des espèces de faune et de flore
sauvages menacées d'extinction

Compiled by the/Compilada por el/Compilée par le
UNEP World Conservation Monitoring Centre
PNUMA Centro de Monitoreo de la Conservación Mundial
PNUE Centre de surveillance continue de la conservation mondiale de la nature

Edited by/Revisada y corregida por/Revue et corrigée par Tim Inskipp & Harriet J. Gillett

With financial support from the
**Secretariat of the Convention on International Trade
in Endangered Species of Wild Fauna and Flora,**
the **European Commission**
and the **UK Joint Nature Conservation Committee**

Con el concurso financiero de la
**Secretaría de la Convención sobre el Comercio Internacional
de Especies Amenazadas de Fauna y Flora Silvestres,**
de la **Comisión Europea**
y del **UK Joint Nature Conservation Committee**

Avec l'appui financier du
**Secrétariat de la Convention sur le commerce international des espèces
de faune et de flore sauvages menacées d'extinction,**
de la **Commission Européenne**
et du **UK Joint Nature Conservation Committee**

2003

The **UNEP World Conservation Monitoring Centre** (UNEP-WCMC) is the biodiversity assessment and policy implementation arm of the United Nations Environment Programme, the world's foremost intergovernmental environmental organization. UNEP-WCMC aims to help decision-makers recognize the value of biodiversity to people everywhere, and to apply this knowledge in all that they do. The Centre's challenge is to transform complex data into policy-relevant information, to build tools and systems for analysis and integration of these data, and to support the needs of nations and the international community as they engage in joint programmes of action.

El **PNUMA Centro de Monitoreo de la Conservación Mundial** (UNEP-WCMC) es el brazo del Programa de las Naciones Unidas del Medio Ambiente, la principal organización intergubernamental ambiental en el mundo, encargado de evaluar la biodiversidad y la implementación de políticas ambientales. El UNEP-WCMC aspira a ayudar a tomadores de decisiones a reconocer el valor de la biodiversidad para la gente de todo el mundo, y a aplicar este conocimiento en todo lo que hacen. El desafío del Centro es transformar datos complejos en información relevante para la formulación de políticas de gestión, desarrollar instrumentos y sistemas para el análisis y la integración de esos datos, y apoyar las necesidades de las naciones y de la comunidad internacional en general en sus esfuerzos por desarrollar programas de acción conjunta.

Le **PNUE Centre de Surveillance Continue pour la Conservation de la Nature Mondiale** (UNEP-WCMC) est l'agence chargée de l'évaluation de la diversité biologique et de la mise en oeuvre des directives du Programme des Nations Unies pour l'Environnement, la principale organisation intergouvernementale environnementale au monde. Le Centre aspire à aider les gouvernements à reconnaître l'importance de la diversité biologique pour les êtres humains du monde entier et à appliquer cette connaissance à toutes leurs activités. Le défi du Centre consiste à transformer et simplifier des données complexes en informations pertinentes afin de trouver des outils et d'établir des systèmes permettant leur intégration et leur analyse dans la politique de tous les jours. Le Centre vise à appuyer les besoins des nations et de la communauté internationale dans leurs activités et programmes communs environnementaux.

ENGLISH

ESPAÑOL

FRANÇAIS

CHECKLIST OF CITES SPECIES

**A reference to the Appendices to the
Convention on International Trade in Endangered Species
of Wild Fauna and Flora**

INTRODUCTION

Compiled by:	UNEP World Conservation Monitoring Centre
Prepared for:	CITES Secretariat

With financial support from:	CITES Secretariat, European Commission and the Joint Nature Conservation Committee of the United Kingdom
Published by:	CITES Secretariat/UNEP World Conservation Monitoring Centre
Copyright:	2003 CITES Secretariat/UNEP World Conservation Monitoring Centre

The geographical designations employed in this book do not imply the expression of any opinion whatsoever on the part of the compilers or the CITES Secretariat concerning the legal status of any country, territory or area, or concerning the delimitation of its frontiers or boundaries.

Citation:	Inskipp, T. & Gillett, H. J. (Eds.) 2003. *Checklist of CITES Species*. Compiled by UNEP-WCMC. CITES Secretariat, Geneva, Switzerland and UNEP-WCMC, Cambridge, UK. 339pp. & CD-ROM
ISBN:	1 899628 23 1
Cover design by:	Michael Edwards
Printed by:	Unwin Brothers, Martins Printing Group, Old Woking, Surrey.
Available from:	CITES Secretariat
	15, Chemin des Anémones
	CH-1219 Châtelaine-Genève
	Switzerland

Tel:	+41 (22) 917 81 39/40
Fax:	+41 (22) 797 34 17
E-mail:	cites@unep.ch
Web:	www.cites.org

CONTENTS

Foreword

This edition of the *Checklist of CITES Species* takes into account the amendments to the CITES Appendices and the changes in nomenclature adopted at the 12th meeting of the Conference of the Parties to CITES (Santiago, 2002).

At its 12th meeting, the Conference of the Parties adopted the Checklist and its updates accepted by the Nomenclature Committee as the standard nomenclature to the names of species listed in the CITES Appendices. We are most grateful to the UNEP World Conservation Monitoring Centre (UNEP-WCMC) for undertaking the production of this Checklist once again, and particularly to the staff responsible for the meticulous work involved.

The costs of preparation and production of this Checklist have been borne by the European Commission, the Joint Nature Conservation Committee (United Kingdom) and UNEP-WCMC, as well as by the CITES Secretariat, and we wish to thank our partners very much for their important contributions.

We know that this Checklist is widely used and appreciated by Management Authorities, Scientific Authorities, Customs officers and other people involved in the implementation of CITES, as well as by non-governmental organizations, academics, the press and others. We are conscious, however, that we must continue to try to meet the changing needs of the users of this guide. For this reason in particular, we welcome the comments and suggestions of all users on ways to improve it in the future.

CITES Secretariat
Geneva
2003

Acknowledgements

This publication was prepared on behalf of the CITES Secretariat by the UNEP World Conservation Monitoring Centre (UNEP-WCMC). It was edited by Tim Inskipp and Harriet Gillett, supported by Alice Davies and Joan Field. Technical support was provided by James O'Carroll, Paul Birrel and Phill Fox. The project was supervised by Gerardo Fragoso.

The production team are most grateful to the staff of the CITES Secretariat for their advice and assistance. UNEP-WCMC also wishes to acknowledge the financial support of the European Commission and of the Joint Nature Conservation Committee of the United Kingdom, which has made possible the production of this book and CD-ROM.

Introduction

CITES-listed fauna and flora

This book and CD-ROM provide a Checklist of the fauna and the flora listed in Appendices I, II and III of CITES as adopted by the Conference of the Parties, valid from 13 February 2003. The CD-ROM also includes the Annotated Appendices, which have an index to family names and common names. It is hoped that these lists will act as an aid to Management and Scientific Authorities, Customs officials, and all others involved in implementing and enforcing the Convention.

General note

The names used in the CITES Appendices are the scientific names approved by the CITES Nomenclature Committee. Common names in the Checklist and Annotated Appendices are included only for reference. If the common name of an animal or plant included in the CITES Appendices is not included, it should be looked for under its scientific name or under another common name.

Species included in the Checklist and Annotated Appendices are referred to:

a)   by the name of the species; or
b)   as being all of the species included in a higher taxon or designated part thereof.

Other references to taxa above the specific level are for the purposes of information or classification only.

Further details relating to each taxon, including distribution and author names, are included in the CITES-species database available on the CITES website (www.cites.org).

Checklist

The Checklist of CITES-listed species comprises an alphabetical list of fauna followed by flora. There are three types of entry: scientific name, common name and scientific synonym. The common name and synonym entries serve as indexes to the adopted scientific name entries, where CITES-related information is provided.

Scientific name

The Checklist contains the scientific names, in alphabetical order, of all animal and plant taxa listed in the CITES Appendices, with the exception of Appendix-II listed orchids, for which only the name of the genus is included, e.g. *Cattleya* spp.

Format   1)   The scientific name
             2)   Optional – English (E), French (F) and Spanish (S) common names;
             3)   Optional – the symbol #1-#8 (see *Interpretation* below);

4) The Appendix or Appendices in which the species is listed, I, II or III, or 'NC' for taxa that are not, or only partly, covered by CITES listings[1]. Some taxa may be split-listed, that is they may be included partly in one Appendix and partly in another. For a taxon listed in both Appendix I and II, for instance, this would be indicated by 'I/II'. In other cases only certain populations are listed whilst others are not covered by the provisions of the Convention. For a taxon partly listed in Appendix I and partly not listed, for instance, this would be indicated by 'I/NC';

5) For fauna, the family in capital letters and a two-letter code for the class in which the species is included. The following codes are used:

Ac = Actinopterygii
Am = Amphibia
An = Anthozoa
Ar = Arachnida
Av = Aves
Bi = Bivalvia
El = Elasmobranchii
Ga = Gastropoda
Hi = Hirudinoidea
Hy = Hydrozoa
In = Insecta
Ma = Mammalia
Re = Reptilia
Sa = Sarcopterygii

Examples   *Abeillia abeillei*: (E) Emerald-chinned hummingbird, (S) Colibrí barbiesmeralda, (F) Colibri d'Abeillé **II** TROCHILIDAE Av
Cattleya spp. #7 **II** ORCHIDACEAE

Common name

Where available, English, Spanish and French common names are provided.

Format   The common name, either English (E), Spanish (S) or French (F), is followed by the corresponding scientific name. There is only one entry for each common name, e.g. there is an entry for 'Golden Eagle' but not for 'Eagle, Golden'.

Examples   Parrots (E): PSITTACIFORMES spp.
Slipper orchids (E): *Paphiopedilum* spp./ *Phragmipedium* spp.
Emerald-chinned humingbird (E): *Abeillia abeillei*

---

[1] A few species not listed in the CITES Appendices are included for information, namely two species of Psittaciformes: *Melopsittacus undulatus* and *Nymphicus hollandicus*, and four species of Falconiformes: *Cathartes aura*, *Cathartes burrovianus*, *Cathartes melambrotus* and *Coragyps atratus* – these are the only species in these large orders not to be covered by CITES provisions. Similarly, *Aloe vera* is the only species of *Aloe* not listed in the Appendices.

Scientific synonym

Some synonyms of scientific names are listed, but these are not comprehensive.

Format   A scientific synonym is followed by = and then the adopted scientific name. The latter name should be looked up alphabetically to find the other relevant information about the species.

Example   *Tirucallia goetzei = Euphorbia goetzei*

Annotated Appendices and reservations
(CD-ROM only)

Information is provided on all taxa currently or previously included in the CITES Appendices. The original listing date is given for all taxa (orders, families, genera, species, subspecies) and populations specifically named in the current Appendices, or in earlier versions of the Appendices. All reservations made by Parties are listed, with the dates on which they entered into force and, in the case of past reservations, the dates on which they were withdrawn.

The information is arranged in taxonomic order, with common names provided for higher taxa, e.g. URSIDAE (bears). In cases where only one or a few species are listed in a family, the common name of a relevant species is provided, e.g. ESCHRICHTIIDAE (Grey Whale). These common names are included in the index.

Note: The Checklist has many more English, French and Spanish common names of species linked to the corresponding scientific species names, and also to the appropriate family name, than the Annotated Appendices. As an example, to locate the Big-headed Sideneck, first use the Checklist, where the name will be found linked to *Peltocephalus dumeriliana*, then search for *Peltocephalus dumeriliana* in the Annotated Appendices.

Five columns provide information on: Scientific name, CITES Appendix, ISO codes, Dates and Notes, as follows:

Scientific name

This column contains the scientific names of the taxa that are, or have been, listed in the Appendices. These names may be at various taxonomic levels: order, family, genus, species, subspecies or variety. Orders and families are given in the same taxonomic sequence as that used in the CITES Appendices. Species (and subspecies) are listed in alphabetical sequence within each family. Higher taxon names given in bold are provided for information only.

CITES Appendix

The next three columns list the Appendix or Appendices in which the taxa are or were listed. Reservations made by Parties are indicated by adding 'r' to the Appendix number, to signify the entry into force, and 'w' to signify the withdrawal of the reservation. If both Appendix I and Appendix II are applicable to a particular taxon on one date, Appendix I appears first in the list. 'Del' in one of the three columns, instead of an Appendix number, indicates that the taxon was deleted from that Appendix on the given date.

ISO codes

This column provides the ISO code of every Party or territory mentioned in relation to inclusions in Appendix III, to reservations and to species that are split-listed or only partially listed.

AF	Afghanistan	GH	Ghana	NP	Nepal
AR	Argentina	GR	Greece	NZ	New Zealand
AT	Austria	GT	Guatemala	PE	Peru
AU	Australia	HK	Hong Kong	PG	Papua New Guinea
BD	Bangladesh	HN	Honduras	PK	Pakistan
BE	Belgium	ID	Indonesia	PT	Portugal
BF	Burkina Faso	IN	India	RU	Russian Federation
BN	Brunei	IS	Iceland	SA	Saudi Arabia
BO	Bolivia	IT	Italy	SC	Seychelles
BR	Brazil	JP	Japan	SD	Sudan
BT	Bhutan	KR	Korea, Republic of	SE	Sweden
BW	Botswana	LI	Liechtenstein	SG	Singapore
CA	Canada	LU	Luxembourg	SN	Senegal
CF	Central African Republic	MA	Morocco	SO	Somalia
CG	Congo	MG	Madagascar	SR	Suriname
CH	Switzerland	MK	Macedonia	SU	former USSR
CL	Chile	ML	Mali	TD	Chad
CM	Cameroon	MM	Myanmar	TH	Thailand
CN	China	MN	Mongolia	TN	Tunisia
CO	Colombia	MR	Mauritania	TZ	United Republic of
CR	Costa Rica	MU	Mauritius		Tanzania
CU	Cuba	MW	Malawi	UG	Uganda
DE	Germany	MX	Mexico	US	United States
DK	Denmark	MY	Malaysia	UY	Uruguay
DZ	Algeria	MZ	Mozambique	VC	Saint Vincent and the
ES	Spain	NA	Namibia		Grenadines
ET	Ethiopia	NE	Niger	ZA	South Africa
FI	Finland	NG	Nigeria	ZM	Zambia
FR	France	NL	Netherlands	ZW	Zimbabwe
GB	United Kingdom	NO	Norway		

Dates

This column contains the dates when changes to the Appendices in relation to the species concerned came into effect. The dates are listed chronologically (as day/month/year, e.g. 01/07/75 = 1 July 1975), with the earliest date first. The subsequent listing history of the taxon or population can be determined by examining the following lines. Where populations of a taxon are split between Appendix I and Appendix II, both Appendices are indicated against every date when a change has taken place, with notes indicating the status of all populations each Appendix.

Notes

The final column contains any extra information. This may relate to the changes and the situation after each change has taken place. Where separate populations are involved the history is provided in a cumulative manner, so that any changes to the listings between the various Appendices can be tracked by reading the lines that refer to each change. References to populations are indicated by the use of two-letter ISO country or territory codes (see above). Other notes provide further information about the listed taxa, e.g. scientific synonyms. The term 'Included with…' indicates that the taxon concerned was originally listed separately but has subsequently been subsumed in a higher taxon. The term 'Listed under…' indicates that the taxon or population concerned was originally part of a higher taxon listing but has subsequently been treated separately, either through a transfer to another Appendix or a reservation.

As an example, if one looks at the listing history of the population of Malawi of *Crocodylus niloticus*, one will see that the first entry for this species shows that the species (i.e. all populations) was listed in Appendix I on 1 July 1975. Below this are a number of entries referring to transfer of various populations between Appendix I and Appendix II. One of these indicates that the population of Malawi (MW) was transferred to Appendix II on 1 August 1985. A further entry shows that on 18 January 1990 an Appendix-II ranching programme for this species came into effect, and the final entry summarizes the current situation for the species, confirming that the ranched population of Malawi is still in Appendix II.

Key to annotations

I	=	listed on Appendix I	spp.	=	all species of a higher taxon
II	=	listed on Appendix II	ssp.	=	subspecies
III	=	listed on Appendix III	syn.	=	synonym
Del	=	deleted from Appendices	var.	=	variety
f.	=	forma	w	=	reservation withdrawn by the named Party
p.e.	=	possibly extinct			
popn(s)	=	population(s)	#1-#8	=	refers to *Interpretation* (see below)
r	=	reservation entered by the named Party			

Interpretation

In accordance with Article I, paragraph (b), sub-paragraph (iii), of the Convention, the symbol (#) followed by a number placed against the name of a species or higher taxon included in Appendix II or III designates parts or derivatives which are specified in relation thereto for the purposes of the Convention as follows:

#1   Designates all parts and derivatives, except: seeds, spores and pollen (including pollinia);
- a) seedling or tissue cultures obtained *in vitro*, in solid or liquid media, transported in sterile containers; and
- b) cut flowers of artificially propagated plants.

#2   Designates all parts and derivatives, except:
- a) seeds and pollen;
- b) seedling or tissue cultures obtained *in vitro*, in solid or liquid media, transported in sterile containers;
- c) cut flowers of artificially propagated plants; and
- d) chemical derivatives and finished pharmaceutical products.

#3   Designates whole and sliced roots and parts of roots, excluding manufactured parts or derivatives such as powders, pills, extracts, tonics, teas and confectionery.

#4   Designates all parts and derivatives, except:
- a) seeds, except those from Mexican cacti originating in Mexico, and pollen;
- b) seedling or tissue cultures obtained in vitro, in solid or liquid media, transported in sterile containers;
- c) cut flowers of artificially propagated plants;
- d) fruits and parts and derivatives thereof of naturalized or artificially propagated plants; and
- e) separate stem joints (pads) and parts and derivatives thereof of naturalized or artificially propagated plants of the genus *Opuntia* subgenus *Opuntia*.

#5   Designates logs, sawn wood and veneer sheets.

#6   Designates logs, sawn wood, veneer sheets and plywood.

#7   Designates logs, wood-chips and unprocessed broken material.

#8   Designates all parts and derivatives, except:
- a) seeds and pollen (including pollinia);
- b) seedling or tissue cultures obtained in vitro, in solid or liquid media, transported in sterile containers;
- c) cut flowers of artificially propagated plants; and
- d) fruits and parts and derivatives thereof of artificially propagated plants of the genus *Vanilla*.

LISTA DE ESPECIES CITES

**Una referencia a los Apéndices
de la Convención sobre el Comercio Internacional
de Especies Amenazadas de Fauna y Flora Silvestres**

INTRODUCCIÓN

Compilación: PNUMA Centro de Monitoreo de la Conservación Mundial

Para: La Secretaría de la CITES

Concurso   La Secretaría de la CITES, la Comisión Europea y el *Joint Nature*
financiero: *Conservation Committee*

Publicación: La Secretaría de la CITES/PNUMA Centro de Monitoreo de la
                    Conservación Mundial

Copyright: 2003 La Secretaría de la CITES/PNUMA Centro de Monitoreo de la
                    Conservación Mundial

Citación: Inskipp, T. & Gillett, H. J. (Eds.) 2003. *Lista de Especies CITES.* Compiladas por UNEP-WCMC. Secretaría de la CITES, Ginebra, Suiza, y UNEP-WCMC, Cambridge, Reino Unido. 339pp. & CD-ROM

ISBN: 1 899628 23 1

Diseño de portada: Michael Edwards

Impresión: Unwin Brothers, Martins Printing Group, Old Woking, Surrey.

Disponible: Secretaría de la CITES
                    15, Chemin des Anémones
                    CH-1219 Châtelaine Genève
                    Suiza
                    Tel: +41 (22) 917 8139/40
                    Fax: +41 (22) 797 3417
                    E-mail: cites@unep.ch
                    Web: www.cites.org

ÍNDICE

Prólogo

En esta versión de la *Lista de Especies CITES* se han incluido las enmiendas a los Apéndices de la CITES y las modificaciones en la nomenclatura aprobadas en la 12a. reunión de la Conferencia de las Partes en la Convención (Santiago, noviembre de 2002).

En su 12a. reunión, la Conferencia de las Partes adoptó la Lista y sus actualizaciones aceptadas por el Comité de Nomenclatura como la referencia normalizada para los nombres de las especies incluidas en los Apéndices de la CITES. Expresamos nuestro agradecimiento al PNUMA-Centro de Monitoreo de la Conservación Mundial (UNEP-WCMC) por haber producido nuevamente esta Lista y, en particular, al personal encargado de esta meticulosa labor.

Los gastos de preparación y producción de esta Lista fueron sufragados por la Comisión Europea, el *Joint Nature Conservation Committee* (Reino Unido) y el UNEP-WCMC, así como por la Secretaría de la CITES. Deseamos dar las gracias a nuestros colaboradores por sus importantes contribuciones.

Sabemos que esta Lista es ampliamente utilizada y apreciada por las Autoridades Administrativas y Científicas, los funcionarios de aduanas y otras personas interesadas en la aplicación de la CITES, así como por las organizaciones no gubernamentales, los medios académicos, la prensa y otras entidades. Somos conscientes, sin embargo, de que debemos seguir tratando de satisfacer las necesidades cambiantes de los usuarios de esta guía. Por esta razón, acogemos con beneplácito los comentarios y sugerencias de todos los usuarios sobre la forma de mejorarla en el futuro.

Secretaría de la CITES
Ginebra
2003

Agradecimientos

Esta publicación fue preparada en nombre de la Secretaría de la CITES por el PNUMA Centro de Monitoreo de la Conservación Mundial (UNEP-WCMC). Fue compilada por Tim Inskipp y Harriet Gillett, con el apoyo de Alice Davies y Joan Field. James O'Carroll, Paul Birrel y Phill Fox prestaron apoyo técnico. Gerardo Fragoso se encargó de la supervisión de este proyecto.

El equipo de producción expresa su agradecimiento al personal de la Secretaría de la CITES por su asesoramiento y asistencia. El UNEP-WCMC desea dar asimismo las gracias a la Comisión Europea y al *Joint Nature Conservation Committee* del Reino Unido por su concurso financiero, que ha hecho posible la producción de esta publicación y del CD-ROM.

Introducción

Especies de fauna y flora incluidas en los Apéndices de la CITES

En esta publicación y CD-ROM se presenta una Lista de especies de fauna y de flora incluidas en los Apéndices I, II y III de la CITES, tal como fue aprobada por la Conferencia de las Partes, válida a partir del 13 de febrero de 2003. En el CD-ROM se incluyen también los Apéndices anotados, con un índice de los nombres de las familias y los nombres comunes. Se alberga la esperanza de que sea útil para las Autoridades Administrativas y Científicas, los funcionarios de aduana y otras personas interesadas en la aplicación y observancia de la Convención.

Observación general

En los Apéndices de la CITES se utilizan los nombres científicos aprobados por el Comité de Nomenclatura de la CITES. En esta Lista y en los Apéndices anotados, se incluyen los nombres comunes a título de referencia. Si no se aparece el nombre común de un animal o planta incluido en los Apéndices de la CITES, debería buscarse bajo su nombre científico o bajo otro nombre común.

Las especies que figuran en la Lista y en los Apéndices anotados se clasifican:

a) con arreglo al nombre de las especies; o
b) como si todas las especies estuviesen incluidas en un taxón superior o en una parte designada del mismo.

Otras referencias a los taxa superiores de la especie se indican únicamente a título de información o de clasificación.

En la base de datos de las especies CITES, disponible en el sitio web de la CITES (www.cites.org), se presenta mayor información sobre cada taxón, incluida la distribución y los nombres de los autores.

Lista de especies CITES

La Lista de especies CITES consta de una lista alfabética de la fauna, seguida por la flora. Hay tres tipos de entradas: el nombre científico, el nombre común y el sinónimo científico. Los nombres comunes y los sinónimos remiten a los nombres científicos adoptados, donde se porporciona la información conexa CITES.

Nombre científico

La Lista contiene los nombres científicos, por orden alfabético, de todos los taxa animales y vegetales incluidos en los Apéndices de la CITES, a la excepción de las orquídeas incluidas en el Apéndice II, para las que solamente se incluye el nombre del género, por ejemplo, *Cattleya* spp.

Formato   1)   Nombre científico
               2)   Optativo - nombres comunes en español (S), francés (F) e inglés (E)
               3)   Optativo – el símbolo #1-#8 (véase la *Interpretación* abajo);

4)   Los Apéndices I, II o III en que está incluida la especie, o 'NC' para taxa que no están, o están parcialmente, incluidos en los Apéndices de la CITES [1]). Algunos taxa son objeto de inclusión dividida, lo que significa que pueden estar parcialmente incluidas en un Apéndice y parcialmente en otro. Cuando un taxón está incluido en el Apéndice I y II, por ejemplo, se indicará mediante 'I/II'. En ocasiones, solo están incluidas ciertas poblaciones, mientras que otras no están amparadas por la Convención. Para un taxón parcialmente incluido en el Apéndice I y parcialmente no incluido en otro Apéndice, se indicará mediante 'I/NC';

5)   Para la fauna, la familia en letras mayúsculas y un código de dos letras para la clase en que está incluida la especie. Se utilizan los siguientes códigos:

Ac = Actinopterygii
Am = Amphibia
An = Anthozoa
Ar = Arachnida
Av = Aves
Bi = Bivalvia
El = Elasmobranchii
Ga = Gastropoda
Hi = Hirudinoidea
Hy = Hydrozoa
In = Insecta
Ma = Mammalia
Re = Reptilia
Sa = Sarcopterygii

Ejemplos   *Abeillia abeillei*: (E) Emerald-chinned hummingbird, (S) Colibrí barbiesmeralda, (F) Colibri d'Abeillé **II** TROCHILIDAE Av
Cattleya spp. #7 **II** Orchidaceae

Nombre común

En la medida de lo posible, se indican los nombres comunes en español, francés e inglés.

Formato   El nombre común, ya sea en inglés (E), español (S) o francés (F), va seguido por el correspondiente nombre científico. Solo hay una entrada para cada nombre común, así, pues, solo hay una entrada para 'águila real', pero no para 'real, águila'.

Ejemplos   Loros (S): PSITTACIFORMES spp.
Slipper orchids (E): *Paphiopedilum* spp., *Phragmipedium* spp.
Colibrí barbiesmeralda (S): *Abeillia abeillei*

---

[1] A título informativo, se incluyen algunas especies que no figuran en los Apéndices de la CITES, concretamente dos especies de Psittaciformes: *Melopsittacus undulatus* y *Nymphicus hollandicus*, y cuatro especies de Falconiformes: *Cathartes aura*, *Cathartes burrovianus*, *Cathartes melambrotus* y *Coragyps atratus*. Son las únicas especies de estos amplios órdenes que no están amparadas por la CITES. De igual modo, *Aloe vera* es la única especie de *Aloe* que no está incluida en los Apéndices.

Sinónimos científicos

Se incluyen algunos sinónimos de los nombres científicos, pero la lista no es exhaustiva.

Formato   Un sinónimo científico va seguido por '=' y por el nombre científico aceptado. Para acceder a mayor información sobre la especie, debe consultarse este último, por orden alfabético.

Ejemplo   *Tirucallia goetzei = Euphorbia goetzei*

Apéndices y reservas anotados de la CITES
(únicamente CD-ROM)

Se incluye información sobre todos los taxa incluidos actual o anteriormente en los Apéndices de la CITES. Se indica la fecha de inclusión de todos los taxa (órden, familia, género, especie, subespecie) y las poblaciones citadas en los Apéndices en vigor, o en anteriores versiones de los Apéndices. Se indican también todas las reservas formuladas por las Partes, con la fecha en que entraron en vigor y, en el caso de antiguas reservas, la fecha en que se retiraron.

La información se presenta por orden taxonómico, con los nombres comunes para los taxa superiores, p.e. URSIDAE (osos). En casos en que solo una o varias especies están incluidas en una familia, se indica el nombre común de una especie relevante, p.e. ESCHRICHTIIDAE (ballena gris). Estos nombres, y los nombres de la familia, se incluyen en el índice.

Nota: En la Lista figuran muchos más nombres comunes de especies en español, francés e inglés, con conexión con los correspondientes nombres científicos, que en los Apéndices anotados. Por ejemplo, para encontrar la especie cabezón, consulte primero la Lista, donde ese nombre aparece asociado a *Peltocephalus dumeriliana*. Busque luego *Peltocephalus dumeriliana* en los Apéndices anotados.

En cinco columnas se ofrece información sobre: el nombre científico, el Apéndice de la CITES, el código ISO, las fechas y las notas, como sigue:

Nombre científico

En la primera columna figuran los nombres científicos de los taxa que están incluidos o han estado incluidos en los Apéndices. Estos nombres pueden referirse a diversos niveles taxonómicos: orden, familia, género y/o especie, subspecie. Los órdenes y las familias figuran en el mismo orden de sucesión taxonómica que la utilizada en los Apéndices oficiales de la CITES (salvo para las familias de anfibios, que se incluyen por orden alfabético dentro de los dos órdenes, como en el Manual de Identificación de la CITES). Las especies (y las subspecies) se indican por orden de sucesión alfabética dentro de cada familia. Obsérvese que los nombres del taxón superior que aparecen en negrita se indican únicamente a título informativo.

Apéndice de la CITES

En las tres columnas siguientes figuran los Apéndices en los que están o estaban incluidos los taxa. Las reservas formuladas por las Partes se indican añadiendo "/r" al número del Apéndice, para señalar la fecha de entrada en vigor y "/w" para indicar que la reserva fue retirada. Si el Apéndice I y el Apéndice II se aplican a un taxón determinado en una fecha, se indica en primer lugar el Apéndice I. Cuando aparece la letra "Del" en una de las tres columnas, en vez del número del Apéndice, significa que el taxón se suprimió de dicho Apéndice en la fecha señalada.

Código ISO

En esta columna se presenta el código ISO de cada Parte o territorio mencionado en relación con una inclusión en el Apéndice III, las reservas y las especies objeto de inclusión dividida o parcial.

AF	Afganistán	GH	Ghana	NP	Nepal
AR	Argentina	GR	Grecia	NZ	Nueva Zelandia
AT	Austria	GT	Guatemala	PE	Perú
AU	Australia	HK	Hong Kong	PG	Papua Nueva Guinea
BD	Bangladesh	HN	Honduras	PK	Pakistán
BE	Bélgica	ID	Indonesia	PT	Portugal
BF	Burkina Faso	IN	India	RU	Federación de Rusia
BN	Brunei Darussalam	IS	Islandia	SA	Arabia Saudita
BO	Bolivia	IT	Italia	SC	Seychelles
BR	Brasil	JP	Japón	SD	Sudán
BT	Bhután	KR	República de Corea	SE	Suecia
BW	Botswana	LI	Liechtenstein	SG	Singapur
CA	Canadá	LU	Luxemburgo	SN	Senegal
CF	República Centroafricana	MA	Marruecos	SO	Somalia
CG	Congo	MG	Madagascar	SR	Suriname
CH	Suiza	MK	Macedonia	SU	Ex USSR
CL	Chile	ML	Malí	TD	Chad
CM	Camerún	MM	Myanmar	TH	Tailandia
CN	China	MN	Mongolia	TN	Túnez
CO	Colombia	MR	Mauritania	TZ	República Unida de
CR	Costa Rica	MU	Mauricio		Tanzanía
CU	Cuba	MW	Malawi	UG	Uganda
DE	Alemania	MX	México	US	Estados Unidos de
DK	Dinamarca	MY	Malasia		América
DZ	Argelia	MZ	Mozambique	UY	Uruguay
ES	España	NA	Namibia	VC	San Vicente y las
ET	Etiopía	NE	Níger		Granadinas
FI	Finlandia	NG	Nigeria	ZA	Sudáfrica
FR	Francia	NL	Países Bajos	ZM	Zambia
GB	Reino Unido	NO	Noruega	ZW	Zimbabwe

Fechas

En esta columna aparecen las fechas en que entraron en vigor los cambios en los Apéndices en relación con las especies. La fechas aparecen por orden cronológico (día/mes/año, es decir, 01/07/75 = 1 de julio de 1975), indicándose en primer lugar la fecha más antigua. La evolución de la inclusión de un taxón/población puede determinarse examinando las líneas siguientes. Cuando las poblaciones de un taxón están divididas entre el Apéndice I y el Apéndice II, ambos Apéndices figuran al lado de cada fecha cuando se produjo un cambio, con notas en las que se indica el estado de todas las poblaciones en cada uno de los Apéndices.

Notas

La última columna contiene toda la información complementaria sobre los cambios y la situación después de cada cambio. Cuando se trata de poblaciones separadas, se muestra la evolución de modo que cualquier cambio en la inclusión entre varios Apéndices pueda determinarse leyendo las dos líneas que se refieren a cada cambio. Las referencias a las poblaciones se indican utilizando el código ISO de dos letras de cada país (véase *supra*). En otras notas se ofrece información complementaria sobre los taxa incluidos, por ejemplo, los sinónimos científicos. El término "Incluido con...." significa que el taxón en cuestión fue inicialmente incluido de forma separada pero fue posteriormente incluido en un taxón superior. El término "Incluido bajo ..." significa que el taxón en cuestión formaba parte inicialmente de un taxón superior pero fue posteriormente tratado por separado, bien sea transferido a otro Apéndice o sujeto a una reserva.

A modo de ejemplo, si se examina la historia de la inclusión en los Apéndices de la población de *Crocodylus niloticus* de Malawi, puede observarse que en la primera entrada para esta especie se indica que la especie (es decir, todas las poblaciones) se incluyó en el Apéndice I el 1 de julio de 1975. A continuación hay un número de entradas que se refieren a la transferencia de diversas poblaciones entre el Apéndice I y el Apéndice II. En una de ellas se indica que la población de Malawi (MW) fue transferida al Apéndice II el 1 de agosto de 1985. En otra entrada se indica que el 18 de enero de 1990 entró en vigor un programa de cría en granjas para esta especie y en la última entrada se resume la situación actual de esta especie, donde se confirma que la población de especímenes criados en granjas de Malawi sigue estando en el Apéndice II

Explicación de las anotaciones

I	=	incluida en el Apéndice I	spp.	=	todas las especies de un taxón superior
II	=	incluida en el Apéndice II			
III	=	incluida en el Apéndice III	ssp.	=	subspecies
Del	=	suprimida de los Apéndices	syn.	=	sinónimo
f	=	forma	var.	=	variedad
p.e.	=	posiblemente extinguida	w	=	reserva retirada por la Parte correspondiente
popn(s)	=	población(es)			
r	=	reserva formulada por la Parte correspondiente	#1–#8	=	se refiere a la *Interpretación* (véase abajo)

Interpretación

De conformidad con las disposiciones del párrafo b(iii) del Artículo I de la Convención, el signo (#) seguido de un número colocado junto al nombre de una especie o de un taxón superior incluido en el Apéndice II o III designa las partes o derivados provenientes de esa especie o de ese taxón y se indican como sigue a los efectos de la Convención:

#1   Designa todas las partes y derivados, excepto:
- a) las semillas, las esporas y el polen (inclusive las polinias);
- b) los cultivos de plántulas o de tejidos obtenidos in vitro, en medios sólidos o líquidos, que se transportan en envases estériles; y
- c) las flores cortadas de plantas reproducidas artificialmente.

#2   Designa todas las partes y derivados, excepto:
- a) las semillas y el polen;
- b) los cultivos de plántulas o de tejidos obtenidos *in vitro*, en medios sólidos o líquidos, que se transportan en envases estériles;
- c) las flores cortadas de plantas reproducidas artificialmente; y
- d) los derivados químicos y productos farmacéuticos acabados.

#3   Designa las raíces enteras o en rodajas o partes de las raíces, excluidas las partes o derivados manufacturados, tales como polvos, pastillas, extractos, tónicos, tés y otros preparados.

#4   Designa todas las partes y derivados, excepto:
- a) las semillas, excepto las de las cactáceas mexicanas originarias de México, y el polen;
- b) los cultivos de plántulas o de tejidos obtenidos *in vitro*, en medios sólidos o líquidos, que se transportan en envases estériles;
- c) las flores cortadas de plantas reproducidas artificialmente;
- d) los frutos, y sus partes y derivados, de plantas aclimatadas o reproducidas artificialmente; y
- e) los elementos del tallo (ramificaciones), y sus partes y derivados, de plantas del género *Opuntia* subgénero *Opuntia* aclimatadas o reproducidas artificialmente.

#5   Designa trozas, madera aserrada y láminas de chapa de madera.

#6   Designa trozas, madera aserrada, láminas de chapa de madera y madera contrachapada.

#7   Designa trozas, troceados de madera y material fragmentado no elaborado.

#8   Designa todas las partes y derivados, excepto:
- a) las semillas y el polen (inclusive las polinias);
- b) los cultivos de plántulas o de tejidos obtenidos *in vitro*, en medios sólidos o líquidos, que se transportan en envases estériles;
- c) las flores cortadas de ejemplares reproducidos artificialmente; y
- d) los frutos, y sus partes y derivados, de plantas del género *Vanilla* reproducidas artificialmente.

LISTE DES ESPECES CITES

**Référence aux annexes de la
Convention sur le commerce international des espèces de faune et de flore
sauvages menacées d'extinction**

INTRODUCTION

Compilation: PNUE Centre de surveillance continue de la conservation mondiale de la nature

Pour: le Secrétariat CITES

Appui financier: Secrétariat CITES, Commission européene et *Joint Nature Conservation Committee*

Publication: Secrétariat CITES/PNUE Centre de surveillance continue de la conservation mondiale de la nature

Citation: Inskipp, T. & Gillett, H. J. (Eds.) 2003. *Liste des espèces CITES*. Compilée par le PNUE-WCMC. Secrétariat CITES, Genève, Suisse et PNUE-WCMC, Cambridge, R.-U. 339pp. & CD-ROM

ISBN: 1 899628 23 1

Couverture: Michael Edwards

Imprimerie: Unwin Brothers, Martins Printing Group, Old Woking, Surrey.

Disponible au: Secrétariat CITES
                    15, Chemin des Anémones
                    CH-1219 Châtelaine-Genève
                    Suisse

                    Tél.:   +41 (22) 917 8139/40
                    Fax: +41 (22) 797 3417
                    Courriel: cites@unep.ch
                    Internet: www.cites.org

TABLE DES MATIERES

Avant-propos

Cette édition de la *Liste des espèces CITES* intègre les amendements aux annexes CITES et les changements de nomenclature adoptés à la 12ᵉ session de la Conférence des Parties à la CITES (Santiago, 2002).

A sa 12ᵉ session, la Conférence des Parties a adopté la Liste et ses mises à jour acceptées par le Comité de la nomenclature comme nomenclature normalisée des noms des espèces inscrites aux annexes CITES. Nous sommes très reconnaissants au PNUE Centre de surveillance continue de la conservation mondiale de la nature (PNUE-WCMC) de s'être de nouveau attelé à cette tâche; nous adressons des remerciements particuliers au personnel qui a été chargé de ce travail méticuleux.

Les frais de préparation et de production de la Liste ont été pris en charge par la Commission européenne, le *Joint Nature Conservation Committee* (Royaume-Uni) et le PNUE-WCMC, ainsi que par le Secrétariat CITES; nous remercions vivement nos partenaires pour leur importante contribution.

Nous savons que la Liste des espèces CITES est largement utilisée et très appréciée par les organes de gestion, les autorités scientifiques, les douanes et les personnes impliquées dans la mise en œuvre de la CITES, ainsi que par les organisations non gouvernementales, les scientifiques, la presse et autres entités. Nous sommes par ailleurs conscients que nous devons continuer de nous adapter aux besoins nouveaux des utilisateurs de ce guide. C'est pour cette raison, entre autres, que nous souhaitons connaître les réactions et les suggestions des utilisateurs de cet ouvrage sur la manière dont nous pourrions l'améliorer à l'avenir.

Secrétariat CITES
Genève
2003

Remerciements

Cette publication a été préparée au nom du Secrétariat CITES par le PNUE Centre de surveillance continue de la conservation mondiale de la nature (PNUE-WCMC). Elle a été revue et corrigée par Tim Inskipp et Harriet Gillett avec l'assistance d'Alice Davies et de Joan Field et l'appui technique de James O'Carroll, Paul Birrel et Phill Fox. Gerardo Fragoso a géré le projet.

L'équipe chargée de la production de la Liste est très reconnaissance au personnel du Secrétariat CITES pour ses conseils et son assistance. Le PNUE-WCMC remercie également la Commission européenne pour son appui financier et le *Joint Nature Conservation Committee*, du Royaume-Uni, qui a rendu possible la production de ce livre et de son CD-ROM.

Introduction

Faune et flore CITES

Ce livre et son CD-ROM donnent la liste des espèces animales et végétales inscrites aux Annexes I, II et III de la CITES adoptée par la Conférence des Parties et valable à compter du 13 février 2003. Le CD-ROM inclut aussi les annexes annotées comportant un index des noms des familles et des noms communs en anglais. Les compilateurs espèrent qu'ils seront utiles au personnel des organes de gestion et des autorités scientifiques, ainsi qu'aux douaniers et à toutes les personnes chargées d'appliquer la Convention ou de la faire respecter.

Remarque générale

Les noms utilisés dans les annexes CITES sont les noms scientifiques acceptés par le Comité CITES de la nomenclature. Les noms communs figurant dans la Liste des espèces CITES et annexes et réserves CITES annotées sont donnés pour référence. Si l'utilisateur ne trouve pas le nom commun d'une plante ou d'un animal couvert par la CITES, il devra le rechercher sous son nom scientifique ou sous un autre nom commun.

Les espèces figurant dans la Liste des espèces CITES et annexes et réserves CITES annotées sont indiquées:

a) par le nom de l'espèce; ou
b) par l'ensemble des espèces appartenant à un taxon supérieur ou à une partie désignée dudit taxon.

Les autres références à des taxons supérieurs à l'espèce sont données uniquement à titre d'information ou à des fins de classification.

Le lecteur trouvera d'autres détails concernant chaque taxon, comme le nom de l'auteur et la répartition géographique, sur le site officiel de la CITES: http://www.cites.org

Liste des espèces CITES

La Liste des espèces CITES comprend une liste alphabétique d'espèces animales et une liste alphabétique d'espèces végétales. Il y a trois types d'entrées: le nom scientifique, le nom commun et le synonyme scientifique. Noms communs et synonymes renvoient aux noms scientifiques, où figurent les informations CITES.

Nom scientifique

La Liste contient, dans l'ordre alphabétique, tous les taxons animaux et végétaux inscrits aux annexes CITES – à l'exception des orchidées de l'Annexe II, pour lesquelles seul le nom du genre est inscrit – *Cattleya* spp., par exemple.

Présentation   1)   Nom scientifique
                   2)   Noms communs en anglais (E), en espagnol (S) et en français (F), s'ils sont connus;

3) Symbole #1 à #8 s'il y a lieu (Voir *Interprétation* ci-dessous);

4) Annexe(s) I, II, III, auxquelles l'espèce est inscrite, ou "NC" pour signaler les taxons partiellement inscrits ou non inscrits aux annexes CITES[1]. Certains taxons font l'objet d'une inscription scindée; cela signifie qu'ils sont inscrits en partie à une annexe et en partie à une autre. Lorsqu'un taxon est inscrit à la fois à l'Annexe I et à l'Annexe II, par exemple, il est signalé par "I/II". Parfois, seules certaines populations sont inscrites alors que d'autres ne sont pas couvertes par la Convention. Un taxon en partie inscrit à l'Annexe I et en partie non inscrit, par exemple, est signalé par "I/NC".

5) Pour la faune, famille en majuscules et code à deux lettres indiquant la classe à laquelle appartient l'espèce. Les codes suivants sont utilisés:

Ac = Actinopterygii
Am = Amphibia
An = Anthozoa
Ar = Arachnida
Av = Aves
Bi = Bivalvia
El = Elasmobranchii
Ga = Gastropoda
Hi = Hirudinoidea
Hy = Hydrozoa
In = Insecta
Ma = Mammalia
Re = Reptilia
Sa = Sarcopterygii

Exemples *Abeillia abeillei*: (E) Emerald-chinned hummingbird, (S) Colibrí barbiesmeralda, (F) Colibri d'Abeillé **II** TROCHILIDAE Av
Cattleya spp. #7 **II** ORCHIDACEAE

Nom commun

Quand ils sont connus, les noms communs en anglais, en espagnol et en français sont donnés pour référence.

Présentation Le nom commun en anglais (E), en espagnol (S) ou en français (F) est suivi du nom scientifique. Il y a une seule entrée pour chaque nom commun: il y en a une pour "Aigle doré" mais pas pour "Doré, Aigle".

Exemples Perroquets (F): PSITTACIFORMES spp.
Slipper orchids (E): *Paphiopedilum* spp., *Phragmipedium* spp.
Colibri d'Abeillé (F): *Abeillia abeillei*

---

[1] Quelques espèces non inscrites aux annexes CITES ont été incluses pour information: deux espèces de Psittaciformes: *Melopsittacus undulatus* et *Nymphicus hollandicus*, et quatre espèces de Falconiformes: *Cathartes aura*, *Cathartes burrovianus*, *Cathartes melambrotus* et *Coragyps atratus*. Ce sont les seules espèces de ces grands ordres à ne pas être couvertes par la CITES. De même, *Aloe vera* est la seule espèce d'*Aloe* non inscrite aux annexes.

Synonyme scientifique

Certains synonymes de noms scientifiques apparaissent dans la liste mais pas tous.

Présentation   Synonyme scientifique suivi de "=" puis du nom scientifique accepté. C'est ce dernier qu'il faut chercher, en suivant l'ordre alphabétique, pour trouver les autres renseignements sur l'espèce.

Exemple   *Tirucallia goetzei = Euphorbia goetzei*

Annexes et réserves CITES annotées
(CD-ROM uniquement)

Des informations sont fournies sur tous les taxons actuellement ou antérieurement inscrits aux annexes CITES. La date de l'inscription originale est indiquée pour tous les taxons (ordre, famille, genre, espèce, sous-espèce) et les populations spécifiquement nommés dans les annexes actuelles ou dans des versions antérieures. Toutes les réserves faites par les Parties sont signalées avec la date d'entrée en vigueur et, dans le cas de réserves passées, la date de retrait.

Les informations sont disposées en suivant l'ordre taxonomique et incluent les noms communs pour les taxons supérieurs. Exemple: URSIDAE (ours). Lorsqu'il n'y a qu'une seule ou quelques espèces d'une famille qui sont inscrites, leurs noms communs sont indiqués. Exemple: ESCHRICHTIIDAE (baleine grise). Ces noms communs et noms de famille sont inclus dans l'index.

Remarque: Il y a dans la Liste plus de noms communs d'espèces en anglais, en espagnol et en français donnés au niveau du nom scientifique correspondant et du nom de famille approprié qu'il n'y en a dans les annexes annotées. Pour trouver podocnémide de Duméril, par exemple, consultez d'abord la Liste, où vous trouverez ce nom sous *Peltocephalus dumeriliana*. Cherchez ensuite *Peltocephalus dumeriliana* dans les annexes annotées.

Des informations sont fournies dans les cinq colonnes suivantes: Nom scientifique, Annexe CITES, Code ISO, Dates et Notes, comme suit:

Nom scientifique

Cette colonne donne le nom scientifique des taxons qui sont, ou ont été, inscrits aux annexes. Ces noms peuvent être situés à divers niveaux taxonomiques: ordre, famille, genre, espèce, sous-espèce ou variété. Les ordres et les familles sont donnés dans la même séquence taxonomique que celle utilisée dans les annexes CITES. Les espèces (et les sous-espèces) sont indiquées par ordre alphabétique dans chaque famille. Les noms des taxons supérieurs, figurant en caractères gras, sont communiqués pour information.

Annexe CITES

Dans les trois colonnes suivantes figurent la ou les annexes auxquelles les taxons sont ou étaient inscrits. Les réserves faites par les Parties sont signalées en ajoutant "r" au numéro de l'annexe pour indiquer que la réserve est entrée en vigueur, ou "w" pour indiquer qu'elle a été retirée. Si les Annexes I et II sont toutes deux applicables à un taxon à une certaine date, l'Annexe I est indiquée en premier. La mention "Del" remplaçant un numéro d'annexe dans une des trois colonnes signale que le taxon a été supprimé de l'annexe à la date indiquée.

Code ISO

Cette colonne donne le code ISO de toute Partie et de tout territoire mentionné dans le contexte d'une inscription à l'Annexe III, des réserves et des espèces faisant l'objet d'une inscription scindée ou partielle.

AF	Afghanistan	GH	Ghana	NP	Népal
AR	Argentine	GR	Grèce	NZ	Nouvelle-Zélande
AT	Autriche	GT	Guatemala	PE	Pérou
AU	Australie	HK	Hong Kong	PG	Papouasie-Nouvelle-
BD	Bangladesh	HN	Honduras		Guinée
BE	Belgique	ID	Indonésie	PK	Pakistan
BF	Burkina Faso	IN	Inde	PT	Portugal
BN	Brunéi Darussalam	IS	Islande	RU	Fédération de Russie
BO	Bolivie	IT	Italie	SA	Arabie saoudite
BR	Brésil	JP	Japon	SC	Seychelles
BT	Bhoutan	KR	République de Corée	SD	Soudan
BW	Botswana	LI	Liechtenstein	SE	Suède
CA	Canada	LU	Luxembourg	SG	Singapour
CF	République	MA	Maroc	SN	Sénégal
	centrafricaine	MG	Madagascar	SO	Somalie
CG	Congo	MK	Macédoine	SR	Suriname
CH	Suisse	ML	Mali	SU	Ex-URSS
CL	Chili	MM	Myanmar	TD	Tchad
CM	Cameroun	MN	Mongolie	TH	Thaïlande
CN	Chine	MR	Mauritanie	TN	Tunisie
CO	Colombie	MU	Maurice	TZ	République-Unie de
CR	Costa Rica	MW	Malawi		Tanzanie
CU	Cuba	MX	Mexique	UG	Ouganda
DE	Allemagne	MY	Malaisie	US	Etats-Unis d'Amérique
DK	Danemark	MZ	Mozambique	UY	Uruguay
DZ	Algérie	NA	Namibie	VC	Saint-Vincent-et-les
ES	Espagne	NE	Niger		Grenadines
ET	Ethiopie	NG	Nigéria	ZA	Afrique du Sud
FI	Finlande	NL	Pays-Bas	ZM	Zambie
FR	France	NO	Norvège	ZW	Zimbabwe
GB	Royaume-Uni				

Dates

Cette colonne donne les dates d'entrée en vigueur des changements survenus dans les annexes concernant l'espèce en question. Les dates sont indiquées dans l'ordre chronologique (jour/mois/année; exemple: 01/07/75 = 1er juillet 1975), la date la plus ancienne étant citée la première. Les inscriptions ultérieures d'un taxon ou d'une population figurent aux lignes suivantes. Lorsque les populations d'un taxon sont scindées entre l'Annexe I et l'Annexe II, les deux annexes sont indiquées après chaque date à laquelle un changement a eu lieu, avec des notes indiquant le statut de toutes les populations à chaque annexe.

Notes

La dernière colonne contient toute information supplémentaire, par exemple sur les changements et la situation après chaque changement. Pour les populations isolées, le déroulement des faits est indiqué de manière que tout changement d'annexe peut être repéré en lisant les lignes se référant à chaque changement. Les références aux populations sont indiquées par le code ISO à deux lettres des pays ou territoires (voir plus haut). D'autres notes donnent des informations complémentaires sur les taxons inscrits (synonymes scientifiques, par exemple). Les mots "inclus dans..." indiquent que le taxon a d'abord été inscrit séparément puis englobé dans un taxon supérieur. Les mots "inscrit sous..." indiquent que le taxon faisait d'abord partie d'un taxon supérieur inscrit puis a été traité séparément, soit qu'il ait été transféré à une autre annexe, ou qu'il ait fait l'objet d'une réserve.

Voici un exemple: si l'on examine les différentes étapes de l'inscription aux annexes de la population de *Crocodylus niloticus* du Malawi, l'on constate que la première entrée pour cette espèce indique que l'espèce entière (toutes ses populations) a été inscrite à l'Annexe I le 1er juillet 1975. On trouve ensuite, sous cette entrée, un certain nombre d'autres entrées indiquant le transfert de diverses populations de l'Annexe I à l'Annexe II. L'une d'elles signale que la population du Malawi (MW) a été transférée à l'Annexe II le 1er août 1985. Une autre indique que le 18 janvier 1990, un programme d'élevage en ranch d'espèces de l'annexe II a commencé pour cette espèce; la dernière entrée résume la situation actuelle de l'espèce et indique que la population de *C. niloticus* du Malawi élevée en ranch est toujours inscrite à l'Annexe II.

Clé aux annotations

I	=	inscrite à l'Annexe I	spp.	=	toutes les espèces d'un taxon supérieur
II	=	inscrite à l'Annexe II			
III	=	inscrite à l'Annexe III	ssp.	=	sous-espèce
Del	=	retirée des annexes	syn.	=	synonyme
f.	=	forme	var.	=	variété
p.e.	=	peut-être éteinte	w	=	réserve retirée par la Partie nommée
popn(s)	=	population(s)			
r	=	réserve faite par la Partie nommée	#1–#8	=	renvoit à *Interprétation* (voir ci-dessous)

Interprétation

Conformément aux dispositions de l'Article I, paragraphe b, alinéa iii), de la Convention, le signe (#) suivi d'un nombre placé après le nom d'une espèce ou d'un taxon supérieur inscrit à l'Annexe II ou à l'Annexe III sert à désigner des parties ou produits obtenus à partir de cette espèce ou de ce taxon et qui sont mentionnés comme suit aux fins de la Convention:

#1   Sert à désigner toutes les parties et tous les produits, sauf les graines, les spores et le pollen (y compris les pollinies);
   - a)   les cultures de plantules ou de tissus obtenues in vitro en milieu solide ou liquide et transportées en conteneurs stériles; et
   - b)   les fleurs coupées des plantes reproduites artificiellement.

#2   Sert à désigner toutes les parties et tous les produits, sauf:
   - a)   les graines et le pollen;
   - b)   les cultures de plantules ou de tissus obtenues *in vitro* en milieu solide ou liquide et transportées en conteneurs stériles;
   - c)   les fleurs coupées des plantes reproduites artificiellement; et
   - d)   les produits chimiques et les produits pharmaceutiques finis.

#3   Sert à désigner les racines entières et tranchées et les parties de racines, à l'exception des parties et produits transformés tels que poudres, pilules, extraits, toniques, tisanes et autres préparations.

#4   Sert à désigner toutes les parties et tous les produits, sauf:
   - a)   les graines, sauf celles des cactus mexicains provenant du Mexique, et le pollen;
   - b)   les cultures de plantules ou de tissus obtenues *in vitro* en milieu solide ou liquide et transportées en conteneurs stériles;
   - c)   les fleurs coupées des plantes reproduites artificiellement;
   - d)   les fruits, et leurs parties et produits, des plantes acclimatées ou reproduites artificiellement; et
   - e)   les éléments de troncs (raquettes), et leurs parties et produits, de plantes du genre *Opuntia* sous-genre *Opuntia* acclimatées ou reproduites artificiellement.

#5   Sert à désigner les grumes, les bois sciés et les placages.

#6   Sert à désigner les grumes, les bois sciés, les placages et les contreplaqués.

#7   Sert à désigner les grumes, les copeaux et les matériaux déchiquetés non transformés.

#8   Sert à désigner toutes les parties et tous les produits, sauf:
   - a)   les graines et le pollen (y compris les pollinies);
   - b)   les cultures de plantules ou de tissus obtenues *in vitro* en milieu solide ou liquide et transportées en conteneurs stériles;
   - c)   les fleurs coupées des plantes reproduites artificiellement; et
   - d)   les fruits, et leurs parties et produits, de plantes du genre *Vanilla* reproduites artificiellement.

Nomenclature and taxonomy

The nomenclature and taxonomy followed here are the same as for the CITES Appendices. In most cases where the Appendices list only the name of an order, family or genus, the names of the individual species in that higher taxon have been included in this Checklist. Where a standard reference has been adopted by the Nomenclature Committee [CoP12 Doc. 10.3 (Rev. 1) Annex 3] the names of those species follow the relevant publications below. However, species lists are not included for Orchidaceae spp. listed in Appendix II and the *CITES Orchid Checklists* (Roberts *et al.* 1995, 1997, 2001) should be consulted for those names at species or lower levels. Where no standard reference has been adopted (as noted in the appropriate places below) the names of species in higher taxa are those currently used in the UNEP-WCMC database and have been extracted from a number of publications.

The Conference of the Parties to CITES has adopted this Checklist as the standard reference for species included in the Appendices to the extent that it is accepted by the Nomenclature Committee. Therefore, it should be noted that the Nomenclature Committee has only accepted the scientific names of species in the standard references listed below. The two references for invertebrates have not been adopted as standard references and are included for information only.

Nomenclatura y taxonomía

La nomenclatura y la taxonomía seguidas aquí son las utilizadas en los Apéndices de la CITES. En la mayoría de los casos en que en los Apéndices se cita únicamente el nombre de un orden, familia o género, los nombres de las especies es ese taxón superior se han incluido en esta Lista. Cuando el Comité de Nomenclatura ha adoptado una referencia normalizada [CoP12 Doc. 10.3 (Rev. 1), Anexo 3] los nombres de esas especies son los utilizados en las correspondientes publicaciones que figuran a continuación. Sin embargo, no se incluyen las listas de especies para Orchidaceae spp. que figuran en el Apéndice II; los nombres a nivel de especie o niveles inferiores pueden encontrarse consultado la Lista de Orquídeas CITES (Roberts *et al.* 1995, 1997, 2001). Cuando no se haya adoptado una referencia normalizada (como se indica a continuación) los nombres de las especies de un taxa superior son los utilizados normalmente en la base de datos del UNEP-WCMC, que se han extraido de diversas publaciones.

La Conferencia de las Partes en la CITES adoptó esta Lista como la referencia normalizada para las especies incluidas en los Apéndices en la medida en que ha sido aceptada por el Comité de Nomenclatura. En consecuencia, cabe señalar que el Comité de Nomenclatura sólo ha aceptado los nombres científicos de las especies en las referencias normalizadas que figuran a continuación. Las dos referencias para los invertebrados no han sido adoptadas como referencias normalizadas y se incluyen únicamente a título informativo.

38

Nomenclature et taxonomie

La nomenclature et la taxonomie suivies ici sont celles utilisées dans les annexes CITES. Dans la plupart des cas où les annexes n'incluent que le nom d'un ordre, d'une famille ou d'un genre, les noms des espèces individuelles de ce taxon supérieur ont été inclus dans la Liste. Lorsqu'une référence normalisée a été adoptée par le Comité de la nomenclature [CoP12 Doc. 10.3 (Rev. 1) Annexe 3], les noms de ces espèces sont ceux utilisés dans les publications pertinentes signalées ci-dessous. Toutefois, les listes d'espèces ne sont pas incluses pour Orchidaceae spp. figurant à l'Annexe II; ces noms au niveau de l'espèce ou à un niveau inférieur peuvent être trouvés en consultant les Listes CITES des Orchidaceae (Roberts *et al.* 1995, 1997, 2001). Lorsqu'aucune référence normalisée n'a été adoptée (comme signalé ci-dessous aux endroits appropriés) les noms d'espèces de taxons supérieurs sont ceux actuellement utilisés dans la base de données du PNUE-WCMC et proviennent de diverses publications.

La Conférence des Parties à la CITES a adopté cette Liste comme référence normalisée pour les espèces inscrites aux annexes dans la mesure où elle a été acceptée par le Comité de la nomenclature. Il convient donc de noter que le Comité de la nomenclature n'a accepté que les noms scientifiques des espèces figurant ci-après dans les références normalisées. Les deux références relatives aux invertébrés n'ont pas été adoptées comme références normalisées; elles ont été incluses ici pour information.

References/Referencias/Références: Fauna/Faune

Mammalia

Wilson, D. E. and Reeder, D. M. 1993. *Mammal Species of the World: a Taxonomic and Geographic Reference.* Second edition. Smithsonian Institution Press, Washington. [for all mammals – with the exception of the recognition of the following names for wild forms of species (in preference to names for domestic forms)/para todos los mamíferos – a excepción del reconocimiento de los nombres siguientes para las formas silvestres de las especies (se prefieren a los nombres de las formas domesticadas)/Pour les mammifères, à l'exception de l'acceptation des noms suivants pour les formes sauvages des espèces (de préférence aux noms des formes domestiquées): *Bos gaurus, Bos mutus, Bubalus arnee, Equus africanus, Equus przewalskii, Ovis orientalis ophion*]

Alperin, R. 1993. *Callithrix argentata* (Linnaeus, 1771): taxonomic observations and description of a new subspecies. *Boletim do Museu Paraense Emilio Goeldi, Serie Zoologia* 9: 317-328. [for/para/pour *Callithrix marcai*]

Dalebout, M. L., Mead, J. G., Baker, C. S., Baker, A. N. and van Helden, A. L. 2002. A new species of beaked whale *Mesoplodon perrini* sp. n. (Cetacea: Ziphiidae) discovered through phylogenetic analyses of mitochondrial DNA sequences. *Marine Mammal Science* 18: 577-608. [for/para/pour *Mesoplodon perrini*]

Ferrari, S. F. and Lopes, M. A. 1992. A new species of marmoset, genus *Callithrix* Erxleben 1777 (Callitrichidae, Primates) from western Brazilian Amazonia. *Goeldiana Zoologia* 12: 1-13. [for/para/pour *Callithrix nigriceps*]

Flannery, T. F. and Groves, C. P. 1998. A revision of the genus *Zaglossus* (Monotremata, Tachyglossidae), with description of new species and subspecies. *Mammalia* 62: 367-396. [for/para/pour *Zaglossus attenboroughi*]

Groves, C. P. 2000. The genus *Cheirogaleus*: unrecognized biodiversity in dwarf lemurs. *International Journal of Primatology* 21: 943-962. [for/para/pour *Cheirogaleus minusculus* & *Cheirogaleus ravus*]

van Helden, A. L., Baker, A. N., Dalebout, M. L., Reyes, J. C., van Waerebeek, K. and Baker, C. S. 2002. Resurrection of *Mesoplodon traversii* (Gray, 1874), senior synonym of *M. bahamondi* Reyes, van Waerebeek, Cárdenas and Yáñez, 1995 (Cetacea: Ziphiidae). *Marine Mammal Science* 18: 609-621. [for/para/pour *Mesoplodon traversii*]

Honess, P. E. and Bearder, S. K. 1997. Descriptions of the dwarf galago species of Tanzania. *African Primates* 2: 75-79. [for/para/pour *Galagoides rondoensis* & *Galagoides udzungwensis*]

Kobayashi, S. and Langguth, A. 1999. A new species of titi monkey, *Callicebus* Thomas, from north-eastern Brazil (Primates, Cebidae). *Revista Brasileira de Zoologia* 16: 531-551. [for/para/pour *Callicebus coimbrai*]

Mittermeier, R. A., Schwarz, M. and Ayres, J. M. 1992. A new species of marmoset, genus *Callithrix* Erxleben, 1777 (Callitrichidae, Primates) from the Rio Maues Region, State of Amazonas, central Brazilian Amazonia. *Goeldiana Zoologia* 14: 1-17. [for/para/pour *Callithrix mauesi*]

Rasoloarison, R. M., Goodman, S. M. and Ganzhorn, J. U. 2000. Taxonomic revision of mouse lemurs (*Microcebus*) in the western portions of Madagascar. *International Journal of Primatology* 21: 963-1019. [for/para/pour *Microcebus berthae, Microcebus sambiranensis & Microcebus tavaratra*]

Rice, D. W. 1998. *Marine Mammals of the World. Systematics and distribution.* Special Publication Number 4: i-ix, 1-231. The Society for Marine Mammals. [for/para/pour *Balaenoptera*]

Richards, G. C. and Hall, L. S. 2002. A new flying-fox of the genus *Pteropus* (Chiroptera: Pteropodidae) from Torres Strait, Australia. *Australian Zoologist* 32: 69-75. [for/para/pour *Pteropus banakrisi*]

van Roosmalen, M. G. M., van Roosmalen, T., Mittermeier, R. A. and Rylands, A. B. 2000. Two new species of marmoset, genus *Callithrix* Erxleben, 1777 (Callitrichidae, Primates), from the Tapajós/Madeira interfluvium, south Central Amazonia, Brazil. *Neotropical Primates* 10 (Suppl.): 2-18. [for/para/pour *Callicebus bernhardi & Callicebus stephennashi*]

van Roosmalen, M. G. M, van Roosmalen, T., Mittermeier, R. A. and da Fonseca, G. A. B. 1998. A new and distinctive species of marmoset (Callitrichidae, Primates) from the lower Rio Aripuana, State of Amazonas, central Brazilian Amazonia. *Goeldiana Zoologia* 22: 1-27. [for/para/pour *Callithrix humilis*]

van Roosmalen, M. G. M., van Roosmalen, T., Mittermeier, R. A. and Rylands, A. B. 2000. Two new species of marmoset, genus *Callithrix* Erxleben, 1777 (Callitrichidae, Primates), from the Tapajós/Madeira interfluvium, south Central Amazonia, Brazil. *Neotropical Primates* 8: 2-18. [for/para/pour *Callithrix acariensis & Callithrix manicorensis*]

Schwartz, J. H. 1996. *Pseudopotto martini*: a new genus and species of extant lorisiform primate. *Anthropological Papers of the American Museum of Natural History* 78: 1-14. [for/para/pour *Pseudopotto martini*]

Silva Jr, J. and Noronha, M. 1996. Discovery of a new species of marmoset in the Brazilian Amazon. *Neotropical Primates* 4: 58-59. [for/para/pour *Callithrix saterei*]

Thalmann, U. and Geissmann, T. 2000. Distributions and geographic variation in the western woolly lemur (*Avahi occidentalis*) with description of a new species (*A. unicolor*). *International Journal of Primatology* 21: 915-941. [for/para/pour *Avahi unicolor*]

Zimmerman, E., Cepok, S., Rakotoarison, N., Zietemann, V. and Radespiel, U. 1998. Sympatric mouse lemurs in north west Madagascar: a new rufous mouse lemur species (*Microcebus ravelobensis*). *Folia Primatologica* 69: 106-114. [for/para/pour *Microcebus ravelobensis*]

Aves

Morony, J. J., Bock, W. J. and Farrand, J., Jr. 1975. *A Reference List of the Birds of the World*. American Museum of Natural History. [for order- and family-level names for birds/para los nombres de las aves a nivel de orden y familia/pour les noms d'oiseaux aux niveaux de l'ordre et de la famille]

Sibley, C. G. and Monroe, B. L., Jr. 1990. *Distribution and Taxonomy of Birds of the World*. Yale University Press, New Haven.

Sibley, C. G. and Monroe, B. L., Jr. 1993. *Supplement to the Distribution and Taxonomy of Birds of the World*. Yale University Press, New Haven. [for bird species, except for/para las especies de aves, excepto para/pour les espèces aviennes sauf Psittaciformes & Trochilidae]

Collar, N. J. 1997. Family Psittacidae (Parrots). Pp. 280-477 in del Hoyo, J., Elliot, A. and Sargatal, J. eds. *Handbook of the Birds of the World*. Vol. 4. Sandgrouse to Cuckoos. Lynx Edicions, Barcelona. [for/para/pour Psittacidae]

Howell, S. N. G. and Robbins, M. B. 1995. Species limits of the Least Pygmy-Owl (*Glaucidium minutissimum*) complex. *Wilson Bulletin* 107: 7-25. [for/para/pour *Glaucidium parkeri*]

Lafontaine, R. M. and Moulaert, N. 1998. A new species of scops owl (*Otus*: Aves): taxonomy and conservation status. *Journal of African Zoology* 112: 163-169. [for/para/pour *Otus moheliensis*]

Lambert, F. R. and Rasmussen, P. C. 1998. A new scops owl from Sangihe Island, Indonesia. *Bulletin of the British Ornithologists' Club* 204-217. [for/para/pour *Otus collari*]

Rasmussen, P. C. 1998. A new scops-owl from Great Nicobar Island. *Bulletin of the British Ornithologists' Club* 118: 141-153. [for/para/pour *Otus alius*]

Rasmussen, P. C. 1999. A new species of hawk-owl *Ninox* from North Sulawesi, Indonesia. *Wilson Bulletin* 111: 457-464. [for/para/pour *Ninox ios*]

Robbins, M. B. and Stiles, F. G. 1999. A new species of pygmy-owl (Strigidae: *Glaucidium*) from the Pacific slope of the northern Andes. *Auk* 116: 305-315. [for/para/pour *Glaucidium nubicola*]

Rowley, I. 1997. Family Cacatuidae (Cockatoos). Pp. 246-279 in del Hoyo, J., Elliot, A. and Sargatal, J. eds. *Handbook of the Birds of the World*. Vol. 4. Sandgrouse to Cuckoos. Lynx Edicions, Barcelona. [for/para/pour Cacatuidae=Psittacidae]

Schuchmann, K. L. 1999. Family Trochilidae (Hummingbirds). Pp. 468-680 in del Hoyo, J., Elliot, A. and Sargatal, J. eds. *Handbook of the Birds of the World*. Vol. 5. Barn-owls to Hummingbirds. Lynx Edicions, Barcelona. [for/para/pour Trochilidae]

Reptilia

Note that no standard references have been adopted for/Sírvase tomar nota de que no se han adoptado referencias normalizadas para/Notez qu'aucune référence normalisée n'a été adoptée pour *Phelsuma* spp., *Uromastyx* spp., *Brachylophus* spp., *Conolophus* spp., *Cyclura* spp., *Iguana* spp., *Dracaena* spp. & *Heloderma* spp.

Andreone, F., Mattioli, F., Jesu, R. and Randrianirina, J. E. 2001. Two new chameleons of the genus *Calumma* from north-east Madagascar, with observations on hemipenial morphology in the *Calumma furcifer* group (Reptilia, Squamata, Chamaeleonidae). *Herpetological Journal* 11: 53-68. [for/para/pour *Calumma vatosoa* & *Calumma vencesi*]

Avila Pires, T. C. S. 1995. Lizards of Brazilian Amazonia. *Zool. Verh.* 299: 706 pp. [for/para/pour *Tupinambis*]

Böhme, W. 1997. Eine neue Chamäleon art aus der *Calumma gastrotaenia* - Verwandtschaft Ost-Madagaskars. *Herpetofauna* (Weinstadt) 19 (107): 5-10. [for/para/pour *Calumma glawi*]

Böhme, W. 2002. Draft checklist of the living monitor lizards of the world (family Varanidae). CoP12 Inf. 6 Annex. Now published: 2003. Checklist of the living monitor lizards of the world (family Varanidae). *Zool. Verh.* Leiden 341: 4-43. [for/para/pour *Varanus*]

Broadley, D. G. 2002. CITES Standard reference for the species of *Cordylus* (Cordylidae, Reptilia) prepared at the request of the CITES Nomenclature Committee. CoP12 Inf. 14. [for/para/pour *Cordylus*]

Cei, J. M. 1993. *Reptiles del noroeste, nordeste y este de la Argentina – herpetofauna de las selvas subtropicales, puna y pampa*. Monografie XIV, Museo Regionale di Scienze Naturali. [for/para/pour *Tupinambis*]

Colli, G. R., Péres, A. K. and da Cunha, H. J. 1998. A new species of *Tupinambis* (Squamata: Teiidae) from central Brazil, with an analysis of morphological and genetic variation in the genus. *Herpetologica* 54: 477-492. [for/para/pour *Tupinambis cerradensis*]

Dirksen, L. 2002. *Anakondas*. NTV Wissenschaft. [for/para/pour *Eunectes beniensis*]

Harvey, M. B., Barker, D. B., Ammerman, L. K. and Chippindale, P. T. 2000. Systematics of pythons of the *Morelia amethistina* complex (Serpentes: Boidae) with the description of three new species. Herpetological Monographs 14: 139-185. [for/para/pour *Morelia clastolepis*, *Morelia nauta* & *Morelia tracyae*, and elevation to species level of/y elevación a nivel de especie de/et élévation au niveau de l'espèce de *Morelia kinghorni*].

Hedges, B. S., Estrada, A. R. and Diaz, L. M. 1999. New snake (*Tropidophis*) from western Cuba. *Copeia* 1999(2): 376-381. [for/para/pour *Tropidophis celiae*]

Hedges, S. B. and Garrido, O. 1999. A new snake of the genus *Tropidophis* (Tropidophiidae) from central Cuba. *Journal of Herpetology* 33: 436-441. [for/para/pour *Tropidophis spiritus*]

Hedges, B. S., Garrido, O. and Diaz, L. M. 2001. A new banded snake of the genus *Tropidophis* (Tropidophiidae) from north-central Cuba. *Journal of Herpetology* 35: 615-617. [for/para/pour *Tropidophis morenoi*]

Jesu, R., Mattioli, F. and Schimenti, G. 1999. On the discovery of a new large chameleon inhabiting the limestone outcrops of western Madagascar: *Furcifer nicosiai* sp. nov. (Reptilia, Chamaeleonidae). Doriana 7(311): 1-14. [for/para/pour *Furcifer nicosiai*]

Keogh, J. S., Barker, D. G. and Shine, R. 2001. Heavily exploited but poorly known: systematics and biogeography of commercially harvested pythons (*Python curtus* group) in Southeast Asia. *Biological Journal of the Linnean Society* 73: 113-129. [for/para/pour *Python breitensteini* & *Python brongersmai*]

Klaver, C. J. J. and Böhme, W. 1997. Chamaeleonidae. *Das Tierreich* 112: 85 pp. [for/para/pour *Bradypodion, Brookesia, Calumma, Chamaeleo* & *Furcifer* – except for the recognition of/excepto para el reconocimiento de/sauf pour la reconnaissance de *Calumma andringitaensis, C. guillaumeti, C. hilleniusi* & *C. marojezensis* as valid species/como especies válidas/en tant qu'espèces valides]

Manzani, P. R. and Abe, A. S. 1997. A new species of *Tupinambis* Daudin, 1802 (Squamata, Teiidae) from central Brazil. *Boletim do Museu Nacional* Nov. Ser. Zool. 382: 1-10. [for/para/pour *Tupinambis quadrilineatus*]

Massary, J.-C. de and Hoogmoed, M. 2001. The valid name for *Crocodilurus lacertinus* auctorum (nec Daudin, 1802) (Squamata: Teiidae). *Journal of Herpetology* 35: 353-357. [for/para/pour *Crocodilurus amazonicus*]

McCord, W. P., Iverson, J. B., Spinks, P. Q. and Shaffer, H. B. 2000. A new genus of Geoemydid turtle from Asia. *Hamadryad* 25: 86-90. [for/para/pour *Leucocephalon*]

McDiarmid, R. W., Campbell, J. A. and Touré, T. A. 1999. *Snake Species of the World. A Taxonomic and Geographic Reference.* Volume 1. The Herpetologists' League, Washington, DC. [for/para/pour Loxocemidae, Pythonidae, Boidae, Bolyeriidae, Tropidophiidae & Viperidae – except for the retention of the genera/excepto para la retención de los géneros/sauf pour le maintien des genres *Acrantophis, Sanzinia, Calabaria* & *Lichanura* and the recognition of *Epicrates maurus* as a valid species/y el reconocimiento de *Epicrates maurus* como especie válida/et la reconnaissance d'*Epicrates maurus* en tant qu'espèce valide]

Perälä, J. 2001. A new species of *Testudo* (Testudines: Testudinidae) from the Middle East, with implications for conservation. *Journal of Herpetology* 35: 567-582. [for/para/pour *Testudo werneri*]

Pough, F. H., Andrews, R. M., Cadle, J. E., Crump, M. L., Savitzky, A. H. and Wells, K. D. 1998. *Herpetology.* [for delimitation of families within the Sauria/para delimitar las familias dentro de Sauria/pour délimiter les familles au sein de Sauria]

Slowinski, J. B. and Wüster, W. 2000. A new cobra (Elapidae: *Naja*) from Myanmar (Burma). *Herpetologica* 56: 257-270. [for/para/pour *Naja mandalayensis*]

Tilbury, C. 1998. Two new chameleons (Sauria: Chamaeleonidae) from isolated Afromontane forests in Sudan and Ethiopia. *Bonner Zoologische Beiträge* 47: 293-299. [for/para/pour *Chamaeleo balebicornutus* & *Chamaeleo conirostratus*]

Wermuth, H. and Mertens, R. 1996 (reprint). *Schildkröte, Krokodile, Brückenechsen.* Gustav Fischer Verlag, Jena. [for/para/pour Crocodylia, Testudinata & Rhynchocephalia]

Wüster, W. 1996. Taxonomic change and toxinology: systematic revisions of the Asiatic cobras *Naja naja* species complex. *Toxicon* 34: 339-406. [for/para/pour *Naja atra*, *Naja kaouthia*, *Naja oxiana*, *Naja philippinensis*, *Naja sagittifera*, *Naja samarensis*, *Naja siamensis*, *Naja sputatrix* & *Naja sumatrana*]

Amphibia

Frost, D. R., ed. 2002. *Amphibian Species of the World: a taxonomic and geographic reference.* http://research.amnh.org/herpetology/amphibia/index.html as of 23 August 2002/a partir de 23 agosto de 2002/à partir de 23 août 2002

Fishes/Peces/Poissons

Eschmeier, W. N. 1998. *Catalog of Fishes.* 3 vols. California Academy of Sciences. [for all fishes / para todos los peces / pour tous les poissons]

Invertebrata

Note that no standard references have been adopted for *Brachypelma* spp., *Colophon* spp., *Bhutanitis* spp., Tridacnidae spp., *Achatinella* spp., Antipatharia spp., Scleractinia spp., Milleporidae spp. and Stylasteridae spp. The following two references have been used as a basis for the last three groups:

Sírvase tomar nota de que no se han adoptado referencias normalizadas para *Brachypelma* spp., *Colophon* spp., *Bhutanitis* spp., Tridacnidae spp., *Achatinella* spp., Antipatharia spp., Scleractinia spp., Milleporidae spp. y Stylasteridae spp. Las dos siguientes referencias se han utilizado como base para los tres últimos grupos:

Notez qu'aucune référence normalisée n'a été adoptée pour *Brachypelma* spp., *Colophon* spp., *Bhutanitis* spp., Tridacnidae spp., *Achatinella* spp., Antipatharia spp., Scleractinia spp., Milleporidae spp. et Stylasteridae spp. Les deux références suivantes ont été utilisées comme base pour les trois derniers groupes:

Cairns, S. D., Hoeksema, B. W. and van der Land, J. 1999. List of extant stony corals. *Atoll Research Bulletin* 459: 13-46. [for/para/pour Cnidaria: Scleractinia, Milleporina & Stylasterina]; supplemented by/completado por/complété par

Veron, J. E. N. 2000. *Corals of the world.* 3 vols. Australian Institute of Marine Science and CRR Qld Pty Ltd. [for/para/pour Scleractinia]

References/Referencias/Références: Flora/Flore

Genera/Géneros/Genres

Mabberley, D. J. 1997. *The Plant-Book*. Second edition. Cambridge University Press, Cambridge. (reprinted with corrections 1998) [for generic names, unless superseded by standard checklists listed below/para los nombres genéricos, salvo que hayan sido reemplazados por las listas normalizadas citadas a continuación/Pour les noms de genres, à moins qu'ils ne soient remplacés par les listes normalisées indiquées ci-dessous]

Willis, J. C. 1973. *A Dictionary of Flowering Plants and Ferns*. Eighth edition, revised by H. K. Airy Shaw. Cambridge University Press, Cambridge. [for generic synonyms not mentioned in Mabberley (1997)/para los sinónimos genéricos no mencionados en Mabberley (1997)/pour les synonymes génériques ne figurant pas dans Mabberley (1997)]

Species/Especies/Espèces

Note that no standard references have been adopted for/Sírvase tomar nota de que no se han adoptado referencias normalizadas para/Notez qu'aucune référence normalisée n'a été adoptée pour Cyatheaceae spp., *Dicksonia* spp., Didiereaceae spp., *Anacampseros* spp., *Avonia* spp., *Gonystylus* spp. & *Guaiacum* spp.

Arx, B. von, Schlauer, J. and Groves, M. 2001. *CITES Carnivorous Plant Checklist*. Royal Botanic Gardens, Kew. [for/para/pour *Dionaea, Nepenthes* & *Sarracenia*]

Carter, S. and Eggli, U. 1997. *The CITES Checklist of Succulent* Euphorbia *Taxa (Euphorbiaceae)*. German Federal Agency for Nature Conservation. [for succulent/para suculentas/pour les succulentes *Euphorbia*]

Davis, A. P. and McGough, N. 1999. *CITES Bulb Checklist*. Royal Botanic Gardens, Kew. [for/para/pour *Cyclamen, Galanthus* & *Sternbergia*]

Eggli, U. ed. 2001. *CITES* Aloe *and* Pachypodium *Checklist*. Royal Botanic Gardens, Kew. [for/para/pour *Aloe* & *Pachypodium*]

Farjon, A. 2001. *World Checklist and Bibliography of Conifers*. Second edition. Royal Botanic Gardens, Kew. [for/para/pour *Taxus*]

Hunt, D. 1999. *CITES Cactaceae Checklist*. Second edition. Royal Botanic Gardens, Kew. [for/para/pour Cactaceae. Synonyms not complete/sinónimos no exhaustivos/ Synonymes non exhaustifs]

Lobin, W. and Schippmann, U. 2002. *Dicksonia* checklist. Unpublished. [The CITES Nomenclature Committee is considering this as a standard reference, to be recommended for adoption at the next Conference of the Parties. It is included here for guidance on *Dicksonia* species of the Americas./El Comité de Nomenclatura de la CITES está considerando esta publicación como una referencia normalizada y recomendará su adopción en la próxima reunión de la Conferencia de las Partes. Se incluye aquí como orientación sobre las especies *Dicksonia* de las Américas./Le Comité CITES de la nomenclature considère cette liste comme une référence normalisée dont l'adoption devrait être recommandée à la prochaine session de la Conférence des Parties. Elle est incluse ici comme orientation sur les espèces de *Dicksonia* d'Amérique.]

Roberts, J. A., Anuku, S., Burdon, J., Mathew, P., McGough, H. N. and Newman, A. 2001. *CITES Orchid Checklist*. Volume 3. Royal Botanic Gardens, Kew. [for/para/pour **Aerangis, *Angraecum, *Ascocentrum, *Bletilla, *Brassavola, *Calanthe, *Catasetum, *Miltonia, *Miltonioides, *Miltoniopsis, *Renanthera, *Renantherella, *Rhynchostylis, *Rossioglossum, *Vanda, & *Vandopsis*]

Roberts, J. A., Beale, C. R., Benseler, J. C., McGough, H. N. and Zappi, D. C. 1995. *CITES Orchid Checklist*. Volume 1. Royal Botanic Gardens, Kew. [for/para/pour **Cattleya, *Cypripedium, *Laelia, Paphiopedilum, *Phalaenopsis, Phragmipedium, *Pleione, & *Sophronitis*]

Roberts, J.A., Allman, L.R., Beale, C.R., Butter, R.W., Crook, K.R. and McGough, H.N. 1997. *CITES Orchid Checklist*. Volume 2. Royal Botanic Gardens, Kew. [for/para/pour **Cymbidium, *Dendrobium* (selected sections only/únicamente las partes seleccionadas/uniquement les parties sélectionnées), **Disa, *Dracula, & *Encyclia*]

Stevenson, D. W., Osborne, R. and Hill, K. D. 1995. A world list of cycads. Pp. 55-64 in P. Vorster (ed.) *Proceedings of the Third International Conference on Cycad Biology*. Cycad Society of South Africa. [for/para/pour Cycadaceae, Stangeriaceae & Zamiaceae]

* Only the Appendix-I listed species from these Orchidaceae genera are included in the Checklist. Users should refer to the three cited volumes of the *CITES Orchid Checklist* for details of the Appendix-II listed species.

* En la Lista figuran únicamente las especies incluidas en el Apéndice I de estos géneros de Orchidaceae. Para información sobre las especies incluidas en el Apéndice II, se ruega consulten los tres volúmenes citados de la Lista de Orquídeas CITES.

* Seules les espèces inscrites à l'Annexe I de ces genres d'Orchidaceae sont incluses dans la Liste. L'utilisateur consultera avec profit les trois Listes CITES des Orchidaceae citées, où il trouvera des détails sur les espèces inscrites à l'Annexe II.

CHECKLIST OF FAUNA

LISTA DE ESPECIES DE FAUNA

LISTE DES ESPECES ANIMALES

Checklist of fauna/Lista de especies de fauna/Liste des espèces animales

Aardwolf (E): *Proteles cristatus*
Abaco Island Boa (E): *Epicrates exsul*
Abbé Allotte's Birdwing (E): *Ornithoptera allottei*
Abbott's Booby (E): *Papasula abbotti*
Abbott's Day Gecko (E): *Phelsuma abbotti*
Abeillia abeillei : (E) Emerald-chinned Hummingbird, (S) Colibrí barbiesmeralda, (F) Colibri d'Abeillé, **II** TROCHILIDAE Av
Abejero colilargo (S): *Henicopernis longicauda*
Abejero de Célebes (S): *Pernis celebensis*
Abejero europeo (S): *Pernis apivorus*
Abejero negro (S): *Henicopernis infuscatus*
Abejero oriental (S): *Pernis ptilorhyncus*
Abolí (S): *Euoticus elegantulus*
Aboma (F): *Epicrates cenchria*
Abruzzo Chamois (E): *Rupicapra pyrenaica ornata*
Aburria jacutinga = *Pipile jacutinga*
Aburria pipile ssp. *pipile* = *Pipile pipile*
Abyssinian long-eared owl (E): *Asio abyssinicus*
Abyssinian Lovebird (E): *Agapornis taranta*
Abyssinian Owl (E): *Asio abyssinicus*
Acanthastrea amakusensis : **II** MUSSIDAE An
Acanthastrea bowerbanki : **II** MUSSIDAE An
Acanthastrea brevis : **II** MUSSIDAE An
Acanthastrea echinata : **II** MUSSIDAE An
Acanthastrea faviaformis : **II** MUSSIDAE An
Acanthastrea hemprichii : **II** MUSSIDAE An
Acanthastrea hillae : **II** MUSSIDAE An
Acanthastrea ishigakiensis : **II** MUSSIDAE An
Acanthastrea lordhowensis : **II** MUSSIDAE An
Acanthastrea maxima : **II** MUSSIDAE An
Acanthastrea minuta : **II** MUSSIDAE An
Acanthastrea regularis : **II** MUSSIDAE An
Acanthastrea rotundoflora : **II** MUSSIDAE An
Acanthastrea subechinata : **II** MUSSIDAE An
Acanthophyllia deshayesiana : **II** MUSSIDAE An
Acapulco Lesser Orange Tarantula (E): *Brachypelmides klaasi*
Accipiter albogularis : (E) Pied Goshawk, Pied Sparrowhawk, (S) Gavilán pío, (F) Autour pie, **II** ACCIPITRIDAE Av
Accipiter badius : (E) Little Banded Sparrowhawk, Shikra, (S) Gavilán chikra, (F) Épervier shikra, **II** ACCIPITRIDAE Av
Accipiter bicolor : (E) Bicolored Hawk, Bicolored Sparrowhawk, (S) Azor bicolor, Esparvero bicolor, Gavilán bicolor, Gavilán pantalón, (F) Épervier bicolore, **II** ACCIPITRIDAE Av
Accipiter brachyurus : (E) New Britain Sparrowhawk, Red-collared Sparrowhawk, (S) Gavilancito de Nueva Bretaña, (F) Épervier de Nouvelle-Bretagne, **II** ACCIPITRIDAE Av
Accipiter brevipes : (E) Levant Sparrowhawk, (S) Gavilán griego, (F) Épervier à pieds courts, **II** ACCIPITRIDAE Av
Accipiter buergersi = *Erythrotriorchis buergersi*
Accipiter butleri : (E) Nicobar Shikra, Nicobar Sparrowhawk, (S) Gavilán de Nicobar, (F) Épervier des Nicobar, **II** ACCIPITRIDAE Av
Accipiter castanilius : (E) Chestnut-bellied Sparrowhawk, Chestnut-flanked Sparrowhawk, (S) Gavilán flanquirrojo, Gavilán pechirrojo, (F) Autour à flancs roux, **II** ACCIPITRIDAE Av
Accipiter chilensis = *Accipiter bicolor*
Accipiter chionogaster : (E) White-breasted Hawk, (S) Gavilán pechiblanco, Gavilán ventriblanco, (F) Épervier à poitrine blanche, **II** ACCIPITRIDAE Av
Accipiter cirrocephalus : (E) Collared Sparrowhawk, (S) Gavilán acollarado, (F) Épervier à collier roux, **II** ACCIPITRIDAE Av
Accipiter collaris : (E) Semicollared Hawk, Semi-collared Hawk, Semi-collared Sparrowhawk, (S) Azer semicollarejo, Gavilán acollarado, Gavilancito torcaz, (F) Épervier à collier interrompu, **II** ACCIPITRIDAE Av

Accipiter cooperii : (E) Cooper's Hawk, (S) Gavilán de Cooper, (F) Épervier de Cooper, **II** ACCIPITRIDAE Av
Accipiter doriae = *Megatriorchis doriae*
Accipiter erythrauchen : **II** ACCIPITRIDAE Av
Accipiter erythronemius : (E) Red-thighed Hawk, Rufous-thighed Hawk, (F) Épervier à cuisses rouges, Épervier à cuisses rousses, **II** ACCIPITRIDAE Av
Accipiter erythropus : (E) Red-thighed Sparrowhawk, (S) Gavilancito de Hartlaub, Gavilancito muslirrojo, (F) Autour minulle, Épervier de Hartlaub, **II** ACCIPITRIDAE Av
Accipiter fasciatus : (E) Australasian Goshawk, Brown Goshawk, (S) Azor australiano, (F) Autour australien, **II** ACCIPITRIDAE Av
Accipiter francesii : (E) Frances's Goshawk, Frances's Sparrowhawk, (S) Gavilán de Frances, (F) Épervier de Frances, **II** ACCIPITRIDAE Av
Accipiter gentilis : (E) Goshawk, Northern Goshawk, (S) Azor, Azor común, Gavilán azor, (F) Autour des palombes, **II** ACCIPITRIDAE Av
Accipiter griseiceps : (E) Celebes Crested Goshawk, Sulawesi Goshawk, (S) Gavilán de Célebes, (F) Autour des Célèbes, **II** ACCIPITRIDAE Av
Accipiter griseogularis = *Accipiter novaehollandiae*
Accipiter gularis : (E) Japanese Lesser Sparrowhawk, Japanese Sparrowhawk, (S) Gavilancito japonés, (F) Épervier du Japon, **II** ACCIPITRIDAE Av
Accipiter gundlachi : (E) Gundlach's Hawk, Gundlach's Sparrowhawk, (S) Gavilán cubano, (F) Épervier de Cuba, **II** ACCIPITRIDAE Av
Accipiter haplochrous : (E) New Caledonia Goshawk, White-bellied Goshawk, (S) Gavilán de Nueva Caledonia, (F) Autour à ventre blanc, **II** ACCIPITRIDAE Av
Accipiter henicogrammus : (E) Gray's Goshawk, Moluccan Barred Sparrowhawk, Moluccan Goshawk, (S) Azor moluqueño, (F) Autour des Moluques, **II** ACCIPITRIDAE Av
Accipiter henstii : (E) Henst's Goshawk, (S) Azor malgache, (F) Autour de Henst, **II** ACCIPITRIDAE Av
Accipiter hiogaster = *Accipiter novaehollandiae*
Accipiter imitator : (E) Imitator Sparrowhawk, (S) Gavilán imitador, (F) Autour imitateur, **II** ACCIPITRIDAE Av
Accipiter luteoschistaceus : (E) Blue-and-grey Sparrowhawk, Slaty-backed Goshawk, Slaty-mantled Sparrowhawk, (S) Gavilán de Nueva Bretaña, (F) Autour bleu et gris, **II** ACCIPITRIDAE Av
Accipiter madagascariensis : (E) Madagascar Sparrowhawk, (S) Gavilán malgache, (F) Épervier de Madagascar, **II** ACCIPITRIDAE Av
Accipiter melanochlamys : (E) Black-mantled Goshawk, Black-mantled Hawk, (S) Gavilán rufinegro, (F) Autour à manteau noir, **II** ACCIPITRIDAE Av
Accipiter melanoleucus : (E) Black Goshawk, Black Sparrowhawk, Great Sparrowhawk, (S) Azor blanquinegro, (F) Autour noir, Épervier pie, **II** ACCIPITRIDAE Av
Accipiter meyerianus : (E) Meyer's Goshawk, Meyer's Hawk, Papuan Goshawk, (S) Azor de Meyer, (F) Autour de Meyer, **II** ACCIPITRIDAE Av
Accipiter minullus : (E) African Little Sparrowhawk, Little Sparrowhawk, (S) Gavilancito chico, (F) Épervier minule, **II** ACCIPITRIDAE Av
Accipiter nanus : (E) Celebes Sparrowhawk, Small Sparrowhawk, (S) Gavilancito de Célebes, (F) Épervier des Célèbes, **II** ACCIPITRIDAE Av
Accipiter nisus : (E) Eurasian Sparrowhawk, Sparrowhawk, (S) Gavilán común, (F) Épervier d'Europe, **II** ACCIPITRIDAE Av

Accipiter novaehollandiae : (E) Grey Goshawk, Grey-throated Goshawk, Variable Goshawk, White Goshawk, (S) Azor variable, (F) Autour blanc, **II** ACCIPITRIDAE Av

Accipiter ovampensis : (E) Ovambo Sparrowhawk, Ovampo Sparrowhawk, (S) Gavilán de Ovampo, (F) Épervier de l'Ovampo, **II** ACCIPITRIDAE Av

Accipiter poliocephalus : (E) Grey-headed Goshawk, Grey-headed Sparrowhawk, New Guinea Grey-headed Goshawk, (S) Gavilán cabecigrís, (F) Autour à tête grise, **II** ACCIPITRIDAE Av

Accipiter poliogaster : (E) Grey-bellied Goshawk, Grey-bellied Hawk, (S) Azor pechigrís, Azor ventigrís, Esparvero pechigrís, Gavilán vientrigris, (F) Autour à ventre gris, **II** ACCIPITRIDAE Av

Accipiter princeps : (E) Grey-headed Goshawk, New Britain Goshawk, (S) Azor de Nueva Bretaña, (F) Autour de Mayr, **II** ACCIPITRIDAE Av

Accipiter radiatus = Erythrotriorchis radiatus

Accipiter rhodogaster : (E) Vinous-breasted Sparrowhawk, (S) Gavilán pechirrojo, (F) Épervier à poitrine rousse, **II** ACCIPITRIDAE Av

Accipiter rufitorques : (E) Fiji Goshawk, Fiji Sparrowhawk, (S) Gavilán de las Fiji, (F) Autour des Fidji, **II** ACCIPITRIDAE Av

Accipiter rufiventris : (E) Rufous-chested Sparrowhawk, (S) Gavilán papirrufo, (F) Épervier menu, **II** ACCIPITRIDAE Av

Accipiter soloensis : (E) Chinese Goshawk, Chinese Sparrowhawk, Grey Frog Hawk, (S) Gavilán ranero, (F) Épervier de Horsfield, **II** ACCIPITRIDAE Av

Accipiter striatus : (E) Sharp-shinned Hawk, (S) Azor chico, Esparvero chico, Gavilán americano, Gavilán arrastrador, Gavilán pajarero, (F) Épervier brun, **II** ACCIPITRIDAE Av

Accipiter striatus ssp. *chionogaster = Accipiter chionogaster*

Accipiter striatus ssp. *erythronemius = Accipiter erythronemius*

Accipiter striatus ssp. *ventralis = Accipiter ventralis*

Accipiter superciliosus : (E) Tiny Hawk, Tiny Sparrowhawk, (S) Azor gris, Esparvero gris, Gavilán enano, Gavilancito americano, (F) Épervier nain, **II** ACCIPITRIDAE Av

Accipiter tachiro : (E) African Goshawk, (S) Azor tachiro, (F) Autour tachiro, **II** ACCIPITRIDAE Av

Accipiter tachiro ssp. *toussenelii = Accipiter toussenelii*

Accipiter toussenelii : (E) Red-chested Goshawk, Red-chested Hawk, (S) Azor de Toussenel, Gavilán pechirroseo, (F) Autour de Toussenel, **II** ACCIPITRIDAE Av

Accipiter trinotatus : (E) Spot-tailed Goshawk, Spot-tailed Sparrowhawk, (S) Gavilán colipinto, (F) Épervier à queue tachetée, **II** ACCIPITRIDAE Av

Accipiter trivirgatus : (E) Asian Crested Goshawk, Crested Goshawk, (S) Azor moñudo, (F) Autour huppé, **II** ACCIPITRIDAE Av

Accipiter ventralis : (E) Plain-breasted Hawk, (S) Azor pechillano, Gavilán andino, (F) Épervier à gorge rayée, **II** ACCIPITRIDAE Av

Accipiter virgatus : (E) Besra, Besra Sparrowhawk, Besra-sperwer, (S) Gavilán besra, (F) Épervier besra, **II** ACCIPITRIDAE Av

Accipiter virgatus ssp. *gularis = Accipiter gularis*

Acerodon spp.: (E) Flying-foxes, (S) Zorros voladores, (F) Renards volants, Roussettes, **I/II** PTEROPODIDAE Ma

Acerodon celebensis : (E) Signal-winged Acerodon, Sulawesi Flying-fox, Sulawesi Fruit Bat, (S) Zorro volador de las Célebes, **II** PTEROPODIDAE Ma

Acerodon humilis : (E) Talaud Acerodon, Talaud Flying-fox, Talaud Fruit Bat, (S) Zorro volador de Talaud, **II** PTEROPODIDAE Ma

Acerodon jubatus : (E) Golden-capped Fruit Bat, (S) Zorro volador filipino, **I** PTEROPODIDAE Ma

Acerodon leucotis : (E) Palawan Flying-fox, Palawan Fruit Bat, (S) Zorro volador de Calamian, **II** PTEROPODIDAE Ma

Acerodon lucifer : (E) Panay Flying-fox, Panay Giant Fruit Bat, Panay Golden-capped Fruit Bat, (S) Zorro volador de la isla Panay, **I** PTEROPODIDAE Ma

Acerodon mackloti : (E) Lesser Sunda Flying-fox, Sunda Flying-fox, Sunda Fruit Bat, (S) Zorro volador de Macklot, **II** PTEROPODIDAE Ma

Aceros spp.: (E) Hornbills, (S) Buceros, Cálaos, (F) Calaos, **I/II** BUCEROTIDAE Av

Aceros cassidix : (E) Buton Hornbill, Celebes Hornbill, Greater Sulawesi Hornbill, Knobbed Hornbill, Red-knobbed Hornbill, Sulawesi Wrinkled Hornbill, (S) Cálao grande de Célebes, (F) Calao à cimier, **II** BUCEROTIDAE Av

Aceros comatus : (E) Asian White-crested Hornbill, Long-crested Hornbill, White-crested Hornbill, White-crowned Hornbill, (S) Cálao crestiblanco, (F) Calao coiffé, **II** BUCEROTIDAE Av

Aceros corrugatus : (E) Sunda Wrinkled Hornbill, Wrinkled Hornbill, (S) Cálao arrugado, (F) Calao à casque rouge, **II** BUCEROTIDAE Av

Aceros everetti : (E) Sumba Hornbill, Sumba Wreathed Hornbill, (S) Cálao de la Sumba, (F) Calao de Sumba, **II** BUCEROTIDAE Av

Aceros leucocephalus : (E) Mindanao Wrinkled Hornbill, White-headed Hornbill, Writhed Hornbill, (S) Cálao grande de Mindanao, (F) Calao de Vieillot, **II** BUCEROTIDAE Av

Aceros leucocephalus ssp. *waldeni = Aceros waldeni*

Aceros narcondami : (E) Narcondam Hornbill, (S) Cálao de la Narcondam, (F) Calao de Narcondam, **II** BUCEROTIDAE Av

Aceros nipalensis : (E) Rufous-cheeked Hornbill, Rufous-necked Hornbill, (S) Cálao del Nepal, (F) Calao à cou roux, Calao de montagne, **I** BUCEROTIDAE Av

Aceros plicatus : (E) Kokomo, New Guinea Hornbill, New Guinea Wreathed Hornbill, Papuan Hornbill, Plicated Hornbill, (F) Calao papou, **II** BUCEROTIDAE Av

Aceros plicatus ssp. *subruficollis = Aceros subruficollis*

Aceros subruficollis : (E) Blyth's Hornbill, Blyth's Wreathed Hornbill, Burmese Hornbill, Plain-pouched Hornbill, Plain-pouched Wreathed Hornbill, (S) Cálao gorgiclaro, (F) Calao à gorge claire, Calao à poche unie, **I** BUCEROTIDAE Av

Aceros undulatus : (E) Bar-pouched Wreathed Hornbill, Bar-throated Wreathed Hornbill, Northern Waved Hornbill, Wreathed Hornbill, (S) Cálao gorginegro, (F) Calao festonné, **II** BUCEROTIDAE Av

Aceros waldeni : (E) Panay Wrinkled Hornbill, Rufous-headed Hornbill, Visayan Wrinkled Hornbill, Writhed-billed Hornbill, (S) Cálao grande de Panay, (F) Calao de Walden, **II** BUCEROTIDAE Av

Acestrura astreans = Chaetocercus astreans

Acestrura berlepschi = Chaetocercus berlepschi

Acestrura bombus = Chaetocercus bombus

Acestrura heliodor = Chaetocercus heliodor

Acestrura heliodor ssp. *astreans = Chaetocercus astreans*

Acestrura mulsant = Chaetocercus mulsant

Achatinella spp.: (E) Little agate shells, Oahu tree snails **I** ACHATINELLIDAE Ga

Achatinella abbreviata : **I** ACHATINELLIDAE Ga

Achatinella apexfulva : **I** ACHATINELLIDAE Ga

Achatinella bellula : **I** ACHATINELLIDAE Ga

Achatinella buddii : **I** ACHATINELLIDAE Ga

Achatinella bulimoides : **I** ACHATINELLIDAE Ga

Achatinella byronii : **I** ACHATINELLIDAE Ga

Achatinella caesia : **I** ACHATINELLIDAE Ga

Achatinella casta : **I** ACHATINELLIDAE Ga

Achatinella cestus : **I** ACHATINELLIDAE Ga

Achatinella concavospira : **I** ACHATINELLIDAE Ga

Achatinella curta : **I** ACHATINELLIDAE Ga

Achatinella decipiens : **I** ACHATINELLIDAE Ga

Achatinella decora : **I** ACHATINELLIDAE Ga

Checklist of fauna/Lista de especies de fauna/Liste des espèces animales

Achatinella dimorpha : **I** ACHATINELLIDAE Ga
Achatinella elegans : **I** ACHATINELLIDAE Ga
Achatinella fulgens : **I** ACHATINELLIDAE Ga
Achatinella fuscobasis : **I** ACHATINELLIDAE Ga
Achatinella juddii : **I** ACHATINELLIDAE Ga
Achatinella juncea : **I** ACHATINELLIDAE Ga
Achatinella lehuiensis : **I** ACHATINELLIDAE Ga
Achatinella leucorrhaphe : **I** ACHATINELLIDAE Ga
Achatinella lila : **I** ACHATINELLIDAE Ga
Achatinella livida : **I** ACHATINELLIDAE Ga
Achatinella lorata : **I** ACHATINELLIDAE Ga
Achatinella mustelina : **I** ACHATINELLIDAE Ga
Achatinella papyracea : **I** ACHATINELLIDAE Ga
Achatinella phaeozona : **I** ACHATINELLIDAE Ga
Achatinella pulcherrima : **I** ACHATINELLIDAE Ga
Achatinella pupukanioe : **I** ACHATINELLIDAE Ga
Achatinella sowerbyana : **I** ACHATINELLIDAE Ga
Achatinella spaldingi : **I** ACHATINELLIDAE Ga
Achatinella stewartii : **I** ACHATINELLIDAE Ga
Achatinella swiftii : **I** ACHATINELLIDAE Ga
Achatinella taeniolata : **I** ACHATINELLIDAE Ga
Achatinella thaanumi : **I** ACHATINELLIDAE Ga
Achatinella turgida : **I** ACHATINELLIDAE Ga
Achatinella valida : **I** ACHATINELLIDAE Ga
Achatinella viridans : **I** ACHATINELLIDAE Ga
Achatinella vulpina : **I** ACHATINELLIDAE Ga
Achoque (E): *Ambystoma dumerilii*
Acinixys planicauda = Pyxis planicauda
Acinonyx jubatus : (E) Cheetah, Hunting Leopard, (S) Chita, Guepardo, (F) Guépard, **I** FELIDAE Ma
Acipenser aculeatus = Acipenser gueldenstaedtii
Acipenser albula = Huso huso
Acipenser aleutensis = Acipenser transmontanus
Acipenser baerii : (E) Siberian Sturgeon, (F) Esturgeon sibérien, **II** ACIPENSERIDAE Ac
Acipenser brachyrhynchus = Acipenser transmontanus
Acipenser brandtii = Huso huso
Acipenser brevirostrum : (E) Shortnose sturgeon, Short-nosed little sturgeon, (S) Esturión chato, Esturión hociquicorto, (F) Esturgeon à museau court, Esturgeon à nez court, **I** ACIPENSERIDAE Ac
Acipenser carbonarius = Acipenser fulvescens
Acipenser cataphractus = Scaphirhynchus platorynchus
Acipenser dabryanus : (E) Dabry's Sturgeon, Yangtze Sturgeon, **II** ACIPENSERIDAE Ac
Acipenser dauricus = Huso dauricus
Acipenser dubius = Acipenser ruthenus
Acipenser fulvescens : (E) Lake Sturgeon, (S) Esturión lacustre, (F) Esturgeon jaune, **II** ACIPENSERIDAE Ac
Acipenser glaber = Acipenser nudiventris
Acipenser gmelini = Acipenser ruthenus
Acipenser grisescens = Acipenser ruthenus
Acipenser gueldenstaedtii : (E) Azov-Black Sea Sturgeon, Danube Sturgeon, Kura sturgeon, Osetr, Persian sturgeon, Russian Sturgeon, (S) Esturión del Danubio, (F) Esturgeon du Danube, **II** ACIPENSERIDAE Ac
Acipenser heckelii = Acipenser naccarii
Acipenser helops = Acipenser stellatus
Acipenser heptipus = Acipenser fulvescens
Acipenser huso = Huso huso
Acipenser husoniformis = Huso huso
Acipenser jeniscensis = Acipenser ruthenus
Acipenser kamensis = Acipenser ruthenus
Acipenser kikuchii = Acipenser sinensis
Acipenser ladanus = Acipenser naccarii
Acipenser laevis = Acipenser fulvescens
Acipenser legenarius = Acipenser fulvescens
Acipenser leucotica = Acipenser ruthenus
Acipenser liopeltis = Acipenser fulvescens
Acipenser macropthalmus = Acipenser gueldenstaedtii
Acipenser maculosus = Acipenser fulvescens
Acipenser mantschuricus = Huso dauricus
Acipenser marsiglii = Acipenser ruthenus

Acipenser medirostris : (E) Barbel Sturgeon, Green Japanese sturgeon, Green sturgeon, (S) Esturión verde, (F) Esturgeon vert, **II** ACIPENSERIDAE Ac
Acipenser medius = Acipenser gueldenstaedtii
Acipenser mikadoi : (E) Sakhalin Sturgeon, **II** ACIPENSERIDAE Ac
Acipenser multiscutatus = Acipenser schrenckii
Acipenser muricatus = Acipenser fulvescens
Acipenser naccarii : (E) Adriatic Sturgeon, (S) Esturión del Adriático, (F) Esturgeon de l'Adriatique, **II** ACIPENSERIDAE Ac
Acipenser nardoi = Acipenser naccarii
Acipenser nasus = Acipenser naccarii
Acipenser nudiventris : (E) Barbel sturgeon, Bastard Sturgeon, Fringebarbel sturgeon, Ship, Ship Sturgeon, Spiny Sturgeon, Thorn Sturgeon, (S) Esturión barba de flecos, (F) Esturgeon à barbillons frangés, Ship, **II** ACIPENSERIDAE Ac
Acipenser obtusirostris = Acipenser ruthenus
Acipenser orientalis = Huso dauricus
Acipenser oxyrinchus : (E) Atlantic Sturgeon, (S) Esturión del Atlántico, (F) Esturgeon de l'Atlantique, **II** ACIPENSERIDAE Ac
Acipenser persicus : (E) Persian Sturgeon, **II** ACIPENSERIDAE Ac
Acipenser platorynchus = Scaphirhynchus platorynchus
Acipenser platycephalus = Acipenser naccarii
Acipenser primigenius = Acipenser ruthenus
Acipenser pygmaeus = Acipenser gueldenstaedtii
Acipenser pygmaeus = Acipenser ruthenus
Acipenser ratzeburgii = Acipenser stellatus
Acipenser rhynchaeus = Acipenser fulvescens
Acipenser rostratus = Acipenser gueldenstaedtii
Acipenser rubicundus = Acipenser fulvescens
Acipenser rupertianus = Acipenser fulvescens
Acipenser ruthenus : (E) Sterlet, Sterlet sturgeon, (S) Esterlete, Esturión de Siberia, (F) Esturgeon de Sibérie, Sterlet, **II** ACIPENSERIDAE Ac
Acipenser ruzskyi = Acipenser ruthenus
Acipenser schrenckii : (E) Amur Sturgeon, **II** ACIPENSERIDAE Ac
Acipenser schypa = Acipenser nudiventris
Acipenser seuruga = Acipenser stellatus
Acipenser shipa = Acipenser nudiventris
Acipenser shyp = Acipenser nudiventris
Acipenser shypa = Acipenser nudiventris
Acipenser sinensis : (E) Chinese Sturgeon **II** ACIPENSERIDAE Ac
Acipenser stellatus : (E) Sevruga, Star Sturgeon, Starry sturgeon, Stellate Sturgeon, (S) Esturión estrellado, (F) Esturgeon étoilé, Sevruga, **II** ACIPENSERIDAE Ac
Acipenser stenorrhynchus = Acipenser baerii
Acipenser sterlet = Acipenser ruthenus
Acipenser sturio : (E) Atlantic Sturgeon, Baltic Sturgeon, Common Sturgeon, European sturgeon, Sea sturgeon, Sturgeon, (S) Esturión, Esturión común, Marion, Sollo, Sollo real, Sulio, (F) Astourion, Créa, Créac, Créach, Estourioun, Esturgeon, Esturgeon Atlantique, Esturgeon Atlantique d'Europe, Esturgeon Baltique, Esturgeon commun, Esturgeon d'Europe, Esturgeon d'Europe occidentale, Esturien, Esturio, Esturjon, Esturjoun, Étrugeon, Sturion, Sturk, **I** ACIPENSERIDAE Ac
Acipenser sturionellus = Acipenser naccarii
Acipenser transmontanus : (E) Columbia sturgeon, Oregon sturgeon, Pacific sturgeon, Sacramento sturgeon, White sturgeon, (S) Esturión blanco, (F) Esturgeon blanc, **II** ACIPENSERIDAE Ac
Acipenser tuecka = Acipenser gueldenstaedtii
Acipenser turritus = Acipenser nudiventris
Acipenser vallisnerii = Huso huso
ACIPENSERIFORMES spp. : (E) Sturgeons, (S) Esturións, (F) Esturgeons, **I/II** Ac
Acoupa de MacDonald (F): *Cynoscion macdonaldi*

Acrantophis spp.: (E) Madagascar ground boas, (F) Boas des savanes de Madagascar, **I** BOIDAE Re

Acrantophis dumerili : (E) Duméril's Boa, Madagascar Ground Boa, (S) Boa de Duméril, (F) Boa de Duméril, Boa des savanes de Dumeril, **I** BOIDAE Re

Acrantophis madagascariensis : (E) Madagascar Boa, Malagasy Ground Boa, (S) Boa de Madagascar meridional, (F) Boa de Madagascar, Boa des savanes de Madagascar, **I** BOIDAE Re

Acrhelia horrescens : (E) Scalpel Coral, **II** OCULINIDAE An

Acrocephalus rodericanus = Bebrornis rodericanus

Acropora abrolhosensis : **II** ACROPORIDAE An

Acropora abrotanoides : **II** ACROPORIDAE An

Acropora acervata = Acropora humilis

Acropora aculeus : **II** ACROPORIDAE An

Acropora acuminata : **II** ACROPORIDAE An

Acropora akajimensis : **II** ACROPORIDAE An

Acropora angulata = Acropora horrida

Acropora anthocercis : **II** ACROPORIDAE An

Acropora appressa : **II** ACROPORIDAE An

Acropora arabensis : **II** ACROPORIDAE An

Acropora aspera : **II** ACROPORIDAE An

Acropora austera : **II** ACROPORIDAE An

Acropora awi : **II** ACROPORIDAE An

Acropora azurea : **II** ACROPORIDAE An

Acropora batunai : **II** ACROPORIDAE An

Acropora bifurcata : **II** ACROPORIDAE An

Acropora branchi : **II** ACROPORIDAE An

Acropora brueggemanni : **II** ACROPORIDAE An

Acropora bushyensis : **II** ACROPORIDAE An

Acropora canalis = Acropora nobilis

Acropora cardenae : **II** ACROPORIDAE An

Acropora carduus : **II** ACROPORIDAE An

Acropora caroliniana : **II** ACROPORIDAE An

Acropora cerealis : **II** ACROPORIDAE An

Acropora cervicornis : (E) Staghorn Coral, (F) Corail cornes de cerf, **II** ACROPORIDAE An

Acropora chesterfieldensis : **II** ACROPORIDAE An

Acropora clathrata : **II** ACROPORIDAE An

Acropora convexa : **II** ACROPORIDAE An

Acropora cophodactyla : **II** ACROPORIDAE An

Acropora copiosa : **II** ACROPORIDAE An

Acropora corymbosa = Acropora cytherea

Acropora crateriformis : **II** ACROPORIDAE An

Acropora cuneata : **II** ACROPORIDAE An

Acropora cylindrica : **II** ACROPORIDAE An

Acropora cytherea : (E) Table Coral, **II** ACROPORIDAE An

Acropora danai : **II** ACROPORIDAE An

Acropora dendrum : **II** ACROPORIDAE An

Acropora derawanensis : **II** ACROPORIDAE An

Acropora desalwii : **II** ACROPORIDAE An

Acropora diffusa = Acropora acuminata

Acropora digitifera : **II** ACROPORIDAE An

Acropora diomedeae = Acropora nasuta

Acropora divaricata : **II** ACROPORIDAE An

Acropora donei : **II** ACROPORIDAE An

Acropora downingi : **II** ACROPORIDAE An

Acropora echinata : **II** ACROPORIDAE An

Acropora efflorescens : **II** ACROPORIDAE An

Acropora elegans : **II** ACROPORIDAE An

Acropora elegantula : **II** ACROPORIDAE An

Acropora elizabethensis : **II** ACROPORIDAE An

Acropora elseyi : (E) Christmas Coral, **II** ACROPORIDAE An

Acropora eurystoma : **II** ACROPORIDAE An

Acropora exquisita : **II** ACROPORIDAE An

Acropora fastigiata : **II** ACROPORIDAE An

Acropora fenneri : **II** ACROPORIDAE An

Acropora filiformis : **II** ACROPORIDAE An

Acropora florida : **II** ACROPORIDAE An

Acropora formosa : **II** ACROPORIDAE An

Acropora forskalii : **II** ACROPORIDAE An

Acropora gemmifera : **II** ACROPORIDAE An

Acropora glauca : **II** ACROPORIDAE An

Acropora globiceps : **II** ACROPORIDAE An

Acropora gomezi : **II** ACROPORIDAE An

Acropora grandis : **II** ACROPORIDAE An

Acropora granulosa : **II** ACROPORIDAE An

Acropora haimei : **II** ACROPORIDAE An

Acropora halmaherae : **II** ACROPORIDAE An

Acropora hemprichii : **II** ACROPORIDAE An

Acropora hoeksemai : **II** ACROPORIDAE An

Acropora horrida : **II** ACROPORIDAE An

Acropora humilis : **II** ACROPORIDAE An

Acropora hyacinthus : **II** ACROPORIDAE An

Acropora indiana : **II** ACROPORIDAE An

Acropora indonesia : **II** ACROPORIDAE An

Acropora inermis : **II** ACROPORIDAE An

Acropora insignis : **II** ACROPORIDAE An

Acropora intermedia : **II** ACROPORIDAE An

Acropora irregularis : **II** ACROPORIDAE An

Acropora jacquelineae : **II** ACROPORIDAE An

Acropora japonica : **II** ACROPORIDAE An

Acropora kimbeensis : **II** ACROPORIDAE An

Acropora kirstyae : **II** ACROPORIDAE An

Acropora kosurini : **II** ACROPORIDAE An

Acropora lamarcki : **II** ACROPORIDAE An

Acropora latistella : **II** ACROPORIDAE An

Acropora lianae : **II** ACROPORIDAE An

Acropora listeri : **II** ACROPORIDAE An

Acropora loisetteae : **II** ACROPORIDAE An

Acropora lokani : **II** ACROPORIDAE An

Acropora longicyathus : **II** ACROPORIDAE An

Acropora loripes : (E) Bluetip Coral , **II** ACROPORIDAE An

Acropora lovelli : **II** ACROPORIDAE An

Acropora lutkeni : **II** ACROPORIDAE An

Acropora luzonica = Acropora aspera

Acropora macrostoma : **II** ACROPORIDAE An

Acropora magnifica : **II** ACROPORIDAE An

Acropora maryae : **II** ACROPORIDAE An

Acropora massawensis : **II** ACROPORIDAE An

Acropora meridiana : **II** ACROPORIDAE An

Acropora microclados : **II** ACROPORIDAE An

Acropora microphthalma : **II** ACROPORIDAE An

Acropora millepora : **II** ACROPORIDAE An

Acropora minuta : **II** ACROPORIDAE An

Acropora mirabilis : **II** ACROPORIDAE An

Acropora monticulosa : **II** ACROPORIDAE An

Acropora mossambica : **II** ACROPORIDAE An

Acropora multiacuta : **II** ACROPORIDAE An

Acropora nana : **II** ACROPORIDAE An

Acropora nasuta : **II** ACROPORIDAE An

Acropora natalensis : **II** ACROPORIDAE An

Acropora navini : **II** ACROPORIDAE An

Acropora nobilis : **II** ACROPORIDAE An

Acropora ocellata : **II** ACROPORIDAE An

Acropora orbicularis : **II** ACROPORIDAE An

Acropora pagoensis = Acropora eurystoma

Acropora palifera : **II** ACROPORIDAE An

Acropora palmata : (E) Elkhorn Coral, (F) Corail cornes d'élan, **II** ACROPORIDAE An

Acropora palmerae : **II** ACROPORIDAE An

Acropora paniculata : **II** ACROPORIDAE An

Acropora papillare : **II** ACROPORIDAE An

Acropora parahemprichii : **II** ACROPORIDAE An

Acropora parapharaonis : **II** ACROPORIDAE An

Acropora parilis : **II** ACROPORIDAE An

Acropora pectinatus : **II** ACROPORIDAE An

Acropora pharaonis : **II** ACROPORIDAE An

Acropora pichoni : **II** ACROPORIDAE An

Acropora pinguis : **II** ACROPORIDAE An

Acropora plana : **II** ACROPORIDAE An

Acropora plantaginea : **II** ACROPORIDAE An

Acropora platycyathus = Acropora humilis

Acropora plumosa : **II** ACROPORIDAE An

Acropora pocilloporina : **II** ACROPORIDAE An

Acropora polystoma : **II** ACROPORIDAE An

Checklist of fauna/Lista de especies de fauna/Liste des espèces animales

Acropora profusa = *Acropora florida*
Acropora prolifera : (E) Fused Staghorn Coral, **II** ACROPORIDAE An
Acropora prostrata : **II** ACROPORIDAE An
Acropora proximalis : **II** ACROPORIDAE An
Acropora pruinosa : **II** ACROPORIDAE An
Acropora pulchra : **II** ACROPORIDAE An
Acropora rambleri : **II** ACROPORIDAE An
Acropora rayneri = *Acropora granulosa*
Acropora retusa : **II** ACROPORIDAE An
Acropora robusta : **II** ACROPORIDAE An
Acropora rosaria : **II** ACROPORIDAE An
Acropora roseni : **II** ACROPORIDAE An
Acropora rudis : **II** ACROPORIDAE An
Acropora rufus : **II** ACROPORIDAE An
Acropora russelli : **II** ACROPORIDAE An
Acropora samoensis : **II** ACROPORIDAE An
Acropora sarmentosa : **II** ACROPORIDAE An
Acropora scandens = *Acropora pharaonis*
Acropora scherzeriana : **II** ACROPORIDAE An
Acropora schmitti : **II** ACROPORIDAE An
Acropora secale : **II** ACROPORIDAE An
Acropora sekiseiensis : **II** ACROPORIDAE An
Acropora selago : **II** ACROPORIDAE An
Acropora seriata : **II** ACROPORIDAE An
Acropora simplex : **II** ACROPORIDAE An
Acropora solitaryensis : **II** ACROPORIDAE An
Acropora sordiensis : **II** ACROPORIDAE An
Acropora speciosa : **II** ACROPORIDAE An
Acropora spicifera : **II** ACROPORIDAE An
Acropora splendida = *Acropora valencennesii*
Acropora squamosa = *Acropora millepora*
Acropora squarrosa : **II** ACROPORIDAE An
Acropora stoddarti : **II** ACROPORIDAE An
Acropora striata : **II** ACROPORIDAE An
Acropora subglabra : **II** ACROPORIDAE An
Acropora subulata : **II** ACROPORIDAE An
Acropora suharsonoi : **II** ACROPORIDAE An
Acropora sukarnoi : **II** ACROPORIDAE An
Acropora syringodes = *Acropora nana*
Acropora tanegashimensis : **II** ACROPORIDAE An
Acropora tenella : **II** ACROPORIDAE An
Acropora tenuis : **II** ACROPORIDAE An
Acropora teres : **II** ACROPORIDAE An
Acropora tizardi : **II** ACROPORIDAE An
Acropora togianensis : **II** ACROPORIDAE An
Acropora torihalimeda : **II** ACROPORIDAE An
Acropora torresiana : **II** ACROPORIDAE An
Acropora tortuosa : **II** ACROPORIDAE An
Acropora tubigera = *Acropora aculeus*
Acropora tumida : **II** ACROPORIDAE An
Acropora turaki : **II** ACROPORIDAE An
Acropora turbinata = *Acropora hyacinthus*
Acropora tutuilensis : **II** ACROPORIDAE An
Acropora valencennesii : **II** ACROPORIDAE An
Acropora valida : **II** ACROPORIDAE An
Acropora variabilis : **II** ACROPORIDAE An
Acropora variolosa : **II** ACROPORIDAE An
Acropora vaughani : **II** ACROPORIDAE An
Acropora vermiculata : **II** ACROPORIDAE An
Acropora verweyi : **II** ACROPORIDAE An
Acropora walindii : **II** ACROPORIDAE An
Acropora wallaceae : **II** ACROPORIDAE An
Acropora willisae : **II** ACROPORIDAE An
Acropora yongei : **II** ACROPORIDAE An
Acuá (S): *Herpetotheres cachinnans*
Adalbert's Eagle (E): *Aquila adalberti*
Adanson's Hinged Terrapin (E): *Pelusios adansonii*
Adanson's Mud Turtle (E): *Pelusios adansonii*
Addax (E/S/F): *Addax nasomaculatus*
Addax à nez tacheté (F): *Addax nasomaculatus*
Addax nasomaculatus : (E) Addax, (S) Addax, (F) Addax, Addax à nez tacheté, Antilope blanche, **I** BOVIDAE Ma
Addra Gazelle (E): *Gazella dama*

Adelaide Parakeet (E): *Platycercus adelaidae*
Adelaide Rosella (E): *Platycercus adelaidae*
Adelochelys crassa = *Orlitia borneensis*
Adelomyia melanogenys : (E) Speckled Hummingbird, (S) Colibrí jaspeado, Colibrí serrano gargantiazul, Picaflor gargantiazul, (F) Colibri moucheté, **II** TROCHILIDAE Av
Adelopora crassilabrum : **II** STYLASTERIDAE Hy
Adelopora fragilis : **II** STYLASTERIDAE Hy
Adelopora moseleyi : **II** STYLASTERIDAE Hy
Adelopora pseudothyron : **II** STYLASTERIDAE Hy
Admiralty Flying-fox (E): *Pteropus admiralitatum*
Admiralty Hawk-Owl (E): *Ninox meeki*
Admiralty island Hawk-owl (E): *Ninox meeki*
Adorable Coquette (E): *Lophornis adorabilis*
Adriatic Sturgeon (E): *Acipenser naccarii*
Aegolius acadicus : (E) Northern Saw-whet Owl, Saw-whet Owl, (S) Mochuelo cabezón, Tecolote-abetero norteño, (F) Petite nyctale, **II** STRIGIDAE Av
Aegolius funereus : (E) Boreal Owl, Tengmalm's Owl, (S) Lechuza de Tengmalm, Mochuelo boreal, (F) Chouette de Tengmalm, Engoulevent d'Europe, Nyctale de Tengmalm, **II** STRIGIDAE Av
Aegolius harrisii : (E) Buff-fronted Owl, (S) Carburé acanelado, Curucucú barriga amarilla, Lechucita acanelada, Mochuelo canela, (F) Chouette de Harris, Nyctale de Harris, **II** STRIGIDAE Av
Aegolius ridgwayi : (E) Unspotted Saw-whet Owl, (S) Mochuelo moreno, (F) Nyctale immaculée, **II** STRIGIDAE Av
Aegypius calvus = *Sarcogyps calvus*
Aegypius monachus : (E) Black Vulture, Cinereous Vulture, (S) Buitre negro, (F) Vautour moine, **II** ACCIPITRIDAE Av
Aegypius occipitalis = *Trigonoceps occipitalis*
Aegypius tracheliotus = *Torgos tracheliotus*
Afep Pigeon (E): *Columba unicincta*
Afghan Fox (E): *Vulpes cana*
Afghan Tortoise (E): *Testudo horsfieldii*
African Ass (E): *Equus africanus*
African Barred Owlet (E): *Glaucidium capense*
African Bay Owl (E): *Phodilus prigoginei*
African Baza (E): *Aviceda cuculoides*
African Black Eagle (E): *Aquila verreauxii*
African Black Terrapin (E): *Pelusios niger*
African Blind Barb Fish (E): *Caecobarbus geertsi*
African Burrowing Python (E): *Calabaria reinhardtii*
African Caracal (E): *Caracal caracal*
African Chameleon (E): *Chamaeleo africanus*
African Civet (E): *Civettictis civetta*
African Clawless Otter (E): *Aonyx capensis*
African Collared-Dove (E): *Streptopelia roseogrisea*
African Crocodile (E): *Crocodylus niloticus*
African Crowned Eagle (E): *Stephanoaetus coronatus*
African Cuckoo-Falcon (E): *Aviceda cuculoides*
African Cuckoo-Hawk (E): *Aviceda cuculoides*
African Dwarf Crocodile (E): *Osteolaemus tetraspis*
African Eagle (E): *Hieraaetus spilogaster*
African Eagle-Owl (E): *Bubo africanus*
African Elephant (E): *Loxodonta africana*
African Firefinch (E): *Lagonosticta rubricata*
African Fish-Eagle (E): *Haliaeetus vocifer*
African Forest Turtle (E): *Pelusios gabonensis*
African Golden Cat (E): *Profelis aurata*
African Goshawk (E): *Accipiter tachiro*
African Grass-Owl (E): *Tyto capensis*
African Green-Pigeon (E): *Treron calva*
African Gymnogene (E): *Polyboroides typus*
African Harrier-Hawk (E): *Polyboroides typus*
African Hawk-Eagle (E): *Hieraaetus spilogaster*
African Helmeted Turtle (E): *Pelomedusa subrufa*
African Hobby (E): *Falco cuvierii*
African Large-grain Lizard (E): *Varanus exanthematicus*
African Little Sparrowhawk (E): *Accipiter minullus*
African Long-tailed Hawk (E): *Urotriorchis macrourus*

Checklist of fauna/Lista de especies de fauna/Liste des espèces animales

African Manatee (E): *Trichechus senegalensis*
African Marsh Owl (E): *Asio capensis*
African Marsh-Harrier (E): *Circus ranivorus*
African Mourning Dove (E): *Streptopelia decipiens*
African Orange-bellied Parrot (E): *Poicephalus rufiventris*
African Penguin (E): *Spheniscus demersus*
African Pygmy Falcon (E): *Polihierax semitorquatus*
African Pygmy-goose (E): *Nettapus auritus*
African Python (E): *Python sebae*
African Quailfinch (E): *Ortygospiza atricollis*
African Red-tailed Buzzard (E): *Buteo auguralis*
African Rock Python (E): *Python sebae*
African Savanna Monitor (E): *Varanus exanthematicus*
African Savannah Elephant (E): *Loxodonta africana*
African Scops-Owl (E): *Otus scops*
African Serpent-Eagle (E): *Dryotriorchis spectabilis*
African Serrated Tortoise (E): *Psammobates oculiferus*
African Sharp-nosed Crocodile (E): *Crocodylus cataphractus*
African Silverbill (E): *Lonchura cantans*
African Slender-snouted Crocodile (E): *Crocodylus cataphractus*
African Small-grain Lizard (E): *Varanus niloticus*
African Softshell Turtle (E): *Trionyx triunguis*
African Spiny-tailed Lizard (E): *Cordylus polyzonus*
African Spurred Tortoise (E): *Geochelone sulcata*
African Swallow-tailed Kite (E): *Chelictinia riocourii*
African Tent Tortoise (E): *Psammobates tentorius*
African viviparous toads (E): *Nectophrynoides* spp.
African White-backed Vulture (E): *Gyps africanus*
African Wild Ass (E): *Equus africanus*
African Wood-Owl (E): *Strix woodfordii*
African Wood-Pigeon (E): *Columba unicincta*
Afro-Australian Fur Seal (E): *Arctocephalus pusillus*
Afrotis atra = *Eupodotis afra*
Agapornis canus : (E) Grey-headed Lovebird, Madagascar Lovebird, (S) Inseparable malgache, (F) Inséparable à tête grise, **II** PSITTACIDAE Av
Agapornis fischeri : (E) Fischer's Lovebird, (S) Inseparable de Fischer, (F) Inséparable de Fischer, Perruche de Fischer, **II** PSITTACIDAE Av
Agapornis lilianae : (E) Lilian's Lovebird, Nyasa Lovebird, (S) Inseparable del Nyasa, (F) Inséparable de Lilian, Perruche de Lilian, **II** PSITTACIDAE Av
Agapornis lilianae ssp. *nigrigenis* = *Agapornis nigrigenis*
Agapornis nigrigenis : (E) Black-cheeked Lovebird, (S) Inseparable cachetón, (F) Inséparable à joues noires, Perruche à joue noire, **II** PSITTACIDAE Av
Agapornis personatus : (E) Black-masked Lovebird, Masked Lovebird, Yellow-collared Lovebird, (S) Inseparable cabecinegro, (F) Inséparable masqué, Perruche masqué, **II** PSITTACIDAE Av
Agapornis pullarius : (E) Red-faced Lovebird, Red-headed Lovebird, (S) Inseparable carirrojo, (F) Inséparable à tête rouge, Perruche à tête rouge, **II** PSITTACIDAE Av
Agapornis roseicollis : (E) Peach-faced Lovebird, Rosy-faced Lovebird, (S) Inseparable de Namibia, (F) Inséparable à face rose, Inséparable rosegorge, Perruche à face rose, **II** PSITTACIDAE Av
Agapornis swindernianus : (E) Black-collared Lovebird, (S) Inseparable acollarado, Inseparable de collera, (F) Inséparable à collier noir, Inséparable de Swindern, Perruche de Swindern, **II** PSITTACIDAE Av
Agapornis taranta : (E) Abyssinian Lovebird, Black-winged Lovebird, (S) Inseparable Abisinio, (F) Inséparable d'Abyssinie, **II** PSITTACIDAE Av
Agaricia agaricites : (E) Leaf Coral, Lettuce Coral, **II** AGARICIIDAE An
Agaricia fragilis : (E) Fragile Saucer Coral, **II** AGARICIIDAE An
Agaricia grahamae : (E) Graham's Sheet Coral, **II** AGARICIIDAE An
Agaricia humilis : (E) Lowrelief Lettuce Coral, **II** AGARICIIDAE An

Agaricia lamarcki : (E) Lamarck's Sheet Coral, **II** AGARICIIDAE An
Agaricia tenuifolia : (E) Ribbon Coral, Thin-leaf Lettuce Coral, **II** AGARICIIDAE An
Agaricia undata : (E) Scroll Coral, **II** AGARICIIDAE An
Agelaius flavus : (E) Saffron-cowled Blackbird, (S) Dragón, Mirlo americano pechiamarillo, Tordo amarillo, Tordo de cabeza amarilla, (F) Carouge safran, Ictéride à tête jaune, **I** ICTERIDAE Av
Agelastes meleagrides : (E) White-breasted Guineafowl, (S) Pintada de pechuga blanca, Pintada pechiblanca, Pintado de pecho blanco, (F) Pintade à poitrine blanche, **III** PHASIANIDAE Av
Agile Gibbon (E): *Hylobates agilis*
Agile Mangabey (E): *Cercocebus agilis*
Aglaeactis aliciae : (E) Purple-backed Sunbeam, (S) Colibrí de Alicia, (F) Colibri d'Alice, **II** TROCHILIDAE Av
Aglaeactis castelnaudii : (E) White-tufted Sunbeam, (S) Colibrí condecorado, (F) Colibri de Castelneau, **II** TROCHILIDAE Av
Aglaeactis cupripennis : (E) Shining Sunbeam, (S) Colibrí cobrizo, Rayito brillante, (F) Colibri étincelant, **II** TROCHILIDAE Av
Aglaeactis pamela : (E) Black-hooded Sunbeam, (S) Colibrí negrito, (F) Colibri paméla, **II** TROCHILIDAE Av
Aglaiocercus berlepschi : (E) Venezuelan Sylph, **II** TROCHILIDAE Av
Aglaiocercus coelestis : (E) Violet-tailed Sylph, (S) Silfo celeste, Silfo colivioleta, (F) Sylphe à queue violette, **II** TROCHILIDAE Av
Aglaiocercus emmae = *Aglaiocercus kingi*
Aglaiocercus kingi : (E) Long-tailed Sylph, (S) Colibrí coludo azul, Silfo coludo, Silfo de King, (F) Sylphe à queue d'azur, **II** TROCHILIDAE Av
Agouti (F): *Agouti paca*
Agouti paca : (E) Paca, Spotted Paca, (S) Paca, (F) Agouti, Paca, **III** AGOUTIDAE Ma
Agouti ponctué (F): *Dasyprocta punctata*
Agoutí rojizo (S): *Dasyprocta punctata*
Agra Lizard (E): *Varanus griseus*
Agra Monitor (E): *Varanus griseus*
Agriocharis ocellata : (E) Ocellated Turkey, (S) Guajolote ocelado, Pavo ocelado, (F) Dindon ocellé, **III** PHASIANIDAE Av
Agrionemys horsfieldii = *Testudo horsfieldii*
Aguara guazu (S): *Chrysocyon brachyurus*
Aguila arpía (S): *Harpia harpyja*
Aguila audaz (S): *Aquila audax*
Aguila blanca (S): *Leucopternis polionota*
Aguila blanquinegra (S): *Spizastur melanoleucus*
Aguila cabeciblanca (S): *Haliaeetus leucocephalus*
Aguila cabeza blanca (S): *Haliaeetus leucocephalus*
Aguila cafre (S): *Aquila verreauxii*
Aguila calzada (S): *Hieraaetus pennatus*
Aguila castaña (S): *Oroaetus isidori*
Aguila colorada (S): *Busarellus nigricollis*
Aguila comemonos (S): *Pithecophaga jefferyi*
Aguila copetuda africana (S): *Lophaetus occipitalis*
Aguila coronada (S): *Harpyhaliaetus coronatus*
Aguila coronada (S): *Stephanoaetus coronatus*
Aguila coronada rabuda (S): *Stephanoaetus coronatus*
Aguila crestada (S): *Morphnus guianensis*
Aguila crestilarga (S): *Lophaetus occipitalis*
Aguila culebrera (S): *Circaetus gallicus*
Aguila culebrera colilarga (S): *Dryotriorchis spectabilis*
Aguila culebrera culiblanca (S): *Circaetus cinerascens*
Aguila culebrera de Brown (S): *Circaetus cinereus*
Aguila de Azara (S): *Harpyhaliaetus coronatus*
Aguila de Bonelli (S): *Hieraaetus fasciatus*
Aguila de Copete (S): *Oroaetus isidori*
Aguila de Penacho (S): *Spizaetus ornatus*
Aguila de Walhberg (S): *Aquila wahlbergi*
Aguila elegante (S): *Spizaetus ornatus*

Checklist of fauna/Lista de especies de fauna/Liste des espèces animales

Aguila escudada (S): *Geranoaetus melanoleucus*
Aguila Esteparia (S): *Aquila rapax*
Aguila harpía (S): *Harpia harpyja*
Aguila imperial (S): *Aquila heliaca*
Aguila imperial ibérica (S): *Aquila adalberti*
Aguila Imperial Oriental (S): *Aquila heliaca*
Aguila marcial (S): *Polemaetus bellicosus*
Aguila milana (S): *Ictinaetus malayensis*
Aguila moluqueña (S): *Aquila gurneyi*
Aguila monera (S): *Morphnus guianensis*
Àguila monera (S): *Pithecophaga jefferyi*
Aguila mora (S): *Geranoaetus melanoleucus*
Aguila Moteada (S): *Aquila clanga*
Aguila negra (S): *Buteogallus urubitinga*
Aguila perdicera (S): *Hieraaetus fasciatus*
Aguila perdicera africana (S): *Hieraaetus spilogaster*
Aguila Pescadora (S): *Pandion haliaetus*
Aguila poma (S): *Oroaetus isidori*
Aguila Pomerana (S): *Aquila pomarina*
Aguila Rapáz (S): *Aquila rapax*
Aguila Real (S): *Aquila chrysaetos/ Geranoaetus melanoleucus*
Aguila sangual (S): *Pandion haliaetus*
Aguila solitaria (S): *Harpyhaliaetus solitarius*
Aguila tirana (S): *Spizaetus tyrannus*
Aguila volatinera (S): *Terathopius ecaudatus*
Aguila-azor africana (S): *Hieraaetus spilogaster*
Aguila-azor blanca (S): *Spizaetus ornatus*
Aguila-azor blanquinegra (S): *Spizastur melanoleucus*
Aguila-azor chica (S): *Spizastur melanoleucus*
Aguila-azor congoleña (S): *Spizaetus africanus*
Aguila-azor de Ayres (S): *Hieraaetus ayresii*
Aguila-azor de Célebes (S): *Spizaetus lanceolatus*
Aguila-azor de Java (S): *Spizaetus bartelsi*
Aguila-azor de Wallace (S): *Spizaetus nanus*
Aguila-azor filipina (S): *Spizaetus philippensis*
Aguila-azor galana (S): *Spizaetus ornatus*
Aguila-azor Indonesia (S): *Spizaetus alboniger*
Aguila-azor montañesa (S): *Spizaetus nipalensis*
Aguila-azor negra (S): *Spizaetus tyrannus*
Aguila-azor perdicera (S): *Hieraaetus fasciatus*
Aguila-azor variable (S): *Spizaetus cirrhatus*
Aguila-azor ventrirroja (S): *Hieraaetus kienerii*
Aguilila blanca (S): *Leucopternis albicollis*
Aguililla aluda (S): *Buteo platypterus*
Aguililla artica (S): *Buteo lagopus*
Aguililla aura (S): *Buteo albonotatus*
Aguililla australiana (S): *Hieraaetus morphnoides*
Aguililla calzada (S): *Hieraaetus pennatus*
Aguililla caminera (S): *Buteo magnirostris*
Aguililla coliblanca (S): *Buteo albicaudatus*
Aguililla colicorta (S): *Buteo brachyurus*
Aguililla colirroja (S): *Buteo jamaicensis*
Aguililla de Harris (S): *Parabuteo unicinctus*
Aguililla de Swainson (S): *Buteo swainsoni*
Aguililla gris (S): *Asturina plagiata*
Aguililla langostera (S): *Butastur rufipennis*
Aguililla negra mayor (S): *Buteogallus urubitinga*
Aguililla negra menor (S): *Buteogallus anthracinus*
Aguililla pechirroja (S): *Buteo lineatus*
Aguililla real (S): *Buteo regalis*
Aguilucho cabecinegro (S): *Buteo albicaudatus*
Aguilucho Cenizo (S): *Circus pygargus*
Aguilucho chico (S): *Buteo albigula*
Aguilucho cola colorada (S): *Buteo ventralis*
Aguilucho cola corta (S): *Buteo brachyurus*
Aguilucho colorada (S): *Buteogallus meridionalis*
Aguilucho común (S): *Buteo polyosoma*
Aguilucho de azara (S): *Circus buffoni*
Aguilucho de ciénaga (S): *Circus buffoni*
Aguilucho gris (S): *Asturina nitida*
Aguilucho lagunero (S): *Circus aeruginosus*
Aguilucho lagunero del pacifico (S): *Circus approximans*
Aguilucho lagunero etiópico (S): *Circus ranivorus*
Aguilucho lagunero malgache (S): *Circus maillardi*

Aguilucho lagunero occidental (S): *Circus aeruginosus*
Aguilucho lagunero oriental (S): *Circus spilonotus*
Aguilucho langostero (S): *Buteo swainsoni*
Aguilucho Lanunero del Pacifico (S): *Circus approximans*
Aguilucho moteado (E): *Circus assimilis*
Aguilucho negro (S): *Circus maurus*
Aguilucho pálido (S): *Circus cyaneus*
Aguilucho papialbo (S): *Circus macrourus*
Aguilucho pío (S): *Circus melanoleucos*
Aguilucho puna (S): *Buteo poecilochrous*
Aguilucho sabanero (S): *Buteogallus meridionalis*
Aguilucho vari (S): *Circus cinereus*
Aguilucho variado (S): *Buteo polyosoma*
Aguilucho-caricalvo común (S): *Polyboroides typus*
Aguilucho-caricalvo malgache (S): *Polyboroides radiatus*
Agutí de América Central (S): *Dasyprocta punctata*
Agyrtria brevirostris : (E) White-chested Emerald, (S) Amazilia pechiblanca, Diamante colidorado, (F) Ariane à poitrine blanche, **II** TROCHILIDAE Av
Agyrtria candida : (E) White-bellied Emerald, (S) Amazilia cándida, Esmeralda viente-blanco, (F) Ariane candide, **II** TROCHILIDAE Av
Agyrtria cyanocephala : (E) Azure-crowned Hummingbird, Pied-billed Azurecrown, (S) Amazilia coroniazul, Colibrí coroniazul, (F) Ariane à couronne azur, **II** TROCHILIDAE Av
Agyrtria franciae : (E) Andean Emerald, (S) Amazilia andina, (F) Ariane de Francia, **II** TROCHILIDAE Av
Agyrtria leucogaster : (E) Plain-bellied Emerald, (S) Amazilia ventriblanca, Diamante ventriblanco, (F) Ariane vert-doré, **II** TROCHILIDAE Av
Agyrtria rondoniae : (E) Rondônia Emerald, **II** TROCHILIDAE Av
Agyrtria versicolor : (E) Versicolored Emerald, (S) Amazilia versicolor, Diamante multicolor, Picaflor pequeño verde, (F) Ariane versicolore, **II** TROCHILIDAE Av
Agyrtria violiceps : (E) Violet-crowned Hummingbird, (S) Amazilia coronivioleta, Colibrí corona-violeta, (F) Ariane à couronne violette, **II** TROCHILIDAE Av
Agyrtria viridifrons : (E) Green-fronted Hummingbird, (S) Amazilia frentiverde, Colibrí corona-verde, (F) Ariane à front vert, **II** TROCHILIDAE Av
Aï de Bolivie (F): *Bradypus variegatus*
Aigle à épaules blanches (F): *Aquila adalberti*
Aigle à tête blanche (F): *Haliaeetus leucocephalus*
Aigle à ventre roux (F): *Hieraaetus kienerii*
Aigle blanchard (F): *Stephanoaetus coronatus*
Aigle botté (F): *Hieraaetus pennatus*
Aigle couronné (F): *Stephanoaetus coronatus*
Aigle criard (F): *Aquila clanga*
Aigle d'Australie (F): *Aquila audax*
Aigle d'Ayres (F): *Hieraaetus ayresii*
Aigle de Blyth (F): *Spizaetus alboniger*
Aigle de Bonelli (F): *Hieraaetus fasciatus*
Aigle de Cassin (F): *Spizaetus africanus*
Aigle de Gurney (F): *Aquila gurneyi*
Aigle de Java (F): *Spizaetus bartelsi*
Aigle de Nouvelle-Guinée (F): *Harpyopsis novaeguineae*
Aigle de Verreaux (F): *Aquila verreauxii*
Aigle de Wahlberg (F): *Aquila wahlbergi*
Aigle de Wallace (F): *Spizaetus nanus*
Aigle des Célèbes (F): *Spizaetus lanceolatus*
Aigle des Philippines (F): *Spizaetus philippensis/ Pithecophaga jefferyi*
Aigle des singes (F): *Pithecophaga jefferyi*
Aigle des steppes (F): *Aquila nipalensis*
Aigle d'Isidore (F): *Oroaetus isidori*
Aigle doré (F): *Aquila chrysaetos*
Aigle fascié (F): *Hieraaetus spilogaster*
Aigle harpie (F): *Harpia harpyja*
Aigle huppard (F): *Lophaetus occipitalis*
Aigle huppé (F): *Spizaetus cirrhatus*
Aigle ibérique (F): *Aquila adalberti*
Aigle impérial (F): *Aquila heliaca*

Checklist of fauna/Lista de especies de fauna/Liste des espèces animales

Aigle impérial espagnol (F): *Aquila adalberti*
Aigle mangeur de singes (F): *Pithecophaga jefferyi*
Aigle martial (F): *Polemaetus bellicosus*
Aigle montagnard (F): *Spizaetus nipalensis*
Aigle nain (F): *Hieraaetus morphnoides*
Aigle noir (F): *Ictinaetus malayensis*
Aigle noir et blanc (F): *Spizastur melanoleucus*
Aigle orné (F): *Spizaetus ornatus*
Aigle pêcheur (F): *Pandion haliaetus*
Aigle pêcheur africain (F): *Haliaeetus vocifer*
Aigle pomarin (F): *Aquila pomarina*
Aigle ravisseur (F): *Aquila rapax*
Aigle royal (F): *Aquila chrysaetos*
Aigle serpentaire (F): *Dryotriorchis spectabilis/ Eutriorchis astur*
Aigle tyran (F): *Spizaetus tyrannus*
Aigle-autour fascié (F): *Hieraaetus spilogaster*
Aigrette garzette (F): *Egretta garzetta*
Ailuropoda melanoleuca : (E) Giant Panda, (S) Panda gigante, (F) Panda, Panda géant, **I** URSIDAE Ma
Ailurus fulgens : (E) Lesser Panda, Red Cat-bear, Red Panda, (S) Panda chico, Panda rojo, Pequeño panda, (F) Panda éclatant, Petit panda, **I** URSIDAE Ma
Ailurus ochraceus = Ailurus fulgens
Ajolote de lago Pátzquaro (S): *Ambystoma dumerilii*
Ajolote mexicano (S): *Ambystoma mexicanum*
Akun Eagle-Owl (E): *Bubo leucostictus*
Ala de sable anteado (S): *Campylopterus duidae*
Ala de sable gris (S): *Campylopterus largipennis*
Ala de sable pechivioleta (S): *Campylopterus falcatus*
Ala de sable rufo (S): *Campylopterus hyperythrus*
Ala de sable verde (S): *Campylopterus ensipennis*
Alabama Lamp Pearly Mussel (E): *Lampsilis virescens*
Alabama Lampmussel (E): *Lampsilis virescens*
Alabama Sturgeon (E): *Scaphirhynchus suttkusi*
Alagoas Curassow (E): *Mitu mitu*
Alajuela Toad (E): *Bufo periglenes*
Alasable azulino (S): *Campylopterus falcatus*
Alasable del Napo (S): *Campylopterus largipennis*
Alatotrochus rubescens : **II** TURBINOLIIDAE An
Alazafiro grande (S): *Pterophanes cyanopterus*
Albatros (S): *Diomedea albatrus*
Albatros à queue courte (F): *Diomedea albatrus*
Albatros colicorto (S): *Diomedea albatrus*
Albatros de Steller (F): *Diomedea albatrus*
Albatros rabón (S): *Diomedea albatrus*
Albertine Owlet (E): *Glaucidium albertinum*
Albert's Curassow (E): *Crax alberti*
Alcaraván Americana (S): *Burhinus bistriatus*
Alcaraván Venozolano (S): *Burhinus bistriatus*
Alcatraz de Abbott (S): *Papasula abbotti*
Alcotán (S): *Falco subbuteo*
Alcotán africano (S): *Falco cuvierii*
Alcotán australiano (S): *Falco longipennis*
Alcotán cuellirrojo (S): *Falco chicquera*
Alcotán europeo (S): *Falco subbuteo*
Alcotán filipino (S): *Falco severus*
Alcotán turumti (S): *Falco chicquera*
Aldabra Day Gecko (E): *Phelsuma abbotti*
Aldabra Flying-fox (E): *Pteropus aldabrensis*
Aldabra Giant Tortoise (E): *Geochelone gigantea*
Aldabrachelys elephantina = Geochelone gigantea
Alder Parrot (E): *Amazona tucumana*
Alecto à bec blanc (F): *Bubalornis albirostris*
Aleutian Canada Goose (E): *Branta canadensis leucopareia*
Aleutian Goose (E): *Branta canadensis leucopareia*
Alexandra's Parrot (E): *Polytelis alexandrae*
Alexandrine Parakeet (E): *Psittacula eupatria*
Aligátor de China (S): *Alligator sinensis*
Aligator del Mississippi (S): *Alligator mississippiensis*
Aligators (S): CROCODYLIA spp. Re
Alimoche (S): *Neophron percnopterus*
Alimoche Común (S): *Neophron percnopterus*
Alimoche sombrío (S): *Necrosyrtes monachus*

Alisterus amboinensis : (E) Ambon King-Parrot, Moluccan King-Parrot, (S) Papagayo Moluqueño, (F) Perruche tricolore, **II** PSITTACIDAE Av
Alisterus chloropterus : (E) Green-winged King-Parrot, Papuan King-Parrot, (S) Papagayo papú, (F) Perruche à ailes vertes, **II** PSITTACIDAE Av
Alisterus scapularis : (E) Australian King-Parrot, (S) Papagayo australiano, (F) Perruche royale, **II** PSITTACIDAE Av
Allamand's Grison (E): *Galictis vittata*
Allenopithecus nigroviridis : (E) Allen's Swamp Monkey, (F) Cercopithèque de Allen, **II** CERCOPITHECIDAE Ma
Allen's Bushbaby (E): *Galago alleni*
Allen's Galago (E): *Galago alleni*
Allen's Hummingbird (E): *Selasphorus sasin*
Allen's Squirrel Galago (E): *Galago alleni*
Allen's Swamp Monkey (E): *Allenopithecus nigroviridis*
Alligator américain (F): *Alligator mississippiensis*
Alligator de Chine (F): *Alligator sinensis*
Alligator du Mississippi (F): *Alligator mississippiensis*
Alligator mississippiensis : (E) American Alligator, (S) Aligator del Mississippi, (F) Alligator américain, Alligator du Mississippi, **II** ALLIGATORIDAE Re
Alligator sinensis : (E) China Alligator, Chinese Alligator, (S) Aligátor de China, (F) Alligator de Chine, **I** ALLIGATORIDAE Re
Alligators (E): CROCODYLIA spp. Re
Allobates femoralis = Epipedobates femoralis
Allocèbe (F): *Allocebus trichotis*
Allocebus trichotis : (E) Hairy-eared Dwarf Lemur, (S) Lemur orejipeludo, (F) Allocèbe, Chirogale aux oreilles poilues, **I** CHEIROGALEIDAE Ma
Allopathes desbonni : **II** ANTIPATHIDAE An
Alopochen aegyptiacus : (E) Egyptian Goose, (S) Ganso del Nilo, Oca del Nilo, (F) Oie d'Égypte, Ouette d'Égypte, **III** ANATIDAE Av
Alouatta arctoidea = Alouatta seniculus
Alouatta belzebul : (E) Black-and-red Howling Monkey, Red-handed Howler, Red-handed Howling Monkey, (F) Hurleur à mains rousses, **II** CEBIDAE Ma
Alouatta beniensis = Alouatta fusca
Alouatta caraya : (E) Black Howler, Black Howling Monkey, (F) Hurleur noir, **II** CEBIDAE Ma
Alouatta coibensis : (E) Coiba Island Howling Monkey **I** CEBIDAE Ma
Alouatta fusca : (E) Brown Howler, Brown Howling Monkey, (F) Hurleur brun, **II** CEBIDAE Ma
Alouatta guariba = Alouatta fusca
Alouatta guariba ssp. *guariba = Alouatta fusca*
Alouatta nigerrima = Alouatta belzebul
Alouatta palliata : (E) Mantled Howler, Mantled Howling Monkey, (S) Aullado, Guariba Peludo, Mono aullador de Guatemala, Mono congo, Mono negro, Mono saraguato, Zaraguate, (F) Hurleur du Guatemala, **I** CEBIDAE Ma
Alouatta palliata ssp. *coibensis = Alouatta coibensis*
Alouatta pigra : (E) Guatemalan Howler, Guatemalan Howling Monkey, (S) Araguato de Guatemala, (F) Hurleur du Guatemala, **I** CEBIDAE Ma
Alouatta sara : (E) Bolivian Red Howling Monkey, **II** CEBIDAE Ma
Alouatta seniculus : (E) Red Howler, Red Howling Monkey, (F) Hurleur roux, **II** CEBIDAE Ma
Alouatta seniculus ssp. *sara = Alouatta sara*
Alouatta villosa = Alouatta pigra
Alpine Musk Deer (E): *Moschus chrysogaster*
Alpine Weasel (E): *Mustela altaica*
Altiphrynoides spp.: (E) Ethiopian toads, (S) Sapos vivíparos, (F) Crapauds vivipares, Grenouille dorée du Panamà, **I** BUFONIDAE Am
Altiphrynoides malcolmi : (E) Malcolm's Ethiopian Toad, (S) Sapo vivíparo de Malcolm, (F) Nectophrynoide de Malcolm, **I** BUFONIDAE Am
Alto de Buey Poison Frog (E): *Minyobates altobueyensis*

Alveopora allingi : **II** PORITIDAE An
Alveopora catalai : **II** PORITIDAE An
Alveopora daedalea : **II** PORITIDAE An
Alveopora excelsa : **II** PORITIDAE An
Alveopora fenestrata : **II** PORITIDAE An
Alveopora gigas : **II** PORITIDAE An
Alveopora japonica : **II** PORITIDAE An
Alveopora marionensis : **II** PORITIDAE An
Alveopora minuta : **II** PORITIDAE An
Alveopora ocellata : **II** PORITIDAE An
Alveopora spongiosa : **II** PORITIDAE An
Alveopora tizardi : **II** PORITIDAE An
Alveopora verrilliana : **II** PORITIDAE An
Alveopora viridis : **II** PORITIDAE An
Amadina fasciata : (E) Cut-throat, Ribbon Finch, (S) Amadina gorgirroja, (F) Amadine cou-coupé, Cou-coupé, **III** ESTRILDIDAE Av
Amadina gorgirroja (S): *Amadina fasciata*
Amadine cou-coupé (F): *Amadina fasciata*
Amandava formosa : (E) Green Avadavat, (S) Estrilda verde, (F) Bengali vert, **II** ESTRILDIDAE Av
Amandava subflava : (E) Golden-breasted Waxbill, Orange-breasted Waxbill, Zebra Waxbill, (S) Astrilda pechigualda, (F) Bengali zébré, Ventre orange, **III** ESTRILDIDAE Av
Amapola (S): *Amazona viridigenalis*
Amarante à ventre noir (F): *Lagonosticta rara*
Amarante commun (F): *Lagonosticta senegala*
Amarante du Sénégal (F): *Lagonosticta senegala*
Amarante flambé (F): *Lagonosticta rubricata*
Amarante foncé (F): *Lagonosticta rubricata*
Amarante masqué (F): *Lagonosticta vinacea*
Amarante pointé (F): *Lagonosticta rufopicta*
Amarante rare (F): *Lagonosticta rara*
Amarante vineux (F): *Lagonosticta vinacea*
Amazilia alticola : (E) Loja Hummingbird, **II** TROCHILIDAE Av
Amazilia amabilis = Polyerata amabilis
Amazilia amabilis ssp. *decora = Polyerata amabilis*
Amazilia amable (S): *Polyerata amabilis*
Amazilia amazilia : (E) Amazilia Hummingbird, (S) Amazilia costeña, Amazilia ventrirrufa, (F) Ariane de Lesson, **II** TROCHILIDAE Av
Amazilia andina (S): *Agyrtria franciae*
Amazilia berilina (S): *Saucerottia beryllina*
Amazilia beryllina = Saucerottia beryllina
Amazilia boucardi = Polyerata boucardi
Amazilia bronceada coliazul (S): *Saucerottia tobaci*
Amazilia cándida (S): *Agyrtria candida*
Amazilia candida = Agyrtria candida
Amazilia canela (S): *Amazilia rutila*
Amazilia capiazul (S): *Saucerottia cyanifrons*
Amazilia castaneiventris : (E) Chestnut-bellied Hummingbird, (S) Amazilia ventricastaña, (F) Ariane à ventre roux, **II** TROCHILIDAE Av
Amazilia chionogaster = Leucippus chionogaster
Amazilia chionopectus = Agyrtria brevirostris
Amazilia coliazul (S): *Saucerottia cyanura*
Amazilia colimorada (S): *Saucerottia viridigaster*
Amazilia colirrufa (S): *Amazilia tzacatl*
Amazilia coroniazul (S): *Agyrtria cyanocephala*
Amazilia coronivioleta (S): *Agyrtria violiceps*
Amazilia costeña (S): *Amazilia amazilia*
Amazilia cyanifrons = Saucerottia cyanifrons
Amazilia cyanocephala = Agyrtria cyanocephala
Amazilia cyanura = Saucerottia cyanura
Amazilia de Edward (S): *Saucerottia edward*
Amazilia de manglar (S): *Polyerata boucardi*
Amazilia de Rosenberg (S): *Polyerata rosenbergi*
Amazilia de Tobago (S): *Saucerottia tobaci*
Amazilia decora = Polyerata amabilis
Amazilia edward = Saucerottia edward
Amazilia fimbriata = Polyerata fimbriata
Amazilia franciae = Agyrtria franciae
Amazilia frentiverde (S): *Agyrtria viridifrons*

Amazilia gorjibrillante (S): *Polyerata fimbriata*
Amazilia handleyi = Amazilia tzacatl
Amazilia Hondureña (S): *Polyerata luciae*
Amazilia Hummingbird (E): *Amazilia amazilia*
Amazilia lactea = Polyerata lactea
Amazilia leucogaster = Agyrtria leucogaster
Amazilia listada (S): *Polyerata fimbriata*
Amazilia luciae = Polyerata luciae
Amazilia microrhyncha = Agyrtria cyanocephala
Amazilia pechiazul (S): *Polyerata amabilis*
Amazilia pechiblanca (S): *Agyrtria brevirostris*
Amazilia pechimorada (S): *Polyerata rosenbergi*
Amazilia rondoniae = Agyrtria rondoniae
Amazilia rosenbergi = Polyerata rosenbergi
Amazilia rutila : (E) Cinnamon Hummingbird, (S) Amazilia canela, Colibrí canelo, (F) Ariane cannelle, **II** TROCHILIDAE Av
Amazilia saucerrottei = Saucerottia saucerrottei
Amazilia tobaci = Saucerottia tobaci
Amazilia tzacatl (S): *Amazilia tzacatl*
Amazilia tzacatl : (E) Rufous-tailed Hummingbird, (S) Amazilia colirrufa, Amazilia tzacatl, Colibrí colirrufo, (F) Ariane à ventre gris, **II** TROCHILIDAE Av
Amazilia ventriblanca (S): *Agyrtria leucogaster*
Amazilia ventricastaña (S): *Amazilia castaneiventris*
Amazilia ventrirrufa (S): *Amazilia amazilia*
Amazilia verdiazul (S): *Saucerottia saucerrottei*
Amazilia versicolor (S): *Agyrtria versicolor*
Amazilia versicolor = Agyrtria versicolor
Amazilia violiceps = Agyrtria violiceps
Amazilia viridicauda = Leucippus viridicauda
Amazilia viridifrons = Agyrtria viridifrons
Amazilia viridigaster = Saucerottia viridigaster
Amazilia wagneri = Agyrtria viridifrons
Amazilia yucatanensis : (E) Buff-bellied Hummingbird, Fawn-breasted Hummingbird, (S) Amazilia yucateca, Colibrí vientre-canelo, (F) Ariane du Yucatan, **II** TROCHILIDAE Av
Amazilia yucateca (S): *Amazilia yucatanensis*
Amazilia zafirina (S): *Polyerata lactea*
Amazon River Dolphin (E): *Inia geoffrensis*
Amazon Tree Boa (E): *Corallus hortulanus*
Amazona aestiva : (E) Blue-fronted Amazon, Blue-fronted Parrot, Turquoise-fronted Parrot, (S) Amazona frentiazul, Loro hablador, (F) Amazone à front bleu, **II** PSITTACIDAE Av
Amazona agilis : (E) Black-billed Amazon, Black-billed Parrot, (S) Amazona Jamaicana piquioscura, Amazonico activo, Amazonico jamaica, Amazonico todo verde, (F) Amazone agile, Amazone verte, **II** PSITTACIDAE Av
Amazona albifrons : (E) White-fronted Amazon, White-fronted Parrot, (S) Amazona frentialba, Loro frente blanca, Perico manglero, (F) Amazone à front blanc, **II** PSITTACIDAE Av
Amazona alinaranja (S): *Amazona amazonica*
Amazona amazonica : (E) Orange-winged Amazon, Orange-winged Parrot, (S) Amazona alinaranja, Loro guaro, (F) Amazone à ailes oranges, Amazone à ailes vertes, Amazone aourou, **II** PSITTACIDAE Av
Amazona arausiaca : (E) Jacquot, Red-necked Amazon, Red-necked Parrot, (S) Amazona cabenazul, Amazona cabeza azul, Amazona gorgirroja, (F) Amazone à cou rouge, Amazone de Bouquet, **I** PSITTACIDAE Av
Amazona auropalliata = Amazona ochrocephala ssp. *auropalliata*
Amazona autumnalis : (E) Red-lored Amazon, Red-lored Parrot, (S) Amazona frentirroja, Cotorra cucha, Loro frente roja, Loro frentirrojo, (F) Amazone à joues jaunes, Amazone diadème, **II** PSITTACIDAE Av

Amazona barbadensis : (E) Yellow-shouldered Amazon, Yellow-shouldered Parrot, (S) Amazona de espalda amarilla, Amazona hombrogualda, Cotorra cabeciamarilla, Loro de Barbados, (F) Amazone à épaulettes jaunes, Amazone de la Barbade, **I** PSITTACIDAE Av

Amazona brasiliensis : (E) Red-tailed Amazon, Red-tailed Parrot, (S) Amazona colirroja, Loro brasileño, Loro cariazul, Papagayo de cara roja, (F) Amazone à joues bleues, Amazone à queue rouge, Amazone du Brésil, **I** PSITTACIDAE Av

Amazona cabecirroja (S): *Amazona pretrei*

Amazona cabenazul (S): *Amazona arausiaca*

Amazona cabeza azul (S): *Amazona arausiaca*

Amazona cariazul (S): *Amazona dufresniana*

Amazona charao (S): *Amazona pretrei*

Amazona colirroja (S): *Amazona brasiliensis*

Amazona collaria : (E) Yellow-billed Amazon, Yellow-billed Parrot, (S) Amazona Jamaicana piquiclara, Loro de Jamaica, (F) Amazone de la Jamaïque, Amazone sasabé, **II** PSITTACIDAE Av

Amazona coronirroja (S): *Amazona rhodocorytha*

Amazona crestirroja (S): *Amazona rhodocorytha*

Amazona Cubana (S): *Amazona leucocephala*

Amazona de cara amarilla (S): *Amazona xanthops*

Amazona de Cuba (S): *Amazona leucocephala*

Amazona de espalda amarilla (S): *Amazona barbadensis*

Amazona de Kawall (S): *Amazona kawalli*

Amazona de la Española (S): *Amazona ventralis*

Amazona de Puerto Rico (S): *Amazona vittata*

Amazona de San Vincente (S): *Amazona guildingii*

Amazona de Santa Lucía (S): *Amazona versicolor*

Amazona del cerrado (S): *Amazona xanthops*

Amazona dufresniana : (E) Blue-cheeked Amazon, Blue-cheeked Parrot, (S) Amazona cariazul, Loro cariazul, (F) Amazone à joues bleues, Amazone de Dufresne, **II** PSITTACIDAE Av

Amazona dufresniana ssp. *rhodocorytha = Amazona rhodocorytha*

Amazona farinosa : (E) Mealy Amazon, Mealy Parrot, (S) Amazona harinosa, Loro burrón, Loro cabeza azul, Loro verde, (F) Amazone farineuse, Amazone poudrée, **II** PSITTACIDAE Av

Amazona festiva (S): *Amazona festiva*

Amazona festiva : (E) Festive Amazon, Festive Parrot, (S) Amazona festiva, Loro lomirrojo, (F) Amazone festive, Amazone tavoua, **II** PSITTACIDAE Av

Amazona finschi : (E) Lilac-crowned Amazon, Lilac-crowned Parrot, (S) Amazona guayabera, Cotorra frente roja, Loro corona-violeta, (F) Amazone à couronne lilas, Amazone de Finsch, **II** PSITTACIDAE Av

Amazona frentialba (S): *Amazona albifrons*

Amazona frentiazul (S): *Amazona aestiva*

Amazona frentirroja (S): *Amazona autumnalis*

Amazona gorgirroja (S): *Amazona arausiaca*

Amazona guayabera (S): *Amazona finschi*

Amazona guildingii : (E) Saint Vincent Amazon, Saint Vincent Parrot, St Vincent Amazon, (S) Amazona de San Vincente, Loro de San Vicente, (F) Amazone de Guilding, Amazone de Saint-Vincent, **I** PSITTACIDAE Av

Amazona harinosa (S): *Amazona farinosa*

Amazona hombrogualda (S): *Amazona barbadensis*

Amazona imperial (S): *Amazona imperialis*

Amazona imperialis : (E) Imperial Amazon, Imperial Parrot, (S) Amazona imperial, Loro imperial, (F) Amazone impériale, **I** PSITTACIDAE Av

Amazona Jamaicana piquiclara (S): *Amazona collaria*

Amazona Jamaicana piquioscura (S): *Amazona agilis*

Amazona kawalli : (E) Kawall's Amazon, Kawall's Parrot, White-faced Amazon, (S) Amazona de Kawall, (F) Amazone de Kawall, **II** PSITTACIDAE Av

Amazona leucocephala : (E) Bahamas Parrot, Caribbean Amazon, Cuban Amazon, Cuban Parrot, (S) Amazona Cubana, Amazona de Cuba, Loro de cabeza blanca, (F) Amazone à tête blanche, Amazone de Cuba, **I** PSITTACIDAE Av

Amazona mercenaria (S): *Amazona mercenaria*

Amazona mercenaria : (E) Scaly-naped Amazon, Scaly-naped Parrot, (S) Amazona mercenaria, Loro verde, (F) Amazone mercenaire, **II** PSITTACIDAE Av

Amazona ochrocephala : (E) Yellow-crowned Amazon, Yellow-crowned Parrot, Yellow-fronted Amazon, (S) Amazona real, Loro cabeza amarilla, Loro mona amarilla, Loro nuca amarilla, Loro real, (F) Amazone à front jaune, **I/II** PSITTACIDAE Av

Amazona ochrocephala auropalliata : (E) Yellow-naped Amazon, Yellow-naped Parrot, (S) Loro nuquiamarillo, (F) Amazone à nuque d'or, **I** PSITTACIDAE Av

Amazona ochrocephala belizensis : **I** PSITTACIDAE Av

Amazona ochrocephala caribaea : **I** PSITTACIDAE Av

Amazona ochrocephala oratrix : (E) Yellow-headed Amazon, Yellow-headed Parrot, (S) Loro cabeciamarillo, (F) Amazone à tête jaune, **I** PSITTACIDAE Av

Amazona ochrocephala parvipes : **I** PSITTACIDAE Av

Amazona ochrocephala tresmariae : **I** PSITTACIDAE Av

Amazona oratrix = Amazona ochrocephala ssp. *oratrix*

Amazona pechivinosa (S): *Amazona vinacea*

Amazona Portorriqueña (S): *Amazona vittata*

Amazona pretrei : (E) Red-spectacled Amazon, Red-spectacled Parrot, (S) Amazona cabecirroja, Amazona charao, Lora de cara roja, Loro cabecirrojo, Loro de cabeza roja, (F) Amazone de Prêtre, **I** PSITTACIDAE Av

Amazona real (S): *Amazona ochrocephala*

Amazona rhodocorytha : (E) Red-browed Amazon, Red-browed Parrot, Red-topped Amazon, Red-topped Parrot, (S) Amazona coronirroja, Amazona crestirroja, Loro de mejillas azules, (F) Amazone à cronne rouge, Amazone à sourcils rouges, **I** PSITTACIDAE Av

Amazona Tamaulipeca (S): *Amazona viridigenalis*

Amazona tucumana (S): *Amazona tucumana*

Amazona tucumana : (E) Alder Parrot, Tucuman Amazon, Tucuman Parrot, (S) Amazona tucumana, Loro alisero, (F) Amazone de Tucuman, **I** PSITTACIDAE Av

Amazona ventralis : (E) Hispaniolan Amazon, Hispaniolan Parrot, (S) Amazona de la Española, Cotorra, Loro de Hispaniola, (F) Amazone de San Domingo, Amazone d'Hispaniola, **II** PSITTACIDAE Av

Amazona versicolor : (E) Saint Lucia Amazon, Saint Lucia Parrot, St Lucia Amazon, St Lucia Parrot, (S) Amazona de Santa Lucía, Loro multicolor, (F) Amazone de Sainte-Lucie, Amazone versicolore, **I** PSITTACIDAE Av

Amazona vinacea : (E) Vinaceous Amazon, Vinaceous Parrot, (S) Amazona pechivinosa, Amazona vinosa, Loro malva, Loro pechivinoso, Loro pecho vinoso, (F) Amazone bourgogne, Amazone vineuse, **I** PSITTACIDAE Av

Amazona vinosa (S): *Amazona vinacea*

Amazona viridigenalis : (E) Green-cheeked Amazon, Green-cheeked Parrot, Red-crowned Amazon, Red-crowned Parrot, (S) Amapola, Amazona Tamaulipeca, Loro cabeza roja, (F) Amazone à joues vertes, **I** PSITTACIDAE Av

Amazona vittata : (E) Puerto Rican Amazon, Puerto Rican Parrot, Red-fronted Amazon, (S) Amazona de Puerto Rico, Amazona Portorriqueña, Loro de banda roja, (F) Amazone à bandeau rouge, Amazone de Porto Rico, **I** PSITTACIDAE Av

Amazona xantholora : (E) Yellow-lored Amazon, Yellow-lored Parrot, Yucatan Parrot, (S) Amazona Yucateca, Loro yucateci, Loro yucateco, (F) Amazone à lores jaunes, Amazone du Yucatan, **II** PSITTACIDAE Av

Amazona xanthops : (E) Yellow-faced Amazon, Yellow-faced Parrot, (S) Amazona de cara amarilla, Amazona del cerrado, (F) Amazone à face jaune, **II** PSITTACIDAE Av

Amazona Yucateca (S): *Amazona xantholora*

Amazone à ailes oranges (F): *Amazona amazonica*

Amazone à ailes vertes (F): *Amazona amazonica*

Amazone à bandeau rouge (F): *Amazona vittata*

Amazone à cou rouge (F): *Amazona arausiaca*

Amazone à couronne lilas (F): *Amazona finschi*

Amazone à cronne rouge (F): *Amazona rhodocorytha*

Amazone à épaulettes jaunes (F): *Amazona barbadensis*

Amazone à face jaune (F): *Amazona xanthops*

Amazone à front blanc (F): *Amazona albifrons*

Amazone à front bleu (F): *Amazona aestiva*

Amazone à front jaune (F): *Amazona ochrocephala*

Amazone à joues bleues (F): *Amazona brasiliensis/ Amazona dufresniana*

Amazone à joues jaunes (F): *Amazona autumnalis*

Amazone à joues vertes (F): *Amazona viridigenalis*

Amazone à lores jaunes (F): *Amazona xantholora*

Amazone à nuque d'or (F): *Amazona ochrocephala auropalliata*

Amazone à queue rouge (F): *Amazona brasiliensis*

Amazone à sourcils rouges (F): *Amazona rhodocorytha*

Amazone à tête blanche (F): *Amazona leucocephala*

Amazone à tête jaune (F): *Amazona ochrocephala oratrix*

Amazone agile (F): *Amazona agilis*

Amazone aourou (F): *Amazona amazonica*

Amazone bourgogne (F): *Amazona vinacea*

Amazone de Bouquet (F): *Amazona arausiaca*

Amazone de Cuba (F): *Amazona leucocephala*

Amazone de Dufresne (F): *Amazona dufresniana*

Amazone de Finsch (F): *Amazona finschi*

Amazone de Guilding (F): *Amazona guildingii*

Amazone de Kawall (F): *Amazona kawalli*

Amazone de la Barbade (F): *Amazona barbadensis*

Amazone de la Jamaïque (F): *Amazona collaria*

Amazone de Porto Rico (F): *Amazona vittata*

Amazone de Prêtre (F): *Amazona pretrei*

Amazone de Sainte-Lucie (F): *Amazona versicolor*

Amazone de Saint-Vincent (F): *Amazona guildingii*

Amazone de San Domingo (F): *Amazona ventralis*

Amazone de Tucuman (F): *Amazona tucumana*

Amazone d'Hispaniola (F): *Amazona ventralis*

Amazone diadème (F): *Amazona autumnalis*

Amazone du Brésil (F): *Amazona brasiliensis*

Amazone du Yucatan (F): *Amazona xantholora*

Amazone farineuse (F): *Amazona farinosa*

Amazone festive (F): *Amazona festiva*

Amazone impériale (F): *Amazona imperialis*

Amazone mercenaire (F): *Amazona mercenaria*

Amazone poudrée (F): *Amazona farinosa*

Amazone sasabé (F): *Amazona collaria*

Amazone tavoua (F): *Amazona festiva*

Amazone versicolore (F): *Amazona versicolor*

Amazone verte (F): *Amazona agilis*

Amazone vineuse (F): *Amazona vinacea*

Amazonian Manatee (E): *Trichechus inunguis*

Amazonian Parakeet (E): *Nannopsittaca dachilleae*

Amazonian Parrotlet (E): *Nannopsittaca dachilleae*

Amazonian Poison Frog (E): *Dendrobates ventrimaculatus*

Amazonian Poison-Arrow Frog (E): *Dendrobates quinquevittatus*

Amazonian River Dolphin (E): *Sotalia fluviatilis*

Amazonian Umbrellabird (E): *Cephalopterus ornatus*

Amazonico activo (S): *Amazona agilis*

Amazonico jamaica (S): *Amazona agilis*

Amazonico todo verde (S): *Amazona agilis*

Ambergris Cay Dwarf Boa (E): *Tropidophis greenwayi*

Ambiky Chameleon (E): *Furcifer tuzetae*

Amblonyx cinereus : (E) Oriental Small-clawed Otter, Small-clawed Otter, (S) Nutria cenicienta, Nutria inerme asiatica, (F) Loutre cendrée, **II** MUSTELIDAE Ma

Amblyospiza albifrons : (E) Grosbeak Weaver, Thick-billed Weaver, White-fronted Grosbeak, (S) Tejedor picogordo, (F) Amblyospize à front blanc, Gros-bec à front blanc, **III** PLOCEIDAE Av

Amblyospize à front blanc (F): *Amblyospiza albifrons*

Amblyrhynche à crête (F): *Amblyrhynchus cristatus*

Amblyrhynchus cristatus : (E) Galapagos Marine Iguana, Marine Iguana, Sea Iguana, (S) Iguana marina, (F) Amblyrhynche à crête, Iguane marin, **II** IGUANIDAE Re

Ambon Flying-fox (E): *Pteropus argentatus/ Pteropus chrysoproctus*

Ambon King-Parrot (E): *Alisterus amboinensis*

Ambon Lizard (E): *Varanus indicus*

Ambystoma dumerilii : (E) Achoque, Lake Patzcuaro Salamander, (S) Ajolote de lago Pátzquaro, Salamandra del lago Patzcuaro, (F) Salamandre du lac Pàtzcuaro, **II** AMBYSTOMATIDAE Am

Ambystoma mexicanum : (E) Axolotl, (S) Ajolote mexicano, Salamandra mexicana, (F) Ambystome du Mexique, Axolotl, Salamandre du Mexique, **II** AMBYSTOMATIDAE Am

Ambystome du Mexique (F): *Ambystoma mexicanum*

American Alligator (E): *Alligator mississippiensis*

American Black Bear (E): *Ursus americanus*

American box turtles (E): *Terrapene* spp.

American Crocodile (E): *Crocodylus acutus*

American Flamingo (E): *Phoenicopterus ruber*

American Harpy Eagle (E): *Harpia harpyja*

American Kestrel (E): *Falco sparverius*

American Lynx (E): *Lynx canadensis*

American Manatee (E): *Trichechus manatus*

American Swallow-tailed Kite (E): *Elanoides forficatus*

Amethyst Woodstar (E): *Calliphlox amethystina*

Amethystine (Rock) Python (E): *Morelia amethistina*

Amethyst-throated Hummingbird (E): *Lampornis amethystinus*

Amethyst-throated Sunangel (E): *Heliangelus amethysticollis*

Ammotragus lervia : (E) Aoudad, Barbary Sheep, Uaddan, (S) Arruí, Muflón del Atlas, (F) Aoudad, Mouflon à manchettes, **II** BOVIDAE Ma

Ampalagua (E): *Boa constrictor*

Amphelia oculata = *Madrepora oculata*

Amsterdam Island Fur Seal (E): *Arctocephalus tropicalis*

Amu Darya shovelnose sturgeon (E): *Pseudoscaphirhynchus kaufmanni*

Amu Darya sturgeon (E): *Pseudoscaphirhynchus kaufmanni*

Amur Falcon (E): *Falco amurensis*

Amur Sturgeon (E): *Acipenser schrenckii*

Amzonian Pygmy-Owl (E): *Glaucidium hardyi*

Anaconda (E/S/F): *Eunectes murinus*

Anaconda à taches sombres (F): *Eunectes deschauenseei*

Anaconda amarilla (S): *Eunectes notaeus*

Anaconda commun (F): *Eunectes murinus*

Anaconda de Deschauensee (F): *Eunectes deschauenseei*

Anaconda du Paraguay (F): *Eunectes notaeus*

Anaconda jaune (F): *Eunectes notaeus*

Anaconda vert (F): *Eunectes murinus*

Anacropora forbesi : **II** ACROPORIDAE An

Anacropora gracilis = *Anacropora forbesi*

Anacropora matthai : **II** ACROPORIDAE An

Anacropora puertogalerae : **II** ACROPORIDAE An

Anacropora reptans = *Anacropora forbesi*

Anacropora reticulata : **II** ACROPORIDAE An

Anacropora spinosa : **II** ACROPORIDAE An

Anacropora spumosa : **II** ACROPORIDAE An

Anade rabudo (S): *Anas acuta*

Anade silbón (S): *Anas penelope*

Anamolure de Beecroft (F): *Anomalurus beecrofti*

Anamolure de Derby (F): *Anomalurus derbianus*

Anamolure de Pel (F): *Anomalurus pelii*

Anamolure nain (F): *Idiurus macrotis*

Anaplectes melanotis = *Anaplectes rubriceps*

Checklist of fauna/Lista de especies de fauna/Liste des espèces animales

Anaplectes rubriceps : (E) Red-headed Weaver, (S) Mailmbo capirotado, (F) Tisserin à ailes rouges, Tisserin écarlate, **III** PLOCEIDAE Av

Anas (S): *Conepatus humboldtii*

Anas acuta : (E) Common Pintail, Northern Pintail, Pintail, (S) Anade rabudo, Pato golondrino norteño, Pato rabudo, (F) Canard pilet, Pilet, **III** ANATIDAE Av

Anas aucklandica : (E) Brown Teal, Flightless Teal, (S) Cerceta alicorta de Auckland, Cerceta Maorí, (F) Sarcelle aptère, Sarcelle brune, Sarcelle de Nouvelle-Zélande, Sarcelle terrestre des îles Auckland, **I** ANATIDAE Av

Anas bernieri : (E) Bernier's Teal, Madagascar Teal, (S) Cerceta de Madagascar, Cerceta malgache, Cerceta malgache de Bernier, Pato de Bernier, (F) Canard de Bernier, Sarcelle de Bernier, Sarcelle de Madagascar, Sarcelle malgache de Bernier, **II** ANATIDAE Av

Anas capensis : (E) Cape Teal, Cape Wigeon, (S) Cerceta del Cabo, (F) Canard du Cap, Sarcelle du Cap, **III** ANATIDAE Av

Anas carolinensis = Anas crecca

Anas chlorotis = Anas aucklandica ssp. *chlorotis*

Anas clypeata : (E) Northern Shoveler, Shoveler, (S) Cuchara común, Pato chucara, Pato cuchara, Pato cucharón norteño, (F) Canard souchet, Souchet, **III** ANATIDAE Av

Anas crecca : (E) Common Teal, Green-winged Teal, Teal, (S) Cerceta aliverde, Cerceta común, (F) Sarcelle d'hiver, **III** ANATIDAE Av

Anas formosa : (E) Baikal Teal, (S) Cerceta del Baikal, (F) Sarcelle élégante, Sarcelle formose, **II** ANATIDAE Av

Anas laysanensis : (E) Laysan Duck, Laysan Teal, (S) Pato de Laysan, Pato real de Laysan, (F) Canard de Laysan, Sarcelle de Laysan, **I** ANATIDAE Av

Anas nesiotis = Anas aucklandica ssp. *nesiotis*

Anas oustaleti : (E) Marianas Island Duck, Marianas Mallard, Oustalet's Grey Duck, (S) Pato de Oustalet, Pato real marismeno, (F) Canard aberrant, Canard des Mariannes, Canard d'Oustalet, **I** ANATIDAE Av

Anas penelope : (E) Eurasian Wigeon, Wigeon, (S) Anade silbón, Pato silbón, Silbón Europeo, (F) Canard siffleur, **III** ANATIDAE Av

Anas platyrhychos ssp. *"oustaleti" = Anas oustaleti*

Anas platyrhynchos ssp. *laysanensis = Anas laysanensis*

Anas querquedula : (E) Garganey, Garganey Teal, (S) Cerceta carretona, Cerceta cejiblanca, (F) Sarcelle d'été, **III** ANATIDAE Av

Anathana ellioti : (E) Indian Treeshrew, Madras Treeshrew, (S) Musaraña arborícola de la India, (F) Toupaïe d'Elliot, **II** TUPAIIDAE Ma

Anca de Llanura (S): *Bubalus depressicornis*

Anchieta's Chameleon (E): *Chamaeleo anchietae*

Anchor Coral (E): *Euphyllia ancora*

Andaman Boobook (E): *Ninox affinis*

Andaman Cobra (E): *Naja sagittifera*

Andaman Dark Serpent-Eagle (E): *Spilornis elgini*

Andaman Day Gecko (E): *Phelsuma andamanensis*

Andaman Hawk-Owl (E): *Ninox affinis*

Andaman Scops-Owl (E): *Otus balli*

Andaman Serpent-Eagle (E): *Spilornis elgini*

Andean Bear (E): *Tremarctos ornatus*

Andean Cat (E): *Oreailurus jacobita*

Andean Cock-of-the-rock (E): *Rupicola peruviana*

Andean Condor (E): *Vultur gryphus*

Andean Emerald (E): *Agyrtria franciae*

Andean Flamingo (E): *Phoenicopterus andinus*

Andean Hairy Armadillo (E): *Chaetophractus nationi*

Andean Hillstar (E): *Oreotrochilus estella*

Andean Night Monkey (E): *Aotus miconax*

Andean Parakeet (E): *Bolborhynchus orbygnesius*

Andean Poison Frog (E): *Minyobates opisthomelas*

Andean Pygmy-Owl (E): *Glaucidium jardinii*

Andean Tapir (E): *Tapirus pinchaque*

Andean Titi Monkey (E): *Callicebus oenanthe*

Andean Wolf (E): *Pseudalopex culpaeus*

Andrews' Frigatebird (E): *Fregata andrewsi*

Andrews's Beaked Whale (E): *Mesoplodon bowdoini*

Andrias spp.: (E) Giant salamanders, (S) Salamandra gigante, Salamandras gigantes, (F) Salamandre géante, **I** CRYPTOBRANCHIDAE Am

Andrias davidianus : (E) Chinese Giant Salamander, (S) Salamandra gigante de China, (F) Salamandre du Père David, Salamandre géante de Chine, **I** CRYPTOBRANCHIDAE Am

Andrias japonicus : (E) Japanese Giant Salamander, (S) Salamandra gigante de Japón, (F) Salamandre géante du Japon, **I** CRYPTOBRANCHIDAE Am

Androdon aequatorialis : (E) Tooth-billed Hummingbird, (S) Colibrí piquidentado, (F) Colibri d'Équateur, **II** TROCHILIDAE Av

Ane sauvage d'Afrique (F): *Equus africanus*

Ane sauvage d'Asie (F): *Equus hemionus*

Ane sauvage de l'Inde (F): *Equus onager khur*

Ane sauvage de Mongolie (F): *Equus hemionus hemionus*

Ane sauvage du Tibet (F): *Equus kiang*

Anegada Ground Iguana (E): *Cyclura pinguis*

Anegada Island Iguana (E): *Cyclura pinguis*

Anegada Rock Iguana (E): *Cyclura pinguis*

Angel de Sol amatista (S): *Heliangelus amethysticollis*

Angel de Sol cuelliocre (S): *Heliangelus mavors*

Angel's Chameleon (E): *Furcifer angeli*

Angola Chameleon (E): *Chamaeleo anchietae*

Angola Pied Colobus (E): *Colobus angolensis*

Angolan Black-and-white Colobus (E): *Colobus angolensis*

Angolan Colobus (E): *Colobus angolensis*

Angolan Girdled Lizard (E): *Cordylus angolensis*

Angolan Python (E): *Python anchietae*

Angolan Spiny-tailed Lizard (E): *Cordylus angolensis*

Angonoka (E): *Geochelone yniphora*

Angulated Tortoise (E): *Chersina angulata*

Angwantibo (E/F): *Arctocebus calabarensis*

Annam Leaf Turtle (E): *Annamemys annamensis*

Annam Pond Turtle (E): *Annamemys annamensis*

Annamemys annamensis : (E) Annam Leaf Turtle, Annam pond Turtle, (F) Emyde d'Annam, **II** EMYDIDAE Re

Annamemys merkleni = Annamemys annamensis

Anna's Hummingbird (E): *Calypte anna*

Annulated Tree Boa (E): *Corallus annulatus*

Anoa (E): *Bubalus depressicornis*

Anoa de Ilanura (S): *Bubalus depressicornis*

Anoa de montaña (S): *Bubalus quarlesi*

Anoa de Quarle (F): *Bubalus quarlesi*

Anoa depressicornis = Bubalus depressicornis

Anoa des montagnes (F): *Bubalus quarlesi*

Anoa des plaines (F): *Bubalus depressicornis*

Anoa mindorensis = Bubalus mindorensis

Anoa quarlesi = Bubalus quarlesi

Anodorhynchus spp.: (E) Blue macaws, (F) Aras bleus, Aras de Lear, Aras glauques, Aras hyacinthes, **I** PSITTACIDAE Av

Anodorhynchus glaucus : (E) Glaucous Macaw, (S) Ara azul, Guacamayo glauco, Guacamayo violáceo, (F) Ara bleu, Ara glauque, **I** PSITTACIDAE Av

Anodorhynchus hyacinthinus : (E) Hyacinth Macaw, (S) Guacamayo azul, Guacamayo jacinto, (F) Ara bleu, Ara hyacinthe, Ara jacinthe, **I** PSITTACIDAE Av

Anodorhynchus leari : (E) Indigo Macaw, Lear's Macaw, (S) Guacamayo cobalto, Guacamayo de Lear, (F) Ara cobalt, Ara de Lear, **I** PSITTACIDAE Av

Anomalospiza imberbis : (E) Cuckoo Weaver, Parasitic Weaver, (F) Anomalospize parasite, Tisserin coucou, Tisserin covcau, **III** PLOCEIDAE Av

Anomalospize parasite (F): *Anomalospiza imberbis*

Anomalurops beecrofti = Anomalurus beecrofti

Anomalurus beecrofti : (E) Beecroft's Flying Squirrel, Beecroft's Scaly-tailed Squirrel, (F) Anamolure de Beecroft, Écureuil volant de Beecroft, **III** ANOMALURIDAE Ma

Checklist of fauna/Lista de especies de fauna/Liste des espèces animales

Anomalurus derbianus : (E) Lord Derby's Flying Squirrel, Lord Derby's Scaly-tailed Squirrrel, (F) Anamolure de Derby, Écureuil volant de Derby, **III** ANOMALURIDAE Ma

Anomalurus pelii : (E) Pel's Flying Squirrel, Pel's Scaly-tailed Squirrel, (F) Anamolure de Pel, Écureuil volant de Pel, **III** ANOMALURIDAE Ma

Anomalurus schoutedeni = Anomalurus beecrofti

Anomastraea irregularis : **II** SIDERASTREIDAE An

Anomocora carinata : **II** CARYOPHYLLIIDAE An

Anomocora fecunda : **II** CARYOPHYLLIIDAE An

Anomocora gigas : **II** CARYOPHYLLIIDAE An

Anomocora marchadi : **II** CARYOPHYLLIIDAE An

Anomocora prolifera : **II** CARYOPHYLLIIDAE An

Anopetia gounellei : (E) Broad-tipped Hermit, (S) Ermitaño coliancho, (F) Ermite de Gounelle, **II** TROCHILIDAE Av

Anorrhinus spp.: (E) Hornbills, (S) Buceros, Cálaos, (F) Calaos, Calaos à huppe touffue, **II** BUCEROTIDAE Av

Anorrhinus austeni = Anorrhinus tickelli

Anorrhinus galeritus : (E) Bushy-crested Hornbill, (S) Cálao crestado, (F) Calao largup, **II** BUCEROTIDAE Av

Anorrhinus tickelli : (E) Assam Brown-backed Hornbill, Brown Hornbill, Tickell's Brown Hornbill, (S) Cálao pardo de Tickell, (F) Calao brun, **II** BUCEROTIDAE Av

Anserelle naine (F): *Nettapus auritus*

Anta (S): *Tapirus terrestris*

Anta brasileña (S): *Tapirus terrestris*

Antaceus ayresii = Acipenser transmontanus

Antaceus buffalo = Acipenser fulvescens

Antaceus caryi = Acipenser transmontanus

Antaceus cincinnati = Acipenser fulvescens

Antaceus putnami = Acipenser transmontanus

Antanosy Day Gecko (E): *Phelsuma antanosy*

Antarctic Fur Seal (E): *Arctocephalus gazella*

Antarctic Minke Whale (E): *Balaenoptera bonaerensis*

Antaresia childreni : (E) Children's (Rock) Python, (S) Pitón enana, (F) Python de Children, **II** PYTHONIDAE Re

Antaresia maculosa : (E) Spotted Python, (F) Python tacheté, **II** PYTHONIDAE Re

Antaresia perthensis : (E) Perth Pygmy Python, Pygmy Python, (F) Python pygmée de Perth, **II** PYTHONIDAE Re

Antaresia stimsoni : (E) Large-blotched Python, Stimson's Python, (F) Python à large tache, Python de Stimson, **II** PYTHONIDAE Re

Anteburro (S): *Tapirus bairdii*

Antechinomys longicaudata = Sminthopsis longicaudata

Anthemiphyllia dentata : **II** ANTHEMIPHYLLIIDAE An

Anthemiphyllia frustum : **II** ANTHEMIPHYLLIIDAE An

Anthemiphyllia macrolobata : **II** ANTHEMIPHYLLIIDAE An

Anthemiphyllia multidentata : **II** ANTHEMIPHYLLIIDAE An

Anthemiphyllia pacifica : **II** ANTHEMIPHYLLIIDAE An

Anthemiphyllia patera : **II** ANTHEMIPHYLLIIDAE An

Anthemiphyllia patera costata : **II** ANTHEMIPHYLLIIDAE An

Anthemiphyllia patera patera : **II** ANTHEMIPHYLLIIDAE An

Anthemiphyllia spinifera : **II** ANTHEMIPHYLLIIDAE An

Anthocephala floriceps : (E) Blossomcrown, (S) Colibrí florido, (F) Colibri à tête rose, **II** TROCHILIDAE Av

Anthracoceros spp.: (E) Hornbills, (S) Buceros, Cálaos, (F) Calao pics, Calaos, **II** BUCEROTIDAE Av

Anthracoceros albirostris : (E) Indian Pied Hornbill, Malaysian Pied-Hornbill, Northern Pied-Hornbill, Oriental Pied-Hornbill, Sunda Pied Hornbill, (S) Cálao cariblanco, (F) Calao pie, **II** BUCEROTIDAE Av

Anthracoceros convexus = Anthracoceros albirostris

Anthracoceros coronatus : (E) Malabar Pied-Hornbill, Pied Hornbill, (F) Calao de Malabar, **II** BUCEROTIDAE Av

Anthracoceros malabaricus = Anthracoceros coronatus

Anthracoceros malayanus : (E) Asian Black Hornbill, Black Hornbill, Malaysian Black Hornbill, (S) Cálao Malayo, (F) Calao charbonnier, **II** BUCEROTIDAE Av

Anthracoceros marchei : (E) Palawan Hornbill, (S) Cálao de Palawan, (F) Calao de Palawan, **II** BUCEROTIDAE Av

Anthracoceros montani : (E) Sulu Hornbill, (S) Cálao de las Sulu, (F) Calao des Sulu, **II** BUCEROTIDAE Av

Anthracothorax dominicus : (E) Antillean Mango, Dominican Mango, (S) Mango Antillano, Zumbador grande, (F) Mango doré, **II** TROCHILIDAE Av

Anthracothorax mango : (E) Jamaican Mango, (S) Mango Jamaicano, (F) Mango de la Jamaïque, **II** TROCHILIDAE Av

Anthracothorax nigricollis : (E) Black-throated Mango, (S) Mango, Mango gorginegro, Mango pechinegro, Picaflor ventrinegro, (F) Mango à cravate noire, **II** TROCHILIDAE Av

Anthracothorax prevostii : (E) Green-breasted Mango, (S) Mango pechiverde, (F) Mango de Prévost, **II** TROCHILIDAE Av

Anthracothorax recurvirostris : (E) Fiery-tailed Awlbill, (S) Colibrí pico lezna, Mango picolezna, (F) Colibri avocette, **II** TROCHILIDAE Av

Anthracothorax veraguensis : (E) Veraguan Mango, (S) Mango de Veragua, (F) Mango de Veragua, **II** TROCHILIDAE Av

Anthracothorax viridigula : (E) Green-throated Mango, (S) Mango gargantiverde, Mango gorgiverde, (F) Mango à cravate verte, **II** TROCHILIDAE Av

Anthracothorax viridis : (E) Green Mango, (S) Mango portorriqueño, (F) Mango vert, **II** TROCHILIDAE Av

Anthropoides paradisea = Grus paradisea

Anthropoides virgo = Grus virgo

Antillean Crested Hummingbird (E): *Orthorhyncus cristatus*

Antillean Mango (E): *Anthracothorax dominicus*

Antilocapra americana : (E) Mexican Pronghorn, Pronghorn, (S) Berrendo, (F) Antilocapre, Antilocapre de Californie, Antilope américaine, Pronghorn, **I/NC** ANTILOCAPRIDAE Ma

Antilocapre (F): *Antilocapra americana*

Antilocapre de Californie (F): *Antilocapra americana*

Antilope américaine (F): *Antilocapra americana*

Antilope amizclero enano de agua (S): *Hyemoschus aquaticus*

Antilope blanche (F): *Addax nasomaculatus*

Antilope cervicapra : (E) Blackbuck, Sasin, (S) Antílope negro indio, Cervicapra, (F) Antilope cervicapre, Cervicapre, **III** BOVIDAE Ma

Antilope cervicapre (F): *Antilope cervicapra*

Antílope de cuatrocuernos (S): *Tetracerus quadricornis*

Antílope del Tibet (S): *Pantholops hodgsonii*

Antilope du Tibet (F): *Pantholops hodgsonii*

Antílope negro gigante (S): *Hippotragus niger variani*

Antílope negro indio (S): *Antilope cervicapra*

Antílope sable negro (S): *Hippotragus niger variani*

Antílope saiga (S): *Saiga tatarica*

Antílope tibetano (S): *Pantholops hodgsonii*

ANTIPATHARIA spp. : (E) Black corals, (S) Corales negros, (F) Coraux noirs, **II** An

Antipathella aperta : **II** ANTIPATHIDAE An

Antipathella fiordensis : **II** ANTIPATHIDAE An

Antipathella strigosa : **II** ANTIPATHIDAE An

Antipathella subpinnata : **II** ANTIPATHIDAE An

Antipathella wollastonii : **II** ANTIPATHIDAE An

Antipathes abies = Cupressopathes abies

Antipathes aculeata : **II** ANTIPATHIDAE An

Antipathes alata : **II** ANTIPATHIDAE An

Antipathes alopecuroides : **II** ANTIPATHIDAE An
Antipathes americana : **II** ANTIPATHIDAE An
Antipathes antrocrada = *Myriopathes antrocrada*
Antipathes aperta = *Antipathella aperta*
Antipathes arborea : **II** ANTIPATHIDAE An
Antipathes assimilis : **II** ANTIPATHIDAE An
Antipathes atlantica : **II** ANTIPATHIDAE An
Antipathes barbadensis = *Tanacetipathes barbadensis*
Antipathes bifaria = *Myriopathes bifaria*
Antipathes boscii : **II** ANTIPATHIDAE An
Antipathes brooki = *Antipathes atlantica*
Antipathes caribbeana : **II** ANTIPATHIDAE An
Antipathes catharinae : **II** ANTIPATHIDAE An
Antipathes ceylonensis : **II** ANTIPATHIDAE An
Antipathes chamaemorus : **II** ANTIPATHIDAE An
Antipathes chota : **II** ANTIPATHIDAE An
Antipathes columnaris : **II** ANTIPATHIDAE An
Antipathes contorta : **II** ANTIPATHIDAE An
Antipathes crispa : **II** ANTIPATHIDAE An
Antipathes cupressus : **II** ANTIPATHIDAE An
Antipathes curvata : **II** ANTIPATHIDAE An
Antipathes cylindrica : **II** ANTIPATHIDAE An
Antipathes delicatula : **II** ANTIPATHIDAE An
Antipathes densa : **II** ANTIPATHIDAE An
Antipathes dichotoma : **II** ANTIPATHIDAE An
Antipathes dubia : **II** ANTIPATHIDAE An
Antipathes elegans : **II** ANTIPATHIDAE An
Antipathes ericoides : **II** ANTIPATHIDAE An
Antipathes erinaceus : **II** ANTIPATHIDAE An
Antipathes eupteridea : **II** ANTIPATHIDAE An
Antipathes expansa : **II** ANTIPATHIDAE An
Antipathes fernandezii = *Plumapathes fernandezii*
Antipathes fiordensis = *Antipathella fiordensis*
Antipathes flabellum : **II** ANTIPATHIDAE An
Antipathes fragilis : **II** ANTIPATHIDAE An
Antipathes fruticosa : **II** ANTIPATHIDAE An
Antipathes furcata : **II** ANTIPATHIDAE An
Antipathes galapagensis : **II** ANTIPATHIDAE An
Antipathes gallensis : **II** ANTIPATHIDAE An
Antipathes glutinata : **II** ANTIPATHIDAE An
Antipathes gracilis = *Cupressopathes gracilis*
Antipathes gracilis = *Stichopathes gracilis*
Antipathes grandiflora : **II** ANTIPATHIDAE An
Antipathes grandis : **II** ANTIPATHIDAE An
Antipathes grayi : **II** ANTIPATHIDAE An
Antipathes hirta = *Tanacetipathes hirta*
Antipathes hypnoides : **II** ANTIPATHIDAE An
Antipathes indistincta : **II** ANTIPATHIDAE An
Antipathes intermedia : **II** ANTIPATHIDAE An
Antipathes japonica = *Myriopathes japonica*
Antipathes lata = *Myriopathes lata*
Antipathes lenta : **II** ANTIPATHIDAE An
Antipathes lentipinna : **II** ANTIPATHIDAE An
Antipathes longibrachiata : **II** ANTIPATHIDAE An
Antipathes mediterranea : **II** ANTIPATHIDAE An
Antipathes minor : **II** ANTIPATHIDAE An
Antipathes myriophylla = *Myriopathes myriophylla*
Antipathes nilanduensis : **II** ANTIPATHIDAE An
Antipathes panamensis = *Myriopathes panamensis*
Antipathes paniculata = *Cupressopathes paniculata*
Antipathes pauroclema : **II** ANTIPATHIDAE An
Antipathes pectinata : **II** ANTIPATHIDAE An
Antipathes pedata : **II** ANTIPATHIDAE An
Antipathes pennacea = *Plumapathes pennacea*
Antipathes plana : **II** ANTIPATHIDAE An
Antipathes plantagenista : **II** ANTIPATHIDAE An
Antipathes pluma : **II** ANTIPATHIDAE An
Antipathes pseudodichotoma : **II** ANTIPATHIDAE An
Antipathes pumila = *Cupressopathes pumila*
Antipathes punctata : **II** ANTIPATHIDAE An
Antipathes reticulata : **II** ANTIPATHIDAE An
Antipathes rhipidion : **II** ANTIPATHIDAE An
Antipathes rigida : **II** ANTIPATHIDAE An
Antipathes robillardi : **II** ANTIPATHIDAE An
Antipathes rugosa = *Myriopathes rugosa*

Antipathes salicoides : **II** ANTIPATHIDAE An
Antipathes salix : **II** ANTIPATHIDAE An
Antipathes sarothamnoides : **II** ANTIPATHIDAE An
Antipathes sarothrum : **II** ANTIPATHIDAE An
Antipathes sealarki : **II** ANTIPATHIDAE An
Antipathes sibogae : **II** ANTIPATHIDAE An
Antipathes simplex : **II** ANTIPATHIDAE An
Antipathes speciosa : **II** ANTIPATHIDAE An
Antipathes spinescens = *Tanacetipathes spinescens*
Antipathes spinosa = *Myriopathes spinosa*
Antipathes squamosa : **II** ANTIPATHIDAE An
Antipathes stechowi = *Myriopathes stechowi*
Antipathes strigosa = *Antipathella strigosa*
Antipathes subpinnata = *Antipathella subpinnata*
Antipathes tanacetum = *Tanacetipathes tanacetum*
Antipathes tenuispina : **II** ANTIPATHIDAE An
Antipathes ternatensis : **II** ANTIPATHIDAE An
Antipathes thamnea = *Tanacetipathes thamnea*
Antipathes thamnoides : **II** ANTIPATHIDAE An
Antipathes tristis : **II** ANTIPATHIDAE An
Antipathes ulex = *Myriopathes ulex*
Antipathes umbratica : **II** ANTIPATHIDAE An
Antipathes valdiviae : **II** ANTIPATHIDAE An
Antipathes verticillata : **II** ANTIPATHIDAE An
Antipathes viminalis : **II** ANTIPATHIDAE An
Antipathes virgata : **II** ANTIPATHIDAE An
Antipathes wollastonii = *Antipathella wollastonii*
Antipathes zoothallus : **II** ANTIPATHIDAE An
Antipodes Green Parakeet (E): *Cyanoramphus unicolor*
Antipodes Parakeet (E): *Cyanoramphus unicolor*
Antler Coral (E): *Pocillopora eydouxi*
Antler Lettuce Coral (E): *Pectinia alcicornis*
Antsingy Leaf Chameleon (E): *Brookesia perarmata*
Aonyx capensis : (E) African Clawless Otter, Cape
    Clawless Otter, (S) Nutria africana, Nutria de cuello
    blanco, (F) Loutre à joues blanches, **II**
    MUSTELIDAE Ma
Aonyx cinerea = *Amblonyx cinereus*
Aonyx congicus : (E) Cameroon Clawless Otter, Congo
    Clawless Otter, Small-clawed Otter, Small-toothed
    Clawless Otter, Swamp Otter, Zaire Clawless Otter,
    (S) Nutria inerme de Camerún, (F) Loutre à joues
    blanches du Cameroun, Loutre à joues blanches du
    Congo, Paraonyx tacheté, **I/II** MUSTELIDAE Ma
Aonyx microdon = *Aonyx congicus*
Aonyx philippsi = *Aonyx congicus*
Aotus azarai : (E) Azara's Night Monkey, **II** CEBIDAE
    Ma
Aotus bipunctatus = *Aotus lemurinus*
Aotus brumbacki : (E) Brumback's Night Monkey, **II**
    CEBIDAE Ma
Aotus hershkovitzi : (E) Hershkovitz's Night Monkey, **II**
    CEBIDAE Ma
Aotus infulatus : (E) Feline Night Monkey, **II** CEBIDAE
    Ma
Aotus lemurinus : (E) Lemurine Night Monkey, **II**
    CEBIDAE Ma
Aotus lemurinus ssp. *brumbacki* = *Aotus brumbacki*
Aotus miconax : (E) Andean Night Monkey, **II** CEBIDAE
    Ma
Aotus nancymaae : (E) Ma's Night Monkey, **II** CEBIDAE
    Ma
Aotus nigriceps : (E) Black-headed Night Monkey,
    Peruvian Night Monkey, **II** CEBIDAE Ma
Aotus trivirgatus : (E) Douroucouli, Night Monkey, Owl
    Monkey, (F) Douroucouli, Singe de nuit, **II**
    CEBIDAE Ma
Aotus trivirgatus ssp. *azarai* = *Aotus azarai*
Aotus trivirgatus ssp. *brumbacki* = *Aotus brumbacki*
Aotus trivirgatus ssp. *hershkovitzi* = *Aotus hershkovitzi*
Aotus trivirgatus ssp. *infulatus* = *Aotus infulatus*
Aotus trivirgatus ssp. *lemurinus* = *Aotus lemurinus*
Aotus trivirgatus ssp. *miconax* = *Aotus miconax*
Aotus trivirgatus ssp. *nancymaae* = *Aotus nancymaae*
Aotus trivirgatus ssp. *nigriceps* = *Aotus nigriceps*

Checklist of fauna/Lista de especies de fauna/Liste des espèces animales

Aotus trivirgatus ssp. *vociferans = Aotus vociferans*
Aotus vociferans : **II** CEBIDAE Ma
Aoudad (E/F): *Ammotragus lervia*
Apalone ater : (E) Cuatro Cienegas Softshell, (S) Tortuga negra, (F) Tortue molle noire, Trionyx noir , **I** TRIONYCHIDAE Re
Apalone spinifera ssp. *ater = Apalone ater*
Apaporis River Caiman (E): *Caiman crocodilus apaporiensis*
Apennine Chamois (E): *Rupicapra pyrenaica ornata*
Apes (E): PRIMATES spp. Ma
Aphanipathes abietina : **II** ANTIPATHIDAE An
Aphanipathes cancellata : **II** ANTIPATHIDAE An
Aphanipathes filix : **II** ANTIPATHIDAE An
Aphanipathes hancocki : **II** ANTIPATHIDAE An
Aphanipathes humilis : **II** ANTIPATHIDAE An
Aphanipathes reticulata : **II** ANTIPATHIDAE An
Aphanipathes somervillei : **II** ANTIPATHIDAE An
Aphanipathes thyoides : **II** ANTIPATHIDAE An
Aphanipathes undulata : **II** ANTIPATHIDAE An
Aphantochroa cirrochloris = Campylopterus cirrochloris
Aphonopelma albiceps : **II** THERAPHOSIDAE Ar
Aphonopelma pallidum : (E) Chihuahua Rose-grey Tarantula, Mexican Grey Tarantula, (S) Tarantula Mexicana gris, (F) Tarantule gris du Mexique, **II** THERAPHOSIDAE Ar
Aplomado Falcon (E): *Falco femoralis*
Apodora papuana : (E) Papuan Python, (S) Pitón acuática de Papua, (F) Python de Papouasie, **II** PYTHONIDAE Re
Apollo (E): *Parnassius apollo*
Apollo Butterfly (E): *Parnassius apollo*
Apolo (S): *Parnassius apollo*
Appalachian Monkeyface (E): *Quadrula sparsa*
Appalachian Monkey-face Pearly Mussel (E): *Quadrula sparsa*
Aprosmictus erythropterus : (E) Red-winged Parrot, (S) Papagayo alirrojo, (F) Perruche érythroptère, **II** PSITTACIDAE Av
Aprosmictus jonquillaceus : (E) Olive-shouldered Parrot, Timor Red-winged Parrot, (S) Papagayo de Timor, (F) Perruche jonquille, **II** PSITTACIDAE Av
Aquatic Box Turtle (E): *Terrapene coahuila*
Aquila adalberti : (E) Adalbert's Eagle, Spanish Imperial Eagle, White-shouldered Eagle , (S) Aguila imperial ibérica, (F) Aigle à épaules blanches, Aigle ibérique, Aigle impérial espagnol, Aquila imperiale iberica, **I** ACCIPITRIDAE Av
Aquila audax : (E) Wedge-tailed Eagle, (S) Aguila audaz, (F) Aigle d'Australie, **II** ACCIPITRIDAE Av
Aquila chrysaetos : (E) Golden Eagle, (S) Aguila Real, (F) Aigle doré, Aigle royal, **II** ACCIPITRIDAE Av
Aquila clanga : (E) Greater Spotted Eagle, Spotted Eagle, (S) Aguila Moteada, (F) Aigle criard, **II** ACCIPITRIDAE Av
Aquila Esteparia (S): *Aquila nipalensis*
Aquila gurneyi : (E) Gurney's Eagle, (S) Aguila moluqueña, (F) Aigle de Gurney, **II** ACCIPITRIDAE Av
Aquila heliaca : (E) Eastern Imperial Eagle, Imperial Eagle, (S) Aguila imperial, Aguila Imperial Oriental, (F) Aigle impérial, **I** ACCIPITRIDAE Av
Aquila heliaca ssp. *adalberti = Aquila adalberti*
Aquila imperiale iberica (F): *Aquila adalberti*
Aquila nipalensis : (E) Steppe Eagle, (S) Aquila Esteparia, (F) Aigle des steppes, **II** ACCIPITRIDAE Av
Aquila orientalis = Aquila nipalensis
Aquila pomarina : (E) Lesser Spotted Eagle, (S) Aguila Pomerana, (F) Aigle pomarin, **II** ACCIPITRIDAE Av
Aquila rapax : (E) Steppe Eagle , Tawny Eagle, (S) Aguila Esteparia, Aguila Rapáz, (F) Aigle ravisseur, **II** ACCIPITRIDAE Av
Aquila verreauxii : (E) African Black Eagle, Black Eagle, Verreaux's Eagle, (S) Aguila cafre, (F) Aigle de Verreaux, **II** ACCIPITRIDAE Av

Aquila vindhiana = Aquila rapax
Aquila wahlbergi : (E) Wahlberg's Eagle, (S) Aguila de Walhberg, (F) Aigle de Wahlberg, **II** ACCIPITRIDAE Av
Ara à collier jaune (F): *Propyrrhura auricollis*
Ara à face grise (F): *Cyanopsitta spixii*
Ara à gorge bleue (F): *Ara glaucogularis*
Ara à nuque d'or (F): *Propyrrhura auricollis*
Ara ambigua : (E) Buffon's Macaw, Great Green Macaw, (S) Guacamayo ambiguo, Guacamayo verde mayor, (F) Ara de Buffon, **I** PSITTACIDAE Av
Ara ararauna : (E) Blue-and-gold Macaw, Blue-and-yellow Macaw, (S) Guacamayo azul y amarillo, Guacamayo azulamarillo, (F) Ara bleu, **II** PSITTACIDAE Av
Ara auricollis = Propyrrhura auricollis
Ara azul (S): *Anodorhynchus glaucus*
Ara bleu (F): *Anodorhynchus glaucus/Anodorhynchus hyacinthinus/ Ara ararauna*
Ara canindé (F): *Ara glaucogularis*
Ara chloroptera : (E) Green-winged Macaw, Red-and-green Macaw, (S) Guacamayo aliverde, Guacamayo rojo, (F) Ara chloroptère, **II** PSITTACIDAE Av
Ara chloroptère (F): *Ara chloroptera*
Ara cobalt (F): *Anodorhynchus leari*
Ara couloni = Propyrrhura couloni
Ara de Buffon (F): *Ara ambigua*
Ara de Coulon (F): *Propyrrhura couloni*
Ara de Fresnaye (F): *Ara rubrogenys*
Ara de Lafresnaye (F): *Ara rubrogenys*
Ara de Lear (F): *Anodorhynchus leari*
Ara de Spix (F): *Cyanopsitta spixii*
Ara d'Illiger (F): *Propyrrhura maracana*
Ara glaucogularis : (E) Blue-throated Macaw, (S) Guacamayo amarillo, Guacamayo barbazul, Guacamayo caninde, (F) Ara à gorge bleue, Ara canindé, **I** PSITTACIDAE Av
Ara glauque (F): *Anodorhynchus glaucus*
Ara hyacinthe (F): *Anodorhynchus hyacinthinus*
Ara jacinthe (F): *Anodorhynchus hyacinthinus*
Ara macao (F): *Ara macao*
Ara macao : (E) Scarlet Macaw, (S) Guacamayo bandera, Guacamayo macao, Lapa azul, (F) Ara macao, Ara rouge, **I** PSITTACIDAE Av
Ara macavouanne (F): *Orthopsittaca manilata*
Ara manilata = Orthopsittaca manilata
Ara maracana = Propyrrhura maracana
Ara militaire (F): *Ara militaris*
Ara militaris : (E) Military Macaw, (S) Guacamayo militar, Guacamayo verde, (F) Ara militaire, **I** PSITTACIDAE Av
Ara miracana (F): *Propyrrhura maracana*
Ara nobilis = Diopsittaca nobilis
Ara noble (F): *Diopsittaca nobilis*
Ara rouge (F): *Ara macao*
Ara rubrogenys : (E) Red-fronted Macaw, (S) Guacamayo de Cochabamba, Guacamayo frentirroja, (F) Ara de Fresnaye, Ara de Lafresnaye, **I** PSITTACIDAE Av
Ara severa : (E) Chestnut-fronted Macaw, Severe Macaw, (S) Guacamayo severo, (F) Ara sévère, Ara vert, **II** PSITTACIDAE Av
Ara sévère (F): *Ara severa*
Ara vert (F): *Ara severa*
Arabian Bustard (E): *Ardeotis arabs*
Arabian Chameleon (E): *Chamaeleo arabicus*
Arabian Oryx (E): *Oryx leucoryx*
Arabian Sand Boa (E): *Eryx jayakari*
Araçari à cou noir (F): *Pteroglossus aracari*
Araçari à oreillons roux (F): *Pteroglossus castanotis*
Araçari grigri (F): *Pteroglossus aracari*
Araçari vert (F): *Pteroglossus viridis*
Araguato de Guatemala (S): *Alouatta pigra*
Arakan Forest Turtle (E): *Heosemys depressa*
Arapaima (E/S): *Arapaima gigas*
Arapaïma (F): *Arapaima gigas*

Arapaima gigas : (E) Arapaima, Giant arapaima, Pirarucu, (S) Arapaima, Paiche, (F) Arapaïma, Paiche, Pirarucu, **II** OSTEOGLOSSIDAE Ac

Aras bleus (F): *Anodorhynchus* spp.

Aras de Lear (F): *Anodorhynchus* spp.

Aras glauques (F): *Anodorhynchus* spp.

Aras hyacinthes (F): *Anodorhynchus* spp.

Arasari orejicastano (S): *Pteroglossus castanotis*

Aratinga acuticaudata : (E) Blue-crowned Conure, Blue-crowned Parakeet, (S) Aratinga cabeciazul, Carapaico, Cotorra de los Palos, (F) Conure à tête bleue, **II** PSITTACIDAE Av

Aratinga astec = Aratinga nana ssp. *astec*

Aratinga aurea : (E) Golden-crowned Conure, Peach-fronted Conure, Peach-fronted Parakeet, (S) Aratinga frentidorada, Cotorra frentidorada, (F) Conure couronnée, Perruche à front doré, **II** PSITTACIDAE Av

Aratinga auricapilla : (E) Golden-capped Conure, Golden-capped Parakeet, (S) Aratinga testadorada, (F) Conure à tête d'or, **II** PSITTACIDAE Av

Aratinga brevipes : (E) Socorro Parakeet, (S) Aratinga de Socorro, (F) Conure de Socorro, **II** PSITTACIDAE Av

Aratinga cabeciazul (S): *Aratinga acuticaudata*

Aratinga cabecifusca (S): *Aratinga weddellii*

Aratinga cactácea (S): *Aratinga cactorum*

Aratinga cactorum : (E) Caatinga Parakeet, Cactus Conure, Cactus Parakeet, (S) Aratinga cactácea, (F) Conure des cactus, **II** PSITTACIDAE Av

Aratinga canicularis : (E) Orange-fronted Conure, Orange-fronted Parakeet, (S) Aratinga frentinaranja, Perico frentinaranja, (F) Conure à front rouge, **II** PSITTACIDAE Av

Aratinga chloroptera : (E) Hispaniolan Conure, Hispaniolan Parakeet, (S) Aratinga de la Española, Perico, (F) Conure maîtresse, **II** PSITTACIDAE Av

Aratinga Cubana (S): *Aratinga euops*

Aratinga de Finsch (S): *Aratinga finschi*

Aratinga de Guayaquil (S): *Aratinga erythrogenys*

Aratinga de la Española (S): *Aratinga chloroptera*

Aratinga de pinceles (S): *Leptosittaca branickii*

Aratinga de Socorro (S): *Aratinga brevipes*

Aratinga de Wagler (S): *Aratinga wagleri*

Aratinga erythrogenys : (E) Red-masked Conure, Red-masked Parakeet, (S) Aratinga de Guayaquil, Perico caretirrojo, (F) Conure à tête rouge, **II** PSITTACIDAE Av

Aratinga euops : (E) Cuban Conure, Cuban Parakeet, (S) Aratinga Cubana, (F) Conure de Cuba, **II** PSITTACIDAE Av

Aratinga finschi : (E) Crimson-fronted Conure, Crimson-fronted Parakeet, Finsch's Conure, (S) Aratinga de Finsch, (F) Conure de Finsch, **II** PSITTACIDAE Av

Aratinga frentidorada (S): *Aratinga aurea*

Aratinga frentinaranja (S): *Aratinga canicularis*

Aratinga gorgirroja (S): *Aratinga rubritorquis*

Aratinga guarouba = Guarouba guarouba

Aratinga guaruba (S): *Guarouba guarouba*

Aratinga holochlora : (E) Green Conure, Green Parakeet, (S) Aratinga verde, Perico verde, (F) Conure verte, **II** PSITTACIDAE Av

Aratinga holochlora ssp. *brevipes = Aratinga brevipes*

Aratinga jandaya (S): *Aratinga jandaya*

Aratinga jandaya : (E) Jandaya Conure, Jandaya Parakeet, Yellow-headed Parakeet, (S) Aratinga jandaya, (F) Conure jandaya, Perruche de Jenday, **II** PSITTACIDAE Av

Aratinga leucophthalmus : (E) White-eyed Conure, White-eyed Parakeet, Witoogaratinga, (S) Aratinga ojiblanca, Cotorra verde, Perico ojo blanco, (F) Conure pavouane, **II** PSITTACIDAE Av

Aratinga mitrada (S): *Aratinga mitrata*

Aratinga mitrata : (E) Mitred Conure, Mitred Parakeet, (S) Aratinga mitrada, Cotorra carirroja, (F) Conure mitrée, **II** PSITTACIDAE Av

Aratinga nana : (E) Aztec Parakeet, Olive-throated Conure, Olive-throated Parakeet, (S) Aratinga pechisucia, Perico pechisucio, (F) Conure aztèque, **II** PSITTACIDAE Av

Aratinga ñanday (S): *Nandayus nenday*

Aratinga ojiblanca (S): *Aratinga leucophthalmus*

Aratinga orejigualda (S): *Ognorhynchus icterotis*

Aratinga pechisucia (S): *Aratinga nana*

Aratinga pertinax : (E) Brown-throated Conure, Brown-throated Parakeet, (S) Aratinga pertinaz, Perico cara sucia, (F) Conure cuivrée, **II** PSITTACIDAE Av

Aratinga pertinaz (S): *Aratinga pertinax*

Aratinga rubritorquis : (E) Red-throated Parakeet, (S) Aratinga gorgirroja, (F) Conure à gorge rouge, **II** PSITTACIDAE Av

Aratinga sol (S): *Aratinga solstitialis*

Aratinga solstitialis : (E) Sun Conure, Sun Parakeet, (S) Aratinga sol, Perico dorado, (F) Conure soleil, Perruche du soleil, **II** PSITTACIDAE Av

Aratinga strenua = Aratinga holochlora

Aratinga testadorada (S): *Aratinga auricapilla*

Aratinga verde (S): *Aratinga holochlora*

Aratinga wagleri : (E) Red-fronted Conure, Scarlet-fronted Parakeet, (S) Aratinga de Wagler, Chacaraco, (F) Conure de Wagler, **II** PSITTACIDAE Av

Aratinga weddellii : (E) Dusky-headed Conure, Dusky-headed Parakeet, (S) Aratinga cabecifusca, Perico cabecioscuro, (F) Conure de Weddell, **II** PSITTACIDAE Av

Arboreal Mantella (E): *Mantella laevigata*

Arborófila de Sumatra (S): *Arborophila orientalis*

Arborófila pechicastaña (S): *Arborophila charltonii*

Arborophila charltonii : (E) Chestnut-breasted Tree-Partridge, Chestnut-necklaced Partridge, (S) Arborófila pechicastaña, Perdiz de bosque de Charlton, (F) Torquéole à poitrine châtaine, Torquéole de Merlin, Torquéole des bois, **III** PHASIANIDAE Av

Arborophila orientalis : (E) Bar-backed Partridge, Grey-breasted Partridge, (S) Arborófila de Sumatra, (F) Torquéole à poitrine brune, Torquéole de Sumatra, **III** PHASIANIDAE Av

Arch-beaked Whale (E): *Mesoplodon carlhubbsi*

Archer's Buzzard (E): *Buteo archeri*

Archibebe manchado (S): *Tringa guttifer*

Archibebe moteado (S): *Tringa guttifer*

Archilochus alexandri : (E) Black-chinned Hummingbird, (S) Colibrí barbinegro, Colibrí gorgirubí, (F) Colibri à gorge noire, **II** TROCHILIDAE Av

Archilochus anna = Calypte anna

Archilochus calliope = Stellula calliope

Archilochus colubris : (E) Ruby-throated Hummingbird, (S) Colibrí gorjirrubí, (F) Colibri à gorge rubis, **II** TROCHILIDAE Av

Archohelia rediviva : **II** OCULINIDAE An

Arctictis binturong : (E) Binturong, (S) Binturong, (F) Binturong, **III** VIVERRIDAE Ma

Arctocèbe (F): *Arctocebus calabarensis*

Arctocebus aureus : (E) Golden Potto **II** LORIDAE Ma

Arctocebus calabarensis : (E) Angwantibo, (S) Poto dorado, (F) Angwantibo, Arctocèbe, Potto de Calabar, **II** LORIDAE Ma

Arctocebus calabarensis ssp. *aureus = Arctocebus aureus*

Arctocéphale d'Afrique du Sud (F): *Arctocephalus pusillus*

Arctocéphale d'Australie (F): *Arctocephalus tropicalis*

Arctocéphale de Guadalupe (F): *Arctocephalus townsendi*

Arctocéphale de Juan Fernandez (F): *Arctocephalus philippii*

Arctocéphale de Kerguelen (F): *Arctocephalus gazella*

Arctocéphale des Galapagos (F): *Arctocephalus galapagoensis*

Arctocéphales du Sud (F): *Arctocephalus* spp.

Arctocephalus spp.: (E) Fur seals, Southern fur seals, (S) Osos marinos, (F) Arctocéphales du Sud, Otaries à fourrure, Otaries à fourrure du Sud, **I/II** OTARIIDAE Ma

Arctocephalus australis : (E) South American Fur Seal, Southern Fur Seal, (S) Lobo fino sudamericano, Oso marino austral, (F) Otarie à fourrure australe, **II** OTARIIDAE Ma

Arctocephalus doriferus = Arctocephalus pusillus

Arctocephalus forsteri : (E) New Zealand Fur Seal, (S) Oso marino de Nueva Zelanda **II** OTARIIDAE Ma

Arctocephalus galapagoensis : (E) Galapagos Fur Seal, Galapagos Islands Fur Seal, (S) Oso marino de las Galápagos, (F) Arctocéphale des Galapagos, **II** OTARIIDAE Ma

Arctocephalus gazella : (E) Antarctic Fur Seal, Kerguelen Fur Seal, (F) Arctocéphale de Kerguelen, **II** OTARIIDAE Ma

Arctocephalus philippii : (E) Juan Fernández Fur Seal, (S) Oso marino de Chile, (F) Arctocéphale de Juan Fernandez, **II** OTARIIDAE Ma

Arctocephalus pusillus : (E) Afro-Australian Fur Seal, Cape Fur Seal, South African Fur Seal, (F) Arctocéphale d'Afrique du Sud, **II** OTARIIDAE Ma

Arctocephalus tasmanicus = Arctocephalus pusillus

Arctocephalus townsendi : (E) Guadalupe Fur Seal, Lower Californian Fur Seal, (S) Oso marino de Guadalupe, Otaria americano, (F) Arctocéphale de Guadalupe, Otarie à fourrure d'Amérique, **I** OTARIIDAE Ma

Arctocephalus tropicalis : (E) Amsterdam Island Fur Seal, Subantarctic Fur Seal, (F) Arctocéphale d'Australie, **II** OTARIIDAE Ma

Ardea goliath : (E) Goliath Heron, (S) Garza goliat, (F) Héron goliath, **III** ARDEIDAE Av

Ardeola ibis = Bubulcus ibis

Ardeotis arabs : (E) Arabian Bustard, (S) Avutarda árabe, (F) Grande outarde arabe, Outarde arabe, **II** OTIDIDAE Av

Ardeotis australis : (E) Australian Bustard, (S) Avutarda australiana, (F) Outarde australienne, Outarde d'Australie, **II** OTIDIDAE Av

Ardeotis kori : (E) Kori Bustard, (S) Avutarda kori, (F) Outarde kori, **II** OTIDIDAE Av

Ardeotis nigriceps : (E) Great Indian Bustard, Indian Bustard, (S) Avutarda de la India, Avutarda india, Avutarda índica, (F) Outarde à tête noire, Outarde de l'Inde, **I** OTIDIDAE Av

Ardilla costarricense (S): *Sciurus deppei*

Ardilla de Deppe (S): *Sciurus deppei*

Ardilla de las palmeras (S): *Epixerus ebii*

Ardilla de los pinos (S): *Sciurus deppei*

Ardilla de palmera (S): *Epixerus ebii*

Ardilla voladera de orejas largas (S): *Idiurus macrotis*

Ardilla voladora enana (S): *Idiurus macrotis*

Ardillas gigantes (S): *Ratufa* spp.

Areolated Tortoise (E): *Homopus areolatus*

Arfak Astrapia (E): *Astrapia nigra*

Arfak Parotia (E): *Parotia sefilata*

Argali (E/F): *Ovis ammon*

Argalí (S): *Ovis ammon*

Argalí del Himalaya (S): *Ovis ammon hodgsonii*

Argentine Boa Constrictor (E): *Boa constrictor occidentalis*

Argentine Grey Fox (E): *Pseudalopex griseus*

Argentine Teju (E): *Tupinambis rufescens*

Argentine Tortoise (E): *Geochelone chilensis*

Argos gigante (S): *Argusianus argus*

Argos real (S): *Argusianus argus*

Argus géant (F): *Argusianus argus*

Argus ocellé (F): *Rheinardia ocellata*

Argus Pheasant (E): *Argusianus argus*

Argusianus argus : (E) Argus Pheasant, Great Argus, (S) Argos gigante, Argos real, Faisán argos, (F) Argus géant, **II** PHASIANIDAE Av

Ariane à couronne azur (F): *Agyrtria cyanocephala*

Ariane à couronne violette (F): *Agyrtria violiceps*

Ariane à front bleu (F): *Saucerottia cyanifrons*

Ariane à front vert (F): *Agyrtria viridifrons*

Ariane à poitrine blanche (F): *Agyrtria brevirostris*

Ariane à queue bleue (F): *Saucerottia cyanura*

Ariane à ventre blanc (F): *Leucippus chionogaster*

Ariane à ventre gris (F): *Amazilia tzacatl*

Ariane à ventre roux (F): *Amazilia castaneiventris*

Ariane à ventre vert (F): *Saucerottia viridigaster*

Ariane aimable (F): *Polyerata amabilis*

Ariane béryl (F): *Saucerottia beryllina*

Ariane candide (F): *Agyrtria candida*

Ariane cannelle (F): *Amazilia rutila*

Ariane de Boucard (F): *Polyerata boucardi*

Ariane de Félicie (F): *Saucerottia tobaci*

Ariane de Francia (F): *Agyrtria franciae*

Ariane de Lesson (F): *Amazilia amazilia*

Ariane de Linné (F): *Polyerata fimbriata*

Ariane de Lucy (F): *Polyerata luciae*

Ariane de Rosenberg (F): *Polyerata rosenbergi*

Ariane de Sophie (F): *Saucerottia saucerrottei*

Ariane d'Edward (F): *Saucerottia edward*

Ariane du Pérou (F): *Leucippus viridicauda*

Ariane du Yucatan (F): *Amazilia yucatanensis*

Ariane saphirine (F): *Polyerata lactea*

Ariane versicolore (F): *Agyrtria versicolor*

Ariane vert-doré (F): *Agyrtria leucogaster*

Arid Monitor (E): *Varanus tristis*

Arirai (S): *Pteronura brasiliensis*

Armadillo gigante (S): *Priodontes maximus*

Armadillo Girdled Lizard (E): *Cordylus cataphractus*

Armadillo peludo andino (S): *Chaetophractus nationi*

Armadillo Spiny-tailed Lizard (E): *Cordylus cataphractus*

Armado de zapilots (S): *Cabassous centralis*

Armoured Teyou (E): *Dracaena guianensis*

Arni (F): *Bubalus arnee*

Arnoux's Beaked Whale (E): *Berardius arnuxii*

Arowana (E): *Scleropages formosus*

Arpía (S): *Harpia harpyja*

Arpía mayor (S): *Harpia harpyja*

Arpía menor (S): *Morphnus guianensis*

Arpía papúa (S): *Harpyopsis novaeguineae*

Arrau (E): *Podocnemis expansa*

Arruí (S): *Ammotragus lervia*

Artichoke Coral (E): *Scolymia cubensis*

Ascagne (F): *Cercopithecus ascanius*

Ashy-faced Owl (E): *Tyto glaucops*

Ashy-headed Flying-fox (E): *Pteropus caniceps*

Asian Arowana (E): *Scleropages formosus*

Asian Barred Owlet (E): *Glaucidium cuculoides*

Asian Baza (E): *Aviceda jerdoni*

Asian Black Eagle (E): *Ictinaetus malayensis*

Asian Black Hornbill (E): *Anthracoceros malayanus*

Asian Black Vulture (E): *Sarcogyps calvus*

Asian Bonytongue (E): *Scleropages formosus*

Asian box turtles (E): *Cuora* spp.

Asian Caracal (E): *Caracal caracal*

Asian Cobra (E): *Naja naja*

Asian Crested Goshawk (E): *Accipiter trivirgatus*

Asian Elephant (E): *Elephas maximus*

Asian Giant Softshell Turtle (E): *Pelochelys cantorii*

Asian Giant Tortoise (E): *Manouria emys*

Asian King Vulture (E): *Sarcogyps calvus*

Asian Palm Civet (E): *Paradoxurus hermaphroditus*

Asian Tapir (E): *Tapirus indicus*

Asian Tortoise (E): *Manouria emys*

Asian White-backed Vulture (E): *Gyps bengalensis*

Asian White-crested Hornbill (E): *Aceros comatus*

Asian Wild Ass (E): *Equus hemionus*

Asian Wild Sheep (E): *Ovis ammon*

Asiatic Black Bear (E): *Ursus thibetanus*

Asiatic Cobra (E): *Naja naja*

Asiatic Golden Cat (E): *Catopuma temminckii*

Asiatic Lion (E): *Panthera leo persica*

Asiatic Rock Python (E): *Python molurus*

Asiatic Water Snake (E): *Xenochrophis piscator*
Asiatic Wild Ass (E): *Equus hemionus*
Asiatic Wild Dog (E): *Cuon alpinus*
Asio abyssinicus : (E) Abyssinian long-eared owl, Abyssinian Owl, (S) Búho Abisinio, (F) Hibou d'Abyssinie, **II** STRIGIDAE Av
Asio capensis : (E) African Marsh Owl, Marsh Owl, (S) Búho moro, Lechuza mora, (F) Hibou du Cap, **II** STRIGIDAE Av
Asio clamator : (E) Striped Owl, (S) Búho gritón, Búho-cornudo cariblanco, Lechuza listada, Lechuzón, Lechuzón orejas largas, Lechuzón orejudo, (F) Hibou criard, Hibou strié, **II** STRIGIDAE Av
Asio flammeus : (E) Short-eared Owl, (S) Búho campestre, Búho orejicorto, Lechuza campestre, Lechuza orejicorta, Lechuzón campestre, (F) Hibou brachyote, Hibou des marais, **II** STRIGIDAE Av
Asio madagascariensis : (E) Madagascar Owl, (S) Búho Malgache, Lechuza orejita de Madagascar, (F) Hibou de Madgascar, Hibou malgache, **II** STRIGIDAE Av
Asio otus : (E) Long-eared Owl, (S) Búho chico, Búho-cornudo caricafe, (F) Hibou moyen-duc, **II** STRIGIDAE Av
Asio otus ssp. *abyssinicus = Asio abyssinicus*
Asio stygius : (E) Stygian Owl, (S) Búho negruzco, Búho-cornudo oscuro, Lechuza estigia, Lechuzón negruzco, (F) Hibou maître-bois, **II** STRIGIDAE Av
Asno salvaje de Africa (S): *Equus africanus*
Aspideretes gangeticus : (E) Indian Softshell Turtle, (S) Tortuga del Ganges, **I** TRIONYCHIDAE Re
Aspideretes hurum : (E) Indian Peacock Softshell Turtle, Peacock Soft-shell Turtle, (S) Tortuga pavo, **I** TRIONYCHIDAE Re
Aspideretes nigricans : (E) Black Softshell Turtle, Bostami Turtle, (S) Tortuga sombría, **I** TRIONYCHIDAE Re
Aspidites melanocephalus : (E) Black-headed Python, (S) Pitón de cabeza negra, (F) Python à tête noire d'Australie, Woma, **II** PYTHONIDAE Re
Aspidites ramsayi : (E) Ramsay's Python, Woma, (S) Pitón de Ramsay, (F) Python de Ramsay, Woma, **II** PYTHONIDAE Re
Assam Brown-backed Hornbill (E): *Anorrhinus tickelli*
Assam Macaque (E): *Macaca assamensis*
Assam Rabbit (E): *Caprolagus hispidus*
Assam Roofed Turtle (E): *Kachuga sylhetensis*
Assamese Macaque (E): *Macaca assamensis*
Asterochelys radiata = Geochelone radiata
Asterochelys yniphora = Geochelone yniphora
Asterosmilia gigas = Anomocora gigas
Asterosmilia marchadi = Anomocora marchadi
Asterosmilia prolifera = Anomocora prolifera
Astourion (F): *Acipenser sturio*
Astraeosmilia connata : **II** FAVIIDAE An
Astrangia atrata : **II** RHIZANGIIDAE An
Astrangia browni : **II** RHIZANGIIDAE An
Astrangia caboensis = Astrangia haimei
Astrangia californica : **II** RHIZANGIIDAE An
Astrangia concepcionensis = Astrangia haimei
Astrangia concinna = Astrangia haimei
Astrangia conferta : **II** RHIZANGIIDAE An
Astrangia cortezi = Astrangia haimei
Astrangia costata : **II** RHIZANGIIDAE An
Astrangia dentata : **II** RHIZANGIIDAE An
Astrangia epithecata = Astrangia solitaria
Astrangia equatorialis : **II** RHIZANGIIDAE An
Astrangia haimei : **II** RHIZANGIIDAE An
Astrangia hancocki = Astrangia haimei
Astrangia howardi : **II** RHIZANGIIDAE An
Astrangia lajollaensis = Astrangia haimei
Astrangia macrodentata : **II** RHIZANGIIDAE An
Astrangia mercatoris : **II** RHIZANGIIDAE An
Astrangia minuta = Astrangia solitaria
Astrangia oaxacensis = Astrangia haimei
Astrangia pedersenii = Astrangia haimei

Astrangia poculata : (E) Northern Star Coral **II** RHIZANGIIDAE An
Astrangia pulchella = Astrangia haimei
Astrangia rathbuni : **II** RHIZANGIIDAE An
Astrangia sanfelipensis = Astrangia haimei
Astrangia solitaria : **II** RHIZANGIIDAE An
Astrangia tangolaensis = Astrangia californica
Astrangia woodsi : **II** RHIZANGIIDAE An
Astrapia mayeri : (E) Ribbon-tailed Astrapia, Ribbon-tailed Bird-of-paradise, (F) Paradisier à rubans, **II** PARADISAEIDAE Av
Astrapia nigra : (E) Arfak Astrapia, (F) Hausse-col doré, Paradisier à gorge noire, **II** PARADISAEIDAE Av
Astrapia rothschildi : (E) Huon Astrapia, (F) Hausse-col de Rothschild, Paradisier de Rothschild, **II** PARADISAEIDAE Av
Astrapia splendidissima : (E) Splendid Astrapia, (F) Hausse-col splendide, Paradisier splendide, **II** PARADISAEIDAE Av
Astrapia stephaniae : (E) Princess Stephanie's Bird-of-paradise, Stephanie's Astrapia, (F) Hausse-col à queue rubanée, Paradisier de la princesse Stéphanie, Paradisier de Stéphanie, **II** PARADISAEIDAE Av
Astreopora spp.: (E) Moon corals, Porous star corals, **II** ACROPORIDAE An
Astreopora cucullata : **II** ACROPORIDAE An
Astreopora elliptica = Astreopora myriophthalma
Astreopora expansa : **II** ACROPORIDAE An
Astreopora explanata : **II** ACROPORIDAE An
Astreopora gracilis : **II** ACROPORIDAE An
Astreopora incrustans : **II** ACROPORIDAE An
Astreopora lambertsi : **II** ACROPORIDAE An
Astreopora listeri : **II** ACROPORIDAE An
Astreopora macrostoma : **II** ACROPORIDAE An
Astreopora moretonensis : **II** ACROPORIDAE An
Astreopora myriophthalma : **II** ACROPORIDAE An
Astreopora ocellata : **II** ACROPORIDAE An
Astreopora randalli : **II** ACROPORIDAE An
Astreopora scabra : **II** ACROPORIDAE An
Astreopora suggesta : **II** ACROPORIDAE An
Astrild à joues oranges (F): *Estrilda melpoda*
Astrild caille (F): *Ortygospiza atricollis*
Astrild cendré (F): *Estrilda troglodytes*
Astrild fourmilier (F): *Parmoptila rubrifrons*
Astrild mésange (F): *Pholidornis rushiae*
Astrild ondulé (F): *Estrilda astrild*
Astrild queue-de-vinaigre (F): *Estrilda caerulescens*
Astrild vert pointillé (F): *Mandingoa nitidula*
Astrilda aperdizada (S): *Ortygospiza atricollis*
Astrilda carirroja (S): *Estrilda melpoda*
Astrilda ceniza del Senegal (S): *Estrilda caerulescens*
Astrilda común (S): *Estrilda astrild*
Astrilda culinegra (S): *Estrilda troglodytes*
Astrilda pechigualda (S): *Amandava subflava*
Astrild-caille à lunettes (F): *Ortygospiza atricollis*
Astroides calycularis : **II** DENDROPHYLLIIDAE An
Astropsammia pedersenii = Tubastraea coccinea
Asturina nitida : (E) Grey-lined Hawk, (S) Aguilucho gris, Busardo gris, Gavilán gris, (F) Buse cendrée, **II** ACCIPITRIDAE Av
Asturina plagiata : (E) Grey Hawk, (S) Aguililla gris, (F) Buse grise, **II** ACCIPITRIDAE Av
Astya aspidopora : **II** STYLASTERIDAE Hy
Astya subviridis : **II** STYLASTERIDAE Hy
Atèle à tête brune (F): *Ateles fusciceps*
Atèle arachnoïde (F): *Brachyteles arachnoides*
Atèle belzébuth (F): *Ateles belzebuth*
Atèle de Geoffroy (F): *Ateles geoffroyi*
Atèle de Geoffroy du Panama (F): *Ateles geoffroyi panamensis*
Atèle du Costa Rica (F): *Ateles geoffroyi frontatus*
Atèle du Panama (F): *Ateles geoffroyi panamensis*
Atèle noir (F): *Ateles paniscus*

Checklist of fauna/Lista de especies de fauna/Liste des espèces animales

Ateles belzebuth : (E) Long-haired Spider Monkey, White-bellied Spider Monkey, (F) Atèle belzébuth, **II** CEBIDAE Ma

Ateles belzebuth ssp. *marginatus* = *Ateles marginatus*

Ateles chamek : (E) Black-faced Black Spider Monkey, **II** CEBIDAE Ma

Ateles de Geoffroy (S): *Ateles geoffroyi*

Ateles de Panamá (S): *Ateles geoffroyi panamensis*

Ateles fusciceps : (E) Brown-headed Spider Monkey, (F) Atèle à tête brune, **II** CEBIDAE Ma

Ateles geoffroyi : (E) Black-handed Spider Monkey, Geoffroy's Spider Monkey, Mono colorado, (S) Ateles de Geoffroy, (F) Atèle de Geoffroy, **I/II** CEBIDAE Ma

Ateles geoffroyi frontatus : (E) Black-browed Spider Monkey, Red-bellied Spider Monkey, (S) Mono araña maninegro, (F) Atèle du Costa Rica, Singe araignée du Panama, Singe-araignée aux mains noires, **I** CEBIDAE Ma

Ateles geoffroyi panamensis : (E) Panama Spider Monkey, Red Spider Monkey, (S) Ateles de Panamá, Mono araña de panamá, (F) Atèle de Geoffroy du Panama, Atèle du Panama, **I** CEBIDAE Ma

Ateles marginatus : (E) White-whiskered Spider Monkey, **II** CEBIDAE Ma

Ateles paniscus : (E) Red-faced Black Spider Monkey, (F) Atèle noir, **II** CEBIDAE Ma

Ateles paniscus ssp. *chamek* = *Ateles chamek*

Atelope variable du Panama (F): *Atelopus zeteki*

Atelopus varius ssp. *zeteki* = *Atelopus zeteki*

Atelopus zeteki : (E) Cerro Campana Stubfoot Toad, Golden Arrow Poison Frog, Golden Frog, Zetek's Golden Frog, (S) Rana dorada, Rana dorada de Panamá, Rana venenosa de Zetek, (F) Atelope variable du Panama, Crapaud orange, Grenouille de Zetek, **I** BUFONIDAE Am

Athene blewitti : (E) Forest Little Owl, Forest Owlet, Forest Spotted Owlet, (S) Mochuelo de Blewitt, Mochuelo de los bosques, Mochuelo forestal, (F) Chevêche forestière, Chouette des forêts, **I** STRIGIDAE Av

Athene brama : (E) Spotted Little Owl, Spotted Owlet, (S) Mochuelo brahmán, (F) Chevêche brame, **II** STRIGIDAE Av

Athene cunicularia = *Speotyto cunicularia*

Athene noctua : (E) Little Owl, Northern Little Owl, Tibet Owlet, (S) Mochuelo común, Mochuelo Europeo, (F) Chevêche d'Athéna, Chouette Chevêche, **II** STRIGIDAE Av

Atitlan Grebe (E): *Podilymbus gigas*

Atlantic Coral Snake (E): *Micrurus diastema*

Atlantic Dolphin (E): *Delphinus delphis*

Atlantic Humpbacked Dolphin (E): *Sousa teuszii*

Atlantic Mushroom Coral (E): *Scolymia lacera*

Atlantic Ridley (E): *Lepidochelys kempi*

Atlantic Spinner Dolphin (E): *Stenella clymene*

Atlantic Spotted Dolphin (E): *Stenella frontalis*

Atlantic Sturgeon (E): *Acipenser oxyrinchus/ Acipenser sturio*

Atlantic White-sided Dolphin (E): *Lagenorhynchus acutus*

Atlas Deer (E): *Cervus elaphus barbarus*

Atretium schistosum : (E) Olivaceous Keelback, Olive Keelback, Split Keelback, (F) Serpent à caréné olive, Serpent ardoisé, **III** COLUBRIDAE Re

Atrichorne bruyant (F): *Atrichornis clamosus*

Atrichornis clamosus : (E) Noisy Scrub-bird, Western Scrub-bird, Corredor chillón, Pájaro de los matorrales, (F) Atrichorne bruyant, Oiseau bruyant des buissons, **I** ATRICHORNITHIDAE Av

Atrophaneura jophon : (E) Sri Lankan Rose, **II** PAPILIONIDAE In

Atrophaneura pandiyana : **II** PAPILIONIDAE In

Atthis ellioti : (E) Wine-throated Hummingbird, (S) Colibrí de Elliot, Zimbador centroamericano, (F) Colibri d'Elliot, **II** TROCHILIDAE Av

Atthis heloisa : (E) Bumblebee Hummingbird, (S) Colibrí de Eloísa, Zimbador mexicano, (F) Colibri héloïse, **II** TROCHILIDAE Av

Attwater's Prairie-chicken (E): *Tympanuchus cupido attwateri*

Augastes geoffroyi : (E) Wedge-billed Hummingbird, (S) Colibrí pico de cuña, Colibrí picocuña, Colibrí piquicunna, (F) Colibri de Geoffroy, **II** TROCHILIDAE Av

Augastes lumachella : (E) Hooded Visorbearer, (S) Colibrí lumaquela, (F) Colibri lumachelle, **II** TROCHILIDAE Av

Augastes scutatus : (E) Hyacinth Visorbearer, (S) Colibrí colaceleste, (F) Colibri superbe, **II** TROCHILIDAE Av

Augur Buzzard (E): *Buteo augur*

Aullado (S): *Alouatta palliata*

Aulocyathus atlanticus : **II** CARYOPHYLLIIDAE An

Aulocyathus juvenescens : **II** CARYOPHYLLIIDAE An

Aulocyathus matricidus : **II** CARYOPHYLLIIDAE An

Aulocyathus recidivus : **II** CARYOPHYLLIIDAE An

Aura gallipavo (S): *Cathartes aura*

Aura sabanera (S): *Cathartes burrovianus*

Aura selvática (S): *Cathartes melambrotus*

Aurora Finch (E): *Pytilia phoenicoptera*

Austral Conure (E): *Enicognathus ferrugineus*

Austral Parakeet (E): *Enicognathus ferrugineus*

Austral Pygmy-Owl (E): *Glaucidium nanum*

Australasian Goshawk (E): *Accipiter fasciatus*

Australasian Harrier (E): *Circus approximans*

Australian Black-shouldered Kite (E): *Elanus axillaris*

Australian Bustard (E): *Ardeotis australis*

Australian Fresh-water Crocodile (E): *Crocodylus johnsoni*

Australian Hobby (E): *Falco longipennis*

Australian Kestrel (E): *Falco cenchroides*

Australian King-Parrot (E): *Alisterus scapularis*

Australian Lungfish (E): *Neoceratodus forsteri*

Australian Masked-Owl (E): *Tyto novaehollandiae*

Australian Ringneck (E): *Barnardius zonarius*

Australocyathus vincentinus : **II** TURBINOLIIDAE An

Australogyra zelli : **II** FAVIIDAE An

Australomussa rowleyensis : **II** MUSSIDAE An

Australophocaena dioptrica : (E) Spectacled Porpoise, (S) Marsopa de anteojo, (F) Marsouin à lunettes, Marsouin de Lahille, **II** PHOCOENIDAE Ma

Autillo (S): *Otus scops*

Autillo Africano (S): *Otus scops*

Autillo barbudo (S): *Otus barbarus*

Autillo bigotudo (S): *Otus trichopsis*

Autillo Californiano (S): *Otus kennicottii*

Autillo capirotado (S): *Otus atricapillus*

Autillo cariblanco (S): *Otus leucotis*

Autillo chino (S): *Otus bakkamoena*

Autillo chóliba (S): *Otus choliba*

Autillo Cubano (S): *Otus lawrencii*

Autillo de Andamán (S): *Otus balli*

Autillo de Célebes (S): *Otus manadensis*

Autillo de Guerney (S): *Mimizuku gurneyi*

Autillo de Java (S): *Otus angelinae*

Autillo de Koepcke (S): *Otus koepckeae*

Autillo de la Mantanani (S): *Otus mantananensis*

Autillo de la Sangihe (S): *Otus collari*

Autillo de la Simeulue (S): *Otus umbra*

Autillo de la Sonda (S): *Otus bakkamoena*

Autillo de las Comores (S): *Otus pauliani*

Autillo de las Mentawai (S): *Otus mentawi*

Autillo de las Palau (S): *Otus podarginus*

Autillo de Luzón (S): *Otus longicornis*

Autillo de Marshall (S): *Otus marshalli*

Autillo de Mindanao (S): *Otus mirus*

Autillo de Mindoro (S): *Otus mindorensis*

Autillo de Moheli (S): *Otus moheliensis*

Autillo de Nicobar (S): *Otus alius*

Autillo de Palawan (S): *Otus fuliginosus*

Autillo de Santa Catarina (S): *Otus sanctaecatarinae*
Autillo de Santo Tomé (S): *Otus hartlaubi*
Autillo de Sokoke (S): *Otus ireneae*
Autillo de Wallace (S): *Otus silvicola*
Autillo del Amazonas (S): *Otus watsonii*
Autillo elegante (S): *Otus elegans*
Autillo europeo (S): *Otus scops*
Autillo Filipino (S): *Otus megalotis*
Autillo flamulado (S): *Otus flammeolus*
Autillo frentiblanco (S): *Otus sagittatus*
Autillo gorgiblanco (S): *Otus albogularis*
Autillo Indio (S): *Otus bakkamoena*
Autillo Malgache (S): *Otus rutilus*
Autillo Moluqueño (S): *Otus magicus*
Autillo montano (S): *Otus spilocephalus*
Autillo Oriental (S): *Otus scops*
Autillo pálido (S): *Otus ingens*
Autillo Persa (S): *Otus brucei*
Autillo peruano (S): *Otus roboratus*
Autillo piquigualdo (S): *Otus icterorhynchus*
Autillo Portorriqueño (S): *Otus nudipes*
Autillo Rajá (S): *Otus brookii*
Autillo roborado (S): *Otus roboratus*
Autillo rojizo (S): *Otus rufescens*
Autillo serrano (S): *Otus clarkii*
Autillo vermiculado (S): *Otus vermiculatus*
Autillo yanqui (S): *Otus asio*
Autour à ailes grises (F): *Melierax poliopterus*
Autour à flancs roux (F): *Accipiter castanilius*
Autour à longue queue (F): *Urotriorchis macrourus*
Autour à manteau noir (F): *Accipiter melanochlamys*
Autour à tête grise (F): *Accipiter poliocephalus*
Autour à ventre blanc (F): *Accipiter haplochrous*
Autour à ventre gris (F): *Accipiter poliogaster*
Autour australien (F): *Accipiter fasciatus*
Autour blanc (F): *Accipiter novaehollandiae*
Autour bleu et gris (F): *Accipiter luteoschistaceus*
Autour chanteur (F): *Melierax canorus*
Autour de Bürger (F): *Erythrotriorchis buergersi*
Autour de Doria (F): *Megatriorchis doriae*
Autour de Henst (F): *Accipiter henstii*
Autour de Mayr (F): *Accipiter princeps*
Autour de Meyer (F): *Accipiter meyerianus*
Autour de Toussenel (F): *Accipiter tousseneli*
Autour des Célèbes (F): *Accipiter griseiceps*
Autour des Fidji (F): *Accipiter rufitorques*
Autour des Moluques (F): *Accipiter henicogrammus*
Autour des palombes (F): *Accipiter gentilis*
Autour gabar (F): *Melierax gabar*
Autour huppé (F): *Accipiter trivirgatus*
Autour imitateur (F): *Accipiter imitator*
Autour minulle (F): *Accipiter erythropus*
Autour noir (F): *Accipiter melanoleucus*
Autour pie (F): *Accipiter albogularis*
Autour rouge (F): *Erythrotriorchis radiatus*
Autour sombre (F): *Melierax metabates*
Autour tachiro (F): *Accipiter tachiro*
Autour unibande (F): *Kaupifalco monogrammicus*
Autruche d'Afrique (F): *Struthio camelus*
Avahi (E/F): *Avahi laniger*
Avahi laineux (F): *Avahi laniger*
Avahi laniger : (E) Avahi, Woolly Indris, Woolly Lemur, (S) Indri lanudo, (F) Avahi, Avahi laineux, Maki à bourre, **I** INDRIDAE Ma
Avahi occidentalis = Avahi laniger
Avahi unicolor : (E) Unicolor Avahi, **I** INDRIDAE Ma
Avahis (F): INDRIDAE spp.
Ave de anteojos de pecho blanco (S): *Zosterops albogularis*
Aves de rapiña (S): FALCONIFORMES spp. Av
Aves del paraíso (S): PARADISAEIDAE spp.
Avestruz (S): *Rhea americana/ Struthio camelus*
Avestruz de Magallanes (S): *Rhea pennata*

Aviceda cuculoides : (E) African Baza, African Cuckoo-Falcon, African Cuckoo-Hawk, (S) Baza africano, (F) Baza coucou, Faucon-coucou, **II** ACCIPITRIDAE Av
Aviceda jerdoni : (E) Asian Baza, Jerdon's Baza, (S) Baza oriental, (F) Baza de Jerdon, **II** ACCIPITRIDAE Av
Aviceda leuphotes : (E) Black Baza, (S) Baza negro, (F) Baza huppard, **II** ACCIPITRIDAE Av
Aviceda madagascariensis : (E) Madagascar Baza, Madagascar Cuckoo-Falcon, Madagascar Cuckoo-Hawk, (S) Baza malgache, (F) Baza malgache, **II** ACCIPITRIDAE Av
Aviceda subcristata : (E) Crested Baza, Pacific Baza, (S) Baza australiano, (F) Baza huppé, **II** ACCIPITRIDAE Av
Avocettula recurvirostris = Anthracothorax recurvirostris
Avutarda (S): *Otis tarda*
Avutarda árabe (S): *Ardeotis arabs*
Avutarda australiana (S): *Ardeotis australis*
Avutarda bengalí (S): *Eupodotis bengalensis*
Avutarda cafre (S): *Neotis denhami*
Avutarda Común (S): *Otis tarda*
Avutarda de Bengala (S): *Eupodotis bengalensis*
Avutarda de Burchell (S): *Neotis denhami*
Avutarda de Denham (S): *Neotis denhami*
Avutarda de Heuglin (S): *Neotis heuglinii*
Avutarda de la India (S): *Ardeotis nigriceps*
Avutarda de Ludwig (S): *Neotis ludwigii*
Avutarda de Namibia (S): *Neotis ludwigii*
Avutarda de Savile (S): *Eupodotis savilei*
Avutarda euroasiática (S): *Otis tarda*
Avutarda hubara (S): *Chlamydotis undulata*
Avutarda india (S): *Ardeotis nigriceps*
Avutarda índica (S): *Ardeotis nigriceps*
Avutarda kori (S): *Ardeotis kori*
Avutarda núbica (S): *Neotis nuba*
Avutarda somalí (S): *Neotis heuglinii*
Avutardas (S): OTIDIDAE spp.
Awash Chameleon (E): *Chamaeleo calcaricarens*
Axis calamianensis : (E) Calamian Deer, Calamian Hog Deer, (S) Ciervo de los Calamianes, Ciervo porquerizo de los Calamianes, (F) Cerf-cochon calamien, **I** CERVIDAE Ma
Axis kuhlii : (E) Bawean Deer, Kuhl's Hog Deer, (S) Cerdo de Kuhl, Ciervo de Kuhl, Ciervo de Marjal, Ciervo porquerizo de Kuhl, (F) Cerf-cochon de Bawean, Cerfcochon de Kuhl, **I** CERVIDAE Ma
Axis porcinus annamiticus : (E) Ganges Hog Deer, Indochinese Hog Deer, Thai Hog Deer, (S) Cerdo tailandés, Ciervo porquerizo de Indochina, (F) Cerfcochon de Thaïlande, Cerf-cochon d'Indochine, **I** CERVIDAE Ma
Axolotl (E/F): *Ambystoma mexicanum*
Aye-aye (E/S/F): *Daubentonia madagascariensis*
Ayres's Eagle (E): *Hieraaetus ayresii*
Ayres's Hawk-Eagle (E): *Hieraaetus ayresii*
Aythya nyroca : (E) Ferruginous Duck, Ferruginous Pochard, White-eyed Pochard, (S) Porrón pardo, (F) Fuligule nyroca, **III** ANATIDAE Av
Azara's Night Monkey (E): *Aotus azarai*
Azara's Zorro (E): *Pseudalopex gymnocercus*
Azer semicollarejo (S): *Accipiter collaris*
Azor (S): *Accipiter gentilis*
Azor australiano (S): *Accipiter fasciatus*
Azor bicolor (S): *Accipiter bicolor*
Azor blanquinegro (S): *Accipiter melanoleucus*
Azor chico (S): *Accipiter striatus*
Azor común (S): *Accipiter gentilis*
Azor culebrero (S): *Polyboroides radiatus*
Azor de Bürgers (S): *Erythrotriorchis buergersi*
Azor de Doria (S): *Megatriorchis doriae*
Azor de Meyer (S): *Accipiter meyerianus*
Azor de Nueva Bretaña (S): *Accipiter princeps*
Azor de Toussenel (S): *Accipiter tousselenii*
Azor gris (S): *Accipiter superciliosus*
Azor lagartijero oscuro (S): *Melierax metabates*

Checklist of fauna/Lista de especies de fauna/Liste des espèces animales

Azor malgache (S): *Accipiter henstii*
Azor moluqueño (S): *Accipiter henicogrammus*
Azor moñudo (S): *Accipiter trivirgatus*
Azor pechigrís (S): *Accipiter poliogaster*
Azor pechillano (S): *Accipiter ventralis*
Azor rabilargo (S): *Urotriorchis macrourus*
Azor rojo (S): *Erythrotriorchis radiatus*
Azor tachiro (S): *Accipiter tachiro*
Azor variable (S): *Accipiter novaehollandiae*
Azor ventigrís (S): *Accipiter poliogaster*
Azor zancón (S): *Geranospiza caerulescens*
Azor-lagartijero claro (S): *Melierax canorus*
Azor-lagartijero somalí (S): *Melierax poliopterus*
Azov-Black Sea Sturgeon (E): *Acipenser gueldenstaedtii*
Aztec Parakeet (E): *Aratinga nana*
Azure-crowned Hummingbird (E): *Agyrtria cyanocephala*
Azure-rumped Parrot (E): *Tanygnathus sumatranus*
Babiroussa (E/F): *Babyrousa babyrussa*
Babirusa (E/S): *Babyrousa babyrussa*
Babisuri (S): *Bassariscus sumichrasti*
Babouin anubis (F): *Papio hamadryas*
Babouin chacma (F): *Papio hamadryas*
Babouin de Guinée (F): *Papio hamadryas*
Babouin jaune (F): *Papio hamadryas*
Baby Python (E): *Gongylophis conicus*
Babyrousa babyrussa : (E) Babiroussa, Babirusa, Deer Hog, (S) Babirusa, (F) Babiroussa, **I** SUIDAE Ma
Bactrian Deer (E): *Cervus elaphus bactrianus*
Bactrian Red Deer (E): *Cervus elaphus bactrianus*
Bactrian Wapiti (E): *Cervus elaphus bactrianus*
Baghdad Small-grain Lizard (E): *Varanus griseus*
Bahama Woodstar (E): *Calliphlox evelynae*
Bahamas Iguana (E): *Cyclura cychlura*
Bahamas Islands Boa (E): *Epicrates chrysogaster*
Bahamas Parrot (E): *Amazona leucocephala*
Bahamas Rock Iguana (E): *Cyclura carinata/ Cyclura cychlura*
Baiji (E/S/F): *Lipotes vexillifer*
Baikal Teal (E): *Anas formosa*
Baillonius bailloni : (E) Saffron Toucanet, (F) Toucan de Baillon, **III** RAMPHASTIDAE Av
Baird's Beaked Whale (E): *Berardius bairdii*
Baird's Tapir (E): *Tapirus bairdii*
Baka Indigobird (E): *Vidua larvaticola*
Balaena glacialis = *Eubalaena glacialis*
Balaena glacialis ssp. *australis* = *Eubalaena australis*
Balaena glacialis ssp. *glacialis* = *Eubalaena glacialis*
Balaena mysticetus : (E) Bowhead Whale, Greenland Right Whale, (S) Ballena boreal, (F) Baleine de grande baie, Baleine du Groenland, **I** BALAENIDAE Ma
Balaeniceps rex : (E) Shoebill, Whale-headed Stork, (S) Picozapato, (F) Baléniceps roi, Bec-en-sabot, Bec-en-sabot du Nil, **II** BALAENICIPITIDAE Av
Balaenoptera acutorostrata : (E) Lesser Rorqual, Little Piked Whale, Minke Whale, Northern Minke Whale, (S) Ballena minke, Rorcual menor, (F) Baleinoptère à museau pointu, Petit rorqual, **I/II** BALAENOPTERIDAE Ma
Balaenoptera bonaerensis : (E) Antarctic Minke Whale, Southern Minke Whale, (S) Rorcual enano del antarctica, (F) Petite Rorqual de l'Antarctique, **I** BALAENOPTERIDAE Ma
Balaenoptera borealis : (E) Coalfish Whale, Pollack Whale, Rudophi's Rorqual, Sei Whale, (S) Ballena boba, Ballena sei, Rorcual boreal, Rorcual de Rudolphi, Rorcual norteno, (F) Baleinoptère de Rudolphi, Rorqual boréal, Rorqual de Rudolphi, Rorqual sei, **I** BALAENOPTERIDAE Ma
Balaenoptera edeni : (E) Bryde's Whale, Tropical Whale, (S) Ballena de Bryde, (F) Baleinoptère de Bryde, Rorqual de Bryde, Rorqual d'Eden, Rorqual tropical, **I** BALAENOPTERIDAE Ma

Balaenoptera musculus : (E) Blue Whale, Sibbald's Rorqual, Sulphur-bottom Whale, (S) Ballena azul, Rorcual azul, (F) Baleine bleue, Baleine d'Ostende, Baleinoptère bleue, Rorqual à ventre cannelé, Rorqual bleu, Rorqual de Sibbold, **II** BALAENOPTERIDAE Ma
Balaenoptera physalus : (E) Common Rorqual, Fin Whale, Finback, Fin-backed Whale, Finner, Herring Whale, Razorback, (S) Ballena aleta, Ballena boba, Rorcual común, (F) Baleine à nageoires, Baleine fin, Baleinoptère commun, Rorqual commun, **I** BALAENOPTERIDAE Ma
Balanophyllia bairdiana : **II** DENDROPHYLLIIDAE An
Balanophyllia bayeri : **II** DENDROPHYLLIIDAE An
Balanophyllia bonaespei : **II** DENDROPHYLLIIDAE An
Balanophyllia brevis = *Balanophyllia regia*
Balanophyllia buccina : **II** DENDROPHYLLIIDAE An
Balanophyllia capensis : **II** DENDROPHYLLIIDAE An
Balanophyllia caribbeana : **II** DENDROPHYLLIIDAE An
Balanophyllia carinata : **II** DENDROPHYLLIIDAE An
Balanophyllia cedrosensis : **II** DENDROPHYLLIIDAE An
Balanophyllia cellulosa : **II** DENDROPHYLLIIDAE An
Balanophyllia chnous : **II** DENDROPHYLLIIDAE An
Balanophyllia corniculans : **II** DENDROPHYLLIIDAE An
Balanophyllia cornu : **II** DENDROPHYLLIIDAE An
Balanophyllia crassiseptum : **II** DENDROPHYLLIIDAE An
Balanophyllia crassitheca : **II** DENDROPHYLLIIDAE An
Balanophyllia cumingii : **II** DENDROPHYLLIIDAE An
Balanophyllia cyathoides : **II** DENDROPHYLLIIDAE An
Balanophyllia dentata : **II** DENDROPHYLLIIDAE An
Balanophyllia desmophyllioides : **II** DENDROPHYLLIIDAE An
Balanophyllia diademata : **II** DENDROPHYLLIIDAE An
Balanophyllia diffusa : **II** DENDROPHYLLIIDAE An
Balanophyllia dilatata = *Balanophyllia dentata*
Balanophyllia dineta : **II** DENDROPHYLLIIDAE An
Balanophyllia diomedeae : **II** DENDROPHYLLIIDAE An
Balanophyllia dubia : **II** DENDROPHYLLIIDAE An
Balanophyllia elegans : **II** DENDROPHYLLIIDAE An
Balanophyllia elliptica : **II** DENDROPHYLLIIDAE An
Balanophyllia elongata : **II** DENDROPHYLLIIDAE An
Balanophyllia europaea : **II** DENDROPHYLLIIDAE An
Balanophyllia floridana : (E) Porous Cup Coral **II** DENDROPHYLLIIDAE An
Balanophyllia galapagensis : **II** DENDROPHYLLIIDAE An
Balanophyllia gemma : **II** DENDROPHYLLIIDAE An
Balanophyllia gemmifera : **II** DENDROPHYLLIIDAE An
Balanophyllia generatrix : **II** DENDROPHYLLIIDAE An
Balanophyllia gigas : **II** DENDROPHYLLIIDAE An
Balanophyllia grandis = *Balanophyllia pittieri*
Balanophyllia hadros : **II** DENDROPHYLLIIDAE An
Balanophyllia imperialis : **II** DENDROPHYLLIIDAE An
Balanophyllia iwayamaensis : **II** DENDROPHYLLIIDAE An
Balanophyllia laysanensis : **II** DENDROPHYLLIIDAE An
Balanophyllia malouinensis : **II** DENDROPHYLLIIDAE An
Balanophyllia nouhuysi = *Dendrophyllia arbuscula*
Balanophyllia palifera : **II** DENDROPHYLLIIDAE An
Balanophyllia parallela : **II** DENDROPHYLLIIDAE An
Balanophyllia parvula : **II** DENDROPHYLLIIDAE An
Balanophyllia pittieri : **II** DENDROPHYLLIIDAE An
Balanophyllia ponderosa : **II** DENDROPHYLLIIDAE An
Balanophyllia profundicella : **II** DENDROPHYLLIIDAE An
Balanophyllia rediviva : **II** DENDROPHYLLIIDAE An
Balanophyllia regalis : **II** DENDROPHYLLIIDAE An

Balanophyllia regia : (E) Scarlet-and-gold Star Coral **II** DENDROPHYLLIIDAE An
Balanophyllia scabra : **II** DENDROPHYLLIIDAE An
Balanophyllia serrata : **II** DENDROPHYLLIIDAE An
Balanophyllia stimpsonii : **II** DENDROPHYLLIIDAE An
Balanophyllia taprobanae : **II** DENDROPHYLLIIDAE An
Balanophyllia tenuis : **II** DENDROPHYLLIIDAE An
Balanophyllia teres : **II** DENDROPHYLLIIDAE An
Balanophyllia thalassae : **II** DENDROPHYLLIIDAE An
Balanophyllia verrucaria = Balanophyllia europaea
Balanophyllia wellsi : **II** DENDROPHYLLIIDAE An
Balanophyllia yongei : **II** DENDROPHYLLIIDAE An
Balbugard fluviatile (F): *Pandion haliaetus*
Balbuzard pêcheur (F): *Pandion haliaetus*
Bald Eagle (E): *Haliaeetus leucocephalus*
Bald Ibis (E): *Geronticus eremita/ Geronticus calvus*
Bald-faced Saki (E): *Pithecia irrorata*
Bald-headed Uacari (E): *Cacajao calvus*
Bale Mountains Heather Chameleon (E): *Chamaeleo harennae*
Bale Mountains Two-horned Chameleon (E): *Chamaeleo balebicornutus*
Balearic Lizard (E): *Podarcis lilfordi*
Balearica pavonina : (E) Black Crowned-Crane, West African Crowned Crane, (S) Grulla coronada, Grulla coronada cuellinegra, Grulla coronada del Africa Occidental, (F) Grue couronnée, Grue couronnée de l'Afrique del'Ouest et du Soudan, **II** GRUIDAE Av
Balearica regulorum : (E) Grey Crowned-Crane, South African Crowned Crane, (S) Grulla coronada cuelligris, Grulla coronada sudafricana, (F) Grue couronnée de Cap, Grue couronnée de l'Afrique du Sud et de l'Est, Grue royale, **II** GRUIDAE Av
Baleine à bosse (F): *Megaptera novaeangliae*
Baleine à nageoires (F): *Balaenoptera physalus*
Baleine à six bosses (F): *Eschrichtius robustus*
Baleine à taquet (F): *Megaptera novaeangliae*
Baleine australe (F): *Eubalaena australis*
Baleine bleue (F): *Balaenoptera musculus*
Baleine de Biscaye (F): *Eubalaena glacialis*
Baleine de grande baie (F): *Balaena mysticetus*
Baleine des Basques (F): *Eubalaena glacialis*
Baleine d'Ostende (F): *Balaenoptera musculus*
Baleine du Groenland (F): *Balaena mysticetus*
Baleine fin (F): *Balaenoptera physalus*
Baleine franche (F): *Eubalaena glacialis*
Baleine grise (F): *Eschrichtius robustus*
Baleine pygmée (F): *Caperea marginata*
Baleines (F): CETACEA spp. Ma
Baleines à bec (F): *Berardius* spp.
Baleines franches (F): *Eubalaena* spp.
Baleines noires (F): *Eubalaena* spp.
Baleinoptère à museau pointu (F): *Balaenoptera acutorostrata*
Baleinoptère bleue (F): *Balaenoptera musculus*
Baleinoptère commun (F): *Balaenoptera physalus*
Baleinoptère de Bryde (F): *Balaenoptera edeni*
Baleinoptère de Rudolphi (F): *Balaenoptera borealis*
Baléniceps roi (F): *Balaeniceps rex*
Bali Myna (E): *Leucopsar rothschildi*
Bali Starling (E): *Leucopsar rothschildi*
Ball Python (E): *Python regius*
Ballena (S): *Eubalaena glacialis*
Ballena aleta (S): *Balaenoptera physalus*
Ballena azul (S): *Balaenoptera musculus*
Ballena blanca (S): *Delphinapterus leucas*
Ballena boba (S): *Balaenoptera borealis/ Balaenoptera physalus*
Ballena boreal (S): *Balaena mysticetus*
Ballena de Bryde (S): *Balaenoptera edeni*
Ballena de Cuvier (S): *Ziphius cavirostris*
Ballena de pico de Andrew (S): *Mesoplodon bowdoini*
Ballena de pico de Arnoux (S): *Berardius arnuxii*
Ballena de pico de Baird (S): *Berardius bairdii*

Ballena de pico de Blainville (S): *Mesoplodon densirostris*
Ballena de pico de Gervais (S): *Mesoplodon europaeus*
Ballena de pico de Gray (S): *Mesoplodon grayi*
Ballena de pico de Héctor (S): *Mesoplodon hectori*
Ballena de pico de Hubbs (S): *Mesoplodon carlhubbsi*
Ballena de pico de Layard (S): *Mesoplodon layardii*
Ballena de pico de Longman (S): *Indopacetus pacificus*
Ballena de pico de Sowerby (S): *Mesoplodon bidens*
Ballena de pico de Stejneger (S): *Mesoplodon stejnegeri*
Ballena de pico de True (S): *Mesoplodon mirus*
Ballena de Shepherd (S): *Tasmacetus shepherdi*
Ballena esperma (S): *Physeter catodon*
Ballena franca (S): *Eubalaena australis*
Ballena franca del Norte (S): *Eubalaena glacialis*
Ballena franca pigmea (S): *Caperea marginata*
Ballena gris (S): *Eschrichtius robustus*
Ballena hocico de botella del norte (S): *Hyperoodon ampullatus*
Ballena hocico de botella del sur (S): *Hyperoodon planifrons*
Ballena jorobada (S): *Megaptera novaeangliae*
Ballena minke (S): *Balaenoptera acutorostrata*
Ballena sei (S): *Balaenoptera borealis*
Ballenas (S): CETCAEA spp. Ma
Ballenas de pico (S): *Berardius* spp.
Ballenas hocico de botella (S): *Hyperoodon* spp.
Ballenga (S): *Eubalaena glacialis*
Baltic Sturgeon (E): *Acipenser sturio*
Banana Boa (E): *Ungaliophis continentalis*
Band-bellied Owl (E): *Pulsatrix melanota*
Banded Cotinga (E): *Cotinga maculata*
Banded Day Gecko (E): *Phelsuma standingi*
Banded Duiker (E): *Cephalophus zebra*
Banded Dwarf Boa (E): *Tropidophis semicinctus*
Banded Eagle-Owl (E): *Bubo shelleyi*
Banded Hare-wallaby (E): *Lagostrophus fasciatus*
Banded Kestrel (E): *Falco zoniventris*
Banded Langur (E): *Presbytis femoralis*
Banded Leaf Monkey (E): *Presbytis femoralis*
Banded Linsang (E): *Prionodon linsang*
Banded Musang (E): *Hemigalus derbyanus*
Banded Palm Civet (E): *Hemigalus derbyanus*
Banded Pitta (E): *Pitta guajana*
Banded Snake-Eagle (E): *Circaetus cinerascens*
Banded Tegu (E): *Tupinambis teguixin*
Banderón caballo (S): *Myrmecophaga tridactyla*
Bandicoot à pied de porc (F): *Chaeropus ecaudatus*
Bandicoot de Bougainville (F): *Perameles bougainville*
Bandicoot pieds de cochon (F): *Chaeropus ecaudatus*
Bandicootlapin (F): *Macrotis lagotis*
Bandicoot-lapin à queue blanche (F): *Macrotis leucura*
Bandicoot-lapin mineur (F): *Macrotis leucura*
Bandicoot conejo (S): *Macrotis lagotis*
Bandicot conejo de cola blanca (S): *Macrotis leucura*
Bandicot de Bouganville (S): *Perameles bougainville*
Bandicot de pies porcinos (S): *Chaeropus ecaudatus*
Band-tailed Barbthroat (E): *Threnetes ruckeri*
Band-tailed Fish-Eagle (E): *Haliaeetus leucoryphus*
Band-tailed Owl (E): *Pulsatrix melanota*
Banks Flying-fox (E): *Pteropus fundatus*
Bannerman's Turaco (E): *Tauraco bannermani*
Barabattoia amicorum : **II** FAVIIDAE An
Barabattoia laddi : **II** FAVIIDAE An
Barabattoia mirabilis : **II** FAVIIDAE An
Barasinga (F/S): *Cervus duvaucelii*
Barasingha (E/F): *Cervus duvaucelii*
Bar-backed Partridge (E): *Arborophila orientalis*
Barbary Ape (E): *Macaca sylvanus*
Barbary Deer (E): *Cervus elaphus barbarus*
Barbary Falcon (E): *Falco pelegrinoides*
Barbary Macaque (E): *Macaca sylvanus*
Barbary Red Deer (E): *Cervus elaphus barbarus*
Barbary Sheep (E): *Ammotragus lervia*
Barbary Stag (E): *Cervus elaphus barbarus*
Barbeau de Jullien (F): *Probarbus jullieni*

Checklist of fauna/Lista de especies de fauna/Liste des espèces animales

Barbel Sturgeon (E): *Acipenser medirostris/ Acipenser nudiventris*
Barberton Girdled Lizard (E): *Cordylus barbertonensis*
Barbita colibandeada (S): *Threnetes ruckeri*
Barbita colipalida (S): *Threnetes niger*
Barbour's Day Gecko (E): *Phelsuma barbouri*
Barbour's Seahorse (E): *Hippocampus barbouri*
Bar-breasted Firefinch (E): *Lagonosticta rufopicta*
Bar-breasted Waxbill (E): *Lagonosticta rufopicta*
Barbu aveugle (F): *Caecobarbus geertsi*
Bare-eyed Cockatoo (E): *Cacatua sanguinea*
Bare-faced Tamarin (E): *Saguinus bicolor*
Bare-headed Rockfowl (E): *Picathartes gymnocephalus*
Bare-legged Owl (E): *Otus lawrencii*
Bare-legged Owlch-Owl (E): *Otus lawrencii*
Bare-shanked Screech-Owl (E): *Otus clarkii*
Bargibant's Seahorse (E): *Hippocampus bargibanti*
Baribal (F): *Ursus americanus*
Barizo dorsirrojo (S): *Saimiri oerstedii*
Barking Owl (E): *Ninox connivens*
Barn Owl (E): *Tyto alba*
Barnacla cuellirroja (S): *Branta ruficollis*
Barnacla de las Aleutianas (S): *Branta canadensis leucopareia*
Barnacla hawaiana (S): *Branta sandvicensis*
Barnacla nené (S): *Branta sandvicensis*
Barnardius barnardi : (E) Barnard's Parakeet, Mallee Ringneck, (S) Perico de Barnard, (F) Perruche de Barnard, **II** PSITTACIDAE Av
Barnardius zonarius : (E) Australian Ringneck, Port Lincoln Ringneck, Twenty-eight Parakeet, (S) Perico de Port Lincoln, (F) Perruche à collier jaune, **II** PSITTACIDAE Av
Barnard's Parakeet (E): *Barnardius barnardi*
Bar-pouched Wreathed Hornbill (E): *Aceros undulatus*
Barraband Parakeet (E): *Polytelis swainsonii*
Barraband's Parrot (E): *Pionopsitta barrabandi*
Barred Bandicoot (E): *Perameles bougainville*
Barred Eagle-Owl (E): *Bubo sumatranus*
Barred Forest-Falcon (E): *Micrastur ruficollis*
Barred Hawk (E): *Leucopternis princeps*
Barred Honey-buzzard (E): *Pernis celebensis*
Barred Jungle Owlet (E): *Glaucidium radiatum*
Barred Kestrel (E): *Falco zoniventris*
Barred Owl (E): *Strix varia*
Barred Owlet (E): *Glaucidium capense*
Barred Parakeet (E): *Bolborhynchus lineola*
Barred Python (E): *Bothrochilus boa*
Barrington Land Iguana (E): *Conolophus pallidus*
Bar-throated Wreathed Hornbill (E): *Aceros undulatus*
Bartsch's Iguana (E): *Cyclura carinata*
Basáride (S): *Bassariscus sumichrasti*
Basilinna leucotis : (E) White-eared Hummingbird, (S) Colibrí orejiblanco, (F) Saphir à oreilles blanches, **II** TROCHILIDAE Av
Basilinna xantusii : (E) Black-fronted Hummingbird, Xantus's Hummingbird, (S) Colibrí de Xantus, (F) Saphir de Xantus, **II** TROCHILIDAE Av
Basket Coral (E): *Sandalolitha robusta*
Basking Shark (E): *Cetorhinus maximus*
Bassarai rusé (F): *Bassariscus sumichrasti*
Bassaricyon gabbii : (E) Bushy-tailed Olingo, Olingo, (S) Chosna pericote, Cuataquil, Cuchumbi, Lingo, Olingo, (F) Cataquil, Olingo, **III** PROCYONIDAE Ma
Bassaris d'Amérique centrale (F): *Bassariscus sumichrasti*
Bassariscus sumichrasti : (E) Cacomistle, Central American Cacomistle, (S) Babisuri, Basáride, Cacomistle, Mico de noche, Mico rayado, (F) Bassarai rusé, Bassaris d'Amérique centrale, **III** PROCYONIDAE Ma
Bastard Sturgeon (E): *Acipenser nudiventris*
Bat Falcon (E): *Falco rufigularis*
Bat Hawk (E): *Macheiramphus alcinus*
Bat Kite (E): *Macheiramphus alcinus*

Batagur (E): *Batagur baska*
Batagur baska : (E) Batagur, Common Batagur, Four-toed Terrapin, River Terrapin, (S) Galápago Batagur, Galápago indio, (F) Batagur malais, Émyde fluviale indienne, **I** EMYDIDAE Re
Batagur elliotí = Kachuga kachuga
Batagur malais (F): *Batagur baska*
Batagur smithii = Kachuga smithii
Bateleur (E/F): *Terathopius ecaudatus*
Bateleur des savanes (F): *Terathopius ecaudatus*
Bateleur Eagle (E): *Terathopius ecaudatus*
Bathelia candida : **II** OCULINIDAE An
Bathycyathus chilensis : **II** CARYOPHYLLIIDAE An
Bathypathes alternata : **II** ANTIPATHIDAE An
Bathypathes bifida : **II** ANTIPATHIDAE An
Bathypathes erotema : **II** ANTIPATHIDAE An
Bathypathes euantha : **II** ANTIPATHIDAE An
Bathypathes galatheae : **II** ANTIPATHIDAE An
Bathypathes heterorhodzos : **II** ANTIPATHIDAE An
Bathypathes lyra : **II** ANTIPATHIDAE An
Bathypathes patula : **II** ANTIPATHIDAE An
Bathypathes platycaulus : **II** ANTIPATHIDAE An
Bathypathes quadribrachiata : **II** ANTIPATHIDAE An
Bathypathes scoparia : **II** ANTIPATHIDAE An
Bathypathes tenuis : **II** ANTIPATHIDAE An
Bathypsammia fallosocialis : **II** DENDROPHYLLIIDAE An
Bathypsammia tintinnabulum : **II** DENDROPHYLLIIDAE An
Battersby's Dwarf Boa (E): *Tropidophis battersbyi*
Bawean Deer (E): *Axis kuhlii*
Bay Cat (E): *Catopuma badia*
Bay Duiker (E): *Cephalophus dorsalis*
Bay Lynx (E): *Lynx rufus*
Bay Owl (E): *Phodilus badius*
Bay-winged Hawk (E): *Parabuteo unicinctus*
Baza africano (S): *Aviceda cuculoides*
Baza australiano (S): *Aviceda subcristata*
Baza coucou (F): *Aviceda cuculoides*
Baza de Jerdon (F): *Aviceda jerdoni*
Baza huppard (F): *Aviceda leuphotes*
Baza huppé (F): *Aviceda subcristata*
Baza malgache (S/F): *Aviceda madagascariensis*
Baza negro (S): *Aviceda leuphotes*
Baza oriental (S): *Aviceda jerdoni*
Beaded Lizard (E): *Heloderma horridum*
Beaked Cape Tortoise (E): *Homopus areolatus*
Beaked whales (E): *Berardius* spp.
Beak-head (E): *Sphenodon punctatus*
Bear Macaque (E): *Macaca arctoides*
Bear Paw Clam (E): *Hippopus hippopus*
Bearded Helmetcrest (E): *Oxypogon guerinii*
Bearded Mountaineer (E): *Oreonympha nobilis*
Bearded Saki (E): *Chiropotes satanas*
Bearded Screech-Owl (E): *Otus barbarus*
Bearded Vulture (E): *Gypaetus barbatus*
Bears (E): URSIDAE spp.
Beaudouin's Snake-Eagle (E): *Circaetus gallicus*
Beaumarquet (F): *Pytilia phoenicoptera*
Beaumarquet à ailes jaunes (F): *Pytilia hypogrammica*
Beaumarquet aurore (F): *Pytilia phoenicoptera*
Beautiful Hummingbird (E): *Calothorax pulcher*
Beautiful Parakeet (E): *Psephotus pulcherrimus*
Beautiful Parrot (E): *Pionopsitta pulchra*
Beautiful-breasted Poison Frog (E): *Epipedobates pulchripectus*
Bebrornis rodericanus : (E) Rodrigues Brush-Warbler, Rodrigues Warbler, Rodriguez Brush-Warbler, (F) Rousserolle de Rodriguez, **III** MUSCICAPIDAE Av
Bec de corail cendré (F): *Estrilda troglodytes*
Bec-d'argent (F): *Lonchura cantans*
Bec-en-faucille aigle (F): *Eutoxeres aquila*
Bec-en-faucille de la Condamine (F): *Eutoxeres condamini*
Bec-en-sabot (F): *Balaeniceps rex*
Bec-en-sabot du Nil (F): *Balaeniceps rex*

73

Bee Hummingbird (E): *Mellisuga helenae*
Beecroft's Flying Squirrel (E): *Anomalurus beecrofti*
Beecroft's Scaly-tailed Squirrel (E): *Anomalurus beecrofti*
Belalanda Chameleon (E): *Furcifer belalandaensis*
Belette à ventre jaune (F): *Mustela kathiah*
Belette alpine (F): *Mustela altaica*
Belette de Sibérie (F): *Mustela sibirica*
Belette des Alpes (F): *Mustela altaica*
Belize Crocodile (E): *Crocodylus moreletii*
Bellia borneensis = Orlitia borneensis
Bell's Dabb Lizard (E): *Uromastyx acanthinura*
Bell's Hinged Tortoise (E): *Kinixys belliana*
Bell's Hinged-backed Tortoise (E): *Kinixys belliana*
Bélouga (F): *Delphinapterus leucas*
Beluga (E): *Delphinapterus leucas*
Beluga (E/S/F): *Huso huso*
Bengal Black Lizard (E): *Varanus bengalensis*
Bengal Bustard (E): *Eupodotis bengalensis*
Bengal Eyed Terrapin (E): *Morenia ocellata*
Bengal Florican (E): *Eupodotis bengalensis*
Bengal Fox (E): *Vulpes bengalensis*
Bengal Leopard Cat (E): *Prionailurus bengalensis
bengalensis*
Bengal Lizard (E): *Varanus bengalensis*
Bengal Monitor (E): *Varanus bengalensis*
Bengal Roof Turtle (E): *Kachuga kachuga*
Bengalí carinegro (S): *Lagonosticta vinacea*
Bengalí de Fraser (S): *Lagonosticta rufopicta*
Bengalí de Lichtenstein (S): *Lagonosticta rubricata*
Bengalí senegalés (S): *Lagonosticta senegala*
Bengali vert (F): *Amandava formosa*
Bengali zébré (F): *Amandava subflava*
Benguela Dolphin (E): *Cephalorhynchus heavisidii*
Beni Titi Monkey (E): *Callicebus ollalae*
Bénitier de Rosewater (F): *Tridacna rosewateri*
Bénitier de Tevoro (F): *Tridacna tevoroa*
Bénitier géant (F): *Tridacna gigas*
Bénitiers (F): TRIDACNIDAE spp.
Bent's Mastigure (E): *Uromastyx benti*
Bérardien d'Arnoux (F): *Berardius arnuxii*
Bérardien de Baird (F): *Berardius bairdii*
Berardius spp.: (E) Beaked whales, (S) Ballenas de pico,
(F) Baleines à bec, Bérards, **I** ZIPHIIDAE Ma
Berardius arnuxii : (E) Arnoux's Beaked Whale, Southern
Four-toothed Whale, (S) Ballena de pico de Arnoux,
(F) Bérardien d'Arnoux, **I** ZIPHIIDAE Ma
Berardius bairdii : (E) Baird's Beaked Whale, Giant
Bottle-nosed Whale, Northern Four-toothed Whale,
(S) Ballena de pico de Baird, (F) Bérardien de Baird, **I**
ZIPHIIDAE Ma
Bérards (F): *Berardius* spp.
Berenicornis comatus = Aceros comatus
Berger's Cape Tortoise (E): *Homopus bergeri*
Berlandier's Tortoise (E): *Gopherus berlandieri*
Bernache à cou roux (F): *Branta ruficollis*
Bernache des Aléoutiennes (F): *Branta canadensis
leucopareia*
Bernache des Iles Sandwich (F): *Branta sandvicensis*
Bernache d'Hawaï (F): *Branta sandvicensis*
Bernache du Canada aléoute (F): *Branta canadensis
leucopareia*
Bernache néné (F): *Branta sandvicensis*
Bernhard's Mantella (E): *Mantella bernhardi*
Bernier's Teal (E): *Anas bernieri*
Berrendo (S): *Antilocapra americana*
Berthe's Mouse Lemur (E): *Microcebus berthae*
Berylline Hummingbird (E): *Saucerottia beryllina*
Besra (E): *Accipiter virgatus*
Besra Sparrowhawk (E): *Accipiter virgatus*
Besra-sperwer (E): *Accipiter virgatus*
Betsileo Golden Frog (E): *Mantella betsileo*
Bettongia spp.: (E) Bettongs, Rat kangaroos, (S) Canguro-
ratas, Rata canguro, (F) Kangourou-rats, **I**
POTOROIDAE Ma

Bettongia gaimardi : (E) Eastern Bettong, Tasmanian
Bettong, Tasmanian Rat Kangaroo, (S) Canguro-rata
de Tasmania, (F) Kangourou-rat de Tasmanie, **I**
POTOROIDAE Ma
Bettongia lesueur : (E) Boodie, Burrowing Bettong,
Lesueur's Rat Kangaroo, (S) Canguro-rata de Lesueur,
(F) Bettongie de Lesueur, Kangourou-rat de Lesueur,
I POTOROIDAE Ma
Bettongia penicillata : (E) Brush-tailed Bettong, Brush-
tailed Rat Kangaroo, Woylie, (S) Canguro-rata
colipeludo, (F) Bettongie à queue touffue, Kangourou-
rat à queue touffue, **I** POTOROIDAE Ma
Bettongia tropica = Bettongia penicillata
Bettongie à queue touffue (F): *Bettongia penicillata*
Bettongie de Lesueur (F): *Bettongia lesueur*
Bettongs (E): *Bettongia* spp.
Bhutan Glory (E): *Bhutanitis lidderdalii*
Bhutan swallowtails (E): *Bhutanitis* spp.
Bhutanitis spp.: (E) Bhutan swallowtails, (F) Macaones, **II**
PAPILIONIDAE In
Bhutanitis lidderdalii : (E) Bhutan Glory, **II**
PAPILIONIDAE In
Bhutanitis ludlowi : (E) Ludlow's Bhutan Swallowtail, **II**
PAPILIONIDAE In
Bhutanitis mansfieldi : (E) Mansfield's Three-tailed
Swallowtail, **II** PAPILIONIDAE In
Bhutanitis nigrilima = Bhutanitis thaidina
Bhutanitis thaidina : (E) Chinese Three-tailed Swallowtail,
II PAPILIONIDAE In
Bhutanitis yulongensis = Bhutanitis thaidina
Biak Red Lory (E): *Eos cyanogenia*
Bichichi (S): *Saguinus oedipus*
Bicolored Hawk (E): *Accipiter bicolor*
Bicolored Sparrowhawk (E): *Accipiter bicolor*
Big Amu-Darya shovelnose (E): *Pseudoscaphirhynchus
kaufmanni*
Big-bellied Seahorse (E): *Hippocampus abdominalis*
Big-belly Seahorse (E): *Hippocampus abdominalis*
Big-eared Flying-fox (E): *Pteropus macrotis*
Big-headed Amazon River Turtle (E): *Peltocephalus
dumeriliana*
Big-headed Sideneck (E): *Peltocephalus dumeriliana*
Big-headed Sideneck Turtle (E): *Peltocephalus
dumeriliana*
Big-headed Turtle (E): *Platysternon megacephalum*
Bighorn (F): *Ovis canadensis*
Bighorn Sheep (E): *Ovis canadensis*
Big-nosed Chameleon (E): *Calumma nasuta*
Bilby (E): *Macrotis lagotis*
Binturong (E/S/F): *Arctictis binturong*
Biolat Poison Frog (E): *Dendrobates biolat*
Birds-of-paradise (E): PARADISAEIDAE spp.
Birds of prey (E): FALCONIFORMES spp. Av
Birdsnest corals (E): *Seriatopora* spp.
Birdwing butterflies (E): *Ornithoptera* spp. / *Trogonoptera*
spp./ *Troides* spp.
Birdwing Pearly Mussel (E): *Conradilla caelata*
Bismarck Boobook (E): *Ninox variegata*
Bismarck Flying-fox (E): *Pteropus neohibernicus*
Bismarck Hawk-Owl (E): *Ninox variegata*
Bismarck Masked-Owl (E): *Tyto aurantia*
Bismarck Ringed Python (E): *Bothrochilus boa*
Bison bison athabascae : (E) Wood Bison, (S) Bisonte
americano de bosque, Bisonte selváticoo de
Athabascal, (F) Bison des forêts, **II** BOVIDAE Ma
Bison des forêts (F): *Bison bison athabascae*
Bisonte americano de bosque (S): *Bison bison athabascae*
Bisonte selváticoo de Athabascal (S): *Bison bison
athabascae*
Black Baza (E): *Aviceda leuphotes*
Black Bustard (E): *Eupodotis afra*
Black Caiman (E): *Melanosuchus niger*
Black Caracara (E): *Daptrius ater*
Black Chachalaca (E): *Penelopina nigra*
Black Colobus (E): *Colobus satanas*

Checklist of fauna/Lista de especies de fauna/Liste des espèces animales

Black corals (E): ANTIPATHARIA spp. An
Black Crowned-Crane (E): *Balearica pavonina*
Black Dolphin (E): *Cephalorhynchus eutropia*
Black Eagle (E): *Ictinaetus malayensis/ Aquila verreauxii*
Black Falcon (E): *Falco subniger*
Black Finless Porpoise (E): *Neophocaena phocaenoides*
Black Flying-fox (E): *Pteropus alecto*
Black Giant Squirrel (E): *Ratufa bicolor*
Black Giant Tortoise (E): *Manouria emys*
Black Gibbon (E): *Hylobates concolor*
Black Girdled Lizard (E): *Cordylus niger*
Black Golden Frog (E): *Mantella cowani*
Black Goshawk (E): *Accipiter melanoleucus*
Black Harrier (E): *Circus maurus*
Black Hawk-Eagle (E): *Spizaetus tyrannus*
Black Honey-buzzard (E): *Henicopernis infuscatus*
Black Hornbill (E): *Anthracoceros malayanus*
Black Howler (E): *Alouatta caraya*
Black Howling Monkey (E): *Alouatta caraya*
Black Inca (E): *Coeligena prunellei*
Black Jacobin (E): *Florisuga fusca*
Black Kite (E): *Milvus migrans*
Black Korhaan (E): *Eupodotis afra*
Black Leaf Monkey (E): *Trachypithecus johnii*
Black Lemur (E): *Eulemur macaco*
Black Lion Tamarin (E): *Leontopithecus chrysopygus*
Black Lory (E): *Chalcopsitta atra*
Black Marsh Turtle (E): *Siebenrockiella crassicollis*
Black Metaltail (E): *Metallura phoebe*
Black Muntjac (E): *Muntiacus crinifrons*
Black Musk Deer (E): *Moschus fuscus*
Black Pajuil (E): *Penelopina nigra*
Black Parrot (E): *Coracopsis nigra*
Black Partridge (E): *Melanoperdix nigra*
Black Penelopina (E): *Penelopina nigra*
Black Pond Turtle (E): *Geoclemys hamiltonii*
Black Porpoise (E): *Phocoena spinipinnis*
Black Python (E): *Morelia boeleni*
Black Rhinoceros (E): *Diceros bicornis*
Black Right Whale (E): *Eubalaena glacialis*
Black Saki (E): *Chiropotes satanas*
Black Sand Monitor (E): *Varanus rosenbergi*
Black Seahorse (E): *Hippocampus erectus/ Hippocampus hippocampus/ Hippocampus kuda*
Black Sicklebill (E): *Epimachus fastuosus*
Black Side-necked Turtle (E): *Pelusios niger*
Black Softshell Turtle (E): *Aspideretes nigricans*
Black Solitary Eagle (E): *Harpyhaliaetus solitarius*
Black Sparrowhawk (E): *Accipiter melanoleucus*
Black Spiny-tailed Lizard (E): *Uromastyx acanthinura*
Black Spotted Turtle (E): *Geoclemys hamiltonii*
Black Stork (E): *Ciconia nigra*
Black Tegu (E): *Tupinambis teguixin*
Black Tree-kangaroo (E): *Dendrolagus ursinus*
Black Turret Coral (E): *Tubastraea micranthus*
Black Uacari (E): *Cacajao melanocephalus*
Black Vulture (E): *Aegypius monachus/ Coragyps atratus*
Black Wire Coral (E): *Stichopathes lutkeni*
Black Wood-Partridge (E): *Melanoperdix nigra*
Black-and-chestnut Eagle (E): *Oroaetus isidori*
Black-and-gold Birdwing (E): *Troides helena*
Black-and-red Howling Monkey (E): *Alouatta belzebul*
Black-and-red Tamarin (E): *Saguinus nigricollis*
Black-and-white Hawk-Eagle (E): *Spizaetus alboniger/ Spizaetus bartelsi/ Spizastur melanoleucus*
Black-and-white Mannikin (E): *Lonchura bicolor*
Black-and-white Munia (E): *Lonchura bicolor*
Black-and-white Owl (E): *Strix nigrolineata*
Black-and-white Saki (E): *Pithecia albicans*
Black-and-white Tassel-ear Marmoset (E): *Callithrix humeralifer*
Black-backed Thornbill (E): *Ramphomicron dorsale*
Black-banded Coral Snake (E): *Micrurus nigrocinctus*
Black-banded Owl (E): *Strix huhula*
Black-bearded Flying-fox (E): *Pteropus melanopogon*

Black-bellied Bustard (E): *Eupodotis melanogaster*
Black-bellied Dwarf Boa (E): *Tropidophis nigriventris*
Black-bellied Firefinch (E): *Lagonosticta rara*
Black-bellied Hummingbird (E): *Eupherusa nigriventris*
Black-bellied Korhaan (E): *Eupodotis melanogaster*
Black-bellied Pangolin (E): *Manis tetradactyla*
Black-bellied Seedcracker (E): *Pyrenestes ostrinus*
Black-bellied Thorntail (E): *Discosura langsdorffi*
Black-bellied Waxbill (E): *Lagonosticta rara*
Black-bellied Whistling-Duck (E): *Dendrocygna autumnalis*
Black-billed Amazon (E): *Amazona agilis*
Black-billed Hanging-Parrot (E): *Loriculus stigmatus*
Black-billed Parrot (E): *Amazona agilis*
Black-billed Sicklebill (E): *Epimachus albertisi*
Black-billed Streamertail (E): *Trochilus scitulus*
Black-billed Turaco (E): *Tauraco schuettii*
Black-billed Wood-Dove (E): *Turtur abyssinicus*
Black-billed Wood-Duck (E): *Dendrocygna arborea*
Black-breasted Buzzard (E): *Hamirostra melanosternon*
Black-breasted Buzzard-Kite (E): *Hamirostra melanosternon/ Harpagus bidentatus*
Black-breasted Harrier-Eagle (E): *Circaetus pectoralis*
Black-breasted Hillstar (E): *Oreotrochilus melanogaster*
Black-breasted Kite (E): *Hamirostra melanosternon*
Black-breasted Pitta (E): *Pitta gurneyi*
Black-breasted Puffleg (E): *Eriocnemis nigrivestis*
Black-breasted Snake-Eagle (E): *Circaetus pectoralis*
Black-brested Buzzard (E): *Hamirostra melanosternon*
Black-browed Spider Monkey (E): *Ateles geoffroyi frontatus*
Blackbuck (E): *Antilope cervicapra*
Black-capped Capuchin (E): *Cebus apella*
Black-capped Conure (E): *Pyrrhura rupicola*
Black-capped Lory (E): *Lorius lory*
Black-capped Parakeet (E): *Pyrrhura rupicola*
Black-capped Screech-Owl (E): *Otus atricapillus*
Black-cheeked Lovebird (E): *Agapornis nigrigenis*
Black-cheeked White-nosed Monkey (E): *Cercopithecus ascanius*
Black-chested Buzzard-Eagle (E): *Geranoaetus melanoleucus*
Black-chested Eagle (E): *Geranoaetus melanoleucus*
Black-chested Hawk (E): *Leucopternis princeps*
Black-chested Snake-Eagle (E): *Circaetus pectoralis*
Blackchin Dolphin (E): *Lagenorhynchus australis*
Black-chinned Hummingbird (E): *Archilochus alexandri*
Black-collared Hawk (E): *Busarellus nigricollis*
Black-collared Lovebird (E): *Agapornis swindernianus*
Black-crested Coquette (E): *Lophornis helenae*
Black-eared Fairy (E): *Heliothryx aurita*
Black-eared Flying-fox (E): *Pteropus melanotus*
Black-eared Kite (E): *Milvus lineatus*
Black-eared Parrot (E): *Hapalopsittaca melanotis*
Black-eared Parrotlet (E): *Touit melanonota*
Black-eyed Gecko (E): *Hoplodactylus kahutarae*
Black-faced Black Spider Monkey (E): *Ateles chamek*
Black-faced Firefinch (E): *Lagonosticta vinacea*
Black-faced Firefinch Indigobird (E): *Vidua larvaticola*
Black-faced Hawk (E): *Leucopternis melanops*
Black-faced Lion Tamarin (E): *Leontopithecus caissara*
Black-footed Cat (E): *Felis nigripes*
Black-footed Ferret (E): *Mustela nigripes*
Black-footed Penguin (E): *Spheniscus demersus*
Black-fronted Curassow (E): *Pipile jacutinga*
Black-fronted Hummingbird (E): *Basilinna xantusii*
Black-fronted Piping-Guan (E): *Pipile jacutinga*
Black-handed Spider Monkey (E): *Ateles geoffroyi*
Black-headed Caique (E): *Pionites melanocephala*
Black-headed Conure (E): *Nandayus nenday*
Black-headed Marmoset (E): *Callithrix nigriceps*
Black-headed Monitor (E): *Varanus tristis*
Black-headed Night Monkey (E): *Aotus nigriceps*
Black-headed Parakeet (E): *Nandayus nenday*
Black-headed Parrot (E): *Pionites melanocephala*

Checklist of fauna/Lista de especies de fauna/Liste des espèces animales

Black-headed Python (E): *Aspidites melanocephalus*
Black-headed Squirrel Monkey (E): *Saimiri boliviensis*
Black-headed Tragopan (E): *Tragopan melanocephalus*
Black-headed Uacari (E): *Cacajao melanocephalus*
Black-headed Weaver (E): *Ploceus melanocephalus*
Black-hooded Sunbeam (E): *Aglaeactis pamela*
Blackish Squirrel Monkey (E): *Saimiri vanzolinii*
Black-legged Falconet (E): *Microhierax fringillarius*
Black-legged Poison Frog (E): *Phyllobates bicolor*
Black-lored Parrot (E): *Tanygnathus gramineus*
Black-mantled Goshawk (E): *Accipiter melanochlamys*
Black-mantled Hawk (E): *Accipiter melanochlamys*
Black-mantled Tamarin (E): *Saguinus nigricollis*
Black-masked Lovebird (E): *Agapornis personatus*
Black-necked Aracari (E): *Pteroglossus aracari*
Black-necked Crane (E): *Grus nigricollis*
Black-necked Swan (E): *Cygnus melanocorypha*
Black-necked Weaver (E): *Ploceus nigricollis*
Black-pencilled Marmoset (E): *Callithrix penicillata*
Black-rumped Waxbill (E): *Estrilda troglodytes*
Black-shouldered Kite (E): *Elanus axillaris/ Elanus caeruleus*
Black-sided Falconet (E): *Microhierax fringillarius*
Black-tailed Marmoset (E): *Callithrix argentata*
Black-tailed Trainbearer (E): *Lesbia victoriae*
Black-thighed Falconet (E): *Microhierax fringillarius*
Black-thighed Puffleg (E): *Eriocnemis derbyi*
Black-throated Brilliant (E): *Heliodoxa schreibersii*
Black-throated Hermit (E): *Phaethornis atrimentalis*
Black-throated Malimbe (E): *Malimbus cassini*
Black-throated Mango (E): *Anthracothorax nigricollis*
Black-tip Crested Turaco (E): *Tauraco macrorhynchus*
Black-tufted-ear Marmoset (E): *Callithrix penicillata*
Black-winged Bishop (E): *Euplectes hordeaceus*
Black-winged Kite (E): *Elanus caeruleus*
Black-winged Lory (E): *Eos cyanogenia*
Black-winged Lovebird (E): *Agapornis taranta*
Black-winged Parrot (E): *Hapalopsittaca melanotis*
Bladder Coral (E): *Plerogyra sinuosa*
Blade Chameleon (E): *Calumma gallus*
Bladed Fire Coral (E): *Millepora complanata*
Blainville's Beaked Whale (E): *Mesoplodon densirostris*
Blakiston's Fish-Owl (E): *Ketupa blakistoni*
Blanc's Leaf Chameleon (E): *Brookesia betschi*
Blanford's Fox (E): *Vulpes cana*
Blastocerus dichotomus : (E) Marsh Deer, (S) Ciervo de los pantanos, Ciervo marismeño, (F) Cerf des marais, **I** CERVIDAE Ma
Blastomussa merleti : **II** MUSSIDAE An
Blastomussa wellsi : **II** MUSSIDAE An
Blastotrochus nutrix : **II** FLABELLIDAE An
Blaze-winged Conure (E): *Pyrrhura devillei*
Blaze-winged Parakeet (E): *Pyrrhura devillei*
Bleeding Heart Dove (E): *Gallicolumba luzonica*
Bleeding Heart Pigeon (E): *Gallicolumba luzonica*
Blood Pheasant (E): *Ithaginis cruentus*
Blood Python (E): *Python brongersmai*
Blood-eared Parakeet (E): *Pyrrhura hoematotis*
Blossomcrown (E): *Anthocephala floriceps*
Blossom-headed Parakeet (E): *Psittacula roseata*
Blue Bird-of-paradise (E): *Paradisaea rudolphi*
Blue Bustard (E): *Eupodotis caerulescens*
Blue Coral (E): *Heliopora coerulea*
Blue Crane (E): *Grus paradisea*
Blue Crowned-Pigeon (E): *Goura cristata*
Blue Crust Coral (E): *Porites branneri*
Blue Duiker (E): *Cephalophus monticola*
Blue Korhaan (E): *Eupodotis caerulescens*
Blue Lorikeet (E): *Vini peruviana*
Blue macaws (E): *Anodorhynchus* spp.
Blue Monkey (E): *Cercopithecus mitis*
Blue Plantain-eater (E): *Corythaeola cristata*
Blue Poison Frog (E): *Dendrobates azureus*
Blue Whale (E): *Balaenoptera musculus*
Blue-and-gold Macaw (E): *Ara ararauna*

Blue-and-grey Sparrowhawk (E): *Accipiter luteoschistaceus*
Blue-and-yellow Macaw (E): *Ara ararauna*
Blue-backed Parrot (E): *Tanygnathus sumatranus*
Blue-bellied Parrot (E): *Triclaria malachitacea*
Blue-bellied Poison Frog (E): *Minyobates minutus*
Blue-billed Curassow (E): *Crax alberti*
Blue-billed Firefinch (E): *Lagonosticta rubricata*
Blue-billed Malimbe (E): *Malimbus nitens*
Blue-billed Mannikin (E): *Lonchura bicolor*
Blue-billed Weaver (E): *Spermophaga haematina*
Bluebonnet (E): *Northiella haematogaster*
Blue-breasted Poison Frog (E): *Epipedobates pulchripectus*
Blue-capped Hummingbird (E): *Eupherusa cyanophrys*
Blue-capped Puffleg (E): *Eriocnemis glaucopoides*
Blue-cheeked Amazon (E): *Amazona dufresniana*
Blue-cheeked Parrot (E): *Amazona dufresniana*
Blue-chested Hummingbird (E): *Polyerata amabilis*
Blue-chested Parakeet (E): *Pyrrhura cruentata*
Blue-chinned Sapphire (E): *Chlorostilbon notatus*
Blue-collared Parrot (E): *Geoffroyus simplex*
Blue-crowned Conure (E): *Aratinga acuticaudata*
Blue-crowned Hanging-Parrot (E): *Loriculus galgulus*
Blue-crowned Lorikeet (E): *Vini australis*
Blue-crowned Parakeet (E): *Aratinga acuticaudata*
Blue-crowned Racquet-tail (E): *Prioniturus discurus*
Blue-crowned Woodnymph (E): *Thalurania colombica*
Blue-eared Lory (E): *Eos semilarvata*
Blue-eyed Cockatoo (E): *Cacatua ophthalmica*
Blue-fronted Amazon (E): *Amazona aestiva*
Blue-fronted Lancebill (E): *Doryfera johannae*
Blue-fronted Lorikeet (E): *Charmosyna toxopei*
Blue-fronted Parrot (E): *Amazona aestiva*
Blue-fronted Parrotlet (E): *Touit dilectissima*
Blue-headed Dove (E): *Turtur brehmeri*
Blue-headed Hummingbird (E): *Cyanophaia bicolor*
Blue-headed Macaw (E): *Propyrrhura couloni*
Blue-headed Parrot (E): *Pionus menstruus*
Blue-headed Racquet-tail (E): *Prioniturus platenae*
Blue-headed Sapphire (E): *Hylocharis grayi*
Blue-headed Wood-Dove (E): *Turtur brehmeri*
Blue-knobbed Curassow (E): *Crax alberti*
Blue-legged Mantella (E): *Mantella expectata*
Blue-mantled Thornbill (E): *Chalcostigma stanleyi*
Blue-naped Parrot (E): *Tanygnathus lucionensis*
Blue-rumped Parrot (E): *Psittinus cyanurus*
Blue-rumped Parrotlet (E): *Forpus cyanopygius*
Blue-spotted Girdled Lizard (E): *Cordylus coeruleopunctatus*
Blue-spotted Spiny-tailed Lizard (E): *Cordylus coeruleopunctatus*
Blue-spotted Wood-Dove (E): *Turtur afer*
Blue-streaked Lory (E): *Eos reticulata*
Blue-tailed Day Gecko (E): *Phelsuma cepediana*
Blue-tailed Emerald (E): *Chlorostilbon mellisugus*
Blue-tailed Hummingbird (E): *Saucerottia cyanura*
Blue-tailed Monitor (E): *Varanus doreanus*
Blue-tailed Pitta (E): *Pitta guajana*
Blue-throated Goldentail (E): *Hylocharis eliciae*
Blue-throated Hummingbird (E): *Lampornis clemenciae*
Blue-throated Macaw (E): *Ara glaucogularis*
Blue-throated Parakeet (E): *Pyrrhura cruentata*
Blue-throated Starfrontlet (E): *Coeligena helianthea*
Bluetip Coral (E): *Acropora loripes*
Blue-topped Hanging-Parrot (E): *Loriculus galgulus*
Blue-tufted Starthroat (E): *Heliomaster furcifer*
Blue-vented Hummingbird (E): *Saucerottia saucerottei*
Blue-winged Grass-Parakeet (E): *Neophema chrysostoma*
Blue-winged Macaw (E): *Propyrrhura maracana*
Blue-winged Parrot (E): *Neophema chrysostoma*
Blue-winged Parrotlet (E): *Forpus crassirostris*
Blue-winged Racquet-tail (E): *Prioniturus verticalis*
Blumenbach's Curassow (E): *Crax blumenbachii*
Blunt-tailed Sand Boa (E): *Eryx johnii*

Blushing Star Coral (E): *Stephanocoenia intersepta*
Blyth's Hawk-Eagle (E): *Spizaetus alboniger*
Blyth's Hornbill (E): *Aceros subruficollis*
Blyth's Parakeet (E): *Psittacula caniceps*
Blyth's Tragopan (E): *Tragopan blythii*
Blyth's Wreathed Hornbill (E): *Aceros subruficollis*
Boa à trois bandes (F): *Lichanura trivirgata*
Boa annelé (F): *Corallus annulatus*
Boa annulata = Corallus annulatus
Boa arborícola anillada (S): *Corallus annulatus*
Boa arborícola de jardín (S): *Corallus hortulanus*
Boa arborícola de Madagascar (S): *Sanzinia madagascariensis*
Boa arboricole annelé (F): *Corallus annulatus*
Boa arboricole d'Amazonie (F): *Corallus hortulanus*
Boa arboricole gracile (F): *Epicrates gracilis*
Boa arc-en-ciel (F): *Epicrates cenchria*
Boa canin (F): *Corallus caninus*
Boa canina = Corallus caninus
Boa caoutchouc (F): *Charina bottae*
Boa Constrictor (E/S/F): *Boa constrictor*
Boa constrictor : (E) Ampalagua, Boa Constrictor, Giboya, Masacuate, (S) Boa constrictor, (F) Boa constrictor, **I/II** BOIDAE Re
Boa constrictor occidental (F): *Boa constrictor occidentalis*
Boa constrictor occidentalis : (E) Argentine Boa Constrictor, (F) Boa constrictor occidental, **I** BOIDAE Re
Boa cookii = Corallus cookii
Boa costera de Brasil (S): *Corallus cropanii*
Boa de arena de Egipto (S): *Gongylophis colubrinus*
Boa de arena de la India (S): *Eryx johnii*
Boa de arena de Müller (S): *Gongylophis muelleri*
Boa de arena de Sri Lanka (S): *Gongylophis conicus*
Boa de arena de Whitaker (S): *Eryx whitakeri*
Boa de arena somalí (S): *Eryx somalicus*
Boa de bosque (S): *Tropidophis melanurus*
Boa de Cook (F): *Corallus hortulanus*
Boa de Cropan (F): *Corallus cropanii*
Boa de Cuba (S/F): *Epicrates angulifer*
Boa de Duméril (S/F): *Acrantophis dumerili*
Boa de Fiji (S): *Candoia bibroni*
Boa de Ford (F): *Epicrates fordii*
Boa de Gomme (S): *Charina bottae*
Boa de Jamaica (S): *Epicrates subflavus*
Boa de la Jamaïque (F): *Epicrates subflavus*
Boa de l'île Abaco (F): *Epicrates exsul*
Boa de l'île Mona (F): *Epicrates monensis*
Boa de l'Ile Ronde de Dussumier (F): *Casarea dussumieri*
Boa de l'île Turk (F): *Epicrates chrysogaster*
Boa de Madagascar (F): *Acrantophis madagascariensis*
Boa de Madagascar meridional (S): *Acrantophis madagascariensis*
Boa de Mauricio (S): *Bolyeria multocarinata*
Boa de Mona (F): *Epicrates monensis*
Boa de Nueva Guinea (S): *Candoia aspera*
Boa de Porto Rico (F): *Epicrates inornatus*
Boa de Puerto Rico (S): *Epicrates inornatus*
Boa de Round Island (S): *Casarea dussumieri*
Boa del Pacífico (S): *Candoia carinata*
Boa des forêts de Madagascar (F): *Sanzinia madagascariensis*
Boa des jardins (F): *Corallus hortulanus*
Boa des sables à écailles rugueuses (F): *Gongylophis conicus*
Boa des sables brun (F): *Eryx johnii*
Boa des sables couleuvrin (F): *Gongylophis colubrinus*
Boa des sables d'Arabie (F): *Eryx jayakari*
Boa des sables d'Asie centrale (F): *Eryx elegans*
Boa des sables de Müller (F): *Gongylophis muelleri*
Boa des sables de Somalie (F): *Eryx somalicus*
Boa des sables de Tatarie (F): *Eryx tataricus*
Boa des sables de Whitaker (F): *Eryx whitakeri*
Boa des sables d'Egypte (F): *Gongylophis colubrinus*

Boa des sables des Indes (F): *Gongylophis conicus*
Boa des sables du Kenya (F): *Gongylophis colubrinus*
Boa des sables élégant (F): *Eryx elegans*
Boa des sables miliaire (F): *Eryx miliaris*
Boa des sables nain (F): *Eryx miliaris*
Boa des sables occidental (F): *Eryx jaculus*
Boa des savanes de Dumeril (F): *Acrantophis dumerili*
Boa des savanes de Madagascar (F): *Acrantophis madagascariensis*
Boa d'Haïti (F): *Epicrates striatus*
Boa d'Hispaniola (F): *Epicrates gracilis*
Boa dumerili = Acrantophis dumerili
Boa émeraude (F): *Corallus caninus*
Boa enana de las Bahamas (S): *Tropidophis canus*
Boa enana de las islas Caimán (S): *Tropidophis caymanensis*
Boa enana del norte de centroamérica (S): *Ungaliophis continentalis*
Boa enana mexicana (S): *Exiliboa placata*
Boa esmerelda (S): *Corallus caninus*
Boa excavadora de Round Island (S): *Bolyeria multocarinata*
Boa forestier à queue noire de l'île Navassa (F): *Tropidophis melanurus*
Boa forestier à ventre noir (F): *Tropidophis nigriventris*
Boa forestier annelé (F): *Tropidophis semicinctus*
Boa forestier brun (F): *Tropidophis fuscus*
Boa forestier d'Ambergris Cay (F): *Tropidophis greenwayi*
Boa forestier de Battersby (F): *Tropidophis battersbyi*
Boa forestier de Feick (F): *Tropidophis feicki*
Boa forestier de l'île du Grand Inagua (F): *Tropidophis canus*
Boa forestier de Pilsbry (F): *Tropidophis pilsbryi*
Boa forestier de Taczanowsky (F): *Tropidophis taczanowskyi*
Boa forestier de Wright (F): *Tropidophis wrighti*
Boa forestier des îles Cayman (F): *Tropidophis caymanensis*
Boa forestier d'Haïti (F): *Tropidophis haetianus*
Boa forestier du Brésil (F): *Tropidophis paucisquamis*
Boa forestier léopard (F): *Tropidophis pardalis*
Boa forestier tacheté (F): *Tropidophis maculatus*
Boa fouisseur de l'île Maurice (F): *Bolyeria multocarinata*
Boa fouisseur de l'Ile Ronde (F): *Bolyeria multocarinata*
Boa hortulana = Corallus hortulanus
Boa irisada (S): *Epicrates cenchria*
Boa jabalina (S): *Eryx jaculus*
Boa madagascariensis = Acrantophis madagascariensis
Boa manditra = Sanzinia madagascariensis
Boa mexicana rosada (S): *Lichanura trivirgata*
Boa nain à carènes (F): *Candoia carinata*
Boa nain à queue noire de l'île Navassa (F): *Tropidophis melanurus*
Boa nain à ventre noir (F): *Tropidophis nigriventris*
Boa nain annelé (F): *Tropidophis semicinctus*
Boa nain brun (F): *Tropidophis fuscus*
Boa nain d'Ambergris Cay (F): *Tropidophis greenwayi*
Boa nain d'Amérique centrale (F): *Ungaliophis continentalis*
Boa nain de Battersby (F): *Tropidophis battersbyi*
Boa nain de Bibron (F): *Candoia bibroni*
Boa nain de Boulenger (F): *Trachyboa boulengeri*
Boa nain de Feick (F): *Tropidophis feicki*
Boa nain de l'Equateur (F): *Trachyboa gularis*
Boa nain de l'île du Grand Inagua (F): *Tropidophis canus*
Boa nain de Pilsbry (F): *Tropidophis pilsbryi*
Boa nain de Taczanowsky (F): *Tropidophis taczanowskyi*
Boa nain de Wright (F): *Tropidophis wrighti*
Boa nain des îles Cayman (F): *Tropidophis caymanensis*
Boa nain des îles du Pacifique (F): *Candoia bibroni*
Boa nain des Salomons (F): *Candoia carinata*
Boa nain d'Haïti (F): *Tropidophis haetianus*
Boa nain d'Oaxaca (F): *Exiliboa placata*
Boa nain du Brésil (F): *Tropidophis paucisquamis*
Boa nain du Panama (F): *Ungaliophis panamensis*

Checklist of fauna/Lista de especies de fauna/Liste des espèces animales

Boa nain léopard (F): *Tropidophis pardalis*
Boa nain tacheté (F): *Tropidophis maculatus*
Boa rose (F): *Lichanura trivirgata*
Boa rugosa (S): *Trachyboa boulengeri*
Boa rugosa de Ecuador (S): *Trachyboa gularis*
Boa rugueux de Boulenger (F): *Trachyboa boulengeri*
Boa rugueux de l'Equateur (F): *Trachyboa gularis*
Boa sobre (F): *Epicrates inornatus*
Boa-javelot (F): *Eryx jaculus*
Boas (E/S/F): BOIDAE spp./ TROPIDOPHIIDAE spp.
Boas de l'Ile Ronde de Dussumier (F): *Bolyeria multocarinata*
Boas des savanes de Madagascar (F): *Acrantophis spp.*
Boa-vipère de Nouvelle Guinée (F): *Candoia aspera*
Bobcat (E): *Lynx rufus*
Bocage's Chameleon (E): *Chamaeleo quilensis*
Bockadam (E): *Cerberus rhynchops*
Boelen's Python (E): *Morelia boeleni*
Boella tenella = Epicrates inornatus
Boettger's Chameleon (E): *Calumma boettgeri*
Boettger's Day Gecko (E): *Phelsuma v-nigra*
Bog Turtle (E): *Clemmys muhlenbergii*
Bogert's Boa (E): *Exiliboa placata*
Bogert's Monitor (E): *Varanus bogerti*
Bogotá Sunangel (E): *Heliangelus zusii*
BOIDAE spp.: (E) Boas (S) Boas, (F) Boas, **I/II** Re
Boissonneaua flavescens : (E) Buff-tailed Coronet, (S) Colibrí cabecidorado, Colibrí colihabano, Coronita colihabana, (F) Colibri flavescent, **II** TROCHILIDAE Av
Boissonneaua jardini : (E) Velvet-purple Coronet, (S) Colibrí sietecolores, Coronita aterciopelada, (F) Colibri de Jardine, **II** TROCHILIDAE Av
Boissonneaua matthewsii : (E) Chestnut-breasted Coronet, (S) Colibrí pechirrojo, Coronita pechicastaña, (F) Colibri de Matthews, **II** TROCHILIDAE Av
Bokharan Deer (E): *Cervus elaphus bactrianus*
Bolbopsittacus lunulatus : (E) Guaiabero, (S) Lorito guayabero, (F) Perruche lunulée, **II** PSITTACIDAE Av
Bolborhynchus aurifrons = Psilopsiagon aurifrons
Bolborhynchus aymara = Psilopsiagon aymara
Bolborhynchus ferrugineifrons : (E) Rufous-fronted Parakeet, (S) Catita frentirrufa, (F) Toui à front roux, **II** PSITTACIDAE Av
Bolborhynchus lineola : (E) Barred Parakeet, (S) Catita barrada, Perico barreteado, Periquito barrado, (F) Toui catherine, **II** PSITTACIDAE Av
Bolborhynchus orbygnesius : (E) Andean Parakeet, (S) Catita andina, (F) Toui d'Orbigny, **II** PSITTACIDAE Av
Bolivian Hairy Armadillo (E): *Chaetophractus nationi*
Bolivian Poison Frog (E): *Epipedobates bolivianus*
Bolivian Red Howling Monkey (E): *Alouatta sara*
Bolivian Three-toed Sloth (E): *Bradypus variegatus*
Bolson Tortoise (E): *Gopherus flavomarginatus*
Bolyeria multocarinata : (E) Round Island Burrowing Boa, (S) Boa de Mauricio, Boa excavadora de Round Island, (F) Boa fouisseur de l'île Maurice, Boa fouisseur de l'Ile Ronde, Boas de l'Ile Ronde de Dussumier, Bolyeride, **I** BOLYERIIDAE Re
Bolyeride (F): *Bolyeria multocarinata*
BOLYERIIDAE spp.: (E) Round Island boas **I** Re
Bondrée à longue queue (F): *Henicopernis longicauda*
Bondrée apivore (F): *Pernis apivorus*
Bondrée des Célèbes (F): *Pernis celebensis*
Bondrée noire (F): *Henicopernis infuscatus*
Bondrée orientale (F): *Pernis ptilorhyncus*
Bone shark (E): *Cetorhinus maximus*
Bonelli's Eagle (E): *Hieraaetus fasciatus*
Bongo (E/S/F): *Tragelaphus eurycerus*
Bonin Flying-fox (F): *Pteropus pselaphon*
Bonin Fruit Bat (E): *Pteropus pselaphon*
Boninastrea boninensis : **II** MERULINIDAE An
Bonnet Macaque (E): *Macaca radiata*

Bonneted Langur (E): *Trachypithecus pileatus*
Bonobo (E/F): *Pan paniscus*
Bontebok (E/S/F): *Damaliscus pygargus pygargus*
Boocercus eurycerus = Tragelaphus eurycerus
Boodie (E): *Bettongia lesueur*
Booted Eagle (E): *Hieraaetus pennatus*
Booted Macaque (E): *Macaca ochreata*
Booted Racket-tail (E): *Ocreatus underwoodii*
Boreal Owl (E): *Aegolius funereus*
Boring Clam (E): *Tridacna crocea*
Bornean Falconet (E): *Microhierax latifrons*
Bornean Gibbon (E): *Hylobates muelleri*
Bornean Marbled Cat (E): *Catopuma badia*
Bornean Peacock-pheasant (E): *Polyplectron schleiermacheri*
Bornean River Turtle (E): *Orlitia borneensis*
Bornean Smooth-tailed Treeshrew (E): *Dendrogale melanura*
Bornean Treeshrew (E): *Tupaia longipes*
Borneo Short-tailed Python (E): *Python breitensteini*
Borner's Day Gecko (E): *Phelsuma minuthi*
Borrego cimarrón (S): *Ovis canadensis*
Bos frontalis = Bos gaurus
Bos gaurus : (E) Gaur, Indian Bison, Indian Wild Ox, Saladang, (S) Gaur, Gauru, (F) Gaur, **I** BOVIDAE Ma
Bos grunniens = Bos mutus
Bos mutus : (E) Wild Yak, (S) Yak, Yak salvaje, (F) Yack sauvage, **I** BOVIDAE Ma
Bos sauveli : (E) Kouprey, (S) Kouprey, Toro cuprey, (F) Kouprey, **I** BOVIDAE Ma
Bosc's Monitor (E): *Varanus exanthematicus*
Bostami Turtle (E): *Aspideretes nigricans*
Bostrychia hagedash : (E) Hadada Ibis, (S) Ibis hadada, Ibis hagedash, (F) Ibis hagedash, **III** THRESKIORNITHIDAE Av
Bostrychia rara : (E) Spot-breasted Ibis, (S) Ibis moteado, Ibis rara, (F) Ibis vermiculé, **III** THRESKIORNITHIDAE Av
Bothrochile (F): *Bothrochilus boa*
Bothrochilus boa : (E) Barred Python, Bismarck Ringed Python, Ringed Python, (S) Pitón anillada de Bismarck, (F) Bothrochile, **II** PYTHONIDAE Re
Boto (E): *Inia geoffrensis*
Bottlehead (E): *Hyperoodon ampullatus*
Bottlenose Dolphin (E): *Tursiops truncatus*
Bottlenose whales (E): *Hyperoodon* spp.
Bottle-nosed Dolphin (E): *Tursiops truncatus*
Boulder Brain Coral (E): *Colpophyllia natans*
Boulder corals (E): *Porites spp.*
Boulder Star Coral (E): *Montastraea annularis*
Boulenger's Cape Tortoise (E): *Homopus boulengeri*
Boulenger's Padloper (E): *Homopus boulengeri*
Bouquet corals (E): *Euphyllia* spp.
Bouquetin du Népal (F): *Naemorhedus goral*
Bourke's Parrot (E): *Neopsephotus bourkii*
Bourneotrochus stellulatus : **II** CARYOPHYLLIIDAE An
Boutu (E): *Inia geoffrensis*
Bowhead Whale (E): *Balaena mysticetus*
Bowl Coral (E): *Turbinaria peltata/ Halomitra pileus*
Bowsprit Tortoise (E): *Chersina angulata*
Box turtles (E): *Cuora spp./ Terrapene spp.*
Brace's Emerald (E): *Chlorostilbon bracei*
Brachlyophes (F): *Brachylophus* spp.
Brachylophus spp.: (E) Fijian iguanas, (S) Iguanas de Fiji, (F) Brachlyophes, Iguanes des Fidji, **I** IGUANIDAE Re
Brachylophus brevicephalus = Brachylophus fasciatus
Brachylophus fasciatus : (E) Fiji Banded Iguana, South Pacific Banded Iguana, (F) Iguane à bandes de Fidji, **I** IGUANIDAE Re
Brachylophus vitiensis : (E) Fiji Crested Iguana, (S) Iguana crestada de Fiji, (F) Iguane à crête de Fidji, **I** IGUANIDAE Re
Brachypelma spp.: (E) Tarantulas, (S) Tarántulas, (F) Mygales, Tarentules, **II** THERAPHOSIDAE Ar

Checklist of fauna/Lista de especies de fauna/Liste des espèces animales

Brachypelma albopilosum : (E) Curly-hair Tarantula, (S) Tarantula de pelo crespo, (F) Tarantule frisée, **II** THERAPHOSIDAE Ar

Brachypelma angustum : (E) Costa Rican Red Tarantula, (S) Tarantula roja de Costa Rica, (F) Tarantule rouge du Costa Rica, **II** THERAPHOSIDAE Ar

Brachypelma auratum : (E) Mexican Flameknee Tarantula, (S) Tarantula Mexicana rodilla de llama, (F) Tarantule à genux de peu du Mexique, **II** THERAPHOSIDAE Ar

Brachypelma aureoceps : (E) Florida Golden Chestnut Tarantula, **II** THERAPHOSIDAE Ar

Brachypelma baumgarteni : (E) Mexican Orangebeauty Tarantula, Michoacan Orange Tarantula, (S) Tarantula Mexicana naranja, (F) Tarantule orange du Mexique, **II** THERAPHOSIDAE Ar

Brachypelma boehmei : (E) Guerrero Orange Legs Tarantula, Mexican Fireleg Tarantula, (S) Tarantula Mexicana pierna naranja oscuro, (F) Tarantule du Mexique à pattes rouille, **II** THERAPHOSIDAE Ar

Brachypelma embrithes : **II** THERAPHOSIDAE Ar

Brachypelma emilia : (E) Mexican Blackcap Tarantula, Mexican Redleg Tarantula, Orange-knee Tarantula, True Red Leg Tarantula, (S) Tarantula Mexicana pierna roja, (F) Tarantule du Mexique à pattes rouge, **II** THERAPHOSIDAE Ar

Brachypelma epicureanum : (E) Yucatan Rusty-rumped Tarantula, **II** THERAPHOSIDAE Ar

Brachypelma fossorium : (E) Filadelfia Rusty Brown Tarantula, **II** THERAPHOSIDAE Ar

Brachypelma klaasi = Brachypelmides klaasi

Brachypelma mesomelas : **II** THERAPHOSIDAE Ar

Brachypelma pallidum = Aphonopelma pallidum

Brachypelma sabulosum : (E) Guatemalan Red-rumped Tarantula, **II** THERAPHOSIDAE Ar

Brachypelma smithi : (E) Mexican Redknee Tarantula, (S) Tarantula Mexicana pierna roja, (F) Tarantule à genoux rouges du Mexique, **II** THERAPHOSIDAE Ar

Brachypelma vagans : (E) Mexican Redrump Tarantula, (S) Tarantula Mexicana cadera roja, (F) Tarantule à croupion rouge du Mexique, **II** THERAPHOSIDAE Ar

Brachypelmides klaasi : (E) Acapulco Lesser Orange Tarantula, **II** THERAPHOSIDAE Ar

Brachyteles arachnoides : (E) Muriqui, Woolly Spider Monkey, (S) Mono araña, Mono grande, Muriki, (F) Atèle arachnoïde, Eroïde, Singe-araignée laineux, **I** CEBIDAE Ma

Brachyteles hypoxanthus = Brachyteles arachnoides

Bradype (F): *Bradypus variegatus*

Bradypodion spp.: (E) Chameleons, Dwarf chameleons, (S) Camaleónes enanos, (F) Caméléons nain, **II** CHAMAELEONIDAE Re

Bradypodion adolfifriderici : (E) Ituri Chameleon, Ituri Forest Chameleon, (F) Caméléon nain d'Ituri, **II** CHAMAELEONIDAE Re

Bradypodion carpenteri : (E) Carpenter's Chameleon, Ruwenzori Mountain Chameleon, (F) Caméléon nain de Carpenter, **II** CHAMAELEONIDAE Re

Bradypodion dracomontanum : (E) Drakensberg Dwarf Chameleon, (F) Caméléon nain du Drakensberg, **II** CHAMAELEONIDAE Re

Bradypodion excubitor = Bradypodion fischeri

Bradypodion fischeri : (E) Fischer's Chameleon, Uluguru Two-horned Chameleon, Usambara Two-horned Chameleon, (F) Caméléon nain de Fischer, **II** CHAMAELEONIDAE Re

Bradypodion mlanjense : (E) Mlanje Mountain Chameleon, (F) Caméléon nain du Zululand, **II** CHAMAELEONIDAE Re

Bradypodion nemorale : (E) Zululand Dwarf Chameleon, (F) Caméléon nain à nez rouge, **II** CHAMAELEONIDAE Re

Bradypodion oxyrhinum : (E) Red-nosed Dwarf Chameleon, Uluguru One-horned Chameleon, (F) Caméléon nain du Cap, **II** CHAMAELEONIDAE Re

Bradypodion pumilum : (E) Cape Dwarf Chameleon, Variegated Dwarf Chameleon, (F) Caméléon nain de Setaro, **II** CHAMAELEONIDAE Re

Bradypodion setaroi : (E) Setaro's Dwarf Chameleon, (F) Caméléon nain épineux, **II** CHAMAELEONIDAE Re

Bradypodion spinosum : (E) Prickly Chameleon, Rosette-nosed Chameleon, Spiny Chameleon, (F) Caméléon nain de Smith, **II** CHAMAELEONIDAE Re

Bradypodion tavetanum : (E) Mt Kilimanjaro Two-horned Chameleon, (F) Caméléon nain de Matschie, **II** CHAMAELEONIDAE Re

Bradypodion tenue : (E) Matschie's Dwarf Chameleon, Single Soft-nosed Chameleon, Slender Chameleon, Usambara Soft-horned Chameleon, (F) Caméléon à corne molle des monts Usambara, **II** CHAMAELEONIDAE Re

Bradypodion thamnobates : (E) Natal Midlands Dwarf Chameleon, (F) Caméléon nain du Transvaal, **II** CHAMAELEONIDAE Re

Bradypodion uthmoelleri : (E) Hanang Hornless Chameleon, Müller's Leaf Chameleon, (F) Caméléon nain du sud et du Namaqua, **II** CHAMAELEONIDAE Re

Bradypodion xenorhinum : (E) Single Welded-horn Chameleon, Strange-horned Chameleon, Strange-nosed Chameleon, (F) Caméléon de Rüppell, **II** CHAMAELEONIDAE Re

Bradypus boliviensis = Bradypus variegatus

Bradypus griseus = Bradypus variegatus

Bradypus infuscatus = Bradypus variegatus

Bradypus variegatus : (E) Bolivian Three-toed Sloth, Brown-throated Sloth, Brown-throated Three-toed Sloth, (S) Perezoso grisaceo, Perezoso o tridáctilo de Bolivia, Perezoso tridáctilo, Perico ligero, (F) Aï de Bolivie, Bradype, Paresseux tridactyle, Paresseux tridactyle de Bolivie, **II** BRADYPODIDAE Ma

Brahminy Kite (E): *Haliastur indus*

Brain corals (E): *Platygyra* spp.

Branched Finger Coral (E): *Porites furcata*

Branching Anchor Coral (E): *Euphyllia paraancora*

Branching Coral (E): *Porites cylindrica*

Branta canadensis leucopareia : (E) Aleutian Canada Goose, Aleutian Goose, (S) Barnacla de las Aleutianas, Ganso canadiense aleutiana, (F) Bernache des Aléoutiennes, Bernache du Canada aléoute, **I** ANATIDAE Av

Branta ruficollis : (E) Red-breasted Goose, (S) Barnacla cuellirroja, (F) Bernache à cou roux, **II** ANATIDAE Av

Branta sandvicensis : (E) Hawaiian Goose, Nene, (S) Barnacla hawaiana, Barnacla nené, Ganso né, Né, (F) Bernache des Iles Sandwich, Bernache d'Hawaï, Bernache néné, Oie néné, **I** ANATIDAE Av

Brazilian Dwarf Boa (E): *Tropidophis paucisquamis*

Brazilian Giant Tortoise (E): *Geochelone denticulata*

Brazilian Poison Frog (E): *Dendrobates vanzolinii*

Brazilian Pygmy-Owl (E): *Glaucidium minutissimum*

Brazilian Ruby (E): *Clytolaema rubricauda*

Brazilian Smooth Snake (E): *Cyclagras gigas*

Brazilian Tapir (E): *Tapirus terrestris*

Brazilian Teju (E): *Tupinambis teguixin*

Brazilian Water Cobra (E): *Cyclagras gigas*

Brazil-nut Poison Frog (E): *Dendrobates castaneoticus*

Brehm's Tiger-Parrot (E): *Psittacella brehmii*

Brelich's Snub-nosed Monkey (E): *Pygathrix brelichi*

Brève à queue bleue (F): *Pitta guajana*

Brève azurine (F): *Pitta guajana*

Brève de Gurney (F): *Pitta gurneyi*

Brève de Koch (F): *Pitta kochi*

Brève du Japon (F): *Pitta nympha*

Brève migratrice (F): *Pitta nympha*

Bridled Dolphin (E): *Stenella attenuata*

Checklist of fauna/Lista de especies de fauna/Liste des espèces animales

Bridled Nailtail Wallaby (E): *Onychogalea fraenata*
Bridled Wallaby (E): *Onychogalea fraenata*
Bright-eyed Day Gecko (E): *Phelsuma dubia*
Brillant à bandeau bleu (F): *Heliodoxa aurescens*
Brillant à couronne verte (F): *Heliodoxa xanthogonys*
Brillant à front violet (F): *Heliodoxa leadbeateri*
Brillant à gorge noire (F): *Heliodoxa schreibersii*
Brillant à gorge rose (F): *Heliodoxa gularis*
Brillant de Branicki (F): *Heliodoxa branickii*
Brillant fer-de-lance (F): *Heliodoxa jacula*
Brillant impératrice (F): *Heliodoxa imperatrix*
Brillant rubinoïde (F): *Heliodoxa rubinoides*
Brillante alicanela (S): *Heliodoxa branickii*
Brillante coroniverde (S): *Heliodoxa jacula*
Brillante de Tepui (S): *Heliodoxa xanthogonys*
Brillante emperador (S): *Heliodoxa imperatrix*
Brillante frentivioleta (S): *Heliodoxa leadbeateri*
Brillante gorgirrosado (S): *Heliodoxa gularis*
Brillante gorjinegro (S): *Heliodoxa schreibersii*
Brillante pechianteado (S): *Heliodoxa rubinoides*
Brillante pechicastaño (S): *Heliodoxa aurescens*
Brillante pechigamuza (S): *Heliodoxa rubinoides*
Brillante ventinegro (S): *Heliodoxa schreibersii*
Brilliant-thighed Poison Frog (E): *Epipedobates femoralis*
Broad-billed Hummingbird (E): *Cynanthus latirostris*
Broad-headed Snake (E): *Hoplocephalus bungaroides*
Broad-nosed Caiman (E): *Caiman latirostris*
Broad-nosed Gentle Lemur (E): *Hapalemur simus*
Broad-snouted Caiman (E): *Caiman latirostris*
Broad-snouted Crocodile (E): *Crocodylus palustris*
Broad-tailed Hummingbird (E): *Selasphorus platycercus*
Broad-tipped Hermit (E): *Anopetia gounellei*
Broad-winged Hawk (E): *Buteo platypterus*
Brolga (E): *Grus rubicunda*
Bronze Mannikin (E): *Lonchura cucullata*
Bronze Munia (E): *Lonchura cucullata*
Bronze-tailed Barbthroat (E): *Threnetes niger*
Bronze-tailed Comet (E): *Polyonymus caroli*
Bronze-tailed Plumeleteer (E): *Chalybura urochrysia*
Bronze-tailed Thornbill (E): *Chalcostigma heteropogon*
Bronze-winged Mannikin (E): *Lonchura cucullata*
Bronze-winged Parrot (E): *Pionus chalcopterus*
Bronzy Hermit (E): *Glaucis aenea*
Bronzy Inca (E): *Coeligena coeligena*
Brookesia spp.: (E) Leaf chameleons, (F) Brookésies, **I/II** CHAMAELEONIDAE Re
Brookesia ambreensis : **II** CHAMAELEONIDAE Re
Brookesia antakarana : **II** CHAMAELEONIDAE Re
Brookesia antoetrae = *Brookesia thieli*
Brookesia bekolosy : **II** CHAMAELEONIDAE Re
Brookesia betschi : (E) Blanc's Leaf Chameleon, **II** CHAMAELEONIDAE Re
Brookesia bonsi : **II** CHAMAELEONIDAE Re
Brookesia brygooi : **II** CHAMAELEONIDAE Re
Brookesia decaryi : (E) Spiny Leaf Chameleon, (F) Brookésie épineuse, **II** CHAMAELEONIDAE Re
Brookesia dentata : (E) Toothed Leaf Chameleon, **II** CHAMAELEONIDAE Re
Brookesia ebenaui : (E) Northern Leaf Chameleon, (F) Brookésie d'Ebenau, **II** CHAMAELEONIDAE Re
Brookesia exarmata : **II** CHAMAELEONIDAE Re
Brookesia griveaudi : (E) Marojejy Leaf Chameleon, **II** CHAMAELEONIDAE Re
Brookesia karchei : (E) Naturelle Leaf Chameleon, **II** CHAMAELEONIDAE Re
Brookesia lambertoni : (E) Fito Leaf Chameleon, **II** CHAMAELEONIDAE Re
Brookesia legendrei = *Brookesia ebenaui*
Brookesia lineata : **II** CHAMAELEONIDAE Re
Brookesia lolontany : **II** CHAMAELEONIDAE Re
Brookesia minima : (E) Minute Leaf Chameleon, (F) Brookésie naine, **II** CHAMAELEONIDAE Re
Brookesia nasus : (E) Elongate Leaf Chameleon, **II** CHAMAELEONIDAE Re

Brookesia perarmata : (E) Antsingy Leaf Chameleon, (F) Brookésie d'Antsingy, **I** CHAMAELEONIDAE Re
Brookesia peyrierasi = *Brookesia minima*
Brookesia ramanantsoai = *Brookesia dentata*
Brookesia stumpffi : (E) Plated Leaf Chameleon, (F) Brookésie de Stumpff, **II** CHAMAELEONIDAE Re
Brookesia superciliaris : (E) Brown Leaf Chameleon, (F) Brookésie commune, **II** CHAMAELEONIDAE Re
Brookesia therezieni : (E) Perinet Leaf Chameleon, **II** CHAMAELEONIDAE Re
Brookesia thieli : (E) Domergue's Leaf Chameleon, (F) Brookésie de Domergue, **II** CHAMAELEONIDAE Re
Brookesia tuberculata = *Brookesia minima*
Brookesia vadoni : (E) Iaraka River Leaf Chameleon, **II** CHAMAELEONIDAE Re
Brookesia valerieae : (E) Raxworthy's Leaf Chameleon, **II** CHAMAELEONIDAE Re
Brookésie commune (F): *Brookesia superciliaris*
Brookésie d'Antsingy (F): *Brookesia perarmata*
Brookésie de Domergue (F): *Brookesia thieli*
Brookésie de Stumpff (F): *Brookesia stumpffi*
Brookésie d'Ebenau (F): *Brookesia ebenaui*
Brookésie épineuse (F): *Brookesia decaryi*
Brookésie naine (F): *Brookesia minima*
Brookésies (F): *Brookesia* spp.
Brother Islands Tuatara (E): *Sphenodon gunatheri*
Brotogeris chiriri : (E) Yellow-chevroned Parakeet, (S) Catita chiriri, (F) Toui à ailes jaunes, **II** PSITTACIDAE Av
Brotogeris chrysopterus : (E) Golden-winged Parakeet, (S) Catita alidorada, Periquito ala dorada, (F) Toui para, **II** PSITTACIDAE Av
Brotogeris cyanoptera : (E) Cobalt-winged Parakeet, (S) Catita aliazul, Periquito azul, (F) Toui de Deville, **II** PSITTACIDAE Av
Brotogeris jugularis : (E) Orange-chinned Parakeet, (S) Catita churica, Churica, Periquito barbinaranja, (F) Perruche tovi, Toui à menton d'or, **II** PSITTACIDAE Av
Brotogeris pyrrhopterus : (E) Grey-cheeked Parakeet, (S) Catita macareña, Perico cachetigris, Perico macareño, (F) Perruche orangé, Toui flamboyant, **II** PSITTACIDAE Av
Brotogeris sanctithomae : (E) Tui Parakeet, (S) Catita frentigualda, Perico tui, (F) Toui à front d'or, **II** PSITTACIDAE Av
Brotogeris tirica : (E) Plain Parakeet, (S) Catita tirica, (F) Toui tirica, **II** PSITTACIDAE Av
Brotogeris versicolurus : (E) Canary-winged Parakeet, (S) Catita aliamarilla, Catita versicolor, (F) Toui à ailes variées, **II** PSITTACIDAE Av
Brotogeris versicolurus ssp. *chiriri* = *Brotogeris chiriri*
Brow-antlered Deer (E): *Cervus eldii*
Brown Bear (E): *Ursus arctos*
Brown Boobook (E): *Ninox scutulata*
Brown Caiman (E): *Caiman crocodilus*
Brown Eared-pheasant (E): *Crossoptilon mantchuricum*
Brown Falcon (E): *Falco berigora*
Brown Fish-Owl (E): *Ketupa zeylonensis*
Brown Goshawk (E): *Accipiter fasciatus*
Brown Harrier-Eagle (E): *Circaetus cinereus*
Brown Hawk-Owl (E): *Ninox scutulata*
Brown Hornbill (E): *Anorrhinus tickelli*
Brown Howler (E): *Alouatta fusca*
Brown Howling Monkey (E): *Alouatta fusca*
Brown Inca (E): *Coeligena wilsoni*
Brown Leaf Chameleon (E): *Brookesia superciliaris*
Brown Lemur (E): *Eulemur fulvus*
Brown Lory (E): *Chalcopsitta duivenbodei*
Brown Mantella (E): *Mantella betsileo*
Brown Monitor (E): *Varanus primordius*
Brown Mouse-lemur (E): *Microcebus rufus*
Brown Pale-fronted Capuchin (E): *Cebus albifrons*
Brown Parrot (E): *Poicephalus meyeri*

Brown River Turtle (E): *Kachuga smithii*
Brown Roofed Turtle (E): *Kachuga smithii*
Brown Sand Boa (E): *Eryx johnii*
Brown Seahorse (E): *Hippocampus erectus*
Brown Sicklebill (E): *Epimachus meyeri*
Brown Snake-Eagle (E): *Circaetus cinereus*
Brown Teal (E): *Anas aucklandica*
Brown Violet-ear (E): *Colibri delphinae*
Brown Wood-Owl (E): *Strix leptogrammica*
Brown-backed Firefinch (E): *Lagonosticta rubricata*
Brown-backed Parrotlet (E): *Touit melanonota*
Brown-blossom Naiad (E): *Epioblasma walkeri*
Brown-blossom Pearly Mussel (E): *Epioblasma walkeri*
Brown-breasted Parakeet (E): *Pyrrhura calliptera*
Brown-headed Parrot (E): *Poicephalus cryptoxanthus*
Brown-headed Spider Monkey (E): *Ateles fusciceps*
Brown-headed Tamarin (E): *Saguinus fuscicollis*
Brown-hooded Parrot (E): *Pionopsitta haematotis*
Brown-necked Parrot (E): *Poicephalus robustus*
Brown-throated Conure (E): *Aratinga pertinax*
Brown-throated Parakeet (E): *Aratinga pertinax*
Brown-throated Sloth (E): *Bradypus variegatus*
Brown-throated Three-toed Sloth (E): *Bradypus variegatus*
Browse Rhinoceros (E): *Diceros bicornis*
Bruce's Green-Pigeon (E): *Treron waalia*
Brumback's Night Monkey (E): *Aotus brumbacki*
Brush corals (E): *Seriatopora* spp.
Brush-tailed Bettong (E): *Bettongia penicillata*
Brush-tailed Rat Kangaroo (E): *Bettongia penicillata*
Bryde's Whale (E): *Balaenoptera edeni*
Brygoo's Chameleon (E): *Calumma peyrierasi*
Bubalornis albirostris : (E) White-billed Buffalo-Weaver, (F) Alecto à bec blanc, **III** PLOCEIDAE Av
Bubalus arnee : (E) Wild Asiatic Buffalo, Wild Water Buffalo, (S) Búfalo acuático, Búfalo arni, Caraboa, (F) Arni, Buffle d'Asie , Buffle de l'Inde, Buffle d'eau, **III** BOVIDAE Ma
Bubalus depressicornis : (E) Anoa, Lowland Anoa, (S) Anca de Llanura, Anoa de Ilanura, (F) Anoa des plaines, **I** BOVIDAE Ma
Bubalus mindorensis : (E) Tamaraw, Tamarou, (S) Búfalo de Mindoro, Tamarao, Tamarau, (F) Tamarau, **I** BOVIDAE Ma
Bubalus quarlesi : (E) Mountain Anoa, (S) Anoa de montaña, (F) Anoa de Quarle, Anoa des montagnes, **I** BOVIDAE Ma
Bubble corals (E): *Physogyra* spp./ *Plerogyra* spp.
Bubo africanus : (E) African Eagle-Owl, Spotted Eagle-Owl, (S) Búho Africano, Búho Africano chico, (F) Grand-duc africain, **II** STRIGIDAE Av
Bubo ascalaphus : (E) Pharaoh Eagle-Owl, (S) Búho desértico, (F) Grand-duc ascalaphe, Grand-duc du désert, **II** STRIGIDAE Av
Bubo bengalensis : (E) Rock Eagle-Owl, (S) Búho Bengalí, (F) Grand-duc indien, **II** STRIGIDAE Av
Bubo blakistoni = Ketupa blakistoni
Bubo bubo : (E) Eagle Owl, Eurasian Eagle-Owl, (S) Buho real, Búho real, (F) Grand-duc d'Europe, Hibou grand-duc, **II** STRIGIDAE Av
Bubo bubo ssp. *ascalaphus = Bubo ascalaphus*
Bubo bubo ssp. *bengalensis = Bubo bengalensis*
Bubo capensis : (E) Cape Eagle-Owl, Mackinder's Eagle-Owl, Mountain Eagle-Owl, (S) Búho de El Cabo, (F) Grand-duc du Cap, **II** STRIGIDAE Av
Bubo cinerascens = Bubo africanus
Bubo coromandus : (E) Dusky Eagle-Owl, (S) Búho de Coromandel, (F) Grand-duc de Coromandel, **II** STRIGIDAE Av
Bubo flavipes = Ketupa flavipes
Bubo ketupu = Ketupa ketupu
Bubo lacteus : (E) Giant Eagle-Owl, Milky Eagle-Owl, Verreaux's Eagle-Owl, (S) Búho lechoso, Gran búho etiópico, (F) Grand-duc de Verreaux, **II** STRIGIDAE Av

Bubo leucostictus : (E) Akun Eagle-Owl, Sooty Eagle-Owl, (S) Búho de Akún, (F) Grand-duc tacheté, **II** STRIGIDAE Av
Bubo magellanicus = Bubo virginianus
Bubo nipalensis : (E) Forest Eagle-Owl, Spot-bellied Eagle-Owl, (S) Búho Nepalí, (F) Grand-duc du Népal, **II** STRIGIDAE Av
Bubo philippensis : (E) Philippine Eagle-Owl, (S) Búho Filipino, (F) Grand-duc des Philippines, **II** STRIGIDAE Av
Bubo poensis : (E) Fraser's Eagle-Owl, (S) Búho de Guinea, (F) Grand-duc à aigrettes, **II** STRIGIDAE Av
Bubo poensis ssp. *vosseleri = Bubo vosseleri*
Bubo shelleyi : (E) Banded Eagle-Owl, Shelley's Eagle-Owl, (S) Búho barrado, (F) Grand-duc de Shelley, **II** STRIGIDAE Av
Bubo sumatranus : (E) Barred Eagle-Owl, (S) Búho Malayo, (F) Grand-duc bruyant, **II** STRIGIDAE Av
Bubo virginianus : (E) Great Horned Owl, (S) Búho, Búho Americano, Búho cornudo, Lechuzón orejudo, Nacurutú, (F) Grand-duc d'Amérique, **II** STRIGIDAE Av
Bubo vosseleri : (E) Usambara Eagle-Owl, (S) Búho de Usambara, (F) Grand-duc des Usambara, **II** STRIGIDAE Av
Bubo zeylonensis = Ketupa zeylonensis
Bubulcus ibis : (E) Buff-backed Heron, Cattle Egret, (S) Espulgabueyes, Garcilla bueyera, Garcita resnera, Garza ganadera, (F) Héron garde-boeufs, **III** ARDEIDAE Av
Buceros (S): *Aceros* spp./ *Anorrhinus* spp./ *Anthracoceros* spp./ *Buceros* spp./ *Penelopides* spp.
Buceros spp.: (E) Hornbills, (S) Buceros, Cálaos, (F) Calao rhinocéros, Calao roux de Luzon, Calaos, **I/II** BUCEROTIDAE Av
Buceros bicornis : (E) Concave-casqued Hornbill, Great Hornbill, Great Indian Hornbill, Great Pied Hornbill, Indian Concave-casqued Hornbill, Indian Hornbill, (S) Cálao bicorne, Cálao grande, (F) Calao bicorne, **I** BUCEROTIDAE Av
Buceros hydrocorax : (E) Rufous Hornbill, (S) Cálao Filipino grande, Cálao rojipardo, (F) Calao à casque plat, Calao des Philippines, **II** BUCEROTIDAE Av
Buceros rhinoceros : (E) Rhinoceros Hornbill, (S) Cálao rinoceronte, (F) Calao rhinocéros, **II** BUCEROTIDAE Av
Buceros vigil : (E) Helmeted Hornbill, (S) Cálao de casco, Cálao de yelmo, (F) Calao à casque, Calao à casque rond, **I** BUCEROTIDAE Av
Buckley's Forest-Falcon (E): *Micrastur buckleyi*
Budeng (F): *Trachypithecus cristatus*
Budgerigar (E): *Melopsittacus undulatus*
Budgerigar ondulado (S): *Melopsittacus undulatus*
Budorcas taxicolor : (E) Takin, (S) Takin, (F) Takin, **II** BOVIDAE Ma
Búfalo acuático (S): *Bubalus arnee*
Búfalo arni (S): *Bubalus arnee*
Búfalo de Mindoro (S): *Bubalus mindorensis*
Bufeo (S): *Inia geoffrensis*
Bufeo africano (S): *Sousa teuszii*
Bufeo asiático (S): *Sousa chinensis*
Bufeo negro (S): *Sotalia fluviatilis*
Bufeos (S): *Sotalia* spp.
Buff-backed Heron (E): *Bubulcus ibis*
Buff-bellied Hermit (E): *Phaethornis subochraceus*
Buff-bellied Hummingbird (E): *Amazilia yucatanensis*
Buff-breasted Sabrewing (E): *Campylopterus duidae*
Buff-cheeked Gibbon (E): *Hylobates gabriellae*
Buff-crested Bustard (E): *Eupodotis gindiana*
Buff-faced Pygmy-Parrot (E): *Micropsitta pusio*
Buff-fronted Owl (E): *Aegolius harrisii*
Buffle d'Asie (F): *Bubalus arnee*
Buffle de l'Inde (F): *Bubalus arnee*
Buffle d'eau (F): *Bubalus arnee*
Buff-nosed Rat-kangaroo (E): *Caloprymnus campestris*

Buffon's Macaw (E): *Ara ambigua*
Buff-tailed Coronet (E): *Boissonneaua flavescens*
Buff-tailed Sicklebill (E): *Eutoxeres condamini/ Epimachus albertisi*
Buff-thighed Puffleg (E): *Haplophaedia assimilis*
Buff-winged Starfrontlet (E): *Coeligena lutetiae*
Buffy Fish-Owl (E): *Ketupa ketupu*
Buffy Hummingbird (E): *Leucippus fallax*
Buffy Saki (E): *Pithecia albicans*
Buffy-headed Marmoset (E): *Callithrix flaviceps*
Buffy-tufted-ear Marmoset (E): *Callithrix aurita*
Bufo negro (S): *Sotalia fluviatilis*
Bufo osgoodi = Spinophrynoides osgoodi
Bufo periglenes : (E) Alajuela Toad, Golden Toad, Monte Verde Toad, Orange Toad, (S) Sapo dorado, Sapo dorado de Monteverde, (F) Crapaud doré, **I** BUFONIDAE Am
Bufo superciliaris : (E) Cameroon Toad, Zaire Toad, (S) Sapo del Camerún, (F) Crapaud du Cameroun, **I** BUFONIDAE Am
Bugeranus carunculatus = Grus carunculatus
Buhito en Pernetas (S): *Otus clarkii*
Búho (S): *Bubo virginianus*
Búho Abisinio (S): *Asio abyssinicus*
Búho Africano (S): *Bubo africanus*
Búho Africano chico (S): *Bubo africanus*
Búho Americano (S): *Bubo virginianus*
Búho barrado (S): *Bubo shelleyi*
Búho barrado (S): *Strix varia*
Búho Bengalí (S): *Bubo bengalensis*
Búho blanquinegro (S): *Strix nigrolineata*
Búho café (S): *Strix virgata*
Búho campestre (S): *Asio flammeus*
Búho chico (S): *Asio otus*
Búho corniblanco (S): *Lophostrix cristata*
Búho cornudo (S): *Bubo virginianus/ Lophostrix cristata*
Búho de Akún (S): *Bubo leucostictus*
Búho de anteojos (S): *Pulsatrix perspicillata*
Búho de Coromandel (S): *Bubo coromandus*
Búho de Crin (S): *Jubula lettii*
Búho de El Cabo (S): *Bubo capensis*
Búho de Guinea (S): *Bubo poensis/ Jubula lettii*
Búho de Jamaica (S): *Pseudoscops grammicus*
Búho de las Salomón (S): *Nesasio solomonensis*
Búho de Mindanao (S): *Mimizuku gurneyi*
Búho de Usambara (S): *Bubo vosseleri*
Búho desértico (S): *Bubo ascalaphus*
Búho Filipino (S): *Bubo philippensis*
Búho fulvo (S): *Strix fulvescens*
Búho gavilán (S): *Surnia ulula*
Búho gritón (S): *Asio clamator*
Búho Jamaicano (S): *Pseudoscops grammicus*
Búho lechoso (S): *Bubo lacteus*
Búho llanero (S): *Speotyto cunicularia*
Búho Malayo (S): *Bubo sumatranus*
Búho Malgache (S): *Asio madagascariensis*
Búho manchado (S): *Strix occidentalis*
Búho Manchú (S): *Ketupa blakistoni*
Búho moro (S): *Asio capensis*
Búho negruzco (S): *Asio stygius*
Búho Nepalí (S): *Bubo nipalensis*
Búho Nival (S): *Nyctea scandiaca*
Búho orejicorto (S): *Asio flammeus*
Búho pequeño de bigotes alargados (S): *Xenoglaux loweryi*
Búho pescador (S): *Ketupa flavipes*
Búho pescador de Ceilán (S): *Ketupa zeylonensis*
Búho pescador leonado (S): *Ketupa flavipes*
Búho pescador Malayo (S): *Ketupa ketupu*
Búho pescador rojizo (S): *Scotopelia ussheri*
Búho real (S): *Bubo bubo*
Búho-cornudo cariblanco (S): *Asio clamator*
Búho-cornudo caricafe (S): *Asio otus*
Búho-cornudo oscuro (S): *Asio stygius*
Buitre cabeciblanco (S): *Trigonoceps occipitalis*

Buitre cabecirrojo (S): *Sarcogyps calvus*
Buitre común (S): *Gyps fulvus*
Buitre del Himalaya (S): *Gyps himalayensis*
Buitre dorsiblanco africano (S): *Gyps africanus*
Buitre dorsiblanco bengalí (S): *Gyps bengalensis*
Buitre el cabo (S): *Gyps coprotheres*
Buitre leonado (S): *Gyps fulvus*
Buitre leonado bengalés (S): *Gyps bengalensis*
Buitre leonado común (S): *Gyps fulvus*
Buitre moteado (S): *Gyps rueppellii*
Buitre negro (S): *Aegypius monachus*
Buitre orejudo (S): *Torgos tracheliotus*
Buitre palmero (S): *Gypohierax angolensis*
Buitre picofino (S): *Gyps indicus*
Buitre piquirrojo (S): *Trigonoceps occipitalis*
Bulbul à tête jaune (F): *Pycnonotus zeylanicus*
Bulbul bigotudo (S): *Pycnonotus zeylanicus*
Bullneck Seahorse (E): *Hippocampus minotaur*
Bumblebee Hummingbird (E): *Atthis heloisa*
Bunch (E): *Megaptera novaeangliae*
Bungarra (E): *Varanus gouldii*
Bunopithecus hoolock = Hylobates hoolock
Bürger's Sparrowhawk (E): *Erythrotriorchis buergersi*
Burhinus bistriatus : (E) Double-striped Thick-knee, (S) Alcaraván Americana, Alcaraván Venozolano, Dara, (F) Oedicnème américain, Oedicnème bistrié, **III** BURHINIDAE Av
Burmeister's Porpoise (E): *Phocoena spinipinnis*
Burmese Brown Tortoise (E): *Manouria emys*
Burmese Eyed Turtle (E): *Morenia ocellata*
Burmese Hornbill (E): *Aceros subruficollis*
Burmese Mountain Tortoise (E): *Manouria emys*
Burmese Python (E): *Python molurus*
Burmese Roofed Turtle (E): *Kachuga trivittata*
Burmese Starred Tortoise (E): *Geochelone platynota*
Burmese swamp turtle (E): *Morenia ocellata*
Burrowing Bettong (E): *Bettongia lesueur*
Burrowing Owl (E): *Speotyto cunicularia*
Burrowing Parakeet (E): *Cyanoliseus patagonus*
Burrowing Python (E): *Loxocemus bicolor*
Buru Opalescent Birdwing (E): *Troides prattorum*
Buru Racquet-tail (E): *Prioniturus mada*
Busard bariolé (F): *Circus cinereus*
Busard cendré (F): *Circus pygargus*
Busard de Buffon (F): *Circus buffoni*
Busard de Gould (F): *Circus approximans*
Busard de Maillard (F): *Circus maillardi*
Busard de montagne (F): *Circus pygargus*
Busard de Wilson (F): *Chondrohierax uncinatus wilsonii*
Busard des roseaux (F): *Circus aeruginosus*
Busard d'Orient (F): *Circus spilonotus*
Busard grenouillard (F): *Circus ranivorus*
Busard maure (F): *Circus maurus*
Busard pâle (F): *Circus macrourus*
Busard Saint-Martin (F): *Circus cyaneus*
Busard tacheté (F): *Circus assimilis*
Busard tchoug (F): *Circus melanoleucos*
Busardo aliancho (S): *Buteo platypterus*
Busardo alirrufo (S): *Butastur liventer*
Busardo augur meridional (S): *Buteo rufofuscus*
Busardo augur oriental (S): *Buteo augur*
Busardo augur somalí (S): *Buteo archeri*
Busardo aura (S): *Buteo albonotatus*
Busardo azoreño (S): *Leucopternis princeps*
Busardo blanco (S): *Leucopternis albicollis*
Busardo blanquinegro (S): *Leucopternis polionota*
Busardo calzado (S): *Buteo lagopus*
Busardo caminero (S): *Buteo magnirostris*
Busardo carigrís (S): *Butastur indicus*
Busardo carinegro (S): *Leucopternis melanops*
Busardo cejiblanco (S): *Leucopternis kuhli*
Busardo chapulinero (S): *Buteo swainsoni*
Busardo coliblanco (S): *Buteo albicaudatus*
Busardo colicorto (S): *Buteo brachyurus*
Busardo colirrojo (S): *Buteo jamaicensis*

Checklist of fauna/Lista de especies de fauna/Liste des espèces animales

Busardo colorado (S): *Busarellus nigricollis*
Busardo cuelliblanco (S): *Leucopternis lacernulata*
Busardo cuellirrojo (S): *Buteo auguralis*
Busardo culiblanco (S): *Buteo leucorrhous*
Busardo de Galápagos (S): *Buteo galapagoensis*
Busardo de la española (S): *Buteo ridgwayi*
Busardo de Wilson (S): *Chondrohierax uncinatus wilsonii*
Busardo dorsi (S): *Leucopternis occidentalis*
Busardo dorsigrís (S): *Leucopternis occidentalis*
Busardo dorsirrojo (S): *Buteo polyosoma*
Busardo gavilán (S): *Kaupifalco monogrammicus*
Busardo gorgiblanco (S): *Buteo albigula*
Busardo gris (S): *Asturina nitida*
Busardo hawaiano (S): *Buteo solitarius*
Busardo herrumbroso (S): *Buteo regalis*
Busardo hombrorrojo (S): *Buteo lineatus*
Busardo langostero (S): *Butastur rufipennis*
Busardo malgache (S): *Buteo brachypterus*
Busardo mixto (S): *Parabuteo unicinctus*
Busardo mongol (S): *Buteo hemilasius*
Busardo montañés (S): *Buteo oreophilus*
Busardo moro (S): *Buteo rufinus*
Busardo patagón (S): *Buteo ventralis*
Busardo pizarroso (S): *Leucopternis schistacea*
Busardo plomizo (S): *Leucopternis plumbea*
Busardo puneño (S): *Buteo poecilochrous*
Busardo ratonero (S): *Buteo buteo*
Busardo sabanero (S): *Buteogallus meridionalis*
Busardo semiplomizo (S): *Leucopternis semiplumbea*
Busardo tisa (S): *Butastur teesa*
Busardo-negro del atlántico (S): *Buteogallus aequinoctialis*
Busardo-negro del pacifico (S): *Buteogallus subtilis*
Busardo-negro norteño (S): *Buteogallus anthracinus*
Busardo-negro urubitinga (S): *Buteogallus urubitinga*
Busarellus nigricollis : (E) Black-collared Hawk, Collared Fishing Hawk, (S) Aguila colorada, Busardo colorado, Gavilán colorado, (F) Buse à tête blanche, **II** ACCIPITRIDAE Av
Busautour à joues grises (F): *Butastur indicus*
Busautour aux yeux blancs (F): *Butastur teesa*
Busautour des sauterelles (F): *Butastur rufipennis*
Busautour pâle (F): *Butastur liventer*
Buse à dos gris (F): *Leucopternis occidentalis*
Buse à épaulettes (F): *Buteo lineatus*
Buse à face noire (F): *Leucopternis melanops*
Buse à gorge blanche (F): *Buteo albigula*
Buse à gros bec (F): *Buteo magnirostris*
Buse à queue barrée (F): *Buteo albonotatus*
Buse à queue blanche (F): *Buteo albicaudatus*
Buse à queue courte (F): *Buteo brachyurus*
Buse à queue rousse (F): *Buteo auguralis/ Buteo jamaicensis*
Buse à sourcils blancs (F): *Leucopternis kuhli*
Buse à tête blanche (F): *Busarellus nigricollis*
Buse aguia (F): *Geranoaetus melanoleucus*
Buse ardoisée (F): *Leucopternis schistacea*
Buse augure (F): *Buteo augur*
Buse barrée (F): *Leucopternis princeps*
Buse blanche (F): *Leucopternis albicollis*
Buse buson (F): *Buteogallus aequinoctialis*
Buse cendrée (F): *Asturina nitida*
Buse couronnée (F): *Harpyhaliaetus coronatus*
Buse cul-blanc (F): *Buteo leucorrhous*
Buse d'Afrique (F): *Buteo auguralis*
Buse d'Archer (F): *Buteo archeri*
Buse de Chine (F): *Buteo hemilasius*
Buse de Harris (F): *Parabuteo unicinctus*
Buse de Madagascar (F): *Buteo brachypterus*
Buse de Patagonie (F): *Buteo ventralis*
Buse de Ridgway (F): *Buteo ridgwayi*
Buse de Swainson (F): *Buteo swainsoni*
Buse des Galapagos (F): *Buteo galapagoensis*
Buse des îles Galapagos (F): *Buteo galapagoensis*
Buse des mangroves (F): *Buteogallus subtilis*

Buse d'Hawaï (F): *Buteo solitarius*
Buse du puna (F): *Buteo poecilochrous*
Buse échasse (F): *Geranospiza caerulescens*
Buse féroce (F): *Buteo rufinus*
Buse grise (F): *Asturina plagiata*
Buse lacernulée (F): *Leucopternis lacernulata*
Buse mantelée (F): *Leucopternis polionota*
Buse montagnarde (F): *Buteo oreophilus*
Buse noire (F): *Buteogallus anthracinus*
Buse pattue (F): *Buteo lagopus*
Buse plombée (F): *Leucopternis plumbea*
Buse rouilleuse (F): *Buteo regalis*
Buse rounoir (F): *Buteo rufofuscus*
Buse roussâtre (F): *Buteogallus meridionalis*
Buse semiplombée (F): *Leucopternis semiplumbea*
Buse solitaire (F): *Harpyhaliaetus solitarius*
Buse tricolore (F): *Buteo polyosoma*
Buse urubu (F): *Buteogallus urubitinga*
Buse variable (F): *Buteo buteo*
Bush corals (E): *Stylophora* spp.
Bush Dog (E): *Speothos venaticus*
Bush Petronia (E): *Petronia dentata*
Bush Sparrow (E): *Petronia dentata*
Bushy-crested Hornbill (E): *Anorrhinus galeritus*
Bushy-tailed Olingo (E): *Bassaricyon gabbii*
Bustards (E): OTIDIDAE spp.
Butastur indicus : (E) Grey-faced Buzzard, Grey-faced Buzzard-Eagle, (F) Busardo carigrís, (F) Busautour à joues grises, **II** ACCIPITRIDAE Av
Butastur liventer : (E) Rufous-winged Buzzard, Rufous-winged Buzzard-Eagle, (S) Busardo alirrufo, (F) Busautour pâle, **II** ACCIPITRIDAE Av
Butastur rufipennis : (E) Grasshopper Buzzard, Grasshopper Buzzard-Eagle, (S) Aguililla langostera, Busardo langostero, (F) Busautour des sauterelles, **II** ACCIPITRIDAE Av
Butastur teesa : (E) White-eyed Buzzard, (S) Busardo tisa, (F) Busautour aux yeux blancs, **II** ACCIPITRIDAE Av
Buteo albicaudatus : (E) White-tailed Hawk, (S) Aguililla coliblanca, Aguilucho cabecinegro, Busardo coliblanco, Gavilán tejé, (F) Buse à queue blanche, **II** ACCIPITRIDAE Av
Buteo albigula : (E) White-throated Hawk, (S) Aguilucho chico, Busardo gorgiblanco, Gavilán gargantiblanco, (F) Buse à gorge blanche, **II** ACCIPITRIDAE Av
Buteo albonotatus : (E) Zone-tailed Hawk, (S) Aguililla aura, Busardo aura, Gavilán albonotatus, Gavilán colifajeado, (F) Buse à queue barrée, **II** ACCIPITRIDAE Av
Buteo archeri : (E) Archer's Buzzard, (S) Busardo augur somali, (F) Buse d'Archer, **II** ACCIPITRIDAE Av
Buteo augur : (E) Augur Buzzard, (S) Busardo augur oriental, (F) Buse augure, **II** ACCIPITRIDAE Av
Buteo augur ssp. *archeri = Buteo archeri*
Buteo auguralis : (E) African Red-tailed Buzzard, Red-necked Buzzard, Red-tailed Buzzard, (S) Busardo cuellirrojo, Ratonero cuellirrojo, (F) Buse à queue rousse, Buse d'Afrique, **II** ACCIPITRIDAE Av
Buteo bannermani = Buteo buteo
Buteo brachypterus : (E) Madagascar Buzzard, (S) Busardo malgache, (F) Buse de Madagascar, **II** ACCIPITRIDAE Av
Buteo brachyurus : (E) Short-tailed Hawk, (S) Aguililla colicorta, Aguilucho cola corta, Busardo colicorto, Gavilán cola corta, (F) Buse à queue courte, **II** ACCIPITRIDAE Av
Buteo brachyurus ssp. *albigula = Buteo albigula*
Buteo buteo : (E) Buzzard, Common Buzzard, Eurasian Buzzard, (S) Busardo ratonero, Ratonero común, (F) Buse variable, **II** ACCIPITRIDAE Av
Buteo galapagoensis : (E) Galapagos Hawk, (S) Busardo de Galápagos, Gavilán de Galapagos, (F) Buse des Galapagos, Buse des îles Galapagos, **II** ACCIPITRIDAE Av

Buteo hemilasius : (E) Upland Buzzard, (S) Busardo mongol, (F) Buse de Chine, **II** ACCIPITRIDAE Av

Buteo jamaicensis : (E) Red-tailed Hawk, (S) Aguililla colirroja, Busardo colirrojo, Guaraguao, (F) Buse à queue rousse, **II** ACCIPITRIDAE Av

Buteo lagopus : (E) Rough-legged Buzzard, Rough-legged Hawk, (S) Aguililla artica, Busardo calzado, Ratonero calzado, (F) Buse pattue, **II** ACCIPITRIDAE Av

Buteo leucorrhous : (E) Rufous-thighed Hawk, White-rumped Hawk, (S) Busardo culiblanco, Gavilán negro, Gavilán rabadilla blanca, (F) Buse cul-blanc, **II** ACCIPITRIDAE Av

Buteo lineatus : (E) Red-shouldered Hawk, (S) Aguililla pechirroja, Busardo hombrorrojo, (F) Buse à épaulettes, **II** ACCIPITRIDAE Av

Buteo magnirostris : (E) Roadside Hawk, (S) Aguililla caminera, Busardo caminero, Gavilán alirrojizo, Gavilán común, Gavilán habado, (F) Buse à gros bec, **II** ACCIPITRIDAE Av

Buteo nitidus = Asturina nitida

Buteo nitidus ssp. *plagiatus = Asturina plagiata*

Buteo oreophilus : (E) Forest Buzzard, Mountain Buzzard, (S) Busardo montañés, (F) Buse montagnarde, **II** ACCIPITRIDAE Av

Buteo platypterus : (E) Broad-winged Hawk, (S) Aguililla aluda, Busardo aliancho, Gavilán bebehumo, (F) Petite buse, **II** ACCIPITRIDAE Av

Buteo poecilochrous : (E) Gurney's Hawk, Puna Hawk, Variable Hawk, (S) Aguilucho puna, Busardo puneño, Gavilán punenno, (F) Buse du puna, **II** ACCIPITRIDAE Av

Buteo polyosoma : (E) Red-backed Hawk, (S) Aguilucho común, Aguilucho variado, Busardo dorsirrojo, (F) Buse tricolore, **II** ACCIPITRIDAE Av

Buteo regalis : (E) Ferruginous Hawk, (S) Aguililla real, Busardo herrumbroso, (F) Buse rouilleuse, **II** ACCIPITRIDAE Av

Buteo ridgwayi : (E) Hispaniolan Hawk, Ridgway's Hawk, (S) Busardo de la española, (F) Buse de Ridgway, **II** ACCIPITRIDAE Av

Buteo rufinus : (E) Long-legged Buzzard, (S) Busardo moro, Ratonero moro, (F) Buse féroce, **II** ACCIPITRIDAE Av

Buteo rufofuscus : (E) Jackal Buzzard, (S) Busardo augur meridional, (F) Buse rounoir, **II** ACCIPITRIDAE Av

Buteo solitarius : (E) Hawaiian Hawk, (S) Busardo hawaiano, (F) Buse d'Hawaï, **II** ACCIPITRIDAE Av

Buteo swainsoni : (E) Swainson's Hawk, (S) Aguililla de Swainson, Aguilucho langostero, Busardo chapulinero, Gavilán langostero, (F) Buse de Swainson, **II** ACCIPITRIDAE Av

Buteo tachardus = Buteo oreophilus

Buteo ventralis : (E) Red-tailed Hawk, Rufous-tailed Hawk, (S) Aguilucho cola colorada, Busardo patagón, (F) Buse de Patagonie, **II** ACCIPITRIDAE Av

Buteogallus aequinoctialis : (E) Rufous Crab-Hawk, (S) Busardo-negro del atlántico, Gavilán de Manglares, (F) Buse buson, **II** ACCIPITRIDAE Av

Buteogallus anthracinus : (E) Common Black-Hawk, Cuban Black Hawk, Lesser Black-Hawk, (S) Aguililla negra menor, Busardo-negro norteño, Gavilán cangrejero, (F) Buse noire, **II** ACCIPITRIDAE Av

Buteogallus meridionalis : (E) Savanna Hawk, (S) Aguilucho colorada, Aguilucho sabanero, Busardo sabanero, Gavilán pita venado, Gavilán sabanero, (F) Buse roussâtre, **II** ACCIPITRIDAE Av

Buteogallus subtilis : (E) Mangrove Black-Hawk, Pacific Black Hawk, (S) Busardo-negro del pacifico, Gavilán negro común, (F) Buse des mangroves, **II** ACCIPITRIDAE Av

Buteogallus urubitinga : (E) Great Black-Hawk, (S) Aguila negra, Aguililla negra mayor, Busardo-negro urubitinga, Gavilán negro grande, (F) Buse urubu, **II** ACCIPITRIDAE Av

Buton Hornbill (E): *Aceros cassidix*

Butterfly of Paradise (E): *Ornithoptera paradisea*

Button Coral (E): *Heteropsammia cochlea/ Scolymia australis*

Buzzard (E): *Buteo buteo*

Caatinga Parakeet (E): *Aratinga cactorum*

Caballito de mar (S): *Hippocampus erectus/ Hippocampus guttulatus/ Hippocampus hippocampus/ Hippocampus ingens*

Caballito de mar (S): *Hippocampus zosterae*

Caballito de mar del Pacífico (S): *Hippocampus ingens*

Caballito erecto (S): *Hippocampus erectus*

Caballito oliváceo (S): *Hippocampus zosterae*

Caballito punteado (S): *Hippocampus erectus*

Caballitos de mar (S): *Hippocampus* spp.

Caballo de Przewalski (S): *Equus przewalskii*

Caballo marino (S): *Hippocampus hippocampus*

Caballo salvaje (S): *Equus przewalskii*

Cabalo de mar (S): *Hippocampus hippocampus*

Cabassous centralis : (E) Northern Naked-tailed Armadillo, (S) Armado de zapilots, Tatú de América central, (F) Tatou, Tatou d'Amérique centrale, **III** DASYPODIDAE Ma

Cabassous gymnurus = Cabassous tatouay

Cabassous tatouay : (E) Greater Naked-tailed Armadillo, (S) Cabasu de orejas largas, Tatú cabasú, Tatú de rabo mol, Tatú de rabo molle, (F) Tatou à queue nue, Tatou gumnure, **III** DASYPODIDAE Ma

Cabasu de orejas largas (S): *Cabassous tatouay*

Cabbage Coral (E): *Merulina* spp.

Cabeza de viejo (S): *Eira barbara*

Cabezón (S): *Peltocephalus dumeriliana*

Cabézon toucan (F): *Semnornis ramphastinus*

Caburé (S): *Glaucidium brasilianum/ Micrastur ruficollis*

Caburé patagónico (S): *Glaucidium nanum*

Cacajao (S): *Cacajao calvus*

Cacajao spp.: (E) Uakaris, (S) Cacajú, (F) Ouakaris, **I** CEBIDAE Ma

Cacajao calvus : (E) Bald-headed Uacari, Red-and-white Uacari, (S) Cacajao, Cacayao, Huapo colorado, Huapo rojo, Uacaries, (F) Ouakari chauve, **I** CEBIDAE Ma

Cacajao melanocephalus : (E) Black Uacari, Black-headed Uacari, (F) Ouakari à tête noire, **I** CEBIDAE Ma

Cacajú (S): *Cacajao* spp.

Cacapo (S): *Strigops habroptilus*

Cacatoès à bec gracile (F): *Cacatua tenuirostris*

Cacatoès à huppe blanche (F): *Cacatua alba*

Cacatoès à huppe jaune (F): *Cacatua galerita*

Cacatoès à huppe rouge (F): *Cacatua moluccensis*

Cacatoès à lores rouges (F): *Cacatua pastinator*

Cacatoès à oeil bleu (F): *Cacatua ophthalmica*

Cacatoès à oreilles blanches (F): *Calyptorhynchus funereus*

Cacatoès à oreilles jaunes (F): *Calyptorhynchus funereus*

Cacatoès à rectrices blanches (F): *Calyptorhynchus latirostris*

Cacatoès à tête brune (F): *Calyptorhynchus lathami*

Cacatoès à tête rouge (F): *Callocephalon fimbriatum*

Cacatoès à ventre rouge (F): *Cacatua haematuropygia*

Cacatoès aux yeux bleus (F): *Cacatua ophthalmica*

Cacatoès aux yeux nus (F): *Cacatua pastinator*

Cacatoès banksien (F): *Calyptorhynchus banksii*

Cacatoès blanc (F): *Cacatua alba*

Cacatoès casqué (F): *Callocephalon fimbriatum*

Cacatoès corella (F): *Cacatua sanguinea*

Cacatoès de Banks (F): *Calyptorhynchus banksii*

Cacatoès de Baudin (F): *Calyptorhynchus baudinii*

Cacatoès de Ducorps (F): *Cacatua ducorpsii*

Cacatoès de Goffin (F): *Cacatua goffini*

Cacatoès de Latham (F): *Calyptorhynchus lathami*

Cacatoès de Leadbeater (F): *Cacatua leadbeateri*

Cacatoès des Moluques (F): *Cacatua moluccensis*

Cacatoès des Philippines (F): *Cacatua haematuropygia*

Cacatoès funèbre (F): *Calyptorhynchus funereus*

Cacatoès laboureur (F): *Cacatua pastinator*

Checklist of fauna/Lista de especies de fauna/Liste des espèces animales

Cacatoès nasique (F): *Cacatua tenuirostris*
Cacatoès noir (F): *Probosciger aterrimus*
Cacatoès rosalbin (F): *Eolophus roseicapillus*
Cacatoès soufré (F): *Cacatua sulphurea*
Cacatúa alba (S): *Cacatua alba*
Cacatua alba : (E) Umbrella Cockatoo, White Cockatoo, (S) Cacatúa alba, Cacatúa blanca, (F) Cacatoès à huppe blanche, Cacatoès blanc, **II** PSITTACIDAE Av
Cacatúa blanca (S): *Cacatua alba*
Cacatúa de alas doradas (S): *Psephotus chrysopterygius*
Cacatúa de cabeza roja (S): *Callocephalon fimbriatum*
Cacatúa de cola roja (S): *Calyptorhynchus banksii*
Cacatúa de cola sangrante (S): *Cacatua haematuropygia*
Cacatúa de cresta amarilla grande (S): *Cacatua galerita*
Cacatúa de Ducorps (S): *Cacatua ducorpsii*
Cacatúa de Forbes (S): *Cyanoramphus forbesi*
Cacatúa de Goffin (S): *Cacatua goffini*
Cacatúa de las Molucas (S): *Cacatua moluccensis*
Cacatúa de Leadbeater (S): *Cacatua leadbeateri*
Cacatúa de pico afilado (S): *Cacatua pastinator*
Cacatúa de pico afilado anaranjada (S): *Cacatua tenuirostris*
Cacatúa de vientre naranja (S): *Neophema chrysogaster*
Cacatúa del collar de Mauricio (S): *Psittacula echo*
Cacatúa del paraíso (S): *Psephotus pulcherrimus*
Cacatúa dorada (S): *Guarouba guarouba*
Cacatua ducorpsii : (E) Ducorps's Cockatoo, (S) Cacatúa de Ducorps, (F) Cacatoès de Ducorps, **II** PSITTACIDAE Av
Cacatúa enlutada (S): *Probosciger aterrimus*
Cacatua galerita : (E) Greater Sulphur-crested Cockatoo, Sulphur-crested Cockatoo, (S) Cacatúa de cresta amarilla grande, (F) Cacatoès à huppe jaune, Grand cacatoès à huppe jaune, **II** PSITTACIDAE Av
Cacatua goffini : (E) Goffin's Cockatoo, Tanimbar Cockatoo, Tanimbar Corella, (S) Cacatúa de Goffin, (F) Cacatoès de Goffin, **I** PSITTACIDAE Av
Cacatua haematuropygia : (E) Philippine Cockatoo, Red-vented Cockatoo, (S) Cacatúa de cola sangrante, (F) Cacatoès à ventre rouge, Cacatoès des Philippines, **I** PSITTACIDAE Av
Cacatúa Inca (S): *Cacatua leadbeateri*
Cacatua leadbeateri : (E) Leadbeater's Cockatoo, Major Mitchell's Cockatoo, Pink Cockatoo, (S) Cacatúa de Leadbeater, Cacatúa Inca, (F) Cacatoès de Leadbeater, **II** PSITTACIDAE Av
Cacatua moluccensis : (E) Moluccan Cockatoo, Salmon-crested Cockatoo, (S) Cacatúa de las Molucas, (F) Cacatoès à huppe rouge, Cacatoès des Moluques, **I** PSITTACIDAE Av
Cacatúa negra de cola amarilla (S): *Calyptorhynchus funereus*
Cacatúa negra de cola roja (S): *Calyptorhynchus banksii*
Cacatúa negra de Latham (S): *Calyptorhynchus lathami*
Cacatúa nocturna (S): *Geopsittacus occidentalis*
Cacatúa oftálmica (S): *Cacatua ophthalmica*
Cacatua ophthalmica : (E) Blue-eyed Cockatoo, (S) Cacatúa oftálmica, (F) Cacatoès à oeil bleu, Cacatoès aux yeux bleus, **II** PSITTACIDAE Av
Cacatua pastinator : (E) Western Corella, (S) Cacatúa de pico afilado, (F) Cacatoès à lores rouges, Cacatoès aux yeux nus, Cacatoès laboureur, **II** PSITTACIDAE Av
Cacatúa rosada (S): *Eolophus roseicapillus*
Cacatua roseicapilla = *Eolophus roseicapillus*
Cacatua sanguinea : (E) Bare-eyed Cockatoo, Little Cockatoo, Little Corella, (F) Cacatoès corella **II** PSITTACIDAE Av
Cacatua sulphurea : (E) Lesser Sulphur-crested Cockatoo, Yellow-crested Cockatoo, (F) Cacatoès soufré, Petit cacatoès à huppe jaune, **II** PSITTACIDAE Av
Cacatua tenuirostris : (E) Long-billed Corella, (S) Cacatúa de pico afilado anaranjada, (F) Cacatoès à bec gracile, Cacatoès nasique, **II** PSITTACIDAE Av
Cacatua tenuirostris ssp. *pastinator* = *Cacatua pastinator*

Cacatúa terrera (S): *Pezoporus wallicus*
Cacayao (S): *Cacajao calvus*
Cachalot (F): *Physeter catodon*
Cachalot nain (F): *Kogia simus*
Cachalot pygmée (F): *Kogia breviceps*
Cachalote (S): *Physeter catodon*
Cachalote cabeza chica (S): *Kogia breviceps*
Cachalote enano (S): *Kogia simus*
Cachalote pigmeo (S): *Kogia breviceps*
Cachelot (E): *Physeter catodon*
Cachorro de mato vinagre (S): *Speothos venaticus*
Cachorro vinagre (S): *Speothos venaticus*
Cacomistle (E/S): *Bassariscus sumichrasti*
Cactus Conure (E): *Aratinga cactorum*
Cactus Coral (E): *Pavona decussata*
Cactus Parakeet (E): *Aratinga cactorum*
Caebézon toucan (F): *Semnornis ramphastinus*
Caecobarbus geertsi : (E) African Blind Barb Fish, Congo Blind Barb, (F) Barbu aveugle, Poisson cavernicole d'Afrique, **II** CYPRINIDAE Ac
Caica Parrot (E): *Pionopsitta caica*
Caimán (S): *Caiman crocodilus*
Caïman à lunettes (F): *Caiman crocodilus*
Caïman à museau large (F): *Caiman latirostris*
Caïman à paupières osseuses (F): *Palaeosuchus palpebrosus*
Caimán americano (S): *Crocodylus acutus*
Caiman crocodilus : (E) Brown Caiman, Common Caiman, Spectacled Caiman, (S) Caimán, (F) Caïman à lunettes, **I/II** ALLIGATORIDAE Re
Caiman crocodilus apaporiensis : (E) Apaporis River Caiman, Rio Apaporis (Spectacled) Caiman, (S) Caimán del Río Apaporis, (F) Caïman du Rio Apaporis, **I** ALLIGATORIDAE Re
Caiman crocodilus ssp. *chiapasius* = *Caiman crocodilus* ssp. *fuscus*
Caiman crocodilus ssp. *matogrossiensis* = *Caiman yacare*
Caiman crocodilus ssp. *paraguaiensis* = *Caiman yacare*
Caiman crocodilus ssp. *yacare* = *Caiman yacare*
Caimán de Cuba (S): *Crocodylus rhombifer*
Caimán de hocico ancho (S): *Caiman latirostris*
Caimán de Morelet (S): *Crocodylus moreletii*
Caimán del Orinoco (S): *Crocodylus intermedius*
Caimán del Río Apaporis (S): *Caiman crocodilus apaporiensis*
Caïman du Rio Apaporis (F): *Caiman crocodilus apaporiensis*
Caimán enano (S): *Palaeosuchus palpebrosus*
Caimán frentiplano (S): *Palaeosuchus trigonatus*
Caïman hérissé (F): *Palaeosuchus trigonatus*
Caimán hociquiancho (S): *Caiman latirostris*
Caiman latirostris : (E) Broad-nosed Caiman, Broad-snouted Caiman, (S) Caimán de hocico ancho, Caimán hociquiancho, Yacaré de hocico ancho, Yacaré overo, (F) Caïman à museau large, **I/II** ALLIGATORIDAE Re
Caiman lizards (E): *Dracaena* spp.
Caimán negro (S): *Melanosuchus niger*
Caïman noir (F): *Melanosuchus niger*
Caiman sclerops = *Caiman crocodilus*
Caiman sclerops ssp. *apaporiensis* = *Caiman crocodilus* ssp. *apaporiensis*
Caïman yacare (F): *Caiman yacare*
Caiman yacare : (E) Yacare Caiman, (S) Yacaré, (F) Caïman yacare, **II** ALLIGATORIDAE Re
Caïque à ailes noires (F): *Hapalopsittaca melanotis*
Caïque à capuchon (F): *Pionopsitta haematotis*
Caïque à face rouge (F): *Hapalopsittaca amazonina*
Caïque à joues roses (F): *Pionopsitta pulchra*
Caïque à queue courte (F): *Graydidascalus brachyurus*
Caïque à tête noire (F): *Pionopsitta caica*
Caïque à ventre blanc (F): *Pionites leucogaster*
Caïque de Barraband (F): *Pionopsitta barrabandi*
Caïque de Bonaparte (F): *Pionopsitta pyrilia*
Caïque de Fuertes (F): *Hapalopsittaca fuertesi*

Checklist of fauna/Lista de especies de fauna/Liste des espèces animales

Caïque de Salvin (F): *Hapalopsittaca pyrrhops*
Caïque maïpourri (F): *Pionites melanocephala*
Caïque mitré (F): *Pionopsitta pileata*
Caïque vautourin (F): *Pionopsitta vulturina*
Cairina hartlaubii = Pteronetta hartlaubii
Cairina moschata : (E) Muscovy Duck, (S) Pato criollo, Pato real, (F) Canard de Barbarie, Canard musqué, **III** ANATIDAE Av
Cairina scutulata : (E) White-winged Duck, White-winged Wood Duck, (S) Pato aliblanco, Pato almizclero aliblanco, Pato de jungla, (F) Canard à ailes blanches, Canard musqué à ailes blanches, **I** ANATIDAE Av
Calabar Ground Python (E): *Calabaria reinhardtii*
Calabare de Reinhardt (F): *Calabaria reinhardtii*
Calabaria de Reinhardt (F): *Calabaria reinhardtii*
Calabaria reinhardtii : (E) African Burrowing Python, Calabar Ground Python, (S) Pitón de Calabar, (F) Calabare de Reinhardt, Calabaria de Reinhardt, **II** BOIDAE Re
Calamian Deer (E): *Axis calamianensis*
Calamian Hog Deer (E): *Axis calamianensis*
Calao à casque (F): *Buceros vigil*
Calao à casque plat (F): *Buceros hydrocorax*
Calao à casque rond (F): *Buceros vigil*
Calao à casque rouge (F): *Aceros corrugatus*
Calao à cimier (F): *Aceros cassidix*
Calao à cou roux (F): *Aceros nipalensis*
Calao à gorge claire (F): *Aceros subruficollis*
Calao à poche unie (F): *Aceros subruficollis*
Cálao arrugado (S): *Aceros corrugatus*
Cálao bicorne (F): *Buceros bicornis*
Cálao bicorne (S): *Buceros bicornis*
Calao brun (F): *Anorrhinus tickelli*
Cálao cariblanco (F): *Anthracoceros albirostris*
Calao charbonnier (F): *Anthracoceros malayanus*
Cálao chico de Célebes (S): *Penelopides exarhatus*
Cálao chico de Luzón (S): *Penelopides manillae*
Cálao chico de Mindanao (S): *Penelopides affinis*
Cálao chico de Mindoro (S): *Penelopides mindorensis*
Cálao chico de Panay (S): *Penelopides panini*
Calao coiffé (F): *Aceros comatus*
Cálao crestado (S): *Anorrhinus galeritus*
Cálao crestiblanco (S): *Aceros comatus*
Cálao de casco (S): *Buceros vigil*
Cálao de la Narcondam (S): *Aceros narcondami*
Cálao de la Sumba (S): *Aceros everetti*
Cálao de las Sulu (S): *Anthracoceros montani*
Calao de Malabar (F): *Anthracoceros coronatus*
Calao de Manille (F): *Penelopides manillae*
Calao de Mindanao (F): *Penelopides affinis*
Caïao de Mindoro (F): *Penelopides mindorensis*
Calao de montagne (F): *Aceros nipalensis*
Calao de Narcondam (F): *Aceros narcondami*
Cálao de Palawan (F): *Anthracoceros marchei*
Cálao de Palawan (S): *Anthracoceros marchei*
Calao de Samar (F): *Penelopides samarensis*
Calao de Sumba (F): *Aceros everetti*
Calao de Vieillot (F): *Aceros leucocephalus*
Calao de Walden (F): *Aceros waldeni*
Cálao de yelmo (S): *Buceros vigil*
Cálao del Nepal (S): *Aceros nipalensis*
Calao des Célèbes (F): *Penelopides exarhatus*
Calao des Philippines (F): *Buceros hydrocorax*
Calao des Sulu (F): *Anthracoceros montani*
Calao festonné (F): *Aceros undulatus*
Cálao Filipino grande (S): *Buceros hydrocorax*
Cálao gorgiclaro (S): *Aceros subruficollis*
Cálao gorginegro (S): *Aceros undulatus*
Cálao grande (S): *Buceros bicornis*
Cálao grande de Célebes (S): *Aceros cassidix*
Cálao grande de Mindanao (S): *Aceros leucocephalus*
Cálao grande de Panay (S): *Aceros waldeni*
Calao largup (F): *Anorrhinus galeritus*
Cálao Malayo (S): *Anthracoceros malayanus*
Calao papou (F): *Aceros plicatus*

Cálao pardo de Tickell (S): *Anorrhinus tickelli*
Calao pics (F): *Anthracoceros* spp.
Calao pie (F): *Anthracoceros albirostris*
Calao rhinocéros (F): *Buceros rhinoceros*
Cálao rinoceronte (S): *Buceros rhinoceros*
Cálao rojipardo (S): *Buceros hydrocorax*
Calao tarictic (F): *Penelopides panini*
Calaos (F): *Aceros* spp./ *Anorrhinus* spp./ *Anthracoceros* spp./ *Buceros* spp./ *Penelopides* spp.
Cálaos (S): *Aceros* spp./ *Anorrhinus* spp./ *Anthracoceros* spp./ *Buceros* spp./ *Penelopides* spp.
Calaos à canelure des Célèbes (F): *Penelopides exarhatus*
Calaos à huppe touffue (F): *Anorrhinus* spp.
Calcutta Oval-grain Lizard (E): *Varanus flavescens*
Caldrón negro (S): *Globicephala macrorhynchus/ Globicephala melas*
California Condor (E): *Gymnogyps californianus*
California Sea Otter (E): *Enhydra lutris nereis*
Callagur borneoensis : (E) Painted Batagur, Painted Terrapin, Saw-jawed Turtle, Three-striped Batagur, (S) Galápago pintado, (F) Émyde peinte de Bornéo, **II** EMYDIDAE Re
Callicebus baptista = Callicebus hoffmannsi
Callicebus bernhardi : **II** CEBIDAE Ma
Callicebus brunneus : **II** CEBIDAE Ma
Callicebus caligatus : **II** CEBIDAE Ma
Callicebus cinerascens : **II** CEBIDAE Ma
Callicebus coimbrai : **II** CEBIDAE Ma
Callicebus cupreus : **II** CEBIDAE Ma
Callicebus discolor = Callicebus cupreus
Callicebus donacophilus : **II** CEBIDAE Ma
Callicebus dubius : **II** CEBIDAE Ma
Callicebus hoffmannsi : (E) Hoffmanns's Titi Monkey **II** CEBIDAE Ma
Callicebus lugens = Callicebus torquatus
Callicebus modestus : **II** CEBIDAE Ma
Callicebus moloch : (E) Dusky Titi, (F) Titi molock **II** CEBIDAE Ma
Callicebus moloch ssp. *brunneus = Callicebus brunneus*
Callicebus moloch ssp. *caligatus = Callicebus caligatus*
Callicebus moloch ssp. *cinerascens = Callicebus cinerascens*
Callicebus moloch ssp. *cupreus = Callicebus cupreus*
Callicebus moloch ssp. *donacophilus = Callicebus donacophilus*
Callicebus moloch ssp. *dubius = Callicebus dubius*
Callicebus moloch ssp. *hoffmannsi = Callicebus hoffmannsi*
Callicebus moloch ssp. *modestus = Callicebus modestus*
Callicebus moloch ssp. *oenanthe = Callicebus oenanthe*
Callicebus moloch ssp. *olallae = Callicebus olallae*
Callicebus oenanthe : (E) Andean Titi Monkey **II** CEBIDAE Ma
Callicebus olallae : (E) Beni Titi Monkey **II** CEBIDAE Ma
Callicebus pallescens = Callicebus donacophilus
Callicebus personatus : (E) Masked Titi, (F) Titi à masque **II** CEBIDAE Ma
Callicebus purinus = Callicebus torquatus
Callicebus regulus = Callicebus torquatus
Callicebus stephennashi : **II** CEBIDAE Ma
Callicebus torquatus : (E) Collared Titi, Widow Titi, (F) Titi à collier **II** CEBIDAE Ma
Callimico goeldii : (E) Goeldi's Marmoset, Goeldi's Monkey, Goeldi's Tamarin, (S) Pichico negro, Tamarín de Goeldi, Tití de Goeldi, (F) Tamarin de Goeldi, Tamarin sauteur, **I** CALLITRICHIDAE Ma
Calliope Hummingbird (E): *Stellula calliope*
Calliphlox amethystina : (E) Amethyst Woodstar, (S) Colibrí amatista, Estrellita amatista, Picaflor amatista, Tucusito amatista, (F) Colibri améthyste, **II** TROCHILIDAE Av
Calliphlox bryantae : (E) Magenta-throated Woodstar, (S) Colibrí magenta, (F) Colibri magenta, **II** TROCHILIDAE Av

Checklist of fauna/Lista de especies de fauna/Liste des espèces animales

Calliphlox evelynae : (E) Bahama Woodstar, (S) Colibrí de las Bahamas, (F) Colibri des Bahamas, **II** TROCHILIDAE Av

Calliphlox mitchellii : (E) Purple-throated Woodstar, (S) Colibrí de Mitchell, Estrellita gorjipurpura, (F) Colibri de Mitchell, **II** TROCHILIDAE Av

Calliste superbe (F): *Tangara fastuosa*

Callithrix acariensis : (E) Rio Acarí Marmoset **II** CALLITRICHIDAE Ma

Callithrix argentata : (E) Black-tailed Marmoset, Silvery Marmoset, (F) Ouistiti argenté **II** CALLITRICHIDAE Ma

Callithrix aurita : (E) Buffy-tufted-ear Marmoset, White-eared Marmoset, (S) Callitrix de orejas blancas, (F) Marmouset à oreilles blanches, Oustiti à oreilles blanches, Oustiti oreillard, **I** CALLITRICHIDAE Ma

Callithrix chrysoleuca = Callithrix humeralifer

Callithrix emiliae = Callithrix argentata

Callithrix flaviceps : (E) Buffy-headed Marmoset, (S) Callitrix de cabeza amarilla, (F) Ouistiti à tête jaune, **I** CALLITRICHIDAE Ma

Callithrix geoffroyi : (E) Geoffroy's Tufted-ear Marmoset, White-fronted Marmoset, (S) Tití de caba blanca **II** CALLITRICHIDAE Ma

Callithrix humeralifer : (E) Black-and-white Tassel-ear Marmoset, Tassel-eared Marmoset, (F) Marmoset Santarem **II** CALLITRICHIDAE Ma

Callithrix humilis : **II** CALLITRICHIDAE Ma

Callithrix intermedia = Callithrix argentata

Callithrix jacchus : (E) Common Marmoset, White-tufted-ear Marmoset, (F) Ouistiti **II** CALLITRICHIDAE Ma

Callithrix jacchus ssp. *aurita = Callithrix aurita*

Callithrix jacchus ssp. *flaviceps = Callithrix flaviceps*

Callithrix jacchus ssp. *geoffroyi = Callithrix geoffroyi*

Callithrix jacchus ssp. *kuhlii = Callithrix kuhlii*

Callithrix jacchus ssp. *penicillata = Callithrix penicillata*

Callithrix kuhlii : (E) Wied's Black-tufted-ear Marmoset, Wied's Marmoset **II** CALLITRICHIDAE Ma

Callithrix manicorensis : (E) Rio Manicoré Marmoset **II** CALLITRICHIDAE Ma

Callithrix marcai : (E) Marca's Marmoset **II** CALLITRICHIDAE Ma

Callithrix mauesi : (E) Maués Marmoset **II** CALLITRICHIDAE Ma

Callithrix melanura = Callithrix argentata

Callithrix nigriceps : (E) Black-headed Marmoset **II** CALLITRICHIDAE Ma

Callithrix penicillata : (E) Black-pencilled Marmoset, Black-tufted-ear Marmoset **II** CALLITRICHIDAE Ma

Callithrix pygmaea : (E) Pygmy Marmoset, (F) Ouistiti mignon **II** CALLITRICHIDAE Ma

Callithrix saterei : (E) Sateré Marmoset **II** CALLITRICHIDAE Ma

Callitrix de cabeza amarilla (S): *Callithrix flaviceps*

Callitrix de orejas blancas (S): *Callithrix aurita*

Callocephalon fimbriatum : (E) Gang-gang Cockatoo, (S) Cacatúa de cabeza roja, Gan-Gan, (F) Cacatoès à tête rouge, Cacatoès casqué, **II** PSITTACIDAE Av

Caloenas nicobarica : (E) Nicobar Dove, Nicobar Pigeon, (S) Paloma calva, Paloma de Nicobar, (F) Nicobar à camail, Pigeon à camail, Pigeon à collerette, Pigeon de Nicobar, **I** COLUMBIDAE Av

Caloperdix oculea : (E) Ferruginous Partridge, Ferruginous Wood-Partridge, (S) Perdicilla herrumbrosa, Perdiz de bosque ferruginosa, (F) Rouloul ocellé, **III** PHASIANIDAE Av

Caloprymnus campestris : (E) Buff-nosed Rat-kangaroo, Desert Rat-kangaroo, Plains Rat-kangaroo, (S) Canguro del desierto, Canguro-rata desértico, (F) Kangourou-rat du désert, **I** POTOROIDAE Ma

Calopsitte élégante (F): *Nymphicus hollandicus*

Calothorax eliza = Doricha eliza

Calothorax enicura = Doricha enicura

Calothorax lucifer : (E) Lucifer Hummingbird, (S) Colibrí lucifer, Tijereta nortena, (F) Colibri lucifer, **II** TROCHILIDAE Av

Calothorax pulcher : (E) Beautiful Hummingbird, (S) Colibrí bonito, Tijereta Oaxaquena, (F) Colibri charmant, **II** TROCHILIDAE Av

Calumma spp.: (E) Chameleons, (S) Camaleónes, (F) Caméléons, **II** CHAMAELEONIDAE Re

Calumma andringitaensis : **II** CHAMAELEONIDAE Re

Calumma boettgeri : (E) Boettger's Chameleon, (S) Camaleón de Boettger, (F) Caméléon de Boettger, **II** CHAMAELEONIDAE Re

Calumma brevicornis : (E) Short-horned Chameleon, (F) Caméléon à cornes courtes **II** CHAMAELEONIDAE Re

Calumma capuroni : (E) Madagascar Chameleon, (F) Caméléon de Madagascar **II** CHAMAELEONIDAE Re

Calumma cucullata : (E) Hooded Chameleon, (F) Caméléon à capuchon **II** CHAMAELEONIDAE Re

Calumma fallax : (E) Deceptive Chameleon, (F) Caméléon de Mocquard **II** CHAMAELEONIDAE Re

Calumma furcifer : (E) Forked Chameleon, Fork-nosed Chameleon, (F) Caméléon à nez fourchu **II** CHAMAELEONIDAE Re

Calumma gallus : (E) Blade Chameleon, (F) Caméléon épée **II** CHAMAELEONIDAE Re

Calumma gastrotaenia : (E) Perinet Chameleon, (F) Caméléon de Perinet **II** CHAMAELEONIDAE Re

Calumma glawi : **II** CHAMAELEONIDAE Re

Calumma globifer : (E) Flat-casqued Chameleon, (F) Caméléon à casque plat **II** CHAMAELEONIDAE Re

Calumma guibei : (E) Guibe's Chameleon, North-western Chameleon, (F) Caméléon de Guibé **II** CHAMAELEONIDAE Re

Calumma guillaumeti : **II** CHAMAELEONIDAE Re

Calumma hilleniusi : **II** CHAMAELEONIDAE Re

Calumma linota : (E) Maroantsetra Chameleon, (F) Caméléon de Maroantsetra **II** CHAMAELEONIDAE Re

Calumma malthe : (E) Yellow-green Chameleon, (F) Caméléon vert-et-jaune **II** CHAMAELEONIDAE Re

Calumma marojezensis : **II** CHAMAELEONIDAE Re

Calumma nasuta : (E) Big-nosed Chameleon, (F) Caméléon nasique **II** CHAMAELEONIDAE Re

Calumma oshaughnessyi : (E) O'Shaughnessy's Chameleon, (F) Caméléon d'O'Shaughnessy **II** CHAMAELEONIDAE Re

Calumma parsonii : (E) Parson's Giant Chameleon, (S) Camaleón de Parson, (F) Caméléon de Parson, **II** CHAMAELEONIDAE Re

Calumma peyrierasi : (E) Brygoo's Chameleon, (F) Caméléon de Peyrieras **II** CHAMAELEONIDAE Re

Calumma tigris : (E) Tiger Chameleon, (F) Caméléon tigre **II** CHAMAELEONIDAE Re

Calumma tsaratananensis : (E) Tsaratanan Chameleon, (F) Caméléon de Tsaratana **II** CHAMAELEONIDAE Re

Calumma vatosoa : **II** CHAMAELEONIDAE Re

Calumma vencesi : **II** CHAMAELEONIDAE Re

Calypte anna : (E) Anna's Hummingbird, (S) Colibrí de Anna, (F) Colibri d'Anna, **II** TROCHILIDAE Av

Calypte costae : (E) Costa's Hummingbird, (S) Colibrí de Costa, (F) Colibri de Costa, **II** TROCHILIDAE Av

Calypte helenae = Mellisuga helenae

Calyptopora reticulata : **II** STYLASTERIDAE Hy

Calyptopora sinuosa : **II** STYLASTERIDAE Hy

Calyptorhynchus banksii : (E) Red-tailed Black-Cockatoo, (S) Cacatúa de cola roja, Cacatúa negra de cola roja, (F) Cacatoès banksien, Cacatoès de Banks, **II** PSITTACIDAE Av

Calyptorhynchus baudinii : (E) Long-billed Black-Cockatoo, White-tailed Black-Cockatoo, (F) Cacatoès de Baudin **II** PSITTACIDAE Av

Calyptorhynchus funereus : (E) Yellow-tailed Black-Cockatoo, (S) Cacatúa negra de cola amarilla, (F) Cacatoès à oreilles blanches, Cacatoès à oreilles jaunes, Cacatoès funèbre, **II** PSITTACIDAE Av
Calyptorhynchus funereus ssp. *baudinii* = *Calyptorhynchus baudinii*
Calyptorhynchus lathami : (E) Glossy Black-Cockatoo, (S) Cacatúa negra de Latham, (F) Cacatoès à tête brune, Cacatoès de Latham, **II** PSITTACIDAE Av
Calyptorhynchus latirostris : (E) Short-billed Black-Cockatoo, Slender-billed Black-Cockatoo, (F) Cacatoès à rectrices blanches **II** PSITTACIDAE Av
Calyptorhynchus magnificus = *Calyptorhynchus banksii*
Calzadito admirable (S): *Eriocnemis mirabilis*
Calzadito canoso (S): *Haplophaedia lugens*
Calzadito cobrizo (S): *Eriocnemis cupreoventris*
Calzadito colilargo norteño (S): *Eriocnemis luciani*
Calzadito de Mosquera (S): *Eriocnemis mosquera*
Calzadito frentiazul (S): *Eriocnemis glaucopoides*
Calzadito patinegro (S): *Eriocnemis derbyi*
Calzadito pechiblanco (S): *Eriocnemis alinae*
Calzadito pechinegro (S): *Eriocnemis nigrivestis*
Calzadito reluciente (S): *Eriocnemis vestitus*
Calzadito turquesa (S): *Eriocnemis godini*
Calzadito verdoso norteño (S): *Haplophaedia aureliae*
Calzonario colibronceado (S): *Chalybura buffonii*
Camaleón (S): *Chamaeleo* spp.
Camaleón africano (S): *Chamaeleo africanus*
Camaleón común (S): *Chamaeleo chamaeleon*
Camaleón crestado (S): *Chamaeleo cristatus*
Camaleón cuadricorne (S): *Chamaeleo quadricornis*
Camaleón de Boettger (S): *Calumma boettgeri*
Camaleón de casco (S): *Chamaeleo hoehnelii*
Camaleón de dos bandas (S): *Chamaeleo bitaeniatus*
Camaleón de Elliot (S): *Chamaeleo ellioti*
Camaleón de Fuelleborn (S): *Chamaeleo fuelleborni*
Camaleón de Jackson (S): *Chamaeleo jacksonii*
Camaleón de Johnston (S): *Chamaeleo johnstoni*
Camaleón de Meller (S): *Chamaeleo melleri*
Camaleón de montaña (S): *Chamaeleo montium*
Camaleón de Oustalet (S): *Furcifer oustaleti*
Camaleón de Owen (S): *Chamaeleo oweni*
Camaleón de Parson (S): *Calumma parsonii*
Camaleón de Petter (S): *Furcifer petteri*
Camaleón de Pfeffer (S): *Chamaeleo pfefferi*
Camaleón de Schouteden (S): *Chamaeleo schoutedeni*
Camaleón de Schubotz (S): *Chamaeleo schubotzi*
Camaleón de Sri Lanka (S): *Chamaeleo zeylanicus*
Camaleón de Werner (S): *Chamaeleo werneri*
Camaleón de Wiedersheim (S): *Chamaeleo wiedersheimi*
Camaleón del Senegal (S): *Chamaeleo senegalensis*
Camaleón grácil (S): *Chamaeleo gracilis*
Camaleón lobulado (S): *Chamaeleo dilepis*
Camaleón rinoceronte (S): *Furcifer rhinoceratus*
Camaleón verrugoso (S): *Furcifer verrucosus*
Camaleónes (S): *Calumma* spp./ *Chamaeleo* spp. / *Furcifer* spp.
Camaleónes enanos (S): *Bradypodion* spp.
Caméléon à bandes latérales (F): *Furcifer lateralis*
Caméléon à capuchon (F): *Calumma cucullata*
Caméléon à casque élevé (F): *Chamaeleo hoehnelii*
Caméléon à casque plat (F): *Calumma globifer*
Caméléon à cornes courtes (F): *Calumma brevicornis*
Caméléon à corne molle des monts Usambara (F): *Bradypodion tenue*
Caméléon à deux bandes (F): *Chamaeleo bitaeniatus*
Caméléon à deux cornes (F): *Furcifer bifidus*
Caméléon à écailles doubles (F): *Chamaeleo anchietae*
Caméléon à lignes blanches (F): *Furcifer antimena*
Caméléon à nez fourchu (F): *Calumma furcifer*
Caméléon à nez fourchu (F): *Furcifer bifidus*
Caméléon à quatre cornes (F): *Chamaeleo quadricornis*
Caméléon à une corne (F): *Furcifer monoceras*
Caméléon à voile du Cameroun (F): *Chamaeleo montium*
Caméléon africain (F): *Chamaeleo africanus*

Caméléon américain (F): *Chamaeleo affinis*
Caméléon bilobé (F): *Chamaeleo dilepis*
Caméléon casqué (F): *Chamaeleo calyptratus*
Caméléon commun (F): *Chamaeleo chamaeleon*
Caméléon común (S): *Chamaeleo chamaeleon*
Caméléon crêté (F): *Chamaeleo cristatus*
Caméléon d'Andrenalamivola (F): *Furcifer tuzetae*
Caméléon d'Angel (F): *Furcifer angeli*
Caméléon d'Angola (F): *Chamaeleo anchietae*
Caméléon d'Arabie (F): *Chamaeleo arabicus*
Caméléon de Belalanda (F): *Furcifer belalandaensis*
Caméléon de Bocage (F): *Chamaeleo quilensis*
Caméléon de Boettger (F): *Calumma boettgeri*
Caméléon de Ceylan (F): *Chamaeleo zeylanicus*
Caméléon de Chapin (F): *Chamaeleo chapini*
Caméléon de Fea (F): *Chamaeleo feae*
Caméléon de Goetze (F): *Chamaeleo goetzei*
Caméléon de Guibé (F): *Calumma guibei*
Caméléon de Günther (F): *Furcifer minor*
Caméléon de Jackson (F): *Chamaeleo jacksonii*
Caméléon de Johnston (F): *Chamaeleo johnstoni*
Caméléon de la canopée (F): *Furcifer willsii*
Caméléon de Leach (F): *Chamaeleo dilepis*
Caméléon de Madagascar (F): *Calumma capuroni*
Caméléon de Maroantsetra (F): *Calumma linota*
Caméléon de Mayotte (F): *Furcifer polleni*
Caméléon de Meller (F): *Chamaeleo melleri*
Caméléon de Mocquard (F): *Calumma fallax*
Caméléon de Parson (F): *Calumma parsonii*
Caméléon de Perinet (F): *Calumma gastrotaenia*
Caméléon de Petter (F): *Furcifer petteri*
Caméléon de Peyrieras (F): *Calumma peyrierasi*
Caméléon de Pfeffer (F): *Chamaeleo pfefferi*
Caméléon de Rüppell (F): *Bradypodion xenorhinum*
Caméléon de Schoudeten (F): *Chamaeleo schoutedeni*
Caméléon de Schubotz (F): *Chamaeleo schubotzi*
Caméléon de Tilbury (F): *Chamaeleo marsabitensis*
Caméléon de Tsaratana (F): *Calumma tsaratananensis*
Caméléon de Werner (F): *Chamaeleo werneri*
Caméléon de Wills (F): *Furcifer willsii*
Caméléon d'Eisentraut (F): *Chamaeleo eisentrauti*
Caméléon d'Elliot (F): *Chamaeleo ellioti*
Caméléon des Comores (F): *Furcifer cephalolepis*
Caméléon des montagnes de Tanzanie (F): *Chamaeleo tempeli*
Caméléon des Monts Uzungwe (F): *Chamaeleo laterispinis*
Caméléon d'Ilolo (F): *Chamaeleo goetzei*
Caméléon d'O'Shaughnessy (F): *Calumma oshaughnessyi*
Caméléon d'Oustalet (F): *Furcifer oustaleti*
Caméléon d'Owen (F): *Chamaeleo oweni*
Caméléon du Cameroun (F): *Chamaeleo camerunensis*
Caméléon du Mont Lefo (F): *Chamaeleo wiedersheimi*
Caméléon du Mont Poroto (F): *Chamaeleo incornutus*
Caméléon du Namaqua (F): *Chamaeleo namaquensis*
Caméléon du Sénégal (F): *Chamaeleo senegalensis*
Caméléon du volcan Ngosi (F): *Chamaeleo fuelleborni*
Caméléon du Yémen (F): *Chamaeleo calcaricarens*
Caméléon épée (F): *Calumma gallus*
Caméléon forestier (F): *Furcifer balteatus*
Caméléon forestier de Madagascar (F): *Furcifer campani*
Caméléon gracile (F): *Chamaeleo gracilis*
Caméléon gris (F): *Chamaeleo chapini*
Caméléon nain à nez rouge (F): *Bradypodion nemorale*
Caméléon nain de Carpenter (F): *Bradypodion carpenteri*
Caméléon nain de Fischer (F): *Bradypodion fischeri*
Caméléon nain de Matschie (F): *Bradypodion tavetanum*
Caméléon nain de Setaro (F): *Bradypodion pumilum*
Caméléon nain de Smith (F): *Bradypodion spinosum*
Caméléon nain d'Ituri (F): *Bradypodion adolfifriderici*
Caméléon nain du Cap (F): *Bradypodion oxyrhinum*
Caméléon nain du Drakensberg (F): *Bradypodion dracomontanum*
Caméléon nain du sud et du Namaqua (F): *Bradypodion uthmoelleri*

Caméléon nain du Transvaal (F): *Bradypodion thamnobates*
Caméléon nain du Zululand (F): *Bradypodion mlanjense*
Caméléon nain épineux (F): *Bradypodion setaroi*
Caméléon nasique (F): *Calumma nasuta*
Caméléon ondulé (F): *Chamaeleo deremensis*
Caméléon panthère (F): *Furcifer pardalis*
Caméléon rhinocéros (F): *Furcifer rhinoceratus*
Caméléon rude (F): *Chamaeleo rudis*
Caméléon tigre (F): *Calumma tigris*
Caméléon verruqueux (F): *Furcifer verrucosus*
Caméléon vert-et-jaune (F): *Calumma malthe*
Caméléon vulgaire (F): *Chamaeleo chamaeleon*
Caméléon-joyau (F): *Furcifer lateralis*
Caméléon-moine (F): *Chamaeleo monachus*
Caméléons (F): *Calumma* spp./ *Chamaeleo* spp. / *Furcifer* spp.
Caméléons nain (F): *Bradypodion* spp.
Caméléons vrais (F): *Chamaeleo* spp.
Cameroon Clawless Otter (E): *Aonyx congicus*
Cameroon Sailfin Chameleon (E): *Chamaeleo montium*
Cameroon Toad (E): *Bufo superciliaris*
Campbell's Girdled Lizard (E): *Cordylus campbelli*
Campbell's Guenon (E): *Cercopithecus campbelli*
Campbell's Monkey (E): *Cercopithecus campbelli*
Campbell's Spiny-tailed Lizard (E): *Cordylus campbelli*
Campephilus imperialis : (E) Imperial Woodpecker, (S) Carpintero gigante, Pito imperial, Pitorreal ocotero, (F) Pic impérial, **I** PICIDAE Av
Campyloptère à queue blanche (F): *Campylopterus ensipennis*
Campyloptère à ventre gris (F): *Campylopterus largipennis*
Campyloptère de Wetmore (F): *Campylopterus excellens*
Campyloptère des Santa Marta (F): *Campylopterus phainopeplus*
Campyloptère du Napo (F): *Campylopterus villaviscensio*
Campyloptère lazulite (F): *Campylopterus falcatus*
Campyloptère montagnard (F): *Campylopterus duidae*
Campyloptère pampa (F): *Campylopterus curvipennis*
Campyloptère rougeâtre (F): *Campylopterus hyperythrus*
Campyloptère roux (F): *Campylopterus rufus*
Campyloptère violet (F): *Campylopterus hemileucurus*
Campylopterus cirrochloris : (E) Sombre Hummingbird, (S) Colibrí apagado, (F) Colibri vert et gris, **II** TROCHILIDAE Av
Campylopterus curvipennis : (E) Wedge-tailed Sabrewing, (S) Colibrí ruiseñor, Fandangero colicuna, (F) Campyloptère pampa, **II** TROCHILIDAE Av
Campylopterus cuvierii : (E) Scaly-breasted Hummingbird, (S) Colibrí de Cuvier, Fandangero pechiescamosa, (F) Colibri de Cuvier, **II** TROCHILIDAE Av
Campylopterus duidae : (E) Buff-breasted Sabrewing, (S) Ala de sable anteado, Colibrí del Duida, (F) Campyloptère montagnard, **II** TROCHILIDAE Av
Campylopterus ensipennis : (E) White-tailed Sabrewing, (S) Ala de sable verde, Colibrí coliblanco, (F) Campyloptère à queue blanche, **II** TROCHILIDAE Av
Campylopterus excellens = Campylopterus curvipennis
Campylopterus falcatus : (E) Lazuline Sabrewing, (S) Ala de sable pechivioleta, Alasable azulino, Colibrí lazulita, (F) Campyloptère lazulite, **II** TROCHILIDAE Av
Campylopterus hemileucurus : (E) Violet Sabrewing, (S) Colibrí morado, Fandangero morado, (F) Campyloptère violet, **II** TROCHILIDAE Av
Campylopterus hyperythrus : (E) Rufous-breasted Sabrewing, (S) Ala de sable rufo, Colibrí rojizo Venezolano, (F) Campyloptère rougeâtre, **II** TROCHILIDAE Av

Campylopterus largipennis : (E) Grey-breasted Sabrewing, (S) Ala de sable gris, Alasable del Napo, Colibrí pechigrís, (F) Campyloptère à ventre gris, **II** TROCHILIDAE Av
Campylopterus macrourus : (E) Swallow-tailed Hummingbird, (S) Colibrí golondrina, (F) Colibri hirondelle, **II** TROCHILIDAE Av
Campylopterus phainopeplus : (E) Santa Marta Sabrewing, (S) Colibrí de Santa Marta, (F) Campyloptère des Santa Marta, **II** TROCHILIDAE Av
Campylopterus rufus : (E) Rufous Sabrewing, (S) Colibrí rojizo Mexicano, Fandangero rufo, (F) Campyloptère roux, **II** TROCHILIDAE Av
Campylopterus villaviscensio : (E) Napo Sabrewing, (S) Colibrí del Napo, (F) Campyloptère du Napo, **II** TROCHILIDAE Av
Canada Lynx (E): *Lynx canadensis*
Canal (S): *Dermochelys coriacea*
Canard à ailes blanches (F): *Cairina scutulata*
Canard à bosse (F): *Sarkidiornis melanotos*
Canard à bosse bronzé (F): *Sarkidiornis melanotos*
Canard à tête rose (F): *Rhodonessa caryophyllacea*
Canard aberrant (F): *Anas oustaleti*
Canard armé (F): *Plectropterus gambensis*
Canard coronculé (F): *Sarkidiornis melanotos*
Canard de Barbarie (F): *Cairina moschata*
Canard de Bernier (F): *Anas bernieri*
Canard de Hartlaub (F): *Pteronetta hartlaubii*
Canard de Laysan (F): *Anas laysanensis*
Canard des Mariannes (F): *Anas oustaleti*
Canard d'Oustalet (F): *Anas oustaleti*
Canard du Cap (F): *Anas capensis*
Canard musqué (F): *Cairina moschata*
Canard musqué à ailes blanches (F): *Cairina scutulata*
Canard pilet (F): *Anas acuta*
Canard siffleur (F): *Anas penelope*
Canard souchet (F): *Anas clypeata*
Canario de Mozambique (S): *Serinus mozambicus*
Canary-winged Parakeet (E): *Brotogeris versicolurus*
Candoia aspera : (E) New Guinea Viper Boa, Papuan Ground Boa, (S) Boa de Nueva Guinea, (F) Boa-vipère de Nouvelle Guinée, **II** BOIDAE Re
Candoia bibroni : (E) Pacific Boa, (S) Boa de Fiji, (F) Boa nain de Bibron, Boa nain des îles du Pacifique, **II** BOIDAE Re
Candoia carinata : (E) Solomon Ground Boa, Tree Boa, (S) Boa del Pacífico, (F) Boa nain à carènes, Boa nain des Salomons, **II** BOIDAE Re
Cangurito narigudo coliblanco (S): *Macrotis leucura*
Cangurito narigudo grande (S): *Macrotis lagotis*
Cangurito piedecerdo (S): *Chaeropus ecaudatus*
Canguro arbóreo gris (S): *Dendrolagus inustus*
Canguro arbóreo negro (S): *Dendrolagus ursinus*
Canguro arborícola gris (S): *Dendrolagus inustus*
Canguro arborícola negro (S): *Dendrolagus ursinus*
Canguro del desierto (S): *Caloprymnus campestris*
Canguro rabipelado occidental (S): *Onychogalea lunata*
Canguro rabipelado oriental (S): *Onychogalea fraenata*
Canguro-liebre peludo (S): *Lagorchestes hirsutus*
Canguro-liebre rayado (S): *Lagostrophus fasciatus*
Canguro-rata colipeludo (S): *Bettongia penicillata*
Canguro-rata de Lesueur (S): *Bettongia lesueur*
Canguro-rata de Tasmania (S): *Bettongia gaimardi*
Canguro-rata desértico (S): *Caloprymnus campestris*
Canguro-ratas (S): *Bettongia* spp.
Canis aureus : (E) Common Jackal, Golden Jackal, (S) Chacal, (F) Chacal commun, Chacal doré, **III** CANIDAE Ma
Canis lupus : (E) Common Wolf, Grey Wolf, Timber Wolf, Wolf, (S) Lobo, Lobo común, (F) Loup, Loup gris, Loup vulgaire, **I/II** CANIDAE Ma
Canopy Chameleon (E): *Furcifer willsii*
Cantharellus doederleini : **II** FUNGIIDAE An
Cantharellus jebbi : **II** FUNGIIDAE An
Cantharellus noumeae : **II** FUNGIIDAE An

Checklist of fauna/Lista de especies de fauna/Liste des espèces animales

Cantil coral (S): *Micrurus diastema*
Cantor's Giant Softshell Turtle (E): *Pelochelys cantorii*
Caouanne (F): *Caretta caretta*
Cape Clawless Otter (E): *Aonyx capensis*
Cape Dwarf Chameleon (E): *Bradypodion pumilum*
Cape Eagle-Owl (E): *Bubo capensis*
Cape Fur Seal (E): *Arctocephalus pusillus*
Cape Girdled Lizard (E): *Cordylus cordylus*
Cape Griffon (E): *Gyps coprotheres*
Cape Mountain Zebra (E): *Equus zebra zebra*
Cape Pangolin (E): *Manis temminckii*
Cape Parrot (E): *Poicephalus robustus*
Cape Seahorse (E): *Hippocampus capensis*
Cape stag beetles (E): *Colophon* spp.
Cape Teal (E): *Anas capensis*
Cape Vulture (E): *Gyps coprotheres*
Cape Wigeon (E): *Anas capensis*
Caperea marginata : (E) Pygmy Right Whale, (S) Ballena
     franca pigmea, (F) Baleine pygmée, **I**
     NEOBALAENIDAE Ma
Capped Gibbon (E): *Hylobates pileatus*
Capped Langur (E): *Trachypithecus pileatus*
Capped Leaf Monkey (E): *Trachypithecus pileatus*
Capped Monkey (E): *Trachypithecus pileatus*
Capra aegagrus ssp. *chialtanensis = Capra falconeri* ssp.
     chialtanensis
Capra falconeri : (E) Markhor, (S) Markhor, (F) Markhor,
     I BOVIDAE Ma
Capricorne de Sumatra (F): *Naemorhedus sumatraensis*
Capricornis sumatraensis = Naemorhedus sumatraensis
Capricornis sumatraensis ssp. *maritimus = Naemorhedus
     sumatraensis*
Capricornis sumatraensis ssp. *milneedwardsii =
     Naemorhedus sumatraensis*
Capricornis sumatraensis ssp. *rubidus = Naemorhedus
     sumatraensis*
Capricornis sumatraensis ssp. *sumatraensis =
     Naemorhedus sumatraensis*
Capricornis sumatraensis ssp. *thar = Naemorhedus
     sumatraensis*
Caprolagus hispidus : (E) Assam Rabbit, Hispid Hare,
     Hispid Rabbit, (S) Conejo de Assam, (F) Lapin de
     l'Assam, **I** LEPORIDAE Ma
Capucin bec-d'argent (F): *Lonchura cantans*
Capucin bicolore (F): *Lonchura bicolor*
Capucin nonnette (F): *Lonchura cucullata*
Capucin pie (F): *Lonchura fringilloides*
Cárabo (S): *Strix aluco*
Cárabo Africano (S): *Strix woodfordii*
Cárabo árabe (S): *Strix butleri*
Cárabo bataraz (S): *Strix rufipes*
Cárabo blanquinegro (S): *Strix nigrolineata*
Cárabo Brasileño (S): *Strix hylophila*
Cárabo café (S): *Strix virgata*
Cárabo Californiano (S): *Strix occidentalis*
Cárabo común (S): *Strix aluco*
Cárabo de Hume (S): *Strix butleri*
Cárabo de las pagodas (S): *Strix seloputo*
Cárabo de Sichuán (S): *Strix davidi*
Cárabo de Sudamérica (S): *Strix nigrolineata*
Cárabo gavilán (S): *Surnia ulula*
Cárabo Guatemalteco (S): *Strix fulvescens*
Cárabo Lapón (S): *Strix nebulosa*
Cárabo negro (S): *Strix huhula*
Cárabo norteamericano (S): *Strix varia*
Cárabo ocelado (S): *Strix ocellata*
Cárabo oriental (S): *Strix leptogrammica*
Cárabo patiblanco (S): *Strix albitarsus*
Cárabo pescador común (S): *Scotopelia peli*
Cárabo pescador rojizo (S): *Scotopelia ussheri*
Cárabo pescador vermiculado (S): *Scotopelia bouvieri*
Cárabo uralense (S): *Strix uralensis*
Caraboa (S): *Bubalus arnee*
Caracal (E/S/F): *Caracal caracal*

Caracal caracal : (E) African Caracal, Asian Caracal,
     Caracal, Desert Lynx, (S) Caracal, Lince africano,
     Lince caracal, (F) Caracal, Lynx du désert, **I/II**
     FELIDAE Ma
Caracara à gorge blanche (F): *Phalcoboenus albogularis*
Caracara à gorge rouge (F): *Daptrius americanus*
Caracara à tête jaune (F): *Milvago chimachima*
Caracara à ventre rouge (F): *Daptrius americanus*
Caracara andino (S): *Phalcoboenus megalopterus*
Caracara araucano (S): *Phalcoboenus albogularis*
Caracara austral (S/F): *Phalcoboenus australis*
Caracara carancho (S): *Polyborus plancus*
Caracara caronculé (F): *Phalcoboenus carunculatus*
Caracara carunculado (S): *Phalcoboenus carunculatus*
Caracara cheriway = Polyborus plancus
Caracara chimachima (S/F): *Milvago chimachima*
Caracara chimango (S/F): *Milvago chimango*
Caracara comecacao (S): *Daptrius americanus*
Caracara commun (F): *Polyborus plancus*
Caracara común (S): *Polyborus plancus*
Caracara de Guadalupe (F): *Polyborus lutosus*
Caracara funèbre (F): *Phalcoboenus australis*
Caracara gorgirrojo (S): *Daptrius americanus*
Caracara huppé (F): *Polyborus plancus*
Caracara lutosus = Polyborus lutosus
Caracara montagnard (F): *Phalcoboenus megalopterus*
Caracara negro (S): *Daptrius ater*
Caracara noir (F): *Daptrius ater*
Caracara plancus = Polyborus plancus
Carachupa Manan (S): *Priodontes maximus*
Caracolero (S): *Rostrhamus hamatus*
Caracolero plomizo (S): *Rostrhamus hamatus*
Carancho (S): *Polyborus plancus*
Carancho andino (S): *Phalcoboenus megalopterus*
Carancho de Guadalupe (S): *Polyborus lutosus*
Carancho negro (S): *Daptrius ater*
Carancho ventri-blanco (S): *Daptrius americanus*
Carapaico (S): *Aratinga acuticaudata*
Carburé acanelado (S): *Aegolius harrisii*
Carcharodon carcharias : (E) Great White Shark, Man-
     eater shark, Mango-taniwha, Mango-ururoa, White
     death, White pointer, White shark, (S) Devorador de
     hombres, Jaquentón blanco, Jaquetón, Jaquetón
     blanco, Jaquetón de ley, Marrajo, Tiburón
     antropófago, Tiburón blanco, (F) Grand requin blanc,
     Lamie , Mangeur d'hommes, Requin blanc, **III**
     LAMNIDAE El
Carcoramphe roi (F): *Sarcoramphus papa*
Cardenal amarillo (S): *Gubernatrix cristata*
Cardenal cabecirrojo (S): *Paroaria capitata*
Cardenal copetón (S): *Paroaria coronata*
Cardenalito (S): *Carduelis cucullata*
Cardinal gris (F): *Paroaria coronata*
Cardinal Lory (E): *Chalcopsitta cardinalis*
Cardinal vert (F): *Gubernatrix cristata*
Carduelis cucullata : (E) Red Siskin, (S) Cardenalito,
     Jilguero rojo, Lúgano cardenalito, Lúgano
     encapuchado, (F) Chardonneret rouge, Tarin rouge du
     Venezuela, Tatin rouge du Venezuela, **I**
     FRINGILLIDAE Av
Carduelis yarrellii : (E) Yellow-faced Siskin, (S) Jilguero
     cara amarilla, Jilguero de Yarrell, Lúgano de Yarrell,
     (F) Chardonneret de Yarrell, Tarin de Yarell, Tatin de
     Yarrell, **II** FRINGILLIDAE Av
Caret (F): *Eretmochelys imbricata*
Caretta caretta : (E) Loggerhead, (S) Cayuma, Tortuga
     boba, (F) Caouanne, Cayunne, Coffre, Tortue à bahut,
     Tortue caouanne, Tortue caret, **I** CHELONIIDAE Re
Caribbean Amazon (E): *Amazona leucocephala*
Caribbean Flamingo (E): *Phoenicopterus ruber*
Caribbean Horn Coral (E): *Caryophyllia ambrosia
     caribbeana*
Caribbean Manatee (E): *Trichechus manatus*
Caribbean Monk Seal (E): *Monachus tropicalis*
Caricare encrestado (S): *Polyborus plancus*

Checklist of fauna/Lista de especies de fauna/Liste des espèces animales

Caricare sabanero (S): *Milvago chimachima*
Carnation Coral (E): *Pectinia lactuca*
Carnation corals (E): *Pectinia* spp.
Carnero del Canadá (S): *Ovis canadensis*
Carnero salvaje (S): *Ovis canadensis*
Carnifex à ailes tachetées (F): *Spiziapteryx circumcinctus*
Carnifex à collier (F): *Micrastur semitorquatus*
Carnifex à cou roux (F): *Micrastur ruficollis*
Carnifex à gorge cendrée (F): *Micrastur gilvicollis*
Carnifex ardoisé (F): *Micrastur mirandollei*
Carnifex barré (F): *Micrastur ruficollis*
Carnifex de Buckley (F): *Micrastur buckleyi*
Carnifex de Traylor (F): *Micrastur buckleyi*
Carnifex plombé (F): *Micrastur plumbeus*
Carocolero común (S): *Rostrhamus sociabilis*
Carola's Parotia (E): *Parotia carolae*
Caroline Flying-fox (E): *Pteropus molossinus*
Carouge safran (F): *Agelaius flavus*
Carpenter's Chameleon (E): *Bradypodion carpenteri*
Carpet Chameleon (E): *Furcifer lateralis*
Carpet Python (E): *Morelia spilota*
Carpilla ikan temoleh (S): *Probarbus jullieni*
Carpintero gigante (S): *Campephilus imperialis*
Carpophage de Mindoro (F): *Ducula mindorensis*
Carunculated Caracara (E): *Phalcoboenus carunculatus*
Carunculina cylindrellus = Toxolasma cylindrellus
Caryophyllia abrupta : **II** CARYOPHYLLIIDAE An
Caryophyllia abyssorum : **II** CARYOPHYLLIIDAE An
Caryophyllia alaskensis : **II** CARYOPHYLLIIDAE An
Caryophyllia alberti : **II** CARYOPHYLLIIDAE An
Caryophyllia ambrosia : **II** CARYOPHYLLIIDAE An
Caryophyllia ambrosia ambrosia : **II** CARYOPHYLLIIDAE An
Caryophyllia ambrosia caribbeana : (E) Caribbean Horn Coral **II** CARYOPHYLLIIDAE An
Caryophyllia antarctica : **II** CARYOPHYLLIIDAE An
Caryophyllia antillarum : **II** CARYOPHYLLIIDAE An
Caryophyllia arnoldi : **II** CARYOPHYLLIIDAE An
Caryophyllia atlantica : **II** CARYOPHYLLIIDAE An
Caryophyllia balaenacea : **II** CARYOPHYLLIIDAE An
Caryophyllia barbadensis : **II** CARYOPHYLLIIDAE An
Caryophyllia berteriana : **II** CARYOPHYLLIIDAE An
Caryophyllia burchae = Trochocyathus burchae
Caryophyllia calveri : **II** CARYOPHYLLIIDAE An
Caryophyllia capensis : **II** CARYOPHYLLIIDAE An
Caryophyllia cincticulatus : **II** CARYOPHYLLIIDAE An
Caryophyllia clavus = Caryophyllia smithii
Caryophyllia compressa = Premocyathus dentiformis
Caryophyllia cornuformis = Premocyathus cornuformis
Caryophyllia cornulum : **II** CARYOPHYLLIIDAE An
Caryophyllia corrugata : **II** CARYOPHYLLIIDAE An
Caryophyllia crosnieri : **II** CARYOPHYLLIIDAE An
Caryophyllia crypta : **II** CARYOPHYLLIIDAE An
Caryophyllia cultrifera = Caryophyllia scobinosa
Caryophyllia cyathus : **II** CARYOPHYLLIIDAE An
Caryophyllia decamera : **II** CARYOPHYLLIIDAE An
Caryophyllia dentata : **II** CARYOPHYLLIIDAE An
Caryophyllia dentiformis = Premocyathus dentiformis
Caryophyllia diomedeae : **II** CARYOPHYLLIIDAE An
Caryophyllia elongata = Caryophyllia crosnieri
Caryophyllia eltaninae : **II** CARYOPHYLLIIDAE An
Caryophyllia ephyala : **II** CARYOPHYLLIIDAE An
Caryophyllia epithecata = Caryophyllia smithii
Caryophyllia foresti : **II** CARYOPHYLLIIDAE An
Caryophyllia grandis : **II** CARYOPHYLLIIDAE An
Caryophyllia grayi : **II** CARYOPHYLLIIDAE An
Caryophyllia hawaiiensis : **II** CARYOPHYLLIIDAE An
Caryophyllia horologium : **II** CARYOPHYLLIIDAE An
Caryophyllia inornata : **II** CARYOPHYLLIIDAE An
Caryophyllia japonica : **II** CARYOPHYLLIIDAE An
Caryophyllia jogashimaensis : **II** CARYOPHYLLIIDAE An
Caryophyllia karubarica : **II** CARYOPHYLLIIDAE An
Caryophyllia lamellifera : **II** CARYOPHYLLIIDAE An
Caryophyllia mabahithi : **II** CARYOPHYLLIIDAE An

Caryophyllia marmorea : **II** CARYOPHYLLIIDAE An
Caryophyllia octonaria : **II** CARYOPHYLLIIDAE An
Caryophyllia octopali : **II** CARYOPHYLLIIDAE An
Caryophyllia panda = Caryophyllia atlantica
Caryophyllia paradoxus : **II** CARYOPHYLLIIDAE An
Caryophyllia paucipalata : **II** CARYOPHYLLIIDAE An
Caryophyllia pauciseptata : **II** CARYOPHYLLIIDAE An
Caryophyllia perculta : **II** CARYOPHYLLIIDAE An
Caryophyllia planilamellata : **II** CARYOPHYLLIIDAE An
Caryophyllia polygona : **II** CARYOPHYLLIIDAE An
Caryophyllia profunda : **II** CARYOPHYLLIIDAE An
Caryophyllia quadragenaria : **II** CARYOPHYLLIIDAE An
Caryophyllia quangdongensis : **II** CARYOPHYLLIIDAE An
Caryophyllia ralphae : **II** CARYOPHYLLIIDAE An
Caryophyllia rugosa : **II** CARYOPHYLLIIDAE An
Caryophyllia sarsiae : **II** CARYOPHYLLIIDAE An
Caryophyllia scillaemorpha : **II** CARYOPHYLLIIDAE An
Caryophyllia scobinosa : **II** CARYOPHYLLIIDAE An
Caryophyllia secta : **II** CARYOPHYLLIIDAE An
Caryophyllia seguenzae : **II** CARYOPHYLLIIDAE An
Caryophyllia smithii : (E) Devonshire Cup Coral **II** CARYOPHYLLIIDAE An
Caryophyllia solida : **II** CARYOPHYLLIIDAE An
Caryophyllia spinicarens : **II** CARYOPHYLLIIDAE An
Caryophyllia spinigera : **II** CARYOPHYLLIIDAE An
Caryophyllia squiresi : **II** CARYOPHYLLIIDAE An
Caryophyllia stellula : **II** CARYOPHYLLIIDAE An
Caryophyllia transversalis : **II** CARYOPHYLLIIDAE An
Caryophyllia unicristata : **II** CARYOPHYLLIIDAE An
Caryophyllia valdiviae : **II** CARYOPHYLLIIDAE An
Caryophyllia zanzibarensis : **II** CARYOPHYLLIIDAE An
Caryophyllia zopyros : **II** CARYOPHYLLIIDAE An
Casarea dussumieri : (E) Round Island Keel-scaled Boa, (S) Boa de Round Island, (F) Boa de l'Ile Ronde de Dussumier, **I** BOLYERIIDAE Re
Cascabel (E/F): *Crotalus durissus*
Cascabel Rattlesnake (E): *Crotalus durissus*
Cascavelle (S/F): *Crotalus durissus*
Casmerodius albus : (E) Great Egret, Great White Egret, (S) Garceta grande, Garcilla grande, Garza blanca real, Garzetta grande, (F) Grande aigrette, **III** ARDEIDAE Av
Caspian Snowcock (E): *Tetraogallus caspius*
Cassin's Hawk-Eagle (E): *Spizaetus africanus*
Cassin's Malimbe (E): *Malimbus cassini*
Castle Coral (E): *Pachyseris rugosa*
Catagonus wagneri : (E) Chacoan Peccary, Tagua, (S) Chaco argentino, Quimilero, (F) Pécari du Chaco, **I** TAYASSUIDAE Ma
Catalaphyllia jardinei : (E) Elegant Coral **II** CARYOPHYLLIIDAE An
Cataquil (F): *Bassaricyon gabbii*
Cathartes aura : (E) Turkey Vulture, (S) Aura gallipavo, (F) Urubu à tête rouge, **NC** CATHARTIDAE Av
Cathartes burrovianus : (E) Lesser Yellow-headed Vulture, (S) Aura sabanera, (F) Urubu à tête jaune, **NC** CATHARTIDAE Av
Cathartes melambrotus : (E) Greater Yellow-headed Vulture, (S) Aura selvática, (F) Grand Urubu, **NC** CATHARTIDAE Av
Catita aimará (S): *Psilopsiagon aymara*
Catita aliamarilla (S): *Brotogeris versicolurus*
Catita aliazul (S): *Brotogeris cyanoptera*
Catita alidorada (S): *Brotogeris chrysopterus*
Catita andina (S): *Bolborhynchus orbygnesius*
Catita barrada (S): *Bolborhynchus lineola*
Catita chiriri (S): *Brotogeris chiriri*
Catita churica (S): *Brotogeris jugularis*
Catita común (S): *Myiopsitta monachus*
Catita enana (S): *Forpus crassirostris*
Catita frentidorada (S): *Psilopsiagon aurifrons*

91

Checklist of fauna/Lista de especies de fauna/Liste des espèces animales

Catita frentigualda (S): *Brotogeris sanctithomae*
Catita frentirrufa (S): *Bolborhynchus ferrugineifrons*
Catita macareña (S): *Brotogeris pyrrhopterus*
Catita serrana común (S): *Psilopsiagon aymara*
Catita serrana verde (S): *Psilopsiagon aurifrons*
Catita tirica (S): *Brotogeris tirica*
Catita versicolor (S): *Brotogeris versicolurus*
Catopuma badia : (E) Bay Cat, Bornean Marbled Cat, (F) Chat bai **II** FELIDAE Ma
Catopuma temminckii : (E) Asiatic Golden Cat, Golden Cat, Temminck's Cat, (S) Gato dorado asiático, (F) Chat de Temminck, Chat doré d'Asie, **I** FELIDAE Ma
Catreus wallichii : (E) Cheer Pheasant, Chir Pheasant, Wallich's Pheasant, (S) Faisán chir, Faisán de Wallich, (F) Faisan de l'Himalaya, Faisan de Wallich, **I** PHASIANIDAE Av
Cats (E): FELIDAE spp.
Cat's-eye Coral (E): *Cynarina lacrymalis*
Cattle Egret (E): *Bubulcus ibis*
Cauca Poison Frog (E): *Minyobates bombetes*
Caucasian Sand Boa (E): *Eryx jaculus*
Caucel (S): *Leopardus tigrinus/ Leopardus wiedii*
Caulastraea spp.: (E) Torch corals, Trumpet corals **II** FAVIIDAE An
Caulastraea connata = Astraeosmilia connata
Caulastraea curvata : **II** FAVIIDAE An
Caulastraea echinulata : **II** FAVIIDAE An
Caulastraea furcata : **II** FAVIIDAE An
Caulastraea plana = Caulastraea tumida
Caulastraea tumida : **II** FAVIIDAE An
Cauliflower Coral (E): *Pocillopora damicornis*
Cavernous Star Coral (E): *Montastraea cavernosa*
Caviar (E): *Huso huso*
Caviare (E): *Huso huso*
Cayenne Kite (E): *Leptodon cayanensis*
Cayman Islands Dwarf Boa (E): *Tropidophis caymanensis*
Cayman Islands Ground Iguana (E): *Cyclura nubila*
Caymans Ground Boa (E): *Tropidophis caymanensis*
Cayuma (S): *Caretta caretta*
Cayunne (F): *Caretta caretta/ Natator depressus*
Cebra de Grévy (S): *Equus grevyi*
Cebra de Hartmann (S): *Equus zebra hartmannae*
Cebra de montaña del Cabo (S): *Equus zebra zebra*
Cebra montanesa del Cabo (S): *Equus zebra zebra*
Cebuella pygmaea = Callithrix pygmaea
Cebus albifrons : (E) Brown Pale-fronted Capuchin, White-fronted Capuchin, (F) Sajou à front blanc **II** CEBIDAE Ma
Cebus apella : (E) Black-capped Capuchin, Tufted Capuchin, (F) Sajou apelle **II** CEBIDAE Ma
Cebus capucinus : (E) White-faced Capuchin, White-throated Capuchin, (S) Mono capuchino, (F) Sajou à gorge blanche, **II** CEBIDAE Ma
Cebus griseus = Cebus olivaceus
Cebus libidinosus = Cebus apella
Cebus nigritus = Cebus apella
Cebus nigrivittatus = Cebus olivaceus
Cebus olivaceus : (E) Weeper Capuchin **II** CEBIDAE Ma
Cecko de la isla Serpiente (S): *Cyrtodactylus serpensinsula*
Cefalofo silvicultor (S): *Cephalophus silvicultor*
Cefalofos (S): *Cephalophus dorsalis*
Cefelofo azul (S): *Cephalophus monticola*
Celebes Black Macaque (E): *Macaca nigra*
Celebes Crested Goshawk (E): *Accipiter griseiceps*
Celebes Crested Macaque (E): *Macaca nigra*
Celebes Hornbill (E): *Aceros cassidix/ Penelopides exarhatus*
Celebes Macaque (E): *Macaca maura*
Celebes Maleo (E): *Macrocephalon maleo*
Celebes Scops-Owl (E): *Otus manadensis*
Celebes Serpent-Eagle (E): *Spilornis rufipectus*
Celebes Sparrowhawk (E): *Accipiter nanus*
Celebes Tarictic Hornbill (E): *Penelopides exarhatus*
Celebes Tortoise (E): *Indotestudo forstenii*

Celecanto (S): *Latimeria chalumnae*
Celestial Parrotlet (E): *Forpus coelestis*
Central American Agouti (E): *Dasyprocta punctata*
Central American Cacomistle (E): *Bassariscus sumichrasti*
Central American Coral Snake (E): *Micrurus nigrocinctus*
Central American Dwarf Boa (E): *Ungaliophis panamensis*
Central American Puma (E): *Puma concolor costaricensis*
Central American River Turtle (E): *Dermatemys mawii*
Central American Squirrel Monkey (E): *Saimiri oerstedii*
Central American Tapir (E): *Tapirus bairdii*
Central Asian Cobra (E): *Naja oxiana*
Central Asian Sand Boa (E): *Eryx elegans*
Central Asian Stone Marten (E): *Martes foina intermedia*
Central Asian Tortoise (E): *Testudo horsfieldii*
Central Flying-fox (E): *Pteropus alecto*
Central Rock Rat (E): *Zyzomys pedunculatus*
Central Thick-tailed Rock Rat (E): *Zyzomys pedunculatus*
Central Tree Gecko (E): *Naultinus poecilochlorus*
Céphalophe à bande dorsale noire (F): *Cephalophus dorsalis*
Céphalophe à dos jaune (F): *Cephalophus silvicultor*
Céphalophe bai (F): *Cephalophus dorsalis*
Céphalophe bleu (F): *Cephalophus monticola*
Céphalophe de Jentink (F): *Cephalophus jentinki*
Céphalophe d'Ogilby (F): *Cephalophus ogilbyi*
Céphalophe géant (F): *Cephalophus silvicultor*
Céphalophe rayé (F): *Cephalophus zebra*
Céphalophe zèbré (F): *Cephalophus zebra*
Cephalophus brookei = Cephalophus ogilbyi
Cephalophus dorsalis : (E) Bay Duiker, (S) Cefalofos, Duiquero bayo, (F) Céphalophe à bande dorsale noire, Céphalophe bai, **II** BOVIDAE Ma
Cephalophus jentinki : (E) Jentink's Duiker, (S) Duiquero de Jentink, (F) Céphalophe de Jentink, **I** BOVIDAE Ma
Cephalophus monticola : (E) Blue Duiker, (S) Cefelofo azul, Duiquero azul, (F) Céphalophe bleu, **II** BOVIDAE Ma
Cephalophus ogilbyi : (E) Ogilby's Duiker, (S) Duiquero de Ogilby, (F) Céphalophe d'Ogilby, **II** BOVIDAE Ma
Cephalophus silvicultor : (E) Yellow-backed Duiker, (S) Cefalofo silvicultor, Duiquero de lomo amarillo, (F) Céphalophe à dos jaune, Céphalophe géant, **II** BOVIDAE Ma
Cephalophus sylvicultor = Cephalophus silvicultor
Cephalophus zebra : (E) Banded Duiker, Zebra Antelope, Zebra Duiker, (S) Duiquero cebrado, (F) Céphalophe rayé, Céphalophe zèbré, **II** BOVIDAE Ma
Cephalopterus ornatus : (E) Amazonian Umbrellabird, Ornate Umbrellabird, (S) Pájaro-paraguas amazónico, Pájaros paraguas, (F) Coracine ornée, **III** COTINGIDAE Av
Cephalopterus penduliger : (E) Long-wattled Umbrellabird, (S) Pájaro paraguas bigotudo, Pájaro-paraguas longuipendulo, (F) Coracine casquée, **III** COTINGIDAE Av
Cephalorhynchus commersonii : (E) Commerson's Dolphin, Piebald Dolphin, (S) Jacobita, Tunina overa, (F) Dauphin de Commerson, **II** DELPHINIDAE Ma
Cephalorhynchus eutropia : (E) Black Dolphin, Chilean Dolphin, White-bellied Dolphin, (S) Delfín negro, Tunina de vientre blanco, (F) Dauphin noir du Chili, **II** DELPHINIDAE Ma
Cephalorhynchus heavisidii : (E) Benguela Dolphin, Heaviside's Dolphin, (S) Tunina de Heaviside, (F) Dauphin de Heaviside, **II** DELPHINIDAE Ma
Cephalorhynchus hectori : (E) Hector's Dolphin, New Zealand Dolphin, White-headed Dolphin, (S) Delfín de Héctor, Tunina de Héctor, (F) Dauphin d'Hector, **II** DELPHINIDAE Ma
Cératode (F): *Neoceratodus forsteri*
Ceratodus (E): *Neoceratodus forsteri*

Ceratotherium simum : (E) Grass Rhinoceros, Square-lipped Rhinoceros, White Rhinoceros, (S) Rinoceronte blanco, (F) Rhinocéros blanc, **I/II** RHINOCEROTIDAE Ma

Ceratotherium simum simum : (E) Southern Square-lipped Rhinoceros, Southern White Rhinoceros, (S) Rinoceronte blanco, (F) Rhinocéros blanc du Sud, **I/II** RHINOCEROTIDAE Ma

Ceratotrochus franciscana : **II** CARYOPHYLLIIDAE An

Ceratotrochus magnaghii : **II** CARYOPHYLLIIDAE An

Cerberus rhynchops : (E) Bockadam, Dog-faced Water Snake, (F) Serpent d'eau à museau de chien, Serpent d'eau à ventre blanc **III** COLUBRIDAE Re

Cerceta alicorta de Auckland (S): *Anas aucklandica*

Cerceta aliverde (S): *Anas crecca*

Cerceta carretona (S): *Anas querquedula*

Cerceta cejiblanca (S): *Anas querquedula*

Cerceta común (S): *Anas crecca*

Cerceta de Madagascar (S): *Anas bernieri*

Cerceta del Baikal (S): *Anas formosa*

Cerceta del Cabo (S): *Anas capensis*

Cerceta malgache (S): *Anas bernieri*

Cerceta malgache de Bernier (S): *Anas bernieri*

Cerceta Maorí (S): *Anas aucklandica*

Cercocebe a crete (F): *Cercocebus galeritus*

Cercocèbe agile (F): *Cercocebus agilis*

Cercocebus agilis : (E) Agile Mangabey, (F) Cercocèbe agile, Mangabey agile **II** CERCOPITHECIDAE Ma

Cercocebus albigena = *Lophocebus albigena*

Cercocebus galeritus : (E) Crested Mangabey, (S) Mangabey crestado, (F) Cercocebe a crete, Mangabe, **I/II** CERCOPITHECIDAE Ma

Cercocebus galeritus galeritus : (E) Tana River Mangabey, (S) Mangabey crestado ventriblanco, (F) Mangabey à crête, Mangabey de la Tana, **I** CERCOPITHECIDAE Ma

Cercocebus galeritus ssp. *agilis* = *Cercocebus agilis*

Cercocebus torquatus : (E) Collared Mangabey, Red-capped Mangabey, Sooty Mangabey, White-collared Mangabey, (S) Mangabey de collar blanco, (F) Mangabey couronné, Mangabey enfumé, **II** CERCOPITHECIDAE Ma

Cercopiteco de Diana (S): *Cercopithecus diana*

Cercopithecus aethiops = *Chlorocebus aethiops*

Cercopithecus albogularis = *Cercopithecus mitis*

Cercopithecus ascanius : (E) Black-cheeked White-nosed Monkey, Redtail Monkey, Red-tailed Monkey, Schmidt's Guenon, (F) Ascagne **II** CERCOPITHECIDAE Ma

Cercopithecus campbelli : (E) Campbell's Guenon, Campbell's Monkey, (F) Cercopithèque de Campbell **II** CERCOPITHECIDAE Ma

Cercopithecus cephus : (E) Moustached Monkey, (F) Moustac bleu **II** CERCOPITHECIDAE Ma

Cercopithecus denti = *Cercopithecus wolfi*

Cercopithecus diana : (E) Diana Guenon, Diana Monkey, (S) Cercopiteco de Diana, Diana, (F) Cercopithèque diane, **I** CERCOPITHECIDAE Ma

Cercopithecus dryas : (E) Dryas Guenon, Dryas Monkey, (S) Mono dryas **II** CERCOPITHECIDAE Ma

Cercopithecus erythrogaster : (E) Red-bellied Guenon, Red-bellied Monkey, White-throated Guenon, White-throated Monkey, (F) Cercopithèque à ventre roux **II** CERCOPITHECIDAE Ma

Cercopithecus erythrotis : (E) Red-eared Guenon, Red-eared Monkey, Russet-eared Guenon, (S) Mono de orejas rojas, (F) Moustac à oreilles rouges, **II** CERCOPITHECIDAE Ma

Cercopithecus erythrotis ssp. *sclateri* = *Cercopithecus sclateri*

Cercopithecus hamlyni : (E) Owl-faced Guenon, Owl-faced Monkey, (F) Cercopithèque d'Hamlyn **II** CERCOPITHECIDAE Ma

Cercopithecus lhoesti : (E) L'Hoest's Monkey, Mountain Monkey, (F) Cercopithèque de l'Hoest **II** CERCOPITHECIDAE Ma

Cercopithecus lhoesti ssp. *preussi* = *Cercopithecus preussi*

Cercopithecus lowei = *Cercopithecus campbelli*

Cercopithecus mitis : (E) Blue Monkey, Diademed Monkey, Gentle Monkey, Sykes's Monkey, (F) Cercopithèque à diadème **II** CERCOPITHECIDAE Ma

Cercopithecus mona : (E) Mona Monkey, (F) Cercopithèque mone **II** CERCOPITHECIDAE Ma

Cercopithecus neglectus : (E) De Brazza's Monkey, (F) Cercopithèque de Brazza **II** CERCOPITHECIDAE Ma

Cercopithecus nictitans : (E) Greater White-nosed Monkey, Putty-nosed Monkey, Spot-nosed Guenon, White-nosed Guenon, (F) Hocheur **II** CERCOPITHECIDAE Ma

Cercopithecus nigroviridis = *Allenopithecus nigroviridis*

Cercopithecus patas = *Erythrocebus patas*

Cercopithecus petaurista : (E) Lesser Spot-nosed Guenon, Lesser White-nosed Guenon, Lesser White-nosed Monkey, Spot-nosed Monkey, (F) Hocheur du Ghana **II** CERCOPITHECIDAE Ma

Cercopithecus pogonias : (E) Crowned Guenon, Crowned Monkey, Golden-bellied Guenon, Golden-bellied Monkey, (S) Mono coronado, (F) Guenon couronnée, Mone, **II** CERCOPITHECIDAE Ma

Cercopithecus pogonias ssp. *wolfi* = *Cercopithecus wolfi*

Cercopithecus preussi : (E) Preuss's Guenon, Preuss's Monkey, (S) Mono de Preuss **II** CERCOPITHECIDAE Ma

Cercopithecus pygerythrus = *Chlorocebus aethiops*

Cercopithecus sabaeus = *Chlorocebus aethiops*

Cercopithecus salongo = *Cercopithecus dryas*

Cercopithecus sclateri : (E) Sclater's Guenon, White-throated Guenon, (S) Mono de Sclater **II** CERCOPITHECIDAE Ma

Cercopithecus solatus : (E) Sun-tailed Guenon, Sun-tailed Monkey, (S) Mono del Gabón, (F) Cercopithèque à queue de soleil, **II** CERCOPITHECIDAE Ma

Cercopithecus talapoin = *Miopithecus talapoin*

Cercopithecus tantalus = *Chlorocebus aethiops*

Cercopithecus thomasi = *Cercopithecus lhoesti*

Cercopithecus wolfi : (E) Wolf's Monkey, (S) Mono de Wolf, (F) Mone de Wolf, **II** CERCOPITHECIDAE Ma

Cercopithèque à diadème (F): *Cercopithecus mitis*

Cercopithèque à queue de soleil (F): *Cercopithecus solatus*

Cercopithèque à ventre roux (F): *Cercopithecus erythrogaster*

Cercopithèque de Allen (F): *Allenopithecus nigroviridis*

Cercopithèque de Brazza (F): *Cercopithecus neglectus*

Cercopithèque de Campbell (F): *Cercopithecus campbelli*

Cercopithèque de l'Hoest (F): *Cercopithecus lhoesti*

Cercopithèque d'Hamlyn (F): *Cercopithecus hamlyni*

Cercopithèque diane (F): *Cercopithecus diana*

Cercopithèque mone (F): *Cercopithecus mona*

Cerdo de Kuhl (S): *Axis kuhlii*

Cerdo tailandés (S): *Axis porcinus annamiticus*

Cerdocyon thous : (E) Common Zorro, Crab-eating Zorro, Forest Fox, (S) Zorro cangrejero, Zorro de monte, (F) Renard crabier, **II** CANIDAE Ma

Cerf de Bactriane (F): *Cervus elaphus bactrianus*

Cerf de Barbarie (F): *Cervus elaphus barbarus*

Cerf de Duvaucel (F): *Cervus duvaucelii*

Cerf d'Eld (F): *Cervus eldii*

Cerf des Andes méridionales (F): *Hippocamelus bisulcus*

Cerf des Andes septentrionales (F): *Hippocamelus antisensis*

Cerf des marais (F): *Blastocerus dichotomus*

Cerf des pampas (F): *Ozotoceros bezoarticus*

Cerf du Turkestan (F): *Cervus elaphus bactrianus*

Cerf élaphe du Cachemire (F): *Cervus elaphus hanglu*

Cerf élaphe du Turkestan (F): *Cervus elaphus bactrianus*

Checklist of fauna/Lista de especies de fauna/Liste des espèces animales

Cerf porte-musc (F): *Moschus moschiferus*
Cerf rouge du Turkestan (F): *Cervus elaphus bactrianus*
Cerf-cochon calamien (F): *Axis calamianensis*
Cerf-cochon de Bawean (F): *Axis kuhlii*
Cerfcochon de Kuhl (F): *Axis kuhlii*
Cerfcochon de Thaïlande (F): *Axis porcinus annamiticus*
Cerf-cochon d'Indochine (F): *Axis porcinus annamiticus*
Cerfs des Andes (F): *Hippocamelus* spp.
Cerise-throated Hummingbird (E): *Selasphorus flammula*
Cernícalo (S): *Gampsonyx swainsonii*
Cernícalo americano (S): *Falco sparverius*
Cernícalo australiano (S): *Falco cenchroides*
Cernícalo común (S): *Falco tinnunculus*
Cernícalo de Aldabra (S): *Falco newtoni*
Cernícalo de Dickinson (S): *Falco dickinsoni*
Cernícalo de la isla Aldabra (S): *Falco newtoni*
Cernícalo de la Mauricio (S): *Falco punctatus*
Cernícalo de las Molucas (S): *Falco moluccensis*
Cernícalo de las Seychelles (S): *Falco araea*
Cernícalo de Madagascar (S): *Falco newtoni*
Cernícalo de Mauricio (S): *Falco punctatus*
Cernícalo del Amur (S): *Falco amurensis*
Cernícalo dorsinegro (S): *Falco dickinsoni*
Cernícalo gris (S): *Falco ardosiaceus*
Cernícalo malgache (S): *Falco zoniventris*
Cernícalo Moluqueño (S): *Falco moluccensis*
Cernícalo ojiblanco (S): *Falco rupicoloides*
Cernícalo ojiblanco de Africa (S): *Falco rupicoloides*
Cernícalo patirrojo (S): *Falco vespertinus*
Cernícalo pizarroso (S): *Falco ardosiaceus*
Cernícalo primilla (S): *Falco naumanni*
Cernícalo primito (S): *Falco sparverius*
Cernícalo vulgar (S): *Falco tinnunculus*
Cernícalo zorruno (S): *Falco alopex*
Cerro Campana Stubfoot Toad (E): *Atelopus zeteki*
Cervatillo almizclero acuático (S): *Hyemoschus aquaticus*
Cervicapra (S): *Antilope cervicapra*
Cervicapre (F): *Antilope cervicapra*
Cervus dama ssp. *mesopotamicus* = *Dama mesopotamica*
Cervus duvaucelii : (E) Barasingha, Swamp Deer, (S) Barasinga, Ciervo de Duvaucel, (F) Barasinga, Barasingha, Cerf de Duvaucel, I CERVIDAE Ma
Cervus elaphus bactrianus : (E) Bactrian Deer, Bactrian Red Deer, Bactrian Wapiti, Bokharan Deer, (S) Ciervo bactriano, Ciervo del Turquestán, (F) Cerf de Bactriane, Cerf du Turkestan, Cerf élaphe du Turkestan, Cerf rouge du Turkestan, II CERVIDAE Ma
Cervus elaphus barbarus : (E) Atlas Deer, Barbary Deer, Barbary Red Deer, Barbary Stag, (S) Ciervo de la Berberia, (F) Cerf de Barbarie, III CERVIDAE Ma
Cervus elaphus hanglu : (E) Hangul, Kashmir Deer, Kashmir Red Deer, Kashmir Stag, (S) Ciervo de Cachemira, (F) Cerf élaphe du Cachemire, Hangul, I CERVIDAE Ma
Cervus eldii : (E) Brow-antlered Deer, Eld's Deer, Thamin, (S) Ciervo de Eld, (F) Cerf d'Eld, I CERVIDAE Ma
Cervus porcinus ssp. *annamiticus* = *Axis porcinus annamiticus*
Cervus porcinus ssp. *calamianensis* = *Axis calamianensis*
Cervus porcinus ssp. *kuhlii* = *Axis kuhlii*
CETACEA spp. : (E) Cetaceans, Dolphins, Porpoises, Whales, (S) Ballenas, Cetáceos, (F) Baleines, I/II Ma
Cetaceans (E): CETACEA spp. Ma
Cetáceos (E): CETACEA spp. Ma
Cetorhinus blainvillei = *Cetorhinus maximus*
Cetorhinus maccoyi = *Cetorhinus maximus*
Cetorhinus maximus : (E) Basking Shark, Bone shark, Elephant shark, Hoe-mother, Sun-fish, (S) Colayo, Marrajo ballenato, Marrajo gigante, Peje vaca, Peregrino, Pez elefante, Tiburón canasta, Tiburón peregrino, (F) Pèlerin, Poisson à voiles, Requin pèlerin, Squale géant, Squale-pèlerin, II CETORHINIDAE El
Ceylon Hanging-Parrot (E): *Loriculus beryllinus*

Chacal (S): *Canis aureus*
Chacal commun (F): *Canis aureus*
Chacal doré (F): *Canis aureus*
Chacaraco (S): *Aratinga wagleri*
Chachalaca (E): *Ortalis vetula*
Chachalaca cornuda (S): *Oreophasis derbianus*
Chachalaca de la Trinidad (S): *Pipile pipile*
Chachalaca de los Llenos (S): *Ortalis vetula*
Chachalaca de remiges blancas (S): *Penelope albipennis*
Chachalaca manchada (S): *Pipile jacutinga*
Chachalaca negra (S): *Penelopina nigra*
Chachalaca norteña (S): *Ortalis vetula*
Chacma Baboon (E): *Papio hamadryas*
Chaco argentino (S): *Catagonus wagneri*
Chaco Tortoise (E): *Geochelone chilensis*
Chacoan Peccary (E): *Catagonus wagneri*
Chaeropus ecaudatus : (E) Pig-footed Bandicoot, (S) Bandicot de pies porcinos, Cangurito piedecerdo, (F) Bandicoot à pied de porc, Bandicoot pieds de cochon, I PERAMELIDAE Ma
Chaetocercus astreans : (E) Santa Marta Woodstar, (S) Colibrí astral, (F) Colibri des Santa Marta, II TROCHILIDAE Av
Chaetocercus berlepschi : (E) Esmeraldas Woodstar, (S) Colibrí de Esmeraldas, Estrellita esmeraldeña, (F) Colibri de Berlepsch, II TROCHILIDAE Av
Chaetocercus bombus : (E) Little Woodstar, (S) Colibrí abejorro, Estrellita chica, (F) Colibri bourdon, II TROCHILIDAE Av
Chaetocercus heliodor : (E) Gorgeted Woodstar, (S) Colibrí heliodoro, Estrella cuellirrojo, Estrellita de gorguera, (F) Colibri héliodore, II TROCHILIDAE Av
Chaetocercus jourdanii : (E) Rufous-shafted Woodstar, (S) Colibrí de Jourdan, Tucusito garganta rosa, (F) Colibri de Jourdan, II TROCHILIDAE Av
Chaetocercus mulsant : (E) White-bellied Woodstar, (S) Colibrí de Mulsant, Estrellita ventriblanca, (F) Colibri de Mulsant, II TROCHILIDAE Av
Chaetophractus nationi : (E) Andean Hairy Armadillo, Bolivian Hairy Armadillo, Hairy armadillo, (S) Armadillo peludo andino, Quirquincho andino, (F) Tatou à 9 bandes, II DASYPODIDAE Ma
Chagrin (F): *Rhincodon typus*
Chalcopsitta atra : (E) Black Lory, (S) Lori negro, (F) Lori noir, II PSITTACIDAE Av
Chalcopsitta cardinalis : (E) Cardinal Lory, (S) Lori cardenal, (F) Lori cardinal, II PSITTACIDAE Av
Chalcopsitta duivenbodei : (E) Brown Lory, Duyvenbode's Lory, (S) Lori pardo, (F) Lori de Duyvenbode, II PSITTACIDAE Av
Chalcopsitta scintillata : (E) Greater Streaked Lory, Yellow-streaked Lory, (S) Lori chispeado, (F) Lori flamméché, II PSITTACIDAE Av
Chalcostigma herrani : (E) Rainbow-bearded Thornbill, (S) Colibrí de Herrán, Picoespina arcoiris, (F) Métallure arc-en-ciel, II TROCHILIDAE Av
Chalcostigma heteropogon : (E) Bronze-tailed Thornbill, (S) Colibrí picoespina, Pico espina bronceado, (F) Métallure à queue bronzée, II TROCHILIDAE Av
Chalcostigma olivaceum : (E) Olivaceous Thornbill, (S) Colibrí olivaceo, (F) Métallure olivâtre, II TROCHILIDAE Av
Chalcostigma ruficeps : (E) Rufous-capped Thornbill, (S) Colibrí capirrufo, Picoespina gorrirrufa, (F) Métallure à tête rousse, II TROCHILIDAE Av
Chalcostigma stanleyi : (E) Blue-mantled Thornbill, (S) Colibrí de Stanley, Picoespina dorsiazul, (F) Métallure de Stanley, II TROCHILIDAE Av
Chalybura buffonii : (E) White-vented Plumeleteer, (S) Calzonario colibronceado, Colibrí de Buffon, Colibrí grande colinegro, (F) Colibri de Buffon, II TROCHILIDAE Av

Chalybura urochrysia : (E) Bronze-tailed Plumeleteer, (S) Colibrí patirrojo, (F) Colibri à queue bronzée, **II** TROCHILIDAE Av

Chamaeleo spp.: (E) Chameleons, (S) Camaleón, Camaleónes, (F) Caméléons, Caméléons vrais, **II** CHAMAELEONIDAE Re

Chamaeleo adolfifriderici = Bradypodion adolfifriderici

Chamaeleo affinis : (E) Ethiopian Highland Chameleon, Rüppell's Desert Chameleon, (F) Caméléon américain **II** CHAMAELEONIDAE Re

Chamaeleo africanus : (E) African Chameleon, Sahel Chameleon, (S) Camaleón africano, (F) Caméléon africain, **II** CHAMAELEONIDAE Re

Chamaeleo anchietae : (E) Anchieta's Chameleon, Angola Chameleon, Double-scaled Chameleon, (F) Caméléon à écailles doubles, Caméléon d'Angola **II** CHAMAELEONIDAE Re

Chamaeleo angeli = Furcifer angeli

Chamaeleo antimena = Furcifer antimena

Chamaeleo arabicus : (E) Arabian Chameleon, (F) Caméléon d'Arabie **II** CHAMAELEONIDAE Re

Chamaeleo balebicornutus : (E) Bale Mountains Two-horned Chameleon **II** CHAMAELEONIDAE Re

Chamaeleo balteatus = Furcifer balteatus

Chamaeleo belalandaensis = Furcifer belalandaensis

Chamaeleo bifidus = Furcifer bifidus

Chamaeleo bifidus ssp. *balteatus = Furcifer balteatus*

Chamaeleo bitaeniatus : (E) Montane Chameleon, Side-striped Chameleon, Two-lined Chameleon, (S) Camaleón de dos bandas, (F) Caméléon à deux bandes, **II** CHAMAELEONIDAE Re

Chamaeleo bitaeniatus ssp. *ellioti = Chamaeleo ellioti*

Chamaeleo bitaeniatus ssp. *kinetensis = Chamaeleo kinetensis*

Chamaeleo boettgeri = Calumma boettgeri

Chamaeleo brevicornis = Calumma brevicornis

Chamaeleo calcaricarens : (E) Awash Chameleon, (F) Caméléon du Yémen **II** CHAMAELEONIDAE Re

Chamaeleo calyptratus : (E) Veiled Chameleon, (F) Caméléon casqué **II** CHAMAELEONIDAE Re

Chamaeleo camerunensis : (F) Caméléon du Cameroun **II** CHAMAELEONIDAE Re

Chamaeleo campani = Furcifer campani

Chamaeleo capuroni = Calumma capuroni

Chamaeleo carpenteri = Bradypodion carpenteri

Chamaeleo cephalolepis = Furcifer cephalolepis

Chamaeleo chamaeleon : (E) Common Chameleon, European Chameleon, Mediterranean Chameleon, (S) Camaleón común, Caméleon común, (F) Caméléon commun, Caméléon vulgaire, **II** CHAMAELEONIDAE Re

Chamaeleo chamaeleon ssp. *zeylanicus = Chamaeleo zeylanicus*

Chamaeleo chapini : (E) Grey Chameleon, (F) Caméléon de Chapin, Caméléon gris **II** CHAMAELEONIDAE Re

Chamaeleo conirostratus : **II** CHAMAELEONIDAE Re

Chamaeleo cristatus : (E) Crested Chameleon, (S) Camaleón crestado, (F) Caméléon crêté, **II** CHAMAELEONIDAE Re

Chamaeleo cucullatus = Calumma cucullata

Chamaeleo deremensis : (E) Usambara Three-horned Chameleon, Wavy Chameleon, (F) Caméléon ondulé **II** CHAMAELEONIDAE Re

Chamaeleo dilepis : (E) Flap-necked Chameleon, (S) Camaleón lobulado, (F) Caméléon bilobé, Caméléon de Leach, **II** CHAMAELEONIDAE Re

Chamaeleo eisentrauti : (F) Caméléon d'Eisentraut **II** CHAMAELEONIDAE Re

Chamaeleo ellioti : (E) Montane Side-striped Chameleon, Mountain Dwarf Chameleon, (S) Camaleón de Elliot, (F) Caméléon d'Elliot, **II** CHAMAELEONIDAE Re

Chamaeleo excubitor = Bradypodion fischeri

Chamaeleo fallax = Calumma fallax

Chamaeleo feae : (F) Caméléon de Fea **II** CHAMAELEONIDAE Re

Chamaeleo fischeri = Bradypodion fischeri

Chamaeleo fischeri ssp. *uthmoelleri = Bradypodion uthmoelleri*

Chamaeleo fuelleborni : (E) Ngosi Volcano Chameleon, Poroto Three-horned Chameleon, (S) Camaleón de Fuelleborn, (F) Caméléon du volcan Ngosi, **II** CHAMAELEONIDAE Re

Chamaeleo furcifer = Calumma furcifer

Chamaeleo gallus = Calumma gallus

Chamaeleo gastrotaenia = Calumma gastrotaenia

Chamaeleo globifer = Calumma globifer

Chamaeleo goetzei : (E) Goetze's Chameleon, Ilolo Chameleon, Tanganyika Chameleon, (F) Caméléon de Goetze, Caméléon d'Ilolo **II** CHAMAELEONIDAE Re

Chamaeleo gracilis : (E) Graceful Chameleon, Gracile Chameleon, Slender Chameleon, Spur-heeled Chameleon, (S) Camaleón grácil, (F) Caméléon gracile, **II** CHAMAELEONIDAE Re

Chamaeleo guentheri = Furcifer pardalis

Chamaeleo guibei = Calumma guibei

Chamaeleo harennae : (E) Bale Mountains Heather Chameleon, Harenna Chameleon **II** CHAMAELEONIDAE Re

Chamaeleo hilleniusi = Calumma brevicornis

Chamaeleo hoehnelii : (E) Helmeted Chameleon, High-casqued Chameleon, Von Höhnel's Chameleon, (S) Camaleón de casco, (F) Caméléon à casque élevé, **II** CHAMAELEONIDAE Re

Chamaeleo incornutus : (E) Poroto Mountain Chameleon, Ukinga Hornless Chameleon, (F) Caméléon du Mont Poroto **II** CHAMAELEONIDAE Re

Chamaeleo ituriensis : (E) Ituri Forest Chameleon **II** CHAMAELEONIDAE Re

Chamaeleo jacksonii : (E) Jackson's Three-horned Chameleon, (S) Camaleón de Jackson, (F) Caméléon de Jackson, **II** CHAMAELEONIDAE Re

Chamaeleo jacksonii merumontanus : **II** CHAMAELEONIDAE Re

Chamaeleo johnstoni : (E) Johnston's Chameleon, Ruwenzori Three-horned Chameleon, (S) Camaleón de Johnston, (F) Caméléon de Johnston, **II** CHAMAELEONIDAE Re

Chamaeleo kinetensis : **II** CHAMAELEONIDAE Re

Chamaeleo laevigatus : (E) Smooth Chameleon **II** CHAMAELEONIDAE Re

Chamaeleo lateralis = Furcifer lateralis

Chamaeleo laterispinis : (E) Spine-sided Chameleon, Spiny-flanked Chameleon, Uzungwe Mountain Chameleon, (F) Caméléon des Monts Uzungwe **II** CHAMAELEONIDAE Re

Chamaeleo linotus = Calumma linota

Chamaeleo malthe = Calumma malthe

Chamaeleo marsabitensis : (E) Mount Marsabit Chameleon, Tilbury's Chameleon, (F) Caméléon de Tilbury **II** CHAMAELEONIDAE Re

Chamaeleo melleri : (E) Giant One-horned Chameleon, Meller's Chameleon, (S) Camaleón de Meller, (F) Caméléon de Meller, **II** CHAMAELEONIDAE Re

Chamaeleo minor = Furcifer minor

Chamaeleo mlanjensis = Bradypodion mlanjense

Chamaeleo monachus : (E) Monarch Chameleon, Socotra Chameleon, (F) Caméléon-moine **II** CHAMAELEONIDAE Re

Chamaeleo monoceras = Furcifer monoceras

Chamaeleo montium : (E) Cameroon Sailfin Chameleon, Mountain Chameleon, (S) Camaleón de montaña, (F) Caméléon à voile du Cameroun, **II** CHAMAELEONIDAE Re

Chamaeleo montium ssp. *feae = Chamaeleo feae*

Chamaeleo namaquensis : (E) Desert Chameleon, Namaqua Chameleon, (F) Caméléon du Namaqua **II** CHAMAELEONIDAE Re

Checklist of fauna/Lista de especies de fauna/Liste des espèces animales

Chamaeleo nasutus = Calumma nasuta
Chamaeleo oshaughnessyi = Calumma oshaughnessyi
Chamaeleo oustaleti = Furcifer oustaleti
Chamaeleo oweni : (E) Owen's Three-horned Chameleon, (S) Camaleón de Owen, (F) Caméléon d'Owen, **II** CHAMAELEONIDAE Re
Chamaeleo oxyrhinus = Bradypodion oxyrhinum
Chamaeleo pardalis = Furcifer pardalis
Chamaeleo parsonii = Calumma parsonii
Chamaeleo petteri = Furcifer petteri
Chamaeleo peyrierasi = Calumma peyrierasi
Chamaeleo pfefferi : (E) Pfeffer's Chameleon, (S) Camaleón de Pfeffer, (F) Caméléon de Pfeffer, **II** CHAMAELEONIDAE Re
Chamaeleo polleni = Furcifer polleni
Chamaeleo pumilus = Bradypodion pumilum
Chamaeleo quadricornis : (E) Four-horned Chameleon, (S) Camaleón cuadricorne, (F) Caméléon à quatre cornes, **II** CHAMAELEONIDAE Re
Chamaeleo quilensis : (E) Bocage's Chameleon, (F) Caméléon de Bocage **II** CHAMAELEONIDAE Re
Chamaeleo rhinoceratus = Furcifer rhinoceratus
Chamaeleo rudis : (E) Coarse Chameleon, Ruwenzori Side-striped Chameleon, (F) Caméléon rude **II** CHAMAELEONIDAE Re
Chamaeleo rudis ssp. *schoutedeni = Chamaeleo schoutedeni*
Chamaeleo rudis ssp. *schubotzi = Chamaeleo schubotzi*
Chamaeleo ruspolii = Chamaeleo dilepis
Chamaeleo schoutedeni : (E) Schouteden's Chameleon, (S) Camaleón de Schouteden, (F) Caméléon de Schoudeten, **II** CHAMAELEONIDAE Re
Chamaeleo schubotzi : (E) Mt Kenya Side-striped Chameleon, Schubotz's Chameleon, (S) Camaleón de Schubotz, (F) Caméléon de Schubotz, **II** CHAMAELEONIDAE Re
Chamaeleo senegalensis : (E) Senegal Chameleon, (S) Camaleón del Senegal, (F) Caméléon du Sénégal, **II** CHAMAELEONIDAE Re
Chamaeleo senegalensis ssp. *laevigatus = Chamaeleo laevigatus*
Chamaeleo spinosus = Bradypodion spinosum
Chamaeleo tavetanus = Bradypodion tavetanum
Chamaeleo tempeli : (E) Tanzania Mountain Chameleon, Tubercle-nosed Chameleon, (F) Caméléon des montagnes de Tanzanie **II** CHAMAELEONIDAE Re
Chamaeleo tenuis = Bradypodion tenue
Chamaeleo tigris = Calumma tigris
Chamaeleo tremperi : (E) Eldama Ravine Chameleon **II** CHAMAELEONIDAE Re
Chamaeleo tsaratananensis = Calumma tsaratananensis
Chamaeleo tuzetae = Furcifer tuzetae
Chamaeleo uthmoelleri = Bradypodion uthmoelleri
Chamaeleo verrucosus = Furcifer verrucosus
Chamaeleo werneri : (E) Uzungwe Three-horned Chameleon, Werner's Chameleon, Werner's Three-horned Chameleon, (S) Camaleón de Werner, (F) Caméléon de Werner, **II** CHAMAELEONIDAE Re
Chamaeleo wiedersheimi : (E) Mount Lefo Chameleon, (S) Camaleón de Wiedersheim, (F) Caméléon du Mont Lefo, **II** CHAMAELEONIDAE Re
Chamaeleo willsii = Furcifer willsii
Chamaeleo xenorhinus = Bradypodion xenorhinum
Chamaeleo zeylanicus : (E) Indian Chameleon, (S) Camaleón de Sri Lanka, (F) Caméléon de Ceylan, **II** CHAMAELEONIDAE Re
Chameleons (E): *Bradypodion* spp./ *Chamaeleo* spp.
Chamois des Abruzzes (F): *Rupicapra pyrenaica ornata*
Changeable Hawk-Eagle (E): *Spizaetus cirrhatus*
Changjiang Dolphin (E): *Lipotes vexillifer*
Channel-billed Toucan (E): *Ramphastos vitellinus*
Chanteur d'Afrique (F): *Serinus leucopygius*
Chardonneret de Yarrell (F): *Carduelis yarrellii*
Chardonneret rouge (F): *Carduelis cucullata*

Charina bottae : (E) Rubber Boa, (S) Boa de Gomme, (F) Boa caoutchouc, Serpent gomme, **II** BOIDAE Re
Charina reinhardtii = Calabaria reinhardtii
Charina trivirgata = Lichanura trivirgata
Charmosyna amabilis : (E) Red-throated Lorikeet, (S) Lori gorgirrojo, (F) Lori à gorge rouge, **II** PSITTACIDAE Av
Charmosyna diadema : (E) New Caledonian Lorikeet, (S) Lori diadema, (F) Lori à diadème, Lori de Nouvelle-Calédonie, **II** PSITTACIDAE Av
Charmosyna josefinae : (E) Josephine's Lorikeet, Josephine's Lory, (S) Lori de Josefina, (F) Lori de Joséphine, **II** PSITTACIDAE Av
Charmosyna margarethae : (E) Duchess Lorikeet, (S) Lori de Margarita, (F) Lori de Margaret, Lori de Marguerite, **II** PSITTACIDAE Av
Charmosyna meeki : (E) Meek's Lorikeet, (S) Lori de Meek, (F) Lori de Meek, **II** PSITTACIDAE Av
Charmosyna multistriata : (E) Streaked Lorikeet, Striated Lorikeet, (S) Lori estriado, (F) Lori strié, **II** PSITTACIDAE Av
Charmosyna palmarum : (E) Palm Lorikeet, (S) Lori palmero, (F) Lori des palmiers, **II** PSITTACIDAE Av
Charmosyna papou : (E) Papuan Lorikeet, (S) Lori rabilargo, (F) Lori de Papouasie, Lori papou, **II** PSITTACIDAE Av
Charmosyna placentis : (E) Red-flanked Lorikeet, (S) Lori flanquirrojo, (F) Lori coquet, Lori croquet, Lori splendide, **II** PSITTACIDAE Av
Charmosyna pulchella : (E) Fairy Lorikeet, Little Red Lorikeet, (S) Lori lindo, (F) Lori féérique, **II** PSITTACIDAE Av
Charmosyna rubrigularis : (E) Red-chinned Lorikeet, (S) Lori barbirrojo, (F) Lori à menton rouge, **II** PSITTACIDAE Av
Charmosyna rubronotata : (E) Red-fronted Lorikeet, Red-spotted Lorikeet, (S) Lori frentirrojo, (F) Lori à front rouge, **II** PSITTACIDAE Av
Charmosyna toxopei : (E) Blue-fronted Lorikeet, (S) Lori de Buru, (F) Lori de Buru, Lori de l'île Buru, **II** PSITTACIDAE Av
Charmosyna wilhelminae : (E) Pygmy Lorikeet, Wilhelmina's Lorikeet, (S) Lori pigmeo, (F) Lori de Wilhelmina, **II** PSITTACIDAE Av
Chasmistes cujus : (E) Cui-ui, (S) Cui, Cui ui, (F) Cuiui, **I** CATOSTOMIDAE Ac
Chat à pieds noirs (F): *Felis nigripes*
Chat à tête plate (F): *Prionailurus planiceps*
Chat bai (F): *Catopuma badia*
Chat de Biet (F): *Felis bieti*
Chat de Chine (F): *Prionailurus bengalensis*
Chat de Geoffroy (F): *Oncifelis geoffroyi*
Chat de jungle (F): *Felis chaus*
Chat de Temminck (F): *Catopuma temminckii*
Chat des Andes (F): *Oreailurus jacobita*
Chat des marais (F): *Felis chaus*
Chat des pampas (F): *Oncifelis colocolo*
Chat des sables (F): *Felis margarita*
Chat doré (F): *Profelis aurata*
Chat doré d'Asie (F): *Catopuma temminckii*
Chat manul (F): *Otocolobus manul*
Chat marbré (F): *Pardofelis marmorata*
Chat orné (F): *Felis silvestris*
Chat pêcheur (F): *Prionailurus viverrinus*
Chat rougeâtre (F): *Prionailurus rubiginosus*
Chat rubigineux (F): *Prionailurus rubiginosus*
Chat sauvage (F): *Felis silvestris/ Lynx rufus*
Chatham Island Yellow-fronted Parakeet (E): *Cyanoramphus forbesi*
Chat-léopard de Chine (F): *Prionailurus bengalensis bengalensis*
Chat-léopard de l'Inde (F): *Prionailurus rubiginosus*
Chat-léopard du Bengale (F): *Prionailurus bengalensis*
Chat-tacheté (F): *Leopardus tigrinus*
Chattering Lory (E): *Lorius garrulus*

Checklist of fauna/Lista de especies de fauna/Liste des espèces animales

Chat-tigre (F): *Leopardus tigrinus/ Leptailurus serval*
Chat-tigre du Bengale (F): *Prionailurus bengalensis bengalensis*
Cheer Pheasant (E): *Catreus wallichii*
Cheetah (E): *Acinonyx jubatus*
Cheiloporidion pulvinatum : **II** STYLASTERIDAE Hy
Cheirogale moyen (F): *Cheirogaleus medius*
CHEIROGALEIDAE spp.: (E) Dwarf lemurs, (S) Makis, (F) Chirogales, **I** Ma
Cheirogaleus major : (E) Greater Dwarf Lemur, (S) Gran lemur ardilla, Lemur enano mayor, Maki coligordo, (F) Grand cheirogale, **I** CHEIROGALEIDAE Ma
Cheirogaleus medius : (E) Fat-tailed Dwarf Lemur, (S) Lemur ardilla coligrueso, Lemur enano coligrueso, Maki coligordo, (F) Cheirogale moyen, Petit cheirogale, **I** CHEIROGALEIDAE Ma
Cheirogaleus minusculus : (E) Lesser Iron-grey Dwarf Lemur **I** CHEIROGALEIDAE Ma
Cheirogaleus ravus : (E) Large Iron-grey Dwarf Lemur **I** CHEIROGALEIDAE Ma
Cheirogaleus trichotis = Allocebus trichotis
Chelictinia riocourii : (E) African Swallow-tailed Kite, Scissor-tailed Kite, (S) Elanio golondrina, (F) Élanion naucler, **II** ACCIPITRIDAE Av
Chelonée à dos plat (F): *Natator depressus*
Chelonia depressa = Natator depressus
Chelonia mydas : (E) Green Turtle, (S) Tortuga blanca, Tortuga verde, (F) Tortue comestible, Tortue franche, Tortue verte, **I** CHELONIIDAE Re
CHELONIIDAE spp.: (E) Marine turtles, (S) Tortugas marinas, (F) Tortues de mer, **I** Re
Chelonoides carbonaria = Geochelone carbonaria
Chelonoides chilensis = Geochelone chilensis
Chelonoides denticulata = Geochelone denticulata
Chelonoides elegans = Geochelone elegans
Chelonoides gigantea = Geochelone gigantea
Chelonoides nigra = Geochelone nigra
Chequered Keelback (E): *Xenochrophis piscator*
Chersina angulata : (E) Angulated Tortoise, Bowsprit Tortoise, South African Bowsprit Tortoise, (S) Tortuga ariete, Tortuga de pechera, (F) Tortue à soc d'Afrique du Sud, **II** TESTUDINIDAE Re
Chestnut Hawk-Owl (E): *Ninox theomacha*
Chestnut Owlet (E): *Glaucidium castaneum*
Chestnut Terrapin (E): *Pelusios castaneus*
Chestnut-backed Owlet (E): *Glaucidium castanonotum*
Chestnut-bellied Hawk-Eagle (E): *Hieraaetus kienerii*
Chestnut-bellied Hummingbird (E): *Amazilia castaneiventris*
Chestnut-bellied Sparrowhawk (E): *Accipiter castanilius*
Chestnut-breasted Coronet (E): *Boissonneaua matthewsii*
Chestnut-breasted Negrofinch (E): *Nigrita bicolor*
Chestnut-breasted Tree-Partridge (E): *Arborophila charltonii*
Chestnut-crowned Sparrow-Weaver (E): *Plocepasser superciliosus*
Chestnut-eared Aracari (E): *Pteroglossus castanotis*
Chestnut-flanked Sparrowhawk (E): *Accipiter castanilius*
Chestnut-fronted Macaw (E): *Ara severa*
Chestnut-mantled Goshawk (E): *Erythrotriorchis buergersi*
Chestnut-necklaced Partridge (E): *Arborophila charltonii*
Chestnut-shouldered Goshawk (E): *Erythrotriorchis buergersi*
Chestnut-shouldered Hawk (E): *Erythrotriorchis buergersi*
Cheval de mer (F): *Hippocampus hippocampus/ Hippocampus histrix*
Cheval de Przewalski (F): *Equus przewalskii*
Cheval marin (F): *Hippocampus guttulatus/ Hippocampus kuda*
Chevalier à gouttelette (F): *Tringa guttifer*
Chevalier tacheté (F): *Tringa guttifer*
Chevaux de mer (F): *Hippocampus* spp.
Chevêche brame (F): *Athene brama*
Chevêche d'Athéna (F): *Athene noctua*

Chevêche des terriers (F): *Speotyto cunicularia*
Chevêche forestière (F): *Athene blewitti*
Chevêchette à collier (F): *Glaucidium brodiei*
Chevêchette à dos marron (F): *Glaucidium castanonotum*
Chevêchette à pieds jaunes (F): *Glaucidium tephronotum*
Chevêchette à queue barrée (F): *Glaucidium sjostedti*
Chevêchette australe (F): *Glaucidium nanum*
Chevêchette brune (F): *Glaucidium brasilianum*
Chevêchette cabouré (F): *Glaucidium minutissimum*
Chevêchette châtaine (F): *Glaucidium castaneum*
Chevêchette cuculoïde (F): *Glaucidium cuculoides*
Chevêchette d'Amazonie (F): *Glaucidium hardyi*
Chevêchette de Cuba (F): *Glaucidium siju*
Chevêchette de jungle (F): *Glaucidium radiatum*
Chevêchette de Ngami (F): *Glaucidium ngamiense*
Chevêchette de Parker (F): *Glaucidium parkeri*
Chevêchette de Scheffler (F): *Glaucidium scheffleri*
Chevêchette des Andes (F): *Glaucidium jardinii*
Chevêchette des Rocheuses (F): *Glaucidium californicum*
Chevêchette des saguaros (F): *Micrathene whitneyi*
Chevêchette des yungas (F): *Glaucidium bolivianum*
Chevêchette d'Europe (F): *Glaucidium passerinum*
Chevêchette du Cap (F): *Glaucidium capense*
Chevêchette du Graben (F): *Glaucidium albertinum*
Chevêchette du Pérou (F): *Glaucidium peruanum*
Chevêchette naine (F): *Glaucidium gnoma*
Chevêchette nimbée (F): *Xenoglaux loweryi*
Chevêchette perlée (F): *Glaucidium perlatum*
Chevêchette spadicée (F): *Glaucidium castanopterum*
Chevêchette-elfe (F): *Micrathene whitneyi*
Chevrotain aquatique (F): *Hyemoschus aquaticus*
Chevrotain porte-musc (F): *Moschus moschiferus*
Chevrotains porte-musc (F): *Moschus* spp.
Chiapan Boa (E): *Ungaliophis continentalis*
Chichimen (S): *Lontra felina*
Chico Grey Fox (E): *Pseudalopex griseus*
Chien de prairie du Mexique (F): *Cynomys mexicanus*
Chien des buissons (F): *Speothos venaticus*
Chien sauvage d'Asie (F): *Cuon alpinus*
Chihuahua Rose-grey Tarantula (E): *Aphonopelma pallidum*
Children's (Rock) Python (E): *Antaresia childreni*
Chilean Cat (E): *Oncifelis guigna*
Chilean Dolphin (E): *Cephalorhynchus eutropia*
Chilean Flamingo (E): *Phoenicopterus chilensis*
Chilean Guemal (E): *Hippocamelus bisulcus*
Chilean Huemul (E): *Hippocamelus bisulcus*
Chilean Pampa Cat (E): *Oncifelis colocolo*
Chilean Pudu (E): *Pudu puda*
Chilean Woodstar (E): *Myrtis yarrellii*
Chilka Seahorse (E): *Hippocampus fuscus*
Chilla (S): *Pseudalopex griseus*
Chillón de Sundevall (S): *Petronia dentata*
Chiloe Fox (E): *Pseudalopex griseus*
Chimachima (S): *Milvago chimachima*
Chimaera Birdwing (E): *Ornithoptera chimaera*
Chimango (S): *Milvago chimango*
Chimango Caracara (E): *Milvago chimango*
Chimpancé (S): *Pan troglodytes*
Chimpancé pigmeo (S): *Pan paniscus*
Chimpancés (S): *Pan* spp.
Chimpanzé (F): *Pan troglodytes*
Chimpanzé nain (F): *Pan paniscus*
Chimpanzé pygmée (F): *Pan paniscus*
Chimpanzee (E): *Pan troglodytes*
Chimpanzees (E): *Pan* spp.
Chimpanzés (F): *Pan* spp.
Chimpire (S): *Podocnemis erythrocephala*
China Alligator (E): *Alligator sinensis*
China Clam (E): *Hippopus porcellanus*
Chinalinda (S): *Phalcoboenus albogularis*
Chinaman's Hat (E): *Zoopilus echinatus*
Chinchay (S): *Oreailurus jacobita*
Chinchilla à longue queue (F): *Chinchilla lanigera*
Chinchilla à queue courte (F): *Chinchilla brevicaudata*

Chinchilla spp.: (E) Chinchillas, (S) Chinchillas, (F) Chinchillas, **I** CHINCHILLIDAE Ma
Chinchilla brevicaudata : (E) Short-tailed Chinchilla, (S) Chinchilla de cola corta, (F) Chinchilla à queue courte, **I** CHINCHILLIDAE Ma
Chinchilla costina (S): *Chinchilla lanigera*
Chinchilla de cola corta (S): *Chinchilla brevicaudata*
Chinchilla de cola larga (S): *Chinchilla lanigera*
Chinchilla lanigera : (E) Long-tailed Chinchilla, (S) Chinchilla costina, Chinchilla de cola larga, (F) Chinchilla à longue queue, **I** CHINCHILLIDAE Ma
Chinchillas (E/S/F): *Chinchilla* spp.
Chinchimen (S): *Lontra felina*
Chinese Alligator (E): *Alligator sinensis*
Chinese Barred-backed Pheasant (E): *Syrmaticus el.loti*
Chinese Box Turtle (E): *Cuora flavomarginata*
Chinese Cobra (E): *Naja atra*
Chinese Crocodile Lizard (E): *Shinisaurus crocodilurus*
Chinese Desert Cat (E): *Felis bieti*
Chinese Forest Musk Deer (E): *Moschus berezovskii*
Chinese Giant Salamander (E): *Andrias davidianus*
Chinese Goral (E): *Naemorhedus caudatus*
Chinese Goshawk (E): *Accipiter soloensis*
Chinese Impeyan (E): *Lophophorus lhuysii*
Chinese Lake Dolphin (E): *Lipotes vexillifer*
Chinese Monal (E): *Lophophorus lhuysii*
Chinese Paddlefish (E): *Psephurus gladius*
Chinese Pangolin (E): *Manis pentadactyla*
Chinese Sparrowhawk (E): *Accipiter soloensis*
Chinese Spitting Cobra (E): *Naja atra*
Chinese Sturgeon (E): *Acipenser sinensis*
Chinese Swordfish (E): *Psephurus gladius*
Chinese Three-striped Box Turtle (E): *Cuora trifasciata*
Chinese Three-tailed Swallowtail (E): *Bhutanitis thaidina*
Chinese Xenosaur (E): *Shinisaurus crocodilurus*
Chingue de la Patagonia (S): *Conepatus humboldtii*
Chingungo (E): *Lontra felina*
Chir Pheasant (E): *Catreus wallichii*
Chiribiquete Emerald (E): *Chlorostilbon olivaresi*
Chirica (S): *Nannopsittaca panychlora*
Chiripepé común (S): *Pyrrhura frontalis*
Chiripepé salteño (S): *Pyrrhura molinae*
Chirogale aux oreilles poilues (F): *Allocebus trichotis*
Chirogales (F): CHEIROGALEIDAE spp.
Chiropotes albinasus : (E) Red-nosed Saki, White-nosed Bearded Saki, White-nosed Saki, (S) Saki de nariz blanca, Saki nariblanco, (F) Saki à nez blanc, **I** CEBIDAE Ma
Chiropotes satanas : (E) Bearded Saki, Black Saki, (F) Saki noir **II** CEBIDAE Ma
Chiru (E): *Pantholops hodgsonii*
Chita (S): *Acinonyx jubatus*
Chitra spp.: (E) Narrow-headed softshell turtles, **II** TRIONYCHIDAE Re
Chitra chitra : (E) Southeast Asian Narrow-headed Softshell Turtle, Striped Giant Soft-shelled Turtle, Striped Narrow-headed Softshell Turtle **II** TRIONYCHIDAE Re
Chitra indica : (E) Indian Narrow-headed Softshell Turtle **II** TRIONYCHIDAE Re
Chivito de los Páramos (S): *Oxypogon guerinii*
Chlamydotis macqueenii = Chlamydotis undulata
Chlamydotis undulata : (E) Houbara, Houbara Bustard, (S) Avutarda hubara, Hubara, (F) Houbara ondulé, Outarde houbara, **I** OTIDIDAE Av
Chlorestes notatus = Chlorostilbon notatus
Chlorocebus aethiops : (E) Green Monkey, Grivet Monkey, Savanna Monkey, Tantalus Monkey, Vervet Monkey, (S) Mono verde, (F) Singe vert, **II** CERCOPITHECIDAE Ma
Chlorocebus pygerythrus = Chlorocebus aethiops
Chlorocebus sabaeus = Chlorocebus aethiops
Chlorocebus tantalus = Chlorocebus aethiops

Chlorostilbon alice : (E) Green-tailed Emerald, (S) Esmeralda coliverde, (F) Émeraude alice, **II** TROCHILIDAE Av
Chlorostilbon assimilis = Chlorostilbon mellisugus
Chlorostilbon auratus = Chlorostilbon poortmani
Chlorostilbon aureoventris : (E) Glittering-bellied Emerald, (S) Esmeralda ventridorada, Picaflor común, (F) Émeraude splendide, **II** TROCHILIDAE Av
Chlorostilbon bracei : (E) Brace's Emerald, Grace's Emerald, (F) Émeraude de New Providence **II** TROCHILIDAE Av
Chlorostilbon canivetii = Chlorostilbon mellisugus
Chlorostilbon canivetii ssp. *assimilis = Chlorostilbon mellisugus*
Chlorostilbon elegans : (E) Gould's Emerald **II** TROCHILIDAE Av
Chlorostilbon forficatus = Chlorostilbon mellisugus
Chlorostilbon gibsoni = Chlorostilbon mellisugus
Chlorostilbon inexpectatus = Chlorostilbon poortmani
Chlorostilbon maugaeus : (E) Puerto Rican Emerald, (S) Esmeralda Portorriqueña, (F) Émeraude de Porto Rico, **II** TROCHILIDAE Av
Chlorostilbon maugeus ssp. *bracei = Chlorostilbon bracei*
Chlorostilbon melanorhynchus = Chlorostilbon mellisugus
Chlorostilbon mellisugus : (E) Blue-tailed Emerald, (S) Esmeralda coliazul, (F) Émeraude orvert, **II** TROCHILIDAE Av
Chlorostilbon notatus : (E) Blue-chinned Sapphire, (S) Colibrí verdecito, Esmeralda gorgiazul, Zafiro barbiazul, (F) Colibri à menton bleu, **II** TROCHILIDAE Av
Chlorostilbon olivaresi : (E) Chiribiquete Emerald, (S) Esmeralda del Chiribiquete, (F) Émeraude d'Olivares, **II** TROCHILIDAE Av
Chlorostilbon poortmani : (E) Short-tailed Emerald, (S) Esmeralda colicorta, (F) Émeraude à queue courte, **II** TROCHILIDAE Av
Chlorostilbon ricordii : (E) Cuban Emerald, (S) Esmeralda zunzún, (F) Émeraude de Ricord, **II** TROCHILIDAE Av
Chlorostilbon russatus : (E) Coppery Emerald, (S) Esmeralda bronceada, (F) Émeraude cuivrée, **II** TROCHILIDAE Av
Chlorostilbon salvini = Chlorostilbon mellisugus
Chlorostilbon stenurus : (E) Narrow-tailed Emerald, (S) Esmeralda cola de alambre, Esmeralda colifina, (F) Émeraude à queue étroite, **II** TROCHILIDAE Av
Chlorostilbon swainsonii : (E) Hispaniolan Emerald, (S) Esmeralda de la Española, Zumbador, (F) Émeraude d'Hispaniola, **II** TROCHILIDAE Av
Choeropsis liberiensis = Hexaprotodon liberiensis
Choloepus hoffmanni : (E) Hoffmann's Two-toed Sloth, (S) Perezoso, Unau, Unau o perezoso de Hoffman, (F) Paresseux d'Hoffmann, Unau , Unau d'Hoffmann, **III** MEGALONYCHIDAE Ma
Chondrohierax uncinatus : (E) Hook-billed Kite, (S) Gavilán pico ganchudo, Milano picogarfio, (F) Milan bec-en-croc, **I/II** ACCIPITRIDAE Av
Chondrohierax uncinatus wilsonii : (E) Cuban Hook-billed Kite, (S) Busardo de Wilson, (F) Busard de Wilson, Milan de Cuba, Milan de Wilson, **I** ACCIPITRIDAE Av
Chondrohierax wilsonii = Chondrohierax uncinatus ssp. *wilsonii*
Chondropython viridis = Morelia viridis
Choriotis arabs = Ardeotis arabs
Choriotis australis = Ardeotis australis
Choriotis kori = Ardeotis kori
Choriotis nigriceps = Ardeotis nigriceps
Chorlito esquimal (S): *Numenius borealis*
Chorlo polar (S): *Numenius borealis*
Chosna (S): *Potos flavus*
Chosna pericote (S): *Bassaricyon gabbii*
Chouette à collier (F): *Pulsatrix melanota*
Chouette à joues blanches (F): *Sceloglaux albifacies*

98

Checklist of fauna/Lista de especies de fauna/Liste des espèces animales

Chouette à lignes noires (F): *Strix nigrolineata*
Chouette à lunettes (F): *Pulsatrix perspicillata*
Chouette à sourcils jaunes (F): *Pulsatrix koeniswaldiana*
Chouette africaine (F): *Strix woodfordii*
Chouette baie (F): *Phodilus badius*
Chouette boobok (F): *Ninox novaeseelandiae*
Chouette boobok de l'île Norfolk (F): *Ninox novaeseelandiae undulata*
Chouette Chevêche (F): *Athene noctua*
Chouette chevêchette (F): *Glaucidium passerinum*
Chouette coucou (F): *Ninox novaeseelandiae*
Chouette de Butler (F): *Strix butleri*
Chouette de Cuba (F): *Otus lawrencii*
Chouette de Harris (F): *Aegolius harrisii*
Chouette de Koeniswald (F): *Pulsatrix koeniswaldiana*
Chouette de l'Oural (F): *Strix uralensis*
Chouette de Nouvelle-Guinée (F): *Uroglaux dimorpha*
Chouette de Sitchouan (F): *Strix davidi*
Chouette de Tengmalm (F): *Aegolius funereus*
Chouette de terrier (F): *Speotyto cunicularia*
Chouette des forêts (F): *Athene blewitti*
Chouette des îles Salomons (F): *Nesasio solomonensis*
Chouette des Moluques (F): *Ninox squamipila*
Chouette des pagodes (F): *Strix seloputo*
Chouette dryade (F): *Strix hylophila*
Chouette du Sitchouan (F): *Strix davidi*
Chouette d'Ussher (F): *Scotopelia ussheri*
Chouette effraie (F): *Tyto alba*
Chouette épervière (F): *Ninox squamipila/ Surnia ulula*
Chouette épervière de l'île Christmas (F): *Ninox squamipila natalis*
Chouette fasciée (F): *Strix albitarsus*
Chouette fauve (F): *Strix fulvescens*
Chouette harfang (F): *Nyctea scandiaca*
Chouette huhul (F): *Strix huhula*
Chouette hulotte (F): *Strix aluco*
Chouette hulotte de Hume (F): *Strix butleri*
Chouette lapone (F): *Strix nebulosa*
Chouette leptogramme (F): *Strix leptogrammica*
Chouette masquée (F): *Strix rufipes*
Chouette mouchetée (F): *Strix virgata*
Chouette noire et blanche (F): *Strix nigrolineata*
Chouette ocellée (F): *Strix ocellata*
Chouette pêcheuse (F): *Scotopelia peli*
Chouette rayée (F): *Strix varia*
Chouette tachetée (F): *Strix occidentalis*
Chouette-pêcheuse de Bouvier (F): *Scotopelia bouvieri*
Chouette-pêcheuse de Pel (F): *Scotopelia peli*
Chouette-pêcheuse rousse (F): *Scotopelia ussheri*
Chousingha (E): *Tetracerus quadricornis*
Christmas Coral (E): *Acropora elseyi*
Christmas Frigatebird (E): *Fregata andrewsi*
Christmas Hawk-Owl (E): *Ninox squamipila natalis*
Christmas Island Flying-fox (E): *Pteropus melanotus*
Christmas Island Frigatebird (E): *Fregata andrewsi*
Christmas Island Hawk-Owl (E): *Ninox squamipila natalis*
Chrysocyon brachyurus : (E) Maned Wolf, (S) Aguara guazu, Lobo de crin, (F) Loup à crinière, **II** CANIDAE Ma
Chrysolampis mosquitus : (E) Ruby-topaz Hummingbird, (S) Colibrí rubí, Tucusito rubí, (F) Colibri rubis-topaze, **II** TROCHILIDAE Av
Chrysuronia oenone : (E) Golden-tailed Sapphire, (S) Colibrí cola de oro, Zafiro colidorado, (F) Saphir oenone, **II** TROCHILIDAE Av
Chuckwalla de San Esteban (F): *Sauromalus varius*
Chungungo (E/S/F): *Lontra felina*
Chupacacao negro (S): *Daptrius ater*
Chupacacao ventriblanco (S): *Daptrius americanus*
Churica (S): *Brotogeris jugularis*
Churiquita (S): *Touit dilectissima*
Chuuk Flying-fox (E): *Pteropus insularis*
Cibeta africana (S): *Civettictis civetta*
Cibeta atigrada (S): *Prionodon linsang*
Cibeta de Madagascar (S): *Fossa fossana*

Cibeta moteada (S): *Prionodon pardicolor*
Cibeta nutria (S): *Cynogale bennettii*
Cibeta palmirayada (S): *Hemigalus derbyanus*
Ciccaba albitarsus = Strix albitarsus
Ciccaba huhula = Strix huhula
Ciccaba nigrolineata = Strix nigrolineata
Ciccaba virgata = Strix virgata
Ciccaba woodfordii = Strix woodfordii
Cicinnurus magnificus : (E) Magnificent Bird-of-paradise, (F) Paradisier magnifique **II** PARADISAEIDAE Av
Cicinnurus regius : (E) King Bird-of-paradise, (F) Paradisier royal **II** PARADISAEIDAE Av
Cicinnurus respublica : (E) Wilson's Bird-of-paradise, (F) Paradisier républicain **II** PARADISAEIDAE Av
Ciconia boyciana : (E) Japanese White Stork, Oriental Stork, Oriental White Stork, (S) Cigüeña blanca coreana, Cigüeña del Japón, Cigüeña oriental, (F) Cigogne à bec noir, Cigogne blanche de Corée, Cigogne blanche du Japon, Cigogne blanche orientale, Cigogne orientale, **I** CICONIIDAE Av
Ciconia ciconia ssp. *boyciana = Ciconia boyciana*
Ciconia nigra : (E) Black Stork, (S) Cigüeña negra, (F) Cigogne noire, **II** CICONIIDAE Av
Cicupa (S): *Pulsatrix melanota*
Ciervo almizclero (S): *Moschus moschiferus*
Ciervo andino meridional (S): *Hippocamelus bisulcus*
Ciervo andino septentrional (S): *Hippocamelus antisensis*
Ciervo bactriano (S): *Cervus elaphus bactrianus*
Ciervo de Cachemira (S): *Cervus elaphus hanglu*
Ciervo de Duvaucel (S): *Cervus duvaucelii*
Ciervo de Eld (S): *Cervus eldii*
Ciervo de Kuhl (S): *Axis kuhlii*
Ciervo de la Berberia (S): *Cervus elaphus barbarus*
Ciervo de las Pampas (S): *Ozotoceros bezoarticus*
Ciervo de los Calamianes (S): *Axis calamianensis*
Ciervo de los pantanos (S): *Blastocerus dichotomus*
Ciervo de Marjal (S): *Axis kuhlii*
Ciervo del Turquestán (S): *Cervus elaphus bactrianus*
Ciervo enano (S): *Pudu puda*
Ciervo marismeño (S): *Blastocerus dichotomus*
Ciervo mazama (S): *Hippocamelus* spp.
Ciervo pampero (S): *Ozotoceros bezoarticus*
Ciervo porquerizo de Indochina (S): *Axis porcinus annamiticus*
Ciervo porquerizo de Kuhl (S): *Axis kuhlii*
Ciervo porquerizo de los Calamianes (S): *Axis calamianensis*
Ciervos almizcleros (S): *Moschus* spp.
Ciervos andinos (S): *Hippocamelus* spp.
Cigogne à bec noir (F): *Ciconia boyciana*
Cigogne blanche de Corée (F): *Ciconia boyciana*
Cigogne blanche du Japon (F): *Ciconia boyciana*
Cigogne blanche orientale (F): *Ciconia boyciana*
Cigogne noire (F): *Ciconia nigra*
Cigogne orientale (F): *Ciconia boyciana*
Cigüeña blanca coreana (S): *Ciconia boyciana*
Cigüeña del Japón (S): *Ciconia boyciana*
Cigüeña ensillada (S): *Ephippiorhynchus senegalensis*
Cigüeña Negra (S): *Ciconia nigra*
Cigüeña oriental (S): *Ciconia boyciana*
Cinereous Harrier (E): *Circus cinereus*
Cinereous Vulture (E): *Aegypius monachus*
Cinnabar Hawk-Owl (E): *Ninox ios*
Cinnamon Hummingbird (E): *Amazilia rutila*
Cinnamon-throated Hermit (E): *Phaethornis nattereri*
Circaète à poitrine noire (F): *Circaetus pectoralis*
Circaète barré (F): *Circaetus fasciolatus*
Circaète brun (F): *Circaetus cinereus*
Circaète cendré (F): *Circaetus cinerascens*
Circaète Jean-le-Blanc (F): *Circaetus gallicus*
Circaetus beaudouini = Circaetus gallicus
Circaetus cinerascens : (E) Banded Snake-Eagle, Smaller Banded Snake-Eagle, (S) Aguila culebrera culiblanca, Culebrera coliblanca, (F) Circaète cendré, **II** ACCIPITRIDAE Av

Checklist of fauna/Lista de especies de fauna/Liste des espèces animales

Circaetus cinereus : (E) Brown Harrier-Eagle, Brown Snake-Eagle, (S) Aguila culebrera de Brown, Culebrera sombría, (F) Circaète brun, **II** ACCIPITRIDAE Av

Circaetus fasciolatus : (E) Fasciated Snake-Eagle, Southern Banded Snake-Eagle, (F) Circaète barré **II** ACCIPITRIDAE Av

Circaetus gallicus : (E) Beaudouin's Snake-Eagle, Short-toed Eagle, Short-toed Snake-Eagle, (S) Aguila culebrera, Culebrera barreada, Culebrera europea, (F) Circaète Jean-le-Blanc, **II** ACCIPITRIDAE Av

Circaetus pectoralis : (E) Black-breasted Harrier-Eagle, Black-breasted Snake-Eagle, Black-chested Snake-Eagle, (S) Culebrera pechinegra, (F) Circaète à poitrine noire, **II** ACCIPITRIDAE Av

Circus aeruginosus : (E) Eurasian Marsh-Harrier, Marsh Harrier, Western Marsh-Harrier, (S) Aguilucho lagunero, Aguilucho lagunero occidental, (F) Busard des roseaux, **II** ACCIPITRIDAE Av

Circus aeruginosus ssp. *approximans* = *Circus approximans*

Circus aeruginosus ssp. *maillardi* = *Circus maillardi*

Circus aeruginosus ssp. *spilonotus* = *Circus spilonotus*

Circus approximans : (E) Australasian Harrier, Pacific Marsh-Harrier, Swamp Harrier, (S) Aguilucho lagunero del pacifico, Aguilucho Lanunero del Pacifico, (F) Busard de Gould, **II** ACCIPITRIDAE Av

Circus assimilis : (E) Aguilucho moteado, Spotted Harrier, (F) Busard tacheté **II** ACCIPITRIDAE Av

Circus buffoni : (E) Long-winged Harrier, (S) Aguilucho de azara, Aguilucho de ciénaga, Gavilán grande, (F) Busard de Buffon, **II** ACCIPITRIDAE Av

Circus cinereus : (E) Cinereous Harrier, (S) Aguilucho vari, Gavilán ceniciento, (F) Busard bariolé, **II** ACCIPITRIDAE Av

Circus cyaneus : (E) Hen Harrier, Marsh Hawk, Northern Harrier, (S) Aguilucho pálido, Gavilán rastrero, (F) Busard Saint-Martin, **II** ACCIPITRIDAE Av

Circus macrourus : (E) Pale Harrier, Pallid Harrier, (S) Aguilucho papialbo, (F) Busard pâle, **II** ACCIPITRIDAE Av

Circus maillardi : (E) Madagascar Harrier, Madagascar Marsh-Harrier, Malagasy Marsh-Harrier, Réunion Harrier, Réunion Marsh-Harrier, (S) Aguilucho lagunero malgache, (F) Busard de Maillard, **II** ACCIPITRIDAE Av

Circus maurus : (E) Black Harrier, (S) Aguilucho negro, (F) Busard maure, **II** ACCIPITRIDAE Av

Circus melanoleucos : (E) Pied Harrier, (S) Aguilucho pío, (F) Busard tchoug, **II** ACCIPITRIDAE Av

Circus pygargus : (E) Montagu's Harrier, (S) Aguilucho Cenizo, (F) Busard cendré, Busard de montagne, **II** ACCIPITRIDAE Av

Circus ranivorus : (E) African Marsh-Harrier, (S) Aguilucho lagunero etiópico, (F) Busard grenouillard, **II** ACCIPITRIDAE Av

Circus spilonotus : (E) Eastern Marsh-Harrier, Papuan Harrier, Spotted Marsh-Harrier, Spotted-backed Harrier, (S) Aguilucho lagunero oriental, (F) Busard d'Orient, **II** ACCIPITRIDAE Av

Cirrhipathes aggregata : **II** ANTIPATHIDAE An

Cirrhipathes anguina : **II** ANTIPATHIDAE An

Cirrhipathes contorta : **II** ANTIPATHIDAE An

Cirrhipathes musculosa : **II** ANTIPATHIDAE An

Cirrhipathes nana : **II** ANTIPATHIDAE An

Cirrhipathes rumphii : **II** ANTIPATHIDAE An

Cirrhipathes saccula : **II** ANTIPATHIDAE An

Cirrhipathes semiglabra = *Stichopathes semiglabra*

Cirrhipathes sinensis : **II** ANTIPATHIDAE An

Cirrhipathes solorensis : **II** ANTIPATHIDAE An

Cirrhipathes spiralis : **II** ANTIPATHIDAE An

Cirrhipathes translucens : **II** ANTIPATHIDAE An

Cirrhipathes variabilis : **II** ANTIPATHIDAE An

Cisne coscoroba (S): *Coscoroba coscoroba*

Cisne cuellinegro (S): *Cygnus melanocorypha*

Cistoclemmys galbinifrons = *Cuora galbinifrons*

Civeta (S): *Civettictis civetta/ Fossa fossana*

Civeta de Derby (S): *Hemigalus derbyanus*

Civeta de palmera común (S): *Paradoxurus hermaphroditus*

Civeta de palmera de Jerdon (S): *Paradoxurus jerdoni*

Civeta de palmera enmascarada (S): *Paguma larvata*

Civeta de Sumatra (S): *Cynogale bennettii*

Civeta franjeada (S): *Prionodon linsang*

Civette (F): *Civettictis civetta*

Civette à bandes (F): *Prionodon linsang*

Civette à grandes taches (F): *Viverra civettina*

Civette africaine (F): *Civettictis civetta*

Civette d'Afrique (F): *Civettictis civetta*

Civette fossane (F): *Fossa fossana*

Civette malgache (F): *Fossa fossana*

Civette palmiste à bandes de Derby (F): *Hemigalus derbyanus*

Civette palmiste à masque (F): *Paguma larvata*

Civette palmiste de Jerdon (F): *Paradoxurus jerdoni*

Civette palmiste hermaphrodite (F): *Paradoxurus hermaphroditus*

Civette palmiste rayée (F): *Hemigalus derbyanus*

Civette-loutre de Sumatra (F): *Cynogale bennettii*

Civettictis civetta : (E) African Civet, (S) Cibeta africana, Civeta, (F) Civette, Civette africaine, Civette d'Afrique, **III** VIVERRIDAE Ma

Cladangia exusta : **II** RHIZANGIIDAE An

Cladangia gemmans : **II** RHIZANGIIDAE An

Cladocora arbuscula : (E) Ivory Tube Coral **II** CARYOPHYLLIIDAE An

Cladocora caespitosa : **II** CARYOPHYLLIIDAE An

Cladocora debilis : (E) Thin Tube Coral **II** CARYOPHYLLIIDAE An

Cladocora pacifica : **II** CARYOPHYLLIIDAE An

Cladopathes plumosa : **II** ANTIPATHIDAE An

Cladopsammia echinata : **II** DENDROPHYLLIIDAE An

Cladopsammia eguchii : **II** DENDROPHYLLIIDAE An

Cladopsammia gracilis : **II** DENDROPHYLLIIDAE An

Cladopsammia manuelensis : **II** DENDROPHYLLIIDAE An

Cladopsammia rolandi : **II** DENDROPHYLLIIDAE An

Cladopsammia willeyi : **II** DENDROPHYLLIIDAE An

Clelia clelia : (E) Mussurana, (S) Masurana, Mussurana, (F) Mussurana, Mussurana d'Amérique du sud, **II** COLUBRIDAE Re

Clelia occipitolutea = *Clelia clelia*

Clemmyde de Muhlenberg (F): *Clemmys muhlenbergii*

Clemmyde sculptée (F): *Clemmys insculpta*

Clemmys gibbera = *Orlitia borneensis*

Clemmys insculpta : (E) Wood Turtle, (F) Clemmyde sculptée **II** EMYDIDAE Re

Clemmys muhlenbergii : (E) Bog Turtle, Muhlenberg's Turtle, (S) Galápago de Muhlenberg, (F) Clemmyde de Muhlenberg, Tortue de Muhlenberg, Tortue des marécages, **I** EMYDIDAE Re

Clemmys mutica = *Mauremys mutica*

Cliff Parakeet (E): *Myiopsitta luchsi*

Cloete's Girdled Lizard (E): *Cordylus cloetei*

Clouded Leopard (E): *Neofelis nebulosa*

Cloud-forest Screech-Owl (E): *Otus marshalli*

Club Finger Coral (E): *Porites porites*

Club finger corals (E): *Stylophora* spp.

Clubshell (E): *Pleurobema clava*

Clubshell Pearly Mussel (E): *Pleurobema clava*

Clubtip Finger Coral (E): *Porites porites*

Cluster Coral (E): *Stylophora pistillata*

Clymene Dolphin (E): *Stenella clymene*

Clytolaema rubricauda : (E) Brazilian Ruby, (S) Colibrí colirrojo, (F) Colibri rubis-émeraude, **II** TROCHILIDAE Av

Cnemophilus loriae : (E) Loria's Bird-of-paradise, (F) Paradisier de Loria, Paradisier loria **II** PARADISAEIDAE Av

Checklist of fauna/Lista de especies de fauna/Liste des espèces animales

Cnemophilus macgregorii : (E) Crested Bird-of-paradise, (F) Paradisier huppé **II** PARADISAEIDAE Av
Coahuila Box Turtle (E): *Terrapene coahuila*
Coahuila Turtle (E): *Terrapene coahuila*
Coalfish Whale (E): *Balaenoptera borealis*
Coarse Chameleon (E): *Chamaeleo rudis*
Coast Horned Lizard (E): *Phrynosoma coronatum*
Coastal Spiny-tailed Lizard (E): *Cordylus macropholis*
Coati (S/F): *Nasua narica*
Coati à museau blanc (F): *Nasua narica*
Coati brun (F): *Nasua narica*
Coati roux (F): *Nasua nasua solitaria*
Cobalt-winged Parakeet (E): *Brotogeris cyanoptera*
Cobe lechwe (F): *Kobus leche*
Cobo de Lechwe (S): *Kobus leche*
Cobra à lunettes (F): *Naja naja*
Cobra común asiática (S): *Naja naja*
Cobra de anteojos (S): *Naja naja*
Cobra des Indes (F): *Naja naja*
Cobra escupidora asiática (S): *Naja naja*
Cobra indien (F): *Naja naja*
Cobra real (S): *Ophiophagus hannah*
Cobra royal (F): *Ophiophagus hannah*
Cobra spectacled de la India (S): *Naja naja*
Cochito (E/S/F): *Phocoena sinus*
Cockatiel (E): *Nymphicus hollandicus*
Cocks-of-the-rock (E): *Rupicola* spp.
Cocodrilo americano (S): *Crocodylus acutus*
Cocodrilo australiano (S): *Crocodylus johnsoni*
Cocodrilo chico africano (S): *Osteolaemus tetraspis*
Cocodrilo de Cuba (S): *Crocodylus rhombifer*
Cocodrilo de hocico corto (S): *Osteolaemus tetraspis*
Cocodrilo de Mindoro (S): *Crocodylus mindorensis*
Cocodrilo de Morelet (S): *Crocodylus moreletii*
Cocodrilo de Nueva Guinea (S): *Crocodylus novaeguineae*
Cocodrilo de Siam (S): *Crocodylus siamensis*
Cocodrilo del Marjal (S): *Crocodylus palustris*
Cocodrilo del Nilo (S): *Crocodylus niloticus*
Cocodrilo del Orinoco (S): *Crocodylus intermedius*
Cocodrilo hociquifino africano (S): *Crocodylus cataphractus*
Cocodrilo marismeño (S): *Crocodylus palustris*
Cocodrilo poroso (S): *Crocodylus porosus*
Cocodrilos (S): CROCODYLIA spp. Re
Coelacanth (E): *Latimeria chalumnae*
Coelacanthe (F): *Latimeria chalumnae*
Coelacanthes (F): *Latimeria* spp.
Coeligena bonapartei : (E) Golden-bellied Starfrontlet, (S) Colibrí inca dorado, Inca ventridorado, (F) Inca de Bonaparte, **II** TROCHILIDAE Av
Coeligena coeligena : (E) Bronzy Inca, (S) Colibrí inca bronceado, Inca bronceado, (F) Inca céleste, **II** TROCHILIDAE Av
Coeligena eos : (E) Golden Starfrontlet **II** TROCHILIDAE Av
Coeligena helianthea : (E) Blue-throated Starfrontlet, (S) Colibrí inca ventrivioleta, Inca ventrivioleta, (F) Inca porphyre, **II** TROCHILIDAE Av
Coeligena inca : (E) Gould's Inca, (S) Inca de Gould, (F) Inca de Gould, **II** TROCHILIDAE Av
Coeligena iris : (E) Rainbow Starfrontlet, (S) Frentiestrella arcoiris, Inca arcoiris, (F) Inca iris, **II** TROCHILIDAE Av
Coeligena lutetiae : (E) Buff-winged Starfrontlet, (S) Frentiestrella alihabano, Inca alihabano, (F) Inca à gemme bleue, **II** TROCHILIDAE Av
Coeligena orina = *Coeligena bonapartei*
Coeligena phalerata : (E) White-tailed Starfrontlet, (S) Inca coliblanco, (F) Inca à queue blanche, **II** TROCHILIDAE Av
Coeligena prunellei : (E) Black Inca, (S) Inca negro, (F) Inca noir, **II** TROCHILIDAE Av
Coeligena torquata : (E) Collared Inca, (S) Colibrí inca acollarado, Inca acollarado, (F) Inca à collier, **II** TROCHILIDAE Av

Coeligena violifer : (E) Violet-throated Starfrontlet, (S) Inca gorgimorado, (F) Inca violifère, **II** TROCHILIDAE Av
Coeligena wilsoni : (E) Brown Inca, (S) Inca café, Inca pardo, (F) Inca brun, **II** TROCHILIDAE Av
Coeloseris mayeri : **II** AGARICIIDAE An
Coenangia conferta = *Astrangia conferta*
Coendou épineux (F): *Sphiggurus spinosus*
Coendou mexicanus = *Sphiggurus mexicanus*
Coendou paragayensis = *Sphiggurus spinosus*
Coendou spinosus = *Sphiggurus spinosus*
Coendu espinoso (S): *Sphiggurus spinosus*
Coenocyathus anthophyllites : **II** CARYOPHYLLIIDAE An
Coenocyathus bowersi : **II** CARYOPHYLLIIDAE An
Coenocyathus brooki : **II** CARYOPHYLLIIDAE An
Coenocyathus caribbeana : **II** CARYOPHYLLIIDAE An
Coenocyathus cylindricus : **II** CARYOPHYLLIIDAE An
Coenocyathus dohrni = *Caryophyllia inornata*
Coenocyathus giesbrechti = *Caryophyllia inornata*
Coenocyathus goreaui : **II** CARYOPHYLLIIDAE An
Coenocyathus humanni : **II** CARYOPHYLLIIDAE An
Coenocyathus parvulus : **II** CARYOPHYLLIIDAE An
Coenocyathus sagamiensis = *Rhizosmilia sagamiensis*
Coenopsammia aequiserialis = *Tubastraea micranthus*
Coenopsammia affinis = *Tubastraea coccinea*
Coenopsammia manni = *Tubastraea coccinea*
Coenopsammia radiata = *Tubastraea coccinea*
Coenosmilia arbuscula : **II** CARYOPHYLLIIDAE An
Coenosmilia inordinata : **II** CARYOPHYLLIIDAE An
Coffre (F): *Caretta caretta/ Natator depressus*
Coiba Island Howling Monkey (E): *Alouatta coibensis*
Cola de pescado (S): *Huso huso*
Colacerda crestuda (S): *Discosura popelairii*
Colacerda ventrinegra (S): *Discosura langsdorffi*
Colacerda verde (S): *Discosura conversii*
Colacinta colinegra (S): *Lesbia victoriae*
Colacinta coliverde (S): *Lesbia nuna*
Colaespatula zamarrito (S): *Ocreatus underwoodii*
Colangia immersa : (E) Lesser Speckled Cup Coral **II** CARYOPHYLLIIDAE An
Colangia jamaicaensis : **II** CARYOPHYLLIIDAE An
Colangia moseleyi : **II** CARYOPHYLLIIDAE An
Colangia multipalifera : **II** CARYOPHYLLIIDAE An
Colapinto ecuatoriano (S): *Phlogophilus hemileucurus*
Colasisi (E): *Loriculus philippensis*
Colayo (S): *Cetorhinus maximus*
Coliazul bengalí (S): *Uraeginthus bengalus*
Colibri à ailes saphir (F): *Pterophanes cyanopterus*
Colibri à bec incurvé (F): *Glaucis dohrnii*
Colibri à bec noir (F): *Trochilus scitulus*
Colibri à calotte violette (F): *Goldmania violiceps*
Colibri à coiffe blanche (F): *Microchera albocoronata*
Colibri à dos noir (F): *Ramphomicron dorsale*
Colibri à épaulettes (F): *Eupherusa eximia*
Colibri à flancs blancs (F): *Oreotrochilus leucopleurus*
Colibri à gorge améthyste (F): *Lampornis amethystinus*
Colibri à gorge blanche (F): *Leucochloris albicollis*
Colibri à gorge bleue (F): *Lampornis clemenciae*
Colibri à gorge grenat (F): *Lamprolaima rhami*
Colibri à gorge lilas (F): *Lampornis hemileucus*
Colibri à gorge noire (F): *Archilochus alexandri*
Colibri à gorge rubis (F): *Archilochus colubris*
Colibri à menton bleu (F): *Chlorostilbon notatus*
Colibri à petit bec (F): *Ramphomicron microrhynchum*
Colibri à plastron noir (F): *Oreotrochilus melanogaster*
Colibri à poitrine violette (F): *Sternoclyta cyanopectus*
Colibri à queue bronzée (F): *Chalybura urochrysia*
Colibri à queue courte (F): *Myrmia micrura*
Colibri à queue en ciseaux (F): *Hylonympha macrocerca*
Colibri à queue large (F): *Selasphorus platycercus*
Colibri à queue mi-blanche (F): *Phlogophilus hemileucurus*
Colibri à queue singulière (F): *Doricha enicura*
Colibri à queue verte (F): *Leucippus chlorocercus*

Checklist of fauna/Lista de especies de fauna/Liste des espèces animales

Colibri à sous-caudales rousses (F): *Urosticte ruficrissa*
Colibri à tête bleue (F): *Cyanophaia bicolor*
Colibri à tête cuivrée (F): *Elvira cupreiceps*
Colibri à tête noire (F): *Trochilus polytmus*
Colibri à tête rose (F): *Anthocephala floriceps*
Colibri à tête violette (F): *Klais guimeti*
Colibri à ventre blanc (F): *Colibri serrirostris*
Colibri à ventre châtain (F): *Lampornis castaneoventris*
Colibri à ventre noir (F): *Eupherusa nigriventris*
Colibri abejorro (S): *Chaetocercus bombus*
Colibri adèle (F): *Oreotrochilus adela*
Colibrí admirable (S): *Loddigesia mirabilis*
Colibrí aliazul (S): *Pterophanes cyanopterus*
Colibri alicastaño (S): *Lamprolaima rhami*
Colibrí amatista (S): *Calliphlox amethystina*
Colibrí amatistino (S): *Lampornis amethystinus*
Colibri améthyste (F): *Calliphlox amethystina*
Colibri anaïs (F): *Colibri coruscans*
Colibri ante (S): *Leucippus fallax*
Colibri anteado (S): *Leucippus fallax*
Colibrí apagado (S): *Campylopterus cirrochloris*
Colibri ardent (F): *Selasphorus ardens*
Colibrí ardiente (S): *Selasphorus ardens*
Colibrí astral (S): *Chaetocercus astreans*
Colibrí aterciopelado (S): *Lafresnaya lafresnayi*
Colibrí austral (S): *Sephanoides sephaniodes*
Colibri aux huppes d'or (F): *Heliactin bilopha*
Colibri avocette (F): *Anthracothorax recurvirostris*
Colibri avocettin (F): *Opisthoprora euryptera*
Colibrí barbiesmeralda (S): *Abeillia abeillei*
Colibrí barbinegro (S): *Archilochus alexandri*
Colibri bicolor (S): *Cyanophaia bicolor*
Colibrí blancioliva (S): *Leucippus chlorocercus*
Colibrí blanquiverde (S): *Leucippus viridicauda*
Colibrí bonito (S): *Calothorax pulcher*
Colibri bourdon (F): *Chaetocercus bombus*
Colibrí cabeciazul (S): *Klais guimeti*
Colibrí cabecidorado (S): *Boissonneaua flavescens*
Colibrí cabecivioleta (S): *Klais guimeti*
Colibrí calíope (S): *Stellula calliope*
Colibrí calliope (F): *Stellula calliope*
Colibrí canelo (S): *Amazilia rutila*
Colibrí capirrufo (S): *Chalcostigma ruficeps*
Colibrí caribeño gorgimorado (S): *Eulampis jugularis*
Colibrí caribeño gorgiverde (S): *Eulampis holosericeus*
Colibri casqué (F): *Oxypogon guerinii*
Colibrí centelleante (S): *Selasphorus scintilla*
Colibri charmant (F): *Calothorax pulcher*
Colibrí chivito (S): *Oxypogon guerinii*
Colibri circé (F): *Cynanthus latirostris*
Colibrí cobrizo (S): *Aglaeactis cupripennis*
Colibrí cola de hoja (S): *Ocreatus underwoodii*
Colibrí cola de oro (S): *Chrysuronia oenone*
Colibrí colaceleste (S): *Augastes scutatus*
Colibrí coliancho (S): *Selasphorus platycercus*
Colibrí coliazul (S): *Saucerottia cyanura*
Colibrí coliblanco (S): *Campylopterus ensipennis*
Colibrí colibronce (S): *Polyonymus caroli*
Colibrí colicorto (S): *Myrmia micrura*
Colibrí colihabano (S): *Boissonneaua flavescens*
Colibrí colilargo mayor (S): *Lesbia victoriae*
Colibrí colilargo menor (S): *Lesbia nuna*
Colibrí colipinto Ecuatoriano (S): *Phlogophilus hemileucurus*
Colibrí colipinto Peruano (S): *Phlogophilus harterti*
Colibrí colirraro (S): *Doricha enicura*
Colibrí colirrayado (S): *Eupherusa eximia*
Colibrí colirrojo (S): *Clytolaema rubricauda*
Colibrí colirrufo (S): *Amazilia tzacatl*
Colibrí colpinto (S): *Tilmatura dupontii*
Colibrí coludo azul (S): *Aglaiocercus kingi*
Colibrí coludo verde (S): *Lesbia nuna*
Colibrí cometa (S): *Sappho sparganura*
Colibrí comète (F): *Taphrolesbia griseiventris*
Colibrí condecorado (S): *Aglaeactis castelnaudii*

Colibrí copetón (S): *Stephanoxis lalandi*
Colibri cora (F): *Thaumastura cora*
Colibri cora (S): *Thaumastura cora*
Colibrí cordillerano (S): *Oreotrochilus leucopleurus*
Colibri corinne (F): *Heliomaster longirostris*
Colibrí cornudito (S): *Heliactin bilopha*
Colibrí corona-verde (S): *Agyrtria viridifrons*
Colibrí corona-violeta (S): *Agyrtria violiceps*
Colibrí coroniazul (S): *Agyrtria cyanocephala*
Colibrí coroniblanco (S): *Microchera albocoronata*
Colibri coruscans : (E) Sparkling Violet-ear, (S) Colibrí orejivioleta grande, Colibrí rutilante, Picaflor ventriazul, (F) Colibri anaïs, II TROCHILIDAE Av
Colibrí crestado (S): *Orthorhyncus cristatus*
Colibrí cuellicastaño (S): *Heliodoxa aurescens*
Colibri d'Abeillé (F): *Abeillia abeillei*
Colibri d'Alice (F): *Aglaeactis aliciae*
Colibri d'Allen (F): *Selasphorus sasin*
Colibri d'Angèle (F): *Heliomaster furcifer*
Colibri d'Anna (F): *Calypte anna*
Colibri d'Arica (F): *Myrtis yarrellii*
Colibrí de Alicia (S): *Aglaeactis aliciae*
Colibrí de Allen (S): *Selasphorus sasin*
Colibrí de Anna (S): *Calypte anna*
Colibrí de Arica (S): *Myrtis yarrellii*
Colibrí de Barbijo (S): *Heliomaster furcifer*
Colibri de Benjamin (F): *Urosticte benjamini*
Colibrí de Berilo (S): *Saucerottia beryllina*
Colibrí de Berlepsch (F): *Chaetocercus berlepschi*
Colibri de Bouguer (F): *Urochroa bougueri*
Colibrí de Bouguer (S): *Urochroa bougueri*
Colibri de Bourcier (F): *Polyonymus caroli*
Colibri de Buffon (F): *Chalybura buffonii*
Colibrí de Buffon (S): *Chalybura buffonii*
Colibri de Burmeister (F): *Microstilbon burmeisteri*
Colibrí de Burmeister (S): *Microstilbon burmeisteri*
Colibri de Castelneau (F): *Aglaeactis castelnaudii*
Colibrí de Cochabamba (S): *Oreotrochilus adela*
Colibri de Constant (F): *Heliomaster constantii*
Colibri de Costa (F): *Calypte costae*
Colibrí de Costa (S): *Calypte costae*
Colibri de Cuvier (F): *Campylopterus cuvierii*
Colibrí de Cuvier (S): *Campylopterus cuvierii*
Colibri de Delalande (F): *Stephanoxis lalandi*
Colibri de Delphine (F): *Colibri delphinae*
Colibri de Dohrn (F): *Glaucis dohrnii*
Colibrí de Dupont (S): *Tilmatura dupontii*
Colibrí de Elisa (S): *Doricha eliza*
Colibrí de Elliot (S): *Atthis ellioti*
Colibrí de Eloísa (S): *Atthis heloisa*
Colibrí de Esmeraldas (S): *Chaetocercus berlepschi*
Colibri de Geoffroy (F): *Augastes geoffroyi*
Colibrí de Goldman (S): *Goldmania violiceps*
Colibri de Goudot (F): *Lepidopyga goudoti*
Colibrí de Goudot (S): *Lepidopyga goudoti*
Colibrí de Guerrero (S): *Eupherusa poliocerca*
Colibri de Hartert (F): *Phlogophilus harterti*
Colibrí de Herrán (S): *Chalcostigma herrani*
Colibri de Jardine (F): *Boissonneaua jardini*
Colibri de Jourdan (F): *Chaetocercus jourdanii*
Colibrí de Jourdan (S): *Chaetocercus jourdanii*
Colibrí de Juan Fernández (S): *Sephanoides fernandensis*
Colibrí de Julia (S): *Damophila julie*
Colibri de Lafresnaye (F): *Lafresnaya lafresnayi*
Colibrí de las Bahamas (S): *Calliphlox evelynae*
Colibri de Lillian (F): *Lepidopyga lilliae*
Colibrí de Marte (S): *Heliangelus mavors*
Colibri de Matthews (F): *Boissonneaua matthewsii*
Colibri de Mitchell (F): *Calliphlox mitchellii*
Colibrí de Mitchell (S): *Calliphlox mitchellii*
Colibri de Mulsant (F): *Chaetocercus mulsant*
Colibrí de Mulsant (S): *Chaetocercus mulsant*
Colibrí de Perijá (S): *Metallura iracunda*
Colibrí de pico recurvado (S): *Glaucis dohrnii*
Colibrí de raquetas (S): *Ocreatus underwoodii*

Checklist of fauna/Lista de especies de fauna/Liste des espèces animales

Colibri de Rivoli (F): *Eugenes fulgens*
Colibrí de Santa Marta (S): *Campylopterus phainopeplus*
Colibrí de Sibila (S): *Lampornis sybillae*
Colibrí de Stanley (S): *Chalcostigma stanleyi*
Colibri de Sybil (F): *Lampornis sybillae*
Colibri de Taczanowski (F): *Leucippus taczanowskii*
Colibrí de Taczanowski (S): *Leucippus taczanowskii*
Colibrí de tepui (S): *Polytmus milleri*
Colibrí de Teresa (S): *Polytmus theresiae*
Colibri de Tumbes (F): *Leucippus baeri*
Colibrí de Tumbes (S): *Leucippus baeri*
Colibrí de Xantus (S): *Basilinna xantusii*
Colibrí del Atacama (S): *Rhodopis vesper*
Colibrí del Chimborazo (S): *Oreotrochilus chimborazo*
Colibrí del Duida (S): *Campylopterus duidae*
Colibrí del Napo (S): *Campylopterus villaviscensio*
Colibrí del Pirre (S): *Goethalsia bella*
Colibri d'Elliot (F): *Atthis ellioti*
Colibri delphinae : (E) Brown Violet-ear, (S) Colibrí
    pardo, Orejavioleta café, Orejivioleta marrón, (F)
    Colibri de Delphine, II TROCHILIDAE Av
Colibri demi-deuil (F): *Florisuga fusca*
Colibri d'Équateur (F): *Androdon aequatorialis*
Colibri des Bahamas (F): *Calliphlox evelynae*
Colibri des Santa Marta (F): *Chaetocercus astreans*
Colibri des tépuis (F): *Polytmus milleri*
Colibri d'Helen (F): *Mellisuga helenae*
Colibri d'Oaxaca (F): *Eupherusa cyanophrys*
Colibri du Chili (F): *Sephanoides sephaniodes*
Colibri du Chimborazo (F): *Oreotrochilus chimborazo*
Colibri du Guerrero (F): *Eupherusa poliocerca*
Colibri du Pirré (F): *Goethalsia bella*
Colibri élise (F): *Doricha eliza*
Colibri elvire (F): *Elvira chionura*
Colibri escamoso (S): *Heliomaster squamosus*
Colibri estelle (F): *Oreotrochilus estella*
Colibri estrella picolargo (S): *Heliomaster longirostris*
Colibri étincelant (F): *Aglaeactis cupripennis*
Colibri falle-vert (F): *Eulampis holosericeus*
Colibri fanny (F): *Myrtis fanny*
Colibri faux-saphir (F): *Lepidopyga coeruleogularis*
Colibri féérique (F): *Heliothryx barroti*
Colibri flammule (F): *Selasphorus flammula*
Colibri flavescent (F): *Boissonneaua flavescens*
Colibrí florido (S): *Anthocephala floriceps*
Colibrí frentiverde (S): *Heliodoxa xanthogonys*
Colibrí gargantidorado (S): *Polytmus guainumbi*
Colibrí gargantilla (S): *Leucochloris albicollis*
Colibri géant (F): *Patagona gigas*
Colibrí gigante (S): *Patagona gigas*
Colibrí golondrina (S): *Campylopterus macrourus*
Colibrí gorgiamatista (S): *Heliangelus amethysticollis*
Colibrí gorgiazul (S): *Lampornis clemenciae*
Colibrí gorgiescamoso (S): *Lampornis viridipallens*
Colibrí gorgirrubí (S): *Archilochus alexandri*
Colibrí gorgivioleta (S): *Lampornis hemileucus*
Colibrí gorgizafiro (S): *Lepidopyga coeruleogularis*
Colibrí gorjirrubí (S): *Archilochus colubris*
Colibri grande colinegro (S): *Chalybura buffonii*
Colibri grivelé (F): *Leucippus hypostictus*
Colibri guaïnumbi (F): *Polytmus guainumbi*
Colibrí guainumbí (S): *Polytmus guainumbi*
Colibrí guerrerense (S): *Eupherusa poliocerca*
Colibrí hada occidental (S): *Heliothryx barroti*
Colibrí hada orejazul (S): *Heliothryx aurita*
Colibrí hada oriental (S): *Heliothryx aurita*
Colibri héliodore (F): *Chaetocercus heliodor*
Colibrí heliodoro (S): *Chaetocercus heliodor*
Colibri héloïse (F): *Atthis heloisa*
Colibri hirondelle (F): *Campylopterus macrourus*
Colibri huppé (F): *Orthorhyncus cristatus*
Colibrí inca acollarado (S): *Coeligena torquata*
Colibrí inca bronceado (S): *Coeligena coeligena*
Colibrí inca dorado (S): *Coeligena bonapartei*
Colibrí inca ventrivioleta (S): *Coeligena helianthea*

Colibri insigne (F): *Panterpe insignis*
Colibrí insigne (S): *Panterpe insignis*
Colibri jacobin (F): *Florisuga mellivora*
Colibrí jaspeado (S): *Adelomyia melanogenys*
Colibri julie (F): *Damophila julie*
Colibri lacero (S): *Heliangelus micraster*
Colibri lazulita (S): *Campylopterus falcatus*
Colibri lucifer (F): *Calothorax lucifer*
Colibri lucifer (S): *Calothorax lucifer*
Colibri lumachelle (F): *Augastes lumachella*
Colibri lumaquela (S): *Augastes lumachella*
Colibri madère (F): *Eulampis jugularis*
Colibri magenta (F): *Calliphlox bryantae*
Colibri magenta (S): *Calliphlox bryantae*
Colibrí magnífico (S): *Eugenes fulgens*
Colibri médiastin (F): *Heliomaster squamosus*
Colibrí morado (S): *Campylopterus hemileucurus*
Colibrí moteado (S): *Leucippus hypostictus*
Colibri moucheté (F): *Adelomyia melanogenys*
Colibrí multipunteado (S): *Leucippus hypostictus*
Colibrí myrtis (S): *Myrtis fanny*
Colibri nain (F): *Mellisuga minima*
Colibrí negrito (S): *Aglaeactis pamela*
Colibrí negro (S): *Florisuga fusca*
Colibri noble (F): *Oreonympha nobilis*
Colibrí noble (S): *Oreonympha nobilis*
Colibrí nuquiblanco (S): *Florisuga mellivora*
Colibrí Oaxaqueño (S): *Eupherusa cyanophrys*
Colibrí oliváceo (S): *Chalcostigma olivaceum*
Colibrí olivipunteado (S): *Leucippus chlorocercus*
Colibri oreillard (F): *Heliothryx aurita*
Colibrí orejiblanco (S): *Basilinna leucotis*
Colibrí orejimorado (S): *Colibri serrirostris*
Colibrí orejivioleta grande (S): *Colibri coruscans*
Colibrí orejivioleta verde (S): *Colibri thalassinus*
Colibri paméla (F): *Aglaeactis pamela*
Colibrí pantalón cobrizo (S): *Eriocnemis cupreoventris*
Colibrí pantalón verde (S): *Eriocnemis vestitus*
Colibrí pardo (S): *Colibri delphinae*
Colibrí patirrojo (S): *Chalybura urochrysia*
Colibrí pechiazul (S): *Sternoclyta cyanopectus*
Colibrí pechigrís (S): *Campylopterus largipennis*
Colibrí pechinegro (S): *Oreotrochilus melanogaster*
Colibrí pechirrojo (S): *Boissonneaua matthewsii*
Colibrí pecho canela (S): *Glaucis hirsuta*
Colibrí pectoral (S): *Heliangelus strophianus*
Colibrí pico de cuña (S): *Augastes geoffroyi*
Colibrí pico espina (S): *Ramphomicron microrhynchum*
Colibrí pico lezna (S): *Anthracothorax recurvirostris*
Colibrí picocuña (S): *Augastes geoffroyi*
Colibrí picoespada (S): *Ensifera ensifera*
Colibrí picoespina (S): *Chalcostigma heteropogon*
Colibrí picolanza mayor (S): *Doryfera ludovicae*
Colibrí picolanza menor (S): *Doryfera johannae*
Colibrí picolezna (S): *Opisthoprora euryptera*
Colibrí picosierra chico (S): *Glaucis dohrnii*
Colibrí piquiancho (S): *Cynanthus latirostris*
Colibrí piquiavoceta (S): *Opisthoprora euryptera*
Colibrí piquicorto común (S): *Ramphomicron
    microrhynchum*
Colibrí piquicorto dorsinegro (S): *Ramphomicron dorsale*
Colibrí piquicunna (S): *Augastes geoffroyi*
Colibrí piquidentado (S): *Androdon aequatorialis*
Colibrí piquilargo (S): *Heliomaster longirostris*
Colibrí pochotero (S): *Heliomaster constantii*
Colibrí portacintas (S): *Trochilus polytmus*
Colibrí portacintas piquinegro (S): *Trochilus scitulus*
Colibri porte-épée (F): *Ensifera ensifera*
Colibrí prieto (S): *Cynanthus sordidus*
Colibrí puneño (S): *Oreotrochilus estella*
Colibrí puntablanca occidental (S): *Urosticte benjamini*
Colibrí puntablanca oriental (S): *Urosticte ruficrissa*
Colibrí real (S): *Heliangelus regalis*
Colibri robinson (F): *Sephanoides fernandensis*
Colibrí rojizo Mexicano (S): *Campylopterus rufus*

Colibrí rojizo Venezolano (S): *Campylopterus hyperythrus*
Colibri roux (F): *Selasphorus rufus*
Colibrí rubí (S): *Chrysolampis mosquitus*
Colibri rubis-émeraude (F): *Clytolaema rubricauda*
Colibri rubis-topaze (F): *Chrysolampis mosquitus*
Colibri rufo (S): *Selasphorus rufus*
Colibri ruiseñor (S): *Campylopterus curvipennis*
Colibri rutilante (S): *Colibri coruscans*
Colibri sapho (F): *Sappho sparganura*
Colibri scintillant (F): *Selasphorus scintilla*
Colibrí serrano gargantiazul (S): *Adelomyia melanogenys*
Colibri serrirostris : (E) White-vented Violet-ear, (S) Colibrí orejimorado, Picaflor ventriverde, (F) Colibri à ventre blanc, II TROCHILIDAE Av
Colibri sietecolores (S): *Boissonneaua jardini*
Colibri sombre (F): *Cynanthus sordidus*
Colibri superbe (F): *Augastes scutatus*
Colibri tacheté (F): *Ramphodon naevius*
Colibri terciopelo (S): *Lafresnaya lafresnayi*
Colibri thalassin (F): *Colibri thalassinus*
Colibri thalassinus : (E) Green Violet-ear, (S) Colibrí orejivioleta verde, Colibrí verdemar, Picaflor orejiazul, (F) Colibri thalassin, II TROCHILIDAE Av
Colibri tijereta (S): *Hylonympha macrocerca*
Colibri topacio (S): *Topaza pella*
Colibri topaze (F): *Topaza pella*
Colibri tout-vert (F): *Polytmus theresiae*
Colibri trompeur (F): *Leucippus fallax*
Colibrí turmalina (S): *Heliangelus exortis*
Colibrí variable (S): *Lampornis castaneoventris*
Colibrí ventigrís (S): *Taphrolesbia griseiventris*
Colibrí ventrinegro (S): *Eupherusa nigriventris*
Colibrí ventriníveo (S): *Leucippus chionogaster*
Colibrí ventrivioleta (S): *Damophila julie*
Colibrí ventrizafiro (S): *Lepidopyga lilliae*
Colibrí verde colirrojo (S): *Metallura tyrianthina*
Colibrí verdecito (S): *Chlorostilbon notatus*
Colibrí verdemar (S): *Colibri thalassinus*
Colibri vert et gris (F): *Campylopterus cirrochloris*
Colibri vert-d'eau (F): *Lampornis viridipallens*
Colibri vesper (F): *Rhodopis vesper*
Colibrí vientre-canelo (S): *Amazilia yucatanensis*
Colibrí violeta (S): *Heliangelus viola*
Colibrí volcanero (S): *Selasphorus flammula*
Colibri zémès (F): *Tilmatura dupontii*
Colibrí zumbadorcito (S): *Mellisuga minima*
Colibrí zunzuncito (S): *Mellisuga helenae*
Colibries (S): TROCHILIDAE spp.
Colibris (F): TROCHILIDAE spp.
Colibrí-serrano gorjiamatisto (S): *Lampornis amethystinus*
Colibrí-serrano gorjiazul (S): *Lampornis clemenciae*
Colibrí-serrano gorjiverde (S): *Lampornis viridipallens*
Colibrí-serrano pechiverde (S): *Lampornis sybillae*
Colin de Ridgway (F): *Colinus virginianus ridgwayi*
Colin de Virginie masqué (F): *Colinus virginianus ridgwayi*
Colín virginiano de Ridgway (S): *Colinus virginianus ridgwayi*
Colinus virginianus ridgwayi : (E) Masked Bobwhite, (S) Colín virginiano de Ridgway, (F) Colin de Ridgway, Colin de Virginie masqué, I PHASIANIDAE Av
Coliuspasser ardens = Euplectes ardens
Coliuspasser macrourus = Euplectes macrourus
Collared Falconet (E): *Microhierax caerulescens*
Collared Fishing Hawk (E): *Busarellus nigricollis*
Collared Forest-Falcon (E): *Micrastur semitorquatus*
Collared Inca (E): *Coeligena torquata*
Collared Lory (E): *Phigys solitarius*
Collared Mangabey (E): *Cercocebus torquatus*
Collared Owlet (E): *Glaucidium brodiei*
Collared Peccary (E): *Pecari tajacu*
Collared Pygmy-Owl (E): *Glaucidium brodiei*
Collared Scops-Owl (E): *Otus bakkamoena*
Collared Sparrowhawk (E): *Accipiter cirrocephalus*
Collared Titi (E): *Callicebus torquatus*

Collins's Poison Frog (E): *Minyobates abditus*
Colobe (F): *Colobus angolensis*
Colobe à camail (F): *Colobus polykomos*
Colobe à épaules blanches (F): *Colobus guereza*
Colobe à huppé (F): *Procolobus verus*
Colobe à longs poils (F): *Colobus polykomos*
Colobe bai (F): *Procolobus badius/ Procolobus pennantii*
Colobe bai d'Afrique occidentale (F): *Procolobus badius*
Colobe bai de la Tana (F): *Procolobus rufomitratus*
Colobe bai de Zanzibar (F): *Procolobus pennantii kirkii*
Colobe bai du Cameroun (F): *Procolobus preussi*
Colobe blanc et noir d'Afrique occidentale (F): *Colobus polykomos*
Colobe de l'Abyssinie (F): *Colobus guereza*
Colobe de Van Beneden (F): *Procolobus verus*
Colobe ferrugineux (F): *Procolobus badius*
Colobe guéréza (F): *Colobus guereza*
Colobe magistrat (F): *Colobus polykomos*
Colobe roux de la Tana (F): *Procolobus rufomitratus*
Colobe vert (F): *Procolobus verus*
Colobe vrai (F): *Procolobus verus*
Colobo blanco y negro de Africa occidental (S): *Colobus polykomos*
Colobo de Tana (S): *Procolobus rufomitratus*
Colobo herrumbroso occidental (S): *Procolobus badius*
Colobo negro (S): *Colobus satanas*
Colobo rojo (S): *Procolobus pennantii*
Colobo rojo de Camerún (S): *Procolobus preussi*
Colobo rojo de Zanzíbar (S): *Procolobus pennantii kirkii*
Colobo rojo guereza (S): *Colobus guereza*
Colobo rojo mitrado (S): *Procolobus rufomitratus*
Colobo verde (S): *Procolobus verus*
Colobus abyssinicus = Colobus guereza
Colobus angolensis : (E) Angola Pied Colobus, Angolan Black-and-white Colobus, Angolan Colobus, (F) Colobe II CERCOPITHECIDAE Ma
Colobus badius = Procolobus badius
Colobus badius ssp. *kirkii = Procolobus pennantii* ssp. *kirkii*
Colobus badius ssp. *preussi = Procolobus preussi*
Colobus guereza : (E) Eastern Black-and-white Colobus, Guereza, Magistrate Colobus, (S) Colobo rojo guereza, (F) Colobe à épaules blanches, Colobe de l'Abyssinie, Colobe guéréza, II CERCOPITHECIDAE Ma
Colobus pennantii = Procolobus pennantii
Colobus polykomos : (E) King Colobus, Western Black-and-white Colobus, Western Pied Colobus, (S) Colobo blanco y negro de Africa occidental, (F) Colobe à camail, Colobe à longs poils, Colobe blanc et noir d'Afrique occidentale, Colobe magistrat, II CERCOPITHECIDAE Ma
Colobus preussi = Procolobus preussi
Colobus rufomitratus = Procolobus rufomitratus
Colobus satanas : (E) Black Colobus, (S) Colobo negro II CERCOPITHECIDAE Ma
Colobus vellerosus = Colobus polykomos
Colobus verus = Procolobus verus
Colombar à front nu (F): *Treron calva*
Colombar waalia (F): *Treron waalia*
Colombe poignardée (F): *Gallicolumba luzonica*
Colombian Screech-Owl (E): *Otus ingens*
Colophon spp.: (E) Cape stag beetles III LUCANIDAE In
Colophon barnardi : III LUCANIDAE In
Colophon berrisfordi : III LUCANIDAE In
Colophon cameroni : III LUCANIDAE In
Colophon cassoni : III LUCANIDAE In
Colophon eastmani : III LUCANIDAE In
Colophon haughtoni : III LUCANIDAE In
Colophon izardi : III LUCANIDAE In
Colophon montisatris : III LUCANIDAE In
Colophon neli : III LUCANIDAE In
Colophon oweni : III LUCANIDAE In
Colophon primosi : III LUCANIDAE In
Colophon stokoei : III LUCANIDAE In

Colophon thunbergi : **III** LUCANIDAE In
Colophon westwoodi : **III** LUCANIDAE In
Colophon whitei : **III** LUCANIDAE In
Colorful Puffleg (E): *Eriocnemis mirabilis*
Colostethus festae = Epipedobates parvulus
Coloured Seahorse (E): *Hippocampus kuda*
Colourful Puffleg (E): *Eriocnemis mirabilis*
Colpeo Fox (E): *Pseudalopex culpaeus*
Colpophyllia amaranthus : **II** FAVIIDAE An
Colpophyllia breviserialis : **II** FAVIIDAE An
Colpophyllia natans : (E) Boulder Brain Coral **II** FAVIIDAE An
Coluber mucosus = Ptyas mucosus
Columba guinea : (E) Speckled Pigeon, Speckled Rock Pigeon, Triangular-spotted Pigeon, (S) Paloma de Guinea, (F) Pigeon de Guinée, Pigeon roussard, **III** COLUMBIDAE Av
Columba iriditorques : (E) Western Bronze-naped Pigeon, (S) Paloma nuquibronceada, (F) Pigeon à nuque bronzée, **III** COLUMBIDAE Av
Columba livia : (E) Common Pigeon, Feral Pigeon, Rock Dove, Rock Pigeon, (S) Paloma Bravía, Paloma Doméstica, (F) Pigeon biset, Pigeon domestique, **III** COLUMBIDAE Av
Columba mayeri : (E) Pink Pigeon, (S) Paloma de Mauricio, (F) Pigeon rose, **III** COLUMBIDAE Av
Columba unicincta : (E) Afep Pigeon, African Wood-Pigeon, Grey Wood-Pigeon, (S) Paloma afep, Paloma del Congo, (F) Pigeon gris, Pigeon gris écailleux, **III** COLUMBIDAE Av
Columbia Sturgeon (E): *Acipenser transmontanus*
Comadreja de montaña (S): *Mustela altaica*
Comadreja de Siberia (S): *Mustela sibirica*
Comadreja de vientre amarillo (S): *Mustela kathiah*
Comb Duck (E): *Sarkidiornis melanotos*
Combassou de Baka (F): *Vidua larvaticola*
Combassou de Jambandu (F): *Vidua raricola*
Combassou de Wilson (F): *Vidua wilsoni*
Combassou du Sénégal (F): *Vidua chalybeata*
Combassou noir (F): *Vidua wilsoni*
Commandeur huppé (F): *Gubernatrix cristata*
Commerson's Dolphin (E): *Cephalorhynchus commersonii*
Common Barn-Owl (E): *Tyto alba*
Common Batagur (E): *Batagur baska*
Common Bay-Owl (E): *Phodilus badius*
Common Birdwing (E): *Ornithoptera priamus/ Troides helena*
Common Black-Hawk (E): *Buteogallus anthracinus*
Common Box Turtle (E): *Terrapene carolina*
Common Brain Coral (E): *Diploria labyrinthiformis*
Common Buzzard (E): *Buteo buteo*
Common Caiman (E): *Caiman crocodilus*
Common Caracara (E): *Polyborus plancus*
Common Chachalaca (E): *Ortalis vetula*
Common Chameleon (E): *Chamaeleo chamaeleon*
Common Cock-of-the-Rock (E): *Rupicola rupicola*
Common Crane (E): *Grus grus*
Common Crowned Pigeon (E): *Goura cristata*
Common Cuscus (E): *Phalanger orientalis*
Common Dolphin (E): *Delphinus delphis*
Common Gibbon (E): *Hylobates lar*
Common Girdled Lizard (E): *Cordylus cordylus*
Common Green Birdwing (E): *Ornithoptera priamus*
Common Hill Myna (E): *Gracula religiosa*
Common Iguana (E): *Iguana iguana*
Common Jackal (E): *Canis aureus*
Common Kestrel (E): *Falco tinnunculus*
Common Langur (E): *Semnopithecus entellus*
Common Marmoset (E): *Callithrix jacchus*
Common Monitor (E): *Varanus bengalensis*
Common Otter (E): *Lutra lutra*
Common Palm Civet (E): *Paradoxurus hermaphroditus*
Common Peacock-Pheasant (E): *Polyplectron bicalcaratum*
Common Phalanger (E): *Phalanger orientalis*

Common Pigeon (E): *Columba livia*
Common Pintail (E): *Anas acuta*
Common Porpoise (E): *Phocoena phocoena*
Common Rat Snake (E): *Ptyas mucosus*
Common Rhea (E): *Rhea americana*
Common Rorqual (E): *Balaenoptera physalus*
Common Scaled Water Snake (E): *Xenochrophis piscator*
Common Scops-Owl (E): *Otus scops*
Common Spiny-tailed Lizard (E): *Cordylus cordylus*
Common Spotted Cuscus (E): *Spilocuscus maculatus*
Common Squirrel Monkey (E): *Saimiri sciureus*
Common Sturgeon (E): *Acipenser sturio*
Common Teal (E): *Anas crecca*
Common Tegu (E): *Tupinambis teguixin*
Common Tortoise (E): *Kinixys erosa/ Testudo graeca*
Common Tree Monitor (E): *Varanus varius*
Common Water Monitor (E): *Varanus salvator*
Common Waxbill (E): *Estrilda astrild*
Common Wolf (E): *Canis lupus*
Common Woolly Monkey (E): *Lagothrix lagotricha*
Common Zorro (E): *Cerdocyon thous*
Comoro Black Flying-fox (E): *Pteropus livingstonei*
Comoro Day Gecko (E): *Phelsuma comorensis*
Comoro Islands Chameleon (E): *Furcifer cephalolepis*
Comoro Scops-Owl (E): *Otus pauliani*
Compact Ivory Bush Coral (E): *Oculina arbuscula*
Compact Weaver (E): *Pachyphantes superciliosus*
Concave-casqued Hornbill (E): *Buceros bicornis*
Concentrotheca laevigata : **II** CARYOPHYLLIIDAE An
Concentrotheca vaughani : **II** CARYOPHYLLIIDAE An
Concha reina del Caribe (S): *Strombus gigas*
Conchodromus dromas = Dromus dromas
Cóndor (S): *Vultur gryphus*
Cóndor andino (S): *Vultur gryphus*
Cóndor californiano (S): *Gymnogyps californianus*
Cóndor de California (S): *Gymnogyps californianus*
Condor de Californie (F): *Gymnogyps californianus*
Cóndor de los Andes (S): *Vultur gryphus*
Condor des Andes (F): *Vultur gryphus*
Conejo de Assam (S): *Caprolagus hispidus*
Conejo de Díaz (S): *Romerolagus diazi*
Conejo de los volcanes (S): *Romerolagus diazi*
Conepatus castaneus = Conepatus humboldtii
Conepatus humboldtii : (E) Humboldt's Hog-nosed Skunk, Patagonian Hog-nosed Skunk, (S) Anas, Chingue de la Patagonia, Mofeta de Patagonia, Zorrillo, Zorrino de la Patagonia, (F) Moufette à nez de cochon, Moufette de Patagonie, **II** MUSTELIDAE Ma
Confluphyllia juncta : **II** CARYOPHYLLIIDAE An
Confusing Poison Frog (S): *Epipedobates maculatus*
Congo Bay-Owl (E): *Phodilus prigoginei*
Congo Blind Barb (E): *Caecobarbus geertsi*
Congo Clawless Otter (E): *Aonyx congicus*
Congo Serpent-Eagle (E): *Dryotriorchis spectabilis*
Conocyathus compressus = Platytrochus compressus
Conocyathus gracilis : **II** TURBINOLIIDAE An
Conocyathus zelandiae : **II** TURBINOLIIDAE An
Conolophes (F): *Conolophus* spp.
Conolophus spp.: (E) Land iguanas, (S) Iguanas terrestres, (F) Conolophes, Iguanes terrestres, Iguanes terrestres des Galapagos, **II** IGUANIDAE Re
Conolophus pallidus : (E) Barrington Land Iguana, Santa Fe Land Iguana, (S) Iguana terrestre de Barrington, (F) Iguane terrestre de l'île Santa Fe, **II** IGUANIDAE Re
Conolophus subcristatus : (E) Galapagos Land Iguana, (S) Iguana terrestre de las Galápagos, (F) Iguane terrestre des Galapagos, **II** IGUANIDAE Re
Conondale Gastric-brooding Frog (E): *Rheobatrachus silus*
Conopora adeta : **II** STYLASTERIDAE Hy
Conopora anthohelia : **II** STYLASTERIDAE Hy
Conopora candelabrum : **II** STYLASTERIDAE Hy
Conopora dura : **II** STYLASTERIDAE Hy
Conopora gigantea : **II** STYLASTERIDAE Hy

Conopora laevis : **II** STYLASTERIDAE Hy
Conopora major = Conopora verrucosa
Conopora tetrastichopora : **II** STYLASTERIDAE Hy
Conopora unifacialis : **II** STYLASTERIDAE Hy
Conopora verrucosa : **II** STYLASTERIDAE Hy
Conotrochus asymmetros : **II** CARYOPHYLLIIDAE An
Conotrochus brunneus : **II** CARYOPHYLLIIDAE An
Conotrochus funicolumna : **II** CARYOPHYLLIIDAE An
Conradilla caelata : (E) Birdwing Pearly Mussel, Rimose Naiad **I** UNIONIDAE Bi
Constrictor constrictor = Boa constrictor
Constrictor constrictor ssp. *occidentalis = Boa constrictor* ssp. *occidentalis*
Conure à cape noire (F): *Pyrrhura rupicola*
Conure à col blanc (F): *Pyrrhura albipectus*
Conure à front brun (F): *Rhynchopsitta terrisi*
Conure à front rouge (F): *Aratinga canicularis*
Conure à gorge bleue (F): *Pyrrhura cruentata*
Conure à gorge rouge (F): *Aratinga rubritorquis*
Conure à gros bec (F): *Rhynchopsitta pachyrhyncha*
Conure à joues d'or (F): *Ognorhynchus icterotis*
Conure à long bec (F): *Enicognathus leptorhynchus*
Conure à oreilles jaunes (F): *Ognorhynchus icterotis*
Conure à oreillons (F): *Pyrrhura hoematotis*
Conure à pinceaux d'or (F): *Leptosittaca branickii*
Conure à poitrine brune (F): *Pyrrhura calliptera*
Conure à tête bleue (F): *Aratinga acuticaudata*
Conure à tête d'or (F): *Aratinga auricapilla*
Conure à tête rouge (F): *Aratinga erythrogenys*
Conure à ventre rouge (F): *Pyrrhura perlata*
Conure aile-de-feu (F): *Pyrrhura egregia*
Conure aztèque (F): *Aratinga nana*
Conure couronnée (F): *Aratinga aurea*
Conure cuivrée (F): *Aratinga pertinax*
Conure de Cuba (F): *Aratinga euops*
Conure de Deville (F): *Pyrrhura devillei*
Conure de Finsch (F): *Aratinga finschi*
Conure de Hoffmann (F): *Pyrrhura hoffmanni*
Conure de la Reine de Bavière (F): *Guarouba guarouba*
Conure de Molina (F): *Pyrrhura molinae*
Conure de Patagonie (F): *Cyanoliseus patagonus*
Conure de Socorro (F): *Aratinga brevipes*
Conure de Souancé (F): *Pyrrhura melanura*
Conure de Vieillot (F): *Pyrrhura frontalis*
Conure de Wagler (F): *Aratinga wagleri*
Conure de Weddell (F): *Aratinga weddellii*
Conure des cactus (F): *Aratinga cactorum*
Conure des rochers (F): *Myiopsitta luchsi*
Conure des Santa Marta (F): *Pyrrhura viridicata*
Conure d'Orcès (F): *Pyrrhura orcesi*
Conure dorée (F): *Guarouba guarouba*
Conure emma (F): *Pyrrhura leucotis*
Conure jandaya (F): *Aratinga jandaya*
Conure magellanique (F): *Enicognathus ferrugineus*
Conure maîtresse (F): *Aratinga chloroptera*
Conure mitrée (F): *Aratinga mitrata*
Conure nanday (F): *Nandayus nenday*
Conure pavouane (F): *Aratinga leucophthalmus*
Conure perlée (F): *Pyrrhura lepida*
Conure soleil (F): *Aratinga solstitialis*
Conure tête-de-feu (F): *Pyrrhura rhodocephala*
Conure tiriba (F): *Pyrrhura cruentata*
Conure versicolore (F): *Pyrrhura picta*
Conure verte (F): *Aratinga holochlora*
Conure veuve (F): *Myiopsitta monachus*
Cook Strait Tuatara (E): *Sphenodon punctatus*
Cook's Tree Boa (E): *Corallus hortulanus*
Cooper's Hawk (E): *Accipiter cooperii*
Copper-rumped Hummingbird (E): *Saucerottia tobaci*
Copper-tailed Hummingbird (E): *Saucerottia cupreicauda*
Coppery Emerald (E): *Chlorostilbon russatus*
Coppery Metaltail (E): *Metallura theresiae*
Coppery Thorntail (E): *Discosura letitiae*
Coppery-bellied Puffleg (E): *Eriocnemis cupreoventris*
Coppery-headed Emerald (E): *Elvira cupreiceps*

Coppery-naped Puffleg (E): *Eriocnemis sapphiropygia*
Coq de Bois (F): *Terpsiphone bourbonnensis*
Coq de Sonnerat (F): *Gallus sonneratii*
Coq-de-roche de Guyane (F): *Rupicola rupicola*
Coq-de-roche orange (F): *Rupicola rupicola*
Coq-de-roche péruvien (F): *Rupicola peruviana*
Coqs-de-roche (F): *Rupicola* spp.
Coquerel's Dwarf Lemur (E): *Microcebus coquereli*
Coquerel's Mouse-lemur (E): *Microcebus coquereli*
Coqueta abanico canela (S): *Lophornis ornatus*
Coqueta abanico pavo real (S): *Lophornis pavoninus*
Coqueta abanico puntiblanco (S): *Lophornis chalybeus*
Coqueta adorable (S): *Lophornis adorabilis*
Coqueta adornada (S): *Lophornis ornatus*
Coqueta cola de Lira (S): *Discosura langsdorffi*
Coqueta cola raqueta (S): *Discosura longicauda*
Coqueta coronada (S): *Lophornis stictolophus*
Coqueta cresticorta (S): *Lophornis brachylophus*
Coqueta crestinegra (S): *Lophornis helenae*
Coqueta crestirrufa (S): *Lophornis delattrei*
Coqueta de Guerrero (S): *Lophornis brachylophus*
Coqueta festiva (S): *Lophornis chalybeus*
Coqueta lentejuelada (S): *Lophornis stictolophus*
Coqueta magnifica (S): *Lophornis magnificus*
Coqueta moteada (S): *Lophornis gouldii*
Coqueta pavonina (S): *Lophornis pavoninus*
Coqueta verde (S): *Lophornis chalybeus*
Coquette à queue fine (F): *Discosura conversii*
Coquette à raquettes (F): *Discosura longicauda*
Coquette adorable (F): *Lophornis adorabilis*
Coquette chalybée (F): *Lophornis chalybeus*
Coquette de Delattre (F): *Lophornis delattrei*
Coquette de Gould (F): *Lophornis gouldii*
Coquette de Langsdorff (F): *Discosura langsdorffi*
Coquette de Létitia (F): *Discosura letitiae*
Coquette de Popelaire (F): *Discosura popelairii*
Coquette d'Hélène (F): *Lophornis helenae*
Coquette du Guerrero (F): *Lophornis brachylophus*
Coquette huppe-col (F): *Lophornis ornatus*
Coquette magnifique (F): *Lophornis magnificus*
Coquette pailletée (F): *Lophornis stictolophus*
Coquette paon (F): *Lophornis pavoninus*
Coracine casquée (F): *Cephalopterus penduliger*
Coracine ornée (F): *Cephalopterus ornatus*
Coracopsis barklyi = Coracopsis nigra
Coracopsis nigra : (E) Black Parrot, (S) Loro negro, (F) Perroquet noir, Perroquet petit vasa, **II** PSITTACIDAE Av
Coracopsis vasa : (E) Vasa Parrot, (S) Loro vasa, (F) Perroquet vaza, Vasa géant, **II** PSITTACIDAE Av
Corail cornes de cerf (F): *Acropora cervicornis*
Corail cornes d'élan (F): *Acropora palmata*
Corail de feu (F): MILLEPORIDAE spp.
Corail limace (F): *Herpolitha limax*
Corail orgue(F): TUBIPORIDAE spp.
Coral anillado (S): *Micrurus diastema*
Corales negros (S): ANTIPATHARIA spp. An
Corallus annulatus : (E) Annulated Tree Boa, (S) Boa arborícola anillada, (F) Boa annelé, Boa arboricole annelé, **II** BOIDAE Re
Corallus caninus : (E) Emerald Tree Boa, (S) Boa esmerelda, (F) Boa canin, Boa émeraude, Faux jacquot, **II** BOIDAE Re
Corallus cookii : **II** BOIDAE Re
Corallus cropanii : (E) Cropan's Boa, (S) Boa costera de Brasil, (F) Boa de Cropan, **II** BOIDAE Re
Corallus enydris = Corallus hortulanus
Corallus grenadensis : **II** BOIDAE Re
Corallus hortulanus : (E) Amazon Tree Boa, Cook's Tree Boa, Garden Tree Boa, (S) Boa arborícola de jardín, (F) Boa arboricole d'Amazonie, Boa de Cook, Boa des jardins, **II** BOIDAE Re
Corallus ruschenbergerii : **II** BOIDAE Re
Coraux champignon (F): *Fungia* spp.
Coraux de feu (F): *Millepora spp.*

Checklist of fauna/Lista de especies de fauna/Liste des espèces animales

Coraux noirs (F): ANTIPATHARIA spp. An
Cordon bleu à joures rouges (F): *Uraeginthus bengalus*
Cordonbleu (E/F): *Uraeginthus bengalus*
Cordonbleu à joues rouges (F): *Uraeginthus bengalus*
Cordyle à larges écailles (F): *Cordylus macropholis*
Cordyle à pustules (F): *Cordylus pustulatus*
Cordyle à taches bleues (F): *Cordylus coeruleopunctatus*
Cordyle africain (F): *Cordylus polyzonus*
Cordyle commun (F): *Cordylus cordylus*
Cordyle d'Armadillo (F): *Cordylus cataphractus*
Cordyle de Campbell (F): *Cordylus campbelli*
Cordyle de Cope (F): *Cordylus tropidosternum*
Cordyle de Hewitt (F): *Cordylus peersi*
Cordyle de Jordan (F): *Cordylus jordani*
Cordyle de Lawrence (F): *Cordylus lawrenci*
Cordyle de McLachlan (F): *Cordylus mclachlani*
Cordyle de Reichenow (F): *Cordylus vittifer*
Cordyle de Rhodésie (F): *Cordylus rhodesianus*
Cordyle de Tasman (F): *Cordylus tasmani*
Cordyle de Warren (F): *Cordylus warreni*
Cordyle d'Oelofsen (F): *Cordylus oelofseni*
Cordyle du Namaqua (F): *Cordylus namaquensis*
Cordyle d'Ukinga (F): *Cordylus ukingensis*
Cordyle géant (F): *Cordylus giganteus*
Cordyle noir (F): *Cordylus niger*
Cordyles (F): *Cordylus* spp.
Cordylus spp.: (E) Crag lizards, Girdled lizards, Spiny-tailed lizards, (S) Falsos lagartos armadillos, Lagartos armadillos, Lézards à fausse ceinture, (F) Cordyles, Lézard épineux d'Afrique australe, Lézards à queue épineuse d'Afrique Australe, Pseudocordyles, II CORDYLIDAE Re
Cordylus angolensis : (E) Angolan Girdled Lizard, Angolan Spiny-tailed Lizard II CORDYLIDAE Re
Cordylus aridus : (E) Dwarf Karoo Girdled Lizard II CORDYLIDAE Re
Cordylus barbertonensis : (E) Barberton Girdled Lizard II CORDYLIDAE Re
Cordylus beraduccii : (E) Maasai Girdled Lizard II CORDYLIDAE Re
Cordylus breyeri : (E) Waterberg Girdled Lizard II CORDYLIDAE Re
Cordylus campbelli : (E) Campbell's Girdled Lizard, Campbell's Spiny-tailed Lizard, (F) Cordyle de Campbell, Lézard à queue épineuse de Campbell II CORDYLIDAE Re
Cordylus capensis : (E) False Girdled Lizard, Graceful Crag Lizard, (S) Falso lagarto armadillo del cabo, (F) Lézard à fausse ceinture du Cap, Pseudocordyle du Cap, II CORDYLIDAE Re
Cordylus cataphractus : (E) Armadillo Girdled Lizard, Armadillo Spiny-tailed Lizard, (F) Cordyle d'Armadillo, Lézard à queue épineuse d'Armadillo II CORDYLIDAE Re
Cordylus cloetei : (E) Cloete's Girdled Lizard II CORDYLIDAE Re
Cordylus coeruleopunctatus : (E) Blue-spotted Girdled Lizard, Blue-spotted Spiny-tailed Lizard, (F) Cordyle à taches bleues, Lézard à queue épineuse à taches bleues II CORDYLIDAE Re
Cordylus cordylus : (E) Cape Girdled Lizard, Common Girdled Lizard, Common Spiny-tailed Lizard, Rough-scaled Girdled Lizard, (F) Cordyle commun, Lézard à queue épineuse commun II CORDYLIDAE Re
Cordylus cordylus ssp. *lawrenci* = *Cordylus lawrenci*
Cordylus cordylus ssp. *minor* = *Cordylus minor*
Cordylus cordylus ssp. *niger* = *Cordylus niger*
Cordylus cordylus ssp. *pustulatus* = *Cordylus pustulatus*
Cordylus cordylus ssp. *rhodesianus* = *Cordylus rhodesianus*
Cordylus cordylus ssp. *tasmani* = *Cordylus tasmani*
Cordylus cordylus ssp. *tropidosternum* = *Cordylus tropidosternum*
Cordylus depressus : (E) Zoutpansberg Girdled Lizard II CORDYLIDAE Re

Cordylus fasciatus : (E) Eastern Cape Crag Lizard II CORDYLIDAE Re
Cordylus giganteus : (E) Giant Girdled Lizard, Giant Spiny-tailed Lizard, Giant Zonure, Sungazer, (F) Cordyle géant, Lézard à queue épineuse géant II CORDYLIDAE Re
Cordylus imkae : (E) Rooiberg Girdled Lizard II CORDYLIDAE Re
Cordylus jonesii : (E) Limpopo Girdled Lizard II CORDYLIDAE Re
Cordylus jordani : (E) Jordan's Girdled Lizard, (F) Cordyle de Jordan, Lézard à queue épineuse de Jordan II CORDYLIDAE Re
Cordylus langi : (E) Lang's Crag Lizard, Lang's Girdled Lizard, (S) Falso lagarto armadillo de Lang, (F) Lézard à fausse ceinture de Lang, Pseudocordyle de Lang, II CORDYLIDAE Re
Cordylus lawrenci : (E) Lawrence's Girdled Lizard, (F) Cordyle de Lawrence, Lézard à queue épineuse de Lawrence II CORDYLIDAE Re
Cordylus machadoi : (E) Machado's Girdled Lizard II CORDYLIDAE Re
Cordylus macropholis : (E) Coastal Spiny-tailed Lizard, Large-scaled Girdled Lizard, (F) Cordyle à larges écailles, Lézard à queue épineuse à larges écailles II CORDYLIDAE Re
Cordylus mclachlani : (E) McLachlan's Girdled Lizard, McLachlan's Spiny-tailed Lizard, (F) Cordyle de McLachlan, Lézard à queue épineuse de McLachlan II CORDYLIDAE Re
Cordylus melanotus : (E) Drakensberg Crag Lizard, Highveld Crag Lizard, (F) Lézard des rochers du Drakensberg, Pseudocordyle du Drakensberg II CORDYLIDAE Re
Cordylus microlepidotus : (E) Western Cape Crag Lizard, (F) Lézard à fausse ceinture des rochers, Lézard des rochers, Pseudocordyle des rochers II CORDYLIDAE Re
Cordylus minor : (E) Dwarf Girdled Lizard, (F) Petit cordyle, Petit lézard à queue épineuse II CORDYLIDAE Re
Cordylus mossambicus : II CORDYLIDAE Re
Cordylus namaquensis : (E) Namaqua Girdled Lizard, Namaqua Spiny-tailed Lizard, (F) Cordyle du Namaqua, Lézard à queue épineuse du Namaqua II CORDYLIDAE Re
Cordylus nebulosus : (E) Dwarf Crag Lizard II CORDYLIDAE Re
Cordylus niger : (E) Black Girdled Lizard, (F) Cordyle noir, Lézard à queue épineuse noir II CORDYLIDAE Re
Cordylus nyikae : II CORDYLIDAE Re
Cordylus oelofseni : (E) Oelofsen's Girdled Lizard, (F) Cordyle d'Oelofsen, Lézard à queue épineuse d'Oelofsen II CORDYLIDAE Re
Cordylus peersi : (E) Hewitt's Spiny-tailed Lizard, Peers's Girdled Lizard, (F) Cordyle de Hewitt, Lézard à queue épineuse de Hewitt II CORDYLIDAE Re
Cordylus polyzonus : (E) African Spiny-tailed Lizard, Karoo Girdled Lizard, (F) Cordyle africain, Lézard à queue épineuse africain II CORDYLIDAE Re
Cordylus polyzonus ssp. *jordani* = *Cordylus jordani*
Cordylus pustulatus : (E) Herero Girdled Lizard, (F) Cordyle à pustules, Lézard à queue épineuse à pustules II CORDYLIDAE Re
Cordylus regius : (E) Regal Girdled Lizard II CORDYLIDAE Re
Cordylus rhodesianus : (E) Rhodesian Girdled Lizard, Zimbabwe Girdled Lizard, (F) Cordyle de Rhodésie, Lézard à queue épineuse de Rhodésie II CORDYLIDAE Re
Cordylus rivae : II CORDYLIDAE Re

Checklist of fauna/Lista de especies de fauna/Liste des espèces animales

Cordylus spinosus : (E) Prickly Girdled Lizard, Spiny Crag Lizard, (S) Falso lagarto armadillo espinoso, (F) Lézard à ceinture épineuse, Pseudocordyle épineux, **II** CORDYLIDAE Re

Cordylus subviridis : (E) Drakensberg Crag Lizard **II** CORDYLIDAE Re

Cordylus tasmani : (E) Tasman's Girdled Lizard, (F) Cordyle de Tasman, Lézard à queue épineuse de Tasman **II** CORDYLIDAE Re

Cordylus transvaalensis : (E) Northern Crag Lizard **II** CORDYLIDAE Re

Cordylus tropidosternum : (E) East African Spiny-tailed Lizard, Tropical Girdled Lizard, Tropical Spiny-tailed Lizard, (F) Cordyle de Cope, Lézard à queue épineuse de Cope **II** CORDYLIDAE Re

Cordylus ukingensis : (E) Ukinga Girdled Lizard, Ukinga Spiny-tailed Lizard, (F) Cordyle d'Ukinga, Lézard à queue épineuse d'Ukinga **II** CORDYLIDAE Re

Cordylus vandami : (E) Van Dam's Girdled Lizard **II** CORDYLIDAE Re

Cordylus vittifer : (E) Reichenow's Spiny-tailed Lizard, Transvaal Girdled Lizard, (F) Cordyle de Reichenow, Lézard à queue épineuse de Reichenow **II** CORDYLIDAE Re

Cordylus warreni : (E) Warren's Girdled Lizard, Warren's Spiny-tailed Lizard, (F) Cordyle de Warren, Lézard à queue épineuse de Warren **II** CORDYLIDAE Re

Cordylus warreni ssp. *breyeri* = *Cordylus breyeri*

Cordylus warreni ssp. *vandami* = *Cordylus vandami*

Corneille de paradis (F): *Lycocorax pyrrhopterus*

Corocoro colorado (S): *Eudocimus ruber*

Corocoro rojo (S): *Eudocimus ruber*

Coronita aterciopelada (S): *Boissonneaua jardini*

Coronita colihabana (S): *Boissonneaua flavescens*

Coronita pechicastaña (S): *Boissonneaua matthewsii*

Corredor chillón (S): *Atrichornis clamosus*

Corsac (E): *Vulpes cana*

Corsican Swallowtail (E): *Papilio hospiton*

Corucia zebrata : (E) Prehensile-tailed Skink, Solomon Islands Giant Skink, (S) Eslizón de las Islas Salomón, (F) Scinque à queue préhensile des Iles Salomons, Scinque arboricole des Iles Salomons, Scinque géant des Iles Salomons, **II** SCINCIDAE Re

Coryllis à front orange (F): *Loriculus aurantiifrons*

Coryllis à gorge jaune (F): *Loriculus pusillus*

Coryllis à tête bleue (F): *Loriculus galgulus*

Coryllis de Ceylan (F): *Loriculus beryllinus*

Coryllis de Wallace (F): *Loriculus flosculus*

Coryllis del Sula (F): *Loriculus sclateri*

Coryllis des Bismarck (F): *Loriculus tener*

Coryllis des Célèbes (F): *Loriculus stigmatus*

Coryllis des Moluques (F): *Loriculus amabilis*

Coryllis des Philippines (F): *Loriculus philippensis*

Coryllis des Sangi (F): *Loriculus catamene*

Coryllis vernal (F): *Loriculus vernalis*

Coryllis vert (F): *Loriculus exilis*

Corythaeola cristata : (E) Blue Plantain-eater, Great Blue Turaco, (S) Turaco gigante, (F) Touraco géant, **III** MUSOPHAGIDAE Av

Coscinastrea columna : **II** SIDERASTREIDAE An

Coscinastrea crassa : **II** SIDERASTREIDAE An

Coscinastrea exesa : **II** SIDERASTREIDAE An

Coscinastrea fossata : **II** SIDERASTREIDAE An

Coscinastrea hahazimaensis : **II** SIDERASTREIDAE An

Coscinastrea marshae : **II** SIDERASTREIDAE An

Coscinastrea mcneilli : **II** SIDERASTREIDAE An

Coscinastrea monile : **II** SIDERASTREIDAE An

Coscinastrea wellsi : **II** SIDERASTREIDAE An

Coscoroba blanc (F): *Coscoroba coscoroba*

Coscoroba coscoroba : (E) Coscoroba Swan, (S) Cisne coscoroba, Ganso blanco, (F) Coscoroba blanc, Cygne coscoroba, **II** ANATIDAE Av

Coscoroba Swan (E): *Coscoroba coscoroba*

Costa Rican Puma (E): *Puma concolor costaricensis*

Costa Rican Red Tarantula (E): *Brachypelma angustum*

Costa's Hummingbird (E): *Calypte costae*

Cotinga à ailes blanches (F): *Xipholena atropurpurea*

Cotinga à bandeau (F): *Cotinga maculata*

Cotinga aliblanca (S): *Xipholena atropurpurea*

Cotinga cordonbleu (F): *Cotinga maculata*

Cotinga de corbata (S): *Cotinga maculata*

Cotinga maculata : (E) Banded Cotinga, Spotted Cotinga, (S) Cotinga de corbata, Cotinga manchado, (F) Cotinga à bandeau, Cotinga cordonbleu, Cotinga maculé, **I** COTINGIDAE Av

Cotinga maculé (F): *Cotinga maculata*

Cotinga manchado (S): *Cotinga maculata*

Cotinga porphyrion (F): *Xipholena atropurpurea*

Cotorra (S): *Amazona ventralis*

Cotorra (S): *Lepidochelys kempi*

Cotorra alejandrina (S): *Psittacula eupatria*

Cotorra amarilla (S): *Guarouba guarouba*

Cotorra Argentina (S): *Myiopsitta monachus*

Cotorra austral (S): *Enicognathus ferrugineus*

Cotorra Boliviana (S): *Myiopsitta luchsi*

Cotorra cabeciamarilla (S): *Amazona barbadensis*

Cotorra cabeciazul (S): *Pionus menstruus*

Cotorra cabeciblanca (S): *Pionus tumultuosus*

Cotorra cabecinegra (S): *Nandayus nenday*

Cotorra cachaña (S): *Enicognathus ferrugineus*

Cotorra capirotada (S): *Pyrrhura rupicola*

Cotorra cariparda (S): *Pyrrhura leucotis*

Cotorra carirroja (S): *Aratinga mitrata*

Cotorra carirrosa (S): *Psittacula roseata*

Cotorra catana (S): *Pyrrhura hoffmanni*

Cotorra chiripepé (S): *Pyrrhura frontalis*

Cotorra choroy (S): *Enicognathus leptorhynchus*

Cotorra ciruela (S): *Psittacula cyanocephala*

Cotorra colilarga (S): *Psittacula longicauda*

Cotorra colinegra (S): *Pyrrhura melanura*

Cotorra colirroja (S): *Pyrrhura hoematotis*

Cotorra coronirroja (S): *Pyrrhura rhodocephala*

Cotorra cucha (S): *Amazona autumnalis*

Cotorra cuelliblanca (S): *Pyrrhura albipectus*

Cotorra de ceilán (S): *Psittacula calthropae*

Cotorra de Derby (S): *Psittacula derbiana*

Cotorra de Deville (S): *Pyrrhura devillei*

Cotorra de El Oro (S): *Pyrrhura orcesi*

Cotorra de Finsch (S): *Psittacula finschii*

Cotorra de Kramer (S): *Psittacula krameri*

Cotorra de los Palos (S): *Aratinga acuticaudata*

Cotorra de Malabar (S): *Psittacula columboides*

Cotorra de Mauricio (S): *Psittacula echo*

Cotorra de Molina (S): *Pyrrhura molinae*

Cotorra de Nicobar (S): *Psittacula caniceps*

Cotorra de Santa Marta (S): *Pyrrhura viridicata*

Cotorra del Himalaya (S): *Psittacula himalayana*

Cotorra egregia (S): *Pyrrhura egregia*

Cotorra frente roja (S): *Amazona finschi*

Cotorra frentidorada (S): *Aratinga aurea*

Cotorra intermedia (S): *Psittacula intermedia*

Cotorra morada (S): *Pionus fuscus*

Cotorra negra (S): *Pionus chalcopterus*

Cotorra pechiparda (S): *Pyrrhura calliptera*

Cotorra pechirroja (S): *Psittacula alexandri*

Cotorra perlada (S): *Pyrrhura lepida*

Cotorra pintada (S): *Pyrrhura picta*

Cotorra tiriba (S): *Pyrrhura cruentata*

Cotorra ventrirroja (S): *Pyrrhura perlata*

Cotorra verde (S): *Aratinga leucophthalmus*

Cotorra-serrana occidental (S): *Rhynchopsitta pachyrhyncha*

Cotorra-serrana oriental (S): *Rhynchopsitta terrisi*

Cotorrita aliazul (S): *Forpus crassirostris*

Cotorrita alipinta (S): *Touit stictoptera*

Cotorrita alirroja (S): *Touit huetii*

Cotorrita amazónica (S): *Nannopsittaca dachilleae*

Cotorrita cariazul (S): *Touit dilectissima*

Cotorrita carigualda (S): *Forpus xanthops*

Cotorrita Costarricense (S): *Touit costaricensis*

Cotorrita culiverde (S): *Forpus passerinus*
Cotorrita de Anteojos (S): *Forpus conspicillatus*
Cotorrita de Piura (S): *Forpus coelestis*
Cotorrita de Sclater (S): *Forpus sclateri*
Cotorrita dorsinegra (S): *Touit melanonota*
Cotorrita Mexicana (S): *Forpus cyanopygius*
Cotorrita purpurada (S): *Touit purpurata*
Cotorrita sietecolores (S): *Touit batavica*
Cotorrita sorda (S): *Touit surda*
Cotorrita tepuí (S): *Nannopsittaca panychlora*
Cotton-headed Tamarin (E): *Saguinus oedipus*
Cotton-top Marmoset (E): *Saguinus geoffroyi*
Cotton-top Tamarin (E): *Saguinus oedipus*
Cotunto (S): *Otus lawrencii*
Cou-coupé (F): *Amadina fasciata*
Cougar (E): *Puma concolor*
Cougar de Floride (F): *Puma concolor coryi*
Cougouar (F): *Puma concolor couguar*
Couleuvre à damier (F): *Xenochrophis piscator*
Couleuvre aquatique (F): *Xenochrophis piscator*
Couleuvre de Westermann (F): *Elachistodon westermanni*
Couleuvre d'eau asiatique (F): *Xenochrophis piscator*
Couleuvre lisse du Brésil (F): *Cyclagras gigas*
Couleuvre pêcheuse (F): *Xenochrophis piscator*
Count Raggi's Bird-of-paradise (E): *Paradisaea raggiana*
Courlis à bec grêle (F): *Numenius tenuirostris*
Courlis esquimau (F): *Numenius borealis*
Couscous de la Sonde (F): *Phalanger orientalis*
Couscous gris (F): *Phalanger orientalis*
Couscous tacheté (F): *Spilocuscus maculatus*
Cowan's Mantella (E): *Mantella cowani*
Coxen's Blue-browed Fig Parrot (E): *Cyclopsitta diophthalma coxeni*
Coxen's Double-eyed Fig-Parrot (E): *Cyclopsitta diophthalma coxeni*
Coxen's Two-eyed Fig Parrot (E): *Cyclopsitta diophthalma coxeni*
Crab-eating Macaque (E): *Macaca fascicularis*
Crab-eating Mongoose (E): *Herpestes urva*
Crab-eating Zorro (E): *Cerdocyon thous*
Crag lizards (E): *Cordylus* spp.
Crane (E): *Grus grus*
Crane Hawk (E): *Geranospiza caerulescens*
Cranes (E): GRUIDAE spp.
Crapaud doré (F): *Bufo periglenes*
Crapaud du Cameroun (F): *Bufo superciliaris*
Crapaud orange (F): *Atelopus zeteki*
Crapaud rouge de Madagascar (F): *Dyscophus antongilii*
Crapauds vivipares (F): *Altiphrynoides* spp./ *Nectophrynoides* spp./ *Nimbaphrynoides* spp./ *Spinophrynoides* spp.
Crapauds vivipares du Mont Nimba (F): *Nimbaphrynoides* spp.
Crater Coral (E): *Trachyphyllia geoffroyi*
Crax alberti : (E) Albert's Curassow, Blue-billed Curassow, Blue-knobbed Curassow, Prince Albert's Curassow, (S) Hocco piguiazul, Paují de pico azul, Pavón piquiazul, (F) Hocco à bec bleu, Hocco d'Albert, **III** CRACIDAE Av
Crax blumenbachii : (E) Blumenbach's Curassow, Mutum, Red-billed Curassow, (S) Haco piguirojo, Muitú mamaco, Mutum-do-sudeste, Paují piquirrojo, Pavón piquirrojo, (F) Hocco à bec rouge, Hocco de Blumenbach, **I** CRACIDAE Av
Crax daubentoni : (E) Daubenton's Curassow, Yellow-knobbed Curassow, (S) Hoco de Daubenton, Paují de Copete, Pavón porú, (F) Hocco de Daubenton, **III** CRACIDAE Av
Crax globulosa : (E) Wattled Curassow, Yarrell's Curassow, (S) Hoco barbado, Pavón carunculado, (F) Hocco globuleux, Hoco caroncule, **III** CRACIDAE Av
Crax mitu ssp. *mitu* = *Mitu mitu*
Crax pauxi = *Pauxi pauxi*

Crax rubra : (E) Globose Curassow, Great Curassow, Mexican Curassow, (S) Hoco grande, Hocofaisan, Pavón grande, Pavón norteño, (F) Grand hocco, **III** CRACIDAE Av
Créa (F): *Acipenser sturio*
Créac (F): *Acipenser sturio*
Créach (F): *Acipenser sturio*
Cream-coloured Giant Squirrel (E): *Ratufa affinis*
Crécerelle américaine (F): *Falco sparverius*
Crécerelle australienne (F): *Falco cenchroides*
Crécerelle aux yeux blancs (F): *Falco rupicoloides*
Crécerelle d'Aldabra (F): *Falco newtoni*
Crécerelle d'Amérique (F): *Falco sparverius*
Crécerelle d'Australie (F): *Falco cenchroides*
Crécerelle de Maurice (F): *Falco punctatus*
Crécerelle des Moluques (F): *Falco moluccensis*
Crécerelle des Seychelles (F): *Falco araea*
Crécerelle katitie (F): *Falco araea*
Crécerelle malgache (F): *Falco newtoni*
Crécerelle renard (F): *Falco alopex*
Crescent Nailtail Wallaby (E): *Onychogalea lunata*
Crested Argus (E): *Rheinardia ocellata*
Crested Baza (E): *Aviceda subcristata*
Crested Bird-of-paradise (E): *Cnemophilus macgregorii*
Crested Caracara (E): *Polyborus plancus*
Crested Chameleon (E): *Chamaeleo cristatus*
Crested Eagle (E): *Morphnus guianensis*
Crested Fireback (E): *Lophura ignita*
Crested Gibbon (E): *Hylobates concolor*
Crested Goshawk (E): *Accipiter trivirgatus*
Crested Guan (E): *Penelope purpurascens*
Crested Hawk-Eagle (E): *Spizaetus cirrhatus*
Crested Ibis (E): *Nipponia nippon*
Crested Korhaan (E): *Eupodotis ruficrista*
Crested Malimbe (E): *Malimbus malimbicus*
Crested Mangabey (E): *Cercocebus galeritus*
Crested Owl (E): *Lophostrix cristata*
Crested Partridge (E): *Rollulus rouloul*
Crested Peacock-Pheasant (E): *Polyplectron malacense*
Crested Porcupine (E): *Hystrix cristata*
Crested Serpent-Eagle (E): *Spilornis cheela*
Crested Turaco (E): *Tauraco macrorhynchus*
Crestless Fireback (E): *Lophura erythrophthalma*
Crestless Monal (E): *Lophophorus sclateri*
Crevice Monitor (E): *Varanus kingorum*
Crevice Tortoise (E): *Malacochersus tornieri*
Crick à ventre bleu (F): *Triclaria malachitacea*
Crimson Horned-Pheasant (E): *Tragopan satyra*
Crimson Rosella (E): *Platycercus elegans*
Crimson Shining-parrot (E): *Prosopeia splendens*
Crimson Topaz (E): *Topaza pella*
Crimson-bellied Conure (E): *Pyrrhura perlata*
Crimson-bellied Parakeet (E): *Pyrrhura perlata*
Crimson-fronted Conure (E): *Aratinga finschi*
Crimson-fronted Parakeet (E): *Aratinga finschi*
Crimson-winged Pytilia (E): *Pytilia phoenicoptera*
Crinifer piscator : (E) Grey Plantain-eater, Western Grey Plantain-eater, (S) Turaco de Crin occidental, Turaco gris occidental, (F) Touraco gris, **III** MUSOPHAGIDAE Av
Crinkle-collared Manucode (E): *Manucodia chalybata*
Crispatotrochus cornu : **II** CARYOPHYLLIIDAE An
Crispatotrochus curvatus : **II** CARYOPHYLLIIDAE An
Crispatotrochus foxi : **II** CARYOPHYLLIIDAE An
Crispatotrochus galapagensis : **II** CARYOPHYLLIIDAE An
Crispatotrochus inornatus : **II** CARYOPHYLLIIDAE An
Crispatotrochus irregularis : **II** CARYOPHYLLIIDAE An
Crispatotrochus niinoi : **II** CARYOPHYLLIIDAE An
Crispatotrochus rubescens : **II** CARYOPHYLLIIDAE An
Crispatotrochus rugosus : **II** CARYOPHYLLIIDAE An
Crispatotrochus squiresi : **II** CARYOPHYLLIIDAE An
Crispatotrochus tydemani = *Crispatotrochus rubescens*
Crispatotrochus woodsi : **II** CARYOPHYLLIIDAE An

Crispy Crust Coral (E): *Merulina ampliata*
Crocea Clam (E): *Tridacna crocea*
Crocodile à front large (F): *Osteolaemus tetraspis*
Crocodile à museau allongé d'Afrique (F): *Crocodylus cataphractus*
Crocodile à museau court (F): *Osteolaemus tetraspis*
Crocodile à museau étroit (F): *Crocodylus cataphractus*
Crocodile à nuque cuirassée (F): *Osteolaemus tetraspis*
Crocodile américain (F): *Crocodylus acutus*
Crocodile d'Amérique (F): *Crocodylus acutus*
Crocodile de Cuba (F): *Crocodylus rhombifer*
Crocodile de Johnstone (F): *Crocodylus johnsoni*
Crocodile de l'Orénoque (F): *Crocodylus intermedius*
Crocodile de Mindoro (F): *Crocodylus mindorensis*
Crocodile de Morelet (F): *Crocodylus moreletii*
Crocodile de Nouvelle Guinée (F): *Crocodylus novaeguineae*
Crocodile des marais (F): *Crocodylus palustris*
Crocodile des Philippines (F): *Crocodylus mindorensis*
Crocodile d'estuaire (F): *Crocodylus porosus*
Crocodile du Nil (F): *Crocodylus niloticus*
Crocodile du Siam (F): *Crocodylus siamensis*
Crocodile lézardet (F): *Crocodilurus amazonicus*
Crocodile marin (F): *Crocodylus porosus*
Crocodile Monitor (E): *Varanus salvadorii*
Crocodile nain africain (F): *Osteolaemus tetraspis*
Crocodile paludéen (F): *Crocodylus palustris*
Crocodile palustre (F): *Crocodylus palustris*
Crocodile Tegu (E): *Crocodilurus amazonicus*
Crocodiles (E): CROCODYLIA spp. Re
Crocodilians (E): CROCODYLIA spp. Re
Crocodilurus amazonicus : (E) Crocodile Tegu, Dragon Lizard, Dragon Lizardet, (F) Crocodile lézardet, Téju-Crocodile **II** TEIIDAE Re
Crocodilurus lacertinus auct. = *Crocodilurus amazonicus*
CROCODYLIA spp. : (E) Alligators, Crocodiles, Crocodilians, (S) Aligators, Cocodrilos, (F) Alligators, Crocodiles, **I/II** Re
Crocodylus acutus : (E) American Crocodile, (S) Caimán americano, Cocodrilo americano, (F) Crocodile américain, Crocodile d'Amérique, **I** CROCODYLIDAE Re
Crocodylus cataphractus : (E) African Sharp-nosed Crocodile, African Slender-snouted Crocodile, Long-snouted Crocodile, (S) Cocodrilo hociquifino africano, Falso gavial africano, (F) Crocodile à museau allongé d'Afrique, Crocodile à museau étroit, Faux-gavial d'Afrique, **I** CROCODYLIDAE Re
Crocodylus intermedius : (E) Orinoco Crocodile, (S) Caimán del Orinoco, Cocodrilo del Orinoco, (F) Crocodile de l'Orénoque, **I** CROCODYLIDAE Re
Crocodylus johnsoni : (E) Australian Fresh-water Crocodile, Johnstone's Crocodile, (S) Cocodrilo australiano, (F) Crocodile de Johnstone, **II** CROCODYLIDAE Re
Crocodylus johnstoni = *Crocodylus johnsoni*
Crocodylus mindorensis : (E) Mindoro Crocodile, Philippine Crocodile, (S) Cocodrilo de Mindoro, (F) Crocodile de Mindoro, Crocodile des Philippines, **I** CROCODYLIDAE Re
Crocodylus moreletii : (E) Belize Crocodile, Morelet's Crocodile, (S) Caimán de Morelet, Cocodrilo de Morelet, (F) Crocodile de Morelet, **I** CROCODYLIDAE Re
Crocodylus niloticus : (E) African Crocodile, Nile Crocodile, (S) Cocodrilo del Nilo, (F) Crocodile du Nil, **I/II** CROCODYLIDAE Re
Crocodylus novaeguineae : (E) New Guinea Crocodile, (S) Cocodrilo de Nueva Guinea, (F) Crocodile de Nouvelle Guinée, **II** CROCODYLIDAE Re
Crocodylus novaeguineae ssp. *mindorensis* = *Crocodylus mindorensis*

Crocodylus palustris : (E) Broad-snouted Crocodile, Marsh Crocodile, Mugger, Mugger Crocodile, (S) Cocodrilo del Marjal, Cocodrilo marismeño, (F) Crocodile des marais, Crocodile paludéen, Crocodile palustre, **I** CROCODYLIDAE Re
Crocodylus porosus : (E) Estuarine Crocodile, Salt-water Crocodile, (S) Cocodrilo poroso, (F) Crocodile d'estuaire, Crocodile marin, **I/II** CROCODYLIDAE Re
Crocodylus raninus = *Crocodylus porosus*
Crocodylus rhombifer : (E) Cuban Crocodile, (S) Caimán de Cuba, Cocodrilo de Cuba, (F) Crocodile de Cuba, **I** CROCODYLIDAE Re
Crocodylus siamensis : (E) Siamese Crocodile, (S) Cocodrilo de Siam, (F) Crocodile du Siam, **I** CROCODYLIDAE Re
Croco-Teju (E): *Dracaena guianensis*
Crocus Clam (E): *Tridacna crocea*
Cropan's Boa (E): *Corallus cropanii*
Crossoptilon crossoptilon : (E) White Eared-Pheasant, (S) Faisán orejudo blanco, Faisán orejudo tibetano, Hoki blanco, (F) Faisan oreillard blanc, Hokki blanc, **I** PHASIANIDAE Av
Crossoptilon crossoptilon ssp. *harmani* = *Crossoptilon harmani*
Crossoptilon harmani : (E) Tibetan Eared-Pheasant, (F) Hokki de Harman, Hokki du Tibet **I** PHASIANIDAE Av
Crossoptilon mantchuricum : (E) Brown Eared-Pheasant, Manchurian Eared-Pheasant, (S) Faisán orejudo de Manchuria, Faisán orejudo pardo, Hoki pardo, (F) Faisan oreillard brun, Hokki brun, **I** PHASIANIDAE Av
Crotale des tropiques (F): *Crotalus durissus*
Crotale durisse (F): *Crotalus durissus*
Crotalus durissus : (E) Cascabel, Cascabel Rattlesnake, Neotropical Rattlesnake, (S) Cascavelle, (F) Cascabel, Cascavelle, Crotale des tropiques, Crotale durisse, Durisse, Serpent à sonnette tropical, **III** VIPERIDAE Re
Crotalus pifanorum = *Crotalus durissus*
Crowned Eagle (E): *Harpyhaliaetus coronatus/ Stephanoaetus coronatus*
Crowned Gibbon (E): *Hylobates pileatus*
Crowned Guenon (E): *Cercopithecus pogonias*
Crowned Hawk-Eagle (E): *Stephanoaetus coronatus*
Crowned Lemur (E): *Eulemur coronatus*
Crowned Monkey (E): *Cercopithecus pogonias*
Crowned Seahorse (E): *Hippocampus coronatus*
Crowned Solitary Eagle (E): *Harpyhaliaetus coronatus*
Crowned-pigeons (E): *Goura* spp.
Crypthelia affinis : **II** STYLASTERIDAE Hy
Crypthelia balia : **II** STYLASTERIDAE Hy
Crypthelia clausa : **II** STYLASTERIDAE Hy
Crypthelia cryptotrema : **II** STYLASTERIDAE Hy
Crypthelia curvata : **II** STYLASTERIDAE Hy
Crypthelia cymas : **II** STYLASTERIDAE Hy
Crypthelia dactylopoma : **II** STYLASTERIDAE Hy
Crypthelia eueides : **II** STYLASTERIDAE Hy
Crypthelia floridana : **II** STYLASTERIDAE Hy
Crypthelia formosa : **II** STYLASTERIDAE Hy
Crypthelia fragilis : **II** STYLASTERIDAE Hy
Crypthelia gigantea : **II** STYLASTERIDAE Hy
Crypthelia glebulenta : **II** STYLASTERIDAE Hy
Crypthelia glossopoma : **II** STYLASTERIDAE Hy
Crypthelia insolita : **II** STYLASTERIDAE Hy
Crypthelia japonica : **II** STYLASTERIDAE Hy
Crypthelia lacunosa : **II** STYLASTERIDAE Hy
Crypthelia medioatlantica : **II** STYLASTERIDAE Hy
Crypthelia micropoma : **II** STYLASTERIDAE Hy
Crypthelia papillosa : **II** STYLASTERIDAE Hy
Crypthelia peircei : **II** STYLASTERIDAE Hy
Crypthelia platypoma : **II** STYLASTERIDAE Hy
Crypthelia polypoma : **II** STYLASTERIDAE Hy
Crypthelia pudica : **II** STYLASTERIDAE Hy

Crypthelia ramosa : **II** STYLASTERIDAE Hy
Crypthelia robusta : **II** STYLASTERIDAE Hy
Crypthelia stenopoma : **II** STYLASTERIDAE Hy
Crypthelia studeri : **II** STYLASTERIDAE Hy
Crypthelia tenuiseptata : **II** STYLASTERIDAE Hy
Crypthelia trophostega : **II** STYLASTERIDAE Hy
Crypthelia vascomarquesi : **II** STYLASTERIDAE Hy
Cryptophyllobates azureiventris = Epipedobates azureiventris
Cryptoprocta ferox : (E) Fosa, Fossa, (S) Gato fossa de Madagascar, (F) Cryptoprocte féroce, Fossa, Foussa, **II** VIVERRIDAE Ma
Cryptoprocte féroce (F): *Cryptoprocta ferox*
Cryptotrochus brevipalus : **II** TURBINOLIIDAE An
Cryptotrochus carolinensis : **II** TURBINOLIIDAE An
Cryptotrochus javanus : **II** TURBINOLIIDAE An
Cryptotrochus venustus = Pleotrochus venustus
Crystal corals (E): *Galaxea spp.*
Ctenactis albitentaculata : **II** FUNGIIDAE An
Ctenactis crassa : **II** FUNGIIDAE An
Ctenactis echinata : **II** FUNGIIDAE An
Ctenella chagius : **II** MEANDRINIIDAE An
Ctenella laxa = Gyrosmilia interrupta
Cuataquil (S): *Bassaricyon gabbii*
Cuatro Cienegas Softshell (E): *Apalone ater*
Cuban Amazon (E): *Amazona leucocephala*
Cuban Black Hawk (E): *Buteogallus anthracinus*
Cuban Black-tailed Dwarf Boa (E): *Tropidophis melanurus*
Cuban Boa (E): *Epicrates angulifer*
Cuban Conure (E): *Aratinga euops*
Cuban Crocodile (E): *Crocodylus rhombifer*
Cuban Emerald (E): *Chlorostilbon ricordii*
Cuban Ground Iguana (E): *Cyclura nubila*
Cuban Hook-billed Kite (E): *Chondrohierax uncinatus wilsonii*
Cuban Iguana (E): *Cyclura nubila*
Cuban Parakeet (E): *Aratinga euops*
Cuban Parrot (E): *Amazona leucocephala*
Cuban Pygmy-Owl (E): *Glaucidium siju*
Cuban Sandhill Crane (E): *Grus canadensis nesiotes*
Cuban Screech-Owl (E): *Otus lawrencii*
Cuban Tree Boa (E): *Epicrates angulifer*
Cuban Tree-Duck (E): *Dendrocygna arborea*
Cuchara común (S): *Anas clypeata*
Cuchumbi (S): *Potos flavus/ Bassaricyon gabbii*
Cuckoo Owlet (E): *Glaucidium cuculoides*
Cuckoo Weaver (E): *Anomalospiza imberbis*
Cuco (S): *Otus lawrencii*
Cucú (S): *Speotyto cunicularia*
Cuervo calvo de cuello blanco (S): *Picathartes gymnocephalus*
Cuervo calvo de cuello gris (S): *Picathartes oreas*
Cui (S): *Chasmistes cujus*
Cui ui (S): *Chasmistes cujus*
Cúiu cúiu (S): *Pionopsitta pileata*
Cui-ui (E): *Chasmistes cujus*
Cuiui (F): *Chasmistes cujus*
Culebra boba (S): *Tropidophis melanurus*
Culebra comedora de huevos (S): *Elachistodon westermanni*
Culebra ratera oriental (S): *Ptyas mucosus*
Culebra tragahuevos india (S): *Elachistodon westermanni*
Culebrera azor (S): *Eutriorchis astur*
Culebrera barreada (S): *Circaetus gallicus*
Culebrera chiíla (S): *Spilornis cheela*
Culebrera coliblanca (S): *Circaetus cinerascens*
Culebrera congoleña (S): *Dryotriorchis spectabilis*
Culebrera de Andamán (S): *Spilornis elgini*
Culebrera de Célebes (S): *Spilornis rufipectus*
Culebrera de Nicobar (S): *Spilornis minimus*
Culebrera del Kinabalu (S): *Spilornis kinabaluensis*
Culebrera europea (S): *Circaetus gallicus*
Culebrera filipina (S): *Spilornis holospilus*
Culebrera pechinegra (S): *Circaetus pectoralis*

Culebrera sombría (S): *Circaetus cinereus*
Culicia australiensis : **II** RHIZANGIIDAE An
Culicia cuticulata : **II** RHIZANGIIDAE An
Culicia excavata : **II** RHIZANGIIDAE An
Culicia fragilis : **II** RHIZANGIIDAE An
Culicia hoffmeisteri : **II** RHIZANGIIDAE An
Culicia japonica = Culicia stellata
Culicia quinaria : **II** RHIZANGIIDAE An
Culicia rubeola : **II** RHIZANGIIDAE An
Culicia smithii : **II** RHIZANGIIDAE An
Culicia stellata : **II** RHIZANGIIDAE An
Culicia subaustraliensis : **II** RHIZANGIIDAE An
Culicia tenella : **II** RHIZANGIIDAE An
Culicia tenella natalensis : **II** RHIZANGIIDAE An
Culicia tenella tenella : **II** RHIZANGIIDAE An
Culicia tenuisepes : **II** RHIZANGIIDAE An
Culicia truncata = Culicia stellata
Culicia verreauxii : **II** RHIZANGIIDAE An
Culpeo (E/S): *Pseudalopex culpaeus*
Cumberland Bean (E): *Villosa trabalis*
Cumberland Bean Pearly Mussel (E): *Villosa trabalis*
Cumberland Monkeyface (E): *Quadrula intermedia*
Cumberland Monkey-face Pearly Mussel (E): *Quadrula intermedia*
Cuniculus paca = Agouti paca
Cuon alpinus : (E) Asiatic Wild Dog, Dhole, Indian Wild Dog, Red Dog, (S) Cuon asiático, Perro salvaje asiático, (F) Chien sauvage d'Asie, Cuon d'Asie, Dhole, **II** CANIDAE Ma
Cuon asiático (S): *Cuon alpinus*
Cuon d'Asie (F): *Cuon alpinus*
Cuora spp.: (E) Asian box turtles, Box turtles, (F) Tortue-boites, **II** EMYDIDAE Re
Cuora amboinensis : (E) Malaysian Box Turtle, South Asian Box Turtle, (F) Tortue boite d'Asie orientale **II** EMYDIDAE Re
Cuora aurocapitata : (E) Golden-headed Box Turtle, Yellow-headed Box Turtle, (F) Tortue-boite à tete jaune **II** EMYDIDAE Re
Cuora chriskarannarum = Cuora pani
Cuora flavomarginata : (E) Chinese Box Turtle, Yellow-margined Box Turtle, (F) Tortue-boite à bords jaune **II** EMYDIDAE Re
Cuora galbinifrons : (E) Indochinese Box Turtle, (F) Tortue-boite à front jaune **II** EMYDIDAE Re
Cuora hainanensis = Cuora galbinifrons
Cuora mccordi : (E) McCord's Box Turtle, (F) Tortue-boite de McCord **II** EMYDIDAE Re
Cuora pallidicephala = Cuora zhoui
Cuora pani : (E) Pan's Box Turtle, (F) Tortue-boite de Pan **II** EMYDIDAE Re
Cuora serrata = Cuora galbinifrons
Cuora trifasciata : (E) Chinese Three-striped Box Turtle, (F) Tortue-boite à trois bandes **II** EMYDIDAE Re
Cuora yunnanensis : (E) Yunnan Box Turtle, (F) Tortue-boite du Yunnan **II** EMYDIDAE Re
Cuora zhoui : (E) Zhou's Box Turtle, (F) Tortue-boite du Guangxi **II** EMYDIDAE Re
Cupiso (S): *Podocnemis sextuberculata*
Cupressopathes abies : **II** MYRIOPATHIDAE An
Cupressopathes gracilis : **II** MYRIOPATHIDAE An
Cupressopathes paniculata : **II** MYRIOPATHIDAE An
Cupressopathes pumila : **II** MYRIOPATHIDAE An
Curl-crested Manucode (E): *Manucodia comrii*
Curly-hair Tarantula (E): *Brachypelma albopilosum*
Curruca bigotuda piquilarga (S): *Dasyornis longirostris*
Curruca bigotuda rojiza (S): *Dasyornis broadbenti litoralis*
Curtis' Pearly Mussel (E): *Epioblasma curtisii*
Curtis' Rifleshell (E): *Epioblasma curtisii*
Curucucú barriga amarilla (S): *Aegolius harrisii*
Curucucú común (S): *Otus choliba*
Curucucú gargantiblanco (S): *Otus albogularis*
Curucucú orejudo (S): *Otus watsonii*
Curucucú pálido (S): *Otus ingens*
Curucucú vermiculado (S): *Otus atricapillus*

Checklist of fauna/Lista de especies de fauna/Liste des espèces animales

Cuscús gris (S): *Phalanger orientalis*
Cuscús manchado (S): *Spilocuscus maculatus*
Cuscús moteado (S): *Spilocuscus maculatus*
Cuscús oriental (S): *Phalanger orientalis*
Cuspon (S): *Priodontes maximus*
Cusumbi (S): *Potos flavus*
Cut-throat (E): *Amadina fasciata*
Cuvier's Beaked Whale (E): *Ziphius cavirostris*
Cuvier's Gazelle (E): *Gazella cuvieri*
Cuvier's Smooth-fronted Caiman (E): *Palaeosuchus palpebrosus*
Cyanoliseus patagonus : (E) Burrowing Parakeet, Patagonian Conure, (S) Loro barranquero, (F) Conure de Patagonie, **II** PSITTACIDAE Av
Cyanophaia bicolor : (E) Blue-headed Hummingbird, (S) Colibrí bicolor, (F) Colibri à tête bleue, **II** TROCHILIDAE Av
Cyanopsitta spixii : (E) Little Blue Macaw, Spix's Macaw, (S) Guacamayito azul, Guacamayo de Spix, (F) Ara à face grise, Ara de Spix, **I** PSITTACIDAE Av
Cyanoramphus auriceps : (E) Yellow-crowned Parakeet, Yellow-fronted Kakariki, Yellow-fronted Parakeet, (S) Perico maori cabecigualdo, (F) Perruche à front jaune, Perruche à tête d'or, **II** PSITTACIDAE Av
Cyanoramphus auriceps ssp. *forbesi* = *Cyanoramphus forbesi*
Cyanoramphus cookii = *Cyanoramphus novaezelandiae*
Cyanoramphus forbesi : (E) Chatham Island Yellow-fronted Parakeet, Forbes's Kakariki, Forbes's Parakeet, (S) Cacatúa de Forbes, Perico de las Chatham, Periquito frentiamarillo de Forbes, (F) Perruche à front jaune de Forbes, Perruche à tête d'or de Forbes, Perruche des îles Chatham, **I** PSITTACIDAE Av
Cyanoramphus malherbi : (E) Malherbe's Parakeet, Orange-fronted Parakeet, (S) Perico maori montano, (F) Perruche de Malherbe, **II** PSITTACIDAE Av
Cyanoramphus novaezelandiae : (E) New Zealand Parakeet, Red-crowned Parakeet, Red-fronted Kakariki, Red-fronted Parakeet, (S) Perico maori cabecirrojo, Periquito cabecirrojo, (F) Perruche à bandeau rouge, Perruche de Nouvelle-Zélande, Perruche de Sparrman, **I** PSITTACIDAE Av
Cyanoramphus saisseti = *Cyanoramphus novaezelandiae*
Cyanoramphus unicolor : (E) Antipodes Green Parakeet, Antipodes Parakeet, (S) Perico de las Antípodas, (F) Perruche des Antipodes, Perruche unicolore, **II** PSITTACIDAE Av
Cyathelia axillaris : **II** OCULINIDAE An
Cyathoceras foxi = *Crispatotrochus foxi*
Cyathoceras quaylei = *Labyrinthocyathus quaylei*
Cyathotrochus herdmani : **II** TURBINOLIIDAE An
Cyathotrochus nascornatus : **II** TURBINOLIIDAE An
Cyathotrochus pileus : **II** TURBINOLIIDAE An
Cyclagras gigas : (E) Brazilian Smooth Snake, Brazilian Water Cobra, False Cobra, False Water Cobra, Surucucu, (S) Falsa cobra, Falsa cobra acuatica, Nakamina, (F) Couleuvre lisse du Brésil, Faux cobra, Faux cobra aquatique du Brésil, **II** COLUBRIDAE Re
Cyclemys annamensis = *Annamemys annamensis*
Cyclemys annandalii = *Hieremys annandalii*
Cyclemys mouhotii = *Pyxidea mouhotii*
Cyclemys yunnanensis = *Cuora yunnanensis*
Cyclohelia lamellata : **II** STYLASTERIDAE Hy
Cyclopsitta diophthalma : (E) Double-eyed Fig-Parrot, Dwarf Fig-Parrot, (S) Lorito dobleojo, (F) Perroquet masqué, Psittacule double-oeil, **I/II** PSITTACIDAE Av
Cyclopsitta diophthalma coxeni : (E) Coxen's Blue-browed Fig Parrot, Coxen's Double-eyed Fig-Parrot, Coxen's Two-eyed Fig Parrot, (S) Lorito de Coxen, Lorito emmascarado de Coxen, (F) Perroquet masqué de Coxen, Psittacule à double-oeil de Coxen, **I** PSITTACIDAE Av

Cyclopsitta gulielmitertii : (E) Orange-breasted Fig-Parrot, (S) Lorito pechinaranja, (F) Psittacule à poitrine orange, **II** PSITTACIDAE Av
Cycloseris colini : **II** FUNGIIDAE An
Cycloseris costulata = *Fungia costulata*
Cycloseris curvata = *Fungia curvata*
Cycloseris cyclolites = *Fungia cyclolites*
Cycloseris erosa = *Fungia erosa*
Cycloseris hexagonalis = *Fungia hexagonalis*
Cycloseris patelliformis = *Fungia patelliformis*
Cycloseris sinensis = *Fungia sinensis*
Cycloseris tenuis = *Fungia tenuis*
Cycloseris vaughani = *Fungia vaughani*
Cyclura spp.: (E) Ground iguanas, (S) Iguanas cornuda, Iguanas terrestres, (F) Cyclures, Iguanes cornus, Iguanes rhinocéros, **I** IGUANIDAE Re
Cyclura baelopha = *Cyclura cychlura*
Cyclura carinata : (E) Bahamas Rock Iguana, Bartsch's Iguana, Turks and Caicos Ground Iguana, Turks and Caicos Iguana, (F) Cyclure des îles Turks et Caïques, Iguane terrestre des îles Turks et Caïques **I** IGUANIDAE Re
Cyclura collei : (E) Jamaica Ground Iguana, Jamaican Iguana, (F) Cyclure terrestre de la Jamaïque, Iguane terrestre de la Jamaïque **I** IGUANIDAE Re
Cyclura cornuta : (E) Rhinoceros Iguana, (F) Cyclure cornu, Iguane cornu, Iguane terrestre cornu **I** IGUANIDAE Re
Cyclura cychlura : (E) Bahamas Iguana, Bahamas Rock Iguana **I** IGUANIDAE Re
Cyclura lophoma = *Cyclura collei*
Cyclura macleayi = *Cyclura nubila*
Cyclura nubila : (E) Cayman Islands Ground Iguana, Cuban Ground Iguana, Cuban Iguana, (F) Cyclure des Iles Cayman, Iguane terrestre des Iles Cayman **I** IGUANIDAE Re
Cyclura pinguis : (E) Anegada Ground Iguana, Anegada Island Iguana, Anegada Rock Iguana, (F) Cyclure de l'Ile Anegada, Iguane terrestre de l'Ile Anegada **I** IGUANIDAE Re
Cyclura ricordi : (E) Hispaniolan Ground Iguana, Ricord's Ground Iguana, Ricord's Iguana, (F) Cyclure de Ricord, Cyclure d'Hispaniola, Iguane terrestre d'Hispaniola **I** IGUANIDAE Re
Cyclura rileyi : (E) San Salvador Ground Iguana, San Salvador Iguana, Watling Island Iguana, White Cay Ground Iguana, (F) Cyclure des Bahamas, Iguane terrestre des Bahamas **I** IGUANIDAE Re
Cyclure cornu (F): *Cyclura cornuta*
Cyclure de l'Ile Anegada (F): *Cyclura pinguis*
Cyclure de Ricord (F): *Cyclura ricordi*
Cyclure des Bahamas (F): *Cyclura rileyi*
Cyclure des Iles Cayman (F): *Cyclura nubila*
Cyclure des îles Turks et Caïques (F): *Cyclura carinata*
Cyclure d'Hispaniola (F): *Cyclura ricordi*
Cyclure terrestre de la Jamaïque (F): *Cyclura collei*
Cyclures (F): *Cyclura* spp.
Cygne à cou noir (F): *Cygnus melanocorypha*
Cygne chanteur (F): *Cygnus melanocorypha*
Cygne coscoroba (F): *Coscoroba coscoroba*
Cygnus melanocorypha : (E) Black-necked Swan, (S) Cisne cuellinegro, (F) Cygne à cou noir, Cygne chanteur, **II** ANATIDAE Av
Cynanthus doubledayi = *Cynanthus latirostris*
Cynanthus latirostris : (E) Broad-billed Hummingbird, (S) Colibrí piquiancho, (F) Colibri circé, **II** TROCHILIDAE Av
Cynanthus lawrencei = *Cynanthus latirostris*
Cynanthus sordidus : (E) Dusky Hummingbird, (S) Colibrí prieto, (F) Colibri sombre, **II** TROCHILIDAE Av
Cynarina lacrymalis : (E) Cat's-eye Coral, Pacific Rose Coral **II** MUSSIDAE An
Cynogale bennettii : (E) Otter-civet, Sunda Otter-civet, (S) Cibeta nutria, Civeta de Sumatra, (F) Civette-loutre de Sumatra, **II** VIVERRIDAE Ma

Checklist of fauna/Lista de especies de fauna/Liste des espèces animales

Cynogale lowei = Cynogale bennettii
Cynomolgus Monkey (E): *Macaca fascicularis*
Cynomys mexicanus : (E) Mexican Prairie Marmot, Mexican Prairie-dog, (S) Perrito de la pradera mexicano, Perrito de las praderas, Perrito llanero Mejicano, (F) Chien de prairie du Mexique, **I** SCIURIDAE Ma
Cynopithèque nègre (F): *Macaca nigra*
Cynoscion macdonaldi : (E) MacDonald's Weakfish, Totoaba, (S) Totoba, (F) Acoupa de MacDonald, **I** SCIAENIDAE Ac
Cyornis ruckii : (E) Rueck's Blue-Flycatcher, Rueck's Niltava, (S) Papamoscas de Rueck, (F) Gobemouche bleu de Rueck, Gobemouche de Rueck, **II** MUSCICAPIDAE Av
Cyphastrea spp.: (E) Knob corals, Lesser knob corals **II** FAVIIDAE An
Cyphastrea agassizi : **II** FAVIIDAE An
Cyphastrea chalcidicum : **II** FAVIIDAE An
Cyphastrea decadia : **II** FAVIIDAE An
Cyphastrea hexasepta : **II** FAVIIDAE An
Cyphastrea japonica : **II** FAVIIDAE An
Cyphastrea microphthalma : **II** FAVIIDAE An
Cyphastrea ocellina : **II** FAVIIDAE An
Cyphastrea serailia : **II** FAVIIDAE An
Cyphastrea tanabensis = Cyphastrea japonica
Cyprian Wild Sheep (E): *Ovis orientalis ophion*
Cyprogenia aberti : (E) Edible Naiad, Edible Pearly Mussel, Western Fanshell, Western Fanshell Mussel **II** UNIONIDAE Bi
Cyprus Mouflon (E): *Ovis orientalis ophion*
Cyrtodactyle de l'île de Serpent (F): *Cyrtodactylus serpensinsula*
Cyrtonaias tampicoensis ssp. *tecomatensis = Unio tampicoensis* ssp. *tecomatensis*

Dabb Lizard (E): *Uromastyx aegyptia*
Dabb's Mastigure (E): *Uromastyx acanthinura*
Daboia russelii : (E) Russell's Viper, (F) Dabois, Vipère de Russell **III** VIPERIDAE Re
Dabois (F): *Daboia russelii*
Dabry's Sturgeon (E): *Acipenser dabryanus*
Dactylotrochus cervicornis : **II** CARYOPHYLLIIDAE An
Daim de Mésopotamie (F): *Dama mesopotamica*
Daisy corals (E): *Goniopora spp./ Tubastraea spp.*
D'Albert's Python (E): *Leiopython albertisii*
Dalgyte (E): *Macrotis lagotis*
Dall's Porpoise (E): *Phocoenoides dalli*
Dalmatian Pelican (E): *Pelecanus crispus*
Dama dama ssp. *mesopotamica = Dama mesopotamica*
Dama Gazelle (E): *Gazella dama*
Dama mesopotamica : (E) Mesopotamian Fallow Deer, Persian Fallow Deer, (S) Dama pérsico, Gacela de Irán, Gamo de Mesopotamia, (F) Daim de Mésopotamie, **I** CERVIDAE Ma
Dama pérsico (S): *Dama mesopotamica*
Damaliscus lunatus : (E) Topi, Tsessebe, Tsessebi, (S) Sasabi , Tiang, (F) Damalisque, Hirola, Korrigum, Sassaby, Topi, **III** BOVIDAE Ma
Damaliscus pygargus pygargus : (E) Bontebok, (S) Bontebok, Topi gacela, (F) Bontebok, **II** BOVIDAE Ma
Damalisque (F): *Damaliscus lunatus*
Damara Korhaan (E): *Eupodotis rueppellii*
Dámero (S): *Rhincodon typus*
Damonia hamiltonii = Geoclemys hamiltonii
Damophila julie : (E) Violet-bellied Hummingbird, (S) Colibrí de Julia, Colibrí ventrivioleta, (F) Colibri julie, **II** TROCHILIDAE Av
Danta (S): *Tapirus terrestris*
Danta cordillerana (S): *Tapirus pinchaque*
Danta lanuda (S): *Tapirus pinchaque*
Danta negra (S): *Tapirus pinchaque*
Dante (S): *Tapirus bairdii*
Danube Sturgeon (E): *Acipenser gueldenstaedtii*

Daptrius americanus : (E) Red-throated Caracara, (S) Caracara comecacao, Caracara gorgirrojo, Carancho ventri-blanco, Chupacacao ventriblanco, (F) Caracara à gorge rouge, Caracara à ventre rouge, **II** FALCONIDAE Av
Daptrius ater : (E) Black Caracara, Yellow-throated Caracara, (S) Caracara negro, Carancho negro, Chupacacao negro, (F) Caracara noir, **II** FALCONIDAE Av
Dara (S): *Burhinus bistriatus*
Dark Chanting-Goshawk (E): *Melierax metabates*
Dark Flying-fox (E): *Pteropus subniger*
Dark Serpent-Eagle (E): *Spilornis elgini*
Dark-handed Gibbon (E): *Hylobates agilis*
Dark-spotted Anaconda (E): *Eunectes deschauenseei*
Darwin's Rhea (E): *Rhea pennata*
Dasmosmilia lymani : (E) Splitting Cup Coral **II** CARYOPHYLLIIDAE An
Dasmosmilia pacifica = Dasmosmilia lymani
Dasmosmilia valida : **II** CARYOPHYLLIIDAE An
Dasmosmilia variegata : **II** CARYOPHYLLIIDAE An
Dasyorne à long bec (F): *Dasyornis longirostris*
Dasyornerousse de l'Ouest (F): *Dasyornis broadbenti litoralis*
Dasyornis brachypterus ssp. *longirostris = Dasyornis longirostris*
Dasyornis broadbenti litoralis : (E) Lesser Rufous Bristlebird, Rufous Bristlebird, Rufous-headed Bristlebird, Western Rufous Bristlebird, (S) Curruca bigotuda rojiza, Papamoscas rosa occidental, (F) Dasyornerousse de l'Ouest, Fauvette rousse de l'Ouest, **I** MUSCICAPIDAE Av
Dasyornis longirostris : (E) Long-billed Bristlebird, Western Bristlebird, (S) Curruca bigotuda piquilarga, Papamoscas piquilargo, (F) Dasyorne à long bec, Fauvette à long bec, Fauvette brune à long bec, Malure occidental, **I** MUSCICAPIDAE Av
Dasyprocta punctata : (E) Central American Agouti, (S) Agoutí rojizo, Agutí de América Central, (F) Agouti ponctué, **III** DASYPROCTIDAE Ma
Dasyprocta variegata = Dasyprocta punctata
Daubentonia madagascariensis : (E) Aye-aye, (S) Aye-aye, (F) Aye-aye, **I** DAUBENTONIIDAE Ma
Daubenton's Curassow (E): *Crax daubentoni*
Dauphin à bosse de l'Atlantique (F): *Sousa teuszii*
Dauphin à bosse de l'Indo-Pacifique (F): *Sousa chinensis*
Dauphin aptère austral (F): *Lissodelphis peronii*
Dauphin aptère boréal (F): *Lissodelphis borealis*
Dauphin blanc (F): *Delphinapterus leucas*
Dauphin bleu et blanc (F): *Stenella coeruleoalba*
Dauphin commun (F): *Delphinus delphis*
Dauphin crucigère (F): *Lagenorhynchus cruciger*
Dauphin de Clymène (F): *Stenella clymene*
Dauphin de Commerson (F): *Cephalorhynchus commersonii*
Dauphin de Fraser (F): *Lagenodelphis hosei*
Dauphin de Heaviside (F): *Cephalorhynchus heavisidii*
Dauphin de la Plata (F): *Pontoporia blainvillei*
Dauphin de l'Amazone (F): *Inia geoffrensis*
Dauphin de Risso (F): *Grampus griseus*
Dauphin d'Hector (F): *Cephalorhynchus hectori*
Dauphin fluviatile de Chine (F): *Lipotes vexillifer*
Dauphin longirostre (F): *Stenella longirostris*
Dauphin noir du Chili (F): *Cephalorhynchus eutropia*
Dauphin rayé (F): *Stenella coeruleoalba*
Dauphin tacheté de l'Atlantique (F): *Stenella frontalis*
Dauphin tacheté pantropical (F): *Stenella attenuata*
Dauphins blancs (F): *Sousa* spp.
Dauphins de rivière (F): *Sotalia* spp.
David's Owl (E): *Strix davidi*
Day geckos (E): *Phelsuma* spp.
De Brazza's Monkey (E): *Cercopithecus neglectus*
Deceptive Chameleon (E): *Calumma fallax*
Deepsea Star Coral (E): *Deltocyathus calcar*
Deer Hog (E): *Babyrousa babyrussa*

Deer Tiger (E): *Puma concolor*
Delcourt's Sticky-toed Gecko (E): *Hoplodactylus delcourti*
Delfín austral (S): *Lagenorhynchus australis*
Delfín blanco africano (S): *Sousa teuszii*
Delfín blanco de China (S): *Sousa chinensis*
Delfín blanco y azul (S): *Stenella coeruleoalba*
Delfín común (S): *Delphinus delphis*
Delfín cruzado (S): *Lagenorhynchus cruciger*
Delfín de Borneo (S): *Lagenodelphis hosei*
Delfín de China (S): *Lipotes vexillifer*
Delfín de flancos blancos (S): *Lagenorhynchus acutus*
Delfín de Héctor (S): *Cephalorhynchus hectori*
Delfín de la Plata (S): *Pontoporia blainvillei*
Delfín de pico blanco (S): *Lagenorhynchus albirostris*
Delfín de pico largo (S): *Steno bredanensis*
Delfín de Risso (S): *Grampus griseus*
Delfín del Ganges (S): *Platanista gangetica*
Delfín del Indo (S): *Platanista minor*
Delfín del Irrawaddy (S): *Orcaella brevirostris*
Delfín lagenor ringo (S): *Lagenorhynchus obliquidens*
Delfín liso (S): *Lissodelphis borealis/ Lissodelphis peronii*
Delfín listado (S): *Lagenorhynchus obscurus*
Delfín manchado (S): *Stenella attenuata*
Delfín manchado del Atlántico (S): *Stenella frontalis*
Delfín mular (S): *Tursiops truncatus*
Delfín negro (S): *Cephalorhynchus eutropia*
Delfín pintado (S): *Stenella attenuata*
Delfín tornillón (S): *Stenella longirostris*
Delfines blancos (S): *Sousa* spp.
Delicate Ivory Bush Coral (E): *Oculina tenella*
Delphinaptère blanc (F): *Delphinapterus leucas*
Delphinapterus leucas : (E) Beluga, White Whale, (S)
    Ballena blanca, (F) Bélouga, Dauphin blanc,
    Delphinaptère blanc, **II** MONODONTIDAE Ma
Delphinus capensis = Delphinus delphis
Delphinus delphis : (E) Atlantic Dolphin, Common
    Dolphin, Pacific Dolphin, Saddle-backed Dolphin,
    Short-beaked Saddleback Dolphin, (S) Delfín común,
    (F) Dauphin commun, **II** DELPHINIDAE Ma
Delphinus tropicalis = Delphinus delphis
Deltocyathoides orientalis : **II** TURBINOLIIDAE An
Deltocyathoides stimpsonii : **II** TURBINOLIIDAE An
Deltocyathus agassizii : **II** CARYOPHYLLIIDAE An
Deltocyathus andamanicus : **II** CARYOPHYLLIIDAE An
Deltocyathus calcar : (E) Deepsea Star Coral **II**
    CARYOPHYLLIIDAE An
Deltocyathus cameratus : **II** CARYOPHYLLIIDAE An
Deltocyathus conicus = Deltocyathus italicus
Deltocyathus corrugatus : **II** CARYOPHYLLIIDAE An
Deltocyathus crassiseptum : **II** CARYOPHYLLIIDAE An
Deltocyathus eccentricus : **II** CARYOPHYLLIIDAE An
Deltocyathus formosus = Deltocyathus suluensis
Deltocyathus halianthus : **II** CARYOPHYLLIIDAE An
Deltocyathus heteroclitus : **II** CARYOPHYLLIIDAE An
Deltocyathus italicus : **II** CARYOPHYLLIIDAE An
Deltocyathus magnificus : **II** CARYOPHYLLIIDAE An
Deltocyathus moseleyi : **II** CARYOPHYLLIIDAE An
Deltocyathus murrayi : **II** CARYOPHYLLIIDAE An
Deltocyathus ornatus : **II** CARYOPHYLLIIDAE An
Deltocyathus parvulus : **II** CARYOPHYLLIIDAE An
Deltocyathus philippinensis : **II** CARYOPHYLLIIDAE
    An
Deltocyathus pourtalesi : **II** CARYOPHYLLIIDAE An
Deltocyathus rotulus : **II** CARYOPHYLLIIDAE An
Deltocyathus sarsi : **II** CARYOPHYLLIIDAE An
Deltocyathus stella : **II** CARYOPHYLLIIDAE An
Deltocyathus suluensis : **II** CARYOPHYLLIIDAE An
Deltocyathus taiwanicus : **II** CARYOPHYLLIIDAE An
Deltocyathus varians : **II** CARYOPHYLLIIDAE An
Deltocyathus vaughani : **II** CARYOPHYLLIIDAE An
Deltocyathus vincentinus = Australocyathus vincentinus
Demidoff's Dwarf Galago (E): *Galagoides demidoff*
Demidoff's Galago (E): *Galagoides demidoff*
Demoiselle Crane (E): *Grus virgo*
Demoiselle de Numidie (F): *Grus virgo*

Demonic Poison Frog (E): *Minyobates steyermarki*
Dendrobate à cinq bandes (F): *Dendrobates
    quinquevittatus*
Dendrobate à tapirer (F): *Dendrobates tinctorius*
Dendrobate à trois bandes (F): *Epipedobates trivittatus*
Dendrobate arboricole (F): *Dendrobates arboreus*
Dendrobate au ventre tacheté (F): *Dendrobates
    ventrimaculatus*
Dendrobate biolat (F): *Dendrobates biolat*
Dendrobate bleu (F): *Dendrobates azureus*
Dendrobate de Bassler (F): *Epipedobates bassleri*
Dendrobate de Lamas (F): *Dendrobates lamasi*
Dendrobate de Lehman (F): *Dendrobates lehmanni*
Dendrobate de Silverstone (F): *Epipedobates silverstonei*
Dendrobate de Sira (F): *Dendrobates imitator*
Dendrobate de Vanzolini (F): *Dendrobates vanzolinii*
Dendrobate doré (F): *Dendrobates auratus*
Dendrobate du Rio Magdalena (F): *Dendrobates truncatus*
Dendrobate du Rio Santiago (F): *Dendrobates captivus*
Dendrobate du Tapajos (F): *Dendrobates galactonotus*
Dendrobate du Xingu (F): *Dendrobates castaneticus*
Dendrobate fantastique (F): *Dendrobates fantasticus*
Dendrobate granuleux (F): *Dendrobates granuliferus*
Dendrobate imitateur (F): *Dendrobates imitator*
Dendrobate jaune et noir (F): *Dendrobates leucomelas*
Dendrobate labié (F): *Dendrobates labialis*
Dendrobate mystérieux (F): *Dendrobates mysteriosus*
Dendrobate occulté (F): *Dendrobates occultator*
Dendrobate pumilio (F): *Dendrobates pumilio*
Dendrobate réticulé (F): *Dendrobates reticulatus*
Dendrobate rougeâtre (F): *Epipedobates rufulus*
Dendrobate variable (F): *Dendrobates ventrimaculatus*
Dendrobates (F): *Dendrobates* spp. / *Epipedobates* spp./
    Minyobates spp.
Dendrobates spp.: (E) Poison frogs, (S) Ranas de puntas
    de flechas, (F) Dendrobates, **II** DENDROBATIDAE
    Am
Dendrobates abditus = Minyobates abditus
Dendrobates altobueyensis = Minyobates altobueyensis
Dendrobates andinus = Epipedobates andinus
Dendrobates anthonyi = Epipedobates tricolor
Dendrobates arboreus : (E) Polkadot Poison Frog, (S)
    Rana de punta de flecha arbórea, (F) Dendrobate
    arboricole, **II** DENDROBATIDAE Am
Dendrobates auratus : (E) Green Poison Frog, Green-and-
    black Poison Frog, (F) Dendrobate doré **II**
    DENDROBATIDAE Am
Dendrobates azureiventris = Epipedobates azureiventris
Dendrobates azureus : (E) Blue Poison Frog, Giant Poison
    Frog, (S) Rana de punta de flecha azul, (F)
    Dendrobate bleu, **II** DENDROBATIDAE Am
Dendrobates bassleri = Epipedobates bassleri
Dendrobates biolat : (E) Biolat Poison Frog, (F)
    Dendrobate biolat **II** DENDROBATIDAE Am
Dendrobates bolivianus = Epipedobates bolivianus
Dendrobates bombetes = Minyobates bombetes
Dendrobates boulengeri = Epipedobates boulengeri
Dendrobates captivus : (E) Rio Santiago Poison Frog, (F)
    Dendrobate du Rio Santiago **II** DENDROBATIDAE
    Am
Dendrobates castaneoticus : (E) Brazil-nut Poison Frog,
    (F) Dendrobate du Xingu **II** DENDROBATIDAE Am
Dendrobates claudiae : **II** DENDROBATIDAE Am
Dendrobates erythromos = Epipedobates erythromos
Dendrobates espinosai = Epipedobates espinosai
Dendrobates fantasticus : (E) Red-headed Poison Frog, (S)
    Rana de punta de flecha fantástica, (F) Dendrobate
    fantastique, **II** DENDROBATIDAE Am
Dendrobates femoralis = Epipedobates femoralis
Dendrobates fulguritus = Minyobates fulguritus
Dendrobates galactonotus : (E) Splash-backed Poison
    Frog, (F) Dendrobate du Tapajos **II**
    DENDROBATIDAE Am

Checklist of fauna/Lista de especies de fauna/Liste des espèces animales

Dendrobates granuliferus : (S) Rana de punta de flecha granulosa, (F) Dendrobate granuleux, Granular Poison Frog, **II** DENDROBATIDAE Am

Dendrobates histrionicus : (E) Harlequin Poison Frog, Red-and-black Poison Frog, (S) Rana de punta de flecha histriónica **II** DENDROBATIDAE Am

Dendrobates imitator : (E) Mimic Poison Frog, Sira Poison Frog, (F) Dendrobate de Sira, Dendrobate imitateur **II** DENDROBATIDAE Am

Dendrobates ingeri = *Epipedobates ingeri*

Dendrobates labialis : (F) Dendrobate labié **II** DENDROBATIDAE Am

Dendrobates lamasi : (E) Pasco Poison Frog, (F) Dendrobate de Lamas **II** DENDROBATIDAE Am

Dendrobates lehmanni : (E) Lehmann's Poison Frog, Red-banded Poison Frog, (S) Rana de punta de flecha de Lehmann, (F) Dendrobate de Lehman, **II** DENDROBATIDAE Am

Dendrobates leucomelas : (E) Yellow-banded Poison Frog, (S) Rana de punta de flecha de bandas amarillas, (F) Dendrobate jaune et noir, **II** DENDROBATIDAE Am

Dendrobates maculatus = *Epipedobates maculatus*

Dendrobates minutus = *Minyobates minutus*

Dendrobates myersi = *Epipedobates myersi*

Dendrobates mysteriosus : (E) Maranon Poison Frog, (S) Rana de punta de flecha misteriosa, (F) Dendrobate mystérieux, **II** DENDROBATIDAE Am

Dendrobates occultator : (E) La Brea Poison Frog, (F) Dendrobate occulté **II** DENDROBATIDAE Am

Dendrobates opisthomelas = *Minyobates opisthomelas*

Dendrobates parvulus = *Epipedobates parvulus*

Dendrobates petersi = *Epipedobates petersi*

Dendrobates pictus = *Epipedobates pictus*

Dendrobates pulchripectus = *Epipedobates pulchripectus*

Dendrobates pumilio : (E) Flaming Poison Frog, Red-and-blue Poison Frog, (S) Rana de punta de flecha roja, (F) Dendrobate pumilio, Strawberry Poison Frog, **II** DENDROBATIDAE Am

Dendrobates quinquevittatus : (E) Amazonian Poison-Arrow Frog, Rio Madeira Poison Frog, (S) Rana de punta de flecha pentaestriada, (F) Dendrobate à cinq bandes, **II** DENDROBATIDAE Am

Dendrobates reticulatus : (E) Red-backed Poison Frog, Reticulated Poison Frog, (S) Rana de punta de flecha reticulada, (F) Dendrobate réticulé, **II** DENDROBATIDAE Am

Dendrobates rufulus = *Epipedobates rufulus*

Dendrobates silverstonei = *Epipedobates silverstonei*

Dendrobates sirensis = *Dendrobates imitator*

Dendrobates smaragdinus = *Epipedobates smaragdinus*

Dendrobates speciosus : (E) Splendid Poison Frog, (F) Epipedobate brillant **II** DENDROBATIDAE Am

Dendrobates steyermarki = *Minyobates steyermarki*

Dendrobates tinctorius : (E) Dyeing Poison Frog, (F) Dendrobate à tapirer **II** DENDROBATIDAE Am

Dendrobates tricolor = *Epipedobates tricolor*

Dendrobates trivittatus = *Epipedobates trivittatus*

Dendrobates truncatus : (E) Yellow-striped Poison Frog, (S) Rana de punta de flecha truncada, (F) Dendrobate du Rio Magdalena, **II** DENDROBATIDAE Am

Dendrobates vanzolinii : (E) Brazilian Poison Frog, (S) Rana de punta de flecha de Vanzolini, (F) Dendrobate de Vanzolini, **II** DENDROBATIDAE Am

Dendrobates variabilis = *Dendrobates ventrimaculatus*

Dendrobates ventrimaculatus : (E) Amazonian Poison Frog, (S) Rana de punta de flecha de variable, (F) Dendrobate au ventre tacheté, Dendrobate variable, **II** DENDROBATIDAE Am

Dendrobates vicentei : **II** DENDROBATIDAE Am

Dendrobates viridis = *Minyobates viridis*

Dendrobates virolensis = *Minyobates virolensis*

Dendrobates zaparo = *Epipedobates zaparo*

Dendrocygna arborea : (E) Black-billed Wood-Duck, Cuban Tree-Duck, West Indian Tree-Duck, West Indian Whistling-Duck, (S) Gïririri de pico negro, Pato silbón de Cuba, Suirirí yaguaza, (F) Dendrocygne à bec noir, Dendrocygne des Antilles, **II** ANATIDAE Av

Dendrocygna autumnalis : (E) Black-bellied Whistling-Duck, Red-billed Whistling-Duck, (S) Guirirí, Pato silbón ventrinegro, Pijiji aliblanco, Suirirí piquirrojo, (F) Dendrocygne à bec rouge, Dendrocygne à ventre noir, **III** ANATIDAE Av

Dendrocygna bicolor : (E) Fulvous Tree-Duck, Fulvous Whistling-Duck, (S) Pato silbón común, Pijiji canelo, Suirirí bicolor, Suirirí leonado, Yaguaso colorado, (F) Dendrocygne fauve, **III** ANATIDAE Av

Dendrocygna fulva = *Dendrocygna bicolor*

Dendrocygna viduata : (E) White-faced Tree-Duck, White-faced Whistling-Duck, (S) Pato silbón cariblanco, Suirirí cariblanco, Yagouaso cariblanco, (F) Dendrocygne veuf, **III** ANATIDAE Av

Dendrocygne à bec noir (F): *Dendrocygna arborea*

Dendrocygne à bec rouge (F): *Dendrocygna autumnalis*

Dendrocygne à ventre noir (F): *Dendrocygna autumnalis*

Dendrocygne des Antilles (F): *Dendrocygna arborea*

Dendrocygne fauve (F): *Dendrocygna bicolor*

Dendrocygne veuf (F): *Dendrocygna viduata*

Dendrogale melanura : (E) Bornean Smooth-tailed Treeshrew, (S) Tupaya de Borneo **II** TUPAIIDAE Ma

Dendrogale murina : (E) Northern Smooth-tailed Treeshrew, (F) Toupaïe murin **II** TUPAIIDAE Ma

Dendrogyra cylindrus : (E) Pillar Coral **II** MEANDRINIIDAE An

Dendrolague gris (F): *Dendrolagus inustus*

Dendrolague noir (F): *Dendrolagus ursinus*

Dendrolagus inustus : (E) Grizzled Tree-kangaroo, (S) Canguro arbóreo gris, Canguro arborícola gris, (F) Dendrolague gris, **II** MACROPODIDAE Ma

Dendrolagus ursinus : (E) Black Tree-kangaroo, Vogelkop Tree-kangaroo, White-throated Tree-kangaroo, (S) Canguro arbóreo negro, Canguro arborícola negro, (F) Dendrolague noir, **II** MACROPODIDAE Ma

Dendrophyllia aculeata : **II** DENDROPHYLLIIDAE An

Dendrophyllia alcocki : **II** DENDROPHYLLIIDAE An

Dendrophyllia alternata : **II** DENDROPHYLLIIDAE An

Dendrophyllia arbuscula : **II** DENDROPHYLLIIDAE An

Dendrophyllia atrata = *Astrangia atrata*

Dendrophyllia boschmai : **II** DENDROPHYLLIIDAE An

Dendrophyllia boschmai boschmai : **II** DENDROPHYLLIIDAE An

Dendrophyllia boschmai cyathelioides : **II** DENDROPHYLLIIDAE An

Dendrophyllia californica : **II** DENDROPHYLLIIDAE An

Dendrophyllia cladonia : **II** DENDROPHYLLIIDAE An

Dendrophyllia coarctata = *Cladopsammia gracilis*

Dendrophyllia cornigera : **II** DENDROPHYLLIIDAE An

Dendrophyllia cornucopia = *Eguchipsammia cornucopia*

Dendrophyllia cribrosa : **II** DENDROPHYLLIIDAE An

Dendrophyllia danae = *Tubastraea coccinea*

Dendrophyllia dilatata : **II** DENDROPHYLLIIDAE An

Dendrophyllia elegans = *Cladopsammia gracilis*

Dendrophyllia fistula = *Eguchipsammia fistula*

Dendrophyllia florulenta : **II** DENDROPHYLLIIDAE An

Dendrophyllia gaditana = *Eguchipsammia gaditana*

Dendrophyllia horsti = *Dendrophyllia arbuscula*

Dendrophyllia ijimai : **II** DENDROPHYLLIIDAE An

Dendrophyllia incisa : **II** DENDROPHYLLIIDAE An

Dendrophyllia indica : **II** DENDROPHYLLIIDAE An

Dendrophyllia japonica = *Eguchipsammia japonica*

Dendrophyllia johnsoni : **II** DENDROPHYLLIIDAE An

Dendrophyllia klunzingeri = *Dendrophyllia robusta*

Dendrophyllia laboreli : **II** DENDROPHYLLIIDAE An

Dendrophyllia minuscula : **II** DENDROPHYLLIIDAE An

Dendrophyllia oahensis = *Eguchipsammia fistula*

Dendrophyllia oldroydae : **II** DENDROPHYLLIIDAE An

Dendrophyllia praecipua = *Eguchipsammia gaditana*
Dendrophyllia ramea : **II** DENDROPHYLLIIDAE An
Dendrophyllia robusta : **II** DENDROPHYLLIIDAE An
Dendrophyllia serpentina = *Eguchipsammia serpentina*
Dendrophyllia velata : **II** DENDROPHYLLIIDAE An
Denham's Bustard (E): *Neotis denhami*
Deppe's Squirrel (E): *Sciurus deppei*
Derasa Clam (E): *Tridacna derasa*
Derbyan Parakeet (E): *Psittacula derbiana*
Derby's Guan (E): *Oreophasis derbianus*
Dermatemyde de Mawe (F): *Dermatemys mawii*
Dermatemys mawii : (E) Central American River Turtle, (S) Plana, Tortuga blanca, (F) Dermatemyde de Mawe, Tortue de Tabasco, **II** DERMATEMYDIDAE Re
Dermochelys coriacea : (E) Leatherback, Leathery Turtle, Luth, Trunkback turtle, (S) Canal, Tinglada, Tortuga laud, (F) Tortue luth, **I** DERMOCHELYIDAE Re
Deroptyus accipitrinus : (E) Hawk-headed Parrot, Red-fan Parrot, (S) Loro cacique, (F) Papegeai maillé, **II** PSITTACIDAE Av
Deschauensee's Anaconda (E): *Eunectes deschauenseei*
Desert Chameleon (E): *Chamaeleo namaquensis*
Desert Lynx (E): *Caracal caracal*
Desert Monitor (E): *Varanus griseus*
Desert Owl (E): *Strix butleri*
Desert Pygmy Monitor (E): *Varanus eremius*
Desert Rat-kangaroo (E): *Caloprymnus campestris*
Desert Sand Boa (E): *Eryx miliaris*
Desert Tortoise (E): *Gopherus agassizii*
Desmarest's Fig-Parrot (E): *Psittaculirostris desmaresti*
Desmophyllum cristagalli = *Desmophyllum dianthus*
Desmophyllum dianthus : **II** CARYOPHYLLIIDAE An
Desmophyllum striatum : **II** CARYOPHYLLIIDAE An
Desmophyllum tenuescens = *Thalamophyllia tenuescens*
Devil Fish (E): *Eschrichtius robustus*
Devonshire Cup Coral (E): *Caryophyllia smithii*
Devorador de hombres (S): *Carcharodon carcharias*
Dhaman (E): *Ptyas mucosus*
Dhiho's Seahorse (E): *Hippocampus sindonis*
Dhole (E/F): *Cuon alpinus*
Dhongoka Roofed Turtle (E): *Kachuga dhongoka*
Diademed Monkey (E): *Cercopithecus mitis*
Diademed Sifaka (E): *Propithecus diadema*
Diamant à bavette (F): *Poephila cincta cincta*
Diamant à face rouge (F): *Pytilia hypogrammica*
Diamant aurore (F): *Pytilia phoenicoptera*
Diamante colidorado (S): *Agyrtria brevirostris*
Diamante de pecho negro (S): *Poephila cincta cincta*
Diamante gargantiverde (S): *Polyerata fimbriata*
Diamante multicolor (S): *Agyrtria versicolor*
Diamante pechizafiro (S): *Polyerata lactea*
Diamante ventriblanco (S): *Agyrtria leucogaster*
Diamond Python (E): *Morelia spilota*
Diana (S): *Cercopithecus diana*
Diana Guenon (E): *Cercopithecus diana*
Diana Monkey (E): *Cercopithecus diana*
Dian's Tarsier (E): *Tarsius dianae*
Diaseris distorta = *Fungia distorta*
Diaseris fragilis = *Fungia fragilis*
Dicerorhinus sumatrensis : (E) Sumatran Rhinoceros, (S) Rinoceronte de Sumatra, (F) Rhinocéros de Sumatra, **I** RHINOCEROTIDAE Ma
Diceros bicornis : (E) Black Rhinoceros, Browse Rhinoceros, Hook-lipped Rhinoceros, (S) Rinoceronte negro, (F) Rhinocéros noir, **I** RHINOCEROTIDAE Ma
Dichocoenia stellaris : (E) Elliptical Star Coral, Pancake Star Coral **II** MEANDRINIIDAE An
Dichocoenia stokesii : (E) Pineapple Coral **II** MEANDRINIIDAE An
Dichopsammia granulosa : **II** DENDROPHYLLIIDAE An
Dickinson's Kestrel (E): *Falco dickinsoni*
Dicotyles tajacu = *Pecari tajacu*

Didermocerus sumatrensis = *Dicerorhinus sumatrensis*
Diffuse Ivory Bush Coral (E): *Oculina diffusa*
Dindon ocellé (F): *Agriocharis ocellata*
Dinectus truncatus = *Acipenser fulvescens*
Diomedea albatrus : (E) Short-tailed Albatross, Steller's Albatross, (S) Albatros, Albatros colicorto, Albatros rabón, (F) Albatros à queue courte, Albatros de Steller, **I** DIOMEDEIDAE Av
Diopsittaca nobilis : (E) Hahn's Macaw, Noble Macaw, Red-shouldered Macaw, (S) Guacamayo enano, Guacamayo noble, (F) Ara noble, Petit perruche-ara, **II** PSITTACIDAE Av
Diostedé pico acanelado (S): *Ramphastos vitellinus*
Diphyllodes magnificus = *Cicinnurus magnificus*
Diphyllodes respublica = *Cicinnurus respublica*
Diploastrea heliopora : **II** FAVIIDAE An
Diploria clivosa : (E) Knobby Brain Coral **II** FAVIIDAE An
Diploria labyrinthiformis : (E) Common Brain Coral, Grooved Brain Coral **II** FAVIIDAE An
Diploria strigosa : (E) Symmetrical Brain Coral **II** FAVIIDAE An
Dipneuste (F): *Neoceratodus forsteri*
Dipnoo (S): *Neoceratodus forsteri*
Dipsochelys abrupta = *Geochelone gigantea*
Dipsochelys arnoldi = *Geochelone gigantea*
Dipsochelys daudinii = *Geochelone gigantea*
Dipsochelys dussumieri = *Geochelone gigantea*
Dipsochelys elephantina = *Geochelone gigantea*
Dipsochelys grandidieri = *Geochelone gigantea*
Dipsochelys hololissa = *Geochelone gigantea*
Discophus antongilii = *Dyscophus antongilii*
Discosura conversii : (E) Green Thorntail, (S) Colacerda verde, Rabudito verde, (F) Coquette à queue fine, **II** TROCHILIDAE Av
Discosura langsdorffi : (E) Black-bellied Thorntail, (S) Colacerda ventrinegra, Coqueta cola de Lira, Rabudito ventrinegro, (F) Coquette de Langsdorff, **II** TROCHILIDAE Av
Discosura letitiae : (E) Coppery Thorntail, (S) Rabudito cobrizo, (F) Coquette de Létitia, **II** TROCHILIDAE Av
Discosura longicauda : (E) Racket-tailed Coquette, (S) Coqueta cola raqueta, Rabudito de raquetas, (F) Coquette à raquettes, **II** TROCHILIDAE Av
Discosura popelairii : (E) Wire-crested Thorntail, (S) Colacerda crestuda, Rabudito crestado, (F) Coquette de Popelaire, **II** TROCHILIDAE Av
Disk Coral (E): *Heliofungia actiniformis*
Distichopora anceps : **II** STYLASTERIDAE Hy
Distichopora anomala : **II** STYLASTERIDAE Hy
Distichopora barbadensis : **II** STYLASTERIDAE Hy
Distichopora borealis : **II** STYLASTERIDAE Hy
Distichopora borealis borealis : **II** STYLASTERIDAE Hy
Distichopora borealis japonica : **II** STYLASTERIDAE Hy
Distichopora cervina : **II** STYLASTERIDAE Hy
Distichopora coccinea : **II** STYLASTERIDAE Hy
Distichopora contorta : **II** STYLASTERIDAE Hy
Distichopora dispar : **II** STYLASTERIDAE Hy
Distichopora foliacea : **II** STYLASTERIDAE Hy
Distichopora gracilis : **II** STYLASTERIDAE Hy
Distichopora irregularis : **II** STYLASTERIDAE Hy
Distichopora laevigranulosa : **II** STYLASTERIDAE Hy
Distichopora livida : **II** STYLASTERIDAE Hy
Distichopora nitida : **II** STYLASTERIDAE Hy
Distichopora profunda : **II** STYLASTERIDAE Hy
Distichopora providentiae : **II** STYLASTERIDAE Hy
Distichopora rosalindae : **II** STYLASTERIDAE Hy
Distichopora serpens : **II** STYLASTERIDAE Hy
Distichopora sulcata : **II** STYLASTERIDAE Hy
Distichopora uniserialis : **II** STYLASTERIDAE Hy
Distichopora vervoorti : **II** STYLASTERIDAE Hy
Distichopora violacea : **II** STYLASTERIDAE Hy
Distichopora yucatanensis : **II** STYLASTERIDAE Hy

Checklist of fauna/Lista de especies de fauna/Liste des espèces animales

Dob (F): *Uromastyx acanthinura*
Dog Fox (E): *Vulpes cana*
Dog-faced Water Snake (E): *Cerberus rhynchops*
Dolphins (E): CETACEA spp. Ma
Dome Coral (E): *Halomitra pileus*
Domergue's Leaf Chameleon (E): *Brookesia thieli*
Dominican Mango (E): *Anthracothorax dominicus*
Don't coraux récifaux (F): SCLERACTINIA spp. An
Dorcas Gazelle (E): *Gazella dorcas*
Doria's Goshawk (E): *Megatriorchis doriae*
Doricha eliza : (E) Mexican Sheartail, (S) Colibrí de Elisa, Tijereta yucateca, (F) Colibri élise, **II** TROCHILIDAE Av
Doricha enicura : (E) Slender Sheartail, (S) Colibrí colirraro, Tijereta centroamericana, (F) Colibri à queue singulière, **II** TROCHILIDAE Av
Doryfera johannae : (E) Blue-fronted Lancebill, (S) Colibrí picolanza menor, Pico lanza frentiazul, (F) Porte-lance de Jeanne, **II** TROCHILIDAE Av
Doryfera ludovicae : (E) Green-fronted Lancebill, (S) Colibrí picolanza mayor, Pico lanza frentiverde, (F) Porte-lance de Louise, **II** TROCHILIDAE Av
Dos-vert à joues blanches (F): *Nesocharis capistrata*
Dot-eared Coquette (E): *Lophornis gouldii*
Double-eyed Fig-Parrot (E): *Cyclopsitta diophthalma*
Double-scaled Chameleon (E): *Chamaeleo anchietae*
Double-striped Thick-knee (E): *Burhinus bistriatus*
Double-toothed Kite (E): *Harpagus bidentatus*
Douc (E/F): *Pygathrix nemaeus*
Douc Langur (E): *Pygathrix nemaeus*
Douc Monkey (E): *Pygathrix nemaeus*
Doucs (F): *Pygathrix* spp.
Doughnut Coral (E): *Scolymia vitiensis*
Douroucouli (E/F): *Aotus trivirgatus*
Dracaena spp.: (E) Caiman lizards, (S) Jacaruxi, Lagartos dragóns, (F) Dracènes, Lézards caïman, **II** TEIIDAE Re
Dracaena guianensis : (E) Armoured Teyou, Croco-Teju, Four-foot Caiman, Guyanan Caiman Lizard, Jacuruxi, (F) Dracène de Guyane, Lézard-caïman de Guyane **II** TEIIDAE Re
Dracaena paraguayensis : (E) Paraguayan Caiman Lizard, (F) Dracène du Paraguay, Lézard-caïman du Paraguay **II** TEIIDAE Re
Dracène de Guyane (F): *Dracaena guianensis*
Dracène du Paraguay (F): *Dracaena paraguayensis*
Dracènes (F): *Dracaena* spp.
Dragón (S): *Agelaius flavus*
Dragón de Komodo (S): *Varanus komodoensis*
Dragon des Komodos (F): *Varanus komodoensis*
Dragon Lizard (E): *Crocodilurus amazonicus*
Dragon Lizardet (E): *Crocodilurus amazonicus*
Dragonfish (E): *Scleropages formosus*
Drakensberg Crag Lizard (E): *Cordylus melanotus/ Cordylus subviridis*
Drakensberg Dwarf Chameleon (E): *Bradypodion dracomontanum*
Drepanornis albertisi = Epimachus albertisi
Drepanornis bruijnii = Epimachus bruijnii
Drépanornis d'Albertis (F): *Epimachus albertisi*
Drépanornis de Bruijn (F): *Epimachus bruijnii*
Dril (S): *Mandrillus leucophaeus*
Drill (E/S/F): *Mandrillus leucophaeus*
Droguera (F): *Papio hamadryas*
Dromedary Naiad (E): *Dromus dromas*
Dromedary Pearly Mussel (E): *Dromus dromas*
Dromus dromas : (E) Dromedary Naiad, Dromedary Pearly Mussel **I** UNIONIDAE Bi
Dryade à queue fourchue (F): *Thalurania furcata*
Dryade couronnée (F): *Thalurania colombica*
Dryade de Fanny (F): *Thalurania fannyi*
Dryade de Waterton (F): *Thalurania watertonii*
Dryade du Mexique (F): *Thalurania ridgwayi*
Dryade glaucope (F): *Thalurania glaucopis*
Dryas Guenon (E): *Cercopithecus dryas*

Dryas Monkey (E): *Cercopithecus dryas*
Dry-bush Weasel Lemur (E): *Lepilemur leucopus*
Dryocopus javensis richardsi : (E) Tristram's Woodpecker, (S) Pito de vientre blanco de Corea, Pito ventriblanco de Corea, (F) Pic à ventre blanc de Corée, Pic de Tristram, **I** PICIDAE Av
Dryotriorchis spectabilis : (E) African Serpent-Eagle, Congo Serpent-Eagle, (S) Aguila culebrera colilarga, Culebrera congoleña, (F) Aigle serpentaire, Serpentaire du Congo, **II** ACCIPITRIDAE Av
Duc à aigrettes (F): *Lophostrix cristata*
Duc à crinière (F): *Jubula lettii*
Duchess Lorikeet (E): *Charmosyna margarethae*
Duck Hawk (E): *Falco peregrinus*
Duckbill Cat (E): *Polyodon spathula*
Ducorps's Cockatoo (E): *Cacatua ducorpsii*
Dúcula de Mindoro (S): *Ducula mindorensis*
Ducula mindorensis : (E) Mindoro Imperial-Pigeon, Mindoro Zone-tailed Pigeon, (S) Dúcula de Mindoro, Paloma de Mindoro, (F) Carpophage de Mindoro, Pigeon de Mindoro, **I** COLUMBIDAE Av
Dugon (S): *Dugong dugon*
Dugong (E/S/F): *Dugong dugon*
Dugong dugon : (E) Dugong, Sea Cow, (S) Dugon, Dugong, Dugongo, (F) Dugong, **I** DUGONGIDAE Ma
Dugongo (S): *Dugong dugon*
Duiquero azul (S): *Cephalophus monticola*
Duiquero bayo (S): *Cephalophus dorsalis*
Duiquero cebrado (S): *Cephalophus zebra*
Duiquero de Jentink (S): *Cephalophus jentinki*
Duiquero de lomo amarillo (S): *Cephalophus silvicultor*
Duiquero de Ogilby (S): *Cephalophus ogilbyi*
Dull-green Day Gecko (E): *Phelsuma dubia*
Dumerilia madagascariensis = Erymnochelys madagascariensis
Duméril's Boa (E): *Acrantophis dumerili*
Duméril's Monitor (E): *Varanus dumerilii*
Duncanopsammia axifuga : (E) Whisker Coral **II** DENDROPHYLLIIDAE An
Dunocyathus parasiticus : **II** TURBINOLIIDAE An
Dura Turtle (E): *Kachuga tecta*
Durisse (F): *Crotalus durissus*
D'Urville's Birdwing (E): *Ornithoptera urvillianus*
Dusicyon culpaeus = Pseudalopex culpaeus
Dusicyon griseus = Pseudalopex griseus
Dusicyon gymnocercus = Pseudalopex gymnocercus
Dusicyon thous = Cerdocyon thous
Dusky Dolphin (E): *Lagenorhynchus obscurus*
Dusky Eagle-Owl (E): *Bubo coromandus*
Dusky Flying-fox (E): *Pteropus brunneus*
Dusky Hummingbird (E): *Cynanthus sordidus*
Dusky Leaf Monkey (E): *Trachypithecus obscurus*
Dusky Lory (E): *Pseudeos fuscata*
Dusky Musk Deer (E): *Moschus fuscus*
Dusky Parrot (E): *Pionus fuscus*
Dusky Tamarin (E): *Saguinus inustus*
Dusky Titi (E): *Callicebus moloch*
Dusky-billed Parrotlet (E): *Forpus sclateri*
Dusky-headed Conure (E): *Aratinga weddellii*
Dusky-headed Parakeet (E): *Aratinga weddellii*
Dusky-throated Hermit (E): *Phaethornis squalidus*
Duvaucel's Gecko (E): *Holpodactylus duvaucelii*
Duyvenbode's Lory (E): *Chalcopsitta duivenbodei*
Dwarf Bushbaby (E): *Galagoides demidoff*
Dwarf Caiman (E): *Palaeosuchus palpebrosus*
Dwarf chameleons (E): *Bradypodion* spp.
Dwarf Chimpanzee (E): *Pan paniscus*
Dwarf Crag Lizard (E): *Cordylus nebulosus*
Dwarf Day Gecko (E): *Phelsuma pusilla*
Dwarf Fig-Parrot (E): *Cyclopsitta diophthalma*
Dwarf Flying-fox (E): *Pteropus woodfordi*
Dwarf Galago (E): *Galagoides demidoff*
Dwarf Gibbon (E): *Hylobates klossii*
Dwarf Girdled Lizard (E): *Cordylus minor*

Checklist of fauna/Lista de especies de fauna/Liste des espèces animales

Dwarf Karoo Girdled Lizard (E): *Cordylus aridus*
Dwarf lemurs (E): CHEIROGALEIDAE spp.
Dwarf Marginated Tortoise (E): *Testudo weissingeri*
Dwarf Monitor (E): *Varanus storri*
Dwarf Musk Deer (E): *Moschus berezovskii*
Dwarf Sand Boa (E): *Eryx miliaris*
Dwarf Seahorse (E): *Hippocampus zosterae*
Dwarf Sperm Whale (E): *Kogia simus*
Dwarf Sturgeon (E): *Pseudoscaphirhynchus hermanni*
Dyeing Poison Frog (E): *Dendrobates tinctorius*
Dyscophus antongilii : (E) Tomato Frog, (F) Crapaud
    rouge de Madagascar, Grenouille tomate **I**
    MICROHYLIDAE Am
Dysnomia florentina ssp. *florentina* = *Epioblasma*
    florentina ssp. *florentina*
Dysnomia florentina ssp. *walkeri* = *Epioblasma walkeri*
Dysnomia lefevrei = *Epioblasma turgidula*
Dysnomia sampsonii = *Epioblasma sampsonii*
Dysnomia torulosa ssp. *gubernaculum* = *Epioblasma*
    torulosa ssp. *gubernaculum*
Dysnomia torulosa ssp. *rangiana* = *Epioblasma torulosa*
    ssp. *rangiana*
Dysnomia torulosa ssp. *torulosa* = *Epioblasma torulosa*
    ssp. *torulosa*
Dysnomia turgidula = *Epioblasma turgidula*
Dziggetai (E): *Equus hemionus hemionus*

Eagle Owl (E): *Bubo bubo*
East African Sand Boa (E): *Gongylophis colubrinus*
East African Spiny-tailed Lizard (E): *Cordylus*
    tropidosternum
Eastern Bettong (E): *Bettongia gaimardi*
Eastern Black-and-white Colobus (E): *Colobus guereza*
Eastern Black-capped Lory (E): *Lorius hypoinochrous*
Eastern Box Turtle (E): *Terrapene carolina*
Eastern Cape Crag Lizard (E): *Cordylus fasciatus*
Eastern Chanting-Goshawk (E): *Melierax poliopterus*
Eastern Cougar (E): *Puma concolor couguar*
Eastern Golden Frog (E): *Mantella crocea*
Eastern Grass-Owl (E): *Tyto longimembris*
Eastern Imperial Eagle (E): *Aquila heliaca*
Eastern Long-tailed Hermit (E): *Phaethornis superciliosus*
Eastern Marsh-Harrier (E): *Circus spilonotus*
Eastern Needle-clawed Bushbaby (E): *Galago matschiei*
Eastern Needle-clawed Galago (E): *Galago matschiei*
Eastern Panther (E): *Puma concolor couguar*
Eastern Parotia (E): *Parotia helenae*
Eastern Potbelly Seahorse (E): *Hippocampus abdominalis*
Eastern Puma (E): *Puma concolor couguar*
Eastern Red Colobus (E): *Procolobus pennantii*
Eastern Red-footed Falcon (E): *Falco amurensis*
Eastern Riflebird (E): *Ptiloris intercedens*
Eastern Rosella (E): *Platycercus eximius*
Eastern Screech-Owl (E): *Otus asio*
Eastern Tarsier (E): *Tarsius spectrum*
Ebian's Palm Squirrel (E): *Epixerus ebii*
Ebony Leaf Monkey (E): *Trachypithecus auratus*
Echidné à bec courbe (F): *Zaglossus bruijni*
Echidné de Nouvelle-Guinée (F): *Zaglossus bruijni*
Echidnos narilargos (S): *Zaglossus bruijni*
Echinomorpha nishihirai = *Echinophyllia nishihirai*
Echinophyllia aspera : **II** PECTINIIDAE An
Echinophyllia costata : **II** PECTINIIDAE An
Echinophyllia echinata : **II** PECTINIIDAE An
Echinophyllia echinoporoides : **II** PECTINIIDAE An
Echinophyllia maxima : **II** PECTINIIDAE An
Echinophyllia nishihirai : **II** PECTINIIDAE An
Echinophyllia orpheensis : **II** PECTINIIDAE An
Echinophyllia patula : **II** PECTINIIDAE An
Echinophyllia pectinata : **II** PECTINIIDAE An
Echinophyllia taylorae : **II** PECTINIIDAE An
Echinophyllia tosaensis : **II** PECTINIIDAE An
Echinopora ashmorensis : **II** FAVIIDAE An
Echinopora forskaliana : **II** FAVIIDAE An
Echinopora fruticulosa : **II** FAVIIDAE An

Echinopora gemmacea : **II** FAVIIDAE An
Echinopora hirsutissima : **II** FAVIIDAE An
Echinopora horrida : **II** FAVIIDAE An
Echinopora irregularis : **II** FAVIIDAE An
Echinopora lamellosa : **II** FAVIIDAE An
Echinopora mammiformis : **II** FAVIIDAE An
Echinopora pacificus : **II** FAVIIDAE An
Echinopora robusta : **II** FAVIIDAE An
Echinopora tiranensis : **II** FAVIIDAE An
Echnidé à bec courbe (F): *Zaglossus* spp.
Eclectus Parrot (E): *Eclectus roratus*
Eclectus roratus : (E) Eclectus Parrot, (S) Loro ecléctico,
    (F) Grand Éclectus, **II** PSITTACIDAE Av
Ecuadorian Dwarf Boa (E): *Tropidophis battersbyi*
Ecuadorian Eyelash Boa (E): *Trachyboa gularis*
Ecuadorian Hillstar (E): *Oreotrochilus chimborazo*
Ecuadorian Piedtail (E): *Phlogophilus hemileucurus*
Écureuil de Deppe (F): *Sciurus deppei*
Écureuil de Raffles (F): *Ratufa affinis*
Écureuil d'Ebi (F): *Epixerus ebii*
Écureuil des palmiers (F): *Epixerus ebii*
Écureuil des pins (F): *Sciurus deppei*
Écureuil géant commun (F): *Ratufa affinis*
Écureuil géant de Ceylan (F): *Ratufa macroura*
Écureuil géant de l'Inde (F): *Ratufa indica*
Écureuil géant de Malaisie (F): *Ratufa bicolor*
Écureuil géant gris (F): *Ratufa macroura*
Écureuil palmiste (F): *Epixerus ebii*
Écureuil volant de Beecroft (F): *Anomalurus beecrofti*
Écureuil volant de Derby (F): *Anomalurus derbianus*
Écureuil volant de Pel (F): *Anomalurus pelii*
Écureuils géants (F): *Ratufa* spp.
Écureuils volants (F): *Anomalurus* spp.
Edible Naiad (E): *Cyprogenia aberti*
Edible Pearly Mussel (E): *Cyprogenia aberti*
Edmi Gazelle (E): *Gazella cuvieri*
Edwards's Fig-Parrot (E): *Psittaculirostris edwardsii*
Edwards's Pheasant (E): *Lophura edwardsi*
Effraie africaine (F): *Tyto alba*
Effraie de Manus (F): *Tyto manusi*
Effraie de Minahassa (F): *Tyto inexspectata*
Effraie de prairie (F): *Tyto longimembris*
Effraie de Soumagne (F): *Tyto soumagnei*
Effraie de Taliabu (F): *Tyto nigrobrunnea*
Effraie de Tasmanie (F): *Tyto castanops*
Effraie des Célèbes (F): *Tyto rosenbergii*
Effraie des clochers (F): *Tyto alba*
Effraie des Tanimbar (F): *Tyto sororcula*
Effraie d'Hispaniola (F): *Tyto glaucops*
Effraie dorée (F): *Tyto aurantia*
Effraie du Cap (F): *Tyto capensis*
Effraie masquée (F): *Tyto novaehollandiae*
Effraie ombrée (F): *Tyto tenebricosa*
Effraie piquetée (F): *Tyto multipunctata*
Effraie rousse de Madagascar (F): *Tyto soumagnei*
Egretta alba = *Casmerodius albus*
Egretta garzetta : (E) Little Egret, (S) Garceta común, (F)
    Aigrette garzette, **III** ARDEIDAE Av
Eguchipsammia cornucopia : **II** DENDROPHYLLIIDAE
    An
Eguchipsammia fistula : **II** DENDROPHYLLIIDAE An
Eguchipsammia gaditana : **II** DENDROPHYLLIIDAE An
Eguchipsammia japonica : **II** DENDROPHYLLIIDAE An
Eguchipsammia serpentina : **II** DENDROPHYLLIIDAE
    An
Eguchipsammia strigosa : **II** DENDROPHYLLIIDAE An
Eguchipsammia wellsi : **II** DENDROPHYLLIIDAE An
Egyptian Goose (E): *Alopochen aegyptiacus*
Egyptian Mastigure (E): *Uromastyx aegyptia*
Egyptian Spiny-tailed Lizard (E): *Uromastyx aegyptia*
Egyptian Tortoise (E): *Testudo kleinmanni*
Egyptian Vulture (E): *Neophron percnopterus*
Eight-ray Finger Coral (E): *Madracis formosa*

Checklist of fauna/Lista de especies de fauna/Liste des espèces animales

Eira barbara : (E) Tayra, (S) Cabeza de viejo, Gato cutarra, Gato negro, Hurón mayor, Manco, Tejón, Tolumuco, Ucati, Ulamá, (F) Tayra, **III** MUSTELIDAE Ma

El Oro Conure (E): *Pyrrhura orcesi*

El Oro Parakeet (E): *Pyrrhura orcesi*

Elachistodon (F): *Elachistodon westermanni*

Elachistodon westermanni : (E) Indian Egg-eater, Indian Egg-eating Snake, Westermann's Snake, (S) Culebra comedora de huevos, Culebra tragahuevos india, (F) Couleuvre de Westermann, Elachistodon, Mangeur d'oeufs indien, Mangeur d'oeufs indien de Westermann, Mangeur d'úufs asiatique, **II** COLUBRIDAE Re

Élançon blanc (F): *Elanus caeruleus*

Elanio australiano (S): *Elanus axillaris*

Elanio azul (S): *Elanus caeruleus*

Elanio bidentado (S): *Harpagus bidentatus*

Elanio blanco (S): *Elanus leucurus*

Elanio chico (S): *Gampsonyx swainsonii*

Elanio Común (S): *Elanus caeruleus*

Elanio del Mississipí (S): *Ictinia mississippiensis*

Elanio enano (S): *Gampsonyx swainsonii*

Elanio escrito (S): *Elanus scriptus*

Elanio golondrina (S): *Chelictinia riocourii*

Elanio maromero (S): *Elanus leucurus*

Elanio muslirrufo (S): *Harpagus diodon*

Elanio plomizo (S): *Ictinia plumbea*

Elanio tijereta (S): *Elanoides forficatus*

Élanion à queue blanche (F): *Elanus leucurus*

Élanion blanc (F): *Elanus caeruleus*

Élanion d'Australie (F): *Elanus axillaris*

Élanion lettré (F): *Elanus scriptus*

Élanion naucler (F): *Chelictinia riocourii*

Élanion perle (F): *Gampsonyx swainsonii*

Elanoides forficatus : (E) American Swallow-tailed Kite, Swallow-tailed Kite, (S) Elanio tijereta, Gavilán tijereta, Milano tijereta, (F) Milan à queue fourchue, **II** ACCIPITRIDAE Av

Elanus axillaris : (E) Australian Black-shouldered Kite, Black-shouldered Kite, (S) Elanio australiano, (F) Élanion d'Australie, **II** ACCIPITRIDAE Av

Elanus caeruleus : (E) Black-shouldered Kite, Black-winged Kite, (S) Elanio azul, Elanio Común, (F) Élançon blanc, Élanion blanc, **II** ACCIPITRIDAE Av

Elanus caeruleus ssp. *leucurus = Elanus leucurus*

Elanus leucurus : (E) White-tailed Kite, (S) Elanio blanco, Elanio maromero, Gavilán maromero, Milano coliblanco, (F) Élanion à queue blanche, **II** ACCIPITRIDAE Av

Elanus notatus = Elanus axillaris

Elanus riocourii = Chelictinia riocourii

Elanus scriptus : (E) Letter-winged Kite, (S) Elanio escrito, (F) Élanion lettré, **II** ACCIPITRIDAE Av

Eldama Ravine Chameleon (E): *Chamaeleo tremperi*

Eld's Deer (E): *Cervus eldii*

Electra (S): *Peponocephala electra*

Elefante africano (S): *Loxodonta africana*

Elefante asiático (S): *Elephas maximus*

Elefante marino del sur (S): *Mirounga leonina*

Elefantes marinos (S): *Mirounga leonina*

Elegance Coral (E): *Euphyllia picteti*

Elegant Coral (E): *Catalaphyllia jardinei*

Elegant Galago (E): *Euoticus elegantulus*

Elegant Grass-Parakeet (E): *Neophema elegans*

Elegant Parrot (E): *Neophema elegans*

Elegant Sand Boa (E): *Eryx elegans*

Elegant Scops-Owl (E): *Otus elegans*

Eleonora's Falcon (E): *Falco eleonorae*

Eléphant africain (F): *Loxodonta africana*

Eléphant d'Afrique (F): *Loxodonta africana*

Eléphant d'Asie (F): *Elephas maximus*

Eléphant de mer du sud (F): *Mirounga leonina*

Eléphant de mer méridional (F): *Mirounga leonina*

Eléphant d'Inde (F): *Elephas maximus*

Elephant Shark (E): *Cetorhinus maximus*

Elephas maximus : (E) Asian Elephant, Indian Elephant, (S) Elefante asiático, (F) Eléphant d'Asie, Eléphant d'Inde, **I** ELEPHANTIDAE Ma

Elf Owl (E): *Micrathene whitneyi*

Elkhorn Coral (E): *Acropora palmata*

Elliot's Pheasant (E): *Syrmaticus ellioti*

Elliptical Star Coral (E): *Dichocoenia stellaris*

Elongate Leaf Chameleon (E): *Brookesia nasus*

Elongated Tortoise (E): *Indotestudo elongata*

Elvira chionura : (E) White-tailed Emerald, (S) Esmeralda elvira, (F) Colibri elvire, **II** TROCHILIDAE Av

Elvira cupreiceps : (E) Coppery-headed Emerald, (S) Esmeralda capirotada, (F) Colibri à tête cuivrée, **II** TROCHILIDAE Av

Emei Shan Liocichla (E): *Liocichla omeiensis*

Emerald Green Snail (E): *Papustyla pulcherrima*

Emerald Lorikeet (E): *Neopsittacus pullicauda*

Emerald Monitor (E): *Varanus prasinus*

Emerald Poison Frog (E): *Epipedobates smaragdinus*

Emerald Tree Boa (E): *Corallus caninus*

Emerald-bellied Puffleg (E): *Eriocnemis alinae*

Emerald-chinned Hummingbird (E): *Abeillia abeillei*

Emerald-collared Parakeet (E): *Psittacula calthropae*

Émeraude à queue courte (F): *Chlorostilbon poortmani*

Émeraude à queue étroite (F): *Chlorostilbon stenurus*

Émeraude alice (F): *Chlorostilbon alice*

Émeraude cuivrée (F): *Chlorostilbon russatus*

Émeraude de Canivet (F): *Chlorostilbon canivetii*

Émeraude de New Providence (F): *Chlorostilbon bracei*

Émeraude de Porto Rico (F): *Chlorostilbon maugaeus*

Émeraude de Ricord (F): *Chlorostilbon ricordii*

Émeraude d'Hispaniola (F): *Chlorostilbon swainsonii*

Émeraude d'Olivares (F): *Chlorostilbon olivaresi*

Émeraude orvert (F): *Chlorostilbon mellisugus*

Émeraude splendide (F): *Chlorostilbon aureoventris*

Emerauldine à bec noir (F): *Turtur abyssinicus*

Emerauldine à bec rouge (F): *Turtur afer*

Emmons' Black Bear (E): *Ursus americanus emmonsii*

Emouchel des Seychelles (F): *Falco araea*

Emperor Bird-of-paradise (E): *Paradisaea guilielmi*

Emperor of Germany's Bird-of-paradise (E): *Paradisaea guilielmi*

Emperor Scorpion (E): *Pandinus imperator*

Emperor Tamarin (E): *Saguinus imperator*

Empress Brilliant (E): *Heliodoxa imperatrix*

Émyde à ocelles de Birmanie (F): *Morenia ocellata*

Émyde d'Annam (F): *Annamemys annamensis*

Émyde en toit (F): *Geoclemys hamiltonii*

Émyde fluviale indienne (F): *Batagur baska*

Émyde géante de Borneo (F): *Orlitia borneensis*

Émyde indienne à trois carènes (F): *Melanochelys tricarinata*

Émyde ocellée de Birmanie (F): *Melanochelys tricarinata*

Émyde peinte de Bornéo (F): *Callagur borneoensis*

Émyde tricarénée (F): *Kachuga tecta*

Emys crassicollis = Siebenrockiella crassicollis

Emys dhongoka = Kachuga dhongoka

Emys duvaucelii = Kachuga dhongoka

Emys kachuga = Kachuga kachuga

Emys lineata = Kachuga kachuga

Emys mutica = Mauremys mutica

Emys spinosa = Heosemys spinosa

Emys tectum var. *intermedia = Kachuga tentoria*

Emys tentoria = Kachuga tentoria

Emys trivittata = Kachuga trivittata

Enallopsammia marenzelleri = Enallopsammia pusilla

Enallopsammia profunda : **II** DENDROPHYLLIIDAE An

Enallopsammia pusilla : **II** DENDROPHYLLIIDAE An

Enallopsammia rostrata : **II** DENDROPHYLLIIDAE An

Endocyathopora laticostata : **II** TURBINOLIIDAE An

Endopachys australiae = Platytrochus hastatus

Endopachys bulbosa : **II** DENDROPHYLLIIDAE An

Endopachys grayi : **II** DENDROPHYLLIIDAE An

Endopachys japonicum = Endopachys grayi

Endopsammia philippensis : **II** DENDROPHYLLIIDAE An

Endopsammia pourtalesi : **II** DENDROPHYLLIIDAE An

Endopsammia regularis : **II** DENDROPHYLLIIDAE An

Engoulevent d'Europe (F): *Aegolius funereus*

Enhydra lutris : (E) Sea Otter, (S) Nutria del Kamtchatka, Nutria marina, (F) Loutre de mer, **I/II** MUSTELIDAE Ma

Enhydra lutris nereis : (E) California Sea Otter, Southern Sea Otter, (S) Nutria de mar californiana, (F) Loutre de mer de Californie, Loutre de mer méridionale, **I** MUSTELIDAE Ma

Enicognathus ferrugineus : (E) Austral Conure, Austral Parakeet, (S) Cotorra austral, Cotorra cachaña, (F) Conure magellanique, Perruche émeraude, **II** PSITTACIDAE Av

Enicognathus leptorhynchus : (E) Slender-billed Conure, Slender-billed Parakeet, (S) Cotorra choroy, (F) Conure à long bec, Perruche à bec gracile, **II** PSITTACIDAE Av

Ensifera ensifera : (E) Sword-billed Hummingbird, (S) Colibrí picoespada, (F) Colibri porte-épée, **II** TROCHILIDAE Av

Entelle (F): *Semnopithecus entellus*

Entelle de Pagi (F): *Nasalis concolor*

Entelle dorée (F): *Trachypithecus geei*

Entelle pileuse (F): *Trachypithecus pileatus*

Entellus Langur (E): *Semnopithecus entellus*

Enygrus asper = *Candoia aspera*

Enygrus bibroni = *Candoia bibroni*

Enygrus carinata = *Candoia carinata*

Eolophus roseicapillus : (E) Galah, Roseate Cockatoo, (S) Cacatúa rosada, (F) Cacatoès rosalbin, **II** PSITTACIDAE Av

Eos bornea : (E) Moluccan Lory, Red Lory, (S) Lori rojo, (F) Lori écarlate, **II** PSITTACIDAE Av

Eos cyanogenia : (E) Biak Red Lory, Black-winged Lory, (S) Lori alinegro, (F) Lori à joues bleues, **II** PSITTACIDAE Av

Eos histrio : (E) Red-and-blue Lory, (S) Lori de Sangir, (F) Lori arlequin, **I** PSITTACIDAE Av

Eos reticulata : (E) Blue-streaked Lory, (S) Lori de las Tanimbar, (F) Lori réticulé, **II** PSITTACIDAE Av

Eos rubra = *Eos bornea*

Eos semilarvata : (E) Blue-eared Lory, (S) Lori de Seram, (F) Lori masqué, **II** PSITTACIDAE Av

Eos squamata : (E) Moluccan Red Lory, Violet-necked Lory, (S) Lori escamoso, (F) Lori écaillé, **II** PSITTACIDAE Av

Epaulard (F): *Orcinus orca*

Epaulard pygmée (F): *Feresa attenuata*

Éperonnier chinquis (F): *Polyplectron bicalcaratum*

Éperonnier de Bornéo (F): *Polyplectron schleiermacheri*

Éperonnier de Germain (F): *Polyplectron germaini*

Éperonnier de Hardwick (F): *Polyplectron malacense*

Éperonnier de Malaisie (F): *Polyplectron malacense*

Éperonnier de Palawan (F): *Polyplectron emphanum*

Éperonnier de Rothschild (F): *Polyplectron inopinatum*

Éperonnier gris (F): *Polyplectron bicalcaratum*

Éperonnier malais (F): *Polyplectron malacense*

Éperonnier Napoléon (F): *Polyplectron emphanum*

Épervier à collier interrompu (F): *Accipiter collaris*

Épervier à collier roux (F): *Accipiter cirrocephalus*

Épervier à cuisses rouges (F): *Accipiter erythronemius*

Épervier à cuisses rousses (F): *Accipiter erythronemius*

Épervier à gorge grise (F): *Accipiter erythrauchen*

Épervier à gorge rayée (F): *Accipiter ventralis*

Épervier à pieds courts (F): *Accipiter brevipes*

Épervier à poitrine blanche (F): *Accipiter chionogaster*

Épervier à poitrine rousse (F): *Accipiter rhodogaster*

Épervier à queue tachetée (F): *Accipiter trinotatus*

Épervier besra (F): *Accipiter virgatus*

Épervier bicolore (F): *Accipiter bicolor*

Épervier brun (F): *Accipiter striatus*

Épervier de Cooper (F): *Accipiter cooperii*

Épervier de Cuba (F): *Accipiter gundlachi*

Épervier de Frances (F): *Accipiter francesii*

Épervier de Hartlaub (F): *Accipiter erythropus*

Épervier de Horsfield (F): *Accipiter soloensis*

Épervier de l'Ovampo (F): *Accipiter ovampensis*

Épervier de Madagascar (F): *Accipiter madagascariensis*

Épervier de Nouvelle-Bretagne (F): *Accipiter brachyurus*

Épervier des Célèbes (F): *Accipiter nanus*

Épervier des Nicobar (F): *Accipiter butleri*

Épervier d'Europe (F): *Accipiter nisus*

Épervier du Japon (F): *Accipiter gularis*

Épervier menu (F): *Accipiter rufiventris*

Épervier minule (F): *Accipiter minullus*

Épervier nain (F): *Accipiter superciliosus*

Épervier pie (F): *Accipiter melanoleucus*

Épervier shikra (F): *Accipiter badius*

Ephippiorhynchus senegalensis : (E) Saddlebill Stork, Saddle-billed Stork, (S) Cigüeña ensillada, Jabirú, Jabirú Africano, (F) Jabiru, Jabiru africain, Jabiru d'Afrique, Jabiru du Sénégal, **III** CICONIIDAE Av

Epicrates angulifer : (E) Cuban Boa, Cuban Tree Boa, (S) Boa de Cuba, Maja de Sta. María, (F) Boa de Cuba, **II** BOIDAE Re

Epicrates cenchria : (E) Rainbow Boa, (S) Boa irisada, (F) Aboma, Boa arc-en-ciel, **II** BOIDAE Re

Epicrates cenchria ssp. *maurus* = *Epicrates maurus*

Epicrates chrysogaster : (E) Bahamas Islands Boa, Turks Islands Boa, (F) Boa de l'île Turk **II** BOIDAE Re

Epicrates exsul : (E) Abaco Island Boa, (F) Boa de l'île Abaco **II** BOIDAE Re

Epicrates fordii : (E) Ford's Boa, (F) Boa de Ford **II** BOIDAE Re

Epicrates gracilis : (E) Haitian Vine Boa, Hispaniolan Boa, (F) Boa arboricole gracile, Boa d'Hispaniola **II** BOIDAE Re

Epicrates gracilis ssp. *monensis* = *Epicrates monensis*

Epicrates inornatus : (E) Puerto Rican Boa, Yellow Tree Boa, (S) Boa de Puerto Rico, (F) Boa de Porto Rico, Boa sobre, **I** BOIDAE Re

Epicrates inornatus ssp. *fordii* = *Epicrates fordii*

Epicrates maurus : **II** BOIDAE Re

Epicrates monensis : (E) Mona Island Boa, Virgin Islands Tree Boa, (F) Boa de l'île Mona, Boa de Mona **I** BOIDAE Re

Epicrates striatus : (E) Fischer's Tree Boa, Haitian Boa, (F) Boa d'Haïti **II** BOIDAE Re

Epicrates striatus ssp. *chrysogaster* = *Epicrates chrysogaster*

Epicrates subflavus : (E) Jamaican Boa, (S) Boa de Jamaica, (F) Boa de la Jamaïque, **I** BOIDAE Re

Epimachus albertisi : (E) Black-billed Sicklebill, Buff-tailed Sicklebill, (F) Drépanornis d'Albertis, Paradisier d'Albertis **II** PARADISAEIDAE Av

Epimachus bruijnii : (E) Pale-billed Sicklebill, White-billed Sicklebill, (F) Drépanornis de Bruijn, Paradisier à bec blanc **II** PARADISAEIDAE Av

Epimachus fastuosus : (E) Black Sicklebill, (F) Epimaque fastueux, Paradisier fastueux **II** PARADISAEIDAE Av

Epimachus meyeri : (E) Brown Sicklebill, (F) Epimaque de Mayer, Paradisier de Meyer **II** PARADISAEIDAE Av

Epimaque de Mayer (F): *Epimachus meyeri*

Epimaque fastueux (F): *Epimachus fastuosus*

Epioblasma curtisii : (E) Curtis' Pearly Mussel, Curtis' Riffleshell **I** UNIONIDAE Bi

Epioblasma florentina : (E) Yellow Blossom, Yellow Riffleshell, Yellow-blossom Pearly Mussel **I** UNIONIDAE Bi

Epioblasma florentina florentina : **I** UNIONIDAE Bi

Epioblasma florentina ssp. *walkeri* = *Epioblasma walkeri*

Epioblasma lefevrei = *Epioblasma turgidula*

Epioblasma rangiana = *Epioblasma torulosa* ssp. *rangiana*

Epioblasma sampsonii : (E) Sampson's Naiad, Sampson's Pearly Mussel, Sampson's Riffleshell, Wabash Riffleshell **I** UNIONIDAE Bi

Epioblasma torulosa gubernaculum : (E) Green Blossom, Green Riffle Shell, Green-blossom Pearly Mussel **I** UNIONIDAE Bi

Epioblasma torulosa rangiana : (E) Northern Riffleshell, Tan-blossom Pearly Mussel **II** UNIONIDAE Bi

Epioblasma torulosa torulosa : (E) Tubercled Blossom, Tubercled-blossom Pearly Mussel, Turberculed Riffle Shell **I** UNIONIDAE Bi

Epioblasma turgidula : (E) Turgid Blossom, Turgid Riffle Shell, Turgid-blossom Pearly Mussel **I** UNIONIDAE Bi

Epioblasma walkeri : (E) Brown-blossom Naiad, Brown-blossom Pearly Mussel, Tan Riffleshell **I** UNIONIDAE Bi

Epipedobate andin (F): *Epipedobates andinus*

Epipedobate au ventre bleu (F): *Epipedobates azureiventris*

Epipedobate bolivien (F): *Epipedobates bolivianus*

Epipedobate brillant (F): *Dendrobates speciosus*

Epipedobate calisterne (F): *Epipedobates pulchripectus*

Epipedobate de Bolivie (F): *Epipedobates bolivianus*

Epipedobate de Boulenger (F): *Epipedobates boulengeri*

Epipedobate de Myers (F): *Epipedobates myersi*

Epipedobate de Peters (F): *Epipedobates petersi*

Epipedobate d'Espinosa (F): *Epipedobates espinosai*

Epipedobate d'Inger (F): *Epipedobates ingeri*

Epipedobate du Rio Palenque (F): *Epipedobates erythromos*

Epipedobate émeraude (F): *Epipedobates smaragdinus*

Epipedobate fémorale (F): *Epipedobates femoralis*

Epipedobate minime (F): *Epipedobates parvulus*

Epipedobate peint (F): *Epipedobates pictus*

Epipedobate simisimi (F): *Epipedobates femoralis*

Epipedobate tacheté (F): *Epipedobates maculatus*

Epipedobate tricolore (F): *Epipedobates tricolor*

Epipedobate zaparo (F): *Epipedobates zaparo*

Epipedobates spp.: (E) Poison frogs, (S) Ranas de puntas de flechas, (F) Dendrobates, **II** DENDROBATIDAE Am

Epipedobates andinus : (E) La Planada Poison Frog, (S) Rana de punta de flecha andino, (F) Epipedobate andin, **II** DENDROBATIDAE Am

Epipedobates anthonyi = Epipedobates tricolor

Epipedobates azureiventris : (E) Sky-blue Poison Frog, (S) Rana de punta de flecha de vientre azul, (F) Epipedobate au ventre bleu, **II** DENDROBATIDAE Am

Epipedobates bassleri : (E) Pleasing Poison Frog, (S) Rana de punta de flecha de Bassler, (F) Dendrobate de Bassler, Phobobate de Bassler, **II** DENDROBATIDAE Am

Epipedobates bilinguis : **II** DENDROBATIDAE Am

Epipedobates bolivianus : (E) Bolivian Poison Frog, (S) Rana de punta de flecha boliviana, (F) Epipedobate bolivien, Epipedobate de Bolivie, **II** DENDROBATIDAE Am

Epipedobates boulengeri : (E) Marbled Poison Frog, (S) Rana de punta de flecha de Boulenger, (F) Epipedobate de Boulenger, **II** DENDROBATIDAE Am

Epipedobates braccatus = Epipedobates pictus

Epipedobates cainarachi : **II** DENDROBATIDAE Am

Epipedobates erythromos :, (F) Epipedobate du Rio Palenque **II** DENDROBATIDAE Am

Epipedobates espinosai : (E) Espinosa Poison Frog, Turquoise-bellied Poison Frog, (F) Epipedobate d'Espinosa **II** DENDROBATIDAE Am

Epipedobates femoralis : (E) Brilliant-thighed Poison Frog, (F) Epipedobate fémorale, Epipedobate simisimi, Simisimi, **II** DENDROBATIDAE Am

Epipedobates flavopictus = Epipedobates pictus

Epipedobates hahneli = Epipedobates pictus

Epipedobates ingeri : (E) Niceforo's Poison Frog, (S) Rana de punta de flecha de Inger, (F) Epipedobate d'Inger, **II** DENDROBATIDAE Am

Epipedobates macero : **II** DENDROBATIDAE Am

Epipedobates maculatus : (S) Confusing Poison Frog, Rana de punta de flecha maculada, (F) Epipedobate tacheté, **II** DENDROBATIDAE Am

Epipedobates myersi : (E) Myers's Poison Frog, (S) Rana de punta de flecha de Myers, (F) Epipedobate de Myers, **II** DENDROBATIDAE Am

Epipedobates parvulus : (S) Ruby Poison Frog, (F) Epipedobate minime, **II** DENDROBATIDAE Am

Epipedobates petersi : (E) Peruvian Poison Frog, (S) Rana de punta de flecha de Peters, (F) Epipedobate de Peters, **II** DENDROBATIDAE Am

Epipedobates pictus : (E) Spot-legged Poison Frog, (F) Epipedobate peint, Rana de punta de flecha picta **II** DENDROBATIDAE Am

Epipedobates planipaleae : **II** DENDROBATIDAE Am

Epipedobates pulchripectus : (E) Beautiful-breasted Poison Frog, Blue-breasted Poison Frog, (F) Epipedobate calisterne **II** DENDROBATIDAE Am

Epipedobates rubriventris : **II** DENDROBATIDAE Am

Epipedobates rufulus : (E) Gorzula's Poison Frog, (F) Dendrobate rougeâtre **II** DENDROBATIDAE Am

Epipedobates silverstonei : (E) Silverstone's Poison Frog, (S) Rana de punta de flecha de Silverstone, (F) Dendrobate de Silverstone, Phobobate de Silverstone, **II** DENDROBATIDAE Am

Epipedobates simulans : **II** DENDROBATIDAE Am

Epipedobates smaragdinus : (E) Emerald Poison Frog, (S) Rana de punta de flecha esmeralda, (F) Epipedobate émeraude, **II** DENDROBATIDAE Am

Epipedobates tricolor : (E) Phantasmal Poison Frog, (S) Rana de punta de flecha tricolor, (F) Epipedobate tricolore, **II** DENDROBATIDAE Am

Epipedobates trivittatus : (E) Three-striped Poison Frog, (F) Dendrobate à trois bandes, Phobobate à trois bandes **II** DENDROBATIDAE Am

Epipedobates zaparo : (E) Sanguine Poison Frog, Zaparo's Poison Frog, (F) Epipedobate zaparo **II** DENDROBATIDAE Am

Epixerus ebii : (E) Ebian's Palm Squirrel, Temminck's Giant Squirrel, Western Palm Squirrel, (S) Ardilla de las palmeras, Ardilla de palmera, (F) Écureuil d'Ebi, Écureuil des palmiers, Écureuil palmiste, **III** SCIURIDAE Ma

Equatorial Saki (E): *Pithecia aequatorialis*

Equatorial Spitting Cobra (E): *Naja sumatrana*

Equidna (S): *Zaglossus* spp.

Equidna de Nueva Guinea (S): *Zaglossus bruijni*

Equus africanus : (E) African Ass, African Wild Ass, (S) Asno salvaje de Africa, (F) Ane sauvage d'Afrique, **I** EQUIDAE Ma

Equus caballus ssp. *przewalskii = Equus przewalskii*

Equus ferus ssp. *przewalskii = Equus przewalskii*

Equus grevyi : (E) Grevy's Zebra, (S) Cebra de Grévy, (F) Zèbre de Grévy, **I** EQUIDAE Ma

Equus hemionus : (E) Asian Wild Ass, Asiatic Wild Ass, Kulan, (S) Hemiono, (F) Ane sauvage d'Asie, Hémione, **I/II** EQUIDAE Ma

Equus hemionus hemionus : (E) Dziggetai, Mongolian Wild Ass, North Mongolian Kulan, (S) Hemiono mongol, (F) Ane sauvage de Mongolie, **I** EQUIDAE Ma

Equus hemionus ssp. *khur = Equus onager* ssp. *khur*

Equus hemionus ssp. *kiang = Equus kiang*

Equus hemionus ssp. *onager = Equus onager*

Equus kiang : (E) Kiang, (S) Kiang, (F) Ane sauvage du Tibet, Kiang, **II** EQUIDAE Ma

Equus onager : (E) Onager, (S) Onagro, (F) Onagre, **I/II** EQUIDAE Ma

Equus onager khur : (E) Ghor-khar, Indian Wild Ass, Khur, (S) Hemiono indostánico, Khur, Onagro de la India, (F) Ane sauvage de l'Inde, Hémione de l'Inde, **I** EQUIDAE Ma

Equus przewalskii : (E) Mongolian Wild Horse, Przewalski's Horse, Przewalski's Wild Horse, Takh, (S) Caballo de Przewalski, Caballo salvaje, (F) Cheval de Przewalski, **I** EQUIDAE Ma

Equus zebra : (E) Mountain Zebra **I/II** EQUIDAE Ma

Equus zebra hartmannae : (E) Hartmann's Mountain Zebra, (S) Cebra de Hartmann, (F) Zèbre de Hartmann, Zèbre de montagne de Hartmann, **II** EQUIDAE Ma

Equus zebra zebra : (E) Cape Mountain Zebra, (S) Cebra de montaña del Cabo, Cebra montanesa del Cabo, (F) Zèbre de montagne du Cap, **I** EQUIDAE Ma

Eretmochelys imbricata : (E) Hawksbill Turtle, (S) Tortuga carey, Tortuga de carey, (F) Caret, Tortue à bec de faucon, Tortue à écailles, Tortue imbriquée, **I** CHELONIIDAE Re

Ericiocyathus echinatus : **II** CARYOPHYLLIIDAE An

Eriocnemis alinae : (E) Emerald-bellied Puffleg, (S) Calzadito pechiblanco, Zamarrito pechiblanco, (F) Érione d'Aline, **II** TROCHILIDAE Av

Eriocnemis cupreoventris : (E) Coppery-bellied Puffleg, (S) Calzadito cobrizo, Colibrí pantalón cobrizo, (F) Érione à ventre cuivré, **II** TROCHILIDAE Av

Eriocnemis derbyi : (E) Black-thighed Puffleg, (S) Calzadito patinegro, Zamarrito muslinegro, (F) Érione de Derby, **II** TROCHILIDAE Av

Eriocnemis glaucopoides : (E) Blue-capped Puffleg, (S) Calzadito frentiazul, Picaflor frentivioleta, (F) Érione à front bleu, **II** TROCHILIDAE Av

Eriocnemis godini : (E) Turquoise-throated Puffleg, (S) Calzadito turquesa, Zamarrito gorjiturquesa, (F) Érione turquoise, **II** TROCHILIDAE Av

Eriocnemis luciani : (E) Sapphire-vented Puffleg, (S) Calzadito colilargo norteño, Zamarrito colilargo, (F) Érione Catherine, **II** TROCHILIDAE Av

Eriocnemis mirabilis : (E) Colorful Puffleg, Colourful Puffleg, (S) Calzadito admirable, (F) Érione multicolore, **II** TROCHILIDAE Av

Eriocnemis mosquera : (E) Golden-breasted Puffleg, (S) Calzadito de Mosquera, Zamarrito pechidorado, (F) Érione à poitrine d'or, **II** TROCHILIDAE Av

Eriocnemis nigrivestis : (E) Black-breasted Puffleg, (S) Calzadito pechinegro, Zamarrito pechinegro, (F) Érione à robe noire, **II** TROCHILIDAE Av

Eriocnemis sapphiropygia : (E) Coppery-naped Puffleg **II** TROCHILIDAE Av

Eriocnemis vestitus : (E) Glowing Puffleg, (S) Calzadito reluciente, Colibrí pantalón verde, Zamarrito luciente, (F) Érione pattue, **II** TROCHILIDAE Av

Érione à front bleu (F): *Eriocnemis glaucopoides*
Érione à poitrine d'or (F): *Eriocnemis mosquera*
Érione à robe noire (F): *Eriocnemis nigrivestis*
Érione à ventre cuivré (F): *Eriocnemis cupreoventris*
Érione Catherine (F): *Eriocnemis luciani*
Érione d'Aline (F): *Eriocnemis alinae*
Érione d'Aurélie (F): *Haplophaedia aureliae*
Érione de Derby (F): *Eriocnemis derbyi*
Érione givrée (F): *Haplophaedia lugens*
Érione multicolore (F): *Eriocnemis mirabilis*
Érione pattue (F): *Eriocnemis vestitus*
Érione turquoise (F): *Eriocnemis godini*
Érismature à tête blanche (F): *Oxyura leucocephala*
Ermitañito barbigrís (S): *Phaethornis griseogularis*
Ermitañito gargantifusco (S): *Phaethornis squalidus*
Ermitañito pequeño (S): *Phaethornis longuemareus*
Ermitañito rufo (S): *Phaethornis ruber*
Ermitaño barbiblanco (S): *Phaethornis hispidus*
Ermitaño barbigris (S): *Phaethornis griseogularis*
Ermitaño barbudo (S): *Threnetes ruckeri*
Ermitaño barbudo colibandeado (S): *Threnetes ruckeri*
Ermitaño bigotiblanco (S): *Phaethornis yaruqui*

Ermitaño Boliviano (S): *Phaethornis stuarti*
Ermitaño bronceado (S): *Glaucis aenea*
Ermitaño carinegro (S): *Phaethornis anthophilus*
Ermitaño chico (S): *Phaethornis longuemareus*
Ermitaño coliancho (S): *Anopetia gounellei*
Ermitaño colilargo (S): *Phaethornis superciliosus*
Ermitaño colilargo común (S): *Phaethornis superciliosus*
Ermitaño colilargo norteño (S): *Phaethornis longirostris*
Ermitaño de Espirito Santo (S): *Glaucis dohrnii*
Ermitaño de Koepcke (S): *Phaethornis koepckeae*
Ermitaño de Natterer (S): *Phaethornis nattereri*
Ermitaño de picorrecto (S): *Phaethornis bourcieri*
Ermitaño de Yaruqui (S): *Phaethornis yaruqui*
Ermitaño del planalto (S): *Phaethornis pretrei*
Ermitaño escamoso (S): *Phaethornis eurynome*
Ermitaño escuálido (S): *Phaethornis squalidus*
Ermitaño frentrinegro (S): *Phaethornis pretrei*
Ermitaño gorgiestriado (S): *Phaethornis striigularis*
Ermitaño guayanés (S): *Phaethornis superciliosus*
Ermitaño hirsuto (S): *Glaucis hirsuta*
Ermitaño limpiacasa (S): *Phaethornis augusti*
Ermitaño manchado (S): *Phaethornis eurynome*
Ermitaño ocráceo (S): *Phaethornis subochraceus*
Ermitaño pechicanelo (S): *Glaucis hirsuta*
Ermitaño picoaguja (S): *Phaethornis philippii*
Ermitaño picogrande (S): *Phaethornis malaris*
Ermitaño picosierra (S): *Ramphodon naevius*
Ermitaño pigmeo (S): *Phaethornis idaliae*
Ermitaño piquirrecto (S): *Phaethornis bourcieri*
Ermitaño rojizo (S): *Phaethornis ruber*
Ermitaño ventrihabano (S): *Phaethornis syrmatophorus*
Ermitaño ventripálido (S): *Phaethornis anthophilus*
Ermitaño verde (S): *Phaethornis guy*
Ermite à brins blancs (F): *Phaethornis superciliosus*
Ermite à gorge grise (F): *Phaethornis griseogularis*
Ermite à gorge rayée (F): *Phaethornis striigularis*
Ermite à long bec (F): *Phaethornis malaris*
Ermite à longue queue (F): *Phaethornis longirostris*
Ermite à queue blanche (F): *Threnetes niger*
Ermite à ventre fauve (F): *Phaethornis syrmatophorus*
Ermite anthophile (F): *Phaethornis anthophilus*
Ermite bronzé (F): *Glaucis aenea*
Ermite d'Auguste (F): *Phaethornis augusti*
Ermite de Bourcier (F): *Phaethornis bourcieri*
Ermite de Dohrn (F): *Glaucis dohrnii*
Ermite de Dohrnou à bec incurvé (F): *Glaucis dohrnii*
Ermite de Filippi (F): *Phaethornis philippii*
Ermite de Gounelle (F): *Anopetia gounellei*
Ermite de Koepcke (F): *Phaethornis koepckeae*
Ermite de Natterer (F): *Phaethornis nattereri*
Ermite de Prêtre (F): *Phaethornis pretrei*
Ermite de Rucker (F): *Threnetes ruckeri*
Ermite de Stuart (F): *Phaethornis stuarti*
Ermite d'Idalie (F): *Phaethornis idaliae*
Ermite d'Osery (F): *Phaethornis hispidus*
Ermite eurynome (F): *Phaethornis eurynome*
Ermite hirsute (F): *Glaucis hirsuta*
Ermite nain (F): *Phaethornis longuemareus*
Ermite ocré (F): *Phaethornis subochraceus*
Ermite roussâtre (F): *Phaethornis ruber*
Ermite terne (F): *Phaethornis squalidus*
Ermite vert (F): *Phaethornis guy*
Ermite yaruqui (F): *Phaethornis yaruqui*
Eroïde (F): *Brachyteles arachnoides*
Errina altispina : **II** STYLASTERIDAE Hy
Errina antarctica : **II** STYLASTERIDAE Hy
Errina aspera : **II** STYLASTERIDAE Hy
Errina atlantica : **II** STYLASTERIDAE Hy
Errina bicolor : **II** STYLASTERIDAE Hy
Errina boschmai : **II** STYLASTERIDAE Hy
Errina capensis : **II** STYLASTERIDAE Hy
Errina chathamensis : **II** STYLASTERIDAE Hy
Errina cheilopora : **II** STYLASTERIDAE Hy
Errina cochleata : **II** STYLASTERIDAE Hy
Errina cooki : **II** STYLASTERIDAE Hy

Checklist of fauna/Lista de especies de fauna/Liste des espèces animales

Errina cruenta = *Errina novaezelandiae*
Errina cyclopora : **II** STYLASTERIDAE Hy
Errina dabneyi : **II** STYLASTERIDAE Hy
Errina dendyi : **II** STYLASTERIDAE Hy
Errina fissurata : **II** STYLASTERIDAE Hy
Errina gracilis : **II** STYLASTERIDAE Hy
Errina japonica : **II** STYLASTERIDAE Hy
Errina kerguelensis : **II** STYLASTERIDAE Hy
Errina laevigata : **II** STYLASTERIDAE Hy
Errina laterorifa : **II** STYLASTERIDAE Hy
Errina macrogastra : **II** STYLASTERIDAE Hy
Errina novaezelandiae : **II** STYLASTERIDAE Hy
Errina porifera : **II** STYLASTERIDAE Hy
Errina reticulata : **II** STYLASTERIDAE Hy
Errina rubra = *Errina dendyi*
Errina sinuosa : **II** STYLASTERIDAE Hy
Errinopora cestoporina : **II** STYLASTERIDAE Hy
Errinopora latifundata : **II** STYLASTERIDAE Hy
Errinopora nanneca : **II** STYLASTERIDAE Hy
Errinopora pourtalesii : **II** STYLASTERIDAE Hy
Errinopora stylifera : **II** STYLASTERIDAE Hy
Errinopora zarhyncha : **II** STYLASTERIDAE Hy
Errinopsis fenestrata : **II** STYLASTERIDAE Hy
Errinopsis reticulum : **II** STYLASTERIDAE Hy
Erymnochelys madagascariensis : (E) Madagascar Big-
    headed Turtle, Madagascar Sideneck Turtle, (F)
    Podocnémide de Madagascar **II** PELOMEDUSIDAE
    Re
Erythrastrea flabellata : **II** FAVIIDAE An
Erythrocebus patas : (E) Patas Monkey, (F) Patas **II**
    CERCOPITHECIDAE Ma
Erythrotriorchis buergersi : (E) Bürger's Sparrowhawk,
    Chestnut-mantled Goshawk, Chestnut-shouldered
    Goshawk, Chestnut-shouldered Hawk, (S) Azor de
    Bürgers, (F) Autour de Bürger, **II** ACCIPITRIDAE
    Av
Erythrotriorchis radiatus : (E) Red Goshawk, (S) Azor
    rojo, (F) Autour rouge, **II** ACCIPITRIDAE Av
Eryx colubrinus = *Gongylophis colubrinus*
Eryx conicus = *Gongylophis conicus*
Eryx elegans : (E) Central Asian Sand Boa, Elegant Sand
    Boa, (F) Boa des sables d'Asie centrale, Boa des
    sables élégant **II** BOIDAE Re
Eryx jaculus : (E) Caucasian Sand Boa, Javelin Sand Boa,
    Spotted Sand Boa, (S) Boa jabalina, (F) Boa des
    sables occidental, Boa-javelot, Eryx javelot, **II**
    BOIDAE Re
Eryx javelot (F): *Eryx jaculus*
Eryx jayakari : (E) Arabian Sand Boa, Jayakar's Sand Boa,
    (F) Boa des sables d'Arabie **II** BOIDAE Re
Eryx johnii : (E) Blunt-tailed Sand Boa, Brown Sand Boa,
    Indian Sand Boa, (S) Boa de arena de la India, (F) Boa
    des sables brun, **II** BOIDAE Re
Eryx loveridgei = *Gongylophis colubrinus*
Eryx miliaire (F): *Eryx miliaris*
Eryx miliaris : (E) Desert Sand Boa, Dwarf Sand Boa, (F)
    Boa des sables miliaire, Boa des sables nain, Eryx
    miliaire **II** BOIDAE Re
Eryx muelleri = *Gongylophis muelleri*
Eryx somalicus : (E) Somali Sand Boa, (S) Boa de arena
    somalí, (F) Boa des sables de Somalie, **II** BOIDAE Re
Eryx tataricus : (E) Tartary Sand Boa, (F) Boa des sables
    de Tatarie **II** BOIDAE Re
Eryx whitakeri : (E) Whitaker's Boa, (S) Boa de arena de
    Whitaker, (F) Boa des sables de Whitaker, **II**
    BOIDAE Re
Eschrichtius gibbosus = *Eschrichtius robustus*
Eschrichtius glaucus = *Eschrichtius robustus*
Eschrichtius robustus : (E) Devil Fish, Gray Back, Grey
    Whale, Hard Head, Mussel Digger, Rip Sack, (S)
    Ballena gris, (F) Baleine à six bosses, Baleine grise, **I**
    ESCHRICHTIIDAE Ma
Escorpión (S): *Heloderma horridum*
Escorpión de Gambia (S): *Pandinus gambiensis*
Escorpión emperador (S): *Pandinus imperator*

Escorpión gigante (S): *Pandinus imperator*
Escorpión magnifico (S): *Pandinus dictator*
Eskimo Curlew (E): *Numenius borealis*
Eslizón de las Islas Salomón (S): *Corucia zebrata*
Esmeralda bronceada (S): *Chlorostilbon russatus*
Esmeralda capirotada (S): *Elvira cupreiceps*
Esmeralda cola de alambre (S): *Chlorostilbon stenurus*
Esmeralda coliazul (S): *Chlorostilbon mellisugus*
Esmeralda colicorta (S): *Chlorostilbon poortmani*
Esmeralda colifina (S): *Chlorostilbon stenurus*
Esmeralda coliverde (S): *Chlorostilbon alice*
Esmeralda de Canivet (S): *Chlorostilbon canivetii*
Esmeralda de la Española (S): *Chlorostilbon swainsonii*
Esmeralda del Chiribiquete (S): *Chlorostilbon olivaresi*
Esmeralda elvira (S): *Elvira chionura*
Esmeralda gorgiazul (S): *Chlorostilbon notatus*
Esmeralda Hondurena (S): *Polyerata luciae*
Esmeralda Portorriqueña (S): *Chlorostilbon maugaeus*
Esmeralda ventridorada (S): *Chlorostilbon aureoventris*
Esmeralda viente-blanco (S): *Agyrtria candida*
Esmeralda zunzún (S): *Chlorostilbon ricordii*
Esmeraldas Woodstar (E): *Chaetocercus berlepschi*
Esmerejón (S): *Falco columbarius*
Esok (E): *Probarbus jullieni*
Espadarte (S): *Orcinus orca*
Esparvero bicolor (S): *Accipiter bicolor*
Esparvero chico (S): *Accipiter striatus*
Esparvero gris (S): *Accipiter superciliosus*
Esparvero pechigrís (S): *Accipiter poliogaster*
Espátula (S): *Platalea leucorodia*
Espátula blanca (S): *Platalea leucorodia*
Espátula común (S): *Platalea leucorodia*
Espermófaga hematina (S): *Spermophaga haematina*
Espinosa Poison Frog (E): *Epipedobates espinosai*
Espolonero chinquis (S): *Polyplectron bicalcaratum*
Espolonero de Borneo (S): *Polyplectron schleiermacheri*
Espolonero de Germain (S): *Polyplectron germaini*
Espolonero de Palawan (S): *Polyplectron emphanum*
Espolonero de Rothschild (S): *Polyplectron inopinatum*
Espolonero Malayo (S): *Polyplectron malacense*
Espulgabueyes (S): *Bubulcus ibis*
Esterlete (S): *Acipenser ruthenus*
Estornino de Rothschild (S): *Leucopsar rothschildi*
Estourioun (F): *Acipenser sturio*
Estrella coliblanca (S): *Urochroa bougueri*
Estrella cuellirrojo (S): *Chaetocercus heliodor*
Estrella ecuatoriana (S): *Oreotrochilus chimborazo*
Estrellita amatista (S): *Calliphlox amethystina*
Estrellita chica (S): *Chaetocercus bombus*
Estrellita colicorta (S): *Myrmia micrura*
Estrellita de gorguera (S): *Chaetocercus heliodor*
Estrellita esmeraldeña (S): *Chaetocercus berlepschi*
Estrellita gargantillada (S): *Myrtis fanny*
Estrellita gorjipurpura (S): *Calliphlox mitchellii*
Estrellita ventriblanca (S): *Chaetocercus mulsant*
Estrilda astrild : (E) Common Waxbill, Saint Helena
    Waxbill, (S) Astrilda común, Pico de Coral, (F)
    Astrild ondulé, Senegal ondulé, **III** ESTRILDIDAE
    Av
Estrilda bengala = *Uraeginthus bengalus*
Estrilda caerulescens : (E) Lavender Firefinch, Lavender
    Waxbill, (S) Astrilda ceniza del Senegal, (F) Astrild
    queue-de-vinaigre, Queue de vinaigre, **III**
    ESTRILDIDAE Av
Estrilda formosa = *Amandava formosa*
Estrilda melpoda : (E) Orange-cheeked Waxbill, (S)
    Astrilda carirroja, (F) Astrild à joues oranges, Joues-
    oranges, **III** ESTRILDIDAE Av
Estrilda subflava = *Amandava subflava*
Estrilda troglodytes : (E) Black-rumped Waxbill, Pink-
    cheeked Waxbill, Red-eared Waxbill, (S) Astrilda
    culinegra, (F) Astrild cendré, Bec de corail cendré, **III**
    ESTRILDIDAE Av
Estrilda verde (S): *Amandava formosa*
Estuarine Crocodile (E): *Crocodylus porosus*

Estuarine Dolphin (E): *Sotalia fluviatilis*
Esturgeon (F): *Acipenser sturio*
Esturgeon à barbillons frangés (F): *Acipenser nudiventris*
Esturgeon à museau court (F): *Acipenser brevirostrum*
Esturgeon à nez court (F): *Acipenser brevirostrum*
Esturgeon Atlantique (F): *Acipenser sturio*
Esturgeon Atlantique d'Europe (F): *Acipenser sturio*
Esturgeon Baltique (F): *Acipenser sturio*
Esturgeon blanc (F): *Acipenser transmontanus*
Esturgeon commun (F): *Acipenser sturio*
Esturgeon de l'Adriatique (F): *Acipenser naccarii*
Esturgeon de l'Atlantique (F): *Acipenser oxyrinchus*
Esturgeon de Sibérie (F): *Acipenser ruthenus*
Esturgeon d'Europe (F): *Acipenser sturio*
Esturgeon d'Europe occidentale (F): *Acipenser sturio*
Esturgeon du Danube (F): *Acipenser gueldenstaedtii*
Esturgeon étoilé (F): *Acipenser stellatus*
Esturgeon jaune (F): *Acipenser fulvescens*
Esturgeon sibérien (F): *Acipenser baerii*
Esturgeon vert (F): *Acipenser medirostris*
Esturgeons (F): ACIPENSERIFORMES spp. Ac
Esturien (F): *Acipenser sturio*
Esturio (F): *Acipenser sturio*
Esturión (S): *Huso huso*/ *Acipenser sturio*
Esturión barba de flecos (S): *Acipenser nudiventris*
Esturión beluga (S): *Huso huso*
Esturión blanco (S): *Acipenser transmontanus*
Esturión chato (S): *Acipenser brevirostrum*
Esturión común (S): *Acipenser sturio*
Esturión de Siberia (S): *Acipenser ruthenus*
Esturión del Adriático (S): *Acipenser naccarii*
Esturión del Atlántico (S): *Acipenser oxyrinchus*
Esturión del Danubio (S): *Acipenser gueldenstaedtii*
Esturión estrellado (S): *Acipenser stellatus*
Esturión hociquicorto (S): *Acipenser brevirostrum*
Esturión lacustre (S): *Acipenser fulvescens*
Esturión verde (S): *Acipenser medirostris*
Esturións (S): ACIPENSERIFORMES spp. Ac
Esturjon (F): *Acipenser sturio*
Esturjoun (F): *Acipenser sturio*
Ethiopian Highland Chameleon (E): *Chamaeleo affinis*
Ethiopian toads (E): *Altiphrynoides* spp. / *Spinophrynoides* spp.
Étourneau de Rothschild (F): *Leucopsar rothschildi*
Étrugeon (F): *Acipenser sturio*
Eubalaena spp.: (E) Right whales, (F) Baleines franches, Baleines noires I BALAENIDAE Ma
Eubalaena australis : (E) Southern Right Whale, (S) Ballena franca, (F) Baleine australe, I BALAENIDAE Ma
Eubalaena glacialis : (E) Black Right Whale, Northern Right Whale, Right Whale, (S) Ballena, Ballena franca del Norte, Ballenga, (F) Baleine de Biscaye, Baleine des Basques, Baleine franche, I BALAENIDAE Ma
Eudocimus ruber : (E) Scarlet Ibis, (S) Corocoro colorado, Corocoro rojo, Ibis escarlata, (F) Ibis rouge, II THRESKIORNITHIDAE Av
Eugenes fulgens : (E) Magnificent Hummingbird, Rivoli's Hummingbird, (S) Colibrí magnífico, (F) Colibri de Rivoli, II TROCHILIDAE Av
Eulampis holosericeus : (E) Green-throated Carib, (S) Colibrí caribeño gorgiverde, (F) Colibri falle-vert, II TROCHILIDAE Av
Eulampis jugularis : (E) Purple-throated Carib, (S) Colibrí caribeño gorgimorado, (F) Colibri madère, II TROCHILIDAE Av
Eulemur coronatus : (E) Crowned Lemur, (S) Lemur coronado, (F) Lémur à couronne, I LEMURIDAE Ma
Eulemur fulvus : (E) Brown Lemur, (S) Lemur leonado, (F) Lémur brun, Maki brun, I LEMURIDAE Ma
Eulemur macaco : (E) Black Lemur, (S) Lemur negro, (F) Lémur macaco, Lémur noir, Maki noir, I LEMURIDAE Ma

Eulemur mongoz : (E) Mongoose Lemur, (S) Lemur mangosta, (F) Lémur mongoz, Maki mongoz, I LEMURIDAE Ma
Eulemur mongoz ssp. *coronatus* = *Eulemur coronatus*
Eulemur rubriventer : (E) Red-bellied Lemur, (S) Lemur de vientre rojo, (F) Lémur à ventre rouge, I LEMURIDAE Ma
Eulidia yarrellii = *Myrtis yarrellii*
Eunectes barbouri = *Eunectes murinus*
Eunectes beniensis : II BOIDAE Re
Eunectes deschauenseei : (E) Dark-spotted Anaconda, Deschauensee's Anaconda, (F) Anaconda à taches sombres, Anaconda de Deschauensee II BOIDAE Re
Eunectes murinus : (E) Anaconda, Green Anaconda, Water Boa, (S) Anaconda, Sucury, (F) Anaconda, Anaconda commun, Anaconda vert, II BOIDAE Re
Eunectes notaeus : (E) Yellow Anaconda, (S) Anaconda amarilla, (F) Anaconda du Paraguay, Anaconda jaune, II BOIDAE Re
Eungella Gastric-brooding Frog (E): *Rheobatrachus vitellinus*
Eunymphicus cornutus : (E) Horned Parakeet, (S) Perico cornudo, (F) Perruche cornue, Perruche huppée, I PSITTACIDAE Av
Eunymphicus uvaeensis = *Eunymphicus cornutus*
Euodice cantans = *Lonchura cantans*
Euoticus elegantulus : (E) Elegant Galago, Western Needle-clawed Bushbaby, Western Needle-clawed Galago, (S) Abolí, Gálago elegante, (F) Galago élégant, II GALAGONIDAE Ma
Euoticus inustus = *Galago matschiei*
Euoticus pallidus : (E) Northern Needle-clawed Bushbaby, Northern Needle-clawed Galago II GALAGONIDAE Ma
Eupetomena macroura = *Campylopterus macrourus*
Eupherusa cyanophrys : (E) Blue-capped Hummingbird, Oaxaca Hummingbird, (S) Colibrí Oaxaqueño, (F) Colibri d'Oaxaca, II TROCHILIDAE Av
Eupherusa eximia : (E) Stripe-tailed Hummingbird, (S) Colibrí colirrayado, (F) Colibri à épaulettes, II TROCHILIDAE Av
Eupherusa nigriventris : (E) Black-bellied Hummingbird, (S) Colibrí ventrinegro, (F) Colibri à ventre noir, II TROCHILIDAE Av
Eupherusa poliocerca : (E) White-tailed Hummingbird, (S) Colibrí de Guerrero, Colibrí guerrerense, (F) Colibri du Guerrero, II TROCHILIDAE Av
Euphlyctis hexadactylus : (E) Six-fingered Frog, (F) Grenouille du Bengale, Grenouille hexadactyle II RANIDAE Am
Euphractus nationi = *Chaetophractus nationi*
Euphrosyne Dolphin (E): *Stenella coeruleoalba*
Euphyllia ancora : (E) Anchor Coral, Hammer Coral II CARYOPHYLLIIDAE An
Euphyllia cristata : (E) White Grape Coral II CARYOPHYLLIIDAE An
Euphyllia divisa : (E) Frogspawn Coral II CARYOPHYLLIIDAE An
Euphyllia fimbriata : II CARYOPHYLLIIDAE An
Euphyllia glabrescens : II CARYOPHYLLIIDAE An
Euphyllia paraancora : (E) Branching Anchor Coral II CARYOPHYLLIIDAE An
Euphyllia paradivisa : II CARYOPHYLLIIDAE An
Euphyllia paraglabrescens : II CARYOPHYLLIIDAE An
Euphyllia yaeyamaensis : II CARYOPHYLLIIDAE An
Euplecte à dos d'or (F): *Euplectes macrourus*
Euplecte franciscain (F): *Euplectes franciscanus*
Euplecte monseigneur (F): *Euplectes hordeaceus*
Euplecte veuve-noire (F): *Euplectes ardens*
Euplecte vorabé (F): *Euplectes afer*
Euplectes afer : (E) Golden Bishop, Napoleon Weaver, Yellow-crowned Bishop, (S) Euplectes amarillo, (F) Euplecte vorabé, Vorabé, III PLOCEIDAE Av
Euplectes alinegro (S): *Euplectes hordeaceus*
Euplectes amarillo (S): *Euplectes afer*

Euplectes ardens : (E) Red-collared Whydah, Red-collared Widowbird, (S) Falsa viuda pechirroja, (F) Euplecte veuve-noire, Veuve-noire, **III** PLOCEIDAE Av

Euplectes franciscanus : (E) Orange Bishop, Orange Weaver, (S) Euplectes rojo, (F) Euplecte franciscain, Ignicolor, Ignicolore, **III** PLOCEIDAE Av

Euplectes hordeaceus : (E) Black-winged Bishop, Fire-crowned Bishop, (S) Euplectes alinegro, (F) Euplecte monseigneur, Monseigneur, **III** PLOCEIDAE Av

Euplectes macrourus : (E) Yellow-backed Whydah, Yellow-mantled Whydah, Yellow-mantled Widowbird, Yellow-shouldered Widowbird, (S) Falsa viuda dorsigualda, (F) Euplecte à dos d'or, Veuve à dos d'or, **III** PLOCEIDAE Av

Euplectes orix ssp. *franciscanus = Euplectes franciscanus*

Euplectes rojo (S): *Euplectes franciscanus*

Euplère de Goudot (F): *Eupleres goudotii*

Eupleres goudotii : (E) Falanouc, Malagasy Mongoose, Slender Fanalouc, Small-toothed Mongoose, (S) Fanaloca, Mangosta dentipequeno, (F) Euplère de Goudot, **II** VIVERRIDAE Ma

Eupleres major = Eupleres goudotii

Eupodotis afra : (E) Black Bustard, Black Korhaan, (S) Sisón negro, Sisón negro alioscuro, (F) Outarde korhaan, Outarde noire, **II** OTIDIDAE Av

Eupodotis afra ssp. *afraoides = Eupodotis afraoides*

Eupodotis afraoides : (E) White-quilled Bustard, (S) Sisón negro aliclaro, (F) Outarde à miroir blanc, **II** OTIDIDAE Av

Eupodotis bengalensis : (E) Bengal Bustard, Bengal Florican, (S) Avutarda bengalí, Avutarda de Bengala, Sisón bengali, (F) Outarde du Bengale, **I** OTIDIDAE Av

Eupodotis caerulescens : (E) Blue Bustard, Blue Korhaan, (S) Sisón azul, Sisón azulado, (F) Outarde plombée, **II** OTIDIDAE Av

Eupodotis gindiana : (E) Buff-crested Bustard, (S) Sisón moñudo etiope, (F) Outarde d'Oustalet, **II** OTIDIDAE Av

Eupodotis hartlaubii : (E) Hartlaub's Bustard, (S) Sisón de Hartlaub, Sisón ventrinegro de Hartlaub, (F) Outarde de Hartlaub, **II** OTIDIDAE Av

Eupodotis humilis : (E) Little Brown Bustard, (S) Sisón somalí, (F) Outarde somalienne, **II** OTIDIDAE Av

Eupodotis indica : (E) Lesser Florican, Likh, (S) Sisón de penacho, Sisón indio, (F) Outarde naine de l'Inde, Outarde passarage, **II** OTIDIDAE Av

Eupodotis melanogaster : (E) Black-bellied Bustard, Black-bellied Korhaan, (S) Sisón ventrinegro, Sisón ventrinegro común, (F) Outarde à ventre noir, **II** OTIDIDAE Av

Eupodotis rueppellii : (E) Damara Korhaan, Rueppell's Bustard, (S) Sisón de Damaraland, Sisón de Rüppell, (F) Outarde de Rüppell, **II** OTIDIDAE Av

Eupodotis ruficrista : (E) Crested Korhaan, Red-crested Bustard, (S) Sisón moñirrojo, Sisón moñudo austral, (F) Outarde houppette, Outarde naine, **II** OTIDIDAE Av

Eupodotis ruficrista ssp. *gindiana = Eupodotis gindiana*

Eupodotis savilei : (E) Savile's Bustard, (S) Avutarda de Savile, Sisón moñudo de saheliano, (F) Outarde de Savile, **II** OTIDIDAE Av

Eupodotis senegalensis : (E) Senegal Bustard, White-bellied Bustard, White-bellied Korhaan, (S) Sisón senegalés, (F) Outarde du Sénégal, **II** OTIDIDAE Av

Eupodotis vigorsii : (E) Karoo Bustard, Karoo Korhaan, Vigors's Bustard, (S) Sisón de Vigors, Sisón del karroo, (F) Outarde de Vigors, **II** OTIDIDAE Av

Eupsammia regalis = Balanophyllia regalis

Eurasian Buzzard (E): *Buteo buteo*

Eurasian Eagle-Owl (E): *Bubo bubo*

Eurasian Griffon (E): *Gyps fulvus*

Eurasian Griffon Vulture (E): *Gyps fulvus*

Eurasian Hobby (E): *Falco subbuteo*

Eurasian Kestrel (E): *Falco tinnunculus*

Eurasian Lynx (E): *Lynx lynx*

Eurasian Marsh-Harrier (E): *Circus aeruginosus*

Eurasian Otter (E): *Lutra lutra*

Eurasian Pygmy-Owl (E): *Glaucidium passerinum*

Eurasian Scops-Owl (E): *Otus scops*

Eurasian Sparrowhawk (E): *Accipiter nisus*

Eurasian Spoonbill (E): *Platalea leucorodia*

Eurasian Wigeon (E): *Anas penelope*

Eurochelidon sirintarae = Pseudochelidon sirintarae

European Chameleon (E): *Chamaeleo chamaeleon*

European Honey-buzzard (E): *Pernis apivorus*

European Otter (E): *Lutra lutra*

European River Otter (E): *Lutra lutra*

European Sturgeon (E): *Huso huso/ Acipenser sturio*

European Turtle-Dove (E): *Streptopelia turtur*

Eurypelma emilia = Brachypelma emilia

Eusmilia aspera = Eusmilia fastigiata

Eusmilia fastigiata : (E) Smooth Flower Coral **II** CARYOPHYLLIIDAE An

Eutoxeres aquila : (E) White-tipped Sicklebill, (S) Pico-de-Hoz puntiblanco, Picohoz coliverde, (F) Bec-en-faucille aigle, **II** TROCHILIDAE Av

Eutoxeres condamini : (E) Buff-tailed Sicklebill, (S) Pico-de-Hoz colihabano, Picohoz colicanela, (F) Bec-en-faucille de la Condamine, **II** TROCHILIDAE Av

Eutriorchis astur : (E) Madagascar Serpent-Eagle, (S) Culebrera azor, (F) Aigle serpentaire, Serpentaire de Madagascar, **II** ACCIPITRIDAE Av

Everglade Kite (E): *Rostrhamus sociabilis*

Exiliboa placata : (E) Bogert's Boa, Oaxacan Boa, Oaxacan Dwarf Boa, (S) Boa enana mexicana, (F) Boa nain d'Oaxaca, **II** TROPIDOPHIIDAE Re

Eyed Dabb Lizard (E): *Uromastyx ocellata*

Eyra Cat (E): *Herpailurus yaguarondi*

Fabo calderón (S): *Grampus griseus*

Fairy Lorikeet (E): *Charmosyna pulchella*

Fairy Pitta (E): *Pitta nympha*

Faisan à queue barrée (F): *Syrmaticus humiae*

Faisan à queue rousse (F): *Lophura erythrophthalma*

Faisán argos (S): *Argusianus argus*

Faisán chir (S): *Catreus wallichii*

Faisán colicanelo (S): *Lophura erythrophthalma*

Faisan de Birmanie (F): *Syrmaticus humiae*

Faisán de carúncula azul (S): *Lophura erythrophthalma*

Faisán de carúncula azul crestado (S): *Lophura ignita*

Faisán de cola ocelada de Germain (S): *Polyplectron germaini*

Faisán de cola ocelada gris (S): *Polyplectron bicalcaratum*

Faisán de cola ocelada indómito (S): *Polyplectron inopinatum*

Faisán de cola ocelada malayo (S): *Polyplectron malacense*

Faisan de cuerno rojo (S): *Oreophasis derbianus*

Faisán de Edwards (S): *Lophura edwardsi*

Faisán de Elliot (S): *Syrmaticus ellioti*

Faisán de espolones de Borneo (S): *Polyplectron schleiermacheri*

Faisán de espolones de Germain (S): *Polyplectron germaini*

Faisán de espolones de Palawan (S): *Polyplectron emphanum*

Faisán de espolones gris (S): *Polyplectron bicalcaratum*

Faisán de espolones malayo (S): *Polyplectron malacense*

Faisán de Formosa (S): *Lophura swinhoii*

Faisan de Formose (F): *Lophura swinhoii*

Faisan de Hume (F): *Syrmaticus humiae*

Faisán de Hume (S): *Syrmaticus humiae*

Faisan de l'Himalaya (F): *Catreus wallichii*

Faisán de Rheinard (S): *Rheinardia ocellata*

Faisan de Swinhoe (F): *Lophura swinhoii*

Faisán de Swinhoe (S): *Lophura swinhoii*

Faisan de Wallich (F): *Catreus wallichii*

Faisán de Wallich (S): *Catreus wallichii*

Faisan d'Edwards (F): *Lophura edwardsi*

Faisan d'Elliot (F): *Syrmaticus ellioti*
Faisán ensangrentado (S): *Ithaginis cruentus*
Faisan impérial (F): *Lophura imperialis*
Faisán imperial (S): *Lophura imperialis*
Faisan mikado (F): *Syrmaticus mikado*
Faisán mikado (S): *Syrmaticus mikado*
Faisán monal chino (S): *Lophophorus lhuysii*
Faisán monal de Sclater (S): *Lophophorus sclateri*
Faisán monal del Himalaya (S): *Lophophorus impejanus*
Faisan noble (F): *Lophura ignita*
Faisán noble (S): *Lophura ignita*
Faisan oreillard blanc (F): *Crossoptilon crossoptilon*
Faisan oreillard brun (F): *Crossoptilon mantchuricum*
Faisán orejudo blanco (S): *Crossoptilon crossoptilon*
Faisán orejudo de Manchuria (S): *Crossoptilon mantchuricum*
Faisán orejudo pardo (S): *Crossoptilon mantchuricum*
Faisán orejudo tibetano (S): *Crossoptilon crossoptilon*
Faisán real de Germain (S): *Polyplectron germaini*
Faisán real de Palaguán (S): *Polyplectron emphanum*
Faisán real gris (S): *Polyplectron bicalcaratum*
Faisán real malayo (S): *Polyplectron malacense*
Faisán sangrante (S): *Ithaginis cruentus*
Faisan sanguin (F): *Ithaginis cruentus*
Faisán sanguineo (S): *Ithaginis cruentus*
Falanouc (E): *Eupleres goudotii*
Falcatoflabellum raoulensis : **II** FLABELLIDAE An
Falco alexanderi = Falco tinnunculus
Falco alopex : (E) Fox Kestrel, (S) Cernícalo zorruno, (F) Crécerelle renard, Faucon-renard, **II** FALCONIDAE Av
Falco altaicus = Falco cherrug
Falco amurensis : (E) Amur Falcon, Eastern Red-footed Falcon, Manchurian Red-footed Falcon, (S) Cernícalo del Amur, (F) Faucon de l'Amour, **II** FALCONIDAE Av
Falco araea : (E) Seychelles Kestrel, (S) Cernícalo de las Seychelles, (F) Crécerelle des Seychelles, Crécerelle katitie, Emouchel des Seychelles, Faucon crécerelle des Seychelles, **I** FALCONIDAE Av
Falco ardosiaceus : (E) Grey Kestrel, (S) Cernícalo gris, Cernícalo pizarroso, (F) Faucon ardoisé, **II** FALCONIDAE Av
Falco berigora : (E) Brown Falcon, (S) Halcón berigora, (F) Faucon bérigora, **II** FALCONIDAE Av
Falco biarmicus : (E) Lanner, Lanner Falcon, (S) Halcón borní, (F) Faucon lanier, **II** FALCONIDAE Av
Falco cenchroides : (E) Australian Kestrel, Nankeen Kestrel, (S) Cernícalo australiano, (F) Crécerelle australienne, Crécerelle d'Australie, **II** FALCONIDAE Av
Falco cherrug : (E) Saker, Saker Falcon, (S) Halcón sacre, (F) Faucon sacre, **II** FALCONIDAE Av
Falco chicquera : (E) Red-headed Falcon, Red-headed Merlin, Red-necked Falcon, (S) Alcotán cuellirrojo, Alcotán turumti, Halcón de cabeza roja, (F) Faucon à cou roux, Faucon chicquera, **II** FALCONIDAE Av
Falco columbarius : (E) Merlin, Pigeon Hawk, (S) Esmerejón, Halcón migratorio, Halcón palomero, (F) Faucon émerillon, **II** FALCONIDAE Av
Falco concolor : (E) Sooty Falcon, (S) Halcón pardo, Halcón pizarroso, (F) Faucon concolore, **II** FALCONIDAE Av
Falco cuvierii : (E) African Hobby, (S) Alcotán africano, Halcón de Cuvier, (F) Faucon de Cuvier, Hobereau africain, **II** FALCONIDAE Av
Falco deiroleucus : (E) Orange-breasted Falcon, (S) Halcón pechianaranjado, Halcón pechirrojo, Halcón pechirrufo, Halcón plomizo, (F) Faucon orangé, **II** FALCONIDAE Av
Falco dickinsoni : (E) Dickinson's Kestrel, White-rumped Kestrel, (S) Cernícalo de Dickinson, Cernícalo dorsinegro, (F) Faucon de Dickinson, **II** FALCONIDAE Av

Falco eleonorae : (E) Eleonora's Falcon, (S) Halcón de Eleonor, Halcón de Eleonora, (F) Faucon d'Éléonore, **II** FALCONIDAE Av
Falco fasciinucha : (E) Taita Falcon, Teita Falcon, (S) Halcón taita, (F) Faucon taita, **II** FALCONIDAE Av
Falco femoralis : (E) Aplomado Falcon, (S) Halcón aleto, Halcón aplomado, Halcón azulado, Halcón perdiguero, (F) Faucon aplomado, **II** FALCONIDAE Av
Falco hypoleucos : (E) Grey Falcon, (S) Halcón gris, Halcón gris de Australia, (F) Faucon gris, **II** FALCONIDAE Av
Falco jugger : (E) Laggar Falcon, (S) Halcón yággar, (F) Faucon laggar, **I** FALCONIDAE Av
Falco kreyenborgi = Falco peregrinus
Falco longipennis : (E) Australian Hobby, Little Falcon, (S) Alcotán australiano, Halconcito australiano, (F) Petit faucon, **II** FALCONIDAE Av
Falco madens = Falco peregrinus
Falco mexicanus : (E) Prairie Falcon, (S) Halcón de las praderas, Halcón mejicano, Halcón pradeño, (F) Faucon des prairies, **II** FALCONIDAE Av
Falco moluccensis : (E) Moluccan Kestrel, Spotted Kestrel, (S) Cernícalo de las Molucas, Cernícalo Moluqueño, (F) Crécerelle des Moluques, **II** FALCONIDAE Av
Falco naumanni : (E) Lesser Kestrel, (S) Cernícalo primilla, (F) Faucon crécerellette, **II** FALCONIDAE Av
Falco neglectus = Falco tinnunculus
Falco newtoni : (E) Madagascar Kestrel, Newton's Kestrel, (S) Cernícalo de Aldabra, Cernícalo de la isla Aldabra, Cernícalo de Madagascar, (F) Crécerelle d'Aldabra, Crécerelle malgache, Faucon de Newton d'Aldabra, **I/II** FALCONIDAE Av
Falco novaeseelandiae : (E) New Zealand Falcon, (S) Halcón de Nueva Zelandia, Halcón maori, (F) Faucon de Nouvelle-Zélande, **II** FALCONIDAE Av
Falco pelegrinoides : (E) Barbary Falcon, (S) Halcón de Berbería, Halcón peregrino de Babilonia, (F) Faucon de Barbarie, **I** FALCONIDAE Av
Falco peregrinus : (E) Duck Hawk, Peregrine, Peregrine Falcon, (S) Halcón blancuzco, Halcón común, Halcón peregrino, Halcón real, Halcón viajero, (F) Faucon pèlerin, **I** FALCONIDAE Av
Falco peregrinus ssp. *babylonicus = Falco pelegrinoides* ssp. *babylonicus*
Falco peregrinus ssp. *pelegrinoides = Falco pelegrinoides*
Falco punctatus : (E) Mauritius Kestrel, (S) Cernícalo de la Mauricio, Cernícalo de Mauricio, (F) Crécerelle de Maurice, Faucon de l'île Maurice, **I** FALCONIDAE Av
Falco rufigularis : (E) Bat Falcon, (S) Halcón golondrina, Halcón murcielaguero, Halcón plomizo menor, (F) Faucon des chauves-souris, **II** FALCONIDAE Av
Falco rupicoloides : (E) Greater Kestrel, White-eyed Kestrel, (S) Cernícalo ojiblanco, Cernícalo ojiblanco de Africa, (F) Crécerelle aux yeux blancs, **II** FALCONIDAE Av
Falco rusticolus : (E) Gyr Falcon, Gyrfalcon, (S) Halcón gerifalte, (F) Faucon gerfaut, Gerfaut, **I** FALCONIDAE Av
Falco severus : (E) Oriental Hobby, (S) Alcotán filipino, (F) Faucon aldrovandin, Hobereau à poitrine rousse, **II** FALCONIDAE Av
Falco sparverius : (E) American Kestrel, (S) Cernícalo americano, Cernícalo primito, Halcón primito, Halconcito, Halconcito común, (F) Crécerelle américaine, Crécerelle d'Amérique, **II** FALCONIDAE Av
Falco subbuteo : (E) Eurasian Hobby, Hobby, Northern Hobby, (S) Alcotán, Alcotán europeo, (F) Faucon hobereau, **II** FALCONIDAE Av

Checklist of fauna/Lista de especies de fauna/Liste des espèces animales

Falco subniger : (E) Black Falcon, (S) Halcón negro,
Halcón negro de Australia, (F) Faucon noir, **II**
FALCONIDAE Av
Falco tinnunculus : (E) Common Kestrel, Eurasian
Kestrel, Kestrel, (S) Cernícalo común, Cernícalo
vulgar, (F) Faucon crécerelle, **II** FALCONIDAE Av
Falco vespertinus : (E) Red-footed Falcon, Western Red-
footed Falcon, (S) Cernícalo patirrojo, (F) Faucon
kobez, **II** FALCONIDAE Av
Falco zoniventris : (E) Banded Kestrel, Barred Kestrel, (S)
Cernícalo malgache, (F) Faucon à ventre rayé, **II**
FALCONIDAE Av
Falconete acollarado (S): *Microhierax caerulescens*
Falconete de Borneo (S): *Microhierax latifrons*
Falconete filipino (S): *Microhierax erythrogenys*
Falconete indonesio (S): *Microhierax fringillarius*
Falconete pío (S): *Microhierax melanoleucos*
FALCONIFORMES spp. : (E) Birds of prey, Raptors, (S)
Aves de rapiña, (F) Rapaces diurnes, **I/II/III/NC** Av
Falsa cobra (S): *Cyclagras gigas*
Falsa cobra acuatica (S): *Cyclagras gigas*
Falsa rata de agua (S): *Xeromys myoides*
Falsa viuda dorsigualda (S): *Euplectes macrourus*
Falsa viuda pechirroja (S): *Euplectes ardens*
False Cobra (E): *Cyclagras gigas*
False Gavial (E): *Tomistoma schlegelii*
False Gharial (E): *Tomistoma schlegelii*
False Girdled Lizard (E): *Cordylus capensis*
False Killer Whale (E): *Pseudorca crassidens*
False Potto (E): *Pseudopotto martini*
False Shovelnose Sturgeon (E): *Pseudoscaphirhynchus
kaufmanni*
False Swamp Rat (E): *Xeromys myoides*
False Water Cobra (E): *Cyclagras gigas*
False Water Rat (E): *Xeromys myoides*
Falso gavial africano (S): *Crocodylus cataphractus*
Falso gavial malayo (S): *Tomistoma schlegelii*
Falso lagarto armadillo de Lang (S): *Cordylus langi*
Falso lagarto armadillo del cabo (S): *Cordylus capensis*
Falso lagarto armadillo espinoso (S): *Cordylus spinosus*
Falso ratón de la Bahía de Shark (S): *Pseudomys praeconis*
Falso vampiro del Uruguay (S): *Platyrrhinus lineatus*
Falsos lagartos armadillos (S): *Cordylus* spp.
Fanaloca (S): *Eupleres goudotii*
Fanaloka (E/F): *Fossa fossana*
Fandangero colicuna (S): *Campylopterus curvipennis*
Fandangero colilargo (S): *Campylopterus excellens*
Fandangero morado (S): *Campylopterus hemileucurus*
Fandangero pechiescamosa (S): *Campylopterus cuvierii*
Fandangero rufo (S): *Campylopterus rufus*
Fan-tailed Day Gecko (E): *Phelsuma serraticauda*
Fasciated Snake-Eagle (E): *Circaetus fasciolatus*
Fat Pocketbook (E): *Potamilus capax*
Fat Pocketbook Pearly Mussel (E): *Potamilus capax*
Fat-tailed Dwarf Lemur (E): *Cheirogaleus medius*
Faucon à cou roux (F): *Falco chicquera*
Faucon à ventre rayé (F): *Falco zoniventris*
Faucon aldrovandin (F): *Falco severus*
Faucon aplomado (F): *Falco femoralis*
Faucon ardoisé (F): *Falco ardosiaceus*
Faucon bérigora (F): *Falco berigora*
Faucon chicquera (F): *Falco chicquera*
Faucon concolore (F): *Falco concolor*
Faucon crécerelle (F): *Falco tinnunculus*
Faucon crécerelle des Seychelles (F): *Falco araea*
Faucon crécerellette (F): *Falco naumanni*
Faucon de Barbarie (F): *Falco pelegrinoides*
Faucon de Cuvier (F): *Falco cuvierii*
Faucon de Dickinson (F): *Falco dickinsoni*
Faucon de l'Amour (F): *Falco amurensis*
Faucon de l'île Maurice (F): *Falco punctatus*
Faucon de Newton d'Aldabra (F): *Falco newtoni*
Faucon de Nouvelle-Zélande (F): *Falco novaeseelandiae*
Faucon d'Éléonore (F): *Falco eleonorae*
Faucon des chauves-souris (F): *Falco rufigularis*

Faucon des prairies (F): *Falco mexicanus*
Faucon émerillon (F): *Falco columbarius*
Faucon gerfaut (F): *Falco rusticolus*
Faucon gris (F): *Falco hypoleucos*
Faucon hobereau (F): *Falco subbuteo*
Faucon kobez (F): *Falco vespertinus*
Faucon laggar (F): *Falco jugger*
Faucon lanier (F): *Falco biarmicus*
Faucon noir (F): *Falco subniger*
Faucon orangé (F): *Falco deiroleucus*
Faucon pèlerin (F): *Falco peregrinus*
Faucon sacre (F): *Falco cherrug*
Faucon taita (F): *Falco fasciinucha*
Faucon-coucou (F): *Aviceda cuculoides*
Fauconnet à collier (F): *Microhierax caerulescens*
Fauconnet à pattes jaunes (F): *Polihierax insignis*
Fauconnet d'Afrique (F): *Polihierax semitorquatus*
Fauconnet d'Amérique (F): *Spiziapteryx circumcinctus*
Fauconnet de Bornéo (F): *Microhierax latifrons*
Fauconnet des Philippines (F): *Microhierax erythrogenys*
Fauconnet moineau (F): *Microhierax fringillarius*
Fauconnet noir-et-blanc (F): *Microhierax melanoleucos*
Faucon-renard (F): *Falco alopex*
Fausse souris de la baie de Shark (F): *Pseudomys
praeconis*
Fauvette à long bec (F): *Dasyornis longirostris*
Fauvette brune à long bec (F): *Dasyornis longirostris*
Fauvette rousse de l'Ouest (F): *Dasyornis broadbenti
litoralis*
Faux cobra (F): *Cyclagras gigas*
Faux cobra aquatique du Brésil (F): *Cyclagras gigas*
Faux gavial malais (F): *Tomistoma schlegelii*
Faux jacquot (F): *Corallus caninus*
Faux rat d'eau (F): *Xeromys myoides*
Faux-gavial d'Afrique (F): *Crocodylus cataphractus*
Faux-orque (F): *Pseudorca crassidens*
Favia affinis = Favia favus
Favia albidus : **II** FAVIIDAE An
Favia danae : **II** FAVIIDAE An
Favia danai : **II** FAVIIDAE An
Favia favus : **II** FAVIIDAE An
Favia fragum : (E) Golfball Coral, Small Star Coral **II**
FAVIIDAE An
Favia gravida : **II** FAVIIDAE An
Favia helianthoides : **II** FAVIIDAE An
Favia lacuna : **II** FAVIIDAE An
Favia laxa : **II** FAVIIDAE An
Favia leptophylla : **II** FAVIIDAE An
Favia lizardensis : **II** FAVIIDAE An
Favia maritima : **II** FAVIIDAE An
Favia marshae : **II** FAVIIDAE An
Favia matthaii : **II** FAVIIDAE An
Favia maxima : **II** FAVIIDAE An
Favia pallida : **II** FAVIIDAE An
Favia rosaria : **II** FAVIIDAE An
Favia rotumana : **II** FAVIIDAE An
Favia rotundata : **II** FAVIIDAE An
Favia speciosa : **II** FAVIIDAE An
Favia stelligera : **II** FAVIIDAE An
Favia truncatus : **II** FAVIIDAE An
Favia veroni : **II** FAVIIDAE An
Favia vietnamensis : **II** FAVIIDAE An
Favia whitfieldi = Favia fragum
Favia wisseli : **II** FAVIIDAE An
Favites spp.: (E) Larger star corals, Pineapple corals **II**
FAVIIDAE An
Favites abdita : (E) Honeycomb Coral **II** FAVIIDAE An
Favites acuticollis : **II** FAVIIDAE An
Favites bestae : **II** FAVIIDAE An
Favites chinensis : **II** FAVIIDAE An
Favites complanata : **II** FAVIIDAE An
Favites flexuosa : **II** FAVIIDAE An
Favites halicora : **II** FAVIIDAE An
Favites micropentagona : **II** FAVIIDAE An
Favites paraflexuosa : **II** FAVIIDAE An

Favites pentagona : **II** FAVIIDAE An
Favites peresi : **II** FAVIIDAE An
Favites russelli : **II** FAVIIDAE An
Favites spinosa : **II** FAVIIDAE An
Favites stylifera : **II** FAVIIDAE An
Favites vasta : **II** FAVIIDAE An
Favites virens = Favites abdita
Fawn-breasted Brilliant (E): *Heliodoxa rubinoides*
Fawn-breasted Hummingbird (E): *Amazilia yucatanensis*
Fearful Owl (E): *Nesasio solomonensis*
Feather Coral (E): *Polyphyllia talpina*
Feather-toed Hawk-Eagle (E): *Spizaetus nipalensis*
Feick's Dwarf Boa (E): *Tropidophis feicki*
FELIDAE spp.: (E) Cats, (S) Felinos, (F) Félidés, Félins
    I/II Ma
Félidés (F): FELIDAE spp.
Feline Night Monkey (E): *Aotus infulatus*
Felinos (S): FELIDAE spp.
Félins (F): FELIDAE spp.
Felis aurata = Profelis aurata
Felis badia = Catopuma badia
Felis bengalensis = Prionailurus bengalensis
Felis bengalensis ssp. *bengalensis = Prionailurus*
    bengalensis ssp. *bengalensis*
Felis bieti : (E) Chinese Desert Cat, (S) Gato de Biet, Gato
    del desierto de China, (F) Chat de Biet, **II** FELIDAE
    Ma
Felis canadensis = Lynx canadensis
Felis caracal = Caracal caracal
Felis chaus : (E) Jungle Cat, Reed Cat, Swamp Cat, (S)
    Gato de la jungla, Gato de los pantanos, (F) Chat de
    jungle, Chat des marais, **II** FELIDAE Ma
Felis colocolo = Oncifelis colocolo
Felis colocolo ssp. *budinii = Oncifelis colocolo* ssp. *budini*
Felis colocolo ssp. *crespoi = Oncifelis colocolo* ssp.
    crespoi
Felis colocolo ssp. *pajeros = Oncifelis colocolo* ssp.
    pajeros
Felis concolor = Puma concolor
Felis concolor ssp. *coryi = Puma concolor* ssp. *coryi*
Felis concolor ssp. *costaricensis = Puma concolor* ssp.
    costaricensis
Felis concolor ssp. *couguar = Puma concolor* ssp.
    couguar
Felis geoffroyi = Oncifelis geoffroyi
Felis guigna = Oncifelis guigna
Felis iriomotensis = Prionailurus bengalensis ssp.
    iriomotensis
Felis jacobita = Oreailurus jacobita
Felis libyca = Felis silvestris
Felis lybica = Felis silvestris ssp. *lybica*
Felis lynx = Lynx lynx
Felis lynx ssp. *isabellina = Lynx lynx* ssp. *isabellinus*
Felis lynx ssp. *pardinus = Lynx pardinus*
Felis manul = Otocolobus manul
Felis margarita : (E) Sand Cat, Sand Dune Cat, (S) Gato
    de las arenas, Gato del Sahara, (F) Chat des sables, **II**
    FELIDAE Ma
Felis marmorata = Pardofelis marmorata
Felis nigripes : (E) Black-footed Cat, Small-spotted Cat,
    (S) Gato de pies negros, Gato patinegro, (F) Chat à
    pieds noirs, **I** FELIDAE Ma
Felis ornata = Felis silvestris
Felis pardalis = Leopardus pardalis
Felis pardina = Lynx pardinus
Felis planiceps = Prionailurus planiceps
Felis rubiginosa = Prionailurus rubiginosus
Felis rufa = Lynx rufus
Felis serval = Leptailurus serval
Felis silvestris : (E) Wild Cat, Wildcat, (S) Gato montés,
    Gato silvestre, (F) Chat orné, Chat sauvage, **II**
    FELIDAE Ma
Felis temminckii = Catopuma temminckii
Felis tigrina = Leopardus tigrinus
Felis viverrina = Prionailurus viverrinus

Felis wiedii = Leopardus wiedii
Felis yaguarondi = Herpailurus yaguarondi
Fennec (S/F): *Vulpes zerda*
Fennec Fox (E): *Vulpes zerda*
Fennecus zerda = Vulpes zerda
Fenocoptéridos (S): PHOENICOPTERIDAE spp.
Feral Pigeon (E): *Columba livia*
Feresa attenuata : (E) Pygmy Killer Whale, Slender
    Blackfish, (S) Orca pigmeo, (F) Epaulard pygmée,
    Orque pygmée, **II** DELPHINIDAE Ma
Feresa occulta = Feresa attenuata
Ferruginous Duck (E): *Aythya nyroca*
Ferruginous Hawk (E): *Buteo regalis*
Ferruginous Partridge (E): *Caloperdix oculea*
Ferruginous Pochard (E): *Aythya nyroca*
Ferruginous Pygmy-Owl (E): *Glaucidium brasilianum*
Ferruginous Wood-Partridge (E): *Caloperdix oculea*
Festive Amazon (E): *Amazona festiva*
Festive Coquette (E): *Lophornis chalybeus*
Festive Parrot (E): *Amazona festiva*
Field Adder (E): *Vipera ursinii*
Fielden's Falconet (E): *Polihierax insignis*
Fierce Snake (E): *Hoplocephalus bungaroides*
Fiery-shouldered Conure (E): *Pyrrhura egregia*
Fiery-shouldered Parakeet (E): *Pyrrhura egregia*
Fiery-tailed Awlbill (E): *Anthracothorax recurvirostris*
Fiery-throated Hummingbird (E): *Panterpe insignis*
Fiji Banded Iguana (E): *Brachylophus fasciatus*
Fiji Crested Iguana (E): *Brachylophus vitiensis*
Fiji Goshawk (E): *Accipiter rufitorques*
Fiji Sparrowhawk (E): *Accipiter rufitorques*
Fijian iguanas (E): *Brachylophus* spp.
Filadelfia Rusty Brown Tarantula (E): *Brachypelma*
    fossorium
Fin Whale (E): *Balaenoptera physalus*
Finback (E): *Balaenoptera physalus*
Fin-backed Whale (E): *Balaenoptera physalus*
Fine-rayed Pigtoe (E): *Fusconaia cuneolus*
Fine-rayed Pigtoe Pearly Mussel (E): *Fusconaia cuneolus*
Finger Coral (E): *Porites cylindrica/ Millepora alcicornis*
Finless Black Porpoise (E): *Neophocaena phocaenoides*
Finless Porpoise (E): *Neophocaena phocaenoides*
Finner (E): *Balaenoptera physalus*
Finsch's Conure (E): *Aratinga finschi*
Finsch's Pygmy-Parrot (E): *Micropsitta finschii*
Fire corals (E): MILLEPORIDAE spp.
Fire-crowned Bishop (E): *Euplectes hordeaceus*
Fire-throated Metaltail (E): *Metallura eupogon*
Fischer's Chameleon (E): *Bradypodion fischeri*
Fischer's Lovebird (E): *Agapornis fischeri*
Fischer's Tree Boa (E): *Epicrates striatus*
Fischer's Turaco (E): *Tauraco fischeri*
Fish Lizard (E): *Varanus dumerilii*
Fish-eating Crocodile (E): *Gavialis gangeticus*
Fisher's Seahorse (E): *Hippocampus fisheri*
Fishing Cat (E): *Prionailurus viverrinus*
Fishing Snake (E): *Xenochrophis piscator*
Fito Leaf Chameleon (E): *Brookesia lambertoni*
Flabellum alabastrum : **II** FLABELLIDAE An
Flabellum angulare : **II** FLABELLIDAE An
Flabellum angustum : **II** FLABELLIDAE An
Flabellum aotearoa : **II** FLABELLIDAE An
Flabellum apertum apertum : **II** FLABELLIDAE An
Flabellum apertum borealis : **II** FLABELLIDAE An
Flabellum arcuatile : **II** FLABELLIDAE An
Flabellum areum : **II** FLABELLIDAE An
Flabellum atlanticum : **II** FLABELLIDAE An
Flabellum australe : **II** FLABELLIDAE An
Flabellum campanulatum : **II** FLABELLIDAE An
Flabellum chunii : **II** FLABELLIDAE An
Flabellum conuis : **II** FLABELLIDAE An
Flabellum curvatum : **II** FLABELLIDAE An
Flabellum daphnense : **II** FLABELLIDAE An
Flabellum deludens : **II** FLABELLIDAE An
Flabellum dens = Truncatoflabellum dens

Checklist of fauna/Lista de especies de fauna/Liste des espèces animales

Flabellum flexuosum : **II** FLABELLIDAE An
Flabellum floridanum : **II** FLABELLIDAE An
Flabellum folkesoni : **II** FLABELLIDAE An
Flabellum fragile = Flabellum floridanum
Flabellum gardineri : **II** FLABELLIDAE An
Flabellum hoffmeisteri : **II** FLABELLIDAE An
Flabellum impensum : **II** FLABELLIDAE An
Flabellum japonicum : **II** FLABELLIDAE An
Flabellum knoxi : **II** FLABELLIDAE An
Flabellum lamellulosum : **II** FLABELLIDAE An
Flabellum lowekeyesi : **II** FLABELLIDAE An
Flabellum macandrewi : (E) Scarlet Crisp Coral, Splitting
    Fan Coral **II** FLABELLIDAE An
Flabellum magnificum : **II** FLABELLIDAE An
Flabellum marcus : **II** FLABELLIDAE An
Flabellum marenzelleri : **II** FLABELLIDAE An
Flabellum messum : **II** FLABELLIDAE An
Flabellum moseleyi : **II** FLABELLIDAE An
Flabellum ongulense : **II** FLABELLIDAE An
Flabellum patens : **II** FLABELLIDAE An
Flabellum pavoninum : **II** FLABELLIDAE An
Flabellum politum : **II** FLABELLIDAE An
Flabellum raukawaensis = Flabellum apertum ssp.
    apertum
Flabellum sexcostatum : **II** FLABELLIDAE An
Flabellum sibogae : **II** FLABELLIDAE An
Flabellum thouarsii : **II** FLABELLIDAE An
Flabellum transversale : **II** FLABELLIDAE An
Flabellum transversale conicum : **II** FLABELLIDAE An
Flabellum transversale transversale : **II** FLABELLIDAE
    An
Flabellum transversale triangulare : **II** FLABELLIDAE
    An
Flabellum truncum = Truncatoflabellum truncum
Flabellum tuthilli : **II** FLABELLIDAE An
Flabellum vaughani : **II** FLABELLIDAE An
Flamant de Cuba (F): *Phoenicopterus ruber*
Flamant de James (F): *Phoenicopterus jamesi*
Flamant des Andes (F): *Phoenicopterus andinus*
Flamant du Chili (F): *Phoenicopterus chilensis*
Flamant nain (F): *Phoenicopterus minor*
Flamant rose (F): *Phoenicopterus ruber*
Flamant rouge (F): *Phoenicopterus ruber*
Flamants (S): PHOENICOPTERIDAE spp.
Flamenco (S): *Phoenicopterus ruber*
Flamenco andino (S): *Phoenicopterus andinus*
Flamenco andino chico (S): *Phoenicopterus jamesi*
Flamenco Chileno (S): *Phoenicopterus chilensis*
Flamenco común (S): *Phoenicopterus ruber*
Flamenco común de Chile (S): *Phoenicopterus chilensis*
Flamenco de Cuba (S): *Phoenicopterus ruber*
Flamenco de James (S): *Phoenicopterus jamesi*
Flamenco enano (S): *Phoenicopterus minor*
Flamenco rojo (S): *Phoenicopterus ruber*
Flamencos (S): PHOENICOPTERIDAE spp.
Flame-winged Conure (E): *Pyrrhura calliptera*
Flame-winged Parakeet (E): *Pyrrhura calliptera*
Flaming Poison Frog (E): *Dendrobates pumilio*
Flamingos (S): PHOENICOPTERIDAE spp.
Flammulated Owl (E): *Otus flammeolus*
Flaphe de l'Inde (F): *Ptyas mucosus*
Flap-necked Chameleon (E): *Chamaeleo dilepis*
Flatback (E): *Natator depressus*
Flatback Tortoise (E): *Geochelone platynota*
Flat-backed Spider Tortoise (E): *Pyxis planicauda*
Flat-casqued Chameleon (E): *Calumma globifer*
Flat-faced Seahorse (E): *Hippocampus trimaculatus*
Flat-headed Cat (E): *Prionailurus planiceps*
Flat-shelled Spider Tortoise (E): *Pyxis planicauda*
Flat-tailed Day Gecko (E): *Phelsuma laticauda*
Flightless Teal (E): *Anas aucklandica*
Flores Hanging-Parrot (E): *Loriculus flosculus*
Floricans (E): OTIDIDAE spp.

Florida Cougar (E): *Puma concolor coryi*
Florida Golden Chestnut Tarantula (E): *Brachypelma*
    aureoceps
Florida Panther (E): *Puma concolor coryi*
Florida Puma (E): *Puma concolor coryi*
Florisuga fusca : (E) Black Jacobin, (S) Colibrí negro,
    Picaflor negro, (F) Colibri demi-deuil, **II**
    TROCHILIDAE Av
Florisuga mellivora : (E) White-necked Jacobin, (S)
    Colibrí nuquiblanco, Jacobino collarejo, Jacobino
    nuquiblanco, (F) Colibri jacobin, **II** TROCHILIDAE
    Av
Flower Lizard (E): *Varanus indicus*
Flowerpot corals (E): *Goniopora spp.*
Fluted Clam (E): *Tridacna squamosa*
Fluted Giant Clam (E): *Tridacna squamosa*
Flying-foxes (E): *Acerodon* spp./ *Pteropus* spp.
Foca fraile de Hawaii (S): *Monachus schauinslandi*
Foca fraile del Caribe (S): *Monachus tropicalis*
Foca monje (S): *Monachus monachus*
Foca monje del Mediterráneo (S): *Monachus monachus*
Focas fraile (S): *Monachus* spp.
Focas monje (S): *Monachus* spp.
Folded Coral (E): *Trachyphyllia geoffroyi*
Folohy Golden Frog (E): *Mantella laevigata*
Forbes's Kakariki (E): *Cyanoramphus forbesi*
Forbes's Parakeet (E): *Cyanoramphus forbesi*
Ford's Boa (E): *Epicrates fordii*
Forest Buzzard (E): *Buteo oreophilus*
Forest Eagle-Owl (E): *Bubo nipalensis*
Forest Fox (E): *Cerdocyon thous*
Forest Hinged Terrapin (E): *Pelusios gabonensis*
Forest Hinged Tortoise (E): *Kinixys erosa*
Forest Little Owl (E): *Athene blewitti*
Forest Musk Deer (E): *Moschus berezovskii*
Forest Owlet (E): *Athene blewitti*
Forest Spotted Owlet (E): *Athene blewitti*
Forest Tortoise (E): *Geochelone denticulata*
Forked Chameleon (E): *Calumma furcifer*
Fork-marked Lemur (E): *Phaner furcifer*
Fork-marked Mouse-lemur (E): *Phaner furcifer*
Fork-nosed Chameleon (E): *Calumma furcifer*
Fork-tailed Emerald (E): *Chlorostilbon canivetii*
Fork-tailed Woodnymph (E): *Thalurania furcata*
Formosan Rock Macaque (E): *Macaca cyclopis*
Forpus coelestis : (E) Celestial Parrotlet, Pacific Parrotlet,
    (S) Cotorrita de Piura, Periquito del Pacífico, (F) Toui
    céleste, **II** PSITTACIDAE Av
Forpus conspicillatus : (E) Spectacled Parrotlet, (S)
    Cotorrita de Anteojos, Periquito ojiazul, (F) Toui à
    lunettes, **II** PSITTACIDAE Av
Forpus crassirostris : (E) Blue-winged Parrotlet, (S) Catita
    enana, Cotorrita aliazul, Periquito aliazul, (F) Toui de
    Spix, **II** PSITTACIDAE Av
Forpus cyanopygius : (E) Blue-rumped Parrotlet, Mexican
    Parrotlet, (S) Cotorrita Mexicana, Periquito mexicano,
    (F) Toui du Mexique, **II** PSITTACIDAE Av
Forpus passerinus : (E) Green-rumped Parrotlet, (S)
    Cotorrita culiverde, Periquito, (F) Perruche aux ailes
    bleues, Toui été, **II** PSITTACIDAE Av
Forpus sclateri : (E) Dusky-billed Parrotlet, Sclater's
    Parrotlet, (S) Cotorrita de Sclater, Periquito obscuro,
    (F) Toui de Sclater, **II** PSITTACIDAE Av
Forpus xanthops : (E) Yellow-faced Parrotlet, (S)
    Cotorrita carigualda, (F) Toui à tête jaune, **II**
    PSITTACIDAE Av
Forpus xanthopterygius = Forpus crassirostris
Forsten's Tortoise (E): *Indotestudo forstenii*
Forster's Caracara (E): *Phalcoboenus australis*
Fosa (E): *Cryptoprocta ferox*
Fossa (E/f): *Cryptoprocta ferox*
Fossa fossana : (E) Fanaloka, Malagasy Civet, Striped
    Civet, (S) Cibeta de Madagascar, Civeta, (F) Civette
    fossane, Civette malgache, Fanaloka, Fossana, **II**
    VIVERRIDAE Ma

Checklist of fauna/Lista de especies de fauna/Liste des espèces animales

Fossana (F): *Fossa fossana*
Fou d'Abbott (F): *Papasula abbotti*
Fouette-queue de Bent (F): *Uromastyx benti*
Fouette-queue de Hardwick (F): *Uromastyx hardwickii*
Fouette-queue de Mésopotamie (F): *Uromastyx loricata*
Fouette-queue de Thomas (F): *Uromastyx thomasi*
Fouette-queue d'Egypte (F): *Uromastyx aegyptia*
Fouette-queue d'Iran (F): *Uromastyx asmussi*
Fouette-queue d'O'Shaughnessy (F): *Uromastyx princeps*
Fouette-queue du Sahara (F): *Uromastyx geyri*
Fouette-queue épineux (F): *Uromastyx acanthinura*
Fouette-queue indien (F): *Uromastyx hardwickii*
Fouette-queue ocellé (F): *Uromastyx ocellata*
Fouettes-queue princier (F): *Uromastyx princeps*
Fouettes-queue (F): *Uromastyx* spp.
Fouine (F): *Martes foina intermedia*
Four-foot Caiman (E): *Dracaena guianensis*
Four-horned Antelope (E): *Tetracerus quadricornis*
Four-horned Chameleon (E): *Chamaeleo quadricornis*
Four-spot Day Gecko (E): *Phelsuma quadriocellata*
Four-toed Terrapin (E): *Batagur baska*
Four-toed Tortoise (E): *Testudo horsfieldii*
Foussa (F): *Cryptoprocta ferox*
Foveolocyathus alternans : **II** TURBINOLIIDAE An
Foveolocyathus verconis : **II** TURBINOLIIDAE An
Fox Kestrel (E): *Falco alopex*
Fragata de las islas Christmas (S): *Fregata andrewsi*
Fragile Saucer Coral (E): *Agaricia fragilis*
Frances's Goshawk (E): *Accipiter francesii*
Frances's Sparrowhawk (E): *Accipiter francesii*
Franciscana (E): *Pontoporia blainvillei*
François's Langur (E): *Trachypithecus francoisi*
François's Leaf Monkey (E): *Trachypithecus francoisi*
Fraser's Dolphin (E): *Lagenodelphis hosei*
Fraser's Eagle-Owl (E): *Bubo poensis*
Freckled Monitor (E): *Varanus tristis*
Fregata andrewsi : (E) Andrews' Frigatebird, Christmas
    Frigatebird, Christmas Island Frigatebird, (S) Fragata
    de las islas Christmas, Rabihorcado de la Christmas,
    Rabihorcado ventriblanco, (F) Frégate d'Andrews,
    Frégate de l'île Christmas, **I** FREGATIDAE Av
Frégate d'Andrews (F): *Fregata andrewsi*
Frégate de l'île Christmas (F): *Fregata andrewsi*
Frentiestrella alihabano (S): *Coeligena lutetiae*
Frentiestrella arcoiris (S): *Coeligena iris*
Frentijoya (S): *Heliodoxa aurescens*
Frilled Coquette (E): *Lophornis magnificus*
Frilly Lettuce Coral (E): *Pectinia lactuca*
Fringebarbel sturgeon (E): *Acipenser nudiventris*
Frog-faced Giant Softshell Turtle (E): *Pelochelys cantorii*
Frogspawn Coral (E): *Euphyllia divisa*
Frogspawn corals (E): *Euphyllia* spp.
Fuertes's Parrot (E): *Hapalopsittaca fuertesi*
Fuligule nyroca (F): *Aythya nyroca*
Fulvous Owl (E): *Strix fulvescens*
Fulvous Tree-Duck (E): *Dendrocygna bicolor*
Fulvous Whistling-Duck (E): *Dendrocygna bicolor*
Fungia concinna : **II** FUNGIIDAE An
Fungia corona : **II** FUNGIIDAE An
Fungia costulata : **II** FUNGIIDAE An
Fungia curvata : **II** FUNGIIDAE An
Fungia cyclolites : **II** FUNGIIDAE An
Fungia danae : **II** FUNGIIDAE An
Fungia distorta : **II** FUNGIIDAE An
Fungia erosa : **II** FUNGIIDAE An
Fungia fragilis : **II** FUNGIIDAE An
Fungia fralinae : **II** FUNGIIDAE An
Fungia fungites : (E) Mushroom Coral **II** FUNGIIDAE An
Fungia granulosa : **II** FUNGIIDAE An
Fungia gravis : **II** FUNGIIDAE An
Fungia hexagonalis : **II** FUNGIIDAE An
Fungia horrida : **II** FUNGIIDAE An
Fungia klunzingeri : **II** FUNGIIDAE An
Fungia moluccensis : **II** FUNGIIDAE An
Fungia patelliformis : **II** FUNGIIDAE An

Fungia paumotensis : **II** FUNGIIDAE An
Fungia puishani : **II** FUNGIIDAE An
Fungia repanda : **II** FUNGIIDAE An
Fungia scabra : **II** FUNGIIDAE An
Fungia scruposa : **II** FUNGIIDAE An
Fungia scutaria : **II** FUNGIIDAE An
Fungia seychellensis : **II** FUNGIIDAE An
Fungia sinensis : **II** FUNGIIDAE An
Fungia somervillei : **II** FUNGIIDAE An
Fungia spinifer : **II** FUNGIIDAE An
Fungia taiwanensis : **II** FUNGIIDAE An
Fungia tenuis : **II** FUNGIIDAE An
Fungia vaughani : **II** FUNGIIDAE An
Fungiacyathus aleuticus = *Fungiacyathus marenzelleri*
Fungiacyathus crispus : **II** FUNGIACYATHIDAE An
Fungiacyathus dennanti : **II** FUNGIACYATHIDAE An
Fungiacyathus durus = *Fungiacyathus marenzelleri*
Fungiacyathus fissidiscus : **II** FUNGIACYATHIDAE An
Fungiacyathus fissilis : **II** FUNGIACYATHIDAE An
Fungiacyathus fragilis : **II** FUNGIACYATHIDAE An
Fungiacyathus granulosus : **II** FUNGIACYATHIDAE An
Fungiacyathus hydra : **II** FUNGIACYATHIDAE An
Fungiacyathus marenzelleri : **II** FUNGIACYATHIDAE
    An
Fungiacyathus margaretae : **II** FUNGIACYATHIDAE
    An
Fungiacyathus multicarinatus : **II** FUNGIACYATHIDAE
    An
Fungiacyathus paliferus : **II** FUNGIACYATHIDAE An
Fungiacyathus pliciseptus : **II** FUNGIACYATHIDAE An
Fungiacyathus pseudostephanus : **II**
    FUNGIACYATHIDAE An
Fungiacyathus pusillus : **II** FUNGIACYATHIDAE An
Fungiacyathus pusillus pacificus : **II**
    FUNGIACYATHIDAE An
Fungiacyathus pusillus pusillus : **II**
    FUNGIACYATHIDAE An
Fungiacyathus sandoi : **II** FUNGIACYATHIDAE An
Fungiacyathus sibogae : **II** FUNGIACYATHIDAE An
Fungiacyathus stephanus : **II** FUNGIACYATHIDAE An
Fungiacyathus symmetricus : **II** FUNGIACYATHIDAE
    An
Fungiacyathus turbinolioides : **II** FUNGIACYATHIDAE
    An
Fungiacyathus variegatus : **II** FUNGIACYATHIDAE An
Fur seals (E): *Arctocephalus* spp.
Furcifer spp.: (E) Chameleons, (S) Camaleónes, (F)
    Caméléons, **II** CHAMAELEONIDAE Re
Furcifer angeli : (E) Angel's Chameleon, (F) Caméléon
    d'Angel **II** CHAMAELEONIDAE Re
Furcifer antimena : (E) White-lined Chameleon, (F)
    Caméléon à lignes blanches **II** CHAMAELEONIDAE
    Re
Furcifer balteatus : (E) Rainforest Chameleon, Two-
    banded Chameleon, (F) Caméléon forestier **II**
    CHAMAELEONIDAE Re
Furcifer belalandaensis : (E) Belalanda Chameleon, (F)
    Caméléon de Belalanda **II** CHAMAELEONIDAE Re
Furcifer bifidus : (E) Two-horned Chameleon, (F)
    Caméléon à deux cornes, Caméléon à nez fourchu **II**
    CHAMAELEONIDAE Re
Furcifer campani : (E) Madagascar Forest Chameleon, (F)
    Caméléon forestier de Madagascar **II**
    CHAMAELEONIDAE Re
Furcifer cephalolepis : (E) Comoro Islands Chameleon,
    (F) Caméléon des Comores **II** CHAMAELEONIDAE
    Re
Furcifer lateralis : (E) Carpet Chameleon, Jewelled
    Chameleon, (F) Caméléon à bandes latérales,
    Caméléon-joyau **II** CHAMAELEONIDAE Re
Furcifer minor : (E) South-central Chameleon, (F)
    Caméléon de Günther **II** CHAMAELEONIDAE Re
Furcifer monoceras : (E) One-horned Chameleon, (F)
    Caméléon à une corne **II** CHAMAELEONIDAE Re
Furcifer nicosiai : **II** CHAMAELEONIDAE Re

Checklist of fauna/Lista de especies de fauna/Liste des espèces animales

Furcifer oustaleti : (E) Malagasy Giant Chameleon, Oustalet's Giant Chameleon, (S) Camaleón de Oustalet, (F) Caméléon d'Oustalet, **II** CHAMAELEONIDAE Re

Furcifer pardalis : (E) Panther Chameleon, (F) Caméléon panthère **II** CHAMAELEONIDAE Re

Furcifer petteri : (E) Petter's Chameleon, (S) Camaleón de Petter, (F) Caméléon de Petter, **II** CHAMAELEONIDAE Re

Furcifer polleni : (E) Mayotte Chameleon, (F) Caméléon de Mayotte **II** CHAMAELEONIDAE Re

Furcifer rhinoceratus : (E) Rhinoceros Chameleon, (S) Camaleón rinoceronte, (F) Caméléon rhinocéros, **II** CHAMAELEONIDAE Re

Furcifer tuzetae : (E) Ambiky Chameleon, (F) Caméléon d'Andrenalamivola **II** CHAMAELEONIDAE Re

Furcifer verrucosus : (E) Madagascar Giant Chameleon, Madagascar Giant Spiny Chameleon, Warty Chameleon, (S) Camaleón verrugoso, (F) Caméléon verruqueux, **II** CHAMAELEONIDAE Re

Furcifer willsii : (E) Canopy Chameleon, (F) Caméléon de la canopée, Caméléon de Wills **II** CHAMAELEONIDAE Re

Furculachelys nabeulensis = *Testudo graeca*
Furculachelys whitei = *Testudo graeca*

Fusconaia cuneolus : (E) Fine-rayed Pigtoe, Fine-rayed Pigtoe Pearly Mussel **I** UNIONIDAE Bi

Fusconaia edgariana : (E) Shiny Pigtoe, Shiny Pigtoe Pearly Mussel **I** UNIONIDAE Bi

Fused Staghorn Coral (E): *Acropora prolifera*

Gabar Goshawk (E): *Melierax gabar*
Gabon Terrapin (E): *Pelusios gabonensis*
Gabon Turtle (E): *Pelusios gabonensis*
Gacela de Cuvier (S): *Gazella cuvieri*
Gacela de Irán (S): *Dama mesopotamica*
Gacela dorcas (S): *Gazella dorcas*
Gafudo gorgiblanco (S): *Zosterops albogularis*
Galago à queue touffue (F): *Otolemur crassicaudatus*
Galago alleni : (E) Allen's Bushbaby, Allen's Galago, Allen's Squirrel Galago, (S) Gálago de Allen, (F) Galago d'Allen, **II** GALAGONIDAE Ma

Galago crassicaudatus = *Otolemur crassicaudatus*
Galago d'Allen (F): *Galago alleni*
Gálago de Allen (S): *Galago alleni*
Gálago de cola gruesa (S): *Otolemur crassicaudatus*
Galago de Demidoff (F): *Galagoides demidoff*
Gálago de Senegal (S): *Galago senegalensis*
Gálago de Zanzíbar (S): *Galagoides zanzibaricus*
Galago demidovii = *Galagoides demidoff*
Galago du Congo (F): *Galago matschiei*
Galago du Sénégal (F): *Galago senegalensis*
Galago élégant (F): *Euoticus elegantulus*
Gálago elegante (S): *Euoticus elegantulus*
Galago elegantulus = *Euoticus elegantulus*
Galago elegantulus ssp. *pallidus* = *Euoticus pallidus*
Gálago enano (S): *Galagoides demidoff*
Gálago etíope (S): *Galago gallarum*
Galago gabonensis = *Galago alleni*
Galago gallarum : (E) Somali Galago, (S) Gálago etíope **II** GALAGONIDAE Ma

Galago granti = *Galagoides zanzibaricus*
Galago inustus = *Galago matschiei*
Galago matschiei : (E) Eastern Needle-clawed Bushbaby, Eastern Needle-clawed Galago, Lesser Needle-clawed Galago, Matschie's Galago, Spectacled Galago, (F) Galago du Congo **II** GALAGONIDAE Ma

Galago moholi : (E) Mohol Galago, South African Lesser Galago **II** GALAGONIDAE Ma

Galago orinus = *Galagoides demidoff*
Galago rondoensis = *Galagoides rondoensis*
Galago senegalensis : (E) Lesser Bushbaby, Lesser Galago, Senegal Galago, (S) Gálago de Senegal, (F) Galago du Sénégal, **II** GALAGONIDAE Ma

Galago senegalensis ssp. *gallarum* = *Galago gallarum*

Galago senegalensis ssp. *moholi* = *Galago moholi*
Galago senegalensis ssp. *zanzibaricus* = *Galagoides zanzibaricus*
Galago zanzibaricus = *Galagoides zanzibaricus*
Galagoides alleni = *Galago alleni*
Galagoides demidoff : (E) Demidoff's Dwarf Galago, Demidoff's Galago, Dwarf Bushbaby, Dwarf Galago, (S) Gálago enano, (F) Galago de Demidoff, **II** GALAGONIDAE Ma

Galagoides granti = *Galagoides zanzibaricus*
Galagoides orinus = *Galagoides demidoff*
Galagoides rondoensis : (E) Rondo Dwarf Galago, Rondo Galago **II** GALAGONIDAE Ma

Galagoides thomasi = *Galagoides demidoff*
Galagoides udzungwensis : (E) Matundu Dwarf Galago **II** GALAGONIDAE Ma

Galagoides zanzibaricus : (E) Zanzibar Bushbaby, Zanzibar Galago, (S) Gálago de Zanzíbar **II** GALAGONIDAE Ma

Galah (E): *Eolophus roseicapillus*
Galápago acuático encajado (S): *Terrapene coahuila*
Galápago Batagur (S): *Batagur baska*
Galápago caja Mexicano (S): *Terrapene coahuila*
Galápago cubierto de la India (S): *Kachuga tecta*
Galápago de Birmania (S): *Morenia ocellata*
Galápago de Hamilton (S): *Geoclemys hamiltonii*
Galápago de Muhlenberg (S): *Clemmys muhlenbergii*
Galápago indio (S): *Batagur baska*
Galápago ocelado de Birmania (S): *Morenia ocellata*
Galápago pintado (S): *Callagur borneoensis*
Galápago rayado (S): *Geoclemys hamiltonii*
Galápago terrestre (S): *Melanochelys tricarinata*
Galápago tricarenado (S): *Melanochelys tricarinata*
Galápagos (S): *Podocnemis* spp.
Galápagos cajas (S): *Terrapene* spp.
Galápagos cubiertos (S): *Kachuga* spp.
Galapagos Fur Seal (E): *Arctocephalus galapagoensis*
Galapagos Giant Tortoise (E): *Geochelone nigra*
Galapagos Hawk (E): *Buteo galapagoensis*
Galapagos Islands Fur Seal (E): *Arctocephalus galapagoensis*
Galapagos Land Iguana (E): *Conolophus subcristatus*
Galapagos Marine Iguana (E): *Amblyrhynchus cristatus*
Galaxea spp.: (E) Crystal corals, Galaxy corals, Starburst corals, Tooth corals **II** OCULINIDAE An
Galaxea acrhelia : **II** OCULINIDAE An
Galaxea alta : **II** OCULINIDAE An
Galaxea astreata : **II** OCULINIDAE An
Galaxea cryptoramosa : **II** OCULINIDAE An
Galaxea fascicularis : **II** OCULINIDAE An
Galaxea horrescens = *Acrhelia horrescens*
Galaxea longisepta : **II** OCULINIDAE An
Galaxea paucisepta : **II** OCULINIDAE An
Galaxy corals (E): *Galaxea* spp.
Galictis allamandi = *Galictis vittata*
Galictis vittata : (E) Allamand's Grison, Greater Grison, (S) Grisón, Hurón, Hurón grange, Tejón, (F) Grison, Grison d'Allemand, **III** MUSTELIDAE Ma
Gallicolombe poignardée (F): *Gallicolumba luzonica*
Gallicolumba luzonica : (E) Bleeding Heart Dove, Bleeding Heart Pigeon, Luzon Bleeding-heart, Paloma apuñalada, Paloma apuñalada de Luzón, (F) Colombe poignardée, Gallicolombe poignardée, **II** COLUMBIDAE Av
Gallina de palo (S): *Iguana iguana*
Gallinazo rey (S): *Sarcoramphus papa*
Gallirallus sylvestris : (E) Lord Howe Island Rail, Lord Howe Island Woodhen, Lord Howe Rail, (S) Rascón de la isla de Lord Howe, Rascón de la Lord Howe, (F) Râle de l'île Lord Howe, Râle sylvestre, **I** RALLIDAE Av
Gallirex porphyreolophus = *Musophaga porphyreolopha*
Gallito de las Rocas (S): *Rupicola rupicola*
Gallito de las Sierras (S): *Rupicola peruviana*
Gallito de pradera (S): *Tympanuchus cupido attwateri*

Checklist of fauna/Lista de especies de fauna/Liste des espèces animales

Gallito de roca anaranjado (S): *Rupicola rupicola*
Gallito de roca peruano (S): *Rupicola peruviana*
Gallitos de las rocas (S): *Rupicola* spp.
Gallo de Sonnerat (S): *Gallus sonneratii*
Gallo gris (S): *Gallus sonneratii*
Gallo lira (S): *Tetrax tetrax*
Gallo lira del Caspio (S): *Tetraogallus caspius*
Gallo lira del Tíbet (S): *Tetraogallus tibetanus*
Gallo salvaje del Caspio (S): *Tetraogallus caspius*
Gallo salvaje del Tibet (S): *Tetraogallus tibetanus*
Gallotia simonyi : (E) Hierro Giant Lizard, (S) Lagarto gigante del Hierro, (F) Lézard de Simony, Lézard géant de Hierro, **I** LACERTIDAE Re
Gallus sonneratii : (E) Grey Junglefowl, Sonnerat's Junglefowl, (S) Gallo de Sonnerat, Gallo gris, (F) Coq de Sonnerat, **II** PHASIANIDAE Av
Gamo de Mesopotamia (S): *Dama mesopotamica*
Gampsonyx swainsonii : (E) Pearl Kite, (S) Cernícalo, Elanio chico, Elanio enano, (F) Élanion perle, **II** ACCIPITRIDAE Av
Gamuza alpina (S): *Rupicapra pyrenaica ornata*
Gamuza de los Abruzzos (S): *Rupicapra pyrenaica ornata*
Gan-Gan (S): *Callocephalon fimbriatum*
Ganges Hog Deer (E): *Axis porcinus annamiticus*
Ganges River Dolphin (E): *Platanista gangetica*
Ganges Susu (E): *Platanista gangetica*
Gang-gang Cockatoo (E): *Callocephalon fimbriatum*
Gansito Africano (S): *Nettapus auritus*
Ganso blanco (S): *Coscoroba coscoroba*
Ganso canadiense aleutiana (S): *Branta canadensis leucopareia*
Ganso de Gambia (S): *Plectropterus gambensis*
Ganso del Nilo (S): *Alopochen aegyptiacus*
Ganso espolonado (S): *Plectropterus gambensis*
Ganso né (S): *Branta sandvicensis*
Garceta común (S): *Egretta garzetta*
Garceta grande (S): *Casmerodius albus*
Garcilla bueyera (S): *Bubulcus ibis*
Garcilla grande (S): *Casmerodius albus*
Garcita resnera (S): *Bubulcus ibis*
Garden Tree Boa (E): *Corallus hortulanus*
Gardineria antarctica = Paraconotrochus antarctica
Gardineria capensis = Paraconotrochus capense
Gardineria hawaiiensis : **II** GARDINERIIDAE An
Gardineria minor : **II** GARDINERIIDAE An
Gardineria musorstomica = Gardineria hawaiiensis
Gardineria paradoxa : **II** GARDINERIIDAE An
Gardineria philippinensis : **II** GARDINERIIDAE An
Gardineria simplex : **II** GARDINERIIDAE An
Gardineroseris planulata : **II** AGARICIIDAE An
Garganey (E): *Anas querquedula*
Garganey Teal (E): *Anas querquedula*
Garganta de oro coliverde (S): *Polytmus theresiae*
Garganta lanza coliblanca (S): *Threnetes niger*
Garnet-throated Hummingbird (E): *Lamprolaima rhami*
Garnett's Greater Galago (E): *Otolemur garnettii*
Garrulax canorus : (E) Hwamei, Melodious Laughingthrush, (F) Garrulaxe hoamy **II** MUSCICAPIDAE Av
Garrulaxe de l'Omei (F): *Liocichla omeiensis*
Garrulaxe hoamy (F): *Garrulax canorus*
Garza blanca real (S): *Casmerodius albus*
Garza ganadera (S): *Bubulcus ibis*
Garza goliat (S): *Ardea goliath*
Garzetta grande (S): *Casmerodius albus*
Garzón soldado (S): *Jabiru mycteria*
Gastric-brooding frogs (E): *Rheobatrachus* spp.
Gato andino (S): *Oreailurus jacobita*
Gato atigrado (S): *Leopardus tigrinus*
Gato bengalí (S): *Prionailurus bengalensis*
Gato cabeciancho (S): *Prionailurus planiceps*
Gato colorado (S): *Herpailurus yaguarondi*
Gato cutarra (S): *Eira barbara*
Gato de agua (S): *Lontra longicaudis*
Gato de Bengala (S): *Prionailurus bengalensis*

Gato de Biet (S): *Felis bieti*
Gato de cabeza plana (S): *Prionailurus planiceps*
Gato de la jungla (S): *Felis chaus*
Gato de las arenas (S): *Felis margarita*
Gato de los pajonales (S): *Oncifelis colocolo*
Gato de los pantanos (S): *Felis chaus*
Gato de mar (S): *Lontra felina*
Gato de mato (S): *Oncifelis geoffroyi*
Gato de Pallas (S): *Otocolobus manul*
Gato de pies negros (S): *Felis nigripes*
Gato del desierto de China (S): *Felis bieti*
Gato del Sahara (S): *Felis margarita*
Gato dorado (S): *Profelis aurata*
Gato dorado asiático (S): *Catopuma temminckii*
Gato fossa de Madagascar (S): *Cryptoprocta ferox*
Gato jaspeado (S): *Pardofelis marmorata*
Gato leopardo chino (S): *Prionailurus bengalensis bengalensis*
Gato leopardo de la India (S): *Prionailurus rubiginosus*
Gato lince (S): *Oreailurus jacobita*
Gato manul (S): *Otocolobus manul*
Gato marino (S): *Lontra felina*
Gato montés (S): *Leopardus wiedii/ Felis silvestris/ Lynx rufus*
Gato montés común (S): *Oncifelis geoffroyi*
Gato moro (S): *Herpailurus yaguarondi*
Gato negro (S): *Eira barbara*
Gato onza (S): *Leopardus pardalis*
Gato pajero (S): *Oncifelis colocolo*
Gato patinegro (S): *Felis nigripes*
Gato pescador (S): *Prionailurus viverrinus*
Gato rojizo (S): *Prionailurus rubiginosus*
Gato rubiginosa (S): *Prionailurus rubiginosus*
Gato silvestre (S): *Felis silvestris*
Gato tigre (S): *Leopardus tigrinus*
Gato tigrillo (S): *Leopardus tigrinus*
Gaur (E/S/F): *Bos gaurus*
Gauru (S): *Bos gaurus*
Gavial (E): *Gavialis gangeticus*
Gavial del Ganges (S): *Gavialis gangeticus*
Gavial du Gange (F): *Gavialis gangeticus*
Gavialis gangeticus : (E) Fish-eating Crocodile, Gavial, Gharial, Long-nosed Crocodile, (S) Gavial del Ganges, (F) Gavial du Gange, **I** GAVIALIDAE Re
Gavilán acollarado (S): *Accipiter cirrocephalus/ Accipiter collaris*
Gavilán albonotatus (S): *Buteo albonotatus*
Gavilán alirrojizo (S): *Buteo magnirostris*
Gavilán americano (S): *Accipiter striatus*
Gavilán andapié (S): *Parabuteo unicinctus*
Gavilán andino (S): *Accipiter ventralis*
Gavilán arrastrador (S): *Accipiter striatus*
Gavilán azor (S): *Accipiter gentilis*
Gavilán azul (S): *Leucopternis schistacea*
Gavilán bebehumo (S): *Buteo platypterus*
Gavilán besra (S): *Accipiter virgatus*
Gavilán bicolor (S): *Accipiter bicolor*
Gavilán bidente (S): *Harpagus bidentatus*
Gavilán blanco (S): *Leucopternis albicollis*
Gavilán cabecigrís (S): *Accipiter poliocephalus*
Gavilán cangrejero (S): *Buteogallus anthracinus*
Gavilán caracolero (S): *Rostrhamus sociabilis*
Gavilán carinegro (S): *Leucopternis melanops*
Gavilán ceniciento (S): *Circus cinereus*
Gavilán chikra (S): *Accipiter badius*
Gavilán cola corta (S): *Buteo brachyurus*
Gavilán colifajeado (S): *Buteo albonotatus*
Gavilán colipinto (S): *Accipiter trinotatus*
Gavilán colorado (S): *Busarellus nigricollis*
Gavilán Común (S): *Accipiter nisus/ Buteo magnirostris*
Gavilán cubano (S): *Accipiter gundlachi*
Gavilán cueillirojo (S): *Micrastur ruficollis*
Gavilán de Célebes (S): *Accipiter griseiceps*
Gavilán de collar (S): *Micrastur gilvicollis*
Gavilán de Cooper (S): *Accipiter cooperii*

Checklist of fauna/Lista de especies de fauna/Liste des espèces animales

Gavilán de Frances (S): *Accipiter francesii*
Gavilán de Galapagos (S): *Buteo galapagoensis*
Gavilán de las Fiji (S): *Accipiter rufitorques*
Gavilán de Manglares (S): *Buteogallus aequinoctialis*
Gavilán de Nicobar (S): *Accipiter butleri*
Gavilán de Nueva Bretaña (S): *Accipiter luteoschistaceus*
Gavilán de Nueva Caledonia (S): *Accipiter haplochrous*
Gavilán de Ovampo (S): *Accipiter ovampensis*
Gavilán de Traylor (S): *Micrastur buckleyi*
Gavilán dorsigris (S): *Leucopternis occidentalis*
Gavilán enano (S): *Accipiter superciliosus*
Gavilán flanquirrojo (S): *Accipiter castanilius*
Gavilán gabar (S): *Melierax gabar*
Gavilán gargantiblanco (S): *Buteo albigula*
Gavilán grande (S): *Circus buffoni*
Gavilán griego (S): *Accipiter brevipes*
Gavilán gris (S): *Asturina nitida*
Gavilán habado (S): *Buteo magnirostris*
Gavilán imitador (S): *Accipiter imitator*
Gavilán langostero (S): *Buteo swainsoni*
Gavilán malgache (S): *Accipiter madagascariensis*
Gavilán maromero (S): *Elanus leucurus*
Gavilán mixto (S): *Parabuteo unicinctus*
Gavilán negro (S): *Buteo leucorrhous*
Gavilán negro común (S): *Buteogallus subtilis*
Gavilán negro grande (S): *Buteogallus urubitinga*
Gavilán pajarero (S): *Accipiter striatus*
Gavilán palomero (S): *Leptodon cayanensis*
Gavilán pantalón (S): *Accipiter bicolor*
Gavilán papirrufo (S): *Accipiter rufiventris*
Gavilán patilargo (S): *Geranospiza caerulescens*
Gavilán pechiblanco (S): *Accipiter chionogaster*
Gavilán pechirrojo (S): *Accipiter castanilius/ Accipiter rhodogaster*
Gavilán pechirroseo (S): *Accipiter toussenelii*
Gavilán pescador (S): *Pandion haliaetus*
Gavilán pico de Hoz (S): *Rostrhamus hamatus*
Gavilán pico ganchudo (S): *Chondrohierax uncinatus*
Gavilán pío (S): *Accipiter albogularis*
Gavilán pita venado (S): *Buteogallus meridionalis*
Gavilán pizarroso (S): *Leucopternis schistacea*
Gavilán plomizo (S): *Ictinia plumbea/ Leucopternis plumbea*
Gavilán principe (S): *Leucopternis princeps*
Gavilán punenno (S): *Buteo poecilochrous*
Gavilán rabadilla blanca (S): *Buteo leucorrhous*
Gavilán ranero (S): *Accipiter soloensis*
Gavilán rastrero (S): *Circus cyaneus*
Gavilán rufinegro (S): *Accipiter melanochlamys*
Gavilán sabanero (S): *Buteogallus meridionalis*
Gavilán semiplomizo (S): *Leucopternis semiplumbea*
Gavilán tejé (S): *Buteo albicaudatus*
Gavilán tijereta (S): *Elanoides forficatus*
Gavilán ventriblanco (S): *Accipiter chionogaster*
Gavilán vientrigris (S): *Accipiter poliogaster*
Gavilán zancón (S): *Geranospiza caerulescens*
Gavilán zancudo (S): *Geranospiza caerulescens*
Gavilancito americano (S): *Accipiter superciliosus*
Gavilancito chico (S): *Accipiter minullus*
Gavilancito de Célebes (S): *Accipiter nanus*
Gavilancito de Hartlaub (S): *Accipiter erythropus*
Gavilancito de Nueva Bretaña (S): *Accipiter brachyurus*
Gavilancito japonés (S): *Accipiter gularis*
Gavilancito moluqueño (S): *Accipiter erythrauchen*
Gavilancito muslirrojo (S): *Accipiter erythropus*
Gavilancito torcaz (S): *Accipiter collaris*
Gavilán-reloj (S): *Micrastur semitorquatus*
Gaviota de Mongolia (S): *Larus relictus*
Gaviota relicta (S): *Larus relictus*
Gazella cuvieri : (E) Cuvier's Gazelle, Edmi Gazelle, Idmi, (S) Gacela de Cuvier, (F) Gazelle de Cuvier, **III** BOVIDAE Ma
Gazella dama : (E) Addra Gazelle, Dama Gazelle, (F) Gazelle dama **I** BOVIDAE Ma

Gazella dorcas : (E) Dorcas Gazelle, (S) Gacela dorcas, (F) Gazelle dorcas, **III** BOVIDAE Ma
Gazella leptoceros : (E) Rhim Gazelle, Sand Gazelle, Slender-horned Gazelle, (S) Rhim, (F) Gazelle à cornes fines, Gazelle leptocère, Rhim, **III** BOVIDAE Ma
Gazelle à cornes fines (F): *Gazella leptoceros*
Gazelle dama (F): *Gazella dama*
Gazelle de Cuvier (F): *Gazella cuvieri*
Gazelle dorcas (F): *Gazella dorcas*
Gazelle leptocère (F): *Gazella leptoceros*
Gecko de l'île Serpent (F): *Cyrtodactylus serpensinsula*
Gecko diurne à bandes noires (F): *Phelsuma nigristriata*
Gecko diurne à courte tête (F): *Phelsuma breviceps*
Gecko diurne à gorge jaune (F): *Phelsuma flavigularis*
Gecko diurne à large queue (F): *Phelsuma laticauda*
Gecko diurne à quatre ocelles (F): *Phelsuma quadriocellata*
Gecko diurne à queue bleue (F): *Phelsuma cepediana*
Gecko diurne à queue charnue (F): *Phelsuma mutabilis*
Gecko diurne à queue plate (F): *Phelsuma serraticauda*
Gecko diurne à tête jaune (F): *Phelsuma klemmeri*
Gecko diurne à trois lignes (F): *Phelsuma trilineata*
Gecko diurne d'Aldabra (F): *Phelsuma abbotti*
Gecko diurne de Barbour (F): *Phelsuma barbouri*
Gecko diurne de Befotaka (F): *Phelsuma befotakensis*
Gecko diurne de Boettger (F): *Phelsuma v-nigra*
Gecko diurne de Borner (F): *Phelsuma minuthi*
Gecko diurne de Bourbon (F): *Phelsuma borbonica*
Gecko diurne de Cheke (F): *Phelsuma chekei*
Gecko diurne de Grandidier (F): *Phelsuma mutabilis*
Gecko diurne de Klemmer (F): *Phelsuma klemmeri*
Gecko diurne de la région Antanosy (F): *Phelsuma antanosy*
Gecko diurne de la Réunion (F): *Phelsuma borbonica*
Gecko diurne de l'Ile Maurice (F): *Phelsuma guimbeaui*
Gecko diurne de l'Ile Pemba (F): *Phelsuma parkeri*
Gecko diurne de l'Ile Ronde (F): *Phelsuma guentheri*
Gecko diurne de Madagascar (F): *Phelsuma madagascariensis*
Gecko diurne de Meier (F): *Phelsuma nigristriata*
Gecko diurne de Minuth (F): *Phelsuma minuthi*
Gecko diurne de Parker (F): *Phelsuma parkeri*
Gecko diurne de Peacock (F): *Phelsuma quadriocellata*
Gecko diurne de Robert Mertens (F): *Phelsuma robertmertensi*
Gecko diurne de Rodrigues (F): *Phelsuma edwardnewtonii*
Gecko diurne de Seipp (F): *Phelsuma seippi*
Gecko diurne de Standing (F): *Phelsuma standingi*
Gecko diurne de Zanzibar (F): *Phelsuma dubia*
Gecko diurne des Comores (F): *Phelsuma comorensis*
Gecko diurne des Iles Andaman (F): *Phelsuma andamanensis*
Gecko diurne des Seychelles (F): *Phelsuma astriata/ Phelsuma longinsulae*
Gecko diurne du Nord de Madagascar (F): *Phelsuma chekei*
Gecko diurne du nord-ouest de Madagascar (F): *Phelsuma befotakensis*
Gecko diurne du sud-ouest de Madagascar (F): *Phelsuma leiogaster*
Gecko diurne géant de Rodrigues (F): *Phelsuma gigas*
Gecko diurne géant des Seychelles (F): *Phelsuma sundbergi*
Gecko diurne ligné (F): *Phelsuma lineata*
Gecko diurne modeste (F): *Phelsuma modesta*
Gecko diurne nain (F): *Phelsuma pusilla*
Gecko diurne ocellé (F): *Phelsuma ocellata*
Gecko diurne orné de l'Ile Maurice (F): *Phelsuma ornata*
Gecko diurne poussière-d'or (F): *Phelsuma laticauda*
Gecko diurne rayé (F): *Phelsuma lineata*
Gecko diurne sombre (F): *Phelsuma dubia*
Gecko diurne tacheté (F): *Phelsuma guttata*
Geckos diurnes (F): *Phelsuma* spp.
Geckos diurnes de l'Océan Indien (F): *Phelsuma* spp.

Checklist of fauna/Lista de especies de fauna/Liste des espèces animales

Geco diurne de Abbott (S): *Phelsuma abbotti*
Geco diurno de Andaman (S): *Phelsuma andamanensis*
Geco diurno de bandas (S): *Phelsuma lineata*
Geco diurno de Barbour (S): *Phelsuma barbouri*
Geco diurno de cola azul (S): *Phelsuma cepediana*
Geco diurno de cola dentada (S): *Phelsuma serraticauda*
Geco diurno de cola gruesa (S): *Phelsuma laticauda*
Geco diurno de estrias negras (S): *Phelsuma nigristriata*
Geco diurno de garganta amarilla (S): *Phelsuma flavigularis*
Geco diurno de Guenther (S): *Phelsuma guentheri*
Geco diurno de Guimbeau (S): *Phelsuma guimbeaui*
Geco diurno de Klemmer (S): *Phelsuma klemmeri*
Geco diurno de las Comores (S): *Phelsuma comorensis*
Geco diurno de Madagascar (S): *Phelsuma madagascariensis*
Geco diurno de Robert Mertens (S): *Phelsuma robertmertensi*
Geco diurno de Standing (S): *Phelsuma standingi*
Geco diurno de Sundberg (S): *Phelsuma sundbergi*
Geco diurno de tres bandas (S): *Phelsuma trilineata*
Geco diurno de Zanzibar (S): *Phelsuma dubia*
Geco diurno ocelado (S): *Phelsuma ocellata*
Geco diurno ornado (S): *Phelsuma ornata*
Gecos diurnos (S): *Phelsuma* spp.
Geelvink Bay Flying-fox (E): *Pteropus pohlei*
Geelvink Pygmy-Parrot (E): *Micropsitta geelvinkiana*
Gelada (F): *Theropithecus gelada*
Gelada Baboon (E): *Theropithecus gelada*
Gentle Monkey (E): *Cercopithecus mitis*
Geochelone carbonaria : (E) Red-footed Tortoise, Wood Tortoise, (S) Jabuti, Karumbé, Tortuga de patas rojas, (F) Tortue charbonnière, **II** TESTUDINIDAE Re
Geochelone chilensis : (E) Argentine Tortoise, Chaco Tortoise, Southern Wood Tortoise, (S) Tortuga terrestre argentina, (F) Tortue de la Pampa, **II** TESTUDINIDAE Re
Geochelone denticulata : (E) Brazilian Giant Tortoise, Forest Tortoise, South American Tortoise, South American Yellow-footed Tortoise, Yellow-footed Tortoise, (S) Morrocoy, Motelo, (F) Tortue de l'Amérique du Sud, Tortue dentelée, Tortue denticulée, **II** TESTUDINIDAE Re
Geochelone donosobarrosi = Geochelone chilensis
Geochelone elegans : (E) Indian Star Tortoise, Star Tortoise, (S) Tortuga estrellada de la India, (F) Tortue étoilée de l'Inde, **II** TESTUDINIDAE Re
Geochelone elephantopus = Geochelone nigra
Geochelone elongata = Indotestudo elongata
Geochelone emys = Manouria emys
Geochelone forstenii = Indotestudo forstenii
Geochelone gigantea : (E) Aldabra Giant Tortoise, (S) Tortuga gigante de Aldabra, (F) Tortue géante, Tortue géante d'Aldabra, **II** TESTUDINIDAE Re
Geochelone impressa = Manouria impressa
Geochelone nigra : (E) Galapagos Giant Tortoise, (S) Tortuga de las Galápagos, Tortuga gigante de las Galápagos, (F) Tortue éléphantine, Tortue géante des Galapagos, **I** TESTUDINIDAE Re
Geochelone pardalis : (E) Leopard Tortoise, Mountain Tortoise, (S) Tortuga leopardo, (F) Tortue-léopard du Cap, **II** TESTUDINIDAE Re
Geochelone petersi = Geochelone chilensis
Geochelone platynota : (E) Burmese Starred Tortoise, Flatback Tortoise, (S) Tortuga estrellada de Burma, (F) Tortue étoilée de Birmanie, **II** TESTUDINIDAE Re
Geochelone radiata : (E) Radiated Tortoise, (S) Tortuga estrellada de Madagascar, Tortuga rayada, (F) Tortue radiée de Madagascar, Tortue rayonnée, **I** TESTUDINIDAE Re
Geochelone sulcata : (E) African Spurred Tortoise, Grooved Tortoise, (S) Tortuga con púas, (F) Tortue sillonnée, **II** TESTUDINIDAE Re
Geochelone travancorica = Indotestudo forstenii

Geochelone yniphora : (E) Angonoka, Madagascar Angulated Tortoise, Madagascar Tortoise, (S) Tortuga de espolones, Tortuga de Madagascar, Tortuga globulosa malagache, (F) Tortue à éperon, Tortue à plastron éperonné, Tortue à soc, Tortue à soc de Madagascar, Tortue de Madagascar, **I** TESTUDINIDAE Re
Géoclemmyde d' Hamilton (F): *Geoclemys hamiltonii*
Geoclemys hamiltonii : (E) Black Pond Turtle, Black Spotted Turtle, Hamilton's Terrapin, Spotted Pond Turtle, (S) Galápago de Hamilton, Galápago rayado, (F) Émyde en toit, Géoclemmyde d' Hamilton, Tortue à toit de l'inde , Tortue de Hamilton, **I** EMYDIDAE Re
Geoemyda arakana = Heosemys depressa
Geoemyda depressa = Heosemys depressa
Geoemyda grandis = Heosemys grandis
Geoemyda leytensis = Heosemys leytensis
Geoemyda spinosa = Heosemys spinosa
Geoemyda tricarinata = Melanochelys tricarinata
Geoemyda yuwonoi = Leucocephalon yuwonoi
Géoémyde de Célèbes (F): *Leucocephalon yuwonoi*
Géoémyde tricarénée (F): *Melanochelys tricarinata*
Geoffroy's Cat (E): *Oncifelis geoffroyi*
Geoffroy's Spider Monkey (E): *Ateles geoffroyi*
Geoffroy's Tamarin (E): *Saguinus geoffroyi*
Geoffroy's Tufted-ear Marmoset (E): *Callithrix geoffroyi*
Geoffroyus geoffroyi : (E) Red-cheeked Parrot, (S) Lorito carirrojo, (F) Perruche de Geoffroy, **II** PSITTACIDAE Av
Geoffroyus heroclitus : (E) Singing Parrot, (S) Lorito heteróclito, (F) Perruche hétéroclite, **II** PSITTACIDAE Av
Geoffroyus simplex : (E) Blue-collared Parrot, (S) Lorito acollarado, (F) Perruche à col bleu, **II** PSITTACIDAE Av
Geometric Tortoise (E): *Psammobates geometricus*
Geopsittacus occidentalis : (E) Night Parrot, (S) Cacatúa nocturna, Loro nocturno, Perico nocturno, (F) Perruche nocturne, **I** PSITTACIDAE Av
Geranoaetus melanoleucus : (E) Black-chested Buzzard-Eagle, Black-chested Eagle, Grey Buzzard-Eagle, (S) Aguila escudada, Aguila mora, Aguila real, (F) Buse aguia, **II** ACCIPITRIDAE Av
Geranospiza caerulescens : (E) Crane Hawk, (S) Azor zancón, Gavilán patilargo, Gavilán zancón, Gavilán zancudo, (F) Buse échasse, **II** ACCIPITRIDAE Av
Gerfaut (F): *Falco rusticolus*
Germain's Peacock-pheasant (E): *Polyplectron germaini*
Geronticus calvus : (E) Bald Ibis, Southern Bald Ibis, (S) Ibis calvo, Ibis calvo de Àfrica del Sur, (F) Ibis chauve de l'Afrique du Sud, Ibis du Cap, Ibis noir, **II** THRESKIORNITHIDAE Av
Geronticus eremita : (E) Bald Ibis, Hermit Ibis, Northern Bald Ibis, Waldrapp, (S) Ibis eremita, (F) Ibis chauve, **I** THRESKIORNITHIDAE Av
Gervais's Beaked Whale (E): *Mesoplodon europaeus*
Gharial (E): *Gavialis gangeticus*
Ghor-khar (E): *Equus onager khur*
Giant Anteater (E): *Myrmecophaga tridactyla*
Giant Arapaima (E): *Arapaima gigas*
Giant Armadillo (E): *Priodontes maximus*
Giant Asian Pond Turtle (E): *Heosemys grandis*
Giant Bottle-nosed Whale (E): *Berardius bairdii*
Giant Brazilian Otter (E): *Pteronura brasiliensis*
Giant Catfish (E): *Pangasianodon gigas*
Giant Clam (E): *Tridacna gigas*
Giant clams (E): TRIDACNIDAE spp.
Giant Day Gecko (E): *Phelsuma gigas*
Giant Eagle-Owl (E): *Bubo lacteus*
Giant Girdled Lizard (E): *Cordylus giganteus*
Giant Grebe (E): *Podilymbus gigas*
Giant Ground Pangolin (E): *Manis gigantea*
Giant Hummingbird (E): *Patagona gigas*
Giant Muntjac (E): *Megamuntiacus vuquanghensis*

Giant One-horned Chameleon (E): *Chamaeleo melleri*
Giant Otter (E): *Pteronura brasiliensis*
Giant Panda (E): *Ailuropoda melanoleuca*
Giant Pangolin (E): *Manis gigantea*
Giant Pied-billed Grebe (E): *Podilymbus gigas*
Giant Poison Frog (E): *Dendrobates azureus*
Giant River Carp (E): *Probarbus jullieni*
Giant Sable Antelope (E): *Hippotragus niger variani*
Giant salamanders (E): *Andrias* spp.
Giant Scops-Owl (E): *Mimizuku gurneyi*
Giant Seahorse (E): *Hippocampus ingens*
Giant Senegalese Scorpion (E): *Pandinus gambiensis*
Giant softshell turtles (E): *Pelochelys* spp.
Giant South American Turtle (E): *Podocnemis expansa*
Giant Spiny-tailed Lizard (E): *Cordylus giganteus*
Giant squirrels (E): *Ratufa* spp.
Giant Sturgeon (E): *Huso huso*
Giant Zonure (E): *Cordylus giganteus*
Gibbon à favoris blancs (F): *Hylobates concolor*
Gibbon à mains blanches (F): *Hylobates lar*
Gibbon agile (F): *Hylobates agilis*
Gibbon cendré (F): *Hylobates moloch*
Gibbon de Muller (F): *Hylobates muelleri*
Gibbon lar (F): *Hylobates lar*
Gibbon noir (F): *Hylobates concolor*
Gibbons (E/F): HYLOBATIDAE spp.
Gibón ceniciento (S): *Hylobates moloch*
Gibón de cresta negra (S): *Hylobates pileatus*
Gibón de manos blancas (S): *Hylobates lar*
Gibón de Mueller (S): *Hylobates muelleri*
Gibón hulock (S): *Hylobates hoolock*
Gibones (S): HYLOBATIDAE spp.
Giboya (E): *Boa constrictor*
Gigas Clam (E): *Tridacna gigas*
Gila Monster (E): *Heloderma suspectum*
Gilded Hummingbird (E): *Hylocharis chrysura*
Gilliard's Flying-fox (E): *Pteropus gilliardi*
Ginger Coral (E): *Millepora alcicornis*
Ginkgo-toothed Beaked Whale (E): *Mesoplodon ginkgodens*
Giraffe Seahorse (E): *Hippocampus camelopardalis*
Girdled lizards (E): *Cordylus* spp.
Gïririri de pico negro (S): *Dendrocygna arborea*
Gladostomus stellatus = *Acipenser stellatus*
Glaucidium albertinum : (E) Albertine Owlet, Prigogine's Owlet, (S) Mochuelo del Alberto, (F) Chevêchette du Graben, **II** STRIGIDAE Av
Glaucidium bolivianum : (E) Yungas Pygmy-Owl, (S) Mochuelo Boliviano, (F) Chevêchette des yungas, **II** STRIGIDAE Av
Glaucidium brasilianum : (E) Ferruginous Pygmy-Owl, (S) Caburé, Mochuelo caburé, Pavita ferruginea, Tecolotito común, (F) Chevêchette brune, **II** STRIGIDAE Av
Glaucidium brodiei : (E) Collared Owlet, Collared Pygmy-Owl, (S) Mochuelo acollarado, (F) Chevêchette à collier, **II** STRIGIDAE Av
Glaucidium californicum : (E) Northern Pygmy-Owl, (S) Mochuelo Californiano, Tecolotito del cabo, (F) Chevêchette des Rocheuses, **II** STRIGIDAE Av
Glaucidium capense : (E) African Barred Owlet, Barred Owlet, (S) Mochuelo de El Cabo, (F) Chevêchette du Cap, **II** STRIGIDAE Av
Glaucidium capense ssp. *castaneum* = *Glaucidium castaneum*
Glaucidium capense ssp. *ngamiense* = *Glaucidium ngamiense*
Glaucidium capense ssp. *scheffleri* = *Glaucidium scheffleri*
Glaucidium castaneum : (E) Chestnut Owlet, (S) Mochuelo castaño, (F) Chevêchette châtaine, **II** STRIGIDAE Av
Glaucidium castanonotum : (E) Chestnut-backed Owlet, (S) Mochuelo de Ceilán, (F) Chevêchette à dos marron, **II** STRIGIDAE Av

Glaucidium castanopterum : (E) Javan Owlet, (S) Mochuelo de Java, (F) Chevêchette spadicée, **II** STRIGIDAE Av
Glaucidium cuculoides : (E) Asian Barred Owlet, Cuckoo Owlet, (S) Mochuelo cuco, (F) Chevêchette cuculoïde, **II** STRIGIDAE Av
Glaucidium gnoma : (E) Mountain Pygmy-Owl, (S) Mochuelo gnomo, Tecolotito serano, (F) Chevêchette naine, **II** STRIGIDAE Av
Glaucidium gnoma ssp. *californicum* = *Glaucidium californicum*
Glaucidium griseiceps = *Glaucidium minutissimum*
Glaucidium hardyi : (E) Amzonian Pygmy-Owl, Hardy's Pygmy-Owl, (F) Chevêchette d'Amazonie, **II** STRIGIDAE Av
Glaucidium hoskinsii = *Glaucidium gnoma*
Glaucidium jardinii : (E) Andean Pygmy-Owl, (S) Mochuelo andino, Pavita andina, (F) Chevêchette des Andes, **II** STRIGIDAE Av
Glaucidium minutissimum : (E) Brazilian Pygmy-Owl, Least Pygmy-Owl, (S) Mochuelo minimo, (F) Chevêchette cabouré, **II** STRIGIDAE Av
Glaucidium nanum : (E) Austral Pygmy-Owl, (S) Caburé patagónico, Mochuelo Patagón, (F) Chevêchette australe, **II** STRIGIDAE Av
Glaucidium ngamiense : (E) Ngami Owlet, (F) Chevêchette de Ngami **II** STRIGIDAE Av
Glaucidium nubicola : **II** STRIGIDAE Av
Glaucidium palmarum = *Glaucidium minutissimum*
Glaucidium parkeri : (E) Subtropical Pygmy-Owl, (S) Mochuelo de Parker, (F) Chevêchette de Parker, **II** STRIGIDAE Av
Glaucidium passerinum : (E) Eurasian Pygmy-Owl, Pygmy Owl, (S) Mochuelo alpino, Mochuelo chico, (F) Chevêchette d'Europe, Chouette chevêchette, **II** STRIGIDAE Av
Glaucidium perlatum : (E) Pearl-spotted Owlet, (S) Mochuelín perlado, Mochuelo perlado, (F) Chevêchette perlée, **II** STRIGIDAE Av
Glaucidium peruanum : (E) Pacific Pygmy-Owl, Peruvian Pygmy-Owl, Peruvian Pygmy-Owl, (S) Mochuelo Peruano, (F) Chevêchette du Pérou, **II** STRIGIDAE Av
Glaucidium radiatum : (E) Barred Jungle Owlet, Jungle Owlet, (S) Mochuelo de jungla, (F) Chevêchette de jungle, **II** STRIGIDAE Av
Glaucidium radiatum ssp. *castanonotus* = *Glaucidium castanonotum*
Glaucidium sanchezi = *Glaucidium minutissimum*
Glaucidium scheffleri : (E) Scheffler's Owlet, (F) Chevêchette de Scheffler **II** STRIGIDAE Av
Glaucidium siju : (E) Cuban Pygmy-Owl, (S) Mochuelo sijú, Siju, Sijucito, (F) Chevêchette de Cuba, **II** STRIGIDAE Av
Glaucidium sjostedti : (E) Sjostedt's Owlet, (S) Mochelo de Sjöstedt, Mochuelo chico, Mochuelo del Congo, (F) Chevêchette à queue barrée, **II** STRIGIDAE Av
Glaucidium tephronotum : (E) Red-chested Owlet, Yellow-legged Owlet, (S) Mochuelo pechirrojo, (F) Chevêchette à pieds jaunes, **II** STRIGIDAE Av
Glaucis aenea : (E) Bronzy Hermit, (S) Ermitaño bronceado, (F) Ermite bronzé, **II** TROCHILIDAE Av
Glaucis dohrnii : (E) Hook-billed Hermit, (S) Colibrí de pico recurvado, Colibrí picosierra chico, Ermitaño de Espirito Santo, (F) Colibri à bec incurvé, Colibri de Dohrn, Ermite de Dohrn, Ermite de Dohrnou à bec incurvé, **I** TROCHILIDAE Av
Glaucis hirsuta : (E) Rufous-breasted Hermit, (S) Colibrí pecho canela, Ermitaño hirsuto, Ermitaño pechicanelo, (F) Ermite hirsute, **II** TROCHILIDAE Av
Glaucous Macaw (E): *Anodorhynchus glaucus*
Glauert's Monitor (E): *Varanus glauerti*
Glittering-bellied Emerald (E): *Chlorostilbon aureoventris*
Glittering-throated Emerald (E): *Polyerata fimbriata*

Checklist of fauna/Lista de especies de fauna/Liste des espèces animales

Globicephala edwardii = Globicephala melas
Globicephala macrorhynchus : (E) Pacific Pilot Whale, Short-finned Pilot Whale, (S) Caldrón negro, (F) Globicéphale tropical, **II** DELPHINIDAE Ma
Globicephala melaena = Globicephala melas
Globicephala melas : (E) Long-finned Pilot Whale, (S) Caldrón negro, (F) Globicéphale commun, **II** DELPHINIDAE Ma
Globicephala sieboldii = Globicephala macrorhynchus
Globicéphale commun (F): *Globicephala melas*
Globicéphale tropical (F): *Globicephala macrorhynchus*
Globose Curassow (E): *Crax rubra*
Glossopsitta concinna : (E) Musk Lorikeet, (S) Lori almizclero, (F) Lori à bandeau rouge, Lori musc, **II** PSITTACIDAE Av
Glossopsitta porphyrocephala : (E) Purple-crowned Lorikeet, (S) Lori coronipúrpura, (F) Lori à couronne pourpre, **II** PSITTACIDAE Av
Glossopsitta pusilla : (E) Little Lorikeet, (S) Lori carirrojo, (F) Lori à masque rouge, Petit lori musc, **II** PSITTACIDAE Av
Glossy Black-cockatoo (E): *Calyptorhynchus lathami*
Glossy-mantled Manucode (E): *Manucodia atra*
Glowing Puffleg (E): *Eriocnemis vestitus*
Glow-throated Hummingbird (E): *Selasphorus ardens*
Goanna Monitor (E): *Varanus acanthurus*
Goazu (F): *Ozotoceros bezoarticus*
Gobemouche bleu de Rueck (F): *Cyornis ruckii*
Gobemouche de Rueck (F): *Cyornis ruckii*
Gobemouches (F): *Terpsiphone bourbonnensis*
Godoy (S): *Potos flavus*
Goéland de Mongolie (F): *Larus relictus*
Goéland relique (F): *Larus relictus*
Goeldi's Marmoset (E): *Callimico goeldii*
Goeldi's Monkey (E): *Callimico goeldii*
Goeldi's Tamarin (E): *Callimico goeldii*
Goethalsia bella : (E) Rufous-cheeked Hummingbird, (S) Colibrí del Pirre, (F) Colibri du Pirré, **II** TROCHILIDAE Av
Goetze's Chameleon (E): *Chamaeleo goetzei*
Goffin's Cockatoo (E): *Cacatua goffini*
Goldbreast Indigobird (E): *Vidua raricola*
Gold-dust Day Gecko (E): *Phelsuma laticauda*
Golden Arowana (E): *Scleropages formosus*
Golden Arrow Poison Frog (E): *Atelopus zeteki*
Golden Bamboo Lemur (E): *Hapalemur aureus*
Golden Birdwing (E): *Troides aeacus/ Troides amphrysus/ Troides cuneifer*
Golden Bishop (E): *Euplectes afer*
Golden Cat (E): *Profelis aurata/ Catopuma temminckii*
Golden Conure (E): *Guarouba guarouba*
Golden Dragon Fish (E): *Scleropages formosus*
Golden Eagle (E): *Aquila chrysaetos*
Golden Frog (E): *Mantella aurantiaca/ Atelopus zeteki*
Golden frogs (E): *Mantella* spp.
Golden Jackal (E): *Canis aureus*
Golden Kaiserihind (E): *Teinopalpus aureus*
Golden Langur (E): *Trachypithecus geei*
Golden Leaf Monkey (E): *Trachypithecus geei*
Golden Lemur (E): *Hapalemur aureus*
Golden Lion Tamarin (E): *Leontopithecus rosalia*
Golden Mantella (E): *Mantella aurantiaca*
Golden Owl (E): *Tyto aurantia*
Golden Parakeet (E): *Guarouba guarouba*
Golden Poison Frog (E): *Minyobates altobueyensis/ Phyllobates terribilis*
Golden Potto (E): *Arctocebus aureus*
Golden Snub-nosed Monkey (E): *Pygathrix roxellana*
Golden Spitting Cobra (E): *Naja sumatrana*
Golden Starfrontlet (E): *Coeligena eos*
Golden Sticky-toed Gecko (E): *Hoplodactylus chrysosireticus*
Golden Toad (E): *Bufo periglenes*
Golden-backed Squirrel Monkey (E): *Saimiri ustus*
Golden-backed Weaver (E): *Ploceus preussi*

Golden-bellied Guenon (E): *Cercopithecus pogonias*
Golden-bellied Monkey (E): *Cercopithecus pogonias*
Golden-bellied Starfrontlet (E): *Coeligena bonapartei*
Golden-bellied Treeshrew (E): *Tupaia chrysogaster*
Golden-breasted Puffleg (E): *Eriocnemis mosquera*
Golden-breasted Waxbill (E): *Amandava subflava*
Golden-brown Mouse Lemur (E): *Microcebus ravelobensis*
Golden-capped Conure (E): *Aratinga auricapilla*
Golden-capped Fruit Bat (E): *Acerodon jubatus*
Golden-capped Parakeet (E): *Aratinga auricapilla*
Golden-collared Macaw (E): *Propyrrhura auricollis*
Golden-crowned Conure (E): *Aratinga aurea*
Golden-crowned Sifaka (E): *Propithecus tattersalli*
Golden-fronted Parakeet (E): *Psilopsiagon aurifrons*
Golden-headed Box Turtle (E): *Cuora aurocapitata*
Golden-headed Fig-Parrot (E): *Psittaculirostris desmarestii*
Golden-headed Lion Tamarin (E): *Leontopithecus chrysomela*
Golden-mantled Racquet-tail (E): *Prioniturus platurus*
Golden-mantled Rosella (E): *Platycercus eximius*
Golden-mantled Saddle-back Tamarin (E): *Saguinus tripartitus*
Golden-plumed Conure (E): *Leptosittaca branickii*
Golden-plumed Parakeet (E): *Leptosittaca branickii*
Golden-rumped Lion Tamarin (E): *Leontopithecus chrysopygus*
Golden-shouldered Parrot (E): *Psephotus chrysopterygius*
Gold-striped Gecko (E): *Hoplodactylus chrysosireticus*
Golden-tailed Parrotlet (E): *Touit surda*
Golden-tailed Sapphire (E): *Chrysuronia oenone*
Golden-winged Parakeet (E): *Brotogeris chrysopterus*
Goldie's Bird-of-paradise (E): *Paradisaea decora*
Goldie's Lorikeet (E): *Psitteuteles goldiei*
Goldmania violiceps : (E) Violet-capped Hummingbird, (S) Colibrí de Goldman, (F) Colibri à calotte violette, **II** TROCHILIDAE Av
Golfball Coral (E): *Favia fragum*
Golfodulcean Poison Frog (E): *Phyllobates vittatus*
Goliath Birdwing (E): *Ornithoptera goliath*
Goliath Heron (E): *Ardea goliath*
Golondrina de anteojos (S): *Pseudochelidon sirintarae*
Gombessa (E): *Latimeria chalumnae*
Gongylophis colubrinus : (E) East African Sand Boa, Kenyan Sand Boa, Theban Sand Boa, (S) Boa de arena de Egipto, (F) Boa des sables couleuvrin, Boa des sables d'Egypte, Boa des sables du Kenya, **II** BOIDAE Re
Gongylophis conicus : (E) Baby Python, Indian Sand Boa, Rough-scaled Sand Boa, Russell's Sand Boa, (S) Boa de arena de Sri Lanka, (F) Boa des sables à écailles rugueuses, Boa des sables des Indes, **II** BOIDAE Re
Gongylophis muelleri : (E) Müller's Sand Boa, West African Sand Boa, (S) Boa de arena de Müller, (F) Boa des sables de Müller, **II** BOIDAE Re
Goniastrea aspera : **II** FAVIIDAE An
Goniastrea australensis : **II** FAVIIDAE An
Goniastrea columella : **II** FAVIIDAE An
Goniastrea deformis : **II** FAVIIDAE An
Goniastrea edwardsi : **II** FAVIIDAE An
Goniastrea favulus : **II** FAVIIDAE An
Goniastrea minuta : **II** FAVIIDAE An
Goniastrea palauensis : **II** FAVIIDAE An
Goniastrea pectinata : **II** FAVIIDAE An
Goniastrea peresi = Favites peresi
Goniastrea ramosa : **II** FAVIIDAE An
Goniastrea retiformis : **II** FAVIIDAE An
Goniastrea spectabilis = Goniastrea aspera
Goniastrea thecata : **II** FAVIIDAE An
Goniocorella dumosa : **II** CARYOPHYLLIIDAE An
Goniopora spp.: (E) Daisy corals, Flowerpot corals, Sunflower corals **II** PORITIDAE An
Goniopora albiconus : **II** PORITIDAE An
Goniopora burgosi : **II** PORITIDAE An

Checklist of fauna/Lista de especies de fauna/Liste des espèces animales

Goniopora cellulosa : **II** PORITIDAE An
Goniopora ciliatus : **II** PORITIDAE An
Goniopora columna : **II** PORITIDAE An
Goniopora djiboutiensis : **II** PORITIDAE An
Goniopora eclipsensis : **II** PORITIDAE An
Goniopora fruticosa : **II** PORITIDAE An
Goniopora lobata : **II** PORITIDAE An
Goniopora minor : **II** PORITIDAE An
Goniopora norfolkensis : **II** PORITIDAE An
Goniopora palmensis : **II** PORITIDAE An
Goniopora pandoraensis : **II** PORITIDAE An
Goniopora pearsoni : **II** PORITIDAE An
Goniopora pendulus : **II** PORITIDAE An
Goniopora planulata : **II** PORITIDAE An
Goniopora polyformis : **II** PORITIDAE An
Goniopora pulvinula = Goniopora djiboutiensis
Goniopora savignii : **II** PORITIDAE An
Goniopora somaliensis : **II** PORITIDAE An
Goniopora stokesi : **II** PORITIDAE An
Goniopora stutchburyi : **II** PORITIDAE An
Goniopora sultani : **II** PORITIDAE An
Goniopora tenella : **II** PORITIDAE An
Goniopora tenuidens : **II** PORITIDAE An
Goniopora traceyi = Goniopora lobata
Goniopora viridis = Alveopora viridis
Goose-beaked Whale (E): *Ziphius cavirostris*
Gopher Tortoise (E): *Gopherus polyphemus*
Gophère (F): *Gopherus flavomarginatus*
Gophère à bords jaunes (F): *Gopherus flavomarginatus*
Gophère d'Agassiz (F): *Gopherus agassizii*
Gophère du Texas (F): *Gopherus berlandieri*
Gophère polyphème (F): *Gopherus polyphemus*
Gopherus agassizii : (E) Desert Tortoise, (S) Tortuga del desierto, (F) Gophère d'Agassiz, Tortue d'Agassiz, **II** TESTUDINIDAE Re
Gopherus berlandieri : (E) Berlandier's Tortoise, Texas Tortoise, (S) Tortuga de Texas, (F) Gophère du Texas, Tortue du Texas, **II** TESTUDINIDAE Re
Gopherus flavomarginatus : (E) Bolson Tortoise, Mexican Giant Tortoise, Yellow-bordered Tortoise, (S) Tortuga grande, Tortuga llanero, Tortuga topo, (F) Gophère , Gophère à bords jaunes, Tortue à bords jaunes, Tortue du Mexique, Tortue fouisseuse du Mexique, **I** TESTUDINIDAE Re
Gopherus polyphemus : (E) Gopher Tortoise, (S) Tortuga terrestre de Florida, (F) Gophère polyphème, Tortue de la Floride, Tortue gaufrée, **II** TESTUDINIDAE Re
Gopherus polyphemus ssp. *agassizii = Gopherus agassizii*
Gopherus polyphemus ssp. *berlandieri = Gopherus berlandieri*
Goral (E/S/F): *Naemorhedus goral*
Goral à queue longue (F): *Naemorhedus caudatus*
Goral rouge (F): *Naemorhedus baileyi*
Gorgeted Sunangel (E): *Heliangelus strophianus*
Gorgeted Woodstar (E): *Chaetocercus heliodor*
Gorila (S): *Gorilla gorilla*
Gorilla (E): *Gorilla gorilla*
Gorilla gorilla : (E) Gorilla, (S) Gorila, (F) Gorille, **I** HOMINIDAE Ma
Gorille (F): *Gorilla gorilla*
Gorontalo Macaque (E): *Macaca nigra*
Gorrión de Java (S): *Padda oryzivora*
Gorrión pardillo (S): *Passer griseus*
Gorzula's Poison Frog (E): *Epipedobates rufulus*
Goshawk (E): *Accipiter gentilis*
Gould's Emerald (E): *Chlorostilbon elegans*
Gould's Inca (E): *Coeligena inca*
Gould's Jewelfront (E): *Heliodoxa aurescens*
Gould's Monitor (E): *Varanus gouldii*
Goura couronné (F): *Goura cristata*
Goura cristata : (E) Blue Crowned-Pigeon, Common Crowned Pigeon, Great Goura, Western Crowned-Pigeon, (S) Gura occidental, Paloma crestada azul, (F) Goura couronné, **II** COLUMBIDAE Av
Goura de Scheepmaker (F): *Goura scheepmakeri*

Goura de Sclater (F): *Goura scheepmakeri*
Goura de Victoria (F): *Goura victoria*
Goura scheepmakeri : (E) Maroon-breasted Crowned-Pigeon, Masked Goura, Scheepmaker's Crowned-Pigeon, Southern Crowned-Pigeon, (S) Gura sureña, Paloma crestada de Scheepmaker, (F) Goura de Scheepmaker, Goura de Sclater, **II** COLUMBIDAE Av
Goura spp.: (E) Crowned-pigeons, Gouras, (S) Palomas crestadas, (F) Gouras, Pigeons couronnés , **II** COLUMBIDAE Av
Goura victoria : (E) Victoria Crowned-Pigeon, Victoria Goura, (S) Gura Victoria, Paloma crestada victoria, (F) Goura de Victoria, **II** COLUMBIDAE Av
Gouras (E/F): *Goura* spp.
Graceful Chameleon (E): *Chamaeleo gracilis*
Graceful Crag Lizard (E): *Cordylus capensis*
Grace's Emerald (E): *Chlorostilbon bracei*
Gracile Chameleon (E): *Chamaeleo gracilis*
Gracula enganensis = Gracula religiosa
Gracula indica = Gracula religiosa
Gracula religiosa : (E) Common Hill Myna, Hill Myna, (S) Miná de la India, Miná religioso, (F) Mainate religieux, Merles des Indes, **II** STURNIDAE Av
Gracula robusta = Gracula religiosa
Graham's Sheet Coral (E): *Agaricia grahamae*
Grampus (F): *Grampus griseus*
Grampus griseus : (E) Grey Dolphin, Risso's Dolphin, (S) Delfín de Risso, Fabo calderón, (F) Dauphin de Risso, Grampus, **II** DELPHINIDAE Ma
Gran autillo veliblanco (S): *Otus leucotis*
Gran búho etiópico (S): *Bubo lacteus*
Gran civeta de la India (S): *Viverra zibetha*
Gran lemur ardilla (S): *Cheirogaleus major*
Gran sifaka blanco (S): *Propithecus verreauxi*
Grand bandicoot-lapin (F): *Macrotis lagotis*
Grand cacatoès à huppe jaune (F): *Cacatua galerita*
Grand cheirogale (F): *Cheirogaleus major*
Grand Comoro Scops-Owl (E): *Otus pauliani*
Grand Dauphin (F): *Tursiops truncatus*
Grand Éclectus (F): *Eclectus roratus*
Grand esturgeon (F): *Huso huso*
Grand fourmilier (F): *Myrmecophaga tridactyla*
Grand galago (F): *Otolemur crassicaudatus*
Grand hapalémur (F): *Hapalemur simus*
Grand hippocampe (F): *Hippocampus kuda*
Grand hocco (F): *Crax rubra*
Grand hocco à bec rasoir (F): *Mitu mitu*
Grand lépilémur (F): *Lepilemur mustelinus*
Grand pangolin (F): *Manis gigantea*
Grand pangolin de l'Inde (F): *Manis crassicaudata*
Grand paradisier (F): *Paradisaea apoda*
Grand requin blanc (F): *Carcharodon carcharias*
Grand scorpian du Sénégal (F): *Pandinus gambiensis*
Grand serpent ratier de l'Indie (F): *Ptyas mucosus*
Grand téju (F): *Tupinambis teguixin*
Grand téjus (F): *Tupinambis* spp.
Grand Urubu (F): *Cathartes melambrotus*
Grand-duc à aigrettes (F): *Bubo poensis*
Grand-duc africain (F): *Bubo africanus*
Grand-duc ascalaphe (F): *Bubo ascalaphus*
Grand-duc bruyant (F): *Bubo sumatranus*
Grand-duc d'Amérique (F): *Bubo virginianus*
Grand-duc de Blakiston (F): *Ketupa blakistoni*
Grand-duc de Coromandel (F): *Bubo coromandus*
Grand-duc de Shelley (F): *Bubo shelleyi*
Grand-duc de Verreaux (F): *Bubo lacteus*
Grand-duc des Philippines (F): *Bubo philippensis*
Grand-duc des Usambara (F): *Bubo vosseleri*
Grand-duc d'Europe (F): *Bubo bubo*
Grand-duc du Cap (F): *Bubo capensis*
Grand-duc du désert (F): *Bubo ascalaphus*
Grand-duc du Népal (F): *Bubo nipalensis*
Grand-duc indien (F): *Bubo bengalensis*
Grand-duc tacheté (F): *Bubo leucostictus*

Checklist of fauna/Lista de especies de fauna/Liste des espèces animales

Grande aigrette (F): *Casmerodius albus*
Grande civette de l'Inde (F): *Viverra zibetha*
Grande mélampitte (F): *Melampitta gigantea*
Grande Outarde (F): *Otis tarda*
Grande outarde arabe (F): *Ardeotis arabs*
Grande toupaïe (F): *Tupaia tana*
Granular Poison Frog (F): *Dendrobates granuliferus*
Granulated Gecko (E): *Hoplodactylus granulatus*
Grape corals (E): *Euphyllia* spp.
Grass Owl (E): *Tyto capensis*
Grass Rhinoceros (E): *Ceratotherium simum*
Grasshopper Buzzard (E): *Butastur rufipennis*
Grasshopper Buzzard-Eagle (E): *Butastur rufipennis*
Gray Back (E): *Eschrichtius robustus*
Graydidascalus brachyurus : (E) Short-tailed Parrot, (S) Lorito colicorto, Loro colicorto, (F) Caïque à queue courte, **II** PSITTACIDAE Av
Gray's Beaked Whale (E): *Mesoplodon grayi*
Gray's Brush-turkey (E): *Macrocephalon maleo*
Gray's Goshawk (E): *Accipiter henicogrammus*
Gray's Malimbe (E): *Malimbus nitens*
Gray's Monitor (E): *Varanus olivaceus*
Gray's Sticky-toed Gecko (E): *Hoplodactylus granulatus*
Gray's Tree Gecko (E): *Naultinus grayii*
Great Argus (E): *Argusianus argus*
Great Black-Hawk (E): *Buteogallus urubitinga*
Great Blue Turaco (E): *Corythaeola cristata*
Great Bustard (E): *Otis tarda*
Great Curassow (E): *Crax rubra*
Great Egret (E): *Casmerodius albus*
Great Flying-fox (E): *Pteropus neohibernicus*
Great Goura (E): *Goura cristata*
Great Green Macaw (E): *Ara ambigua*
Great Grey Owl (E): *Strix nebulosa*
Great Hornbill (E): *Buceros bicornis*
Great Horned Owl (E): *Bubo virginianus*
Great Inagua Island Dwarf Boa (E): *Tropidophis canus*
Great Indian Bustard (E): *Ardeotis nigriceps*
Great Indian Hornbill (E): *Buceros bicornis*
Great Indian Rhinoceros (E): *Rhinoceros unicornis*
Great Philippine Eagle (E): *Pithecophaga jefferyi*
Great Pied Hornbill (E): *Buceros bicornis*
Great Sapphirewing (E): *Pterophanes cyanopterus*
Great Seahorse (E): *Hippocampus kelloggi*
Great Siberian Sturgeon (E): *Huso dauricus*
Great Sparrowhawk (E): *Accipiter melanoleucus*
Great Star Coral (E): *Montastraea cavernosa*
Great Sturgeon (E): *Huso huso*
Great Tibetan Sheep (E): *Ovis ammon hodgsonii*
Great White Egret (E): *Casmerodius albus*
Great White Shark (E): *Carcharodon carcharias*
Great-billed Hermit (E): *Phaethornis malaris*
Great-billed Parrot (E): *Tanygnathus megalorynchos*
Greater Bamboo Lemur (E): *Hapalemur simus*
Greater Bilby (E): *Macrotis lagotis*
Greater Bird-of-paradise (E): *Paradisaea apoda*
Greater Bushbaby (E): *Otolemur crassicaudatus*
Greater Dwarf Lemur (E): *Cheirogaleus major*
Greater Flamingo (E): *Phoenicopterus ruber*
Greater Grison (E): *Galictis vittata*
Greater Kestrel (E): *Falco rupicoloides*
Greater Mascarene Flying-fox (E): *Pteropus niger*
Greater Melampitta (E): *Melampitta gigantea*
Greater Naked-tailed Armadillo (E): *Cabassous tatouay*
Greater Padloper (E): *Homopus femoralis*
Greater Rabbit-eared Bandicoot (E): *Macrotis lagotis*
Greater Rhea (E): *Rhea americana*
Greater Sooty-Owl (E): *Tyto tenebricosa*
Greater Sportive Lemur (E): *Lepilemur mustelinus*
Greater Spotted Eagle (E): *Aquila clanga*
Greater Stick-nest Rat (E): *Leporillus conditor*
Greater Streaked Lory (E): *Chalcopsitta scintillata*
Greater Sulawesi Hornbill (E): *Aceros cassidix*
Greater Sulphur-crested Cockatoo (E): *Cacatua galerita*
Greater Weasel Lemur (E): *Lepilemur mustelinus*

Greater White-nosed Monkey (E): *Cercopithecus nictitans*
Greater Yellow-headed Vulture (E): *Cathartes melambrotus*
Grèbe de l'Atitlan (F): *Podilymbus gigas*
Grèbe du lac Atitlan (F): *Podilymbus gigas*
Grèbe géant (F): *Podilymbus gigas*
Greek Tortoise (E): *Testudo graeca*
Green Anaconda (E): *Eunectes murinus*
Green Aracari (E): *Pteroglossus viridis*
Green Avadavat (E): *Amandava formosa*
Green Blossom (E): *Epioblasma torulosa gubernaculum*
Green Cactus Coral (E): *Madracis decactis*
Green Conure (E): *Aratinga holochlora*
Green Golden Frog (E): *Mantella viridis*
Green Hanging-Parrot (E): *Loriculus exilis*
Green Hermit (E): *Phaethornis guy*
Green Iguana (E): *Iguana iguana*
Green Indigobird (E): *Vidua chalybeata*
Green Japanese Sturgeon (E): *Acipenser medirostris*
Green Leek Parrot (E): *Polytelis swainsonii*
Green Mango (E): *Anthracothorax viridis*
Green Mantella (E): *Mantella viridis*
Green Monkey (E): *Chlorocebus aethiops*
Green Parakeet (E): *Aratinga holochlora*
Green Peafowl (E): *Pavo muticus*
Green Poison Frog (E): *Dendrobates auratus/ Minyobates viridis*
Green Racquet-tail (E): *Prioniturus luconensis*
Green Riffle Shell (E): *Epioblasma torulosa gubernaculum*
Green Rosella (E): *Platycercus caledonicus*
Green Singing Finch (E): *Serinus mozambicus*
Green Sturgeon (E): *Acipenser medirostris*
Green Thorntail (E): *Discosura conversii*
Green Tree Gecko (E): *Naultinus elegans*
Green Tree Python (E): *Morelia viridis*
Green Tree Snail (E): *Papustyla pulcherrima*
Green Turtle (E): *Chelonia mydas*
Green Twinspot (E): *Mandingoa nitidula*
Green Violet-ear (E): *Colibri thalassinus*
Green-and-black Poison Frog (E): *Dendrobates auratus*
Green-and-white Hummingbird (E): *Leucippus viridicauda*
Green-backed Firecrown (E): *Sephanoides sephaniodes*
Green-backed Twinspot (E): *Mandingoa nitidula*
Green-bellied Hummingbird (E): *Saucerottia viridigaster*
Green-blossom Pearly Mussel (E): *Epioblasma torulosa gubernaculum*
Green-breasted Mango (E): *Anthracothorax prevostii*
Green-breasted Mountain-gem (E): *Lampornis sybillae*
Green-cheeked Amazon (E): *Amazona viridigenalis*
Green-cheeked Conure (E): *Pyrrhura molinae*
Green-cheeked Parakeet (E): *Pyrrhura molinae*
Green-cheeked Parrot (E): *Amazona viridigenalis*
Green-crowned Brilliant (E): *Heliodoxa jacula*
Green-crowned Racket-tailed Parrot (E): *Prioniturus luconensis*
Green-crowned Woodnymph (E): *Thalurania fannyi*
Green-fronted Hanging-Parrot (E): *Loriculus tener*
Green-fronted Hummingbird (E): *Agyrtria viridifrons*
Green-fronted Lancebill (E): *Doryfera ludovicae*
Green-headed Hillstar (E): *Oreotrochilus stolzmanni*
Green-headed Racket-tailed Parrot (E): *Prioniturus luconensis*
Greenish Puffleg (E): *Haplophaedia aureliae*
Greenland Right Whale (E): *Balaena mysticetus*
Green-naped Lorikeet (E): *Trichoglossus haematodus*
Green-necked Peafowl (E): *Pavo muticus*
Green-rumped Parrotlet (E): *Forpus passerinus*
Green-tailed Emerald (E): *Chlorostilbon alice*
Green-tailed Goldenthroat (E): *Polytmus theresiae*
Green-tailed Trainbearer (E): *Lesbia nuna*
Green-throated Carib (E): *Eulampis holosericeus*
Green-throated Mango (E): *Anthracothorax viridigula*

Checklist of fauna/Lista de especies de fauna/Liste des espèces animales

Green-throated Mountain-gem (E): *Lampornis viridipallens*
Green-winged King-Parrot (E): *Alisterus chloropterus*
Green-winged Macaw (E): *Ara chloroptera*
Green-winged Teal (E): *Anas crecca*
Grenedera (S): *Penelope purpurascens*
Grenouille de Zetek (F): *Atelopus zeteki*
Grenouille dorée du Panamà (F): *Altiphrynoides* spp.
Grenouille du Bengale (F): *Euphlyctis hexadactylus*
Grenouille hexadactyle (F): *Euphlyctis hexadactylus*
Grenouille plate à incubation gastrique (F): *Rheobatrachus silus*
Grenouille tigre (F): *Hoplobatrachus tigerinus*
Grenouille tigrée (F): *Hoplobatrachus tigerinus*
Grenouille tomate (F): *Dyscophus antongilii*
Grenouilles à incubation gastrique (F): *Rheobatrachus* spp.
Grevy's Zebra (E): *Equus grevyi*
Grey Buzzard-Eagle (E): *Geranoaetus melanoleucus*
Grey Canary (E): *Serinus leucopygius*
Grey Chameleon (E): *Chamaeleo chapini*
Grey Crowned-Crane (E): *Balearica regulorum*
Grey Cuscus (E): *Phalanger orientalis*
Grey Dolphin (E): *Grampus griseus/ Sotalia fluviatilis*
Grey Falcon (E): *Falco hypoleucos*
Grey Flying-fox (E): *Pteropus griseus*
Grey Frog Hawk (E): *Accipiter soloensis*
Grey Gentle Lemur (E): *Hapalemur griseus*
Grey Gibbon (E): *Hylobates muelleri*
Grey Goshawk (E): *Accipiter novaehollandiae*
Grey Hawk (E): *Asturina plagiata*
Grey Junglefowl (E): *Gallus sonneratii*
Grey Kestrel (E): *Falco ardosiaceus*
Grey Langur (E): *Semnopithecus entellus*
Grey Leaf Monkey (E): *Presbytis hosei*
Grey Monitor (E): *Varanus griseus*
Grey Mouse-lemur (E): *Microcebus murinus*
Grey Owl (E): *Strix nebulosa*
Grey Parrot (E): *Psittacus erithacus*
Grey Peacock-Pheasant (E): *Polyplectron bicalcaratum*
Grey Plantain-eater (E): *Crinifer piscator*
Grey Sea Eagle (E): *Haliaeetus albicilla*
Grey Singing Finch (E): *Serinus leucopygius*
Grey Snub-nosed Monkey (E): *Pygathrix brelichi*
Grey Whale (E): *Eschrichtius robustus*
Grey Wolf (E): *Canis lupus*
Grey Wood-Pigeon (E): *Columba unicincta*
Grey Zorro (E): *Pseudalopex griseus*
Grey-backed Hawk (E): *Leucopternis occidentalis*
Grey-backed Sportive Lemur (E): *Lepilemur dorsalis*
Grey-bellied Comet (E): *Taphrolesbia griseiventris*
Grey-bellied Goshawk (E): *Accipiter poliogaster*
Grey-bellied Hawk (E): *Accipiter poliogaster*
Grey-bellied Tragopan (E): *Tragopan blythii*
Grey-breasted Parakeet (E): *Myiopsitta monachus*
Grey-breasted Partridge (E): *Arborophila orientalis*
Grey-breasted Sabrewing (E): *Campylopterus largipennis*
Grey-cheeked Mangabey (E): *Lophocebus albigena*
Grey-cheeked Parakeet (E): *Brotogeris pyrrhopterus*
Grey-chinned Hermit (E): *Phaethornis griseogularis*
Grey-crowned Negrofinch (E): *Nigrita canicapilla*
Grey-faced Buzzard (E): *Butastur indicus*
Grey-faced Buzzard-Eagle (E): *Butastur indicus*
Grey-headed Fish-eagle (E): *Ichthyophaga ichthyaetus*
Grey-headed Fishing Eagle (E): *Ichthyophaga ichthyaetus*
Grey-headed Flying-fox (E): *Pteropus poliocephalus*
Grey-headed Goshawk (E): *Accipiter poliocephalus/ Accipiter princeps*
Grey-headed Kite (E): *Leptodon cayanensis*
Grey-headed Lovebird (E): *Agapornis canus*
Grey-headed Negrofinch (E): *Nigrita canicapilla*
Grey-headed Oliveback (E): *Nesocharis capistrata*
Grey-headed Parakeet (E): *Psittacula finschii*
Grey-headed Sparrow (E): *Passer griseus*
Grey-headed Sparrowhawk (E): *Accipiter poliocephalus*
Grey-hooded Parakeet (E): *Psilopsiagon aymara*

Grey-lined Hawk (E): *Asturina nitida*
Grey-necked Picathartes (E): *Picathartes oreas*
Grey-necked Rockfowl (E): *Picathartes oreas*
Grey-throated Goshawk (E): *Accipiter novaehollandiae*
Griffon Vulture (E): *Gyps fulvus*
Grison (F): *Galictis vittata*
Grisón (S): *Galictis vittata*
Grison d'Allemand (F): *Galictis vittata*
Grivet Monkey (E): *Chlorocebus aethiops*
Grizzled Giant Squirrel (E): *Ratufa macroura*
Grizzled Leaf Monkey (E): *Presbytis comata*
Grizzled Tree-kangaroo (E): *Dendrolagus inustus*
Grizzly (F): *Ursus arctos*
Grizzly Bear (E): *Ursus arctos*
Grooved Brain Coral (E): *Diploria labyrinthiformis*
Grooved Mountain Tortoise (E): *Homopus areolatus*
Grooved Tortoise (E): *Geochelone sulcata*
Grosbeak Weaver (E): *Amblyospiza albifrons*
Gros-bec à front blanc (F): *Amblyospiza albifrons*
Gros-bec ponceau à ventre noir (F): *Pyrenestes ostrinus*
Gros-bec sanguin (F): *Spermophaga haematina*
Grosse cateau verte de Maurice (F): *Psittacula echo*
Ground iguanas (E): *Cyclura* spp.
Ground Parakeet (E): *Pezoporus wallicus*
Ground Parrot (E): *Pezoporus wallicus*
Ground Python (E): *Loxocemus bicolor*
Grue à cou blanc (F): *Grus vipio*
Grue à cou noir (F): *Grus nigricollis*
Grue antigone (F): *Grus antigone*
Grue antigone tropicale (F): *Grus antigone*
Grue blanche (F): *Grus americana*
Grue blanche américaine (F): *Grus americana*
Grue blanche asiatique (F): *Grus leucogeranus*
Grue blanche d'Amérique (F): *Grus americana*
Grue blanche d'Asie (F): *Grus leucogeranus*
Grue blanche du Japon (F): *Grus japonensis*
Grue bleue (F): *Grus paradisea*
Grue brolga (F): *Grus rubicunda*
Grue canadienne (F): *Grus canadensis*
Grue canadienne de Cuba (F): *Grus canadensis nesiotes*
Grue canadienne du Mississippi (F): *Grus canadensis pulla*
Grue caronculée (F): *Grus carunculatus*
Grue cendrée (F): *Grus grus*
Grue couronnée (F): *Balearica pavonina*
Grue couronnée de Cap (F): *Balearica regulorum*
Grue couronnée de l'Afrique del'Ouest et du Soudan (F): *Balearica pavonina*
Grue couronnée de l'Afrique du Sud et de l'Est (F): *Balearica regulorum*
Grue d'Australie (F): *Grus rubicunda*
Grue de Mandchourie (F): *Grus japonensis*
Grue de paradis (F): *Grus paradisea*
Grue de Sibérie (F): *Grus leucogeranus*
Grue demoiselle (F): *Grus virgo*
Grue du Canada (F): *Grus canadensis*
Grue du Japon (F): *Grus japonensis*
Grue grise (F): *Grus canadensis*
Grue moine (F): *Grus monacha*
Grue royale (F): *Balearica regulorum*
Grues (F): GRUIDAE spp.
GRUIDAE spp.: (E) Cranes, (S) Grúidos, Grullas, (F) Grues, **I/II** Av
Grúidos (S): GRUIDAE spp.
Grulla americana (S): *Grus americana*
Grulla australiana (S): *Grus rubicunda*
Grulla azul (S): *Grus paradisea*
Grulla blanca asiática (S): *Grus leucogeranus*
Grulla blanco cuello (S): *Grus antigone*
Grulla brolga (S): *Grus rubicunda*
Grulla canadiense (S): *Grus canadensis*
Grulla carunculada (S): *Grus carunculatus*
Grulla cenicienta (S): *Grus canadensis*
Grulla cenicienta de Cuba (S): *Grus canadensis nesiotes*
Grulla cenicienta del Misisipí (S): *Grus canadensis pulla*

Grulla Común (S): *Grus grus*
Grulla coronada (S): *Balearica pavonina*
Grulla coronada cuelligris (S): *Balearica regulorum*
Grulla coronada cuellinegra (S): *Balearica pavonina*
Grulla coronada del Africa Occidental (S): *Balearica pavonina*
Grulla coronada sudafricana (S): *Balearica regulorum*
Grulla cuelliblanca (S): *Grus vipio*
Grulla cuellinegra (S): *Grus nigricollis*
Grulla damisela (S): *Grus virgo*
Grulla de Cuba (S): *Grus canadensis*
Grulla de Manchuria (S): *Grus japonensis*
Grulla de paraiso (S): *Grus paradisea*
Grulla gritona (S): *Grus americana*
Grulla manchú (S): *Grus japonensis*
Grulla monje (S): *Grus monacha*
Grulla monjita (S): *Grus monacha*
Grulla moruna (S): *Grus virgo*
Grulla sarus (S): *Grus antigone*
Grulla siberiana (S): *Grus leucogeranus*
Grulla siberiana blanca (S): *Grus leucogeranus*
Grulla trompetera (S): *Grus americana*
Grulla zarzo (S): *Grus carunculatus*
Grullas (S): GRUIDAE spp.
Grus americana : (E) Whooping Crane, (S) Grulla americana, Grulla gritona, Grulla trompetera, (F) Grue blanche, Grue blanche américaine, Grue blanche d'Amérique, **I** GRUIDAE Av
Grus antigone : (E) Sarus Crane, (S) Grulla blanco cuello, Grulla sarus, (F) Grue antigone, Grue antigone tropicale, **II** GRUIDAE Av
Grus canadensis : (E) Sandhill Crane, (S) Grulla canadiense, Grulla cenicienta, Grulla de Cuba, (F) Grue canadienne, Grue du Canada, Grue grise, **II** GRUIDAE Av
Grus canadensis nesiotes : (E) Cuban Sandhill Crane, (S) Grulla cenicienta de Cuba, (F) Grue canadienne de Cuba, **I** GRUIDAE Av
Grus canadensis pulla : (E) Mississippi Sandhill Crane, (S) Grulla cenicienta del Misisipí, (F) Grue canadienne du Mississippi, **I** GRUIDAE Av
Grus carunculatus : (E) Wattled Crane, (S) Grulla carunculada, Grulla zarzo, (F) Grue caronculée, **II** GRUIDAE Av
Grus grus : (E) Common Crane, Crane, (S) Grulla común, (F) Grue cendrée, **II** GRUIDAE Av
Grus japonensis : (E) Japanese Crane, Manchurian Crane, Red-crowned Crane, (S) Grulla de Manchuria, Grulla manchú, (F) Grue blanche du Japon, Grue de Mandchourie, Grue du Japon, **I** GRUIDAE Av
Grus leucogeranus : (E) Siberian Crane, Siberian White Crane, Snow Crane, (S) Grulla blanca asiática, Grulla siberiana, Grulla siberiana blanca, (F) Grue blanche asiatique , Grue blanche d'Asie, Grue de Sibérie, Leucogéranne, **I** GRUIDAE Av
Grus monacha : (E) Hooded Crane, (S) Grulla monje, Grulla monjita, (F) Grue moine, **I** GRUIDAE Av
Grus nigricollis : (E) Black-necked Crane, Tibetan Crane, (S) Grulla cuellinegra, (F) Grue à cou noir, **I** GRUIDAE Av
Grus paradisea : (E) Blue Crane, Stanley Crane, (S) Grulla azul, Grulla de paraiso, (F) Grue bleue, Grue de paradis, **II** GRUIDAE Av
Grus rubicunda : (E) Brolga, (S) Grulla australiana, Grulla brolga, (F) Grue brolga, Grue d'Australie, **II** GRUIDAE Av
Grus vipio : (E) White-naped Crane, White-necked Crane, (S) Grulla cuelliblanca, (F) Grue à cou blanc, **I** GRUIDAE Av
Grus virgo : (E) Demoiselle Crane, (S) Grulla damisela, Grulla moruna, (F) Demoiselle de Numidie, Grue demoiselle, **II** GRUIDAE Av
Guacamayito azul (S): *Cyanopsitta spixii*
Guacamayo acollarado (S): *Propyrrhura auricollis*
Guacamayo aliverde (S): *Ara chloroptera*

Guacamayo amarillo (S): *Ara glaucogularis*
Guacamayo ambiguo (S): *Ara ambigua*
Guacamayo azul (S): *Anodorhynchus hyacinthinus*
Guacamayo azul y amarillo (S): *Ara ararauna*
Guacamayo azulamarillo (S): *Ara ararauna*
Guacamayo bandera (S): *Ara macao*
Guacamayo barbazul (S): *Ara glaucogularis*
Guacamayo barriga roja (S): *Orthopsittaca manilata*
Guacamayo cabeciazul (S): *Propyrrhura couloni*
Guacamayo caninde (S): *Ara glaucogularis*
Guacamayo cobalto (S): *Anodorhynchus leari*
Guacamayo de Cochabamba (S): *Ara rubrogenys*
Guacamayo de Illiger (S): *Propyrrhura maracana*
Guacamayo de Lear (S): *Anodorhynchus leari*
Guacamayo de Spix (S): *Cyanopsitta spixii*
Guacamayo enano (S): *Diopsittaca nobilis*
Guacamayo frentirroja (S): *Ara rubrogenys*
Guacamayo glauco (S): *Anodorhynchus glaucus*
Guacamayo jacinto (S): *Anodorhynchus hyacinthinus*
Guacamayo macao (S): *Ara macao*
Guacamayo maracaná (S): *Propyrrhura maracana*
Guacamayo militar (S): *Ara militaris*
Guacamayo noble (S): *Diopsittaca nobilis*
Guacamayo rojo (S): *Ara chloroptera*
Guacamayo severo (S): *Ara severa*
Guacamayo ventrirrojo (S): *Orthopsittaca manilata*
Guacamayo verde (S): *Ara militaris*
Guacamayo verde mayor (S): *Ara ambigua*
Guacamayo violáceo (S): *Anodorhynchus glaucus*
Guadalupe Caracara (E): *Polyborus lutosus*
Guadalupe Fur Seal (E): *Arctocephalus townsendi*
Guaiabero (E): *Bolbopsittacus lunulatus*
Guajolote ocelado (S): *Agriocharis ocellata*
Guam Flying-fox (E): *Pteropus tokudae*
Guam Fruit Bat (E): *Pteropus tokudae*
Guan aliblanco (S): *Penelope albipennis*
Guan comun de Trinidad (S): *Pipile pipile*
Guan cornudo (S): *Oreophasis derbianus*
Guan de frente negre (S): *Pipile jacutinga*
Guan negro (S): *Penelopina nigra*
Guanaco (E/S/F): *Lama guanicoe*
Guaraguao (S): *Buteo jamaicensis*
Guarahuau cordillerano (S): *Phalcoboenus albogularis*
Guariba Peludo (S): *Alouatta palliata*
Guarouba (F): *Guarouba guarouba*
Guarouba guarouba : (E) Golden Conure, Golden Parakeet, Queen of Bavaria's Conure, (S) Aratinga guaruba, Cacatúa dorada, Cotorra amarilla, (F) Conure de la Reine de Bavière, Conure dorée, Guarouba, Perruche dorée, **I** PSITTACIDAE Av
Guatemalan Howler (E): *Alouatta pigra*
Guatemalan Howling Monkey (E): *Alouatta pigra*
Guatemalan Red Brocket (E): *Mazama americana cerasina*
Guatemalan Red-rumped Tarantula (E): *Brachypelma sabulosum*
Guatemalan White-tailed Deer (E): *Odocoileus virginianus mayensis*
Gubarte (S): *Megaptera novaeangliae*
Gubernatrix cristata : (E) Yellow Cardinal, (S) Cardenal amarillo, (F) Cardinal vert, Commandeur huppé, **II** EMBERIZIDAE Av
Guemal (S): *Hippocamelus antisensis*
Guémal péruvien (F): *Hippocamelus antisensis*
Guémaux (F): *Hippocamelus* spp.
Guenon couronnée (F): *Cercopithecus pogonias*
Guépard (F): *Acinonyx jubatus*
Guepardo (S): *Acinonyx jubatus*
Guereza (E): *Colobus guereza*
Guerrero Orange Legs Tarantula (E): *Brachypelma boehmei*
Guianan Cock-of-the-rock (E): *Rupicola rupicola*
Guianan Crested Eagle (E): *Morphnus guianensis*
Guianian River Dolphin (E): *Sotalia fluviatilis*
Guib d'eau (F): *Tragelaphus spekii*

Checklist of fauna/Lista de especies de fauna/Liste des espèces animales

Guibe's Chameleon (E): *Calumma guibei*
Guigna (F): *Oncifelis guigna*
Guina (S): *Oncifelis guigna*
Guincho (S): *Pandion haliaetus*
Guinea Baboon (E): *Papio hamadryas*
Guinea Turaco (E): *Tauraco persa*
Guiriri (S): *Dendrocygna autumnalis*
Guizhou Snub-nosed Monkey (E): *Pygathrix brelichi*
Gulf of California Harbour Porpoise (E): *Phocoena sinus*
Gulf Porpoise (E): *Phocoena sinus*
Gulf Ridley (E): *Lepidochelys kempi*
Gulf Stream Beaked Whale (E): *Mesoplodon europaeus*
Gundlach's Hawk (E): *Accipiter gundlachi*
Gundlach's Sparrowhawk (E): *Accipiter gundlachi*
Gura occidental (S): *Goura cristata*
Gura sureña (S): *Goura scheepmakeri*
Gura Victoria (S): *Goura victoria*
Gurney's Eagle (E): *Aquila gurneyi*
Gurney's Hawk (E): *Buteo poecilochrous*
Gurney's Pitta (E): *Pitta gurneyi*
Guyanan Caiman Lizard (E): *Dracaena guianensis*
Guynia annulata : **II** GUYNIIDAE An
Gymnogene (E): *Polyboroides typus*
Gymnogène d'Afrique (F): *Polyboroides typus*
Gymnogène de Madagascar (F): *Polyboroides radiatus*
Gymnoglaux lawrencii = Otus lawrencii
Gymnogyps californianus : (E) California Condor, (S)
    Cóndor californiano, Cóndor de California, (F)
    Condor de Californie, **I** CATHARTIDAE Av
Gypaète barbu (F): *Gypaetus barbatus*
Gypaetus barbatus : (E) Bearded Vulture, Lammergeier,
    (S) Quebrantahuesos, (F) Gypaète barbu, **II**
    ACCIPITRIDAE Av
Gypohierax angolensis : (E) Palm-nut Vulture, Vulturine
    Fish-Eagle, (S) Buitre palmero, (F) Palmiste africain,
    II ACCIPITRIDAE Av
Gypopsitta vulturina = Pionopsitta vulturina
Gyps africain (F): *Gyps bengalensis*
Gyps africanus : (E) African White-backed Vulture,
    White-backed Vulture, (S) Buitre dorsiblanco
    africano, (F) Vautour africain, **II** ACCIPITRIDAE Av
Gyps bengalensis : (E) Asian White-backed Vulture,
    Oriental White-backed Vulture, White-backed
    Vulture, White-rumped Vulture, (S) Buitre
    dorsiblanco bengalí, Buitre leonado bengalés, (F)
    Gyps africain, Vautour chaugoun, **II** ACCIPITRIDAE
    Av
Gyps coprotheres : (E) Cape Griffon, Cape Vulture, (S)
    Buitre el cabo, (F) Vautour chassefiente, **II**
    ACCIPITRIDAE Av
Gyps fulvus : (E) Eurasian Griffon, Eurasian Griffon
    Vulture, Griffon Vulture, (S) Buitre común, Buitre
    leonado, Buitre leonado común, (F) Vautour fauve, **II**
    ACCIPITRIDAE Av
Gyps himalayensis : (E) Himalayan Griffon, Himalayan
    Griffon Vulture, (S) Buitre del Himalaya, (F) Vautour
    de l'Himalaya, **II** ACCIPITRIDAE Av
Gyps indicus : (E) Long-billed Griffon, Long-billed
    Vulture, (S) Buitre picofino, (F) Vautour indien, **II**
    ACCIPITRIDAE Av
Gyps rueppellii : (E) Rueppell's Griffon, Rueppell's
    Griffon Vulture, Rueppell's Vulture, (S) Buitre
    moteado, (F) Vautour de Rüppell, **II** ACCIPITRIDAE
    Av
Gyr Falcon (E): *Falco rusticolus*
Gyrfalcon (E): *Falco rusticolus*
Gyropora africana : **II** STYLASTERIDAE Hy
Gyrosmilia interrupta : **II** CARYOPHYLLIIDAE An

Haco piguirojo (S): *Crax blumenbachii*
Hada coronimorada (S): *Heliothryx barroti*
Hada gorrimorada (S): *Heliothryx barroti*
Hada orejinegro (S): *Heliothryx aurita*
Hadada Ibis (E): *Bostrychia hagedash*
Hagedashia hagedash = Bostrychia hagedash

Hahn's Macaw (E): *Diopsittaca nobilis*
Hairy armadillo (E): *Chaetophractus nationi*
Hairy-eared Dwarf Lemur (E): *Allocebus trichotis*
Hairy-nosed Otter (E): *Lutra sumatrana*
Haitian Boa (E): *Epicrates striatus*
Haitian Dwarf Boa (E): *Tropidophis haetianus*
Haitian Ground Boa (E): *Tropidophis haetianus*
Haitian Vine Boa (E): *Epicrates gracilis*
Halcón abejero (S): *Pernis apivorus*
Halcón aleto (S): *Falco femoralis*
Halcón aplomado (S): *Falco femoralis*
Halcón azulado (S): *Falco femoralis*
Halcón berigora (S): *Falco berigora*
Halcón blancuzco (S): *Falco peregrinus*
Halcón borní (S): *Falco biarmicus*
Halcón común (S): *Falco peregrinus*
Halcón cuellirrufo (S): *Micrastur ruficollis*
Halcón de Berbería (S): *Falco pelegrinoides*
Halcón de cabeza roja (S): *Falco chicquera*
Halcón de Cuvier (S): *Falco cuvierii*
Halcón de Eleonor (S): *Falco eleonorae*
Halcón de Eleonora (S): *Falco eleonorae*
Halcón de las praderas (S): *Falco mexicanus*
Halcón de lomo pizarreño (S): *Micrastur mirandollei*
Halcón de Nueva Zelandia (S): *Falco novaeseelandiae*
Halcón enano de la India (S): *Microhierax caerulescens*
Halcón gerifalte (S): *Falco rusticolus*
Halcón golondrina (S): *Falco rufigularis*
Halcón gris (S): *Falco hypoleucos*
Halcón gris de Australia (S): *Falco hypoleucos*
Halcón guaco (S): *Herpetotheres cachinnans*
Halcón guaicurú (S): *Herpetotheres cachinnans*
Halcón macagua (S): *Herpetotheres cachinnans*
Halcón maori (S): *Falco novaeseelandiae*
Halcón mejicano (S): *Falco mexicanus*
Halcón migratorio (S): *Falco columbarius*
Halcón murcielaguero (S): *Falco rufigularis*
Halcón negro (S): *Falco subniger*
Halcón negro de Australia (S): *Falco subniger*
Halcón palomero (S): *Falco columbarius/ Micrastur*
    ruficollis
Halcón palomero del sur (S): *Micrastur gilvicollis*
Halcón pardo (S): *Falco concolor*
Halcón pechianaranjado (S): *Falco deiroleucus*
Halcón pechirrojo (S): *Falco deiroleucus*
Halcón pechirrufo (S): *Falco deiroleucus*
Halcón perdiguero (S): *Falco femoralis*
Halcón peregrino (S): *Falco peregrinus*
Halcón peregrino de Babilonia (S): *Falco pelegrinoides*
Halcón pizarroso (S): *Falco concolor*
Halcón plomizo (S): *Falco deiroleucus*
Halcón plomizo menor (S): *Falco rufigularis*
Halcón pradeño (S): *Falco mexicanus*
Halcón primito (S): *Falco sparverius*
Halcón real (S): *Falco peregrinus*
Halcón reidor (S): *Herpetotheres cachinnans*
Halcón sacre (S): *Falco cherrug*
Halcón semiacollarado (S): *Micrastur semitorquatus*
Halcón taita (S): *Falco fasciinucha*
Halcón viajero (S): *Falco peregrinus*
Halcón yággar (S): *Falco jugger*
Halconcito (S): *Falco sparverius*
Halconcito africano (S): *Polihierax semitorquatus*
Halconcito argentino (S): *Spiziapteryx circumcinctus*
Halconcito asiático (S): *Polihierax insignis*
Halconcito australiano (S): *Falco longipennis*
Halconcito colilargo de Asia (S): *Polihierax insignis*
Halconcito común (S): *Falco sparverius*
Halconcito de Borneo (S): *Microhierax latifrons*
Halconcito de las Filipinas (S): *Microhierax erythrogenys*
Halconcito gris (S): *Spiziapteryx circumcinctus*
Halconcito gris americano (S): *Spiziapteryx circumcinctus*
Halconcito malayo (S): *Microhierax fringillarius*
Halcón-montés agavilanado (S): *Micrastur ruficollis*
Halcón-montés cabecigrís (S): *Micrastur gilvicollis*

Checklist of fauna/Lista de especies de fauna/Liste des espèces animales

Halcón-montés collarejo (S): *Micrastur semitorquatus*
Halcón-montés de Buckley (S): *Micrastur buckleyi*
Halcón-montés dorsigrís (S): *Micrastur mirandollei*
Halcón-montés plomizo (S): *Micrastur plumbeus*
Halcón-selvático collarejo (S): *Micrastur semitorquatus*
Haliaeetus albicilla : (E) Grey Sea Eagle, White-tailed Eagle, (S) Pigargo, Pigargo coliblanco, Pigargo coliblanco de Groenlandia, Pigargo común, Pigargo europeo, (F) Pygargue à queue blanche, Pygargue commun, **I** ACCIPITRIDAE Av
Haliaeetus leucocephalus : (E) Bald Eagle, White-headed Eagle, (S) Aguila cabeciblanca, Aguila cabeza blanca, Pigargo americano, Pigargo cabeciblanco, Pigargo cabeciblanco meridional, (F) Aigle à tête blanche, Pygargue à tête blanche, **I** ACCIPITRIDAE Av
Haliaeetus leucogaster : (E) White-bellied Fish-Eagle, White-bellied Sea-Eagle, (S) Pigargo de vientre blanco, Pigargo oriental, (F) Pygargue à ventre blanc, Pygargue blagre, **II** ACCIPITRIDAE Av
Haliaeetus leucoryphus : (E) Band-tailed Fish-Eagle, Pallas's Fish-Eagle, Pallas's Sea-Eagle, (S) Pigargo de Pallas, (F) Pygargue de Pallas, **II** ACCIPITRIDAE Av
Haliaeetus pelagicus : (E) Steller's Sea-Eagle, (S) Pigargo de Steller, Pigargo gigante, (F) Pygargue de Steller, Pygargue empereur, **II** ACCIPITRIDAE Av
Haliaeetus sanfordi : (E) Sanford's Fish-eagle, Sanford's Sea-Eagle, Solomon Fish-Eagle, Solomon Sea-Eagle, (S) Pigargo de las Salomón, Pigargo de Sanford, (F) Pygargue de Sanford, **II** ACCIPITRIDAE Av
Haliaeetus vocifer : (E) African Fish-Eagle, River Eagle, (S) Pigargo vocinglero, (F) Aigle pêcheur africain, Pygargue vocifer, Pygargue vocifère, **II** ACCIPITRIDAE Av
Haliaeetus vociferoides : (E) Madagascar Fish-Eagle, (S) Pigargo de Madagascar, Pigargo malgache, (F) Pygargue de Madagascar, **II** ACCIPITRIDAE Av
Haliastur indus : (E) Brahminy Kite, Red-backed Kite, Red-backed Sea Eagle, White-headed Sea Eagle, (S) Milano brahmán, (F) Milan sacré, **II** ACCIPITRIDAE Av
Haliastur sphenurus : (E) Whistling Eagle, Whistling Hawk, Whistling Kite, (S) Milano silbador, (F) Milan siffleur, **II** ACCIPITRIDAE Av
Halomitra clavator : **II** FUNGIIDAE An
Halomitra meierae : **II** FUNGIIDAE An
Halomitra pileus : (E) Bowl Coral, Dome Coral, Helmet Coral, Neptune's Cap Coral **II** FUNGIIDAE An
Halsydrus pontoppidani = Cetorhinus maximus
Hamadryad (E): *Ophiophagus hannah*
Hamadryade (F): *Ophiophagus hannah*
Hamadryas (F): *Ophiophagus hannah*
Hamadryas Baboon (E): *Papio hamadryas*
Hamilton's Terrapin (E): *Geoclemys hamiltonii*
Hamirostra melanosternon : (E) Black-breasted Buzzard, Black-breasted Buzzard-Kite, Black-breasted Kite, Black-brested Buzzard, (S) Milano pechinegro, (F) Milan à plastron, **II** ACCIPITRIDAE Av
Hammer Coral (E): *Euphyllia ancora*
Hanang Hornless Chameleon (E): *Bradypodion uthmoelleri*
Hangul (E/F): *Cervus elaphus hanglu*
Hanuman Langur (E): *Semnopithecus entellus*
Hapalemur aureus : (E) Golden Bamboo Lemur, Golden Lemur, (S) Lemur cariancho, (F) Hapalémur doré, **I** LEMURIDAE Ma
Hapalémur doré (F): *Hapalemur aureus*
Hapalémur gris (F): *Hapalemur griseus*
Hapalemur griseus : (E) Grey Gentle Lemur, (S) Lemur cariancho, (F) Hapalémur gris, Petit hapalémur, **I** LEMURIDAE Ma
Hapalémur simien (F): *Hapalemur simus*
Hapalemur simus : (E) Broad-nosed Gentle Lemur, Greater Bamboo Lemur, (S) Lemur cariancho, (F) Grand hapalémur, Hapalémur simien, **I** LEMURIDAE Ma

Hapalopsittaca amazonina : (E) Rusty-faced Parrot, (S) Lorito amazonino, Perico multicolor, (F) Caïque à face rouge, **II** PSITTACIDAE Av
Hapalopsittaca amazonina ssp. *fuertesi = Hapalopsittaca fuertesi*
Hapalopsittaca amazonina ssp. *pyrrhops = Hapalopsittaca pyrrhops*
Hapalopsittaca fuertesi : (E) Fuertes's Parrot, Indigo-winged Parrot, (S) Lorito de Fuertes, (F) Caïque de Fuertes, **II** PSITTACIDAE Av
Hapalopsittaca melanotis : (E) Black-eared Parrot, Black-winged Parrot, (S) Lorito alinegro, (F) Caïque à ailes noires, **II** PSITTACIDAE Av
Hapalopsittaca pyrrhops : (E) Red-faced Parrot, (S) Lorito ecuatoriano, (F) Caïque de Salvin, **II** PSITTACIDAE Av
Haplophaedia assimilis : (E) Buff-thighed Puffleg **II** TROCHILIDAE Av
Haplophaedia aureliae : (E) Greenish Puffleg, (S) Calzadito verdoso norteño, Zamarrito verdoso, (F) Érione d'Aurélie, **II** TROCHILIDAE Av
Haplophaedia lugens : (E) Hoary Puffleg, (S) Calzadito canoso, Zamarrito canoso, (F) Érione givrée, **II** TROCHILIDAE Av
Haraldmeier's Mantella (E): *Mantella haraldmeieri*
Harbour Porpoise (E): *Phocoena phocoena*
Hard corals (E): SCLERACTINIA spp. An
Hard Head (E): *Eschrichtius robustus*
Hardella baileyi = Orlitia borneensis
Hardwick's Civet (E): *Hemigalus derbyanus*
Hardwick's Spiny-tailed Lizard (E): *Uromastyx hardwickii*
Hardy's Pygmy-Owl (E): *Glaucidium hardyi*
Harenna Chameleon (E): *Chamaeleo harennae*
Harfang des neiges (F): *Nyctea scandiaca*
Harlequin Gecko (E): *Hoplodactylus rakiurae*
Harlequin Monitor (E): *Varanus rudicollis*
Harlequin Poison Frog (E): *Dendrobates histrionicus*
Harpagus bidentatus : (E) Black-breasted Buzzard-kite, Double-toothed Kite, (S) Elanio bidentado, Gavilán bidente, Milano bidentado, (F) Milan bidenté, **II** ACCIPITRIDAE Av
Harpagus diodon : (E) Rufous-thighed Kite, (S) Elanio muslirrufo, Milano dentado, Milano muslirrufo, (F) Milan diodon, **II** ACCIPITRIDAE Av
Harpía (S): *Harpia harpyja*
Harpia harpyja : (E) American Harpy Eagle, Harpy Eagle, (S) Aguila arpía, Aguila harpía, Arpía, Arpía mayor, Harpía, (F) Aigle harpie, Harpie, Harpie féroce, **I** ACCIPITRIDAE Av
Harpie (F): *Harpia harpyja*
Harpie féroce (F): *Harpia harpyja*
Harpie huppée (F): *Morphnus guianensis*
Harpy Eagle (E): *Harpia harpyja*
Harpyhaliaetus coronatus : (E) Crowned Eagle, Crowned Solitary Eagle, (S) Aguila coronada, Aguila de Azara, (F) Buse couronnée, **II** ACCIPITRIDAE Av
Harpyhaliaetus solitarius : (E) Black Solitary Eagle, Solitary Eagle, (S) Aguila solitaria, (F) Buse solitaire, **II** ACCIPITRIDAE Av
Harpyopsis novaeguineae : (E) New Guinea Eagle, New Guinea Harpy Eagle, (S) Arpía papúa, (F) Aigle de Nouvelle-Guinée, **II** ACCIPITRIDAE Av
Harris's Hawk (E): *Parabuteo unicinctus*
Hartlaub's Bustard (E): *Eupodotis hartlaubii*
Hartlaub's Duck (E): *Pteronetta hartlaubii*
Hartlaub's Turaco (E): *Tauraco hartlaubi*
Hartmann's Mountain Zebra (E): *Equus zebra hartmannae*
Hatteria de Günther (F): *Sphenodon guntheri*
Hatteria ponctué (F): *Sphenodon punctatus*
Hatterias (F): *Sphenodon* spp.
Hausse-col à queue rubanée (F): *Astrapia stephaniae*
Hausse-col de Rothschild (F): *Astrapia rothschildi*
Hausse-col doré (F): *Astrapia nigra*
Hausse-col splendide (F): *Astrapia splendidissima*
Haut-de-chausses à palettes (F): *Ocreatus underwoodii*

Hawaiian Goose (E): *Branta sandvicensis*
Hawaiian Hawk (E): *Buteo solitarius*
Hawaiian Monk Seal (E): *Monachus schauinslandi*
Hawk Owl (E): *Surnia ulula*
Hawk-headed Parrot (E): *Deroptyus accipitrinus*
Hawksbill Turtle (E): *Eretmochelys imbricata*
Heaviside's Dolphin (E): *Cephalorhynchus heavisidii*
Hector's Beaked Whale (E): *Mesoplodon hectori*
Hector's Dolphin (E): *Cephalorhynchus hectori*
Hedgehog Seahorse (E): *Hippocampus spinosissimus*
Helarctos malayanus : (E) Malayan Sun Bear, Sun Bear, (S) Oso de los cocoteros, Oso de sol, Oso malayo, (F) Ours des cocotiers, Ours malais, **I** URSIDAE Ma
Heliactin bilopha : (E) Horned Sungem, (S) Colibrí cornudito, (F) Colibri aux huppes d'or, **II** TROCHILIDAE Av
Heliactin ornata = Heliactin bilopha
Héliange à gorge améthyste (S): *Heliangelus amethysticollis*
Héliange à queue bleue (F): *Heliangelus strophianus*
Héliange clarisse (F): *Heliangelus amethysticollis*
Héliange mars (F): *Heliangelus mavors*
Héliange menu (F): *Heliangelus micraster*
Héliange royale (F): *Heliangelus regalis*
Héliange tourmaline (F): *Heliangelus exortis*
Héliange violette (F): *Heliangelus viola*
Heliangelus amethysticollis : (E) Amethyst-throated Sunangel, (S) Angel de Sol amatista, Colibrí gorgiamatista, Héliange à gorge améthyste, Solangel gorjiamatista, (F) Héliange clarisse, **II** TROCHILIDAE Av
Heliangelus clarisse : (E) Longuemare's Sunangel **II** TROCHILIDAE Av
Heliangelus exortis : (E) Little Sunangel, Tourmaline Sunangel, (S) Colibrí turmalina, Solangel turmalino, (F) Héliange tourmaline, **II** TROCHILIDAE Av
Heliangelus mavors : (E) Orange-throated Sunangel, (S) Angel de Sol cuelliocre, Colibrí de Marte, (F) Héliange mars, **II** TROCHILIDAE Av
Heliangelus micraster : (E) Little Sunangel, (S) Colibrí lacero, (F) Héliange menu, **II** TROCHILIDAE Av
Heliangelus regalis : (E) Royal Sunangel, (S) Colibrí real, (F) Héliange royale, **II** TROCHILIDAE Av
Heliangelus spencei = Heliangelus clarisse
Heliangelus strophianus : (E) Gorgeted Sunangel, (S) Colibrí pectoral, Solangel de gorguera, (F) Héliange à queue bleue, **II** TROCHILIDAE Av
Heliangelus viola : (E) Purple-throated Sunangel, (S) Colibrí violeta, Solangel gorjipurpura, (F) Héliange violette, **II** TROCHILIDAE Av
Heliangelus zusii : (E) Bogotá Sunangel **II** TROCHILIDAE Av
Helicolestes hamatus = Rostrhamus hamatus
Heliodoxa aurescens : (E) Gould's Jewelfront, (S) Brillante pechicastaño, Colibrí cuellicastaño, Frentijoya, (F) Brillant à bandeau bleu, **II** TROCHILIDAE Av
Heliodoxa branickii : (E) Rufous-webbed Brilliant, (S) Brillante alicanela, (F) Brillant de Branicki, **II** TROCHILIDAE Av
Heliodoxa frentiazul (S): *Heliodoxa leadbeateri*
Heliodoxa gularis : (E) Pink-throated Brilliant, (S) Brillante gorrirrosado, (F) Brillant à gorge rose, **II** TROCHILIDAE Av
Heliodoxa imperatrix : (E) Empress Brilliant, (S) Brillante emperador, (F) Brillant impératrice, **II** TROCHILIDAE Av
Heliodoxa jacula : (E) Green-crowned Brilliant, (S) Brillante coroniverde, (F) Brillant fer-de-lance, **II** TROCHILIDAE Av
Heliodoxa leadbeateri : (E) Violet-fronted Brilliant, (S) Brillante frentivioleta, Heliodoxa frentiazul, (F) Brillant à front violet, **II** TROCHILIDAE Av

Heliodoxa rubinoides : (E) Fawn-breasted Brilliant, (S) Brillante pechianteado, Brillante pechigamuza, (F) Brillant rubinoïde, **II** TROCHILIDAE Av
Heliodoxa schreibersii : (E) Black-throated Brilliant, (S) Brillante gorjinegro, Brillante ventinegro, (F) Brillant à gorge noire, **II** TROCHILIDAE Av
Heliodoxa xanthogonys : (E) Velvet-browed Brilliant, Velvet-crowned Brilliant, (S) Brillante de Tepui, Colibrí frentiverde, (F) Brillant à couronne verte, **II** TROCHILIDAE Av
Heliofungia actiniformis : (E) Disk Coral, Mushroom Coral, Sunflower Coral **II** FUNGIIDAE An
Heliomaster constantii : (E) Plain-capped Starthroat, (S) Colibrí pochotero, Picolargo coronioscuro, (F) Colibri de Constant, **II** TROCHILIDAE Av
Heliomaster furcifer : (E) Blue-tufted Starthroat, (S) Colibrí de Barbijo, Picaflor de Barbijo, (F) Colibri d'Angèle, **II** TROCHILIDAE Av
Heliomaster longirostris : (E) Long-billed Starthroat, (S) Colibrí estrella picolargo, Colibrí piquilargo, Heliomaster piquilargo, Picolargo coroniazul, (F) Colibri corinne, **II** TROCHILIDAE Av
Heliomaster piquilargo (S): *Heliomaster longirostris*
Heliomaster squamosus : (E) Stripe-breasted Starthroat, (S) Colibrí escamoso, Picaflor escamado, (F) Colibri médiastin, **II** TROCHILIDAE Av
Heliopora coerulea : (E) Blue Coral **II** HELIOPORIDAE An
Helioseris cucullata : (E) Sunray Lettuce Coral **II** AGARICIIDAE An
Heliothryx aurita : (E) Black-eared Fairy, (S) Colibrí hada orejazul, Colibrí hada oriental, Hada orejinegro, (F) Colibri oreillard, **II** TROCHILIDAE Av
Heliothryx barroti : (E) Purple-crowned Fairy, (S) Colibrí hada occidental, Hada coronimorada, Hada gorrimorada, (F) Colibri féérique, **II** TROCHILIDAE Av
Heliotrope-throated Hummingbird (E): *Selasphorus flammula*
Helmet Coral (E): *Halomitra pileus*
Helmet Dolphin (E): *Stenella clymene*
Helmeted Chameleon (E): *Chamaeleo hoehnelii*
Helmeted Curassow (E): *Pauxi pauxi*
Helmeted Honeyeater (E): *Lichenostomus melanops cassidix*
Helmeted Hornbill (E): *Buceros vigil*
Helmeted Turaco (E): *Tauraco corythaix*
Helmeted Turtle (E): *Pelomedusa subrufa*
Heloderma spp.: (E) Poisonous lizards, (S) Helodermas, (F) Hélodermes, Lézards perlés, Lézards venimeux, **II** HELODERMATIDAE Re
Heloderma horridum : (E) Beaded Lizard, (S) Escorpión, Lagarto de Cuentas, (F) Héloderme granuleux, Héloderme horrible, **II** HELODERMATIDAE Re
Heloderma suspectum : (E) Gila Monster, (S) Monstruo de Gila, (F) Lézard perlé, Monstre de Gila, **II** HELODERMATIDAE Re
Helodermas (S): *Heloderma* spp.
Héloderme granuleux (F): *Heloderma horridum*
Héloderme horrible (F): *Heloderma horridum*
Hélodermes (F): *Heloderma* spp.
Helops stellatus = Acipenser stellatus
Hémigale de Derby (F): *Hemigalus derbyanus*
Hemigalus derbyanus : (E) Banded Musang, Banded Palm Civet, Hardwick's Civet, (S) Cibeta palmirayada, Civeta de Derby, (F) Civette palmiste à bandes de Derby, Civette palmiste rayée, Hémigale de Derby, **II** VIVERRIDAE Ma
Hémione (F): *Equus hemionus*
Hémione de l'Inde (F): *Equus onager khur*
Hemiono (S): *Equus hemionus*
Hemiono indostánico (S): *Equus onager khur*
Hemiono mongol (S): *Equus hemionus hemionus*
Hen Harrier (E): *Circus cyaneus*
Henderson Lorikeet (E): *Vini stepheni*

Henicopernis infuscatus : (E) Black Honey-buzzard, New
   Britain Honey-buzzard, (S) Abejero negro, (F)
   Bondrée noire, **II** ACCIPITRIDAE Av
Henicopernis longicauda : (E) Long-tailed Honey-
   buzzard, Papuan Honey-buzzard, (S) Abejero
   colilargo, (F) Bondrée à longue queue, **II**
   ACCIPITRIDAE Av
Henst's Goshawk (E): *Accipiter henstii*
Héosémyde de l'Arakan (F): *Heosemys depressa*
Héosémyde de Leyte (F): *Heosemys leytensis*
Héosémyde épineuse (F): *Heosemys spinosa*
Héosémyde géante (F): *Heosemys grandis*
Heosemys depressa : (E) Arakan Forest Turtle, (F)
   Héosémyde de l'Arakan, **II** EMYDIDAE Re
Heosemys grandis : (E) Giant Asian Pond Turtle, (F)
   Héosémyde géante, **II** EMYDIDAE Re
Heosemys leytensis : (E) Leyte Pond Turtle, Philippine
   Pond Turtle, (F) Héosémyde de Leyte, **II**
   EMYDIDAE Re
Heosemys spinosa : (E) Spiny Terrapin, Spiny Turtle,
   Sunburst Turtle, (F) Héosémyde épineuse, **II**
   EMYDIDAE Re
Heosemys yuwonoi = Leucocephalon yuwonoi
Herero Girdled Lizard (E): *Cordylus pustulatus*
Hermann's Tortoise (E): *Testudo hermanni*
Hermit Ibis (E): *Geronticus eremita*
Héron garde-bœufs (F): *Bubulcus ibis*
Héron goliath (F): *Ardea goliath*
Herpailurus yaguarondi : (E) Eyra Cat, Jaguarundi, (S)
   Gato colorado, Gato moro, León brenero, Leoncillo,
   Onza, Tigrillo, Yaguarundí, (F) Jaguarundi, **I/II**
   FELIDAE Ma
Herpestes auropunctatus = Herpestes javanicus ssp.
   auropunctatus
Herpestes brachyurus fuscus : (E) Indian Brown
   Mongoose, (S) Mangosta colicorta oscura, (F)
   Mangouste à queue courte de l'Inde, **III**
   HERPESTIDAE Ma
Herpestes edwardsii : (E) Indian Grey Mongoose, (S)
   Mangosta gris de la India, (F) Mangouste d'Edwards,
   Mangouste grise de l'Inde, **III** HERPESTIDAE Ma
Herpestes fuscus = Herpestes brachyurus ssp. *fuscus*
Herpestes fuscus ssp. *fuscus = Herpestes brachyurus* ssp.
   fuscus
Herpestes javanicus auropunctatus : (E) Small Indian
   Mongoose, (S) Mangosta de manchas doradas, (F)
   Petite mangouste indienne, **III** HERPESTIDAE Ma
Herpestes smithii : (E) Ruddy Mongoose, (S) Mangosta
   roja de la India, (F) Mangouste de Smith, **III**
   HERPESTIDAE Ma
Herpestes urva : (E) Crab-eating Mongoose, (S) Mangosta
   cangrejera, (F) Mangouste crabière, **III**
   HERPESTIDAE Ma
Herpestes vitticollis : (E) Stripe-necked Mongoose, (S)
   Mangosta de nuca rayada, (F) Mangouste à cou rayé,
   III HERPESTIDAE Ma
Herpetotheres cachinnans : (E) Laughing Falcon, (S)
   Acuá, Halcón guaco, Halcón guaicurú, Halcón
   macagua, Halcón reidor, (F) Macagua rieur, **II**
   FALCONIDAE Av
Herpolitha spp.: (E) Mole corals **II** FUNGIIDAE An
Herpolitha limax : (E) Slipper Coral, Tongue Coral, (F)
   Corail limace **II** FUNGIIDAE An
Herpolitha weberi : **II** FUNGIIDAE An
Herring Whale (E): *Balaenoptera physalus*
Hershkovitz's Night Monkey (E): *Aotus hershkovitzi*
Heterocyathus aequicostatus : **II** CARYOPHYLLIIDAE
   An
Heterocyathus alternatus : **II** CARYOPHYLLIIDAE An
Heterocyathus hemisphaericus : **II** CARYOPHYLLIIDAE
   An
Heterocyathus sulcatus : **II** CARYOPHYLLIIDAE An
Heterometrus roeseli = Pandinus imperator
Heteropsammia cochlea : (E) Button Coral **II**
   DENDROPHYLLIIDAE An

Heteropsammia eupsammides : **II**
   DENDROPHYLLIIDAE An
Heterospizias meridionalis = Buteogallus meridionalis
Heuglin's Bustard (E): *Neotis heuglinii*
Heuglin's Masked-Weaver (E): *Ploceus heuglini*
Hewitt's Spiny-tailed Lizard (E): *Cordylus peersi*
Hexapathes heterosticha : **II** ANTIPATHIDAE An
Hexaprotodon liberiensis : (E) Pygmy Hippopotamus, (S)
   Hipopótamo enano, Hipopótamo pigmeo, (F)
   Hippopotame nain, Hippopotame pygmée, **II**
   HIPPOPOTAMIDAE Ma
Hibiscus corals (E): *Pectinia* spp.
Hibou à bec jaune (F): *Jubula lettii*
Hibou à casque (F): *Lophostrix cristata*
Hibou brachyote (F): *Asio flammeus*
Hibou criard (F): *Asio clamator*
Hibou d'Abyssinie (F): *Asio abyssinicus*
Hibou de la Jamaïque (F): *Pseudoscops grammicus*
Hibou de Madagascar (F): *Asio madagascariensis*
Hibou de Tweeddale (F): *Mimizuku gurneyi*
Hibou des marais (F): *Asio flammeus*
Hibou du Cap (F): *Asio capensis*
Hibou grand-duc (F): *Bubo bubo*
Hibou maître-bois (F): *Asio stygius*
Hibou malgache (F): *Asio madagascariensis*
Hibou moyen-duc (F): *Asio otus*
Hibou pêcheur roux (F): *Ketupa flavipes*
Hibou petit-duc (F): *Otus scops*
Hibou redoutable (F): *Nesasio solomonensis*
Hibou strié (F): *Asio clamator*
Hieraaetus ayresii : (E) Ayres's Eagle, Ayres's Hawk-
   Eagle, (S) Aguila-azor de Ayres, (F) Aigle d'Ayres, **II**
   ACCIPITRIDAE Av
Hieraaetus bellicosus = Polemaetus bellicosus
Hieraaetus dubius = Hieraaetus ayresii
Hieraaetus fasciatus : (E) Bonelli's Eagle, (S) Aguila de
   Bonelli, Aguila perdicera, Aguila-azor perdicera, (F)
   Aigle de Bonelli, **II** ACCIPITRIDAE Av
Hieraaetus fasciatus ssp. *spilogaster = Hieraaetus
   spilogaster*
Hieraaetus kienerii : (E) Chestnut-bellied Hawk-Eagle,
   Rufous-bellied Eagle, (S) Aguila-azor ventrirroja, (F)
   Aigle à ventre roux, **II** ACCIPITRIDAE Av
Hieraaetus morphnoides : (E) Little Eagle, (S) Aguililla
   australiana, (F) Aigle nain, **II** ACCIPITRIDAE Av
Hieraaetus pennatus : (E) Booted Eagle, (S) Aguila
   calzada, Aguililla calzada, (F) Aigle botté, **II**
   ACCIPITRIDAE Av
Hieraaetus spilogaster : (E) African Eagle, African Hawk-
   Eagle, (S) Aguila perdicera africana, Aguila-azor
   africana, (F) Aigle fascié, Aigle-autour fascié, **II**
   ACCIPITRIDAE Av
Hieremys annandalii : (E) Yellow-headed Temple Turtle
   II EMYDIDAE Re
Hierro Giant Lizard (E): *Gallotia simonyi*
Higgins Eye (E): *Lampsilis higginsii*
Higgins' Eye Pearly Mussel (E): *Lampsilis higginsii*
High-casqued Chameleon (E): *Chamaeleo hoehnelii*
Highland Guan (E): *Penelopina nigra*
Highveld Crag Lizard (E): *Cordylus melanotus*
Hill Myna (E): *Gracula religiosa*
Hillopathes ramosa : **II** ANTIPATHIDAE An
Himalayan Black Bear (E): *Ursus thibetanus*
Himalayan Brown Bear (E): *Ursus arctos isabellinus*
Himalayan Goral (E): *Naemorhedus goral*
Himalayan Griffon (E): *Gyps himalayensis*
Himalayan Griffon Vulture (E): *Gyps himalayensis*
Himalayan Marmot (E): *Marmota himalayana*
Himalayan Monal (E): *Lophophorus impejanus*
Himalayan Musk Deer (E): *Moschus chrysogaster*
Hipopótamo anfibio (S): *Hippopotamus amphibius*
Hipopótamo enano (S): *Hexaprotodon liberiensis*
Hipopótamo pigmeo (S): *Hexaprotodon liberiensis*

Hippocamelus spp.: (E) Huemuls, (S) Ciervo mazama, Ciervos andinos, Huemules, (F) Cerfs des Andes, Guémaux, **I** CERVIDAE Ma

Hippocamelus antisensis : (E) North Andean Deer, North Andean Huemul, Peruvian Guemal, Peruvian Huemul, Taruca, (S) Ciervo andino septentrional, Guemal, Huemul, Taruca, Taruka de los Andes septentrionales, (F) Cerf des Andes septentrionales, Guémal péruvien, Huémul des Andes septentrionales, **I** CERVIDAE Ma

Hippocamelus bisulcus : (E) Chilean Guemal, Chilean Huemul, South Andean Deer, South Andean Huemul, (S) Ciervo andino meridional, Huemul, (F) Cerf des Andes méridionales, Huémul des Andes méridionales, **I** CERVIDAE Ma

Hippocampe (F): *Hippocampus camelopardalis/ Hippocampus hippocampus/ Hippocampus histrix*

Hippocampe à museau court (F): *Hippocampus hippocampus*

Hippocampe couronné (F): *Hippocampus coronatus*

Hippocampe de kuda (F): *Hippocampus kuda*

Hippocampe doré (F): *Hippocampus kuda*

Hippocampe du Pacifique (F): *Hippocampus kuda*

Hippocampe épineux (F): *Hippocampus histrix*

Hippocampe long-nez (F): *Hippocampus reidi*

Hippocampe marin (F): *Hippocampus ingens*

Hippocampe moucheté (F): *Hippocampus erectus/ Hippocampus guttulatus*

Hippocampe nain (F): *Hippocampus zosterae*

Hippocampe rayé (F): *Hippocampus erectus*

Hippocampes (F): *Hippocampus* spp.

Hippocampus spp. : (E) Horsefishes, seahorses, sea ponies, (S) Caballitos de mar (F) Chevaux de mer, Hippocampes, **II** (from 15/05/2004) SYNGNATHIDAE Ac

Hippocampus abdominalis : (E) Big-bellied Seahorse, Big-belly Seahorse, Eastern Potbelly Seahorse, Pot-bellied seahorse, Seahorse Fish **II** (from 15/05/2004) SYNGNATHIDAE Ac

Hippocampus agnesae = *Hippocampus abdominalis*

Hippocampus alatus : **II** (from 15/05/2004) SYNGNATHIDAE Ac

Hippocampus algiricus : (E) West African Seahorse **II** (from 15/05/2004) SYNGNATHIDAE Ac

Hippocampus angustus : (E) Narrow-bellied Seahorse, Western Australian seahorse, Western Spiny Seahorse **II** (from 15/05/2004) SYNGNATHIDAE Ac

Hippocampus antiquorum = *Hippocampus hippocampus*

Hippocampus antiquus = *Hippocampus hippocampus*

Hippocampus aterrimus = *Hippocampus kuda*

Hippocampus atrichus = *Hippocampus guttulatus*

Hippocampus barbouri : (E) Barbour's Seahorse **II** (from 15/05/2004) SYNGNATHIDAE Ac

Hippocampus bargibanti : (E) Bargibant's Seahorse, Pygmy Seahorse **II** (from 15/05/2004) SYNGNATHIDAE Ac

Hippocampus biocellatus = *Hippocampus trimaculatus*

Hippocampus bleekeri = *Hippocampus abdominalis*

Hippocampus borboniensis : (E) Réunion Seahorse **II** (from 15/05/2004) SYNGNATHIDAE Ac

Hippocampus breviceps : (E) Knobby seahorse, Short-head Seahorse, Short-headed seahorse, Short-snouted seahorse **II** (from 15/05/2004) SYNGNATHIDAE Ac

Hippocampus brevirostris = *Hippocampus hippocampus*

Hippocampus brunneus = *Hippocampus erectus*

Hippocampus camelopardalis : (E) Giraffe Seahorse, (F) Hippocampe **II** (from 15/05/2004) SYNGNATHIDAE Ac

Hippocampus capensis : (E) Cape Seahorse, Knysna Seahorse **II** (from 15/05/2004) SYNGNATHIDAE Ac

Hippocampus chinensis = *Hippocampus kuda*

Hippocampus comes : (E) Tiger-tail Seahorse **II** (from 15/05/2004) SYNGNATHIDAE Ac

Hippocampus coronatus : (E) Crowned Seahorse, (F) Hippocampe couronné **II** (from 15/05/2004) SYNGNATHIDAE Ac

Hippocampus dahli = *Hippocampus trimaculatus*

Hippocampus deanei = *Hippocampus algiricus*

Hippocampus ecuadorensis = *Hippocampus ingens*

Hippocampus elongatus = *Hippocampus subelongatus*

Hippocampus erectus : (E) Black Seahorse, Brown Seahorse, Horsefish, Lined Seahorse, Northern Seahorse, Spotted Seahorse, Yellow Seahorse, (S) Caballo de mar, Caballito erecto, Caballito punteado, (F) Hippocampe moucheté, Hippocampe rayé, **II** (from 15/05/2004) SYNGNATHIDAE Ac

Hippocampus europaeus = *Hippocampus hippocampus*

Hippocampus fasciatus = *Hippocampus coronatus*

Hippocampus fascicularis = *Hippocampus erectus*

Hippocampus filamentosus = *Hippocampus guttulatus*

Hippocampus fisheri : (E) Fisher's Seahorse **II** (from 15/05/2004) SYNGNATHIDAE Ac

Hippocampus fuscus : (E) Chilka Seahorse, Sea Pony **II** (from 15/05/2004) SYNGNATHIDAE Ac

Hippocampus graciliformis = *Hippocampus abdominalis*

Hippocampus gracilis = *Hippocampus ingens*

Hippocampus grandiceps : **II** (from 15/05/2004) SYNGNATHIDAE Ac

Hippocampus guttulatus : (E) Long-snouted Seahorse, (S) Caballito de mar, (F) Cheval marin, Hippocampe moucheté, **II** (from 15/05/2004) SYNGNATHIDAE Ac

Hippocampus hendriki : **II** (from 15/05/2004) SYNGNATHIDAE Ac

Hippocampus heptagonus = *Hippocampus hippocampus*

Hippocampus hildebrandi = *Hippocampus ingens*

Hippocampus hilonis = *Hippocampus kuda*

Hippocampus hippocampus : (E) Black Seahorse, Sea Horse, Short-snouted Seahorse, (S) Caballito de mar, Caballo marino, Cabalo de mar, (F) Cheval de mer, Hippocampe, Hippocampe à museau court, **II** (from 15/05/2004) SYNGNATHIDAE Ac

Hippocampus histrix : (E) Seahorse, Spiny Seahorse, Thorny Seahorse, (F) Cheval de mer, Hippocampe, Hippocampe épineux **II** (from 15/05/2004) SYNGNATHIDAE Ac

Hippocampus hudsonius = *Hippocampus erectus*

Hippocampus ingens : (E) Giant Seahorse, Pacific Seahorse, (S) Caballito de mar, Caballito de mar del Pacífico, (F) Hippocampe marin, **II** (from 15/05/2004) SYNGNATHIDAE Ac

Hippocampus jayakari : (E) Jayakar's Seahorse **II** (from 15/05/2004) SYNGNATHIDAE Ac

Hippocampus jubatus = *Hippocampus guttulatus*

Hippocampus jugumus : **II** (from 15/05/2004) SYNGNATHIDAE Ac

Hippocampus kampylotrachelos = *Hippocampus trimaculatus*

Hippocampus kelloggi : (E) Great Seahorse, Kellog's Seahorse, Offshore Seahorse **II** (from 15/05/2004) SYNGNATHIDAE Ac

Hippocampus kincaidi = *Hippocampus erectus*

Hippocampus kuda : (E) Black Seahorse, Coloured Seahorse, Oceanic Seahorse, Spotted Seahorse, Yellow Seahorse, (F) Cheval marin, Grand hippocampe, Hippocampe de kuda , Hippocampe doré, Hippocampe du Pacifique **II** (from 15/05/2004) SYNGNATHIDAE Ac

Hippocampus kuda ssp. *multiannularis* = *Hippocampus kuda*

Hippocampus laevicaudatus = *Hippocampus erectus*

Hippocampus lenis = *Hippocampus trimaculatus*

Hippocampus lichtensteinii : (E) Lichtenstein's Seahorse **II** (from 15/05/2004) SYNGNATHIDAE Ac

Hippocampus longirostris = *Hippocampus guttulatus*

Hippocampus macleayana = *Hippocampus abdominalis*

Hippocampus manadensis = *Hippocampus trimaculatus*

Hippocampus mannulus = *Hippocampus trimaculatus*

Hippocampus marginalis = *Hippocampus erectus*

Hippocampus melanospilos = *Hippocampus kuda*

Hippocampus microcoronatus = *Hippocampus guttulatus*

Hippocampus microstephanus = *Hippocampus guttulatus*
Hippocampus minotaur : (E) Bullneck Seahorse **II** (from 15/05/2004) SYNGNATHIDAE Ac
Hippocampus mohnikei : (E) Japanese Seahorse **II** (from 15/05/2004) SYNGNATHIDAE Ac
Hippocampus moluccensis = *Hippocampus kuda*
Hippocampus montebelloensis : **II** (from 15/05/2004) SYNGNATHIDAE Ac
Hippocampus multiannularis = *Hippocampus guttulatus*
Hippocampus multispinus : **II** (from 15/05/2004) SYNGNATHIDAE Ac
Hippocampus natalensis = *Hippocampus kuda*
Hippocampus novaehebudorum = *Hippocampus kuda*
Hippocampus novaehollandiae = *Hippocampus whitei*
Hippocampus obscurus = *Hippocampus fuscus*
Hippocampus obtusus = *Hippocampus reidi*
Hippocampus pentagonus = *Hippocampus hippocampus*
Hippocampus poeyi = *Hippocampus reidi*
Hippocampus polytaenia = *Hippocampus kuda*
Hippocampus procerus = *Hippocampus whitei*
Hippocampus punctulatus = *Hippocampus algiricus*
Hippocampus punctulatus = *Hippocampus erectus*
Hippocampus queenslandicus : **II** (from 15/05/2004) SYNGNATHIDAE Ac
Hippocampus raji = *Hippocampus kuda*
Hippocampus regulus = *Hippocampus zosterae*
Hippocampus reidi : (E) Longsnout Seahorse, Slender Seahorse, (F) Hippocampe long-nez **II** (from 15/05/2004) SYNGNATHIDAE Ac
Hippocampus rhynchomacer = *Hippocampus kuda*
Hippocampus ringens = *Hippocampus ingens*
Hippocampus rondeletii = *Hippocampus hippocampus*
Hippocampus rosaceus = *Hippocampus guttulatus*
Hippocampus rosamondae = *Hippocampus zosterae*
Hippocampus sexmaculatus = *Hippocampus trimaculatus*
Hippocampus semispinosus : **II** (from 15/05/2004) SYNGNATHIDAE Ac
Hippocampus sindonis : (E) Dhiho's Seahorse **II** (from 15/05/2004) SYNGNATHIDAE Ac
Hippocampus spinosissimus : (E) Hedgehog Seahorse **II** (from 15/05/2004) SYNGNATHIDAE Ac
Hippocampus stylifer = *Hippocampus erectus*
Hippocampus subcoronatus = *Hippocampus camelopardalis*
Hippocampus subelongatus : (E) Tiger-snout Seahorse, West Australian Seahorse **II** (from 15/05/2004) SYNGNATHIDAE Ac
Hippocampus suezensis = *Hippocampus kelloggi*
Hippocampus taeniopterus = *Hippocampus kuda*
Hippocampus tetragonus = *Hippocampus erectus*
Hippocampus trimaculatus : (E) Flat-faced Seahorse, Longnose Seahorse, Low-crowned Seahorse, Three-spot Seahorse, Three-spotted Seahorse **II** (from 15/05/2004) SYNGNATHIDAE Ac
Hippocampus tuberculatus = *Hippocampus breviceps*
Hippocampus valentini = *Hippocampus kuda*
Hippocampus villosus = *Hippocampus erectus*
Hippocampus vulgaris = *Hippocampus hippocampus*
Hippocampus whitei : (E) New Holland seahorse, Sydney seahorse, White's Seahorse **II** (from 15/05/2004) SYNGNATHIDAE Ac
Hippocampus zebra : (E) Zebra Seahorse **II** (from 15/05/2004) SYNGNATHIDAE Ac
Hippocampus zosterae : (E) Dwarf Seahorse, (S) Caballito de mar, Caballito oliváceo, (F) Hippocampe nain, **II** (from 15/05/2004) SYNGNATHIDAE Ac
Hippopotame (F): *Hippopotamus amphibius*
Hippopotame amphibie (F): *Hippopotamus amphibius*
Hippopotame nain (F): *Hexaprotodon liberiensis*
Hippopotame pygmée (F): *Hexaprotodon liberiensis*
Hippopotamus (E): *Hippopotamus amphibius*
Hippopotamus amphibius : (E) Hippopotamus, Large Hippo, (S) Hipopótamo anfibio, (F) Hippopotame, Hippopotame amphibie, **II** HIPPOPOTAMIDAE Ma

Hippopus hippopus : (E) Bear Paw Clam, Horse's Hoof Clam, Strawberry Clam **II** TRIDACNIDAE Bi
Hippopus porcellanus : (E) China Clam **II** TRIDACNIDAE Bi
Hippotrague géant de l'Angola (F): *Hippotragus niger variani*
Hippotrague noir géant (F): *Hippotragus niger variani*
Hippotragus niger variani : (E) Giant Sable Antelope, (S) Antílope negro gigante, Antílope sable negro, (F) Hippotrague géant de l'Angola, Hippotrague noir géant, **I** BOVIDAE Ma
Hirola (F): *Damaliscus lunatus*
Hirondelle à lunettes (F): *Pseudochelidon sirintarae*
Hirudo medicinalis : (E) Medicinal Leech, (S) Sanguijuela, (F) Sangsue médicinale, Sangsue officinale, **II** HIRUDINIDAE Hi
Hispaniolan Amazon (E): *Amazona ventralis*
Hispaniolan Boa (E): *Epicrates gracilis*
Hispaniolan Conure (E): *Aratinga chloroptera*
Hispaniolan Emerald (E): *Chlorostilbon swainsonii*
Hispaniolan Ground Iguana (E): *Cyclura ricordi*
Hispaniolan Hawk (E): *Buteo ridgwayi*
Hispaniolan Parakeet (E): *Aratinga chloroptera*
Hispaniolan Parrot (E): *Amazona ventralis*
Hispid Hare (E): *Caprolagus hispidus*
Hispid Rabbit (E): *Caprolagus hispidus*
Hoary Fox (E): *Vulpes cana*
Hoary Puffleg (E): *Haplophaedia lugens*
Hobby (E): *Falco subbuteo*
Hobereau à poitrine rousse (F): *Falco severus*
Hobereau africain (F): *Falco cuvierii*
Hocco à bec bleu (F): *Crax alberti*
Hocco à bec rouge (F): *Crax blumenbachii*
Hocco à pierre (F): *Pauxi pauxi*
Hocco d'Albert (F): *Crax alberti*
Hocco de Blumenbach (F): *Crax blumenbachii*
Hocco de Daubenton (F): *Crax daubentoni*
Hocco globuleux (F): *Crax globulosa*
Hocco huppé (F): *Oreophasis derbianus*
Hocco mitou (F): *Mitu mitu*
Hocco piguiazul (S): *Crax alberti*
Hocheur (F): *Cercopithecus nictitans*
Hocheur du Ghana (F): *Cercopithecus petaurista*
Hoco barbado (S): *Crax globulosa*
Hoco caroncule (F): *Crax globulosa*
Hoco de casco (S): *Pauxi pauxi*
Hoco de Daubenton (S): *Crax daubentoni*
Hoco de pico navaja (S): *Mitu mitu*
Hoco grande (S): *Crax rubra*
Hoco mitu (S): *Mitu mitu*
Hocofaisan (S): *Crax rubra*
Hodgson's Hawk-Eagle (E): *Spizaetus nipalensis*
Hoe-mother (E): *Cetorhinus maximus*
Hoffmann's Conure (E): *Pyrrhura hoffmanni*
Hoffmann's Two-toed Sloth (E): *Choloepus hoffmanni*
Hoffmanns's Titi Monkey (E): *Callicebus hoffmannsi*
Hoki blanco (S): *Crossoptilon crossoptilon*
Hoki pardo (S): *Crossoptilon mantchuricum*
Hokki blanc (F): *Crossoptilon crossoptilon*
Hokki brun (F): *Crossoptilon mantchuricum*
Hokki de Harman (F): *Crossoptilon harmani*
Hokki du Tibet (F): *Crossoptilon harmani*
Holcotrochus crenulatus : **II** TURBINOLIIDAE An
Holcotrochus scriptus : **II** TURBINOLIIDAE An
Homerus Swallowtail (E): *Papilio homerus*
Home's Hinge-back Tortoise (E): *Kinixys homeana*
Home's Hinged Tortoise (E): *Kinixys homeana*
Home's Hinged-backed Tortoise (E): *Kinixys homeana*
Homopode à éperon (F): *Homopus femoralis*
Homopode aréolé (F): *Homopus areolatus*
Homopode de Boulenger (F): *Homopus boulengeri*
Homopode de Namibie (F): *Homopus bergeri*
Homopode éperonné (F): *Homopus femoralis*
Homopode marqué (F): *Homopus signatus*

146

Homopus areolatus : (E) Areolated Tortoise, Beaked Cape Tortoise, Grooved Mountain Tortoise, Parrot-beaked Tortoise, (S) Tortuga pico de loro, (F) Homopode aréolé, **II** TESTUDINIDAE Re

Homopus bergeri : (E) Berger's Cape Tortoise, (F) Homopode de Namibie **II** TESTUDINIDAE Re

Homopus boulengeri : (E) Boulenger's Cape Tortoise, Boulenger's Padloper, Karoo Padloper, (S) Tortuga terrestre, (F) Homopode de Boulenger, **II** TESTUDINIDAE Re

Homopus femoralis : (E) Greater Padloper, Karoo Cape Tortoise, (F) Homopode à éperon, Homopode éperonné **II** TESTUDINIDAE Re

Homopus signatus : (E) Speckled Cape Tortoise, Speckled Padloper, Speckled Tortoise, (S) Tortuga manchada, (F) Homopode marqué, **II** TESTUDINIDAE Re

Honduran Emerald (E): *Polyerata luciae*

Honey Badger (E): *Mellivora capensis*

Honey Buzzard (E): *Pernis apivorus*

Honeycomb Coral (E): *Favites abdita*

Honeycomb Plate Coral (E): *Porites colonensis*

Hooded Chameleon (E): *Calumma cucullata*

Hooded Crane (E): *Grus monacha*

Hooded Parrot (E): *Psephotus dissimilis*

Hooded Visorbearer (E): *Augastes lumachella*

Hooded Vulture (E): *Necrosyrtes monachus*

Hook-billed Hermit (E): *Glaucis dohrnii*

Hook-billed Kite (E): *Chondrohierax uncinatus*

Hooked-beaked Terrapin (E): *Pelusios niger*

Hook-lipped Rhinoceros (E): *Diceros bicornis*

Hoolock (F): *Hylobates hoolock*

Hoolock Gibbon (E): *Hylobates hoolock*

Hoplangia durotrix : (E) Weymouth Carpet Coral **II** CARYOPHYLLIIDAE An

Hoplobatrachus tigerinus : (E) Indian Bullfrog, Tiger Frog, (F) Grenouille tigre, Grenouille tigrée **II** RANIDAE Am

Hoplocéphale à large tête (F): *Hoplocephalus bungaroides*

Hoplocéphale de Schlegel (F): *Hoplocephalus bungaroides*

Hoplocephalus bungaroides : (E) Broad-headed Snake, Fierce Snake, (F) Hoplocéphale à large tête, Hoplocéphale de Schlegel **II** ELAPIDAE Re

Hoplodactylus spp. : (E) Sticky-toed geckos **III** GEKKONIDAE Re

Hoplodactylus chrysosireticus : (E) Golden Sticky-toed Gecko, Gold-striped Gecko **III** GEKKONIDAE Re

Hoplodactylus delcourti : (E) Delcourt's Sticky-toed Gecko **III** GEKKONIDAE Re

Hoplodactylus duvaucelii : (E) Duvaucel's Gecko, Northern Sticky-toed Gecko **III** GEKKONIDAE Re

Hoplodactylus granulatus : (E) Granulated Gecko, Gray's Sticky-toed Gecko **III** GEKKONIDAE Re

Hoplodactylus kahutarae : (E) Black-eyed Gecko, Whitaker's Sticky-toed Gecko **III** GEKKONIDAE Re

Hoplodactylus maculatus : (E) Spotted Sticky-toed Gecko **III** GEKKONIDAE Re

Hoplodactylus nebulosus : **III** GEKKONIDAE Re

Hoplodactylus pacificus : (E) Pacific Sticky-toed Gecko **III** GEKKONIDAE Re

Hoplodactylus rakiurae : (E) Harlequin Gecko, Stewart's Sticky-toed Gecko **III** GEKKONIDAE Re

Hoplodactylus stephensi : (E) Stephens's Island Gecko, Stephens's Sticky-toed Gecko **III** GEKKONIDAE Re

Horastrea indica : **II** SIDERASTREIDAE An

Hormiguero gigante (S): *Myrmecophaga tridactyla*

Horn Coral (E): *Hydnophora spp.*

Horn Lizard (E): *Uromastyx asmussi*

Hornbills (E): *Aceros* spp./ *Anorrhinus* spp. / *Anthracoceros* spp./ *Buceros* spp.

Horned Guan (E): *Oreophasis derbianus*

Horned Parakeet (E): *Eunymphicus cornutus*

Horned Sungem (E): *Heliactin bilopha*

Horsefish (E): *Hippocampus erectus*

Horsefishes (E): *Hippocampus* spp.

Horse's Hoof Clam (E): *Hippopus hippopus*

Horsfield's Tarsier (E): *Tarsius bancanus*

Horsfield's Tortoise (E): *Testudo horsfieldii*

Hose's Leaf Monkey (E): *Presbytis hosei*

Houbara (E): *Chlamydotis undulata*

Houbara Bustard (E): *Chlamydotis undulata*

Houbara ondulé (F): *Chlamydotis undulata*

Houbaropsis bengalensis = Eupodotis bengalensis

Houleman (F): *Semnopithecus entellus*

Houlemán (S): *Semnopithecus entellus*

Hourglass Dolphin (E): *Lagenorhynchus cruciger*

House-building Rat (E): *Leporillus conditor*

Huallaca (S): *Lontra felina*

Huapo colorado (S): *Cacajao calvus*

Huapo rojo (S): *Cacajao calvus*

Hubara (S): *Chlamydotis undulata*

Hubbs's Beaked Whale (E): *Mesoplodon carlhubbsi*

Huemul (S): *Hippocamelus antisensis/ Hippocamelus bisulcus*

Huémul des Andes méridionales (F): *Hippocamelus bisulcus*

Huémul des Andes septentrionales (F): *Hippocamelus antisensis*

Huemules (S): *Hippocamelus* spp.

Huemuls (E): *Hippocamelus* spp.

Huillin (E/F): *Lontra provocax*

Huillín (S): *Lontra provocax*

Hulotte africaine (F): *Strix woodfordii*

Hulotte chathuant (F): *Strix aluco*

Humboldt Penguin (E): *Spheniscus humboldti*

Humboldt's Hog-nosed Skunk (E): *Conepatus humboldtii*

Humboldt's Woolly Monkey (E): *Lagothrix lagotricha*

Hume's Bar-tailed Pheasant (E): *Syrmaticus humiae*

Hume's Owl (E): *Strix butleri*

Hume's Pheasant (E): *Syrmaticus humiae*

Hume's Tawny Owl (E): *Strix butleri*

Hume's Wood-Owl (E): *Strix butleri*

Hummingbirds (E): TROCHILIDAE spp.

Hump Whale (E): *Megaptera novaeangliae*

Humpback dolphins (E): *Sousa* spp.

Humpback Whale (E): *Megaptera novaeangliae*

Hunchbacked Whale (E): *Megaptera novaeangliae*

Hunting Leopard (E): *Acinonyx jubatus*

Huon Astrapia (E): *Astrapia rothschildi*

Hurleur à mains rousses (F): *Alouatta belzebul*

Hurleur brun (F): *Alouatta fusca*

Hurleur du Guatemala (F): *Alouatta palliata/ Alouatta pigra*

Hurleur noir (F): *Alouatta caraya*

Hurleur roux (F): *Alouatta seniculus*

Hurón (S): *Galictis vittata*

Hurón grange (S): *Galictis vittata*

Hurón mayor (S): *Eira barbara*

Hurria rynchops = Cerberus rhynchops

Huso anasimos = Acipenser fulvescens

Huso anthracinus = Acipenser fulvescens

Huso atelaspis = Acipenser fulvescens

Huso copei = Acipenser fulvescens

Huso dauricus : (E) Great Siberian sturgeon, Huso sturgeon, Kaluga **II** ACIPENSERIDAE Ac

Huso honneymani = Acipenser fulvescens

Huso huso : (E) Beluga, Caviar, Caviare, European Sturgeon, Giant Sturgeon, Great Sturgeon, Isinglass, Russian Sturgeon, (S) Beluga, Cola de pescado, Esturión, Esturión beluga, (F) Beluga, Grand esturgeon, Ichtyocolle, **II** ACIPENSERIDAE Ac

Huso ichthyocolla = Huso huso

Huso kaluschka = Huso dauricus

Huso kirtlandi = Acipenser fulvescens

Huso lamarii = Acipenser fulvescens

Huso mertinianus = Acipenser fulvescens

Huso paranasimos = Acipenser fulvescens

Huso platyrhinus = Acipenser fulvescens

Huso rafinesquii = Acipenser fulvescens

Huso rauchii = Acipenser fulvescens

Checklist of fauna/Lista de especies de fauna/Liste des espèces animales

Huso richardsonii = Acipenser fulvescens
Huso rosarium = Acipenser fulvescens
Huso Sturgeon (E): *Huso dauricus*
Hwamei (E): *Garrulax canorus*
Hyacinth Macaw (E): *Anodorhynchus hyacinthinus*
Hyacinth Visorbearer (E): *Augastes scutatus*
Hydnophora spp.: (E) Horn Coral , Spine Coral **II**
 MERULINIDAE An
Hydnophora bonsai : **II** MERULINIDAE An
Hydnophora exesa : **II** MERULINIDAE An
Hydnophora grandis : **II** MERULINIDAE An
Hydnophora microconos : **II** MERULINIDAE An
Hydnophora pilosa : **II** MERULINIDAE An
Hydnophora rigida : **II** MERULINIDAE An
Hydrictis maculicollis = Lutra maculicollis
Hydrodynastes gigas = Cyclagras gigas
Hyemoschus aquaticus : (E) Water Chevrotain, (S)
 Antilope amizclero enano de agua, Cervatillo
 almizclero acuático, (F) Chevrotain aquatique, **III**
 TRAGULIDAE Ma
Hylobates agilis : (E) Agile Gibbon, Dark-handed Gibbon,
 (F) Gibbon agile **I** HYLOBATIDAE Ma
Hylobates concolor : (E) Black Gibbon, Crested Gibbon,
 Indochinese Gibbon, (F) Gibbon à favoris blancs,
 Gibbon noir **I** HYLOBATIDAE Ma
Hylobates concolor ssp. *gabriellae = Hylobates gabriellae*
Hylobates concolor ssp. *leucogenys = Hylobates
 leucogenys*
Hylobates gabriellae : (E) Buff-cheeked Gibbon **I**
 HYLOBATIDAE Ma
Hylobates hoolock : (E) Hoolock Gibbon, (S) Gibón
 hulock, (F) Hoolock, **I** HYLOBATIDAE Ma
Hylobates klossii : (E) Dwarf Gibbon, Kloss's Gibbon,
 Mentawai Gibbon, (S) Siamang de Kloss, Siamang
 enano, (F) Siamang de Kloss, **I** HYLOBATIDAE Ma
Hylobates lar : (E) Common Gibbon, Lar Gibbon, White-
 handed Gibbon, (S) Gibón de manos blancas, (F)
 Gibbon à mains blanches, Gibbon lar, **I**
 HYLOBATIDAE Ma
Hylobates lar ssp. *agilis = Hylobates agilis*
Hylobates lar ssp. *moloch = Hylobates moloch*
Hylobates lar ssp. *muelleri = Hylobates muelleri*
Hylobates lar ssp. *pileatus = Hylobates pileatus*
Hylobates leucogenys : (E) White-cheeked Gibbon **I**
 HYLOBATIDAE Ma
Hylobates leucogenys ssp. *gabriellae = Hylobates
 gabriellae*
Hylobates moloch : (E) Javan Gibbon, Silvery Gibbon, (S)
 Gibón ceniciento, (F) Gibbon cendré, **I**
 HYLOBATIDAE Ma
Hylobates muelleri : (E) Bornean Gibbon, Grey Gibbon,
 Müller's Gibbon, (S) Gibón de Mueller, (F) Gibbon de
 Muller, **I** HYLOBATIDAE Ma
Hylobates pileatus : (E) Capped Gibbon, Crowned
 Gibbon, Pileated Gibbon, (S) Gibón de cresta negra **I**
 HYLOBATIDAE Ma
Hylobates syndactylus : (E) Siamang, (S) Siamang, (F)
 Siamang, **I** HYLOBATIDAE Ma
HYLOBATIDAE spp.: (E) Gibbons, (S) Gibones, (F)
 Gibbons, **I** Ma
Hylocharis chrysura : (E) Gilded Hummingbird, (S)
 Picaflor bronceado, Picaflor dorado, Zafiro
 bronceado, (F) Saphir à queue d'or, **II**
 TROCHILIDAE Av
Hylocharis cyanus : (E) White-chinned Sapphire, (S)
 Picaflor cabeciazul, Zafiro cabecimorado, Zafiro
 gorgiblanco, (F) Saphir azuré, **II** TROCHILIDAE Av
Hylocharis eliciae : (E) Blue-throated Goldentail, (S)
 Zafiro de Elicia, Zafiro gorjiazul, (F) Saphir d'Elicia,
 II TROCHILIDAE Av
Hylocharis grayi : (E) Blue-headed Sapphire, (S) Zafiro
 cabeciazul, (F) Saphir ulysse, **II** TROCHILIDAE Av
Hylocharis humboldtii = Hylocharis grayi
Hylocharis leucotis = Basilinna leucotis

Hylocharis sapphirina : (E) Rufous-throated Sapphire, (S)
 Picaflor pechiazul, Zafiro gargantirrufo, Zafiro
 gorgirrojo, (F) Saphir à gorge rousse, **II**
 TROCHILIDAE Av
Hylocharis xantusii = Basilinna xantusii
Hylonympha macrocerca : (E) Scissor-tailed
 Hummingbird, (S) Colibrí tijereta, (F) Colibri à queue
 en ciseaux, **II** TROCHILIDAE Av
Hypargos nitidula = Mandingoa nitidula
Hyperoodon spp.: (E) Bottlenose whales, (S) Ballenas
 hocico de botella **I** ZIPHIIDAE Ma
Hyperoodon ampullatus : (E) Bottlehead, Northern
 Bottlenose Whale, (S) Ballena hocico de botella del
 norte, (F) Hyperoodon boréal, **I** ZIPHIIDAE Ma
Hyperoodon austral (F): *Hyperoodon planifrons*
Hyperoodon boréal (F): *Hyperoodon ampullatus*
Hyperoodon planifrons : (E) Southern Bottlenose Whale,
 (S) Ballena hocico de botella del sur, (F) Hyperoodon
 austral, **I** ZIPHIIDAE Ma
Hyperoodon rostratus = Hyperoodon ampullatus
Hypochera chalybeata = Vidua chalybeata
Hypochera wilsoni = Vidua wilsoni
Hystrix cristata : (E) Crested Porcupine, North African
 Crested Porcupine, (S) Puercoespín, (F) Porc-épic à
 crête, Porc-épic du nord de l'Afrique, **III**
 HYSTRICIDAE Ma
Iaça (S): *Podocnemis sextuberculata*
Iaraka River Leaf Chameleon (E): *Brookesia vadoni*
Iberian Lynx (E): *Lynx pardinus*
Ibis à crête du Japon (F): *Nipponia nippon*
Ibis blanc (F): *Nipponia nippon*
Ibis blanc du Japon (F): *Nipponia nippon*
Ibis blanco japonés (S): *Nipponia nippon*
Ibis calvo (S): *Geronticus calvus*
Ibis calvo de Àrica del Sur (S): *Geronticus calvus*
Ibis chauve (F): *Geronticus eremita*
Ibis chauve de l'Afrique du Sud (F): *Geronticus calvus*
Ibis du Cap (F): *Geronticus calvus*
Ibis eremita (S): *Geronticus eremita*
Ibis escarlata (S): *Eudocimus ruber*
Ibis hadada (S): *Bostrychia hagedash*
Ibis hagedash (S/F): *Bostrychia hagedash*
Ibis moñudo japonés (S): *Nipponia nippon*
Ibis moteado (S): *Bostrychia rara*
Ibis nipón (S): *Nipponia nippon*
Ibis nippon (F): *Nipponia nippon*
Ibis noir (F): *Geronticus calvus*
Ibis rara (S): *Bostrychia rara*
Ibis rouge (F): *Eudocimus ruber*
Ibis sacré (F): *Threskiornis aethiopicus*
Ibis sagrado (S): *Threskiornis aethiopicus*
Ibis vermiculé (F): *Bostrychia rara*
Ibiza Wall Lizard (E): *Podarcis pityusensis*
Ibycter americanus = Daptrius americanus
Ichthyophaga humilis : (E) Lesser Fish-eagle, Lesser
 Fishing Eagle, (S) Pigarguillo menor, (F) Pygargue
 nain, **II** ACCIPITRIDAE Av
Ichthyophaga ichthyaetus : (E) Grey-headed Fish-eagle,
 Grey-headed Fishing Eagle, (S) Pigarguillo común,
 (F) Pygargue à tête grise, **II** ACCIPITRIDAE Av
Ichthyophaga nana = Ichthyophaga humilis
Ichtyocolle (F): *Huso huso*
Ictéride à tête jaune (F): *Agelaius flavus*
Icterus xantholaemus = Agelaius flavus
Ictinaetus malayensis : (E) Asian Black Eagle, Black
 Eagle, Indian Black Eagle, (S) Aguila milana, (F)
 Aigle noir, **II** ACCIPITRIDAE Av
Ictinia mississippiensis : (E) Mississippi Kite, (S) Elanio
 del Mississipí, Milano del Misisipi, Milano
 misisipero, (F) Milan du Mississippi, **II**
 ACCIPITRIDAE Av
Ictinia plumbea : (E) Plumbeous Kite, (S) Elanio plomizo,
 Gavilán plomizo, Milano plomizo, (F) Milan bleuâtre,
 II ACCIPITRIDAE Av
Idiotrochus emarciatus : **II** TURBINOLIIDAE An

148

Checklist of fauna/Lista de especies de fauna/Liste des espèces animales

Idiotrochus kikutii : **II** TURBINOLIIDAE An
Idiotrochus perexigua = Idiotrochus emarciatus
Idiurus kivuensis = Idiurus macrotis
Idiurus macrotis : (E) Long-eared Flying Mouse, Long-eared Flying Squirrel, Long-eared Scaly-tailed Flying Squirrel, (S) Ardilla voladera de orejas largas, Ardilla voladora enana, (F) Anamolure nain, **III** ANOMALURIDAE Ma
Idmi (E): *Gazella cuvieri*
Ignicolor (F): *Euplectes franciscanus*
Ignicolore (F): *Euplectes franciscanus*
Iguana cornuda (S): *Phrynosoma coronatum*
Iguana crestada de Fiji (S): *Brachylophus vitiensis*
Iguana spp.: (E) Iguanas, (S) Iguanas, (F) Iguanes communs, Iguanes vrais, **II** IGUANIDAE Re
Iguana delicatissima : (E) Lesser Antillean Iguana, West Indian Iguana, (F) Iguane des Antilles **II** IGUANIDAE Re
Iguana iguana : (E) Common Iguana, Green Iguana, (S) Gallina de palo, (F) Iguane commun, Iguane vert, **II** IGUANIDAE Re
Iguana marina (S): *Amblyrhynchus cristatus*
Iguana rhinolopha = Iguana iguana
Iguana terrestre de Barrington (S): *Conolophus pallidus*
Iguana terrestre de las Galápagos (S): *Conolophus subcristatus*
Iguanas (E/S): *Iguana* spp.
Iguanas cornuda (S): *Cyclura* spp.
Iguanas de Fiji (S): *Brachylophus* spp.
Iguanas terrestres (S): *Cyclura* spp./ *Conolophus* spp.
Iguane à bandes de Fidji (F): *Brachylophus fasciatus*
Iguane à crête de Fidji (F): *Brachylophus vitiensis*
Iguane commun (F): *Iguana iguana*
Iguane cornu (F): *Cyclura cornuta*
Iguane des Antilles (F): *Iguana delicatissima*
Iguane marin (F): *Amblyrhynchus cristatus*
Iguane terrestre cornu (F): *Cyclura cornuta*
Iguane terrestre de la Jamaïque (F): *Cyclura collei*
Iguane terrestre de l'Ile Anegada (F): *Cyclura pinguis*
Iguane terrestre de l'île Santa Fe (F): *Conolophus pallidus*
Iguane terrestre des Bahamas (F): *Cyclura rileyi*
Iguane terrestre des Galapagos (F): *Conolophus subcristatus*
Iguane terrestre des Iles Cayman (F): *Cyclura nubila*
Iguane terrestre des îles Turks et Caïques (F): *Cyclura carinata*
Iguane terrestre d'Hispaniola (F): *Cyclura ricordi*
Iguane vert (F): *Iguana iguana*
Iguanes communs (F): *Iguana* spp.
Iguanes cornus (F): *Cyclura* spp.
Iguanes des Fidji (F): *Brachylophus* spp.
Iguanes rhinocéros (F): *Cyclura* spp.
Iguanes terrestres (F): *Conolophus* spp.
Iguanes terrestres des Galapagos (F): *Conolophus* spp.
Iguanes vrais (F): *Iguana* spp.
Ikan temoleh (E): *Probarbus jullieni*
Illiger's Macaw (E): *Propyrrhura maracana*
Ilolo Chameleon (E): *Chamaeleo goetzei*
Imitator Sparrowhawk (E): *Accipiter imitator*
Imperial Amazon (E): *Amazona imperialis*
Imperial Eagle (E): *Aquila heliaca*
Imperial Parrot (E): *Amazona imperialis*
Imperial Pheasant (E): *Lophura imperialis*
Imperial Woodpecker (E): *Campephilus imperialis*
Impeyan Pheasant (E): *Lophophorus impejanus*
Impressed Tortoise (E): *Manouria impressa*
Inca à collier (F): *Coeligena torquata*
Inca à gemme bleue (F): *Coeligena lutetiae*
Inca à queue blanche (F): *Coeligena phalerata*
Inca acollarado (S): *Coeligena torquata*
Inca alihabano (S): *Coeligena lutetiae*
Inca arcoiris (S): *Coeligena iris*
Inca bronceado (S): *Coeligena coeligena*
Inca brun (F): *Coeligena wilsoni*
Inca café (S): *Coeligena wilsoni*

Inca céleste (F): *Coeligena coeligena*
Inca coliblanco (S): *Coeligena phalerata*
Inca de Bonaparte (F): *Coeligena bonapartei*
Inca de Gould (S/F): *Coeligena inca*
Inca gorgimorado (S): *Coeligena violifer*
Inca iris (F): *Coeligena iris*
Inca negro (S): *Coeligena prunellei*
Inca noir (F): *Coeligena prunellei*
Inca pardo (S): *Coeligena wilsoni*
Inca porphyre (F): *Coeligena helianthea*
Inca ventridorado (S): *Coeligena bonapartei*
Inca ventrivioleta (S): *Coeligena helianthea*
Inca violifère (F): *Coeligena violifer*
Indian Bison (E): *Bos gaurus*
Indian Black Eagle (E): *Ictinaetus malayensis*
Indian Black Vulture (E): *Sarcogyps calvus*
Indian Brown Mongoose (E): *Herpestes brachyurus fuscus*
Indian Bullfrog (E): *Hoplobatrachus tigerinus*
Indian Bustard (E): *Ardeotis nigriceps*
Indian Chameleon (E): *Chamaeleo zeylanicus*
Indian Cobra (E): *Naja naja*
Indian Concave-casqued Hornbill (E): *Buceros bicornis*
Indian Egg-eater (E): *Elachistodon westermanni*
Indian Egg-eating Snake (E): *Elachistodon westermanni*
Indian Elephant (E): *Elephas maximus*
Indian Flapshell Turtle (E): *Lissemys punctata*
Indian Flying-fox (E): *Pteropus giganteus*
Indian Giant Squirrel (E): *Ratufa indica*
Indian Grey Mongoose (E): *Herpestes edwardsii*
Indian Hornbill (E): *Buceros bicornis*
Indian King Vulture (E): *Sarcogyps calvus*
Indian Lion (E): *Panthera leo persica*
Indian Mastigure (E): *Uromastyx hardwickii*
Indian Monitor (E): *Varanus bengalensis*
Indian Narrow-headed Softshell Turtle (E): *Chitra indica*
Indian Oval-grain Lizard (E): *Varanus flavescens*
Indian Pangolin (E): *Manis crassicaudata*
Indian Peacock Softshell Turtle (E): *Aspideretes hurum*
Indian Pied Hornbill (E): *Anthracoceros albirostris*
Indian Pond Turtle (E): *Kachuga tecta*
Indian Python (E): *Python molurus molurus*
Indian Roofed Turtle (E): *Kachuga tecta*
Indian Sand Boa (E): *Eryx johnii / Gongylophis conicus*
Indian Sawback Turtle (E): *Kachuga tecta*
Indian Scops-Owl (E): *Otus bakkamoena*
Indian Small-grain Lizard (E): *Varanus bengalensis*
Indian Smooth-coated Otter (E): *Lutrogale perspicillata*
Indian Softshell Turtle (E): *Aspideretes gangeticus*
Indian Spectacled Cobra (E): *Naja naja*
Indian Star Tortoise (E): *Geochelone elegans*
Indian Tapir (E): *Tapirus indicus*
Indian Tent Turtle (E): *Kachuga tentoria*
Indian Tragopan (E): *Tragopan satyra*
Indian Treeshrew (E): *Anathana ellioti*
Indian Wild Ass (E): *Equus onager khur*
Indian Wild Dog (E): *Cuon alpinus*
Indian Wild Ox (E): *Bos gaurus*
Indigo Macaw (E): *Anodorhynchus leari*
Indigo-capped Hummingbird (E): *Saucerottia cyanifrons*
Indigo-winged Parrot (E): *Hapalopsittaca fuertesi*
Indochinese Box Turtle (E): *Cuora galbinifrons*
Indochinese Gibbon (E): *Hylobates concolor*
Indochinese Hog Deer (E): *Axis porcinus annamiticus*
Indochinese Spitting Cobra (E): *Naja siamensis*
Indo-Gangetic Flap-shell (E): *Lissemys punctata*
Indonesian Cobra (E): *Naja sputatrix*
Indopacetus pacificus : (E) Indo-pacific Beaked Whale, Longman's Beaked Whale, (S) Ballena de pico de Longman, (F) Mesoplodon de Longman, **II** ZIPHIIDAE Ma
Indo-pacific Beaked Whale (E): *Indopacetus pacificus*
Indo-pacific Humpbacked Dolphin (E): *Sousa chinensis*

Indophyllia macassarensis : **II** MUSSIDAE An

Indotestudo elongata : (E) Elongated Tortoise, Pineapple Tortoise, Red-nosed Tortoise, Yellow Tortoise, Yellow-headed Tortoise, (F) Tortue à tête jaune **II** TESTUDINIDAE Re

Indotestudo forstenii : (E) Celebes Tortoise, Forsten's Tortoise, Travancore Tortoise, (S) Tortuga marrón de la India, (F) Tortue de Tranvancore, Tortue des Celèbes, **II** TESTUDINIDAE Re

Indotestudo travancorica = Indotestudo forstenii

Indri (F): *Indri indri*

Indri à queue courte (F): *Indri indri*

Indri colicorto (S): *Indri indri*

Indri indri : (E) Indris, (S) Indri colicorto, (F) Indri, Indri à queue courte, **I** INDRIDAE Ma

Indri lanudo (S): *Avahi laniger*

INDRIDAE spp.: (E) Indris, Sifakas (S) Indris, Sifakas, (F) Avahis, Propithéques, **I** Ma

Indris (E): *Indri indri*

Indris (E/S): INDRIDAE spp.

Indris sifaca (S): *Propithecus diadema/ Propithecus tattersalli/ Propithecus verreauxi*

Indus Dolphin (E): *Platanista minor*

Indus River Dolphin (E): *Platanista minor*

Inferiolabiata labiata : **II** STYLASTERIDAE Hy

Inferiolabiata lowei : **II** STYLASTERIDAE Hy

Inferiolabiata spinosa : **II** STYLASTERIDAE Hy

Inia (F): *Inia geoffrensis*

Inia boliviensis = Inia geoffrensis

Inia geoffrensis : (E) Amazon River Dolphin, Boto, Boutu, (S) Bufeo, (F) Dauphin de l'Amazone, Inia, **II** PLATANISTIDAE Ma

Inséparable à collier noir (F): *Agapornis swindernianus*

Inséparable à face rose (F): *Agapornis roseicollis*

Inséparable à joues noires (F): *Agapornis nigrigenis*

Inséparable à tête grise (F): *Agapornis canus*

Inséparable à tête rouge (F): *Agapornis pullarius*

Inseparable Abisinio (S): *Agapornis taranta*

Inseparable acollarado (S): *Agapornis swindernianus*

Inseparable cabecinegro (S): *Agapornis personatus*

Inseparable cachetón (S): *Agapornis nigrigenis*

Inseparable carirrojo (S): *Agapornis pullarius*

Inséparable d'Abyssinie (F): *Agapornis taranta*

Inséparable de collera (S): *Agapornis swindernianus*

Inséparable de Fischer (F): *Agapornis fischeri*

Inseparable de Fischer (S): *Agapornis fischeri*

Inséparable de Lilian (F): *Agapornis lilianae*

Inseparable de Namibia (S): *Agapornis roseicollis*

Inséparable de Swindern (F): *Agapornis swindernianus*

Inseparable del Nyasa (S): *Agapornis lilianae*

Inseparable malgache (S): *Agapornis canus*

Inséparable masqué (F): *Agapornis personatus*

Inséparable rosegorge (F): *Agapornis roseicollis*

Insular Flying-fox (E): *Pteropus tonganus*

Intermediate Parakeet (E): *Psittacula intermedia*

Iranian Mastigure (E): *Uromastyx asmussi*

Irbis (F): *Uncia uncia*

Iris Lorikeet (E): *Psitteuteles iris*

Iris Lory (E): *Psitteuteles iris*

Iris Peacock-Pheasant (E): *Polyplectron bicalcaratum*

Irrawaddy Dolphin (E): *Orcaella brevirostris*

Isidor's Eagle (E): *Oroaetus isidori*

Isinglass (E): *Huso huso*

Island Day Gecko (E): *Phelsuma nigristriata*

Isok barb (E): *Probarbus jullieni*

Isophyllastrea rigida : (E) Rough Star Coral **II** MUSSIDAE An

Isophyllia multiflora = Isophyllia sinuosa

Isophyllia rigida = Isophyllastrea rigida

Isophyllia sinuosa : (E) Sinuous Cactus Coral **II** MUSSIDAE An

Isthmian Dwarf Boa (E): *Ungaliophis continentalis*

Ithagine ensanglantée (F): *Ithaginis cruentus*

Ithagines (F): *Ithaginis cruentus*

Ithaginis cruentus : (E) Blood Pheasant, (S) Faisán ensangrentado, Faisán sangrante, Faisán sanguineo, (F) Faisan sanguin, Ithagine ensanglantée, Ithagines, **II** PHASIANIDAE Av

Itombwe Owl (E): *Phodilus prigoginei*

Ituri Chameleon (E): *Bradypodion adolfifriderici*

Ituri Forest Chameleon (E): *Bradypodion adolfifriderici/ Chamaeleo ituriensis*

Ivory Tree Coral (E): *Oculina valenciennesi*

Ivory Tube Coral (E): *Cladocora arbuscula*

Jabalí enano (S): *Sus salvanius*

Jabalí pigmeo (S): *Sus salvanius*

Jabiru (E): *Jabiru mycteria/ Ephippiorhynchus senegalensis*

Jabirú (S): *Jabiru mycteria/ Ephippiorhynchus senegalensis*

Jabiru africain (F): *Ephippiorhynchus senegalensis*

Jabirú Africano (S): *Ephippiorhynchus senegalensis*

Jabiru américain (F): *Jabiru mycteria*

Jabirú Americano (S): *Jabiru mycteria*

Jabiru d'Afrique (F): *Ephippiorhynchus senegalensis*

Jabiru d'Amérique (F): *Jabiru mycteria*

Jabiru du Sénégal (F): *Ephippiorhynchus senegalensis*

Jabiru mycteria : (E) Jabiru, (S) Garzón soldado, Jabirú, Jabirú Americano, (F) Jabiru américain, Jabiru d'Amérique, **I** CICONIIDAE Av

Jabuti (S): *Geochelone carbonaria*

Jacaruxi (S): *Dracaena* spp.

Jackal Buzzard (E): *Buteo rufofuscus*

Jackass Penguin (E): *Spheniscus demersus*

Jacko (F): *Psittacus erithacus*

Jackson's Three-horned Chameleon (E): *Chamaeleo jacksonii*

Jacobino collarejo (S): *Florisuga mellivora*

Jacobino nuquiblanco (S): *Florisuga mellivora*

Jacobita (S): *Cephalorhynchus commersonii*

Jacotinga (S): *Pipile jacutinga*

Jacquot (E): *Amazona arausiaca/ Psittacus erithacus*

Jacuruxi (E): *Dracaena guianensis*

Jagged-shelled Turtle (E): *Pyxidea mouhotii*

Jaguar (E/S/F): *Panthera onca*

Jaguarundi (E/F): *Herpailurus yaguarondi*

Jamaica Ground Iguana (E): *Cyclura collei*

Jamaican Boa (E): *Epicrates subflavus*

Jamaican Iguana (E): *Cyclura collei*

Jamaican Mango (E): *Anthracothorax mango*

Jamaican Owl (E): *Pseudoscops grammicus*

Jambandu Indigobird (E): *Vidua raricola*

James' Flamingo (E): *Phoenicopterus jamesi*

Jameson's Antpecker (E): *Parmoptila rubrifrons*

James's Flamingo (E): *Phoenicopterus jamesi*

Jandaya Conure (E): *Aratinga jandaya*

Jandaya Parakeet (E): *Aratinga jandaya*

Japanese Crane (E): *Grus japonensis*

Japanese Crested Ibis (E): *Nipponia nippon*

Japanese Giant Salamander (E): *Andrias japonicus*

Japanese Lesser Sparrowhawk (E): *Accipiter gularis*

Japanese Macaque (E): *Macaca fuscata*

Japanese Seahorse (E): *Hippocampus mohnikei*

Japanese Sparrowhawk (E): *Accipiter gularis*

Japanese White Stork (E): *Ciconia boyciana*

Jaquentón blanco (S): *Carcharodon carcharias*

Jaquetón (S): *Carcharodon carcharias*

Jaquetón blanco (S): *Carcharodon carcharias*

Jaquetón de ley (S): *Carcharodon carcharias*

Jardine's Parrot (E): *Poicephalus gulielmi*

Jasmine Coral (E): *Plerogyra turbida*

Java Leaf Monkey (E): *Presbytis comata*

Java Rock Python (E): *Python reticulatus*

Java Sparrow (E): *Padda oryzivora*

Javan Gibbon (E): *Hylobates moloch*

Javan Hawk-Eagle (E): *Spizaetus bartelsi*

Javan Owlet (E): *Glaucidium castanopterum*

Javan Rhinoceros (E): *Rhinoceros sondaicus*

Javan Scops-Owl (E): *Otus angelinae*
Javan Treeshrew (E): *Tupaia javanica*
Javania antarctica : **II** FLABELLIDAE An
Javania borealis : **II** FLABELLIDAE An
Javania cailleti : **II** FLABELLIDAE An
Javania californica : **II** FLABELLIDAE An
Javania exserta : **II** FLABELLIDAE An
Javania fusca : **II** FLABELLIDAE An
Javania insignis : **II** FLABELLIDAE An
Javania lamprotichum : **II** FLABELLIDAE An
Javania pachytheca = Javania fusca
Javania pseudoalabastra : **II** FLABELLIDAE An
Javelin Sand Boa (E): *Eryx jaculus*
Jayakar's Sand Boa (E): *Eryx jayakari*
Jayakar's Seahorse (E): *Hippocampus jayakari*
Jentink's Duiker (E): *Cephalophus jentinki*
Jerdonella sylhetensis = Kachuga sylhetensis
Jerdon's Baza (E): *Aviceda jerdoni*
Jerdon's Palm Civet (E): *Paradoxurus jerdoni*
Jewelled Chameleon (E): *Furcifer lateralis*
Jilguero cara amarilla (S): *Carduelis yarrellii*
Jilguero de Yarrell (S): *Carduelis yarrellii*
Jilguero rojo (S): *Carduelis cucullata*
Jobi Manucode (E): *Manucodia jobiensis*
John's Langur (E): *Trachypithecus johnii*
Johnstone's Crocodile (E): *Crocodylus johnsoni*
Johnstone's Lorikeet (E): *Trichoglossus johnstoniae*
Johnston's Chameleon (E): *Chamaeleo johnstoni*
Joker's Boomerang Coral (E): *Polyphyllia talpina*
Jordan's Girdled Lizard (E): *Cordylus jordani*
Jorobada (S): *Megaptera novaeangliae*
Josephine's Lorikeet (E): *Charmosyna josefinae*
Josephine's Lory (E): *Charmosyna josefinae*
Jote real (S): *Sarcoramphus papa*
Joues-oranges (F): *Estrilda melpoda*
Juan Fernández Firecrown (E): *Sephanoides fernandensis*
Juan Fernández Fur Seal (E): *Arctocephalus philippii*
Jubarte (F): *Megaptera novaeangliae*
Jubula lettii : (E) Maned Owl, (S) Búho de Crin, Búho de Guinea, (F) Duc à crinière, Hibou à bec jaune, **II** STRIGIDAE Av
Jullien's Golden Carp (E): *Probarbus jullieni*
Jungle Boobook (E): *Ninox theomacha*
Jungle Cat (E): *Felis chaus*
Jungle Hawk-Owl (E): *Ninox theomacha*
Jungle Owlet (E): *Glaucidium radiatum*

Kachuga à cou rayé (F): *Kachuga dhongoka*
Kachuga à dos en toit (F): *Kachuga tecta*
Kachuga à front rouge (F): *Kachuga kachuga*
Kachuga carénée (F): *Kachuga tentoria*
Kachuga de l'Assam (F): *Kachuga sylhetensis*
Kachuga de Smith (F): *Kachuga smithii*
Kachuga spp.: (E) Roofed turtles, (S) Galápagos cubiertos, (F) Kachugas, **I/II** EMYDIDAE Re
Kachuga dhongoka : (E) Dhongoka Roof Turtle, Three-striped Roofed Turtle, (F) Kachuga à cou rayé, **II** EMYDIDAE Re
Kachuga fusca = Kachuga kachuga/ Kachuga trivittata
Kachuga hardwickii = Kachuga dhongoka
Kachuga intermedia = Kachuga tentoria
Kachuga kachuga : (E) Bengal Roof Turtle, Red-crowned Roofed Turtle, Sail Terrapin, (F) Kachuga à front rouge, **II** EMYDIDAE Re
Kachuga lineata = Kachuga kachuga
Kachuga peguensis = Kachuga trivittata
Kachuga smithii : (E) Brown River Turtle, Brown Roofed Turtle, (F) Kachuga de Smith, **II** EMYDIDAE Re
Kachuga sylhetensis : (E) Assam Roofed Turtle, Sylhet Roofed Turtle, (F) Kachuga de l'Assam, **II** EMYDIDAE Re

Kachuga tecta : (E) Dura Turtle, Indian Pond Turtle, Indian Sawback Turtle, Tent Turtle, (S) Galápago cubierto de la India, Tortuga india de visera, (F) Émyde tricarénée, Kachuga à dos en toit, **I** EMYDIDAE Re
Kachuga tentoria : (E) Indian Roofed Turtle, Indian Tent Turtle, (F) Kachuga carénée, **II** EMYDIDAE Re
Kachuga trilineata = Kachuga trivittata
Kachuga trivittata : (E) Burmese Roofed Turtle **II** EMYDIDAE Re
Kagou (F): *Rhynochetos jubatus*
Kagou huppé (F): *Rhynochetos jubatus*
Kagu (E): *Rhynochetos jubatus*
Kagú (S): *Rhynochetos jubatus*
Kaiserihind (E): *Teinopalpus imperialis*
Kaiserihinds (E): *Teinopalpus* spp.
Kaka (E/S): *Nestor meridionalis*
Kakapo (E/S/F): *Strigops habroptilus*
Kaluga (E): *Huso dauricus*
Kangourou-rat à queue touffue (F): *Bettongia penicillata*
Kangourou-rat de Lesueur (F): *Bettongia lesueur*
Kangourou-rat de Tasmanie (F): *Bettongia gaimardi*
Kangourou-rat du désert (F): *Caloprymnus campestris*
Kangourou-rats (F): *Bettongia* spp.
Kara Tau Argali (E): *Ovis ammon nigrimontana*
Karoo Bustard (E): *Eupodotis vigorsii*
Karoo Cape Tortoise (E): *Homopus femoralis*
Karoo Girdled Lizard (E): *Cordylus polyzonus*
Karoo Korhaan (E): *Eupodotis vigorsii*
Karoo Padloper (E): *Homopus boulengeri*
Karumbé (S): *Geochelone carbonaria*
Kashmir Deer (E): *Cervus elaphus hanglu*
Kashmir Red Deer (E): *Cervus elaphus hanglu*
Kashmir Stag (E): *Cervus elaphus hanglu*
Kaupifalco monogrammicus : (E) Lizard Buzzard, (S) Busardo gavilán, (F) Autour unibande, **II** ACCIPITRIDAE Av
Kawall's Amazon (E): *Amazona kawalli*
Kawall's Parrot (E): *Amazona kawalli*
Kea (E/S/F): *Nestor notabilis*
Keel-backed Turtle (E): *Pyxidea mouhotii*
Keel-billed Toucan (E): *Ramphastos sulfuratus*
Keeled Box Turtle (E): *Pyxidea mouhotii*
Keeled-scaled Python (E): *Morelia carinata*
Kelesa (E): *Scleropages formosus*
Kellog's Seahorse (E): *Hippocampus kelloggi*
Kemp's Ridley (E): *Lepidochelys kempi*
Kenyan Sand Boa (E): *Gongylophis colubrinus*
Kerguelen Fur Seal (E): *Arctocephalus gazella*
Kestrel (E): *Falco tinnunculus*
Kétoupa brun (F): *Ketupa zeylonensis*
Kétoupa de Blakiston (F): *Ketupa blakistoni*
Kétoupa malais (F): *Ketupa ketupu*
Kétoupa roux (F): *Ketupa flavipes*
Ketupa blakistoni : (E) Blakiston's Fish-Owl, (S) Búho Manchú, (F) Grand-duc de Blakiston, Kétoupa de Blakiston, **II** STRIGIDAE Av
Ketupa flavipes : (E) Tawny Fish-Owl, (S) Búho pescador, Búho pescador leonado, (F) Hibou pêcheur roux, Kétoupa roux, **II** STRIGIDAE Av
Ketupa ketupu : (E) Buffy Fish-Owl, Malay Fish-Owl, (S) Búho pescador Malayo, (F) Kétoupa malais, **II** STRIGIDAE Av
Ketupa zeylonensis : (E) Brown Fish Owl, Brown Fish-Owl, (S) Búho pescador de Ceilán, (F) Kétoupa brun, **II** STRIGIDAE Av
Khur (E/S): *Equus onager khur*
Kiang (E/S/F): *Equus kiang*
Killer Whale (E): *Orcinus orca*
Kinabalu Serpent-Eagle (E): *Spilornis kinabaluensis*
King Bird-of-paradise (E): *Cicinnurus regius*
King Cobra (E): *Ophiophagus hannah*
King Colobus (E): *Colobus polykomos*
King Vulture (E): *Sarcoramphus papa*

King-of-Saxony Bird-of-paradise (E): *Pteridophora alberti*

King's Monitor (E): *Varanus kingorum*

Kinixys belliana : (E) Bell's Hinged Tortoise, Bell's Hinged-backed Tortoise, (F) Kinixys de Bell **II** TESTUDINIDAE Re

Kinixys belliana ssp. *natalensis = Kinixys natalensis*

Kinixys de Bell (F): *Kinixys belliana*

Kinixys de Home (F): *Kinixys homeana*

Kinixys du Natal (F): *Kinixys natalensis*

Kinixys erosa : (E) Common Tortoise, Forest Hinged Tortoise, Schweigger's Tortoise, Serrated Hinge-back Tortoise, Serrated Hinge-backed Tortoise, Serrated Tortoise, (F) Kinixys rongée, Tortue articulée d'Afrique **II** TESTUDINIDAE Re

Kinixys homeana : (E) Home's Hinge-back Tortoise, Home's Hinged Tortoise, Home's Hinged-backed Tortoise, (F) Kinixys de Home **II** TESTUDINIDAE Re

Kinixys lobatsiana = Kinixys belliana

Kinixys natalensis : (E) Natal Hinge-back Tortoise, Natal Hinge-backed Tortoise, Natal Hinged Tortoise, (F) Kinixys du Natal **II** TESTUDINIDAE Re

Kinixys rongée (F): *Kinixys erosa*

Kinixys spekii = Kinixys belliana

Kinkajou (E): *Potos flavus*

Kionotrochus suteri : **II** TURBINOLIIDAE An

Kirk's Colobus (E): *Procolobus pennantii kirkii*

Kirk's Red Colobus (E): *Procolobus pennantii kirkii*

Klais guimeti : (E) Violet-headed Hummingbird, (S) Colibrí cabeciazul, Colibrí cabecivioleta, Tucusito cabeza azul, (F) Colibri à tête violette, **II** TROCHILIDAE Av

Kleinmann's Tortoise (E): *Testudo kleinmanni*

Klemmer's Day Gecko (E): *Phelsuma klemmeri*

Kloss's Gibbon (E): *Hylobates klossii*

Knob corals (E): *Cyphastrea spp./ Favia* spp.

Knobbed Hornbill (E): *Aceros cassidix*

Knob-billed Goose (E): *Sarkidiornis melanotos*

Knobby Brain Coral (E): *Diploria clivosa*

Knobby Cactus Coral (E): *Mycetophyllia aliciae*

Knobby Seahorse (E): *Hippocampus breviceps*

Knobby Star Coral (E): *Solenastrea hyades*

Knysna Parrot (E): *Poicephalus robustus*

Knysna Seahorse (E): *Hippocampus capensis*

Knysna Turaco (E): *Tauraco corythaix*

Kobus leche : (E) Lechwe, (S) Cobo de Lechwe, Lechwe, (F) Cobe lechwe, Lechwe, **II** BOVIDAE Ma

Koch's Pitta (E): *Pitta kochi*

Kodkod (E): *Oncifelis guigna*

Koepcke's Hermit (E): *Phaethornis koepckeae*

Koepcke's Screech-Owl (E): *Otus koepckeae*

Kogia breviceps : (E) Pygmy Sperm Whale, (S) Cachalote cabeza chica, Cachalote pigmeo, (F) Cachalot pygmée, **II** PHYSETERIDAE Ma

Kogia simus : (E) Dwarf Sperm Whale, Owen's Pygmy Sperm Whale, (S) Cachalote enano, (F) Cachalot nain, **II** PHYSETERIDAE Ma

Kokoe Poison Frog (E): *Phyllobates aurotaenia*

Kokomo (E): *Aceros plicatus*

Komodo Dragon (E): *Varanus komodoensis*

Komodo Monitor (E): *Varanus komodoensis*

Kori Bustard (E): *Ardeotis kori*

Korrigum (F): *Damaliscus lunatus*

Kouprey (E/S/F): *Bos sauveli*

Kuhl's Hog Deer (E): *Axis kuhlii*

Kuhl's Lorikeet (E): *Vini kuhlii*

Kuhl's Tortoise (E): *Psammobates oculiferus*

Kulan (E): *Equus hemionus*

Kura sturgeon (E): *Acipenser gueldenstaedtii*

La Brea Poison Frog (E): *Dendrobates occultator*

La chimère (F): *Ornithoptera chimaera*

La Planada Poison Frog (E): *Epipedobates andinus*

La plata (F): *Lontra longicaudis*

La Plata River Dolphin (E): *Pontoporia blainvillei*

Laborioso cabecirrojo (S): *Quelea erythrops*

Labyrinthocyathus delicatus : **II** CARYOPHYLLIIDAE An

Labyrinthocyathus facetus : **II** CARYOPHYLLIIDAE An

Labyrinthocyathus langae : **II** CARYOPHYLLIIDAE An

Labyrinthocyathus limatulus : **II** CARYOPHYLLIIDAE An

Labyrinthocyathus quaylei : **II** CARYOPHYLLIIDAE An

Lace corals (E): STYLASTERIDAE spp.

Lace Monitor (E): *Varanus varius*

Lacy Lettuce Coral (E): *Leptoseris cailleti*

Ladakh Urial (E): *Ovis vignei vignei*

La-Digue Day Gecko (E): *Phelsuma sundbergi*

Lafresnaya lafresnayi : (E) Mountain Velvetbreast, (S) Colibrí aterciopelado, Colibrí terciopelo, (F) Colibri de Lafresnaye, **II** TROCHILIDAE Av

Lagarhja de las Pitiusas (S): *Podarcis pityusensis*

Lagartija balear (S): *Podarcis lilfordi*

Lagartija de las Pitiusas (S): *Podarcis pityusensis*

Lagarto cocodrilo chino (S): *Shinisaurus crocodilurus*

Lagarto de cola espinosa común (S): *Uromastyx acanthinura*

Lagarto de cola espinosa de Geyr (S): *Uromastyx geyri*

Lagarto de cola espinosa de Thomas (S): *Uromastyx thomasi*

Lagarto de cola espinosa egipcio (S): *Uromastyx aegyptia*

Lagarto de cola espinosa indo (S): *Uromastyx hardwickii*

Lagarto de cola espinosa ocelado (S): *Uromastyx ocellata*

Lagarto de Cuentas (S): *Heloderma horridum*

Lagarto gigante del Hierro (S): *Gallotia simonyi*

Lagarto negro (S): *Melanosuchus niger*

Lagartos (S): *Tupinambis* spp.

Lagartos armadillos (S): *Cordylus* spp.

Lagartos dragóns (S): *Dracaena* spp.

Lagenodelphis hosei : (E) Fraser's Dolphin, Sarawak Dolphin, (S) Delfín de Borneo, (F) Dauphin de Fraser, **II** DELPHINIDAE Ma

Lagenorhynchus acutus : (E) Atlantic White-sided Dolphin, (S) Delfín de flancos blancos, (F) Lagénorhynque à flanc blanc de l'Atlantique, **II** DELPHINIDAE Ma

Lagenorhynchus albirostris : (E) White-beaked Dolphin, (S) Delfín de pico blanco, (F) Lagénorhynque à bec blanc de l'Atlantique, **II** DELPHINIDAE Ma

Lagenorhynchus australis : (E) Blackchin Dolphin, Peale's Dolphin, (S) Delfín austral, (F) Lagénorhynque de Peale, **II** DELPHINIDAE Ma

Lagenorhynchus cruciger : (E) Hourglass Dolphin, (S) Delfín cruzado, (F) Dauphin crucigère, Lagénorhynque crucigère, **II** DELPHINIDAE Ma

Lagenorhynchus obliquidens : (E) Pacific White-sided Dolphin, (S) Delfín lagenor ringo, (F) Lagénorhynque à flanc blanc du Pacifique, **II** DELPHINIDAE Ma

Lagenorhynchus obscurus : (E) Dusky Dolphin, (S) Delfín listado, (F) Lagénorhynque sombre, **II** DELPHINIDAE Ma

Lagenorhynchus superciliosus = Lagenorhynchus obscurus

Lagénorhynque à bec blanc de l'Atlantique (F): *Lagenorhynchus albirostris*

Lagénorhynque à flanc blanc de l'Atlantique (F): *Lagenorhynchus acutus*

Lagénorhynque à flanc blanc du Pacifique (F): *Lagenorhynchus obliquidens*

Lagénorhynque crucigère (F): *Lagenorhynchus cruciger*

Lagénorhynque de Peale (F): *Lagenorhynchus australis*

Lagénorhynque sombre (F): *Lagenorhynchus obscurus*

Laggar Falcon (E): *Falco jugger*

Lagonosticta larvata ssp. *vinacea = Lagonosticta vinacea*

Lagonosticta rara : (E) Black-bellied Firefinch, Black-bellied Waxbill, (F) Amarante à ventre noir, Amarante rare **III** ESTRILDIDAE Av

Lagonosticta rubricata : (E) African Firefinch, Blue-billed Firefinch, Brown-backed Firefinch, (S) Bengalí de Lichtenstein, (F) Amarante flambé, Amarante foncé, **III** ESTRILDIDAE Av

Lagonosticta rufopicta : (E) Bar-breasted Firefinch, Bar-breasted Waxbill, (S) Bengalí de Fraser, (F) Amarante pointé, **III** ESTRILDIDAE Av

Lagonosticta senegala : (E) Red-billed Firefinch, Senegal Firefinch, (S) Bengalí senegalés, (F) Amarante commun, Amarante du Sénégal, **III** ESTRILDIDAE Av

Lagonosticta vinacea : (E) Black-faced Firefinch, Vinaceous Firefinch, Vinaceous Waxbill, (S) Bengalí carinegro, (F) Amarante masqué, Amarante vineux, **III** ESTRILDIDAE Av

Lagorchestes hirsutus : (E) Ormala, Rufous Hare-wallaby, Western Hare-wallaby, Wurrup, (S) Canguro-liebre peludo, Wallabi rojo, (F) Wallaby-lièvre de l'ouest, Wallaby-lièvre roux, **I** MACROPODIDAE Ma

Lagostrophus fasciatus : (E) Banded Hare-wallaby, Munning, (S) Canguro-liebre rayado, Wallabi rayado, (F) Wallaby-lièvre à bandes, Wallaby-lièvre rayé, **I** MACROPODIDAE Ma

Lagothriche de Humboldt (F): *Lagothrix lagotricha*

Lagothrix flavicauda : (E) Yellow-tailed Woolly Monkey, (F) Singe laineux à queue jaune **I** CEBIDAE Ma

Lagothrix hendeei = Lagothrix flavicauda

Lagothrix lagotricha : (E) Common Woolly Monkey, Humboldt's Woolly Monkey, (F) Lagothriche de Humboldt, Singe laineux **II** CEBIDAE Ma

Lake Patzcuaro Salamander (E): *Ambystoma dumerilii*

Lake Sturgeon (E): *Acipenser fulvescens*

Lama guanicoe : (E) Guanaco, (S) Guanaco, (F) Guanaco, **II** CAMELIDAE Ma

Lamantin d'Afrique (F): *Trichechus senegalensis*

Lamantin d'Amérique du Nord (F): *Trichechus manatus*

Lamantin d'Amérique du Sud (F): *Trichechus inunguis*

Lamantin de l'Amazone (F): *Trichechus inunguis*

Lamantin des Antilles (F): *Trichechus manatus*

Lamantin des Caraïbes (F): *Trichechus manatus*

Lamantin du Sénégal (F): *Trichechus senegalensis*

Lamantin ouest-africain (F): *Trichechus senegalensis*

Lamantino amazónico (S): *Trichechus inunguis*

Lamantino norteamericana (S): *Trichechus manatus*

Lamarck's Sheet Coral (E): *Agaricia lamarcki*

Lambis (F): *Strombus gigas*

Lamie (F): *Carcharodon carcharias*

Lammergeier (E): *Gypaetus barbatus*

Lampornis amethystinus : (E) Amethyst-throated Hummingbird, (S) Colibrí amatistino, Colibrí-serrano gorjiamatisto, (F) Colibri à gorge améthyste, **II** TROCHILIDAE Av

Lampornis calolaema = Lampornis castaneoventris

Lampornis castaneoventris : (E) Purple-throated Mountain-gem, Variable Mountain-gem, White-throated Mountain-gem, (S) Colibrí variable, (F) Colibri à ventre châtain, **II** TROCHILIDAE Av

Lampornis cinereicauda = Lampornis castaneoventris

Lampornis clemenciae : (E) Blue-throated Hummingbird, (S) Colibrí gorgiazul, Colibrí-serrano gorjiazul, (F) Colibri à gorge bleue, **II** TROCHILIDAE Av

Lampornis hemileucus : (E) White-bellied Mountain-gem, (S) Colibrí gorgivioleta, (F) Colibri à gorge lilas, **II** TROCHILIDAE Av

Lampornis sybillae : (E) Green-breasted Mountain-gem, (S) Colibrí de Sibila, Colibrí-serrano pechiverde, (F) Colibri de Sybil, **II** TROCHILIDAE Av

Lampornis viridipallens : (E) Green-throated Mountain-gem, (S) Colibrí gorgiescamoso, Colibrí-serrano gorjiverde, (F) Colibri vert-d'eau, **II** TROCHILIDAE Av

Lampornis viripallens ssp. *sybillae = Lampornis sybillae*

Lampribis rara = Bostrychia rara

Lamprolaima rhami : (E) Garnet-throated Hummingbird, (S) Colibrí alicastaño, (F) Colibri à gorge grenat, **II** TROCHILIDAE Av

Lampsilis higginsii : (E) Higgins Eye, Higgins' Eye Pearly Mussel **I** UNIONIDAE Bi

Lampsilis orbiculata orbiculata : (E) Pinkmucket **I** UNIONIDAE Bi

Lampsilis satur : (E) Plain Pocketbook Pearly Mussel, Sandbank Pocketbook **I** UNIONIDAE Bi

Lampsilis tampicoensis ssp. *tecomatensis = Unio tampicoensis* ssp. *tecomatensis*

Lampsilis virescens : (E) Alabama Lamp Pearly Mussel, Alabama Lampmussel **I** UNIONIDAE Bi

Land iguanas (E): *Conolophus* spp.

Lang's Crag Lizard (E): *Cordylus langi*

Lang's Girdled Lizard (E): *Cordylus langi*

Langur à capuchon (F): *Trachypithecus pileatus*

Langur à queue de cochon (F): *Nasalis concolor*

Langur capuchino (S): *Trachypithecus pileatus*

Langur chato (S): *Pygathrix roxellana*

Langur colilargo (S): *Presbytis potenziani*

Langur común (S): *Semnopithecus entellus*

Langur crestado (S): *Trachypithecus cristatus*

Langur de capa (S): *Trachypithecus pileatus*

Langur de cara roja (S): *Trachypithecus vetulus*

Langur de cresta (S): *Presbytis melalophos*

Langur de François (F): *Trachypithecus francoisi*

Langur de Francois (S): *Trachypithecus francoisi*

Langur de frente blanca (S): *Presbytis frontata*

Langur de Hose (S): *Presbytis hosei*

Langur de Mentawi (S): *Presbytis potenziani*

Langur de Nilgiri (S): *Trachypithecus johnii*

Langur de Thomas (S): *Presbytis thomasi*

Langur des îles Mentawi (F): *Nasalis concolor*

Langur dorado (S): *Trachypithecus geei*

Langur doré (F): *Trachypithecus geei*

Langur douc (S): *Pygathrix nemaeus*

Langur du Nilgiri (F): *Trachypithecus johnii*

Langur gris (S): *Presbytis comata*

Langur hanuman (S): *Semnopithecus entellus*

Langur mitrado (S): *Presbytis femoralis*

Langur obscuro (S): *Trachypithecus obscurus*

Langur rabicerdo (S): *Nasalis concolor*

Langur rubicundo (S): *Presbytis rubicunda*

Lanner (E): *Falco biarmicus*

Lanner Falcon (E): *Falco biarmicus*

Lapa azul (S): *Ara macao*

Lapin de Diaz (F): *Romerolagus diazi*

Lapin de l'Assam (F): *Caprolagus hispidus*

Lapin des volcans (F): *Romerolagus diazi*

Lapland Owl (E): *Strix nebulosa*

Lapp Owl (E): *Strix nebulosa*

Lappet-faced Vulture (E): *Torgos tracheliotus*

Lar Gibbon (E): *Hylobates lar*

Large Amu-Dar Shovelnose Sturgeon (E): *Pseudoscaphirhynchus kaufmanni*

Large Desert Marsupial-Mouse (E): *Sminthopsis psammophila*

Large Fig-Parrot (E): *Psittaculirostris desmarestii*

Large Flower Coral (E): *Mussa angulosa*

Large Flying-fox (E): *Pteropus vampyrus*

Large Hippo (E): *Hippopotamus amphibius*

Large Indian Civet (E): *Viverra zibetha*

Large Iron-grey Dwarf Lemur (E): *Cheirogaleus ravus*

Large Palau Flying-fox (E): *Pteropus pilosus*

Large Treeshrew (E): *Tupaia tana*

Large-blotched Python (E): *Antaresia stimsoni*

Large-eared Flying-fox (E): *Pteropus macrotis*

Large-Eared Greater Galago (E): *Otolemur crassicaudatus*

Larger star corals (E): *Favites* spp.

Large-scaled Girdled Lizard (E): *Cordylus macropholis*

Larus relictus : (E) Relict Gull, (S) Gaviota de Mongolia, Gaviota relicta, (F) Goéland de Mongolie, Goéland relique, Mouette relique, **I** LARIDAE Av

Lasiorhinus barnardi = Lasiorhinus krefftii

Lasiorhinus gillespiei = Lasiorhinus krefftii

Lasiorhinus krefftii : (E) Northern Hairy-nosed Wombat, Queensland Hairy-nosed Wombat, (S) Oso marsupial del Río Moonie, Vombat de Queensland, (F) Wombat à nez poilu de Queensland, **I** VOMBATIDAE Ma

Lathamus discolor : (E) Swift Parrot, (S) Periquito migrador, (F) Perruche de Latham, **II** PSITTACIDAE Av

Latimeria (E): *Latimeria chalumnae*

Latimeria spp.:, (F) Coelacanthes **I** LATIMERIIDAE Sa

Latimeria chalumnae : (E) Coelacanth, Gombessa, Latimeria, Old four legs, (S) Celecanto, (F) Coelacanthe, **I** LATIMERIIDAE Sa

Latimeria menadoensis : (E) Menado Coelacanth **I** LATIMERIIDAE Sa

Laughing Dove (E): *Streptopelia senegalensis*

Laughing Falcon (E): *Herpetotheres cachinnans*

Laughing Owl (E): *Sceloglaux albifacies*

Lavender Firefinch (E): *Estrilda caerulescens*

Lavender Waxbill (E): *Estrilda caerulescens*

Lawes's Parotia (E): *Parotia lawesii*

Lawrence's Girdled Lizard (E): *Cordylus lawrenci*

Layard's Beaked Whale (E): *Mesoplodon layardii*

Layard's Black-headed Weaver (E): *Ploceus cucullatus*

Layard's Parakeet (E): *Psittacula calthropae*

Laysan Duck (E): *Anas laysanensis*

Laysan Teal (E): *Anas laysanensis*

Lazuline Sabrewing (E): *Campylopterus falcatus*

Leadbeater's Cockatoo (E): *Cacatua leadbeateri*

Leaf chameleons (E): *Brookesia* spp.

Leaf Coral (E): *Agaricia agaricites/ Montipora foliosa/ Pavona cactus*

Leaf corals (E): *Pavona* spp.

Lear's Macaw (E): *Anodorhynchus leari*

Least Flying-fox (E): *Pteropus woodfordi*

Least Fruit Bat (E): *Pteropus woodfordi*

Least Pygmy-Owl (E): *Glaucidium minutissimum*

Leatherback (E): *Dermochelys coriacea*

Leathery Turtle (E): *Dermochelys coriacea*

Lechucita acanelada (S): *Aegolius harrisii*

Lechucita común (S): *Otus choliba*

Lechucita común (S): *Speotyto cunicularia*

Lechucita de las viscacheras (S): *Speotyto cunicularia*

Lechucita rojiza (S): *Otus atricapillus*

Lechuza Australiana (S): *Tyto novaehollandiae*

Lechuza bataraz (S): *Strix rufipes*

Lechuza baya de Madagascar (S): *Phodilus badius*

Lechuza blanquinegra (S): *Strix nigrolineata*

Lechuza campestre (S): *Asio flammeus*

Lechuza colilarga (S): *Strix albitarsus*

Lechuza colilarga (S): *Strix virgata*

Lechuza Común (S): *Tyto alba*

Lechuza copetona (S): *Lophostrix cristata*

Lechuza cornuda (S): *Phodilus badius*

Lechuza de campanario (S): *Tyto alba*

Lechuza de Célebes (S): *Tyto rosenbergii*

Lechuza de El Cabo (S): *Tyto capensis*

Lechuza de la Española (S): *Tyto glaucops*

Lechuza de la Manus (S): *Tyto manusi*

Lechuza de la Taliabu (S): *Tyto nigrobrunnea*

Lechuza de las Tanimbar (S): *Tyto sororcula*

Lechuza de Madagascar (S): *Tyto soumagnei*

Lechuza de Minahassa (S): *Tyto inexspectata*

Lechuza de Tengmalm (S): *Aegolius funereus*

Lechuza del Congo (S): *Phodilus prigoginei*

Lechuza dorada (S): *Tyto aurantia*

Lechuza estigia (S): *Asio stygius*

Lechuza gavilana (S): *Surnia ulula*

Lechuza gavilana de las Molucas (S): *Ninox squamipila*

Lechuza gavilana de Norfolk (S): *Ninox novaeseelandiae undulata*

Lechuza listada (S): *Asio clamator*

Lechuza listada (S): *Strix hylophila*

Lechuza Malgache (S): *Tyto soumagnei*

Lechuza mora (S): *Asio capensis*

Lechuza moteada (S): *Tyto multipunctata*

Lechuza negra (S): *Strix huhula*

Lechuza orejicorta (S): *Asio flammeus*

Lechuza orejita de Madagascar (S): *Asio madagascariensis*

Lechuza patiblanca (S): *Strix albitarsus*

Lechuza patilarga (S): *Tyto longimembris*

Lechuza pescadora (S): *Scotopelia peli*

Lechuza tenebrosa (S): *Tyto tenebricosa*

Lechuzas (S): STRIGIFORMES spp. Av

Lechuzón (S): *Asio clamator*

Lechuzón acollarado chico (S): *Pulsatrix koeniswaldiana*

Lechuzón acollarado grande (S): *Pulsatrix melanota*

Lechuzón anteojo (S): *Pulsatrix perspicillata*

Lechuzón anteojo menor (S): *Pulsatrix koeniswaldiana*

Lechuzón campestre (S): *Asio flammeus*

Lechuzón cariblanco (S): *Sceloglaux albifacies*

Lechuzón de Anteojos (S): *Pulsatrix perspicillata*

Lechuzón de Woodford (S): *Strix woodfordii*

Lechuzón negruzco (S): *Asio stygius*

Lechuzón orejas largas (S): *Asio clamator*

Lechuzón orejudo (S): *Asio clamator*

Lechuzón orejudo (S): *Bubo virginianus*

Lechuzón pardo menor (S): *Pulsatrix koeniswaldiana*

Lechwe (E): *Kobus leche*

Lehmann's Poison Frog (E): *Dendrobates lehmanni*

Leiopathes acanthophora : **II** LEIOPATHIDAE An

Leiopathes bullosa : **II** LEIOPATHIDAE An

Leiopathes expansa : **II** LEIOPATHIDAE An

Leiopathes glaberrima : (E) Smooth Black Coral **II** LEIOPATHIDAE An

Leiopathes grimaldii : **II** LEIOPATHIDAE An

Leiopathes secunda : **II** LEIOPATHIDAE An

Leiopython albertisii : (E) D'Albert's Python, White-lipped Python, (S) Pitón de Albert, (F) Python à lèvres blanches, Python de Nouvelle-Guinée, **II** PYTHONIDAE Re

Léiothrix à joues argent (F): *Leiothrix argentauris*

Leiothrix argentauris : (E) Silver-eared Mesia, (S) Mesía, (F) Léiothrix à joues argent, Mésia , **II** MUSCICAPIDAE Av

Léiothrix jaune (F): *Leiothrix lutea*

Leiothrix lutea : (E) Red-billed Leiothrix, Red-billed Mesia, (S) Ruiseñor del bambú, (F) Léiothrix jaune, **II** MUSCICAPIDAE Av

Leith's Tortoise (E): *Testudo kleinmanni*

Lémur à couronne (F): *Eulemur coronatus*

Lémur à ventre rouge (F): *Eulemur rubriventer*

Lemur ardilla coligrueso (S): *Cheirogaleus medius*

Lémur brun (F): *Eulemur fulvus*

Lemur cariancho (S): *Hapalemur aureus*

Lemur cariancho (S): *Hapalemur griseus*

Lemur cariancho (S): *Hapalemur simus*

Lémur catta (F): *Lemur catta*

Lemur catta : (E) Ring-tailed Lemur, (S) Lemur colianillado, (F) Lémur catta, Maki catta, **I** LEMURIDAE Ma

Lemur colianillado (S): *Lemur catta*

Lemur comadreja de Ambanja (S): *Lepilemur dorsalis*

Lemur comadreja de dientes pequeños (S): *Lepilemur microdon*

Lemur comadreja de Edwards (S): *Lepilemur edwardsi*

Lemur comadreja de pies blancos (S): *Lepilemur leucopus*

Lemur comadreja septentrional (S): *Lepilemur septentrionalis*

Lemur coronado (S): *Eulemur coronatus*

Lemur coronatus = Eulemur coronatus

Lemur de collar (S): *Varecia variegata*

Lemur de Gola (S): *Varecia variegata*

Lemur de Gorguera (S): *Varecia variegata*

Lemur de vientre rojo (S): *Eulemur rubriventer*

Lemur enano coligrueso (S): *Cheirogaleus medius*

Lemur enano mayor (S): *Cheirogaleus major*

Lemur fulvus = Eulemur fulvus

Lemur leonado (S): *Eulemur fulvus*

Checklist of fauna/Lista de especies de fauna/Liste des espèces animales

Lémur macaco (F): *Eulemur macaco*
Lemur macaco = Eulemur macaco
Lemur mangosta (S): *Eulemur mongoz*
Lémur mongoz (F): *Eulemur mongoz*
Lemur mongoz = Eulemur mongoz
Lemur negro (S): *Eulemur macaco*
Lémur noir (F): *Eulemur macaco*
Lemur orejipeludo (S): *Allocebus trichotis*
Lemur rubriventer = Eulemur rubriventer
Lémur vari (F): *Varecia variegata*
Lemur variegatus = Varecia variegata
Lemures (S): LEMURIDAE spp.
LEMURIDAE spp.: (E) Lemurs, (S) Lemures, (F) Lémuriens, Lémurs **I** Ma
Lémuriens (F): LEMURIDAE spp.
Lemurine Night Monkey (E): *Aotus lemurinus*
Lemurs (E): LEMURIDAE spp.
Lémurs (F): LEMURIDAE spp.
Lemurs comadreja (S): MEGALADAPIDAE spp.
León (S): *Panthera leo*
León americano (S): *Puma concolor*
León asiático (S): *Panthera leo persica*
León bayo (S): *Puma concolor*
León brenero (S): *Herpailurus yaguarondi*
León costarricense (S): *Puma concolor costaricensis*
León de Florida (S): *Puma concolor coryi*
León indostánico (S): *Panthera leo persica*
Leoncillo (S): *Herpailurus yaguarondi*
Leontideus caissara = Leontopithecus caissara
Leontideus chrysomela = Leontopithecus chrysomela
Leontideus chrysopygus = Leontopithecus chrysopygus
Leontideus rosalia = Leontopithecus rosalia
Leontopithecus caissara : (E) Black-faced Lion Tamarin **I** CALLITRICHIDAE Ma
Leontopithecus chrysomela : (E) Golden-headed Lion Tamarin, (S) Tamarino león de cabeza dorada **I** CALLITRICHIDAE Ma
Leontopithecus chrysopygus : (E) Black Lion Tamarin, Golden-rumped Lion Tamarin **I** CALLITRICHIDAE Ma
Leontopithecus rosalia : (E) Golden Lion Tamarin, (F) Singe-lion, Tamarin soyeux **I** CALLITRICHIDAE Ma
Leontopithecus rosalia ssp. *caissara = Leontopithecus caissara*
Leontopithecus rosalia ssp. *chrysomela = Leontopithecus chrysomela*
Leontopithecus rosalia ssp. *chrysopygus = Leontopithecus chrysopygus*
Leontopithecus rosalia ssp. *rosalia = Leontopithecus rosalia*
Leopard (E): *Panthera pardus*
Léopard (F): *Panthera pardus*
Leopard Cat (E): *Prionailurus bengalensis*
Léopard des neiges (F): *Uncia uncia*
Leopard Dwarf Boa (E): *Tropidophis pardalis*
Leopard Tortoise (E): *Geochelone pardalis*
Leopardo (S): *Panthera pardus*
Leopardo de las nieves (S): *Uncia uncia*
Leopardo nival (S): *Uncia uncia*
Leopardus pardalis : (E) Ocelot, (S) Gato onza, Manigordo, Ocelote, (F) Ocelot, **I** FELIDAE Ma
Leopardus tigrinus : (E) Little Spotted Cat, Oncilla, Tiger Cat, (S) Caucel, Gato atigrado, Gato tigre, Gato tigrillo, Tigrillo, Tirica, (F) Chat-tacheté, Chat-tigre, Oncille, **I** FELIDAE Ma
Leopardus wiedii : (E) Margay, Tree Ocelot, (S) Caucel, Gato montés, Margay, Tigrillo, (F) Margay, **I** FELIDAE Ma
Lépidochelyde de Kemp (F): *Lepidochelys kempi*
Lepidochelys kempi : (E) Atlantic Ridley, Gulf Ridley, Kemp's Ridley, Mexican Ridley, (S) Cotorra, Tortuga iora, Tortuga marina bastarda, (F) Lépidochelyde de Kemp, Ridley de Kemp, Tortue de Kemp, **I** CHELONIIDAE Re

Lepidochelys olivacea : (E) Olive Ridley, Pacific Ridley, (S) Tortuga golfina, Tortuga olivacea, (F) Ridley du Pacifique, Tortue bâtarde, Tortue de Ridley, Tortue olivâtre, **I** CHELONIIDAE Re
Lepidopora acrolophos : **II** STYLASTERIDAE Hy
Lepidopora biserialis : **II** STYLASTERIDAE Hy
Lepidopora carinata : **II** STYLASTERIDAE Hy
Lepidopora clavigera : **II** STYLASTERIDAE Hy
Lepidopora concatenata : **II** STYLASTERIDAE Hy
Lepidopora cryptocymas : **II** STYLASTERIDAE Hy
Lepidopora decipiens : **II** STYLASTERIDAE Hy
Lepidopora dendrostylus : **II** STYLASTERIDAE Hy
Lepidopora diffusa : **II** STYLASTERIDAE Hy
Lepidopora eburnea : **II** STYLASTERIDAE Hy
Lepidopora glabra : **II** STYLASTERIDAE Hy
Lepidopora granulosa : **II** STYLASTERIDAE Hy
Lepidopora hicksoni = Lepidopora eburnea
Lepidopora microstylus : **II** STYLASTERIDAE Hy
Lepidopora polystichopora : **II** STYLASTERIDAE Hy
Lepidopora sarmentosa : **II** STYLASTERIDAE Hy
Lepidopora symmetrica : **II** STYLASTERIDAE Hy
Lepidopyga coeruleogularis : (E) Sapphire-throated Hummingbird, (S) Colibrí gorgizafiro, (F) Colibri faux-saphir, **II** TROCHILIDAE Av
Lepidopyga goudoti : (E) Shining-green Hummingbird, (S) Colibrí de Goudot, Tucusito pico curvo, (F) Colibri de Goudot, **II** TROCHILIDAE Av
Lepidopyga lilliae : (E) Sapphire-bellied Hummingbird, (S) Colibrí ventrizafiro, (F) Colibri de Lillian, **II** TROCHILIDAE Av
Lepidotheca altispina : **II** STYLASTERIDAE Hy
Lepidotheca brochi : **II** STYLASTERIDAE Hy
Lepidotheca cervicornis : **II** STYLASTERIDAE Hy
Lepidotheca chauliostylus : **II** STYLASTERIDAE Hy
Lepidotheca fascicularis : **II** STYLASTERIDAE Hy
Lepidotheca horrida : **II** STYLASTERIDAE Hy
Lepidotheca inconsuta : **II** STYLASTERIDAE Hy
Lepidotheca macropora : **II** STYLASTERIDAE Hy
Lepidotheca pourtalesi : **II** STYLASTERIDAE Hy
Lepidotheca ramosa : **II** STYLASTERIDAE Hy
Lepidotheca robusta : **II** STYLASTERIDAE Hy
Lepidotheca tenuistylus : **II** STYLASTERIDAE Hy
Lepilemur dorsalis : (E) Grey-backed Sportive Lemur, Nossi-bé Sportive Lemur, (S) Lemur comadreja de Ambanja **I** MEGALADAPIDAE Ma
Lepilemur edwardsi : (E) Milne-Edwards's Sportive Lemur, (S) Lemur comadreja de Edwards **I** MEGALADAPIDAE Ma
Lepilemur leucopus : (E) Dry-bush Weasel Lemur, White-footed Sportive Lemur, (S) Lemur comadreja de pies blancos **I** MEGALADAPIDAE Ma
Lepilemur microdon : (E) Light-necked Sportive Lemur, (S) Lemur comadreja de dientes pequeños **I** MEGALADAPIDAE Ma
Lepilemur mustelinus : (E) Greater Sportive Lemur, Greater Weasel Lemur, (F) Grand lépilémur **I** MEGALADAPIDAE Ma
Lepilemur mustelinus ssp. *dorsalis = Lepilemur dorsalis*
Lepilemur mustelinus ssp. *edwardsi = Lepilemur edwardsi*
Lepilemur mustelinus ssp. *leucopus = Lepilemur leucopus*
Lepilemur mustelinus ssp. *microdon = Lepilemur microdon*
Lepilemur mustelinus ssp. *ruficaudatus = Lepilemur ruficaudatus*
Lepilemur mustelinus ssp. *septentrionalis = Lepilemur septentrionalis*
Lepilemur rufescens = Lepilemur edwardsi
Lepilemur ruficaudatus : (E) Lesser Weasel Lemur, Red-tailed Sportive Lemur, (F) Petit lépilémur **I** MEGALADAPIDAE Ma
Lepilemur septentrionalis : (E) Northern Sportive Lemur, (S) Lemur comadreja septentrional **I** MEGALADAPIDAE Ma
Lépilémurs (F): MEGALADAPIDAE spp.

Leporillus conditor : (E) Greater Stick-nest Rat, House-building Rat, (S) Rata arquitecto, (F) Rat architecte, **I** MURIDAE Ma

Leptailurus serval : (E) Serval, (S) Serval, (F) Chat-tigre, Serval, **II** FELIDAE Ma

Leptastrea aequalis : **II** FAVIIDAE An

Leptastrea bewickensis : **II** FAVIIDAE An

Leptastrea bottae : **II** FAVIIDAE An

Leptastrea inaequalis : **II** FAVIIDAE An

Leptastrea pruinosa : **II** FAVIIDAE An

Leptastrea purpurea : **II** FAVIIDAE An

Leptastrea transversa : **II** FAVIIDAE An

Leptodon cayanensis : (E) Cayenne Kite, Grey-headed Kite, (S) Gavilán palomero, Milano blanquigrís, Milano cabecigris, (F) Milan de Cayenne, **II** ACCIPITRIDAE Av

Leptodon forbesi : (E) White-collared Kite, (S) Milano acollarado, (F) Milan de Forbes, **II** ACCIPITRIDAE Av

Leptopenus antarcticus : **II** MICRABACIIDAE An

Leptopenus discus : **II** MICRABACIIDAE An

Leptopenus hypocoelus : **II** MICRABACIIDAE An

Leptopenus solidus : **II** MICRABACIIDAE An

Leptopsammia britannica : **II** DENDROPHYLLIIDAE An

Leptopsammia chevalieri : **II** DENDROPHYLLIIDAE An

Leptopsammia columna : **II** DENDROPHYLLIIDAE An

Leptopsammia crassa : **II** DENDROPHYLLIIDAE An

Leptopsammia formosa : **II** DENDROPHYLLIIDAE An

Leptopsammia microcardia = Leptopsammia pruvoti

Leptopsammia poculum : **II** DENDROPHYLLIIDAE An

Leptopsammia pruvoti : **II** DENDROPHYLLIIDAE An

Leptopsammia queenslandiae : **II** DENDROPHYLLIIDAE An

Leptopsammia stokesiana : **II** DENDROPHYLLIIDAE An

Leptopsammia trinitatis : **II** DENDROPHYLLIIDAE An

Leptoptilos crumeniferus : (E) Marabou Stork, (S) Marabú, Marabú Africano, (F) Marabout, Marabout africain, Marabout d'Afrique, **III** CICONIIDAE Av

Leptoria irregularis : **II** FAVIIDAE An

Leptoria phrygia : **II** FAVIIDAE An

Leptoseris amitoriensis : **II** AGARICIIDAE An

Leptoseris cailleti : (E) Lacy Lettuce Coral **II** AGARICIIDAE An

Leptoseris cucullata = Helioseris cucullata

Leptoseris explanata : **II** AGARICIIDAE An

Leptoseris foliosa : **II** AGARICIIDAE An

Leptoseris fragilis = Leptoseris tenuis

Leptoseris gardineri : **II** AGARICIIDAE An

Leptoseris glabra = Leptoseris explanata

Leptoseris hawaiiensis : **II** AGARICIIDAE An

Leptoseris incrustans : **II** AGARICIIDAE An

Leptoseris mycetoseroides : **II** AGARICIIDAE An

Leptoseris papyracea : **II** AGARICIIDAE An

Leptoseris scabra : **II** AGARICIIDAE An

Leptoseris solida : **II** AGARICIIDAE An

Leptoseris striata : **II** AGARICIIDAE An

Leptoseris tenuis : **II** AGARICIIDAE An

Leptoseris tubulifera : **II** AGARICIIDAE An

Leptoseris yabei : **II** AGARICIIDAE An

Leptosittaca branickii : (E) Golden-plumed Conure, Golden-plumed Parakeet, (S) Aratinga de pinceles, (F) Conure à pinceaux d'or, Perruche de Branicki, **II** PSITTACIDAE Av

Lesbia nuna : (E) Green-tailed Trainbearer, (S) Colacinta coliverde, Colibrí colilargo menor, Colibrí coludo verde, (F) Porte-traîne nouna, **II** TROCHILIDAE Av

Lesbia victoriae : (E) Black-tailed Trainbearer, (S) Colacinta colinegra, Colibrí colilargo mayor, (F) Porte-traîne lesbie, **II** TROCHILIDAE Av

Lesser Antillean Iguana (E): *Iguana delicatissima*

Lesser Beaked Whale (E): *Mesoplodon peruvianus*

Lesser Bilby (E): *Macrotis leucura*

Lesser Bird-of-paradise (E): *Paradisaea minor*

Lesser Black-Hawk (E): *Buteogallus anthracinus*

Lesser Bushbaby (E): *Galago senegalensis*

Lesser Collared Forest-Falcon (E): *Micrastur buckleyi*

Lesser Eagle-Owl (E): *Mimizuku gurneyi*

Lesser Fish-eagle (E): *Ichthyophaga humilis*

Lesser Fishing Eagle (E): *Ichthyophaga humilis*

Lesser Flamingo (E): *Phoenicopterus minor*

Lesser Florican (E): *Eupodotis indica*

Lesser Flying-fox (E): *Pteropus mahaganus*

Lesser Galago (E): *Galago senegalensis*

Lesser Horn Coral (E): *Premocyathus cornuformis*

Lesser Iron-grey Dwarf Lemur (E): *Cheirogaleus minusculus*

Lesser Kestrel (E): *Falco naumanni*

Lesser knob corals (E): *Cyphastrea spp.*

Lesser Mascarene Flying-fox (E): *Pteropus subniger*

Lesser Masked-Owl (E): *Tyto sororcula*

Lesser Melampitta (E): *Melampitta lugubris*

Lesser Mouse-lemur (E): *Microcebus murinus*

Lesser Needle-clawed Galago (E): *Galago matschiei*

Lesser Panda (E): *Ailurus fulgens*

Lesser Rabbit-eared Bandicoot (E): *Macrotis leucura*

Lesser Rhea (E): *Rhea pennata*

Lesser Rorqual (E): *Balaenoptera acutorostrata*

Lesser Rufous Bristlebird (E): *Dasyornis broadbenti litoralis*

Lesser Slow Loris (E): *Nycticebus pygmaeus*

Lesser Sooty-Owl (E): *Tyto multipunctata*

Lesser Speckled Cup Coral (E): *Colangia immersa*

Lesser Spectral Tarsier (E): *Tarsius pumilus*

Lesser Spot-nosed Guenon (E): *Cercopithecus petaurista*

Lesser Spotted Eagle (E): *Aquila pomarina*

Lesser Starlet Coral (E): *Siderastrea radians*

Lesser Sulphur-crested Cockatoo (E): *Cacatua sulphurea*

Lesser Sunda Flying-fox (E): *Acerodon mackloti*

Lesser Sunda Scops-Owl (E): *Otus silvicola*

Lesser Treeshrew (E): *Tupaia minor*

Lesser Weasel Lemur (E): *Lepilemur ruficaudatus*

Lesser White-nosed Guenon (E): *Cercopithecus petaurista*

Lesser White-nosed Monkey (E): *Cercopithecus petaurista*

Lesser Yellow-headed Vulture (E): *Cathartes burrovianus*

Lesueur's Rat Kangaroo (E): *Bettongia lesueur*

Letepsammia fissilis : **II** MICRABACIIDAE An

Letepsammia formosissima : **II** MICRABACIIDAE An

Letepsammia franki : **II** MICRABACIIDAE An

Letepsammia superstes : **II** MICRABACIIDAE An

Letter-winged Kite (E): *Elanus scriptus*

Lettuce Coral (E): *Agaricia agaricites*

Lettuce corals (E): *Pectinia* spp.

Leucippus baeri : (E) Tumbes Hummingbird, (S) Colibrí de Tumbes, (F) Colibri de Tumbes, **II** TROCHILIDAE Av

Leucippus chionogaster : (E) White-bellied Hummingbird, (S) Colibrí ventriníveo, Picaflor ventriblanco, (F) Ariane à ventre blanc, **II** TROCHILIDAE Av

Leucippus chlorocercus : (E) Olive-spotted Hummingbird, (S) Colibrí blancioliva, Colibrí olivipunteado, (F) Colibri à queue verte, **II** TROCHILIDAE Av

Leucippus fallax : (E) Buffy Hummingbird, (S) Colibrí ante, Colibrí anteado, (F) Colibri trompeur, **II** TROCHILIDAE Av

Leucippus hypostictus : (E) Many-spotted Hummingbird, (S) Colibrí moteado, Colibrí multipunteado, (F) Colibri grivelé, **II** TROCHILIDAE Av

Leucippus taczanowskii : (E) Spot-throated Hummingbird, (S) Colibrí de Taczanowski, (F) Colibri de Taczanowski, **II** TROCHILIDAE Av

Leucippus viridicauda : (E) Green-and-white Hummingbird, (S) Colibrí blanquiverde, (F) Ariane du Pérou, **II** TROCHILIDAE Av

Leucocephalon yuwonoi : (E) Sulawesi Forest Turtle, (F) Géoémyde de Célèbes, **II** EMYDIDAE Re

Leucochloris albicollis : (E) White-throated Hummingbird, (S) Colibrí gargantilla, Picaflor cuelliblanco, (F) Colibri à gorge blanche, **II** TROCHILIDAE Av

Leucogéranne (F): *Grus leucogeranus*
Leucopleurus acutus = Lagenorhynchus acutus
Leucopsar rothschildi : (E) Bali Myna, Bali Starling, Rothschild's Myna, Rothschild's Starling, White Starling, (S) Estornino de Rothschild, Miná de Rothschild, (F) Étourneau de Rothschild, Mainate , Mainate de Rothschild, Martin de Rothschild, Sansonnet de Rothschild, **I** STURNIDAE Av
Leucopternis albicollis : (E) White Hawk, (S) Aguilila blanca, Busardo blanco, Gavilán blanco, (F) Buse blanche, **II** ACCIPITRIDAE Av
Leucopternis kuhli : (E) White-browed Hawk, (S) Busardo cejiblanco, (F) Buse à sourcils blancs, **II** ACCIPITRIDAE Av
Leucopternis lacernulata : (E) White-necked Hawk, (S) Busardo cuelliblanco, (F) Buse lacernulée, **II** ACCIPITRIDAE Av
Leucopternis melanops : (E) Black-faced Hawk, Masked Hawk, (S) Busardo carinegro, Gavilán carinegro, (F) Buse à face noire, **II** ACCIPITRIDAE Av
Leucopternis occidentalis : (E) Grey-backed Hawk, (S) Busardo dorsi, Busardo dorsigrís, Gavilán dorsigris, (F) Buse à dos gris, **II** ACCIPITRIDAE Av
Leucopternis plumbea : (E) Plumbeous Hawk, (S) Busardo plomizo, Gavilán plomizo, (F) Buse plombée, **II** ACCIPITRIDAE Av
Leucopternis polionota : (E) Mantled Hawk, (S) Aguila blanca, Busardo blanquinegro, (F) Buse mantelée, **II** ACCIPITRIDAE Av
Leucopternis princeps : (E) Barred Hawk, Black-chested Hawk, (S) Busardo azoreño, Gavilán principe, (F) Buse barrée, **II** ACCIPITRIDAE Av
Leucopternis schistacea : (E) Slate-colored Hawk, (S) Busardo pizarroso, Gavilán azul, Gavilán pizarroso, (F) Buse ardoisée, **II** ACCIPITRIDAE Av
Leucopternis semiplumbea : (E) Semiplumbeous Hawk, (S) Busardo semiplomizo, Gavilán semiplomizo, (F) Buse semiplombée, **II** ACCIPITRIDAE Av
Levaillant's Parrot (E): *Poicephalus robustus*
Levant Sparrowhawk (E): *Accipiter brevipes*
Leyte Pond Turtle (E): *Heosemys leytensis*
Lézard à ceinture épineuse (F): *Cordylus spinosus*
Lézard à fausse ceinture de Lang (F): *Cordylus langi*
Lézard à fausse ceinture des rochers (F): *Cordylus microlepidotus*
Lézard à fausse ceinture du Cap (F): *Cordylus capensis*
Lézard à queue épineuse à larges écailles (F): *Cordylus macropholis*
Lézard à queue épineuse à pustules (F): *Cordylus pustulatus*
Lézard à queue épineuse à taches bleues (F): *Cordylus coeruleopunctatus*
Lézard à queue épineuse africain (F): *Cordylus polyzonus*
Lézard à queue épineuse commun (F): *Cordylus cordylus*
Lézard à queue épineuse d'Armadillo (F): *Cordylus cataphractus*
Lézard à queue épineuse de Campbell (F): *Cordylus campbelli*
Lézard à queue épineuse de Cope (F): *Cordylus tropidosternum*
Lézard à queue épineuse de Hewitt (F): *Cordylus peersi*
Lézard à queue épineuse de Jordan (F): *Cordylus jordani*
Lézard à queue épineuse de Lawrence (F): *Cordylus lawrenci*
Lézard à queue épineuse de McLachlan (F): *Cordylus mclachlani*
Lézard à queue épineuse de Reichenow (F): *Cordylus vittifer*
Lézard à queue épineuse de Rhodésie (F): *Cordylus rhodesianus*
Lézard à queue épineuse de Tasman (F): *Cordylus tasmani*
Lézard à queue épineuse de Warren (F): *Cordylus warreni*
Lézard à queue épineuse d'Oelofsen (F): *Cordylus oelofseni*

Lézard à queue épineuse du Namaqua (F): *Cordylus namaquensis*
Lézard à queue épineuse d'Ukinga (F): *Cordylus ukingensis*
Lézard à queue épineuse géant (F): *Cordylus giganteus*
Lézard à queue épineuse noir (F): *Cordylus niger*
Lézard cornu (F): *Phrynosoma coronatum*
Lézard cornu de San Diego (F): *Phrynosoma coronatum*
Lézard crocodile de Chine (F): *Shinisaurus crocodilurus*
Lézard de Lilford (F): *Podarcis lilfordi*
Lézard de Simony (F): *Gallotia simonyi*
Lézard des Baléares (F): *Podarcis lilfordi*
Lézard des Pityuses (F): *Podarcis pityusensis*
Lézard des rochers (F): *Cordylus microlepidotus*
Lézard des rochers du Drakensberg (F): *Cordylus melanotus*
Lézard d'Ibiza (F): *Podarcis pityusensis*
Lézard épineux d'Afrique australe (F): *Cordylus* spp.
Lézard géant de Hierro (F): *Gallotia simonyi*
Lézard perlé (F): *Heloderma suspectum*
Lézard-caïman de Guyane (F): *Dracaena guianensis*
Lézard-caïman du Paraguay (F): *Dracaena paraguayensis*
Lézards à fausse ceinture (S): *Cordylus* spp.
Lézards à queue épineuse d'Afrique Australe (F): *Cordylus* spp.
Lézards caïman (F): *Dracaena* spp.
Lézards fouette-queue (F): *Uromastyx* spp.
Lézards perlés (F): *Heloderma* spp.
Lézards venimeux (F): *Heloderma* spp.
L'Hoest's Monkey (E): *Cercopithecus lhoesti*
Liasis albertisii = Leiopython albertisii
Liasis amethistinus = Morelia amethistina
Liasis boa = Bothrochilus boa
Liasis boeleni = Morelia boeleni
Liasis carinata = Morelia carinata
Liasis childreni = Antaresia childreni
Liasis fuscus : **II** PYTHONIDAE Re
Liasis fuscus ssp. *albertisii = Leiopython albertisii*
Liasis mackloti : (E) Macklot's Python, Water Python, (S) Pitón de Macklot, (F) Python de Macklot, **II** PYTHONIDAE Re
Liasis maculosus = Antaresia maculosa
Liasis maximus = Apodora papuana
Liasis olivaceus : (E) Olive (Rock) Python, (S) Pitón oliva, (F) Python olive, **II** PYTHONIDAE Re
Liasis papuanus = Apodora papuana
Liasis perthensis = Antaresia perthensis
Liasis savuensis = Liasis mackloti
Liasis taronga = Morelia boeleni
Liberia Nimba Toad (E): *Nimbaphrynoides liberiensis*
Lichanotus laniger = Avahi laniger
Lichanura roseofusca = Lichanura trivirgata
Lichanura trivirgata : (E) Rosy Boa, (S) Boa mexicana rosada, (F) Boa à trois bandes, Boa rose, **II** BOIDAE Re
Lichenostomus cassidix = Lichenostomus melanops ssp. *cassidix*
Lichenostomus melanops cassidix : (E) Helmeted Honeyeater, (S) Melero de casco, Melífago de casco, (F) Méliphage casqué, Méliphage cornu, **I** MELIPHAGIDAE Av
Lichtenstein's Seahorse (E): *Hippocampus lichtensteinii*
Liemys inornata = Orlitia borneensis
Light-necked Sportive Lemur (E): *Lepilemur microdon*
Likh (E): *Eupodotis indica*
Lilac-crowned Amazon (E): *Amazona finschi*
Lilac-crowned Parrot (E): *Amazona finschi*
Lilac-tailed Parrotlet (E): *Touit batavica*
Lilford's Wall Lizard (E): *Podarcis lilfordi*
Lilian's Lovebird (E): *Agapornis lilianae*
Limpiacasa (S): *Phaethornis augusti*
Limpopo Girdled Lizard (E): *Cordylus jonesii*
Lince (S): *Lynx lynx*
Lince africano (S): *Caracal caracal*
Lince boreal (S): *Lynx lynx*

Lince caracal (S): *Caracal caracal*
Lince del Canadá (S): *Lynx canadensis*
Lince europeo (S): *Lynx lynx*
Lince ibérico (S): *Lynx pardinus*
Lince rojo (S): *Lynx rufus*
Lined Day Gecko (E): *Phelsuma lineata*
Lined Forest-Falcon (E): *Micrastur gilvicollis*
Lined Seahorse (E): *Hippocampus erectus*
Lingo (S): *Bassaricyon gabbii*
Linsang à taches (F): *Prionodon pardicolor*
Linsang manchado (S): *Prionodon pardicolor*
Linsang rayado (S): *Prionodon linsang*
Linsang rayé (F): *Prionodon linsang*
Linsang tacheté (F): *Prionodon pardicolor*
Liocichla omeiensis : (E) Emei Shan Liocichla, Mount Omei Liocichla, Omei Shan Liocichla, (S) Liocicla del Monte Omei, (F) Garrulaxe de l'Omei, **II** MUSCICAPIDAE Av
Liocicla del Monte Omei (S): *Liocichla omeiensis*
Lion (E): *Panthera leo*
Lion d'Afrique (F): *Panthera leo*
Lion d'Asie (F): *Panthera leo persica*
Lion tamarins (E): *Leontopithecus spp.*
Lion-tailed Macaque (E): *Macaca silenus*
Lipotes vexillifer : (E) Baiji, Changjiang Dolphin, Chinese Lake Dolphin, White Flag Dolphin, Whitefin Dolphin, Yangtze River Dolphin, (S) Baiji, Delfín de China, (F) Baiji, Dauphin fluviatile de Chine, **I** PLATANISTIDAE Ma
Lissemys punctata : (E) Indian Flapshell Turtle, Indo-Gangetic Flap-shell, Spotted Turtle, (S) Tortuga de concha blanda moteada, Tortuga plana indiana, (F) Lyssémyde ponctuée, Tortue de l'Inde, Tortue molle à clapet de l'Inde, Trionyx de l'Inde, **II** TRIONYCHIDAE Re
Lissodelphis borealis : (E) Northern Right Whale Dolphin, (S) Delfín liso, (F) Dauphin aptère boréal, **II** DELPHINIDAE Ma
Lissodelphis peronii : (E) Southern Right Whale Dolphin, (S) Delfín liso, Tunina sinaleta, (F) Dauphin aptère austral, **II** DELPHINIDAE Ma
Lissotis hartlaubii = Eupodotis hartlaubii
Lissotis melanogaster = Eupodotis melanogaster
Liszt Monkey (E): *Saguinus geoffroyi*
Lithophyllon bistomatum : **II** FUNGIIDAE An
Lithophyllon lobata : **II** FUNGIIDAE An
Lithophyllon mokai : **II** FUNGIIDAE An
Lithophyllon undulatum : **II** FUNGIIDAE An
Little agate shells (E): *Achatinella* spp.
Little Amu-Darya shovelnose (E): *Pseudoscaphirhynchus hermanni*
Little Banded Sparrowhawk (E): *Accipiter badius*
Little Blue Macaw (E): *Cyanopsitta spixii*
Little Brown Bustard (E): *Eupodotis humilis*
Little Bustard (E): *Tetrax tetrax*
Little Cockatoo (E): *Cacatua sanguinea*
Little Corella (E): *Cacatua sanguinea*
Little Eagle (E): *Hieraaetus morphnoides*
Little Egret (E): *Egretta garzetta*
Little Falcon (E): *Falco longipennis*
Little Fox (E): *Pseudalopex griseus*
Little Golden-mantled Flying-fox (E): *Pteropus pumilus*
Little Guan (E): *Penelopina nigra*
Little Hermit (E): *Phaethornis longuemareus*
Little Lorikeet (E): *Glossopsitta pusilla*
Little Owl (E): *Athene noctua*
Little Piked Whale (E): *Balaenoptera acutorostrata*
Little Red Flying-fox (E): *Pteropus scapulatus*
Little Red Lorikeet (E): *Charmosyna pulchella*
Little Shovelnose Sturgeon (E): *Pseudoscaphirhynchus hermanni*
Little Sparrowhawk (E): *Accipiter minullus*
Little Spotted Cat (E): *Leopardus tigrinus*
Little Sunangel (E): *Heliangelus exortis/ Heliangelus micraster*

Little Weaver (E): *Ploceus luteolus*
Little Woodstar (E): *Chaetocercus bombus*
Livingstone's Turaco (E): *Tauraco livingstonii*
Lizard Buzzard (E): *Kaupifalco monogrammicus*
Llanos Sideneck Turtle (E): *Podocnemis vogli*
Lobed Star Coral (E): *Solenastrea hyades*
Lobito de cola ancha (S): *Lontra brasiliensis*
Lobito de Río (S): *Lontra longicaudis*
Lobito del Plata (S): *Lontra longicaudis*
Lobito patagonica (S): *Lontra provocax*
Lobo (S): *Canis lupus*
Lobo común (S): *Canis lupus*
Lobo de crin (S): *Chrysocyon brachyurus*
Lobo de Río Grande (S): *Pteronura brasiliensis*
Lobo de Tasmania (S): *Thylacinus cynocephalus*
Lobo de tierra (S): *Proteles cristatus*
Lobo del río (S): *Pteronura brasiliensis*
Lobo fino sudamericano (S): *Arctocephalus australis*
Lobo gargantilla (S): *Pteronura brasiliensis*
Lobo marsupial (S): *Thylacinus cynocephalus*
Loboparadisea sericea : (E) Wattle-billed Bird-of-paradise, Yellow-breasted Bird-of-paradise, (F) Paradisier soyeux **II** PARADISAEIDAE Av
Lobophyllia corymbosa : **II** MUSSIDAE An
Lobophyllia costata : **II** MUSSIDAE An
Lobophyllia dentatus : **II** MUSSIDAE An
Lobophyllia diminuta : **II** MUSSIDAE An
Lobophyllia flabelliformis : **II** MUSSIDAE An
Lobophyllia hataii : **II** MUSSIDAE An
Lobophyllia hemprichii : **II** MUSSIDAE An
Lobophyllia pachysepta : **II** MUSSIDAE An
Lobophyllia robusta : **II** MUSSIDAE An
Lobophyllia serratus : **II** MUSSIDAE An
Lochmaeotrochus gardineri : **II** CARYOPHYLLIIDAE An
Lochmaeotrochus oculeus : **II** CARYOPHYLLIIDAE An
Loddigesia mirabilis : (E) Marvellous Spatuletail, (S) Colibrí admirable, (F) Loddigésie admirable, **II** TROCHILIDAE Av
Loddigésie admirable (F): *Loddigesia mirabilis*
Lofóforo chino (S): *Lophophorus lhuysii*
Lofóforo de Sclater (S): *Lophophorus sclateri*
Lofóforo del Himalaya (S): *Lophophorus impejanus*
Loggerhead (E): *Caretta caretta*
Loja Hummingbird (E): *Amazilia alticola*
Lombok Flying-fox (E): *Pteropus lombocensis*
Lonchura bicolor : (E) Black-and-white Mannikin, Black-and-white Munia, Blue-billed Mannikin, (F) Capucin bicolore, Spermète à bec bleu **III** ESTRILDIDAE Av
Lonchura cantans : (E) African Silverbill, (S) Monjita pico-de-plata, (F) Bec-d'argent, Capucin bec-d'argent, **III** ESTRILDIDAE Av
Lonchura cucullata : (E) Bronze Mannikin, Bronze Munia, Bronze-winged Mannikin, (S) Negrita bronceada, (F) Capucin nonnette, Spermète nonnette, **III** ESTRILDIDAE Av
Lonchura fringilloides : (E) Magpie Mannikin, Magpie Munia, Pied Mannikin, (S) Negrita picanza, (F) Capucin pie, Spermète pie, **III** ESTRILDIDAE Av
Lonchura malabarica ssp. *cantans = Lonchura cantans*
Lonchura oryzivora = Padda oryzivora
Long-beaked Dolphin (E): *Stenella longirostris*
Long-beaked Echidna (E): *Zaglossus bruijni*
Long-billed Black-Cockatoo (E): *Calyptorhynchus baudinii*
Long-billed Bristlebird (E): *Dasyornis longirostris*
Long-billed Corella (E): *Cacatua tenuirostris*
Long-billed Griffon (E): *Gyps indicus*
Long-billed Partridge (E): *Rhizothera longirostris*
Long-billed Starthroat (E): *Heliomaster longirostris*
Long-billed Vulture (E): *Gyps indicus*
Long-crested Eagle (E): *Lophaetus occipitalis*
Long-crested Hornbill (E): *Aceros comatus*
Long-eared Flying Mouse (E): *Idiurus macrotis*
Long-eared Flying Squirrel (E): *Idiurus macrotis*

Long-eared Owl (E): *Asio otus*
Long-eared Scaly-tailed Flying Squirrel (E): *Idiurus macrotis*
Long-finned Pilot Whale (E): *Globicephala melas*
Long-footed Treeshrew (E): *Tupaia longipes*
Long-haired Spider Monkey (E): *Ateles belzebuth*
Long-legged Buzzard (E): *Buteo rufinus*
Longman's Beaked Whale (E): *Indopacetus pacificus*
Longnose Seahorse (E): *Hippocampus trimaculatus*
Long-nosed Bandicoot (E): *Perameles bougainville*
Long-nosed Crocodile (E): *Gavialis gangeticus*
Long-nosed Echidna (E): *Zaglossus bruijni*
Long-nosed echidnas (E): *Zaglossus* spp.
Long-nosed Monkey (E): *Nasalis larvatus*
Long-nosed Spiny Anteater (E): *Zaglossus bruijni*
Longsnout Seahorse (E): *Hippocampus reidi*
Long-snouted Crocodile (E): *Crocodylus cataphractus*
Long-snouted Dolphin (E): *Stenella longirostris*
Long-snouted Seahorse (E): *Hippocampus guttulatus*
Long-tailed Chinchilla (E): *Chinchilla lanigera*
Long-tailed Dove (E): *Oena capensis*
Long-tailed Dunnart (E): *Sminthopsis longicaudata*
Long-tailed Hawk (E): *Urotriorchis macrourus*
Long-tailed Hermit (E): *Phaethornis superciliosus*
Long-tailed Honey-buzzard (E): *Henicopernis longicauda*
Long-tailed Langur (E): *Presbytis potenziani*
Long-tailed Macaque (E): *Macaca fascicularis*
Long-tailed Marmot (E): *Marmota caudata*
Long-tailed Marsupial-Mouse (E): *Sminthopsis longicaudata*
Long-tailed Otter (E): *Lontra longicaudis*
Long-tailed Pangolin (E): *Manis tetradactyla*
Long-tailed Paradigalla (E): *Paradigalla carunculata*
Long-tailed Paradise-Whydah (E): *Vidua interjecta*
Long-tailed Parakeet (E): *Psittacula longicauda*
Long-tailed Rock Monitor (E): *Varanus glebopalma*
Long-tailed Sabrewing (E): *Campylopterus excellens*
Long-tailed Sminthopsis (E): *Sminthopsis longicaudata*
Long-tailed Sylph (E): *Aglaiocercus kingi*
Long-tailed Woodnymph (E): *Thalurania watertonii*
Long-tufted Screech-Owl (E): *Otus sanctaecatarinae*
Longuemare's Sunangel (E): *Heliangelus clarisse*
Long-wattled Umbrellabird (E): *Cephalopterus penduliger*
Long-whiskered Owlet (E): *Xenoglaux loweryi*
Long-winged Harrier (E): *Circus buffoni*
Lontra annectens = Lontra longicaudis
Lontra canadensis : (E) North American Otter, North American River Otter, Northern River Otter, (S) Nutria de Canadá, Nutria norteamericana, (F) Loutre du Canada, **II** MUSTELIDAE Ma
Lontra enudris = Lontra longicaudis
Lontra felina : (E) Chingungo, Chungungo, Marine Otter, Sea Cat, (S) Chichimen, Chinchimen, Chungungo, Gato de mar, Gato marino, Huallaca, Nutria de mar, Nutria marina, (F) Chungungo, Loutre de mer, **I** MUSTELIDAE Ma
Lontra incarum = Lontra longicaudis
Lontra longicaudis : (E) Long-tailed Otter, Neotropical Otter, Neotropical River Otter, South American River Otter, (S) Gato de agua, Lobito de Río, Lobito del Plata, Nutria de agua, Nutria de cola larga, Perro de agua, Taira, (F) La plata, Loutre à longue queue, Loutre d'Amérique du Sud, **I** MUSTELIDAE Ma
Lontra mesopetes = Lontra longicaudis
Lontra platensis = Lontra longicaudis
Lontra provocax : (E) Huillin, Southern River Otter, (S) Huillín, Lobito patagonica, Nutria chilena, Nutria de Chile, (F) Huillin, Loutre du Chili, **I** MUSTELIDAE Ma
Lophaetus occipitalis : (E) Long-crested Eagle, (S) Aguila copetuda africana, Aguila crestilarga, (F) Aigle huppard, **II** ACCIPITRIDAE Av
Lophelia pertusa : (E) Tuft Coral **II** CARYOPHYLLIIDAE An
Lophelia prolifera = Lophelia pertusa

Lophocebus albigena : (E) Grey-cheeked Mangabey, White-cheeked Mangabey, (S) Mangabey de mejillas grises **II** CERCOPITHECIDAE Ma
Lophoictinia isura : (E) Square-tailed Kite, (S) Milano colicuadrado, (F) Milan à queue carrée, **II** ACCIPITRIDAE Av
Lophophore de Lhuys (F): *Lophophorus lhuysii*
Lophophore de Sclater (F): *Lophophorus sclateri*
Lophophore resplendissant (F): *Lophophorus impejanus*
Lophophorus impejanus : (E) Himalayan Monal, Impeyan Pheasant, Monal Pheasant, (S) Faisán monal del Himalaya, Lofóforo del Himalaya, Monal colirrojo, (F) Lophophore resplendissant, Monal de l'Himalaya, **I** PHASIANIDAE Av
Lophophorus lhuysii : (E) Chinese Impeyan, Chinese Monal, (S) Faisán monal chino, Lofóforo chino, Monal coliverde, (F) Lophophore de Lhuys, Monal chinois, **I** PHASIANIDAE Av
Lophophorus sclateri : (E) Crestless Monal, Sclater's Monal, (S) Faisán monal de Sclater, Lofóforo de Sclater, Monal coliblanco, (F) Lophophore de Sclater, Monal birman, **I** PHASIANIDAE Av
Lophorina superba : (E) Superb Bird-of-paradise, (F) Paradisier superbe **II** PARADISAEIDAE Av
Lophornis adorabilis : (E) Adorable Coquette, White-crested Coquette, (S) Coqueta adorable, (F) Coquette adorable, **II** TROCHILIDAE Av
Lophornis brachylophus : (E) Short-crested Coquette, (S) Coqueta cresticorta, Coqueta de Guerrero, (F) Coquette du Guerrero, **II** TROCHILIDAE Av
Lophornis chalybeus : (E) Festive Coquette, (S) Coqueta abanico puntiblanco, Coqueta festiva, Coqueta verde, Picaflor abanico verde, (F) Coquette chalybée, **II** TROCHILIDAE Av
Lophornis delattrei : (E) Rufous-crested Coquette, (S) Coqueta crestirrufa, (F) Coquette de Delattre, **II** TROCHILIDAE Av
Lophornis delattrei ssp. *brachylophus = Lophornis brachylophus*
Lophornis gouldii : (E) Dot-eared Coquette, (S) Coqueta moteada, (F) Coquette de Gould, **II** TROCHILIDAE Av
Lophornis helenae : (E) Black-crested Coquette, (S) Coqueta crestinegra, (F) Coquette d'Hélène, **II** TROCHILIDAE Av
Lophornis magnificus : (E) Frilled Coquette, (S) Coqueta magnifica, (F) Coquette magnifique, **II** TROCHILIDAE Av
Lophornis ornatus : (E) Tufted Coquette, (S) Coqueta abanico canela, Coqueta adornada, (F) Coquette huppe-col, **II** TROCHILIDAE Av
Lophornis pavoninus : (E) Peacock Coquette, (S) Coqueta abanico pavo real, Coqueta pavonina, (F) Coquette paon, **II** TROCHILIDAE Av
Lophornis stictolophus : (E) Spangled Coquette, (S) Coqueta coronada, Coqueta lentejuelada, (F) Coquette pailletée, **II** TROCHILIDAE Av
Lophostrix cristata : (E) Crested Owl, (S) Búho corniblanco, Búho cornudo, Lechuza copetona, (F) Duc à aigrettes, Hibou à casque, **II** STRIGIDAE Av
Lophostrix lettii = Jubula lettii
Lophotis ruficrista = Eupodotis ruficrista
Lophotis savilei = Eupodotis savilei
Lophura edwardsi : (E) Edwards's Pheasant, (S) Faisán de Edwards, (F) Faisan d'Edwards, **I** PHASIANIDAE Av
Lophura erythrophthalma : (E) Crestless Fireback, Rufous-tailed Pheasant, (S) Faisán colicanelo, Faisán de carúncula azul, (F) Faisan à queue rousse, **III** PHASIANIDAE Av
Lophura ignita : (E) Crested Fireback, Vieillot's Fireback, (S) Faisán de carúncula azul crestado, Faisán noble, (F) Faisan noble, **III** PHASIANIDAE Av
Lophura imperialis : (E) Imperial Pheasant, (S) Faisán imperial, (F) Faisan impérial, **I** PHASIANIDAE Av

Checklist of fauna/Lista de especies de fauna/Liste des espèces animales

Lophura swinhoii : (E) Swinhoe's Pheasant, (S) Faisán de
  Formosa, Faisán de Swinhoe, (F) Faisan de Formose,
  Faisan de Swinhoe, **I** PHASIANIDAE Av
Lora de cara roja (S): *Amazona pretrei*
Lord Derby's Flying Squirrel (E): *Anomalurus derbianus*
Lord Derby's Mountain Pheasant (E): *Oreophasis
  derbianus*
Lord Derby's Scaly-tailed Squirrrel (E): *Anomalurus
  derbianus*
Lord Howe Island Rail (E): *Gallirallus sylvestris*
Lord Howe Island Woodhen (E): *Gallirallus sylvestris*
Lord Howe Rail (E): *Gallirallus sylvestris*
Lori à bandeau rouge (F): *Glossopsitta concinna*
Lori à collier jaune (F): *Lorius chlorocercus*
Lori à couronne pourpre (F): *Glossopsitta
  porphyrocephala*
Lori à diadème (F): *Charmosyna diadema*
Lori à front rouge (F): *Charmosyna rubronotata*
Lori à gorge rouge (F): *Charmosyna amabilis*
Lori à joues bleues (F): *Eos cyanogenia*
Lori à masque rouge (F): *Glossopsitta pusilla*
Lori à menton rouge (F): *Charmosyna rubrigularis*
Lori à nuque blanche (F): *Lorius albidinuchus*
Lori à ventre violet (F): *Lorius hypoinochrous*
Lori acollarado (S): *Lorius chlorocercus*
Lori adornado (S): *Trichoglossus ornatus*
Lori alinegro (S): *Eos cyanogenia*
Lori almizclero (S): *Glossopsitta concinna*
Lori arcoiris (S): *Trichoglossus haematodus*
Lori arlequin (F): *Eos histrio*
Lori barbirrojo (S): *Charmosyna rubrigularis*
Lori bigotudo (S): *Oreopsittacus arfaki*
Lori bridé (F): *Oreopsittacus arfaki*
Lori cardenal (S): *Chalcopsitta cardinalis*
Lori cardinal (F): *Chalcopsitta cardinalis*
Lori carirrojo (S): *Glossopsitta pusilla*
Lori chispeado (S): *Chalcopsitta scintillata*
Lori coquet (F): *Charmosyna placentis*
Lori coronipúrpura (S): *Glossopsitta porphyrocephala*
Lori croquet (F): *Charmosyna placentis*
Lori damisela (S): *Lorius domicella*
Lori de Buru (F/S): *Charmosyna toxopei*
Lori de Duyvenbode (F): *Chalcopsitta duivenbodei*
Lori de Goldie (S): *Psitteuteles goldiei*
Lori de Josefina (S): *Charmosyna josefinae*
Lori de Joséphine (F): *Charmosyna josefinae*
Lori de Kuhl (F): *Vini kuhlii*
Lori de las Tanimbar (S): *Eos reticulata*
Lori de l'île Buru (F): *Charmosyna toxopei*
Lori de Margaret (F): *Charmosyna margarethae*
Lori de Margarita (S): *Charmosyna margarethae*
Lori de Marguerite (F): *Charmosyna margarethae*
Lori de Meek (S/F): *Charmosyna meeki*
Lori de Mindanao (S): *Trichoglossus johnstoniae*
Lori de Musschenbroek (F): *Neopsittacus musschenbroekii*
Lori de Nouvelle-Calédonie (F): *Charmosyna diadema*
Lori de Papouasie (F): *Charmosyna papou*
Lori de Ponapé (S): *Trichoglossus rubiginosus*
Lori de Rimitara (S): *Vini kuhlii*
Lori de Samoa (S): *Vini australis*
Lori de Sangir (S): *Eos histrio*
Lori de Seram (S): *Eos semilarvata*
Lori de Stephen (S/F): *Vini stepheni*
Lori de Wilhelmina (F): *Charmosyna wilhelminae*
Lori des dames (F): *Lorius domicella*
Lori des Fidji (F): *Phigys solitarius*
Lori des Moluques (F): *Lorius lory*
Lori des montagnes (F): *Oreopsittacus arfaki*
Lori des palmiers (F): *Charmosyna palmarum*
Lori diadema (S): *Charmosyna diadema*
Lori écaillé (F): *Eos squamata*
Lori écarlate (F): *Eos bornea*
Lori émeraude (F): *Neopsittacus pullicauda*
Lori escamoso (S): *Eos squamata*
Lori escuamiverde (S): *Trichoglossus chlorolepidotus*

Lori estriado (S): *Charmosyna multistriata*
Lori féérique (F): *Charmosyna pulchella*
Lori flamméché (F): *Chalcopsitta scintillata*
Lori flanquirrojo (S): *Charmosyna placentis*
Lori frentirrojo (S): *Charmosyna rubronotata*
Lori fringillaire (F): *Vini australis*
Lori gárrulo (S): *Lorius garrulus*
Lori gorgirrojo (S): *Charmosyna amabilis*
Lori humilde (S): *Trichoglossus euteles*
Lori iris (S): *Psitteuteles iris*
Lori lindo (S): *Charmosyna pulchella*
Lori masqué (F): *Eos semilarvata*
Lori monjita (S): *Vini peruviana*
Lori montano chico (S): *Neopsittacus pullicauda*
Lori montano grande (S): *Neopsittacus musschenbroekii*
Lori musc (F): *Glossopsitta concinna*
Lori negro (S): *Chalcopsitta atra*
Lori noir (F): *Chalcopsitta atra*
Lori noira (F): *Lorius garrulus*
Lori nonnette (F): *Vini peruviana*
Lori nuquiblanco (S): *Lorius albidinuchus*
Lori orange sombre (F): *Pseudeos fuscata*
Lori palmero (S): *Charmosyna palmarum*
Lori papou (F): *Charmosyna papou*
Lori pardo (S): *Chalcopsitta duivenbodei*
Lori pigmeo (S): *Charmosyna wilhelminae*
Lori rabilargo (S): *Charmosyna papou*
Lori réticulé (F): *Eos reticulata*
Lori rojo (S): *Eos bornea*
Lori solitaire des îles Fidji (F): *Phigys solitarius*
Lori solitario (S): *Phigys solitarius*
Lori sombre (F): *Pseudeos fuscata*
Lori sombrio (S): *Pseudeos fuscata*
Lori splendide (F): *Charmosyna placentis*
Lori strié (F): *Charmosyna multistriata*
Lori tricolor (S): *Lorius lory*
Lori tricolore (F): *Lorius lory*
Lori ultramar (S): *Vini ultramarina*
Lori ultramarin (F): *Vini ultramarina*
Lori ventrivinoso (S): *Lorius hypoinochrous*
Lori verdigualdo (S): *Trichoglossus flavoviridis*
Lori versicolor (S): *Psitteuteles versicolor*
Loria loriae = Cnemophilus loriae
Loria's Bird-of-paradise (E): *Cnemophilus loriae*
Lorículo amable (S): *Loriculus amabilis*
Lorículo coroniazul (S): *Loriculus galgulus*
Lorículo de Ceilán (S): *Loriculus beryllinus*
Lorículo de Célebes (S): *Loriculus stigmatus*
Lorículo de Flores (S): *Loriculus flosculus*
Lorículo de Java (S): *Loriculus pusillus*
Lorículo de la Sangihe (S): *Loriculus catamene*
Lorículo de las Bismarck (S): *Loriculus tener*
Lorículo de las Sula (S): *Loriculus sclateri*
Lorículo exiguo (S): *Loriculus exilis*
Lorículo Filipino (S): *Loriculus philippensis*
Lorículo papú (S): *Loriculus aurantiifrons*
Lorículo vernal (S): *Loriculus vernalis*
Loriculus amabilis : (E) Moluccan Hanging-Parrot, (S)
  Lorículo amable, (F) Coryllis des Moluques, **II**
  PSITTACIDAE Av
Loriculus amabilis ssp. *catamene = Loriculus catamene*
Loriculus aurantiifrons : (E) Orange-fronted Hanging-
  Parrot, Papuan Hanging-Parrot, (S) Lorículo papú, (F)
  Coryllis à front orange, **II** PSITTACIDAE Av
Loriculus beryllinus : (E) Ceylon Hanging-Parrot, Sri
  Lanka Hanging-Parrot, (S) Lorículo de Ceilán, (F)
  Coryllis de Ceylan, **II** PSITTACIDAE Av
Loriculus catamene : (E) Sangihe Hanging-Parrot, (S)
  Lorículo de la Sangihe, (F) Coryllis des Sangi, **II**
  PSITTACIDAE Av
Loriculus exilis : (E) Green Hanging-Parrot, Pygmy
  Hanging-Parrot, Red-billed Hanging-Parrot, (S)
  Lorículo exiguo, (F) Coryllis vert, **II** PSITTACIDAE
  Av

Loriculus flosculus : (E) Flores Hanging-Parrot, Wallace's Hanging-Parrot, (S) Lorículo de Flores, (F) Coryllis de Wallace, **II** PSITTACIDAE Av
Loriculus galgulus : (E) Blue-crowned Hanging-Parrot, Blue-topped Hanging-Parrot, (S) Lorículo coroniazul, (F) Coryllis à tête bleue, Loriculus malais, **II** PSITTACIDAE Av
Loriculus malais (F): *Loriculus galgulus*
Loriculus philippensis : (E) Colasisi, Philippine Hanging-Parrot, (S) Lorículo Filipino, (F) Coryllis des Philippines, **II** PSITTACIDAE Av
Loriculus pusillus : (E) Yellow-throated Hanging-Parrot, (S) Lorículo de Java, (F) Coryllis à gorge jaune, **II** PSITTACIDAE Av
Loriculus sclateri : (E) Sula Hanging-Parrot, (S) Lorículo de las Sula, (F) Coryllis del Sula, **II** PSITTACIDAE Av
Loriculus stigmatus : (E) Black-billed Hanging-Parrot, Maroon-rumped Hanging-Parrot, Sulawesi Hanging-Parrot, (S) Lorículo de Célebes, (F) Coryllis des Célèbes, **II** PSITTACIDAE Av
Loriculus stigmatus ssp. *tener* = *Loriculus tener*
Loriculus tener : (E) Green-fronted Hanging-Parrot, (S) Lorículo de las Bismarck, (F) Coryllis des Bismarck, **II** PSITTACIDAE Av
Loriculus vernalis : (E) Vernal Hanging-Parrot, (S) Lorículo vernal, (F) Coryllis vernal, **II** PSITTACIDAE Av
Loriquet à tête bleue (F): *Trichoglossus haematodus*
Loriquet de Goldie (F): *Psitteuteles goldiei*
Loriquet de Johnstone (F): *Trichoglossus johnstoniae*
Loriquet de Ponapé (F): *Trichoglossus rubiginosus*
Loriquet eutèle (F): *Trichoglossus euteles*
Loriquet iris (F): *Psitteuteles iris*
Loriquet jaune et vert (F): *Trichoglossus flavoviridis*
Loriquet orné (F): *Trichoglossus ornatus*
Loriquet versicolore (F): *Psitteuteles versicolor*
Loriquet vert (F): *Trichoglossus chlorolepidotus*
Loris fino (S): *Loris tardigradus*
Loris grandis = *Loris tardigradus*
Loris grêle (F): *Loris tardigradus*
Loris lent (F): *Nycticebus coucang*
Loris lento (S): *Nycticebus coucang*
Loris lydekkerianus = *Loris tardigradus*
Loris malabaricus = *Loris tardigradus*
Loris nordicus = *Loris tardigradus*
Loris nycticeboides = *Loris tardigradus*
Loris tardigradus : (E) Slender Loris, (S) Loris fino, (F) Loris grêle, **II** LORIDAE Ma
Lorito acollarado (S): *Geoffroyus simplex*
Lorito alinegro (S): *Hapalopsittaca melanotis*
Lorito amazonino (S): *Hapalopsittaca amazonina*
Lorito cabecigualdo (S): *Pionopsitta pyrilia*
Lorito cabecipardo (S): *Poicephalus cryptoxanthus*
Lorito caica (S): *Pionopsitta caica*
Lorito carigualdo (S): *Poicephalus flavifrons*
Lorito carinaranja (S): *Pionopsitta barrabandi*
Lorito carirrojo (S): *Geoffroyus geoffroyi/ Pionopsitta pileata*
Lorito carirrosado (S): *Pionopsitta pulchra*
Lorito chirlecrés (S): *Pionites melanocephala*
Lorito colicorto (S): *Graydidascalus brachyurus*
Lorito de copete (S): *Nymphicus hollandicus*
Lorito de Coxen (S): *Cyclopsitta diophthalma coxeni*
Lorito de Desmarest (S): *Psittaculirostris desmarestii*
Lorito de Edwards (S): *Psittaculirostris edwardsii*
Lorito de Fuertes (S): *Hapalopsittaca fuertesi*
Lorito de Meyer (S): *Poicephalus meyeri*
Lorito de Rüppell (S): *Poicephalus rueppellii*
Lorito de Salvadori (S): *Psittaculirostris salvadorii*
Lorito dobleojo (S): *Cyclopsitta diophthalma*
Lorito dorsiazul (S): *Psittinus cyanurus*
Lorito ecuatoriano (S): *Hapalopsittaca pyrrhops*
Lorito emmascarado de Coxen (S): *Cyclopsitta diophthalma coxeni*

Lorito encapuchado (S): *Pionopsitta haematotis*
Lorito frentirrojo (S): *Poicephalus gulielmi*
Lorito guayabero (S): *Bolbopsittacus lunulatus*
Lorito heteróclito (S): *Geoffroyus heteroclitus*
Lorito niam-niam (S): *Poicephalus crassus*
Lorito orejudo (S): *Pionopsitta pileata*
Lorito pechinaranja (S): *Cyclopsitta gulielmitertii*
Lorito pileado (S): *Pionopsitta pileata*
Lorito piquigrueso (S): *Rhynchopsitta* spp.
Lorito robusto (S): *Poicephalus robustus*
Lorito rubio (S): *Pionites leucogaster*
Lorito Senegalés (S): *Poicephalus senegalus*
Lorito ventrirrojo (S): *Poicephalus rufiventris*
Lorito vulturino (S): *Pionopsitta vulturina*
Lorito-momoto amarillento (S): *Prioniturus flavicans*
Lorito-momoto coroniazul (S): *Prioniturus discurus*
Lorito-momoto de Buru (S): *Prioniturus mada*
Lorito-momoto de las Sulu (S): *Prioniturus verticalis*
Lorito-momoto de Luzón (S): *Prioniturus luconensis*
Lorito-momoto de Mindanao (S): *Prioniturus waterstradti*
Lorito-momoto de Palawan (S): *Prioniturus platenae*
Lorito-momoto dorsidorado (S): *Prioniturus platurus*
Lorito-momoto montano (S): *Prioniturus montanus*
Lorito-tigre de Brehm (S): *Psittacella brehmii*
Lorito-tigre de Madarasz (S): *Psittacella madaraszi*
Lorito-tigre modesto (S): *Psittacella modesta*
Lorito-tigre pintado (S): *Psittacella picta*
Lorius albidinuchus : (E) White-naped Lory, (S) Lori nuquiblanco, (F) Lori à nuque blanche, **II** PSITTACIDAE Av
Lorius chlorocercus : (E) Yellow-bibbed Lory, (S) Lori acollarado, (F) Lori à collier jaune, **II** PSITTACIDAE Av
Lorius domicella : (E) Purple-capped Lory, Purple-naped Lory, (S) Lori damisela, (F) Lori des dames, **II** PSITTACIDAE Av
Lorius garrulus : (E) Chattering Lory, Yellow-backed Lory, (S) Lori gárrulo, (F) Lori noira, **II** PSITTACIDAE Av
Lorius hypoinochrous : (E) Eastern Black-capped Lory, Purple-bellied Lory, (S) Lori ventrivinoso, (F) Lori à ventre violet, **II** PSITTACIDAE Av
Lorius lory : (E) Black-capped Lory, Western Black-capped Lory, (S) Lori tricolor, (F) Lori des Moluques, Lori tricolore, **II** PSITTACIDAE Av
Lorius tibialis = *Lorius domicella*
Loro aguileño (S): *Psittrichas fulgidus*
Loro alibronceado (S): *Pionus chalcopterus*
Loro alisero (S): *Amazona tucumana*
Loro barranquero (S): *Cyanoliseus patagonus*
Loro brasileño (S): *Amazona brasiliensis*
Loro burrón (S): *Amazona farinosa*
Loro cabeciamarillo (S): *Amazona ochrocephala oratrix*
Loro cabeciazul (S): *Pionus menstruus*
Loro cabecirrojo (S): *Amazona pretrei*
Loro cabeza amarilla (S): *Amazona ochrocephala*
Loro cabeza azul (S): *Amazona farinosa*
Loro cabeza roja (S): *Amazona viridigenalis*
Loro cachirrosa (S): *Pionopsitta pulchra*
Loro cacique (S): *Deroptyus accipitrinus*
Loro cariazul (S): *Amazona brasiliensis/ Amazona dufresniana*
Loro caroniblanco (S): *Pionus senilis*
Loro choclero (S): *Pionus maximiliani*
Loro colicorto (S): *Graydidascalus brachyurus*
Loro corona-violeta (S): *Amazona finschi*
Loro de banda roja (S): *Amazona vittata*
Loro de Barbados (S): *Amazona barbadensis*
Loro de Buru (S): *Tanygnathus gramineus*
Loro de cabeza blanca (S): *Amazona leucocephala*
Loro de cabeza roja (S): *Amazona pretrei*
Loro de Hispaniola (S): *Amazona ventralis*
Loro de Jamaica (S): *Amazona collaria*
Loro de mejillas azules (S): *Amazona rhodocorytha*
Loro de Müller (S): *Tanygnathus sumatranus*

Checklist of fauna/Lista de especies de fauna/Liste des espèces animales

Loro de San Vicente (S): *Amazona guildingii*
Loro del paraíso (S): *Psephotus pulcherrimus*
Loro ecléctico (S): *Eclectus roratus*
Loro famaulipeco (S): *Amazona viridigenalis*
Loro frente blanca (S): *Amazona albifrons*
Loro frente roja (S): *Amazona autumnalis*
Loro frentirrojo (S): *Amazona autumnalis*
Loro guaro (S): *Amazona amazonica*
Loro hablador (S): *Amazona aestiva*
Loro hombroamarillo (S): *Psephotus chrysopterygius*
Loro imperial (S): *Amazona imperialis*
Loro lomirrojo (S): *Amazona festiva*
Loro malva (S): *Amazona vinacea*
Loro mona amarilla (S): *Amazona ochrocephala*
Loro morado (S): *Pionus fuscus*
Loro multicolor (S): *Amazona versicolor*
Loro negro (S): *Coracopsis nigra*
Loro nocturno (S): *Geopsittacus occidentalis*
Loro nuca amarilla (S): *Amazona ochrocephala*
Loro nuquiamarillo (S): *Amazona ochrocephala auropalliata*
Loro nuquiazul (S): *Tanygnathus lucionensis*
Loro orejirrojo (S): *Pionopsitta haematotis*
Loro pechivinoso (S): *Amazona vinacea*
Loro pecho vinoso (S): *Amazona vinacea*
Loro picogrodo (S): *Tanygnathus megalorynchos*
Loro piquigordo (S): *Rhynchopsitta pachyrhyncha*
Loro piquirrojo (S): *Pionus sordidus*
Loro rabudo collar (S): *Psittacula krameri*
Loro real (S): *Amazona ochrocephala*
Loro senil (S): *Pionus senilis*
Loro tumultuoso (S): *Pionus tumultuosus*
Loro vasa (S): *Coracopsis vasa*
Loro ventriazul (S): *Triclaria malachitacea*
Loro ventrinaranja (S): *Neophema chrysogaster*
Loro verde (S): *Amazona farinosa/ Amazona mercenaria*
Loro yaco (S): *Psittacus erithacus*
Loro yucateci (S): *Amazona xantholora*
Loro yucateco (S): *Amazona xantholora*
Loros (S): PSITTACIFORMES spp. Av
Loup (F): *Canis lupus*
Loup à crinière (F): *Chrysocyon brachyurus*
Loup gris (F): *Canis lupus*
Loup marsupial (F): *Thylacinus cynocephalus*
Loup vulgaire (F): *Canis lupus*
Loutre à cou tacheté (F): *Lutra maculicollis*
Loutre à joues blanches (F): *Aonyx capensis*
Loutre à joues blanches du Cameroun (F): *Aonyx congicus*
Loutre à joues blanches du Congo (F): *Aonyx congicus*
Loutre à longue queue (F): *Lontra longicaudis*
Loutre cendrée (F): *Amblonyx cinereus*
Loutre commune (F): *Lutra lutra*
Loutre d'Amérique du Sud (F): *Lontra longicaudis*
Loutre d'Asie (F): *Lutrogale perspicillata*
Loutre de mer (F): *Enhydra lutris/ Lontra felina*
Loutre de mer de Californie (F): *Enhydra lutris nereis*
Loutre de mer méridionale (F): *Enhydra lutris nereis*
Loutre de rivière (F): *Lutra lutra*
Loutre de Sumatra (F): *Lutra sumatrana*
Loutre d'Europe (F): *Lutra lutra*
Loutre du Canada (F): *Lontra canadensis*
Loutre du Chili (F): *Lontra provocax*
Loutre géante du Brésil (F): *Pteronura brasiliensis*
Loutres (F): LUTRINAE spp.
Lovely Poison Frog (E): *Phyllobates lugubris*
Low-crowned Seahorse (E): *Hippocampus trimaculatus*
Lower Californian Fur Seal (E): *Arctocephalus townsendi*
Lowland Anoa (E): *Bubalus depressicornis*
Lowland Tapir (E): *Tapirus terrestris*
Lowrelief Lettuce Coral (E): *Agaricia humilis*
Lowridge Cactus Coral (E): *Mycetophyllia daniana*
LOXOCEMIDAE spp.: (E) New World pythons II Re

Loxocemus bicolor : (E) Burrowing Python, Ground Python, New World Python, (S) Pitón excavadora, (F) Python d'Amérique centrale, Python fouisseur du Mexique, II LOXOCEMIDAE Re
Loxodonta africana : (E) African Elephant, African Savannah Elephant, (S) Elefante africano, (F) Eléphant africain, Eléphant d'Afrique, I/II ELEPHANTIDAE Ma
Loxodonta cyclotis = Loxodonta africana
Lucifer Hummingbird (E): *Calothorax lucifer*
Ludlow's Bhutan Swallowtail (E): *Bhutanitis ludlowi*
Ludwig's Bustard (E): *Neotis ludwigii*
Lúgano cardenalito (S): *Carduelis cucullata*
Lúgano de Yarrell (S): *Carduelis yarrellii*
Lúgano encapuchado (S): *Carduelis cucullata*
Luth (E): *Dermochelys coriacea*
Lutra canadensis = Lontra canadensis
Lutra felina = Lontra felina
Lutra longicaudis = Lontra longicaudis
Lutra longicaudis ssp. *longicaudis = Lontra longicaudis*
Lutra lutra : (E) Common Otter, Eurasian Otter, European Otter, European River Otter, Old World Otter, (S) Nutria, Nutria común, Nutria europea, (F) Loutre commune, Loutre de rivière, Loutre d'Europe, I MUSTELIDAE Ma
Lutra maculicollis : (E) Speckle-throated Otter, Spot-necked Otter, Spotted-necked Otter, (S) Nutria de cuello manchado, (F) Loutre à cou tacheté, II MUSTELIDAE Ma
Lutra nippon = Lutra lutra
Lutra perspicillata = Lutrogale perspicillata
Lutra provocax = Lontra provocax
Lutra sumatrana : (E) Hairy-nosed Otter, (S) Nutria de Sumatra, (F) Loutre de Sumatra, II MUSTELIDAE Ma
LUTRINAE spp. : (E) Otters, (S) Nutrias, (F) Loutres, I/II MUSTELIDAE Ma
Lutrogale perspicillata : (E) Indian Smooth-coated Otter, Smooth-coated Otter, (S) Nutria lisa, Nutria simung, (F) Loutre d'Asie, II MUSTELIDAE Ma
Luzon Bleeding-heart (E): *Gallicolumba luzonica*
Luzon Hornbill (E): *Penelopides manillae*
Luzon Peacock Swallowtail (E): *Papilio chikae*
Luzon Racquet-tail (E): *Prioniturus montanus*
Luzon Scops-Owl (E): *Otus longicornis*
Luzon Tarictic Hornbill (E): *Penelopides manillae*
Lycalopex griseus = Pseudalopex griseus
Lycalopex gymnocercus = Pseudalopex gymnocercus
Lycocorax pyrrhopterus : (E) Paradise-Crow, Silky-Crow, (F) Corneille de paradis, Paradisier corvin II PARADISAEIDAE Av
Lyle's Flying-fox (E): *Pteropus lylei*
Lynx (F): *Lynx lynx*
Lynx boréal (F): *Lynx lynx*
Lynx canadensis : (E) American Lynx, Canada Lynx, (S) Lince del Canadá, (F) Lynx du Canada, II FELIDAE Ma
Lynx caracal = Caracal caracal
Lynx d'Espagne (F): *Lynx pardinus*
Lynx d'Eurasie (F): *Lynx lynx*
Lynx du Canada (F): *Lynx canadensis*
Lynx du désert (F): *Caracal caracal*
Lynx lynx : (E) Eurasian Lynx, (S) Lince, Lince boreal, Lince europeo, (F) Lynx, Lynx boréal, Lynx d'Eurasie, II FELIDAE Ma
Lynx lynx ssp. *canadensis = Lynx canadensis*
Lynx lynx ssp. *pardinus = Lynx pardinus*
Lynx pardelle (F): *Lynx pardinus*
Lynx pardinus : (E) Iberian Lynx, Pardel Lynx, Spanish Lynx, (S) Lince ibérico, (F) Lynx d'Espagne, Lynx pardelle, I FELIDAE Ma
Lynx roux (F): *Lynx rufus*
Lynx rufus : (E) Bay Lynx, Bobcat, (S) Gato montés, Lince rojo, (F) Chat sauvage, Lynx roux, II FELIDAE Ma
Lyssémyde ponctuée (F): *Lissemys punctata*

Checklist of fauna/Lista de especies de fauna/Liste des espèces animales

Maasai Girdled Lizard (E): *Cordylus beraduccii*
Macaca arctoides : (E) Bear Macaque, Stumptail Macaque, Stump-tailed Macaque, (S) Macaca ursin, (F) Macaque brun, **II** CERCOPITHECIDAE Ma
Macaca assamensis : (E) Assam Macaque, Assamese Macaque, (S) Macaca del Himalaya, (F) Macaque d' Assam, **II** CERCOPITHECIDAE Ma
Macaca cangrejera (S): *Macaca fascicularis*
Macaca cola de cerdo (S): *Macaca nemestrina*
Macaca crestada de Sulawesi (S): *Macaca ochreata*
Macaca cyclopis : (E) Formosan Rock Macaque, Taiwan Macaque, (S) Macaca de Formosa, (F) Macaque de Formose, **II** CERCOPITHECIDAE Ma
Macaca cynomolgus = Macaca fascicularis
Macaca de Formosa (S): *Macaca cyclopis*
Macaca de Madras (S): *Macaca radiata*
Macaca de Sri Lanka (S): *Macaca sinica*
Macaca de Tonkean (S): *Macaca tonkeana*
Macaca del Himalaya (S): *Macaca assamensis*
Macaca del Tibet (S): *Macaca thibetana*
Macaca fascicularis : (E) Crab-eating Macaque, Cynomolgus Monkey, Long-tailed Macaque, (S) Macaca cangrejera, (F) Macaque crabier, Macaque de Buffon, **II** CERCOPITHECIDAE Ma
Macaca fuscata : (E) Japanese Macaque, (S) Macaca japonesa, (F) Macaque à face rouge, Macaque japonais, **II** CERCOPITHECIDAE Ma
Macaca irus = Macaca fascicularis
Macaca japonesa (S): *Macaca fuscata*
Macaca leonina (S): *Macaca silenus*
Macaca leonina = Macaca nemestrina
Macaca maura : (E) Celebes Macaque, Moor Macaque, (S) Macaca mora, (F) Macaque maure, **II** CERCOPITHECIDAE Ma
Macaca mora (S): *Macaca maura*
Macaca mulatta : (E) Rhesus Macaque, Rhesus Monkey, (S) Mono resus, (F) Macaque rhésus, **II** CERCOPITHECIDAE Ma
Macaca negra (S): *Macaca nigra*
Macaca nemestrina : (E) Pigtail Macaque, Pig-tailed Macaque, (S) Macaca cola de cerdo, (F) Macaque à queue de cochon, **II** CERCOPITHECIDAE Ma
Macaca nigra : (E) Celebes Black Macaque, Celebes Crested Macaque, Gorontalo Macaque, Sulawesi Macaque, (S) Macaca negra, (F) Cynopithèque nègre, Macaque des Célèbes, **II** CERCOPITHECIDAE Ma
Macaca nigrescens = Macaca nigra
Macaca ochreata : (E) Booted Macaque, (S) Macaca crestada de Sulawesi **II** CERCOPITHECIDAE Ma
Macaca pagensis = Macaca nemestrina ssp. *pagensis*
Macaca pagensis ssp. *pagensis = Macaca nemestrina* ssp. *pagensis*
Macaca pagensis ssp. *siberu = Macaca nemestrina*
Macaca radiata : (E) Bonnet Macaque, (S) Macaca de Madras, (F) Macaque bonnet chinois, Macaque commun, **II** CERCOPITHECIDAE Ma
Macaca silenus : (E) Lion-tailed Macaque, Wanderoo, (S) Macaca leonina, Macaco barbudo, Macaco de cola de león, (F) Macaque à queue de lion, Macaque ouandérou, Ouandérou, **I** CERCOPITHECIDAE Ma
Macaca sinica : (E) Toque Macaque, (S) Macaca de Sri Lanka, (F) Macaque couronné, Macaque toque, **II** CERCOPITHECIDAE Ma
Macaca speciosa = Macaca arctoides
Macaca speciosa = Macaca fuscata
Macaca sylvanus : (E) Barbary Ape, Barbary Macaque, (S) Mona de Berbería, Mono de Berberea, Mono de Gibraltar, (F) Macaque de Gibraltar, Magot, Magot commun, **II** CERCOPITHECIDAE Ma
Macaca thibetana : (E) Père David's Macaque, Short-tailed Tibetan Macaque, Tibetan Macaque, (S) Macaca del Tibet, (F) Macaque du Tibet, **II** CERCOPITHECIDAE Ma

Macaca tonkeana : (E) Tonkean Black Macaque, Tonkean Macaque, (S) Macaca de Tonkean, (F) Macaque de Tonkea, **II** CERCOPITHECIDAE Ma
Macaca ursin (S): *Macaca arctoides*
Macaco barbudo (S): *Macaca silenus*
Macaco de cola de león (S): *Macaca silenus*
Macagua rieur (F): *Herpetotheres cachinnans*
Macaón de Córcega (S): *Papilio hospiton*
Macaones (F): *Bhutanitis* spp.
Macaque à face rouge (F): *Macaca fuscata*
Macaque à queue de cochon (F): *Macaca nemestrina*
Macaque à queue de lion (F): *Macaca silenus*
Macaque bonnet chinois (F): *Macaca radiata*
Macaque brun (F): *Macaca arctoides*
Macaque commun (F): *Macaca radiata*
Macaque couronné (F): *Macaca sinica*
Macaque crabier (F): *Macaca fascicularis*
Macaque d' Assam (F): *Macaca assamensis*
Macaque de Buffon (F): *Macaca fascicularis*
Macaque de Formose (F): *Macaca cyclopis*
Macaque de Gibraltar (F): *Macaca sylvanus*
Macaque de Tonkea (F): *Macaca tonkeana*
Macaque des Célèbes (F): *Macaca nigra*
Macaque du Tibet (F): *Macaca thibetana*
Macaque japonais (F): *Macaca fuscata*
Macaque maure (F): *Macaca maura*
Macaque ouandérou (F): *Macaca silenus*
Macaque rhésus (F): *Macaca mulatta*
Macaque toque (F): *Macaca sinica*
MacDonald's Weakfish (E): *Cynoscion macdonaldi*
Macdonnell Range Rock-rat (E): *Zyzomys pedunculatus*
Macgregoria pulchra : (E) Macgregor's Bird-of-paradise, (F) Paradisier de Macgregor **II** PARADISAEIDAE Av
Macgregor's Bird-of-paradise (E): *Macgregoria pulchra*
Machado's Girdled Lizard (E): *Cordylus machadoi*
Machaerhamphus alcinus = Macheiramphus alcinus
Machaon de Luzon (F): *Papilio chikae*
Macheiramphus alcinus : (E) Bat Hawk, Bat Kite, (S) Milano murcielaguero, (F) Milan des chauves-souris, **II** ACCIPITRIDAE Av
Mackinder's Eagle-Owl (E): *Bubo capensis*
Macklot's Python (E): *Liasis mackloti*
Macrocephalon maleo : (E) Celebes Maleo, Gray's Brush-turkey, Malee Fowl, Maleo, Maleo Fowl, Maleo Megapode, (S) Megapodio maleo, Megápodo cabecigrande, Talégalo maleo, (F) Maléo, Mégapode maléo, **I** MEGAPODIIDAE Av
Macrotis lagotis : (E) Bilby, Dalgyte, Greater Bilby, Greater Rabbit-eared Bandicoot, (S) Bandicot conejo, Cangurito narigudo grande, (F) Bandicootlapin, Grand bandicoot-lapin, **I** PERAMELIDAE Ma
Macrotis leucura : (E) Lesser Bilby, Lesser Rabbit-eared Bandicoot, White-tailed Rabbit-eared Bandicoot, Yallara, (S) Bandicot conejo de cola blanca, Cangurito narigudo coliblanco, (F) Bandicoot-lapin à queue blanche, Bandicoot-lapin mineur, Petit bandicoot-lapin, **I** PERAMELIDAE Ma
Macuco (S): *Tinamus solitarius*
Madagascar Angulated Tortoise (E): *Geochelone yniphora*
Madagascar Baza (E): *Aviceda madagascariensis*
Madagascar Big-headed Turtle (E): *Erymnochelys madagascariensis*
Madagascar Boa (E): *Acrantophis madagascariensis*
Madagascar Buzzard (E): *Buteo brachypterus*
Madagascar Chameleon (E): *Calumma capuroni*
Madagascar Cuckoo-Falcon (E): *Aviceda madagascariensis*
Madagascar Cuckoo-Hawk (E): *Aviceda madagascariensis*
Madagascar Day Gecko (E): *Phelsuma madagascariensis*
Madagascar Fish-eagle (E): *Haliaeetus vociferoides*
Madagascar Flat-shelled Tortoise (E): *Pyxis planicauda*
Madagascar Flying-fox (E): *Pteropus rufus*
Madagascar Forest Chameleon (E): *Furcifer campani*
Madagascar Fruit Bat (E): *Pteropus rufus*

Madagascar Giant Chameleon (E): *Furcifer verrucosus*
Madagascar Giant Spiny Chameleon (E): *Furcifer verrucosus*
Madagascar Golden Frog (E): *Mantella madagascariensis*
Madagascar Grass Owl (E): *Tyto soumagnei*
Madagascar Ground Boa (E): *Acrantophis dumerili*
Madagascar ground boas (E): *Acrantophis spp.*
Madagascar Gymnogene (E): *Polyboroides radiatus*
Madagascar Harrier (E): *Circus maillardi*
Madagascar Harrier-Hawk (E): *Polyboroides radiatus*
Madagascar Hawk-Owl (E): *Ninox superciliaris*
Madagascar Kestrel (E): *Falco newtoni*
Madagascar Lovebird (E): *Agapornis canus*
Madagascar Marsh-Harrier (E): *Circus maillardi*
Madagascar Owl (E): *Asio madagascariensis/ Tyto soumagnei*
Madagascar Red Owl (E): *Tyto soumagnei*
Madagascar Scops-Owl (E): *Otus rutilus*
Madagascar Serpent-Eagle (E): *Eutriorchis astur*
Madagascar Sideneck Turtle (E): *Erymnochelys madagascariensis*
Madagascar Sparrowhawk (E): *Accipiter madagascariensis*
Madagascar Teal (E): *Anas bernieri*
Madagascar Tortoise (E): *Geochelone yniphora*
Madagascar Tree Boa (E): *Sanzinia madagascariensis*
Madarasz's Tiger-Parrot (E): *Psittacella madaraszi*
Madracis asanoi : II POCILLOPORIDAE An
Madracis asperula : II POCILLOPORIDAE An
Madracis brueggemanni : II POCILLOPORIDAE An
Madracis decactis : (E) Green Cactus Coral, Ten-ray Star Coral II POCILLOPORIDAE An
Madracis formosa : (E) Eight-ray Finger Coral II POCILLOPORIDAE An
Madracis hellana : II POCILLOPORIDAE An
Madracis interjecta : II POCILLOPORIDAE An
Madracis kauaiensis : II POCILLOPORIDAE An
Madracis kirbyi : II POCILLOPORIDAE An
Madracis mirabilis = *Madracis myriaster*
Madracis myriaster : (E) Striate Finger Coral, Yellow Pencil Coral II POCILLOPORIDAE An
Madracis pharensis : (E) Star Coral II POCILLOPORIDAE An
Madracis profunda : II POCILLOPORIDAE An
Madracis senaria : II POCILLOPORIDAE An
Madracis singularis : II POCILLOPORIDAE An
Madras Treeshrew (E): *Anathana ellioti*
Madrepora arbuscula : II OCULINIDAE An
Madrepora candida = *Madrepora oculata*
Madrepora carolina : II OCULINIDAE An
Madrepora formosa = *Madrepora oculata*
Madrepora kauaiensis : II OCULINIDAE An
Madrepora minutiseptum : II OCULINIDAE An
Madrepora oculata : II OCULINIDAE An
Madrepora porcellana : II OCULINIDAE An
Madrepora vitiae = *Madrepora oculata*
Magdalena River Turtle (E): *Podocnemis lewyana*
Magenta-throated Woodstar (E): *Calliphlox bryantae*
Magistrate Colobus (E): *Colobus guereza*
Magnificent Bird-of-paradise (E): *Cicinnurus magnificus*
Magnificent Hummingbird (E): *Eugenes fulgens*
Magnificent Quetzal (E): *Pharomachrus mocinno*
Magnificent Riflebird (E): *Ptiloris magnificus*
Magot (F): *Macaca sylvanus*
Magot commun (F): *Macaca sylvanus*
Magpie Mannikin (E): *Lonchura fringilloides*
Magpie Munia (E): *Lonchura fringilloides*
Mahali à calotte marron (F): *Plocepasser superciliosus*
Mailmbo capirotado (S): *Anaplectes rubriceps*
Mainate (F): *Leucopsar rothschildi*
Mainate de Rothschild (F): *Leucopsar rothschildi*
Mainate religieux (F): *Gracula religiosa*
Mainland Serow (E): *Naemorhedus sumatraensis*
Maja chico (S): *Tropidophis melanurus*
Maja de Sta. María (S): *Epicrates angulifer*

Major Mitchell's Cockatoo (E): *Cacatua leadbeateri*
Maki à bourre (F): *Avahi laniger*
Maki ardilla (S): *Phaner furcifer*
Maki brun (F): *Eulemur fulvus*
Maki catta (F): *Lemur catta*
Maki coligordo (S): *Cheirogaleus major/ Cheirogaleus medius*
Maki horquilla (S): *Phaner furcifer*
Maki mongoz (F): *Eulemur mongoz*
Maki noir (F): *Eulemur macaco*
Maki ratón (S): *Microcebus murinus/ Microcebus rufus*
Maki ratón de Coquerel (S): *Microcebus coquereli*
Maki vari (F): *Varecia variegata*
Makis (S): CHEIROGALEIDAE spp.
Makisratone (S): *Microcebus coquereli/ Microcebus murinus*
Malabar Civet (E): *Viverra civettina*
Malabar Large-spotted Civet (E): *Viverra civettina*
Malabar Parakeet (E): *Psittacula columboides*
Malabar Pied-Hornbill (E): *Anthracoceros coronatus*
Malacochersus tornieri : (E) Crevice Tortoise, Pancake Tortoise, Softshell Tortoise, Tornier's Tortoise, (S) Tortuga de cuña, (F) Tortue à carapace souple, Tortue de Tornier, II TESTUDINIDAE Re
Malagasy Civet (E): *Fossa fossana*
Malagasy Flat-tailed Tortoise (E): *Pyxis planicauda*
Malagasy Giant Chameleon (E): *Furcifer oustaleti*
Malagasy Ground Boa (E): *Acrantophis madagascariensis*
Malagasy Marsh-Harrier (E): *Circus maillardi*
Malagasy Mongoose (E): *Eupleres goudotii*
Malagasy Scops-Owl (E): *Otus rutilus*
Malay Birdwing (E): *Troides amphrysus*
Malay Fish-Owl (E): *Ketupa ketupu*
Malayan Bonytongue (E): *Scleropages formosus*
Malayan Gharial (E): *Tomistoma schlegelii*
Malayan Monitor (E): *Varanus salvator*
Malayan Pangolin (E): *Manis javanica*
Malayan Peacock-pheasant (E): *Polyplectron malacense*
Malayan Sun Bear (E): *Helarctos malayanus*
Malayan Tapir (E): *Tapirus indicus*
Malaysian Black Hornbill (E): *Anthracoceros malayanus*
Malaysian Box Turtle (E): *Cuora amboinensis*
Malaysian Giant Terrapin (E): *Orlitia borneensis*
Malaysian Giant Turtle (E): *Orlitia borneensis*
Malaysian Pied-Hornbill (E): *Anthracoceros albirostris*
Malaysian Treeshrew (E): *Tupaia glis*
Malcolm's Ethiopian Toad (E): *Altiphrynoides malcolmi*
Malee Fowl (E): *Macrocephalon maleo*
Maleo (E): *Macrocephalon maleo*
Maléo (F): *Macrocephalon maleo*
Maleo Fowl (E): *Macrocephalon maleo*
Maleo Megapode (E): *Macrocephalon maleo*
Malherbe's Parakeet (E): *Cyanoramphus malherbi*
Malimbe à bec bleu (F): *Malimbus nitens*
Malimbe à gorge noire (F): *Malimbus cassini*
Malimbe à queue rouge (F): *Malimbus scutatus*
Malimbe à tête rouge (F): *Malimbus rubricollis*
Malimbe de Cassin (F): *Malimbus cassini*
Malimbe huppé (F): *Malimbus malimbicus*
Malimbo cabecinegro (S): *Malimbus nitens*
Malimbo cuellirrojo (S): *Malimbus rubricollis*
Malimbo culirrojo (S): *Malimbus scutatus*
Malimbo moñudo (S): *Malimbus malimbicus*
Malimbus cassini : (E) Black-throated Malimbe, Cassin's Malimbe, (F) Malimbe à gorge noire, Malimbe de Cassin III PLOCEIDAE Av
Malimbus malimbicus : (E) Crested Malimbe, (S) Malimbo moñudo, (F) Malimbe huppé, III PLOCEIDAE Av
Malimbus nitens : (E) Blue-billed Malimbe, Gray's Malimbe, (S) Malimbo cabecinegro, (F) Malimbe à bec bleu, III PLOCEIDAE Av
Malimbus rubriceps = *Anaplectes rubriceps*

Checklist of fauna/Lista de especies de fauna/Liste des espèces animales

Malimbus rubricollis : (E) Red-headed Malimbe, Red-headed Weaver, (S) Malimbo cuellirrojo, (F) Malimbe à tête rouge, **III** PLOCEIDAE Av

Malimbus scutatus : (E) Red-vented Malimbe, (S) Malimbo culirrojo, (F) Malimbe à queue rouge, **III** PLOCEIDAE Av

Mallee Ringneck (E): *Barnardius barnardi*

Malure occidental (F): *Dasyornis longirostris*

Malvasía (S): *Oxyura leucocephala*

Malvasía cabeciblanca (S): *Oxyura leucocephala*

Manatí amazónico (S): *Trichechus inunguis*

Manatí de Senegal (S): *Trichechus senegalensis*

Manatí norteamericano (S): *Trichechus manatus*

Manchot de Humboldt (F): *Spheniscus humboldti*

Manchot du Cap (F): *Spheniscus demersus*

Manchurian Crane (E): *Grus japonensis*

Manchurian Eared-Pheasant (E): *Crossoptilon mantchuricum*

Manchurian Red-footed Falcon (E): *Falco amurensis*

Manco (S): *Eira barbara*

Mandingoa nitidula : (E) Green Twinspot, Green-backed Twinspot, (F) Astrild vert pointillé, Sénégali vert **III** ESTRILDIDAE Av

Mandril (S): *Mandrillus sphinx*

Mandrill (E/S/F): *Mandrillus sphinx*

Mandrillus leucophaeus : (E) Drill, (S) Dril, Drill, (F) Drill, **I** CERCOPITHECIDAE Ma

Mandrillus sphinx : (E) Mandrill, (S) Mandril, Mandrill, (F) Mandrill, **I** CERCOPITHECIDAE Ma

Man-eater shark (E): *Carcharodon carcharias*

Maned Owl (E): *Jubula lettii*

Maned Wolf (E): *Chrysocyon brachyurus*

Mangabe (F): *Cercocebus galeritus*

Mangabey à crête (F): *Cercocebus galeritus galeritus*

Mangabey agile (F): *Cercocebus agilis*

Mangabey couronné (F): *Cercocebus torquatus*

Mangabey crestado (S): *Cercocebus galeritus*

Mangabey crestado ventriblanco (S): *Cercocebus galeritus galeritus*

Mangabey de collar blanco (S): *Cercocebus torquatus*

Mangabey de la Tana (F): *Cercocebus galeritus galeritus*

Mangabey de mejillas grises (S): *Lophocebus albigena*

Mangabey enfumé (F): *Cercocebus torquatus*

Mangeur d'hommes (F): *Carcharodon carcharias*

Mangeur d'oeufs asiatique (F): *Elachistodon westermanni*

Mangeur d'oeufs indien (F): *Elachistodon westermanni*

Mangeur d'oeufs indien de Westermann (F): *Elachistodon westermanni*

Mango (S): *Anthracothorax nigricollis*

Mango à cravate noire (F): *Anthracothorax nigricollis*

Mango à cravate verte (F): *Anthracothorax viridigula*

Mango Antillano (S): *Anthracothorax dominicus*

Mango de la Jamaïque (F): *Anthracothorax mango*

Mango de Prévost (F): *Anthracothorax prevostii*

Mango de Veragua (S/F): *Anthracothorax veraguensis*

Mango doré (F): *Anthracothorax dominicus*

Mango gargantiverde (S): *Anthracothorax viridigula*

Mango gorginegro (S): *Anthracothorax nigricollis*

Mango gorgiverde (S): *Anthracothorax viridigula*

Mango Jamaicano (S): *Anthracothorax mango*

Mango pechinegro (S): *Anthracothorax nigricollis*

Mango pechiverde (S): *Anthracothorax prevostii*

Mango picolezna (S): *Anthracothorax recurvirostris*

Mango portorriqueño (S): *Anthracothorax viridis*

Mango vert (F): *Anthracothorax viridis*

Mangosta cangrejera (S): *Herpestes urva*

Mangosta colicorta oscura (S): *Herpestes brachyurus fuscus*

Mangosta de manchas doradas (S): *Herpestes javanicus auropunctatus*

Mangosta de nuca rayada (S): *Herpestes vitticollis*

Mangosta dentipequeno (S): *Eupleres goudotii*

Mangosta gris de la India (S): *Herpestes edwardsii*

Mangosta roja de la India (S): *Herpestes smithii*

Mango-taniwha (E): *Carcharodon carcharias*

Mango-ururoa (E): *Carcharodon carcharias*

Mangouste à cou rayé (F): *Herpestes vitticollis*

Mangouste à queue courte de l'Inde (F): *Herpestes brachyurus fuscus*

Mangouste crabière (F): *Herpestes urva*

Mangouste de Smith (F): *Herpestes smithii*

Mangouste d'Edwards (F): *Herpestes edwardsii*

Mangouste grise de l'Inde (F): *Herpestes edwardsii*

Mangrove Black-Hawk (E): *Buteogallus subtilis*

Mangrove Hummingbird (E): *Polyerata boucardi*

Mangrove Monitor (E): *Varanus indicus/ Varanus semiremex*

Manicina areolata : (E) Rose Coral **II** FAVIIDAE An

Manigordo (S): *Leopardus pardalis*

Manis spp.: (E) Pangolins, (S) Pangolines, Pangolínos, (F) Pangolins, **II** MANIDAE Ma

Manis crassicaudata : (E) Indian Pangolin, Thick-tailed Pangolin, (S) Pangolín indio, (F) Grand pangolin de l'Inde, Pangolin à grosse queue, **II** MANIDAE Ma

Manis culionensis = Manis javanica

Manis gigantea : (E) Giant Ground Pangolin, Giant Pangolin, (S) Pangolín gigante, (F) Grand pangolin, Pangolin géant, **II** MANIDAE Ma

Manis javanica : (E) Malayan Pangolin, (S) Pangolín malayo, (F) Pangolin javanais, Pangolin malais, **II** MANIDAE Ma

Manis longicaudata = Manis tetradactyla

Manis pentadactyla : (E) Chinese Pangolin, (S) Pangolín chino, (F) Pangolin à queue courte, Pangolin de Chine, **II** MANIDAE Ma

Manis temminckii : (E) Cape Pangolin, Scaly Anteater, South African Pangolin, Temminck's Ground Pangolin, (S) Pangolín del Cabo, (F) Pangolin de Temminck, Pangolin terrestre du Cap, **II** MANIDAE Ma

Manis tetradactyla : (E) Black-bellied Pangolin, Long-tailed Pangolin, (S) Pangolín de cola larga, (F) Pangolin à longue queue, Pangolin tétradactyle, **II** MANIDAE Ma

Manis tricuspis : (E) Three-cusped Pangolin, Tree Pangolin, White-bellied Pangolin, (F) Pangolin à écailles tricuspides, Pangolin commun, Tricuspide **II** MANIDAE Ma

Manouria emys : (E) Asian Giant Tortoise, Asian Tortoise, Black Giant Tortoise, Burmese Brown Tortoise, Burmese Mountain Tortoise, Six-legged Tortoise, (F) Tortue brune **II** TESTUDINIDAE Re

Manouria impressa : (E) Impressed Tortoise, (S) Tortuga marrón de Burma, (F) Tortue imprimée, **II** TESTUDINIDAE Re

Mansfield's Three-tailed Swallowtail (E): *Bhutanitis mansfieldi*

Mantanani Scops-Owl (E): *Otus mantananensis*

Mantella spp.: (E) Golden frogs, Mantellas, (F) Mantelles, (S) Ranas doradas, **II** MANTELLIDAE Am

Mantella aurantiaca : (E) Golden Frog, Golden Mantella, (S) Rana dorada, Ranita dorada de Madagascar, (F) Mantelle dorée, **II** MANTELLIDAE Am

Mantella aurantiaca ssp. *milotympanum = Mantella milotympanum*

Mantella baroni : **II** MANTELLIDAE Am

Mantella bernhardi : (E) Bernhard's Mantella **II** MANTELLIDAE Am

Mantella betsileo : (E) Betsileo Golden Frog, Brown Mantella **II** MANTELLIDAE Am

Mantella cowani : (E) Black Golden Frog, Cowan's Mantella **II** MANTELLIDAE Am

Mantella cowani ssp. *nigricans = Mantella nigricans*

Mantella crocea : (E) Eastern Golden Frog, Yellow Mantella **II** MANTELLIDAE Am

Mantella expectata : (E) Blue-legged Mantella, Tulear Golden Frog **II** MANTELLIDAE Am

Mantella haraldmeieri : (E) Haraldmeier's Mantella **II** MANTELLIDAE Am

Checklist of fauna/Lista de especies de fauna/Liste des espèces animales

Mantella laevigata : (E) Arboreal Mantella, Folohy
Golden Frog **II** MANTELLIDAE Am
Mantella madagascariensis : (E) Madagascar Golden Frog
II MANTELLIDAE Am
Mantella madagascariensis ssp. *haraldmeieri = Mantella
haraldmeieri*
Mantella manery : **II** MANTELLIDAE Am
Mantella milotympanum : **II** MANTELLIDAE Am
Mantella nigricans : **II** MANTELLIDAE Am
Mantella pulchra : (E) Parker's Golden Frog **II**
MANTELLIDAE Am
Mantella viridis : (E) Green Golden Frog, Green Mantella
II MANTELLIDAE Am
Mantellas (E): *Mantella* spp.
Mantelle dorée (F): *Mantella aurantiaca*
Mantelles (F): *Mantella* spp.
Mantled Hawk (E): *Leucopternis polionota*
Mantled Howler (E): *Alouatta palliata*
Mantled Howling Monkey (E): *Alouatta palliata*
Manucaude de Comrie (F): *Manucodia comrii*
Manucaude de Jobi (F): *Manucodia jobiensis*
Manucaude de Keraudren (F): *Manucodia keraudrenii*
Manucaude noir (F): *Manucodia atra*
Manucaude vert (F): *Manucodia chalybata*
Manucodia atra : (E) Glossy-mantled Manucode, (F)
Manucaude noir, Paradisier noir **II**
PARADISAEIDAE Av
Manucodia chalybata : (E) Crinkle-collared Manucode,
(F) Manucaude vert, Paradisier vert **II**
PARADISAEIDAE Av
Manucodia comrii : (E) Curl-crested Manucode, (F)
Manucaude de Comrie, Paradisier d'Entrecasteaux **II**
PARADISAEIDAE Av
Manucodia jobiensis : (E) Jobi Manucode, (F) Manucaude
de Jobi, Paradisier de Jobi **II** PARADISAEIDAE Av
Manucodia keraudrenii : (E) Trumpet Manucode,
Trumpetbird, (F) Manucaude de Keraudren, Paradisier
de Keraudren **II** PARADISAEIDAE Av
Manus Boobook (E): *Ninox meeki*
Manus Green Tree Snail (E): *Papustyla pulcherrima*
Manus Hawk-Owl (E): *Ninox meeki*
Manus Masked-owl (E): *Tyto manusi*
Many-coloured Parakeet (E): *Psephotus varius*
Many-spotted Hummingbird (E): *Leucippus hypostictus*
Marabou Stork (E): *Leptoptilos crumeniferus*
Marabout (F): *Leptoptilos crumeniferus*
Marabout africain (F): *Leptoptilos crumeniferus*
Marabout d'Afrique (F): *Leptoptilos crumeniferus*
Marabú (S): *Leptoptilos crumeniferus*
Marabú Africano (S): *Leptoptilos crumeniferus*
Maracana cuellidorada (S): *Propyrrhura auricollis*
Maracana dorsirroja (S): *Propyrrhura maracana*
Maranon Poison Frog (E): *Dendrobates mysteriosus*
Marbled Cat (E): *Pardofelis marmorata*
Marbled Poison Frog (E): *Epipedobates boulengeri*
Marca's Marmoset (E): *Callithrix marcai*
Marco Polo Sheep (E): *Ovis ammon*
Margaretta's Hermit (E): *Phaethornis malaris*
Margay (E/S/F): *Leopardus wiedii*
Marginated Tortoise (E): *Testudo marginata*
Margined Tortoise (E): *Testudo marginata*
Marianas Flying-fox (E): *Pteropus mariannus*
Marianas Island Duck (E): *Anas oustaleti*
Marianas Mallard (E): *Anas oustaleti*
Marine Iguana (E): *Amblyrhynchus cristatus*
Marine Otter (E): *Lontra felina*
Marine turtles (E): CHELONIIDAE spp.
Marion (S): *Acipenser sturio*
Mariposa apollo (S): *Parnassius apollo*
Markhor (E/S/F): *Capra falconeri*
Marl (E): *Perameles bougainville*
Marmoset Santarem (F): *Callithrix humeralifer*
Marmota caudata : (E) Long-tailed Marmot, (S) Marmota
de cola larga, (F) Marmote à longue queue, **III**
SCIURIDAE Ma

Marmota de cola larga (S): *Marmota caudata*
Marmota del Himalaya (S): *Marmota himalayana*
Marmota himalayana : (E) Himalayan Marmot, (S)
Marmota del Himalaya, (F) Marmote de l'Himalaya,
III SCIURIDAE Ma
Marmote à longue queue (F): *Marmota caudata*
Marmote de l'Himalaya (F): *Marmota himalayana*
Marmouset à oreilles blanches (F): *Callithrix aurita*
Maroantsetra Chameleon (E): *Calumma linota*
Marojejy Leaf Chameleon (E): *Brookesia griveaudi*
Maroon Langur (E): *Presbytis rubicunda*
Maroon Leaf Monkey (E): *Presbytis rubicunda*
Maroon-bellied Parakeet (E): *Pyrrhura frontalis*
Maroon-breasted Crowned-Pigeon (E): *Goura
scheepmakeri*
Maroon-faced Parakeet (E): *Pyrrhura leucotis*
Maroon-fronted Parrot (E): *Rhynchopsitta terrisi*
Maroon-rumped Hanging-Parrot (E): *Loriculus stigmatus*
Maroon-tailed Conure (E): *Pyrrhura melanura*
Maroon-tailed Parakeet (E): *Pyrrhura melanura*
Marrajo (S): *Carcharodon carcharias*
Marrajo ballenato (S): *Cetorhinus maximus*
Marrajo gigante (S): *Cetorhinus maximus*
Marsh Crocodile (E): *Crocodylus palustris*
Marsh Deer (E): *Blastocerus dichotomus*
Marsh Harrier (E): *Circus aeruginosus*
Marsh Hawk (E): *Circus cyaneus*
Marsh Owl (E): *Asio capensis*
Marsh Terrapin (E): *Pelomedusa subrufa*
Marshbuck (E): *Tragelaphus spekii*
Marsopa común (S): *Phocoena phocoena*
Marsopa de anteojo (S): *Australophocaena dioptrica*
Marsopa de Dall (S): *Phocoenoides dalli*
Marsopa espinosa (S): *Phocoena spinipinnis*
Marsopa negra (S): *Neophocaena phocaenoides*
Marsouin (F): *Phocoena phocoena*
Marsouin à lunettes (F): *Australophocaena dioptrica*
Marsouin aptère (F): *Neophocaena phocaenoides*
Marsouin commun (F): *Phocoena phocoena*
Marsouin de Burmeister (F): *Phocoena spinipinnis*
Marsouin de Dall (F): *Phocoenoides dalli*
Marsouin de Lahille (F): *Australophocaena dioptrica*
Marsouin du Golfe de Californie (F): *Phocoena sinus*
Marsouin sans nageoires (F): *Neophocaena phocaenoides*
Marta (S): *Potos flavus*
Marta de cuello amarillo (S): *Martes flavigula*
Martes flavigula : (E) Yellow-throated Marten, (S) Marta
de cuello amarillo, (F) Martre à gorge jaune, **III**
MUSTELIDAE Ma
Martes flavigula ssp. *gwatkinsii = Martes gwatkinsii*
Martes foina intermedia : (E) Central Asian Stone Marten,
(F) Fouine **III** MUSTELIDAE Ma
Martes gwatkinsii : (E) Nilgiri Marten, (F) Martre de l'Inde
du Sud **III** MUSTELIDAE Ma
Martial Eagle (E): *Polemaetus bellicosus*
Martin de Rothschild (F): *Leucopsar rothschildi*
Martre à gorge jaune (F): *Martes flavigula*
Martre de l'Inde du Sud (F): *Martes gwatkinsii*
Martucha (S): *Potos flavus*
Marvellous Spatuletail (E): *Loddigesia mirabilis*
Ma's Night Monkey (E): *Aotus nancymaae*
Masacuate (E): *Boa constrictor*
Mascarene Paradise-Flycatcher (E): *Terpsiphone
bourbonnensis*
Masked Bobwhite (E): *Colinus virginianus ridgwayi*
Masked Dove (E): *Oena capensis*
Masked Flying-fox (E): *Pteropus personatus*
Masked Fruit Bat (E): *Pteropus personatus*
Masked Goura (E): *Goura scheepmakeri*
Masked Hawk (E): *Leucopternis melanops*
Masked Lovebird (E): *Agapornis personatus*
Masked Owl (E): *Tyto novaehollandiae*
Masked Palm Civet (E): *Paguma larvata*
Masked Shining-Parrot (E): *Prosopeia personata*
Masked Titi (E): *Callicebus personatus*

Checklist of fauna/Lista de especies de fauna/Liste des espèces animales

Massive Starlet Coral (E): *Siderastrea siderea*
Mastigures (E): *Uromastyx* spp.
Masurana (S): *Clelia clelia*
Matamico blanco (S): *Phalcoboenus albogularis*
Matamico cordillerano (S): *Phalcoboenus megalopterus*
Matamico estriado (S): *Phalcoboenus australis*
Matamico grande (S): *Phalcoboenus australis*
Matschie's Dwarf Chameleon (E): *Bradypodion tenue*
Matschie's Galago (E): *Galago matschiei*
Matundu Dwarf Galago (E): *Galagoides udzungwensis*
Maués Marmoset (E): *Callithrix mauesi*
Mauremys annamensis = Annamemys annamensis
Mauremys mutica : (E) Yellow Pond Turtle **II**
　　EMYDIDAE Re
Mauritius Day Gecko (E): *Phelsuma guimbeaui*
Mauritius Greater Day Gecko (E): *Phelsuma cepediana*
Mauritius Kestrel (E): *Falco punctatus*
Mauritius Lowland Forest Day Gecko (E): *Phelsuma guimbeaui*
Mauritius Parakeet (E): *Psittacula echo*
Mauritius Ring-necked Parakeet (E): *Psittacula echo*
Maxima Clam (E): *Tridacna maxima*
Maxwell's Black Weaver (E): *Ploceus albinucha*
Mayotte Chameleon (E): *Furcifer polleni*
Mazama americana cerasina : (E) Guatemalan Red Brocket, Middle American Red Brocket **III** CERVIDAE Ma
Maze Coral (E): *Meandrina maeandrites*
Maze corals (E): *Plerogyra* spp.
McCord's Box Turtle (E): *Cuora mccordi*
McLachlan's Girdled Lizard (E): *Cordylus mclachlani*
McLachlan's Spiny-tailed Lizard (E): *Cordylus mclachlani*
Meadow Viper (E): *Vipera ursinii*
Mealy Amazon (E): *Amazona farinosa*
Mealy Parrot (E): *Amazona farinosa*
Mealy Rosella (E): *Platycercus adscitus*
Meandrina brasiliensis : **II** MEANDRINIIDAE An
Meandrina maeandrites : (E) Maze Coral **II** MEANDRINIIDAE An
Meandrina memorialis = Meandrina maeandrites
Mearns's Flying-fox (E): *Pteropus mearnsi*
Medicinal Leech (E): *Hirudo medicinalis*
Mediterranean Chameleon (E): *Chamaeleo chamaeleon*
Mediterranean Monk Seal (E): *Monachus monachus*
Meek's Lorikeet (E): *Charmosyna meeki*
Meek's Pygmy-Parrot (E): *Micropsitta meeki*
MEGALADAPIDAE spp.: (E) Sportive lemurs, (S) Lemurs comadreja, (F) Lépilémurs, **I** Ma
Megalobatrachus davidianus = Andrias davidianus
Megalobatrachus japonicus = Andrias japonicus
Megalonaias nickliniana = Unio nickliniana
Megamuntiacus vuquanghensis : (E) Giant Muntjac, (S) Muntjac gigante, (F) Muntjac géant, **I** CERVIDAE Ma
Mégapode maléo (F): *Macrocephalon maleo*
Megapodio maleo (S): *Macrocephalon maleo*
Megápodo cabecigrande (S): *Macrocephalon maleo*
Megaptera novaeangliae : (E) Bunch, Hump Whale, Humpback Whale, Hunchbacked Whale, (S) Ballena jorobada, Gubarte, Jorobada, Rorcual jorobado, (F) Baleine à bosse, Baleine à taquet, Jubarte, Mégaptère, Rorqual à bosse, Rorqual du Cap, **I** BALAENOPTERIDAE Ma
Mégaptère (F): *Megaptera novaeangliae*
Megatriorchis doriae : (E) Doria's Goshawk, (S) Azor de Doria, (F) Autour de Doria, **II** ACCIPITRIDAE Av
Melampitta gigantea : (E) Greater Melampitta, (F) Grande mélampitte **II** PARADISAEIDAE Av
Melampitta lugubris : (E) Lesser Melampitta, (F) Petite mélampitte **II** PARADISAEIDAE Av

Melanochelys tricarinata : (E) Three-keeled Land Tortoise, Three-keeled Land Turtle, Tricarinate Hill Turtle, (S) Galápago terrestre, Galápago tricarenado, (F) Émyde indienne à trois carènes, Émyde ocellée de Birmanie, Géoémyde tricarénée, Tortue tricarénée, **I** EMYDIDAE Re
Melanoperdix nigra : (E) Black Partridge, Black Wood-Partridge, (S) Perdiz de bosque negra, Perdiz negra, (F) Perdrix noire, Rouloul noir, **III** PHASIANIDAE Av
Melanosuchus niger : (E) Black Caiman, (S) Caimán negro, Lagarto negro, (F) Caïman noir, **I/II** ALLIGATORIDAE Re
Melanotrochilus fuscus = Florisuga fusca
Meleagris ocellata = Agriocharis ocellata
Melero de casco (S): *Lichenostomus melanops cassidix*
Melierax canorus : (E) Pale Chanting-Goshawk, (S) Azor-lagartijero claro, (F) Autour chanteur, **II** ACCIPITRIDAE Av
Melierax canorus ssp. *poliopterus = Melierax poliopterus*
Melierax gabar : (E) Gabar Goshawk, (S) Gavilán gabar, (F) Autour gabar, **II** ACCIPITRIDAE Av
Melierax metabates : (E) Dark Chanting-Goshawk, (S) Azor lagartijero oscuro, (F) Autour sombre, **II** ACCIPITRIDAE Av
Melierax poliopterus : (E) Eastern Chanting-Goshawk, (S) Azor-lagartijero somalí, (F) Autour à ailes grises, **II** ACCIPITRIDAE Av
Melífago de casco (S): *Lichenostomus melanops cassidix*
Meliphaga cassidix = Lichenostomus melanops ssp. *cassidix*
Méliphage casqué (F): *Lichenostomus melanops cassidix*
Méliphage cornu (F): *Lichenostomus melanops cassidix*
Meller's Chameleon (E): *Chamaeleo melleri*
Mellisuga helenae : (E) Bee Hummingbird, (S) Colibrí zunzuncito, (F) Colibri d'Helen, **II** TROCHILIDAE Av
Mellisuga minima : (E) Vervain Hummingbird, (S) Colibrí zumbadorcito, Zumbadorcito, (F) Colibri nain, **II** TROCHILIDAE Av
Mellivora capensis : (E) Honey Badger, Ratel, (S) Ratel, Tejón melívoro, (F) Ratel, **III** MUSTELIDAE Ma
Melodious Laughingthrush (E): *Garrulax canorus*
Melon-headed Whale (E): *Peponocephala electra*
Melopsittacus undulatus : (E) Budgerigar, (S) Budgerigar ondulado, (F) Perruche inseparable, Peruche ondulée, **NC** PSITTACIDAE Av
Melursus ursinus : (E) Sloth Bear, (S) Oso bezudo, Oso perezoso, (F) Ours à miel , Ours lippu de l'Inde, Ours prochile lippu, **I** URSIDAE Ma
Menado Coelacanth (E): *Latimeria menadoensis*
Mentaur Scops-Owl (E): *Otus umbra*
Mentawai Gibbon (E): *Hylobates klossii*
Mentawai Langur (E): *Presbytis potenziani*
Mentawai Leaf Monkey (E): *Presbytis potenziani*
Mentawai Scops-Owl (E): *Otus mentawi*
Mentawai Serpent-Eagle (E): *Spilornis cheela*
Mentawai Treeshrew (E): *Tupaia chrysogaster*
Mentawi Islands Snub-nosed Langur (E): *Nasalis concolor*
Merles des Indes (F): *Gracula religiosa*
Merlin (E): *Falco columbarius*
Merrin (E): *Onychogalea fraenata*
Mertens's Day Gecko (E): *Phelsuma robertmertensi*
Mertens's Water Monitor (E): *Varanus mertensi*
Merulina ampliata : (E) Crispy Crust Coral, Ruffled Coral **II** MERULINIDAE An
Merulina scabricula : **II** MERULINIDAE An
Merulina scheeri : **II** MERULINIDAE An
Mésangette rayée (F): *Pholidornis rushiae*
Mésia (F): *Leiothrix argentauris*
Mesia (S): *Leiothrix argentauris*
Mesoplodon bahamondi = Mesoplodon traversii
Mesoplodon bidens : (E) Sowerby's Beaked Whale, (S) Ballena de pico de Sowerby, (F) Mesoplodon de Sowerby, **II** ZIPHIIDAE Ma

Mesoplodon bowdoini : (E) Andrews's Beaked Whale, Splaytooth Beaked Whale, (S) Ballena de pico de Andrew, (F) Mesoplodon de Bowdoin, **II** ZIPHIIDAE Ma

Mesoplodon carlhubbsi : (E) Arch-beaked Whale, Hubbs's Beaked Whale, (S) Ballena de pico de Hubbs, (F) Mesoplodon de Hubbs, **II** ZIPHIIDAE Ma

Mesoplodon de Blainville (F): *Mesoplodon densirostris*

Mesoplodon de Bowdoin (F): *Mesoplodon bowdoini*

Mesoplodon de Gervais (F): *Mesoplodon europaeus*

Mesoplodon de Gray (F): *Mesoplodon grayi*

Mesoplodon de Hubbs (F): *Mesoplodon carlhubbsi*

Mesoplodon de Layard (F): *Mesoplodon layardii*

Mesoplodon de Longman (F): *Indopacetus pacificus*

Mesoplodon de Nishiwaki (F): *Mesoplodon ginkgodens*

Mesoplodon de Sowerby (F): *Mesoplodon bidens*

Mesoplodon de Stejneger (F): *Mesoplodon stejnegeri*

Mesoplodon de True (F): *Mesoplodon mirus*

Mesoplodon densirostris : (E) Blainville's Beaked Whale, (S) Ballena de pico de Blainville, (F) Mesoplodon de Blainville, **II** ZIPHIIDAE Ma

Mesoplodon d'Hector (F): *Mesoplodon hectori*

Mesoplodon europaeus : (E) Gervais's Beaked Whale, Gulf Stream Beaked Whale, (S) Ballena de pico de Gervais, (F) Mesoplodon de Gervais, **II** ZIPHIIDAE Ma

Mesoplodon ginkgodens : (E) Ginkgo-toothed Beaked Whale, (F) Mesoplodon de Nishiwaki **II** ZIPHIIDAE Ma

Mesoplodon grayi : (E) Gray's Beaked Whale, Southern Beaked Whale, (S) Ballena de pico de Gray, (F) Mesoplodon de Gray, **II** ZIPHIIDAE Ma

Mesoplodon hectori : (E) Hector's Beaked Whale, Skew-beaked Whale, (S) Ballena de pico de Héctor, (F) Mesoplodon d'Hector, **II** ZIPHIIDAE Ma

Mesoplodon layardii : (E) Layard's Beaked Whale, Strap-toothed Whale, (S) Ballena de pico de Layard, (F) Mesoplodon de Layard, **II** ZIPHIIDAE Ma

Mesoplodon mirus : (E) True's Beaked Whale, (S) Ballena de pico de True, (F) Mesoplodon de True, **II** ZIPHIIDAE Ma

Mesoplodon pacificus = Indopacetus pacificus

Mesoplodon perrini : **II** ZIPHIIDAE Ma

Mesoplodon peruvianus : (E) Lesser Beaked Whale, Pygmy Beaked Whale, (F) Mesoplodon pygmée **II** ZIPHIIDAE Ma

Mesoplodon pygmée (F): *Mesoplodon peruvianus*

Mesoplodon stejnegeri : (E) Stejneger's Beaked Whale, (S) Ballena de pico de Stejneger, (F) Mesoplodon de Stejneger, **II** ZIPHIIDAE Ma

Mesoplodon traversii : **II** ZIPHIIDAE Ma

Mesopotamian Fallow Deer (E): *Dama mesopotamica*

Mesopotamian Mastigure (E): *Uromastyx loricata*

Mesopotamian Spiny-tailed Lizard (E): *Uromastyx loricata*

Messager sagittaire (F): *Sagittarius serpentarius*

Metallura aeneocauda : (E) Scaled Metaltail, (S) Metalura escamosa, (F) Métallure à queue d'airain, **II** TROCHILIDAE Av

Metallura baroni : (E) Violet-throated Metaltail, (S) Metalura de Azuay, Metalura gorjivioleta, (F) Métallure de Baron, **II** TROCHILIDAE Av

Metallura eupogon : (E) Fire-throated Metaltail, (S) Metalura barbafuego, (F) Métallure à gorge feu, **II** TROCHILIDAE Av

Metallura iracunda : (E) Perijá Metaltail, (S) Colibrí de Perijá, Metalura iracunda, (F) Métallure dorée, **II** TROCHILIDAE Av

Metallura malagae = Metallura aeneocauda

Metallura odomae : (E) Neblina Metaltail, (S) Metalura del Chinguela, (F) Métallure du Chinguela, **II** TROCHILIDAE Av

Metallura phoebe : (E) Black Metaltail, (S) Metalura negra, (F) Métallure phébé, **II** TROCHILIDAE Av

Metallura theresiae : (E) Coppery Metaltail, (S) Metalura de Teresa, (F) Métallure de Thérèse, **II** TROCHILIDAE Av

Metallura tyrianthina : (E) Tyrian Metaltail, (S) Colibrí verde colirrojo, Metalura tiria, (F) Métallure émeraude, **II** TROCHILIDAE Av

Metallura williami : (E) Viridian Metaltail, (S) Metalura verde, (F) Métallure verte, **II** TROCHILIDAE Av

Métallure à gorge feu (F): *Metallura eupogon*

Métallure à queue bronzée (F): *Chalcostigma heteropogon*

Métallure à queue d'airain (F): *Metallura aeneocauda*

Métallure à tête rousse (F): *Chalcostigma ruficeps*

Métallure arc-en-ciel (F): *Chalcostigma herrani*

Métallure de Baron (F): *Metallura baroni*

Métallure de Stanley (F): *Chalcostigma stanleyi*

Métallure de Thérèse (F): *Metallura theresiae*

Métallure dorée (F): *Metallura iracunda*

Métallure du Chinguela (F): *Metallura odomae*

Métallure émeraude (F): *Metallura tyrianthina*

Métallure olivâtre (F): *Chalcostigma olivaceum*

Métallure phébé (F): *Metallura phoebe*

Métallure verte (F): *Metallura williami*

Metalura barbafuego (S): *Metallura eupogon*

Metalura de Azuay (S): *Metallura baroni*

Metalura de Teresa (S): *Metallura theresiae*

Metalura del Chinguela (S): *Metallura odomae*

Metalura escamosa (S): *Metallura aeneocauda*

Metalura gorjivioleta (S): *Metallura baroni*

Metalura iracunda (S): *Metallura iracunda*

Metalura negra (S): *Metallura phoebe*

Metalura tiria (S): *Metallura tyrianthina*

Metalura verde (S): *Metallura williami*

Mexican Bighorn Sheep (E): *Ovis canadensis*

Mexican Blackcap Tarantula (E): *Brachypelma emilia*

Mexican Chachalaca (E): *Ortalis vetula*

Mexican Curassow (E): *Crax rubra*

Mexican Fireleg Tarantula (E): *Brachypelma boehmei*

Mexican Flameknee Tarantula (E): *Brachypelma auratum*

Mexican Giant Tortoise (E): *Gopherus flavomarginatus*

Mexican Grey Tarantula (E): *Aphonopelma pallidum*

Mexican Hairy Dwarf Porcupine (E): *Sphiggurus mexicanus*

Mexican Orangebeauty Tarantula (E): *Brachypelma baumgarteni*

Mexican Parrotlet (E): *Forpus cyanopygius*

Mexican Prairie Marmot (E): *Cynomys mexicanus*

Mexican Prairie-dog (E): *Cynomys mexicanus*

Mexican Pronghorn (E): *Antilocapra americana*

Mexican Redknee Tarantula (E): *Brachypelma smithi*

Mexican Redleg Tarantula (E): *Brachypelma emilia*

Mexican Redrump Tarantula (E): *Brachypelma vagans*

Mexican Ridley (E): *Lepidochelys kempi*

Mexican Sheartail (E): *Doricha eliza*

Mexican Tree Porcupine (E): *Sphiggurus mexicanus*

Mexican Woodnymph (E): *Thalurania ridgwayi*

Meyer's Goshawk (E): *Accipiter meyerianus*

Meyer's Hawk (E): *Accipiter meyerianus*

Meyer's Lorikeet (E): *Trichoglossus flavoviridis*

Meyer's Parrot (E): *Poicephalus meyeri*

Michoacan Orange Tarantula (E): *Brachypelma baumgarteni*

Mico acariensis = Callithrix acariensis

Mico argentatus = Callithrix argentata

Mico chrysoleucus = Callithrix humeralifer

Mico de noche (S): *Potos flavus/ Bassariscus sumichrasti*

Mico emiliae = Callithrix argentata

Mico humeralifer = Callithrix humeralifer

Mico humilis = Callithrix humilis

Mico intermedius = Callithrix argentata

Mico manicorensis = Callithrix manicorensis

Mico marcai = Callithrix marcai

Mico mauesi = Callithrix mauesi

Mico melanurus = Callithrix argentata

Mico nigriceps = Callithrix nigriceps

Mico rayado (S): *Bassariscus sumichrasti*

Checklist of fauna/Lista de especies de fauna/Liste des espèces animales

Mico saterei = Callithrix saterei
Micoleón (S): *Potos flavus*
Micrastur buckleyi : (E) Buckley's Forest-Falcon, Lesser
    Collared Forest-Falcon, Traylor's Forest-Falcon, (S)
    Gavilán de Traylor, Halcón-montés de Buckley, (F)
    Carnifex de Buckley, Carnifex de Traylor, **II**
    FALCONIDAE Av
Micrastur gilvicollis : (E) Lined Forest-Falcon, (S)
    Gavilán de collar, Halcón palomero del sur, Halcón-
    montés cabecigrís, (F) Carnifex à gorge cendrée, **II**
    FALCONIDAE Av
Micrastur mirandollei : (E) Slaty-backed Forest-Falcon,
    (S) Halcón de lomo pizarreño, Halcón-montés
    dorsigrís, (F) Carnifex ardoisé, **II** FALCONIDAE Av
Micrastur plumbeus : (E) Plumbeous Forest-Falcon, (S)
    Halcón-montés plomizo, (F) Carnifex plombé, **II**
    FALCONIDAE Av
Micrastur ruficollis : (E) Barred Forest-Falcon, (S)
    Caburé, Gavilán cuellirojo, Halcón cuellirrufo,
    Halcón palomero, Halcón-montés agavilanado, (F)
    Carnifex à cou roux, Carnifex barré, **II**
    FALCONIDAE Av
Micrastur ruficollis ssp. *gilvicollis = Micrastur gilvicollis*
Micrastur semitorquatus : (E) Collared Forest-Falcon, (S)
    Gavilán-reloj, Halcón semiacollarado, Halcón-montés
    collarejo, Halcón-selvático collarejo, (F) Carnifex à
    collier, **II** FALCONIDAE Av
Micrathene whitneyi : (E) Elf Owl, (S) Mochuelo de los
    saguaros, Mochuelo duende, Tecolotito enano, (F)
    Chevêchette des saguaros, Chevêchette-elfe, **II**
    STRIGIDAE Av
Micristodus punctatus = Rhincodon typus
Microcèbe de Coquerel (F): *Microcebus coquereli*
Microcèbe murin (F): *Microcebus murinus*
Microcebus berthae : (E) Berthe's Mouse Lemur **I**
    CHEIROGALEIDAE Ma
Microcebus coquereli : (E) Coquerel's Dwarf Lemur,
    Coquerel's Mouse-lemur, (S) Maki ratón de Coquerel,
    Makisratone, (F) Microcèbe de Coquerel, **I**
    CHEIROGALEIDAE Ma
Microcebus murinus : (E) Grey Mouse-lemur, Lesser
    Mouse-lemur, (S) Maki ratón, Makisratone, (F)
    Microcèbe murin, Petit microcèbe, **I**
    CHEIROGALEIDAE Ma
Microcebus murinus ssp. *rufus = Microcebus rufus*
Microcebus myoxinus = Microcebus murinus
Microcebus ravelobensis : (E) Golden-brown Mouse
    Lemur **I** CHEIROGALEIDAE Ma
Microcebus rufus : (E) Brown Mouse-lemur, Rufous
    Mouse-lemur, Russet Mouse-lemur, (S) Maki ratón **I**
    CHEIROGALEIDAE Ma
Microcebus sambiranensis : (E) Sambirano Mouse Lemur
    I CHEIROGALEIDAE Ma
Microcebus tavaratra : (E) Northern Rufous Mouse Lemur
    I CHEIROGALEIDAE Ma
Microchera albocoronata : (E) Snowcap, (S) Colibrí
    coroniblanco, (F) Colibri à coiffe blanche, **II**
    TROCHILIDAE Av
Microglosse noir (F): *Probosciger aterrimus*
Microhierax caerulescens : (E) Collared Falconet, Red-
    legged Falconet, Red-thighed Falconet, (S) Falconete
    acollarado, Halcón enano de la India, (F) Fauconnet à
    collier, **II** FALCONIDAE Av
Microhierax erythrogenys : (E) Philippine Falconet, (S)
    Falconete filipino, Halconcito de las Filipinas, (F)
    Fauconnet des Philippines, **II** FALCONIDAE Av
Microhierax fringillarius : (E) Black-legged Falconet,
    Black-sided Falconet, Black-thighed Falconet, (S)
    Falconete indonesio, Halconcito malayo, (F)
    Fauconnet moineau, **II** FALCONIDAE Av
Microhierax latifrons : (E) Bornean Falconet, White-
    fronted Falconet, (S) Falconete de Borneo, Halconcito
    de Borneo, (F) Fauconnet de Bornéo, **II**
    FALCONIDAE Av

Microhierax melanoleucos : (E) Pied Falconet, (S)
    Falconete pío, (F) Fauconnet noir-et-blanc, **II**
    FALCONIDAE Av
Microhierax melanoleucus = Microhierax melanoleucos
Microloro de Finsch (S): *Micropsitta finschii*
Microloro de Geelvink (S): *Micropsitta geelvinkiana*
Microloro de las Kai (S): *Micropsitta keiensis*
Microloro de Meek (S): *Micropsitta meeki*
Microloro pechirrojo (S): *Micropsitta bruijnii*
Microloro pusio (S): *Micropsitta pusio*
Micromussa amakusensis = Acanthastrea amakusensis
Micromussa diminuta : **II** MUSSIDAE An
Micromussa minuta = Acanthastrea minuta
Micromya trabalis = Villosa trabalis
Micronesian Flying-fox (E): *Pteropus mariannus*
Micronisus gabar = Melierax gabar
Micropsitta bruijnii : (E) Red-breasted Pygmy-Parrot, (S)
    Microloro pechirrojo, (F) Micropsitte de Bruijn,
    Perruche pygmée de Brujin, **II** PSITTACIDAE Av
Micropsitta finschii : (E) Finsch's Pygmy-Parrot, (S)
    Microloro de Finsch, (F) Micropsitte de Finsch, **II**
    PSITTACIDAE Av
Micropsitta geelvinkiana : (E) Geelvink Pygmy-Parrot, (S)
    Microloro de Geelvink, (F) Micropsitte de Geelvink,
    Perruche pygmée de Schlegel, **II** PSITTACIDAE Av
Micropsitta keiensis : (E) Yellow-capped Pygmy-Parrot,
    (S) Microloro de las Kai, (F) Micropsitte pygmée,
    Perruche pygmée de Salvadori, **II** PSITTACIDAE Av
Micropsitta meeki : (E) Meek's Pygmy-Parrot, (S)
    Microloro de Meek, (F) Micropsitte de Meek,
    Perruche pygmée de Meek, **II** PSITTACIDAE Av
Micropsitta pusio : (E) Buff-faced Pygmy-Parrot, (S)
    Microloro pusio, (F) Micropsitte à tête fauve,
    Perruche pygmée de Sclater, **II** PSITTACIDAE Av
Micropsitte à tête fauve (F): *Micropsitta pusio*
Micropsitte de Bruijn (F): *Micropsitta bruijnii*
Micropsitte de Finsch (F): *Micropsitta finschii*
Micropsitte de Geelvink (F): *Micropsitta geelvinkiana*
Micropsitte de Meek (F): *Micropsitta meeki*
Micropsitte pygmée (F): *Micropsitta keiensis*
Microstilbon burmeisteri : (E) Slender-tailed Woodstar,
    (S) Colibrí de Burmeister, Picaflor enano, (F) Colibri
    de Burmeister, **II** TROCHILIDAE Av
Micrure à bandes noires (F): *Micrurus nigrocinctus*
Micrure distancé (F): *Micrurus diastema*
Micrurus diastema : (E) Atlantic Coral Snake, Variable
    Coral Snake, (S) Cantil coral, Coral anillado, (F)
    Micrure distancé, Serpent corail, **III** ELAPIDAE Re
Micrurus nigrocinctus : (E) Black-banded Coral Snake,
    Central American Coral Snake, (F) Micrure à bandes
    noires, Serpent corail à bandes noires **III** ELAPIDAE
    Re
Micrurus ruatanus = Micrurus nigrocinctus
Middle American Red Brocket (E): *Mazama americana*
    cerasina
Mikado Pheasant (E): *Syrmaticus mikado*
Milan à long bec (F): *Rostrhamus hamatus*
Milan à plastron (F): *Hamirostra melanosternon*
Milan à queue carrée (F): *Lophoictinia isura*
Milan à queue fourchue (F): *Elanoides forficatus*
Milan bec-en-croc (F): *Chondrohierax uncinatus*
Milan bidenté (F): *Harpagus bidentatus*
Milan bleuâtre (F): *Ictinia plumbea*
Milan brun (F): *Milvus lineatus*
Milan de Cayenne (F): *Leptodon cayanensis*
Milan de Cuba (F): *Chondrohierax uncinatus wilsonii*
Milan de Forbes (F): *Leptodon forbesi*
Milan de Wilson (F): *Chondrohierax uncinatus wilsonii*
Milan des chauves-souris (F): *Macheiramphus alcinus*
Milan des marais (F): *Rostrhamus sociabilis*
Milan diodon (F): *Harpagus diodon*
Milan du Mississippi (F): *Ictinia mississippiensis*
Milan noir (F): *Milvus migrans*
Milan royal (F): *Milvus milvus*
Milan sacré (F): *Haliastur indus*

Milan siffleur (F): *Haliastur sphenurus*
Milano acollarado (S): *Leptodon forbesi*
Milano bidentado (S): *Harpagus bidentatus*
Milano blanquigrís (S): *Leptodon cayanensis*
Milano brahmán (S): *Haliastur indus*
Milano cabecigris (S): *Leptodon cayanensis*
Milano caracolero (S): *Rostrhamus sociabilis*
Milano coliblanco (S): *Elanus leucurus*
Milano colicuadrado (S): *Lophoictinia isura*
Milano del Misisipi (S): *Ictinia mississippiensis*
Milano dentado (S): *Harpagus diodon*
Milano misisipero (S): *Ictinia mississippiensis*
Milano murcielaguero (S): *Macheiramphus alcinus*
Milano muslirrufo (S): *Harpagus diodon*
Milano negro (S): *Milvus migrans*
Milano pechinegro (S): *Hamirostra melanosternon*
Milano picogarfio (S): *Chondrohierax uncinatus*
Milano plomizo (S): *Ictinia plumbea*
Milano Real (S): *Milvus milvus*
Milano silbador (S): *Haliastur sphenurus*
Milano tijereta (S): *Elanoides forficatus*
Milanus nigro (S): *Milvus migrans*
Military Macaw (E): *Ara militaris*
Milky Eagle-Owl (E): *Bubo lacteus*
Milky Stork (E): *Mycteria cinerea*
Millepora spp.:, (F) Coraux de feu **II** MILLEPORIDAE Hy
Millepora alcicornis : (E) Finger Coral, Ginger Coral **II** MILLEPORIDAE Hy
Millepora boschmai : **II** MILLEPORIDAE Hy
Millepora braziliensis : **II** MILLEPORIDAE Hy
Millepora complanata : (E) Bladed Fire Coral **II** MILLEPORIDAE Hy
Millepora dichotoma : **II** MILLEPORIDAE Hy
Millepora exaesa : **II** MILLEPORIDAE Hy
Millepora foveolata : **II** MILLEPORIDAE Hy
Millepora intricata : **II** MILLEPORIDAE Hy
Millepora latifolia : **II** MILLEPORIDAE Hy
Millepora murrayi : **II** MILLEPORIDAE Hy
Millepora nitida : **II** MILLEPORIDAE Hy
Millepora platyphylla : **II** MILLEPORIDAE Hy
Millepora plicata = *Millepora alcicornis*
Millepora ramosa = *Millepora alcicornis*
Millepora squarrosa : **II** MILLEPORIDAE Hy
Millepora striata : **II** MILLEPORIDAE Hy
Millepora tenera : **II** MILLEPORIDAE Hy
Millepora tuberosa : **II** MILLEPORIDAE Hy
Millepora xishaensis : **II** MILLEPORIDAE Hy
MILLEPORIDAE spp.: (E) Fire corals, (F) Corail de feu, **II** Hy
Milne-Edwards's Sportive Lemur (E): *Lepilemur edwardsi*
Milvago chimachima : (E) Yellow-headed Caracara, (S) Caracara chimachima, Caricare sabanero, Chimachima, (F) Caracara à tête jaune, Caracara chimachima, **II** FALCONIDAE Av
Milvago chimango : (E) Chimango Caracara, (S) Caracara chimango, Chimango, (F) Caracara chimango, **II** FALCONIDAE Av
Milvus fasciicauda = *Milvus milvus*
Milvus lineatus : (E) Black-eared Kite, (F) Milan brun **II** ACCIPITRIDAE Av
Milvus migrans : (E) Black Kite, Pariah Kite, Yellow-billed Kite, (S) Milano negro, Milanus nigro, (F) Milan noir, **II** ACCIPITRIDAE Av
Milvus migrans ssp. *lineatus* = *Milvus lineatus*
Milvus milvus : (E) Red Kite, (S) Milano real, (F) Milan royal, **II** ACCIPITRIDAE Av
Mimic Poison Frog (E): *Dendrobates imitator*
Mimizuku gurneyi : (E) Giant Scops-Owl, Lesser Eagle-Owl, Mindanao Eagle-Owl, (S) Autillo de Guerney, Búho de Mindanao, (F) Hibou de Tweeddale, Petit-duc de Gurney, Petit-duc géant, Scops géant de Guerney, **I** STRIGIDAE Av
Miná de la India (S): *Gracula religiosa*
Miná de Rothschild (S): *Leucopsar rothschildi*

Miná religioso (S): *Gracula religiosa*
Minahassa Barn-Owl (E): *Tyto inexspectata*
Minahassa Masked-Owl (E): *Tyto inexspectata*
Minahassa Owl (E): *Tyto inexspectata*
Mindanao Eagle-Owl (E): *Mimizuku gurneyi*
Mindanao Hornbill (E): *Penelopides affinis*
Mindanao Lorikeet (E): *Trichoglossus johnstoniae*
Mindanao Racquet-tail (E): *Prioniturus waterstradti*
Mindanao Scops-owl (E): *Otus mirus*
Mindanao Tarictic Hornbill (E): *Penelopides affinis*
Mindanao Treeshrew (E): *Urogale everetti*
Mindanao Wrinkled Hornbill (E): *Aceros leucocephalus*
Mindoro Crocodile (E): *Crocodylus mindorensis*
Mindoro Hornbill (E): *Penelopides mindorensis*
Mindoro Imperial-pigeon (E): *Ducula mindorensis*
Mindoro Scops-Owl (E): *Otus mindorensis*
Mindoro Zone-tailed Pigeon (E): *Ducula mindorensis*
Minke Whale (E): *Balaenoptera acutorostrata*
Minute Hermit (E): *Phaethornis idaliae*
Minute Leaf Chameleon (E): *Brookesia minima*
Minute Tree Toad (E): *Nectophrynoides minutus*
Minyobate bourdonnant (F): *Minyobates bombetes*
Minyobate d'Alto del Buey (F): *Minyobates altobueyensis*
Minyobate de Steyermark (F): *Minyobates steyermarki*
Minyobate étincelant (F): *Minyobates fulguritus*
Minyobate menu (F): *Minyobates minutus*
Minyobate opisthomèle (F): *Minyobates opisthomelas*
Minyobate secret (F): *Minyobates abditus*
Minyobate vert (F): *Minyobates viridis*
Minyobates spp.: (E) Poison frogs, (S) Ranas de puntas de flechas, (F) Dendrobates, **II** DENDROBATIDAE Am
Minyobates abditus : (E) Collins's Poison Frog, (F) Minyobate secret **II** DENDROBATIDAE Am
Minyobates altobueyensis : (E) Alto de Buey Poison Frog, Golden Poison Frog, (F) Minyobate d'Alto del Buey **II** DENDROBATIDAE Am
Minyobates bombetes : (E) Cauca Poison Frog, (F) Minyobate bourdonnant **II** DENDROBATIDAE Am
Minyobates fulguritus : (E) Yellow-bellied Poison Frog, (F) Minyobate étincelant **II** DENDROBATIDAE Am
Minyobates minutus : (E) Blue-bellied Poison Frog, (F) Minyobate menu **II** DENDROBATIDAE Am
Minyobates opisthomelas : (E) Andean Poison Frog, (F) Minyobate opisthomèle **II** DENDROBATIDAE Am
Minyobates steyermarki : (E) Demonic Poison Frog, (S) Rana de punta de flecha de Steyermark, (F) Minyobate de Steyermark, **II** DENDROBATIDAE Am
Minyobates viridis : (E) Green Poison Frog, (S) Rana de punta de flecha verde, (F) Minyobate vert, **II** DENDROBATIDAE Am
Minyobates virolensis : (E) Santander Poison Frog **II** DENDROBATIDAE Am
Miopithecus ogouensis = *Miopithecus talapoin*
Miopithecus talapoin : (E) Southern Talapoin, Talapoin, (S) Talapoin, (F) Talapoin, **II** CERCOPITHECIDAE Ma
Mirlo americano pechiamarillo (S): *Agelaius flavus*
Mirounga leonina : (E) South Atlantic Elephant Seal, Southern Elephant Seal, (S) Elefante marino del sur, Elefantes marinos, (F) Eléphant de mer du sud, Eléphant de mer méridional, **II** PHOCIDAE Ma
Mirza coquereli = *Microcebus coquereli*
Mississippi Paddlefish (E): *Polyodon spathula*
Mississippi Kite (E): *Ictinia mississippiensis*
Mississippi Sandhill Crane (E): *Grus canadensis pulla*
Mitchell's Water Monitor (E): *Varanus mitchelli*
Mitred Conure (E): *Aratinga mitrata*
Mitred Leaf Monkey (E): *Presbytis melalophos*
Mitred Parakeet (E): *Aratinga mitrata*
Mitu (S): *Mitu mitu*
Mitu mitu : (E) Alagoas Curassow, Razor-billed Curassow, (S) Hoco de pico navaja, Hoco mitu, Mitu, Mutum-do-nordeste, Paují de Alagoas, Paují menor, (F) Grand hocco à bec rasoir, Hocco mitou, **I** CRACIDAE Av

Checklist of fauna/Lista de especies de fauna/Liste des espèces animales

Mitzli (S): *Puma concolor*
Mlanje Mountain Chameleon (E): *Bradypodion mlanjense*
Mochelo de Sjöstedt (S): *Glaucidium sjostedti*
Mochuelín perlado (S): *Glaucidium perlatum*
Mochuelo acollarado (S): *Glaucidium brodiei*
Mochuelo alpino (S): *Glaucidium passerinum*
Mochuelo Amazónico (S): *Glaucidium hardyi*
Mochuelo andino (S): *Glaucidium jardinii*
Mochuelo Boliviano (S): *Glaucidium bolivianum*
Mochuelo boreal (S): *Aegolius funereus*
Mochuelo brahmán (S): *Athene brama*
Mochuelo cabezón (S): *Aegolius acadicus*
Mochuelo caburé (S): *Glaucidium brasilianum*
Mochuelo Californiano (S): *Glaucidium californicum*
Mochuelo canela (S): *Aegolius harrisii*
Mochuelo castaño (S): *Glaucidium castaneum*
Mochuelo chico (S): *Glaucidium passerinum/ Glaucidium sjostedti*
Mochuelo común (S): *Athene noctua*
Mochuelo cuco (S): *Glaucidium cuculoides*
Mochuelo cucú (S): *Ninox novaeseelandiae undulata*
Mochuelo de Blewitt (S): *Athene blewitti*
Mochuelo de Ceilán (S): *Glaucidium castanonotum*
Mochuelo de El Cabo (S): *Glaucidium capense*
Mochuelo de Hoyo (S): *Speotyto cunicularia*
Mochuelo de Java (S): *Glaucidium castanopterum*
Mochuelo de jungla (S): *Glaucidium radiatum*
Mochuelo de las Molucas (S): *Ninox squamipila*
Mochuelo de los bosques (S): *Athene blewitti*
Mochuelo de los saguaros (S): *Micrathene whitneyi*
Mochuelo de Madriguera (S): *Speotyto cunicularia*
Mochuelo de Parker (S): *Glaucidium parkeri*
Mochuelo del Alberto (S): *Glaucidium albertinum*
Mochuelo del Congo (S): *Glaucidium sjostedti*
Mochuelo duende (S): *Micrathene whitneyi*
Mochuelo Europeo (S): *Athene noctua*
Mochuelo forestal (S): *Athene blewitti*
Mochuelo gnomo (S): *Glaucidium gnoma*
Mochuelo minimo (S): *Glaucidium minutissimum*
Mochuelo moreno (S): *Aegolius ridgwayi*
Mochuelo Patagón (S): *Glaucidium nanum*
Mochuelo pechirrojo (S): *Glaucidium tephronotum*
Mochuelo peludo (S): *Xenoglaux loweryi*
Mochuelo perlado (S): *Glaucidium perlatum*
Mochuelo Peruano (S): *Glaucidium peruanum*
Mochuelo sijú (S): *Glaucidium siju*
Modest Day Gecko (E): *Phelsuma modesta*
Modest Tiger-Parrot (E): *Psittacella modesta*
Mofeta de Patagonia (S): *Conepatus humboldtii*
Moheli Scops-Owl (E): *Otus moheliensis*
Mohol Galago (E): *Galago moholi*
Moineau gris (F): *Passer griseus*
Moineau quadrillé (F): *Sporopipes frontalis*
Moineau-tisserin (F): *Plocepasser superciliosus*
Mole corals (E): *Herpolitha* spp./ *Polyphyllia* spp.
Moluccan Barred Sparrowhawk (E): *Accipiter henicogrammus*
Moluccan Boobook (E): *Ninox squamipila*
Moluccan Cockatoo (E): *Cacatua moluccensis*
Moluccan Flying-fox (E): *Pteropus chrysoproctus*
Moluccan Goshawk (E): *Accipiter henicogrammus*
Moluccan Hanging-Parrot (E): *Loriculus amabilis*
Moluccan Hawk-Owl (E): *Ninox squamipila*
Moluccan Kestrel (E): *Falco moluccensis*
Moluccan King-Parrot (E): *Alisterus amboinensis*
Moluccan Lory (E): *Eos bornea*
Moluccan Red Lory (E): *Eos squamata*
Moluccan Scops-Owl (E): *Otus magicus*
Moluccan Sparrowhawk (E): *Accipiter erythrauchen*
Mona de Berbería (S): *Macaca sylvanus*
Mona Island Boa (E): *Epicrates monensis*
Mona Monkey (E): *Cercopithecus mona*
Monachus spp.: (E) Monk seals, (S) Focas fraile, Focas monje, (F) Phoque-moines, **I** PHOCIDAE Ma

Monachus monachus : (E) Mediterranean Monk Seal, (S) Foca monje, Foca monje del Mediterráneo, (F) Phoque moine, Phoque-moine méditerranéen, **I** PHOCIDAE Ma
Monachus schauinslandi : (E) Hawaiian Monk Seal, (S) Foca fraile de Hawaii **I** PHOCIDAE Ma
Monachus tropicalis : (E) Caribbean Monk Seal, West Indian Monk Seal, West Indian Seal, (S) Foca fraile del Caribe **I** PHOCIDAE Ma
Monal birman (F): *Lophophorus sclateri*
Monal chinois (F): *Lophophorus lhuysii*
Monal coliblanco (S): *Lophophorus sclateri*
Monal colirrojo (S): *Lophophorus impejanus*
Monal coliverde (S): *Lophophorus lhuysii*
Monal de l'Himalaya (F): *Lophophorus impejanus*
Monal Pheasant (E): *Lophophorus impejanus*
Monarch Chameleon (E): *Chamaeleo monachus*
Mone (F): *Cercopithecus pogonias*
Mone de Wolf (F): *Cercopithecus wolfi*
Mongolian Wild Ass (E): *Equus hemionus hemionus*
Mongolian Wild Horse (E): *Equus przewalskii*
Mongoose Lemur (E): *Eulemur mongoz*
Monitor lizards (E): *Varanus* spp.
Monjita pico-de-plata (S): *Lonchura cantans*
Monk Parakeet (E): *Myiopsitta monachus*
Monk Saki (E): *Pithecia monachus*
Monk seals (E): *Monachus* spp.
Monkey-eating Eagle (E): *Pithecophaga jefferyi*
Monkeys (E): PRIMATES spp. Ma
Mono araña (S): *Brachyteles arachnoides*
Mono araña de panamá (S): *Ateles geoffroyi panamensis*
Mono araña maningro (S): *Ateles geoffroyi frontatus*
Mono aullador de Guatemala (S): *Alouatta palliata*
Mono capuchino (S): *Cebus capucinus*
Mono colorado (E): *Ateles geoffroyi*
Mono congo (S): *Alouatta palliata*
Mono coronado (S): *Cercopithecus pogonias*
Mono de Berberea (S): *Macaca sylvanus*
Mono de Gibraltar (S): *Macaca sylvanus*
Mono de orejas rojas (S): *Cercopithecus erythrotis*
Mono de Preuss (S): *Cercopithecus preussi*
Mono de Sclater (S): *Cercopithecus sclateri*
Mono de Wolf (S): *Cercopithecus wolfi*
Mono del Gabón (S): *Cercopithecus solatus*
Mono dryas (S): *Cercopithecus dryas*
Mono grande (S): *Brachyteles arachnoides*
Mono narigudo (S): *Nasalis larvatus*
Mono negro (S): *Alouatta palliata*
Mono pigatrix (S): *Pygathrix nemaeus*
Mono resus (S): *Macaca mulatta*
Mono saraguato (S): *Alouatta palliata*
Mono tití (S): *Saimiri oerstedii*
Mono verde (S): *Chlorocebus aethiops*
Monos (S): PRIMATES spp. Ma
Monocellate Cobra (E): *Naja kaouthia*
Monocled Cobra (E): *Naja kaouthia*
Monodon monoceros : (E) Narwhal, Unicorn Whale, (S) Narval, (F) Narval, **II** MONODONTIDAE Ma
Monomyces pygmaea : **II** FLABELLIDAE An
Monomyces rubrum : **II** FLABELLIDAE An
Monseigneur (F): *Euplectes hordeaceus*
Monstre de Gila (F): *Heloderma suspectum*
Monstruo de Gila (S): *Heloderma suspectum*
Montagu's Harrier (E): *Circus pygargus*
Montane Chamaeleon (E): *Chamaeleo bitaeniatus*
Montane Racquet-tail (E): *Prioniturus montanus*
Montane Side-striped Chameleon (E): *Chamaeleo ellioti*
Montastraea annularis : (E) Boulder Star Coral, Mountainous Star Coral **II** FAVIIDAE An
Montastraea annuligera : **II** FAVIIDAE An
Montastraea cavernosa : (E) Cavernous Star Coral, Great Star Coral **II** FAVIIDAE An
Montastraea colemani : **II** FAVIIDAE An
Montastraea curta : **II** FAVIIDAE An
Montastraea faveolata : **II** FAVIIDAE An

Montastraea forskaelana = Echinopora gemmacea
Montastraea franksi : **II** FAVIIDAE An
Montastraea magnistellata : **II** FAVIIDAE An
Montastraea multipunctata : **II** FAVIIDAE An
Montastraea salebrosa : **II** FAVIIDAE An
Montastraea serageldini : **II** FAVIIDAE An
Montastraea valenciennesii : **II** FAVIIDAE An
Monte Verde Toad (E): *Bufo periglenes*
Montigyra kenti : **II** CARYOPHYLLIIDAE An
Montipora spp.: (E) Pore corals, Velvet Branch corals,
   Velvet corals **II** ACROPORIDAE An
Montipora aequituberculata : **II** ACROPORIDAE An
Montipora altasepta : **II** ACROPORIDAE An
Montipora angulata : **II** ACROPORIDAE An
Montipora aspergillus : **II** ACROPORIDAE An
Montipora australiensis : **II** ACROPORIDAE An
Montipora berryi = Montipora informis
Montipora cactus : **II** ACROPORIDAE An
Montipora calcarea : **II** ACROPORIDAE An
Montipora caliculata : **II** ACROPORIDAE An
Montipora capitata : **II** ACROPORIDAE An
Montipora capricornis : **II** ACROPORIDAE An
Montipora cebuensis : **II** ACROPORIDAE An
Montipora circumvallata : **II** ACROPORIDAE An
Montipora cocosensis : **II** ACROPORIDAE An
Montipora confusa : **II** ACROPORIDAE An
Montipora corbettensis : **II** ACROPORIDAE An
Montipora crassituberculata : **II** ACROPORIDAE An
Montipora cristagalli = Montipora circumvallata
Montipora cryptus : **II** ACROPORIDAE An
Montipora danae : **II** ACROPORIDAE An
Montipora delicatula : **II** ACROPORIDAE An
Montipora digitata : **II** ACROPORIDAE An
Montipora echinata : **II** ACROPORIDAE An
Montipora edwardsi : **II** ACROPORIDAE An
Montipora efflorescens : **II** ACROPORIDAE An
Montipora effusa : **II** ACROPORIDAE An
Montipora flabellata : **II** ACROPORIDAE An
Montipora florida : **II** ACROPORIDAE An
Montipora floweri : **II** ACROPORIDAE An
Montipora foliosa : (E) Leaf Coral **II** ACROPORIDAE
   An
Montipora foveolata : **II** ACROPORIDAE An
Montipora friabilis : **II** ACROPORIDAE An
Montipora gaimardi : **II** ACROPORIDAE An
Montipora granulosa : **II** ACROPORIDAE An
Montipora grisea : **II** ACROPORIDAE An
Montipora hemispherica : **II** ACROPORIDAE An
Montipora hirsuta : **II** ACROPORIDAE An
Montipora hispida : **II** ACROPORIDAE An
Montipora hodgsonii : **II** ACROPORIDAE An
Montipora hoffmeisteri : **II** ACROPORIDAE An
Montipora incrassata : **II** ACROPORIDAE An
Montipora informis : **II** ACROPORIDAE An
Montipora kellyi : **II** ACROPORIDAE An
Montipora lobulata : **II** ACROPORIDAE An
Montipora mactanensis : **II** ACROPORIDAE An
Montipora maeandrina : **II** ACROPORIDAE An
Montipora malampaya : **II** ACROPORIDAE An
Montipora millepora : **II** ACROPORIDAE An
Montipora mollis : **II** ACROPORIDAE An
Montipora monasteriata : **II** ACROPORIDAE An
Montipora niugini : **II** ACROPORIDAE An
Montipora nodosa : **II** ACROPORIDAE An
Montipora orientalis : **II** ACROPORIDAE An
Montipora pachytuberculata : **II** ACROPORIDAE An
Montipora palawanensis : **II** ACROPORIDAE An
Montipora patula : **II** ACROPORIDAE An
Montipora peltiformis : **II** ACROPORIDAE An
Montipora porites : **II** ACROPORIDAE An
Montipora samarensis : **II** ACROPORIDAE An
Montipora saudii : **II** ACROPORIDAE An
Montipora setosa : **II** ACROPORIDAE An
Montipora solanderi : **II** ACROPORIDAE An
Montipora spongiosa : **II** ACROPORIDAE An

Montipora spongodes : **II** ACROPORIDAE An
Montipora spumosa : **II** ACROPORIDAE An
Montipora stellata : **II** ACROPORIDAE An
Montipora stilosa : **II** ACROPORIDAE An
Montipora striata : **II** ACROPORIDAE An
Montipora taiwanensis : **II** ACROPORIDAE An
Montipora tuberculosa : **II** ACROPORIDAE An
Montipora turgescens : **II** ACROPORIDAE An
Montipora turtlensis : **II** ACROPORIDAE An
Montipora undata : **II** ACROPORIDAE An
Montipora venosa : **II** ACROPORIDAE An
Montipora verrilli : **II** ACROPORIDAE An
Montipora verrucosa : **II** ACROPORIDAE An
Montipora verruculosus : **II** ACROPORIDAE An
Montipora vietnamensis : **II** ACROPORIDAE An
Moon corals (E): *Astreopora* spp./ *Favia* spp.
Moor Macaque (E): *Macaca maura*
Moorish Tortoise (E): *Testudo graeca*
Morden's Scops-Owl (E): *Otus ireneae*
Morelet's Crocodile (E): *Crocodylus moreletii*
Morelia albertisii = Leiopython albertisii
Morelia amethistina : (E) Amethystine (Rock) Python,
   Scrub Python, (S) Pitón ametista, (F) Python
   améthiste, Python de la brousse, Python des rochers,
   II PYTHONIDAE Re
Morelia boa = Bothrochilus boa
Morelia boeleni : (E) Black Python, Boelen's Python, (S)
   Pitón de Boelen, (F) Python de Boelen, **II**
   PYTHONIDAE Re
Morelia bredli : **II** PYTHONIDAE Re
Morelia carinata : (E) Keeled-scaled Python, Rough-
   scaled Python, (F) Python à écailles rugueuses, Python
   caréné **II** PYTHONIDAE Re
Morelia childreni = Antaresia childreni
Morelia clastolepis : **II** PYTHONIDAE Re
Morelia kinghorni : **II** PYTHONIDAE Re
Morelia mackloti = Liasis mackloti
Morelia mackloti ssp. *fusca = Liasis fuscus*
Morelia maculosa = Antaresia maculosa
Morelia nauta : **II** PYTHONIDAE Re
Morelia oenpelliensis : (E) Oenpelli Python, South
   Australian Water Python, (F) Python d'Oenpelli **II**
   PYTHONIDAE Re
Morelia olivacea = Liasis olivaceus
Morelia papuana = Apodora papuana
Morelia perthensis = Antaresia perthensis
Morelia spilota : (E) Carpet Python, Diamond Python, (S)
   Pitón diamantina, (F) Python tapis, **II** PYTHONIDAE
   Re
Morelia stimsoni = Antaresia stimsoni
Morelia tracyae : **II** PYTHONIDAE Re
Morelia variegata = Morelia spilota
Morelia viridis : (E) Green Tree Python, (F) Python
   arboricole vert australien **II** PYTHONIDAE Re
Morenia ocellata : (E) Bengal Eyed Terrapin, Burmese
   Eyed Turtle, Burmese swamp turtle, Peacock Turtle,
   Swamp Turtle, (S) Galápago de Birmania, Galápago
   ocelado de Birmania, (F) Émyde à ocelles de
   Birmanie, Terrapenes , Tortue de Birmanie, Tortues
   boîtes, **I** EMYDIDAE Re
Morepork (E): *Ninox novaeseelandiae*
Morogoro Tree Toad (E): *Nectophrynoides viviparus*
Morphnus guianensis : (E) Crested Eagle, Guianan
   Crested Eagle, (S) Aguila crestada, Aguila monera,
   Arpía menor, (F) Harpie huppée, **II** ACCIPITRIDAE
   Av
Morrocoy (S): *Geochelone denticulata*
Morsa (S): *Odobenus rosmarus*
Morse (F): *Odobenus rosmarus*
Mortlock Flying-fox (E): *Pteropus phaeocephalus*
Mortlock Islands Flying-fox (E): *Pteropus phaeocephalus*
Moschus spp.: (E) Musk deer, (S) Ciervos almizcleros, (F)
   Chevrotains porte-musc, Portemusc, **I/II**
   MOSCHIDAE Ma
Moschus anhuiensis = Moschus berezovskii

Checklist of fauna/Lista de especies de fauna/Liste des espèces animales

Moschus berezovskii : (E) Chinese Forest Musk Deer, Dwarf Musk Deer, Forest Musk Deer **II** MOSCHIDAE Ma

Moschus chrysogaster : (E) Alpine Musk Deer, Himalayan Musk Deer **I/II** MOSCHIDAE Ma

Moschus chrysogaster ssp. *berezovskii* = *Moschus berezovskii*

Moschus chrysogaster ssp. *fuscus* = *Moschus fuscus*

Moschus fuscus : (E) Black Musk Deer, Dusky Musk Deer **I/II** MOSCHIDAE Ma

Moschus moschiferus : (E) Siberian Musk Deer, (S) Ciervo almizclero, (F) Cerf porte-musc, Chevrotain porte-musc, Porte-musc, **I/II** MOSCHIDAE Ma

Moschus sifanicus = *Moschus chrysogaster*

Moseleya latistellata : **II** FAVIIDAE An

Motelo (S): *Geochelone denticulata*

Mottled Owl (E): *Strix virgata*

Mottled Wood-Owl (E): *Strix ocellata*

Mottle-faced Tamarin (E): *Saguinus inustus*

Mouette relique (F): *Larus relictus*

Moufette à nez de cochon (F): *Conepatus humboldtii*

Moufette de Patagonie (F): *Conepatus humboldtii*

Mouflon à manchettes (F): *Ammotragus lervia*

Mouflon d'Amérique (F): *Ovis canadensis*

Mouflon d'Asie (F): *Ovis ammon*

Mouflon de Chypre (F): *Ovis orientalis ophion*

Mouflon de l'Himalaya (F): *Ovis ammon hodgsonii*

Mouflon des montagnes (F): *Ovis ammon hodgsonii*

Mouflon d'Eurasie (F): *Ovis ammon*

Mouflon du Canada (F): *Ovis canadensis*

Mouflon du Ladak (F): *Ovis vignei vignei*

Mouflon méditerranéen (F): *Ovis ammon*

Mouflon pachycère (F): *Ovis canadensis*

Mouflon vrai (F): *Ovis ammon*

Mount Lefo Chameleon (E): *Chamaeleo wiedersheimi*

Mount Marsabit Chameleon (E): *Chamaeleo marsabitensis*

Mount Omei Liocichla (E): *Liocichla omeiensis*

Mountain Anoa (E): *Bubalus quarlesi*

Mountain Apollo (E): *Parnassius apollo*

Mountain Avocetbill (E): *Opisthoprora euryptera*

Mountain Buzzard (E): *Buteo oreophilus*

Mountain Caracara (E): *Phalcoboenus megalopterus*

Mountain Cat (E): *Oreailurus jacobita*

Mountain Chameleon (E): *Chamaeleo montium*

Mountain Dwarf Chameleon (E): *Chamaeleo ellioti*

Mountain Eagle-Owl (E): *Bubo capensis*

Mountain Hawk-Eagle (E): *Spizaetus nipalensis*

Mountain Lion (E): *Puma concolor*

Mountain Monkey (E): *Cercopithecus lhoesti*

Mountain Parakeet (E): *Psilopsiagon aurifrons*

Mountain Peacock-pheasant (E): *Polyplectron inopinatum*

Mountain Pygmy-Owl (E): *Glaucidium gnoma*

Mountain Scops-Owl (E): *Otus spilocephalus*

Mountain Serpent-Eagle (E): *Spilornis kinabaluensis*

Mountain Sheep (E): *Ovis canadensis*

Mountain Tapir (E): *Tapirus pinchaque*

Mountain Tortoise (E): *Geochelone pardalis*

Mountain Treeshrew (E): *Tupaia montana*

Mountain Velvetbreast (E): *Lafresnaya lafresnayi*

Mountain Weasel (E): *Mustela altaica*

Mountain Zebra (E): *Equus zebra*

Mountainous Star Coral (E): *Montastraea annularis*

Mournful Tree Monitor (E): *Varanus tristis*

Mourning Collared-Dove (E): *Streptopelia decipiens*

Moustac à oreilles rouges (F): *Cercopithecus erythrotis*

Moustac bleu (F): *Cercopithecus cephus*

Moustached Monkey (E): *Cercopithecus cephus*

Moustached Parakeet (E): *Psittacula alexandri*

Moustached Tamarin (E): *Saguinus mystax*

Mrs Hume's Pheasant (E): *Syrmaticus humiae*

Mt Kenya Side-striped Chameleon (E): *Chamaeleo schubotzi*

Mt Kilimanjaro Two-horned Chameleon (E): *Bradypodion tavetanum*

Mt Nimba Viviparous Toad (E): *Nimbaphrynoides occidentalis*

Muflón (S): *Ovis ammon*

Muflón Argal (S): *Ovis ammon*

Muflón Argal Tibetano (S): *Ovis ammon hodgsonii*

Muflón de Chipre (S): *Ovis orientalis ophion*

Muflón de Marco Polo (S): *Ovis ammon*

Muflón del Atlas (S): *Ammotragus lervia*

Mugger (E): *Crocodylus palustris*

Mugger Crocodile (E): *Crocodylus palustris*

Muhlenberg's Turtle (E): *Clemmys muhlenbergii*

Muitú mamaco (S): *Crax blumenbachii*

Mulga Parrot (E): *Psephotus varius*

Müller's Gibbon (E): *Hylobates muelleri*

Müller's Leaf Chameleon (E): *Bradypodion uthmoelleri*

Müller's Parrot (E): *Tanygnathus sumatranus*

Müller's Sand Boa (E): *Gongylophis muelleri*

Munning (E): *Lagostrophus fasciatus*

Muntiacus crinifrons : (E) Black Muntjac, (S) Muntjac negro, (F) Muntjac noir, **I** CERVIDAE Ma

Muntiacus vuquanghensis = *Megamuntiacus vuquanghensis*

Muntjac géant (F): *Megamuntiacus vuquanghensis*

Muntjac gigante (S): *Megamuntiacus vuquanghensis*

Muntjac negro (S): *Muntiacus crinifrons*

Muntjac noir (F): *Muntiacus crinifrons*

Murciélago de estrias blancas (S): *Platyrrhinus lineatus*

Muriki (S): *Brachyteles arachnoides*

Muriqui (E): *Brachyteles arachnoides*

Musaraña arborícola coliplumada (S): *Ptilocercus lowii*

Musaraña arborícola de Filipinas (S): *Urogale everetti*

Musaraña arborícola de la India (S): *Anathana ellioti*

Musaraña común (S): *Tupaia glis*

Musaraña grande (S): *Tupaia tana*

Musaraña pigmea (S): *Tupaia minor*

Muscicapa ruecki = *Cyornis ruckii*

Muscovy Duck (E): *Cairina moschata*

Mushroom Coral (E): *Heliofungia actiniformis/ Fungia fungites*

Mushroom corals (E): *Fungia* spp.

Musk deer (E): *Moschus* spp.

Musk Lorikeet (E): *Glossopsitta concinna*

Musophaga porphyreolopha : (E) Purple-crested Turaco, Violet-crested Turaco, (S) Turaco crestimorado, Turaco crestivioleta, (F) Touraco à huppe pourprée, Touraco à huppe splendide, Touraco à huppe violette, Touraco violet, **II** MUSOPHAGIDAE Av

Musophaga violacea : (E) Violet Plantain-eater, Violet Turaco, (S) Turaco azul, Turaco violáceo, (F) Touraco violet, **III** MUSOPHAGIDAE Av

Mussa angulosa : (E) Large Flower Coral, Spiny Flower Coral **II** MUSSIDAE An

Mussa cerebriformis = *Lobophyllia hemprichii*

Musschenbroek's Lorikeet (E): *Neopsittacus musschenbroekii*

Mussel Digger (E): *Eschrichtius robustus*

Mussismilia braziliensis : **II** MUSSIDAE An

Mussismilia harttii : **II** MUSSIDAE An

Mussismilia hispida : **II** MUSSIDAE An

Mussurana (E/S/F): *Clelia clelia*

Mussurana d'Amérique du sud (F): *Clelia clelia*

Mustard Hill Coral (E): *Porites astreoides*

Mustela altaica : (E) Alpine Weasel, Mountain Weasel, (S) Comadreja de montaña, (F) Belette alpine, Belette des Alpes, **III** MUSTELIDAE Ma

Mustela erminea ferghanae : **III** MUSTELIDAE Ma

Mustela kathiah : (E) Yellow-bellied Weasel, (S) Comadreja de vientre amarillo, (F) Belette à ventre jaune, **III** MUSTELIDAE Ma

Mustela nigripes : (E) Black-footed Ferret, (S) Turón de patas negras, Turón patinegro americano, (F) Putois à pieds noirs, **I** MUSTELIDAE Ma

Mustela sibirica : (E) Siberian Weasel, (S) Comadreja de Siberia, (F) Belette de Sibérie, Vison sibérien, **III** MUSTELIDAE Ma

Checklist of fauna/Lista de especies de fauna/Liste des espèces animales

Mutum (E): *Crax blumenbachii*
Mutum-do-nordeste (S): *Mitu mitu*
Mutum-do-sudeste (S): *Crax blumenbachii*
Mycedium elephantotus : **II** PECTINIIDAE An
Mycedium mancaoi : **II** PECTINIIDAE An
Mycedium robokaki : **II** PECTINIIDAE An
Mycedium steeni : **II** PECTINIIDAE An
Mycedium umbra : **II** PECTINIIDAE An
Mycetophyllia aliciae : (E) Knobby Cactus Coral **II**
    MUSSIDAE An
Mycetophyllia daniana : (E) Lowridge Cactus Coral **II**
    MUSSIDAE An
Mycetophyllia ferox : (E) Rough Cactus Coral **II**
    MUSSIDAE An
Mycetophyllia lamarckiana : (E) Ridged Cactus Coral **II**
    MUSSIDAE An
Mycetophyllia reesi : (E) Ridgeless Cactus Coral **II**
    MUSSIDAE An
Mycteria cinerea : (E) Milky Stork, (S) Tántalo Malayo,
    (F) Tantale blanc, **I** CICONIIDAE Av
Myers's Poison Frog (E): *Epipedobates myersi*
Mygale emilia = *Brachypelma emilia*
Mygales (F): *Brachypelma* spp.
Myiopsitta luchsi : (E) Cliff Parakeet, (S) Cotorra
    Boliviana, (F) Conure des rochers, **II** PSITTACIDAE
    Av
Myiopsitta monachus : (E) Grey-breasted Parakeet, Monk
    Parakeet, Quaker Parakeet, (S) Catita común, Cotorra
    Argentina, (F) Conure veuve, Perruche-souris, **II**
    PSITTACIDAE Av
Myriopathes antrocrada : **II** MYRIOPATHIDAE An
Myriopathes bifaria : **II** MYRIOPATHIDAE An
Myriopathes japonica : **II** MYRIOPATHIDAE An
Myriopathes lata : **II** MYRIOPATHIDAE An
Myriopathes myriophylla : **II** MYRIOPATHIDAE An
Myriopathes panamensis : **II** MYRIOPATHIDAE An
Myriopathes rugosa : **II** MYRIOPATHIDAE An
Myriopathes spinosa : **II** MYRIOPATHIDAE An
Myriopathes stechowi : **II** MYRIOPATHIDAE An
Myriopathes ulex : **II** MYRIOPATHIDAE An
Myrmecophaga tridactyla : (E) Giant Anteater, (S)
    Banderón caballo, Hormiguero gigante, Oso caballo,
    Oso hormiguero, (F) Grand fourmilier, Tamanoir, **II**
    MYRMECOPHAGIDAE Ma
Myrmia micrura : (E) Short-tailed Woodstar, (S) Colibrí
    colicorto, Estrellita colicorta, (F) Colibri à queue
    courte, **II** TROCHILIDAE Av
Myrtis fanny : (E) Purple-collared Woodstar, (S) Colibrí
    myrtis, Estrellita gargantillada, (F) Colibri fanny, **II**
    TROCHILIDAE Av
Myrtis yarrellii : (E) Chilean Woodstar, (S) Colibrí de
    Arica, (F) Colibri d'Arica, **II** TROCHILIDAE Av

Nacurutú (S): *Bubo virginianus*
Naemorhedus baileyi : (E) Red Goral, (F) Goral rouge **I**
    BOVIDAE Ma
Naemorhedus caudatus : (E) Chinese Goral, (F) Goral à
    queue longue **I** BOVIDAE Ma
Naemorhedus goral : (E) Goral, Himalayan Goral, (S)
    Goral, (F) Bouquetin du Népal, Goral, **I** BOVIDAE
    Ma
Naemorhedus goral ssp. *baileyi* = *Naemorhedus baileyi*
Naemorhedus goral ssp. *caudatus* = *Naemorhedus*
    caudatus
Naemorhedus sumatraensis : (E) Mainland Serow, Serow,
    (S) Serau, Serow de Sumatra, (F) Capricorne de
    Sumatra, Serow , **I** BOVIDAE Ma
Naja à lunettes (F): *Naja naja*
Naja atra : (E) Chinese Cobra, Chinese Spitting Cobra **II**
    ELAPIDAE Re
Naja indien (F): *Naja naja*
Naja kaouthia : (E) Monocellate Cobra, Monocled Cobra
    II ELAPIDAE Re
Naja mandalayensis : **II** ELAPIDAE Re

Naja naja : (E) Asian Cobra, Asiatic Cobra, Indian Cobra,
    Indian Spectacled Cobra, (S) Cobra común asiática,
    Cobra de anteojos, Cobra escupidora asiática, Cobra
    spectacled de la India, (F) Cobra à lunettes, Cobra des
    Indes, Cobra indien, Naja à lunettes, Naja indien,
    Serpent à lunetes, **II** ELAPIDAE Re
Naja naja ssp. *atra* = *Naja atra*
Naja naja ssp. *kaouthia* = *Naja kaouthia*
Naja naja ssp. *oxiana* = *Naja oxiana*
Naja naja ssp. *philippinensis* = *Naja philippinensis*
Naja naja ssp. *sagittifera* = *Naja sagittifera*
Naja naja ssp. *samarensis* = *Naja samarensis*
Naja naja ssp. *siamensis* = *Naja siamensis*
Naja naja ssp. *sputatrix* = *Naja sputatrix*
Naja naja ssp. *sumatrana* = *Naja sumatrana*
Naja oxiana : (E) Central Asian Cobra, Oxus Cobra **II**
    ELAPIDAE Re
Naja philippinensis : (E) North Philippine Spitting Cobra,
    Philippine Cobra **II** ELAPIDAE Re
Naja sagittifera : (E) Andaman Cobra **II** ELAPIDAE Re
Naja samarensis : (E) Peters's Cobra, South-east
    Philippine Spitting Cobra **II** ELAPIDAE Re
Naja siamensis : (E) Indochinese Spitting Cobra **II**
    ELAPIDAE Re
Naja sputatrix : (E) Indonesian Cobra, South Indonesian
    Spitting Cobra **II** ELAPIDAE Re
Naja sumatrana : (E) Equatorial Spitting Cobra, Golden
    Spitting Cobra **II** ELAPIDAE Re
Nakamina (S): *Cyclagras gigas*
Namaqua Chameleon (E): *Chamaeleo namaquensis*
Namaqua Day Gecko (E): *Phelsuma ocellata*
Namaqua Dove (E): *Oena capensis*
Namaqua Girdled Lizard (E): *Cordylus namaquensis*
Namaqua Spiny-tailed Lizard (E): *Cordylus namaquensis*
Nanday Conure (E): *Nandayus nenday*
Nanday Parakeet (E): *Nandayus nenday*
Nandayus nenday : (E) Black-headed Conure, Black-
    headed Parakeet, Nanday Conure, Nanday Parakeet,
    (S) Aratinga ñanday, Cotorra cabecinegra, (F) Conure
    nanday, Perruche Nanday, **II** PSITTACIDAE Av
Nandou américain (F): *Rhea americana*
Nandou commun (F): *Rhea americana*
Nandou d'Amérique (F): *Rhea americana*
Nandou de Darwin (F): *Rhea pennata*
Nandou gris (F): *Rhea americana*
Ñandú (S): *Rhea americana*
Ñandú común (S): *Rhea americana*
Ñandú cordillerano (S): *Rhea pennata*
Ñandú de Darwin (S): *Rhea pennata*
Ñandú petizo (S): *Rhea pennata*
Nankeen Kestrel (E): *Falco cenchroides*
Nannopsittaca dachilleae : (E) Amazonian Parakeet,
    Amazonian Parrotlet, (S) Cotorrita amazónica, (F)
    Toui de D'Achille, **II** PSITTACIDAE Av
Nannopsittaca panychlora : (E) Tepui Parakeet, Tepui
    Parrotlet, (S) Chirica, Cotorrita tepuí, (F) Toui des
    tépuis, **II** PSITTACIDAE Av
Napo Sabrewing (E): *Campylopterus villaviscensio*
Napoleon Weaver (E): *Euplectes afer*
Napoleon's Peacock-Pheasant (E): *Polyplectron*
    emphanum
Narcondam Hornbill (E): *Aceros narcondami*
Narrow-bellied Seahorse (E): *Hippocampus angustus*
Narrow-headed softshell turtles (E): *Chitra* spp.
Narrow-snouted Dolphin (E): *Stenella attenuata*
Narrow-tailed Emerald (E): *Chlorostilbon stenurus*
Narval (S/F): *Monodon monoceros*
Narwhal (E): *Monodon monoceros*
Nasalis spp.: (S) Násicos, (F) Nasiques, **I**
    CERCOPITHECIDAE Ma
Nasalis concolor : (E) Mentawi Islands Snub-nosed
    Langur, Pagai Island Langur, Pig-tailed Langur, (S)
    Langur rabicerdo, Násico, (F) Entelle de Pagi, Langur
    à queue de cochon, Langur des îles Mentawi, Nasique,
    I CERCOPITHECIDAE Ma

Checklist of fauna/Lista de especies de fauna/Liste des espèces animales

Nasalis larvatus : (E) Long-nosed Monkey, Proboscis Monkey, (S) Mono narigudo, Násico, (F) Nasique, **I** CERCOPITHECIDAE Ma

Násico (S): *Nasalis concolor/ Nasalis larvatus*

Násicos (S): *Nasalis* spp.

Nasique (F): *Nasalis concolor/ Nasalis larvatus*

Nasiques (F): *Nasalis* spp.

Nasua narica : (E) Northern Coati, White-nosed Coati, (S) Coati, (F) Coati, Coati à museau blanc, Coati brun, **III** PROCYONIDAE Ma

Nasua nasua solitaria : (E) South Brazilian Coati, (F) Coati roux **III** PROCYONIDAE Ma

Nasua nelsoni = Nasua narica

Natal Hinge-back Tortoise (E): *Kinixys natalensis*

Natal Hinge-backed Tortoise (E): *Kinixys natalensis*

Natal Hinged Tortoise (E): *Kinixys natalensis*

Natal Midlands Dwarf Chameleon (E): *Bradypodion thamnobates*

Natator depressus : (E) Flatback, (S) Tortuga franca oriental, (F) Cayunne, Chelonée à dos plat, Coffre, Tortue à bahut, Tortue marine à dos plat, **I** CHELONIIDAE Re

Natrix piscator = Xenochrophis piscator

Natuna Serpent-Eagle (E): *Spilornis cheela*

Natural Tree Gecko (E): *Naultinus rudis*

Naturelle Leaf Chameleon (E): *Brookesia karchei*

Naultinus spp. : (E) New Zealand tree geckos **III** GEKKONIDAE Re

Naultinus elegans : (E) Green Tree Gecko **III** GEKKONIDAE Re

Naultinus gemmeus : (E) South Island Tree Gecko **III** GEKKONIDAE Re

Naultinus grayii : (E) Gray's Tree Gecko **III** GEKKONIDAE Re

Naultinus manukanus : (E) Northern Tree Gecko **III** GEKKONIDAE Re

Naultinus poecilochlorus : (E) Central Tree Gecko **III** GEKKONIDAE Re

Naultinus rudis : (E) Natural Tree Gecko, Rough Gecko **III** GEKKONIDAE Re

Naultinus stellatus : (E) Starry Tree Gecko **III** GEKKONIDAE Re

Naultinus tuberculatus : (E) Warty Tree Gecko **III** GEKKONIDAE Re

Navassa Island Black-tailed Dwarf Boa (E): *Tropidophis melanurus*

Né (S): *Branta sandvicensis*

Neblina Metaltail (E): *Metallura odomae*

Necrosyrtes monachus : (E) Hooded Vulture, (S) Alimoche sombrío, (F) Percnoptère brun, Vautour charognard, **II** ACCIPITRIDAE Av

Nectophrynoide cryptique (F): *Nectophrynoides cryptus*

Nectophrynoide de Malcolm (F): *Altiphrynoides malcolmi*

Nectophrynoide de Tornier (F): *Nectophrynoides tornieri*

Nectophrynoide des Monts Uluguru (F): *Nectophrynoides viviparus*

Nectophrynoide des Monts Usambara (F): *Nectophrynoides tornieri*

Nectophrynoide des Monts Uzungwe (F): *Nectophrynoides wendyae*

Nectophrynoide d'Ethiopie (F): *Spinophrynoides osgoodi*

Nectophrynoide d'Osgood (F): *Spinophrynoides osgoodi*

Nectophrynoide du Liberia (F): *Nimbaphrynoides liberiensis*

Nectophrynoide du Mont Nimba (F): *Nimbaphrynoides occidentalis*

Nectophrynoide menu (F): *Nectophrynoides minutus*

Nectophrynoides (F): *Nectophrynoides* spp.

Nectophrynoides spp.: (E) African viviparous toads, Tree toads, (S) Sapos vivíparos, Sapos vivíparos africanos, (F) Crapauds vivipares, Nectophrynoides, **I** BUFONIDAE Am

Nectophrynoides asperginis : **I** BUFONIDAE Am

Nectophrynoides cryptus : (E) Secret Tree Toad, (F) Nectophrynoide cryptique **I** BUFONIDAE Am

Nectophrynoides liberiensis = Nimbaphrynoides liberiensis

Nectophrynoides malcolmi = Altiphrynoides malcolmi

Nectophrynoides minutus : (E) Minute Tree Toad, (F) Nectophrynoide menu **I** BUFONIDAE Am

Nectophrynoides occidentalis = Nimbaphrynoides occidentalis

Nectophrynoides osgoodi = Spinophrynoides osgoodi

Nectophrynoides tornieri : (E) Tornier's Tree Toad, Usambara Viviparous Toad, (F) Nectophrynoide de Tornier, Nectophrynoide des Monts Usambara **I** BUFONIDAE Am

Nectophrynoides viviparus : (E) Morogoro Tree Toad, Rungwe Viviparous Toad, (F) Nectophrynoide des Monts Uluguru **I** BUFONIDAE Am

Nectophrynoides wendyae : (E) Uzungwe Scarp Tree Toad, (F) Nectophrynoide des Monts Uzungwe **I** BUFONIDAE Am

Needle Coral (E): *Seriatopora hystrix*

Needle-billed Hermit (E): *Phaethornis philippii*

Negrita bronceada (S): *Lonchura cucullata*

Negrita cana (S): *Nigrita canicapilla*

Negrita frentigualda (S): *Nigrita luteifrons*

Negrita pechiblanca (S): *Nigrita fusconota*

Negrita pechirroja (S): *Nigrita bicolor*

Negrita picanza (S): *Lonchura fringilloides*

Negro Tamarin (E): *Saguinus midas*

Nemenzophyllia turbida = Plerogyra turbida

Nene (E): *Branta sandvicensis*

Neoceratodus forsteri : (E) Australian Lungfish, Ceratodus, Queensland Lungfish, (S) Dipnoo, Pez pulmonado australiano, (F) Cératode, Dipneuste, **II** CERATODONTIDAE Sa

Neofelis nebulosa : (E) Clouded Leopard, (S) Pantera del Himalaya, Pantera longibanda, Pantera nebulosa, (F) Panthère longibande, Panthère nébuleuse, **I** FELIDAE Ma

Neohelia porcellana = Madrepora porcellana

Neophema bourkii = Neopsephotus bourkii

Neophema chrysogaster : (E) Orange-bellied Parakeet, Orange-bellied Parrot, (S) Cacatúa de vientre naranja, Loro ventrinaranja, Periquito ventrinaranja, (F) Perruche à lunettes vertes, Perruche à ventre orange, **I** PSITTACIDAE Av

Neophema chrysostoma : (E) Blue-winged Grass-Parakeet, Blue-winged Parrot, (S) Periquito crisóstomo, (F) Perruche à bouche d'or, **II** PSITTACIDAE Av

Neophema elegans : (E) Elegant Grass-Parakeet, Elegant Parrot, (S) Periquito elegante, (F) Perruche élégante, **II** PSITTACIDAE Av

Neophema petrophila : (E) Rock Parrot, (S) Periquito roquero, (F) Perruche des écueils, Perruche des rochers, **II** PSITTACIDAE Av

Neophema pulchella : (E) Turquoise Grass-Parakeet, Turquoise Parrot, (S) Periquito turquesa, (F) Perruche turquoisine, **II** PSITTACIDAE Av

Neophema splendida : (E) Scarlet-chested Parrot, Splendid Grass-Parakeet, (S) Periquito espléndido, (F) Perruche à poitrine écarlate, Perruche splendide, **II** PSITTACIDAE Av

Neophocaena phocaenoides : (E) Black Finless Porpoise, Finless Black Porpoise, Finless Porpoise, (S) Marsopa negra, (F) Marsouin aptère, Marsouin sans nageoires, **I** PHOCOENIDAE Ma

Neophron percnopterus : (E) Egyptian Vulture, (S) Alimoche, Alimoche Común, (F) Percnoptère d'Égypte, Vautour percnoptère, **II** ACCIPITRIDAE Av

Neopsephotus bourkii : (E) Bourke's Parrot, (S) Periquito rosado, (F) Perruche de Bourke, **II** PSITTACIDAE Av

Neopsittacus musschenbroekii : (E) Musschenbroek's Lorikeet, Yellow-billed Lorikeet, (S) Lori montano grande, (F) Lori de Musschenbroek, **II** PSITTACIDAE Av

175

Neopsittacus pullicauda : (E) Emerald Lorikeet, Orange-billed Lorikeet, (S) Lori montano chico, (F) Lori émeraude, **II** PSITTACIDAE Av
Neotis burchellii = Neotis denhami
Neotis cafra = Eupodotis senegalensis
Neotis denhami : (E) Denham's Bustard, Stanley Bustard, (S) Avutarda cafre, Avutarda de Burchell, Avutarda de Denham, (F) Outarde de Burchell, Outarde de Denham, **II** OTIDIDAE Av
Neotis heuglinii : (E) Heuglin's Bustard, (S) Avutarda de Heuglin, Avutarda somalí, (F) Outarde de Heuglin, **II** OTIDIDAE Av
Neotis ludwigii : (E) Ludwig's Bustard, (S) Avutarda de Ludwig, Avutarda de Namibia, (F) Outarde de Ludwig, **II** OTIDIDAE Av
Neotis nuba : (E) Nubian Bustard, (S) Avutarda núbica, (F) Outarde de Nubie, Outarde nubienne, **II** OTIDIDAE Av
Neotropical Otter (E): *Lontra longicaudis*
Neotropical Rattlesnake (E): *Crotalus durissus*
Neotropical River Otter (E): *Lontra longicaudis*
Neptune's Cap Coral (E): *Halomitra pileus*
Nesasio solomonensis : (E) Fearful Owl, (S) Búho de las Salomón, (F) Chouette des îles Salomons, Hibou redoutable, **II** STRIGIDAE Av
Nesocharis capistrata : (E) Grey-headed Oliveback, White-cheeked Olive Weaver, (S) Olivino cariblanco, (F) Dos-vert à joues blanches, Sénégali vert à joues blanches, **III** ESTRILDIDAE Av
Nesochen sandvicensis = Branta sandvicensis
Nesoenas mayeri = Columba mayeri
Nestor de Norfolk (F): *Nestor productus*
Nestor kéa (F): *Nestor notabilis*
Nestor meridionalis : (E) Kaka, New Zealand Kaka, (S) Kaka, (F) Nestor superbe, **II** PSITTACIDAE Av
Nestor notabilis : (E) Kea, (S) Kea, (F) Kea, Nestor kéa, **II** PSITTACIDAE Av
Nestor productus : (E) Norfolk Island Kaka, Norfolk Kaka, (F) Nestor de Norfolk **II** PSITTACIDAE Av
Nestor superbe (F): *Nestor meridionalis*
Nettapus auritus : (E) African Pygmy-goose, (S) Gansito Africano, Patito Africano, (F) Anserelle naine, Sarcelle à oreillons, **III** ANATIDAE Av
Nette à cou rose (F): *Rhodonessa caryophyllacea*
New Britain Flying-fox (E): *Pteropus gilliardi*
New Britain Goshawk (E): *Accipiter princeps*
New Britain Hawk-Owl (E): *Ninox odiosa*
New Britain Honey-buzzard (E): *Henicopernis infuscatus*
New Britain Masked-Owl (E): *Tyto aurantia*
New Britain Sparrowhawk (E): *Accipiter brachyurus*
New Caledonia Flying-fox (E): *Pteropus vetulus*
New Caledonia Goshawk (E): *Accipiter haplochrous*
New Caledonian Lorikeet (E): *Charmosyna diadema*
New Guinea Birdwing (E): *Ornithoptera priamus*
New Guinea Crocodile (E): *Crocodylus novaeguineae*
New Guinea Eagle (E): *Harpyopsis novaeguineae*
New Guinea Giant Softshell Turtle (E): *Pelochelys bibroni*
New Guinea Grey-headed Goshawk (E): *Accipiter poliocephalus*
New Guinea Harpy Eagle (E): *Harpyopsis novaeguineae*
New Guinea Hornbill (E): *Aceros plicatus*
New Guinea Long-nosed Echidna (E): *Zaglossus bruijni*
New Guinea Viper Boa (E): *Candoia aspera*
New Guinea Wreathed Hornbill (E): *Aceros plicatus*
New Holland Seahorse (E): *Hippocampus whitei*
New Ireland Hawk-Owl (E): *Ninox variegata*
New World Python (E): *Loxocemus bicolor*
New World pythons (E): LOXOCEMIDAE spp.
New Zealand Dolphin (E): *Cephalorhynchus hectori*
New Zealand Falcon (E): *Falco novaeseelandiae*
New Zealand Fur Seal (E): *Arctocephalus forsteri*
New Zealand Kaka (E): *Nestor meridionalis*
New Zealand Parakeet (E): *Cyanoramphus novaezelandiae*
Newton's Kestrel (E): *Falco newtoni*
Newton's Parakeet (E): *Psittacula exsul*

Ngami Owlet (E): *Glaucidium ngamiense*
Ngosi Volcano Chameleon (E): *Chamaeleo fuelleborni*
Niam-niam Parrot (E): *Poicephalus crassus*
Nias Serpent-Eagle (E): *Spilornis cheela*
Niceforo's Poison Frog (E): *Epipedobates ingeri*
Nicklin's Pearly Mussel (E): *Unio nickliniana*
Nicobar à camail (F): *Caloenas nicobarica*
Nicobar Dove (E): *Caloenas nicobarica*
Nicobar Flying-fox (E): *Pteropus faunulus*
Nicobar Parakeet (E): *Psittacula caniceps*
Nicobar Pigeon (E): *Caloenas nicobarica*
Nicobar Scops-Owl (E): *Otus alius*
Nicobar Serpent-eagle (E): *Spilornis minimus*
Nicobar Shikra (E): *Accipiter butleri*
Nicobar Sparrowhawk (E): *Accipiter butleri*
Nicobar Treeshrew (E): *Tupaia nicobarica*
Nicoria tricarinata = Melanochelys tricarinata
Nifa mexicana (S): *Thalurania ridgwayi*
Night Monkey (E): *Aotus trivirgatus*
Night Parrot (E): *Geopsittacus occidentalis*
Nigrette à calotte grise (F): *Nigrita canicapilla*
Nigrette à front jaune (F): *Nigrita luteifrons*
Nigrette à ventre blanc (F): *Nigrita fusconota*
Nigrette à ventre roux (F): *Nigrita bicolor*
Nigrita bicolor : (E) Chestnut-breasted Negrofinch, (S) Negrita pechirroja, (F) Nigrette à ventre roux, Sénégali brun à ventre roux, **III** ESTRILDIDAE Av
Nigrita canicapilla : (E) Grey-crowned Negrofinch, Grey-headed Negrofinch, (S) Negrita cana, (F) Nigrette à calotte grise, Sénégali nègre, **III** ESTRILDIDAE Av
Nigrita fusconota : (E) White-breasted Negrofinch, (S) Negrita pechiblanca, (F) Nigrette à ventre blanc, Sénégali brun à ventre blanc, **III** ESTRILDIDAE Av
Nigrita luteifrons : (E) Pale-fronted Negrofinch, (S) Negrita frentigualda, (F) Nigrette à front jaune, Sénégali nègre à front jaune, **III** ESTRILDIDAE Av
Nile Crocodile (E): *Crocodylus niloticus*
Nile Monitor (E): *Varanus niloticus*
Nile Softshell Turtle (E): *Trionyx triunguis*
Nile Soft-shelled Terrapin (E): *Trionyx triunguis*
Nilgiri Langur (E): *Trachypithecus johnii*
Nilgiri Leaf Monkey (E): *Trachypithecus johnii*
Nilgiri Marten (E): *Martes gwatkinsii*
Niltava ruecki = Cyornis ruckii
Nimba toads (E): *Nimbaphrynoides* spp.
Nimbaphrynoides spp.: (E) Nimba toads, (S) Sapos vivíparos, (F) Crapauds vivipares, Crapauds vivipares du Mont Nimba, **I** BUFONIDAE Am
Nimbaphrynoides liberiensis : (E) Liberia Nimba Toad, (S) Sapo vivíparo liberiano, (F) Nectophrynoide du Liberia, **I** BUFONIDAE Am
Nimbaphrynoides occidentalis : (E) Mt Nimba Viviparous Toad, Western Nimba Toad, (S) Sapo vivíparo de Africa occidental, (F) Nectophrynoide du Mont Nimba, **I** BUFONIDAE Am
Ninfa coronada (S): *Thalurania colombica/ Thalurania fannyi*
Ninox affinis : (E) Andaman Boobook, Andaman Hawk Owl, Andaman Hawk-Owl, (S) Nínox de Andamán, (F) Ninoxe des Andaman, **II** STRIGIDAE Av
Nínox Australiano (S): *Ninox boobook*
Ninox boobook : (E) Southern Boobook, (S) Nínox Australiano, (F) Ninoxe d'Australie, **II** STRIGIDAE Av
Ninox connivens : (E) Barking Owl, Winking Owl, (S) Nínox ladrador, (F) Ninoxe aboyeuse, **II** STRIGIDAE Av
Nínox de Andamán (S): *Ninox affinis*
Nínox de la Manus (S): *Ninox meeki*
Nínox de las Bismarck (S): *Ninox variegata*
Nínox de las Solomón (S): *Ninox jacquinoti*
Nínox de Nueva Bretaña (S): *Ninox odiosa*
Nínox de Sumba (S): *Ninox rudolfi*
Nínox Filipino (S): *Ninox philippensis*
Ninox goldii = Ninox theomacha

Nínox halcón (S): *Uroglaux dimorpha*
Ninox ios : (E) Cinnabar Hawk-Owl **II** STRIGIDAE Av
Ninox jacquinoti : (E) Solomon Hawk-Owl, Solomon Islands Boobook, (S) Nínox de las Solomón, (F) Ninoxe de Jacquinot, **II** STRIGIDAE Av
Ninox japonica = Ninox scutulata
Nínox ladrador (S): *Ninox connivens*
Nínox Malgache (S): *Ninox superciliaris*
Nínox Maorí (S): *Ninox novaeseelandiae*
Ninox meeki : (E) Admiralty Hawk-Owl, Admiralty island Hawk-owl, Manus Boobook, Manus Hawk-Owl, (S) Nínox de la Manus, (F) Ninoxe de l'Amirauté, **II** STRIGIDAE Av
Nínox Moluqueño (S): *Ninox squamipila*
Ninox natalis = Ninox squamipila ssp. *natalis*
Ninox novaeseelandiae : (E) Morepork, (S) Nínox Maorí, (F) Chouette boobok, Chouette coucou, Ninoxe boubouk, **I/II** STRIGIDAE Av
Ninox novaeseelandiae ssp. *boobook = Ninox boobook*
Ninox novaeseelandiae ssp. *royana = Ninox novaeseelandiae* ssp. *undulata*
Ninox novaeseelandiae ssp. *rudolfi = Ninox rudolfi*
Ninox novaeseelandiae undulata : (E) Norfolk Boobook, Norfolk Island Boobook Owl, (S) Lechuza gavilana de Norfolk, Mochuelo cucú, (F) Chouette boobok de l'île Norfolk, Ninoxe boubouk de l'île Norfolk, **I** STRIGIDAE Av
Ninox ochracea : (E) Ochre-bellied Boobook, Ochre-bellied Hawk-Owl, (S) Nínox ocráceo, (F) Ninoxe ocrée, **II** STRIGIDAE Av
Nínox ocráceo (S): *Ninox ochracea*
Ninox odiosa : (E) New Britain Hawk-Owl, Russet Boobook, Russet Hawk-Owl, (S) Nínox de Nueva Bretaña, (F) Ninoxe odieuse, **II** STRIGIDAE Av
Nínox Papú (S): *Ninox theomacha*
Nínox pardo (S): *Ninox scutulata*
Ninox perversa = Ninox ochracea
Ninox philippensis : (E) Philippine Boobook, Philippine Hawk-Owl, (S) Nínox Filipino, (F) Ninoxe des Philippines, **II** STRIGIDAE Av
Ninox punctulata : (E) Speckled Boobook, Speckled Hawk-Owl, (S) Nínox punteado, (F) Ninoxe pointillée, **II** STRIGIDAE Av
Nínox punteado (S): *Ninox punctulata*
Ninox randi = Ninox scutulata
Nínox reidor (S): *Sceloglaux albifacies*
Nínox robusto (S): *Ninox strenua*
Nínox rojizo (S): *Ninox rufa*
Ninox rudolfi : (E) Sumba Boobook, (S) Nínox de Sumba, (F) Ninoxe de Sumba, **II** STRIGIDAE Av
Ninox rufa : (E) Rufous Owl, (S) Nínox rojizo, (F) Ninoxe rousse, **II** STRIGIDAE Av
Ninox scutulata : (E) Brown Boobook, Brown Hawk Owl, Brown Hawk-Owl, (S) Nínox pardo, (F) Ninoxe hirsute, **II** STRIGIDAE Av
Ninox solomonis = Ninox variegata
Ninox squamipila : (E) Moluccan Boobook, Moluccan Hawk-Owl, (S) Lechuza gavilana de las Molucas, Mochuelo de las Molucas, Nínox Moluqueño, (F) Chouette des Moluques, Chouette épervière, Ninoxe des Moluques, **I/II** STRIGIDAE Av
Ninox squamipila natalis : (E) Christmas Hawk-Owl, Christmas Island Hawk-Owl, (F) Chouette épervière de l'île Christmas **I** STRIGIDAE Av
Ninox strenua : (E) Powerful Owl, (S) Nínox robusto, (F) Ninoxe puissante, **II** STRIGIDAE Av
Ninox superciliaris : (E) Madagascar Hawk-Owl, White-browed Boobook, White-browed Owl, (S) Nínox Malgache, (F) Ninoxe à sourcils blancs, **II** STRIGIDAE Av
Ninox theomacha : (E) Chestnut Hawk-Owl, Jungle Boobook, Jungle Hawk-Owl, Sooty-backed Hawk-Owl, (S) Nínox Papú, (F) Ninoxe brune, **II** STRIGIDAE Av

Ninox variegata : (E) Bismarck Boobook, Bismarck Hawk-Owl, New Ireland Hawk-Owl, (S) Nínox de las Bismarck, (F) Ninoxe bariolée, **II** STRIGIDAE Av
Ninoxe à sourcils blancs (F): *Ninox superciliaris*
Ninoxe aboyeuse (F): *Ninox connivens*
Ninoxe bariolée (F): *Ninox variegata*
Ninoxe boubouk (F): *Ninox novaeseelandiae*
Ninoxe boubouk de l'île Norfolk (F): *Ninox novaeseelandiae undulata*
Ninoxe brune (F): *Ninox theomacha*
Ninoxe d'Australie (F): *Ninox boobook*
Ninoxe de Jacquinot (F): *Ninox jacquinoti*
Ninoxe de l'Amirauté (F): *Ninox meeki*
Ninoxe de Sumba (F): *Ninox rudolfi*
Ninoxe des Andaman (F): *Ninox affinis*
Ninoxe des Moluques (F): *Ninox squamipila*
Ninoxe des Philippines (F): *Ninox philippensis*
Ninoxe hirsute (F): *Ninox scutulata*
Ninoxe ocrée (F): *Ninox ochracea*
Ninoxe odieuse (F): *Ninox odiosa*
Ninoxe papoue (F): *Uroglaux dimorpha*
Ninoxe pointillée (F): *Ninox punctulata*
Ninoxe puissante (F): *Ninox strenua*
Ninoxe rieuse (F): *Sceloglaux albifacies*
Ninoxe rousse (F): *Ninox rufa*
Nipponia nippon : (E) Crested Ibis, Japanese Crested Ibis, (S) Ibis blanco japonés, Ibis moñudo japonés, Ibis nipón, (F) Ibis à crête du Japon, Ibis blanc, Ibis blanc du Japon, Ibis nippon, **I** THRESKIORNITHIDAE Av
Noble Macaw (E): *Diopsittaca nobilis*
Noisy Scrub-bird (E): *Atrichornis clamosus*
No-mark Lizard (E): *Varanus salvator*
Nomascus concolor = Hylobates concolor
Nomascus gabriellae = Hylobates gabriellae
Nomascus leucogenys = Hylobates leucogenys
Nomlandia californica : **II** CARYOPHYLLIIDAE An
Nordmann's Greenshank (E): *Tringa guttifer*
Norfolk Boobook (E): *Ninox novaeseelandiae undulata*
Norfolk Island Boobook Owl (E): *Ninox novaeseelandiae undulata*
Norfolk Island Kaka (E): *Nestor productus*
Norfolk Kaka (E): *Nestor productus*
North African Crested Porcupine (E): *Hystrix cristata*
North American Manatee (E): *Trichechus manatus*
North American Otter (E): *Lontra canadensis*
North American River Otter (E): *Lontra canadensis*
North Andean Deer (E): *Hippocamelus antisensis*
North Andean Huemul (E): *Hippocamelus antisensis*
North Moluccan Flying-fox (E): *Pteropus caniceps*
North Mongolian Kulan (E): *Equus hemionus hemionus*
North Philippine Spitting Cobra (E): *Naja philippinensis*
Northern Bald Ibis (E): *Geronticus eremita*
Northern Bottlenose Whale (E): *Hyperoodon ampullatus*
Northern Coati (E): *Nasua narica*
Northern Common Cuscus (E): *Phalanger orientalis*
Northern Crag Lizard (E): *Cordylus transvaalensis*
Northern Day Gecko (E): *Phelsuma chekei*
Northern Eyelash Boa (E): *Trachyboa boulengeri*
Northern Four-toothed Whale (E): *Berardius bairdii*
Northern Goshawk (E): *Accipiter gentilis*
Northern Hairy-nosed Wombat (E): *Lasiorhinus krefftii*
Northern Harrier (E): *Circus cyaneus*
Northern Hawk Owl (E): *Surnia ulula*
Northern Helmeted Curassow (E): *Pauxi pauxi*
Northern Hobby (E): *Falco subbuteo*
Northern Leaf Chameleon (E): *Brookesia ebenaui*
Northern Little Owl (E): *Athene noctua*
Northern Minke Whale (E): *Balaenoptera acutorostrata*
Northern Naked-tailed Armadillo (E): *Cabassous centralis*
Northern Needle-clawed Bushbaby (E): *Euoticus pallidus*
Northern Needle-clawed Galago (E): *Euoticus pallidus*
Northern Paradise-Whydah (E): *Vidua orientalis*
Northern Pied-Hornbill (E): *Anthracoceros albirostris*
Northern Pintail (E): *Anas acuta*
Northern Pudu (E): *Pudu mephistophiles*

Checklist of fauna/Lista de especies de fauna/Liste des espèces animales

Northern Pygmy-Owl (E): *Glaucidium californicum*
Northern Riffleshell (E): *Epioblasma torulosa rangiana*
Northern Right Whale (E): *Eubalaena glacialis*
Northern Right Whale Dolphin (E): *Lissodelphis borealis*
Northern River Otter (E): *Lontra canadensis*
Northern Rosella (E): *Platycercus venustus*
Northern Rufous Mouse Lemur (E): *Microcebus tavaratra*
Northern Savanna Monitor (E): *Varanus exanthematicus*
Northern Saw-whet Owl (E): *Aegolius acadicus*
Northern Seahorse (E): *Hippocampus erectus*
Northern Shoveler (E): *Anas clypeata*
Northern Smooth-tailed Treeshrew (E): *Dendrogale murina*
Northern Sportive Lemur (E): *Lepilemur septentrionalis*
Northern Star Coral (E): *Astrangia poculata*
Northern Sticky-toed Gecko (E): *Hoplodactylus duvaucelii*
Northern Tamandua (E): *Tamandua mexicana*
Northern Tree Gecko (E): *Naultinus manukanus*
Northern Treeshrew (E): *Tupaia belangeri*
Northern Waved Hornbill (E): *Aceros undulatus*
Northiella haematogaster : (E) Bluebonnet, (S) Perico cariazul, (F) Perruche à bonnet bleu, **II** PSITTACIDAE Av
North-western Chameleon (E): *Calumma guibei*
North-western Day Gecko (E): *Phelsuma befotakensis*
Nossi-bé Sportive Lemur (E): *Lepilemur dorsalis*
Notocyathus conicus : **II** TURBINOLIIDAE An
Notocyathus venustus : **II** TURBINOLIIDAE An
Notophyllia etheridgi : **II** DENDROPHYLLIIDAE An
Notophyllia piscacauda : **II** DENDROPHYLLIIDAE An
Notophyllia recta : **II** DENDROPHYLLIIDAE An
Novibos sauveli = Bos sauveli
Nubian Bustard (E): *Neotis nuba*
Nubian Vulture (E): *Torgos tracheliotus*
Numenius borealis : (E) Eskimo Curlew, (S) Chorlito esquimal, Chorlo polar, Zarapito boreal, Zarapito esquimal, Zarapito polar, (F) Courlis esquimau, **I** SCOLOPACIDAE Av
Numenius tenuirostris : (E) Slender-billed Curlew, (S) Zarapito fino, (F) Courlis à bec grêle, **I** SCOLOPACIDAE Av
Nutria (S): *Lutra lutra*
Nutria africana (S): *Aonyx capensis*
Nutria brasileña (S): *Pteronura brasiliensis*
Nutria cenicienta (S): *Amblonyx cinereus*
Nutria chilena (S): *Lontra provocax*
Nutria común (S): *Lutra lutra*
Nutria de agua (S): *Lontra longicaudis*
Nutria de Canadá (S): *Lontra canadensis*
Nutria de Chile (S): *Lontra provocax*
Nutria de cola larga (S): *Lontra longicaudis*
Nutria de cuello blanco (S): *Aonyx capensis*
Nutria de cuello manchado (S): *Lutra maculicollis*
Nutria de mar (S): *Lontra felina*
Nutria de mar californiana (S): *Enhydra lutris nereis*
Nutria de Sumatra (S): *Lutra sumatrana*
Nutria del Kamtchatka (S): *Enhydra lutris*
Nutria europea (S): *Lutra lutra*
Nutria gigante (S): *Pteronura brasiliensis*
Nutria inerme asiatica (S): *Amblonyx cinereus*
Nutria inerme de Camerún (S): *Aonyx congicus*
Nutria lisa (S): *Lutrogale perspicillata*
Nutria marina (S): *Enhydra lutris/ Lontra felina*
Nutria norteamericana (S): *Lontra canadensis*
Nutria simung (S): *Lutrogale perspicillata*
Nutrias (S): LUTRINAE spp.
Nyan (E): *Ovis ammon hodgsonii*
Nyasa Lovebird (E): *Agapornis lilianae*
Nyctale de Harris (F): *Aegolius harrisii*
Nyctale de Tengmalm (F): *Aegolius funereus*
Nyctale immaculée (F): *Aegolius ridgwayi*
Nyctea scandiaca : (E) Snowy Owl, (S) Búho Nival, (F) Chouette harfang, Harfang des neiges, **II** STRIGIDAE Av
Nycticebus bengalensis = Nycticebus coucang

Nycticebus coucang : (E) Slow Loris, (S) Loris lento, (F) Loris lent, **II** LORIDAE Ma
Nycticebus intermedius = Nycticebus pygmaeus
Nycticebus javanicus = Nycticebus coucang
Nycticebus menagensis = Nycticebus coucang
Nycticebus pygmaeus : (E) Lesser Slow Loris, Pygmy Loris **II** LORIDAE Ma
Nymphicus hollandicus : (E) Cockatiel, (S) Lorito de copete, (F) Calopsitte élégante, **NC** PSITTACIDAE Av
Nyroca nyroca = Aythya nyroca
Oahu tree snails (E): *Achatinella* spp.
Oasis Hummingbird (E): *Rhodopis vesper*
Oaxaca Hummingbird (E): *Eupherusa cyanophrys*
Oaxacan Boa (E): *Exiliboa placata*
Oaxacan Dwarf Boa (E): *Exiliboa placata*
Obi Birdwing (E): *Ornithoptera aesacus*
Obscure Hermit (E): *Phaethornis idaliae*
Oca del Nilo (S): *Alopochen aegyptiacus*
Oceanic Seahorse (E): *Hippocampus kuda*
Ocellated Day Gecko (E): *Phelsuma ocellata*
Ocellated Mastigure (E): *Uromastyx ocellata*
Ocellated Pheasant (E): *Rheinardia ocellata*
Ocellated Turkey (E): *Agriocharis ocellata*
Ocelot (E/F): *Leopardus pardalis*
Ocelote (S): *Leopardus pardalis*
Ochre-bellied Boobook (E): *Ninox ochracea*
Ochre-bellied Hawk-Owl (E): *Ninox ochracea*
Ochre-marked Parakeet (E): *Pyrrhura cruentata*
Ocreatus underwoodii : (E) Booted Racket-tail, (S) Colaespatula zamarrito, Colibrí cola de hoja, Colibrí de raquetas, (F) Haut-de-chausses à palettes, **II** TROCHILIDAE Av
Oculina arbuscula : (E) Compact Ivory Bush Coral **II** OCULINIDAE An
Oculina diffusa : (E) Diffuse Ivory Bush Coral **II** OCULINIDAE An
Oculina patagonica : **II** OCULINIDAE An
Oculina profunda : **II** OCULINIDAE An
Oculina robusta : (E) Robust Ivory Tree Coral **II** OCULINIDAE An
Oculina tenella : (E) Delicate Ivory Bush Coral **II** OCULINIDAE An
Oculina valenciennesi : (E) Ivory Tree Coral **II** OCULINIDAE An
Oculina varicosa : **II** OCULINIDAE An
Oculina virgosa : **II** OCULINIDAE An
Odobenus rosmarus : (E) Walrus, (S) Morsa, (F) Morse, **III** ODOBENIDAE Ma
Odocoileus bezoarticus = Ozotoceros bezoarticus
Odocoileus virginianus mayensis : (E) Guatemalan White-tailed Deer **III** CERVIDAE Ma
Odontocyathus coronatus = Stephanocyathus coronatus
Odontocyathus sexradiis = Stephanocyathus spiniger
Odontocyathus stella = Stephanocyathus spiniger
Oedicnème américain (F): *Burhinus bistriatus*
Oedicnème bistrié (F): *Burhinus bistriatus*
Oelofsen's Girdled Lizard (E): *Cordylus oelofseni*
Oena capensis : (E) Long-tailed Dove, Masked Dove, Namaqua Dove, (S) Palomita especulada capense, Tortolita rabilarga, (F) Tourtelette masquée, Tourterelle à masque de fer, Tourterelle du Cap, Tourterelle masquée, **III** COLUMBIDAE Av
Oenpelli Python (E): *Morelia oenpelliensis*
Offshore Seahorse (E): *Hippocampus kelloggi*
Ogilby's Duiker (E): *Cephalophus ogilbyi*
Ognorhynchus icterotis : (E) Yellow-eared Conure, Yellow-eared Parrot, (S) Aratinga orejigualda, Periquito orejiamarillo, (F) Conure à joues d'or, Conure à oreilles jaunes, Perruche aux oreilles jaunes, **I** PSITTACIDAE Av
Oie d'Égypte (F): *Alopochen aegyptiacus*
Oie néné (F): *Branta sandvicensis*
Oie-armée de Gambie (F): *Plectropterus gambensis*
Oiseau bruyant des buissons (F): *Atrichornis clamosus*

Checklist of fauna/Lista de especies de fauna/Liste des espèces animales

Oiseaux-mouches (F): TROCHILIDAE spp.
Old four legs (E): *Latimeria chalumnae*
Old World Otter (E): *Lutra lutra*
Olingo (E/S/F): *Bassaricyon gabbii*
Olivaceous Keelback (E): *Atretium schistosum*
Olivaceous Thornbill (E): *Chalcostigma olivaceum*
Olive (Rock) Python (E): *Liasis olivaceus*
Olive Baboon (E): *Papio hamadryas*
Olive Colobus (E): *Procolobus verus*
Olive Keelback (E): *Atretium schistosum*
Olive Ridley (E): *Lepidochelys olivacea*
Olive-headed Lorikeet (E): *Trichoglossus euteles*
Olive-shouldered Parrot (E): *Aprosmictus jonquillaceus*
Olive-spotted Hummingbird (E): *Leucippus chlorocercus*
Olive-throated Conure (E): *Aratinga nana*
Olive-throated Parakeet (E): *Aratinga nana*
Olivino cariblanco (S): *Nesocharis capistrata*
Omei Shan Liocichla (E): *Liocichla omeiensis*
Onager (E): *Equus onager*
Onagre (F): *Equus onager*
Onagro (S): *Equus onager*
Onagro de la India (S): *Equus onager khur*
Once (F): *Uncia uncia*
Oncifelis colocolo : (E) Chilean Pampa Cat, Pampas Cat, (S) Gato de los pajonales, Gato pajero, Osio, (F) Chat des pampas, **II** FELIDAE Ma
Oncifelis geoffroyi : (E) Geoffroy's Cat, (S) Gato de mato, Gato montés común, (F) Chat de Geoffroy, **I** FELIDAE Ma
Oncifelis guigna : (E) Chilean Cat, Kodkod, (S) Guina, (F) Guigna, **II** FELIDAE Ma
Oncifelis pajeros = Oncifelis colocolo ssp. *pajeros*
Oncilla (E): *Leopardus tigrinus*
Oncille (F): *Leopardus tigrinus*
One-horned Chameleon (E): *Furcifer monoceras*
Ontong Java Flying-fox (E): *Pteropus howensis*
Onychogale bridé (F): *Onychogalea fraenata*
Onychogale croissant (F): *Onychogalea lunata*
Onychogalea fraenata : (E) Bridled Nailtail Wallaby, Bridled Wallaby, Merrin, (S) Canguro rabipelado oriental, (F) Onychogale bridé, Onycholage bridé, **I** MACROPODIDAE Ma
Onychogalea lunata : (E) Crescent Nailtail Wallaby, Wurrung, (S) Canguro rabipelado occidental, (F) Onychogale croissant, Onychologe croissant, Wallaby à queue cornée, **I** MACROPODIDAE Ma
Onycholage bridé (F): *Onychogalea fraenata*
Onychologe croissant (F): *Onychogalea lunata*
Onza (S): *Herpailurus yaguarondi*
Onza bermeja (S): *Puma concolor*
Ophiophagus hannah : (E) Hamadryad, King Cobra, (S) Cobra real, (F) Cobra royal, Hamadryade, Hamadryas, **II** ELAPIDAE Re
Opisthoprora euryptera : (E) Mountain Avocetbill, (S) Colibrí picolezna, Colibrí piquiavoceta, (F) Colibri avocettin, **II** TROCHILIDAE Av
Opopsitta diophthalma = Cyclopsitta diophthalma
Opopsitta diophthalma ssp. *coxeni = Cyclopsitta diophthalma* ssp. *coxeni*
Opopsitta gulielmitertii = Cyclopsitta gulielmitertii
Ora (E): *Varanus komodoensis*
Orange Bishop (E): *Euplectes franciscanus*
Orange Cock-of-the-rock (E): *Rupicola rupicola*
Orange Cup Coral (E): *Tubastraea coccinea*
Orange Toad (E): *Bufo periglenes*
Orange Tube Coral (E): *Tubastraea coccinea*
Orange Turret Coral (E): *Tubastraea faulkneri*
Orange Weaver (E): *Euplectes franciscanus/ Ploceus aurantius*
Orange-and-black Poison Frog (E): *Phyllobates vittatus*
Orange-bellied Parakeet (E): *Neophema chrysogaster*
Orange-bellied Parrot (E): *Neophema chrysogaster*
Orange-billed Lorikeet (E): *Neopsittacus pullicauda*
Orange-breasted Falcon (E): *Falco deiroleucus*
Orange-breasted Fig-Parrot (E): *Cyclopsitta gulielmitertii*

Orange-breasted Waxbill (E): *Amandava subflava*
Orange-cheeked Parrot (E): *Pionopsitta barrabandi*
Orange-cheeked Waxbill (E): *Estrilda melpoda*
Orange-chinned Parakeet (E): *Brotogeris jugularis*
Orange-foot Pimpleback (E): *Plethobasus cooperianus*
Orange-footed Pimpleback Mussel (E): *Plethobasus cooperianus*
Orange-fronted Conure (E): *Aratinga canicularis*
Orange-fronted Hanging-Parrot (E): *Loriculus aurantiifrons*
Orange-fronted Parakeet (E): *Aratinga canicularis/ Cyanoramphus malherbi*
Orange-knee Tarantula (E): *Brachypelma emilia*
Orange-spined Hairy Dwarf Porcupine (E): *Sphiggurus spinosus*
Orange-throated Sunangel (E): *Heliangelus mavors*
Orange-winged Amazon (E): *Amazona amazonica*
Orange-winged Parrot (E): *Amazona amazonica*
Orang-outan (F): *Pongo pygmaeus*
Orang-utan (E): *Pongo pygmaeus*
Orangután (S): *Pongo pygmaeus*
Orca (E/S): *Orcinus orca*
Orca falsa (S): *Pseudorca crassidens*
Orca pigmeo (S): *Feresa attenuata*
Orcaella brevirostris : (E) Irrawaddy Dolphin, Snubfin Dolphin, (S) Delfín del Irrawaddy, (F) Orcelle, **II** DELPHINIDAE Ma
Orcelle (F): *Orcaella brevirostris*
Orcinus glacialis = Orcinus orca
Orcinus nanus = Orcinus orca
Orcinus orca : (E) Killer Whale, Orca, (S) Espadarte, Orca, (F) Epaulard, Orque, **II** DELPHINIDAE Ma
Oreailurus jacobita : (E) Andean Cat, Mountain Cat, (S) Chinchay, Gato andino, Gato lince, Osjo, (F) Chat des Andes, **I** FELIDAE Ma
Oregon Sturgeon (E): *Acipenser transmontanus*
Orejavioleta café (S): *Colibri delphinae*
Orejivioleta marrón (S): *Colibri delphinae*
Oreonax flavicauda = Lagothrix flavicauda
Oreonympha nobilis : (E) Bearded Mountaineer, (S) Colibrí noble, (F) Colibri noble, **II** TROCHILIDAE Av
Oréophase cornu (F): *Oreophasis derbianus*
Oreophasis derbianus : (E) Derby's Guan, Horned Guan, Lord Derby's Mountain Pheasant, (S) Chachalaca cornuda, Faisan de cuerno rojo, Guan cornudo, Paují cornudo, Pava pajuil, Pavón, Pavón cornudo, (F) Hocco huppé, Oréophase cornu, Pénélope cornue, Pénélope de Derby, **I** CRACIDAE Av
Oreopsittacus arfaki : (E) Plum-faced Lorikeet, Whiskered Lorikeet, (S) Lori bigotudo, (F) Lori bridé, Lori des montagnes, **II** PSITTACIDAE Av
Oreotrochilus adela : (E) Wedge-tailed Hillstar, (S) Colibrí de Cochabamba, (F) Colibri adèle, **II** TROCHILIDAE Av
Oreotrochilus chimborazo : (E) Ecuadorian Hillstar, (S) Colibrí del Chimborazo, Estrella ecuatoriana, (F) Colibri du Chimborazo, **II** TROCHILIDAE Av
Oreotrochilus estella : (E) Andean Hillstar, (S) Colibrí puneño, Picaflor serrano ventricanela, (F) Colibri estelle, **II** TROCHILIDAE Av
Oreotrochilus estella ssp. *chimborazo = Oreotrochilus chimborazo*
Oreotrochilus leucopleurus : (E) White-sided Hillstar, (S) Colibrí cordillerano, Picaflor serrano ventrinegro, (F) Colibri à flancs blancs, **II** TROCHILIDAE Av
Oreotrochilus melanogaster : (E) Black-breasted Hillstar, (S) Colibrí pechinegro, (F) Colibri à plastron noir, **II** TROCHILIDAE Av
Oreotrochilus stolzmanni : (E) Green-headed Hillstar **II** TROCHILIDAE Av
Organ-pipe Coral (E): *Tubipora musica*
Oricou (F): *Torgos tracheliotus*
Oriental Bay-Owl (E): *Phodilus badius*
Oriental Hobby (E): *Falco severus*

Checklist of fauna/Lista de especies de fauna/Liste des espèces animales

Oriental Honey-buzzard (E): *Pernis ptilorhyncus*
Oriental Pied-Hornbill (E): *Anthracoceros albirostris*
Oriental Rat Snake (E): *Ptyas mucosus*
Oriental Scops-Owl (E): *Otus scops*
Oriental Small-clawed Otter (E): *Amblonyx cinereus*
Oriental Stork (E): *Ciconia boyciana*
Oriental White Stork (E): *Ciconia boyciana*
Oriental White-backed Vulture (E): *Gyps bengalensis*
Orinoco Crocodile (E): *Crocodylus intermedius*
Orix algacel (S): *Oryx dammah*
Orix blanco (S): *Oryx leucoryx*
Orix de Arabia (S): *Oryx leucoryx*
Orix de Cimitarra (S): *Oryx dammah*
Orlitia borneensis : (E) Bornean River Turtle, Malaysian
    Giant Turtle, Malaysian Giant Terrapin, (F) Émyde
    géante de Borneo, **II** EMYDIDAE Re
Ormala (E): *Lagorchestes hirsutus*
Ornate Box Turtle (E): *Terrapene ornata*
Ornate Day Gecko (E): *Phelsuma ornata*
Ornate Flying-fox (E): *Pteropus ornatus*
Ornate Hawk-Eagle (E): *Spizaetus ornatus*
Ornate Lorikeet (E): *Trichoglossus ornatus*
Ornate Lory (E): *Trichoglossus ornatus*
Ornate Umbrellabird (E): *Cephalopterus ornatus*
Ornithoptera spp.: (E) Birdwing butterflies, (F)
    Ornithoptères **I/II** PAPILIONIDAE In
Ornithoptera aesacus : (E) Obi Birdwing, (F) Ornithoptère
    Obi **II** PAPILIONIDAE In
Ornithoptera akakeae : **II** PAPILIONIDAE In
Ornithoptera alexandrae : (E) Queen Alexandra's
    Birdwing, (F) Ornithoptère de la reine Alexandra **I**
    PAPILIONIDAE In
Ornithoptera allottei : (E) Abbé Allotte's Birdwing, (F)
    Ornithoptère de l'abbé Allotte **II** PAPILIONIDAE In
Ornithoptera caelestis : **II** PAPILIONIDAE In
Ornithoptera chimaera : (E) Chimaera Birdwing, (F) La
    chimère, Ornithoptère chimère **II** PAPILIONIDAE In
Ornithoptera croesus : **II** PAPILIONIDAE In
Ornithoptera goliath : (E) Goliath Birdwing, (F)
    Ornithoptère goliath **II** PAPILIONIDAE In
Ornithoptera meridionalis :, (F) Ornithoptère méridional
    II PAPILIONIDAE In
Ornithoptera paradisea : (E) Butterfly of Paradise,
    Paradise Birdwing, Tailed Birdwing, (F) Ornithoptère
    de paradis **II** PAPILIONIDAE In
Ornithoptera priamus : (E) Common Birdwing, Common
    Green Birdwing, New Guinea Birdwing, Priam's
    Birdwing **II** PAPILIONIDAE In
Ornithoptera richmondia : (E) Richmond Birdwing **II**
    PAPILIONIDAE In
Ornithoptera rothschildi : (E) Rothschild's Birdwing **II**
    PAPILIONIDAE In
Ornithoptera tithonus : **II** PAPILIONIDAE In
Ornithoptera urvillianus : (E) D'Urville's Birdwing **II**
    PAPILIONIDAE In
Ornithoptera victoriae : (E) Queen Victoria's Birdwing,
    (F) Ornithoptère de la reine Victoria **II**
    PAPILIONIDAE In
Ornithoptère chimère (F): *Ornithoptera chimaera*
Ornithoptère de Brooke (F): *Trogonoptera brookiana*
Ornithoptère de la reine Alexandra (F): *Ornithoptera*
    alexandrae
Ornithoptère de la reine Victoria (F): *Ornithoptera*
    victoriae
Ornithoptère de l'abbé Allotte (F): *Ornithoptera allottei*
Ornithoptère de paradis (F): *Ornithoptera paradisea*
Ornithoptère goliath (F): *Ornithoptera goliath*
Ornithoptère méridional (F): *Ornithoptera meridionalis*
Ornithoptère Obi (F): *Ornithoptera aesacus*
Ornithoptères (F): *Ornithoptera* spp. / *Trogonoptera* spp.
Oroaetus isidori : (E) Black-and-chestnut Eagle, Isidor's
    Eagle, (S) Aguila castaña, Aguila de Copete, Aguila
    poma, (F) Aigle d'Isidore, **II** ACCIPITRIDAE Av
Orong (E): *Pantholops hodgsonii*
Orque (F): *Orcinus orca*

Orque pygmée (F): *Feresa attenuata*
Orsini's Viper (E): *Vipera ursinii*
Ortalide chacamel (F): *Ortalis vetula*
Ortalide commune (F): *Ortalis vetula*
Ortalide du Mexique (F): *Ortalis vetula*
Ortalis vetula : (E) Chachalaca, Common Chachalaca,
    Mexican Chachalaca, Plain Chachalaca, (S)
    Chachalaca de los Llenos, Chachalaca norteña, (F)
    Ortalide chacamel, Ortalide commune, Ortalide du
    Mexique, **III** CRACIDAE Av
Orthopsittaca manilata : (E) Red-bellied Macaw, (S)
    Guacamayo barriga roja, Guacamayo ventrirrojo, (F)
    Ara macavouanne, **II** PSITTACIDAE Av
Orthorhyncus cristatus : (E) Antillean Crested
    Hummingbird, (S) Colibrí crestado, (F) Colibri huppé,
    II TROCHILIDAE Av
Ortygospiza atricollis : (E) African Quailfinch, (S)
    Astrilda aperdizada, (F) Astrild caille, Astrild-caille à
    lunettes, **III** ESTRILDIDAE Av
Oryx algazelle (F): *Oryx dammah*
Oryx blanc (F): *Oryx leucoryx*
Oryx dammah : (E) Sahara Oryx, Scimitar-horned Oryx,
    White Oryx, (S) Orix algacel, Orix de Cimitarra, (F)
    Oryx algazelle, Oryx de Libye, **I** BOVIDAE Ma
Oryx d'Arabie (F): *Oryx leucoryx*
Oryx de Libye (F): *Oryx dammah*
Oryx leucoryx : (E) Arabian Oryx, White Oryx, (S) Orix
    blanco, Orix de Arabia, (F) Oryx blanc, Oryx
    d'Arabie, **I** BOVIDAE Ma
Oryx tao = *Oryx dammah*
Oryzotrochus stephensoni = *Turbinolia stephensoni*
Osetr (E): *Acipenser gueldenstaedtii*
Osgood's Ethiopian Toad (E): *Spinophrynoides osgoodi*
O'Shaughnessy's Chameleon (E): *Calumma oshaughnessyi*
Osio (S): *Oncifelis colocolo*
Osjo (S): *Oreailurus jacobita*
Oso andino de anteojos (S): *Tremarctos ornatus*
Oso bezudo (S): *Melursus ursinus*
Oso caballo (S): *Myrmecophaga tridactyla*
Oso de anteojos (S): *Tremarctos ornatus*
Oso de collar (S): *Ursus thibetanus*
Oso de los cocoteros (S): *Helarctos malayanus*
Oso de sol (S): *Helarctos malayanus*
Oso frontino (S): *Tremarctos ornatus*
Oso hormiguero (S): *Myrmecophaga tridactyla*
Oso malayo (S): *Helarctos malayanus*
Oso marino austral (S): *Arctocephalus australis*
Oso marino de Chile (S): *Arctocephalus philippii*
Oso marino de Guadalupe (S): *Arctocephalus townsendi*
Oso marino de las Galápagos (S): *Arctocephalus*
    galapagoensis
Oso marino de Nueva Zelanda (S): *Arctocephalus forsteri*
Oso marsupial del Río Moonie (S): *Lasiorhinus krefftii*
Oso negro americano (S): *Ursus americanus*
Oso negro de Asia (S): *Ursus thibetanus*
Oso pardo (S): *Ursus arctos*
Oso pardo del Himalaya (S): *Ursus arctos isabellinus*
Oso perezoso (S): *Melursus ursinus*
Oso polar (S): *Ursus maritimus*
Oso real (S): *Tremarctos ornatus*
Osos (S): URSIDAE spp.
Osos marinos (S): *Arctocephalus* spp.
Osprey (E): *Pandion haliaetus*
Osteolaemus tetraspis : (E) African Dwarf Crocodile,
    West African Dwarf Crocodile, (S) Cocodrilo chico
    africano, Cocodrilo de hocico corto, (F) Crocodile à
    front large, Crocodile à museau court, Crocodile à
    nuque cuirassée, Crocodile nain africain, **I**
    CROCODYLIDAE Re
Ostrich (E): *Struthio camelus*
Otaria americano (S): *Arctocephalus townsendi*
Otarie à fourrure australe (F): *Arctocephalus australis*
Otarie à fourrure d'Amérique (F): *Arctocephalus*
    townsendi
Otaries à fourrure (F): *Arctocephalus* spp.

Checklist of fauna/Lista de especies de fauna/Liste des espèces animales

Otaries à fourrure du Sud (F): *Arctocephalus* spp.

OTIDIDAE spp.: (E) Bustards, Floricans, (S) Avutardas, Otídidos, Sisones, (F) Outardes, **I/II** Av

Otídidos (S): OTIDIDAE spp.

Otis tarda : (E) Great Bustard, (S) Avutarda, Avutarda común, Avutarda euroasiática, (F) Grande Outarde, Outarde barbue, **II** OTIDIDAE Av

Otis tetrax = Tetrax tetrax

Otocolobus manul : (E) Pallas's Cat, (S) Gato de Pallas, Gato manul, (F) Chat manul, **II** FELIDAE Ma

Otolemur crassicaudatus : (E) Greater Bushbaby, Large-Eared Greater Galago, Thick-tailed Bushbaby, (S) Gálago de cola gruesa, (F) Galago à queue touffue, Grand galago, **II** GALAGONIDAE Ma

Otolemur crassicaudatus ssp. *garnettii = Otolemur garnettii*

Otolemur garnettii : (E) Garnett's Greater Galago, Small-eared Greater Galago **II** GALAGONIDAE Ma

Otorongo (S): *Panthera onca*

Otter-civet (E): *Cynogale bennettii*

Otters (E): LUTRINAE spp.

Otus albogularis : (E) White-throated Screech-Owl, (S) Autillo gorgiblanco, Curucucú gargantiblanco, (F) Petit-duc à gorge blanche, **II** STRIGIDAE Av

Otus alius : (E) Nicobar Scops-Owl, (S) Autillo de Nicobar, (F) Petit-duc de Nicobar, **II** STRIGIDAE Av

Otus angelinae : (E) Javan Scops-Owl, (S) Autillo de Java, (F) Petit-duc de Java, **II** STRIGIDAE Av

Otus asio : (E) Eastern Screech-Owl, (S) Autillo yanqui, Tecolote oriental, (F) Petit-duc maculé, **II** STRIGIDAE Av

Otus asio ssp. *kennicottii = Otus kennicottii*

Otus atricapillus : (E) Black-capped Screech-Owl, Variable Screech-Owl, (S) Autillo capirotado, Curucucú vermiculado, Lechucita rojiza, (F) Petit-duc à mèches noires, **II** STRIGIDAE Av

Otus bakkamoena : (E) Collared Scops-Owl, Indian Scops-Owl, Sunda Scops-Owl, (S) Autillo chino, Autillo de la Sonda, Autillo Indio, (F) Petit-duc à collier, Petit-duc de Horsfield, Petit-duc indien, **II** STRIGIDAE Av

Otus bakkamoena ssp. *fuliginosus = Otus fuliginosus*

Otus bakkamoena ssp. *megalotis = Otus megalotis*

Otus bakkamoena ssp. *mentawi = Otus mentawi*

Otus balli : (E) Andaman Scops-Owl, (S) Autillo de Andamán, (F) Petit-duc des Andaman, **II** STRIGIDAE Av

Otus barbarus : (E) Bearded Screech-Owl, Santa Barbara Screech-Owl, (S) Autillo barbudo, Tecolote barbudo, (F) Petit-duc bridé, **II** STRIGIDAE Av

Otus beccarii = Otus magicus

Otus brookii : (E) Rajah Scops-Owl, (S) Autillo Rajá, (F) Petit-duc radjah, **II** STRIGIDAE Av

Otus brucei : (E) Pallid Scops-Owl, Striated Scops-Owl, (S) Autillo Persa, (F) Petit-duc de Bruce, **II** STRIGIDAE Av

Otus capnodes = Otus rutilus

Otus choliba : (E) Tropical Screech-Owl, (S) Autillo chóliba, Curucucú común, Lechucita común, (F) Petit-duc choliba, **II** STRIGIDAE Av

Otus clarkii : (E) Bare-shanked Screech-Owl, (S) Autillo serrano, Buhito en Pernetas, (F) Petit-duc de Clark, **II** STRIGIDAE Av

Otus collari : (E) Sangihe Scops-Owl, (S) Autillo de la Sangihe, (F) Petit-duc de Sangihe, **II** STRIGIDAE Av

Otus colombianus = Otus ingens

Otus cooperi = Otus kennicottii

Otus elegans : (E) Elegant Scops-Owl, Ryukyu Scops-Owl , (S) Autillo elegante, (F) Petit-duc élégant, **II** STRIGIDAE Av

Otus flammeolus : (E) Flammulated Owl, (S) Autillo flamulado, Tecolote flameado, (F) Petit-duc nain, **II** STRIGIDAE Av

Otus fuliginosus : (E) Palawan Scops-Owl, (S) Autillo de Palawan, (F) Petit-duc de Palawan, **II** STRIGIDAE Av

Otus guatemalae = Otus atricapillus

Otus guatemalae ssp. *vermiculatus = Otus vermiculatus*

Otus gurneyi = Mimizuku gurneyi

Otus hartlaubi : (E) Sao Tomé Scops-owl, (S) Autillo de Santo Tomé, (F) Petit-duc de Sao Tomé, **II** STRIGIDAE Av

Otus hoyi = Otus atricapillus

Otus icterorhynchus : (E) Sandy Scops-Owl, (S) Autillo piquigualdo, (F) Petit-duc à bec jaune, **II** STRIGIDAE Av

Otus ingens : (E) Colombian Screech-Owl, Rufescent Screech-Owl, (S) Autillo pálido, Curucucú pálido, (F) Petit-duc de Salvin, **II** STRIGIDAE Av

Otus ireneae : (E) Morden's Scops-Owl, Sokoke Scops-Owl, (S) Autillo de Sokoke, (F) Petit-duc d'Irène, **II** STRIGIDAE Av

Otus kennicottii : (E) Western Screech-Owl, (S) Autillo Californiano, Tecolote occidental, (F) Petit-duc des montagnes, **II** STRIGIDAE Av

Otus koepckeae : (E) Koepcke's Screech-Owl, (S) Autillo de Koepcke, (F) Petit-duc de Koepcke, **II** STRIGIDAE Av

Otus lawrencii : (E) Bare-legged Owl, Bare-legged Owlch-Owl, Cuban Screech-Owl, (S) Autillo Cubano, Cotunto, Cuco, Siju cotunto, (F) Chouette de Cuba, Petit-duc de Cuba, **II** STRIGIDAE Av

Otus lempiji = Otus bakkamoena

Otus leucotis : (E) White-faced Screech-Owl, (S) Autillo cariblanco, Gran autillo veliblanco, (F) Petit-duc à face blanche, **II** STRIGIDAE Av

Otus longicornis : (E) Luzon Scops-Owl, (S) Autillo de Luzón, (F) Petit-duc longicorne, **II** STRIGIDAE Av

Otus madagascariensis = Otus rutilus

Otus magicus : (E) Moluccan Scops-Owl, Papuan Scops-Owl, (S) Autillo Moluqueño, (F) Petit-duc mystérieux, **II** STRIGIDAE Av

Otus manadensis : (E) Celebes Scops-Owl, Sulawesi Scops-Owl, (S) Autillo de Célebes, (F) Petit-duc de Manado, **II** STRIGIDAE Av

Otus manadensis ssp. *magicus = Otus magicus*

Otus mantananensis : (E) Mantanani Scops-Owl, (S) Autillo de la Mantanani, (F) Petit-duc de Mantanani, **II** STRIGIDAE Av

Otus marshalli : (E) Cloud-forest Screech-Owl, (S) Autillo de Marshall, (F) Petit-duc de Marshall, **II** STRIGIDAE Av

Otus mayottensis = Otus rutilus

Otus megalotis : (E) Philippine Scops-Owl, (S) Autillo Filipino, (F) Petit-duc de Luçon, **II** STRIGIDAE Av

Otus mentawi : (E) Mentawai Scops-Owl, (S) Autillo de las Mentawai, (F) Petit-duc des Mentawei, **II** STRIGIDAE Av

Otus mindorensis : (E) Mindoro Scops-Owl, (S) Autillo de Mindoro, (F) Petit-duc de Mindoro, **II** STRIGIDAE Av

Otus mirus : (E) Mindanao Scops-Owl, (S) Autillo de Mindanao, (F) Petit-duc de Mindanao, **II** STRIGIDAE Av

Otus moheliensis : (E) Moheli Scops-Owl, (S) Autillo de Moheli, (F) Petit-duc de Mohéli, **II** STRIGIDAE Av

Otus nudipes : (E) Puerto Rican Screech-Owl, (S) Autillo Portorriqueño, (F) Petit-duc de Porto Rico, **II** STRIGIDAE Av

Otus pauliani : (E) Comoro Scops-Owl, Grand Comoro Scops-Owl, (S) Autillo de las Comores, (F) Petit-duc du Karthala, **II** STRIGIDAE Av

Otus petersoni = Otus marshalli

Otus podarginus : (E) Palau Owl, (S) Autillo de las Palau, (F) Petit-duc des Palau, **II** STRIGIDAE Av

Otus roboratus : (E) Peruvian Screech-Owl, West Peruvian Screech-Owl, (S) Autillo peruano, Autillo roborado, (F) Petit-duc du Pérou, **II** STRIGIDAE Av

Otus rufescens : (E) Reddish Scops-Owl, (S) Autillo rojizo, (F) Petit-duc roussâtre, **II** STRIGIDAE Av

Checklist of fauna/Lista de especies de fauna/Liste des espèces animales

Otus rutilus : (E) Madagascar Scops-Owl, Malagasy
 Scops-Owl, Pemba Scops-Owl, (S) Autillo Malgache,
 (F) Petit-duc malgache, **II** STRIGIDAE Av
Otus rutilus ssp. *pauliani = Otus pauliani*
Otus sagittatus : (E) White-fronted Scops-Owl, (S) Autillo
 frentiblanco, (F) Petit-duc à front blanc, **II**
 STRIGIDAE Av
Otus sanctaecatarinae : (E) Long-tufted Screech-Owl, (S)
 Autillo de Santa Catarina, (F) Petit-duc à aigrettes
 longues, **II** STRIGIDAE Av
Otus scops : (E) African Scops-Owl, Common Scops-Owl,
 Eurasian Scops-Owl, Oriental Scops-Owl, Scops Owl,
 (S) Autillo, Autillo Africano, Autillo europeo, Autillo
 Oriental, (F) Hibou petit-duc, Petit-duc africain, Petit-
 duc scops, **II** STRIGIDAE Av
Otus scops ssp. *elegans = Otus elegans*
Otus scops ssp. *longicornis = Otus longicornis*
Otus scops ssp. *mantananensis = Otus mantananensis*
Otus scops ssp. *mindorensis = Otus mindorensis*
Otus scops ssp. *mirus = Otus mirus*
Otus seductus = Otus kennicottii
Otus senegalensis = Otus scops
Otus silvicola : (E) Lesser Sunda Scops-Owl, Wallace's
 Scops-Owl, (S) Autillo de Wallace, (F) Petit-duc de
 Wallace, **II** STRIGIDAE Av
Otus spilocephalus : (E) Mountain Scops-Owl, Spotted
 Scops-Owl, (S) Autillo montano, (F) Petit-duc tacheté,
 II STRIGIDAE Av
Otus spilocephalus ssp. *angelinae = Otus angelinae*
Otus sunia = Otus scops
Otus trichopsis : (E) Whiskered Screech-Owl, (S) Autillo
 bigotudo, Tecolote bigotudo, (F) Petit-duc à
 moustaches, **II** STRIGIDAE Av
Otus umbra : (E) Mentaur Scops-Owl, Simeulue Scops-
 Owl, (S) Autillo de la Simeulue, (F) Petit-duc de
 Simalur, **II** STRIGIDAE Av
Otus usta = Otus watsonii
Otus vermiculatus : (E) Vermiculated Screech-Owl, (S)
 Autillo vermiculado, (F) Petit-duc vermiculé, **II**
 STRIGIDAE Av
Otus watsonii : (E) Tawny-bellied Screech-Owl, (S)
 Autillo del Amazonas, Curucucú orejudo, (F) Petit-
 duc de Watson, **II** STRIGIDAE Av
Ouakari à tête noire (F): *Cacajao melanocephalus*
Ouakari chauve (F): *Cacajao calvus*
Ouakaris (F): *Cacajao* spp.
Ouandérou (F): *Macaca silenus*
Ouette d'Égypte (F): *Alopochen aegyptiacus*
Ouistiti (F): *Callithrix jacchus*
Ouistiti à tête jaune (F): *Callithrix flaviceps*
Ouistiti argenté (F): *Callithrix argentata*
Ouistiti mignon (F): *Callithrix pygmaea*
Oulangia bradleyi : **II** RHIZANGIIDAE An
Oulangia cyathiformis : **II** RHIZANGIIDAE An
Oulangia stokesiana : **II** RHIZANGIIDAE An
Oulangia stokesiana miltoni : **II** RHIZANGIIDAE An
Oulangia stokesiana stokesiana : **II** RHIZANGIIDAE An
Oulastrea crispata : (E) Zebra Coral **II** FAVIIDAE An
Oulophyllia bennettae : **II** FAVIIDAE An
Oulophyllia crispa : **II** FAVIIDAE An
Oulophyllia levis : **II** FAVIIDAE An
Ounce (E): *Uncia uncia*
Ours (F): URSIDAE spp.
Ours à collier (F): *Ursus thibetanus*
Ours à lunettes (F): *Tremarctos ornatus*
Ours à miel (F): *Melursus ursinus*
Ours andin (F): *Tremarctos ornatus*
Ours blanc (F): *Ursus maritimus*
Ours brun (F): *Ursus arctos*
Ours brun de l'Himalaya (F): *Ursus arctos isabellinus*
Ours brun isabelle (F): *Ursus arctos isabellinus*
Ours de l'Himalaya (F): *Ursus thibetanus*
Ours des cocotiers (F): *Helarctos malayanus*
Ours du Tibet (F): *Ursus thibetanus*
Ours grizzly (F): *Ursus arctos*

Ours isabelle (F): *Ursus arctos isabellinus*
Ours lippu de l'Inde (F): *Melursus ursinus*
Ours malais (F): *Helarctos malayanus*
Ours noir américain (F): *Ursus americanus*
Ours noir d'Asie (F): *Ursus thibetanus*
Ours polaire (F): *Ursus maritimus*
Ours prochile lippu (F): *Melursus ursinus*
Oustalet's Giant Chameleon (E): *Furcifer oustaleti*
Oustalet's Grey Duck (E): *Anas oustaleti*
Ousof à oreilles blanches (F): *Callithrix aurita*
Ousof oreillard (F): *Callithrix aurita*
Outarde à miroir blanc (F): *Eupodotis afraoides*
Outarde à tête noire (F): *Ardeotis nigriceps*
Outarde à ventre noir (F): *Eupodotis melanogaster*
Outarde arabe (F): *Ardeotis arabs*
Outarde australienne (F): *Ardeotis australis*
Outarde barbue (F): *Otis tarda*
Outarde canepetière (F): *Tetrax tetrax*
Outarde d'Australie (F): *Ardeotis australis*
Outarde de Burchell (F): *Neotis denhami*
Outarde de Denham (F): *Neotis denhami*
Outarde de Hartlaub (F): *Eupodotis hartlaubii*
Outarde de Heuglin (F): *Neotis heuglinii*
Outarde de l'Inde (F): *Ardeotis nigriceps*
Outarde de Ludwig (F): *Neotis ludwigii*
Outarde de Nubie (F): *Neotis nuba*
Outarde de Rüppell (F): *Eupodotis rueppellii*
Outarde de Savile (F): *Eupodotis savilei*
Outarde de Vigors (F): *Eupodotis vigorsii*
Outarde d'Oustalet (F): *Eupodotis gindiana*
Outarde du Bengale (F): *Eupodotis bengalensis*
Outarde du Sénégal (F): *Eupodotis senegalensis*
Outarde houbara (F): *Chlamydotis undulata*
Outarde houppette (F): *Eupodotis ruficrista*
Outarde korhaan (F): *Eupodotis afra*
Outarde kori (F): *Ardeotis kori*
Outarde naine (F): *Eupodotis ruficrista*
Outarde naine de l'Inde (F): *Eupodotis indica*
Outarde noire (F): *Eupodotis afra*
Outarde nubienne (F): *Neotis nuba*
Outarde passarage (F): *Eupodotis indica*
Outarde plombée (F): *Eupodotis caerulescens*
Outarde somalienne (F): *Eupodotis humilis*
Outardes (F): OTIDIDAE spp.
Ovambo Sparrowhawk (E): *Accipiter ovampensis*
Ovampo Sparrowhawk (E): *Accipiter ovampensis*
Ovis ammon : (E) Argali, Asian Wild Sheep, Marco Polo
 Sheep, (S) Argalí, Muflón, Muflón Argal, Muflón de
 Marco Polo, (F) Argali, Mouflon d'Asie, Mouflon
 d'Eurasie, Mouflon méditerranéen, Mouflon vrai, **I/II**
 BOVIDAE Ma
Ovis ammon hodgsonii : (E) Great Tibetan Sheep, Nyan,
 Tibetan Argali, (S) Argalí del Himalaya, Muflón
 Argal Tibetano, (F) Mouflon de l'Himalaya, Mouflon
 des montagnes, **I** BOVIDAE Ma
Ovis ammon nigrimontana : (E) Kara Tau Argali **I**
 BOVIDAE Ma
Ovis ammon ssp. *severtzovi = Ovis vignei* ssp. *severtzovi*
Ovis ammon ssp. *vignei = Ovis vignei* ssp. *vignei*
Ovis aries ssp. *ophion = Ovis orientalis* ssp. *ophion*
Ovis canadensis : (E) Bighorn Sheep, Mexican Bighorn
 Sheep, Mountain Sheep, (S) Borrego cimarrón,
 Carnero del Canadá, Carnero salvaje, (F) Bighorn,
 Mouflon d'Amérique, Mouflon du Canada, Mouflon
 pachycère, **II/NC** BOVIDAE Ma
Ovis orientalis ophion : (E) Cyprian Wild Sheep, Cyprus
 Mouflon, (S) Muflón de Chipre, (F) Mouflon de
 Chypre, **I** BOVIDAE Ma
Ovis orientalis ssp. *arkal = Ovis vignei* ssp. *arkal*
Ovis orientalis ssp. *bochariensis = Ovis vignei* ssp.
 bochariensis
Ovis orientalis ssp. *cycloceros = Ovis vignei* ssp.
 cycloceros
Ovis orientalis ssp. *punjabiensis = Ovis vignei* ssp.
 punjabiensis

Ovis orientalis ssp. *severtzovi* = *Ovis vignei* ssp. *severtzovi*
Ovis orientalis ssp. *vignei* = *Ovis vignei* ssp. *vignei*
Ovis vignei : (E) Red Sheep, Shapo, Shapu, Urial, (S) Urial, (F) Urial, **I/II** BOVIDAE Ma
Ovis vignei vignei : (E) Ladakh Urial, (F) Mouflon du Ladak, Urial **I** BOVIDAE Ma
Owen's Pygmy Sperm Whale (E): *Kogia simus*
Owen's Three-horned Chameleon (E): *Chamaeleo oweni*
Owl Monkey (E): *Aotus trivirgatus*
Owl Parrot (E): *Strigops habroptilus*
Owls (E): STRIGIFORMES spp. Av
Owl-faced Guenon (E): *Cercopithecus hamlyni*
Owl-faced Monkey (E): *Cercopithecus hamlyni*
Oxus Cobra (E): *Naja oxiana*
Oxypogon guerinii : (E) Bearded Helmetcrest, (S) Chivito de los Páramos, Colibrí chivito, (F) Colibri casqué, **II** TROCHILIDAE Av
Oxypora convoluta : **II** PECTINIIDAE An
Oxypora crassispinosa : **II** PECTINIIDAE An
Oxypora egyptensis : **II** PECTINIIDAE An
Oxypora glabra : **II** PECTINIIDAE An
Oxypora lacera : **II** PECTINIIDAE An
Oxysmilia circularis : **II** CARYOPHYLLIIDAE An
Oxysmilia corrugata : **II** CARYOPHYLLIIDAE An
Oxysmilia epithecata : **II** CARYOPHYLLIIDAE An
Oxysmilia portoricensis = *Oxysmilia rotundifolia*
Oxysmilia rotundifolia : **II** CARYOPHYLLIIDAE An
Oxyura leucocephala : (E) White-headed Duck, (S) Malvasía, Malvasía cabeciblanca, (F) Érismature à tête blanche, **II** ANATIDAE Av
Ozotoceros bezoarticus : (E) Pampas Deer, (S) Ciervo de las Pampas, Ciervo pampero, Venado campero, Venado de campo, Venado de las Pampas, (F) Cerf des pampas, Goazu, **I** CERVIDAE Ma

Paca (E/S/F): *Agouti paca*
Pachliopta jophon = *Atrophaneura jophon*
Pachliopta pandiyana = *Atrophaneura pandiyana*
Pachyphantes superciliosus : (E) Compact Weaver, (S) Tejedor rollizo, (F) Tisserin gros-bec, **III** PLOCEIDAE Av
Pachyseris carinata = *Pachyseris rugosa*
Pachyseris foliosa : **II** AGARICIIDAE An
Pachyseris gemmae : **II** AGARICIIDAE An
Pachyseris involuta : **II** AGARICIIDAE An
Pachyseris rugosa : (E) Castle Coral **II** AGARICIIDAE An
Pachyseris speciosa : (E) Phonograph Coral **II** AGARICIIDAE An
Pacific Baza (E): *Aviceda subcristata*
Pacific Black Hawk (E): *Buteogallus subtilis*
Pacific Boa (E): *Candoia bibroni*
Pacific Dolphin (E): *Delphinus delphis*
Pacific Flying-fox (E): *Pteropus tonganus*
Pacific Marsh-Harrier (E): *Circus approximans*
Pacific Monitor (E): *Varanus indicus*
Pacific Parrotlet (E): *Forpus coelestis*
Pacific Pilot Whale (E): *Globicephala macrorhynchus*
Pacific Pygmy-Owl (E): *Glaucidium peruanum*
Pacific Ridley (E): *Lepidochelys olivacea*
Pacific Rose Coral (E): *Cynarina lacrymalis*
Pacific Seahorse (E): *Hippocampus ingens*
Pacific Sticky-toed Gecko (E): *Hoplodactylus pacificus*
Pacific Sturgeon (E): *Acipenser transmontanus*
Pacific White-sided Dolphin (E): *Lagenorhynchus obliquidens*
Padda de Java (F): *Padda oryzivora*
Padda oryzivora : (E) Java Sparrow, (S) Gorrión de Java, (F) Padda de Java, **II** ESTRILDIDAE Av
Paddlefish (E): *Polyodon spathula/ Psephurus gladius*
Pagai Island Langur (E): *Nasalis concolor*
Pagoda Coral (E): *Turbinaria mesenterina*
Paguma larvata : (E) Masked Palm Civet, (S) Civeta de palmera enmascarada, (F) Civette palmiste à masque, **III** VIVERRIDAE Ma

Paiche (S/F): *Arapaima gigas*
Painted Batagur (E): *Callagur borneoensis*
Painted Conure (E): *Pyrrhura picta*
Painted Parakeet (E): *Pyrrhura picta*
Painted Terrapin (E): *Callagur borneoensis*
Painted Tiger-Parrot (E): *Psittacella picta*
Painted Treeshrew (E): *Tupaia picta*
Pájaro de los matorrales (S): *Atrichornis clamosus*
Pájaro paraguas bigotudo (S): *Cephalopterus penduliger*
Pájaro-paraguas amazónico (S): *Cephalopterus ornatus*
Pájaro-paraguas longuipendulo (S): *Cephalopterus penduliger*
Pájaros paraguas (S): *Cephalopterus ornatus*
Palaeosuchus palpebrosus : (E) Cuvier's Smooth-fronted Caiman, Dwarf Caiman, (S) Caimán enano, (F) Caïman à paupières osseuses, **II** ALLIGATORIDAE Re
Palaeosuchus trigonatus : (E) Schneider's Smooth-fronted Caiman, (S) Caimán frentiplano, (F) Caïman hérissé, **II** ALLIGATORIDAE Re
Palau Fruit Bat (E): *Pteropus pilosus*
Palau Owl (E): *Otus podarginus*
Palauastrea ramosa : **II** POCILLOPORIDAE An
Palawan Flying-fox (E): *Acerodon leucotis*
Palawan Fruit Bat (E): *Acerodon leucotis*
Palawan Hornbill (E): *Anthracoceros marchei*
Palawan Peacock-pheasant (E): *Polyplectron emphanum*
Palawan Racket-tailed Parrot (E): *Prioniturus discurus*
Palawan Scops-Owl (E): *Otus fuliginosus*
Palawan Treeshrew (E): *Tupaia palawanensis*
Pale Chanting-Goshawk (E): *Melierax canorus*
Pale Giant Squirrel (E): *Ratufa affinis*
Pale Harrier (E): *Circus macrourus*
Pale Lilliput (E): *Toxolasma cylindrellus*
Pale Lilliput Pearly Mussel (E): *Toxolasma cylindrellus*
Pale-bellied Hermit (E): *Phaethornis anthophilus*
Pale-billed Sicklebill (E): *Epimachus bruijnii*
Pale-fronted Negrofinch (E): *Nigrita luteifrons*
Pale-headed Rosella (E): *Platycercus adscitus*
Pale-headed Saki (E): *Pithecia pithecia*
Pale-tailed Barbthroat (E): *Threnetes niger*
Palette à couronne bleue (F): *Prioniturus discurus*
Palette à manteau d'or (F): *Prioniturus platurus*
Palette de Buru (F): *Prioniturus mada*
Palette de Cassin (F): *Prioniturus flavicans*
Palette de Mindanao (F): *Prioniturus waterstradti*
Palette de Palawan (F): *Prioniturus platenae*
Palette des Sulu (F): *Prioniturus verticalis*
Palette momot (F): *Prioniturus montanus*
Palette verte (F): *Prioniturus luconensis*
Pale-winged Indigobird (E): *Vidua wilsoni*
Pallas's Cat (E): *Otocolobus manul*
Pallas's Fish-Eagle (E): *Haliaeetus leucoryphus*
Pallas's Sea-eagle (E): *Haliaeetus leucoryphus*
Pallid Harrier (E): *Circus macrourus*
Pallid Scops-Owl (E): *Otus brucei*
Pallid Sturgeon (E): *Scaphirhynchus albus*
Palm Cockatoo (E): *Probosciger aterrimus*
Palm Dove (E): *Streptopelia senegalensis*
Palm Lettuce Coral (E): *Pectinia paeonia*
Palm Lorikeet (E): *Charmosyna palmarum*
Palmiste africain (F): *Gypohierax angolensis*
Palm-nut Vulture (E): *Gypohierax angolensis*
Paloma afep (S): *Columba unicincta*
Paloma apuñalada (S): *Gallicolumba luzonica*
Paloma apuñalada de Luzón (S): *Gallicolumba luzonica*
Paloma Bravía (S): *Columba livia*
Paloma calva (S): *Caloenas nicobarica*
Paloma crestada azul (S): *Goura cristata*
Paloma crestada de Scheepmaker (S): *Goura scheepmakeri*
Paloma crestada victoria (S): *Goura victoria*
Paloma de Guinea (S): *Columba guinea*
Paloma de Mauricio (S): *Columba mayeri*
Paloma de Mindoro (S): *Ducula mindorensis*

Checklist of fauna/Lista de especies de fauna/Liste des espèces animales

Paloma de Nicobar (S): *Caloenas nicobarica*
Paloma del Congo (S): *Columba unicincta*
Paloma Doméstica (S): *Columba livia*
Paloma nuquibronceada (S): *Columba iriditorques*
Palomas crestadas (S): *Goura* spp.
Palomita aliazul (S): *Turtur afer*
Palomita cabeciazul (S): *Turtur brehmeri*
Palomita especulada abisinica (S): *Turtur abyssinicus*
Palomita especulada africana (S): *Turtur afer*
Palomita especulada capense (S): *Oena capensis*
Palomita especulada cobriza (S): *Turtur brehmeri*
Palomita Saheliana (S): *Turtur abyssinicus*
Palomita tamborilera (S): *Turtur tympanistria*
Pampa Fox (E): *Pseudalopex gymnocercus/ Pseudalopex griseus*
Pampas Cat (E): *Oncifelis colocolo*
Pampas Deer (E): *Ozotoceros bezoarticus*
Pan spp.: (E) Chimpanzees, (S) Chimpancés, (F) Bonobo, Chimpanzés, I HOMINIDAE Ma
Pan paniscus : (E) Bonobo, Dwarf Chimpanzee, Pygmy Chimpanzee, (S) Chimpancé pigmeo, (F) Bonobo, Chimpanzé nain, Chimpanzé pygmée, I HOMINIDAE Ma
Pan troglodytes : (E) Chimpanzee, (S) Chimpancé, (F) Chimpanzé, I HOMINIDAE Ma
Panama Spider Monkey (E): *Ateles geoffroyi panamensis*
Panamanian Dwarf Boa (E): *Ungaliophis panamensis*
Panay Flying-fox (E): *Acerodon lucifer*
Panay Giant Fruit Bat (E): *Acerodon lucifer*
Panay Golden-capped Fruit Bat (E): *Acerodon lucifer*
Panay Tarictic Hornbill (E): *Penelopides panini*
Panay Wrinkled Hornbill (E): *Aceros waldeni*
Pancake Star Coral (E): *Dichocoenia stellaris*
Pancake Tortoise (E): *Malacochersus tornieri*
Panda (F): *Ailuropoda melanoleuca*
Panda chico (S): *Ailurus fulgens*
Panda éclatant (F): *Ailurus fulgens*
Panda géant (F): *Ailuropoda melanoleuca*
Panda gigante (S): *Ailuropoda melanoleuca*
Panda rojo (S): *Ailurus fulgens*
Pandinus africanus = Pandinus imperator
Pandinus dictator : (E) Scorpion, (S) Escorpión magnifico, (F) Scorpion dictateur, II SCORPIONIDAE Ar
Pandinus gambiensis : (E) Giant Senegalese Scorpion, (S) Escorpión de Gambia, (F) Grand scorpian du Sénégal, Scorpion de Gambie , II SCORPIONIDAE Ar
Pandinus imperator : (E) Emperor Scorpion, (S) Escorpión emperador, Escorpión gigante, (F) Scorpion empereur, Scorpion impérial , II SCORPIONIDAE Ar
Pandion haliaetus : (E) Osprey, (S) Aguila Pescadora, Aguila sangual, Gavilán pescador, Guincho, (F) Aigle pêcheur, Balbugard fluviatile, Balbuzard pêcheur, II PANDIONIDAE Av
Pangasianodon gigas : (E) Giant Catfish, (S) Siluro gigante, (F) Silure de verre géant, I PANGASIIDAE Ac
Pangasius gigas = Pangasianodon gigas
Pangolin à écailles tricuspides (F): *Manis tricuspis*
Pangolin à grosse queue (F): *Manis crassicaudata*
Pangolin à longue queue (F): *Manis tetradactyla*
Pangolin à queue courte (F): *Manis pentadactyla*
Pangolín chino (S): *Manis pentadactyla*
Pangolin commun (F): *Manis tricuspis*
Pangolin de Chine (F): *Manis pentadactyla*
Pangolín de cola larga (S): *Manis tetradactyla*
Pangolin de Temminck (F): *Manis temminckii*
Pangolín del Cabo (S): *Manis temminckii*
Pangolin géant (F): *Manis gigantea*
Pangolín gigante (S): *Manis gigantea*
Pangolín indio (S): *Manis crassicaudata*
Pangolin javanais (F): *Manis javanica*
Pangolin malais (F): *Manis javanica*
Pangolín malayo (S): *Manis javanica*
Pangolin terrestre du Cap (F): *Manis temminckii*
Pangolin tétradactyle (F): *Manis tetradactyla*

Pangolines (S): *Manis* spp.
Pangolínos (S): *Manis* spp.
Pangolins (E/F): *Manis* spp.
Pangshura leithii = Kachuga tentoria
Pangshura sylhetensis = Kachuga sylhetensis
Pangshura tentoria = Kachuga tentoria
Pan's Box Turtle (E): *Cuora pani*
Pantera (S): *Panthera pardus*
Pantera de la nieves (S): *Uncia uncia*
Pantera del Himalaya (S): *Neofelis nebulosa*
Pantera longibanda (S): *Neofelis nebulosa*
Pantera nebulosa (S): *Neofelis nebulosa*
Panterpe insignis : (E) Fiery-throated Hummingbird, (S) Colibrí insigne, (F) Colibri insigne, II TROCHILIDAE Av
Panther Chameleon (E): *Furcifer pardalis*
Panthera leo : (E) Lion, (S) León, (F) Lion d'Afrique, I/II FELIDAE Ma
Panthera leo persica : (E) Asiatic Lion, Indian Lion, (S) León asiático, León indostánico, (F) Lion d'Asie, I FELIDAE Ma
Panthera onca : (E) Jaguar, (S) Jaguar, Otorongo, Tigre americano, Tigre real, Yaguar, Yaguarete, (F) Jaguar, I FELIDAE Ma
Panthera pardus : (E) Leopard, (S) Leopardo, Pantera, (F) Léopard, Panthère, I FELIDAE Ma
Panthera tigris : (E) Tiger, (S) Tigre, (F) Tigre, I FELIDAE Ma
Panthera uncia = Uncia uncia
Panthère (F): *Panthera pardus*
Panthère des neiges (F): *Uncia uncia*
Panthère longibande (F): *Neofelis nebulosa*
Panthère nébuleuse (F): *Neofelis nebulosa*
Pantholops hodgsonii : (E) Chiru, Orong, Tibetan Antelope, (S) Antílope del Tibet, Antílope tibetano, (F) Antilope du Tibet, Tchirou, I BOVIDAE Ma
Pantropical Spotted Dolphin (E): *Stenella attenuata*
Paon spicifère (F): *Pavo muticus*
Paon vert (F): *Pavo muticus*
Papagayo alirrojo (S): *Aprosmictus erythropterus*
Papagayo australiano (S): *Alisterus scapularis*
Papagayo de cara roja (S): *Amazona brasiliensis*
Papagayo de Gulielm (S): *Poicephalus gulielmi*
Papagayo de Timor (S): *Aprosmictus jonquillaceus*
Papagayo enmascarado (S): *Prosopeia personata*
Papagayo escarlata (S): *Prosopeia splendens*
Papagayo granate (S): *Prosopeia tabuensis*
Papagayo Moluqueño (S): *Alisterus amboinensis*
Papagayo papú (S): *Alisterus chloropterus*
Papagayo robusto (S): *Poicephalus robustus*
Papagayo senegalés (S): *Poicephalus senegalus*
Papagayos (S): PSITTACIFORMES spp. Av
Papamoscas (S): *Terpsiphone bourbonnensis*
Papamoscas de Rueck (S): *Cyornis ruckii*
Papamoscas piquilargo (S): *Dasyornis longirostris*
Papamoscas rosa occidental (S): *Dasyornis broadbenti litoralis*
Papasula abbotti : (E) Abbott's Booby, (S) Alcatraz de Abbott, Piquero de Abbott, (F) Fou d'Abbott, I SULIDAE Av
Papegeai maillé (F): *Deroptyus accipitrinus*
Paphosia adorabilis = Lophornis adorabilis
Paphosia helenae = Lophornis helenae
Papilio chikae : (E) Luzon Peacock Swallowtail, (F) Machaon de Luzon I PAPILIONIDAE In
Papilio homerus : (E) Homerus Swallowtail, (F) Portequeue Homerus I PAPILIONIDAE In
Papilio hospiton : (E) Corsican Swallowtail, (S) Macaón de Córcega, (F) Portequeue de Corse, Porte-queue de Corse, I PAPILIONIDAE In
Papillose Cup Coral (E): *Paracyathus pulchellus*

Checklist of fauna/Lista de especies de fauna/Liste des espèces animales

Papio hamadryas : (E) Chacma Baboon, Guinea Baboon, Hamadryas Baboon, Olive Baboon, Yellow Baboon, (S) Papión de Guinea, Papión negro, Papión oliva, (F) Babouin anubis, Babouin chacma, Babouin de Guinée, Babouin jaune, Droguera, **II** CERCOPITHECIDAE Ma

Papio leucophaeus = Mandrillus leucophaeus

Papio sphinx = Mandrillus sphinx

Papión de Guinea (S): *Papio hamadryas*

Papión negro (S): *Papio hamadryas*

Papión oliva (S): *Papio hamadryas*

Papuan Boobook (E): *Uroglaux dimorpha*

Papuan Goshawk (E): *Accipiter meyerianus*

Papuan Ground Boa (E): *Candoia aspera*

Papuan Hanging-Parrot (E): *Loriculus aurantiifrons*

Papuan Harrier (E): *Circus spilonotus*

Papuan Hawk-Owl (E): *Uroglaux dimorpha*

Papuan Honey-buzzard (E): *Henicopernis longicauda*

Papuan Hornbill (E): *Aceros plicatus*

Papuan King-Parrot (E): *Alisterus chloropterus*

Papuan Lorikeet (E): *Charmosyna papou*

Papuan Monitor (E): *Varanus salvadorii*

Papuan Python (E): *Apodora papuana*

Papuan Scops-Owl (E): *Otus magicus*

Papuina pulcherrima = Papustyla pulcherrima

Papustyla pulcherrima : (E) Emerald Green Snail, Green Tree Snail, Manus Green Tree Snail **II** CAMAENIDAE Ga

Parabuteo unicinctus : (E) Bay-winged Hawk, Harris's Hawk, (S) Aguililla de Harris, Busardo mixto, Gavilán andapié, Gavilán mixto, (F) Buse de Harris, **II** ACCIPITRIDAE Av

Paraclavarina triangularis : **II** MERULINIDAE An

Paraconotrochus antarctica : **II** CARYOPHYLLIIDAE An

Paraconotrochus capense : **II** CARYOPHYLLIIDAE An

Paraconotrochus zeidleri : **II** CARYOPHYLLIIDAE An

Paracyathus andersoni : **II** CARYOPHYLLIIDAE An

Paracyathus arcuatus : **II** CARYOPHYLLIIDAE An

Paracyathus caeruleus = Paracyathus rotundatus

Paracyathus caltha = Paracyathus stearnsii

Paracyathus cavatus : **II** CARYOPHYLLIIDAE An

Paracyathus conceptus : **II** CARYOPHYLLIIDAE An

Paracyathus ebonensis : **II** CARYOPHYLLIIDAE An

Paracyathus fulvus : **II** CARYOPHYLLIIDAE An

Paracyathus humilis : **II** CARYOPHYLLIIDAE An

Paracyathus indicus : **II** CARYOPHYLLIIDAE An

Paracyathus indicus gracilis : **II** CARYOPHYLLIIDAE An

Paracyathus indicus indicus : **II** CARYOPHYLLIIDAE An

Paracyathus laxus = Trochocyathus rawsonii

Paracyathus lifuensis : **II** CARYOPHYLLIIDAE An

Paracyathus merguiensis = Paracyathus rotundatus

Paracyathus molokensis : **II** CARYOPHYLLIIDAE An

Paracyathus montereyensis : **II** CARYOPHYLLIIDAE An

Paracyathus parvulus : **II** CARYOPHYLLIIDAE An

Paracyathus persicus = Polycyathus persicus

Paracyathus porcellanus : **II** CARYOPHYLLIIDAE An

Paracyathus porphyreus = Trochocyathus porphyreus

Paracyathus profundus : **II** CARYOPHYLLIIDAE An

Paracyathus pruinosus : **II** CARYOPHYLLIIDAE An

Paracyathus pulchellus : (E) Papillose Cup Coral **II** CARYOPHYLLIIDAE An

Paracyathus rotundatus : **II** CARYOPHYLLIIDAE An

Paracyathus stearnsii : **II** CARYOPHYLLIIDAE An

Paracyathus stokesii : **II** CARYOPHYLLIIDAE An

Paracyathus vittatus : **II** CARYOPHYLLIIDAE An

Paradigalla brevicauda : (E) Short-tailed Paradigalla, (F) Paradigalle à queue courte, Paradisier à queue courte **II** PARADISAEIDAE Av

Paradigalla carunculata : (E) Long-tailed Paradigalla, (F) Paradigalle caronculée, Paradisier caronculé **II** PARADISAEIDAE Av

Paradigalle à queue courte (F): *Paradigalla brevicauda*

Paradigalle caronculée (F): *Paradigalla carunculata*

Paradisaea apoda : (E) Greater Bird-of-paradise, (F) Grand paradisier, Paradisier grand-émeraude **II** PARADISAEIDAE Av

Paradisaea decora : (E) Goldie's Bird-of-paradise, (F) Paradisier de Goldie **II** PARADISAEIDAE Av

Paradisaea guilielmi : (E) Emperor Bird-of-paradise, Emperor of Germany's Bird-of-paradise, (F) Paradisier de Guillaume, Paradisier de l'empereur Guillaume **II** PARADISAEIDAE Av

Paradisaea minor : (E) Lesser Bird-of-paradise, (F) Paradisier petit-émeraude, Petit paradisier **II** PARADISAEIDAE Av

Paradisaea raggiana : (E) Count Raggi's Bird-of-paradise, Raggiana Bird-of-paradise, (F) Paradisier de Raggi, Paradisier du comte Raggi **II** PARADISAEIDAE Av

Paradisaea rubra : (E) Red Bird-of-paradise, (F) Paradisier rouge **II** PARADISAEIDAE Av

Paradisaea rudolphi : (E) Blue Bird-of-paradise, (F) Paradisier bleu, Paradisier de Rodolphe **II** PARADISAEIDAE Av

PARADISAEIDAE spp.: (E) Birds-of-paradise, (S) Aves del paraiso, (F) Paradisiers **II** Av

Paradise Birdwing (E): *Ornithoptera paradisea*

Paradise Parrot (E): *Psephotus pulcherrimus*

Paradise Riflebird (E): *Ptiloris paradiseus*

Paradise-Crow (E): *Lycocorax pyrrhopterus*

Paradisier à bec blanc (F): *Epimachus bruijnii*

Paradisier à gorge noire (F): *Astrapia nigra*

Paradisier à queue courte (F): *Paradigalla brevicauda*

Paradisier à rubans (F): *Astrapia mayeri*

Paradisier bleu (F): *Paradisaea rudolphi*

Paradisier caronculé (F): *Paradigalla carunculata*

Paradisier corvin (F): *Lycocorax pyrrhopterus*

Paradisier d'Albert (F): *Pteridophora alberti*

Paradisier d'Albertis (F): *Epimachus albertisi*

Paradisier de Carola (F): *Parotia carolae*

Paradisier de Goldie (F): *Paradisaea decora*

Paradisier de Guillaume (F): *Paradisaea guilielmi*

Paradisier de Jobi (F): *Manucodia jobiensis*

Paradisier de Keraudren (F): *Manucodia keraudrenii*

Paradisier de la princesse Stéphanie (F): *Astrapia stephaniae*

Paradisier de Lawes (F): *Parotia lawesii*

Paradisier de l'empereur Guillaume (F): *Paradisaea guilielmi*

Paradisier de Loria (F): *Cnemophilus loriae*

Paradisier de Macgregor (F): *Macgregoria pulchra*

Paradisier de Meyer (F): *Epimachus meyeri*

Paradisier de Raggi (F): *Paradisaea raggiana*

Paradisier de Rodolphe (F): *Paradisaea rudolphi*

Paradisier de Rothschild (F): *Astrapia rothschildi*

Paradisier de Stéphanie (F): *Astrapia stephaniae*

Paradisier de Victoria (F): *Ptiloris victoriae*

Paradisier de Wahnes (F): *Parotia wahnesi*

Paradisier de Wallace (F): *Semioptera wallacii*

Paradisier d'Entrecasteaux (F): *Manucodia comrii*

Paradisier d'Helena (F): *Parotia helenae*

Paradisier du comte Raggi (F): *Paradisaea raggiana*

Paradisier du prince Albert (F): *Pteridophora alberti*

Paradisier fastueux (F): *Epimachus fastuosus*

Paradisier festonné (F): *Ptiloris paradiseus*

Paradisier gorge-d'acier (F): *Ptiloris magnificus*

Paradisier grand-émeraude (F): *Paradisaea apoda*

Paradisier huppé (F): *Cnemophilus macgregorii*

Paradisier loria (F): *Cnemophilus loriae*

Paradisier magnifique (F): *Cicinnurus magnificus*

Paradisier multifil (F): *Seleucidis melanoleuca*

Paradisier noir (F): *Manucodia atra*

Paradisier petit-émeraude (F): *Paradisaea minor*

Paradisier républicain (F): *Cicinnurus respublica*

Paradisier rouge (F): *Paradisaea rubra*

Paradisier royal (F): *Cicinnurus regius*

Paradisier sifilet (F): *Parotia sefilata*

Checklist of fauna/Lista de especies de fauna/Liste des espèces animales

Paradisier soyeux (F): *Loboparadisea sericea*
Paradisier splendide (F): *Astrapia splendidissima*
Paradisier superbe (F): *Lophorina superba*
Paradisier vert (F): *Manucodia chalybata*
Paradisiers (F): PARADISAEIDAE spp.
Paradoxurus hermaphroditus : (E) Asian Palm Civet,
  Common Palm Civet, (S) Civeta de palmera común,
  (F) Civette palmiste hermaphrodite, **III**
  VIVERRIDAE Ma
Paradoxurus jerdoni : (E) Jerdon's Palm Civet, (S) Civeta
  de palmera de Jerdon, (F) Civette palmiste de Jerdon,
  III VIVERRIDAE Ma
Paradoxurus jorandensis = Paradoxurus hermaphroditus
Paraerrina decipiens : **II** STYLASTERIDAE Hy
Paraguay Hairy Dwarf Porcupine (E): *Sphiggurus spinosus*
Paraguayan Caiman Lizard (E): *Dracaena paraguayensis*
Parantipathes laricides : **II** ANTIPATHIDAE An
Parantipathes larix : **II** ANTIPATHIDAE An
Parantipathes lilliei : **II** ANTIPATHIDAE An
Parantipathes strigosa : **II** ANTIPATHIDAE An
Parantipathes tetrasticha : **II** ANTIPATHIDAE An
Parantipathes tristicha : **II** ANTIPATHIDAE An
Parantipathes wolffi : **II** ANTIPATHIDAE An
Paraonyx microdon = Aonyx congicus
Paraonyx tacheté (F): *Aonyx congicus*
Parascaphirhynchus albus = Scaphirhynchus albus
Parasimplastrea sheppardi : **II** FAVIIDAE An
Parasitic Weaver (E): *Anomalospiza imberbis*
Pardel Lynx (E): *Lynx pardinus*
Pardofelis marmorata : (E) Marbled Cat, (S) Gato
  jaspeado, (F) Chat marbré, **I** FELIDAE Ma
Pardofelis nebulosa = Neofelis nebulosa
Paresseux d'Hoffmann (F): *Choloepus hoffmanni*
Paresseux tridactyle (F): *Bradypus variegatus*
Paresseux tridactyle de Bolivie (F): *Bradypus variegatus*
Pariah Kite (E): *Milvus migrans*
Parihuana (S): *Phoenicopterus chilensis*
Parina chica (S): *Phoenicopterus jamesi*
Parina grande (S): *Phoenicopterus andinus*
Pariona (S): *Phoenicopterus chilensis*
Parker's Day Gecko (E): *Phelsuma parkeri*
Parker's Golden Frog (E): *Mantella pulchra*
Parmoptila rubrifrons : (E) Jameson's Antpecker, Red-
  fronted Antpecker, (F) Astrild fourmilier, Parmoptile
  à front rouge **III** ESTRILDIDAE Av
Parmoptila woodhousei ssp. *rubrifrons = Parmoptila
  rubrifrons*
Parmoptile à front rouge (F): *Parmoptila rubrifrons*
Parnassius apollo : (E) Apollo, Apollo Butterfly,
  Mountain Apollo, (S) Apolo, Mariposa apollo **II**
  PAPILIONIDAE In
Paroare à bec jaune (F): *Paroaria capitata*
Paroare cardinal à bec jaune (F): *Paroaria capitata*
Paroare huppé (F): *Paroaria coronata*
Paroaria capitata : (E) Yellow-billed Cardinal, (S)
  Cardenal cabecirrojo, (F) Paroare à bec jaune, Paroare
  cardinal à bec jaune, **II** EMBERIZIDAE Av
Paroaria coronata : (E) Red-crested Cardinal, (S)
  Cardenal copetón, (F) Cardinal gris, Paroare huppé, **II**
  EMBERIZIDAE Av
Parotia carolae : (E) Carola's Parotia, Queen Carola's
  Parotia, (F) Paradisier de Carola, Sifilet de Carola **II**
  PARADISAEIDAE Av
Parotia helenae : (E) Eastern Parotia, (F) Paradisier
  d'Helena, Sifilet d'Hélène **II** PARADISAEIDAE Av
Parotia lawesii : (E) Lawes's Parotia, (F) Paradisier de
  Lawes, Sifilet de Lawe **II** PARADISAEIDAE Av
Parotia lawesii ssp. *helenae = Parotia helenae*
Parotia sefilata : (E) Arfak Parotia, Six-plumed Parotia,
  Western Parotia, (F) Paradisier sifilet, Sifilet d'Arfak
  II PARADISAEIDAE Av
Parotia wahnesi : (E) Wahnes's Parotia, (F) Paradisier de
  Wahnes, Sifilet de Wahnes **II** PARADISAEIDAE Av
Parrot-beaked Tortoise (E): *Homopus areolatus*
Parrots (S): PSITTACIFORMES spp. Av

Parson's Giant Chameleon (E): *Calumma parsonii*
Pasco Poison Frog (E): *Dendrobates lamasi*
Passer griseus : (E) Grey-headed Sparrow, (S) Gorrión
  pardillo, (F) Moineau gris, **III** PLOCEIDAE Av
Patagona gigas : (E) Giant Hummingbird, (S) Colibrí
  gigante, Picaflor gigante, (F) Colibri géant, **II**
  TROCHILIDAE Av
Patagonian Conure (E): *Cyanoliseus patagonus*
Patagonian Hog-nosed Skunk (E): *Conepatus humboldtii*
Patas (F): *Erythrocebus patas*
Patas Monkey (E): *Erythrocebus patas*
Patito Africano (S): *Nettapus auritus*
Pato aliblanco (S): *Cairina scutulata*
Pato almizclero aliblanco (S): *Cairina scutulata*
Pato cabecirrosa (S): *Rhodonessa caryophyllacea*
Pato chucara (S): *Anas clypeata*
Pato crestado (S): *Sarkidiornis melanotos*
Pato crestón (S): *Sarkidiornis melanotos*
Pato crestudo (S): *Sarkidiornis melanotos*
Pato criollo (S): *Cairina moschata*
Pato cuchara (S): *Anas clypeata*
Pato cucharón norteño (S): *Anas clypeata*
Pato de Bernier (S): *Anas bernieri*
Pato de cabeza rosa (S): *Rhodonessa caryophyllacea*
Pato de Hartlaub (S): *Pteronetta hartlaubii*
Pato de jungla (S): *Cairina scutulata*
Pato de Laysan (S): *Anas laysanensis*
Pato de moco (S): *Sarkidiornis melanotos*
Pato de monte (S): *Sarkidiornis melanotos*
Pato de Oustalet (S): *Anas oustaleti*
Pato golondrino norteño (S): *Anas acuta*
Pato rabudo (S): *Anas acuta*
Pato real (S): *Cairina moschata*
Pato real de Laysan (S): *Anas laysanensis*
Pato real marismeno (S): *Anas oustaleti*
Pato silbón (S): *Anas penelope*
Pato silbón cariblanco (S): *Dendrocygna viduata*
Pato silbón común (S): *Dendrocygna bicolor*
Pato silbón de Cuba (S): *Dendrocygna arborea*
Pato silbón ventrinegro (S): *Dendrocygna autumnalis*
Paují copete de Piedra (S): *Pauxi pauxi*
Paují cornudo (S): *Oreophasis derbianus*
Paují de Alagoas (S): *Mitu mitu*
Paují de Copete (S): *Crax daubentoni*
Paují de pico azul (S): *Crax alberti*
Paují de yelmo (S): *Pauxi pauxi*
Paují menor (S): *Mitu mitu*
Paují piquirrojo (S): *Crax blumenbachii*
Pauxi pauxi : (E) Helmeted Curassow, Northern Helmeted
  Curassow, (S) Hoco de casco, Paují copete de Piedra,
  Paují de yelmo, (F) Hocco à pierre, Pauxi pierre, **III**
  CRACIDAE Av
Pauxi pierre (F): *Pauxi pauxi*
Pava aliblanca (S): *Penelope albipennis*
Pava cojolita (S): *Penelope purpurascens*
Pava culirroja (S): *Penelope purpurascens*
Pava de Trinidad (S): *Pipile pipile*
Pava pajuil (S): *Penelopina nigra/ Oreophasis derbianus*
Pava rajadora (S): *Pipile pipile*
Pava yacutinga (S): *Pipile jacutinga*
Pavita andina (S): *Glaucidium jardinii*
Pavita ferruginea (S): *Glaucidium brasilianum*
Pavo mudo (S): *Pavo muticus*
Pavo muticus : (E) Green Peafowl, Green-necked Peafowl,
  (S) Pavo mudo, Pavo-real cuelliverde, Pavo-real
  verde, (F) Paon spicifère, Paon vert, **II**
  PHASIANIDAE Av
Pavo ocelado (S): *Agriocharis ocellata*
Pavón (S): *Oreophasis derbianus*
Pavón carunculado (S): *Crax globulosa*
Pavón cornudo (S): *Oreophasis derbianus*
Pavón grande (S): *Crax rubra*
Pavón norteño (S): *Crax rubra*
Pavón piquiazul (S): *Crax alberti*
Pavón piquirrojo (S): *Crax blumenbachii*

186

Pavón poría (S): *Crax daubentoni*
Pavón porú (S): *Crax daubentoni*
Pavona bipartita : **II** AGARICIIDAE An
Pavona cactus : (E) Leaf Coral **II** AGARICIIDAE An
Pavona calicifera = Pavona varians
Pavona clavus : (E) Star Column Coral **II** AGARICIIDAE An
Pavona clivosa = Pavona cactus
Pavona danai : **II** AGARICIIDAE An
Pavona decussata : (E) Cactus Coral **II** AGARICIIDAE An
Pavona diffluens : **II** AGARICIIDAE An
Pavona divaricata : **II** AGARICIIDAE An
Pavona duerdeni : **II** AGARICIIDAE An
Pavona explanulata : **II** AGARICIIDAE An
Pavona frondifera : **II** AGARICIIDAE An
Pavona galapagensis = Pavona cactus
Pavona gigantea : **II** AGARICIIDAE An
Pavona intermedia = Pavona varians
Pavona lata : **II** AGARICIIDAE An
Pavona maldivensis : **II** AGARICIIDAE An
Pavona minuta : **II** AGARICIIDAE An
Pavona repens = Pavona varians
Pavona varians : **II** AGARICIIDAE An
Pavona venosa : **II** AGARICIIDAE An
Pavona xarifae : **II** AGARICIIDAE An
Pavo-real cuelliverde (S): *Pavo muticus*
Pavo-real verde (S): *Pavo muticus*
Peach-faced Lovebird (E): *Agapornis roseicollis*
Peach-fronted Conure (E): *Aratinga aurea*
Peach-fronted Parakeet (E): *Aratinga aurea*
Peachthroat Monitor (E): *Varanus jobiensis*
Peacock Coquette (E): *Lophornis pavoninus*
Peacock Day Gecko (E): *Phelsuma quadriocellata*
Peacock Soft-shell Turtle (E): *Aspideretes hurum*
Peacock Turtle (E): *Morenia ocellata*
Peale's Dolphin (E): *Lagenorhynchus australis*
Pearl Bubble Coral (E): *Physogyra lichtensteini*
Pearl Kite (E): *Gampsonyx swainsonii*
Pearl-spotted Owlet (E): *Glaucidium perlatum*
Pearly Conure (E): *Pyrrhura lepida*
Pearly Parakeet (E): *Pyrrhura lepida*
Pécari à barbe blanche (F): *Tayassu pecari*
Pecari à collier (F): *Pecari tajacu*
Pécari aux babines blanches (F): *Tayassu pecari*
Pecarí de collar (S): *Pecari tajacu*
Pecarí de labio blanco (S): *Tayassu pecari*
Pécari du Chaco (F): *Catagonus wagneri*
Pecari tajacu : (E) Collared Peccary, (S) Pecarí de collar, Zaino Javelina, (F) Pecari à collier, **II/NC** TAYASSUIDAE Ma
Pecaries (S): TAYASSUIDAE spp.
Pécaries (F): TAYASSUIDAE spp.
Peccaries (E): TAYASSUIDAE spp.
Pectinia africanus : **II** PECTINIIDAE An
Pectinia alcicornis : (E) Antler Lettuce Coral **II** PECTINIIDAE An
Pectinia ayleni = Physophyllia ayleni
Pectinia elongata : **II** PECTINIIDAE An
Pectinia lactuca : (E) Carnation Coral, Frilly Lettuce Coral **II** PECTINIIDAE An
Pectinia maxima = Echinophyllia maxima
Pectinia paeonia : (E) Palm Lettuce Coral **II** PECTINIIDAE An
Pectinia pygmaeus : **II** PECTINIIDAE An
Pectinia teres : **II** PECTINIIDAE An
Pedicellocyathus keyesi : **II** GUYNIIDAE An
Peers's Girdled Lizard (E): *Cordylus peersi*
Peje vaca (S): *Cetorhinus maximus*
Pelecanus crispus : (E) Dalmatian Pelican, (S) Pelícano ceñudo, Pelícano rizado, (F) Pélican dalmate, Pélican frisé, **I** PELECANIDAE Av
Pélican dalmate (F): *Pelecanus crispus*
Pélican frisé (F): *Pelecanus crispus*
Pelícano ceñudo (S): *Pelecanus crispus*

Pelícano rizado (S): *Pelecanus crispus*
Pelochelys spp.: (E) Giant softshell turtles, **II** TRIONYCHIDAE Re
Pelochelys bibroni : (E) New Guinea Giant Softshell Turtle **II** TRIONYCHIDAE Re
Pelochelys cantorii : (E) Asian Giant Softshell Turtle, Cantor's Giant Softshell Turtle, Frog-faced Giant Softshell Turtle, **II** TRIONYCHIDAE Re
Pelomedusa subrufa : (E) African Helmeted Turtle, Helmeted Turtle, Marsh Terrapin, (S) Tortuga plana, (F) Peloméduse roussâtre, Péloméduse rousse, **III** PELOMEDUSIDAE Re
Peloméduse roussâtre (F): *Pelomedusa subrufa*
Péloméduse rousse (F): *Pelomedusa subrufa*
Pel's Fishing-Owl (E): *Scotopelia peli*
Pel's Flying Squirrel (E): *Anomalurus pelii*
Pel's Scaly-tailed Squirrel (E): *Anomalurus pelii*
Peltocephale de Duméril (F): *Peltocephalus dumeriliana*
Peltocephalus dumeriliana : (E) Big-headed Amazon River Turtle, Big-headed Sideneck, Big-headed Sideneck Turtle, (S) Cabezón, (F) Peltocephale de Duméril, Podocnémide de Duméril, **II** PELOMEDUSIDAE Re
Peltocephalus tracaxa = Peltocephalus dumeriliana
Péluse à bec crochu (F): *Pelusios niger*
Péluse d'Adanson (F): *Pelusios adansonii*
Péluse de Schweigger (F): *Pelusios castaneus*
Péluse du Gabon (F): *Pelusios gabonensis*
Péluse noire (F): *Pelusios niger*
Péluses (F): *Pelusios* spp.
Pelusios adansonii : (E) Adanson's Hinged Terrapin, Adanson's Mud Turtle, Sahelian Terrapin, White-breasted Side-necked Turtle, (S) Tortuga negra de Adanson, (F) Péluse d'Adanson, Pélusios d'Adanson, **III** PELOMEDUSIDAE Re
Pelusios castaneus : (E) Chestnut Terrapin, Schweigger's Terrapin, West African Mud Turtle, (F) Péluse de Schweigger, Pélusios noisette **III** PELOMEDUSIDAE Re
Pélusios d'Adanson (F): *Pelusios adansonii*
Pélusios du Gabon (F): *Pelusios gabonensis*
Pelusios gabonensis : (E) African Forest Turtle, Forest Hinged Terrapin, Gabon Terrapin, Gabon Turtle, Stripe-backed Side-necked Turtle, (S) Tortuga negra del Gabón, (F) Péluse du Gabon, Pélusios du Gabon, **III** PELOMEDUSIDAE Re
Pelusios niger : (E) African Black Terrapin, Black Side-necked Turtle, Hooked-beaked Terrapin, West African Black Forest Turtle, (S) Tortuga negra de Africa occidental, (F) Péluse à bec crochu, Péluse noire, Pélusios noir, **III** PELOMEDUSIDAE Re
Pélusios noir (F): *Pelusios niger*
Pélusios noisette (F): *Pelusios castaneus*
Pemba Day Gecko (E): *Phelsuma parkeri*
Pemba Flying-fox (E): *Pteropus voeltzkowi*
Pemba Scops-Owl (E): *Otus rutilus*
Penang Lizard (E): *Varanus bengalensis*
Pénélope à ailes blanches (F): *Penelope albipennis*
Penelope à Crete (F): *Penelope purpurascens*
Pénélope à front noir (F): *Pipile jacutinga*
Pénélope à plastron (F): *Pipile jacutinga*
Pénélope à ventre blanc (F): *Penelope purpurascens*
Penelope albipennis : (E) White-winged Guan, (S) Chachalaca de remiges blancas, Guan aliblanco, Pava aliblanca, (F) Pénélope à ailes blanches, **I** CRACIDAE Av
Pénélope cornue (F): *Oreophasis derbianus*
Pénélope de Derby (F): *Oreophasis derbianus*
Pénélope huppée (F): *Penelope purpurascens*
Pénélope noire (F): *Penelopina nigra*
Pénélope pajuil (F): *Penelopina nigra*
Pénélope panachée (F): *Penelope purpurascens*

Penelope purpurascens : (E) Crested Guan, Purple Guan, Purplish Guan, (S) Grenedera, Pava cojolita, Pava culirroja, (F) Penelope à Crete, Pénélope à ventre blanc, Pénélope huppée, Pénélope panachée, **III** CRACIDAE Av
Pénélope siffleuse (F): *Pipile jacutinga/ Pipile pipile*
Pénélope siffleuse a gorge bleue (F): *Pipile pipile*
Penelopides spp.: (E) Tarictic hornbills, (S) Buceros, Cálaos, **II** BUCEROTIDAE Av
Penelopides affinis : (E) Mindanao Hornbill, Mindanao Tarictic Hornbill, (S) Cálao chico de Mindanao, (F) Calao de Mindanao, **II** BUCEROTIDAE Av
Penelopides exarhatus : (E) Celebes Hornbill, Celebes Tarictic Hornbill, Sulawesi Dwarf Hornbill, Sulawesi Hornbill, Sulawesi Tarictic Hornbill, (S) Cálao chico de Célèbes, (F) Calao des Célèbes, Calaos à canelure des Célèbes, **II** BUCEROTIDAE Av
Penelopides manillae : (E) Luzon Hornbill, Luzon Tarictic Hornbill, (S) Cálao chico de Luzón, (F) Calao de Manille, **II** BUCEROTIDAE Av
Penelopides mindorensis : (E) Mindoro Hornbill, (S) Cálao chico de Mindoro, (F) Calao de Mindoro, **II** BUCEROTIDAE Av
Penelopides panini : (E) Panay Tarictic Hornbill, Tarictic Hornbill, Visayan Hornbill, (S) Cálao chico de Panay, (F) Calao tarictic, **II** BUCEROTIDAE Av
Penelopides panini ssp. *affinis* = *Penelopides affinis*
Penelopides panini ssp. *manillae* = *Penelopides manillae*
Penelopides panini ssp. *samarensis* = *Penelopides samarensis*
Penelopides samarensis : (E) Samar Hornbill, Samar Tarictic Hornbill, (F) Calao de Samar **II** BUCEROTIDAE Av
Penelopina nigra : (E) Black Chachalaca, Black Pajuil, Black Penelopina, Highland Guan, Little Guan, (S) Chachalaca negra, Guan negro, Pava pajuil, (F) Pénélope noire, Pénélope pajuil, **III** CRACIDAE Av
Pennant's Parakeet (E): *Platycercus elegans*
Pen-tailed Treeshrew (E): *Ptilocercus lowii*
Peponocephala electra : (E) Melon-headed Whale, (S) Electra, (F) Péponocéphale, **II** DELPHINIDAE Ma
Péponocéphale (F): *Peponocephala electra*
Peponocyathus dawsoni : **II** TURBINOLIIDAE An
Peponocyathus folliculus : **II** TURBINOLIIDAE An
Peponocyathus minimus : **II** TURBINOLIIDAE An
Peponocyathus stimpsonii = *Deltocyathoides stimpsonii*
Pequeña civeta de la India (S): *Viverricula indica*
Pequeño panda (S): *Ailurus fulgens*
Perameles bougainville : (E) Barred Bandicoot, Long-nosed Bandicoot, Marl, Western Barred Bandicoot, (S) Bandicot de Bouganville, Tejón marsupial rayado, (F) Bandicoot de Bougainville, **I** PERAMELIDAE Ma
Percnoptère brun (F): *Necrosyrtes monachus*
Percnoptère d'Égypte (F): *Neophron percnopterus*
Perdicilla herrumbrosa (S): *Caloperdix oculea*
Perdigallo caspio (S): *Tetraogallus caspius*
Perdigallo del Caspio (S): *Tetraogallus caspius*
Perdigallo Tibetano (S): *Tetraogallus tibetanus*
Perdiz de bosque crestada (S): *Rollulus rouloul*
Perdiz de bosque de Charlton (S): *Arborophila charltonii*
Perdiz de bosque de pico largo (S): *Rhizothera longirostris*
Perdiz de bosque ferruginosa (S): *Caloperdix oculea*
Perdiz de bosque negra (S): *Melanoperdix nigra*
Perdiz negra (S): *Melanoperdix nigra*
Perdiz piquilarga (S): *Rhizothera longirostris*
Perdiz real del Caspio (S): *Tetraogallus caspius*
Perdiz real del Tibet (S): *Tetraogallus tibetanus*
Perdiz rulrul (S): *Rollulus rouloul*
Perdrix à long bec (F): *Rhizothera longirostris*
Perdrix des neiges de la Caspienne (F): *Tetraogallus caspius*
Perdrix des neiges du Tibet (F): *Tetraogallus tibetanus*
Perdrix noire (F): *Melanoperdix nigra*
Père David's Macaque (E): *Macaca thibetana*

Peregrine (E): *Falco peregrinus*
Peregrine Falcon (E): *Falco peregrinus*
Peregrino (S): *Cetorhinus maximus*
Perentie (E/F): *Varanus giganteus*
Perezoso (S): *Choloepus hoffmanni*
Perezoso grisaceo (S): *Bradypus variegatus*
Perezoso o tridáctilo de Bolivia (S): *Bradypus variegatus*
Perezoso tridáctilo (S): *Bradypus variegatus*
Perfect Lorikeet (E): *Trichoglossus euteles*
Perico (S): *Aratinga chloroptera*
Perico aligualdo (S): *Psephotus chrysopterygius*
Perico barreteado (S): *Bolborhynchus lineola*
Perico cabecidorado (S): *Pionopsitta pyrilia*
Perico cabecinegro (S): *Pionopsitta caica*
Perico cabecioscuro (S): *Aratinga weddellii*
Perico cabecirrojo (S): *Pyrrhura rhodocephala*
Perico cabecirrosado (S): *Pyrrhura picta*
Perico cachete amarillo (S): *Pionopsitta barrabandi*
Perico cachetigris (S): *Brotogeris pyrrhopterus*
Perico calzoncito (S): *Pionites melanocephala*
Perico capelo (S): *Purpureicephalus spurius*
Perico capirotado (S): *Psephotus dissimilis*
Perico cara sucia (S): *Aratinga pertinax*
Perico caretirrojo (S): *Aratinga erythrogenys*
Perico cariazul (S): *Northiella haematogaster*
Perico carigualdo (S): *Platycercus icterotis*
Perico cola negra (S): *Pyrrhura melanura*
Perico cola roja (S): *Pyrrhura hoematotis*
Perico colimorado (S): *Pyrrhura egregia*
Perico cornudo (S): *Eunymphicus cornutus*
Perico de Adelaida (S): *Platycercus adelaidae*
Perico de Barnard (S): *Barnardius barnardi*
Perico de El Oro (S): *Pyrrhura orcesi*
Perico de las Antípodas (S): *Cyanoramphus unicolor*
Perico de las Chatham (S): *Cyanoramphus forbesi*
Perico de Port Lincoln (S): *Barnardius zonarius*
Perico de Tasmania (S): *Platycercus caledonicus*
Perico del Paraíso (S): *Psephotus pulcherrimus*
Perico dorado (S): *Aratinga solstitialis*
Perico dorsirrojo (S): *Psephotus haematonotus*
Perico elegante (S): *Platycercus elegans*
Perico frentinaranja (S): *Aratinga canicularis*
Perico gracioso (S): *Platycercus venustus*
Perico grande (S): *Pyrrhura cruentata*
Perico gualda (S): *Platycercus flaveolus*
Perico ligero (S): *Bradypus variegatus*
Perico macareño (S): *Brotogeris pyrrhopterus*
Perico manglero (S): *Amazona albifrons*
Perico maori cabecigualdo (S): *Cyanoramphus auriceps*
Perico maori cabecirrojo (S): *Cyanoramphus novaezelandiae*
Perico maori montano (S): *Cyanoramphus malherbi*
Perico multicolor (S): *Hapalopsittaca amazonina/ Platycercus eximius*
Perico nocturno (S): *Geopsittacus occidentalis*
Perico ojo blanco (S): *Aratinga leucophthalmus*
Perico pálido (S): *Platycercus adscitus*
Perico pechiblanco (S): *Pyrrhura albipectus*
Perico pechisucio (S): *Aratinga nana*
Perico pico rojo (S): *Pionus sordidus*
Perico pintado (S): *Pyrrhura leucotis*
Perico princesa (S): *Polytelis alexandrae*
Perico regente (S): *Polytelis anthopeplus*
Perico siete colores (S): *Touit batavica*
Perico soberbio (S): *Polytelis swainsonii*
Perico terrestre (S): *Pezoporus wallicus*
Perico tui (S): *Brotogeris sanctithomae*
Perico variado (S): *Psephotus varius*
Perico verde (S): *Aratinga holochlora*
Perijá Metaltail (E): *Metallura iracunda*
Perinet Chameleon (E): *Calumma gastrotaenia*
Perinet Leaf Chameleon (E): *Brookesia therezieni*
Periquito (S): *Forpus passerinus*
Periquito ala dorada (S): *Brotogeris chrysopterus*
Periquito aliazul (S): *Forpus crassirostris*

Checklist of fauna/Lista de especies de fauna/Liste des espèces animales

Periquito alipunteado (S): *Touit stictoptera*
Periquito azul (S): *Brotogeris cyanoptera*
Periquito azul alirrojo (S): *Touit huetii*
Periquito barbinaranja (S): *Brotogeris jugularis*
Periquito barrado (S): *Bolborhynchus lineola*
Periquito cabecirrojo (S): *Cyanoramphus novaezelandiae*
Periquito crisóstomo (S): *Neophema chrysostoma*
Periquito de collar africano (S): *Psittacula krameri*
Periquito de espalda dorada (S): *Psephotus chrysopterygius*
Periquito de pico grueso (S): *Rhynchopsitta pachyrhyncha*
Periquito de tierra (S): *Pezoporus wallicus*
Periquito del Pacífico (S): *Forpus coelestis*
Periquito elegante (S): *Neophema elegans*
Periquito encapuchado (S): *Psephotus dissimilis*
Periquito espléndido (S): *Neophema splendida*
Periquito frentiamarillo de Forbes (S): *Cyanoramphus forbesi*
Periquito frentiazul (S): *Touit dilectissima*
Periquito mexicano (S): *Forpus cyanopygius*
Periquito migrador (S): *Lathamus discolor*
Periquito obscuro (S): *Forpus sclateri*
Periquito ojiazul (S): *Forpus conspicillatus*
Periquito orejiamarillo (S): *Ognorhynchus icterotis*
Periquito rabadilla púrpura (S): *Touit purpurata*
Periquito roquero (S): *Neophema petrophila*
Periquito rosado (S): *Neopsephotus bourkii*
Periquito turquesa (S): *Neophema pulchella*
Periquito ventrinaranja (S): *Neophema chrysogaster*
Pernis apivorus : (E) European Honey-buzzard, Honey Buzzard, (S) Abejero europeo, Halcón abejero, (F) Bondrée apivore, **II** ACCIPITRIDAE Av
Pernis celebensis : (E) Barred Honey-buzzard, (S) Abejero de Célebes, (F) Bondrée des Célèbes, **II** ACCIPITRIDAE Av
Pernis ptilorhyncus : (E) Oriental Honey-buzzard, (S) Abejero oriental, (F) Bondrée orientale, **II** ACCIPITRIDAE Av
Perodicticus potto : (E) Potto, Potto Gibbon, (S) Poto de Bosman, (F) Potto, **II** LORIDAE Ma
Perrito de la pradera mexicano (S): *Cynomys mexicanus*
Perrito de las praderas (S): *Cynomys mexicanus*
Perrito llanero Mejicano (S): *Cynomys mexicanus*
Perro de agua (S): *Lontra longicaudis/ Pteronura brasiliensis*
Perro de los matorrales (S): *Speothos venaticus*
Perro de monte (S): *Speothos venaticus*
Perro salvaje asiático (S): *Cuon alpinus*
Perroquet à calotte rouge (F): *Poicephalus gulielmi*
Perroquet à couronne (F): *Tanygnathus lucionensis*
Perroquet à face jaune (F): *Poicephalus flavifrons*
Perroquet à oreilles (F): *Pionopsitta pileata*
Perroquet à tête brune (F): *Poicephalus cryptoxanthus*
Perroquet à tête grise (F): *Poicephalus senegalus*
Perroquet à ventre rouge (F): *Poicephalus rufiventris*
Perroquet de Meyer (F): *Poicephalus meyeri*
Perroquet de Rüppell (F): *Poicephalus rueppellii*
Perroquet des niam-niam (F): *Poicephalus crassus*
Perroquet du Cap (F): *Poicephalus robustus*
Perroquet gris (F): *Psittacus erithacus*
Perroquet jaco (F): *Psittacus erithacus*
Perroquet masqué (F): *Cyclopsitta diophthalma*
Perroquet masqué de Coxen (F): *Cyclopsitta diophthalma coxeni*
Perroquet nocturne (F): *Strigops habroptilus*
Perroquet noir (F): *Coracopsis nigra*
Perroquet petit vasa (F): *Coracopsis nigra*
Perroquet robuste (F): *Poicephalus robustus*
Perroquet vaza (F): *Coracopsis vasa*
Perroquet vert à calotte rouge (F): *Poicephalus gulielmi*
Perroquet vert du Congo (F): *Poicephalus gulielmi*
Perroquet youyou (F): *Poicephalus senegalus*
Perroquet-hibou (F): *Strigops habroptilus*
Perroquets à gros bec (F): *Rhynchopsitta* spp.
Perruche à ailes d'or (F): *Psephotus chrysopterygius*

Perruche à ailes vertes (F): *Alisterus chloropterus*
Perruche à bandeau rouge (F): *Cyanoramphus novaezelandiae*
Perruche à bec de sang (F): *Tanygnathus megalorynchos*
Perruche à bec gracile (F): *Enicognathus leptorhynchus*
Perruche à bonnet bleu (F): *Northiella haematogaster*
Perruche à bouche d'or (F): *Neophema chrysostoma*
Perruche à calotte bleue (F): *Polytelis alexandrae/ Tanygnathus lucionensis*
Perruche à capuchon (F): *Psephotus dissimilis*
Perruche à capuchon noir (F): *Psephotus dissimilis*
Perruche à col bleu (F): *Geoffroyus simplex*
Perruche à collier (F): *Psittacula krameri*
Perruche à collier de Maurice (F): *Psittacula echo*
Perruche à collier jaune (F): *Barnardius zonarius*
Perruche à croupion bleu (F): *Psittinus cyanurus*
Perruche à croupion rouge (F): *Psephotus haematonotus/ Psephotus varius*
Perruche à dos rouge (F): *Psephotus haematonotus*
Perruche à épaules dorées (F): *Psephotus chrysopterygius*
Perruche à face rose (F): *Agapornis roseicollis*
Perruche à front doré (F): *Aratinga aurea*
Perruche à front jaune (F): *Cyanoramphus auriceps*
Perruche à front jaune de Forbes (F): *Cyanoramphus forbesi*
Perruche à gros bec (F): *Rhynchopsitta pachyrhyncha*
Perruche à joue noire (F): *Agapornis nigrigenis*
Perruche à longs brins (F): *Psittacula longicauda*
Perruche à lunettes vertes (F): *Neophema chrysogaster*
Perruche à moustaches (F): *Psittacula alexandri*
Perruche à oreilles jaunes (F): *Platycercus icterotis*
Perruche à poitrine écarlate (F): *Neophema splendida*
Perruche à tête ardoisée (F): *Psittacula himalayana*
Perruche à tête d'or (F): *Cyanoramphus auriceps*
Perruche à tête d'or de Forbes (F): *Cyanoramphus forbesi*
Perruche à tête pâle (F): *Platycercus adscitus*
Perruche à tête pourpre (F): *Purpureicephalus spurius*
Perruche à tête prune (F): *Psittacula cyanocephala*
Perruche à tête rose (F): *Psittacula roseata*
Perruche à tête rouge (F): *Agapornis pullarius*
Perruche à ventre bleu (F): *Triclaria malachitacea*
Perruche à ventre jaune (F): *Platycercus caledonicus*
Perruche à ventre orange (F): *Neophema chrysogaster*
Perruche alexandre (F): *Psittacula eupatria*
Perruche ara (F): *Rhynchopsitta pachyrhyncha*
Perruche aux ailes bleues (F): *Forpus passerinus*
Perruche aux ailes d'or (F): *Psephotus chrysopterygius*
Perruche aux oreilles jaunes (F): *Ognorhynchus icterotis*
Perruche calédonienne (F): *Platycercus caledonicus*
Perruche cornue (F): *Eunymphicus cornutus*
Perruche d'Adélaïde (F): *Platycercus adelaidae*
Perruche d'Alexandra (F): *Polytelis alexandrae*
Perruche d'Aymara (F): *Psilopsiagon aymara*
Perruche de Barnard (F): *Barnardius barnardi*
Perruche de Barraband (F): *Polytelis swainsonii*
Perruche de Bourke (F): *Neopsephotus bourkii*
Perruche de Branicki (F): *Leptosittaca branickii*
Perruche de Brehm (F): *Psittacella brehmii*
Perruche de Buru (F): *Tanygnathus gramineus*
Perruche de Derby (F): *Psittacula derbiana*
Perruche de Finsch (F): *Psittacula finschii*
Perruche de Fischer (F): *Agapornis fischeri*
Perruche de Geoffroy (F): *Geoffroyus geoffroyi*
Perruche de Jenday (F): *Aratinga jandaya*
Perruche de Latham (F): *Lathamus discolor*
Perruche de Layard (F): *Psittacula calthropae*
Perruche de l'Himalaya (F): *Psittacula himalayana*
Perruche de l'île Maurice (F): *Psittacula echo*
Perruche de Lilian (F): *Agapornis lilianae*
Perruche de Luçon (F): *Tanygnathus lucionensis*
Perruche de Madarasz (F): *Psittacella madaraszi*
Perruche de Malabar (F): *Psittacula columboides*
Perruche de Malherbe (F): *Cyanoramphus malherbi*
Perruche de Maurice (F): *Psittacula echo*
Perruche de Müller (F): *Tanygnathus sumatranus*

Perruche de Newton (F): *Psittacula exsul*
Perruche de Nouvelle-Zélande (F): *Cyanoramphus novaezelandiae*
Perruche de paradis (F): *Psephotus pulcherrimus*
Perruche de Pennant (F): *Platycercus elegans*
Perruche de Sparrman (F): *Cyanoramphus novaezelandiae*
Perruche de Stanley (F): *Platycercus icterotis*
Perruche de Swindern (F): *Agapornis swindernianus*
Perruche de terre (F): *Pezoporus wallicus*
Perruche des Antipodes (F): *Cyanoramphus unicolor*
Perruche des écueils (F): *Neophema petrophila*
Perruche des îles Chatham (F): *Cyanoramphus forbesi*
Perruche des Nicobar (F): *Psittacula caniceps*
Perruche des rochers (F): *Neophema petrophila*
Perruche des Seychelles (F): *Psittacula wardi*
Perruche dorée (F): *Guarouba guarouba*
Perruche du soleil (F): *Aratinga solstitialis*
Perruche écarlate (F): *Prosopeia splendens*
Perruche élégante (F): *Neophema elegans*
Perruche émeraude (F): *Enicognathus ferrugineus*
Perruche érythroptère (F): *Aprosmictus erythropterus*
Perruche flavéole (F): *Platycercus flaveolus*
Perruche gracieuse (F): *Platycercus venustus*
Perruche hétéroclite (F): *Geoffroyus heteroclitus*
Perruche huppée (F): *Eunymphicus cornutus*
Perruche inseparable (F): *Melopsittacus undulatus*
Perruche intermédiaire (F): *Psittacula intermedia*
Perruche jonquille (F): *Aprosmictus jonquillaceus*
Perruche lunulée (F): *Bolbopsittacus lunulatus*
Perruche magnifique (F): *Psephotus pulcherrimus*
Perruche masqué (F): *Agapornis personatus*
Perruche masquée (F): *Prosopeia personata*
Perruche mélanure (F): *Polytelis anthopeplus*
Perruche modeste (F): *Psittacella modesta*
Perruche multicolore (F): *Psephotus varius*
Perruche Nanday (F): *Nandayus nenday*
Perruche nocturne (F): *Geopsittacus occidentalis*
Perruche omnicolore (F): *Platycercus eximius*
Perruche ondulée (F): *Melopsittacus undulatus*
Perruche orangé (F): *Brotogeris pyrrhopterus*
Perruche palliceps (F): *Platycercus adscitus*
Perruche peinte (F): *Psittacella picta*
Perruche pompadour (F): *Prosopeia tabuensis*
Perruche princesse (F): *Polytelis alexandrae*
Perruche pygmée de Brujin (F): *Micropsitta bruijnii*
Perruche pygmée de Meek (F): *Micropsitta meeki*
Perruche pygmée de Salvadori (F): *Micropsitta keiensis*
Perruche pygmée de Schlegel (F): *Micropsitta geelvinkiana*
Perruche pygmée de Sclater (F): *Micropsitta pusio*
Perruche royale (F): *Alisterus scapularis*
Perruche splendide (F): *Neophema splendida*
Perruche terrestre (F): *Pezoporus wallicus*
Perruche tiriba (F): *Pyrrhura cruentata*
Perruche tovi (F): *Brotogeris jugularis*
Perruche tricolore (F): *Alisterus amboinensis*
Perruche turquoisine (F): *Neophema pulchella*
Perruche unicolore (F): *Cyanoramphus unicolor*
Perruches (F): PSITTACIFORMES spp. Av
Perruche-souris (F): *Myiopsitta monachus*
Persian Fallow Deer (E): *Dama mesopotamica*
Persian Sturgeon (E): *Acipenser gueldenstaedtii/ Acipenser persicus*
Perth Pygmy Python (E): *Antaresia perthensis*
Peruvian Cock-of-the-Rock (E): *Rupicola peruviana*
Peruvian Guemal (E): *Hippocamelus antisensis*
Peruvian Huemul (E): *Hippocamelus antisensis*
Peruvian Night Monkey (E): *Aotus nigriceps*
Peruvian Penguin (E): *Spheniscus humboldti*
Peruvian Piedtail (E): *Phlogophilus harterti*
Peruvian Poison Frog (E): *Epipedobates petersi*
Peruvian Pygmy-Owl (E): *Glaucidium peruanum*
Peruvian Pygmy-Owl (E): *Glaucidium peruanum*
Peruvian Screech-Owl (E): *Otus roboratus*
Peruvian Sheartail (E): *Thaumastura cora*

Pesquet's Parrot (E): *Psittrichas fulgidus*
Peters's Cobra (E): *Naja samarensis*
Petit bandicoot-lapin (F): *Macrotis leucura*
Petit cacatoès à huppe jaune (F): *Cacatua sulphurea*
Petit cheirogale (F): *Cheirogaleus medius*
Petit cordyle (F): *Cordylus minor*
Petit faucon (F): *Falco longipennis*
Petit flamant (F): *Phoenicopterus minor*
Petit gecko diurne des Seychelles (F): *Phelsuma astriata*
Petit hapalémur (F): *Hapalemur griseus*
Petit lépilémur (F): *Lepilemur ruficaudatus*
Petit lézard à queue épineuse (F): *Cordylus minor*
Petit lori musc (F): *Glossopsitta pusilla*
Petit microcèbe (F): *Microcebus murinus*
Petit Moineau (F): *Petronia dentata*
Petit moineau soulcie (F): *Petronia dentata*
Petit moineau soulie (F): *Petronia dentata*
Petit panda (F): *Ailurus fulgens*
Petit paradisier (F): *Paradisaea minor*
Petit perruche-ara (F): *Diopsittaca nobilis*
Petit phelsume des Seychelles (F): *Phelsuma astriata*
Petit rorqual (F): *Balaenoptera acutorostrata*
Petit serpentaire (F): *Polyboroides radiatus*
Petit-duc à aigrettes longues (F): *Otus sanctaecatarinae*
Petit-duc à bec jaune (F): *Otus icterorhynchus*
Petit-duc à collier (F): *Otus bakkamoena*
Petit-duc à face blanche (F): *Otus leucotis*
Petit-duc à front blanc (F): *Otus sagittatus*
Petit-duc à gorge blanche (F): *Otus albogularis*
Petit-duc à mèches noires (F): *Otus atricapillus*
Petit-duc à moustaches (F): *Otus trichopsis*
Petit-duc africain (F): *Otus scops*
Petit-duc bridé (F): *Otus barbarus*
Petit-duc choliba (F): *Otus choliba*
Petit-duc de Bruce (F): *Otus brucei*
Petit-duc de Clark (F): *Otus clarkii*
Petit-duc de Cuba (F): *Otus lawrencii*
Petit-duc de Gurney (F): *Mimizuku gurneyi*
Petit-duc de Horsfield (F): *Otus bakkamoena*
Petit-duc de Java (F): *Otus angelinae*
Petit-duc de Koepcke (F): *Otus koepckeae*
Petit-duc de Luçon (F): *Otus megalotis*
Petit-duc de Manado (F): *Otus manadensis*
Petit-duc de Mantanani (F): *Otus mantananensis*
Petit-duc de Marshall (F): *Otus marshalli*
Petit-duc de Mindanao (F): *Otus mirus*
Petit-duc de Mindoro (F): *Otus mindorensis*
Petit-duc de Mohéli (F): *Otus moheliensis*
Petit-duc de Nicobar (F): *Otus alius*
Petit-duc de Palawan (F): *Otus fuliginosus*
Petit-duc de Porto Rico (F): *Otus nudipes*
Petit-duc de Salvin (F): *Otus ingens*
Petit-duc de Sangihe (F): *Otus collari*
Petit-duc de Sao Tomé (F): *Otus hartlaubi*
Petit-duc de Simalur (F): *Otus umbra*
Petit-duc de Wallace (F): *Otus silvicola*
Petit-duc de Watson (F): *Otus watsonii*
Petit-duc des Andaman (F): *Otus balli*
Petit-duc des Mentawei (F): *Otus mentawi*
Petit-duc des montagnes (F): *Otus kennicottii*
Petit-duc des Palau (F): *Otus podarginus*
Petit-duc d'Irène (F): *Otus ireneae*
Petit-duc du Karthala (F): *Otus pauliani*
Petit-duc du Pérou (F): *Otus roboratus*
Petit-duc élégant (F): *Otus elegans*
Petit-duc géant (F): *Mimizuku gurneyi*
Petit-duc indien (F): *Otus bakkamoena*
Petit-duc longicorne (F): *Otus longicornis*
Petit-duc maculé (F): *Otus asio*
Petit-duc malgache (F): *Otus rutilus*
Petit-duc mystérieux (F): *Otus magicus*
Petit-duc nain (F): *Otus flammeolus*
Petit-duc radjah (F): *Otus brookii*
Petit-duc roussâtre (F): *Otus rufescens*
Petit-duc scops (F): *Otus scops*

Petit-duc tacheté (F): *Otus spilocephalus*
Petit-duc vermiculé (F): *Otus vermiculatus*
Petite buse (F): *Buteo platypterus*
Petite civette de l'Inde (F): *Viverricula indica*
Petite mangouste indienne (F): *Herpestes javanicus auropunctatus*
Petite mélampitte (F): *Melampitta lugubris*
Petite nyctale (F): *Aegolius acadicus*
Petite Rorqual de l'Antarctique (F): *Balaenoptera bonaerensis*
Petronia dentata : (E) Bush Petronia, Bush Sparrow, (S) Chillón de Sundevall, (F) Petit Moineau, Petit moineau soulcie, Petit moineau soulie, **III** PLOCEIDAE Av
Petter's Chameleon (E): *Furcifer petteri*
Petterus coronatus = *Eulemur coronatus*
Pez dama (S): *Rhincodon typus*
Pez elefante (S): *Cetorhinus maximus*
Pez espátula (S): *Polyodon spathula*
Pez lengüihueso malayo (S): *Scleropages formosus*
Pez mular (S): *Tursiops truncatus*
Pez pulmonado australiano (S): *Neoceratodus forsteri*
Pezoporus occidentalis = *Geopsittacus occidentalis*
Pezoporus wallicus : (E) Ground Parakeet, Ground Parrot, Swamp Parakeet, (S) Cacatúa terrera, Perico terrestre, Periquito de tierra, (F) Perruche de terre, Perruche terrestre, **I** PSITTACIDAE Av
Pfeffer's Chameleon (E): *Chamaeleo pfefferi*
Phacelocyathus flos : **II** CARYOPHYLLIIDAE An
Phaeochroa cuvierii = *Campylopterus cuvierii*
Phaethornis anthophilus : (E) Pale-bellied Hermit, (S) Ermitaño carinegro, Ermitaño ventripálido, (F) Ermite anthophile, **II** TROCHILIDAE Av
Phaethornis atrimentalis : (E) Black-throated Hermit **II** TROCHILIDAE Av
Phaethornis augusti : (E) Sooty-capped Hermit, (S) Ermitaño limpiacasa, Limpiacasa, (F) Ermite d'Auguste, **II** TROCHILIDAE Av
Phaethornis bourcieri : (E) Straight-billed Hermit, (S) Ermitaño de picorrecto, Ermitaño piquirrecto, (F) Ermite de Bourcier, **II** TROCHILIDAE Av
Phaethornis eurynome : (E) Scale-throated Hermit, (S) Ermitaño escamoso, Ermitaño manchado, (F) Ermite eurynome, **II** TROCHILIDAE Av
Phaethornis gounellei = *Anopetia gounellei*
Phaethornis griseogularis : (E) Grey-chinned Hermit, Porculla Hermit, (S) Ermitañito barbigrís, Ermitaño barbigris, (F) Ermite à gorge grise, **II** TROCHILIDAE Av
Phaethornis guy : (E) Green Hermit, (S) Ermitaño verde, (F) Ermite vert, **II** TROCHILIDAE Av
Phaethornis hispidus : (E) White-bearded Hermit, (S) Ermitaño barbiblanco, (F) Ermite d'Osery, **II** TROCHILIDAE Av
Phaethornis idaliae : (E) Minute Hermit, Obscure Hermit, (S) Ermitaño pigmeo, (F) Ermite d'Idalie, **II** TROCHILIDAE Av
Phaethornis koepckeae : (E) Koepcke's Hermit, (S) Ermitaño de Koepcke, (F) Ermite de Koepcke, **II** TROCHILIDAE Av
Phaethornis longirostris : (E) Western Long-tailed Hermit, (S) Ermitaño colilargo norteño, (F) Ermite à longue queue, **II** TROCHILIDAE Av
Phaethornis longuemareus : (E) Little Hermit, (S) Ermitañito pequeño, Ermitaño chico, (F) Ermite nain, **II** TROCHILIDAE Av
Phaethornis malaris : (E) Great-billed Hermit, Margaretta's Hermit, (S) Ermitaño picogrande, (F) Ermite à long bec, **II** TROCHILIDAE Av
Phaethornis maranhaoensis = *Phaethornis nattereri*
Phaethornis margarettae = *Phaethornis malaris*
Phaethornis mexicanus = *Phaethornis superciliosus*
Phaethornis nattereri : (E) Cinnamon-throated Hermit, (S) Ermitaño de Natterer, (F) Ermite de Natterer, **II** TROCHILIDAE Av

Phaethornis nigrirostris = *Phaethornis eurynome*
Phaethornis philippii : (E) Needle-billed Hermit, (S) Ermitaño picoaguja, (F) Ermite de Filippi, **II** TROCHILIDAE Av
Phaethornis porcullae = *Phaethornis griseogularis*
Phaethornis pretrei : (E) Planalto Hermit, (S) Ermitaño del planalto, Ermitaño frentrinegro, (F) Ermite de Prêtre, **II** TROCHILIDAE Av
Phaethornis ruber : (E) Reddish Hermit, (S) Ermitañito rufo, Ermitaño rojizo, (F) Ermite roussâtre, **II** TROCHILIDAE Av
Phaethornis rupurumii : (E) Streak-throated Hermit **II** TROCHILIDAE Av
Phaethornis squalidus : (E) Dusky-throated Hermit, (S) Ermitañito gargantifusco, Ermitaño escuálido, (F) Ermite terne, **II** TROCHILIDAE Av
Phaethornis striigularis : (E) Stripe-throated Hermit, (S) Ermitaño gorgiestriado, (F) Ermite à gorge rayée, **II** TROCHILIDAE Av
Phaethornis stuarti : (E) White-browed Hermit, (S) Ermitaño Boliviano, (F) Ermite de Stuart, **II** TROCHILIDAE Av
Phaethornis subochraceus : (E) Buff-bellied Hermit, (S) Ermitaño ocráceo, (F) Ermite ocré, **II** TROCHILIDAE Av
Phaethornis superciliosus : (E) Eastern Long-tailed Hermit, Long-tailed Hermit, (S) Ermitaño colilargo, Ermitaño colilargo común, Ermitaño guayanés, (F) Ermite à brins blancs, **II** TROCHILIDAE Av
Phaethornis syrmatophorus : (E) Tawny-bellied Hermit, (S) Ermitaño ventrihabano, (F) Ermite à ventre fauve, **II** TROCHILIDAE Av
Phaethornis yaruqui : (E) White-whiskered Hermit, (S) Ermitaño bigotiblanco, Ermitaño de Yaruqui, (F) Ermite yaruqui, **II** TROCHILIDAE Av
Phalanger maculatus = *Spilocuscus maculatus*
Phalanger mimicus = *Phalanger orientalis*
Phalanger orientalis : (E) Common Cuscus, Common Phalanger, Grey Cuscus, Northern Common Cuscus, (S) Cuscús gris, Cuscús oriental, (F) Couscous de la Sonde, Couscous gris, **II** PHALANGERIDAE Ma
Phalanger tacheté (F): *Spilocuscus maculatus*
Phalangopora regularis : **II** STYLASTERIDAE Hy
Phalcoboenus albogularis : (E) White-throated Caracara, (S) Caracara araucano, Chinalinda, Guarahuau cordillerano, Matamico blanco, (F) Caracara à gorge blanche, **II** FALCONIDAE Av
Phalcoboenus australis : (E) Forster's Caracara, Striated Caracara, (S) Caracara austral, Matamico estriado, Matamico grande, Tiuque cordillerano austral, (F) Caracara austral, Caracara funèbre, **II** FALCONIDAE Av
Phalcoboenus carunculatus : (E) Carunculated Caracara, (S) Caracara carunculado, (F) Caracara caronculé, **II** FALCONIDAE Av
Phalcoboenus megalopterus : (E) Mountain Caracara, (S) Caracara andino, Carancho andino, Matamico cordillerano, (F) Caracara montagnard, **II** FALCONIDAE Av
Phalcoboenus megalopterus ssp. *albogularis* = *Phalcoboenus albogularis*
Phaner (F): *Phaner furcifer*
Phaner furcifer : (E) Fork-marked Lemur, Fork-marked Mouse-lemur, (S) Maki ardilla, Maki horquilla, (F) Phaner, **I** CHEIROGALEIDAE Ma
Phantasmal Poison Frog (E): *Epipedobates tricolor*
Pharaoh Eagle-Owl (E): *Bubo ascalaphus*
Pharomachrus mocinno : (E) Magnificent Quetzal, Resplendent Quetzal, (S) Quetzal, Quetzal centroamericano, Quetzal Guatemalteco, (F) Quetzal resplendissant, Trogon couroucou, **I** TROGONIDAE Av
Phasis wallengrenii = *Ailurus fulgens*
Phataginus gigantea = *Manis gigantea*
Phataginus temminckii = *Manis temminckii*

Phataginus tetradactyla = Manis tetradactyla
Phataginus tricuspis = Manis tricuspis
Phayre's Langur (E): *Trachypithecus phayrei*
Phayre's Leaf Monkey (E): *Trachypithecus phayrei*
Phelsuma spp.: (E) Day geckos, (S) Gecos diurnos, (F) Geckos diurnes, Geckos diurnes de l'Océan Indien, Phelsumes, **II** GEKKONIDAE Re
Phelsuma abbotti : (E) Abbott's Day Gecko, Aldabra Day Gecko, Seychelles Day Gecko, (S) Geco diurne de Abbott, (F) Gecko diurne d'Aldabra, Phelsume d'Aldabra, **II** GEKKONIDAE Re
Phelsuma abbotti ssp. *parkeri = Phelsuma parkeri*
Phelsuma abbotti ssp. *v-nigra = Phelsuma v-nigra*
Phelsuma agalegae = Phelsuma borbonica
Phelsuma andamanensis : (E) Andaman Day Gecko, (S) Geco diurno de Andaman, (F) Gecko diurne des Iles Andaman, Phelsume des Iles Andaman, **II** GEKKONIDAE Re
Phelsuma antanosy : (E) Antanosy Day Gecko, (F) Gecko diurne de la région Antanosy, Phelsume de la région Antanosy **II** GEKKONIDAE Re
Phelsuma astriata : (E) Seychelles Day Gecko, (F) Gecko diurne des Seychelles, Petit gecko diurne des Seychelles, Petit phelsume des Seychelles **II** GEKKONIDAE Re
Phelsuma barbouri : (E) Barbour's Day Gecko, (S) Geco diurno de Barbour, (F) Gecko diurne de Barbour, Phelsume de Barbour, **II** GEKKONIDAE Re
Phelsuma befotakensis : (E) North-western Day Gecko, (F) Gecko diurne de Befotaka, Gecko diurne du nord-ouest de Madagascar, Phelsume de Befotaka **II** GEKKONIDAE Re
Phelsuma berghofi : **II** GEKKONIDAE Re
Phelsuma bimaculata = Phelsuma quadriocellata
Phelsuma borbonica : (E) Réunion Day Gecko, (F) Gecko diurne de Bourbon, Gecko diurne de la Réunion, Phelsume de Bourbon **II** GEKKONIDAE Re
Phelsuma breviceps :, (F) Gecko diurne à courte tête, Phelsume à courte tête **II** GEKKONIDAE Re
Phelsuma cepediana : (E) Blue-tailed Day Gecko, Mauritius Greater Day Gecko, (S) Geco diurno de cola azul, (F) Gecko diurne à queue bleue, Phelsume à queue bleue, **II** GEKKONIDAE Re
Phelsuma cepediana ssp. *borbonica = Phelsuma borbonica*
Phelsuma chekei : (E) Northern Day Gecko, (F) Gecko diurne de Cheke, Gecko diurne du Nord de Madagascar, Phelsume de Cheke **II** GEKKONIDAE Re
Phelsuma comorensis : (E) Comoro Day Gecko, (S) Geco diurno de las Comores, (F) Gecko diurne des Comores, Phelsume des Comores, **II** GEKKONIDAE Re
Phelsuma dubia : (E) Bright-eyed Day Gecko, Dull-green Day Gecko, Zanzibar Day Gecko, (S) Geco diurno de Zanzibar, (F) Gecko diurne de Zanzibar, Gecko diurne sombre, Phelsume de Zanzibar, **II** GEKKONIDAE Re
Phelsuma dubia ssp. *comorensis = Phelsuma comorensis*
Phelsuma edwardnewtonii : (E) Rodrigues Day Gecko, (F) Gecko diurne de Rodrigues, Phelsume de Rodrigues **II** GEKKONIDAE Re
Phelsuma flavigularis : (E) Yellow-throated Day Gecko, (S) Geco diurno de garganta amarilla, (F) Gecko diurne à gorge jaune, Phelsume à gorge jaune, **II** GEKKONIDAE Re
Phelsuma flavigularis ssp. *serraticauda = Phelsuma serraticauda*
Phelsuma gigas : (E) Giant Day Gecko, (F) Gecko diurne géant de Rodrigues, Phelsume de géant Rodrigues **II** GEKKONIDAE Re
Phelsuma guentheri : (E) Round Island Day Gecko, (S) Geco diurno de Guenther, (F) Gecko diurne de l'Ile Ronde, Phelsume de Günther, Phelsume de l'Ile Ronde, **II** GEKKONIDAE Re

Phelsuma guimbeaui : (E) Mauritius Day Gecko, Mauritius Lowland Forest Day Gecko, (S) Geco diurno de Guimbeau, (F) Gecko diurne de l'Ile Maurice, Phelsume de l'Ile Maurice, **II** GEKKONIDAE Re
Phelsuma guttata : (E) Speckled Day Gecko, Spotted Day Gecko, (F) Gecko diurne tacheté, Phelsume tacheté **II** GEKKONIDAE Re
Phelsuma hielscheri : **II** GEKKONIDAE Re
Phelsuma inexpectata = Phelsuma ornata
Phelsuma klemmeri : (E) Klemmer's Day Gecko, (S) Geco diurno de Klemmer, (F) Gecko diurne à tête jaune, Gecko diurne de Klemmer, Phelsume de Klemmer, **II** GEKKONIDAE Re
Phelsuma laticauda : (E) Flat-tailed Day Gecko, Gold-dust Day Gecko, (S) Geco diurno de cola gruesa, (F) Gecko diurne à large queue, Gecko diurne poussière-d'or, Phelsume poussière-d'or, **II** GEKKONIDAE Re
Phelsuma leiogaster :, (F) Gecko diurne du sud-ouest de Madagascar, Phelsume du sud-ouest de Madagascar **II** GEKKONIDAE Re
Phelsuma lineata : (E) Lined Day Gecko, Side-striped Day Gecko, Striped Day Gecko, (S) Geco diurno de bandas, (F) Gecko diurne ligné, Gecko diurne rayé, Phelsume rayé, **II** GEKKONIDAE Re
Phelsuma lineata ssp. *pusilla = Phelsuma pusilla*
Phelsuma longinsulae :, (F) Gecko diurne des Seychelles, Phelsume des Seychelles **II** GEKKONIDAE Re
Phelsuma madagascariensis : (E) Madagascar Day Gecko, (S) Geco diurno de Madagascar, (F) Gecko diurne de Madagascar, Phelsume de Madagascar, **II** GEKKONIDAE Re
Phelsuma malamakibo : **II** GEKKONIDAE Re
Phelsuma masohoala : **II** GEKKONIDAE Re
Phelsuma minuthi : (E) Borner's Day Gecko, (F) Gecko diurne de Borner, Gecko diurne de Minuth, Phelsume de Minuth **II** GEKKONIDAE Re
Phelsuma modesta : (E) Modest Day Gecko, (F) Gecko diurne modeste, Phelsume modeste **II** GEKKONIDAE Re
Phelsuma mutabilis : (E) Thick-tailed Day Gecko, (F) Gecko diurne à queue charnue, Gecko diurne de Grandidier, Phelsume variable **II** GEKKONIDAE Re
Phelsuma mutabilis ssp. *breviceps = Phelsuma breviceps*
Phelsuma newtonii = Phelsuma gigas
Phelsuma nigristriata : (E) Island Day Gecko, (S) Geco diurno de estrias negras, (F) Gecko diurne à bandes noires, Gecko diurne de Meier, Phelsume de Meier, **II** GEKKONIDAE Re
Phelsuma ocellata : (E) Namaqua Day Gecko, Ocellated Day Gecko, Spotted Day Gecko, (S) Geco diurno ocelado, (F) Gecko diurne ocellé, Phelsume ocellé, **II** GEKKONIDAE Re
Phelsuma ornata : (E) Ornate Day Gecko, (S) Geco diurno ornado, (F) Gecko diurne orné de l'Ile Maurice, Phelsume orné de l'Ile Maurice, **II** GEKKONIDAE Re
Phelsuma parkeri : (E) Parker's Day Gecko, Pemba Day Gecko, (F) Gecko diurne de l'Ile Pemba, Gecko diurne de Parker, Phelsume de Parker **II** GEKKONIDAE Re
Phelsuma pronki : (E) Pronk's Day Gecko **II** GEKKONIDAE Re
Phelsuma pusilla : (E) Dwarf Day Gecko, (F) Gecko diurne nain, Phelsume nain **II** GEKKONIDAE Re
Phelsuma quadriocellata : (E) Four-spot Day Gecko, Peacock Day Gecko, (F) Gecko diurne à quatre ocelles, Gecko diurne de Peacock, Phelsume à quatre ocelles **II** GEKKONIDAE Re
Phelsuma robertmertensi : (E) Mertens's Day Gecko, (S) Geco diurno de Robert Mertens, (F) Gecko diurne de Robert Mertens, Phelsume de Robert Mertens, **II** GEKKONIDAE Re
Phelsuma seippi : (E) Seipp's Day Gecko, (F) Gecko diurne de Seipp, Phelsume de Seipp **II** GEKKONIDAE Re

Checklist of fauna/Lista de especies de fauna/Liste des espèces animales

Phelsuma serraticauda : (E) Fan-tailed Day Gecko, Serrated Day Gecko, (S) Geco diurno de cola dentada, (F) Gecko diurne à queue plate, Phelsume à queue plate, **II** GEKKONIDAE Re

Phelsuma standingi : (E) Banded Day Gecko, Standing's Day Gecko, (S) Geco diurno de Standing, (F) Gecko diurne de Standing, Phelsume de Standing, **II** GEKKONIDAE Re

Phelsuma sundbergi : (E) La-Digue Day Gecko, Seychelles Giant Day Gecko, (S) Geco diurno de Sundberg, (F) Gecko diurne géant des Seychelles, Phelsume géant des Seychelles, **II** GEKKONIDAE Re

Phelsuma trilineata : (E) Three-lined Day Gecko, (S) Geco diurno de tres bandas, (F) Gecko diurne à trois lignes, Phelsume à trois lignes, **II** GEKKONIDAE Re

Phelsuma vinsoni = Phelsuma ornata

Phelsuma v-nigra : (E) Boettger's Day Gecko, (F) Gecko diurne de Boettger, Phelsume de Boettger **II** GEKKONIDAE Re

Phelsume à courte tête (F): *Phelsuma breviceps*

Phelsume à gorge jaune (F): *Phelsuma flavigularis*

Phelsume à quatre ocelles (F): *Phelsuma quadriocellata*

Phelsume à queue bleue (F): *Phelsuma cepediana*

Phelsume à queue plate (F): *Phelsuma serraticauda*

Phelsume à trois lignes (F): *Phelsuma trilineata*

Phelsume d'Aldabra (F): *Phelsuma abbotti*

Phelsume de Barbour (F): *Phelsuma barbouri*

Phelsume de Befotaka (F): *Phelsuma befotakensis*

Phelsume de Boettger (F): *Phelsuma v-nigra*

Phelsume de Bourbon (F): *Phelsuma borbonica*

Phelsume de Cheke (F): *Phelsuma chekei*

Phelsume de géant Rodrigues (F): *Phelsuma gigas*

Phelsume de Günther (F): *Phelsuma guentheri*

Phelsume de Klemmer (F): *Phelsuma klemmeri*

Phelsume de la région Antanosy (F): *Phelsuma antanosy*

Phelsume de l'Ile Maurice (F): *Phelsuma guimbeaui*

Phelsume de l'Ile Ronde (F): *Phelsuma guentheri*

Phelsume de Madagascar (F): *Phelsuma madagascariensis*

Phelsume de Meier (F): *Phelsuma nigristriata*

Phelsume de Minuth (F): *Phelsuma minuthi*

Phelsume de Parker (F): *Phelsuma parkeri*

Phelsume de Robert Mertens (F): *Phelsuma robertmertensi*

Phelsume de Rodrigues (F): *Phelsuma edwardnewtonii*

Phelsume de Seipp (F): *Phelsuma seippi*

Phelsume de Standing (F): *Phelsuma standingi*

Phelsume de Zanzibar (F): *Phelsuma dubia*

Phelsume des Comores (F): *Phelsuma comorensis*

Phelsume des Iles Andaman (F): *Phelsuma andamanensis*

Phelsume des Seychelles (F): *Phelsuma longinsulae*

Phelsume du sud-ouest de Madagascar (F): *Phelsuma leiogaster*

Phelsume géant des Seychelles (F): *Phelsuma sundbergi*

Phelsume modeste (F): *Phelsuma modesta*

Phelsume nain (F): *Phelsuma pusilla*

Phelsume ocellé (F): *Phelsuma ocellata*

Phelsume orné de l'Ile Maurice (F): *Phelsuma ornata*

Phelsume poussière-d'or (F): *Phelsuma laticauda*

Phelsume rayé (F): *Phelsuma lineata*

Phelsume tacheté (F): *Phelsuma guttata*

Phelsume variable (F): *Phelsuma mutabilis*

Phelsumes (F): *Phelsuma* spp.

Phigys solitarius : (E) Collared Lory, (S) Lori solitario, (F) Lori des Fidji, Lori solitaire des îles Fidji, **II** PSITTACIDAE Av

Philantomba monticola = Cephalophus monticola

Philippine Boobook (E): *Ninox philippensis*

Philippine Cobra (E): *Naja philippinensis*

Philippine Cockatoo (E): *Cacatua haematuropygia*

Philippine Crocodile (E): *Crocodylus mindorensis*

Philippine Eagle (E): *Pithecophaga jefferyi*

Philippine Eagle-Owl (E): *Bubo philippensis*

Philippine Falconet (E): *Microhierax erythrogenys*

Philippine Grey Flying-fox (E): *Pteropus speciosus*

Philippine Hanging-Parrot (E): *Loriculus philippensis*

Philippine Hawk-Eagle (E): *Spizaetus philippensis*

Philippine Hawk-Owl (E): *Ninox philippensis*

Philippine Pond Turtle (E): *Heosemys leytensis*

Philippine Scops-Owl (E): *Otus megalotis*

Philippine Serpent-Eagle (E): *Spilornis holospilus*

Philippine Tarsier (E): *Tarsius syrichta*

Philippine Treeshrew (E): *Urogale everetti*

Philodice bryantae = Calliphlox bryantae

Philodice dupontii = Tilmatura dupontii

Philodice evelynae = Calliphlox evelynae

Philodice mitchellii = Calliphlox mitchellii

Phlogophilus harterti : (E) Peruvian Piedtail, (S) Colibrí colipinto Peruano, (F) Colibri de Hartert, **II** TROCHILIDAE Av

Phlogophilus hemileucurus : (E) Ecuadorian Piedtail, (S) Colapinto ecuatoriano, Colibrí colipinto Ecuatoriano, (F) Colibri à queue mi-blanche, **II** TROCHILIDAE Av

Phobobate à trois bandes (F): *Epipedobates trivittatus*

Phobobate de Bassler (F): *Epipedobates bassleri*

Phobobate de Silverstone (F): *Epipedobates silverstonei*

Phobobates bassleri = Epipedobates bassleri

Phobobates silverstonei = Epipedobates silverstonei

Phobobates trivittatus = Epipedobates trivittatus

Phocoena dioptrica = Australophocaena dioptrica

Phocoena phocoena : (E) Common Porpoise, Harbour Porpoise, (S) Marsopa común, (F) Marsouin, Marsouin commun, **II** PHOCOENIDAE Ma

Phocoena sinus : (E) Cochito, Gulf of California Harbour Porpoise, Gulf Porpoise, Vaquita, (S) Cochito, Vaquita, (F) Cochito, Marsouin du Golfe de Californie, Vaquita, **I** PHOCOENIDAE Ma

Phocoena spinipinnis : (E) Black Porpoise, Burmeister's Porpoise, (S) Marsopa espinosa, (F) Marsouin de Burmeister, **II** PHOCOENIDAE Ma

Phocoena vomerina = Phocoena phocoena

Phocoenoides dalli : (E) Dall's Porpoise, White-flanked Porpoise, (S) Marsopa de Dall, (F) Marsouin de Dall, **II** PHOCOENIDAE Ma

Phodile calong (F): *Phodilus badius*

Phodile de Prigogine (F): *Phodilus prigoginei*

Phodilus badius : (E) Bay Owl, Common Bay-Owl, Oriental Bay-Owl, (S) Lechuza baya de Madagascar, Lechuza cornuda, (F) Chouette baie, Phodile calong, **II** TYTONIDAE Av

Phodilus prigoginei : (E) African Bay Owl, Congo Bay-Owl, Itombwe Owl, (S) Lechuza del Congo, (F) Phodile de Prigogine, **II** TYTONIDAE Av

Phoebastria albatrus = Diomedea albatrus

Phoeniconaias minor = Phoenicopterus minor

Phoenicoparrus andinus = Phoenicopterus andinus

Phoenicoparrus jamesi = Phoenicopterus jamesi

PHOENICOPTERIDAE spp.: (E) Flamingos (S) Fenocoptéridos, Flamencos, (F) Flamants, **II** Av

Phoenicopterus andinus : (E) Andean Flamingo, (S) Flamenco andino, Parina grande, (F) Flamant des Andes, **II** PHOENICOPTERIDAE Av

Phoenicopterus chilensis : (E) Chilean Flamingo, (S) Flamenco Chileno, Flamenco común de Chile, Parihuana, Pariona, (F) Flamant du Chili, **II** PHOENICOPTERIDAE Av

Phoenicopterus jamesi : (E) James' Flamingo, James's Flamingo, Puna Flamingo, (S) Flamenco andino chico, Flamenco de James, Parina chica, (F) Flamant de James, **II** PHOENICOPTERIDAE Av

Phoenicopterus minor : (E) Lesser Flamingo, (S) Flamenco enano, (F) Flamant nain, Petit flamant, **II** PHOENICOPTERIDAE Av

Phoenicopterus roseus = Phoenicopterus ruber

Phoenicopterus ruber : (E) American Flamingo, Caribbean Flamingo, Greater Flamingo, (S) Flamenco, Flamenco común, Flamenco de Cuba, Flamenco rojo, Tococo, (F) Flamant de Cuba, Flamant rose, Flamant rouge, **II** PHOENICOPTERIDAE Av

Pholidornis rushiae : (E) Tit-hylia, (F) Astrild mésange, Mésangette rayée **III** ESTRILDIDAE Av
Phonograph Coral (E): *Pachyseris speciosa*
Phonygammus keraudrenii = Manucodia keraudrenii
Phoque moine (F): *Monachus monachus*
Phoque-moine méditerranéen (F): *Monachus monachus*
Phoque-moines (F): *Monachus* spp.
Phrynomantis maculatus = Mantella baroni
Phrynosoma cerroense = Phrynosoma coronatum
Phrynosoma coronatum : (E) Coast Horned Lizard, (S) Iguana cornuda, (F) Lézard cornu, Lézard cornu de San Diego, Phrynosome couronné, **II** IGUANIDAE Re
Phrynosome couronné (F): *Phrynosoma coronatum*
Phyllangia americana : **II** CARYOPHYLLIIDAE An
Phyllangia consagensis : **II** CARYOPHYLLIIDAE An
Phyllangia dispersa : **II** CARYOPHYLLIIDAE An
Phyllangia echinosepes : **II** CARYOPHYLLIIDAE An
Phyllangia granulata : **II** CARYOPHYLLIIDAE An
Phyllangia hayamaensis : **II** CARYOPHYLLIIDAE An
Phyllangia mouchezii = Phyllangia americana ssp. *mouchezii*
Phyllangia papuensis : **II** CARYOPHYLLIIDAE An
Phyllangia pequegnatae : **II** CARYOPHYLLIIDAE An
Phyllobate (F): *Phyllobates* spp.
Phyllobate à bande (F): *Phyllobates vittatus*
Phyllobate à bande dorée (F): *Phyllobates aurotaenia*
Phyllobate bicolore (F): *Phyllobates bicolor*
Phyllobate lugubre (F): *Phyllobates lugubris*
Phyllobate terrible (F): *Phyllobates terribilis*
Phyllobates spp.: (E) Poison frogs, (S) Ranas de puntas de flechas, (F) Phyllobate, **II** DENDROBATIDAE Am
Phyllobates aurotaenia : (E) Kokoe Poison Frog, (F) Phyllobate à bande dorée **II** DENDROBATIDAE Am
Phyllobates azureiventris = Epipedobates azureiventris
Phyllobates bicolor : (E) Black-legged Poison Frog, Two-toned Poison Frog, (F) Phyllobate bicolore **II** DENDROBATIDAE Am
Phyllobates espinosai = Epipedobates espinosai
Phyllobates lugubris : (E) Lovely Poison Frog, (S) Rana de punta de flecha lúgubre, (F) Phyllobate lugubre, **II** DENDROBATIDAE Am
Phyllobates petersi = Epipedobates petersi
Phyllobates pulchripectus = Epipedobates pulchripectus
Phyllobates smaragdinus = Epipedobates smaragdinus
Phyllobates terribilis : (E) Golden Poison Frog, (S) Rana de punta de flecha terrible, (F) Phyllobate terrible, **II** DENDROBATIDAE Am
Phyllobates vittatus : (E) Golfodulcean Poison Frog, Orange-and-black Poison Frog, (S) Rana de punta de flecha rayada, (F) Phyllobate à bande, **II** DENDROBATIDAE Am
Phyllobates zaparo = Epipedobates zaparo
Physeter catodon : (E) Cachelot, Pot whale, Sperm Whale, Spermacet whale, (S) Ballena esperma, Cachalote, (F) Cachalot, **I** PHYSETERIDAE Ma
Physeter macrocephalus = Physeter catodon
Physogyra spp.: (E) Bubble corals **II** CARYOPHYLLIIDAE An
Physogyra exerta : **II** CARYOPHYLLIIDAE An
Physogyra lichtensteini : (E) Pearl Bubble Coral, Small Bubble Coral **II** CARYOPHYLLIIDAE An
Physophyllia ayleni : **II** PECTINIIDAE An
Piapoco pico rojo (S): *Ramphastos tucanus*
Piapoco pico verde (S): *Ramphastos sulfuratus*
Pic à ventre blanc de Corée (F): *Dryocopus javensis richardsi*
Pic de Tristram (F): *Dryocopus javensis richardsi*
Pic impérial (F): *Campephilus imperialis*
Picaflor abanico verde (S): *Lophornis chalybeus*
Picaflor amatista (S): *Calliphlox amethystina*
Picaflor bronceado (S): *Hylocharis chrysura*
Picaflor cabeciazul (S): *Hylocharis cyanus*
Picaflor cabeza granate (S): *Sephanoides sephaniodes*
Picaflor coliverde (S): *Polytmus guainumbi*

Picaflor coludo rojo (S): *Sappho sparganura*
Picaflor común (S): *Chlorostilbon aureoventris*
Picaflor copetón (S): *Stephanoxis lalandi*
Picaflor corona azul (S): *Thalurania glaucopis*
Picaflor cuelliblanco (S): *Leucochloris albicollis*
Picaflor de Barbijo (S): *Heliomaster furcifer*
Picaflor dorado (S): *Hylocharis chrysura*
Picaflor enano (S): *Microstilbon burmeisteri*
Picaflor escamado (S): *Heliomaster squamosus*
Picaflor frentivioleta (S): *Eriocnemis glaucopoides*
Picaflor gargantiazul (S): *Adelomyia melanogenys*
Picaflor gargantiverde (S): *Thalurania furcata*
Picaflor gigante (S): *Patagona gigas*
Picaflor negro (S): *Florisuga fusca*
Picaflor orejiazul (S): *Colibri thalassinus*
Picaflor pechiazul (S): *Hylocharis sapphirina*
Picaflor pequeño verde (S): *Agyrtria versicolor*
Picaflor serrano ventricanela (S): *Oreotrochilus estella*
Picaflor serrano ventrinegro (S): *Oreotrochilus leucopleurus*
Picaflor ventriazul (S): *Colibri coruscans*
Picaflor ventriblanco (S): *Leucippus chionogaster*
Picaflor ventrinegro (S): *Anthracothorax nigricollis*
Picaflor ventriverde (S): *Colibri serrirostris*
Picaflores (S): TROCHILIDAE spp.
Picatartes cuelliblanco (S): *Picathartes gymnocephalus*
Picatartes cuelligris (S): *Picathartes oreas*
Picatharte à cou blanc (F): *Picathartes gymnocephalus*
Picatharte à cou gris (F): *Picathartes oreas*
Picatharte à tête rouge (F): *Picathartes oreas*
Picatharte chauve (F): *Picathartes gymnocephalus*
Picatharte de Guinée (F): *Picathartes gymnocephalus*
Picatharte du Cameroun (F): *Picathartes oreas*
Picathartes (F): *Picathartes gymnocephalus*
Picathartes gymnocephalus : (E) Bare-headed Rockfowl, White-necked Picathartes, White-necked Rockfowl, Yellow-headed Rockfowl, (S) Cuervo calvo de cuello blanco, Picatartes cuelliblanco, (F) Picatharte à cou blanc, Picatharte chauve, Picatharte de Guinée, Picathartes, **I** MUSCICAPIDAE Av
Picathartes oreas : (E) Grey-necked Picathartes, Grey-necked Rockfowl, Red-headed Rockfowl, (S) Cuervo calvo de cuello gris, Picatartes cuelligris, (F) Picatharte à cou gris, Picatharte à tête rouge, Picatharte du Cameroun, **I** MUSCICAPIDAE Av
Pichico negro (S): *Callimico goeldii*
Pico de Coral (S): *Estrilda astrild*
Pico espina bronceado (S): *Chalcostigma heteropogon*
Pico lanza frentiazul (S): *Doryfera johannae*
Pico lanza frentiverde (S): *Doryfera ludovicae*
Pico-de-Hoz colihabano (S): *Eutoxeres condamini*
Pico-de-Hoz puntiblanco (S): *Eutoxeres aquila*
Picoespina arcoiris (S): *Chalcostigma herrani*
Picoespina dorsiazul (S): *Chalcostigma stanleyi*
Picoespina dorsipurpura (S): *Ramphomicron microrhynchum*
Picoespina gorrirrufa (S): *Chalcostigma ruficeps*
Picohoz colicanela (S): *Eutoxeres condamini*
Picohoz coliverde (S): *Eutoxeres aquila*
Picolargo coroniazul (S): *Heliomaster longirostris*
Picolargo coronioscuro (S): *Heliomaster constantii*
Picozapato (S): *Balaeniceps rex*
Piebald Chuckwalla (E): *Sauromalus varius*
Piebald Dolphin (E): *Cephalorhynchus commersonii*
Pied Falconet (E): *Microhierax melanoleucos*
Pied Goshawk (E): *Accipiter albogularis*
Pied Harrier (E): *Circus melanoleucos*
Pied Hornbill (E): *Anthracoceros coronatus*
Pied Mannikin (E): *Lonchura fringilloides*
Pied Sparrowhawk (E): *Accipiter albogularis*
Pied Tamarin (E): *Saguinus bicolor*
Pied-billed Azurecrown (E): *Agyrtria cyanocephala*
Pigargo (S): *Haliaeetus albicilla*
Pigargo americano (S): *Haliaeetus leucocephalus*
Pigargo cabeciblanco (S): *Haliaeetus leucocephalus*

Checklist of fauna/Lista de especies de fauna/Liste des espèces animales

Pigargo cabeciblanco meridional (S): *Haliaeetus leucocephalus*
Pigargo coliblanco (S): *Haliaeetus albicilla*
Pigargo coliblanco de Groenlandia (S): *Haliaeetus albicilla*
Pigargo común (S): *Haliaeetus albicilla*
Pigargo de las Salomón (S): *Haliaeetus sanfordi*
Pigargo de Madagascar (S): *Haliaeetus vociferoides*
Pigargo de Pallas (S): *Haliaeetus leucoryphus*
Pigargo de Sanford (S): *Haliaeetus sanfordi*
Pigargo de Steller (S): *Haliaeetus pelagicus*
Pigargo de vientre blanco (S): *Haliaeetus leucogaster*
Pigargo europeo (S): *Haliaeetus albicilla*
Pigargo gigante (S): *Haliaeetus pelagicus*
Pigargo malgache (S): *Haliaeetus vociferoides*
Pigargo oriental (S): *Haliaeetus leucogaster*
Pigargo vocinglero (S): *Haliaeetus vocifer*
Pigarguillo común (S): *Ichthyophaga ichthyaetus*
Pigarguillo menor (S): *Ichthyophaga humilis*
Pigeon à camail (F): *Caloenas nicobarica*
Pigeon à collerette (F): *Caloenas nicobarica*
Pigeon à nuque bronzée (F): *Columba iriditorques*
Pigeon biset (F): *Columba livia*
Pigeon de Guinée (F): *Columba guinea*
Pigeon de Mindoro (F): *Ducula mindorensis*
Pigeon de Nicobar (F): *Caloenas nicobarica*
Pigeon domestique (F): *Columba livia*
Pigeon gris (F): *Columba unicincta*
Pigeon gris écailleux (F): *Columba unicincta*
Pigeon Hawk (E): *Falco columbarius*
Pigeon rose (F): *Columba mayeri*
Pigeon roussard (F): *Columba guinea*
Pigeon vert à épaulettes violettes (F): *Treron waalia*
Pigeon vert à front nu (F): *Streptopelia vinacea*
Pigeons à épaulettes violettes (F): *Treron waalia*
Pigeons couronnés (F): *Goura* spp.
Pig-footed Bandicoot (E): *Chaeropus ecaudatus*
Pigtail Macaque (E): *Macaca nemestrina*
Pig-tailed Langur (E): *Nasalis concolor*
Pig-tailed Macaque (E): *Macaca nemestrina*
Pijiji aliblanco (S): *Dendrocygna autumnalis*
Pijiji canelo (S): *Dendrocygna bicolor*
Pilbara Monitor (E): *Varanus pilbarensis*
Pileated Gibbon (E): *Hylobates pileatus*
Pileated Parakeet (E): *Purpureicephalus spurius*
Pileated Parrot (E): *Pionopsitta pileata*
Pilet (F): *Anas acuta*
Piliocolobus badius = Procolobus badius
Piliocolobus gordonorum = Procolobus pennantii ssp. *gordonorum*
Piliocolobus kirkii = Procolobus pennantii ssp. *kirkii*
Piliocolobus pennantii = Procolobus pennantii
Piliocolobus preussi = Procolobus preussi
Piliocolobus rufomitratus = Procolobus rufomitratus
Pillar Coral (E): *Dendrogyra cylindrus*
Pilsbry's Dwarf Boa (E): *Tropidophis pilsbryi*
Pinchaque (S): *Tapirus pinchaque*
Pinche Marmoset (E): *Saguinus geoffroyi*
Pineapple Coral (E): *Dichocoenia stokesii*
Pineapple corals (E): *Favites* spp.
Pineapple Tortoise (E): *Indotestudo elongata*
Pingüino de Humboldt (S): *Spheniscus humboldti*
Pingüino del Cabo (S): *Spheniscus demersus*
Pink Cockatoo (E): *Cacatua leadbeateri*
Pink Conch (E): *Strombus gigas*
Pink Pigeon (E): *Columba mayeri*
Pink-cheeked Parakeet (E): *Psittacula longicauda*
Pink-cheeked Waxbill (E): *Estrilda troglodytes*
Pink-headed Dove (E): *Streptopelia roseogrisea*
Pink-headed Duck (E): *Rhodonessa caryophyllacea*
Pinkmucket (E): *Lampsilis orbiculata orbiculata*
Pink-throated Brilliant (E): *Heliodoxa gularis*
Pintada de pechuga blanca (S): *Agelastes meleagrides*
Pintada pechiblanca (S): *Agelastes meleagrides*
Pintade à poitrine blanche (F): *Agelastes meleagrides*

Pintado de pecho blanco (S): *Agelastes meleagrides*
Pintail (E): *Anas acuta*
Pin-tailed Whydah (E): *Vidua macroura*
Pione à bec rouge (F): *Pionus sordidus*
Pione à couronne blanche (F): *Pionus senilis*
Pione à tête bleue (F): *Pionus menstruus*
Pione de Maximilien (F): *Pionus maximiliani*
Pione noire (F): *Pionus chalcopterus*
Pione pailletée (F): *Pionus tumultuosus*
Pione violette (F): *Pionus fuscus*
Pionites leucogaster : (E) White-bellied Caique, White-bellied Parrot, (S) Lorito rubio, (F) Caïque à ventre blanc, **II** PSITTACIDAE Av
Pionites melanocephala : (E) Black-headed Caique, Black-headed Parrot, (S) Lorito chirlecrés, Perico calzoncito, (F) Caïque maïpourri, **II** PSITTACIDAE Av
Pionopsitta barrabandi : (E) Barraband's Parrot, Orange-cheeked Parrot, (S) Lorito carinaranja, Perico cachete amarillo, (F) Caïque de Barraband, **II** PSITTACIDAE Av
Pionopsitta caica : (E) Caica Parrot, (S) Lorito caica, Perico cabecinegro, (F) Caïque à tête noire, **II** PSITTACIDAE Av
Pionopsitta haematotis : (E) Brown-hooded Parrot, (S) Lorito encapuchado, Loro orejirrojo, (F) Caïque à capuchon, **II** PSITTACIDAE Av
Pionopsitta pileata : (E) Pileated Parrot, Red-capped Parrot, (S) Cúiu cúiu, Lorito carirrojo, Lorito orejudo, Lorito pileado, (F) Caïque mitré, Perroquet à oreilles, **I** PSITTACIDAE Av
Pionopsitta pulchra : (E) Beautiful Parrot, Rose-faced Parrot, (S) Lorito carirrosado, Loro cachtirrosa, (F) Caïque à joues roses, **II** PSITTACIDAE Av
Pionopsitta pyrilia : (E) Saffron-headed Parrot, (S) Lorito cabecigualdo, Perico cabecidorado, (F) Caïque de Bonaparte, **II** PSITTACIDAE Av
Pionopsitta vulturina : (E) Vulturine Parrot, (S) Lorito vulturino, (F) Caïque vautourin, **II** PSITTACIDAE Av
Pionus chalcopterus : (E) Bronze-winged Parrot, (S) Cotorra negra, Loro alibronceado, (F) Pione noire, **II** PSITTACIDAE Av
Pionus fuscus : (E) Dusky Parrot, (S) Cotorra morada, Loro morado, (F) Pione violette, **II** PSITTACIDAE Av
Pionus maximiliani : (E) Scaly-headed Parrot, (S) Loro choclero, (F) Pione de Maximilien, **II** PSITTACIDAE Av
Pionus menstruus : (E) Blue-headed Parrot, Red-vented Parrot, (S) Cotorra cabeciazul, Loro cabeciazul, (F) Pione à tête bleue, **II** PSITTACIDAE Av
Pionus senilis : (E) White-capped Parrot, White-crowned Parrot, (S) Loro caroniblanco, Loro senil, (F) Pione à couronne blanche, **II** PSITTACIDAE Av
Pionus seniloides = Pionus tumultuosus
Pionus sordidus : (E) Red-billed Parrot, (S) Loro piquirrojo, Perico pico rojo, (F) Pione à bec rouge, **II** PSITTACIDAE Av
Pionus tumultuosus : (E) Plum-crowned Parrot, (S) Cotorra cabeciblanca, Loro tumultuoso, (F) Pione pailletée, **II** PSITTACIDAE Av
Pipile jacutinga : (E) Black-fronted Curassow, Black-fronted Piping-Guan, (S) Chachalaca manchada, Guan de frente negre, Jacotinga, Pava yacutinga, Yacutingá frentinegra, (F) Pénélope à front noir, Pénélope à plastron, Pénélope siffleuse, **I** CRACIDAE Av
Pipile pipile : (E) Trinidad Piping-Guan, Trinidad White-headed Curassow, Trinidad White-headed Piping Guan, (S) Chachalaca de la Trinidad, Guan comun de Trinidad, Pava de Trinidad, Pava rajadora, Yacutinga cariazul, (F) Pénélope siffleuse, Pénélope siffleuse a gorge bleue, Siffleuse de la Trinité, **I** CRACIDAE Av
Piquero de Abbott (S): *Papasula abbotti*
Pirarucu (E/F): *Arapaima gigas*
Pirenestes ventrinegro (S): *Pyrenestes ostrinus*

Checklist of fauna/Lista de especies de fauna/Liste des espèces animales

Pita coliazul (S): *Pitta guajana*
Pita de Gurney (S): *Pitta gurneyi*
Pita de Koch (S): *Pitta kochi*
Pita nympha (S): *Pitta nympha*
Pita rayada (S): *Pitta guajana*
Pithecia aequatorialis : (E) Equatorial Saki **II** CEBIDAE Ma
Pithecia albicans : (E) Black-and-white Saki, Buffy Saki, White Saki, (S) Saki amazónico **II** CEBIDAE Ma
Pithecia hirsuta = Pithecia monachus
Pithecia irrorata : (E) Bald-faced Saki, (S) Saki de cara pelada **II** CEBIDAE Ma
Pithecia monachus : (E) Monk Saki, Red-bearded Saki, (F) Saki chevelu **II** CEBIDAE Ma
Pithecia monachus ssp. *irrorata = Pithecia irrorata*
Pithecia pithecia : (E) Pale-headed Saki, White-faced Saki, (F) Saki à tête pâle **II** CEBIDAE Ma
Pithecophaga jefferyi : (E) Great Philippine Eagle, Monkey-eating Eagle, Philippine Eagle, (S) Aguila comemonos, Águila monera, (F) Aigle des Philippines, Aigle des singes, Aigle mangeur de singes, Pithécophage des Philippines, **I** ACCIPITRIDAE Av
Pithécophage des Philippines (F): *Pithecophaga jefferyi*
Pitilia alirroja (S): *Pytilia phoenicoptera*
Pitiu (S): *Podocnemis sextuberculata*
Pito de vientre blanco de Corea (S): *Dryocopus javensis richardsi*
Pito imperial (S): *Campephilus imperialis*
Pito ventriblanco de Corea (S): *Dryocopus javensis richardsi*
Pitón acuática de Papua (S): *Apodora papuana*
Pitón ametista (S): *Morelia amethistina*
Pitón anillada de Bismarck (S): *Bothrochilus boa*
Pitón de Albert (S): *Leiopython albertisii*
Pitón de Angola (S): *Python anchietae*
Pitón de Boelen (S): *Morelia boeleni*
Pitón de cabeza negra (S): *Aspidites melanocephalus*
Pitón de Calabar (S): *Calabaria reinhardtii*
Pitón de la India (S): *Python molurus molurus*
Pitón de Macklot (S): *Liasis mackloti*
Pitón de Ramsay (S): *Aspidites ramsayi*
Pitón de Seba (S): *Python sebae*
Pitón de Timor (S): *Python timoriensis*
Pitón diamantina (S): *Morelia spilota*
Pitón enana (S): *Antaresia childreni*
Pitón excavadora (S): *Loxocemus bicolor*
Pitón malaya (S): *Python curtus*
Pitón oliva (S): *Liasis olivaceus*
Pitón real (S): *Python regius*
Pitón reticulada (S): *Python reticulatus*
Pitóns (S): PYTHONIDAE spp.
Pitorreal ocotero (S): *Campephilus imperialis*
Pitta brachyura ssp. *nympha = Pitta nympha*
Pitta guajana : (E) Banded Pitta, Blue-tailed Pitta, (S) Pita coliazul, Pita rayada, (F) Brève à queue bleue, Brève azurine, **II** PITTIDAE Av
Pitta gurneyi : (E) Black-breasted Pitta, Gurney's Pitta, (S) Pita de Gurney, (F) Brève de Gurney, **I** PITTIDAE Av
Pitta kochi : (E) Koch's Pitta, Whiskered Pitta, (S) Pita de Koch, (F) Brève de Koch, **I** PITTIDAE Av
Pitta nympha : (E) Fairy Pitta, (S) Pita nympha, (F) Brève du Japon, Brève migratrice, **II** PITTIDAE Av
Plaa eesok (F): *Probarbus jullieni*
Placotrochides alabastrum = Javania lamprotichum
Placotrochides frustum : **II** FLABELLIDAE An
Placotrochides scaphula : **II** FLABELLIDAE An
Placotrochus fuscus = Javania fusca
Placotrochus laevis : **II** FLABELLIDAE An
Placotrochus pedicellatus : **II** FLABELLIDAE An
Plagiola florentina = Epioblasma florentina
Plagiola torulosa = Epioblasma torulosa ssp. *torulosa*
Plain Chachalaca (E): *Ortalis vetula*
Plain Lizard (E): *Varanus salvator*
Plain Parakeet (E): *Brotogeris tirica*

Plain Pocketbook Pearly Mussel (E): *Lampsilis satur*
Plain-bellied Emerald (E): *Agyrtria leucogaster*
Plain-breasted Hawk (E): *Accipiter ventralis*
Plain-capped Starthroat (E): *Heliomaster constantii*
Plain-pouched Hornbill (E): *Aceros subruficollis*
Plain-pouched Wreathed Hornbill (E): *Aceros subruficollis*
Plains Rat-kangaroo (E): *Caloprymnus campestris*
Plan temoleh (F): *Probarbus jullieni*
Plana (S): *Dermatemys mawii*
Planalto Hermit (E): *Phaethornis pretrei*
Platalea leucorodia : (E) Eurasian Spoonbill, Spoonbill, White Spoonbill, (S) Espátula, Espátula blanca, Espátula común, (F) Spatule blanche, **II** THRESKIORNITHIDAE Av
Platanista spp.: (E) Susus, (F) Platanistes, Sousous **I** PLATANISTIDAE Ma
Platanista gangetica : (E) Ganges River Dolphin, Ganges Susu, (S) Delfín del Ganges, (F) Plataniste du Gange, Sousou, **I** PLATANISTIDAE Ma
Platanista gangetica ssp. *gangetica = Platanista gangetica*
Platanista gangetica ssp. *minor = Platanista minor*
Platanista indi = Platanista minor
Platanista minor : (E) Indus Dolphin, Indus River Dolphin, Susu, (S) Delfín del Indo, (F) Plataniste de l'Indus, **I** PLATANISTIDAE Ma
Plataniste de l'Indus (F): *Platanista minor*
Plataniste du Gange (F): *Platanista gangetica*
Platanistes (F): *Platanista* spp.
Plated Leaf Chameleon (E): *Brookesia stumpffi*
Platycercus adelaidae : (E) Adelaide Parakeet, Adelaide Rosella, (S) Perico de Adelaida, (F) Perruche d'Adélaïde, **II** PSITTACIDAE Av
Platycercus adscitus : (E) Mealy Rosella, Pale-headed Rosella, (S) Perico pálido, (F) Perruche à tête pâle, Perruche palliceps, **II** PSITTACIDAE Av
Platycercus barnardi = Barnardius barnardi
Platycercus caledonicus : (E) Green Rosella, Tasmanian Rosella, (S) Perico de Tasmania, (F) Perruche à ventre jaune, Perruche calédonienne, **II** PSITTACIDAE Av
Platycercus elegans : (E) Crimson Rosella, Pennant's Parakeet, (S) Perico elegante, (F) Perruche de Pennant, **II** PSITTACIDAE Av
Platycercus eximius : (E) Eastern Rosella, Golden-mantled Rosella, (S) Perico multicolor, (F) Perruche omnicolore, **II** PSITTACIDAE Av
Platycercus flaveolus : (E) Yellow Rosella, (S) Perico gualda, (F) Perruche flavéole, **II** PSITTACIDAE Av
Platycercus icterotis : (E) Stanley Parakeet, Western Rosella, (S) Perico carigualdo, (F) Perruche à oreilles jaunes, Perruche de Stanley, **II** PSITTACIDAE Av
Platycercus venustus : (E) Northern Rosella, (S) Perico gracioso, (F) Perruche gracieuse, **II** PSITTACIDAE Av
Platycercus zonarius = Barnardius zonarius
Platygyra acuta : **II** FAVIIDAE An
Platygyra carnosus : **II** FAVIIDAE An
Platygyra contorta : **II** FAVIIDAE An
Platygyra crosslandi : **II** FAVIIDAE An
Platygyra daedalea : **II** FAVIIDAE An
Platygyra lamellina : **II** FAVIIDAE An
Platygyra pini : **II** FAVIIDAE An
Platygyra ryukyuensis : **II** FAVIIDAE An
Platygyra sinensis : **II** FAVIIDAE An
Platygyra verweyi : **II** FAVIIDAE An
Platygyra yaeyamaensis : **II** FAVIIDAE An
Platypus Frog (E): *Rheobatrachus silus*
Platyrrhinus lineatus : (E) White-lined Bat, White-lined Broad-nosed Bat, (S) Falso vampiro del Uruguay, Murciélago de estrias blancas, (F) Sténoderme pseudo-vampire, **III** PHYLLOSTOMIDAE Ma
Platysternon megacephalum : (E) Big-headed Turtle **II** PLATYSTERNIDAE Re
Platytrochus compressus : **II** TURBINOLIIDAE An
Platytrochus hastatus : **II** TURBINOLIIDAE An
Platytrochus laevigatus : **II** TURBINOLIIDAE An

Platytrochus parisepta : **II** TURBINOLIIDAE An
Pleasing Poison Frog (E): *Epipedobates bassleri*
Plectropterus gambensis : (E) Spur-winged Goose, (S) Ganso de Gambia, Ganso espolonado, (F) Canard armé, Oie-armée de Gambie, **III** ANATIDAE Av
Pleotrochus venustus : **II** TURBINOLIIDAE An
Pleotrochus zibrowii : **II** TURBINOLIIDAE An
Plerogyra spp.: (E) Bubble corals, Maze corals **II** CARYOPHYLLIIDAE An
Plerogyra discus : **II** CARYOPHYLLIIDAE An
Plerogyra eurysepta : **II** CARYOPHYLLIIDAE An
Plerogyra simplex : **II** CARYOPHYLLIIDAE An
Plerogyra sinuosa : (E) Bladder Coral **II** CARYOPHYLLIIDAE An
Plerogyra turbida : (E) Jasmine Coral **II** CARYOPHYLLIIDAE An
Plesiastrea devantieri : **II** FAVIIDAE An
Plesiastrea versipora : **II** FAVIIDAE An
Plesioseris australiae : **II** SIDERASTREIDAE An
Plethobasus cicatricosus : (E) White Wartyback, White Warty-back Pearly Mussel **I** UNIONIDAE Bi
Plethobasus cooperianus : (E) Orange-foot Pimpleback, Orange-footed Pimpleback Mussel **I** UNIONIDAE Bi
Pleurobema clava : (E) Clubshell, Clubshell Pearly Mussel **II** UNIONIDAE Bi
Pleurobema plenum : (E) Rough Pigtoe, Rough Pigtoe Pearly Mussel **I** UNIONIDAE Bi
Plicated Hornbill (E): *Aceros plicatus*
Pliobothrus echinatus : **II** STYLASTERIDAE Hy
Pliobothrus fistulosus : **II** STYLASTERIDAE Hy
Pliobothrus gracilis : **II** STYLASTERIDAE Hy
Pliobothrus symmetricus : **II** STYLASTERIDAE Hy
Pliobothrus tubulatus : **II** STYLASTERIDAE Hy
Plocepasser superciliosus : (E) Chestnut-crowned Sparrow-Weaver, (S) Tejedor pardal capirotado, (F) Mahali à calotte marron, Moineau-tisserin, **III** PLOCEIDAE Av
Ploceus albinucha : (E) Maxwell's Black Weaver, White-naped Weaver, (S) Tejedor negro albinuca, (F) Tisserin de Maxwell, Tisserin noir de Maxwell, **III** PLOCEIDAE Av
Ploceus aurantius : (E) Orange Weaver, (S) Tejedor naranja, (F) Tisserin orangé, **III** PLOCEIDAE Av
Ploceus capitalis = Ploceus melanocephalus
Ploceus cucullatus : (E) Layard's Black-headed Weaver, Spot-backed Weaver, Village Weaver, (S) Tejedor cogullado, (F) Tisserin gendarme, **III** PLOCEIDAE Av
Ploceus heuglini : (E) Heuglin's Masked-Weaver, (S) Tejedor de Heuglin, (F) Tisserin masqué, **III** PLOCEIDAE Av
Ploceus luteolus : (E) Little Weaver, (S) Sitragra chico común, (F) Tisserin minule, **III** PLOCEIDAE Av
Ploceus melanocephalus : (E) Black-headed Weaver, Yellow-backed Weaver, (S) Tejedor cabecinegro, (F) Tisserin à tête noire, **III** PLOCEIDAE Av
Ploceus nigerrimus : (E) Vieillot's Black Weaver, (S) Tejedor negro de Vieillot, (F) Tisserin noir, Tisserin noir de Vieillot, **III** PLOCEIDAE Av
Ploceus nigriceps = Ploceus cucullatus
Ploceus nigricollis : (E) Black-necked Weaver, (S) Tejedor cuellinegro, (F) Tisserin à cou noir, Tisserin à lunettes, **III** PLOCEIDAE Av
Ploceus pelzelni : (E) Slender-billed Weaver, (S) Sitagra de Pelzeln, (F) Tisserin de Pelzeln, Tisserin nain, **III** PLOCEIDAE Av
Ploceus preussi : (E) Golden-backed Weaver, Preuss's Weaver, Yellow-capped Weaver, (F) Tisserin à dos doré, Tisserin de Preuss **III** PLOCEIDAE Av
Ploceus superciliosus = Pachyphantes superciliosus
Ploceus tricolor : (E) Yellow-mantled Weaver, (S) Tejedor tricolor, (F) Tisserin tricolore, **III** PLOCEIDAE Av
Ploceus velatus ssp. *vitellinus = Ploceus vitellinus*

Ploceus vitellinus : (E) Vitelline Masked-Weaver, (S) Tejedor velado, (F) Tisserin à tête rouge, Tisserin à tête rousse, Tisserin vitellin, **III** PLOCEIDAE Av
Plovercrest (E): *Stephanoxis lalandi*
Plumapathes fernandezii : **II** MYRIOPATHIDAE An
Plumapathes pennacea : **II** MYRIOPATHIDAE An
Plumbeous Forest-falcon (E): *Micrastur plumbeus*
Plumbeous Hawk (E): *Leucopternis plumbea*
Plumbeous Kite (E): *Ictinia plumbea*
Plum-crowned Parrot (E): *Pionus tumultuosus*
Plum-faced Lorikeet (E): *Oreopsittacus arfaki*
Plum-headed Parakeet (E): *Psittacula cyanocephala*
Poc de Atitlán (S): *Podilymbus gigas*
Pocillopora ankeli : **II** POCILLOPORIDAE An
Pocillopora capitata : **II** POCILLOPORIDAE An
Pocillopora damicornis : (E) Cauliflower Coral **II** POCILLOPORIDAE An
Pocillopora danae : **II** POCILLOPORIDAE An
Pocillopora diomedeae = Pocillopora damicornis
Pocillopora effusus : **II** POCILLOPORIDAE An
Pocillopora elegans : **II** POCILLOPORIDAE An
Pocillopora eydouxi : (E) Antler Coral **II** POCILLOPORIDAE An
Pocillopora fungiformis : **II** POCILLOPORIDAE An
Pocillopora indiania : **II** POCILLOPORIDAE An
Pocillopora inflata : **II** POCILLOPORIDAE An
Pocillopora kellereheri : **II** POCILLOPORIDAE An
Pocillopora lacera = Pocillopora damicornis
Pocillopora ligulata : **II** POCILLOPORIDAE An
Pocillopora meandrina : **II** POCILLOPORIDAE An
Pocillopora molokensis : **II** POCILLOPORIDAE An
Pocillopora porosa = Pocillopora verrucosa
Pocillopora robusta = Pocillopora elegans
Pocillopora verrucosa : **II** POCILLOPORIDAE An
Pocillopora woodjonesi : **II** POCILLOPORIDAE An
Pocillopora zelli : **II** POCILLOPORIDAE An
Podabacia crustacea : **II** FUNGIIDAE An
Podabacia lankaensis : **II** FUNGIIDAE An
Podabacia motuporensis : **II** FUNGIIDAE An
Podabacia sinai : **II** FUNGIIDAE An
Podarcis lilfordi : (E) Balearic Lizard, Lilford's Wall Lizard, (S) Lagartija balear, (F) Lézard de Lilford, Lézard des Baléares, **II** LACERTIDAE Re
Podarcis pityusensis : (E) Ibiza Wall Lizard, (S) Lagarhja de las Pitiusas, Lagartija de las Pitiusas, (F) Lézard des Pityuses, Lézard d'Ibiza, **II** LACERTIDAE Re
Podilymbus gigas : (E) Atitlan Grebe, Giant Grebe, Giant Pied-billed Grebe, (S) Poc de Atitlán, Somormujo de Atitlán, Somormujo del lago Atitlán, Zambullidor de Atitlán, Zampullín del Atitlán, (F) Grèbe de l'Atitlan, Grèbe du lac Atitlan, Grèbe géant, **I** PODICIPEDIDAE Av
Podocnémide à tête rouge (F): *Podocnemis erythrocephala*
Podocnémide de Cayenne (F): *Podocnemis unifilis*
Podocnémide de Duméril (F): *Peltocephalus dumeriliana*
Podocnémide de Léwy (F): *Podocnemis lewyana*
Podocnémide de l'Orénoque (F): *Podocnemis vogli*
Podocnémide de Madagascar (F): *Erymnochelys madagascariensis*
Podocnémide de Vogl (F): *Podocnemis vogli*
Podocnémide élargie (F): *Podocnemis expansa*
Podocnémide tuberculée (F): *Podocnemis sextuberculata*
Podocnémides (F): *Podocnemis* spp.
Podocnémides à front sillonné (F): *Podocnemis* spp.
Podocnemis spp.: (E) South American river turtles, (S) Galápagos, (F) Podocnémides, Podocnémides à front sillonné, Tortues fluviatiles, **II** PELOMEDUSIDAE Re
Podocnemis cayennensis = Podocnemis erythrocephala
Podocnemis dumeriliana = Peltocephalus dumeriliana
Podocnemis erythrocephala : (E) Red-headed Amazon River Turtle, Red-headed River Turtle, Red-headed Sideneck, (S) Chimpire, (F) Podocnémide à tête rouge, **II** PELOMEDUSIDAE Re

Podocnemis expansa : (E) Arrau, Giant South American Turtle, South American River Turtle, Tartaruga, (F) Podocnémide élargie **II** PELOMEDUSIDAE Re

Podocnemis lewyana : (E) Magdalena River Turtle, Rio Magdalena River Turtle, (S) Tortuga de agua, (F) Podocnémide de Léwy, **II** PELOMEDUSIDAE Re

Podocnemis madagascariensis = Erymnochelys madagascariensis

Podocnemis sextuberculata : (E) Six-tubercled Amazon River Turtle, Six-tubercled River Turtle, (S) Cupiso, Iaça, Pitiu, (F) Podocnémide tuberculée, **II** PELOMEDUSIDAE Re

Podocnemis unifilis : (E) Yellow-headed Sideneck, Yellow-spotted River Turtle, Yellow-spotted Sideneck Turtle, (S) Terecay, (F) Podocnémide de Cayenne, **II** PELOMEDUSIDAE Re

Podocnemis vogli : (E) Llanos Sideneck Turtle, Savanna Sideneck Turtle, (F) Podocnémide de l'Orénoque, Podocnémide de Vogl **II** PELOMEDUSIDAE Re

Poephila cincta cincta : (E) Southern Black-throated Finch, (S) Diamante de pecho negro, (F) Diamant à bavette, **II** ESTRILDIDAE Av

Pohnpei Flying-fox (E): *Pteropus molossinus*

Pohnpei Lorikeet (E): *Trichoglossus rubiginosus*

Pohnpei Lory (E): *Trichoglossus rubiginosus*

Poicephalus crassus : (E) Niam-niam Parrot, (S) Lorito niam-niam, (F) Perroquet des niam-niam, **II** PSITTACIDAE Av

Poicephalus cryptoxanthus : (E) Brown-headed Parrot, (S) Lorito cabecipardo, (F) Perroquet à tête brune, **II** PSITTACIDAE Av

Poicephalus flavifrons : (E) Yellow-fronted Parrot, (S) Lorito carigualdo, (F) Perroquet à face jaune, **II** PSITTACIDAE Av

Poicephalus gulielmi : (E) Jardine's Parrot, Red-crowned Parrot, Red-fronted Parrot, (S) Lorito frentirrojo, Papagayo de Gulielm, (F) Perroquet à calotte rouge, Perroquet vert à calotte rouge, Perroquet vert du Congo, **II** PSITTACIDAE Av

Poicephalus meyeri : (E) Brown Parrot, Meyer's Parrot, (S) Lorito de Meyer, (F) Perroquet de Meyer, **II** PSITTACIDAE Av

Poicephalus robustus : (E) Brown-necked Parrot, Cape Parrot, Knysna Parrot, Levaillant's Parrot, (S) Lorito robusto, Papagayo robusto, (F) Perroquet du Cap, Perroquet robuste, **II** PSITTACIDAE Av

Poicephalus rueppellii : (E) Rueppell's Parrot, (S) Lorito de Rüppell, Rüppell's Parrot, (F) Perroquet de Rüppell, **II** PSITTACIDAE Av

Poicephalus rufiventris : (E) African Orange-bellied Parrot, Red-bellied Parrot, (S) Lorito ventrirrojo, (F) Perroquet à ventre rouge, **II** PSITTACIDAE Av

Poicephalus senegalus : (E) Senegal Parrot, (S) Lorito Senegalés, Papagayo senegalés, (F) Perroquet à tête grise, Perroquet youyou, Youyou, **II** PSITTACIDAE Av

Poison frogs (E): *Dendrobates* spp./ *Epipedobates* spp. / *Minyobates* spp./ *Phyllobates* spp.

Poisonous lizards (E): *Heloderma* spp.

Poisson à voiles (F): *Cetorhinus maximus*

Poisson cavernicole d'Afrique (F): *Caecobarbus geertsi*

Poisson spatule (F): *Polyodon spathula*

Polar Bear (E): *Ursus maritimus*

Polemaetus bellicosus : (E) Martial Eagle, (S) Aguila marcial, (F) Aigle martial, **II** ACCIPITRIDAE Av

Polihierax insignis : (E) Fielden's Falconet, White-rumped Falcon, White-rumped Falconet, (S) Halconcito asiático, Halconcito colilargo de Asia, (F) Fauconnet à pattes jaunes, **II** FALCONIDAE Av

Polihierax semitorquatus : (E) African Pygmy Falcon, Pygmy Falcon, (S) Halconcito africano, (F) Fauconnet d'Afrique, **II** FALCONIDAE Av

Polkadot Poison Frog (E): *Dendrobates arboreus*

Pollack Whale (E): *Balaenoptera borealis*

Polyboroides radiatus : (E) Madagascar Gymnogene, Madagascar Harrier-Hawk, (S) Aguilucho-caricalvo malgache, Azor culebrero, (F) Gymnogène de Madagascar, Petit serpentaire, **II** ACCIPITRIDAE Av

Polyboroides typus : (E) African Gymnogene, African Harrier-Hawk, Gymnogene, (S) Aguilucho-caricalvo común, (F) Gymnogène d'Afrique, **II** ACCIPITRIDAE Av

Polyborus lutosus : (E) Guadalupe Caracara, (S) Carancho de Guadalupe, (F) Caracara de Guadalupe, **II** FALCONIDAE Av

Polyborus plancus : (E) Common Caracara, Crested Caracara, Southern Caracara, (S) Caracara carancho, Caracara común, Carancho, Caricare encrestado, Traro, (F) Caracara commun, Caracara huppé, **II** FALCONIDAE Av

Polycyathus andamanensis : **II** CARYOPHYLLIIDAE An

Polycyathus atlanticus : **II** CARYOPHYLLIIDAE An

Polycyathus banyulensis = Polycyathus muellerae

Polycyathus conceptus = Paracyathus conceptus

Polycyathus difficilis : **II** CARYOPHYLLIIDAE An

Polycyathus fulvus : **II** CARYOPHYLLIIDAE An

Polycyathus furanaensis : **II** CARYOPHYLLIIDAE An

Polycyathus fuscomarginatus : **II** CARYOPHYLLIIDAE An

Polycyathus hodgsoni : **II** CARYOPHYLLIIDAE An

Polycyathus hondaensis : **II** CARYOPHYLLIIDAE An

Polycyathus isabela : **II** CARYOPHYLLIIDAE An

Polycyathus marigondoni : **II** CARYOPHYLLIIDAE An

Polycyathus mayae : **II** CARYOPHYLLIIDAE An

Polycyathus mediterraneus = Polycyathus muellerae

Polycyathus muellerae : **II** CARYOPHYLLIIDAE An

Polycyathus norfolkensis : **II** CARYOPHYLLIIDAE An

Polycyathus octuplus : **II** CARYOPHYLLIIDAE Av

Polycyathus palifera : **II** CARYOPHYLLIIDAE An

Polycyathus pallidus = Polycyathus fuscomarginatus

Polycyathus persicus : **II** CARYOPHYLLIIDAE An

Polycyathus senegalensis : **II** CARYOPHYLLIIDAE An

Polycyathus verrilli : **II** CARYOPHYLLIIDAE An

Polyerata amabilis : (E) Blue-chested Hummingbird, (S) Amazilia amable, Amazilia pechiazul, (F) Ariane aimable, **II** TROCHILIDAE Av

Polyerata boucardi : (E) Mangrove Hummingbird, (S) Amazilia de manglar, (F) Ariane de Boucard, **II** TROCHILIDAE Av

Polyerata fimbriata : (E) Glittering-throated Emerald, (S) Amazilia gorjibrillante, Amazilia listada, Diamante gargantiverde, (F) Ariane de Linné, **II** TROCHILIDAE Av

Polyerata lactea : (E) Sapphire-spangled Emerald, (S) Amazilia zafirina, Diamante pechizafiro, (F) Ariane saphirine, **II** TROCHILIDAE Av

Polyerata luciae : (E) Honduran Emerald, (S) Amazilia Hondureña, Esmeralda Hondurena, (F) Ariane de Lucy, **II** TROCHILIDAE Av

Polyerata rosenbergi : (E) Purple-chested Hummingbird, (S) Amazilia de Rosenberg, Amazilia pechimorada, (F) Ariane de Rosenberg, **II** TROCHILIDAE Av

Polymyces fragilis : (E) Twelve-root Cup Coral **II** FLABELLIDAE An

Polymyces montereyensis : **II** FLABELLIDAE An

Polymyces tannerensis = Polymyces montereyensis

Polymyces wellsi : **II** FLABELLIDAE An

Polyodon angustifolium = Psephurus gladius

Polyodon gladius = Psephurus gladius

Polyodon spathula : (E) Duckbill Cat, Mississippi paddlefish, Paddlefish, Spadefish, Spoonbill Cat, Spoonbill catfish, (S) Pez espátula, Sollo, (F) Poisson spatule, **II** POLYODONTIDAE Ac

Polyonymus caroli : (E) Bronze-tailed Comet, (S) Colibrí colibronce, (F) Colibri de Bourcier, **II** TROCHILIDAE Av

Polyphyllia novaehiberniae : **II** FUNGIIDAE An

Polyphyllia talpina : (E) Feather Coral, Joker's Boomerang Coral, Sea Mole Coral, Slipper Coral **II** FUNGIIDAE An

Polyplancta aurescens = Heliodoxa aurescens

Polyplectron bicalcaratum : (E) Common Peacock-Pheasant, Grey Peacock-Pheasant, Iris Peacock-Pheasant, (S) Espolonero chinquis, Faisán de cola ocelada gris, Faisán de espolones gris, Faisán real gris, (F) Éperonnier chinquis, Éperonnier gris, **II** PHASIANIDAE Av

Polyplectron emphanum : (E) Napoleon's Peacock-Pheasant, Palawan Peacock-Pheasant, (S) Espolonero de Palawan, Faisán de espolones de Palawan, Faisán real de Palaguán, (F) Éperonnier de Palawan, Éperonnier Napoléon, **I** PHASIANIDAE Av

Polyplectron germaini : (E) Germain's Peacock-Pheasant, (S) Espolonero de Germain, Faisán de cola ocelada de Germain, Faisán de espolones de Germain, Faisán real de Germain, (F) Éperonnier de Germain, **II** PHASIANIDAE Av

Polyplectron inopinatum : (E) Mountain Peacock-Pheasant, Rothschild's Peacock-Pheasant, (S) Espolonero de Rothschild, Faisán de cola ocelada indómito, (F) Éperonnier de Rothschild, **III** PHASIANIDAE Av

Polyplectron katsumatae = Polyplectron bicalcaratum

Polyplectron malacense : (E) Crested Peacock-Pheasant, Malayan Peacock-Pheasant, (S) Espolonero Malayo, Faisán de cola ocelada malayo, Faisán de espolones malayo, Faisán real malayo, (F) Éperonnier de Hardwick, Éperonnier de Malaisie, Éperonnier malais, **II** PHASIANIDAE Av

Polyplectron malacense ssp. *schleiermacheri = Polyplectron schleiermacheri*

Polyplectron napoleonis = Polyplectron emphanum

Polyplectron schleiermacheri : (E) Bornean Peacock-Pheasant, (S) Espolonero de Borneo, Faisán de espolones de Borneo, (F) Éperonnier de Bornéo, **II** PHASIANIDAE Av

Polyprosopus macer = Cetorhinus maximus

Polytelis alexandrae : (E) Alexandra's Parrot, Princess of Wales Parakeet, Princess Parrot, (S) Perico princesa, (F) Perruche à calotte bleue, Perruche d'Alexandra, Perruche princesse, **II** PSITTACIDAE Av

Polytelis anthopeplus : (E) Regent Parrot, Rock Pebbler, (S) Perico regente, (F) Perruche mélanure, **II** PSITTACIDAE Av

Polytelis swainsonii : (E) Barraband Parakeet, Green Leek Parrot, Superb Parrot, (S) Perico soberbio, (F) Perruche de Barraband, **II** PSITTACIDAE Av

Polytmus guainumbi : (E) White-tailed Goldenthroat, (S) Colibrí gargantidorado, Colibrí guainumbí, Picaflor coliverde, (F) Colibri guaïnumbi, **II** TROCHILIDAE Av

Polytmus milleri : (E) Tepui Goldenthroat, (S) Colibrí de tepui, (F) Colibri des tépuis, **II** TROCHILIDAE Av

Polytmus theresiae : (E) Green-tailed Goldenthroat, (S) Colibrí de Teresa, Garganta de oro coliverde, (F) Colibri tout-vert, **II** TROCHILIDAE Av

Pondicherry Vulture (E): *Sarcogyps calvus*

Pongo abelii = Pongo pygmaeus

Pongo pygmaeus : (E) Orang-utan, (S) Orangután, (F) Orang-outan, **I** HOMINIDAE Ma

Pontoporia blainvillei : (E) Franciscana, La Plata River Dolphin, (S) Delfín de la Plata, Tonina, (F) Dauphin de la Plata, **II** PLATANISTIDAE Ma

Popelairia conversii = Discosura conversii

Popelairia langsdorffi = Discosura langsdorffi

Popelairia letitiae = Discosura letitiae

Popelairia popelairii = Discosura popelairii

Porc-épic à crête (F): *Hystrix cristata*

Porc-épic du nord de l'Afrique (F): *Hystrix cristata*

Porc-épic préhensile (F): *Sphiggurus mexicanus*

Porcula Hermit (E): *Phaethornis griseogularis*

Pore corals (E): *Montipora spp./ Porites spp.*

Porites spp.: (E) Boulder corals, Pore corals **II** PORITIDAE An

Porites annae : **II** PORITIDAE An

Porites aranetai : **II** PORITIDAE An

Porites arnaudi : **II** PORITIDAE An

Porites astreoides : (E) Mustard Hill Coral **II** PORITIDAE An

Porites attenuata : **II** PORITIDAE An

Porites australiensis : **II** PORITIDAE An

Porites baueri : **II** PORITIDAE An

Porites branneri : (E) Blue Crust Coral **II** PORITIDAE An

Porites brighami : **II** PORITIDAE An

Porites californica = Porites panamensis

Porites cocosensis : **II** PORITIDAE An

Porites colonensis : (E) Honeycomb Plate Coral **II** PORITIDAE An

Porites columnaris : **II** PORITIDAE An

Porites compressa : **II** PORITIDAE An

Porites cumulatus : **II** PORITIDAE An

Porites cylindrica : (E) Branching Coral, Finger Coral **II** PORITIDAE An

Porites danae = Psammocora contigua

Porites deformis : **II** PORITIDAE An

Porites densa : **II** PORITIDAE An

Porites desilveri : **II** PORITIDAE An

Porites divaricata : (E) Thin Finger Coral **II** PORITIDAE An

Porites echinulata : **II** PORITIDAE An

Porites eridani : **II** PORITIDAE An

Porites evermanni : **II** PORITIDAE An

Porites faustinoi = Porites rus

Porites flavus : **II** PORITIDAE An

Porites furcata : (E) Branched Finger Coral **II** PORITIDAE An

Porites gabonensis : **II** PORITIDAE An

Porites harrisoni : **II** PORITIDAE An

Porites hawaiiensis = Porites rus

Porites heronensis : **II** PORITIDAE An

Porites horizontalata : **II** PORITIDAE An

Porites iwayamaensis : **II** PORITIDAE An

Porites latistellata : **II** PORITIDAE An

Porites lichen : **II** PORITIDAE An

Porites lobata : **II** PORITIDAE An

Porites lutea : **II** PORITIDAE An

Porites mayeri : **II** PORITIDAE An

Porites monticulosa : **II** PORITIDAE An

Porites murrayensis : **II** PORITIDAE An

Porites myrmidonensis : **II** PORITIDAE An

Porites napopora : **II** PORITIDAE An

Porites negrosensis : **II** PORITIDAE An

Porites nigrescens : **II** PORITIDAE An

Porites nodifera : **II** PORITIDAE An

Porites nodulosa = Porites panamensis

Porites okinawensis : **II** PORITIDAE An

Porites ornata : **II** PORITIDAE An

Porites palmata = Porites cylindrica

Porites panamensis : **II** PORITIDAE An

Porites porites : (E) Club Finger Coral, Clubtip Finger Coral **II** PORITIDAE An

Porites profundus : **II** PORITIDAE An

Porites pukoensis : **II** PORITIDAE An

Porites rugosa : **II** PORITIDAE An

Porites rus : **II** PORITIDAE An

Porites sillimaniani : **II** PORITIDAE An

Porites solida : **II** PORITIDAE An

Porites somaliensis : **II** PORITIDAE An

Porites stephensoni : **II** PORITIDAE An

Porites sverdrupi : **II** PORITIDAE An

Porites tuberculosa : **II** PORITIDAE An

Porites undulata : **II** PORITIDAE An

Porites vaughani : **II** PORITIDAE An

Poritipora paliformis : **II** PORITIDAE An

Poroto Mountain Chameleon (E): *Chamaeleo incornutus*

Checklist of fauna/Lista de especies de fauna/Liste des espèces animales

Poroto Three-horned Chameleon (E): *Chamaeleo fuelleborni*
Porous Cup Coral (E): *Balanophyllia floridana*
Porous star corals (E): *Astreopora* spp.
Porpoises (E): CETACEA spp. Ma
Porrón pardo (S): *Aythya nyroca*
Port Lincoln Ringneck (E): *Barnardius zonarius*
Porte-lance de Jeanne (F): *Doryfera johannae*
Porte-lance de Louise (F): *Doryfera ludovicae*
Porte-musc (F): *Moschus moschiferus*
Porte-Musc (F): *Moschus moschiferus moschiferus*
Portemusc (F): *Moschus* spp.
Portequeue de Corse (F): *Papilio hospiton*
Porte-queue de Corse (F): *Papilio hospiton*
Portequeue Homerus (F): *Papilio homerus*
Porte-traîne lesbie (F): *Lesbia victoriae*
Porte-traîne nouna (F): *Lesbia nuna*
Pot whale (E): *Physeter catodon*
Potamilus capax : (E) Fat Pocketbook, Fat Pocketbook Pearly Mussel **I** UNIONIDAE Bi
Potato-chip corals (E): *Pavona* spp.
Pot-bellied Seahorse (E): *Hippocampus abdominalis*
Poto de Bosman (S): *Perodicticus potto*
Poto dorado (S): *Arctocebus calabarensis*
Potos (F): *Potos flavus*
Potos flavus : (E) Kinkajou, (S) Chosna, Cuchumbi, Cusumbi, Godoy, Marta, Martucha, Mico de noche, Micoleón, (F) Potos, **III** PROCYONIDAE Ma
Potto (E/F): *Perodicticus potto*
Potto de Calabar (F): *Arctocebus calabarensis*
Potto Gibbon (E): *Perodicticus potto*
Poudou du nord (F): *Pudu mephistophiles*
Poudou du sud (F): *Pudu puda*
Poule de prairie d'Attwater (F): *Tympanuchus cupido attwateri*
Pourtalocyathus hispidus : **II** GUYNIIDAE An
Pourtalosmilia anthophyllites : **II** CARYOPHYLLIIDAE An
Pourtalosmilia conferta : **II** CARYOPHYLLIIDAE An
Powerful Owl (E): *Ninox strenua*
Prairie Falcon (E): *Falco mexicanus*
Prehensile-tailed Skink (E): *Corucia zebrata*
Premocyathus cornuformis : (E) Lesser Horn Coral **II** CARYOPHYLLIIDAE An
Premocyathus dentiformis : **II** CARYOPHYLLIIDAE An
Presbytis auratus = Trachypithecus auratus
Presbytis aygula = Presbytis comata
Presbytis comata : (E) Grizzled Leaf Monkey, Java Leaf Monkey, (S) Langur gris **II** CERCOPITHECIDAE Ma
Presbytis comata ssp. *hosei = Presbytis hosei*
Presbytis comata ssp. *thomasi = Presbytis thomasi*
Presbytis cristata = Trachypithecus cristatus
Presbytis entellus = Semnopithecus entellus
Presbytis femoralis : (E) Banded Langur, Banded Leaf Monkey, (S) Langur mitrado **II** CERCOPITHECIDAE Ma
Presbytis francoisi = Trachypithecus francoisi
Presbytis frontata : (E) White-faced Langur, White-fronted Leaf Monkey, (S) Langur de frente blanca, (F) Semnopithèque à front blanc, **II** CERCOPITHECIDAE Ma
Presbytis geei = Trachypithecus geei
Presbytis hosei : (E) Grey Leaf Monkey, Hose's Leaf Monkey, (S) Langur de Hose, (F) Semnopithèque de Hose, **II** CERCOPITHECIDAE Ma
Presbytis johnii = Trachypithecus johnii
Presbytis melalophos : (E) Mitred Leaf Monkey, (S) Langur de cresta, (F) Semnopithèque mélalophe, **II** CERCOPITHECIDAE Ma
Presbytis melalophos ssp. *femoralis = Presbytis femoralis*
Presbytis obscura = Trachypithecus obscurus
Presbytis phayrei = Trachypithecus phayrei
Presbytis pileata = Trachypithecus pileatus

Presbytis potenziani: (E) Long-tailed Langur, Mentawai Langur, Mentawai Leaf Monkey, (S) Langur colilargo, Langur de Mentawi, (F) Semnopithèque de Mentawi, **I** CERCOPITHECIDAE Ma
Presbytis rubicunda : (E) Maroon Langur, Maroon Leaf Monkey, (S) Langur rubicundo, (F) Semnopithèque rubicond, **II** CERCOPITHECIDAE Ma
Presbytis senex = Trachypithecus vetulus
Presbytis thomasi : (E) Thomas's Langur, Thomas's Leaf Monkey, (S) Langur de Thomas, (F) Semnopithèque de Thomas, **II** CERCOPITHECIDAE Ma
Presbytis vetulus = Trachypithecus vetulus
Preuss's Colobus (E): *Procolobus preussi*
Preuss's Guenon (E): *Cercopithecus preussi*
Preuss's Monkey (E): *Cercopithecus preussi*
Preuss's Red Colobus (E): *Procolobus preussi*
Preuss's Weaver (E): *Ploceus preussi*
Priam's Birdwing (E): *Ornithoptera priamus*
Prickly Chameleon (E): *Bradypodion spinosum*
Prickly Girdled Lizard (E): *Cordylus spinosus*
Prigogine's Owlet (E): *Glaucidium albertinum*
Primates (E): PRIMATES spp. Ma
PRIMATES spp. : (E) Apes, Monkeys, Primates, (S) Monos, Primates, (F) Primates, **I/II** Ma
Primolius auricollis = Propyrrhura auricollis
Primolius couloni = Propyrrhura couloni
Primolius maracana = Propyrrhura maracana
Prince Albert's Curassow (E): *Crax alberti*
Prince Ruspoli's Turaco (E): *Tauraco ruspolii*
Princely Mastigure (E): *Uromastyx princeps*
Princess of Wales Parakeet (E): *Polytelis alexandrae*
Princess Parrot (E): *Polytelis alexandrae*
Princess Stephanie's Bird-of-paradise (E): *Astrapia stephaniae*
Priodontes giganteus = Priodontes maximus
Priodontes maximus : (E) Giant Armadillo, (S) Armadillo gigante, Carachupa Manan, Cuspon, Tatú carreta, Tatú gigante, Tatú guazú, (F) Tatou géant, **I** DASYPODIDAE Ma
Prionailurus bengalensis : (E) Leopard Cat, (S) Gato bengalí, Gato de Bengala, (F) Chat de Chine, Chat-léopard du Bengale, **I/II** FELIDAE Ma
Prionailurus bengalensis bengalensis : (E) Bengal Leopard Cat, (S) Gato leopardo chino, (F) Chat-léopard de Chine, Chat-tigre du Bengale, **I/II** FELIDAE Ma
Prionailurus iriomotensis = Prionailurus bengalensis ssp. *iriomotensis*
Prionailurus planiceps : (E) Flat-headed Cat, (S) Gato cabeciancho, Gato de cabeza plana, (F) Chat à tête plate, **I** FELIDAE Ma
Prionailurus rubiginosus : (E) Rusty-spotted Cat, (S) Gato leopardo de la India, Gato rojizo, Gato rubiginosa, (F) Chat rougeâtre, Chat rubigineux, Chat-léopard de l'Inde, **I/II** FELIDAE Ma
Prionailurus viverrinus : (E) Fishing Cat, (S) Gato pescador, (F) Chat pêcheur, **II** FELIDAE Ma
Prioniturus discurus : (E) Blue-crowned Racquet-tail, Palawan Racket-tailed Parrot, (S) Lorito-momoto coroniazul, (F) Palette à couronne bleue, **II** PSITTACIDAE Av
Prioniturus discurus ssp. *platenae = Prioniturus platenae*
Prioniturus discurus ssp. *verticalis = Prioniturus verticalis*
Prioniturus flavicans : (E) Yellow-breasted Racquet-tail, Yellowish-breasted Racquet-tail, (S) Lorito-momoto amarillento, (F) Palette de Cassin, **II** PSITTACIDAE Av
Prioniturus luconensis : (E) Green Racquet-tail, Green-crowned Racket-tailed Parrot, Green-headed Racket-tailed Parrot, (S) Lorito-momoto de Luzón, (F) Palette verte, **II** PSITTACIDAE Av
Prioniturus mada : (E) Buru Racquet-tail, (S) Lorito-momoto de Buru, (F) Palette de Buru, **II** PSITTACIDAE Av

Prioniturus montanus : (E) Luzon Racquet-tail, Montane Racquet-tail, (S) Lorito-momoto montano, (F) Palette momot, **II** PSITTACIDAE Av

Prioniturus montanus ssp. *waterstradti* = *Prioniturus waterstradti*

Prioniturus platenae : (E) Blue-headed Racquet-tail, (S) Lorito-momoto de Palawan, (F) Palette de Palawan, **II** PSITTACIDAE Av

Prioniturus platurus : (E) Golden-mantled Racquet-tail, (S) Lorito-momoto dorsidorado, (F) Palette à manteau d'or, **II** PSITTACIDAE Av

Prioniturus verticalis : (E) Blue-winged Racquet-tail, (S) Lorito-momoto de las Sulu, (F) Palette des Sulu, **II** PSITTACIDAE Av

Prioniturus waterstradti : (E) Mindanao Racquet-tail, (S) Lorito-momoto de Mindanao, (F) Palette de Mindanao, **II** PSITTACIDAE Av

Prionodon linsang : (E) Banded Linsang, (S) Cibeta atigrada, Civeta franjeada, Linsang rayado, (F) Civette à bandes, Linsang rayé, **II** VIVERRIDAE Ma

Prionodon pardicolor : (E) Spotted Linsang, Tiger Civet, (S) Cibeta moteada, Linsang manchado, (F) Linsang à taches, Linsang tacheté, **I** VIVERRIDAE Ma

Probarbus jullieni : (E) Esok, Giant river carp, Ikan temoleh, Isok barb, Jullien's Golden Carp, Seven-line barb, Seven-striped Barb, (S) Carpilla ikan temoleh, (F) Barbeau de Jullien, Plaa eesok , Plan temoleh, **I** CYPRINIDAE Ac

Probosciger aterrimus : (E) Palm Cockatoo, (S) Cacatúa enlutada, (F) Cacatoès noir, Microglosse noir, **I** PSITTACIDAE Av

Proboscis Monkey (E): *Nasalis larvatus*

Procolobus badius : (E) Red Colobus, Western Red Colobus, (S) Colobo herrumbroso occidental, (F) Colobe bai, Colobe bai d'Afrique occidentale, Colobe ferrugineux, **II** CERCOPITHECIDAE Ma

Procolobus badius ssp. *gordonorum* = *Procolobus pennantii* ssp. *gordonorum*

Procolobus badius ssp. *kirkii* = *Procolobus pennantii* ssp. *kirkii*

Procolobus badius ssp. *preussi* = *Procolobus preussi*

Procolobus badius ssp. *rufomitratus* = *Procolobus rufomitratus*

Procolobus gordonorum = *Procolobus pennantii* ssp. *gordonorum*

Procolobus kirkii = *Procolobus pennantii* ssp. *kirkii*

Procolobus pennantii : (E) Eastern Red Colobus, (S) Colobo rojo, (F) Colobe bai, **I/II** CERCOPITHECIDAE Ma

Procolobus pennantii kirkii : (E) Kirk's Colobus, Kirk's Red Colobus, Zanzibar Red Colobus, (S) Colobo rojo de Zanzíbar, (F) Colobe bai de Zanzibar, **I** CERCOPITHECIDAE Ma

Procolobus pennantii ssp. *preussi* = *Procolobus preussi*

Procolobus preussi : (E) Preuss's Colobus, Preuss's Red Colobus, (S) Colobo rojo de Camerún, (F) Colobe bai du Cameroun, **II** CERCOPITHECIDAE Ma

Procolobus rufomitratus : (E) Tana River Colobus, (S) Colobo de Tana, Colobo rojo mitrado, (F) Colobe bai de la Tana, Colobe roux de la Tana, **I** CERCOPITHECIDAE Ma

Procolobus rufomitratus ssp. *rufomitratus* = *Procolobus rufomitratus*

Procolobus verus : (E) Olive Colobus, Van Beneden's Colobus, (S) Colobo verde, (F) Colobe à huppé, Colobe de Van Beneden, Colobe vert, Colobe vrai, **II** CERCOPITHECIDAE Ma

Profelis aurata : (E) African Golden Cat, Golden Cat, (S) Gato dorado, (F) Chat doré, **II** FELIDAE Ma

Proméfil (F): *Ptiloris magnificus*

Pronghorn (E/F): *Antilocapra americana*

Pronk's Day Gecko (E): *Phelsuma pronki*

Propithecus diadema : (E) Diademed Sifaka, (S) Indris sifaca, Sifaka diademado, (F) Propithèque à diadème, **I** INDRIDAE Ma

Propithecus tattersalli : (E) Golden-crowned Sifaka, Tattersall's Sifaka, (S) Indris sifaca **I** INDRIDAE Ma

Propithecus verreauxi : (E) Verreaux's Sifaka, (S) Gran sifaka blanco, Indris sifaca, (F) Propithèque de Verreaux, Sifaka, **I** INDRIDAE Ma

Propithèque à diadème (F): *Propithecus diadema*

Propithèque de Verreaux (F): *Propithecus verreauxi*

Propithéques (F): INDRIDAE spp.

Propyrrhura auricollis : (E) Golden-collared Macaw, Yellow-collared Macaw, (S) Guacamayo acollarado, Maracana cuellidorada, (F) Ara à collier jaune, Ara à nuque d'or, **II** PSITTACIDAE Av

Propyrrhura couloni : (E) Blue-headed Macaw, (S) Guacamayo cabeciazul, (F) Ara de Coulon, **I** PSITTACIDAE Av

Propyrrhura maracana : (E) Blue-winged Macaw, Illiger's Macaw, (S) Guacamayo de Illiger, Guacamayo maracaná, Maracana dorsirroja, (F) Ara d'Illiger, Ara miracana, **I** PSITTACIDAE Av

Prosopeia personata : (E) Masked Shining-Parrot, (S) Papagayo enmascarado, (F) Perruche masquée, **II** PSITTACIDAE Av

Prosopeia splendens : (E) Crimson Shining-Parrot, (S) Papagayo escarlata, (F) Perruche écarlate, **II** PSITTACIDAE Av

Prosopeia tabuensis : (E) Red Shining-Parrot, (S) Papagayo granate, (F) Perruche pompadour, **II** PSITTACIDAE Av

Prosopeia tabuensis ssp. *splendens* = *Prosopeia splendens*

Protèle (F): *Proteles cristatus*

Proteles cristatus : (E) Aardwolf, (S) Lobo de tierra, (F) Protèle, **III** HYAENIDAE Ma

Przewalski's Horse (E): *Equus przewalskii*

Przewalski's Wild Horse (E): *Equus przewalskii*

Psammobates geometricus : (E) Geometric Tortoise, (S) Sacafi, Tortuga geométrica, (F) Sakafi, Tortue géométrique, **I** TESTUDINIDAE Re

Psammobates oculiferus : (E) African Serrated Tortoise, Kuhl's Tortoise, Serrated Star Tortoise, Serrated Tent Tortoise, Toothed Cape Tortoise, (S) Tortuga estrellada sudafricana de caparazón, (F) Tortue ocelée, **II** TESTUDINIDAE Re

Psammobates tentorius : (E) African Tent Tortoise, South African Tent Tortoise, (S) Tortuga estrellada sudafricana, (F) Tortue bosselée, **II** TESTUDINIDAE Re

Psammocora brighami : **II** SIDERASTREIDAE An

Psammocora contigua : **II** SIDERASTREIDAE An

Psammocora decussata : **II** SIDERASTREIDAE An

Psammocora digitata : **II** SIDERASTREIDAE An

Psammocora explanulata : **II** SIDERASTREIDAE An

Psammocora haimiana : **II** SIDERASTREIDAE An

Psammocora nierstraszi : **II** SIDERASTREIDAE An

Psammocora obtusangula : **II** SIDERASTREIDAE An

Psammocora profundacella : **II** SIDERASTREIDAE An

Psammocora stellata : **II** SIDERASTREIDAE An

Psammocora superficialis : **II** SIDERASTREIDAE An

Psammocora vaughani : **II** SIDERASTREIDAE An

Psammocora verrilli : **II** SIDERASTREIDAE An

Psephotus chrysopterygius : (E) Golden-shouldered Parrot, (S) Cacatúa de alas doradas, Loro hombroamarillo, Perico aligualdo, Periquito de espalda dorada, (F) Perruche à ailes d'or, Perruche à épaules dorées, Perruche aux ailes d'or, **I** PSITTACIDAE Av

Psephotus chrysopterygius ssp. *dissimilis* = *Psephotus dissimilis*

Psephotus dissimilis : (E) Hooded Parrot, (S) Perico capirotado, Periquito encapuchado, (F) Perruche à capuchon, Perruche à capuchon noir, **I** PSITTACIDAE Av

Psephotus haematogaster = *Northiella haematogaster*

Psephotus haematogaster ssp. *narethae* = *Northiella haematogaster* ssp. *narethae*

201

Psephotus haematonotus : (E) Red-rumped Parrot, (S) Perico dorsirrojo, (F) Perruche à croupion rouge, Perruche à dos rouge, **II** PSITTACIDAE Av

Psephotus pulcherrimus : (E) Beautiful Parakeet, Paradise Parrot, (S) Cacatúa del paraíso, Loro del paraíso, Perico del Paraíso, (F) Perruche de paradis, Perruche magnifique, **I** PSITTACIDAE Av

Psephotus varius : (E) Many-coloured Parakeet, Mulga Parrot, (S) Perico variado, (F) Perruche à croupion rouge, Perruche multicolore, **II** PSITTACIDAE Av

Psephurus gladius : (E) Chinese Paddlefish, Chinese Swordfish, Paddlefish **II** POLYODONTIDAE Ac

Pseudalopex culpaeus : (E) Andean Wolf, Colpeo Fox, Culpeo, Red Fox, (S) Culpeo, Zorro andino, Zorro colorado, (F) Renard colfeo, **II** CANIDAE Ma

Pseudalopex fulvipes = Pseudalopex griseus

Pseudalopex griseus : (E) Argentine Grey Fox, Chico Grey Fox, Chiloe Fox, Grey Zorro, Little Fox, Pampa Fox, (S) Chilla, Zorro chico, Zorro de la Isla Chiloe, Zorro gris argentino, (F) Renard de Chiloé, Renard gris d'Argentine, **II** CANIDAE Ma

Pseudalopex gymnocercus : (E) Azara's Zorro, Pampa Fox, (S) Zorro de la Pampa, (F) Renard d'Azara, Renard de la Pampa, **II** CANIDAE Ma

Pseudemydura umbrina : (E) Western Short-necked Turtle, Western Swamp Turtle, (S) Tortuga occidental de cuello de serpiente, Tortuga serpentina occidental, (F) Pseudémydure de Perth, Tortue à col court, Tortues des étangs de Perth, **I** CHELIDAE Re

Pseudémydure de Perth (F): *Pseudemydura umbrina*

Pseudeos fuscata : (E) Dusky Lory, (S) Lori sombrio, (F) Lori orange sombre, Lori sombre, **II** PSITTACIDAE Av

Pseudoboa clelia = Clelia clelia

Pseudochelidon sirintarae : (E) White-eyed River-Martin, (S) Golondrina de anteojos, (F) Hirondelle à lunettes, Pseudolangrayen d'Asie, **I** HIRUNDINIDAE Av

Pseudocordyle de Lang (F): *Cordylus langi*

Pseudocordyle des rochers (F): *Cordylus microlepidotus*

Pseudocordyle du Cap (F): *Cordylus capensis*

Pseudocordyle du Drakensberg (F): *Cordylus melanotus*

Pseudocordyle épineux (F): *Cordylus spinosus*

Pseudocordyles (F): *Cordylus* spp.

Pseudocordylus capensis = Cordylus capensis

Pseudocordylus langi = Cordylus langi

Pseudocordylus melanotus = Cordylus melanotus

Pseudocordylus microlepidotus = Cordylus microlepidotus

Pseudocordylus microlepidotus ssp. *melanotus = Cordylus melanotus*

Pseudocordylus nebulosus = Cordylus nebulosus

Pseudocordylus spinosus = Cordylus spinosus

Pseudocrypthelia pachypoma : **II** STYLASTERIDAE Hy

Pseudocyathoceras avis : **II** TURBINOLIIDAE An

Pseudolangrayen d'Asie (F): *Pseudochelidon sirintarae*

Pseudomys praeconis : (E) Shark Bay Mouse, (S) Falso ratón de la Bahía de Shark, Ratón bastardo peludo, (F) Fausse souris de la baie de Shark, Souris de la baie de Shark, **I** MURIDAE Ma

Pseudopotto martini : (E) False Potto **II** LORIDAE Ma

Pseudoptynx philippensis = Bubo philippensis

Pseudorca crassidens : (E) False Killer Whale, (S) Orca falsa, (F) Faux-orque, **II** DELPHINIDAE Ma

Pseudoryx nghetinhensis : (E) Saola, Vu Quang Ox, (S) Saola, Ver nota pie de página, (F) Saola, **I** BOVIDAE Ma

Pseudoscaphirhynchus fedtschenkoi : (E) Syr Darya sturgeon, Syr-Dar Shovelnose Sturgeon, Syr-Darya shovelnose **II** ACIPENSERIDAE Ac

Pseudoscaphirhynchus hermanni : (E) Dwarf Sturgeon, Little Amu-Darya shovelnose, Little shovelnose sturgeon, Small Amu-Dar Shovelnose Sturgeon **II** ACIPENSERIDAE Ac

Pseudoscaphirhynchus kaufmanni : (E) Amu Darya shovelnose sturgeon, Amu Darya sturgeon, Big Amu-Darya shovelnose, False Shovelnose Sturgeon, Large Amu-Dar Shovelnose Sturgeon, Shovelfish **II** ACIPENSERIDAE Ac

Pseudoscops grammicus : (E) Jamaican Owl, (S) Búho de Jamaica, Búho Jamaicano, (F) Hibou de la Jamaïque, **II** STRIGIDAE Av

Pseudosiderastrea tayamai : **II** SIDERASTREIDAE An

Psilopsiagon aurifrons : (E) Golden-fronted Parakeet, Mountain Parakeet, (S) Catita frentidorada, Catita serrana verde, (F) Toui à bandeau jaune, **II** PSITTACIDAE Av

Psilopsiagon aymara : (E) Grey-hooded Parakeet, Sierra Parakeet, (S) Catita aimará, Catita serrana común, (F) Perruche d'Aymara, Toui aymara, **II** PSITTACIDAE Av

Psittacella brehmii : (E) Brehm's Tiger-Parrot, (S) Lorito-tigre de Brehm, (F) Perruche de Brehm, **II** PSITTACIDAE Av

Psittacella madaraszi : (E) Madarasz's Tiger-Parrot, (S) Lorito-tigre de Madarasz, (F) Perruche de Madarasz, **II** PSITTACIDAE Av

Psittacella modesta : (E) Modest Tiger-Parrot, (S) Lorito-tigre modesto, (F) Perruche modeste, **II** PSITTACIDAE Av

Psittacella picta : (E) Painted Tiger-Parrot, (S) Lorito-tigre pintado, (F) Perruche peinte, **II** PSITTACIDAE Av

PSITTACIFORMES spp. : (E) Parrots, Psittacines, (S) Loros, Papagayos, (F) Perruches, **I/II/III/NC** Av

Psittacines (E): PSITTACIFORMES spp. Av

Psittacula alexandri : (E) Moustached Parakeet, Red-breasted Parakeet, (S) Cotorra pechirroja, (F) Perruche à moustaches, **II** PSITTACIDAE Av

Psittacula calthropae : (E) Emerald-collared Parakeet, Layard's Parakeet, (S) Cotorra de ceilán, (F) Perruche de Layard, **II** PSITTACIDAE Av

Psittacula caniceps : (E) Blyth's Parakeet, Nicobar Parakeet, (S) Cotorra de Nicobar, (F) Perruche des Nicobar, **II** PSITTACIDAE Av

Psittacula columboides : (E) Malabar Parakeet, (S) Cotorra de Malabar, (F) Perruche de Malabar, **II** PSITTACIDAE Av

Psittacula cyanocephala : (E) Plum-headed Parakeet, (S) Cotorra ciruela, (F) Perruche à tête prune, **II** PSITTACIDAE Av

Psittacula derbiana : (E) Derbyan Parakeet, (S) Cotorra de Derby, (F) Perruche de Derby, **II** PSITTACIDAE Av

Psittacula echo : (E) Mauritius Parakeet, Mauritius Ring-necked Parakeet, (S) Cacatúa del collar de Mauricio, Cotorra de Mauricio, (F) Grosse cateau verte de Maurice, Perruche à collier de Maurice, Perruche de l'île Maurice, Perruche de Maurice, **I** PSITTACIDAE Av

Psittacula eques = Psittacula echo

Psittacula eques ssp. *echo = Psittacula echo*

Psittacula eupatria : (E) Alexandrine Parakeet, (S) Cotorra alejandrina, (F) Perruche alexandre, **II** PSITTACIDAE Av

Psittacula exsul : (E) Newton's Parakeet, (F) Perruche de Newton **II** PSITTACIDAE Av

Psittacula finschii : (E) Grey-headed Parakeet, (S) Cotorra de Finsch, (F) Perruche de Finsch, **II** PSITTACIDAE Av

Psittacula himalayana : (E) Slaty-headed Parakeet, (S) Cotorra del Himalaya, (F) Perruche à tête ardoisée, Perruche de l'Himalaya, **II** PSITTACIDAE Av

Psittacula himalayana ssp. *finschii = Psittacula finschii*

Psittacula intermedia : (E) Intermediate Parakeet, Rothschild's Parakeet, (S) Cotorra intermedia, (F) Perruche intermédiaire, **II** PSITTACIDAE Av

Psittacula krameri : (E) Ring-necked Parakeet, Rose-ringed Parakeet, (S) Cotorra de Kramer, Loro rabudo collar, Periquito de collar africano, (F) Perruche à collier, **III** PSITTACIDAE Av

Psittacula krameri ssp. *echo = Psittacula echo*

Psittacula longicauda : (E) Long-tailed Parakeet, Pink-cheeked Parakeet, (S) Cotorra colilarga, (F) Perruche à longs brins, **II** PSITTACIDAE Av

Psittacula roseata : (E) Blossom-headed Parakeet, (S) Cotorra carirrosa, (F) Perruche à tête rose, **II** PSITTACIDAE Av

Psittacula wardi : (E) Seychelles Parakeet, Seychelles Parrot, (F) Perruche des Seychelles **II** PSITTACIDAE Av

Psittacule à double-oeil de Coxen (F): *Cyclopsitta diophthalma coxeni*

Psittacule à poitrine orange (F): *Cyclopsitta gulielmitertii*

Psittacule de Desmarest (F): *Psittaculirostris desmarestii*

Psittacule de Salvadori (F): *Psittaculirostris salvadorii*

Psittacule d'Edwards (F): *Psittaculirostris edwardsii*

Psittacule double-oeil (F): *Cyclopsitta diophthalma*

Psittaculirostris desmarestii : (E) Desmarest's Fig-Parrot, Golden-headed Fig-Parrot, Large Fig-Parrot, (S) Lorito de Desmarest, (F) Psittacule de Desmarest, **II** PSITTACIDAE Av

Psittaculirostris edwardsii : (E) Edwards's Fig-Parrot, (S) Lorito de Edwards, (F) Psittacule d'Edwards, **II** PSITTACIDAE Av

Psittaculirostris salvadorii : (E) Salvadori's Fig-Parrot, (S) Lorito de Salvadori, (F) Psittacule de Salvadori, **II** PSITTACIDAE Av

Psittacus erithacus : (E) Grey Parrot, (S) Loro yaco, Yaco, (F) Jacko, Jacquot, Perroquet gris, Perroquet jaco, **II** PSITTACIDAE Av

Psittacus erithacus ssp. *princeps = Psittacus erithacus erithacus*

Psitteuteles goldiei : (E) Goldie's Lorikeet, (S) Lori de Goldie, (F) Loriquet de Goldie, **II** PSITTACIDAE Av

Psitteuteles iris : (E) Iris Lorikeet, Iris Lory, (S) Lori iris, (F) Loriquet iris, **II** PSITTACIDAE Av

Psitteuteles versicolor : (E) Varied Lorikeet, (S) Lori versicolor, (F) Loriquet versicolore, **II** PSITTACIDAE Av

Psittinus cyanurus : (E) Blue-rumped Parrot, (S) Lorito dorsiazul, (F) Perruche à croupion bleu, **II** PSITTACIDAE Av

Psittrichas de Pesquet (F): *Psittrichas fulgidus*

Psittrichas fulgidus : (E) Pesquet's Parrot, Vulturine Parrot, (S) Loro aguileño, (F) Psittrichas de Pesquet, **II** PSITTACIDAE Av

Pteridophora alberti : (E) King-of-Saxony Bird-of-paradise, (F) Paradisier d'Albert, Paradisier du prince Albert **II** PARADISAEIDAE Av

Pterocnemia pennata = Rhea pennata

Pteroglossus aracari : (E) Black-necked Aracari, (S) Tilingo cuellinegro, (F) Araçari à cou noir, Araçari grigri, **II** RAMPHASTIDAE Av

Pteroglossus castanotis : (E) Chestnut-eared Aracari, (S) Arasari orejicastano, Tucán tilingo, Tucán-Tilingo verde, (F) Araçari à oreillons roux, **III** RAMPHASTIDAE Av

Pteroglossus viridis : (E) Green Aracari, (S) Tilingo limón, (F) Araçari vert, **II** RAMPHASTIDAE Av

Pteronetta hartlaubii : (E) Hartlaub's Duck, (S) Pato de Hartlaub, (F) Canard de Hartlaub, **III** ANATIDAE Av

Pteronura brasiliensis : (E) Giant Brazilian Otter, Giant Otter, (S) Arirai, Lobito de cola ancha, Lobo de Río Grande, Lobo del río, Lobo gargantilla, Nutria brasileña, Nutria gigante, Perro de agua, (F) Loutre géante du Brésil, **I** MUSTELIDAE Ma

Pterophanes cyanopterus : (E) Great Sapphirewing, (S) Alazafiro grande, Colibrí aliazul, (F) Colibri à ailes saphir, **II** TROCHILIDAE Av

Pteropus spp.: (E) Flying-foxes, (S) Zorros voladores, (F) Renards volants, Roussettes, **I/II** PTEROPODIDAE Ma

Pteropus admiralitatum : (E) Admiralty Flying-fox, (S) Zorro volador de las islas de almirantazgo **II** PTEROPODIDAE Ma

Pteropus aldabrensis : (E) Aldabra Flying-fox, (S) Zorro volador de Aldabra **II** PTEROPODIDAE Ma

Pteropus alecto : (E) Black Flying-fox, Central Flying-fox, (S) Zorro volador negro **II** PTEROPODIDAE Ma

Pteropus anetianus : (E) Vanuatu Flying-fox, White Flying-fox **II** PTEROPODIDAE Ma

Pteropus argentatus : (E) Ambon Flying-fox, Silvery Flying-fox, Silvery Fruit Bat, (S) Zorro volador argénteo **II** PTEROPODIDAE Ma

Pteropus arquatus = Acerodon celebensis

Pteropus balutus = Pteropus pumilus

Pteropus banakrisi : **II** PTEROPODIDAE Ma

Pteropus brunneus : (E) Dusky Flying-fox, (S) Zorro volador de las islas Percy **II** PTEROPODIDAE Ma

Pteropus caniceps : (E) Ashy-headed Flying-fox, North Moluccan Flying-fox, (S) Zorro volador de cabeza ceniciento **II** PTEROPODIDAE Ma

Pteropus capistratus = Pteropus temmincki

Pteropus chrysoproctus : (E) Ambon Flying-fox, Moluccan Flying-fox, (S) Zorro volador de Amboina **II** PTEROPODIDAE Ma

Pteropus cognatus = Pteropus rayneri

Pteropus comorensis = Pteropus seychellensis

Pteropus conspicillatus : (E) Spectacled Flying-fox, (S) Zorro volador de anteojos **II** PTEROPODIDAE Ma

Pteropus dasymallus : (E) Ryukyu Flying-fox, (S) Zorro volador de Ryu-Kyu **II** PTEROPODIDAE Ma

Pteropus faunulus : (E) Nicobar Flying-fox **II** PTEROPODIDAE Ma

Pteropus fundatus : (E) Banks Flying-fox, (S) Zorro volador de las islas Banks **II** PTEROPODIDAE Ma

Pteropus giganteus : (E) Indian Flying-fox, (S) Zorro volador de la India **II** PTEROPODIDAE Ma

Pteropus gilliardi : (E) Gilliard's Flying-fox, New Britain Flying-fox, (S) Zorro volador de Gilliard **II** PTEROPODIDAE Ma

Pteropus gilliardorum = Pteropus gilliardi

Pteropus griseus : (E) Grey Flying-fox, (S) Zorro volador gris **II** PTEROPODIDAE Ma

Pteropus howensis : (E) Ontong Java Flying-fox, (S) Zorro volador de Howens **II** PTEROPODIDAE Ma

Pteropus hypomelanus : (E) Small Flying-fox, Variable Flying-fox, (S) Zorro volador pequeño **II** PTEROPODIDAE Ma

Pteropus hypomelanus ssp. *mearnsi = Pteropus mearnsi*

Pteropus hypomelanus ssp. *santacrucis = Pteropus sanctacrucis*

Pteropus insularis : (E) Chuuk Flying-fox, Ruck Flying-fox, (F) Roussette des îles Truk **I** PTEROPODIDAE Ma

Pteropus intermedius = Pteropus vampyrus

Pteropus leucopterus : (E) White-winged Flying-fox, (S) Zorro volador de Luzón **II** PTEROPODIDAE Ma

Pteropus leucotis = Acerodon leucotis

Pteropus livingstonei : (E) Comoro Black Flying-fox, (S) Zorro volador de Livingston **II** PTEROPODIDAE Ma

Pteropus lombocensis : (E) Lombok Flying-fox, (S) Zorro volador de Lombok **II** PTEROPODIDAE Ma

Pteropus loochoensis = Pteropus mariannus

Pteropus lylei : (E) Lyle's Flying-fox, (S) Zorro volador de Lyle **II** PTEROPODIDAE Ma

Pteropus macrotis : (E) Big-eared Flying-fox, Large-eared Flying-fox, (S) Zorro volador de orejas grandes **II** PTEROPODIDAE Ma

Pteropus macrotis ssp. *pohlei = Pteropus pohlei*

Pteropus mahaganus : (E) Lesser Flying-fox, Sanborn's Flying-fox, (S) Zorro volador de Bougainville **II** PTEROPODIDAE Ma

Pteropus mariannus : (E) Marianas Flying-fox, Micronesian Flying-fox, (F) Roussette des îles Marianes, Roussette des îles Marianne **I** PTEROPODIDAE Ma

Pteropus mearnsi : (E) Mearns's Flying-fox, (S) Zorro volador de Mearns **II** PTEROPODIDAE Ma

Pteropus melanopogon : (E) Black-bearded Flying-fox, (S) Zorro volador de barba negra **II** PTEROPODIDAE Ma

Pteropus melanotus : (E) Black-eared Flying-fox, Christmas Island Flying-fox, (S) Zorro volador de Andaman **II** PTEROPODIDAE Ma

Pteropus molossinus : (E) Caroline Flying-fox, Pohnpei Flying-fox, (F) Renard volant de Ponape **I** PTEROPODIDAE Ma

Pteropus neohibernicus : (E) Bismarck Flying-fox, Great Flying-fox, (S) Zorro volador de Bismarck **II** PTEROPODIDAE Ma

Pteropus niger : (E) Greater Mascarene Flying-fox, (S) Zorro volador negro de Mauricio **II** PTEROPODIDAE Ma

Pteropus nitendiensis : (E) Temotu Flying-fox, (S) Zorro volador de la isla Ndeni **II** PTEROPODIDAE Ma

Pteropus ocularis : (E) Seram Flying-fox, Seram Fruit Bat, (S) Zorro volador de las isla Ceram **II** PTEROPODIDAE Ma

Pteropus ornatus : (E) Ornate Flying-fox, (S) Zorro volador de las islas de la Leal **II** PTEROPODIDAE Ma

Pteropus pelewensis = Pteropus mariannus

Pteropus personatus : (E) Masked Flying-fox, Masked Fruit Bat, (S) Zorro volador enmascarado **II** PTEROPODIDAE Ma

Pteropus phaeocephalus : (E) Mortlock Flying-fox, Mortlock Islands Flying-fox, (F) Roussette de l'île Mortlock **I** PTEROPODIDAE Ma

Pteropus pilosus : (E) Large Palau Flying-fox, Palau Fruit Bat, (S) Zorro volador de las islas Palau, (F) Roussette des îles Palau, **I** PTEROPODIDAE Ma

Pteropus pohlei : (E) Geelvink Bay Flying-fox, (S) Zorro volador de las isla Japen **II** PTEROPODIDAE Ma

Pteropus poliocephalus : (E) Grey-headed Flying-fox, (S) Zorro volador de cabeza gris **II** PTEROPODIDAE Ma

Pteropus pselaphon : (E) Bonin Flying-fox, Bonin Fruit Bat, (S) Zorro volador de las isla Bonin **II** PTEROPODIDAE Ma

Pteropus pumilus : (E) Little Golden-mantled Flying-fox, (S) Zorro volador de Taylor **II** PTEROPODIDAE Ma

Pteropus rayneri : (E) Solomons Flying-fox, (S) Zorro volador de las Salomón **II** PTEROPODIDAE Ma

Pteropus rennelli = Pteropus rayneri

Pteropus rodricensis : (E) Rodrigues Flying-fox, (S) Zorro volador de la isla Rodrígues **II** PTEROPODIDAE Ma

Pteropus rufus : (E) Madagascar Flying-fox, Madagascar Fruit Bat, (S) Zorro volador de Madagascar **II** PTEROPODIDAE Ma

Pteropus samoensis : (E) Samoan Flying-fox, (F) Roussette des îles Samoa **I** PTEROPODIDAE Ma

Pteropus sanctacrucis : (E) Santa Cruz Flying-fox, (S) Zorro volador de la isla Santa Cruz **II** PTEROPODIDAE Ma

Pteropus satyrus = Pteropus hypomelanus

Pteropus scapulatus : (E) Little Red Flying-fox, (S) Zorro volador de Queensland **II** PTEROPODIDAE Ma

Pteropus seychellensis : (E) Seychelles Flying-fox, (S) Zorro volador de las Seychelles **II** PTEROPODIDAE Ma

Pteropus seychellensis aldabrensis = Pteropus aldabrensis

Pteropus speciosus : (E) Philippine Grey Flying-fox, (S) Zorro volador de la isla Malawi **II** PTEROPODIDAE Ma

Pteropus subniger : (E) Dark Flying-fox, Lesser Mascarene Flying-fox, (S) Zorro volador oscuro de Mauricio **II** PTEROPODIDAE Ma

Pteropus tablasi = Pteropus pumilus

Pteropus temmincki : (E) Temminck's Flying-fox, (S) Zorro volador de Temminck **II** PTEROPODIDAE Ma

Pteropus tokudae : (E) Guam Flying-fox, Guam Fruit Bat, (S) Zorro volador de Tokuda **II** PTEROPODIDAE Ma

Pteropus tonganus : (E) Insular Flying-fox, Pacific Flying-fox, (F) Roussette des îles Tonga **I** PTEROPODIDAE Ma

Pteropus tuberculatus : (E) Vanikoro Flying-fox, (S) Zorro volador de la isla Jawi **II** PTEROPODIDAE Ma

Pteropus ualanus = Pteropus mariannus

Pteropus vampyrus : (E) Large Flying-fox, (S) Zorro volador de cuello rojo **II** PTEROPODIDAE Ma

Pteropus vetulus : (E) New Caledonia Flying-fox, (S) Zorro volador de Nueva Caledonia **II** PTEROPODIDAE Ma

Pteropus voeltzkowi : (E) Pemba Flying-fox, (S) Zorro volador de Voeltzkow **II** PTEROPODIDAE Ma

Pteropus woodfordi : (E) Dwarf Flying-fox, Least Flying-fox, Least Fruit Bat, (S) Zorro volador de Woodford **II** PTEROPODIDAE Ma

Pteropus yapensis = Pteropus mariannus

Ptilocercus lowii : (E) Pen-tailed Treeshrew, (S) Musaraña arborícola coliplumada, (F) Ptilocerque de Low, **II** TUPAIIDAE Ma

Ptilocerque de Low (F): *Ptilocercus lowii*

Ptilolaemus tickelli = Anorrhinus tickelli

Ptilopsis granti = Otus leucotis

Ptilopsis leucotis = Otus leucotis

Ptiloris de Victoria (F): *Ptiloris victoriae*

Ptiloris intercedens : (E) Eastern Riflebird **II** PARADISAEIDAE Av

Ptiloris magnificus : (E) Magnificent Riflebird, (F) Paradisier gorge-d'acier, Proméfil **II** PARADISAEIDAE Av

Ptiloris paradis (F): *Ptiloris paradiseus*

Ptiloris paradiseus : (E) Paradise Riflebird, (F) Paradisier festonné, Ptiloris paradis **II** PARADISAEIDAE Av

Ptiloris victoriae : (E) Queen Victoria's Riflebird, Victoria's Riflebird, (F) Paradisier de Victoria, Ptiloris de Victoria **II** PARADISAEIDAE Av

Ptyas mucosus : (E) Common Rat Snake, Dhaman, Oriental Rat Snake, (S) Culebra ratera oriental, (F) Flaphe de l'Inde, Grand serpent ratier de l'Inde, Serpent ratier, Serpent ratier indien, Serpent ratier oriental, **II** COLUBRIDAE Re

Pudu du Nord (F): *Pudu mephistophiles*

Pudu du Sud (F): *Pudu puda*

Pudu mephistophiles : (E) Northern Pudu, (S) Pudu norteño, Sachacabra, Venadito de los páramos, Venado conejo, (F) Poudou du nord, Pudu du Nord, **II** CERVIDAE Ma

Pudu meridional (S): *Pudu puda*

Pudu norteño (S): *Pudu mephistophiles*

Pudu puda : (E) Chilean Pudu, Southern Pudu, (S) Ciervo enano, Pudu meridional, Pudu sureño, Venadito, (F) Poudou du sud, Pudu du Sud, **I** CERVIDAE Ma

Pudu sureño (S): *Pudu puda*

Puercoespín (S): *Hystrix cristata*

Puerto Rican Amazon (E): *Amazona vittata*

Puerto Rican Boa (E): *Epicrates inornatus*

Puerto Rican Emerald (E): *Chlorostilbon maugaeus*

Puerto Rican Parrot (E): *Amazona vittata*

Puerto Rican Screech-Owl (E): *Otus nudipes*

Puffed Coral (E): *Trachyphyllia geoffroyi*

Pulsatrix koeniswaldiana : (E) Tawny-browed Owl, White-chinned Owl, (S) Lechuzón acollarado chico, Lechuzón anteojo menor, Lechuzón pardo menor, (F) Chouette à sourcils jaunes, Chouette de Koeniswald, **II** STRIGIDAE Av

Pulsatrix melanota : (E) Band-bellied Owl, Band-tailed Owl, Rusty-barred Owl, (S) Cicupa, Lechuzón acollarado grande, (F) Chouette à collier, **II** STRIGIDAE Av

Pulsatrix perspicillata : (E) Spectacled Owl, (S) Búho de anteojos, Lechuzón anteojo, Lechuzón de Anteojos, (F) Chouette à lunettes, **II** STRIGIDAE Av

Puma (E/S/F): *Puma concolor*

Checklist of fauna/Lista de especies de fauna/Liste des espèces animales

Puma concolor : (E) Cougar, Deer Tiger, Mountain Lion, Puma, Red Tiger, (S) León americano, León bayo, Mitzli, Onza bermeja, Puma, (F) Puma, **I/II** FELIDAE Ma

Puma concolor coryi : (E) Florida Cougar, Florida Panther, Florida Puma, (S) León de Florida, Puma de Florida, (F) Cougar de Floride, Puma de Floride, **I** FELIDAE Ma

Puma concolor costaricensis : (E) Central American Puma, Costa Rican Puma, (S) León costarricense, Puma costarricense, Puma de América Central, (F) Puma d'Amérique centrale, **I** FELIDAE Ma

Puma concolor couguar : (E) Eastern Cougar, Eastern Panther, Eastern Puma, (S) Puma del este de América del Norte, Puma oriental, (F) Cougouar, Puma de l'est de l'Amérique du Nord, **I** FELIDAE Ma

Puma costarricense (S): *Puma concolor costaricensis*

Puma d'Amérique centrale (F): *Puma concolor costaricensis*

Puma de América Central (S): *Puma concolor costaricensis*

Puma de Florida (S): *Puma concolor coryi*

Puma de Floride (F): *Puma concolor coryi*

Puma de l'est de l'Amérique du Nord (F): *Puma concolor couguar*

Puma del este de América del Norte (S): *Puma concolor couguar*

Puma oriental (S): *Puma concolor couguar*

Puna Flamingo (E): *Phoenicopterus jamesi*

Puna Hawk (E): *Buteo poecilochrous*

Puna Rhea (E): *Rhea pennata*

Punta blanca (S): *Urosticte benjamini*

Purple Guan (E): *Penelope purpurascens*

Purple-backed Sunbeam (E): *Aglaeactis aliciae*

Purple-backed Thornbill (E): *Ramphomicron microrhynchum*

Purple-bellied Lory (E): *Lorius hypoinochrous*

Purple-bellied Parrot (E): *Triclaria malachitacea*

Purple-bibbed Whitetip (E): *Urosticte benjamini*

Purple-capped Lory (E): *Lorius domicella*

Purple-chested Hummingbird (E): *Polyerata rosenbergi*

Purple-collared Woodstar (E): *Myrtis fanny*

Purple-crested Turaco (E): *Musophaga porphyreolopha*

Purple-crowned Fairy (E): *Heliothryx barroti*

Purple-crowned Lorikeet (E): *Glossopsitta porphyrocephala*

Purple-faced Leaf Monkey (E): *Trachypithecus vetulus*

Purple-naped Lory (E): *Lorius domicella*

Purple-throated Carib (E): *Eulampis jugularis*

Purple-throated Mountain-gem (E): *Lampornis castaneoventris*

Purple-throated Sunangel (E): *Heliangelus viola*

Purple-throated Woodstar (E): *Calliphlox mitchellii*

Purplish Guan (E): *Penelope purpurascens*

Purpureicephalus spurius : (E) Pileated Parakeet, Red-capped Parrot, (S) Perico capelo, (F) Perruche à tête pourpre, **II** PSITTACIDAE Av

Putois à pieds noirs (F): *Mustela nigripes*

Putty-nosed Monkey (E): *Cercopithecus nictitans*

Pycnonotus zeylanicus : (E) Straw-crowned Bulbul, Straw-headed Bulbul, (S) Bulbul bigotudo, (F) Bulbul à tête jaune, **II** PYCNONOTIDAE Av

Pygargue à queue blanche (F): *Haliaeetus albicilla*

Pygargue à tête blanche (F): *Haliaeetus leucocephalus*

Pygargue à tête grise (F): *Ichthyophaga ichthyaetus*

Pygargue à ventre blanc (F): *Haliaeetus leucogaster*

Pygargue blagre (F): *Haliaeetus leucogaster*

Pygargue commun (F): *Haliaeetus albicilla*

Pygargue de Madagascar (F): *Haliaeetus vociferoides*

Pygargue de Pallas (F): *Haliaeetus leucoryphus*

Pygargue de Sanford (F): *Haliaeetus sanfordi*

Pygargue de Steller (F): *Haliaeetus pelagicus*

Pygargue empereur (F): *Haliaeetus pelagicus*

Pygargue nain (F): *Ichthyophaga humilis*

Pygargue vocifer (F): *Haliaeetus vocifer*

Pygargue vocifère (F): *Haliaeetus vocifer*

Pygathrix spp.: (E) Snub-nosed monkeys, (F) Doucs, Rhinopithèques **I** CERCOPITHECIDAE Ma

Pygathrix avunculus : (E) Tonkin Snub-nosed Monkey, (F) Rhinopithèque du Tonkin **I** CERCOPITHECIDAE Ma

Pygathrix bieti : (E) Yunnan Snub-nosed Monkey **I** CERCOPITHECIDAE Ma

Pygathrix brelichi : (E) Brelich's Snub-nosed Monkey, Grey Snub-nosed Monkey, Guizhou Snub-nosed Monkey, (F) Rhinopithèque jaune doré **I** CERCOPITHECIDAE Ma

Pygathrix nemaeus : (E) Douc, Douc Langur, Douc Monkey, Red-shanked Douc Langur, (S) Langur douc, Mono pigatrix, (F) Douc, Rhinopithèque douc, **I** CERCOPITHECIDAE Ma

Pygathrix nigripes = *Pygathrix nemaeus*

Pygathrix roxellana : (E) Golden Snub-nosed Monkey, Sichuan Snub-nosed Monkey, (S) Langur chato, (F) Rhinopithèque de Roxellane, Rhinopithèque doré, **I** CERCOPITHECIDAE Ma

Pygathrix roxellana ssp. *bieti* = *Pygathrix bieti*

Pygathrix roxellana ssp. *brelichi* = *Pygathrix brelichi*

Pygmornis longuemareus = *Phaethornis longuemareus*

Pygmornis striigularis = *Phaethornis longuemareus*

Pygmy Beaked Whale (E): *Mesoplodon peruvianus*

Pygmy Chimpanzee (E): *Pan paniscus*

Pygmy Falcon (E): *Polihierax semitorquatus*

Pygmy Hanging-Parrot (E): *Loriculus exilis*

Pygmy Hippopotamus (E): *Hexaprotodon liberiensis*

Pygmy Hog (E): *Sus salvanius*

Pygmy Killer Whale (E): *Feresa attenuata*

Pygmy Lorikeet (E): *Charmosyna wilhelminae*

Pygmy Loris (E): *Nycticebus pygmaeus*

Pygmy Marmoset (E): *Callithrix pygmaea*

Pygmy Mulga Monitor (E): *Varanus gilleni*

Pygmy Owl (E): *Glaucidium passerinum*

Pygmy Python (E): *Antaresia perthensis*

Pygmy Right Whale (E): *Caperea marginata*

Pygmy scaly-tailed flying squirrels (E): *Idiurus* spp.

Pygmy Seahorse (E): *Hippocampus bargibanti*

Pygmy Sperm Whale (E): *Kogia breviceps*

Pygmy Tarsier (E): *Tarsius pumilus*

Pygmy Treeshrew (E): *Tupaia minor*

Pyréneste ponceau (F): *Pyrenestes ostrinus*

Pyrenestes frommi = *Pyrenestes ostrinus*

Pyrenestes maximus = *Pyrenestes ostrinus*

Pyrenestes ostrinus : (E) Black-bellied Seedcracker, (S) Pirenestes ventrinegro, (F) Gros-bec ponceau à ventre noir, Pyréneste ponceau, **III** ESTRILDIDAE Av

Pyrenestes rothschildi = *Pyrenestes ostrinus*

Pyrrhura albipectus : (E) White-breasted Parakeet, White-necked Conure, White-necked Parakeet, (S) Cotorra cuelliblanca, Perico pechiblanco, (F) Conure à col blanc, **II** PSITTACIDAE Av

Pyrrhura calliptera : (E) Brown-breasted Parakeet, Flame-winged Conure, Flame-winged Parakeet, (S) Cotorra pechiparda, (F) Conure à poitrine brune, **II** PSITTACIDAE Av

Pyrrhura cruentata : (E) Blue-chested Parakeet, Blue-throated Parakeet, Ochre-marked Parakeet, Red-eared Conure, (S) Cotorra tiriba, Perico grande, (F) Conure à gorge bleue, Conure tiriba, Perruche tiriba, **I** PSITTACIDAE Av

Pyrrhura devillei : (E) Blaze-winged Conure, Blaze-winged Parakeet, (S) Cotorra de Deville, (F) Conure de Deville, **II** PSITTACIDAE Av

Pyrrhura egregia : (E) Fiery-shouldered Conure, Fiery-shouldered Parakeet, (S) Cotorra egregia, Perico colimorado, (F) Conure aile-de-feu, **II** PSITTACIDAE Av

Pyrrhura frontalis : (E) Maroon-bellied Parakeet, Red-bellied Conure, Reddish-bellied Parakeet, (S) Chiripepé común, Cotorra chiripepé, (F) Conure de Vieillot, **II** PSITTACIDAE Av

Checklist of fauna/Lista de especies de fauna/Liste des espèces animales

Pyrrhura griseipectus = Pyrrhura leucotis

Pyrrhura hoematotis : (E) Blood-eared Parakeet, Red-breasted Conure, Red-eared Parakeet, (S) Cotorra colirroja, Perico cola roja, (F) Conure à oreillons, **II** PSITTACIDAE Av

Pyrrhura hoffmanni : (E) Hoffmann's Conure, Sulphur-winged Parakeet, (S) Cotorra catana, (F) Conure de Hoffmann, **II** PSITTACIDAE Av

Pyrrhura hypoxantha = Pyrrhura molinae

Pyrrhura lepida : (E) Pearly Conure, Pearly Parakeet, (S) Cotorra perlada, (F) Conure perlée, **II** PSITTACIDAE Av

Pyrrhura leucotis : (E) Maroon-faced Parakeet, White-eared Conure, White-eared Parakeet, (S) Cotorra cariparda, Perico pintado, (F) Conure emma, **II** PSITTACIDAE Av

Pyrrhura melanura : (E) Maroon-tailed Conure, Maroon-tailed Parakeet, (S) Cotorra colinegra, Perico cola negra, (F) Conure de Souancé, **II** PSITTACIDAE Av

Pyrrhura molinae : (E) Green-cheeked Conure, Green-cheeked Parakeet, (S) Chiripepé salteño, Cotorra de Molina, (F) Conure de Molina, **II** PSITTACIDAE Av

Pyrrhura orcesi : (E) El Oro Conure, El Oro Parakeet, (S) Cotorra de El Oro, Perico de El Oro, (F) Conure d'Orcès, **II** PSITTACIDAE Av

Pyrrhura perlata : (E) Crimson-bellied Conure, Crimson-bellied Parakeet, (S) Cotorra ventrirroja, (F) Conure à ventre rouge, **II** PSITTACIDAE Av

Pyrrhura pfrimeri = Pyrrhura leucotis

Pyrrhura picta : (E) Painted Conure, Painted Parakeet, (S) Cotorra pintada, Perico cabecirrosado, (F) Conure versicolore, **II** PSITTACIDAE Av

Pyrrhura rhodocephala : (E) Rose-crowned Conure, Rose-headed Conure, Rose-headed Parakeet, (S) Cotorra coronirroja, Perico cabecirrojo, (F) Conure tête-de-feu, **II** PSITTACIDAE Av

Pyrrhura rhodogaster = Pyrrhura perlata

Pyrrhura rupicola : (E) Black-capped Conure, Black-capped Parakeet, Rock Parakeet, (S) Cotorra capirotada, (F) Conure à cape noire, **II** PSITTACIDAE Av

Pyrrhura viridicata : (E) Santa Marta Conure, Santa Marta Parakeet, (S) Cotorra de Santa Marta, (F) Conure des Santa Marta, **II** PSITTACIDAE Av

Pyrroglaux podargina = Otus podarginus

Python à écailles rugueuses (F): *Morelia carinata*

Python à large tache (F): *Antaresia stimsoni*

Python à lèvres blanches (F): *Leiopython albertisii*

Python à tête noire d'Australie (F): *Aspidites melanocephalus*

Python améthiste (F): *Morelia amethistina*

Python amethistinus = Morelia amethistina

Python anchietae : (E) Angolan Python, (S) Pitón de Angola, (F) Python d'Angola, **II** PYTHONIDAE Re

Python arboricole vert australien (F): *Morelia viridis*

Python boeleni = Morelia boeleni

Python bredli = Morelia bredli

Python breitensteini : (E) Borneo Short-tailed Python **II** PYTHONIDAE Re

Python brongersmai : (E) Blood Python, (F) Python sanguin **II** PYTHONIDAE Re

Python caréné (F): *Morelia carinata*

Python curtus : (E) Sumatran Short-tailed Python, (S) Pitón malaya, (F) Python malais, **II** PYTHONIDAE Re

Python curtus breitensteini = Python breitensteini

Python curtus brongersmai = Python brongersmai

Python curtus curtus = Python curtus

Python d'Amérique centrale (F): *Loxocemus bicolor*

Python d'Angola (F): *Python anchietae*

Python de Boelen (F): *Morelia boeleni*

Python de Children (F): *Antaresia childreni*

Python de la brousse (F): *Morelia amethistina*

Python de Macklot (F): *Liasis mackloti*

Python de Nouvelle-Guinée (F): *Leiopython albertisii*

Python de Papouasie (F): *Apodora papuana*

Python de Ramsay (F): *Aspidites ramsayi*

Python de Seba (F): *Python sebae*

Python de Stimson (F): *Antaresia stimsoni*

Python de Timor (F): *Python timoriensis*

Python des rochers (F): *Morelia amethistina*

Python d'Oenpelli (F): *Morelia oenpelliensis*

Python fouisseur du Mexique (F): *Loxocemus bicolor*

Python malais (F): *Python curtus*

Python molure (F): *Python molurus*

Python molure indien (F): *Python molurus molurus*

Python molurus : (E) Asiatic Rock Python, Burmese Python, Tiger Python, (F) Python molure, Python tigre **I/II** PYTHONIDAE Re

Python molurus molurus : (E) Indian Python, (S) Pitón de la India, (F) Python molure indien, **I** PYTHONIDAE Re

Python molurus ssp. *pimbura = Python molurus* ssp. *molurus*

Python natalensis = Python sebae

Python oenpelliensis = Morelia oenpelliensis

Python olive (F): *Liasis olivaceus*

Python pygmée de Perth (F): *Antaresia perthensis*

Python regius : (E) Ball Python, Royal Python, (S) Pitón real, (F) Python royal, **II** PYTHONIDAE Re

Python reticulatus : (E) Java Rock Python, Regal Python, Reticulated Python, (S) Pitón reticulada, (F) Python réticulé, **II** PYTHONIDAE Re

Python réticulé (F): *Python reticulatus*

Python royal (F): *Python regius*

Python sanguin (F): *Python brongersmai*

Python saxuloides = Python sebae

Python sebae : (E) African Python, African Rock Python, (S) Pitón de Seba, (F) Python de Seba, **II** PYTHONIDAE Re

Python spilotus = Morelia spilota

Python tacheté (F): *Antaresia maculosa*

Python tapis (F): *Morelia spilota*

Python tigre (F): *Python molurus*

Python timoriensis : (E) Timor Python, (S) Pitón de Timor, (F) Python de Timor, **II** PYTHONIDAE Re

PYTHONIDAE spp.: (E) Pythons (S) Pitóns, (F) Pythons, **I/II** Re

Pythons (E/F): PYTHONIDAE spp.

Pytilia hypogrammica : (E) Red-faced Pytilia, Yellow-winged Pytilia, (F) Beaumarquet à ailes jaunes, Diamant à face rouge **III** ESTRILDIDAE Av

Pytilia phoenicoptera : (E) Aurora Finch, Crimson-winged Pytilia, Red-winged Pytilia, (S) Pitilia alirroja, (F) Beaumarquet, Beaumarquet aurore, Diamant aurore, **III** ESTRILDIDAE Av

Pyxide à dos plat (F): *Pyxis planicauda*

Pyxide à queue platte (F): *Pyxis planicauda*

Pyxide arachnoide (F): *Pyxis arachnoides*

Pyxidea mouhotii : (E) Keeled Box Turtle, Jagged-shelled Turtle, Keel-backed Turtle, **II** EMYDIDAE Re

Pyxis arachnoides : (E) Spider Tortoise, (S) Tortuga araña, Tortuga de plastrón articulado, (F) Pyxide arachnoide, **II** TESTUDINIDAE Re

Pyxis planicauda : (E) Flat-backed Spider Tortoise, Flat-shelled Spider Tortoise, Madagascar Flat-shelled Tortoise, Malagasy Flat-tailed Tortoise, (S) Tortuga de cola plana, (F) Pyxide à dos plat, Pyxide à queue platte, **I** TESTUDINIDAE Re

Quadrula intermedia : (E) Cumberland Monkeyface, Cumberland Monkey-face Pearly Mussel **I** UNIONIDAE Bi

Quadrula sparsa : (E) Appalachian Monkeyface, Appalachian Monkey-face Pearly Mussel **I** UNIONIDAE Bi

Quadrula striata = Plethobasus cooperianus

Quaker Parakeet (E): *Myiopsitta monachus*

Quebrantahuesos (S): *Gypaetus barbatus*

Queen Alexandra's Birdwing (E): *Ornithoptera alexandrae*

Checklist of fauna/Lista de especies de fauna/Liste des espèces animales

Queen Carola's Parotia (E): *Parotia carolae*
Queen Conch (E): *Strombus gigas*
Queen of Bavaria's Conure (E): *Guarouba guarouba*
Queen Victoria's Birdwing (E): *Ornithoptera victoriae*
Queen Victoria's Riflebird (E): *Ptiloris victoriae*
Queensland Hairy-nosed Wombat (E): *Lasiorhinus krefftii*
Queensland Lungfish (E): *Neoceratodus forsteri*
Quelea erythrops : (E) Red-headed Dioch, Red-headed Quelea, (S) Laborioso cabecirrojo, (F) Travailleur à tête rouge, **III** PLOCEIDAE Av
Quetzal (S): *Pharomachrus mocinno*
Quetzal centroamericano (S): *Pharomachrus mocinno*
Quetzal Guatemalteco (S): *Pharomachrus mocinno*
Quetzal resplendissant (F): *Pharomachrus mocinno*
Queue de vinaigre (F): *Estrilda caerulescens*
Quimilero (S): *Catagonus wagneri*
Quirquincho andino (S): *Chaetophractus nationi*

Rabihorcado de la Christmas (S): *Fregata andrewsi*
Rabihorcado ventriblanco (S): *Fregata andrewsi*
Rabudito cobrizo (S): *Discosura letitiae*
Rabudito crestado (S): *Discosura popelairii*
Rabudito de raquetas (S): *Discosura longicauda*
Rabudito ventrinegro (S): *Discosura langsdorffi*
Rabudito verde (S): *Discosura conversii*
Racket-tailed Coquette (E): *Discosura longicauda*
Radiated Tortoise (E): *Geochelone radiata*
Raggiana Bird-of-paradise (E): *Paradisaea raggiana*
Rainbow Boa (E): *Epicrates cenchria*
Rainbow Lorikeet (E): *Trichoglossus haematodus*
Rainbow Lory (E): *Trichoglossus haematodus*
Rainbow Starfrontlet (E): *Coeligena iris*
Rainbow-bearded Thornbill (E): *Chalcostigma herrani*
Rainforest Chameleon (E): *Furcifer balteatus*
Rajah Brooke's Birdwing (E): *Trogonoptera brookiana*
Rajah Scops-Owl (E): *Otus brookii*
Râle de l'île Lord Howe (F): *Gallirallus sylvestris*
Râle sylvestre (F): *Gallirallus sylvestris*
Ramphastos dicolorus : (E) Red-breasted Toucan, (S) Tucán rojo y amarillo, Tucán verde, (F) Toucan à ventre rouge, **III** RAMPHASTIDAE Av
Ramphastos sulfuratus : (E) Keel-billed Toucan, (S) Piapoco pico verde, Tucán pico-multicolor, (F) Toucan à carène, **II** RAMPHASTIDAE Av
Ramphastos toco : (E) Toco Toucan, (S) Tucán de pico verde, Tucán grande, (F) Toucan toco, **II** RAMPHASTIDAE Av
Ramphastos tucanus : (E) Red-billed Toucan, (S) Piapoco pico rojo, (F) Toucan à bec rouge, **II** RAMPHASTIDAE Av
Ramphastos vitellinus : (E) Channel-billed Toucan, (S) Diostedé pico acanelado, Tucán piquirrojo, (F) Toucan à gorge jaune et blanche, Toucan ariel, **II** RAMPHASTIDAE Av
Ramphodon dohrnii = Glaucis dohrnii
Ramphodon naevius : (E) Saw-billed Hermit, (S) Ermitaño picosierra, (F) Colibri tacheté, **II** TROCHILIDAE Av
Ramphomicron dorsale : (E) Black-backed Thornbill, (S) Colibrí piquicorto dorsinegro, (F) Colibri à dos noir, **II** TROCHILIDAE Av
Ramphomicron microrhynchum : (E) Purple-backed Thornbill, (S) Colibrí pico espina, Colibrí piquicorto común, Picoespina dorsipurpura, (F) Colibri à petit bec, **II** TROCHILIDAE Av
Ramsay's Python (E): *Aspidites ramsayi*
Rana de punta de flecha andino (S): *Epipedobates andinus*
Rana de punta de flecha arbórea (S): *Dendrobates arboreus*
Rana de punta de flecha azul (S): *Dendrobates azureus*
Rana de punta de flecha boliviana (S): *Epipedobates bolivianus*
Rana de punta de flecha de bandas amarillas (S): *Dendrobates leucomelas*
Rana de punta de flecha de Bassler (S): *Epipedobates bassleri*

Rana de punta de flecha de Boulenger (S): *Epipedobates boulengeri*
Rana de punta de flecha de Inger (S): *Epipedobates ingeri*
Rana de punta de flecha de Lehmann (S): *Dendrobates lehmanni*
Rana de punta de flecha de Myers (S): *Epipedobates myersi*
Rana de punta de flecha de Peters (S): *Epipedobates petersi*
Rana de punta de flecha de Silverstone (S): *Epipedobates silverstonei*
Rana de punta de flecha de Steyermark (S): *Minyobates steyermarki*
Rana de punta de flecha de Vanzolini (S): *Dendrobates vanzolinii*
Rana de punta de flecha de vientre azul (S): *Epipedobates azureiventris*
Rana de punta de flecha esmeralda (S): *Epipedobates smaragdinus*
Rana de punta de flecha fantástica (S): *Dendrobates fantasticus*
Rana de punta de flecha granulosa (S): *Dendrobates granuliferus*
Rana de punta de flecha histriónica (S): *Dendrobates histrionicus*
Rana de punta de flecha lúgubre (S): *Phyllobates lugubris*
Rana de punta de flecha maculada (S): *Epipedobates maculatus*
Rana de punta de flecha misteriosa (S): *Dendrobates mysteriosus*
Rana de punta de flecha pentaestriada (S): *Dendrobates quinquevittatus*
Rana de punta de flecha picta (F): *Epipedobates pictus*
Rana de punta de flecha rayada (S): *Phyllobates vittatus*
Rana de punta de flecha reticulada (S): *Dendrobates reticulatus*
Rana de punta de flecha roja (S): *Dendrobates pumilio*
Rana de punta de flecha terrible (S): *Phyllobates terribilis*
Rana de punta de flecha tricolor (S): *Epipedobates tricolor*
Rana de punta de flecha truncada (S): *Dendrobates truncatus*
Rana de punta de flecha variable (S): *Dendrobates ventrimaculatus*
Rana de punta de flecha verde (S): *Minyobates viridis*
Rana dorada (S): *Mantella aurantiaca/ Atelopus zeteki*
Rana dorada de Panamá (S): *Atelopus zeteki*
Rana hexadactyla = Euphlyctis hexadactylus
Rana tigerina = Hoplobatrachus tigerinus
Rana venenosa de Zetek (S): *Atelopus zeteki*
Ranas de puntas de flechas (S): *Dendrobates* spp. / *Epipedobates* spp./ *Minyobates* spp./ *Phyllobates* spp.
Ranas doradas (S): *Mantella* spp.
Ranita dorada de Madagascar (S): *Mantella aurantiaca*
Rapaces diurnes (F): FALCONIFORMES spp. Av
Rapaces nocturnes (F): STRIGIFORMES spp. Av
Raptors (F): FALCONIFORMES spp. Av
Rascón de la isla de Lord Howe (S): *Gallirallus sylvestris*
Rascón de la Lord Howe (S): *Gallirallus sylvestris*
Rat à grosse queue (F): *Zyzomys pedunculatus*
Rat architecte (F): *Leporillus conditor*
Rat kangaroos (E): *Bettongia* spp.
Rata arquitecto (S): *Leporillus conditor*
Rata bastarda de agua (S): *Xeromys myoides*
Rata canguro (S): *Bettongia* spp.
Rata coligorda (S): *Zyzomys pedunculatus*
Ratel (E/S/F): *Mellivora capensis*
Ratón marsupial colilargo (S): *Sminthopsis longicaudata*
Ratón marsupial desértico (S): *Sminthopsis psammophila*
Ratonero calzado (S): *Buteo lagopus*
Ratonero común (S): *Buteo buteo*
Ratonero cuellirrojo (S): *Buteo auguralis*
Ratonero moro (S): *Buteo rufinus*
Ratufa spp.: (E) Giant squirrels, (S) Ardillas gigantes, (F) Écureuils géants, **II** SCIURIDAE Ma

Checklist of fauna/Lista de especies de fauna/Liste des espèces animales

Ratufa affinis : (E) Cream-coloured Giant Squirrel, Pale
Giant Squirrel, (F) Écureuil de Raffles, Écureuil géant
commun, Ratufe dorée **II** SCIURIDAE Ma
Ratufa bicolor : (E) Black Giant Squirrel, (F) Écureuil
géant de Malaisie **II** SCIURIDAE Ma
Ratufa indica : (E) Indian Giant Squirrel, (F) Écureuil
géant de l'Inde **II** SCIURIDAE Ma
Ratufa macroura : (E) Grizzled Giant Squirrel, Sri Lankan
Giant Squirrel, (F) Écureuil géant de Ceylan, Écureuil
géant gris **II** SCIURIDAE Ma
Ratufe dorée (F): *Ratufa affinis*
Raxworthy's Leaf Chameleon (E): *Brookesia valerieae*
Rayito brillante (S): *Aglaeactis cupripennis*
Razorback (E): *Balaenoptera physalus*
Razor-billed Curassow (E): *Mitu mitu*
Rebeco de los Abruzzos (S): *Rupicapra pyrenaica ornata*
Rebeco de los Apeninos (S): *Rupicapra pyrenaica ornata*
Red Bear (E): *Ursus arctos isabellinus*
Red Bird-of-paradise (E): *Paradisaea rubra*
Red Cat-bear (E): *Ailurus fulgens*
Red cave corals (E): *Tubastraea spp.*
Red Cock-of-the-rock (E): *Rupicola peruviana*
Red Colobus (E): *Procolobus badius*
Red Dog (E): *Cuon alpinus*
Red Fox (E): *Pseudalopex culpaeus*
Red Goral (E): *Naemorhedus baileyi*
Red Goshawk (E): *Erythrotriorchis radiatus*
Red Howler (E): *Alouatta seniculus*
Red Howling Monkey (E): *Alouatta seniculus*
Red Kite (E): *Milvus milvus*
Red Lory (E): *Eos bornea*
Red Panda (E): *Ailurus fulgens*
Red Rain Frog (E): *Scaphiophryne gottlebei*
Red Sheep (E): *Ovis vignei*
Red Shining-Parrot (E): *Prosopeia tabuensis*
Red Siskin (E): *Carduelis cucullata*
Red Spider Monkey (E): *Ateles geoffroyi panamensis*
Red Teju (E): *Tupinambis rufescens*
Red Tiger (E): *Puma concolor*
Red-and-black Poison Frog (E): *Dendrobates histrionicus*
Red-and-blue Lory (E): *Eos histrio*
Red-and-blue Poison Frog (E): *Dendrobates pumilio*
Red-and-green Macaw (E): *Ara chloroptera*
Red-and-white Uacari (E): *Cacajao calvus*
Red-backed Hawk (E): *Buteo polyosoma*
Red-backed Kite (E): *Haliastur indus*
Red-backed Poison Frog (E): *Dendrobates reticulatus*
Red-backed Sea Eagle (E): *Haliastur indus*
Red-backed Squirrel Monkey (E): *Saimiri oerstedii*
Red-banded Poison Frog (E): *Dendrobates lehmanni*
Red-bearded Saki (E): *Pithecia monachus*
Red-bellied Conure (E): *Pyrrhura frontalis*
Red-bellied Guenon (E): *Cercopithecus erythrogaster*
Red-bellied Lemur (E): *Eulemur rubriventer*
Red-bellied Macaw (E): *Orthopsittaca manilata*
Red-bellied Monkey (E): *Cercopithecus erythrogaster*
Red-bellied Parrot (E): *Poicephalus rufiventris*
Red-bellied Spider Monkey (E): *Ateles geoffroyi frontatus*
Red-bellied Tamarin (E): *Saguinus labiatus*
Red-billed Curassow (E): *Crax blumenbachii*
Red-billed Firefinch (E): *Lagonosticta senegala*
Red-billed Hanging-Parrot (E): *Loriculus exilis*
Red-billed Leiothrix (E): *Leiothrix lutea*
Red-billed Mesia (E): *Leiothrix lutea*
Red-billed Parrot (E): *Pionus sordidus*
Red-billed Toucan (E): *Ramphastos tucanus*
Red-billed Whistling-Duck (E): *Dendrocygna autumnalis*
Red-billed Wood-Dove (E): *Turtur afer*
Red-breasted Conure (E): *Pyrrhura hoematotis*
Red-breasted Goose (E): *Branta ruficollis*
Red-breasted Parakeet (E): *Psittacula alexandri*
Red-breasted Pygmy-Parrot (E): *Micropsitta bruijnii*
Red-breasted Toucan (E): *Ramphastos dicolorus*
Red-browed Amazon (E): *Amazona rhodocorytha*
Red-browed Parrot (E): *Amazona rhodocorytha*

Red-capped Mangabey (E): *Cercocebus torquatus*
Red-capped Parrot (E): *Purpureicephalus spurius/
Pionopsitta pileata*
Red-cheeked Cordonbleu (E): *Uraeginthus bengalus*
Red-cheeked Parrot (E): *Geoffroyus geoffroyi*
Red-chested Goshawk (E): *Accipiter toussenelii*
Red-chested Hawk (E): *Accipiter toussenelii*
Red-chested Owlet (E): *Glaucidium tephronotum*
Red-chested Tamarin (E): *Saguinus labiatus*
Red-chinned Lorikeet (E): *Charmosyna rubrigularis*
Red-collared Sparrowhawk (E): *Accipiter brachyurus*
Red-collared Whydah (E): *Euplectes ardens*
Red-collared Widowbird (E): *Euplectes ardens*
Red-crested Bustard (E): *Eupodotis ruficrista*
Red-crested Cardinal (E): *Paroaria coronata*
Red-crested Turaco (E): *Tauraco erythrolophus*
Red-crowned Amazon (E): *Amazona viridigenalis*
Red-crowned Crane (E): *Grus japonensis*
Red-crowned Parakeet (E): *Cyanoramphus
novaezelandiae*
Red-crowned Parrot (E): *Amazona viridigenalis/
Poicephalus gulielmi*
Red-crowned Roofed Turtle (E): *Kachuga kachuga*
Reddish Hermit (E): *Phaethornis ruber*
Reddish Scops-Owl (E): *Otus rufescens*
Reddish-bellied Parakeet (E): *Pyrrhura frontalis*
Red-eared Conure (E): *Pyrrhura cruentata*
Red-eared Guenon (E): *Cercopithecus erythrotis*
Red-eared Monkey (E): *Cercopithecus erythrotis*
Red-eared Parakeet (E): *Pyrrhura hoematotis*
Red-eared Waxbill (E): *Estrilda troglodytes*
Red-eyed Dove (E): *Streptopelia semitorquata*
Red-faced Black Spider Monkey (E): *Ateles paniscus*
Red-faced Lovebird (E): *Agapornis pullarius*
Red-faced Parrot (E): *Hapalopsittaca pyrrhops*
Red-faced Pytilia (E): *Pytilia hypogrammica*
Red-fan Parrot (E): *Deroptyus accipitrinus*
Red-flanked Lorikeet (E): *Charmosyna placentis*
Red-footed Falcon (E): *Falco vespertinus*
Red-footed Tortoise (E): *Geochelone carbonaria*
Red-fronted Amazon (E): *Amazona vittata*
Red-fronted Antpecker (E): *Parmoptila rubrifrons*
Red-fronted Conure (E): *Aratinga wagleri*
Red-fronted Kakariki (E): *Cyanoramphus novaezelandiae*
Red-fronted Lorikeet (E): *Charmosyna rubronotata*
Red-fronted Macaw (E): *Ara rubrogenys*
Red-fronted Parakeet (E): *Cyanoramphus novaezelandiae*
Red-fronted Parrot (E): *Poicephalus gulielmi*
Red-fronted Parrotlet (E): *Touit costaricensis*
Red-handed Howler (E): *Alouatta belzebul*
Red-handed Howling Monkey (E): *Alouatta belzebul*
Red-handed Tamarin (E): *Saguinus midas*
Red-headed Amazon River Turtle (E): *Podocnemis
erythrocephala*
Red-headed Dioch (E): *Quelea erythrops*
Red-headed Falcon (E): *Falco chicquera*
Red-headed Lovebird (E): *Agapornis pullarius*
Red-headed Malimbe (E): *Malimbus rubricollis*
Red-headed Merlin (E): *Falco chicquera*
Red-headed Poison Frog (E): *Dendrobates fantasticus*
Red-headed Quelea (E): *Quelea erythrops*
Red-headed River Turtle (E): *Podocnemis erythrocephala*
Red-headed Rockfowl (E): *Picathartes oreas*
Red-headed Sideneck (E): *Podocnemis erythrocephala*
Red-headed Vulture (E): *Sarcogyps calvus*
Red-headed Weaver (E): *Anaplectes rubriceps/ Malimbus
rubricollis*
Red-knobbed Hornbill (E): *Aceros cassidix*
Red-legged Falconet (E): *Microhierax caerulescens*
Red-lored Amazon (E): *Amazona autumnalis*
Red-lored Parrot (E): *Amazona autumnalis*
Red-masked Conure (E): *Aratinga erythrogenys*
Red-masked Parakeet (E): *Aratinga erythrogenys*
Red-necked Amazon (E): *Amazona arausiaca*
Red-necked Buzzard (E): *Buteo auguralis*

Red-necked Falcon (E): *Falco chicquera*
Red-necked Parrot (E): *Amazona arausiaca*
Red-nosed Dwarf Chameleon (E): *Bradypodion oxyrhinum*
Red-nosed Saki (E): *Chiropotes albinasus*
Red-nosed Tortoise (E): *Indotestudo elongata*
Red-rumped Parrot (E): *Psephotus haematonotus*
Red-shanked Douc Langur (E): *Pygathrix nemaeus*
Red-shouldered Hawk (E): *Buteo lineatus*
Red-shouldered Macaw (E): *Diopsittaca nobilis*
Red-spectacled Amazon (E): *Amazona pretrei*
Red-spectacled Parrot (E): *Amazona pretrei*
Red-spotted Lorikeet (E): *Charmosyna rubronotata*
Redtail Monkey (E): *Cercopithecus ascanius*
Red-tailed Amazon (E): *Amazona brasiliensis*
Red-tailed Black-Cockatoo (E): *Calyptorhynchus banksii*
Red-tailed Buzzard (E): *Buteo auguralis*
Red-tailed Comet (E): *Sappho sparganura*
Red-tailed Hawk (E): *Buteo jamaicensis/ Buteo ventralis*
Red-tailed Monkey (E): *Cercopithecus ascanius*
Red-tailed Parrot (E): *Amazona brasiliensis*
Red-tailed Sportive Lemur (E): *Lepilemur ruficaudatus*
Red-thighed Falconet (E): *Microhierax caerulescens*
Red-thighed Hawk (E): *Accipiter erythronemius*
Red-thighed Sparrowhawk (E): *Accipiter erythropus*
Red-throated Caracara (E): *Daptrius americanus*
Red-throated Lorikeet (E): *Charmosyna amabilis*
Red-throated Parakeet (E): *Aratinga rubritorquis*
Red-topped Amazon (E): *Amazona rhodocorytha*
Red-topped Parrot (E): *Amazona rhodocorytha*
Red-vented Cockatoo (E): *Cacatua haematuropygia*
Red-vented Malimbe (E): *Malimbus scutatus*
Red-vented Parrot (E): *Pionus menstruus*
Red-winged Parrot (E): *Aprosmictus erythropterus*
Red-winged Pytilia (E): *Pytilia phoenicoptera*
Reed Cat (E): *Felis chaus*
Regal Girdled Lizard (E): *Cordylus regius*
Regal Python (E): *Python reticulatus*
Regent Parrot (E): *Polytelis anthopeplus*
Reichenow's Spiny-tailed Lizard (E): *Cordylus vittifer*
Relict Gull (E): *Larus relictus*
Renard colfeo (F): *Pseudalopex culpaeus*
Renard crabier (F): *Cerdocyon thous*
Renard d'Azara (F): *Pseudalopex gymnocercus*
Renard de Blanford (F): *Vulpes cana*
Renard de Chiloé (F): *Pseudalopex griseus*
Renard de la Pampa (F): *Pseudalopex gymnocercus*
Renard du Bengale (F): *Vulpes bengalensis*
Renard gris d'Argentine (F): *Pseudalopex griseus*
Renard volant de Ponape (F): *Pteropus molossinus*
Renards volants (F): *Acerodon* spp./ *Pteropus* spp.
Requin baleine (F): *Rhincodon typus*
Requin blanc (F): *Carcharodon carcharias*
Requin pèlerin (F): *Cetorhinus maximus*
Resplendent Quetzal (E): *Pharomachrus mocinno*
Reticulated Poison Frog (E): *Dendrobates reticulatus*
Reticulated Python (E): *Python reticulatus*
Réunion Day Gecko (E): *Phelsuma borbonica*
Réunion Harrier (E): *Circus maillardi*
Réunion Marsh-Harrier (E): *Circus maillardi*
Réunion Seahorse (E): *Hippocampus borboniensis*
Rey zamuro (S): *Sarcoramphus papa*
Rhea americana : (E) Common Rhea, Greater Rhea, (S) Avestruz, Ñandú, Ñandú común, (F) Nandou américain , Nandou commun, Nandou d'Amérique, Nandou gris, **II** RHEIDAE Av
Rhea pennata : (E) Darwin's Rhea, Lesser Rhea, Puna Rhea, (S) Avestruz de Magallanes, Ñandú cordillerano, Ñandú de Darwin, Ñandú petizo, (F) Nandou de Darwin, **I/II** RHEIDAE Av
Rhea pennata pennata : **I/II** RHEIDAE Av
Rheinardia nigrescens = *Rheinardia ocellata*
Rheinardia ocellata : (E) Crested Argus, Ocellated Pheasant, (S) Faisán de Rheinard, (F) Argus ocellé, Rheinarte ocellé, **I** PHASIANIDAE Av
Rheinarte ocellé (F): *Rheinardia ocellata*

Rheobatrachus spp.: (E) Gastric-brooding frogs, (F) Grenouilles à incubation gastrique **II** MYOBATRACHIDAE Am
Rheobatrachus silus : (E) Conondale Gastric-brooding Frog, Platypus Frog, (F) Grenouille plate à incubation gastrique **II** MYOBATRACHIDAE Am
Rheobatrachus vitellinus : (E) Eungella Gastric-brooding Frog, Southern Gastric-brooding Frog **II** MYOBATRACHIDAE Am
Rhesus Macaque (E): *Macaca mulatta*
Rhesus Monkey (E): *Macaca mulatta*
Rhim (F/S): *Gazella leptoceros*
Rhim Gazelle (E): *Gazella leptoceros*
Rhincodon typus : (E) Whale Shark, (S) Dámero, Pez dama, Tiburón ballena, (F) Chagrin, Requin baleine, **II** RHINCODONTIDAE El
Rhinocéros blanc (F): *Ceratotherium simum*
Rhinocéros blanc du Sud (F): *Ceratotherium simum simum*
Rhinoceros Chameleon (E): *Furcifer rhinoceratus*
Rhinocéros de la Sonde (F): *Rhinoceros sondaicus*
Rhinocéros de Sumatra (F): *Dicerorhinus sumatrensis*
Rhinoceros Hornbill (E): *Buceros rhinoceros*
Rhinoceros Iguana (E): *Cyclura cornuta*
Rhinocéros noir (F): *Diceros bicornis*
Rhinoceros sondaicus : (E) Javan Rhinoceros, (S) Rinoceronte de Java, (F) Rhinocéros de la Sonde, **I** RHINOCEROTIDAE Ma
Rhinocéros unicorne de l'Inde (F): *Rhinoceros unicornis*
Rhinoceros unicornis : (E) Great Indian Rhinoceros, (S) Rinoceronte unicornio índico, (F) Rhinocéros unicorne de l'Inde, **I** RHINOCEROTIDAE Ma
Rhinocéros (F): RHINOCEROTIDAE spp.
Rhinoceroses (E): RHINOCEROTIDAE spp.
RHINOCEROTIDAE spp.: (E) Rhinoceroses, (S) Rinocerontes, (F) Rhinocéros, **I/II** Ma
Rhinodon pentalineatus = *Rhincodon typus*
Rhinopithecus avunculus = *Pygathrix avunculus*
Rhinopithecus bieti = *Pygathrix bieti*
Rhinopithecus brelichi = *Pygathrix brelichi*
Rhinopithecus nemaeus = *Pygathrix nemaeus*
Rhinopithecus roxellana = *Pygathrix roxellana*
Rhinopithèque de Roxellane (F): *Pygathrix roxellana*
Rhinopithèque doré (F): *Pygathrix roxellana*
Rhinopithèque douc (F): *Pygathrix nemaeus*
Rhinopithèque du Tonkin (F): *Pygathrix avunculus*
Rhinopithèque jaune doré (F): *Pygathrix brelichi*
Rhinopithèques (F): *Pygathrix* spp.
Rhinoplax vigil = *Buceros vigil*
Rhinoptynx clamator = *Asio clamator*
Rhizopsammia annae : **II** DENDROPHYLLIIDAE An
Rhizopsammia bermudensis : **II** DENDROPHYLLIIDAE An
Rhizopsammia chamissoi = *Rhizopsammia verrilli*
Rhizopsammia compacta : **II** DENDROPHYLLIIDAE An
Rhizopsammia goesi : **II** DENDROPHYLLIIDAE An
Rhizopsammia manuelensis = *Cladopsammia manuelensis*
Rhizopsammia minuta : **II** DENDROPHYLLIIDAE An
Rhizopsammia nuda : **II** DENDROPHYLLIIDAE An
Rhizopsammia pulchra : **II** DENDROPHYLLIIDAE An
Rhizopsammia verrilli : **II** DENDROPHYLLIIDAE An
Rhizopsammia wellingtoni : **II** DENDROPHYLLIIDAE An
Rhizopsammia wettsteini : **II** DENDROPHYLLIIDAE An
Rhizosmilia elata : **II** CARYOPHYLLIIDAE An
Rhizosmilia gerdae : **II** CARYOPHYLLIIDAE An
Rhizosmilia maculata : (E) Speckled Cup Coral **II** CARYOPHYLLIIDAE An
Rhizosmilia multipaliferus : **II** CARYOPHYLLIIDAE An
Rhizosmilia robusta : **II** CARYOPHYLLIIDAE An
Rhizosmilia sagamiensis : **II** CARYOPHYLLIIDAE An
Rhizothera longirostris : (E) Long-billed Partridge, (S) Perdiz de bosque de pico largo, Perdiz piquilarga, (F) Perdrix à long bec, Rouloul à long bec, **III** PHASIANIDAE Av
Rhizotrochus flabelliformis : **II** FLABELLIDAE An

Checklist of fauna/Lista de especies de fauna/Liste des espèces animales

Rhizotrochus levidensis : **II** FLABELLIDAE An
Rhizotrochus niinoi : **II** FLABELLIDAE An
Rhizotrochus radiatus = *Rhizotrochus tuberculatus*
Rhizotrochus tuberculatus : **II** FLABELLIDAE An
Rhizotrochus typus : **II** FLABELLIDAE An
Rhodesian Girdled Lizard (E): *Cordylus rhodesianus*
Rhodonessa caryophyllacea : (E) Pink-headed Duck, (S) Pato cabecirrosa, Pato de cabeza rosa, (F) Canard à tête rose, Nette à cou rose, **I** ANATIDAE Av
Rhodopis vesper : (E) Oasis Hummingbird, (S) Colibrí del Atacama, (F) Colibri vesper, **II** TROCHILIDAE Av
Rhombopsammia niphada : **II** MICRABACIIDAE An
Rhombopsammia squiresi : **II** MICRABACIIDAE An
Rhoptropella ocellata = *Phelsuma ocellata*
Rhynchopsitta spp.: (S) Lorito piquigrueso, (F) Perroquets à gros bec, **I** PSITTACIDAE Av
Rhynchopsitta pachyrhyncha : (E) Thick-billed Parrot, (S) Cotorra-serrana occidental, Loro piquigordo, Periquito de pico grueso, (F) Conure à gros bec, Perruche à gros bec, Perruche ara, **I** PSITTACIDAE Av
Rhynchopsitta pachyrhyncha ssp. *terrisi* = *Rhynchopsitta terrisi*
Rhynchopsitta terrisi : (E) Maroon-fronted Parrot, (S) Cotorra-serrana oriental, (F) Conure à front brun, **I** PSITTACIDAE Av
Rhynochetos jubatus : (E) Kagu, (S) Kagú, (F) Kagou, Kagou huppé, **I** RHYNOCHETIDAE Av
Rhyticeros cassidix = *Aceros cassidix*
Rhyticeros corrugatus = *Aceros corrugatus*
Rhyticeros everetti = *Aceros everetti*
Rhyticeros leucocephalus = *Aceros leucocephalus*
Rhyticeros leucocephalus ssp. *waldeni* = *Aceros waldeni*
Rhyticeros narcondami = *Aceros narcondami*
Rhyticeros plicatus = *Aceros plicatus*
Rhyticeros subruficollis = *Aceros subruficollis*
Rhyticeros undulatus = *Aceros undulatus*
Ribbon Coral (E): *Agaricia tenuifolia*
Ribbon Finch (E): *Amadina fasciata*
Ribbon-tailed Astrapia (E): *Astrapia mayeri*
Ribbon-tailed Bird-of-paradise (E): *Astrapia mayeri*
Rice Lizard (E): *Varanus salvator*
Rice Paddy Snake (E): *Xenochrophis piscator*
Richmond Birdwing (E): *Ornithoptera richmondia*
Ricord's Ground Iguana (E): *Cyclura ricordi*
Ricord's Iguana (E): *Cyclura ricordi*
Ridged Cactus Coral (E): *Mycetophyllia lamarckiana*
Ridgeless Cactus Coral (E): *Mycetophyllia reesi*
Ridge-tailed Monitor (E): *Varanus acanthurus/ Varanus primordius*
Ridgway's Hawk (E): *Buteo ridgwayi*
Ridley de Kemp (F): *Lepidochelys kempi*
Ridley du Pacifique (F): *Lepidochelys olivacea*
Right Whale (E): *Eubalaena glacialis*
Right whales (E): *Eubalaena* spp.
Rimose Naiad (E): *Conradilla caelata*
Ring Lizard (E): *Varanus salvator*
Ringed Python (E): *Bothrochilus boa*
Ring-necked Parakeet (E): *Psittacula krameri*
Ring-tailed Lemur (E): *Lemur catta*
Rinoceronte blanco (S): *Ceratotherium simum*
Rinoceronte de Java (S): *Rhinoceros sondaicus*
Rinoceronte de Sumatra (S): *Dicerorhinus sumatrensis*
Rinoceronte negro (S): *Diceros bicornis*
Rinoceronte unicornio índico (S): *Rhinoceros unicornis*
Rinocerontes (S): RHINOCEROTIDAE spp.
Rio Acarí Marmoset (E): *Callithrix acariensis*
Rio Apaporis (Spectacled) Caiman (E): *Caiman crocodilus apaporiensis*
Rio Madeira Poison Frog (E): *Dendrobates quinquevittatus*
Rio Magdalena River Turtle (E): *Podocnemis lewyana*
Rio Manicoré Marmoset (E): *Callithrix manicorensis*
Rio Napo Tamarin (E): *Saguinus fuscicollis*
Rio Santiago Poison Frog (E): *Dendrobates captivus*
Rip Sack (E): *Eschrichtius robustus*

Risso's Dolphin (E): *Grampus griseus*
River dolphins (E): *Sotalia* spp.
River Eagle (E): *Haliaeetus vocifer*
River Terrapin (E): *Batagur baska*
Rivoli's Hummingbird (E): *Eugenes fulgens*
Roadside Hawk (E): *Buteo magnirostris*
Robust Ivory Tree Coral (E): *Oculina robusta*
Rock Dove (E): *Columba livia*
Rock Eagle-Owl (E): *Bubo bengalensis*
Rock Monitor (E): *Varanus albigularis*
Rock Parakeet (E): *Pyrrhura rupicola*
Rock Parrot (E): *Neophema petrophila*
Rock Pebbler (E): *Polytelis anthopeplus*
Rock Pigeon (E): *Columba livia*
Rodrigues Brush-Warbler (E): *Bebrornis rodericanus*
Rodrigues Day Gecko (E): *Phelsuma edwardnewtonii*
Rodrigues Flying-fox (E): *Pteropus rodricensis*
Rodrigues Warbler (E): *Bebrornis rodericanus*
Roi des vautours (F): *Sarcoramphus papa*
Rollulus rouloul : (E) Crested Partridge, Roulroul, (S) Perdiz de bosque crestada, Perdiz rulrul, (F) Rouloul à couronne, Rouloul couronné, **III** PHASIANIDAE Av
Romerolagus diazi : (E) Volcano Rabbit, (S) Conejo de Díaz, Conejo de los volcanes, Teporingo, Zacatuche, (F) Lapin de Diaz, Lapin des volcans, **I** LEPORIDAE Ma
Rondo Dwarf Galago (E): *Galagoides rondoensis*
Rondo Galago (E): *Galagoides rondoensis*
Rondônia Emerald (E): *Agyrtria rondoniae*
Roofed turtles (E): *Kachuga* spp.
Rooiberg Girdled Lizard (E): *Cordylus imkae*
Rorcual azul (S): *Balaenoptera musculus*
Rorcual boreal (S): *Balaenoptera borealis*
Rorcual común (S): *Balaenoptera physalus*
Rorcual de Rudolphi (S): *Balaenoptera borealis*
Rorcual enano del antarctica (S): *Balaenoptera bonaerensis*
Rorcual jorobado (S): *Megaptera novaeangliae*
Rorcual menor (S): *Balaenoptera acutorostrata*
Rorcual norteno (S): *Balaenoptera borealis*
Rorqual à bosse (F): *Megaptera novaeangliae*
Rorqual à ventre cannelé (F): *Balaenoptera musculus*
Rorqual bleu (F): *Balaenoptera musculus*
Rorqual boréal (F): *Balaenoptera borealis*
Rorqual commun (F): *Balaenoptera physalus*
Rorqual de Bryde (F): *Balaenoptera edeni*
Rorqual de Rudolphi (F): *Balaenoptera borealis*
Rorqual de Sibbold (F): *Balaenoptera musculus*
Rorqual d'Eden (F): *Balaenoptera edeni*
Rorqual du Cap (F): *Megaptera novaeangliae*
Rorqual sei (F): *Balaenoptera borealis*
Rorqual tropical (F): *Balaenoptera edeni*
Rose Coral (E): *Manicina areolata*
Roseate Cockatoo (E): *Eolophus roseicapillus*
Rose-crowned Conure (E): *Pyrrhura rhodocephala*
Rose-faced Parrot (E): *Pionopsitta pulchra*
Rose-grey Dove (E): *Streptopelia roseogrisea*
Rose-headed Conure (E): *Pyrrhura rhodocephala*
Rose-headed Parakeet (E): *Pyrrhura rhodocephala*
Rosenberg's Monitor (E): *Varanus rosenbergi*
Rose-ringed Parakeet (E): *Psittacula krameri*
Rosette-nosed Chameleon (E): *Bradypodion spinosum*
Rosmarus rosmarus = *Odobenus rosmarus*
Rossell Island Tree Monitor (E): *Varanus telenesetes*
Rostrhamus hamatus : (E) Slender-billed Kite, (S) Caracolero, Caracolero plomizo, Gavilán pico de Hoz, (F) Milan à long bec, **II** ACCIPITRIDAE Av
Rostrhamus sociabilis : (E) Everglade Kite, Snail Kite, (S) Carocolero común, Gavilán caracolero, Milano caracolero, (F) Milan des marais, **II** ACCIPITRIDAE Av
Rosy Boa (E): *Lichanura trivirgata*
Rosy-faced Lovebird (E): *Agapornis roseicollis*
Rothschild's Birdwing (E): *Ornithoptera rothschildi*
Rothschild's Myna (E): *Leucopsar rothschildi*

Checklist of fauna/Lista de especies de fauna/Liste des espèces animales

Rothschild's Parakeet (E): *Psittacula intermedia*
Rothschild's Peacock-Pheasant (E): *Polyplectron inopinatum*
Rothschild's Starling (E): *Leucopsar rothschildi*
Rough Cactus Coral (E): *Mycetophyllia ferox*
Rough Gecko (E): *Naultinus rudis*
Rough Pigtoe (E): *Pleurobema plenum*
Rough Pigtoe Pearly Mussel (E): *Pleurobema plenum*
Rough Star Coral (E): *Isophyllastrea rigida*
Rough Starlet Coral (E): *Siderastrea radians*
Rough-legged Buzzard (E): *Buteo lagopus*
Rough-legged Hawk (E): *Buteo lagopus*
Rough-necked Monitor (E): *Varanus rudicollis*
Rough-scaled Boa (E): *Trachyboa boulengeri*
Rough-scaled Girdled Lizard (E): *Cordylus cordylus*
Rough-scaled Python (E): *Morelia carinata*
Rough-scaled Sand Boa (E): *Gongylophis conicus*
Rough-toothed Dolphin (E): *Steno bredanensis*
Rouloul à couronne (F): *Rollulus rouloul*
Rouloul à long bec (F): *Rhizothera longirostris*
Rouloul couronné (F): *Rollulus rouloul*
Rouloul noir (F): *Melanoperdix nigra*
Rouloul ocellé (F): *Caloperdix oculea*
Roulroul (E): *Rollulus rouloul*
Round Island boas (E): BOLYERIIDAE spp.
Round Island Burrowing Boa (E): *Bolyeria multocarinata*
Round Island Day Gecko (E): *Phelsuma guentheri*
Round Island Keel-scaled Boa (E): *Casarea dussumieri*
Rousettes (F): *Acerodon* spp.
Rousserolle de Rodriguez (F): *Bebrornis rodericanus*
Roussette de l'île Mortlock (F): *Pteropus phaeocephalus*
Roussette des îles Marianes (F): *Pteropus mariannus*
Roussette des îles Marianne (F): *Pteropus mariannus*
Roussette des îles Palau (F): *Pteropus pilosus*
Roussette des îles Samoa (F): *Pteropus samoensis*
Roussette des îles Tonga (F): *Pteropus tonganus*
Roussette des îles Truk (F): *Pteropus insularis*
Roussettes (F): *Pteropus* spp.
Royal Python (E): *Python regius*
Royal Sunangel (E): *Heliangelus regalis*
Rubber Boa (E): *Charina bottae*
Ruby Poison Frog (S): *Epipedobates parvulus*
Ruby-throated Hummingbird (E): *Archilochus colubris*
Ruby-topaz Hummingbird (E): *Chrysolampis mosquitus*
Ruck Flying-fox (E): *Pteropus insularis*
Ruddy Mongoose (E): *Herpestes smithii*
Ruddy Snub-nosed Monitor (E): *Varanus flavescens*
Ruddy Treeshrew (E): *Tupaia splendidula*
Rudophi's Rorqual (E): *Balaenoptera borealis*
Rueck's Blue-Flycatcher (E): *Cyornis ruckii*
Rueck's Niltava (E): *Cyornis ruckii*
Rueppell's Bustard (E): *Eupodotis rueppellii*
Rueppell's Griffon (E): *Gyps rueppellii*
Rueppell's Griffon Vulture (E): *Gyps rueppellii*
Rueppell's Parrot (E): *Poicephalus rueppellii*
Rueppell's Vulture (E): *Gyps rueppellii*
Rufescent Screech-Owl (E): *Otus ingens*
Ruffed Lemur (E): *Varecia variegata*
Ruffled Coral (E): *Merulina ampliata*
Rufibrenta ruficollis = *Branta ruficollis*
Rufous Bristlebird (E): *Dasyornis broadbenti litoralis*
Rufous Crab-Hawk (E): *Buteogallus aequinoctialis*
Rufous Fishing-Owl (E): *Scotopelia ussheri*
Rufous Hare-wallaby (E): *Lagorchestes hirsutus*
Rufous Hornbill (E): *Buceros hydrocorax*
Rufous Hummingbird (E): *Selasphorus rufus*
Rufous Mouse-lemur (E): *Microcebus rufus*
Rufous Owl (E): *Ninox rufa*
Rufous Sabrewing (E): *Campylopterus rufus*
Rufous-banded Owl (E): *Strix albitarsus*
Rufous-bellied Eagle (E): *Hieraaetus kienerii*
Rufous-breasted Hermit (E): *Glaucis hirsuta*
Rufous-breasted Sabrewing (E): *Campylopterus hyperythrus*
Rufous-capped Thornbill (E): *Chalcostigma ruficeps*

Rufous-cheeked Hornbill (E): *Aceros nipalensis*
Rufous-cheeked Hummingbird (E): *Goethalsia bella*
Rufous-chested Sparrowhawk (E): *Accipiter rufiventris*
Rufous-crested Coquette (E): *Lophornis delattrei*
Rufous-fronted Parakeet (E): *Bolborhynchus ferrugineifrons*
Rufous-headed Bristlebird (E): *Dasyornis broadbenti litoralis*
Rufous-headed Hornbill (E): *Aceros waldeni*
Rufous-legged Owl (E): *Strix rufipes*
Rufous-naped Tamarin (E): *Saguinus geoffroyi*
Rufous-necked Hornbill (E): *Aceros nipalensis*
Rufous-necked Sparrowhawk (E): *Accipiter erythrauchen*
Rufous-shafted Woodstar (E): *Chaetocercus jourdanii*
Rufous-tailed Hawk (E): *Buteo ventralis*
Rufous-tailed Hummingbird (E): *Amazilia tzacatl*
Rufous-tailed Pheasant (E): *Lophura erythrophthalma*
Rufous-tailed Treeshrew (E): *Tupaia splendidula*
Rufous-thighed Hawk (E): *Accipiter erythronemius/ Buteo leucorrhous*
Rufous-thighed Kite (E): *Harpagus diodon*
Rufous-throated Sapphire (E): *Hylocharis sapphirina*
Rufous-vented Whitetip (E): *Urosticte ruficrissa*
Rufous-webbed Brilliant (E): *Heliodoxa branickii*
Rufous-winged Buzzard (E): *Butastur liventer*
Rufous-winged Buzzard-Eagle (E): *Butastur liventer*
Ruiseñor del bambú (S): *Leiothrix lutea*
Rungwe Viviparous Toad (E): *Nectophrynoides viviparus*
Rupicapra ornata = *Rupicapra pyrenaica* ssp. *ornata*
Rupicapra pyrenaica ornata : (E) Abruzzo Chamois, Apennine Chamois, (S) Gamuza alpina, Gamuza de los Abruzzos, Rebeco de los Abruzzos, Rebeco de los Apeninos, (F) Chamois des Abruzzes, **I** BOVIDAE Ma
Rupicapra rupicapra ssp. *ornata* = *Rupicapra pyrenaica* ssp. *ornata*
Rupicola spp.: (E) Cocks-of-the-rock, (S) Gallitos de las rocas, (F) Coqs-de-roche, **II** COTINGIDAE Av
Rupicola peruviana : (E) Andean Cock-of-the-rock, Peruvian Cock-of-the-Rock, Red Cock-of-the-rock, Scarlet Cock-of-the-rock, (S) Gallito de las Sierras, Gallito de roca peruano, Tunqui, (F) Coq-de-roche péruvien, **II** COTINGIDAE Av
Rupicola rupicola : (E) Common Cock-of-the-Rock, Guianan Cock-of-the-rock, Orange Cock-of-the-rock, Smaller Cock-of-the-rock, (S) Gallito de las Rocas, Gallito de roca anaranjado, (F) Coq-de-roche de Guyane, Coq-de-roche orange, **II** COTINGIDAE Av
Rüppell's Desert Chameleon (E): *Chamaeleo affinis*
Rüppell's Parrot (S): *Poicephalus rueppellii*
Ruspoli's Turaco (E): *Tauraco ruspolii*
Russell's Sand Boa (E): *Gongylophis conicus*
Russell's Viper (E): *Daboia russelii*
Russet Boobook (E): *Ninox odiosa*
Russet Hawk-Owl (E): *Ninox odiosa*
Russet Mouse-lemur (E): *Microcebus rufus*
Russet-eared Guenon (E): *Cercopithecus erythrotis*
Russian Sturgeon (E): *Acipenser gueldenstaedtii/ Huso huso*
Rusty Monitor (E): *Varanus semiremex*
Rusty-barred Owl (E): *Pulsatrix melanota/ Strix hylophila*
Rusty-faced Parrot (E): *Hapalopsittaca amazonina*
Rusty-spotted Cat (E): *Prionailurus rubiginosus*
Ruwenzori Mountain Chameleon (E): *Bradypodion carpenteri*
Ruwenzori Side-striped Chameleon (E): *Chamaeleo rudis*
Ruwenzori Three-horned Chameleon (E): *Chamaeleo johnstoni*
Ryukyu Flying-fox (E): *Pteropus dasymallus*
Ryukyu Scops-Owl (E): *Otus elegans*
Ryukyu Serpent-Eagle (E): *Spilornis cheela*

Sacafi (S): *Psammobates geometricus*
Sachacabra (S): *Pudu mephistophiles*
Sachavaca (S): *Tapirus terrestris*

Checklist of fauna/Lista de especies de fauna/Liste des espèces animales

Sacramento sturgeon (E): *Acipenser transmontanus*
Sacred Ibis (E): *Threskiornis aethiopicus*
Saddle-back Tamarin (E): *Saguinus fuscicollis*
Saddle-backed Dolphin (E): *Delphinus delphis*
Saddlebill Stork (E): *Ephippiorhynchus senegalensis*
Saddle-billed Stork (E): *Ephippiorhynchus senegalensis*
Saffron Toucanet (E): *Baillonius bailloni*
Saffron-coloured Clam (E): *Tridacna crocea*
Saffron-cowled Blackbird (E): *Agelaius flavus*
Saffron-headed Parrot (E): *Pionopsitta pyrilia*
Sagittarius serpentarius : (E) Secretarybird, Secretary-
  bird, (S) Secretario, Serpentario, (F) Messager
  sagittaire, Secrétaire des serpents, Serpentaire, **II**
  SAGITTARIIDAE Av
Sagmatias australis = *Lagenorhynchus australis*
Sagmatias cruciger = *Lagenorhynchus cruciger*
Sagmatias obliquidens = *Lagenorhynchus obliquidens*
Sagmatias obscurus = *Lagenorhynchus obscurus*
Saguinus bicolor : (E) Bare-faced Tamarin, Pied Tamarin,
  (S) Tamarín bicolor, (F) Tamarin bicolore, **I**
  CALLITRICHIDAE Ma
Saguinus fuscicollis : (E) Brown-headed Tamarin, Rio
  Napo Tamarin, Saddle-back Tamarin, (F) Tamarin à
  manteau rouge **II** CALLITRICHIDAE Ma
Saguinus geoffroyi : (E) Cotton-top Marmoset, Geoffroy's
  Tamarin, Liszt Monkey, Pinche Marmoset, Rufous-
  naped Tamarin, (S) Tamarino de Geoffroy, (F)
  Tamarin de Geoffroy, **I** CALLITRICHIDAE Ma
Saguinus graellsi = *Saguinus nigricollis*
Saguinus imperator : (E) Emperor Tamarin, (S) Tamarino
  emperador **II** CALLITRICHIDAE Ma
Saguinus inustus : (E) Dusky Tamarin, Mottle-faced
  Tamarin, (S) Tamarino de caba manchada **II**
  CALLITRICHIDAE Ma
Saguinus labiatus : (E) Red-bellied Tamarin, Red-chested
  Tamarin, White-lipped Tamarin, (S) Tamarino de
  labios blancos **II** CALLITRICHIDAE Ma
Saguinus leucopus : (E) White-footed Tamarin, (S)
  Tamarín de manos blancas, Tamarín de pies blancos,
  (F) Tamarin à pieds blancs, **I** CALLITRICHIDAE Ma
Saguinus martinsi = *Saguinus bicolor*
Saguinus melanoleucus = *Saguinus fuscicollis*
Saguinus midas : (E) Negro Tamarin, Red-handed
  Tamarin, (F) Tamarin aux mains rousses **II**
  CALLITRICHIDAE Ma
Saguinus mystax : (E) Moustached Tamarin, (F) Tamarin à
  moustaches **II** CALLITRICHIDAE Ma
Saguinus niger = *Saguinus midas*
Saguinus nigricollis : (E) Black-and-red Tamarin, Black-
  mantled Tamarin, (F) Tamarin rouge et noir **II**
  CALLITRICHIDAE Ma
Saguinus oedipus : (E) Cotton-headed Tamarin, Cotton-top
  Tamarin, (S) Bichichi, (F) Tamarin à perruque,
  Tamarin d'Oedipe, Tamarin pinché, **I**
  CALLITRICHIDAE Ma
Saguinus oedipus ssp. *geoffroyi* = *Saguinus geoffroyi*
Saguinus pileatus = *Saguinus mystax*
Saguinus tamarin = *Saguinus midas*
Saguinus tripartitus : (E) Golden-mantled Saddle-back
  Tamarin, (S) Tamarino de espalda dorada **II**
  CALLITRICHIDAE Ma
Sahara Mastigure (E): *Uromastyx geyri*
Sahara Oryx (E): *Oryx dammah*
Sahel Chameleon (E): *Chamaeleo africanus*
Sahelian Terrapin (E): *Pelusios adansonii*
Saiga (E/S): *Saiga tatarica*
Saïga (F): *Saiga tatarica*
Saiga Antelope (E): *Saiga tatarica*
Saiga tatarica : (E) Saiga, Saiga Antelope, (S) Antílope
  saiga, Saiga, (F) Saïga, **II/NC** BOVIDAE Ma
Sail Terrapin (E): *Kachuga kachuga*
Saïmiri à dos roux (F): *Saimiri oerstedii*
Saimiri boliviensis : (E) Black-headed Squirrel Monkey **II**
  CEBIDAE Ma
Saimiri dorsirrojo (S): *Saimiri oerstedii*

Saïmiri écureuil (F): *Saimiri sciureus*
Saimiri oerstedii : (E) Central American Squirrel Monkey,
  Red-backed Squirrel Monkey, (S) Barizo dorsirrojo,
  Mono tití, Saimiri dorsirrojo, (F) Saïmiri à dos roux,
  Singe-écureuil à dos rouge, Singe-écureuil à dos roux,
  I CEBIDAE Ma
Saimiri sciureus : (E) Common Squirrel Monkey, (F)
  Saïmiri écureuil **II** CEBIDAE Ma
Saimiri sciureus ssp. *boliviensis* = *Saimiri boliviensis*
Saimiri sciureus ssp. *ustus* = *Saimiri ustus*
Saimiri ustus : (E) Golden-backed Squirrel Monkey **II**
  CEBIDAE Ma
Saimiri vanzolinii : (E) Blackish Squirrel Monkey **II**
  CEBIDAE Ma
Saint Helena Waxbill (E): *Estrilda astrild*
Saint Lucia Amazon (E): *Amazona versicolor*
Saint Lucia Parrot (E): *Amazona versicolor*
Saint Vincent Amazon (E): *Amazona guildingii*
Saint Vincent Parrot (E): *Amazona guildingii*
Sajou à front blanc (F): *Cebus albifrons*
Sajou à gorge blanche (F): *Cebus capucinus*
Sajou apelle (F): *Cebus apella*
Sakafi (F): *Psammobates geometricus*
Saker (E): *Falco cherrug*
Saker Falcon (E): *Falco cherrug*
Sakhalin Sturgeon (E): *Acipenser mikadoi*
Saki à nez blanc (F): *Chiropotes albinasus*
Saki à tête pâle (F): *Pithecia pithecia*
Saki amazónico (S): *Pithecia albicans*
Saki chevelu (F): *Pithecia monachus*
Saki de cara pelada (S): *Pithecia irrorata*
Saki de nariz blanca (S): *Chiropotes albinasus*
Saki nariblanco (S): *Chiropotes albinasus*
Saki noir (F): *Chiropotes satanas*
Saladang (E): *Bos gaurus*
Salamandra del lago Patzcuaro (S): *Ambystoma dumerilii*
Salamandra gigante (S): *Andrias* spp.
Salamandra gigante de China (S): *Andrias davidianus*
Salamandra gigante de Japón (S): *Andrias japonicus*
Salamandra mexicana (S): *Ambystoma mexicanum*
Salamandras gigantes (S): *Andrias* spp.
Salamandre du lac Pàtzcuaro (F): *Ambystoma dumerilii*
Salamandre du Mexique (F): *Ambystoma mexicanum*
Salamandre du Père David (F): *Andrias davidianus*
Salamandre géante (F): *Andrias* spp.
Salamandre géante de Chine (F): *Andrias davidianus*
Salamandre géante du Japon (F): *Andrias japonicus*
Salmon-crested Cockatoo (E): *Cacatua moluccensis*
Salt-water Crocodile (E): *Crocodylus porosus*
Salvadori's Fig-parrot (E): *Psittaculirostris salvadorii*
Samar Hornbill (E): *Penelopides samarensis*
Samar Tarictic Hornbill (E): *Penelopides samarensis*
Sambirano Mouse Lemur (E): *Microcebus sambiranensis*
Samoan Flying-fox (E): *Pteropus samoensis*
Sampson's Naiad (E): *Epioblasma sampsonii*
Sampson's Pearly Mussel (E): *Epioblasma sampsonii*
Sampson's Riffleshell (E): *Epioblasma sampsonii*
San Esteban Island Chuckwalla (E): *Sauromalus varius*
San Salvador Ground Iguana (E): *Cyclura rileyi*
San Salvador Iguana (E): *Cyclura rileyi*
Sanborn's Flying-fox (E): *Pteropus mahaganus*
Sand Cat (E): *Felis margarita*
Sand Dune Cat (E): *Felis margarita*
Sand Gazelle (E): *Gazella leptoceros*
Sand Goanna (E): *Varanus rosenbergi*
Sand Monitor (E): *Varanus gouldii*
Sand Sturgeon (E): *Scaphirhynchus platorynchus*
Sandalolitha africana : **II** FUNGIIDAE An
Sandalolitha dentata : **II** FUNGIIDAE An
Sandalolitha robusta : (E) Basket Coral **II** FUNGIIDAE
  An
Sandbank Pocketbook (E): *Lampsilis satur*
Sandhill Crane (E): *Grus canadensis*
Sandhill Dunnart (E): *Sminthopsis psammophila*
Sandhill Sminthopsis (E): *Sminthopsis psammophila*

Checklist of fauna/Lista de especies de fauna/Liste des espèces animales

Sandy Scops-Owl (E): *Otus icterorhynchus*
Sanford's Fish-eagle (E): *Haliaeetus sanfordi*
Sanford's Sea-Eagle (E): *Haliaeetus sanfordi*
Sangihe Hanging-Parrot (E): *Loriculus catamene*
Sangihe Scops-Owl (E): *Otus collari*
Sanglier nain (F): *Sus salvanius*
Sanglier pygmée (F): *Sus salvanius*
Sangsue médicinale (F): *Hirudo medicinalis*
Sangsue officinale (F): *Hirudo medicinalis*
Sanguijuela (S): *Hirudo medicinalis*
Sanguine Poison Frog (E): *Epipedobates zaparo*
Sansonnet de Rothschild (F): *Leucopsar rothschildi*
Santa Barbara Screech-owl (E): *Otus barbarus*
Santa Cruz Flying-fox (E): *Pteropus sanctacrucis*
Santa Fe Land Iguana (E): *Conolophus pallidus*
Santa Marta Conure (E): *Pyrrhura viridicata*
Santa Marta Parakeet (E): *Pyrrhura viridicata*
Santa Marta Sabrewing (E): *Campylopterus phainopeplus*
Santa Marta Woodstar (E): *Chaetocercus astreans*
Santander Poison Frog (E): *Minyobates virolensis*
Sanzinia (E): *Sanzinia madagascariensis*
Sanzinia madagascariensis : (E) Madagascar Tree Boa, Sanzinia, (S) Boa arborícola de Madagascar, (F) Boa des forêts de Madagascar, **I** BOIDAE Re
Sao Tomé Scops-Owl (E): *Otus hartlaubi*
Saola (E/S/F): *Pseudoryx nghetinhensis*
Saphir à gorge rousse (F): *Hylocharis sapphirina*
Saphir à oreilles blanches (F): *Basilinna leucotis*
Saphir à queue d'or (F): *Hylocharis chrysura*
Saphir azuré (F): *Hylocharis cyanus*
Saphir de Xantus (F): *Basilinna xantusii*
Saphir d'Elicia (F): *Hylocharis eliciae*
Saphir oenome (F): *Chrysuronia oenone*
Saphir ulysse (F): *Hylocharis grayi*
Sapo del Camerún (S): *Bufo superciliaris*
Sapo dorado (S): *Bufo periglenes*
Sapo dorado de Monteverde (S): *Bufo periglenes*
Sapo vivíparo de Africa occidental (S): *Nimbaphrynoides occidentalis*
Sapo vivíparo de Malcolm (S): *Altiphrynoides malcolmi*
Sapo vivíparo de Osgood (S): *Spinophrynoides osgoodi*
Sapo vivíparo liberiano (S): *Nimbaphrynoides liberiensis*
Sapos vivíparos (S): *Altiphrynoides* spp./ *Nectophrynoides* spp./ *Nimbaphrynoides* spp./ *Spinophrynoides* spp.
Sapos vivíparos africanos (S): *Nectophrynoides* spp.
Sapphire-bellied Hummingbird (E): *Lepidopyga lilliae*
Sapphire-rumped Parrotlet (E): *Touit purpurata*
Sapphire-spangled Emerald (E): *Polyerata lactea*
Sapphire-throated Hummingbird (E): *Lepidopyga coeruleogularis*
Sapphire-vented Puffleg (E): *Eriocnemis luciani*
Sappho sparganura : (E) Red-tailed Comet, (S) Colibrí cometa, Picaflor coludo rojo, (F) Colibri sapho, **II** TROCHILIDAE Av
Sarawak Dolphin (E): *Lagenodelphis hosei*
Sarcelle à oreillons (F): *Nettapus auritus*
Sarcelle aptère (F): *Anas aucklandica*
Sarcelle brune (F): *Anas aucklandica*
Sarcelle de Bernier (F): *Anas bernieri*
Sarcelle de Laysan (F): *Anas laysanensis*
Sarcelle de Madagascar (F): *Anas bernieri*
Sarcelle de Nouvelle-Zélande (F): *Anas aucklandica*
Sarcelle d'été (F): *Anas querquedula*
Sarcelle d'hiver (F): *Anas crecca*
Sarcelle du Cap (F): *Anas capensis*
Sarcelle élégante (F): *Anas formosa*
Sarcelle formose (F): *Anas formosa*
Sarcelle malgache de Bernier (F): *Anas bernieri*
Sarcelle terrestre des îles Auckland (F): *Anas aucklandica*
Sarcidiorne à crête (F): *Sarkidiornis melanotos*
Sarcogyps calvus : (E) Asian Black Vulture, Asian King Vulture, Indian Black Vulture, Indian King Vulture, Pondicherry Vulture, Red-headed Vulture, (S) Buitre cabecirrojo, (F) Vautour royal, **II** ACCIPITRIDAE Av

Sarcoramphe roi (F): *Sarcoramphus papa*
Sarcoramphus papa : (E) King Vulture, (S) Gallinazo rey, Jote real, Rey zamuro, Zopilote rey, (F) Carcoramphe roi, Roi des vautours, Sarcoramphe roi, Vautour page, Vautour royal, **III** CATHARTIDAE Av
Sarkidiornis melanotos : (E) Comb Duck, Knob-billed Goose, (S) Pato crestado, Pato crestón, Pato crestudo, Pato de moco, Pato de monte, (F) Canard à bosse, Canard à bosse bronzé, Canard coronculé, Sarcidiorne à crête, **II** ANATIDAE Av
Sarus Crane (E): *Grus antigone*
Sasabi (S): *Damaliscus lunatus*
Sasin (E): *Antilope cervicapra*
Sassaby (F): *Damaliscus lunatus*
Sateré Marmoset (E): *Callithrix saterei*
Satyr Tragopan (E): *Tragopan satyra*
Saucerottia beryllina : (E) Berylline Hummingbird, (S) Amazilia berilina, Colibrí de Berilo, (F) Ariane béryl, **II** TROCHILIDAE Av
Saucerottia cupreicauda : (E) Copper-tailed Hummingbird **II** TROCHILIDAE Av
Saucerottia cyanifrons : (E) Indigo-capped Hummingbird, (S) Amazilia capiazul, (F) Ariane à front bleu, **II** TROCHILIDAE Av
Saucerottia cyanura : (E) Blue-tailed Hummingbird, (S) Amazilia coliazul, Colibrí coliazul, (F) Ariane à queue bleue, **II** TROCHILIDAE Av
Saucerottia edward : (E) Snowy-breasted Hummingbird, (S) Amazilia de Edward, (F) Ariane d'Edward, **II** TROCHILIDAE Av
Saucerottia saucerrottei : (E) Blue-vented Hummingbird, Steely-vented Hummingbird, (S) Amazilia verdiazul, (F) Ariane de Sophie, **II** TROCHILIDAE Av
Saucerottia tobaci : (E) Copper-rumped Hummingbird, (S) Amazilia bronceada coliazul, Amazilia de Tobago, (F) Ariane de Félicie, **II** TROCHILIDAE Av
Saucerottia viridigaster : (E) Green-bellied Hummingbird, (S) Amazilia colimorada, (F) Ariane à ventre vert, **II** TROCHILIDAE Av
Sauromalus varius : (E) Piebald Chuckwalla, San Esteban Island Chuckwalla, (F) Chuckwalla de San Esteban **I** IGUANIDAE Re
Sauvegarde (F): *Tupinambis teguixin*
Savanna Hawk (E): *Buteogallus meridionalis*
Savanna Monkey (E): *Chlorocebus aethiops*
Savanna Sideneck Turtle (E): *Podocnemis vogli*
Savannah Dog (E): *Speothos venaticus*
Savile's Bustard (E): *Eupodotis savilei*
Saw-billed Hermit (E): *Ramphodon naevius*
Saw-jawed Turtle (E): *Callagur borneoensis*
Saw-whet Owl (E): *Aegolius acadicus*
Scaled Metaltail (E): *Metallura aeneocauda*
Scale-throated Hermit (E): *Phaethornis eurynome*
Scalpel Coral (E): *Acrhelia horrescens*
Scaly Anteater (E): *Manis temminckii*
Scaly Clam (E): *Tridacna squamosa*
Scaly-breasted Hummingbird (E): *Campylopterus cuvierii*
Scaly-breasted Lorikeet (E): *Trichoglossus chlorolepidotus*
Scaly-fronted Weaver (E): *Sporopipes frontalis*
Scaly-headed Parrot (E): *Pionus maximiliani*
Scaly-naped Amazon (E): *Amazona mercenaria*
Scaly-naped Parrot (E): *Amazona mercenaria*
Scaly-tailed flying squirrels (E): *Anomalurus* spp.
Scaphiophryne gottlebei : (E) Red Rain Frog **II** MICROHYLIDAE Am
Scaphirhynchus albus : (E) Pallid Sturgeon **II** ACIPENSERIDAE Ac
Scaphirhynchus fedtschenkoi = Pseudoscaphirhynchus fedtschenkoi
Scaphirhynchus hermanni = Pseudoscaphirhynchus hermanni
Scaphirhynchus kaufmanni = Pseudoscaphirhynchus kaufmanni

Checklist of fauna/Lista de especies de fauna/Liste des espèces animales

Scaphirhynchus mexicanus = Scaphirhynchus platorynchus
Scaphirhynchus platorynchus : (E) Sand Sturgeon, Shovelnose Sturgeon **II** ACIPENSERIDAE Ac
Scaphirhynchus rafinesquei = Scaphirhynchus platorynchus
Scaphirhynchus suttkusi : (E) Alabama Sturgeon **II** ACIPENSERIDAE Ac
Scapophyllia cylindrica : **II** MERULINIDAE An
Scaptochelys agassizii = Gopherus agassizii
Scaptochelys berlandieri = Gopherus berlandieri
Scarlet Cock-of-the-rock (E): *Rupicola peruviana*
Scarlet Crisp Coral (E): *Flabellum macandrewi*
Scarlet Ibis (E): *Eudocimus ruber*
Scarlet Macaw (E): *Ara macao*
Scarlet-and-gold Star Coral (E): *Balanophyllia regia*
Scarlet-breasted Lorikeet (E): *Vini kuhlii*
Scarlet-chested Parrot (E): *Neophema splendida*
Scarlet-fronted Parakeet (E): *Aratinga wagleri*
Scarlet-shouldered Parrotlet (E): *Touit huetii*
Sceloglaux albifacies : (E) Laughing Owl, White-faced Owl, (S) Lechuzón cariblanco, Nínox reidor, (F) Chouette à joues blanches, Ninoxe rieuse, **II** STRIGIDAE Av
Schalow's Turaco (E): *Tauraco schalowi*
Scheepmaker's Crowned-Pigeon (E): *Goura scheepmakeri*
Scheffler's Owlet (E): *Glaucidium scheffleri*
Schistes geoffroyi = Augastes geoffroyi
Schizoculina africana : **II** OCULINIDAE An
Schizoculina arbuscula = Oculina arbuscula
Schizoculina fissipara : **II** OCULINIDAE An
Schizocyathus fissilis : **II** GUYNIIDAE An
Schizopathes affinis : **II** ANTIPATHIDAE An
Schizopathes amplispina : **II** ANTIPATHIDAE An
Schizopathes conferta : **II** ANTIPATHIDAE An
Schizopathes crassa : **II** ANTIPATHIDAE An
Schmidt's Guenon (E): *Cercopithecus ascanius*
Schmidt's Monitor (E): *Varanus jobiensis*
Schneider's Smooth-fronted Caiman (E): *Palaeosuchus trigonatus*
Schouteden's Chameleon (E): *Chamaeleo schoutedeni*
Schubotz's Chameleon (E): *Chamaeleo schubotzi*
Schweigger's Terrapin (E): *Pelusios castaneus*
Schweigger's Tortoise (E): *Kinixys erosa*
Scimitar-horned Oryx (E): *Oryx dammah*
Scinque à queue préhensile des Iles Salomons (F): *Corucia zebrata*
Scinque arboricole des Iles Salomons (F): *Corucia zebrata*
Scinque géant des Iles Salomons (F): *Corucia zebrata*
Scintillant Hummingbird (E): *Selasphorus scintilla*
Scissor-tailed Hummingbird (E): *Hylonympha macrocerca*
Scissor-tailed Kite (E): *Chelictinia riocourii*
Sciurus deppei : (E) Deppe's Squirrel, (S) Ardilla costarricense, Ardilla de Deppe, Ardilla de los pinos, (F) Écureuil de Deppe, Écureuil des pins, **III** SCIURIDAE Ma
Sclater's Guenon (E): *Cercopithecus sclateri*
Sclater's Monal (E): *Lophophorus sclateri*
Sclater's Parrotlet (E): *Forpus sclateri*
SCLERACTINIA spp. : (E) Stony corals, Hard Corals, (F) Don't coraux récifaux, **II** An
Sclerhelia dubia : **II** OCULINIDAE An
Sclerhelia hirtella : **II** OCULINIDAE An
Scléropage d'Asie (F): *Scleropages formosus*
Scléropage formosus (F): *Scleropages formosus*
Scleropages formosus : (E) Arowana, Asian Arowana, Asian Bonytongue, Dragon fish, Golden Arowana, Golden Dragon Fish, Kelesa, Malayan bonytongue, (S) Pez lengüihueso malayo, (F) Scléropage d'Asie, Scléropage formosus, **I** OSTEOGLOSSIDAE Ac
Scolymia australis : (E) Button Coral **II** MUSSIDAE An
Scolymia cubensis : (E) Artichoke Coral, Solitary Disk Coral **II** MUSSIDAE An
Scolymia lacera : (E) Atlantic Mushroom Coral **II** MUSSIDAE An

Scolymia vitiensis : (E) Doughnut Coral **II** MUSSIDAE An
Scolymia wellsii : **II** MUSSIDAE An
Scops géant de Guerney (F): *Mimizuku gurneyi*
Scops Owl (E): *Otus scops*
Scorpion (E): *Pandinus dictator*
Scorpion de Gambie (F): *Pandinus gambiensis*
Scorpion dictateur (F): *Pandinus dictator*
Scorpion empereur (F): *Pandinus imperator*
Scorpion impérial (F): *Pandinus imperator*
Scotopelia bouvieri : (E) Vermiculated Fishing-Owl, (S) Cárabo pescador vermiculado, (F) Chouette-pêcheuse de Bouvier, **II** STRIGIDAE Av
Scotopelia peli : (E) Pel's Fishing-Owl, (S) Cárabo pescador común, Lechuza pescadora, (F) Chouette pêcheuse, Chouette-pêcheuse de Pel, **II** STRIGIDAE Av
Scotopelia ussheri : (E) Rufous Fishing-Owl, (S) Búho pescador rojizo, Cárabo pescador rojizo, (F) Chouette d'Usssher, Chouette-pêcheuse rousse, **II** STRIGIDAE Av
Scroll Coral (E): *Agaricia undata*
Scrub Python (E): *Morelia amethistina*
Sea Cat (E): *Lontra felina*
Sea Cow (E): *Dugong dugon*
Sea Horse (E): *Hippocampus hippocampus*
Sea Iguana (E): *Amblyrhynchus cristatus*
Sea Mole Coral (E): *Polyphyllia talpina*
Sea Otter (E): *Enhydra lutris*
Sea ponies (E): *Hippocampus* spp.
Sea Pony (E): *Hippocampus fuscus*
Sea Sturgeon (E): *Acipenser sturio*
Seahorse (E): *Hippocampus histrix*
Seahorse Fish (E): *Hippocampus abdominalis*
Seahorses (E): *Hippocampus* spp.
Secret Tree Toad (E): *Nectophrynoides cryptus*
Secrétaire des serpents (F): *Sagittarius serpentarius*
Secretario (S): *Sagittarius serpentarius*
Secretarybird (E): *Sagittarius serpentarius*
Secretary-bird (E): *Sagittarius serpentarius*
Sei Whale (E): *Balaenoptera borealis*
Seipp's Day Gecko (E): *Phelsuma seippi*
Selachus pennantii = Cetorhinus maximus
Selasphorus ardens : (E) Glow-throated Hummingbird, (S) Colibrí ardiente, (F) Colibri ardent, **II** TROCHILIDAE Av
Selasphorus ellioti = Atthis ellioti
Selasphorus flammula : (E) Cerise-throated Hummingbird, Heliotrope-throated Hummingbird, Volcano Hummingbird, (S) Colibrí volcanero, (F) Colibri flammule, **II** TROCHILIDAE Av
Selasphorus heloisa = Atthis heloisa
Selasphorus platycercus : (E) Broad-tailed Hummingbird, (S) Colibrí coliancho, Zumbador coliancho, (F) Colibri à queue large, **II** TROCHILIDAE Av
Selasphorus rufus : (E) Rufous Hummingbird, (S) Colibrí rufo, Zumbador rufo, (F) Colibri roux, **II** TROCHILIDAE Av
Selasphorus sasin : (E) Allen's Hummingbird, (S) Colibrí de Allen, Zumbador de Allen, (F) Colibri d'Allen, **II** TROCHILIDAE Av
Selasphorus scintilla : (E) Scintillant Hummingbird, (S) Colibrí centelleante, (F) Colibri scintillant, **II** TROCHILIDAE Av
Selasphorus simoni = Selasphorus flammula
Selasphorus torridus = Selasphorus flammula
Selenarctos thibetanus = Ursus thibetanus
Selenidera maculirostris : (E) Spot-billed Toucanet, (S) Tucán de pico acanalado, Tucancito picomaculado, (F) Toucanet à bec tacheté, **III** RAMPHASTIDAE Av
Seleucidis melanoleuca : (E) Twelve-wired Bird-of-paradise, (F) Paradisier multifil **II** PARADISAEIDAE Av
Semi-collared Hawk (E): *Accipiter collaris*
Semi-collared Sparrowhawk (E): *Accipiter collaris*

Checklist of fauna/Lista de especies de fauna/Liste des espèces animales

Semioptera wallacii : (E) Standardwing, Standard-wing Bird-of-paradise, Wallace's Standardwing, (F) Paradisier de Wallace **II** PARADISAEIDAE Av
Semiplumbeous Hawk (E): *Leucopternis semiplumbea*
Semnopithecus entellus : (E) Common Langur, Entellus Langur, Grey Langur, Hanuman Langur, True Langur, (S) Houlemán, Langur común, Langur hanuman, (F) Entelle, Houleman, **I** CERCOPITHECIDAE Ma
Semnopithecus geei = Trachypithecus geei
Semnopithecus hypoleucos = Semnopithecus entellus
Semnopithecus pileatus = Trachypithecus pileatus
Semnopithèque à front blanc (F): *Presbytis frontata*
Semnopithèque blanchâtre (F): *Trachypithecus vetulus*
Semnopithèque de François (F): *Trachypithecus francoisi*
Semnopithèque de Gee (F): *Trachypithecus geei*
Semnopithèque de Hose (F): *Presbytis hosei*
Semnopithèque de Mentawi (F): *Presbytis potenziani*
Semnopithèque de Phayre (F): *Trachypithecus phayrei*
Semnopithèque de Thomas (F): *Presbytis thomasi*
Semnopithèque des Nilgiris (F): *Trachypithecus johnii*
Semnopithèque doré (F): *Trachypithecus geei*
Semnopithèque mélalophe (F): *Presbytis melalophos*
Semnopithèque obscur (F): *Trachypithecus obscurus*
Semnopithèque rubicond (F): *Presbytis rubicunda*
Semnornis ramphastinus : (E) Toucan Barbet, (F) Cabézon toucan, Caebézon toucan, Toucan barbet **III** CAPITONIDAE Av
Senegal Bustard (E): *Eupodotis senegalensis*
Senegal Chameleon (E): *Chamaeleo senegalensis*
Senegal Combassou (E): *Vidua chalybeata*
Senegal Dove (E): *Streptopelia senegalensis*
Senegal Firefinch (E): *Lagonosticta senegala*
Senegal Galago (E): *Galago senegalensis*
Senegal ondulé (F): *Estrilda astrild*
Senegal Parrot (E): *Poicephalus senegalus*
Sénégali brun à ventre blanc (F): *Nigrita fusconota*
Sénégali brun à ventre roux (F): *Nigrita bicolor*
Sénégali nègre (F): *Nigrita canicapilla*
Sénégali nègre à front jaune (F): *Nigrita luteifrons*
Sénégali sanguin (F): *Spermophaga haematina*
Sénégali vert (F): *Mandingoa nitidula*
Sénégali vert à joues blanches (F): *Nesocharis capistrata*
Sephanoides fernandensis : (E) Juan Fernández Firecrown, (S) Colibrí de Juan Fernández, (F) Colibri robinson, **II** TROCHILIDAE Av
Sephanoides sephaniodes : (E) Green-backed Firecrown, (S) Colibrí austral, Picaflor cabeza granate, (F) Colibri du Chili, **II** TROCHILIDAE Av
Sepik Monitor (E): *Varanus jobiensis*
Seram Flying-fox (E): *Pteropus ocularis*
Seram Fruit Bat (E): *Pteropus ocularis*
Serau (S): *Naemorhedus sumatraensis*
Seriatopora aculeata : **II** POCILLOPORIDAE An
Seriatopora caliendrum : **II** POCILLOPORIDAE An
Seriatopora crassa = Seriatopora hystrix
Seriatopora dendritica : **II** POCILLOPORIDAE An
Seriatopora guttatus : **II** POCILLOPORIDAE An
Seriatopora hystrix : (E) Needle Coral **II** POCILLOPORIDAE An
Seriatopora stellata : **II** POCILLOPORIDAE An
Sericotes holosericeus = Eulampis holosericeus
Serin à croupion blanc (F): *Serinus leucopygius*
Serín culiblanco (S): *Serinus leucopygius*
Serin de Mozambique (S): *Serinus mozambicus*
Serin du Mozambique (F): *Serinus mozambicus*
Serin gris à tête blanche (F): *Serinus canicapillus*
Serín mofletudo (S): *Serinus canicapillus*
Serin ouest-africain (F): *Serinus canicapillus*
Serinus canicapillus : (E) West African Seedeater, West African Streaky-headed Seedeater, (S) Serín mofletudo, (F) Serin gris à tête blanche, Serin ouest-africain, **III** FRINGILLIDAE Av
Serinus gularis ssp. *canicapillus = Serinus canicapillus*

Serinus leucopygius : (E) Grey Canary, Grey Singing Finch, White-rumped Seedeater, (S) Serín culiblanco, (F) Chanteur d'Afrique, Serin à croupion blanc, **III** FRINGILLIDAE Av
Serinus mozambicus : (E) Green Singing Finch, Yellow-fronted Canary, (S) Canario de Mozambique, Serin de Mozambique, (F) Serin du Mozambique, **III** FRINGILLIDAE Av
Serow (E/F): *Naemorhedus sumatraensis*
Serow de Sumatra (S): *Naemorhedus sumatraensis*
Serpent à caréné olive (F): *Atretium schistosum*
Serpent à lunetes (F): *Naja naja*
Serpent à sonnette tropical (F): *Crotalus durissus*
Serpent aquatique caréné à damier (F): *Xenochrophis piscator*
Serpent ardoisé (F): *Atretium schistosum*
Serpent corail (F): *Micrurus diastema*
Serpent corail à bandes noires (F): *Micrurus nigrocinctus*
Serpent d'eau à museau de chien (F): *Cerberus rhynchops*
Serpent d'eau à ventre blanc (F): *Cerberus rhynchops*
Serpent gomme (F): *Charina bottae*
Serpent Island Gecko (E): *Cyrtodactylus serpensinsula*
Serpent ratier (F): *Ptyas mucosus*
Serpent ratier indien (F): *Ptyas mucosus*
Serpent ratier oriental (F): *Ptyas mucosus*
Serpentaire (F): *Sagittarius serpentarius*
Serpentaire bacha (F): *Spilornis cheela*
Serpentaire de Madagascar (F): *Eutriorchis astur*
Serpentaire des Andaman (F): *Spilornis elgini*
Serpentaire des Célèbes (F): *Spilornis rufipectus*
Serpentaire des Kinabalu (F): *Spilornis kinabaluensis*
Serpentaire des Nicobar (F): *Spilornis minimus*
Serpentaire des Philippines (F): *Spilornis holospilus*
Serpentaire du Congo (F): *Dryotriorchis spectabilis*
Serpentario (S): *Sagittarius serpentarius*
Serrated Day Gecko (E): *Phelsuma serraticauda*
Serrated Hinge-back Tortoise (E): *Kinixys erosa*
Serrated Hinge-backed Tortoise (E): *Kinixys erosa*
Serrated Star Tortoise (E): *Psammobates oculiferus*
Serrated Tent Tortoise (E): *Psammobates oculiferus*
Serrated Tortoise (E): *Kinixys erosa*
Serval (E/S/F): *Leptailurus serval*
Setaro's Dwarf Chameleon (E): *Bradypodion setaroi*
Seven-colored Parrotlet (E): *Touit batavica*
Seven-colored Tanager (E): *Tangara fastuosa*
Seven-line barb (E): *Probarbus jullieni*
Seven-striped Barb (E): *Probarbus jullieni*
Severe Macaw (E): *Ara severa*
Sevruga (E/F): *Acipenser stellatus*
Seychelles Day Gecko (E): *Phelsuma abbotti/ Phelsuma astriata*
Seychelles Flying-fox (E): *Pteropus seychellensis*
Seychelles Giant Day Gecko (E): *Phelsuma sundbergi*
Seychelles Kestrel (E): *Falco araea*
Seychelles Parakeet (E): *Psittacula wardi*
Seychelles Parrot (E): *Psittacula wardi*
Shapo (E): *Ovis vignei*
Shapu (E): *Ovis vignei*
Shark Bay Mouse (E): *Pseudomys praeconis*
Sharp-shinned Hawk (E): *Accipiter striatus*
Shelley's Eagle-Owl (E): *Bubo shelleyi*
Shepherd's Beaked Whale (E): *Tasmacetus shepherdi*
Shikra (E): *Accipiter badius*
Shining Sunbeam (E): *Aglaeactis cupripennis*
Shining-green Hummingbird (E): *Lepidopyga goudoti*
Shinisaurus crocodilurus : (E) Chinese Crocodile Lizard, Chinese Xenosaur, (S) Lagarto cocodrilo chino, (F) Lézard crocodile de Chine, **II** XENOSAURIDAE Re
Shiny Pigtoe (E): *Fusconaia edgariana*
Shiny Pigtoe Pearly Mussel (E): *Fusconaia edgariana*
Ship (E/F): *Acipenser nudiventris*
Ship Sturgeon (E): *Acipenser nudiventris*
Shoebill (E): *Balaeniceps rex*
Short-beaked Saddleback Dolphin (E): *Delphinus delphis*

Checklist of fauna/Lista de especies de fauna/Liste des espèces animales

Short-billed Black-Cockatoo (E): *Calyptorhynchus latirostris*
Short-crested Coquette (E): *Lophornis brachylophus*
Short-eared Owl (E): *Asio flammeus*
Short-finned Pilot Whale (E): *Globicephala macrorhynchus*
Short-head Seahorse (E): *Hippocampus breviceps*
Short-headed Seahorse (E): *Hippocampus breviceps*
Short-horned Chameleon (E): *Calumma brevicornis*
Shortnose sturgeon (E): *Acipenser brevirostrum*
Short-nosed Little Sturgeon (E): *Acipenser brevirostrum*
Short-snouted Seahorse (E): *Hippocampus breviceps/ Hippocampus hippocampus*
Short-tailed Albatross (E): *Diomedea albatrus*
Short-tailed Chinchilla (E): *Chinchilla brevicaudata*
Short-tailed Emerald (E): *Chlorostilbon poortmani*
Short-tailed Hawk (E): *Buteo brachyurus*
Short-tailed Paradigalla (E): *Paradigalla brevicauda*
Short-tailed Parrot (E): *Graydidascalus brachyurus*
Short-tailed porcupines (E): *Hystrix* spp.
Short-tailed Pygmy Monitor (E): *Varanus brevicauda*
Short-tailed Spotted Cuscus (E): *Spilocuscus maculatus*
Short-tailed Tibetan Macaque (E): *Macaca thibetana*
Short-tailed Woodstar (E): *Myrmia micrura*
Short-toed Eagle (E): *Circaetus gallicus*
Short-toed Snake-Eagle (E): *Circaetus gallicus*
Shoveler (E): *Anas clypeata*
Shovelfish (E): *Pseudoscaphirhynchus kaufmanni*
Shovelnose Sturgeon (E): *Scaphirhynchus platorynchus*
Siamang (E/S/F): *Hylobates syndactylus*
Siamang de Kloss (S/F): *Hylobates klossii*
Siamang enano (S): *Hylobates klossii*
Siamese Crocodile (E): *Crocodylus siamensis*
Sibbald's Rorqual (E): *Balaenoptera musculus*
Siberian Crane (E): *Grus leucogeranus*
Siberian Musk Deer (E): *Moschus moschiferus*
Siberian Sturgeon (E): *Acipenser baerii*
Siberian Weasel (E): *Mustela sibirica*
Siberian White Crane (E): *Grus leucogeranus*
Sibopathes gephura : **II** ANTIPATHIDAE An
Sibopathes macrospina : **II** ANTIPATHIDAE An
Sichuan Snub-nosed Monkey (E): *Pygathrix roxellana*
Sichuan Wood-owl (E): *Strix davidi*
Siderastrea glynni : **II** SIDERASTREIDAE An
Siderastrea radians : (E) Lesser Starlet Coral, Rough Starlet Coral **II** SIDERASTREIDAE An
Siderastrea savignyana : **II** SIDERASTREIDAE An
Siderastrea siderea : (E) Massive Starlet Coral, Smooth Starlet Coral **II** SIDERASTREIDAE An
Siderastrea stellata : **II** SIDERASTREIDAE An
Side-striped Chameleon (E): *Chamaeleo bitaeniatus*
Side-striped Day Gecko (E): *Phelsuma lineata*
Siebenrockiella crassicollis : (E) Black Marsh Turtle **II** EMYDIDAE Re
Sierra Parakeet (E): *Psilopsiagon aymara*
Sifaka (F): *Propithecus verreauxi*
Sifaka diademado (S): *Propithecus diadema*
Sifakas (E/S): INDRIDAE spp.
Siffleuse de la Trinité (F): *Pipile pipile*
Sifilet d'Arfak (F): *Parotia sefilata*
Sifilet de Carola (F): *Parotia carolae*
Sifilet de Lawe (F): *Parotia lawesii*
Sifilet de Wahnes (F): *Parotia wahnesi*
Sifilet d'Hélène (F): *Parotia helenae*
Signal-winged Acerodon (E): *Acerodon celebensis*
Siju (S): *Glaucidium siju*
Siju cotunto (S): *Otus lawrencii*
Sijucito (S): *Glaucidium siju*
Silbón Europeo (S): *Anas penelope*
Silfo celeste (S): *Aglaiocercus coelestis*
Silfo colilargo (S): *Aglaiocercus kingi*
Silfo colivioleta (S): *Aglaiocercus coelestis*
Silfo de King (S): *Aglaiocercus kingi*
Silky-Crow (E): *Lycocorax pyrrhopterus*
Silure de verre géant (F): *Pangasianodon gigas*

Siluro gigante (S): *Pangasianodon gigas*
Silver-eared Mesia (E): *Leiothrix argentauris*
Silvered Langur (E): *Trachypithecus cristatus*
Silvered Leaf Monkey (E): *Trachypithecus cristatus*
Silverstone's Poison Frog (E): *Epipedobates silverstonei*
Silvery Flying-fox (E): *Pteropus argentatus*
Silvery Fruit Bat (E): *Pteropus argentatus*
Silvery Gibbon (E): *Hylobates moloch*
Silvery Marmoset (E): *Callithrix argentata*
Simeulue Scops-Owl (E): *Otus umbra*
Simeulue Serpent-Eagle (E): *Spilornis cheela*
Simias concolor = Nasalis concolor
Simisimi (F): *Epipedobates femoralis*
Simplastrea vesicularis : **II** OCULINIDAE An
Singe araignée du Panama (F): *Ateles geoffroyi frontatus*
Singe de nuit (F): *Aotus trivirgatus*
Singe laineux (F): *Lagothrix lagotricha*
Singe laineux à queue jaune (F): *Lagothrix flavicauda*
Singe vert (F): *Chlorocebus aethiops*
Singe-araignée aux mains noires (F): *Ateles geoffroyi frontatus*
Singe-araignée laineux (F): *Brachyteles arachnoides*
Singe-écureuil à dos rouge (F): *Saimiri oerstedii*
Singe-écureuil à dos roux (F): *Saimiri oerstedii*
Singe-lion (F): *Leontopithecus rosalia*
Singeslions (F): *Leontopithecus* spp.
Singing Parrot (E): *Geoffroyus heteroclitus*
Single Soft-nosed Chameleon (E): *Bradypodion tenue*
Single Welded-horn Chameleon (E): *Bradypodion xenorhinum*
Sinuous Cactus Coral (E): *Isophyllia sinuosa*
Sira Poison Frog (E): *Dendrobates imitator*
Sisón (S): *Tetrax tetrax*
Sisón azul (S): *Eupodotis caerulescens*
Sisón azulado (S): *Eupodotis caerulescens*
Sisón bengali (S): *Eupodotis bengalensis*
Sisón Común (S): *Tetrax tetrax*
Sisón de Damaraland (S): *Eupodotis rueppellii*
Sisón de Hartlaub (S): *Eupodotis hartlaubii*
Sisón de penacho (S): *Eupodotis indica*
Sisón de Rüppell (S): *Eupodotis rueppellii*
Sisón de Vigors (S): *Eupodotis vigorsii*
Sisón del karroo (S): *Eupodotis vigorsii*
Sisón indio (S): *Eupodotis indica*
Sisón moñirrojo (S): *Eupodotis ruficrista*
Sisón moñudo austral (S): *Eupodotis ruficrista*
Sisón moñudo de saheliano (S): *Eupodotis savilei*
Sisón moñudo etiope (S): *Eupodotis gindiana*
Sisón negro (S): *Eupodotis afra*
Sisón negro aliclaro (S): *Eupodotis afraoides*
Sisón negro alioscuro (S): *Eupodotis afra*
Sisón senegalés (S): *Eupodotis senegalensis*
Sisón somalí (S): *Eupodotis humilis*
Sisón ventrinegro (S): *Eupodotis melanogaster*
Sisón ventrinegro común (S): *Eupodotis melanogaster*
Sisón ventrinegro de Hartlaub (S): *Eupodotis hartlaubii*
Sisones (S): OTIDIDAE spp.
Sitagra de Pelzeln (S): *Ploceus pelzelni*
Sitagra luteola = Ploceus luteolus
Sitagra melanocephala = Ploceus melanocephalus
Sitatunga (E/S/F): *Tragelaphus spekii*
Sitragra chico común (S): *Ploceus luteolus*
Six-fingered Frog (E): *Euphlyctis hexadactylus*
Six-legged Tortoise (E): *Manouria emys*
Six-plumed Parotia (E): *Parotia sefilata*
Six-tubercled Amazon River Turtle (E): *Podocnemis sextuberculata*
Six-tubercled River Turtle (E): *Podocnemis sextuberculata*
Sjostedt's Owlet (E): *Glaucidium sjostedti*
Skew-beaked Whale (E): *Mesoplodon hectori*
Sky-blue Poison Frog (E): *Epipedobates azureiventris*
Slate-colored Hawk (E): *Leucopternis schistacea*
Slaty-backed Forest-Falcon (E): *Micrastur mirandollei*
Slaty-backed Goshawk (E): *Accipiter luteoschistaceus*
Slaty-headed Parakeet (E): *Psittacula himalayana*

Checklist of fauna/Lista de especies de fauna/Liste des espèces animales

Slaty-mantled Sparrowhawk (E): *Accipiter luteoschistaceus*
Slender Blackfish (E): *Feresa attenuata*
Slender Chameleon (E): *Bradypodion tenue/ Chamaeleo gracilis*
Slender Fanalouc (E): *Eupleres goudotii*
Slender Loris (E): *Loris tardigradus*
Slender Seahorse (E): *Hippocampus reidi*
Slender Sheartail (E): *Doricha enicura*
Slender Treeshrew (E): *Tupaia gracilis*
Slender-billed Black-cockatoo (E): *Calyptorhynchus latirostris*
Slender-billed Conure (E): *Enicognathus leptorhynchus*
Slender-billed Curlew (E): *Numenius tenuirostris*
Slender-billed Kite (E): *Rostrhamus hamatus*
Slender-billed Parakeet (E): *Enicognathus leptorhynchus*
Slender-billed Weaver (E): *Ploceus pelzelni*
Slender-horned Gazelle (E): *Gazella leptoceros*
Slender-tailed Woodstar (E): *Microstilbon burmeisteri*
Slipper Coral (E): *Herpolitha limax/ Polyphyllia talpina*
Sloth Bear (E): *Melursus ursinus*
Slow Loris (E): *Nycticebus coucang*
Small Amu-Dar Shovelnose Sturgeon (E): *Pseudoscaphirhynchus hermanni*
Small Birdwing (E): *Troides aeacus*
Small Bubble Coral (E): *Physogyra lichtensteini*
Small Flying-fox (E): *Pteropus hypomelanus*
Small Giant Clam (E): *Tridacna maxima*
Small Indian Civet (E): *Viverricula indica*
Small Indian Mongoose (E): *Herpestes javanicus auropunctatus*
Small Serpent-Eagle (E): *Spilornis minimus*
Small Sparrowhawk (E): *Accipiter nanus*
Small Star Coral (E): *Favia fragum*
Small-clawed Otter (E): *Aonyx congicus/ Amblonyx cinereus*
Small-eared Greater Galago (E): *Otolemur garnettii*
Smaller Banded Snake-Eagle (E): *Circaetus cinerascens*
Smaller Cock-of-the-rock (E): *Rupicola rupicola*
Small-spotted Cat (E): *Felis nigripes*
Small-toothed Clawless Otter (E): *Aonyx congicus*
Small-toothed Mongoose (E): *Eupleres goudotii*
Sminthopsis longicaudata : (E) Long-tailed Dunnart, Long-tailed Marsupial-Mouse, Long-tailed Sminthopsis, (S) Ratón marsupial colilargo, (F) Souris marsupiale à longue queue, I DASYURIDAE Ma
Sminthopsis psammophila : (E) Large Desert Marsupial-Mouse, Sandhill Dunnart, Sandhill Sminthopsis, (S) Ratón marsupial desértico, (F) Souris marsupiale du désert, I DASYURIDAE Ma
Smooth Black Coral (E): *Leiopathes glaberrima*
Smooth Chameleon (E): *Chamaeleo laevigatus*
Smooth Flower Coral (E): *Eusmilia fastigiata*
Smooth Star Coral (E): *Solenastrea bournoni*
Smooth Starlet Coral (E): *Siderastrea siderea*
Smooth-coated Otter (E): *Lutrogale perspicillata*
Smooth-ribbed Wedge Coral (E): *Sphenotrochus andrewianus andrewianus*
Smutsia gigantea = Manis gigantea
Smutsia temminckii = Manis temminckii
Snail Kite (E): *Rostrhamus sociabilis*
Snow Crane (E): *Grus leucogeranus*
Snow Leopard (E): *Uncia uncia*
Snowcap (E): *Microchera albocoronata*
Snowy Owl (E): *Nyctea scandiaca*
Snowy-breasted Hummingbird (E): *Saucerottia edward*
Snubfin Dolphin (E): *Orcaella brevirostris*
Snub-nosed monkeys (E): *Pygathrix* spp.
Socorro Parakeet (E): *Aratinga brevipes*
Socotra Chameleon (E): *Chamaeleo monachus*
Softshell Tortoise (E): *Malacochersus tornieri*
Sokoke Scops-Owl (E): *Otus ireneae*
Solangel de gorguera (S): *Heliangelus strophianus*
Solangel gorjiamatista (S): *Heliangelus amethysticollis*
Solangel gorjipurpura (S): *Heliangelus viola*

Solangel turmalino (S): *Heliangelus exortis*
Solenastrea bournoni : (E) Smooth Star Coral II FAVIIDAE An
Solenastrea hyades : (E) Knobby Star Coral, Lobed Star Coral II FAVIIDAE An
Solenosmilia variabilis : II CARYOPHYLLIIDAE An
Solitary Disk Coral (E): *Scolymia cubensis*
Solitary Eagle (E): *Harpyhaliaetus solitarius*
Solitary Tinamou (E): *Tinamus solitarius*
Sollo (S): *Polyodon spathula/ Acipenser sturio*
Sollo real (S): *Acipenser sturio*
Solomon Fish-Eagle (E): *Haliaeetus sanfordi*
Solomon Ground Boa (E): *Candoia carinata*
Solomon Hawk-Owl (E): *Ninox jacquinoti*
Solomon Islands Boobook (E): *Ninox jacquinoti*
Solomon Islands Giant Skink (E): *Corucia zebrata*
Solomon Islands Spiny Monitor (E): *Varanus spinulosus*
Solomon Sea-Eagle (E): *Haliaeetus sanfordi*
Solomons Flying-fox (E): *Pteropus rayneri*
Somali Galago (E): *Galago gallarum*
Somali Sand Boa (E): *Eryx somalicus*
Sombre Hummingbird (E): *Campylopterus cirrochloris*
Somormujo de Atitlán (S): *Podilymbus gigas*
Somormujo del lago Atitlán (S): *Podilymbus gigas*
Sonnerat's Junglefowl (E): *Gallus sonneratii*
Sooty Eagle-Owl (E): *Bubo leucostictus*
Sooty Falcon (E): *Falco concolor*
Sooty Mangabey (E): *Cercocebus torquatus*
Sooty Owl (E): *Tyto tenebricosa*
Sooty-backed Hawk-Owl (E): *Ninox theomacha*
Sooty-capped Hermit (E): *Phaethornis augusti*
Sotalia spp.: (E) River dolphins, (S) Bufeos, Toninas, (F) Dauphins de rivière, Sotalies de l'Amérique du Sud, I DELPHINIDAE Ma
Sotalia brasiliensis = Sotalia fluviatilis
Sotalia fluviatilis : (E) Amazonian River Dolphin, Estuarine Dolphin, Grey Dolphin, Guianian River Dolphin, Tucuxi, (S) Bufeo negro, Bufo negro, (F) Sotalie, I DELPHINIDAE Ma
Sotalia guianensis = Sotalia fluviatilis
Sotalie (F): *Sotalia fluviatilis*
Sotalies africaines et asiatiques (F): *Sousa* spp.
Sotalies de l'Amérique du Sud (F): *Sotalia* spp.
Souchet (F): *Anas clypeata*
Souffleur (F): *Tursiops truncatus*
Soumagne's Owl (E): *Tyto soumagnei*
Souris de la baie de Shark (F): *Pseudomys praeconis*
Souris marsupiale à longue queue (F): *Sminthopsis longicaudata*
Souris marsupiale du désert (F): *Sminthopsis psammophila*
Sousa spp.: (E) Humpback dolphins, (S) Delfines blancos, (F) Dauphins blancs, Sotalies africaines et asiatiques, Sousas, I DELPHINIDAE Ma
Sousa borneensis = Sousa chinensis
Sousa chinensis : (E) Indo-pacific Humpbacked Dolphin, (S) Bufeo asiático, Delfín blanco de China, (F) Dauphin à bosse de l'Indo-Pacifique, I DELPHINIDAE Ma
Sousa lentiginosa = Sousa chinensis
Sousa plumbea = Sousa chinensis
Sousa teuszii : (E) Atlantic Humpbacked Dolphin, (S) Bufeo africano, Delfín blanco africano, (F) Dauphin à bosse de l'Atlantique, I DELPHINIDAE Ma
Sousas (F): *Sousa* spp.
Sousou (F): *Platanista gangetica*
Sousous (F): *Platanista* spp.
South African Bowsprit Tortoise (E): *Chersina angulata*
South African Crowned Crane (E): *Balearica regulorum*
South African Fur Seal (E): *Arctocephalus pusillus*
South African Lesser Galago (E): *Galago moholi*
South African Pangolin (E): *Manis temminckii*
South African Tent Tortoise (E): *Psammobates tentorius*
South American Fur Seal (E): *Arctocephalus australis*
South American Manatee (E): *Trichechus inunguis*
South American River Otter (E): *Lontra longicaudis*

Checklist of fauna/Lista de especies de fauna/Liste des espèces animales

South American River Turtle (E): *Podocnemis expansa*
South American river turtles (E): *Podocnemis* spp.
South American Tapir (E): *Tapirus terrestris*
South American Tortoise (E): *Geochelone denticulata*
South American Yellow-footed Tortoise (E): *Geochelone denticulata*
South Andean Deer (E): *Hippocamelus bisulcus*
South Andean Huemul (E): *Hippocamelus bisulcus*
South Asian Box Turtle (E): *Cuora amboinensis*
South Atlantic Elephant Seal (E): *Mirounga leonina*
South Australian Water Python (E): *Morelia oenpelliensis*
South Brazilian Coati (E): *Nasua nasua solitaria*
South Indonesian Spitting Cobra (E): *Naja sputatrix*
South Island Tree Gecko (E): *Naultinus gemmeus*
South Pacific Banded Iguana (E): *Brachylophus fasciatus*
South-central Chameleon (E): *Furcifer minor*
Southeast Asian Narrow-headed Softshell Turtle (E): *Chitra chitra*
South-east Philippine Spitting Cobra (E): *Naja samarensis*
Southern Bald Ibis (E): *Geronticus calvus*
Southern Banded Snake-eagle (E): *Circaetus fasciolatus*
Southern Beaked Whale (E): *Mesoplodon grayi*
Southern Black-throated Finch (E): *Poephila cincta cincta*
Southern Boobook (E): *Ninox boobook*
Southern Bottlenose Whale (E): *Hyperoodon planifrons*
Southern Caracara (E): *Polyborus plancus*
Southern Crowned-pigeon (E): *Goura scheepmakeri*
Southern Elephant Seal (E): *Mirounga leonina*
Southern Eyelash Boa (E): *Trachyboa gularis*
Southern Four-toothed Whale (E): *Berardius arnuxii*
Southern Fur Seal (E): *Arctocephalus australis*
Southern fur seals (E): *Arctocephalus* spp.
Southern Gastric-brooding Frog (E): *Rheobatrachus vitellinus*
Southern Giant Clam (E): *Tridacna derasa*
Southern Minke Whale (E): *Balaenoptera bonaerensis*
Southern Pudu (E): *Pudu puda*
Southern Right Whale (E): *Eubalaena australis*
Southern Right Whale Dolphin (E): *Lissodelphis peronii*
Southern River Otter (E): *Lontra provocax*
Southern Savanna Monitor (E): *Varanus albigularis*
Southern Sea Otter (E): *Enhydra lutris nereis*
Southern Square-lipped Rhinoceros (E): *Ceratotherium simum simum*
Southern Talapoin (E): *Miopithecus talapoin*
Southern White Rhinoceros (E): *Ceratotherium simum simum*
Southern Wood Tortoise (E): *Geochelone chilensis*
Sowerby's Beaked Whale (E): *Mesoplodon bidens*
Spadefish (E): *Polyodon spathula*
Spangled Coquette (E): *Lophornis stictolophus*
Spanish Imperial Eagle (E): *Aquila adalberti*
Spanish Lynx (E): *Lynx pardinus*
Sparkling Violet-ear (E): *Colibri coruscans*
Sparkling-tailed Barbthroat (E): *Tilmatura dupontii*
Sparkling-tailed Hummingbird (E): *Tilmatura dupontii*
Sparrowhawk (E): *Accipiter nisus*
Spatula clypeata = Anas clypeata
Spatule blanche (F): *Platalea leucorodia*
Speckled Boobook (E): *Ninox punctulata*
Speckled Cape Tortoise (E): *Homopus signatus*
Speckled Cup Coral (E): *Rhizosmilia maculata*
Speckled Day Gecko (E): *Phelsuma guttata*
Speckled Hawk-Owl (E): *Ninox punctulata*
Speckled Hummingbird (E): *Adelomyia melanogenys*
Speckled Padloper (E): *Homopus signatus*
Speckled Pigeon (E): *Columba guinea*
Speckled Rock Pigeon (E): *Columba guinea*
Speckled Tortoise (E): *Homopus signatus*
Speckle-fronted Weaver (E): *Sporopipes frontalis*
Speckle-throated Otter (E): *Lutra maculicollis*
Spectacled Bear (E): *Tremarctos ornatus*
Spectacled Caiman (E): *Caiman crocodilus*
Spectacled Flying-fox (E): *Pteropus conspicillatus*
Spectacled Galago (E): *Galago matschiei*

Spectacled Langur (E): *Trachypithecus obscurus*
Spectacled Leaf Monkey (E): *Trachypithecus obscurus*
Spectacled Owl (E): *Pulsatrix perspicillata*
Spectacled Parrotlet (E): *Forpus conspicillatus*
Spectacled Porpoise (E): *Australophocaena dioptrica*
Spectral Tarsier (E): *Tarsius spectrum*
Spencer's Monitor (E): *Varanus spenceri*
Speothos venaticus : (E) Bush Dog, Savannah Dog, (S) Cachorro de mato vinagre, Cachorro vinagre, Perro de los matorrales, Perro de monte, Umba, Zorro vinagre, (F) Chien des buissons, **I** CANIDAE Ma
Speotyto cunicularia : (E) Burrowing Owl, (S) Búho llanero, Cucú, Lechucita común, Lechucita de las viscacheras, Mochuelo de Hoyo, Mochuelo de Madriguera, (F) Chevêche des terriers, Chouette de terrier, **II** STRIGIDAE Av
Sperm Whale (E): *Physeter catodon*
Spermacet whale (E): *Physeter catodon*
Spermestes bicolor = Lonchura bicolor
Spermestes cucullatus = Lonchura cucullata
Spermestes fringilloides = Lonchura fringilloides
Spermète à bec bleu (F): *Lonchura bicolor*
Spermète nonnette (F): *Lonchura cucullata*
Spermète pie (F): *Lonchura fringilloides*
Spermophaga haematina : (E) Blue-billed Weaver, Western Bluebill, (S) Espermófaga hematina, (F) Gros-bec sanguin, Sénégali sanguin, **III** ESTRILDIDAE Av
Spheniscus demersus : (E) African Penguin, Black-footed Penguin, Jackass Penguin, (S) Pingüino del Cabo, (F) Manchot du Cap, **II** SPHENISCIDAE Av
Spheniscus humboldti : (E) Humboldt Penguin, Peruvian Penguin, (S) Pingüino de Humboldt, (F) Manchot de Humboldt, **I** SPHENISCIDAE Av
Sphenodon (E): *Sphenodon punctatus*
Sphénodon de Günther (F): *Sphenodon guntheri*
Sphenodon spp.: (S) Tuátaras, (F) Hatterias , Sphénodons, Tuataras, **I** SPHENODONTIDAE Re
Sphenodon guntheri : (E) Brother Islands Tuatara, (F) Hatteria de Günther, Sphénodon de Günther **I** SPHENODONTIDAE Re
Sphénodon ponctué (F): *Sphenodon punctatus*
Sphenodon punctatus : (E) Beak-head, Cook Strait Tuatara, Sphenodon, Tuatara, (S) Tuátara, (F) Hatteria ponctué, Sphénodon ponctué, **I** SPHENODONTIDAE Re
Sphénodons (F): *Sphenodon* spp.
Sphenotrochus andrewianus andrewianus : (E) Smooth-ribbed Wedge Coral **II** TURBINOLIIDAE An
Sphenotrochus andrewianus moorei : **II** TURBINOLIIDAE An
Sphenotrochus aurantiacus : **II** TURBINOLIIDAE An
Sphenotrochus auritus : **II** TURBINOLIIDAE An
Sphenotrochus evexicostatus : **II** TURBINOLIIDAE An
Sphenotrochus excavatus : **II** TURBINOLIIDAE An
Sphenotrochus gardineri : **II** TURBINOLIIDAE An
Sphenotrochus gilchristi : **II** TURBINOLIIDAE An
Sphenotrochus hancocki : **II** TURBINOLIIDAE An
Sphenotrochus imbricatocostatus : **II** TURBINOLIIDAE An
Sphenotrochus lindstroemi : **II** TURBINOLIIDAE An
Sphenotrochus ralphae : **II** TURBINOLIIDAE An
Sphenotrochus squiresi : **II** TURBINOLIIDAE An
Sphiggurus mexicanus : (E) Mexican Hairy Dwarf Porcupine, Mexican Tree Porcupine, (F) Porc-épic préhensile **III** ERETHIZONTIDAE Ma
Sphiggurus paragayensis = Sphiggurus spinosus
Sphiggurus spinosus : (E) Orange-spined Hairy Dwarf Porcupine, Paraguay Hairy Dwarf Porcupine, Spiny Tree Porcupine, (S) Coendu espinoso, (F) Coendou épineux, **III** ERETHIZONTIDAE Ma
Spider Tortoise (E): *Pyxis arachnoides*
Spilocuscus kraemeri = Spilocuscus maculatus

Spilocuscus maculatus : (E) Common Spotted Cuscus, Short-tailed Spotted Cuscus, Spotted Phalanger, (S) Cuscús manchado, Cuscus moteado, (F) Couscous tacheté, Phalanger tacheté, **II** PHALANGERIDAE Ma

Spilocuscus papuensis = Spilocuscus maculatus

Spilornis cheela : (E) Crested Serpent-Eagle, Mentawai Serpent-Eagle, Natuna Serpent-Eagle, Nias Serpent-Eagle, Ryukyu Serpent-Eagle, Simeulue Serpent-Eagle, (S) Culebrera chiíla, (F) Serpentaire bacha, **II** ACCIPITRIDAE Av

Spilornis cheela ssp. *holospilus = Spilornis holospilus*

Spilornis cheela ssp. *kinabaluensis = Spilornis kinabaluensis*

Spilornis elgini : (E) Andaman Dark Serpent-Eagle, Andaman Serpent-Eagle, Dark Serpent-Eagle, (S) Culebrera de Andamán, (F) Serpentaire des Andaman, **II** ACCIPITRIDAE Av

Spilornis holospilus : (E) Philippine Serpent-Eagle, (S) Culebrera filipina, (F) Serpentaire des Philippines, **II** ACCIPITRIDAE Av

Spilornis kinabaluensis : (E) Kinabalu Serpent-Eagle, Mountain Serpent-Eagle, (S) Culebrera del Kinabalu, (F) Serpentaire des Kinabalu, **II** ACCIPITRIDAE Av

Spilornis minimus : (E) Nicobar Serpent-Eagle, Small Serpent-Eagle, (S) Culebrera de Nicobar, (F) Serpentaire des Nicobar, **II** ACCIPITRIDAE Av

Spilornis rufipectus : (E) Celebes Serpent-Eagle, Sulawesi Serpent-Eagle, (S) Culebrera de Célebes, (F) Serpentaire des Célèbes, **II** ACCIPITRIDAE Av

Spine Coral (E): *Hydnophora spp.*

Spine-sided Chameleon (E): *Chamaeleo laterispinis*

Spinifex Monitor (E): *Varanus eremius*

Spinner Dolphin (E): *Stenella longirostris*

Spinophrynoides spp.: (E) Ethiopian toads, (S) Sapos vivíparos, (F) Crapauds vivipares, **I** BUFONIDAE Am

Spinophrynoides osgoodi : (E) Osgood's Ethiopian Toad, (S) Sapo vivíparo de Osgood, (F) Nectophrynoide d'Ethiopie, Nectophrynoide d'Osgood, **I** BUFONIDAE Am

Spinus cucullatus = Carduelis cucullata

Spinus yarrellii = Carduelis yarrellii

Spiny Boa (E): *Trachyboa gularis*

Spiny Chameleon (E): *Bradypodion spinosum*

Spiny Crag Lizard (E): *Cordylus spinosus*

Spiny Flower Coral (E): *Mussa angulosa*

Spiny Leaf Chameleon (E): *Brookesia decaryi*

Spiny Seahorse (E): *Hippocampus histrix*

Spiny Sturgeon (E): *Acipenser nudiventris*

Spiny Terrapin (E): *Heosemys spinosa*

Spiny Tree Porcupine (E): *Sphiggurus spinosus*

Spiny Turtle (E): *Heosemys spinosa*

Spiny-flanked Chameleon (E): *Chamaeleo laterispinis*

Spiny-tailed lizards (E): *Cordylus* spp. / *Uromastyx* spp.

Spiny-tailed Pygmy Monitor (E): *Varanus acanthurus*

Spix's Macaw (E): *Cyanopsitta spixii*

Spizaetus africanus : (E) Cassin's Hawk-Eagle, (S) Aguila-azor congoleña, (F) Aigle de Cassin, **II** ACCIPITRIDAE Av

Spizaetus alboniger : (E) Black-and-white Hawk-Eagle, Blyth's Hawk-Eagle, (S) Aguila-azor Indonesia, (F) Aigle de Blyth, **II** ACCIPITRIDAE Av

Spizaetus bartelsi : (E) Black-and-white Hawk-Eagle, Javan Hawk-Eagle, (S) Aguila-azor de Java, (F) Aigle de Java, **II** ACCIPITRIDAE Av

Spizaetus cirrhatus : (E) Changeable Hawk-Eagle, Crested Hawk-Eagle, Sunda Hawk-Eagle, (S) Aguila-azor variable, (F) Aigle huppé, **II** ACCIPITRIDAE Av

Spizaetus coronatus = Stephanoaetus coronatus

Spizaetus isidori = Oroaetus isidori

Spizaetus lanceolatus : (E) Sulawesi Hawk-Eagle, (S) Aguila-azor de Célebes, (F) Aigle des Célèbes, **II** ACCIPITRIDAE Av

Spizaetus nanus : (E) Wallace's Hawk-Eagle, (S) Aguila-azor de Wallace, (F) Aigle de Wallace, **II** ACCIPITRIDAE Av

Spizaetus nipalensis : (E) Feather-toed Hawk-Eagle, Hodgson's Hawk-Eagle, Mountain Hawk-Eagle, (S) Aguila-azor montañesa, (F) Aigle montagnard, **II** ACCIPITRIDAE Av

Spizaetus occipitalis = Lophaetus occipitalis

Spizaetus ornatus : (E) Ornate Hawk-Eagle, (S) Aguila de Penacho, Aguila elegante, Aguila-azor blanca, Aguila-azor galana, (F) Aigle orné, **II** ACCIPITRIDAE Av

Spizaetus philippensis : (E) Philippine Hawk-Eagle, (S) Aguila-azor filipina, (F) Aigle des Philippines, **II** ACCIPITRIDAE Av

Spizaetus tyrannus : (E) Black Hawk-Eagle, Tyrant Hawk-Eagle, (S) Aguila tirana, Aguila-azor negra, (F) Aigle tyran, **II** ACCIPITRIDAE Av

Spizastur melanoleucus : (E) Black-and-white Hawk-Eagle, (S) Aguila blanquinegra, Aguila-azor blanquinegra, Aguila-azor chica, (F) Aigle noir et blanc, **II** ACCIPITRIDAE Av

Spiziapteryx circumcinctus : (E) Spot-winged Falcon, Spot-winged Falconet, (S) Halconcito argentino, Halconcito gris, Halconcito gris americano, (F) Carnifex à ailes tachetées, Fauconnet d'Amérique, **II** FALCONIDAE Av

Splash-backed Poison Frog (E): *Dendrobates galactonotus*

Splaytooth Beaked Whale (E): *Mesoplodon bowdoini*

Splendid Astrapia (E): *Astrapia splendidissima*

Splendid Grass-Parakeet (E): *Neophema splendida*

Splendid Poison Frog (E): *Dendrobates speciosus*

Split Keelback (E): *Atretium schistosum*

Splitting Cup Coral (E): *Dasmosmilia lymani*

Splitting Fan Coral (E): *Flabellum macandrewi*

Spoonbill (E): *Platalea leucorodia*

Spoonbill Cat (E): *Polyodon spathula*

Spoonbill catfish (E): *Polyodon spathula*

Sporadopora dichotoma : **II** STYLASTERIDAE Hy

Sporadopora micropora : **II** STYLASTERIDAE Hy

Sporadopora mortenseni : **II** STYLASTERIDAE Hy

Sporaeginthus subflavus = Amandava subflava

Sporopipe quadrillé (F): *Sporopipes frontalis*

Sporopipes frontalis : (E) Scaly-fronted Weaver, Speckle-fronted Weaver, (S) Tejedorcito punteado, (F) Moineau quadrillé, Sporopipe quadrillé, **III** PLOCEIDAE Av

Sportive lemurs (E): MEGALADAPIDAE spp.

Spot-backed Weaver (E): *Ploceus cucullatus*

Spot-bellied Eagle-Owl (E): *Bubo nipalensis*

Spot-billed Toucanet (E): *Selenidera maculirostris*

Spot-breasted Ibis (E): *Bostrychia rara*

Spot-legged Poison Frog (E): *Epipedobates pictus*

Spot-necked Otter (E): *Lutra maculicollis*

Spot-nosed Guenon (E): *Cercopithecus nictitans*

Spot-nosed Monkey (E): *Cercopithecus petaurista*

Spot-tailed Goshawk (E): *Accipiter trinotatus*

Spot-tailed Sparrowhawk (E): *Accipiter trinotatus*

Spotted Box Turtle (E): *Terrapene nelsoni*

Spotted Cotinga (E): *Cotinga maculata*

Spotted Day Gecko (E): *Phelsuma guttata/ Phelsuma ocellata*

Spotted Dwarf Boa (E): *Tropidophis maculatus*

Spotted Eagle (E): *Aquila clanga*

Spotted Eagle-Owl (E): *Bubo africanus*

Spotted Greenshank (E): *Tringa guttifer*

Spotted Harrier (E): *Circus assimilis*

Spotted Kestrel (E): *Falco moluccensis*

Spotted Linsang (E): *Prionodon pardicolor*

Spotted Little Owl (E): *Athene brama*

Spotted Marsh-Harrier (E): *Circus spilonotus*

Spotted Owl (E): *Strix occidentalis*

Spotted Owlet (E): *Athene brama*

Spotted Paca (E): *Agouti paca*

Spotted Phalanger (E): *Spilocuscus maculatus*

Spotted Pond Turtle (E): *Geoclemys hamiltonii*

Checklist of fauna/Lista de especies de fauna/Liste des espèces animales

Spotted Python (E): *Antaresia maculosa*
Spotted Sand Boa (E): *Eryx jaculus*
Spotted Scops-Owl (E): *Otus spilocephalus*
Spotted Seahorse (E): *Hippocampus erectus/ Hippocampus kuda*
Spotted Sticky-toed Gecko (E): *Hoplodactylus maculatus*
Spotted Tree Monitor (E): *Varanus timorensis*
Spotted Turtle (E): *Lissemys punctata*
Spotted Wood-Owl (E): *Strix seloputo*
Spotted-backed Harrier (E): *Circus spilonotus*
Spotted-necked Otter (E): *Lutra maculicollis*
Spot-throated Hummingbird (E): *Leucippus taczanowskii*
Spot-winged Falcon (E): *Spiziapteryx circumcinctus*
Spot-winged Falconet (E): *Spiziapteryx circumcinctus*
Spot-winged Parrotlet (E): *Touit stictoptera*
Spur-heeled Chameleon (E): *Chamaeleo gracilis*
Spur-thighed Tortoise (E): *Testudo graeca*
Spur-winged Goose (E): *Plectropterus gambensis*
Squale géant (F): *Cetorhinus maximus*
Squale-pèlerin (F): *Cetorhinus maximus*
Squalus cetaceus = Cetorhinus maximus
Squalus elephas = Cetorhinus maximus
Squalus gunneri = Cetorhinus maximus
Squalus gunnerianus = Cetorhinus maximus
Squalus homianus = Cetorhinus maximus
Squalus isodus = Cetorhinus maximus
Squalus pelegrinus = Cetorhinus maximus
Squalus peregrinus = Cetorhinus maximus
Squalus rashleighanus = Cetorhinus maximus
Squalus rhinoceros = Cetorhinus maximus
Square-lipped Rhinoceros (E): *Ceratotherium simum*
Square-tailed Kite (E): *Lophoictinia isura*
Sri Lanka Hanging-Parrot (E): *Loriculus beryllinus*
Sri Lankan Giant Squirrel (E): *Ratufa macroura*
Sri Lankan Rose (E): *Atrophaneura jophon*
St Lucia Amazon (E): *Amazona versicolor*
St Lucia Parrot (E): *Amazona versicolor*
St Vincent Amazon (E): *Amazona guildingii*
Staghorn Coral (E): *Acropora cervicornis*
Standardwing (E): *Semioptera wallacii*
Standard-wing Bird-of-paradise (E): *Semioptera wallacii*
Standing's Day Gecko (E): *Phelsuma standingi*
Stanley Bustard (E): *Neotis denhami*
Stanley Crane (E): *Grus paradisea*
Stanley Parakeet (E): *Platycercus icterotis*
Star Column Coral (E): *Pavona clavus*
Star Coral (E): *Madracis pharensis*
Star Sturgeon (E): *Acipenser stellatus*
Star Tortoise (E): *Geochelone elegans*
Starburst corals (E): *Galaxea spp.*
Starry Sturgeon (E): *Acipenser stellatus*
Starry Tree Gecko (E): *Naultinus stellatus*
Steely-vented Hummingbird (E): *Saucerottia saucerrottei*
Stejneger's Beaked Whale (E): *Mesoplodon stejnegeri*
Stellapora echinata : **II** STYLASTERIDAE Hy
Stellate Sturgeon (E): *Acipenser stellatus*
Steller's Albatross (E): *Diomedea albatrus*
Steller's Sea-Eagle (E): *Haliaeetus pelagicus*
Stellula calliope : (E) Calliope Hummingbird, (S) Colibrí calíope, (F) Colibri calliope, **II** TROCHILIDAE Av
Stenella attenuata : (E) Bridled Dolphin, Narrow-snouted Dolphin, Pantropical Spotted Dolphin, (S) Delfín manchado, Delfín pintado, (F) Dauphin tacheté pantropical, **II** DELPHINIDAE Ma
Stenella attenuata ssp. *frontalis = Stenella frontalis*
Stenella clymene : (E) Atlantic Spinner Dolphin, Clymene Dolphin, Helmet Dolphin, (F) Dauphin de Clymène **II** DELPHINIDAE Ma
Stenella coeruleoalba : (E) Euphrosyne Dolphin, Striped Dolphin, (S) Delfín blanco y azul, (F) Dauphin bleu et blanc, Dauphin rayé, **II** DELPHINIDAE Ma
Stenella dubia = Stenella attenuata
Stenella dubia ssp. *attenuata = Stenella attenuata*

Stenella frontalis : (E) Atlantic Spotted Dolphin, (S) Delfín manchado del Atlántico, (F) Dauphin tacheté de l'Atlantique, **II** DELPHINIDAE Ma
Stenella graffmani = Stenella attenuata
Stenella longirostris : (E) Long-beaked Dolphin, Long-snouted Dolphin, Spinner Dolphin, (S) Delfín tornillón, (F) Dauphin longirostre, **II** DELPHINIDAE Ma
Stenella malayana = Stenella attenuata
Stenella microps = Stenella longirostris
Stenella pernettensis = Stenella frontalis
Stenella plagiodon = Stenella frontalis
Stenella roseiventris = Stenella longirostris
Stenella styx = Stenella coeruleoalba
Sténo (F): *Steno bredanensis*
Steno bredanensis : (E) Rough-toothed Dolphin, (S) Delfín de pico largo, (F) Sténo, **II** DELPHINIDAE Ma
Stenocyathus vermiformis : (E) Worm Coral **II** GUYNIIDAE An
Sténoderme pseudo-vampire (F): *Platyrrhinus lineatus*
Stenohelia concinna : **II** STYLASTERIDAE Hy
Stenohelia conferta : **II** STYLASTERIDAE Hy
Stenohelia echinata : **II** STYLASTERIDAE Hy
Stenohelia maderensis : **II** STYLASTERIDAE Hy
Stenohelia pauciseptata : **II** STYLASTERIDAE Hy
Stenohelia profunda : **II** STYLASTERIDAE Hy
Stenohelia robusta = Stenohelia concinna
Stenohelia tiliata : **II** STYLASTERIDAE Hy
Stenohelia umbonata : **II** STYLASTERIDAE Hy
Stenohelia yabei : **II** STYLASTERIDAE Hy
Stephanie's Astrapia (E): *Astrapia stephaniae*
Stephanoaetus coronatus : (E) African Crowned Eagle, Crowned Eagle, Crowned Hawk-Eagle, (S) Aguila coronada, Aguila coronada rabuda, (F) Aigle blanchard, Aigle couronné, **II** ACCIPITRIDAE Av
Stephanocoenia intersepta : (E) Blushing Star Coral **II** ASTROCOENIIDAE An
Stephanocoenia michelinii = Stephanocoenia intersepta
Stephanocyathus campaniformis : **II** CARYOPHYLLIIDAE An
Stephanocyathus coronatus : **II** CARYOPHYLLIIDAE An
Stephanocyathus crassus : **II** CARYOPHYLLIIDAE An
Stephanocyathus diadema : **II** CARYOPHYLLIIDAE An
Stephanocyathus discoides = Stephanocyathus diadema
Stephanocyathus explanans : **II** CARYOPHYLLIIDAE An
Stephanocyathus laevifundus : **II** CARYOPHYLLIIDAE An
Stephanocyathus moseleyanus : **II** CARYOPHYLLIIDAE An
Stephanocyathus nobilis : **II** CARYOPHYLLIIDAE An
Stephanocyathus paliferus : **II** CARYOPHYLLIIDAE An
Stephanocyathus platypus : **II** CARYOPHYLLIIDAE An
Stephanocyathus regius : **II** CARYOPHYLLIIDAE An
Stephanocyathus spiniger : **II** CARYOPHYLLIIDAE An
Stephanocyathus weberianus : **II** CARYOPHYLLIIDAE An
Stephanohelia praecipua : **II** STYLASTERIDAE Hy
Stephanophyllia complicata : **II** MICRABACIIDAE An
Stephanophyllia fungulus : **II** MICRABACIIDAE An
Stephanophyllia neglecta : **II** MICRABACIIDAE An
Stephanoxis lalandi : (E) Plovercrest, (S) Colibrí copetón, Picaflor copetón, (F) Colibri de Delalande, **II** TROCHILIDAE Av
Stephen's Lorikeet (E): *Vini stepheni*
Stephens's Island Gecko (E): *Hoplodactylus stephensi*
Stephens's Sticky-toed Gecko (E): *Hoplodactylus stephensi*
Steppe Eagle (E): *Aquila nipalensis*
Steppe Fox (E): *Vulpes cana*
Steppe Tortoise (E): *Testudo horsfieldii*
Sterlet (E/F): *Acipenser ruthenus*
Sterlet sturgeon (E): *Acipenser ruthenus*
Sterletus helenae = Acipenser ruthenus

Sterletus kankreni = Acipenser ruthenus
Sterletus macrostomus = Acipenser fulvescens
Sterletus serotimus = Acipenser fulvescens
Sternoclyta cyanopectus : (E) Violet-chested Hummingbird, (S) Colibrí pechiazul, (F) Colibri à poitrine violette, **II** TROCHILIDAE Av
Stewart's Sticky-toed Gecko (E): *Hoplodactylus rakiurae*
Stichopathes abyssicola : **II** ANTIPATHIDAE An
Stichopathes alcocki : **II** ANTIPATHIDAE An
Stichopathes bournei : **II** ANTIPATHIDAE An
Stichopathes ceylonensis : **II** ANTIPATHIDAE An
Stichopathes contorta : **II** ANTIPATHIDAE An
Stichopathes echinulata : **II** ANTIPATHIDAE An
Stichopathes filiformis : **II** ANTIPATHIDAE An
Stichopathes flagellum : **II** ANTIPATHIDAE An
Stichopathes gracilis : **II** ANTIPATHIDAE An
Stichopathes longispina : **II** ANTIPATHIDAE An
Stichopathes lutkeni : (E) Black Wire Coral **II** ANTIPATHIDAE An
Stichopathes papillosa : **II** ANTIPATHIDAE An
Stichopathes paucispina : **II** ANTIPATHIDAE An
Stichopathes regularis : **II** ANTIPATHIDAE An
Stichopathes semiglabra : **II** ANTIPATHIDAE An
Stichopathes seychellensis : **II** ANTIPATHIDAE An
Stichopathes spiessi : **II** ANTIPATHIDAE An
Stichopathes variabilis : **II** ANTIPATHIDAE An
Stimson's Python (E): *Antaresia stimsoni*
Stone Monitor (E): *Varanus baritji*
Stony corals (E): SCLERACTINIA spp. An
Straight-billed Hermit (E): *Phaethornis bourcieri*
Strange-horned Chameleon (E): *Bradypodion xenorhinum*
Strange-nosed Chameleon (E): *Bradypodion xenorhinum*
Strap-toothed Whale (E): *Mesoplodon layardii*
Strawberry Clam (E): *Hippopus hippopus*
Strawberry Poison Frog (F): *Dendrobates pumilio*
Straw-crowned Bulbul (E): *Pycnonotus zeylanicus*
Straw-headed Bulbul (E): *Pycnonotus zeylanicus*
Streaked Lorikeet (E): *Charmosyna multistriata*
Streak-tailed Monitor (E): *Varanus caudolineatus*
Streak-throated Hermit (E): *Phaethornis rupurumii*
Streamertail (E): *Trochilus polytmus*
Streptopelia decipiens : (E) African Mourning Dove, Mourning Collared-Dove, (S) Tórtola engañosa, (F) Tourterelle pleureuse, **III** COLUMBIDAE Av
Streptopelia roseogrisea : (E) African Collared-Dove, Pink-headed Dove, Rose-grey Dove, (S) Tórtola rosigrís, (F) Tourterelle rieuse, **III** COLUMBIDAE Av
Streptopelia semitorquata : (E) Red-eyed Dove, (S) Tórtola ojirroja, Tórtola rizum, (F) Tourterelle à collier, **III** COLUMBIDAE Av
Streptopelia senegalensis : (E) Laughing Dove, Palm Dove, Senegal Dove, (S) Tórtola del Senegal, Tórtola Reidora, Tórtola Senegalesa, (F) Tourterelle des palmiers, Tourterelle maillée, **III** COLUMBIDAE Av
Streptopelia turtur : (E) European Turtle-Dove, Turtle Dove, Western Turtle-Dove, (S) Tórtola común, Tórtola Europea, (F) Tourterelle des bois, **III** COLUMBIDAE Av
Streptopelia vinacea : (E) Vinaceous Dove, (S) Tórtola vinosa, (F) Pigeon vert à front nu, Tourterelle vineuse, **III** COLUMBIDAE Av
Striate Finger Coral (E): *Madracis myriaster*
Striated Caracara (E): *Phalcoboenus australis*
Striated Lorikeet (E): *Charmosyna multistriata*
Striated Scops-Owl (E): *Otus brucei*
STRIGIFORMES spp. : (E) Owls, (S) Lechuzas, (F) Rapaces nocturnes, **I/II** Av
Strigocuscus mimicus = Phalanger orientalis
Strigops habroptilus : (E) Kakapo, Owl Parrot, (S) Cacapo, Kakapo, (F) Kakapo, Perroquet nocturne, Perroquet-hibou, Strigops kakapo, **I** PSITTACIDAE Av
Strigops kakapo (F): *Strigops habroptilus*
Stripe-backed Side-necked Turtle (E): *Pelusios gabonensis*

Stripe-breasted Starthroat (E): *Heliomaster squamosus*
Striped Civet (E): *Fossa fossana*
Striped Day Gecko (E): *Phelsuma lineata*
Striped Dolphin (E): *Stenella coeruleoalba*
Striped Giant Soft-shelled Turtle (E): *Chitra chitra*
Striped Narrow-headed Softshell Turtle (E): *Chitra chitra*
Striped Owl (E): *Asio clamator*
Striped Treeshrew (E): *Tupaia dorsalis*
Stripe-necked Mongoose (E): *Herpestes vitticollis*
Stripe-tailed Hummingbird (E): *Eupherusa eximia*
Stripe-tailed Monitor (E): *Varanus caudolineatus*
Stripe-throated Hermit (E): *Phaethornis striigularis*
Strix albitarsus : (E) Rufous-banded Owl, (S) Cárabo patiblanco, Lechuza colilarga, Lechuza patiblanca, (F) Chouette fasciée, **II** STRIGIDAE Av
Strix aluco : (E) Tawny Owl, Tawny Wood-Owl, (S) Cárabo, Cárabo común, (F) Chouette hulotte, Hulotte chathuant, **II** STRIGIDAE Av
Strix butleri : (E) Desert Owl, Hume's Owl, Hume's Tawny Owl, Hume's Wood-Owl, (S) Cárabo árabe, Cárabo de Hume, (F) Chouette de Butler, Chouette hulotte de Hume, **II** STRIGIDAE Av
Strix chacoensis = Strix rufipes
Strix davidi : (E) David's Owl, Sichuan Wood-Owl, (S) Cárabo de Sichuán, (F) Chouette de Sitchouan, Chouette du Sitchouan, **II** STRIGIDAE Av
Strix fulvescens : (E) Fulvous Owl, (S) Búho fulvo, Cárabo Guatemalteco, (F) Chouette fauve, **II** STRIGIDAE Av
Strix huhula : (E) Black-banded Owl, (S) Cárabo negro, Lechuza negra, (F) Chouette huhul, **II** STRIGIDAE Av
Strix hylophila : (E) Rusty-barred Owl, (S) Cárabo Brasileño, Lechuza listada, (F) Chouette dryade, **II** STRIGIDAE Av
Strix leptogrammica : (E) Brown Wood-Owl, (S) Cárabo oriental, (F) Chouette leptogramme, **II** STRIGIDAE Av
Strix nebulosa : (E) Great Grey Owl, Grey Owl, Lapland Owl, Lapp Owl, (S) Cárabo Lapón, (F) Chouette lapone, **II** STRIGIDAE Av
Strix nigrolineata : (E) Black-and-white Owl, (S) Búho blanquinegro, Cárabo blanquinegro, Cárabo de Sudamérica, Lechuza blanquinegra, (F) Chouette à lignes noires, Chouette noire et blanche, **II** STRIGIDAE Av
Strix occidentalis : (E) Spotted Owl, (S) Búho manchado, Cárabo Californiano, (F) Chouette tachetée, **II** STRIGIDAE Av
Strix ocellata : (E) Mottled Wood-Owl, (S) Cárabo ocelado, (F) Chouette ocellée, **II** STRIGIDAE Av
Strix rufipes : (E) Rufous-legged Owl, (S) Cárabo bataraz, Lechuza bataraz, (F) Chouette masquée, **II** STRIGIDAE Av
Strix seloputo : (E) Spotted Wood-Owl, (S) Cárabo de las pagodas, (F) Chouette des pagodes, **II** STRIGIDAE Av
Strix uralensis : (E) Ural Owl, (S) Cárabo uralense, (F) Chouette de l'Oural, **II** STRIGIDAE Av
Strix uralensis ssp. *davidi = Strix davidi*
Strix varia : (E) Barred Owl, (S) Búho barrado, Cárabo norteamericano, (F) Chouette rayée, **II** STRIGIDAE Av
Strix varia ssp. *fulvescens = Strix fulvescens*
Strix virgata : (E) Mottled Owl, (S) Búho café, Cárabo café, Lechuza colilarga, (F) Chouette mouchetée, **II** STRIGIDAE Av
Strix woodfordii : (E) African Wood-Owl, Woodford's Owl, (S) Cárabo Africano, Lechuzón de Woodford, (F) Chouette africaine, Hulotte africaine, **II** STRIGIDAE Av
Strombe géant (F): *Strombus gigas*
Strombus gigas : (E) Pink Conch, Queen Conch, (S) Concha reina del Caribe, (F) Lambis, Strombe géant, **II** STROMBIDAE Ga

Struthio camelus : (E) Ostrich, (S) Avestruz, (F) Autruche d'Afrique, **I/NC** STRUTHIONIDAE Av
Struthio molybdophanes = Struthio camelus
Stumptail Macaque (E): *Macaca arctoides*
Stump-tailed Macaque (E): *Macaca arctoides*
Sturgeon (E): *Acipenser sturio*
Sturgeons (E): ACIPENSERIFORMES spp. Ac
Sturion (F): *Acipenser sturio*
Sturk (F): *Acipenser sturio*
Stygian Owl (E): *Asio stygius*
Stylantheca papillosa : **II** STYLASTERIDAE Hy
Stylantheca petrograpta : **II** STYLASTERIDAE Hy
Stylantheca porphyra : **II** STYLASTERIDAE Hy
Stylaraea punctata : **II** PORITIDAE An
Stylaster alaskanus : **II** STYLASTERIDAE Hy
Stylaster amphiheloides : **II** STYLASTERIDAE Hy
Stylaster antillarum : **II** STYLASTERIDAE Hy
Stylaster asper : **II** STYLASTERIDAE Hy
Stylaster aurantiacus : **II** STYLASTERIDAE Hy
Stylaster bellus : **II** STYLASTERIDAE Hy
Stylaster bilobatus : **II** STYLASTERIDAE Hy
Stylaster bithalamus : **II** STYLASTERIDAE Hy
Stylaster blatteus : **II** STYLASTERIDAE Hy
Stylaster bocki : **II** STYLASTERIDAE Hy
Stylaster boreopacificus : **II** STYLASTERIDAE Hy
Stylaster boschmai : **II** STYLASTERIDAE Hy
Stylaster brochi : **II** STYLASTERIDAE Hy
Stylaster brunneus : **II** STYLASTERIDAE Hy
Stylaster californicus : **II** STYLASTERIDAE Hy
Stylaster campylecus : **II** STYLASTERIDAE Hy
Stylaster campylecus campylecus : **II** STYLASTERIDAE Hy
Stylaster campylecus parageus : **II** STYLASTERIDAE Hy
Stylaster campylecus trachystomus : **II** STYLASTERIDAE Hy
Stylaster campylecus tylotus : **II** STYLASTERIDAE Hy
Stylaster cancellatus : **II** STYLASTERIDAE Hy
Stylaster carinatus : **II** STYLASTERIDAE Hy
Stylaster cocosensis : **II** STYLASTERIDAE Hy
Stylaster complanatus : **II** STYLASTERIDAE Hy
Stylaster corallium : **II** STYLASTERIDAE Hy
Stylaster crassior : **II** STYLASTERIDAE Hy
Stylaster densicaulis : **II** STYLASTERIDAE Hy
Stylaster dentatus : **II** STYLASTERIDAE Hy
Stylaster divergens : **II** STYLASTERIDAE Hy
Stylaster duchassaingii : **II** STYLASTERIDAE Hy
Stylaster eguchii : **II** STYLASTERIDAE Hy
Stylaster elassotomus : **II** STYLASTERIDAE Hy
Stylaster erubescens : **II** STYLASTERIDAE Hy
Stylaster erubescens britannicus : **II** STYLASTERIDAE Hy
Stylaster erubescens erubescens : **II** STYLASTERIDAE Hy
Stylaster erubescens groenlandicus : **II** STYLASTERIDAE Hy
Stylaster erubescens meteorensis : **II** STYLASTERIDAE Hy
Stylaster eximius : **II** STYLASTERIDAE Hy
Stylaster filogranus : **II** STYLASTERIDAE Hy
Stylaster flabelliformis : **II** STYLASTERIDAE Hy
Stylaster galapagensis : **II** STYLASTERIDAE Hy
Stylaster gemmascens : **II** STYLASTERIDAE Hy
Stylaster gracilis : **II** STYLASTERIDAE Hy
Stylaster granulosus : **II** STYLASTERIDAE Hy
Stylaster hattorii : **II** STYLASTERIDAE Hy
Stylaster horologium : **II** STYLASTERIDAE Hy
Stylaster ibericus : **II** STYLASTERIDAE Hy
Stylaster imbricatus : **II** STYLASTERIDAE Hy
Stylaster incompletus : **II** STYLASTERIDAE Hy
Stylaster incrassitus : **II** STYLASTERIDAE Hy
Stylaster inornatus : **II** STYLASTERIDAE Hy
Stylaster laevigatus : **II** STYLASTERIDAE Hy
Stylaster lonchitis : **II** STYLASTERIDAE Hy
Stylaster marenzelleri : **II** STYLASTERIDAE Hy

Stylaster maroccanus : **II** STYLASTERIDAE Hy
Stylaster marshae : **II** STYLASTERIDAE Hy
Stylaster microstriatus : **II** STYLASTERIDAE Hy
Stylaster miniatus : **II** STYLASTERIDAE Hy
Stylaster moseleyanus : **II** STYLASTERIDAE Hy
Stylaster multiplex : **II** STYLASTERIDAE Hy
Stylaster nobilis : **II** STYLASTERIDAE Hy
Stylaster norvegicus : **II** STYLASTERIDAE Hy
Stylaster papuensis : **II** STYLASTERIDAE Hy
Stylaster polymorphus : **II** STYLASTERIDAE Hy
Stylaster polyorchis : **II** STYLASTERIDAE Hy
Stylaster profundiporus : **II** STYLASTERIDAE Hy
Stylaster profundus : **II** STYLASTERIDAE Hy
Stylaster pulcher : **II** STYLASTERIDAE Hy
Stylaster punctatus = Stylaster roseus
Stylaster purpuratus : **II** STYLASTERIDAE Hy
Stylaster ramosus : **II** STYLASTERIDAE Hy
Stylaster robustus : **II** STYLASTERIDAE Hy
Stylaster rosaceus : **II** STYLASTERIDAE Hy
Stylaster roseus : **II** STYLASTERIDAE Hy
Stylaster sanguineus : **II** STYLASTERIDAE Hy
Stylaster scabiosus : **II** STYLASTERIDAE Hy
Stylaster solidus : **II** STYLASTERIDAE Hy
Stylaster spatula : **II** STYLASTERIDAE Hy
Stylaster stejnegeri : **II** STYLASTERIDAE Hy
Stylaster stellulatus : **II** STYLASTERIDAE Hy
Stylaster subviolaceus : **II** STYLASTERIDAE Hy
Stylaster tenisonwoodsi : **II** STYLASTERIDAE Hy
Stylaster venustus : **II** STYLASTERIDAE Hy
Stylaster verrillii : **II** STYLASTERIDAE Hy
STYLASTERIDAE spp.: (E) Lace corals **II** Hy
Stylocoeniella armata : **II** ASTROCOENIIDAE An
Stylocoeniella cocosensis : **II** ASTROCOENIIDAE An
Stylocoeniella guentheri : **II** ASTROCOENIIDAE An
Stylophora danae : **II** POCILLOPORIDAE An
Stylophora kuehlmanni : **II** POCILLOPORIDAE An
Stylophora madagascariensis : **II** POCILLOPORIDAE An
Stylophora mamillata : **II** POCILLOPORIDAE An
Stylophora mordax : **II** POCILLOPORIDAE An
Stylophora pistillata : (E) Cluster Coral **II** POCILLOPORIDAE An
Stylophora subseriata : **II** POCILLOPORIDAE An
Stylophora wellsi : **II** POCILLOPORIDAE An
Subantarctic Fur Seal (E): *Arctocephalus tropicalis*
Subtropical Pygmy-Owl (E): *Glaucidium parkeri*
Sucury (S): *Eunectes murinus*
Suirirí bicolor (S): *Dendrocygna bicolor*
Suirirí cariblanco (S): *Dendrocygna viduata*
Suirirí leonado (S): *Dendrocygna bicolor*
Suirirí piquirrojo (S): *Dendrocygna autumnalis*
Suirirí yaguaza (S): *Dendrocygna arborea*
Sula abbotti = Papasula abbotti
Sula Barn-Owl (E): *Tyto nigrobrunnea*
Sula Hanging-Parrot (E): *Loriculus sclateri*
Sulawesi Dwarf Hornbill (E): *Penelopides exarhatus*
Sulawesi Flying-fox (E): *Acerodon celebensis*
Sulawesi Forest Turtle (E): *Leucocephalon yuwonoi*
Sulawesi Fruit Bat (E): *Acerodon celebensis*
Sulawesi Goshawk (E): *Accipiter griseiceps*
Sulawesi Hanging-Parrot (E): *Loriculus stigmatus*
Sulawesi Hawk-eagle (E): *Spizaetus lanceolatus*
Sulawesi Hornbill (E): *Penelopides exarhatus*
Sulawesi Macaque (E): *Macaca nigra*
Sulawesi Owl (E): *Tyto rosenbergii*
Sulawesi Scops-Owl (E): *Otus manadensis*
Sulawesi Serpent-Eagle (E): *Spilornis rufipectus*
Sulawesi Tarictic Hornbill (E): *Penelopides exarhatus*
Sulawesi Tarsier (E): *Tarsius spectrum*
Sulawesi Wrinkled Hornbill (E): *Aceros cassidix*
Sulio (S): *Acipenser sturio*
Sulphur-bottom Whale (E): *Balaenoptera musculus*
Sulphur-crested Cockatoo (E): *Cacatua galerita*
Sulphur-winged Parakeet (E): *Pyrrhura hoffmanni*
Sulu Hornbill (E): *Anthracoceros montani*
Sumatran Rhinoceros (E): *Dicerorhinus sumatrensis*

Checklist of fauna/Lista de especies de fauna/Liste des espèces animales

Sumatran Short-tailed Python (E): *Python curtus*
Sumba Boobook (E): *Ninox rudolfi*
Sumba Hornbill (E): *Aceros everetti*
Sumba Wreathed Hornbill (E): *Aceros everetti*
Sun Bear (E): *Helarctos malayanus*
Sun Conure (E): *Aratinga solstitialis*
Sun corals (E): *Tubastraea spp.*
Sun Parakeet (E): *Aratinga solstitialis*
Sunburst Turtle (E): *Heosemys spinosa*
Sunda Flying-fox (E): *Acerodon mackloti*
Sunda Fruit Bat (E): *Acerodon mackloti*
Sunda Hawk-Eagle (E): *Spizaetus cirrhatus*
Sunda Otter-civet (E): *Cynogale bennettii*
Sunda Pied Hornbill (E): *Anthracoceros albirostris*
Sunda Scops-Owl (E): *Otus bakkamoena*
Sunda Wrinkled Hornbill (E): *Aceros corrugatus*
Sun-fish (E): *Cetorhinus maximus*
Sunflower Coral (E): *Heliofungia actiniformis*
Sunflower corals (E): *Goniopora spp.*
Sungazer (E): *Cordylus giganteus*
Sunray Lettuce Coral (E): *Helioseris cucullata*
Sun-tailed Guenon (E): *Cercopithecus solatus*
Sun-tailed Monkey (E): *Cercopithecus solatus*
Superb Bird-of-paradise (E): *Lophorina superba*
Superb Parrot (E): *Polytelis swainsonii*
Surnia ulula : (E) Hawk Owl, Northern Hawk Owl, (S) Búho gavilán, Cárabo gavilán, Lechuza gavilana, (F) Chouette épervière, **II** STRIGIDAE Av
Surucucu (E): *Cyclagras gigas*
Sus salvanius : (E) Pygmy Hog, (S) Jabalí enano, Jabalí pigmeo, (F) Sanglier nain, Sanglier pygmée, **I** SUIDAE Ma
Susu (E): *Platanista minor*
Susus (E): *Platanista* spp.
Swainson's Hawk (E): *Buteo swainsoni*
Swallow-tailed Hummingbird (E): *Campylopterus macrourus*
Swallow-tailed Kite (E): *Elanoides forficatus*
Swamp Cat (E): *Felis chaus*
Swamp Deer (E): *Cervus duvaucelii*
Swamp Harrier (E): *Circus approximans*
Swamp Otter (E): *Aonyx congicus*
Swamp Parakeet (E): *Pezoporus wallicus*
Swamp Turtle (E): *Morenia ocellata*
Swift Parrot (E): *Lathamus discolor*
Swinhoe's Pheasant (E): *Lophura swinhoii*
Sword-billed Hummingbird (E): *Ensifera ensifera*
Sydney Seahorse (E): *Hippocampus whitei*
Sykes's Monkey (E): *Cercopithecus mitis*
Sylhet Roofed Turtle (E): *Kachuga sylhetensis*
Sylphe à queue d'azur (F): *Aglaiocercus kingi*
Sylphe à queue violette (F): *Aglaiocercus coelestis*
Symmetrical Brain Coral (E): *Diploria strigosa*
Symphalangus syndactylus = *Hylobates syndactylus*
Symphyllia agaricia : **II** MUSSIDAE An
Symphyllia erythraea : **II** MUSSIDAE An
Symphyllia hassi : **II** MUSSIDAE An
Symphyllia radians : **II** MUSSIDAE An
Symphyllia recta : **II** MUSSIDAE An
Symphyllia valenciennesii : **II** MUSSIDAE An
Symphyllia wilsoni : **II** MUSSIDAE An
Sympodangia albatrossi : **II** CARYOPHYLLIIDAE An
Sypheotides indica = *Eupodotis indica*
Syr Darya sturgeon (E): *Pseudoscaphirhynchus fedtschenkoi*
Syr-Dar Shovelnose Sturgeon (E): *Pseudoscaphirhynchus fedtschenkoi*
Syr-Darya shovelnose (E): *Pseudoscaphirhynchus fedtschenkoi*
Syrmaticus ellioti : (E) Chinese Barred-backed Pheasant, Elliot's Pheasant, (S) Faisán de Elliot, (F) Faisan d'Elliot, **I** PHASIANIDAE Av

Syrmaticus humiae : (E) Hume's Bar-tailed Pheasant, Hume's Pheasant, Mrs Hume's Pheasant, (S) Faisán de Hume, (F) Faisan à queue barrée, Faisan de Birmanie, Faisan de Hume, **I** PHASIANIDAE Av
Syrmaticus mikado : (E) Mikado Pheasant, (S) Faisán mikado, (F) Faisan mikado, **I** PHASIANIDAE Av
Systemapora ornata : **II** STYLASTERIDAE Hy
Table Coral (E): *Acropora cytherea*
Taczanowsky's Dwarf Boa (E): *Tropidophis taczanowskyi*
Tagua (E): *Catagonus wagneri*
Tahitian Lorikeet (E): *Vini peruviana*
Tailed Birdwing (E): *Ornithoptera paradisea*
Taira (S): *Lontra longicaudis*
Taita Falcon (E): *Falco fasciinucha*
Taiwan Macaque (E): *Macaca cyclopis*
Takh (E): *Equus przewalskii*
Takin (E/S/F): *Budorcas taxicolor*
Talagoya Lizard (E): *Varanus bengalensis*
Talapoin (E/S/F): *Miopithecus talapoin*
Talaud Acerodon (E): *Acerodon humilis*
Talaud Black Birdwing (E): *Troides dohertyi*
Talaud Flying-fox (E): *Acerodon humilis*
Talaud Fruit Bat (E): *Acerodon humilis*
Talégalo maleo (S): *Macrocephalon maleo*
Taliabu Masked-owl (E): *Tyto nigrobrunnea*
Taliabu Owl (E): *Tyto nigrobrunnea*
Tamandua (F): *Tamandua mexicana*
Tamandúa (S): *Tamandua mexicana*
Tamandua mexicana : (E) Northern Tamandua, (S) Tamandúa, (F) Tamandua, **III** MYRMECOPHAGIDAE Ma
Tamanoir (F): *Myrmecophaga tridactyla*
Tamarao (S): *Bubalus mindorensis*
Tamarau (S/F): *Bubalus mindorensis*
Tamaraw (E): *Bubalus mindorensis*
Tamarin à manteau rouge (F): *Saguinus fuscicollis*
Tamarin à moustaches (F): *Saguinus mystax*
Tamarin à perruque (F): *Saguinus oedipus*
Tamarin à pieds blancs (F): *Saguinus leucopus*
Tamarin aux mains rousses (F): *Saguinus midas*
Tamarín bicolor (S): *Saguinus bicolor*
Tamarin bicolore (F): *Saguinus bicolor*
Tamarin de Geoffroy (F): *Saguinus geoffroyi*
Tamarin de Goeldi (F): *Callimico goeldii*
Tamarín de Goeldi (S): *Callimico goeldii*
Tamarín de manos blancas (S): *Saguinus leucopus*
Tamarín de pies blancos (S): *Saguinus leucopus*
Tamarin d'Oedipe (F): *Saguinus oedipus*
Tamarin pinché (F): *Saguinus oedipus*
Tamarin rouge et noir (F): *Saguinus nigricollis*
Tamarin sauteur (F): *Callimico goeldii*
Tamarin soyeux (F): *Leontopithecus rosalia*
Tamarino de caba manchada (S): *Saguinus inustus*
Tamarino de espalda dorada (S): *Saguinus tripartitus*
Tamarino de Geoffroy (S): *Saguinus geoffroyi*
Tamarino de labios blancos (S): *Saguinus labiatus*
Tamarino emperador (S): *Saguinus imperator*
Tamarino león de cabeza dorada (S): *Leontopithecus chrysomela*
Tamarins dorés (F): *Leontopithecus spp.*
Tamarou (E): *Bubalus mindorensis*
Tambourine Dove (E): *Turtur tympanistria*
Tampico Pearly Mussel (E): *Unio tampicoensis tecomatensis*
Tan Riffleshell (E): *Epioblasma walkeri*
Tana (F): *Tupaia tana*
Tana River Colobus (E): *Procolobus rufomitratus*
Tana River Mangabey (E): *Cercocebus galeritus galeritus*
Tanacetipathes barbadensis : **II** MYRIOPATHIDAE An
Tanacetipathes cavernicola : **II** MYRIOPATHIDAE An
Tanacetipathes hirta : **II** MYRIOPATHIDAE An
Tanacetipathes spinescens : **II** MYRIOPATHIDAE An
Tanacetipathes tanacetum : **II** MYRIOPATHIDAE An
Tanacetipathes thamnea : **II** MYRIOPATHIDAE An
Tanacetipathes wirtzi : **II** MYRIOPATHIDAE An

Tan-blossom Pearly Mussel (E): *Epioblasma torulosa rangiana*
Tanganyika Chameleon (E): *Chamaeleo goetzei*
Tángara fastuosa (S): *Tangara fastuosa*
Tangara fastuosa : (E) Seven-colored Tanager, (S) Tángara fastuosa, (F) Calliste superbe, **II** EMBERIZIDAE Av
Tanimbar Cockatoo (E): *Cacatua goffini*
Tanimbar Corella (E): *Cacatua goffini*
Tanimbar Owl (E): *Tyto sororcula*
Tantale blanc (F): *Mycteria cinerea*
Tántalo Malayo (S): *Mycteria cinerea*
Tantalus Monkey (E): *Chlorocebus aethiops*
Tanygnathus gramineus : (E) Black-lored Parrot, (S) Loro de Buru, (F) Perruche de Buru, **II** PSITTACIDAE Av
Tanygnathus heterurus = Tanygnathus sumatranus
Tanygnathus lucionensis : (E) Blue-naped Parrot, (S) Loro nuquiazul, (F) Perroquet à couronne, Perruche à calotte bleue, Perruche de Luçon, **II** PSITTACIDAE Av
Tanygnathus megalorynchos : (E) Great-billed Parrot, (S) Loro picogrodo, (F) Perruche à bec de sang, **II** PSITTACIDAE Av
Tanygnathus sumatranus : (E) Azure-rumped Parrot, Blue-backed Parrot, Müller's Parrot, (S) Loro de Müller, (F) Perruche de Müller, **II** PSITTACIDAE Av
Tanzania Mountain Chameleon (E): *Chamaeleo tempeli*
Taphrolesbia griseiventris : (E) Grey-bellied Comet, (S) Colibrí ventigrís, (F) Colibri comète, **II** TROCHILIDAE Av
Taphrospilus hypostictus = Leucippus hypostictus
Tapir à chabraque (F): *Tapirus indicus*
Tapir à dos blanc (F): *Tapirus indicus*
Tapir andino (S): *Tapirus pinchaque*
Tapir brasileño (S): *Tapirus terrestris*
Tapir centroamericano (S): *Tapirus bairdii*
Tapir d'Amérique (F): *Tapirus terrestris*
Tapir de Baird (F): *Tapirus bairdii*
Tapir de la India (S): *Tapirus indicus*
Tapir de l'Inde (F): *Tapirus indicus*
Tapir des Andes (F): *Tapirus pinchaque*
Tapir malais (F): *Tapirus indicus*
Tapir pinchaque (F): *Tapirus pinchaque*
Tapir terrestre (/F): *Tapirus terrestris*
Tapires (S): TAPIRIDAE spp.
TAPIRIDAE spp.: (E) Tapirs (S) Tapires, (F) Tapirs, **I/II** Ma
Tapirs (E/F): TAPIRIDAE spp.
Tapirus bairdii : (E) Baird's Tapir, Central American Tapir, (S) Anteburro, Dante, Tapir centroamericano, (F) Tapir de Baird, **I** TAPIRIDAE Ma
Tapirus indicus : (E) Asian Tapir, Indian Tapir, Malayan Tapir, (S) Tapir de la India, (F) Tapir à chabraque, Tapir à dos blanc, Tapir de l'Inde, Tapir malais, **I** TAPIRIDAE Ma
Tapirus pinchaque : (E) Andean Tapir, Mountain Tapir, Woolly Tapir, (S) Danta cordillerana, Danta lanuda, Danta negra, Pinchaque, Tapir andino, (F) Tapir des Andes, Tapir pinchaque, **I** TAPIRIDAE Ma
Tapirus roulinii = Tapirus pinchaque
Tapirus terrestris : (E) Brazilian Tapir, Lowland Tapir, South American Tapir, (S) Anta, Anta brasileña, Danta, Sachavaca, Tapir brasileño, Tapir terrestre, (F) Tapir d'Amérique, Tapir terrestre, **II** TAPIRIDAE Ma
Tarantula de pelo crespo (S): *Brachypelma albopilosum*
Tarantula Mexicana cadera roja (S): *Brachypelma vagans*
Tarantula Mexicana gris (S): *Aphonopelma pallidum*
Tarantula Mexicana naranja (S): *Brachypelma baumgarteni*
Tarantula Mexicana pierna naranja oscuro (S): *Brachypelma boehmei*
Tarantula Mexicana pierna roja (S): *Brachypelma emilia/Brachypelma smithi*
Tarantula Mexicana rodilla de llama (S): *Brachypelma auratum*

Tarantula roja de Costa Rica (S): *Brachypelma angustum*
Tarantulas (E): *Brachypelma* spp.
Tarántulas (S): *Brachypelma* spp.
Tarantule à croupion rouge du Mexique (F): *Brachypelma vagans*
Tarantule à genoux rouges du Mexique (F): *Brachypelma smithi*
Tarantule à genux de peu du Mexique (F): *Brachypelma auratum*
Tarantule du Mexique à pattes rouge (F): *Brachypelma emilia*
Tarantule du Mexique à pattes rouille (F): *Brachypelma boehmei*
Tarantule frisée (F): *Brachypelma albopilosum*
Tarantule gris du Mexique (F): *Aphonopelma pallidum*
Tarantule orange du Mexique (F): *Brachypelma baumgarteni*
Tarantule rouge du Costa Rica (F): *Brachypelma angustum*
Tarentules (F): *Brachypelma* spp.
Tarictic Hornbill (E): *Penelopides panini*
Tarictic hornbills (E): *Penelopides* spp.
Tarin de Yarell (F): *Carduelis yarrellii*
Tarin rouge du Venezuela (F): *Carduelis cucullata*
Tarsero piemeno (S): *Tarsius pumilus*
Tarsier de Bornéo (F): *Tarsius bancanus*
Tarsier des Célèbes (F): *Tarsius spectrum*
Tarsier des Philippines (F): *Tarsius syrichta*
Tarsius bancanus : (E) Horsfield's Tarsier, Western Tarsier, (F) Tarsier de Bornéo **II** TARSIIDAE Ma
Tarsius dianae : (E) Dian's Tarsier **II** TARSIIDAE Ma
Tarsius pelengensis = Tarsius spectrum
Tarsius pumilus : (E) Lesser Spectral Tarsier, Pygmy Tarsier, (S) Tarsero piemeno **II** TARSIIDAE Ma
Tarsius sangirensis = Tarsius spectrum
Tarsius spectrum : (E) Eastern Tarsier, Spectral Tarsier, Sulawesi Tarsier, (F) Tarsier des Célèbes **II** TARSIIDAE Ma
Tarsius spectrum ssp. *pumilus = Tarsius pumilus*
Tarsius syrichta : (E) Philippine Tarsier, (F) Tarsier des Philippines **II** TARSIIDAE Ma
Tartaruga (E): *Podocnemis expansa*
Tartary Sand Boa (E): *Eryx tataricus*
Taruca (E/S): *Hippocamelus antisensis*
Taruka de los Andes septentrionales (S): *Hippocamelus antisensis*
Tasmacète (F): *Tasmacetus shepherdi*
Tasmacetus shepherdi : (E) Shepherd's Beaked Whale, Tasman Beaked Whale, Tasman Whale, (S) Ballena de Shepherd, (F) Tasmacète, **II** ZIPHIIDAE Ma
Tasman Beaked Whale (E): *Tasmacetus shepherdi*
Tasman Whale (E): *Tasmacetus shepherdi*
Tasmanian Bettong (E): *Bettongia gaimardi*
Tasmanian Masked-Owl (E): *Tyto castanops*
Tasmanian Rat Kangaroo (E): *Bettongia gaimardi*
Tasmanian Rosella (E): *Platycercus caledonicus*
Tasmanian Tiger (E): *Thylacinus cynocephalus*
Tasmanian Wolf (E): *Thylacinus cynocephalus*
Tasman's Girdled Lizard (E): *Cordylus tasmani*
Tassel-eared Marmoset (E): *Callithrix humeralifer*
Tatin de Yarrell (F): *Carduelis yarrellii*
Tatin rouge du Venezuela (F): *Carduelis cucullata*
Tatou (F): *Cabassous centralis*
Tatou à 9 bandes (F): *Chaetophractus nationi*
Tatou à queue nue (F): *Cabassous tatouay*
Tatou d'Amérique centrale (F): *Cabassous centralis*
Tatou géant (F): *Priodontes maximus*
Tatou gumnure (F): *Cabassous tatouay*
Tattersall's Sifaka (E): *Propithecus tattersalli*
Tatú cabasú (S): *Cabassous tatouay*
Tatú carreta (S): *Priodontes maximus*
Tatú de América central (S): *Cabassous centralis*
Tatú de rabo mol (S): *Cabassous tatouay*
Tatú de rabo molle (S): *Cabassous tatouay*
Tatú gigante (S): *Priodontes maximus*
Tatú guazú (S): *Priodontes maximus*

Tauraco spp.: (E) Turacos, (S) Turacos, (F) Touracos, **II** MUSOPHAGIDAE Av
Tauraco bannermani : (E) Bannerman's Turaco, (S) Turaco de Bannerman, (F) Touraco de Bannerman, Touraco doré, **II** MUSOPHAGIDAE Av
Tauraco corythaix : (E) Helmeted Turaco, Knysna Turaco, (S) Turaco de Knysna, Turaco sudafricano, (F) Touraco louri, Touraco lourie, Touraco vert d'Afrique du Sud, **II** MUSOPHAGIDAE Av
Tauraco corythaix ssp. *fischeri = Tauraco fischeri*
Tauraco corythaix ssp. *livingstonii = Tauraco livingstonii*
Tauraco corythaix ssp. *persa = Tauraco persa*
Tauraco corythaix ssp. *schalowi = Tauraco schalowi*
Tauraco corythaix ssp. *schuettii = Tauraco schuettii*
Tauraco erythrolophus : (E) Red-crested Turaco, (S) Turaco crestirrojo, (F) Touraco pauline, **II** MUSOPHAGIDAE Av
Tauraco fischeri : (E) Fischer's Turaco, (S) Turaco de Fischer, (F) Touraco de Fischer, **II** MUSOPHAGIDAE Av
Tauraco hartlaubi : (E) Hartlaub's Turaco, (S) Turaco de Hartlaub, (F) Touraco de Hartlaub, **II** MUSOPHAGIDAE Av
Tauraco leucolophus : (E) White-crested Turaco, (S) Turaco capucha-blanca, Turaco crestiblanco, (F) Touraco à huppe blanche, **II** MUSOPHAGIDAE Av
Tauraco leucotis : (E) White-cheeked Turaco, (S) Turaco cariblanco, (F) Touraco à joues blanches, **II** MUSOPHAGIDAE Av
Tauraco livingstonii : (E) Livingstone's Turaco, (S) Touraco de Livingstone, Turaco de Livingstone, (F) Touraco de Livingstone, **II** MUSOPHAGIDAE Av
Tauraco macrorhynchus : (E) Black-tip Crested Turaco, Crested Turaco, Verreaux's Turaco, Yellow-billed Turaco, (S) Turaco capucha-franjeada, Turaco piquigualdo, (F) Touraco à gros bec, **II** MUSOPHAGIDAE Av
Tauraco persa : (E) Guinea Turaco, (S) Turaco capucha-verde de Guinea, Turaco de Guinea, Turaco persa, (F) Touraco vert, **II** MUSOPHAGIDAE Av
Tauraco persa ssp. *corythaix = Tauraco corythaix*
Tauraco porphyreolophus = Musophaga porphyreolopha
Tauraco ruspolii : (E) Prince Ruspoli's Turaco, Ruspoli's Turaco, (S) Turaco de Ruspoli, (F) Touraco de Ruspoli, **II** MUSOPHAGIDAE Av
Tauraco schalowi : (E) Schalow's Turaco, (S) Turaco de Schalow, (F) Touraco de Schalow, **II** MUSOPHAGIDAE Av
Tauraco schuettii : (E) Black-billed Turaco, (S) Turaco de Schuett, Turaco piquinegro, (F) Touraco à bec noir, **II** MUSOPHAGIDAE Av
Taurotragus eurycerus = Tragelaphus eurycerus
Tawny Eagle (E): *Aquila rapax*
Tawny Fish-owl (E): *Ketupa flavipes*
Tawny Owl (E): *Strix aluco*
Tawny Wood-Owl (E): *Strix aluco*
Tawny-bellied Hermit (E): *Phaethornis syrmatophorus*
Tawny-bellied Screech-Owl (E): *Otus watsonii*
Tawny-browed Owl (E): *Pulsatrix koeniswaldiana*
Taxipathes recta : **II** ANTIPATHIDAE An
Tayassu pecari : (E) White-lipped Peccary, (S) Pecarí de labio blanco, (F) Pécari à barbe blanche, Pécari aux babines blanches, **II** TAYASSUIDAE Ma
Tayassu tajacu = Pecari tajacu
TAYASSUIDAE spp.: (E) Peccaries (S) Pecaries, (F) Pécaries, **I/II/NC** Ma
Tayra (E/F): *Eira barbara*
Tchirou (F): *Pantholops hodgsonii*
Tchitrea bourbonnensis = Terpsiphone bourbonnensis
Tchitrec des Mascareignes (F): *Terpsiphone bourbonnensis*
Teal (E): *Anas crecca*
Tecolote barbudo (S): *Otus barbarus*
Tecolote bigotudo (S): *Otus trichopsis*
Tecolote flameado (S): *Otus flammeolus*

Tecolote occidental (S): *Otus kennicottii*
Tecolote oriental (S): *Otus asio*
Tecolote-abetero norteño (S): *Aegolius acadicus*
Tecolotito común (S): *Glaucidium brasilianum*
Tecolotito del cabo (S): *Glaucidium californicum*
Tecolotito enano (S): *Micrathene whitneyi*
Tecolotito serano (S): *Glaucidium gnoma*
Tegu (S): *Tupinambis* spp.
Tegu lizards (E): *Tupinambis* spp.
Tégus (F): *Tupinambis* spp.
Teinopalpus spp.: (E) Kaiserihinds **II** PAPILIONIDAE In
Teinopalpus aureus : (E) Golden Kaiserihind **II** PAPILIONIDAE In
Teinopalpus imperialis : (E) Kaiserihind **II** PAPILIONIDAE In
Teita Falcon (E): *Falco fasciinucha*
Tejedor bruñido de Wilson (S): *Vidua wilsoni*
Tejedor bruñido verdoso (S): *Vidua chalybeata*
Tejedor cabecinegro (S): *Ploceus melanocephalus*
Tejedor cogullado (S): *Ploceus cucullatus*
Tejedor cuellinegro (S): *Ploceus nigricollis*
Tejedor de Heuglin (S): *Ploceus heuglini*
Tejedor naranja (S): *Ploceus aurantius*
Tejedor negro albinuca (S): *Ploceus albinucha*
Tejedor negro de Vieillot (S): *Ploceus nigerrimus*
Tejedor pardal capirotado (S): *Plocepasser superciliosus*
Tejedor picogordo (S): *Amblyospiza albifrons*
Tejedor rollizo (S): *Pachyphantes superciliosus*
Tejedor tricolor (S): *Ploceus tricolor*
Tejedor velado (S): *Ploceus vitellinus*
Tejedorcito punteado (S): *Sporopipes frontalis*
Tejón (S): *Eira barbara/ Galictis vittata*
Tejón marsupial rayado (S): *Perameles bougainville*
Tejón melívoro (S): *Mellivora capensis*
Téju à taches noires (F): *Tupinambis teguixin*
Téju noir (F): *Tupinambis teguixin*
Téju rouge (F): *Tupinambis rufescens*
Téju-Crocodile (F): *Crocodilurus amazonicus*
Téjus (F): *Tupinambis* spp.
Temminck's Cat (E): *Catopuma temminckii*
Temminck's Flying-fox (E): *Pteropus temmincki*
Temminck's Giant Squirrel (E): *Epixerus ebii*
Temminck's Ground Pangolin (E): *Manis temminckii*
Temnotrochus kermadecensis : **II** GUYNIIDAE An
Temotu Flying-fox (E): *Pteropus nitendiensis*
Tengmalm's Owl (E): *Aegolius funereus*
Ten-ray Star Coral (E): *Madracis decactis*
Tent Turtle (E): *Kachuga tecta*
Teporingo (S): *Romerolagus diazi*
Tepui Goldenthroat (E): *Polytmus milleri*
Tepui Parakeet (E): *Nannopsittaca panychlora*
Tepui Parrotlet (E): *Nannopsittaca panychlora*
Terathopius ecaudatus : (E) Bateleur, Bateleur Eagle, (S) Aguila volatinera, (F) Bateleur, Bateleur des savanes, **II** ACCIPITRIDAE Av
Terecay (S): *Podocnemis unifilis*
Terpsiphone bourbonnensis : (E) Mascarene Paradise-Flycatcher, (S) Papamoscas, (F) Coq de Bois, Gobemouches, Tchitrec des Mascareignes, **III** MUSCICAPIDAE Av
Terrapene spp.: (E) American box turtles, Box turtles, (S) Galápagos cajas, Tortugas caja, (F) Tortue-boîte aquatique, Tortue-boîtes, **I/II** EMYDIDAE Re
Terrapene carolina : (E) Common Box Turtle, Eastern Box Turtle, (F) Tortue-boîte de Caroline **II** EMYDIDAE Re
Terrapene coahuila : (E) Aquatic Box Turtle, Coahuila Box Turtle, Coahuila Turtle, Water Box Turtle, (S) Galápago acuático encajado, Galápago caja Mexicano, Tortuga Coahuila, (F) Tortue-boîte de Coahuila, Tortue-boîte du Mexique, **I** EMYDIDAE Re
Terrapene nelsoni : (E) Spotted Box Turtle, (F) Tortue-boîte du Mexique **II** EMYDIDAE Re

Checklist of fauna/Lista de especies de fauna/Liste des espèces animales

Terrapene ornata : (E) Ornate Box Turtle, Western Box Turtle, (F) Tortue-boîte ornée commune **II** EMYDIDAE Re

Terrapenes (F): *Morenia ocellata*

TESTUDINIDAE spp.: (E) Tortoises, (S) Testudínidos, Tortugas, (F) Tortues terrestres, **I/II** Re

Testudínidos (S): TESTUDINIDAE spp.

Testudo angulata = Chersina angulata

Testudo elephantopus = Geochelone nigra

Testudo flavominimaralis = Testudo graeca

Testudo geometrica = Psammobates geometricus

Testudo graeca : (E) Common Tortoise, Greek Tortoise, Moorish Tortoise, Spur-thighed Tortoise, (S) Tortuga mora, (F) Tortue grecque , Tortue mauresque, **II** TESTUDINIDAE Re

Testudo hermanni : (E) Hermann's Tortoise, (S) Tortuga mediterránea, (F) Tortue d'Hermann, **II** TESTUDINIDAE Re

Testudo horsfieldii : (E) Afghan Tortoise, Central Asian Tortoise, Four-toed Tortoise, Horsfield's Tortoise, Steppe Tortoise, (S) Tortuga terrestre afgana, (F) Tortue des steppes, Tortue d'Horsfield, **II** TESTUDINIDAE Re

Testudo kleinmanni : (E) Egyptian Tortoise, Kleinmann's Tortoise, Leith's Tortoise, (S) Tortuga de plastrón articulado, (F) Tortue de Kleinmann, Tortue d'Egypte, **I** TESTUDINIDAE Re

Testudo marginata : (E) Marginated Tortoise, Margined Tortoise, (S) Tortuga marginada, (F) Tortue bordée, Tortue marginée, **II** TESTUDINIDAE Re

Testudo nabeulensis = Testudo graeca

Testudo nutapundi = Manouria emys

Testudo planicauda = Pyxis planicauda

Testudo radiata = Geochelone radiata

Testudo weissingeri : (E) Dwarf Marginated Tortoise **II** TESTUDINIDAE Re

Testudo werneri : **I** TESTUDINIDAE Re

Testudo whitei = Testudo graeca

Testudo yniphora = Geochelone yniphora

Tethocyathus cylindraceus : **II** CARYOPHYLLIIDAE An

Tethocyathus minor : **II** CARYOPHYLLIIDAE An

Tethocyathus prahli : **II** CARYOPHYLLIIDAE An

Tethocyathus recurvatus : **II** CARYOPHYLLIIDAE An

Tethocyathus variabilis : **II** CARYOPHYLLIIDAE An

Tethocyathus virgatus : **II** CARYOPHYLLIIDAE An

Tétracère (F): *Tetracerus quadricornis*

Tetracerus quadricornis : (E) Chousingha, Four-horned Antelope, (S) Antílope de cuatrocuernos, (F) Tétracère, **III** BOVIDAE Ma

Tétraogalle de Perse (F): *Tetraogallus caspius*

Tétraogalle du Tibet (F): *Tetraogallus tibetanus*

Tetraogallus caspius : (E) Caspian Snowcock, (S) Gallo lira del Caspio, Gallo salvaje del Caspio, Perdigallo caspio, Perdigallo del Caspio, Perdiz real del Caspio, (F) Perdrix des neiges de la Caspienne, Tétraogalle de Perse, Tétras des neiges de la Caspienne, Tétrogalle de la Caspienne, **I** PHASIANIDAE Av

Tetraogallus tibetanus : (E) Tibetan Snowcock, (S) Gallo lira del Tíbet, Gallo salvaje del Tibet, Perdigallo Tibetano, Perdiz real del Tibet, (F) Perdrix des neiges du Tibet, Tétraogalle du Tibet, Tétras des neiges du Tibet, **I** PHASIANIDAE Av

Tétras cupidon d'Attwater (F): *Tympanuchus cupido attwateri*

Tétras des neiges de la Caspienne (F): *Tetraogallus caspius*

Tétras des neiges du Tibet (F): *Tetraogallus tibetanus*

Tetrax tetrax : (E) Little Bustard, (S) Gallo lira, Sisón, Sisón común, (F) Outarde canepetière, **II** OTIDIDAE Av

Tétrogalle de la Caspienne (F): *Tetraogallus caspius*

Tetroras angiova = Cetorhinus maximus

Tevoro Clam (E): *Tridacna tevoroa*

Texas Tortoise (E): *Gopherus berlandieri*

Textu atrogularis = Ploceus heuglini

Thai Hog Deer (E): *Axis porcinus annamiticus*

Thalamophyllia gasti : **II** CARYOPHYLLIIDAE An

Thalamophyllia gombergi : **II** CARYOPHYLLIIDAE An

Thalamophyllia riisei : **II** CARYOPHYLLIIDAE An

Thalamophyllia tenuescens : **II** CARYOPHYLLIIDAE An

Thalarctos maritimus = Ursus maritimus

Thalurania colombica : (E) Blue-crowned Woodnymph, (S) Ninfa coronada, Zafiro coroniazul, (F) Dryade couronnée, **II** TROCHILIDAE Av

Thalurania colombica ssp. *fannyi = Thalurania fannyi*

Thalurania colombica ssp. *ridgwayi = Thalurania ridgwayi*

Thalurania fannyi : (E) Green-crowned Woodnymph, (S) Ninfa coronada, Zafiro coroniverde, (F) Dryade de Fanny, **II** TROCHILIDAE Av

Thalurania furcata : (E) Fork-tailed Woodnymph, (S) Picaflor gargantiverde, Tucusito moradito, Zafiro golondrina, (F) Dryade à queue fourchue, **II** TROCHILIDAE Av

Thalurania furcata ssp. *colombica = Thalurania colombica*

Thalurania glaucopis : (E) Violet-capped Woodnymph, (S) Picaflor corona azul, Zafiro capirotado, (F) Dryade glaucope, **II** TROCHILIDAE Av

Thalurania ridgwayi : (E) Mexican Woodnymph, (S) Nifa mexicana, Zafiro Mexicano, (F) Dryade du Mexique, **II** TROCHILIDAE Av

Thalurania watertonii : (E) Long-tailed Woodnymph, (S) Zafiro colilargo, (F) Dryade de Waterton, **II** TROCHILIDAE Av

Thamin (E): *Cervus eldii*

Thaumastura cora : (E) Peruvian Sheartail, (S) Colibri Cora, (F) Colibri cora, **II** TROCHILIDAE Av

Theban Sand Boa (E): *Gongylophis colubrinus*

Thecopsammia elongata = Balanophyllia elongata

Thecopsammia gemma = Balanophyllia gemma

Thecopsammia imperfecta = Leptopsammia formosa

Thecopsammia socialis : **II** DENDROPHYLLIIDAE An

Theropithecus gelada : (E) Gelada Baboon, (F) Gelada **II** CERCOPITHECIDAE Ma

Thick-billed Parrot (E): *Rhynchopsitta pachyrhyncha*

Thick-billed Weaver (E): *Amblyospiza albifrons*

Thick-tailed Bushbaby (E): *Otolemur crassicaudatus*

Thick-tailed Day Gecko (E): *Phelsuma mutabilis*

Thick-tailed Pangolin (E): *Manis crassicaudata*

Thin Finger Coral (E): *Porites divaricata*

Thin Tube Coral (E): *Cladocora debilis*

Thin-leaf Lettuce Coral (E): *Agaricia tenuifolia*

Thomas's Langur (E): *Presbytis thomasi*

Thomas's Leaf Monkey (E): *Presbytis thomasi*

Thomas's Mastigure (E): *Uromastyx thomasi*

Thorn Sturgeon (E): *Acipenser nudiventris*

Thorny Seahorse (E): *Hippocampus histrix*

Three-cusped Pangolin (E): *Manis tricuspis*

Three-keeled Land Tortoise (E): *Melanochelys tricarinata*

Three-keeled Land Turtle (E): *Melanochelys tricarinata*

Three-lined Day Gecko (E): *Phelsuma trilineata*

Three-spot Seahorse (E): *Hippocampus trimaculatus*

Three-spotted Seahorse (E): *Hippocampus trimaculatus*

Three-striped Batagur (E): *Callagur borneoensis*

Three-striped Poison Frog (E): *Epipedobates trivittatus*

Three-striped Roofed Turtle (E): *Kachuga dhongoka*

Threnetes cristinae = Threnetes niger

Threnetes grzimeki = Glaucis hirsuta

Threnetes leucurus = Threnetes niger

Threnetes loehkeni = Threnetes niger

Threnetes niger : (E) Bronze-tailed Barbthroat, Pale-tailed Barbthroat, (S) Barbita colipalida, Garganta lanza coliblanca, (F) Ermite à queue blanche, **II** TROCHILIDAE Av

Threnetes ruckeri : (E) Band-tailed Barbthroat, (S) Barbita colibandeada, Ermitaño barbudo, Ermitaño barbudo colibandeado, Tucuso de Barba, (F) Ermite de Rucker, **II** TROCHILIDAE Av

Threskiornis aethiopicus : (E) Sacred Ibis, (S) Ibis sagrado, (F) Ibis sacré, **III** THRESKIORNITHIDAE Av
Thrypticotrochus multilobatus : **II** TURBINOLIIDAE An
Thrypticotrochus petterdi : **II** TURBINOLIIDAE An
Thunder Snake (E): *Tropidophis pardalis*
Thylacine (E/F): *Thylacinus cynocephalus*
Thylacinus cynocephalus : (E) Tasmanian Tiger, Tasmanian Wolf, Thylacine, (S) Lobo de Tasamania, Lobo marsupial, (F) Loup marsupial, Thylacine, **I** THYLACINIDAE Ma
Tiang (S): *Damaliscus lunatus*
Tibet Owlet (E): *Athene noctua*
Tibetan Antelope (E): *Pantholops hodgsonii*
Tibetan Argali (E): *Ovis ammon hodgsonii*
Tibetan Crane (E): *Grus nigricollis*
Tibetan Eared-pheasant (E): *Crossoptilon harmani*
Tibetan Macaque (E): *Macaca thibetana*
Tibetan Snowcock (E): *Tetraogallus tibetanus*
Tiburón antropófago (S): *Carcharodon carcharias*
Tiburón ballena (S): *Rhincodon typus*
Tiburón blanco (S): *Carcharodon carcharias*
Tiburón canasta (S): *Cetorhinus maximus*
Tiburón peregrino (S): *Cetorhinus maximus*
Tickell's Brown Hornbill (E): *Anorrhinus tickelli*
Tiger (E): *Panthera tigris*
Tiger Cat (E): *Leopardus tigrinus*
Tiger Chameleon (E): *Calumma tigris*
Tiger Civet (E): *Prionodon pardicolor*
Tiger Frog (E): *Hoplobatrachus tigerinus*
Tiger Python (E): *Python molurus*
Tiger-snout Seahorse (E): *Hippocampus subelongatus*
Tiger-tail Seahorse (E): *Hippocampus comes*
Tigre (S/F): *Panthera tigris*
Tigre americano (S): *Panthera onca*
Tigre real (S): *Panthera onca*
Tigrillo (S): *Leopardus tigrinus/ Leopardus wiedii/ Herpailurus yaguarondi*
Tijereta centroamericana (S): *Doricha enicura*
Tijereta nortena (S): *Calothorax lucifer*
Tijereta Oaxaquena (S): *Calothorax pulcher*
Tijereta yucateca (S): *Doricha eliza*
Tilbury's Chameleon (E): *Chamaeleo marsabitensis*
Tilingo cuellinegro (S): *Pteroglossus aracari*
Tilingo limón (S): *Pteroglossus viridis*
Tilmatura dupontii : (E) Sparkling-tailed Barbthroat, Sparkling-tailed Hummingbird, (S) Colibrí colpinto, Colibrí de Dupont, (F) Colibri zémès, **II** TROCHILIDAE Av
Timber Wolf (E): *Canis lupus*
Timor Python (E): *Python timoriensis*
Timor Red-winged Parrot (E): *Aprosmictus jonquillaceus*
Timor Tree Monitor (E): *Varanus timorensis*
Tinamou solitaire (F): *Tinamus solitarius*
Tinamu grande (S): *Tinamus solitarius*
Tinamu macuco (S): *Tinamus solitarius*
Tinamú solitario (S): *Tinamus solitarius*
Tinamus solitarius : (E) Solitary Tinamou, (S) Macuco, Tinamu grande, Tinamu macuco, Tinamú solitario, (F) Tinamou solitaire, **I** TINAMIDAE Av
Tinglada (S): *Dermochelys coriacea*
Tiny Hawk (E): *Accipiter superciliosus*
Tiny Sparrowhawk (E): *Accipiter superciliosus*
Tirica (S): *Leopardus tigrinus*
Tisserin à ailes rouges (F): *Anaplectes rubriceps*
Tisserin à cou noir (F): *Ploceus nigricollis*
Tisserin à dos doré (F): *Ploceus preussi*
Tisserin à lunettes (F): *Ploceus nigricollis*
Tisserin à tête noire (F): *Ploceus melanocephalus*
Tisserin à tête rouge (F): *Ploceus vitellinus*
Tisserin à tête rousse (F): *Ploceus vitellinus*
Tisserin coucou (F): *Anomalospiza imberbis*
Tisserin covcou (F): *Anomalospiza imberbis*
Tisserin de Maxwell (F): *Ploceus albinucha*
Tisserin de Pelzeln (F): *Ploceus pelzelni*

Tisserin de Preuss (F): *Ploceus preussi*
Tisserin écarlate (F): *Anaplectes rubriceps*
Tisserin gendarme (F): *Ploceus cucullatus*
Tisserin gros-bec (F): *Pachyphantes superciliosus*
Tisserin masqué (F): *Ploceus heuglini*
Tisserin minule (F): *Ploceus luteolus*
Tisserin nain (F): *Ploceus pelzelni*
Tisserin noir (F): *Ploceus nigerrimus*
Tisserin noir de Maxwell (F): *Ploceus albinucha*
Tisserin noir de Vieillot (F): *Ploceus nigerrimus*
Tisserin orangé (F): *Ploceus aurantius*
Tisserin tricolore (F): *Ploceus tricolor*
Tisserin vitellin (F): *Ploceus vitellinus*
Tit-hylia (E): *Pholidornis rushiae*
Titi à collier (F): *Callicebus torquatus*
Titi à masque (F): *Callicebus personatus*
Tití de caba blanca (S): *Callithrix geoffroyi*
Tití de Goeldi (S): *Callimico goeldii*
Titi molock (F): *Callicebus moloch*
Titis-león (S): *Leontopithecus spp.*
Tiuque cordillerano austral (S): *Phalcoboenus australis*
Toco Toucan (E): *Ramphastos toco*
Tococo (S): *Phoenicopterus ruber*
Togo Paradise-Whydah (E): *Vidua togoensis*
Tolumuco (S): *Eira barbara*
Tomato Frog (E): *Dyscophus antongilii*
Tomistoma (E): *Tomistoma schlegelii*
Tomistoma schlegelii : (E) False Gavial, False Gharial, Malayan Gharial, Tomistoma, (S) Falso gavial malayo, (F) Faux gavial malais, **I** CROCODYLIDAE Re
Tongue Coral (E): *Herpolitha limax*
Tonina (S): *Pontoporia blainvillei*
Toninas (S): *Sotalia* spp.
Tonkean Black Macaque (E): *Macaca tonkeana*
Tonkean Macaque (E): *Macaca tonkeana*
Tonkin Leaf Monkey (E): *Trachypithecus francoisi*
Tonkin Snub-nosed Monkey (E): *Pygathrix avunculus*
Tooth Coral (E): *Euphyllia picteti*
Tooth corals (E): *Galaxea spp./ Lobophyllia* spp.
Tooth-billed Hummingbird (E): *Androdon aequatorialis*
Toothed Cape Tortoise (E): *Psammobates oculiferus*
Toothed Leaf Chameleon (E): *Brookesia dentata*
Topacio candela colicanelo (S): *Topaza pella*
Topacio carmesi (S): *Topaza pella*
Topaza pella : (E) Crimson Topaz, (S) Colibrí topacio, Topacio candela colicanelo, Topacio carmesi, (F) Colibri topaze, **II** TROCHILIDAE Av
Topaza pyra = Topaza pella
Topi (E/F): *Damaliscus lunatus*
Topi gacela (S): *Damaliscus pygargus pygargus*
Toque Macaque (E): *Macaca sinica*
Torch corals (E): *Caulastraea* spp.
Tordo amarillo (S): *Agelaius flavus*
Tordo de cabeza amarilla (S): *Agelaius flavus*
Torgos calvus = Sarcogyps calvus
Torgos tracheliotus : (E) Lappet-faced Vulture, Nubian Vulture, (S) Buitre orejudo, (F) Oricou, Vautour oricou, **II** ACCIPITRIDAE Av
Tornier's Tortoise (E): *Malacochersus tornieri*
Tornier's Tree Toad (E): *Nectophrynoides tornieri*
Toro cuprey (S): *Bos sauveli*
Torquéole à poitrine brune (F): *Arborophila orientalis*
Torquéole à poitrine châtaine (F): *Arborophila charltonii*
Torquéole de Merlin (F): *Arborophila charltonii*
Torquéole de Sumatra (F): *Arborophila orientalis*
Torquéole des bois (F): *Arborophila charltonii*
Tortoises (E): TESTUDINIDAE spp.
Tórtola común (S): *Streptopelia turtur*
Tórtola del Senegal (S): *Streptopelia senegalensis*
Tórtola engañosa (S): *Streptopelia decipiens*
Tórtola Europea (S): *Streptopelia turtur*
Tórtola ojirroja (S): *Streptopelia semitorquata*
Tórtola Reidora (S): *Streptopelia senegalensis*
Tórtola rizum (S): *Streptopelia semitorquata*

Checklist of fauna/Lista de especies de fauna/Liste des espèces animales

Tórtola rosigrís (S): *Streptopelia roseogrisea*
Tórtola Senegalesa (S): *Streptopelia senegalensis*
Tórtola tamborilera (S): *Turtur tympanistria*
Tórtola vinosa (S): *Streptopelia vinacea*
Tortolita rabilarga (S): *Oena capensis*
Tortue à bahut (F): *Caretta caretta/ Natator depressus*
Tortue à bec de faucon (F): *Eretmochelys imbricata*
Tortue à bords jaunes (F): *Gopherus flavomarginatus*
Tortue à carapace souple (F): *Malacochersus tornieri*
Tortue à col court (F): *Pseudemydura umbrina*
Tortue à écailles (F): *Eretmochelys imbricata*
Tortue à éperon (F): *Geochelone yniphora*
Tortue à plastron éperonné (F): *Geochelone yniphora*
Tortue à soc (F): *Geochelone yniphora*
Tortue à soc d'Afrique du Sud (F): *Chersina angulata*
Tortue à soc de Madagascar (F): *Geochelone yniphora*
Tortue à tête jaune (F): *Indotestudo elongata*
Tortue à toit de l'inde (F): *Geoclemys hamiltonii*
Tortue articulée d'Afrique (F): *Kinixys erosa*
Tortue bâtarde (F): *Lepidochelys olivacea*
Tortue boite d'Asie orientale (F): *Cuora amboinensis*
Tortue bordée (F): *Testudo marginata*
Tortue bosselée (F): *Psammobates tentorius*
Tortue brune (F): *Manouria emys*
Tortue caouanne (F): *Caretta caretta*
Tortue caret (F): *Caretta caretta*
Tortue charbonnière (F): *Geochelone carbonaria*
Tortue comestible (F): *Chelonia mydas*
Tortue d'Afrique à carapace molle (F): *Trionyx triunguis*
Tortue d'Agassiz (F): *Gopherus agassizii*
Tortue de Birmanie (F): *Morenia ocellata*
Tortue de Hamilton (F): *Geoclemys hamiltonii*
Tortue de Kemp (F): *Lepidochelys kempi*
Tortue de Kleinmann (F): *Testudo kleinmanni*
Tortue de la Floride (F): *Gopherus polyphemus*
Tortue de la Pampa (F): *Geochelone chilensis*
Tortue de l'Amérique du Sud (F): *Geochelone denticulata*
Tortue de l'Inde (F): *Lissemys punctata*
Tortue de Madagascar (F): *Geochelone yniphora*
Tortue de Muhlenberg (F): *Clemmys muhlenbergii*
Tortue de Ridley (F): *Lepidochelys olivacea*
Tortue de Tabasco (F): *Dermatemys mawii*
Tortue de Tornier (F): *Malacochersus tornieri*
Tortue de Tranvancore (F): *Indotestudo forstenii*
Tortue d'Egypte (F): *Testudo kleinmanni*
Tortue dentelée (F): *Geochelone denticulata*
Tortue denticulée (F): *Geochelone denticulata*
Tortue des Celèbes (F): *Indotestudo forstenii*
Tortue des marécages (F): *Clemmys muhlenbergii*
Tortue des steppes (F): *Testudo horsfieldii*
Tortue d'Hermann (F): *Testudo hermanni*
Tortue d'Horsfield (F): *Testudo horsfieldii*
Tortue du Mexique (F): *Gopherus flavomarginatus*
Tortue du Texas (F): *Gopherus berlandieri*
Tortue éléphantine (F): *Geochelone nigra*
Tortue étoilée de Birmanie (F): *Geochelone platynota*
Tortue étoilée de l'Inde (F): *Geochelone elegans*
Tortue fouisseuse du Mexique (F): *Gopherus flavomarginatus*
Tortue franche (F): *Chelonia mydas*
Tortue gaufrée (F): *Gopherus polyphemus*
Tortue géante (F): *Geochelone gigantea*
Tortue géante d'Aldabra (F): *Geochelone gigantea*
Tortue géante des Galapagos (F): *Geochelone nigra*
Tortue géométrique (F): *Psammobates geometricus*
Tortue grecque (F): *Testudo graeca*
Tortue imbriquée (F): *Eretmochelys imbricata*
Tortue imprimée (F): *Manouria impressa*
Tortue luth (F): *Dermochelys coriacea*
Tortue marginée (F): *Testudo marginata*
Tortue marine à dos plat (F): *Natator depressus*
Tortue mauresque (F): *Testudo graeca*
Tortue molle à clapet de l'Inde (F): *Lissemys punctata*
Tortue molle noire (F): *Apalone ater*
Tortue ocelée (F): *Psammobates oculiferus*

Tortue olivâtre (F): *Lepidochelys olivacea*
Tortue radiée de Madagascar (F): *Geochelone radiata*
Tortue rayonnée (F): *Geochelone radiata*
Tortue sillonnée (F): *Geochelone sulcata*
Tortue tricarénée (F): *Melanochelys tricarinata*
Tortue verte (F): *Chelonia mydas*
Tortue-boite à bords jaune (F): *Cuora flavomarginata*
Tortue-boite à front jaune (F): *Cuora galbinifrons*
Tortue-boite à tete jaune (F): *Cuora aurocapitata*
Tortue-boîte à trois bandes (F): *Cuora trifasciata*
Tortue-boîte aquatique (F): *Terrapene* spp.
Tortue-boîte de Caroline (F): *Terrapene carolina*
Tortue-boîte de Coahuila (F): *Terrapene coahuila*
Tortue-boîte de McCord (F): *Cuora mccordi*
Tortue-boîte de Pan (F): *Cuora pani*
Tortue-boîte du Guangxi (F): *Cuora zhoui*
Tortue-boîte du Mexique (F): *Terrapene nelsoni / Terrapene coahuila*
Tortue-boite du Yunnan (F): *Cuora yunnanensis*
Tortue-boîte ornée commune (F): *Terrapene ornata*
Tortue-boites (F): *Cuora* spp.
Tortue-boîtes (F): *Terrapene* spp.
Tortue-léopard du Cap (F): *Geochelone pardalis*
Tortues boîtes (F): *Morenia ocellata*
Tortues de mer (F): CHELONIIDAE spp.
Tortues des étangs de Perth (F): *Pseudemydura umbrina*
Tortues fluviatiles (F): *Podocnemis* spp.
Tortues terrestres (F): TESTUDINIDAE spp.
Tortuga araña (S): *Pyxis arachnoides*
Tortuga ariete (S): *Chersina angulata*
Tortuga blanca (S): *Chelonia mydas/ Dermatemys mawii*
Tortuga boba (S): *Caretta caretta*
Tortuga carey (S): *Eretmochelys imbricata*
Tortuga Coahuila (S): *Terrapene coahuila*
Tortuga con púas (S): *Geochelone sulcata*
Tortuga de agua (S): *Podocnemis lewyana*
Tortuga de carey (S): *Eretmochelys imbricata*
Tortuga de cola plana (S): *Pyxis planicauda*
Tortuga de concha blanda moteada (S): *Lissemys punctata*
Tortuga de cuña (S): *Malacochersus tornieri*
Tortuga de espolones (S): *Geochelone yniphora*
Tortuga de las Galápagos (S): *Geochelone nigra*
Tortuga de Madagascar (S): *Geochelone yniphora*
Tortuga de patas rojas (S): *Geochelone carbonaria*
Tortuga de pechera (S): *Chersina angulata*
Tortuga de plastrón articulado (S): *Testudo kleinmanni/ Pyxis arachnoides*
Tortuga de Texas (S): *Gopherus berlandieri*
Tortuga del desierto (S): *Gopherus agassizii*
Tortuga del Ganges (S): *Aspideretes gangeticus*
Tortuga del Nilo (S): *Trionyx triunguis*
Tortuga estrellada de Burma (S): *Geochelone platynota*
Tortuga estrellada de la India (S): *Geochelone elegans*
Tortuga estrellada de Madagascar (S): *Geochelone radiata*
Tortuga estrellada sudafricana (S): *Psammobates tentorius*
Tortuga estrellada sudafricana de caparazón (S): *Psammobates oculiferus*
Tortuga franca oriental (S): *Natator depressus*
Tortuga geométrica (S): *Psammobates geometricus*
Tortuga gigante de Aldabra (S): *Geochelone gigantea*
Tortuga gigante de las Galápagos (S): *Geochelone nigra*
Tortuga globulosa malagache (S): *Geochelone yniphora*
Tortuga golfina (S): *Lepidochelys olivacea*
Tortuga grande (S): *Gopherus flavomarginatus*
Tortuga india de visera (S): *Kachuga tecta*
Tortuga iora (S): *Lepidochelys kempi*
Tortuga laud (S): *Dermochelys coriacea*
Tortuga leopardo (S): *Geochelone pardalis*
Tortuga llanero (S): *Gopherus flavomarginatus*
Tortuga manchada (S): *Homopus signatus*
Tortuga marginada (S): *Testudo marginata*
Tortuga marina bastarda (S): *Lepidochelys kempi*
Tortuga marrón de Burma (S): *Manouria impressa*
Tortuga marrón de la India (S): *Indotestudo forstenii*
Tortuga/mediterránea (S): *Testudo hermanni*

Checklist of fauna/Lista de especies de fauna/Liste des espèces animales

Tortuga mora (S): *Testudo graeca*
Tortuga negra (S): *Apalone ater*
Tortuga negra de Adanson (S): *Pelusios adansonii*
Tortuga negra de Africa occidental (S): *Pelusios niger*
Tortuga negra del Gabón (S): *Pelusios gabonensis*
Tortuga occidental de cuello de serpiente (S): *Pseudemydura umbrina*
Tortuga olivacea (S): *Lepidochelys olivacea*
Tortuga pavo (S): *Aspideretes hurum*
Tortuga pico de loro (S): *Homopus areolatus*
Tortuga plana (S): *Pelomedusa subrufa*
Tortuga plana indiana (S): *Lissemys punctata*
Tortuga rayada (S): *Geochelone radiata*
Tortuga serpentina occidental (S): *Pseudemydura umbrina*
Tortuga sombría (S): *Aspideretes nigricans*
Tortuga terrestre (S): *Homopus boulengeri*
Tortuga terrestre afgana (S): *Testudo horsfieldii*
Tortuga terrestre argentina (S): *Geochelone chilensis*
Tortuga terrestre de Florida (S): *Gopherus polyphemus*
Tortuga topo (S): *Gopherus flavomarginatus*
Tortuga verde (S): *Chelonia mydas*
Tortugas (S): TESTUDINIDAE spp.
Tortugas caja (S): *Terrapene* spp.
Tortugas marinas (S): CHELONIIDAE spp.
Totoaba (E): *Cynoscion macdonaldi*
Totoaba macdonaldi = Cynoscion macdonaldi
Totoba (S): *Cynoscion macdonaldi*
Toucan à bec rouge (F): *Ramphastos tucanus*
Toucan à carène (F): *Ramphastos sulfuratus*
Toucan à gorge jaune et blanche (F): *Ramphastos vitellinus*
Toucan à ventre rouge (F): *Ramphastos dicolorus*
Toucan ariel (F): *Ramphastos vitellinus*
Toucan Barbet (E): *Semnornis ramphastinus*
Toucan de Baillon (F): *Baillonius bailloni*
Toucan toco (F): *Ramphastos toco*
Toucanet à bec tacheté (F): *Selenidera maculirostris*
Toui à ailes jaunes (F): *Brotogeris chiriri*
Toui à ailes variées (F): *Brotogeris versicolurus*
Toui à bandeau jaune (F): *Psilopsiagon aurifrons*
Toui à dos noir (F): *Touit melanonota*
Toui à front bleu (F): *Touit dilectissima*
Toui à front d'or (F): *Brotogeris sanctithomae*
Toui à front roux (F): *Bolborhynchus ferrugineifrons*
Toui à lunettes (F): *Forpus conspicillatus*
Toui à menton d'or (F): *Brotogeris jugularis*
Toui à queue d'or (F): *Touit surda*
Toui à queue pourprée (F): *Touit purpurata*
Toui à sept couleurs (F): *Touit batavica*
Toui à tête jaune (F): *Forpus xanthops*
Toui aymara (F): *Psilopsiagon aymara*
Toui catherine (F): *Bolborhynchus lineola*
Toui céleste (F): *Forpus coelestis*
Toui de D'Achille (F): *Nannopsittaca dachilleae*
Toui de Deville (F): *Brotogeris cyanoptera*
Toui de Huet (F): *Touit huetii*
Toui de Sclater (F): *Forpus sclateri*
Toui de Spix (F): *Forpus crassirostris*
Toui des tépuis (F): *Nannopsittaca panychlora*
Toui d'Orbigny (F): *Bolborhynchus orbygnesius*
Toui du Costa Rica (F): *Touit costaricensis*
Toui du Mexique (F): *Forpus cyanopygius*
Toui été (F): *Forpus passerinus*
Toui flamboyant (F): *Brotogeris pyrrhopterus*
Toui para (F): *Brotogeris chrysopterus*
Toui tacheté (F): *Touit stictoptera*
Toui tirica (F): *Brotogeris tirica*
Touit batavica : (E) Lilac-tailed Parrotlet, Seven-colored Parrotlet, (S) Cotorrita sietecolores, Perico siete colores, (F) Toui à sept couleurs, II PSITTACIDAE Av
Touit costaricensis : (E) Red-fronted Parrotlet, (S) Cotorrita Costarricense, (F) Toui du Costa Rica, II PSITTACIDAE Av

Touit dilectissima : (E) Blue-fronted Parrotlet, (S) Churiquita, Cotorrita cariazul, Periquito frentiazul, (F) Toui à front bleu, II PSITTACIDAE Av
Touit dilectissima ssp. *costaricensis = Touit costaricensis*
Touit huetii : (E) Scarlet-shouldered Parrotlet, (S) Cotorrita alirroja, Periquito azul alirrojo, (F) Toui de Huet, II PSITTACIDAE Av
Touit melanonota : (E) Black-eared Parrotlet, Brown-backed Parrotlet, (S) Cotorrita dorsinegra, (F) Toui à dos noir, II PSITTACIDAE Av
Touit purpurata : (E) Sapphire-rumped Parrotlet, (S) Cotorrita purpurada, Periquito rabadilla púrpura, (F) Toui à queue pourprée, II PSITTACIDAE Av
Touit stictoptera : (E) Spot-winged Parrotlet, (S) Cotorrita alipinta, Periquito alipunteado, (F) Toui tacheté, II PSITTACIDAE Av
Touit surda : (E) Golden-tailed Parrotlet, (S) Cotorrita sorda, (F) Toui à queue d'or, II PSITTACIDAE Av
Toupaïe commun (F): *Tupaia glis*
Toupaïe de Java (F): *Tupaia javanica*
Toupaïe de l'île Palawan (F): *Tupaia palawanensis*
Toupaïe de Müller (F): *Tupaia minor*
Toupaïe d'Elliot (F): *Anathana ellioti*
Toupaïe des îles Nicobar (F): *Tupaia nicobarica*
Toupaïe des montagnes (F): *Tupaia montana*
Toupaïe murin (F): *Dendrogale murina*
Touraco à bec noir (F): *Tauraco schuettii*
Touraco à gros bec (F): *Tauraco macrorhynchus*
Touraco à huppe blanche (F): *Tauraco leucolophus*
Touraco à huppe pourprée (F): *Musophaga porphyreolopha*
Touraco à huppe splendide (F): *Musophaga porphyreolopha*
Touraco à huppe violette (F): *Musophaga porphyreolopha*
Touraco à joues blanches (F): *Tauraco leucotis*
Touraco de Bannerman (F): *Tauraco bannermani*
Touraco de Fischer (F): *Tauraco fischeri*
Touraco de Hartlaub (F): *Tauraco hartlaubi*
Touraco de Livingstone (S/F): *Tauraco livingstonii*
Touraco de Ruspoli (F): *Tauraco ruspolii*
Touraco de Schalow (F): *Tauraco schalowi*
Touraco doré (F): *Tauraco bannermani*
Touraco géant (F): *Corythaeola cristata*
Touraco gris (F): *Crinifer piscator*
Touraco louri (F): *Tauraco corythaix*
Touraco lourie (F): *Tauraco corythaix*
Touraco pauline (F): *Tauraco erythrolophus*
Touraco vert (F): *Tauraco persa*
Touraco vert d'Afrique du Sud (F): *Tauraco corythaix*
Touraco violet (F): *Musophaga violacea/ Musophaga porphyreolopha*
Touracos (F): *Tauraco* spp.
Tourmaline Sunangel (E): *Heliangelus exortis*
Tourtelette améthystine (F): *Turtur afer*
Tourtelette d'Abyssinie (F): *Turtur abyssinicus*
Tourtelette demoiselle (F): *Turtur brehmeri*
Tourtelette masquée (F): *Oena capensis*
Tourtelette tambourette (F): *Turtur tympanistria*
Tourterelle à collier (F): *Streptopelia semitorquata*
Tourterelle à masque de fer (F): *Oena capensis*
Tourterelle à tête bleue (F): *Turtur brehmeri*
Tourterelle des bois (F): *Streptopelia turtur*
Tourterelle des palmiers (F): *Streptopelia senegalensis*
Tourterelle du Cap (F): *Oena capensis*
Tourterelle maillée (F): *Streptopelia senegalensis*
Tourterelle masquée (F): *Oena capensis*
Tourterelle pleureuse (F): *Streptopelia decipiens*
Tourterelle rieuse (F): *Streptopelia roseogrisea*
Tourterelle tambourette (F): *Turtur tympanistria*
Tourterelle vineuse (F): *Streptopelia vinacea*
Toxolasma cylindrellus : (E) Pale Lilliput, Pale Lilliput Pearly Mussel I UNIONIDAE Bi

Trachyboa boulengeri : (E) Northern Eyelash Boa, Rough-scaled Boa, (S) Boa rugosa, (F) Boa nain de Boulenger, Boa rugueux de Boulenger, **II** TROPIDOPHIIDAE Re

Trachyboa gularis : (E) Ecuadorian Eyelash Boa, Southern Eyelash Boa, Spiny Boa, (S) Boa rugosa de Ecuador, (F) Boa nain de l'Equateur, Boa rugueux de l'Equateur, **II** TROPIDOPHIIDAE Re

Trachyphyllia geoffroyi : (E) Crater Coral, Folded Coral, Puffed Coral **II** TRACHYPHYLLIIDAE An

Trachypithecus auratus : (E) Ebony Leaf Monkey **II** CERCOPITHECIDAE Ma

Trachypithecus cristatus : (E) Silvered Langur, Silvered Leaf Monkey, (S) Langur crestado, (F) Budeng, **II** CERCOPITHECIDAE Ma

Trachypithecus cristatus ssp. *auratus* = *Trachypithecus auratus*

Trachypithecus francoisi : (E) François's Langur, François's Leaf Monkey, Tonkin Leaf Monkey, (S) Langur de Francois, (F) Langur de François, Semnopithèque de François, **II** CERCOPITHECIDAE Ma

Trachypithecus geei : (E) Golden Langur, Golden Leaf Monkey, (S) Langur dorado, (F) Entelle dorée, Langur doré, Semnopithèque de Gee, Semnopithèque doré, **I** CERCOPITHECIDAE Ma

Trachypithecus johnii : (E) Black Leaf Monkey, John's Langur, Nilgiri Langur, Nilgiri Leaf Monkey, (S) Langur de Nilgiri, (F) Langur du Nilgiri, Semnopithèque des Nilgiris, **II** CERCOPITHECIDAE Ma

Trachypithecus obscurus : (E) Dusky Leaf Monkey, Spectacled Langur, Spectacled Leaf Monkey, (S) Langur obscuro, (F) Semnopithèque obscur, **II** CERCOPITHECIDAE Ma

Trachypithecus phayrei : (E) Phayre's Langur, Phayre's Leaf Monkey, (F) Semnopithèque de Phayre **II** CERCOPITHECIDAE Ma

Trachypithecus pileatus : (E) Bonneted Langur, Capped Langur, Capped Leaf Monkey, Capped Monkey, (S) Langur capuchino, Langur de capa, (F) Entelle pileuse, Langur à capuchon, **I** CERCOPITHECIDAE Ma

Trachypithecus vetulus : (E) Purple-faced Leaf Monkey, (S) Langur de cara roja, (F) Semnopithèque blanchâtre, **I** CERCOPITHECIDAE Ma

Trachypithecus villosus = *Trachypithecus cristatus*

Tragelaphus eurycerus : (E) Bongo, (S) Bongo, (F) Bongo, **III** BOVIDAE Ma

Tragelaphus spekii : (E) Marshbuck, Sitatunga, (S) Sitatunga, (F) Guib d'eau, Sitatunga, **III** BOVIDAE Ma

Tragopan à tête noire (F): *Tragopan melanocephalus*
Tragopan arlequin (F): *Tragopan caboti*
Tragopán arlequín (S): *Tragopan caboti*

Tragopan blythii : (E) Blyth's Tragopan, Grey-bellied Tragopan, (S) Tragopán de Blyth, Tragopán oriental, (F) Tragopan de Blyth, Tragopan de Molesworth, Tragopan oriental, **I** PHASIANIDAE Av

Tragopan caboti : (E) Cabot's Tragopan, Yellow-billed Tragopan, (S) Tragopán arlequín, Tragopán Chino, Tragopán de Cabot, (F) Tragopan arlequin, Tragopan de Cabot, **I** PHASIANIDAE Av

Tragopán Chino (S): *Tragopan caboti*
Tragopan de Blyth (F): *Tragopan blythii*
Tragopán de Blyth (S): *Tragopan blythii*
Tragopán de cabeza negra (S): *Tragopan melanocephalus*
Tragopan de Cabot (F): *Tragopan caboti*
Tragopán de Cabot (S): *Tragopan caboti*
Tragopan de Hastings (F): *Tragopan melanocephalus*
Tragopan de Molesworth (F): *Tragopan blythii*
Tragopán dorsigrís (S): *Tragopan melanocephalus*

Tragopan melanocephalus : (E) Black-headed Tragopan, Western Horned-Pheasant, Western Tragopan, (S) Tragopán de cabeza negra, Tragopán dorsigrís, Tragopán occidental, (F) Tragopan à tête noire, Tragopan de Hastings, Tragopan occidental, **I** PHASIANIDAE Av

Tragopan occidental (F): *Tragopan melanocephalus*
Tragopán occidental (S): *Tragopan melanocephalus*
Tragopan oriental (F): *Tragopan blythii*
Tragopán oriental (S): *Tragopan blythii*
Tragopán sátiro (S): *Tragopan satyra*

Tragopan satyra : (E) Crimson Horned-Pheasant, Indian Tragopan, Satyr Tragopan, (S) Tragopán sátiro, (F) Tragopan satyre, **III** PHASIANIDAE Av

Tragopan satyre (F): *Tragopan satyra*
Transvaal Girdled Lizard (E): *Cordylus vittifer*
Traro (S): *Polyborus plancus*
Travailleur à tête rouge (F): *Quelea erythrops*
Travancore Tortoise (E): *Indotestudo forstenii*
Traylor's Forest-Falcon (E): *Micrastur buckleyi*
Tree Boa (E): *Candoia carinata*
Tree Coral (E): *Tubastraea micranthus*
Tree Crocodile (E): *Varanus salvadorii*
Tree Lizard (E): *Varanus rudicollis*
Tree Ocelot (E): *Leopardus wiedii*
Tree Pangolin (E): *Manis tricuspis*
Tree toads (E): *Nectophrynoides* spp.

Tremarctos ornatus : (E) Andean Bear, Spectacled Bear, (S) Oso andino de anteojos, Oso de anteojos, Oso frontino, Oso real, (F) Ours à lunettes, Ours andin, **I** URSIDAE Ma

Trematotrochus alternans = *Foveolocyathus alternans*
Trematotrochus corbicula : **II** TURBINOLIIDAE An
Trematotrochus hedleyi : **II** TURBINOLIIDAE An
Trematotrochus verconis = *Foveolocyathus verconis*
Treron australis ssp. *calva* = *Treron calva*

Treron calva : (E) African Green-Pigeon, (S) Vinago Africano, Vinago obeng, (F) Colombar à front nu, **III** COLUMBIDAE Av

Treron waalia : (E) Bruce's Green-Pigeon, Yellow-bellied Green-Pigeon, (S) Vinago waalia, (F) Colombar waalia, Pigeon vert à épaulettes violettes, Pigeons à épaulettes violettes, **III** COLUMBIDAE Av

Triangular-spotted Pigeon (E): *Columba guinea*
Tricarinate Hill Turtle (E): *Melanochelys tricarinata*

Trichechus inunguis : (E) Amazonian Manatee, South American Manatee, (S) Lamantino amazónico, Manatí amazónico, Vaca marina amazónica, (F) Lamantin d'Amérique du Sud, Lamantin de l'Amazone, **I** TRICHECHIDAE Ma

Trichechus manatus : (E) American Manatee, Caribbean Manatee, North American Manatee, West Indian Manatee, (S) Lamantino norteamericana, Manatí norteamericano, (F) Lamantin d'Amérique du Nord, Lamantin des Antilles, Lamantin des Caraïbes, **I** TRICHECHIDAE Ma

Trichechus senegalensis : (E) African Manatee, West African Manatee, (S) Manatí de Senegal, (F) Lamantin d'Afrique, Lamantin du Sénégal, Lamantin ouest-africain, **II** TRICHECHIDAE Ma

Trichoglossus chlorolepidotus : (E) Scaly-breasted Lorikeet, (S) Lori escuamiverde, (F) Loriquet vert, **II** PSITTACIDAE Av

Trichoglossus euteles : (E) Olive-headed Lorikeet, Perfect Lorikeet, (S) Lori humilde, (F) Loriquet eutèle, **II** PSITTACIDAE Av

Trichoglossus flavoviridis : (E) Meyer's Lorikeet, Yellow-and-green Lorikeet, (S) Lori verdigualdo, (F) Loriquet jaune et vert, **II** PSITTACIDAE Av

Trichoglossus goldiei = *Psitteuteles goldiei*

Trichoglossus haematodus : (E) Green-naped Lorikeet, Rainbow Lorikeet, Rainbow Lory, (S) Lori arcoiris, (F) Loriquet à tête bleue, **II** PSITTACIDAE Av

Trichoglossus iris = *Psitteuteles iris*

Checklist of fauna/Lista de especies de fauna/Liste des espèces animales

Trichoglossus johnstoniae : (E) Johnstone's Lorikeet, Mindanao Lorikeet, (S) Lori de Mindanao, (F) Loriquet de Johnstone, **II** PSITTACIDAE Av

Trichoglossus ornatus : (E) Ornate Lorikeet, Ornate Lory, (S) Lori adornado, (F) Loriquet orné, **II** PSITTACIDAE Av

Trichoglossus rubiginosus : (E) Pohnpei Lorikeet, Pohnpei Lory, (S) Lori de Ponapé, (F) Loriquet de Ponapé, **II** PSITTACIDAE Av

Trichoglossus rubritorquis = Trichoglossus haematodus

Trichoglossus versicolor = Psitteuteles versicolor

Tricholimnas conditicius = Gallirallus sylvestris

Tricholimnas sylvestris = Gallirallus sylvestris

Triclaria malachitacea : (E) Blue-bellied Parrot, Purple-bellied Parrot, (S) Loro ventriazul, (F) Crick à ventre bleu, Perruche à ventre bleu, **II** PSITTACIDAE Av

Tricuspide (F): *Manis tricuspis*

Tridacna crocea : (E) Boring Clam, Crocea Clam, Crocus Clam, Saffron-coloured Clam **II** TRIDACNIDAE Bi

Tridacna derasa : (E) Derasa Clam, Southern Giant Clam **II** TRIDACNIDAE Bi

Tridacna gigas : (E) Giant Clam, Gigas Clam, (F) Bénitier géant **II** TRIDACNIDAE Bi

Tridacna maxima : (E) Maxima Clam, Small Giant Clam **II** TRIDACNIDAE Bi

Tridacna mbulvuana = Tridacna tevoroa

Tridacna rosewateri :, (F) Bénitier de Rosewater **II** TRIDACNIDAE Bi

Tridacna squamosa : (E) Fluted Clam, Fluted Giant Clam, Scaly Clam **II** TRIDACNIDAE Bi

Tridacna tevoroa : (E) Tevoro Clam, (F) Bénitier de Tevoro **II** TRIDACNIDAE Bi

TRIDACNIDAE spp.: (E) Giant clams, (F) Bénitiers, **II** Bi

Trigonoceps occipitalis : (E) White-headed Vulture, (S) Buitre cabeciblanco, Buitre piquirrojo, (F) Vautour à tête blanche, Vautour huppé, **II** ACCIPITRIDAE Av

Tringa guttifer : (E) Nordmann's Greenshank, Spotted Greenshank, (S) Archibebe manchado, Archibebe moteado, (F) Chevalier à gouttelette, Chevalier tacheté, **I** SCOLOPACIDAE Av

Trinidad Piping-Guan (E): *Pipile pipile*

Trinidad White-headed Curassow (E): *Pipile pipile*

Trinidad White-headed Piping Guan (E): *Pipile pipile*

Trionyx ater = Apalone ater

Trionyx bibroni = Pelochelys bibroni

Trionyx de l'Inde (F): *Lissemys punctata*

Trionyx du Nil (F): *Trionyx triunguis*

Trionyx gangeticus = Aspideretes gangeticus

Trionyx hurum = Aspideretes hurum

Trionyx indicus = Chitra indicus

Trionyx nigricans = Aspideretes nigricans

Trionyx noir (F): *Apalone ater*

Trionyx spiniferus ssp. *ater = Apalone ater*

Trionyx triunguis : (E) African Softshell Turtle, Nile Softshell Turtle, Nile Soft-shelled Terrapin, (S) Tortuga del Nilo, (F) Tortue d'Afrique à carapace molle, Trionyx du Nil, **III** TRIONYCHIDAE Re

Tristram's Woodpecker (E): *Dryocopus javensis richardsi*

TROCHILIDAE spp.: (E) Hummingbirds, (S) Colibries, Picaflores, (F) Colibris, Oiseaux-mouches, **I/II** Av

Trochilus polytmus : (E) Streamertail, (S) Colibrí portacintas, (F) Colibri à tête noire, **II** TROCHILIDAE Av

Trochilus scitulus : (E) Black-billed Streamertail, (S) Colibrí portacintas piquinegro, (F) Colibri à bec noir, **II** TROCHILIDAE Av

Trochocyathus aithoseptatus : **II** CARYOPHYLLIIDAE An

Trochocyathus apertus : **II** CARYOPHYLLIIDAE An

Trochocyathus brevispina : **II** CARYOPHYLLIIDAE An

Trochocyathus burchae : **II** CARYOPHYLLIIDAE An

Trochocyathus caryophylloides : **II** CARYOPHYLLIIDAE An

Trochocyathus cepulla : **II** CARYOPHYLLIIDAE An

Trochocyathus cooperi : **II** CARYOPHYLLIIDAE An

Trochocyathus decamera : **II** CARYOPHYLLIIDAE An

Trochocyathus discus : **II** CARYOPHYLLIIDAE An

Trochocyathus efateensis : **II** CARYOPHYLLIIDAE An

Trochocyathus fasciatus : **II** CARYOPHYLLIIDAE An

Trochocyathus fossulus : **II** CARYOPHYLLIIDAE An

Trochocyathus gardineri : **II** CARYOPHYLLIIDAE An

Trochocyathus gordoni : **II** CARYOPHYLLIIDAE An

Trochocyathus hastatus : **II** CARYOPHYLLIIDAE An

Trochocyathus japonicus : **II** CARYOPHYLLIIDAE An

Trochocyathus laboreli : **II** CARYOPHYLLIIDAE An

Trochocyathus longispina : **II** CARYOPHYLLIIDAE An

Trochocyathus maculatus : **II** CARYOPHYLLIIDAE An

Trochocyathus mauiensis : **II** CARYOPHYLLIIDAE An

Trochocyathus mediterraneus : **II** CARYOPHYLLIIDAE An

Trochocyathus oahensis : **II** CARYOPHYLLIIDAE An

Trochocyathus patelliformis : **II** CARYOPHYLLIIDAE An

Trochocyathus philippinensis : **II** CARYOPHYLLIIDAE An

Trochocyathus porphyreus : **II** CARYOPHYLLIIDAE An

Trochocyathus rawsonii : **II** CARYOPHYLLIIDAE An

Trochocyathus rhombocolumna : **II** CARYOPHYLLIIDAE An

Trochocyathus semperi : **II** CARYOPHYLLIIDAE An

Trochocyathus spinosocostatus : **II** CARYOPHYLLIIDAE An

Trochocyathus tenuicalyx = Trochocyathus rhombocolumna

Trochocyathus vasiformis : **II** CARYOPHYLLIIDAE An

Trochocyathus virgatus = Tethocyathus virgatus

Trochopsammia infundibulum : **II** DENDROPHYLLIIDAE An

Trochopsammia togata : **II** DENDROPHYLLIIDAE An

Trogon couroucou (F): *Pharomachrus mocinno*

Trogonoptera spp.: (E) Birdwing butterflies, (F) Ornithoptères **II** PAPILIONIDAE In

Trogonoptera brookiana : (E) Rajah Brooke's Birdwing, (F) Ornithoptère de Brooke **II** PAPILIONIDAE In

Trogonoptera trojana : **II** PAPILIONIDAE In

Troides spp.: (E) Birdwing butterflies **II** PAPILIONIDAE In

Troides aeacus : (E) Golden Birdwing, Small Birdwing **II** PAPILIONIDAE In

Troides amphrysus : (E) Golden Birdwing, Malay Birdwing **II** PAPILIONIDAE In

Troides andromache : **II** PAPILIONIDAE In

Troides criton : **II** PAPILIONIDAE In

Troides cuneifer : (E) Golden Birdwing **II** PAPILIONIDAE In

Troides darsius : **II** PAPILIONIDAE In

Troides dohertyi : (E) Talaud Black Birdwing **II** PAPILIONIDAE In

Troides haliphron : **II** PAPILIONIDAE In

Troides helena : (E) Black-and-gold Birdwing, Common Birdwing **II** PAPILIONIDAE In

Troides hypolitus : **II** PAPILIONIDAE In

Troides magellanus : **II** PAPILIONIDAE In

Troides minos : **II** PAPILIONIDAE In

Troides miranda : **II** PAPILIONIDAE In

Troides oblongomaculatus : **II** PAPILIONIDAE In

Troides plateni : **II** PAPILIONIDAE In

Troides plato : **II** PAPILIONIDAE In

Troides prattorum : (E) Buru Opalescent Birdwing **II** PAPILIONIDAE In

Troides rhadamantus : **II** PAPILIONIDAE In

Troides riedeli : **II** PAPILIONIDAE In

Troides vandepolli : **II** PAPILIONIDAE In

Tropical Girdled Lizard (E): *Cordylus tropidosternum*

Tropical Screech-Owl (E): *Otus choliba*

Tropical Spiny-tailed Lizard (E): *Cordylus tropidosternum*

Tropical Whale (E): *Balaenoptera edeni*

Tropicoperdix charltonii = Arborophila charltonii

Tropidocyathus labidus : **II** TURBINOLIIDAE An

Tropidocyathus lessonii : **II** TURBINOLIIDAE An

Tropidocyathus pileus = Cyathotrochus pileus
TROPIDOPHIIDAE spp.: (E) Boas (S) Boas, (F) Boas, **II** Re
Tropidophis battersbyi : (E) Battersby's Dwarf Boa, Ecuadorian Dwarf Boa, (F) Boa forestier de Battersby, Boa nain de Battersby **II** TROPIDOPHIIDAE Re
Tropidophis bucculentus = Tropidophis melanurus
Tropidophis canus : (E) Great Inagua Island Dwarf Boa, Wood Snake, (S) Boa enana de las Bahamas, (F) Boa forestier de l'île du Grand Inagua, Boa nain de l'île du Grand Inagua, **II** TROPIDOPHIIDAE Re
Tropidophis caymanensis : (E) Cayman Islands Dwarf Boa, Caymans Ground Boa, (S) Boa enana de las islas Caimán, (F) Boa forestier des îles Cayman, Boa nain des îles Cayman, **II** TROPIDOPHIIDAE Re
Tropidophis celiae : **II** TROPIDOPHIIDAE Re
Tropidophis curtus = Tropidophis canus
Tropidophis feicki : (E) Feick's Dwarf Boa, (F) Boa forestier de Feick, Boa nain de Feick **II** TROPIDOPHIIDAE Re
Tropidophis fuscus :, (F) Boa forestier brun, Boa nain brun **II** TROPIDOPHIIDAE Re
Tropidophis galacelidus = Tropidophis pilsbryi
Tropidophis greenwayi : (E) Ambergris Cay Dwarf Boa, (F) Boa forestier d'Ambergris Cay, Boa nain d'Ambergris Cay **II** TROPIDOPHIIDAE Re
Tropidophis haetianus : (E) Haitian Dwarf Boa, Haitian Ground Boa, (F) Boa forestier d'Haïti, Boa nain d'Haïti **II** TROPIDOPHIIDAE Re
Tropidophis hardyi = Tropidophis nigriventris
Tropidophis jamaicensis = Tropidophis haetianus
Tropidophis maculatus : (E) Spotted Dwarf Boa, (F) Boa forestier tacheté, Boa nain tacheté **II** TROPIDOPHIIDAE Re
Tropidophis melanurus : (E) Cuban Black-tailed Dwarf Boa, Navassa Island Black-tailed Dwarf Boa, Wood Snake, (S) Boa de bosque, Culebra boba, Maja chico, (F) Boa forestier à queue noire de l'île Navassa, Boa nain à queue noire de l'île Navassa, **II** TROPIDOPHIIDAE Re
Tropidophis morenoi : **II** TROPIDOPHIIDAE Re
Tropidophis nigriventris : (E) Black-bellied Dwarf Boa, (F) Boa forestier à ventre noir, Boa nain à ventre noir **II** TROPIDOPHIIDAE Re
Tropidophis pardalis : (E) Leopard Dwarf Boa, Thunder Snake, (F) Boa forestier léopard, Boa nain léopard **II** TROPIDOPHIIDAE Re
Tropidophis parkeri = Tropidophis caymanensis
Tropidophis paucisquamis : (E) Brazilian Dwarf Boa, (F) Boa forestier du Brésil, Boa nain du Brésil **II** TROPIDOPHIIDAE Re
Tropidophis pilsbryi : (E) Pilsbry's Dwarf Boa, (F) Boa forestier de Pilsbry, Boa nain de Pilsbry **II** TROPIDOPHIIDAE Re
Tropidophis schwartzi = Tropidophis caymanensis
Tropidophis semicinctus : (E) Banded Dwarf Boa, (F) Boa forestier annelé, Boa nain annelé **II** TROPIDOPHIIDAE Re
Tropidophis spiritus : **II** TROPIDOPHIIDAE Re
Tropidophis stejnegeri = Tropidophis haetianus
Tropidophis stullae = Tropidophis haetianus
Tropidophis taczanowskyi : (E) Taczanowsky's Dwarf Boa, (F) Boa forestier de Taczanowsky, Boa nain de Taczanowsky **II** TROPIDOPHIIDAE Re
Tropidophis wrighti : (E) Wright's Dwarf Boa, (F) Boa forestier de Wright, Boa nain de Wright **II** TROPIDOPHIIDAE Re
True Langur (E): *Semnopithecus entellus*
True Red Leg Tarantula (E): *Brachypelma emilia*
True's Beaked Whale (E): *Mesoplodon mirus*
Trumpet corals (E): *Caulastraea spp.*
Trumpet Manucode (E): *Manucodia keraudrenii*
Trumpetbird (E): *Manucodia keraudrenii*
Truncatoflabellum aculeatum : **II** FLABELLIDAE An
Truncatoflabellum angiostomum : **II** FLABELLIDAE An

Truncatoflabellum angustum : **II** FLABELLIDAE An
Truncatoflabellum arcuatum : **II** FLABELLIDAE An
Truncatoflabellum australiensis : **II** FLABELLIDAE An
Truncatoflabellum candeanum : **II** FLABELLIDAE An
Truncatoflabellum carinatum : **II** FLABELLIDAE An
Truncatoflabellum crassum : **II** FLABELLIDAE An
Truncatoflabellum cumingii : **II** FLABELLIDAE An
Truncatoflabellum dens : **II** FLABELLIDAE An
Truncatoflabellum formosum : **II** FLABELLIDAE An
Truncatoflabellum gardineri : **II** FLABELLIDAE An
Truncatoflabellum inconstans : **II** FLABELLIDAE An
Truncatoflabellum incrustatum : **II** FLABELLIDAE An
Truncatoflabellum irregulare : **II** FLABELLIDAE An
Truncatoflabellum macroeschara : **II** FLABELLIDAE An
Truncatoflabellum martensii : **II** FLABELLIDAE An
Truncatoflabellum mortenseni : **II** FLABELLIDAE An
Truncatoflabellum multispinosum : **II** FLABELLIDAE An
Truncatoflabellum paripavoninum : **II** FLABELLIDAE An
Truncatoflabellum phoenix : **II** FLABELLIDAE An
Truncatoflabellum pusillum : **II** FLABELLIDAE An
Truncatoflabellum spheniscus : **II** FLABELLIDAE An
Truncatoflabellum stabile : **II** FLABELLIDAE An
Truncatoflabellum stokesii : **II** FLABELLIDAE An
Truncatoflabellum trapezoideum : **II** FLABELLIDAE An
Truncatoflabellum truncum : **II** FLABELLIDAE An
Truncatoflabellum vanuatu : **II** FLABELLIDAE An
Truncatoflabellum veroni : **II** FLABELLIDAE An
Truncatoflabellum vigintifarium : **II** FLABELLIDAE An
Truncatoflabellum zuluense : **II** FLABELLIDAE An
Truncatoguynia irregularis : **II** GUYNIIDAE An
Trunkback turtle (E): *Dermochelys coriacea*
Tsaratanan Chameleon (E): *Calumma tsaratananensis*
Tsessebe (E): *Damaliscus lunatus*
Tsessebi (E): *Damaliscus lunatus*
Tuatara (E): *Sphenodon punctatus*
Tuátara (S): *Sphenodon punctatus*
Tuataras (F): *Sphenodon spp.*
Tuátaras (S): *Sphenodon spp.*
Tubastraea spp.: (E) Daisy corals, Red cave corals, Sun corals, Turret corals **II** DENDROPHYLLIIDAE An
Tubastraea coccinea : (E) Orange Cup Coral, Orange Tube Coral **II** DENDROPHYLLIIDAE An
Tubastraea diaphana : **II** DENDROPHYLLIIDAE An
Tubastraea faulkneri : (E) Orange Turret Coral **II** DENDROPHYLLIIDAE An
Tubastraea floreana : **II** DENDROPHYLLIIDAE An
Tubastraea micranthus : (E) Black Turret Coral, Tree Coral **II** DENDROPHYLLIIDAE An
Tubastraea tagusensis : **II** DENDROPHYLLIIDAE An
Tubercled Blossom (E): *Epioblasma torulosa torulosa*
Tubercled-blossom Pearly Mussel (E): *Epioblasma torulosa torulosa*
Tubercle-nosed Chameleon (E): *Chamaeleo tempeli*
Tubipora musica : (E) Organ-pipe Coral **II** TUBIPORIDAE An
TUBIPORIDAE spp.: (E) Organpipe coral, (F) Corail orgue, **II** An
Tucán de pico acanalado (S): *Selenidera maculirostris*
Tucán de pico verde (S): *Ramphastos toco*
Tucán grande (S): *Ramphastos toco*
Tucán pico-multicolor (S): *Ramphastos sulfuratus*
Tucán piquirrojo (S): *Ramphastos vitellinus*
Tucán rojo y amarillo (S): *Ramphastos dicolorus*
Tucán tilingo (S): *Pteroglossus castanotis*
Tucán verde (S): *Ramphastos dicolorus*
Tucancito picomaculado (S): *Selenidera maculirostris*
Tucán-Tilingo verde (S): *Pteroglossus castanotis*
Tucuman Amazon (E): *Amazona tucumana*
Tucuman Parrot (E): *Amazona tucumana*
Tucusito amatista (S): *Calliphlox amethystina*
Tucusito cabeza azul (S): *Klais guimeti*
Tucusito garganta rosa (S): *Chaetocercus jourdanii*
Tucusito moradito (S): *Thalurania furcata*
Tucusito pico curvo (S): *Lepidopyga goudoti*

Tucusito rubí (S): *Chrysolampis mosquitus*
Tucuso de Barba (S): *Threnetes ruckeri*
Tucuxi (E): *Sotalia fluviatilis*
Tuft Coral (E): *Lophelia pertusa*
Tufted Capuchin (E): *Cebus apella*
Tufted Coquette (E): *Lophornis ornatus*
Tui Parakeet (E): *Brotogeris sanctithomae*
Tulear Golden Frog (E): *Mantella expectata*
Tumbes Hummingbird (E): *Leucippus baeri*
Tunina de Heaviside (S): *Cephalorhynchus heavisidii*
Tunina de Héctor (S): *Cephalorhynchus hectori*
Tunina de vientre blanco (S): *Cephalorhynchus eutropia*
Tunina overa (S): *Cephalorhynchus commersonii*
Tunina sinaleta (S): *Lissodelphis peronii*
Tunqui (S): *Rupicola peruviana*
Tupaia belangeri : (E) Northern Treeshrew, (S) Tupaya norteña **II** TUPAIIDAE Ma
Tupaia chrysogaster : (E) Golden-bellied Treeshrew, Mentawai Treeshrew, (S) Tupaya de vientre dorado **II** TUPAIIDAE Ma
Tupaia de Bornéo (F): *Tupaia tana*
Tupaia dorsalis : (E) Striped Treeshrew, (S) Tupaya rayada **II** TUPAIIDAE Ma
Tupaia glis : (E) Malaysian Treeshrew, (S) Musaraña común, (F) Toupaïe commun, **II** TUPAIIDAE Ma
Tupaia glis ssp. *belangeri* = *Tupaia belangeri*
Tupaia glis ssp. *chrysogaster* = *Tupaia chrysogaster*
Tupaia glis ssp. *longipes* = *Tupaia longipes*
Tupaia glis ssp. *palawanensis* = *Tupaia palawanensis*
Tupaia gracilis : (E) Slender Treeshrew, (S) Tupaya esbelta **II** TUPAIIDAE Ma
Tupaia javanica : (E) Javan Treeshrew, (F) Toupaïe de Java **II** TUPAIIDAE Ma
Tupaia longipes : (E) Bornean Treeshrew, Long-footed Treeshrew, (S) Tupaya de pies largos **II** TUPAIIDAE Ma
Tupaia minor : (E) Lesser Treeshrew, Pygmy Treeshrew, (S) Musaraña pigmea, (F) Toupaïe de Müller, **II** TUPAIIDAE Ma
Tupaia montana : (E) Mountain Treeshrew, (F) Toupaïe des montagnes **II** TUPAIIDAE Ma
Tupaia nicobarica : (E) Nicobar Treeshrew, (F) Toupaïe des îles Nicobar **II** TUPAIIDAE Ma
Tupaia palawanensis : (E) Palawan Treeshrew, (F) Toupaïe de l'île Palawan **II** TUPAIIDAE Ma
Tupaia picta : (E) Painted Treeshrew, (S) Tupaya pintada **II** TUPAIIDAE Ma
Tupaia splendidula : (E) Ruddy Treeshrew, Rufous-tailed Treeshrew, (S) Tupaya de cola marrón **II** TUPAIIDAE Ma
Tupaia tana : (E) Large Treeshrew, (S) Musaraña grande, (F) Grande toupaïe, Tana, Tupaia de Bornéo, **II** TUPAIIDAE Ma
Tupaya de Borneo (S): *Dendrogale melanura*
Tupaya de cola marrón (S): *Tupaia splendidula*
Tupaya de pies largos (S): *Tupaia longipes*
Tupaya de vientre dorado (S): *Tupaia chrysogaster*
Tupaya esbelta (S): *Tupaia gracilis*
Tupaya norteña (S): *Tupaia belangeri*
Tupaya pintada (S): *Tupaia picta*
Tupaya rayada (S): *Tupaia dorsalis*
Tupinambis spp.: (E) Tegu lizards, (S) Lagartos, Tegu, (F) Grand téjus, Tégus, Téjus, **II** TEIIDAE Re
Tupinambis cerradensis : **II** TEIIDAE Re
Tupinambis duseni = *Tupinambis rufescens*
Tupinambis longilineus : **II** TEIIDAE Re
Tupinambis merianae : **II** TEIIDAE Re
Tupinambis nigropunctatus = *Tupinambis teguixin*
Tupinambis quadrilineatus : **II** TEIIDAE Re
Tupinambis rufescens : (E) Argentine Teju, Red Teju, (F) Téju rouge **II** TEIIDAE Re
Tupinambis teguixin : (E) Banded Tegu, Black Tegu, Brazilian Teju, Common Tegu, (F) Grand téju, Sauvegarde, Téju à taches noires, Téju noir **II** TEIIDAE Re

Turaco azul (S): *Musophaga violacea*
Turaco capucha-blanca (S): *Tauraco leucolophus*
Turaco capucha-franjeada (S): *Tauraco macrorhynchus*
Turaco capucha-verde de Guinea (S): *Tauraco persa*
Turaco cariblanco (S): *Tauraco leucotis*
Turaco crestiblanco (S): *Tauraco leucolophus*
Turaco crestimorado (S): *Musophaga porphyreolopha*
Turaco crestirrojo (S): *Tauraco erythrolophus*
Turaco crestivioleta (S): *Musophaga porphyreolopha*
Turaco de Bannerman (S): *Tauraco bannermani*
Turaco de Crin occidentale (S): *Crinifer piscator*
Turaco de Fischer (S): *Tauraco fischeri*
Turaco de Guinea (S): *Tauraco persa*
Turaco de Hartlaub (S): *Tauraco hartlaubi*
Turaco de Knysna (S): *Tauraco corythaix*
Turaco de Livingstone (S): *Tauraco livingstonii*
Turaco de Ruspoli (S): *Tauraco ruspolii*
Turaco de Schalow (S): *Tauraco schalowi*
Turaco de Schuett (S): *Tauraco schuettii*
Turaco gigante (S): *Corythaeola cristata*
Turaco gris occidental (S): *Crinifer piscator*
Turaco persa (S): *Tauraco persa*
Turaco piquigualdo (S): *Tauraco macrorhynchus*
Turaco piquinegro (S): *Tauraco schuettii*
Turaco sudafricano (S): *Tauraco corythaix*
Turaco violáceo (S): *Musophaga violacea*
Turacos (E/S): *Tauraco* spp.
Turberculed Riffle Shell (E): *Epioblasma torulosa torulosa*
Turbinaria aspera = *Turbinaria mesenterina*
Turbinaria bifrons : **II** DENDROPHYLLIIDAE An
Turbinaria conica = *Turbinaria mesenterina*
Turbinaria conspicua : **II** DENDROPHYLLIIDAE An
Turbinaria crater : **II** DENDROPHYLLIIDAE An
Turbinaria elegans = *Turbinaria mesenterina*
Turbinaria frondens : **II** DENDROPHYLLIIDAE An
Turbinaria heronensis : **II** DENDROPHYLLIIDAE An
Turbinaria irregularis : **II** DENDROPHYLLIIDAE An
Turbinaria mesenterina : (E) Pagoda Coral **II** DENDROPHYLLIIDAE An
Turbinaria patula : **II** DENDROPHYLLIIDAE An
Turbinaria peltata : (E) Bowl Coral **II** DENDROPHYLLIIDAE An
Turbinaria quincuncialis = *Turbinaria crater*
Turbinaria radicalis : **II** DENDROPHYLLIIDAE An
Turbinaria reniformis : (E) Yellow Scroll Coral **II** DENDROPHYLLIIDAE An
Turbinaria stellulata : **II** DENDROPHYLLIIDAE An
Turbinolia stephensoni : **II** TURBINOLIIDAE An
Turgid Blossom (E): *Epioblasma turgidula*
Turgid Riffle Shell (E): *Epioblasma turgidula*
Turgid-blossom Pearly Mussel (E): *Epioblasma turgidula*
Turkey Vulture (E): *Cathartes aura*
Turks and Caicos Ground Iguana (E): *Cyclura carinata*
Turks and Caicos Iguana (E): *Cyclura carinata*
Turks Islands Boa (E): *Epicrates chrysogaster*
Turón de patas negras (S): *Mustela nigripes*
Turón patinegro americano (S): *Mustela nigripes*
Turquoise Grass-Parakeet (E): *Neophema pulchella*
Turquoise Parrot (E): *Neophema pulchella*
Turquoise-bellied Poison Frog (E): *Epipedobates espinosai*
Turquoise-fronted Parrot (E): *Amazona aestiva*
Turquoise-throated Puffleg (E): *Eriocnemis godini*
Turret corals (E): *Tubastraea* spp.
Tursión (S): *Tursiops truncatus*
Tursiops (F): *Tursiops truncatus*
Tursiops aduncus = *Tursiops truncatus*
Tursiops gillii = *Tursiops truncatus*
Tursiops nesarnack = *Tursiops truncatus*
Tursiops nuuanu = *Tursiops truncatus*
Tursiops truncatus : (E) Bottlenose Dolphin, Bottle-nosed Dolphin, (S) Delfín mular, Pez mular, Tursión, (F) Grand dauphin, Souffleur, Tursiops, **II** DELPHINIDAE Ma

Turtle Dove (E): *Streptopelia turtur*

Turtur abyssinicus : (E) Black-billed Wood-Dove, (S) Palomita especulada abisinica, Palomita Saheliana, (F) Emerauldine à bec noir, Tourtelette d'Abyssinie, **III** COLUMBIDAE Av

Turtur afer : (E) Blue-spotted Wood-Dove, Red-billed Wood-Dove, (S) Palomita aliazul, Palomita especulada africana, (F) Emerauldine à bec rouge, Tourtelette améthystine, **III** COLUMBIDAE Av

Turtur brehmeri : (E) Blue-headed Dove, Blue-headed Wood-Dove, (S) Palomita cabeciazul, Palomita especulada cobriza, (F) Tourtelette demoiselle, Tourterelle à tête bleue, **III** COLUMBIDAE Av

Turtur tympanistria : (E) Tambourine Dove, (S) Palomita tamborilera, Tórtola tamborilera, (F) Tourtelette tambourette, Tourterelle tambourette, **III** COLUMBIDAE Av

Turturoena iriditorques = Columba iriditorques

Twelve-root Cup Coral (E): *Polymyces fragilis*

Twelve-wired Bird-of-paradise (E): *Seleucidis melanoleuca*

Twenty-eight Parakeet (E): *Barnardius zonarius*

Two-banded Chameleon (E): *Furcifer balteatus*

Two-banded Monitor (E): *Varanus salvator*

Two-horned Chameleon (E): *Furcifer bifidus*

Two-lined Chameleon (E): *Chamaeleo bitaeniatus*

Two-toned Poison Frog (E): *Phyllobates bicolor*

Tympanistria tympanistria = Turtur tympanistria

Tympanuchus cupido attwateri : (E) Attwater's Prairie-chicken, (S) Gallito de pradera, (F) Poule de prairie d'Attwater, Tétras cupidon d'Attwater, **I** PHASIANIDAE Av

Tyrant Hawk-Eagle (E): *Spizaetus tyrannus*

Tyrian Metaltail (E): *Metallura tyrianthina*

Tyto alba : (E) Barn Owl, Common Barn-Owl, (S) Lechuza común, Lechuza de campanario, (F) Chouette effraie, Effraie africaine, Effraie des clochers, **II** TYTONIDAE Av

Tyto alba ssp. *glaucops = Tyto glaucops*

Tyto aurantia : (E) Bismarck Masked-Owl, Golden Owl, New Britain Masked-Owl, (S) Lechuza dorada, (F) Effraie dorée, **II** TYTONIDAE Av

Tyto capensis : (E) African Grass-Owl, Grass Owl, (S) Lechuza de El Cabo, (F) Effraie du Cap, **II** TYTONIDAE Av

Tyto capensis ssp. *longimembris = Tyto longimembris*

Tyto castanops : (E) Tasmanian Masked-Owl, (F) Effraie de Tasmanie **II** TYTONIDAE Av

Tyto detorta = Tyto alba

Tyto glaucops : (E) Ashy-faced Owl, (S) Lechuza de la Española, (F) Effraie d'Hispaniola, **II** TYTONIDAE Av

Tyto inexspectata : (E) Minahassa Barn-Owl, Minahassa Masked-Owl, Minahassa Owl, (S) Lechuza de Minahassa, (F) Effraie de Minahassa, **II** TYTONIDAE Av

Tyto longimembris : (E) Eastern Grass-Owl, (S) Lechuza patilarga, (F) Effraie de prairie, **II** TYTONIDAE Av

Tyto manusi : (E) Manus Masked-Owl, (S) Lechuza de la Manus, (F) Effraie de Manus, **II** TYTONIDAE Av

Tyto multipunctata : (E) Lesser Sooty-Owl, (S) Lechuza moteada, (F) Effraie piquetée, **II** TYTONIDAE Av

Tyto nigrobrunnea : (E) Sula Barn-Owl, Taliabu Masked-Owl, Taliabu Owl, (S) Lechuza de la Taliabu, (F) Effraie de Taliabu, **II** TYTONIDAE Av

Tyto novaehollandiae : (E) Australian Masked-Owl, Masked Owl, (S) Lechuza Australiana, (F) Effraie masquée, **II** TYTONIDAE Av

Tyto novaehollandiae ssp. *castanops = Tyto castanops*

Tyto novaehollandiae ssp. *manusi = Tyto manusi*

Tyto novaehollandiae ssp. *sororcula = Tyto sororcula*

Tyto rosenbergii : (E) Sulawesi Owl, (S) Lechuza de Célebes, (F) Effraie des Célèbes, **II** TYTONIDAE Av

Tyto sororcula : (E) Lesser Masked-Owl, Tanimbar Owl, (S) Lechuza de las Tanimbar, (F) Effraie des Tanimbar, **II** TYTONIDAE Av

Tyto soumagnei : (E) Madagascar Grass Owl, Madagascar Owl, Madagascar Red Owl, Soumange's Owl, (S) Lechuza de Madagascar, Lechuza Malgache, (F) Effraie de Soumagne, Effraie rousse de Madagascar, **I** TYTONIDAE Av

Tyto tenebricosa : (E) Greater Sooty-Owl, Sooty Owl, (S) Lechuza tenebrosa, (F) Effraie ombrée, **II** TYTONIDAE Av

Tyto tenebricosa ssp. *multipunctata = Tyto multipunctata*

Uacaries (S): *Cacajao calvus*

Uaddan (E): *Ammotragus lervia*

Uakaris (E): *Cacajao* spp.

Ucati (S): *Eira barbara*

Uelle Paradise-Whydah (E): *Vidua interjecta*

Ukinga Girdled Lizard (E): *Cordylus ukingensis*

Ukinga Hornless Chameleon (E): *Chamaeleo incornutus*

Ukinga Spiny-tailed Lizard (E): *Cordylus ukingensis*

Ulamá (S): *Eira barbara*

Ultramarine Lorikeet (E): *Vini ultramarina*

Ultramarine Lory (E): *Vini ultramarina*

Uluguru One-horned Chameleon (E): *Bradypodion oxyrhinum*

Uluguru Two-horned Chameleon (E): *Bradypodion fischeri*

Umba (S): *Speothos venaticus*

Umbrella Cockatoo (E): *Cacatua alba*

Unau (S/F): *Choloepus hoffmanni*

Unau d'Hoffmann (F): *Choloepus hoffmanni*

Unau o perezoso de Hoffman (S): *Choloepus hoffmanni*

Uncia uncia : (E) Ounce, Snow Leopard, (S) Leopardo de las nieves, Leopardo nival, Pantera de la nieves, (F) Irbis, Léopard des neiges, Once, Panthère des neiges, **I** FELIDAE Ma

Ungaliophis continentalis : (E) Banana Boa, Chiapan Boa, Isthmian Dwarf Boa, (S) Boa enana del norte de centroamérica, (F) Boa nain d'Amérique centrale, **II** TROPIDOPHIIDAE Re

Ungaliophis panamensis : (E) Central American Dwarf Boa, Panamanian Dwarf Boa, (F) Boa nain du Panama **II** TROPIDOPHIIDAE Re

Ungaliophis paucisquamis = Tropidophis paucisquamis

Unicolor Avahi (E): *Avahi unicolor*

Unicorn Whale (E): *Monodon monoceros*

Unio nickliniana : (E) Nicklin's Pearly Mussel **I** UNIONIDAE Bi

Unio tampicoensis tecomatensis : (E) Tampico Pearly Mussel **I** UNIONIDAE Bi

Unspotted Saw-whet Owl (E): *Aegolius ridgwayi*

Upland Buzzard (E): *Buteo hemilasius*

Uraeginthus bengalus : (E) Cordonbleu, Red-cheeked Cordonbleu, (S) Coliazul bengalí, (F) Cordon bleu à joures rouges, Cordonbleu, Cordonbleu à joues rouges, **III** ESTRILDIDAE Av

Ural Owl (E): *Strix uralensis*

Urial (E/S/F): *Ovis vignei*

Urial (F): *Ovis vignei vignei*

Urochroa bougueri : (E) White-tailed Hillstar, (S) Colibrí de Bouguer, Estrella coliblanca, (F) Colibri de Bouguer, **II** TROCHILIDAE Av

Urogale de Mindanao (F): *Urogale everetti*

Urogale d'Everett (F): *Urogale everetti*

Urogale everetti : (E) Mindanao Treeshrew, Philippine Treeshrew, (S) Musaraña arborícola de Filipinas, (F) Urogale de Mindanao, Urogale d'Everett, **II** TUPAIIDAE Ma

Uroglaux dimorpha : (E) Papuan Boobook, Papuan Hawk-Owl, (S) Nínox halcón, (F) Chouette de Nouvelle-Guinée, Ninoxe papoue, **II** STRIGIDAE Av

Uromanis tetradactyla = Manis tetradactyla

Uromastyx spp.: (E) Mastigures, Spiny-tailed lizards, (F) Fouettes-queue, Lézards fouette-queue **II** AGAMIDAE Re

Uromastyx acanthinura : (E) Bell's Dabb Lizard, Black Spiny-tailed Lizard, Dabb's Mastigure, (S) Lagarto de cola espinosa común, (F) Dob, Fouette-queue épineux, **II** AGAMIDAE Re

Uromastyx aegyptia : (E) Dabb Lizard, Egyptian Mastigure, Egyptian Spiny-tailed Lizard, (S) Lagarto de cola espinosa egipcio, (F) Fouette-queue d'Egypte, **II** AGAMIDAE Re

Uromastyx alfredschmidti : **II** AGAMIDAE Re

Uromastyx asmussi : (E) Horn Lizard, Iranian Mastigure, (F) Fouette-queue d'Iran **II** AGAMIDAE Re

Uromastyx benti : (E) Bent's Mastigure, (F) Fouette-queue de Bent **II** AGAMIDAE Re

Uromastyx dispar : **II** AGAMIDAE Re

Uromastyx flavifasciata = Uromastyx dispar

Uromastyx geyri : (E) Sahara Mastigure, (S) Lagarto de cola espinosa de Geyr, (F) Fouette-queue du Sahara, **II** AGAMIDAE Re

Uromastyx hardwickii : (E) Hardwick's Spiny-tailed Lizard, Indian Mastigure, (S) Lagarto de cola espinosa indo, (F) Fouette-queue de Hardwick, Fouette-queue indien, **II** AGAMIDAE Re

Uromastyx leptieni : **II** AGAMIDAE Re

Uromastyx loricata : (E) Mesopotamian Mastigure, Mesopotamian Spiny-tailed Lizard, (F) Fouette-queue de Mésopotamie **II** AGAMIDAE Re

Uromastyx macfadyeni = Uromastyx ocellata

Uromastyx maliensis = Uromastyx dispar

Uromastyx microlepis = Uromastyx aegyptia

Uromastyx occidentalis : **II** AGAMIDAE Re

Uromastyx ocellata : (E) Eyed Dabb Lizard, Ocellated Mastigure, (S) Lagarto de cola espinosa ocelado, (F) Fouette-queue ocellé, **II** AGAMIDAE Re

Uromastyx ornata = Uromastyx ocellata

Uromastyx philbyi = Uromastyx ocellata

Uromastyx princeps : (E) Princely Mastigure, (F) Fouette-queue d'O'Shaughnessy, Fouette-queue princier **II** AGAMIDAE Re

Uromastyx thomasi : (E) Thomas's Mastigure, (S) Lagarto de cola espinosa de Thomas, (F) Fouette-queue de Thomas, **II** AGAMIDAE Re

Urosticte benjamini : (E) Purple-bibbed Whitetip, (S) Colibrí puntablanca occidental, Punta blanca, (F) Colibri de Benjamin, **II** TROCHILIDAE Av

Urosticte benjamini ssp. *ruficrissa = Urosticte ruficrissa*

Urosticte ruficrissa : (E) Rufous-vented Whitetip, (S) Colibrí puntablanca oriental, (F) Colibri à sous-caudales rousses, **II** TROCHILIDAE Av

Urotriorchis macrourus : (E) African Long-tailed Hawk, Long-tailed Hawk, (S) Azor rabilargo, (F) Autour à longue queue, **II** ACCIPITRIDAE Av

URSIDAE spp.: (E) Bears, (S) Osos, (F) Ours **I/II** Ma

Ursus americanus : (E) American Black Bear, (S) Oso negro americano, (F) Baribal, Ours noir américain, **II** URSIDAE Ma

Ursus arctos : (E) Brown Bear, Grizzly Bear, (S) Oso pardo, (F) Grizzly, Ours brun, Ours grizzly, **I/II** URSIDAE Ma

Ursus arctos isabellinus : (E) Himalayan Brown Bear, Red Bear, (S) Oso pardo del Himalaya, (F) Ours brun de l'Himalaya, Ours brun isabelle, Ours isabelle, **I** URSIDAE Ma

Ursus malayanus = Helarctos malayanus

Ursus maritimus : (E) Polar Bear, (S) Oso polar, (F) Ours blanc, Ours polaire, **II** URSIDAE Ma

Ursus melanoleucus = Ailuropoda melanoleuca

Ursus thibetanus : (E) Asiatic Black Bear, Himalayan Black Bear, (S) Oso de collar, Oso negro de Asia, (F) Ours à collier, Ours de l'Himalaya, Ours du Tibet , Ours noir d'Asie, **I** URSIDAE Ma

Urubu à tête jaune (F): *Cathartes burrovianus*

Urubu à tête rouge (F): *Cathartes aura*

Urubu noir (F): *Coragyps atratus*

Usambara Eagle-Owl (E): *Bubo vosseleri*

Usambara Soft-horned Chameleon (E): *Bradypodion tenue*

Usambara Three-horned Chameleon (E): *Chamaeleo deremensis*

Usambara Two-horned Chameleon (E): *Bradypodion fischeri*

Usambara Viviparous Toad (E): *Nectophrynoides tornieri*

Uzungwe Mountain Chameleon (E): *Chamaeleo laterispinis*

Uzungwe Scarp Tree Toad (E): *Nectophrynoides wendyae*

Uzungwe Three-horned Chameleon (E): *Chamaeleo werneri*

Vaca marina amazónica (S): *Trichechus inunguis*

Vampyrops lineatus = Platyrrhinus lineatus

Van Beneden's Colobus (E): *Procolobus verus*

Van Dam's Girdled Lizard (E): *Cordylus vandami*

Vanikoro Flying-fox (E): *Pteropus tuberculatus*

Vanuatu Flying-fox (E): *Pteropus anetianus*

Vaquita (E/S/F): *Phocoena sinus*

Varan à deux bandes (F): *Varanus salvator*

Varan à gorge blanche (F): *Varanus albigularis*

Varan à queue bleue (F): *Varanus doreanus*

Varan à queue courte (F): *Varanus brevicauda*

Varan à queue épineuse (F): *Varanus acanthurus/ Varanus primordius*

Varan à queue rayée (F): *Varanus caudolineatus*

Varan à tête noire (F): *Varanus tristis*

Varan aquatique commun (F): *Varanus salvator*

Varan aquatique de Mertens (F): *Varanus mertensi*

Varan aquatique de Mitchell (F): *Varanus mitchelli*

Varan arboricole de l'Ile Rossell (F): *Varanus telenesetes*

Varan arboricole tacheté (F): *Varanus timorensis*

Varan bigarré (F): *Varanus varius*

Varan brun (F): *Varanus primordius*

Varan cou rugueux (F): *Varanus rudicollis*

Varan crocodile (F): *Varanus salvadorii*

Varan de Bogert (F): *Varanus bogerti*

Varan de Duméril (F): *Varanus dumerilii*

Varan de Gillen (F): *Varanus gilleni*

Varan de Glauert (F): *Varanus glauerti*

Varan de Gould (F): *Varanus gouldii*

Varan de Gray (F): *Varanus olivaceus*

Varan de Kimberley (F): *Varanus panoptes*

Varan de King (F): *Varanus kingorum*

Varan de Komodo (F): *Varanus komodoensis*

Varan de Papouasie (F): *Varanus salvadorii*

Varan de Pilbara (F): *Varanus pilbarensis*

Varan de Rosenberg (F): *Varanus rosenbergi*

Varan de Schlegel (F): *Varanus tristis*

Varan de Schmidt (F): *Varanus jobiensis*

Varan de Spencer (F): *Varanus spenceri*

Varan de Storr (F): *Varanus storri*

Varan de Timor (F): *Varanus timorensis*

Varan dentelle (F): *Varanus varius*

Varan des cavernes (F): *Varanus eremius*

Varan des crevaces (F): *Varanus kingorum*

Varan des Indes (F): *Varanus indicus*

Varan des mangroves (F): *Varanus indicus/ Varanus semiremex*

Varan des rochers à longue queue (F): *Varanus glebopalma*

Varan des sables noir (F): *Varanus rosenbergi*

Varan des savanes (F): *Varanus exanthematicus*

Varan des spinifex (F): *Varanus eremius*

Varan des steppes (F): *Varanus exanthematicus*

Varan du Bengale (F): *Varanus bengalensis*

Varan du désert (F): *Varanus griseus*

Varan du Nil (F): *Varanus niloticus*

Varan du nord de l'Australie (F): *Varanus similis*

Varan du Yemen (F): *Varanus yemenensis*

Varan émeraude (F): *Varanus prasinus*

Varan épineux des Iles Salomon (F): *Varanus spinulosus*

Varan gigantesque (F): *Varanus giganteus*

Varan gris (F): *Varanus griseus*

Varan jaune (F): *Varanus flavescens*

Varan nain (F): *Varanus storri*

Varan olivâtre (F): *Varanus olivaceus*

Varan pierre (F): *Varanus baritji*
Varan pygmée de Mulga (F): *Varanus gilleni*
Varan rouillé (F): *Varanus semiremex*
Varano amarillo (S): *Varanus flavescens*
Varano arborícola común (S): *Varanus varius*
Varano arborícola manchado (S): *Varanus timorensis*
Varano colicorto (S): *Varanus brevicauda*
Varano colilargo de las rocas (S): *Varanus glauerti*
Varano cuellirugoso (S): *Varanus rudicollis*
Varano de agua de Mertens (S): *Varanus mertensi*
Varano de agua de Mitchell (S): *Varanus mitchelli*
Varano de arena (S): *Varanus gouldii*
Varano de Bengala (S): *Varanus bengalensis*
Varano de cabeza negra (S): *Varanus tristis*
Varano de cola crestada (S): *Varanus acanthurus/ Varanus primordius*
Varano de cola rayada (S): *Varanus caudolineatus*
Varano de dos bandas (S): *Varanus salvator*
Varano de Dumeril (S): *Varanus dumerilii*
Varano de Gillen (S): *Varanus gilleni*
Varano de Gould (S): *Varanus gouldii*
Varano de King (S): *Varanus kingorum*
Varano de Komodo (S): *Varanus komodoensis*
Varano de manglar (S): *Varanus indicus*
Varano de Papua (S): *Varanus salvadorii*
Varano de Rosenberg (S): *Varanus rosenbergi*
Varano de Schmidt (S): *Varanus jobiensis*
Varano de Spencer (S): *Varanus spenceri*
Varano del desierto (S): *Varanus griseus*
Varano del Nilo (S): *Varanus niloticus*
Varano desértico (S): *Varanus griseus*
Varano enano (S): *Varanus storri*
Varano gigante (S): *Varanus giganteus*
Varano pardo (S): *Varanus semiremex*
Varano pigmeo del desierto (S): *Varanus eremius*
Varano verde (S): *Varanus prasinus*
Varanos (S): *Varanus* spp.
Varans (F): *Varanus* spp.
Varanus spp.: (E) Monitor lizards, (S) Varanos, (F) Varans, **I/II** VARANIDAE Re
Varanus acanthurus : (E) Goanna Monitor, Ridge-tailed Monitor, Spiny-tailed Pygmy Monitor, (S) Varano de cola crestada, (F) Varan à queue épineuse, **II** VARANIDAE Re
Varanus acanthurus ssp. *primordius = Varanus primordius*
Varanus albigularis : (E) Rock Monitor, Southern Savanna Monitor, White-throated Monitor, (F) Varan à gorge blanche **II** VARANIDAE Re
Varanus auffenbergi : **II** VARANIDAE Re
Varanus baritji : (E) Stone Monitor, (F) Varan pierre **II** VARANIDAE Re
Varanus beccarii = Varanus prasinus ssp. *beccarii*
Varanus bengalensis : (E) Bengal Black Lizard, Bengal Lizard, Bengal Monitor, Common Monitor, Indian Monitor, Indian Small-grain Lizard, Penang Lizard, Talagoya Lizard, (S) Varano de Bengala, (F) Varan du Bengale, **I** VARANIDAE Re
Varanus bivittatus = Varanus salvator
Varanus bogerti : (E) Bogert's Monitor, (F) Varan de Bogert **II** VARANIDAE Re
Varanus brevicauda : (E) Short-tailed Pygmy Monitor, (S) Varano colicorto, (F) Varan à queue courte, **II** VARANIDAE Re
Varanus bulliwallah = Varanus mertensi
Varanus caerulivirens : **II** VARANIDAE Re
Varanus caudolineatus : (E) Streak-tailed Monitor, Stripe-tailed Monitor, (S) Varano de cola rayada, (F) Varan à queue rayée, **II** VARANIDAE Re
Varanus cerambonensis : **II** VARANIDAE Re
Varanus cumingi = Varanus salvator
Varanus doreanus : (E) Blue-tailed Monitor, (F) Varan à queue bleue **II** VARANIDAE Re

Varanus dumerilii : (E) Duméril's Monitor, Fish Lizard, (S) Varano de Dumeril, (F) Varan de Duméril, **II** VARANIDAE Re
Varanus eremius : (E) Desert Pygmy Monitor, Spinifex Monitor, (S) Varano pigmeo del desierto, (F) Varan des cavernes, Varan des spinifex, **II** VARANIDAE Re
Varanus exanthematicus : (E) African Large-grain Lizard, African Savanna Monitor, Bosc's Monitor, Northern Savanna Monitor, (F) Varan des savanes, Varan des steppes **II** VARANIDAE Re
Varanus exanthematicus ssp. *albigularis = Varanus albigularis*
Varanus finschi : **II** VARANIDAE Re
Varanus flavescens : (E) Calcutta Oval-grain Lizard, Indian Oval-grain Lizard, Ruddy Snub-nosed Monitor, Yellow Land Lizard, Yellow Monitor, (S) Varano amarillo, (F) Varan jaune, **I** VARANIDAE Re
Varanus giganteus : (E) Perentie, (S) Varano gigante, (F) Perentie, Varan gigantesque, **II** VARANIDAE Re
Varanus gilleni : (E) Pygmy Mulga Monitor, (S) Varano de Gillen, (F) Varan de Gillen, Varan pygmée de Mulga, **II** VARANIDAE Re
Varanus glauerti : (E) Glauert's Monitor, (S) Varano colilargo de las rocas, (F) Varan de Glauert, **II** VARANIDAE Re
Varanus glebopalma : (E) Long-tailed Rock Monitor, (F) Varan des rochers à longue queue **II** VARANIDAE Re
Varanus gouldii : (E) Bungarra, Gould's Monitor, Sand Monitor, (S) Varano de arena, Varano de Gould, (F) Varan de Gould, **II** VARANIDAE Re
Varanus grayi = Varanus olivaceus
Varanus griseus : (E) Agra Lizard, Agra Monitor, Baghdad Small-grain Lizard, Desert Monitor, Grey Monitor, (S) Varano del desierto, Varano desértico, (F) Varan du désert, Varan gris, **I** VARANIDAE Re
Varanus indicus : (E) Ambon Lizard, Flower Lizard, Mangrove Monitor, Pacific Monitor, (S) Varano de manglar, (F) Varan des Indes, Varan des mangroves, **II** VARANIDAE Re
Varanus indicus ssp. *spinulosus = Varanus spinulosus*
Varanus irrawadicus = Varanus bengalensis
Varanus jobiensis : (E) Peachthroat Monitor, Schmidt's Monitor, Sepik Monitor, (S) Varano de Schmidt, (F) Varan de Schmidt, **II** VARANIDAE Re
Varanus juxtindicus : **II** VARANIDAE Re
Varanus karlschmidti = Varanus jobiensis
Varanus keithhornei : **II** VARANIDAE Re
Varanus kingorum : (E) Crevice Monitor, King's Monitor, (S) Varano de King, (F) Varan de King, Varan des crevaces, **II** VARANIDAE Re
Varanus komodoensis : (E) Komodo Dragon, Komodo Monitor, Ora, (S) Dragón de Komodo, Varano de Komodo, (F) Dragon des Komodos, Varan de Komodo, **I** VARANIDAE Re .
Varanus kordensis : **II** VARANIDAE Re
Varanus mabitang : **II** VARANIDAE Re
Varanus macraei : **II** VARANIDAE Re
Varanus melinus : **II** VARANIDAE Re
Varanus mertensi : (E) Mertens's Water Monitor, (S) Varano de agua de Mertens, (F) Varan aquatique de Mertens, **II** VARANIDAE Re
Varanus mitchelli : (E) Mitchell's Water Monitor, (S) Varano de agua de Mitchell, (F) Varan aquatique de Mitchell, **II** VARANIDAE Re
Varanus nebulosus : **I** VARANIDAE Re
Varanus niloticus : (E) African Small-grain Lizard, Nile Monitor, (S) Varano del Nilo, (F) Varan du Nil, **II** VARANIDAE Re
Varanus olivaceus : (E) Gray's Monitor, (F) Varan de Gray, Varan olivâtre **II** VARANIDAE Re
Varanus ornatus : **II** VARANIDAE Re
Varanus panoptes :, (F) Varan de Kimberley **II** VARANIDAE Re

Checklist of fauna/Lista de especies de fauna/Liste des espèces animales

Varanus pilbarensis : (E) Pilbara Monitor, (F) Varan de Pilbara **II** VARANIDAE Re
Varanus prasinus : (E) Emerald Monitor, (S) Varano verde, (F) Varan émeraude, **II** VARANIDAE Re
Varanus primordius : (E) Brown Monitor, Ridge-tailed Monitor, (S) Varano de cola crestada, (F) Varan à queue épineuse, Varan brun, **II** VARANIDAE Re
Varanus rosenbergi : (E) Black Sand Monitor, Rosenberg's Monitor, Sand Goanna, (S) Varano de Rosenberg, (F) Varan de Rosenberg, Varan des sables noir, **II** VARANIDAE Re
Varanus rudicollis : (E) Harlequin Monitor, Rough-necked Monitor, Tree Lizard, (S) Varano cuellirugoso, (F) Varan cou rugueux, **II** VARANIDAE Re
Varanus salvadorii : (E) Crocodile Monitor, Papuan Monitor, Tree Crocodile, (S) Varano de Papua, (F) Varan crocodile, Varan de Papouasie, **II** VARANIDAE Re
Varanus salvator : (E) Common Water Monitor, Malayan Monitor, No-mark Lizard, Plain Lizard, Rice Lizard, Ring Lizard, Two-banded Monitor, Water Monitor, (S) Varano de dos bandas, (F) Varan à deux bandes, Varan aquatique commun, **II** VARANIDAE Re
Varanus scalaris : **II** VARANIDAE Re
Varanus semiremex : (E) Mangrove Monitor, Rusty Monitor, (S) Varano pardo, (F) Varan des mangroves, Varan rouillé, **II** VARANIDAE Re
Varanus similis :, (F) Varan du nord de l'Australie **II** VARANIDAE Re
Varanus spenceri : (E) Spencer's Monitor, (S) Varano de Spencer, (F) Varan de Spencer, **II** VARANIDAE Re
Varanus spinulosus : (E) Solomon Islands Spiny Monitor, (F) Varan épineux des Iles Salomon **II** VARANIDAE Re
Varanus storri : (E) Dwarf Monitor, (S) Varano enano, (F) Varan de Storr, Varan nain, **II** VARANIDAE Re
Varanus teleneseses : (E) Rossell Island Tree Monitor, (F) Varan arboricole de l'Ile Rossell **II** VARANIDAE Re
Varanus teriae = Varanus keithhornei
Varanus timorensis : (E) Spotted Tree Monitor, Timor Tree Monitor, (S) Varano arborícola manchado, (F) Varan arboricole tacheté, Varan de Timor, **II** VARANIDAE Re
Varanus timorensis ssp. *scalaris = Varanus scalaris*
Varanus timorensis ssp. *similis = Varanus similis*
Varanus togianus = Varanus salvator
Varanus tristis : (E) Arid Monitor, Black-headed Monitor, Freckled Monitor, Mournful Tree Monitor, (S) Varano de cabeza negra, (F) Varan à tête noire, Varan de Schlegel, **II** VARANIDAE Re
Varanus varius : (E) Common Tree Monitor, Lace Monitor, (S) Varano arborícola común, (F) Varan bigarré, Varan dentelle, **II** VARANIDAE Re
Varanus yemenensis : (E) Yemen Monitor, (F) Varan du Yemen **II** VARANIDAE Re
Varanus yuwonoi : **II** VARANIDAE Re
Varecia variegata : (E) Ruffed Lemur, (S) Lemur de collar, Lemur de Gola, Lemur de Gorguera, (F) Lémur vari, Maki vari, **I** LEMURIDAE Ma
Variable Coral Snake (E): *Micrurus diastema*
Variable Flying-fox (E): *Pteropus hypomelanus*
Variable Goshawk (E): *Accipiter novaehollandiae*
Variable Hawk (E): *Buteo poecilochrous*
Variable Mountain-gem (E): *Lampornis castaneoventris*
Variable Screech-Owl (E): *Otus atricapillus*
Varied Lorikeet (E): *Psitteuteles versicolor*
Variegated Dwarf Chameleon (E): *Bradypodion pumilum*
Vasa géant (F): *Coracopsis vasa*
Vasa Parrot (E): *Coracopsis vasa*
Vase corals (E): *Euphyllia* spp.
Vaughanella concinna : **II** CARYOPHYLLIIDAE An
Vaughanella margaritata : **II** CARYOPHYLLIIDAE An
Vaughanella multipalifera : **II** CARYOPHYLLIIDAE An
Vaughanella oreophila : **II** CARYOPHYLLIIDAE An
Vautour à tête blanche (F): *Trigonoceps occipitalis*

Vautour africain (F): *Gyps africanus*
Vautour charognard (F): *Necrosyrtes monachus*
Vautour chassefiente (F): *Gyps coprotheres*
Vautour chaugoun (F): *Gyps bengalensis*
Vautour de l'Himalaya (F): *Gyps himalayensis*
Vautour de Rüppell (F): *Gyps rueppellii*
Vautour fauve (F): *Gyps fulvus*
Vautour huppé (F): *Trigonoceps occipitalis*
Vautour indien (F): *Gyps indicus*
Vautour moine (F): *Aegypius monachus*
Vautour oricou (F): *Torgos tracheliotus*
Vautour page (F): *Sarcoramphus papa*
Vautour percnoptère (F): *Neophron percnopterus*
Vautour royal (F): *Sarcoramphus papa/ Sarcogyps calvus*
Veiled Chameleon (E): *Chamaeleo calyptratus*
Velvet branch corals (E): *Montipora spp.*
Velvet corals (E): *Montipora spp.*
Velvet-browed Brilliant (E): *Heliodoxa xanthogonys*
Velvet-crowned Brilliant (E): *Heliodoxa xanthogonys*
Velvet-purple Coronet (E): *Boissonneaua jardini*
Venadito (S): *Pudu puda*
Venadito de los páramos (S): *Pudu mephistophiles*
Venado campero (S): *Ozotoceros bezoarticus*
Venado conejo (S): *Pudu mephistophiles*
Venado de campo (S): *Ozotoceros bezoarticus*
Venado de las Pampas (S): *Ozotoceros bezoarticus*
Venezuelan Sylph (E): *Aglaiocercus berlepschi*
Ventre orange (F): *Amandava subflava*
Ver nota pie de página (S): *Pseudoryx nghetinhensis*
Veraguan Mango (E): *Anthracothorax veraguensis*
Vermiculated Fishing-Owl (E): *Scotopelia bouvieri*
Vermiculated Screech-Owl (E): *Otus vermiculatus*
Vernal Hanging-Parrot (E): *Loriculus vernalis*
Verreaux's Eagle (E): *Aquila verreauxii*
Verreaux's Eagle-Owl (E): *Bubo lacteus*
Verreaux's Sifaka (E): *Propithecus verreauxi*
Verreaux's Turaco (E): *Tauraco macrorhynchus*
Versicolored Emerald (E): *Agyrtria versicolor*
Vervain Hummingbird (E): *Mellisuga minima*
Vervet Monkey (E): *Chlorocebus aethiops*
Veuve (F): *Vidua larvaticola/ Vidua raricola*
Veuve à collier d'or (F): *Vidua orientalis*
Veuve à dos d'or (F): *Euplectes macrourus*
Veuve à queue large (F): *Vidua interjecta*
Veuve dominicaine (F): *Vidua macroura*
Veuve du Togo (F): *Vidua togoensis*
Veuve nigérienne (F): *Vidua interjecta*
Veuve paradisier (F): *Vidua orientalis*
Veuve-noire (F): *Euplectes ardens*
Víbora de los Orsini (S): *Vipera ursinii*
Vibora de Wagner (S): *Vipera wagneri*
Vibora del Orsini (S): *Vipera ursinii*
Victoria Crowned-Pigeon (E): *Goura victoria*
Victoria Goura (E): *Goura victoria*
Victoria's Riflebird (E): *Ptiloris victoriae*
Vicugna (E): *Vicugna vicugna*
Vicugna vicugna : (E) Vicugna, Vicuña, (S) Vicuña, (F) Vigogne, **I/II** CAMELIDAE Ma
Vicuña (E/S): *Vicugna vicugna*
Vidua amauropteryx = Vidua chalybeata
Vidua centralis = Vidua chalybeata
Vidua chalybeata : (E) Green Indigobird, Senegal Combassou, Village Indigobird, (S) Tejedor bruñido verdoso, (F) Combassou du Sénégal, **III** PLOCEIDAE Av
Vidua incognita = Vidua wilsoni
Vidua interjecta : (E) Long-tailed Paradise-Whydah, Uelle Paradise-Whydah, (F) Veuve à queue large, Veuve nigérienne **III** PLOCEIDAE Av
Vidua larvaticola : (E) Baka Indigobird, Black-faced Firefinch Indigobird, (F) Combassou de Baka, Veuve **III** PLOCEIDAE Av
Vidua lorenzi = Vidua wilsoni

Checklist of fauna/Lista de especies de fauna/Liste des espèces animales

Vidua macroura : (E) Pin-tailed Whydah, (S) Viuda colicinta, (F) Veuve dominicaine, **III** PLOCEIDAE Av
Vidua neumanni = Vidua chalybeata
Vidua okavangoensis = Vidua chalybeata
Vidua orientalis : (E) Northern Paradise-Whydah, (S) Viuda del paraiso oriental, (F) Veuve à collier d'or, Veuve paradisier, **III** PLOCEIDAE Av
Vidua orientalis ssp. *interjecta = Vidua interjecta*
Vidua orientalis ssp. *togoensis = Vidua togoensis*
Vidua paradisaea ssp. *orientalis = Vidua orientalis*
Vidua raricola : (E) Goldbreast Indigobird, Jambandu Indigobird, (F) Combassou de Jambandu, Veuve **III** PLOCEIDAE Av
Vidua togoensis : (E) Togo Paradise-Whydah, (F) Veuve du Togo **III** PLOCEIDAE Av
Vidua ultramarina = Vidua chalybeata
Vidua wilsoni : (E) Pale-winged Indigobird, Wilson's Indigobird, (S) Tejedor bruñido de Wilson, (F) Combassou de Wilson, Combassou noir, **III** PLOCEIDAE Av
Vieillot's Black Weaver (E): *Ploceus nigerrimus*
Vieillot's Fireback (E): *Lophura ignita*
Vigogne (F): *Vicugna vicugna*
Vigors's Bustard (E): *Eupodotis vigorsii*
Village Indigobird (E): *Vidua chalybeata*
Village Weaver (E): *Ploceus cucullatus*
Villosa trabalis : (E) Cumberland Bean, Cumberland Bean Pearly Mussel **I** UNIONIDAE Bi
Vinaceous Amazon (E): *Amazona vinacea*
Vinaceous Dove (E): *Streptopelia vinacea*
Vinaceous Firefinch (E): *Lagonosticta vinacea*
Vinaceous Parrot (E): *Amazona vinacea*
Vinaceous Waxbill (E): *Lagonosticta vinacea*
Vinago Africano (S): *Treron calva*
Vinago obeng (S): *Treron calva*
Vinago waalia (S): *Treron waalia*
Vini australis : (E) Blue-crowned Lorikeet, (S) Lori de Samoa, (F) Lori fringillaire, **II** PSITTACIDAE Av
Vini kuhlii : (E) Kuhl's Lorikeet, Scarlet-breasted Lorikeet, (S) Lori de Rimitara, (F) Lori de Kuhl, **II** PSITTACIDAE Av
Vini peruviana : (E) Blue Lorikeet, Tahitian Lorikeet, (S) Lori monjita, (F) Lori nonnette, **II** PSITTACIDAE Av
Vini stepheni : (E) Henderson Lorikeet, Stephen's Lorikeet, (S) Lori de Stephen, (F) Lori de Stephen, **II** PSITTACIDAE Av
Vini ultramarina : (E) Ultramarine Lorikeet, Ultramarine Lory, (S) Lori ultramar, (F) Lori ultramarin, **I** PSITTACIDAE Av
Vinous-breasted Sparrowhawk (E): *Accipiter rhodogaster*
Violet Plantain-eater (E): *Musophaga violacea*
Violet Sabrewing (E): *Campylopterus hemileucurus*
Violet Turaco (E): *Musophaga violacea*
Violet-bellied Hummingbird (E): *Damophila julie*
Violet-capped Hummingbird (E): *Goldmania violiceps*
Violet-capped Woodnymph (E): *Thalurania glaucopis*
Violet-chested Hummingbird (E): *Sternoclyta cyanopectus*
Violet-crested Turaco (E): *Musophaga porphyreolopha*
Violet-crowned Hummingbird (E): *Agyrtria violiceps*
Violet-fronted Brilliant (E): *Heliodoxa leadbeateri*
Violet-headed Hummingbird (E): *Klais guimeti*
Violet-necked Lory (E): *Eos squamata*
Violet-tailed Sylph (E): *Aglaiocercus coelestis*
Violet-throated Metaltail (E): *Metallura baroni*
Violet-throated Starfrontlet (E): *Coeligena violifer*
Vipera eriwanensis = Vipera ursinii
Vipera renardi = Vipera ursinii
Vipera russelli = Daboia russelii
Vipera ursinii : (E) Field Adder, Meadow Viper, Orsini's Viper, (S) Víbora de los Orsini, Vibora del Orsini, (F) Vipère des steppes, Vipère d'Orsini, **I/NC** VIPERIDAE Re
Vipera wagneri : (E) Wagner's Viper, (S) Vibora de Wagner, (F) Vipère de Wagner, **II** VIPERIDAE Re

Vipère de Russell (F): *Daboia russelii*
Vipère de Wagner (F): *Vipera wagneri*
Vipère des steppes (F): *Vipera ursinii*
Vipère d'Orsini (F): *Vipera ursinii*
Virgin Islands Tree Boa (E): *Epicrates monensis*
Viridian Metaltail (E): *Metallura williami*
Visayan Hornbill (E): *Penelopides panini*
Visayan Wrinkled Hornbill (E): *Aceros waldeni*
Vison sibérien (F): *Mustela sibirica*
Vitelline Masked-Weaver (E): *Ploceus vitellinus*
Viuda colicinta (S): *Vidua macroura*
Viuda del paraiso oriental (S): *Vidua orientalis*
Viverra civetta = Civettictis civetta
Viverra civettina : (E) Malabar Civet, Malabar Large-spotted Civet, (F) Civette à grandes taches **III** VIVERRIDAE Ma
Viverra megaspila ssp. *civettina = Viverra civettina*
Viverra zibetha : (E) Large Indian Civet, (S) Gran civeta de la India, (F) Grande civette de l'Inde, **III** VIVERRIDAE Ma
Viverricula indica : (E) Small Indian Civet, (S) Pequeña civeta de la India, (F) Petite civette de l'Inde, **III** VIVERRIDAE Ma
Vogelkop Tree-kangaroo (E): *Dendrolagus ursinus*
Volcano Hummingbird (E): *Selasphorus flammula*
Volcano Rabbit (E): *Romerolagus diazi*
Vombat of Queensland (S): *Lasiorhinus krefftii*
Von Höhnel's Chameleon (E): *Chamaeleo hoehnelii*
Vorabé (F): *Euplectes afer*
Vu Quang Ox (E): *Pseudoryx nghetinhensis*
Vulpes bengalensis : (E) Bengal Fox, (S) Zorro de Bengala, (F) Renard du Bengale, **III** CANIDAE Ma
Vulpes cana : (E) Afghan Fox, Blanford's Fox, Corsac, Dog Fox, Hoary Fox, Steppe Fox, (S) Zorro de Blanford, (F) Renard de Blanford, **II** CANIDAE Ma
Vulpes vulpes griffithii : **III** CANIDAE Ma
Vulpes vulpes montana : **III** CANIDAE Ma
Vulpes vulpes pusilla : **III** CANIDAE Ma
Vulpes vulpes ssp. *leucopus = Vulpes vulpes* ssp. *pusilla*
Vulpes zerda : (E) Fennec Fox, (S) Fennec, Zorro del Sahara, (F) Fennec, **II** CANIDAE Ma
Vultur gryphus : (E) Andean Condor, (S) Cóndor, Cóndor andino, Cóndor de los Andes, (F) Condor des Andes, **I** CATHARTIDAE Av
Vulturine Fish-Eagle (E): *Gypohierax angolensis*
Vulturine Parrot (E): *Pionopsitta vulturina/ Psittrichas fulgidus*
Wabash Riffleshell (E): *Epioblasma sampsonii*
Wagner's Viper (E): *Vipera wagneri*
Wahlberg's Eagle (E): *Aquila wahlbergi*
Wahnes's Parotia (E): *Parotia wahnesi*
Waldrapp (E): *Geronticus eremita*
Wallabi rayado (S): *Lagostrophus fasciatus*
Wallabi rojo (S): *Lagorchestes hirsutus*
Wallaby à queue cornée (F): *Onychogalea lunata*
Wallaby-lièvre à bandes (F): *Lagostrophus fasciatus*
Wallaby-lièvre de l'ouest (F): *Lagorchestes hirsutus*
Wallaby-lièvre rayé (F): *Lagostrophus fasciatus*
Wallaby-lièvre roux (F): *Lagorchestes hirsutus*
Wallace's Hanging-Parrot (E): *Loriculus flosculus*
Wallace's Hawk-Eagle (E): *Spizaetus nanus*
Wallace's Scops-Owl (E): *Otus silvicola*
Wallace's Standardwing (E): *Semioptera wallacii*
Wallich's Pheasant (E): *Catreus wallichii*
Walrus (E): *Odobenus rosmarus*
Wanderoo (E): *Macaca silenus*
Warren's Girdled Lizard (E): *Cordylus warreni*
Warren's Spiny-tailed Lizard (E): *Cordylus warreni*
Warty Chameleon (E): *Furcifer verrucosus*
Warty Tree Gecko (E): *Naultinus tuberculatus*
Water Boa (E): *Eunectes murinus*
Water Box Turtle (E): *Terrapene coahuila*
Water Chevrotain (E): *Hyemoschus aquaticus*
Water Monitor (E): *Varanus salvator*
Water Python (E): *Liasis mackloti*

Checklist of fauna/Lista de especies de fauna/Liste des espèces animales

Waterberg Girdled Lizard (E): *Cordylus breyeri*
Watling Island Iguana (E): *Cyclura rileyi*
Wattle-billed Bird-of-paradise (E): *Loboparadisea sericea*
Wattled Crane (E): *Grus carunculatus*
Wattled Curassow (E): *Crax globulosa*
Wavy Chameleon (E): *Chamaeleo deremensis*
Wedge-billed Hummingbird (E): *Augastes geoffroyi*
Wedge-tailed Eagle (E): *Aquila audax*
Wedge-tailed Hillstar (E): *Oreotrochilus adela*
Wedge-tailed Sabrewing (E): *Campylopterus curvipennis*
Weeper Capuchin (E): *Cebus olivaceus*
Wellsophyllia geoffroyi = Trachyphyllia geoffroyi
Wellsophyllia radiata = Trachyphyllia geoffroyi
Werner's Chameleon (E): *Chamaeleo werneri*
Werner's Three-horned Chameleon (E): *Chamaeleo werneri*
West African Black Forest Turtle (E): *Pelusios niger*
West African Crowned Crane (E): *Balearica pavonina*
West African Dwarf Crocodile (E): *Osteolaemus tetraspis*
West African Manatee (E): *Trichechus senegalensis*
West African Mud Turtle (E): *Pelusios castaneus*
West African Sand Boa (E): *Gongylophis muelleri*
West African Seahorse (E): *Hippocampus algiricus*
West African Seedeater (E): *Serinus canicapillus*
West African Streaky-headed Seedeater (E): *Serinus canicapillus*
West Australian Seahorse (E): *Hippocampus subelongatus*
West Indian Iguana (E): *Iguana delicatissima*
West Indian Manatee (E): *Trichechus manatus*
West Indian Monk Seal (E): *Monachus tropicalis*
West Indian Seal (E): *Monachus tropicalis*
West Indian Tree-Duck (E): *Dendrocygna arborea*
West Indian Whistling-duck (E): *Dendrocygna arborea*
West Peruvian Screech-Owl (E): *Otus roboratus*
Westermann's Snake (E): *Elachistodon westermanni*
Western Australian seahorse (E): *Hippocampus angustus*
Western Barred Bandicoot (E): *Perameles bougainville*
Western Black-and-white Colobus (E): *Colobus polykomos*
Western Black-capped Lory (E): *Lorius lory*
Western Bluebill (E): *Spermophaga haematina*
Western Box Turtle (E): *Terrapene ornata*
Western Bristlebird (E): *Dasyornis longirostris*
Western Bronze-naped Pigeon (E): *Columba iriditorques*
Western Cape Crag Lizard (E): *Cordylus microlepidotus*
Western Corella (E): *Cacatua pastinator*
Western Crowned-pigeon (E): *Goura cristata*
Western Fanshell (E): *Cyprogenia aberti*
Western Fanshell Mussel (E): *Cyprogenia aberti*
Western Grey Plantain-eater (E): *Crinifer piscator*
Western Hare-wallaby (E): *Lagorchestes hirsutus*
Western Horned-Pheasant (E): *Tragopan melanocephalus*
Western Long-tailed Hermit (E): *Phaethornis longirostris*
Western Marsh-Harrier (E): *Circus aeruginosus*
Western Needle-clawed Bushbaby (E): *Euoticus elegantulus*
Western Needle-clawed Galago (E): *Euoticus elegantulus*
Western Nimba Toad (E): *Nimbaphrynoides occidentalis*
Western Palm Squirrel (E): *Epixerus ebii*
Western Parotia (E): *Parotia sefilata*
Western Pied Colobus (E): *Colobus polykomos*
Western Red Colobus (E): *Procolobus badius*
Western Red-footed Falcon (E): *Falco vespertinus*
Western Rosella (E): *Platycercus icterotis*
Western Rufous Bristlebird (E): *Dasyornis broadbenti litoralis*
Western Screech-Owl (E): *Otus kennicottii*
Western Scrub-bird (E): *Atrichornis clamosus*
Western Short-necked Turtle (E): *Pseudemydura umbrina*
Western Spiny Seahorse (E): *Hippocampus angustus*
Western Swamp Turtle (E): *Pseudemydura umbrina*
Western Tarsier (E): *Tarsius bancanus*
Western Tragopan (E): *Tragopan melanocephalus*
Western Turtle-Dove (E): *Streptopelia turtur*
Weymouth Carpet Coral (E): *Hoplangia durotrix*

Whale Shark (E): *Rhincodon typus*
Whales (E): CETACEA spp. Ma
Whale-headed Stork (E): *Balaeniceps rex*
Whisker Coral (E): *Duncanopsammia axifuga*
Whiskered Lorikeet (E): *Oreopsittacus arfaki*
Whiskered Pitta (E): *Pitta kochi*
Whiskered Screech-Owl (E): *Otus trichopsis*
Whistling Eagle (E): *Haliastur sphenurus*
Whistling Hawk (E): *Haliastur sphenurus*
Whistling Kite (E): *Haliastur sphenurus*
Whitaker's Boa (E): *Eryx whitakeri*
Whitaker's Sticky-toed Gecko (E): *Hoplodactylus kahutarae*
White Cay Ground Iguana (E): *Cyclura rileyi*
White Cockatoo (E): *Cacatua alba*
White Eared-pheasant (E): *Crossoptilon crossoptilon*
White Flag Dolphin (E): *Lipotes vexillifer*
White Flying-fox (E): *Pteropus anetianus*
White Goshawk (E): *Accipiter novaehollandiae*
White Grape Coral (E): *Euphyllia cristata*
White Hawk (E): *Leucopternis albicollis*
White Oryx (E): *Oryx dammah/ Oryx leucoryx*
White Pointer (E): *Carcharodon carcharias*
White Rhinoceros (E): *Ceratotherium simum*
White Saki (E): *Pithecia albicans*
White Shark (E): *Carcharodon carcharias*
White Spoonbill (E): *Platalea leucorodia*
White Starling (E): *Leucopsar rothschildi*
White Sturgeon (E): *Acipenser transmontanus*
White Wartyback (E): *Plethobasus cicatricosus*
White Warty-back Pearly Mussel (E): *Plethobasus cicatricosus*
White Whale (E): *Delphinapterus leucas*
White-backed Vulture (E): *Gyps africanus/ Gyps bengalensis*
White-beaked Dolphin (E): *Lagenorhynchus albirostris*
White-bearded Hermit (E): *Phaethornis hispidus*
White-bellied Bustard (E): *Eupodotis senegalensis*
White-bellied Caique (E): *Pionites leucogaster*
White-bellied Dolphin (E): *Cephalorhynchus eutropia*
White-bellied Emerald (E): *Agyrtria candida*
White-bellied Fish-Eagle (E): *Haliaeetus leucogaster*
White-bellied Goshawk (E): *Accipiter haplochrous*
White-bellied Hummingbird (E): *Leucippus chionogaster*
White-bellied Korhaan (E): *Eupodotis senegalensis*
White-bellied Mountain-gem (E): *Lampornis hemileucus*
White-bellied Pangolin (E): *Manis tricuspis*
White-bellied Parrot (E): *Pionites leucogaster*
White-bellied Sea-Eagle (E): *Haliaeetus leucogaster*
White-bellied Spider Monkey (E): *Ateles belzebuth*
White-bellied Woodstar (E): *Chaetocercus mulsant*
White-billed Buffalo-Weaver (E): *Bubalornis albirostris*
White-billed Sicklebill (E): *Epimachus bruijnii*
White-breasted Guineafowl (E): *Agelastes meleagrides*
White-breasted Hawk (E): *Accipiter chionogaster*
White-breasted Negrofinch (E): *Nigrita fusconota*
White-breasted Parakeet (E): *Pyrrhura albipectus*
White-breasted Side-necked Turtle (E): *Pelusios adansonii*
White-breasted Silvereye (E): *Zosterops albogularis*
White-breasted White-eye (E): *Zosterops albogularis*
White-browed Boobook (E): *Ninox superciliaris*
White-browed Hawk (E): *Leucopternis kuhli*
White-browed Hermit (E): *Phaethornis stuarti*
White-browed Owl (E): *Ninox superciliaris*
White-capped Parrot (E): *Pionus senilis*
White-cheeked Gibbon (E): *Hylobates leucogenys*
White-cheeked Mangabey (E): *Lophocebus albigena*
White-cheeked Olive Weaver (E): *Nesocharis capistrata*
White-cheeked Turaco (E): *Tauraco leucotis*
White-chested Emerald (E): *Agyrtria brevirostris*
White-chested White-eye (E): *Zosterops albogularis*
White-chinned Owl (E): *Pulsatrix koeniswaldiana*
White-chinned Sapphire (E): *Hylocharis cyanus*
White-collared Kite (E): *Leptodon forbesi*
White-collared Mangabey (E): *Cercocebus torquatus*

Checklist of fauna/Lista de especies de fauna/Liste des espèces animales

White-crested Coquette (E): *Lophornis adorabilis*
White-crested Hornbill (E): *Aceros comatus*
White-crested Turaco (E): *Tauraco leucolophus*
White-crowned Hornbill (E): *Aceros comatus*
White-crowned Parrot (E): *Pionus senilis*
White-death (E): *Carcharodon carcharias*
White-eared Conure (E): *Pyrrhura leucotis*
White-eared Hummingbird (E): *Basilinna leucotis*
White-eared Marmoset (E): *Callithrix aurita*
White-eared Parakeet (E): *Pyrrhura leucotis*
White-eyed Buzzard (E): *Butastur teesa*
White-eyed Conure (E): *Aratinga leucophthalmus*
White-eyed Kestrel (E): *Falco rupicoloides*
White-eyed Parakeet (E): *Aratinga leucophthalmus*
White-eyed Pochard (E): *Aythya nyroca*
White-eyed River-Martin (E): *Pseudochelidon sirintarae*
White-faced Amazon (E): *Amazona kawalli*
White-faced Capuchin (E): *Cebus capucinus*
White-faced Langur (E): *Presbytis frontata*
White-faced Owl (E): *Sceloglaux albifacies*
White-faced Saki (E): *Pithecia pithecia*
White-faced Scops-Owl (E): *Otus leucotis*
White-faced Tree-Duck (E): *Dendrocygna viduata*
White-faced Whistling-Duck (E): *Dendrocygna viduata*
Whitefin Dolphin (E): *Lipotes vexillifer*
White-flanked Porpoise (E): *Phocoenoides dalli*
White-footed Sportive Lemur (E): *Lepilemur leucopus*
White-footed Tamarin (E): *Saguinus leucopus*
White-fronted Amazon (E): *Amazona albifrons*
White-fronted Capuchin (E): *Cebus albifrons*
White-fronted Falconet (E): *Microhierax latifrons*
White-fronted Grosbeak (E): *Amblyospiza albifrons*
White-fronted Leaf Monkey (E): *Presbytis frontata*
White-fronted Marmoset (E): *Callithrix geoffroyi*
White-fronted Parrot (E): *Amazona albifrons*
White-fronted Scops-Owl (E): *Otus sagittatus*
White-handed Gibbon (E): *Hylobates lar*
White-headed Dolphin (E): *Cephalorhynchus hectori*
White-headed Duck (E): *Oxyura leucocephala*
White-headed Eagle (E): *Haliaeetus leucocephalus*
White-headed Hornbill (E): *Aceros leucocephalus*
White-headed Sea Eagle (E): *Haliastur indus*
White-headed Vulture (E): *Trigonoceps occipitalis*
White-lined Bat (E): *Platyrrhinus lineatus*
White-lined Broad-nosed Bat (E): *Platyrrhinus lineatus*
White-lined Chameleon (E): *Furcifer antimena*
White-lipped Peccary (E): *Tayassu pecari*
White-lipped Python (E): *Leiopython albertisii*
White-lipped Tamarin (E): *Saguinus labiatus*
White-naped Crane (E): *Grus vipio*
White-naped Lory (E): *Lorius albidinuchus*
White-naped Weaver (E): *Ploceus albinucha*
White-necked Conure (E): *Pyrrhura albipectus*
White-necked Crane (E): *Grus vipio*
White-necked Hawk (E): *Leucopternis lacernulata*
White-necked Jacobin (E): *Florisuga mellivora*
White-necked Parakeet (E): *Pyrrhura albipectus*
White-necked Picathartes (E): *Picathartes gymnocephalus*
White-necked Rockfowl (E): *Picathartes gymnocephalus*
White-nosed Bearded Saki (E): *Chiropotes albinasus*
White-nosed Coati (E): *Nasua narica*
White-nosed Guenon (E): *Cercopithecus nictitans*
White-nosed Saki (E): *Chiropotes albinasus*
White-quilled Bustard (E): *Eupodotis afraoides*
White-rumped Falcon (E): *Polihierax insignis*
White-rumped Falconet (E): *Polihierax insignis*
White-rumped Hawk (E): *Buteo leucorrhous*
White-rumped Kestrel (E): *Falco dickinsoni*
White-rumped Seedeater (E): *Serinus leucopygius*
White-rumped Vulture (E): *Gyps bengalensis*
White's Seahorse (E): *Hippocampus whitei*
White-shouldered Eagle (E): *Aquila adalberti*
White-sided Hillstar (E): *Oreotrochilus leucopleurus*
White-tailed Black-Cockatoo (E): *Calyptorhynchus baudinii*

White-tailed Eagle (E): *Haliaeetus albicilla*
White-tailed Emerald (E): *Elvira chionura*
White-tailed Goldenthroat (E): *Polytmus guainumbi*
White-tailed Hawk (E): *Buteo albicaudatus*
White-tailed Hillstar (E): *Urochroa bougueri*
White-tailed Hummingbird (E): *Eupherusa poliocerca*
White-tailed Kite (E): *Elanus leucurus*
White-tailed Rabbit-eared Bandicoot (E): *Macrotis leucura*
White-tailed Sabrewing (E): *Campylopterus ensipennis*
White-tailed Starfrontlet (E): *Coeligena phalerata*
White-throated Capuchin (E): *Cebus capucinus*
White-throated Caracara (E): *Phalcoboenus albogularis*
White-throated Guenon (E): *Cercopithecus erythrogaster/ Cercopithecus sclateri*
White-throated Hawk (E): *Buteo albigula*
White-throated Hummingbird (E): *Leucochloris albicollis*
White-throated Monitor (E): *Varanus albigularis*
White-throated Monkey (E): *Cercopithecus erythrogaster*
White-throated Mountain-gem (E): *Lampornis castaneoventris*
White-throated Screech-Owl (E): *Otus albogularis*
White-throated Tree-kangaroo (E): *Dendrolagus ursinus*
White-tipped Sicklebill (E): *Eutoxeres aquila*
White-tufted Sunbeam (E): *Aglaeactis castelnaudii*
White-tufted-ear Marmoset (E): *Callithrix jacchus*
White-vented Plumeleteer (E): *Chalybura buffonii*
White-vented Violet-ear (E): *Colibri serrirostris*
White-whiskered Hermit (E): *Phaethornis yaruqui*
White-whiskered Spider Monkey (E): *Ateles marginatus*
White-winged Cotinga (E): *Xipholena atropurpurea*
White-winged Duck (E): *Cairina scutulata*
White-winged Flying-fox (E): *Pteropus leucopterus*
White-winged Guan (E): *Penelope albipennis*
White-winged Wood Duck (E): *Cairina scutulata*
Whooping Crane (E): *Grus americana*
Widow Titi (E): *Callicebus torquatus*
Wied's Black-tufted-ear Marmoset (E): *Callithrix kuhlii*
Wied's Marmoset (E): *Callithrix kuhlii*
Wigeon (E): *Anas penelope*
Wild Asiatic Buffalo (E): *Bubalus arnee*
Wild Cat (E): *Felis silvestris*
Wild Water Buffalo (E): *Bubalus arnee*
Wild Yak (E): *Bos mutus*
Wildcat (E): *Felis silvestris*
Wilhelmina's Lorikeet (E): *Charmosyna wilhelminae*
Wilson's Bird-of-paradise (E): *Cicinnurus respublica*
Wilson's Indigobird (E): *Vidua wilsoni*
Wine-throated Hummingbird (E): *Atthis ellioti*
Winking Owl (E): *Ninox connivens*
Wire-crested Thorntail (E): *Discosura popelairii*
Witoogaratinga (E): *Aratinga leucophthalmus*
Wolf (E): *Canis lupus*
Wolf's Monkey (E): *Cercopithecus wolfi*
Woma (E/F): *Aspidites ramsayi*
Woma (F): *Aspidites melanocephalus*
Wombat à nez poilu de Queensland (F): *Lasiorhinus krefftii*
Wood Bison (E): *Bison bison athabascae*
Wood Snake (E): *Tropidophis canus/ Tropidophis melanurus*
Wood Tortoise (E): *Geochelone carbonaria*
Wood Turtle (E): *Clemmys insculpta*
Woodford's Owl (E): *Strix woodfordii*
Woolly Indris (E): *Avahi laniger*
Woolly Lemur (E): *Avahi laniger*
Woolly Spider Monkey (E): *Brachyteles arachnoides*
Woolly Tapir (E): *Tapirus pinchaque*
Worm Coral (E): *Stenocyathus vermiformis*
Woylie (E): *Bettongia penicillata*
Wreathed Hornbill (E): *Aceros undulatus*
Wright's Dwarf Boa (E): *Tropidophis wrighti*
Wrinkled Hornbill (E): *Aceros corrugatus*
Writhed Hornbill (E): *Aceros leucocephalus*
Writhed-billed Hornbill (E): *Aceros waldeni*

Checklist of fauna/Lista de especies de fauna/Liste des espèces animales

Wurrung (E): *Onychogalea lunata*
Wurrup (E): *Lagorchestes hirsutus*
Xanthopsar flavus = Agelaius flavus
Xantus's Hummingbird (E): *Basilinna xantusii*
Xenoboa cropanii = Corallus cropanii
Xenochrophis flavipunctatum = Xenochrophis piscator
Xenochrophis piscator : (E) Asiatic Water Snake, Chequered Keelback, Common Scaled Water Snake, Fishing Snake, Rice Paddy Snake, (F) Couleuvre à damier, Couleuvre aquatique, Couleuvre d'eau asiatique, Couleuvre pêcheuse, Serpent aquatique caréné à damier **III** COLUBRIDAE Re
Xenoglaux loweryi : (E) Long-whiskered Owlet, (S) Búho pequeño de bigotes alargados, Mochuelo peludo, (F) Chevêchette nimbée, **II** STRIGIDAE Av
Xerobates agassizii = Gopherus agassizii
Xerobates berlandieri = Gopherus berlandieri
Xeromys myoides : (E) False Swamp Rat, False Water Rat, (S) Falsa rata de agua, Rata bastarda de agua, (F) Faux rat d'eau, **I** MURIDAE Ma
Xipholena atropurpurea : (E) White-winged Cotinga, (S) Cotinga aliblanca, (F) Cotinga a ailes blanches, Cotinga porphyrion, **I** COTINGIDAE Av
Yacaré (S): *Caiman yacare*
Yacare Caiman (E): *Caiman yacare*
Yacaré de hocico ancho (S): *Caiman latirostris*
Yack sauvage (F): *Bos mutus*
Yaco (S): *Psittacus erithacus*
Yacutinga cariazul (S): *Pipile pipile*
Yacutingá frentinegra (S): *Pipile jacutinga*
Yagouaso cariblanco (S): *Dendrocygna viduata*
Yaguar (S): *Panthera onca*
Yaguarete (S): *Panthera onca*
Yaguarundí (S): *Herpailurus yaguarondi*
Yaguaso colorado (S): *Dendrocygna bicolor*
Yak (S): *Bos mutus*
Yak salvaje (S): *Bos mutus*
Yallara (E): *Macrotis leucura*
Yangtze River Dolphin (E): *Lipotes vexillifer*
Yangtze Sturgeon (E): *Acipenser dabryanus*
Yarrell's Curassow (E): *Crax globulosa*
Yellow Anaconda (E): *Eunectes notaeus*
Yellow Baboon (E): *Papio hamadryas*
Yellow Blossom (E): *Epioblasma florentina*
Yellow Cardinal (E): *Gubernatrix cristata*
Yellow Land Lizard (E): *Varanus flavescens*
Yellow Mantella (E): *Mantella crocea*
Yellow Monitor (E): *Varanus flavescens*
Yellow Pencil Coral (E): *Madracis mirabilis/ Madracis myriaster*
Yellow Pond Turtle (E): *Mauremys mutica*
Yellow Riffleshell (E): *Epioblasma florentina*
Yellow Rosella (E): *Platycercus flaveolus*
Yellow Scroll Coral (E): *Turbinaria reniformis*
Yellow Seahorse (E): *Hippocampus erectus/ Hippocampus kuda*
Yellow Tortoise (E): *Indotestudo elongata*
Yellow Tree Boa (E): *Epicrates inornatus*
Yellow-and-green Lorikeet (E): *Trichoglossus flavoviridis*
Yellow-backed Duiker (E): *Cephalophus silvicultor*
Yellow-backed Lory (E): *Lorius garrulus*
Yellow-backed Weaver (E): *Ploceus melanocephalus*
Yellow-backed Whydah (E): *Euplectes macrourus*
Yellow-banded Poison Frog (E): *Dendrobates leucomelas*
Yellow-bellied Green-Pigeon (E): *Treron waalia*
Yellow-bellied Poison Frog (E): *Minyobates fulguritus*
Yellow-bellied Weasel (E): *Mustela kathiah*
Yellow-bibbed Lory (E): *Lorius chlorocercus*
Yellow-billed Amazon (E): *Amazona collaria*
Yellow-billed Cardinal (E): *Paroaria capitata*
Yellow-billed Kite (E): *Milvus migrans*
Yellow-billed Lorikeet (E): *Neopsittacus musschenbroekii*
Yellow-billed Parrot (E): *Amazona collaria*
Yellow-billed Tragopan (E): *Tragopan caboti*

Yellow-billed Turaco (E): *Tauraco macrorhynchus*
Yellow-blossom Pearly Mussel (E): *Epioblasma florentina*
Yellow-bordered Tortoise (E): *Gopherus flavomarginatus*
Yellow-breasted Bird-of-paradise (E): *Loboparadisea sericea*
Yellow-breasted Racquet-tail (E): *Prioniturus flavicans*
Yellow-capped Pygmy-Parrot (E): *Micropsitta keiensis*
Yellow-capped Weaver (E): *Ploceus preussi*
Yellow-chevroned Parakeet (E): *Brotogeris chiriri*
Yellow-collared Lovebird (E): *Agapornis personatus*
Yellow-collared Macaw (E): *Propyrrhura auricollis*
Yellow-crested Cockatoo (E): *Cacatua sulphurea*
Yellow-crowned Amazon (E): *Amazona ochrocephala*
Yellow-crowned Bishop (E): *Euplectes afer*
Yellow-crowned Parakeet (E): *Cyanoramphus auriceps*
Yellow-crowned Parrot (E): *Amazona ochrocephala*
Yellow-eared Conure (E): *Ognorhynchus icterotis*
Yellow-eared Parrot (E): *Ognorhynchus icterotis*
Yellow-faced Amazon (E): *Amazona xanthops*
Yellow-faced Parrot (E): *Amazona xanthops*
Yellow-faced Parrotlet (E): *Forpus xanthops*
Yellow-faced Siskin (E): *Carduelis yarrellii*
Yellow-footed Tortoise (E): *Geochelone denticulata*
Yellow-fronted Amazon (E): *Amazona ochrocephala*
Yellow-fronted Canary (E): *Serinus mozambicus*
Yellow-fronted Kakariki (E): *Cyanoramphus auriceps*
Yellow-fronted Parakeet (E): *Cyanoramphus auriceps*
Yellow-fronted Parrot (E): *Poicephalus flavifrons*
Yellow-green Chameleon (E): *Calumma malthe*
Yellow-headed Amazon (E): *Amazona ochrocephala oratrix*
Yellow-headed Box Turtle (E): *Cuora aurocapitata*
Yellow-headed Caracara (E): *Milvago chimachima*
Yellow-headed Parakeet (E): *Aratinga jandaya*
Yellow-headed Parrot (E): *Amazona ochrocephala oratrix*
Yellow-headed Rockfowl (E): *Picathartes gymnocephalus*
Yellow-headed Sideneck (E): *Podocnemis unifilis*
Yellow-headed Temple Turtle (E): *Hieremys annandalii*
Yellow-headed Tortoise (E): *Indotestudo elongata*
Yellowish-breasted Racquet-tail (E): *Prioniturus flavicans*
Yellow-knobbed Curassow (E): *Crax daubentoni*
Yellow-legged Owlet (E): *Glaucidium tephronotum*
Yellow-lored Amazon (E): *Amazona xantholora*
Yellow-lored Parrot (E): *Amazona xantholora*
Yellow-mantled Weaver (E): *Ploceus tricolor*
Yellow-mantled Whydah (E): *Euplectes macrourus*
Yellow-mantled Widowbird (E): *Euplectes macrourus*
Yellow-margined Box Turtle (E): *Cuora flavomarginata*
Yellow-naped Amazon (E): *Amazona ochrocephala auropalliata*
Yellow-naped Parrot (E): *Amazona ochrocephala auropalliata*
Yellow-shouldered Amazon (E): *Amazona barbadensis*
Yellow-shouldered Parrot (E): *Amazona barbadensis*
Yellow-shouldered Widowbird (E): *Euplectes macrourus*
Yellow-spotted River Turtle (E): *Podocnemis unifilis*
Yellow-spotted Sideneck Turtle (E): *Podocnemis unifilis*
Yellow-streaked Lory (E): *Chalcopsitta scintillata*
Yellow-striped Poison Frog (E): *Dendrobates truncatus*
Yellow-tailed Black-Cockatoo (E): *Calyptorhynchus funereus*
Yellow-tailed Woolly Monkey (E): *Lagothrix flavicauda*
Yellow-throated Caracara (E): *Daptrius ater*
Yellow-throated Day Gecko (E): *Phelsuma flavigularis*
Yellow-throated Hanging-Parrot (E): *Loriculus pusillus*
Yellow-throated Marten (E): *Martes flavigula*
Yellow-winged Pytilia (E): *Pytilia hypogrammica*
Yemen Monitor (E): *Varanus yemenensis*
Youyou (F): *Poicephalus senegalus*
Yucatan Parrot (E): *Amazona xantholora*
Yucatan Rusty-rumped Tarantula (E): *Brachypelma epicureanum*
Yungas Pygmy-Owl (E): *Glaucidium bolivianum*
Yunnan Box Turtle (E): *Cuora yunnanensis*
Yunnan Snub-nosed Monkey (E): *Pygathrix bieti*

Zacatuche (S): *Romerolagus diazi*
Zafiro barbiazul (S): *Chlorostilbon notatus*
Zafiro bronceado (S): *Hylocharis chrysura*
Zafiro cabeciazul (S): *Hylocharis grayi*
Zafiro cabecimorado (S): *Hylocharis cyanus*
Zafiro capirotado (S): *Thalurania glaucopis*
Zafiro colidorado (S): *Chrysuronia oenone*
Zafiro colilargo (S): *Thalurania watertonii*
Zafiro coroniazul (S): *Thalurania colombica*
Zafiro coroniverde (S): *Thalurania fannyi*
Zafiro de Elicia (S): *Hylocharis eliciae*
Zafiro gargantirrufo (S): *Hylocharis sapphirina*
Zafiro golondrina (S): *Thalurania furcata*
Zafiro gorgiblanco (S): *Hylocharis cyanus*
Zafiro gorgirrojo (S): *Hylocharis sapphirina*
Zafiro gorjiazul (S): *Hylocharis eliciae*
Zafiro Mexicano (S): *Thalurania ridgwayi*
Zaglossus spp.: (E) Long-nosed echidnas, (S) Equidna, (F) Echnidé à bec courbe, **II** TACHYGLOSSIDAE Ma
Zaglossus attenboroughi : **II** TACHYGLOSSIDAE Ma
Zaglossus bartoni = Zaglossus bruijni
Zaglossus bruijni : (E) Long-beaked Echidna, Long-nosed Echidna, Long-nosed Spiny Anteater, New Guinea Long-nosed Echidna, (S) Echidnos narilargos, Equidna de Nueva Guinea, (F) Echidné à bec courbe, Echidné de Nouvelle-Guinée, **II** TACHYGLOSSIDAE Ma
Zaino Javelina (S): *Pecari tajacu*
Zaire Clawless Otter (E): *Aonyx congicus*
Zaire Toad (E): *Bufo superciliaris*
Zamarrito canoso (S): *Haplophaedia lugens*
Zamarrito colilargo (S): *Eriocnemis luciani*
Zamarrito gorjiturquesa (S): *Eriocnemis godini*
Zamarrito luciente (S): *Eriocnemis vestitus*
Zamarrito muslinegro (S): *Eriocnemis derbyi*
Zamarrito pechiblanco (S): *Eriocnemis alinae*
Zamarrito pechidorado (S): *Eriocnemis mosquera*
Zamarrito pechinegro (S): *Eriocnemis nigrivestis*
Zamarrito verdoso (S): *Haplophaedia aureliae*
Zambullidor de Atitlán (S): *Podilymbus gigas*
Zampullín del Atitlán (S): *Podilymbus gigas*
Zanzibar Bushbaby (E): *Galagoides zanzibaricus*
Zanzibar Day Gecko (E): *Phelsuma dubia*
Zanzibar Galago (E): *Galagoides zanzibaricus*
Zanzibar Red Colobus (E): *Procolobus pennantii kirkii*
Zaparo's Poison Frog (E): *Epipedobates zaparo*
Zaraguate (S): *Alouatta palliata*
Zarapito boreal (S): *Numenius borealis*
Zarapito esquimal (S): *Numenius borealis*
Zarapito fino (S): *Numenius tenuirostris*
Zarapito polar (S): *Numenius borealis*
Zebra Antelope (E): *Cephalophus zebra*
Zebra Coral (E): *Oulastrea crispata*
Zebra Duiker (E): *Cephalophus zebra*
Zebra Seahorse (E): *Hippocampus zebra*
Zebra Waxbill (E): *Amandava subflava*
Zèbre de Grévy (F): *Equus grevyi*
Zèbre de Hartmann (F): *Equus zebra hartmannae*
Zèbre de montagne de Hartmann (F): *Equus zebra hartmannae*
Zèbre de montagne du Cap (F): *Equus zebra zebra*
Zetek's Golden Frog (E): *Atelopus zeteki*
Zhou's Box Turtle (E): *Cuora zhoui*
Zigzag corals (E): *Euphyllia* spp.
Zimbabwe Girdled Lizard (E): *Cordylus rhodesianus*
Zimbador centroamericano (S): *Atthis ellioti*
Zimbador mexicano (S): *Atthis heloisa*
Ziphio de Cuvier (S): *Ziphius cavirostris*
Ziphius (F): *Ziphius cavirostris*
Ziphius cavirostris : (E) Cuvier's Beaked Whale, Goose-beaked Whale, (S) Ballena de Cuvier, Ziphio de Cuvier, (F) Ziphius, **II** ZIPHIIDAE Ma
Zone-tailed Hawk (E): *Buteo albonotatus*
Zoopilus echinatus : (E) Chinaman's Hat **II** FUNGIIDAE An

Zopilote negro (S): *Coragyps atratus*
Zopilote rey (S): *Sarcoramphus papa*
Zorrillo (S): *Conepatus humboldtii*
Zorrino de la Patagonia (S): *Conepatus humboldtii*
Zorro andino (S): *Pseudalopex culpaeus*
Zorro cangrejero (S): *Cerdocyon thous*
Zorro chico (S): *Pseudalopex griseus*
Zorro colorado (S): *Pseudalopex culpaeus*
Zorro de Bengala (S): *Vulpes bengalensis*
Zorro de Blanford (S): *Vulpes cana*
Zorro de la Isla Chiloe (S): *Pseudalopex griseus*
Zorro de la Pampa (S): *Pseudalopex gymnocercus*
Zorro de monte (S): *Cerdocyon thous*
Zorro del Sahara (S): *Vulpes zerda*
Zorro gris argentino (S): *Pseudalopex griseus*
Zorro vinagre (S): *Speothos venaticus*
Zorro volador argénteo (S): *Pteropus argentatus*
Zorro volador de Aldabra (S): *Pteropus aldabrensis*
Zorro volador de Amboina (S): *Pteropus chrysoproctus*
Zorro volador de Andaman (S): *Pteropus melanotus*
Zorro volador de anteojos (S): *Pteropus conspicillatus*
Zorro volador de barba negra (S): *Pteropus melanopogon*
Zorro volador de Bismarck (S): *Pteropus neohibernicus*
Zorro volador de Bougainville (S): *Pteropus mahaganus*
Zorro volador de cabeza cenicienta (S): *Pteropus caniceps*
Zorro volador de cabeza gris (S): *Pteropus poliocephalus*
Zorro volador de Calamian (S): *Acerodon leucotis*
Zorro volador de cuello rojo (S): *Pteropus vampyrus*
Zorro volador de Gilliard (S): *Pteropus gilliardi*
Zorro volador de Howens (S): *Pteropus howensis*
Zorro volador de la India (S): *Pteropus giganteus*
Zorro volador de la isla Jawi (S): *Pteropus tuberculatus*
Zorro volador de la isla Malawi (S): *Pteropus speciosus*
Zorro volador de la isla Ndeni (S): *Pteropus nitendiensis*
Zorro volador de la isla Panay (S): *Acerodon lucifer*
Zorro volador de la isla Rodrígues (S): *Pteropus rodricensis*
Zorro volador de la isla Santa Cruz (S): *Pteropus sanctacrucis*
Zorro volador de las Célebes (S): *Acerodon celebensis*
Zorro volador de las isla Bonin (S): *Pteropus pselaphon*
Zorro volador de las isla Ceram (S): *Pteropus ocularis*
Zorro volador de las isla Japen (S): *Pteropus pohlei*
Zorro volador de las islas Banks (S): *Pteropus fundatus*
Zorro volador de las islas de almirantazgo (S): *Pteropus admiralitatum*
Zorro volador de las islas de la Leal (S): *Pteropus ornatus*
Zorro volador de las islas Palau (S): *Pteropus pilosus*
Zorro volador de las islas Percy (S): *Pteropus brunneus*
Zorro volador de las Salomón (S): *Pteropus rayneri*
Zorro volador de las Seychelles (S): *Pteropus seychellensis*
Zorro volador de Livingston (S): *Pteropus livingstonei*
Zorro volador de Lombok (S): *Pteropus lombocensis*
Zorro volador de Luzón (S): *Pteropus leucopterus*
Zorro volador de Lyle (S): *Pteropus lylei*
Zorro volador de Macklot (S): *Acerodon mackloti*
Zorro volador de Madagascar (S): *Pteropus rufus*
Zorro volador de Mearns (S): *Pteropus mearnsi*
Zorro volador de Nueva Caledonia (S): *Pteropus vetulus*
Zorro volador de orejas grandes (S): *Pteropus macrotis*
Zorro volador de Queensland (S): *Pteropus scapulatus*
Zorro volador de Ryu-Kyu (S): *Pteropus dasymallus*
Zorro volador de Talaud (S): *Acerodon humilis*
Zorro volador de Taylor (S): *Pteropus pumilus*
Zorro volador de Temminck (S): *Pteropus temmincki*
Zorro volador de Tokuda (S): *Pteropus tokudae*
Zorro volador de Voeltzkow (S): *Pteropus voeltzkowi*
Zorro volador de Woodford (S): *Pteropus woodfordi*
Zorro volador enmascarado (S): *Pteropus personatus*
Zorro volador filipino (S): *Acerodon jubatus*
Zorro volador gris (S): *Pteropus griseus*
Zorro volador negro (S): *Pteropus alecto*
Zorro volador negro de Mauricio (S): *Pteropus niger*
Zorro volador oscuro de Mauricio (S): *Pteropus subniger*

Checklist of fauna/Lista de especies de fauna/Liste des espèces animales

Zorro volador pequeño (S): *Pteropus hypomelanus*
Zorros voladores (S): *Acerodon* spp. / *Pteropus* spp.
Zostérops à gorge blanche de l'île de Norfolk (F):
    Zosterops albogularis
Zostérops à poitrine blanche (F): *Zosterops albogularis*
Zosterops albogularis : (E) White-breasted Silvereye,
    White-breasted White-eye, White-chested White-eye,
    (S) Ave de anteojos de pecho blanco, Gafudo
    gorgiblanco, (F) Zostérops à gorge blanche de l'île de
    Norfolk, Zostérops à poitrine blanche, Zosterops de
    l'île de Norfolk, **I** ZOSTEROPIDAE Av
Zosterops de l'île de Norfolk (F): *Zosterops albogularis*
Zoutpansberg Girdled Lizard (E): *Cordylus depressus*
Zululand Dwarf Chameleon (E): *Bradypodion nemorale*
Zumbador (S): *Chlorostilbon swainsonii*
Zumbador coliancho (S): *Selasphorus platycercus*
Zumbador de Allen (S): *Selasphorus sasin*
Zumbador grande (S): *Anthracothorax dominicus*
Zumbador rufo (S): *Selasphorus rufus*
Zumbadorcito (S): *Mellisuga minima*
Zyzomys pedunculatus : (E) Central Rock Rat, Central
    Thick-tailed Rock Rat, Macdonnell Range Rock-rat,
    (S) Rata coligorda, (F) Rat à grosse queue, **I**
    MURIDAE Ma

CHECKLIST OF FLORA

LISTA DE ESPECIES DE FLORA

LISTE DES ESPECES VEGETALES

Aa spp.: #7 **II** ORCHIDACEAE
Abdominea spp.: #7 **II** ORCHIDACEAE
Abeto mexicano (S): *Abies guatemalensis*
Abies araucana = *Araucaria araucana*
Abies columbaria = *Araucaria araucana*
Abies flinckii = *Abies guatemalensis* var. *jaliscana*
Acanthocalycium glaucum = *Echinopsis glaucina*
Abies guatemalensis: (E) Guatemala fir, (S) Abeto mexicano,
   Pinabete **I** PINACEAE
Abies guatemalensis var. *guatemalensis*: **I** PINACEAE
Abies guatemalensis var. *ixtepejiensis* = *Abies guatemalensis* var.
   guatemalensis
Abies guatemalensis var. *jaliscana*: **I** PINACEAE
Abies guatemalensis var. *longibracteata* = *Abies guatemalensis*
   var. *guatemalensis*
Abies guatemalensis var. *rushforthii* = *Abies guatemalensis* var.
   guatemalensis
Abies guatemalensis var. *tacanensis* = *Abies guatemalensis* var.
   guatemalensis
Abies guatemalensis var. *tamaulipensis* = *Abies guatemalensis* var.
   guatemalensis
Abies religiosa = *Abies guatemalensis* var. *jaliscana*
Abies tacanensis = *Abies guatemalensis* var. *guatemalensis*
Abies zapotekensis = *Abies guatemalensis* var. *guatemalensis*
Abola = *Caucaea*
Aboriginal prickly-apple cactus (E): *Harrisia aboriginum*
Acacallis = *Aganisia*
Acajou d'Amérique (F): *Swietenia macrophylla*
Acajou des Antilles (F): *Swietenia macrophylla*
Acampe spp.: #7 **II** ORCHIDACEAE
Acanthephippium spp.: #7 **II** ORCHIDACEAE
Acanthocalycium andreaeanum = *Eriosyce andreaeana*
Acanthocalycium aurantiacum = *Echinopsis glaucina*
Acanthocalycium brevispinum = *Echinopsis thionantha*
Acanthocalycium catamarcense = *Echinopsis thionantha*
Acanthocalycium chionanthum = *Echinopsis thionantha*
Acanthocalycium ferrarii: #4 **II** CACTACEAE
Acanthocalycium glaucum = *Echinopsis thionantha*
Acanthocalycium griseum = *Echinopsis thionantha*
Acanthocalycium klimpelianum: #4 **II** CACTACEAE
Acanthocalycium peitscherianum = *Acanthocalycium klimpelianum*
Acanthocalycium spiniflorum: #4 **II** CACTACEAE
Acanthocalycium thionanthum = *Echinopsis thionantha*
Acanthocalycium variiflorum = *Acanthocalycium ferrarii*
Acanthocalycium violaceum = *Acanthocalycium spiniflorum*
Acanthocereus albicaulis = *Cereus albicaulis*
Acanthocereus baxaniensis: #4 **II** CACTACEAE
Acanthocereus brasiliensis = *Pseudoacanthocereus brasiliensis*
Acanthocereus colombianus: #4 **II** CACTACEAE
Acanthocereus floridanus = *Acanthocereus tetragonus*
Acanthocereus horridus: #4 **II** CACTACEAE
Acanthocereus maculatus = *Peniocereus maculatus*
Acanthocereus occidentalis: #4 **II** CACTACEAE
Acanthocereus pentagonus = *Acanthocereus tetragonus*
Acanthocereus sicariguensis = *Pseudoacanthocereus sicariguensis*
Acanthocereus subinermis: #4 **II** CACTACEAE
Acanthocereus tetragonus: (E) Barbwire apple-cactus, Liane-
   raquette #4 **II** CACTACEAE
Acanthocereus undulosus = *Dendrocereus undulosus*
Acanthoglossum = *Pholidota*
Acantholobivia incuiensis = *Echinopsis tegeleriana*
Acantholobivia tegeleriana = *Echinopsis tegeleriana*
Acanthophippium = *Acanthephippium*
Acanthorhipsalis brevispina = *Lepismium brevispinum*
Acanthorhipsalis crenata = *Lepismium crenatum*
Acanthorhipsalis houlletiana = *Lepismium houlletianum*
Acanthorhipsalis incachacana = *Lepismium incachacanum*
Acanthorhipsalis incahuasina = *Lepismium monacanthum*
Acanthorhipsalis micrantha = *Lepismium micranthum*
Acanthorhipsalis monacantha = *Lepismium monacanthum*
Acanthorhipsalis paranganiensis = *Lepismium paranganiense*
Acanthorhipsalis samaipatana = *Lepismium monacanthum*
Aceras spp.: #7 **II** ORCHIDACEAE
Aceratorchis spp.: #7 **II** ORCHIDACEAE
Acharagma aguirreana = *Escobaria aguirreana*

Achroanthes = *Malaxis*
Acianthera = *Pleurothallis*
Acianthus spp.: #7 **II** ORCHIDACEAE
Acineta spp.: #7 **II** ORCHIDACEAE
Aclinia = *Dendrobium*
Acoidium = *Trichocentrum*
Acoridium = *Dendrochilum*
Acostaea spp.: #7 **II** ORCHIDACEAE
Acraea = *Pterichis*
Acriopsis spp.: #7 **II** ORCHIDACEAE
Acroanthes = *Malaxis*
Acrochaene = *Monomeria*
Acrolophia spp.: #7 **II** ORCHIDACEAE
Acronia = *Pleurothallis*
Acropera = *Gongora*
Acrorchis spp.: #7 **II** ORCHIDACEAE
Acrostylia = *Cynorkis*
Acuña cactus (E): *Sclerocactus erectocentrus* var. *acunensis*
Ada spp.: #7 **II** ORCHIDACEAE
Adactylus = *Apostasia*
Adelopetalum = *Bulbophyllum*
Adeneleuterophora = *Elleanthus*
Adenium namaquanum = *Pachypodium namaquanum*
Adenochilus spp.: #7 **II** ORCHIDACEAE
Adenoncos spp.: #7 **II** ORCHIDACEAE
Adenostylis = *Zeuxine*
Adipe = *Bifrenaria*
Adnula = *Pelexia*
Adonide du printemps (F): *Adonis vernalis*
Adonis appennina = *Adonis vernalis*
Adonis davurica = *Adonis vernalis*
Adonis helleborus = *Adonis vernalis*
Adonis ircutiana = *Adonis vernalis*
Adonis parviflora = *Adonis vernalis*
Adonis vernalis: (E) Spring adonis, Spring pheasant's-eye, Yellow
   adonis, (S) Sello de oro, Yerba de Adonis (F) Adonide du
   printemps, #2 **II** RANUNCULACEAE
Adrorhizon spp.: #7 **II** ORCHIDACEAE
Aeonia = *Oeonia*
Aerangis alata = *Aerangis ellisii*
Aerangis caulescens = *Aerangis ellisii*
Aerangis cryptodon = *Aerangis ellisii*
Aerangis ellisii: **I** ORCHIDACEAE
Aerangis platyphylla = *Aerangis ellisii*
Aerangis spp.: #7 **II** ORCHIDACEAE
Aeranthes spp.: #7 **II** ORCHIDACEAE
Aerides spp.: #7 **II** ORCHIDACEAE
Aeridium = *Aerides*
Aeridostachya = *Eria*
Aerobion = *Angraecum*
Aetheria = *Stenorrhynchos*
African cherry (E): *Prunus africana*
African teak (E): *Pericopsis elata*
Afrormosia (S): *Pericopsis elata*
Afrormosia elata = *Pericopsis elata*
Aganisia spp.: #7 **II** ORCHIDACEAE
Agarwood (E): *Aquilaria malaccensis*
Agave arizonica: (E) Arizona agave, New River agave **I**
   AGAVACEAE
Agave cactus (E): *Leuchtenbergia principis*
Agave parviflora: (E) Santa Cruz striped agave **I** AGAVACEAE
Agave victoriae-reginae: (E) Queen agave, Queen Victoria agave
   #1 **II** AGAVACEAE
Aggeianthus = *Porpax*
Aglossorhyncha spp.: #7 **II** ORCHIDACEAE
Aguano (S): *Swietenia macrophylla*
Ahuano (S): *Swietenia macrophylla*
Agrostophyllum spp.: #7 **II** ORCHIDACEAE
Aguano (S): *Swietenia macrophylla*
Ajillo (S): *Caryocar costaricense*
Ajo (S): *Caryocar costaricense*
Alabama canebreak pitcher plant (E): *Sarracenia alabamensis*
Alamania spp.: #7 **II** ORCHIDACEAE
Alerce (S): *Fitzroya cupressoides*
Alipsea = *Liparis*

Alismorkis = *Calanthe*
Allochilus = *Goodyera*
Alluaudia ascendens: #1 **II** DIDIEREACEAE
Alluaudia comosa: #1 **II** DIDIEREACEAE
Alluaudia dumosa: #1 **II** DIDIEREACEAE
Alluaudia geayi: #1 **II** DIDIEREACEAE
Alluaudia humbertii: #1 **II** DIDIEREACEAE
Alluaudia montagnacii: #1 **II** DIDIEREACEAE
Alluaudia procera: (F) Arbre pieuvre **II** DIDIEREACEAE
Alluaudias (E): DIDIEREACEAE spp.
Alluaudiopsis fiherenensis: #1 **II** DIDIEREACEAE
Alluaudiopsis marnieriana: #1 **II** DIDIEREACEAE
Almendrillo (S): *Caryocar costaricense*
Almendrón (S): *Caryocar costaricense*
Aloe spp.: (E) aloes, (F) aloès #1 **I/II** LILIACEAE
Aloe aageodonta: #1 **II** LILIACEAE
Aloe abyssicola: #1 **II** LILIACEAE
Aloe abyssinica = *Aloe adigratana*
Aloe abyssinica = *Aloe camperi*
Aloe abyssinica = *Aloe elegans*
Aloe abyssinica var. *peacockii* = *Aloe elegans*
Aloe abyssinica var. *percrassa* = *Aloe percrassa*
Aloe aculeata: #1 **II** LILIACEAE
Aloe acuminata = *Aloe humilis*
Aloe acuminata var. *major* = *Aloe humilis*
Aloe acutissima: #1 **II** LILIACEAE
Aloe acutissima var. *acutissima*: #1 **II** LILIACEAE
Aloe acutissima var. *antanimorensis*: #1 **II** LILIACEAE
Aloe adigratana: #1 **II** LILIACEAE
Aloe aethiopica = *Aloe elegans*
Aloe affinis: #1 **II** LILIACEAE
Aloe africana: #1 **II** LILIACEAE
Aloe africana var. *angustior* = *Aloe africana*
Aloe africana var. *latifolia* = *Aloe africana*
Aloe agrophila = *Aloe boylei*
Aloe ahmarensis: #1 **II** LILIACEAE
Aloe albida: **I** LILIACEAE
Aloe albiflora: **I** LILIACEAE
Aloe albocincta = *Aloe striata* ssp. *striata*
Aloe albopicta = *Aloe camperi*
Aloe albovestita: #1 **II** LILIACEAE
Aloe aldabrensis: #1 **II** LILIACEAE
Aloe alfredii: **I** LILIACEAE
Aloe alooides: #1 **II** LILIACEAE
Aloe amanensis = *Aloe lateritia* var. *lateritia*
Aloe ambigens: #1 **II** LILIACEAE
Aloe amicorum: #1 **II** LILIACEAE
Aloe ammophila = *Aloe zebrina*
Aloe amoena = *Aloe framesii*
Aloe amudatensis: #1 **II** LILIACEAE
Aloe andongensis: #1 **II** LILIACEAE
Aloe andongensis var. *andongensis*: #1 **II** LILIACEAE
Aloe andongensis var. *repens*: #1 **II** LILIACEAE
Aloe andringitrensis: #1 **II** LILIACEAE
Aloe angelica: #1 **II** LILIACEAE
Aloe angiensis = *Aloe wollastonii*
Aloe angiensis var. *kitalensis* = *Aloe wollastonii*
Aloe angolensis: #1 **II** LILIACEAE
Aloe angustifolia = *Aloe africana*
Aloe angustifolia = *Aloe zebrina*
Aloe anivoranoensis: #1 **II** LILIACEAE
Aloe ankaranensis: #1 **II** LILIACEAE
Aloe ankoberensis: #1 **II** LILIACEAE
Aloe antandroi: #1 **II** LILIACEAE
Aloe antsingyensis: #1 **II** LILIACEAE
Aloe arabica = *Aloe pendens*
Aloe arborea = *Aloe arborescens*
Aloe arborescens: (E) Candelabra aloe, Octopus plant, Torch plant #1 **II** LILIACEAE
Aloe arborescens var. *frutescens* = *Aloe arborescens*
Aloe arborescens var. *milleri* = *Aloe arborescens*
Aloe arborescens var. *natalensis* = *Aloe arborescens*
Aloe arborescens var. *pachythyrsa* = *Aloe arborescens*
Aloe archeri: #1 **II** LILIACEAE
Aloe arenicola: #1 **II** LILIACEAE

Aloe argenticauda: #1 **II** LILIACEAE
Aloe aristata: #1 **II** LILIACEAE
Aloe aristata var. *leiophyllia* = *Aloe aristata*
Aloe aristata var. *parvifolia* = *Aloe aristata*
Aloe armatissima: #1 **II** LILIACEAE
Aloe asperifolia: #1 **II** LILIACEAE
Aloe atherstonei = *Aloe pluridens*
Aloe audhalica = *Aloe vacillans*
Aloe aurantiaca = *Aloe striatula* var. *striatula*
Aloe ausana = *Aloe variegata*
Aloe babatiensis: #1 **II** LILIACEAE
Aloe bainesii = *Aloe barberae*
Aloe bainesii var. *barberae* = *Aloe barberae*
Aloe bakeri: **I** LILIACEAE
Aloe ballii: #1 **II** LILIACEAE
Aloe ballii var. *ballii*: #1 **II** LILIACEAE
Aloe ballii var. *makurupiniensis*: #1 **II** LILIACEAE
Aloe ballyi: (E) Rat aloe #1 **II** LILIACEAE
Aloe bamangwatensis = *Aloe zebrina*
Aloe barberae: #1 **II** LILIACEAE
Aloe barbertoniae: #1 **II** LILIACEAE
Aloe bargalensis: #1 **II** LILIACEAE
Aloe barteri = *Aloe buettneri*
Aloe barteri = *Aloe macrocarpa*
Aloe barteri var. *dahomensis* = *Aloe buettneri*
Aloe barteri var. *lutea* = *Aloe schweinfurthii*
Aloe barteri var. *sudanica* = *Aloe buettneri*
Aloe belavenokensis: #1 **II** LILIACEAE
Aloe bella: #1 **II** LILIACEAE
Aloe bellatula: **I** LILIACEAE
Aloe beniensis = *Aloe dawei*
Aloe bequaertii = *Aloe wollastonii*
Aloe berevoana: #1 **II** LILIACEAE
Aloe berhana = *Aloe debrana*
Aloe bernadettae: #1 **II** LILIACEAE
Aloe bertemariae: #1 **II** LILIACEAE
Aloe betsileensis: #1 **II** LILIACEAE
Aloe bicomitum: #1 **II** LILIACEAE
Aloe boastii = *Aloe chortolirioides* var. *chortolirioides*
Aloe boehmii = *Aloe lateritia* var. *lateritia*
Aloe boiteaui: #1 **II** LILIACEAE
Aloe bolusii = *Aloe africana*
Aloe boranensis = *Aloe otallensis*
Aloe boscawenii: #1 **II** LILIACEAE
Aloe bosseri: #1 **II** LILIACEAE
Aloe bowiea: #1 **II** LILIACEAE
Aloe boylei: #1 **II** LILIACEAE
Aloe boylei ssp. *boylei*: #1 **II** LILIACEAE
Aloe boylei ssp. *major*: #1 **II** LILIACEAE
Aloe brachystachys: #1 **II** LILIACEAE
Aloe branddraaiensis: #1 **II** LILIACEAE
Aloe brandhamii: #1 **II** LILIACEAE
Aloe brevifolia = *Aloe distans*
Aloe brevifolia: #1 **II** LILIACEAE
Aloe brevifolia var. *brevifolia*: #1 **II** LILIACEAE
Aloe brevifolia var. *depressa*: #1 **II** LILIACEAE
Aloe brevifolia var. *postgenita*: #1 **II** LILIACEAE
Aloe brevifolia var. *serra* = *Aloe brevifolia* var. *depressa*
Aloe breviscapa: #1 **II** LILIACEAE
Aloe broomii: #1 **II** LILIACEAE
Aloe broomii var. *broomii*: #1 **II** LILIACEAE
Aloe broomii var. *tarkaensis*: #1 **II** LILIACEAE
Aloe brunneodentata: #1 **II** LILIACEAE
Aloe brunneo-punctata = *Aloe nuttii*
Aloe brunneostriata: #1 **II** LILIACEAE
Aloe brunnthaleri = *Aloe microstigma*
Aloe buchananii: #1 **II** LILIACEAE
Aloe buchlohii: #1 **II** LILIACEAE
Aloe buettneri: #1 **II** LILIACEAE
Aloe buhrii: #1 **II** LILIACEAE
Aloe bukobana: #1 **II** LILIACEAE
Aloe bulbicaulis: #1 **II** LILIACEAE
Aloe bulbillifera: #1 **II** LILIACEAE
Aloe bulbillifera var. *bulbillifera*: #1 **II** LILIACEAE
Aloe bulbillifera var. *paulianae*: #1 **II** LILIACEAE

Checklist of flora/Lista de especies de flora/Liste des espèces végétales

Aloe bullockii: #1 **II** LILIACEAE
Aloe burgersfortensis: #1 **II** LILIACEAE
Aloe bussei: #1 **II** LILIACEAE
Aloe calcairophila: **I** LILIACEAE
Aloe calcairophylla = *Aloe calcairophila*
Aloe calidophila: #1 **II** LILIACEAE
Aloe cameronii: #1 **II** LILIACEAE
Aloe cameronii var. *bondana*: #1 **II** LILIACEAE
Aloe cameronii var. *cameronii*: #1 **II** LILIACEAE
Aloe cameronii var. *dedzana*: #1 **II** LILIACEAE
Aloe camperi: #1 **II** LILIACEAE
Aloe campylosiphon = *Aloe lateritia* var. *lateritia*
Aloe canarina: #1 **II** LILIACEAE
Aloe candelabrum = *Aloe ferox*
Aloe candelabrum = *Aloe thraskii*
Aloe cannellii: #1 **II** LILIACEAE
Aloe capitata: #1 **II** LILIACEAE
Aloe capitata var. *capitata*: #1 **II** LILIACEAE
Aloe capitata var. *cipolinicola*: #1 **II** LILIACEAE
Aloe capitata var. *gneissicola*: #1 **II** LILIACEAE
Aloe capitata var. *quartziticola*: #1 **II** LILIACEAE
Aloe capitata var. *silvicola*: #1 **II** LILIACEAE
Aloe capitata var. *trachyticola* = *Aloe trachyticola*
Aloe capmanambatoensis: #1 **II** LILIACEAE
Aloe caricina = *Aloe myriacantha*
Aloe carnea: #1 **II** LILIACEAE
Aloe carowii = *Aloe sladeniana*
Aloe cascandensis = *Aloe striatula* var. *striatula*
Aloe castanea: #1 **II** LILIACEAE
Aloe castellorum: #1 **II** LILIACEAE
Aloe catengiana: #1 **II** LILIACEAE
Aloe cephalophora: #1 **II** LILIACEAE
Aloe cernua = *Aloe capitata* var. *capitata*
Aloe chabaudii: #1 **II** LILIACEAE
Aloe chabaudii var. *chabaudii*: #1 **II** LILIACEAE
Aloe chabaudii var. *mlanjeana*: #1 **II** LILIACEAE
Aloe chabaudii var. *verekeri*: #1 **II** LILIACEAE
Aloe cheranganiensis: #1 **II** LILIACEAE
Aloe chimanimaniensis = *Aloe swynnertonii*
Aloe chlorantha: #1 **II** LILIACEAE
Aloe chortolirioides: #1 **II** LILIACEAE
Aloe chortolirioides var. *boastii* = *Aloe chortolirioides* var. *chortolirioides*
Aloe chortolirioides var. *chortolirioides*: #1 **II** LILIACEAE
Aloe chortolirioides var. *woolliana*: #1 **II** LILIACEAE
Aloe christianii: #1 **II** LILIACEAE
Aloe chrysostachys: #1 **II** LILIACEAE
Aloe ciliaris: #1 **II** LILIACEAE
Aloe ciliaris f. *flanaganii* = *Aloe ciliaris* var. *ciliaris*
Aloe ciliaris f. *gigas* = *Aloe ciliaris* var. *ciliaris*
Aloe ciliaris f. *tidmarshii* = *Aloe ciliaris* var. *tidmarshii*
Aloe ciliaris var. *ciliaris*: #1 **II** LILIACEAE
Aloe ciliaris var. *flanaganii* = *Aloe ciliaris* var. *ciliaris*
Aloe ciliaris var. *redacta*: #1 **II** LILIACEAE
Aloe ciliaris var. *tidmarshii*: #1 **II** LILIACEAE
Aloe citrea: #1 **II** LILIACEAE
Aloe citrina: #1 **II** LILIACEAE
Aloe classenii: #1 **II** LILIACEAE
Aloe claviflora: #1 **II** LILIACEAE
Aloe collenetteae: #1 **II** LILIACEAE
Aloe collina: #1 **II** LILIACEAE
Aloe commixta: #1 **II** LILIACEAE
Aloe commutata = *Aloe macrocarpa*
Aloe comosa: (E) Clanwilliam aloe #1 **II** LILIACEAE
Aloe comosibracteata = *Aloe greatheadii* var. *davyana*
Aloe compacta = *Aloe macrosiphon*
Aloe compressa: **I** LILIACEAE
Aloe compressa var. *compressa*: **I** LILIACEAE
Aloe compressa var. *paucituberculata*: **I** LILIACEAE
Aloe compressa var. *rugosquamosa*: **I** LILIACEAE
Aloe compressa var. *schistophila*: **I** LILIACEAE
Aloe comptonii: #1 **II** LILIACEAE
Aloe concinna = *Aloe squarrosa*
Aloe confusa: #1 **II** LILIACEAE
Aloe congdonii: #1 **II** LILIACEAE

Aloe conifera: #1 **II** LILIACEAE
Aloe contigua = *Aloe imalotensis*
Aloe cooperi: #1 **II** LILIACEAE
Aloe cooperi ssp. *cooperi*: #1 **II** LILIACEAE
Aloe cooperi ssp. *pulchra*: #1 **II** LILIACEAE
Aloe corallina: #1 **II** LILIACEAE
Aloe corbisieri = *Aloe nuttii*
Aloe crassipes: #1 **II** LILIACEAE
Aloe cremersii: #1 **II** LILIACEAE
Aloe cremnophila: #1 **II** LILIACEAE
Aloe cryptoflora: #1 **II** LILIACEAE
Aloe cryptopoda: #1 **II** LILIACEAE
Aloe cyrtophylla: #1 **II** LILIACEAE
Aloe dabenorisana: #1 **II** LILIACEAE
Aloe davyana = *Aloe greatheadii* var. *davyana*
Aloe davyana var. *subolifera* = *Aloe greatheadii* var. *davyana*
Aloe dawei: #1 **II** LILIACEAE
Aloe debrana: #1 **II** LILIACEAE
Aloe decora = *Aloe claviflora*
Aloe decorsei: #1 **II** LILIACEAE
Aloe decurva: #1 **II** LILIACEAE
Aloe decurvidens = *Aloe parvibracteata*
Aloe delphinensis: **I** LILIACEAE
Aloe deltoideodonta: #1 **II** LILIACEAE
Aloe deltoideodonta f. *latifolia* = *Aloe imalotensis*
Aloe deltoideodonta f. *longifolia* = *Aloe imalotensis*
Aloe deltoideodonta subforma *variegata* = *Aloe imalotensis*
Aloe deltoideodonta var. *brevifolia*: #1 **II** LILIACEAE
Aloe deltoideodonta var. *candicans*: #1 **II** LILIACEAE
Aloe deltoideodonta var. *contigua* = *Aloe imalotensis*
Aloe deltoideodonta var. *deltoideodonta*: #1 **II** LILIACEAE
Aloe deltoideodonta var. *intermedia* = *Aloe subacutissima*
Aloe deltoideodonta var. *typica* = *Aloe deltoideodonta* var. *deltoideodonta*
Aloe dependens = *Aloe pendens*
Aloe depressa = *Aloe brevifolia* var. *depressa*
Aloe descoingsii: **I** LILIACEAE
Aloe descoingsii ssp. *augustina*: #1 **II** LILIACEAE
Aloe descoingsii ssp. *descoingsii*: #1 **II** LILIACEAE
Aloe deserti: #1 **II** LILIACEAE
Aloe dewetii: #1 **II** LILIACEAE
Aloe dewinteri: #1 **II** LILIACEAE
Aloe dhalensis = *Aloe vacillans*
Aloe dhufarensis: #1 **II** LILIACEAE
Aloe dichotoma: #1 **II** LILIACEAE
Aloe dichotoma var. *montana* = *Aloe dichotoma*
Aloe dichotoma var. *ramosissima* = *Aloe ramosissima*
Aloe dinteri: #1 **II** LILIACEAE
Aloe diolii: #1 **II** LILIACEAE
Aloe distans: #1 **II** LILIACEAE
Aloe disticha = *Aloe maculata*
Aloe disticha var. *plicatilis* = *Aloe plicatilis*
Aloe divaricata: #1 **II** LILIACEAE
Aloe divaricata var. *divaricata*: #1 **II** LILIACEAE
Aloe divaricata var. *rosea*: #1 **II** LILIACEAE
Aloe doei: #1 **II** LILIACEAE
Aloe doei var. *doei*: #1 **II** LILIACEAE
Aloe doei var. *lavranosii*: #1 **II** LILIACEAE
Aloe dolomitica = *Aloe vryheidensis*
Aloe dominella: #1 **II** LILIACEAE
Aloe dorotheae: #1 **II** LILIACEAE
Aloe duckeri: #1 **II** LILIACEAE
Aloe dumetorum = *Aloe ellenbeckii*
Aloe dyeri: #1 **II** LILIACEAE
Aloe echinata = *Aloe humilis*
Aloe ecklonis: #1 **II** LILIACEAE
Aloe edentata: #1 **II** LILIACEAE
Aloe edulis = *Aloe macrocarpa*
Aloe elata: #1 **II** LILIACEAE
Aloe elegans: #1 **II** LILIACEAE
Aloe elgonica: #1 **II** LILIACEAE
Aloe ellenbeckii: #1 **II** LILIACEAE
Aloe ellenbergeri = *Aloe aristata*
Aloe eminens: #1 **II** LILIACEAE
Aloe engleri = *Aloe secundiflora* var. *secundiflora*

Aloe enotata: #1 **II** LILIACEAE
Aloe eremophila: #1 **II** LILIACEAE
Aloe erensii: #1 **II** LILIACEAE
Aloe ericetorum: #1 **II** LILIACEAE
Aloe erinacea = *Aloe melanacantha* var. *erinacea*
Aloe eru = *Aloe camperi*
Aloe eru f. *erecta* = *Aloe camperi*
Aloe eru f. *glauca* = *Aloe camperi*
Aloe eru f. *maculata* = *Aloe camperi*
Aloe eru f. *parvipunctata* = *Aloe camperi*
Aloe eru var. *cornuta* = *Aloe camperi*
Aloe eru var. *hookeri* = *Aloe adigratana*
Aloe erythrophylla: #1 **II** LILIACEAE
Aloe esculenta: #1 **II** LILIACEAE
Aloe eumassawana: #1 **II** LILIACEAE
Aloe excelsa: #1 **II** LILIACEAE
Aloe excelsa var. *breviflora*: #1 **II** LILIACEAE
Aloe excelsa var. *excelsa*: #1 **II** LILIACEAE
Aloe eylesii = *Aloe rhodesiana*
Aloe falcata: #1 **II** LILIACEAE
Aloe ferox = *Aloe marlothii*
Aloe ferox: (E) Aloe, Cape aloe #1 **II** LILIACEAE
Aloe ferox var. *eyrthrocarpa* = *Aloe ferox*
Aloe ferox var. *galpinii* = *Aloe ferox*
Aloe ferox var. *hanburyi* = *Aloe ferox*
Aloe ferox var. *incurva* = *Aloe ferox*
Aloe ferox var. *subferox* = *Aloe ferox*
Aloe ferox var. *xanthostachys* = *Aloe marlothii*
Aloe fibrosa: #1 **II** LILIACEAE
Aloe fievetii: #1 **II** LILIACEAE
Aloe fimbrialis: #1 **II** LILIACEAE
Aloe flabelliformis = *Aloe plicatilis*
Aloe fleurentinorum: #1 **II** LILIACEAE
Aloe fleuretteana: #1 **II** LILIACEAE
Aloe flexilifolia: #1 **II** LILIACEAE
Aloe floramaculata = *Aloe secundiflora* var. *secundiflora*
Aloe forbesii: #1 **II** LILIACEAE
Aloe fosteri: #1 **II** LILIACEAE
Aloe fouriei: #1 **II** LILIACEAE
Aloe fragilis: **I** LILIACEAE
Aloe framesii: #1 **II** LILIACEAE
Aloe francombei: #1 **II** LILIACEAE
Aloe friisii: #1 **II** LILIACEAE
Aloe frutescens = *Aloe arborescens*
Aloe fruticosa = *Aloe arborescens*
Aloe fulleri: #1 **II** LILIACEAE
Aloe galpinii = *Aloe ferox*
Aloe gariepensis: #1 **II** LILIACEAE
Aloe gariusiana = *Aloe gariepensis*
Aloe gerstneri: #1 **II** LILIACEAE
Aloe gilbertii: #1 **II** LILIACEAE
Aloe gilbertii ssp. *gilbertii*: #1 **II** LILIACEAE
Aloe gilbertii ssp. *megalacanthoides*: #1 **II** LILIACEAE
Aloe gillettii: #1 **II** LILIACEAE
Aloe gillilandii = *Aloe sabaea*
Aloe glabrescens: #1 **II** LILIACEAE
Aloe glauca: #1 **II** LILIACEAE
Aloe glauca var. *elatior* = *Aloe glauca* var. *glauca*
Aloe glauca var. *glauca*: #1 **II** LILIACEAE
Aloe glauca var. *humilior* = *Aloe glauca* var. *glauca*
Aloe glauca var. *major* = *Aloe glauca* var. *glauca*
Aloe glauca var. *minor* = *Aloe glauca* var. *glauca*
Aloe glauca var. *muricata* = *Aloe glauca* var. *spinosior*
Aloe glauca var. *spinosior*: #1 **II** LILIACEAE
Aloe globuligemma: #1 **II** LILIACEAE
Aloe gloveri = *Aloe hildebrandtii*
Aloe gossweileri: #1 **II** LILIACEAE
Aloe gracilicaulis: #1 **II** LILIACEAE
Aloe graciliflora = *Aloe greatheadii* var. *davyana*
Aloe gracilis = *Aloe commixta*
Aloe gracilis: #1 **II** LILIACEAE
Aloe gracilis var. *decumbens*: #1 **II** LILIACEAE
Aloe gracilis var. *gracilis*: #1 **II** LILIACEAE
Aloe graminicola = *Aloe lateritia* var. *graminicola*
Aloe graminifolia = *Aloe myriacantha*

Aloe grandidentata: #1 **II** LILIACEAE
Aloe grata: #1 **II** LILIACEAE
Aloe greatheadii: #1 **II** LILIACEAE
Aloe greatheadii var. *davyana*: #1 **II** LILIACEAE
Aloe greatheadii var. *greatheadii*: #1 **II** LILIACEAE
Aloe greenii: #1 **II** LILIACEAE
Aloe greenwayi = *Aloe leptosiphon*
Aloe grisea: #1 **II** LILIACEAE
Aloe guerrae: #1 **II** LILIACEAE
Aloe guillaumetii: #1 **II** LILIACEAE
Aloe haemanthifolia: #1 **II** LILIACEAE
Aloe hanburyana = *Aloe striata* ssp. *striata*
Aloe hardyi: #1 **II** LILIACEAE
Aloe harlana: #1 **II** LILIACEAE
Aloe harmsii = *Aloe dorotheae*
Aloe haworthioides: **I** LILIACEAE
Aloe haworthioides var. *aurantiaca*: **I** LILIACEAE
Aloe haworthioides var. *haworthioides*: **I** LILIACEAE
Aloe hazeliana: #1 **II** LILIACEAE
Aloe helenae: **I** LILIACEAE
Aloe heliderana: #1 **II** LILIACEAE
Aloe hemmingii: #1 **II** LILIACEAE
Aloe hendrickxii: #1 **II** LILIACEAE
Aloe hereroensis: #1 **II** LILIACEAE
Aloe hereroensis var. *hereroensis* = *Aloe hereroensis*
Aloe heybensis: #1 **II** LILIACEAE
Aloe hijazensis: #1 **II** LILIACEAE
Aloe hildebrandtii: #1 **II** LILIACEAE
Aloe hlangapensis = *Aloe hlangapies*
Aloe hlangapies: #1 **II** LILIACEAE
Aloe hlangapitis = *Aloe hlangapies*
Aloe howmanii: #1 **II** LILIACEAE
Aloe humbertii: #1 **II** LILIACEAE
Aloe humilis: #1 **II** LILIACEAE
Aloe humilis subv. *minor* = *Aloe humilis*
Aloe humilis subv. *semiguttata* = *Aloe humilis*
Aloe humilis var. *acuminata* = *Aloe humilis*
Aloe humilis var. *candolli* = *Aloe humilis*
Aloe humilis var. *echinata* = *Aloe humilis*
Aloe humilis var. *humilis* = *Aloe humilis*
Aloe humilis var. *incurva* = *Aloe humilis*
Aloe humilis var. *suberecta* = *Aloe humilis*
Aloe humilis var. *subtuberculata* = *Aloe humilis*
Aloe ibitiensis: #1 **II** LILIACEAE
Aloe ibityensis = *Aloe ibitiensis*
Aloe imalotensis: #1 **II** LILIACEAE
Aloe immaculata: #1 **II** LILIACEAE
Aloe inamara: #1 **II** LILIACEAE
Aloe inconspicua: #1 **II** LILIACEAE
Aloe incurva = *Aloe humilis*
Aloe inermis: #1 **II** LILIACEAE
Aloe integra: #1 **II** LILIACEAE
Aloe intermedia = *Aloe subacutissima*
Aloe inyangensis: #1 **II** LILIACEAE
Aloe inyangensis var. *inyangensis*: #1 **II** LILIACEAE
Aloe inyangensis var. *kimberleyana*: #1 **II** LILIACEAE
Aloe isaloensis: #1 **II** LILIACEAE
Aloe itremensis: #1 **II** LILIACEAE
Aloe jacksonii: #1 **II** LILIACEAE
Aloe jex-blakeae = *Aloe ruspoliana*
Aloe johnstonii = *Aloe myriacantha*
Aloe jucunda: #1 **II** LILIACEAE
Aloe juttae = *Aloe microstigma*
Aloe juvenna: #1 **II** LILIACEAE
Aloe karasbergensis = *Aloe striata* ssp. *karasbergensis*
Aloe kedongensis: #1 **II** LILIACEAE
Aloe kefaensis: #1 **II** LILIACEAE
Aloe keithii: #1 **II** LILIACEAE
Aloe ketabrowniorum: #1 **II** LILIACEAE
Aloe khamiesensis: (E) Namaqua aloe #1 **II** LILIACEAE
Aloe kilifiensis: #1 **II** LILIACEAE
Aloe kirkii = *Aloe massawana*
Aloe kniphofioides: #1 **II** LILIACEAE
Aloe komaggasensis = *Aloe striata* ssp. *komaggasensis*
Aloe komatiensis = *Aloe parvibracteata*

Checklist of flora/Lista de especies de flora/Liste des espèces végétales

Aloe krapohliana: #1 **II** LILIACEAE
Aloe krapohliana var. *dumoulinii*: #1 **II** LILIACEAE
Aloe krapohliana var. *krapohliana*: #1 **II** LILIACEAE
Aloe krausii: #1 **II** LILIACEAE
Aloe kraussii = Aloe albida
Aloe kraussii var. *minor = Aloe albida*
Aloe kulalensis: #1 **II** LILIACEAE
Aloe labiaflava = Aloe greatheadii var. *davyana*
Aloe labworana: #1 **II** LILIACEAE
Aloe laeta: **I** LILIACEAE
Aloe laeta var. *laeta*: **I** LILIACEAE
Aloe laeta var. *maniaensis*: **I** LILIACEAE
Aloe lanuriensis = Aloe wollastonii
Aloe lastii = Aloe brachystachys
Aloe lateritia: #1 **II** LILIACEAE
Aloe lateritia var. *graminicola*: #1 **II** LILIACEAE
Aloe lateritia var. *kitaliensis = Aloe wollastonii*
Aloe lateritia var. *lateritia*: #1 **II** LILIACEAE
Aloe latifolia = Aloe maculata
Aloe lavranosii: #1 **II** LILIACEAE
Aloe laxiflora = Aloe gracilis var. *gracilis*
Aloe laxissima = Aloe zebrina
Aloe leachii: #1 **II** LILIACEAE
Aloe leandrii: #1 **II** LILIACEAE
Aloe leedalii: #1 **II** LILIACEAE
Aloe lensayuensis: #1 **II** LILIACEAE
Aloe lepida: #1 **II** LILIACEAE
Aloe leptocaulon = Aloe antandroi
Aloe leptophylla = Aloe maculata
Aloe leptophylla var. *stenophylla = Aloe maculata*
Aloe leptosiphon: #1 **II** LILIACEAE
Aloe lettyae: #1 **II** LILIACEAE
Aloe lindenii: #1 **II** LILIACEAE
Aloe linearifolia: #1 **II** LILIACEAE
Aloe lineata: #1 **II** LILIACEAE
Aloe lineata var. *glaucescens = Aloe lineata* var. *lineata*
Aloe lineata var. *lineata*: #1 **II** LILIACEAE
Aloe lineata var. *muirii*: #1 **II** LILIACEAE
Aloe lineata var. *viridis = Aloe lineata* var. *lineata*
Aloe lingua = Aloe plicatilis
Aloe linguaeformis = Aloe plicatilis
Aloe littoralis: #1 **II** LILIACEAE
Aloe lolwensis: #1 **II** LILIACEAE
Aloe lomatophylloides: #1 **II** LILIACEAE
Aloe longiaristata = Aloe aristata
Aloe longibracteata = Aloe greatheadii var. *davyana*
Aloe longistyla: #1 **II** LILIACEAE
Aloe luapulana: #1 **II** LILIACEAE
Aloe lucile-allorgeae: #1 **II** LILIACEAE
Aloe lugardiana = Aloe zebrina
Aloe luntii: #1 **II** LILIACEAE
Aloe lusitanica = Aloe parvibracteata
Aloe lutescens: #1 **II** LILIACEAE
Aloe maclaughlinii = Aloe mcloughlinii
Aloe macleayi: #1 **II** LILIACEAE
Aloe macowanii = Aloe striatula var. *striatula*
Aloe macra: #1 **II** LILIACEAE
Aloe macrocarpa: #1 **II** LILIACEAE
Aloe macrocarpa var. *major = Aloe macrocarpa*
Aloe macroclada: #1 **II** LILIACEAE
Aloe macrosiphon: #1 **II** LILIACEAE
Aloe maculata = Aloe officinalis
Aloe maculata: #1 **II** LILIACEAE
Aloe maculosa = Aloe maculata
Aloe madecassa: #1 **II** LILIACEAE
Aloe madecassa var. *lutea*: #1 **II** LILIACEAE
Aloe madecassa var. *madecassa*: #1 **II** LILIACEAE
Aloe magnidentata = Aloe megalacantha ssp. *megalacantha*
Aloe marginalis = Aloe purpurea
Aloe marginata = Aloe purpurea
Aloe marlothii: #1 **II** LILIACEAE
Aloe marlothii var. *bicolor*: #1 **II** LILIACEAE
Aloe marlothii var. *marlothii*: #1 **II** LILIACEAE
Aloe marlothii var. *orientalis*: #1 **II** LILIACEAE
Aloe marsabitensis = Aloe secundiflora var. *secundiflora*

Aloe marshalli = Aloe kniphofioides
Aloe massawana: #1 **II** LILIACEAE
Aloe mawii: #1 **II** LILIACEAE
Aloe mayottensis: #1 **II** LILIACEAE
Aloe mccoyi: #1 **II** LILIACEAE
Aloe mcloughlinii: #1 **II** LILIACEAE
Aloe medishiana: #1 **II** LILIACEAE
Aloe megalacantha: #1 **II** LILIACEAE
Aloe megalacantha ssp. *alticola*: #1 **II** LILIACEAE
Aloe megalacantha ssp. *megalacantha*: #1 **II** LILIACEAE
Aloe megalocarpa: #1 **II** LILIACEAE
Aloe melanacantha: #1 **II** LILIACEAE
Aloe melanacantha var. *erinacea*: #1 **II** LILIACEAE
Aloe melanacantha var. *melanacantha*: #1 **II** LILIACEAE
Aloe melsetterensis = Aloe swynnertonii
Aloe menachensis: #1 **II** LILIACEAE
Aloe mendesii: #1 **II** LILIACEAE
Aloe menyharthii: #1 **II** LILIACEAE
Aloe menyharthii ssp. *ensifolia*: #1 **II** LILIACEAE
Aloe menyharthii ssp. *menyharthii*: #1 **II** LILIACEAE
Aloe meruana = Aloe chrysostachys
Aloe metallica: #1 **II** LILIACEAE
Aloe meyeri: #1 **II** LILIACEAE
Aloe micracantha = Aloe boylei
Aloe micracantha = Aloe micracantha
Aloe micracantha: #1 **II** LILIACEAE
Aloe microdonta: #1 **II** LILIACEAE
Aloe microstigma: #1 **II** LILIACEAE
Aloe millotii: #1 **II** LILIACEAE
Aloe milne-redheadii: #1 **II** LILIACEAE
Aloe minima = Aloe saundersiae
Aloe minima: #1 **II** LILIACEAE
Aloe minima var. *blyderivierensis*: #1 **II** LILIACEAE
Aloe minima var. *minima*: #1 **II** LILIACEAE
Aloe mitriformis: #1 **II** LILIACEAE
Aloe mitriformis var. *angustior = Aloe distans*
Aloe mitriformis var. *brevifolia = Aloe distans*
Aloe mitriformis var. *elatior = Aloe mitriformis*
Aloe mitriformis var. *humilior = Aloe mitriformis*
Aloe mketiensis = Aloe nuttii
Aloe modesta: #1 **II** LILIACEAE
Aloe molederana: #1 **II** LILIACEAE
Aloe monotropa: #1 **II** LILIACEAE
Aloe montana = Aloe dichotoma
Aloe monticola: #1 **II** LILIACEAE
Aloe morijensis: #1 **II** LILIACEAE
Aloe morogoroensis = Aloe bussei
Aloe mubendiensis: #1 **II** LILIACEAE
Aloe mudenensis: #1 **II** LILIACEAE
Aloe muirii = Aloe lineata var. *muirii*
Aloe multicolor: #1 **II** LILIACEAE
Aloe munchii: #1 **II** LILIACEAE
Aloe muricata = Aloe ferox
Aloe muricata = Aloe glauca var. *spinosior*
Aloe murina: #1 **II** LILIACEAE
Aloe musapana: #1 **II** LILIACEAE
Aloe mutabilis: #1 **II** LILIACEAE
Aloe mutans = Aloe greatheadii var. *davyana*
Aloe mwanzana = Aloe macrosiphon
Aloe myriacantha: #1 **II** LILIACEAE
Aloe myriacantha var. *minor = Aloe albida*
Aloe mzimbana: #1 **II** LILIACEAE
Aloe namibensis: #1 **II** LILIACEAE
Aloe namorokaensis: #1 **II** LILIACEAE
Aloe natalensis = Aloe arborescens
Aloe ngobitensis = Aloe nyeriensis
Aloe ngongensis: #1 **II** LILIACEAE
Aloe niebuhriana: #1 **II** LILIACEAE
Aloe nitens = Aloe rupestris
Aloe nubigena: #1 **II** LILIACEAE
Aloe nuttii: #1 **II** LILIACEAE
Aloe nyeriensis: #1 **II** LILIACEAE
Aloe nyeriensis ssp. *kedongensis = Aloe kedongensis*
Aloe nyeriensis ssp. *nyeriensis*: #1 **II** LILIACEAE
Aloe occidentalis: #1 **II** LILIACEAE

Aloe officinalis: #1 **II** LILIACEAE
Aloe officinalis var. *angustifolia* = *Aloe officinalis*
Aloe oligophylla: #1 **II** LILIACEAE
Aloe oligospila = *Aloe percrassa*
Aloe orientalis: #1 **II** LILIACEAE
Aloe ortholopha: #1 **II** LILIACEAE
Aloe otallensis: #1 **II** LILIACEAE
Aloe otallensis var. *elongata* = *Aloe rugosifolia*
Aloe otallensis var. *otallensis*: #1 **II** LILIACEAE
Aloe pachygaster: #1 **II** LILIACEAE
Aloe paedogona: #1 **II** LILIACEAE
Aloe pallidiflora = *Aloe greatheadii* var. *greatheadii*
Aloe palmiformis: #1 **II** LILIACEAE
Aloe paludicola = *Aloe buettneri*
Aloe paniculata = *Aloe striata* ssp. *striata*
Aloe parallelifolia: **I** LILIACEAE
Aloe parvibracteata: #1 **II** LILIACEAE
Aloe parvibracteata var. *parvibracteata*: #1 **II** LILIACEAE
Aloe parvibracteata var. *zuluensis* = *Aloe parvibracteata*
Aloe parvicapsula: #1 **II** LILIACEAE
Aloe parvicoma: #1 **II** LILIACEAE
Aloe parvidens: #1 **II** LILIACEAE
Aloe parviflora = *Aloe minima* var. *minima*
Aloe parvispina = *Aloe mitriformis*
Aloe parvula = *Aloe perrieri*
Aloe parvula: **I** LILIACEAE
Aloe patersonii: #1 **II** LILIACEAE
Aloe peacockii = *Aloe elegans*
Aloe pearsonii: #1 **II** LILIACEAE
Aloe peckii: #1 **II** LILIACEAE
Aloe peglerae: #1 **II** LILIACEAE
Aloe pembana: #1 **II** LILIACEAE
Aloe pendens: #1 **II** LILIACEAE
Aloe penduliflora: #1 **II** LILIACEAE
Aloe percrassa = *Aloe trichosantha* ssp. *trichosantha*
Aloe percrassa: #1 **II** LILIACEAE
Aloe percrassa var. *albo-picta* = *Aloe trichosantha* ssp. *trichosantha*
Aloe percrassa var. *menachensis* = *Aloe menachensis*
Aloe percrassa var. *saganeitiana* = *Aloe elegans*
Aloe perfoliata = *Aloe ferox*
Aloe perfoliata var. *africana* = *Aloe africana*
Aloe perfoliata var. *alpha* = *Aloe commixta*
Aloe perfoliata var. *beta* = *Aloe africana*
Aloe perfoliata var. *brevifolia* = *Aloe distans*
Aloe perfoliata var. *delta* = *Aloe maculata*
Aloe perfoliata var. *epsilon* = *Aloe ferox*
Aloe perfoliata var. *eta* = *Aloe arborescens*
Aloe perfoliata var. *ferox* = *Aloe ferox*
Aloe perfoliata var. *gamma* = *Aloe ferox*
Aloe perfoliata var. *glauca* = *Aloe glauca* var. *glauca*
Aloe perfoliata var. *humilis* = *Aloe humilis*
Aloe perfoliata var. *kappa* = *Aloe glauca* var. *glauca*
Aloe perfoliata var. *lainda* = *Aloe maculata*
Aloe perfoliata var. *lineata* = *Aloe lineata*
Aloe perfoliata var. *mitriformis* = *Aloe mitriformis*
Aloe perfoliata var. *mu* = *Aloe mitriformis*
Aloe perfoliata var. *purpurascens* = *Aloe succotrina*
Aloe perfoliata var. *saponaria* = *Aloe maculata*
Aloe perfoliata var. *succotrina* = *Aloe succotrina*
Aloe perfoliata var. *theta* = *Aloe maculata*
Aloe perfoliata var. *xi* = *Aloe mitriformis*
Aloe perfoliata var. *xi* = *Aloe succotrina*
Aloe perfoliata var. *zeta* = *Aloe brevifolia* var. *depressa*
Aloe perfoliata var. *zeta* = *Aloe ferox*
Aloe perrieri: #1 **II** LILIACEAE
Aloe perryi: #1 **II** LILIACEAE
Aloe petricola: #1 **II** LILIACEAE
Aloe petrophila: #1 **II** LILIACEAE
Aloe peyrierasii: #1 **II** LILIACEAE
Aloe pictifolia: #1 **II** LILIACEAE
Aloe pienaarii = *Aloe cryptopoda*
Aloe pillansii: (E) Bastard quiver tree **I** LILIACEAE
Aloe pirottae: #1 **II** LILIACEAE

Aloe platyphylla = *Aloe zebrina*
Aloe plicatilis: #1 **II** LILIACEAE
Aloe plicatilis var. *major* = *Aloe plicatilis*
Aloe plowesii: #1 **II** LILIACEAE
Aloe pluridens: #1 **II** LILIACEAE
Aloe pluridens var. *beckeri* = *Aloe pluridens*
Aloe pole-evansii = *Aloe dawei*
Aloe polyphylla: (E) Spiral aloe **I** LILIACEAE
Aloe pongolensis = *Aloe parvibracteata*
Aloe pongolensis var. *zuluensis* = *Aloe parvibracteata*
Aloe porphyrostachys: #1 **II** LILIACEAE
Aloe postgenita = *Aloe brevifolia* var. *postgenita*
Aloe powysiorum: #1 **II** LILIACEAE
Aloe pratensis: #1 **II** LILIACEAE
Aloe pretoriensis: #1 **II** LILIACEAE
Aloe prinslooi: #1 **II** LILIACEAE
Aloe procera: #1 **II** LILIACEAE
Aloe prolifera = *Aloe brevifolia* var. *brevifolia*
Aloe prolifera var. *major* = *Aloe brevifolia* var. *postgenita*
Aloe propagulifera: #1 **II** LILIACEAE
Aloe prostrata: #1 **II** LILIACEAE
Aloe prostrata ssp. *pallida*: #1 **II** LILIACEAE
Aloe pruinosa: #1 **II** LILIACEAE
Aloe pseudoafricana = *Aloe africana*
Aloe pseudoferox = *Aloe ferox*
Aloe pseudorubroviolacea: #1 **II** LILIACEAE
Aloe pubescens: #1 **II** LILIACEAE
Aloe pulcherrima: #1 **II** LILIACEAE
Aloe pulchra = *Aloe bella*
Aloe punctata = *Aloe variegata*
Aloe purpurascens = *Aloe succotrina*
Aloe purpurea: #1 **II** LILIACEAE
Aloe pustuligemma: #1 **II** LILIACEAE
Aloe pycnacantha = *Aloe rupestris*
Aloe rabaiensis: #1 **II** LILIACEAE
Aloe ramosa = *Aloe dichotoma*
Aloe ramosissima: (E) Maiden's quiver tree #1 **II** LILIACEAE
Aloe rauhii: **I** LILIACEAE
Aloe recurvifolia = *Aloe alooides*
Aloe reitzii: #1 **II** LILIACEAE
Aloe reitzii var. *reitzii*: #1 **II** LILIACEAE
Aloe reitzii var. *vernalis*: #1 **II** LILIACEAE
Aloe retrospiciens: #1 **II** LILIACEAE
Aloe reynoldsii: #1 **II** LILIACEAE
Aloe rhodacantha = *Aloe glauca* var. *glauca*
Aloe rhodesiana: #1 **II** LILIACEAE
Aloe rhodocincta = *Aloe striata* ssp. *striata*
Aloe richardsiae: #1 **II** LILIACEAE
Aloe richtersveldensis = *Aloe meyeri*
Aloe rigens: #1 **II** LILIACEAE
Aloe rigens var. *glabrescens* = *Aloe glabrescens*
Aloe rigens var. *mortimeri*: #1 **II** LILIACEAE
Aloe rigens var. *rigens*: #1 **II** LILIACEAE
Aloe rivae: #1 **II** LILIACEAE
Aloe rivierei: #1 **II** LILIACEAE
Aloe rosea: #1 **II** LILIACEAE
Aloe rubriflora: #1 **II** LILIACEAE
Aloe rubrolutea = *Aloe littoralis*
Aloe rubroviolacea: #1 **II** LILIACEAE
Aloe ruffingiana: #1 **II** LILIACEAE
Aloe rufocincta = *Aloe purpurea*
Aloe rugosifolia: #1 **II** LILIACEAE
Aloe rupestris: #1 **II** LILIACEAE
Aloe rupicola: #1 **II** LILIACEAE
Aloe ruspoliana: #1 **II** LILIACEAE
Aloe ruspoliana var. *dracaeniformis* = *Aloe retrospiciens*
Aloe sabaea: #1 **II** LILIACEAE
Aloe sahundra = *Aloe divaricata* var. *divaricata*
Aloe saponaria = *Aloe maculata*
Aloe saponaria var. *brachyphylla* = *Aloe maculata*
Aloe saponaria var. *ficksburgensis* = *Aloe maculata*
Aloe saponaria var. *latifolia* = *Aloe maculata*
Aloe saponaria var. *saponaria* = *Aloe maculata*
Aloe saundersiae: #1 **II** LILIACEAE
Aloe scabrifolia: #1 **II** LILIACEAE

Aloe schelpei: #1 **II** LILIACEAE
Aloe schilliana: #1 **II** LILIACEAE
Aloe schimperi = *Aloe percrassa*
Aloe schinzii = *Aloe littoralis*
Aloe schlechteri = *Aloe claviflora*
Aloe schliebenii = *Aloe brachystachys*
Aloe schmidtiana = *Aloe cooperi* ssp. *cooperi*
Aloe schoelleri: #1 **II** LILIACEAE
Aloe schomeri: #1 **II** LILIACEAE
Aloe schweinfurthii = *Aloe elegans*
Aloe schweinfurthii: #1 **II** LILIACEAE
Aloe schweinfurthii var. *labworana* = *Aloe labworana*
Aloe scobinifolia: #1 **II** LILIACEAE
Aloe scorpioides: #1 **II** LILIACEAE
Aloe secundiflora: #1 **II** LILIACEAE
Aloe secundiflora var. *secundiflora*: #1 **II** LILIACEAE
Aloe secundiflora var. *sobolifera*: #1 **II** LILIACEAE
Aloe sempervivoides = *Aloe parvula*
Aloe seretii: #1 **II** LILIACEAE
Aloe serra = *Aloe brevifolia* var. *depressa*
Aloe serriyensis: #1 **II** LILIACEAE
Aloe sessiliflora = *Aloe spicata*
Aloe shadensis: #1 **II** LILIACEAE
Aloe sheilae: #1 **II** LILIACEAE
Aloe silicicola: #1 **II** LILIACEAE
Aloe simii: #1 **II** LILIACEAE
Aloe sinana: #1 **II** LILIACEAE
Aloe sinkatana: #1 **II** LILIACEAE
Aloe sinuata = *Aloe succotrina*
Aloe sladeniana: #1 **II** LILIACEAE
Aloe soccotrina = *Aloe succotrina*
Aloe soccotrina var. *purpurascens* = *Aloe succotrina*
Aloe socialis: #1 **II** LILIACEAE
Aloe socotorina = *Aloe ferox*
Aloe solaiana = *Aloe lateritia* var. *graminicola*
Aloe somaliensis: #1 **II** LILIACEAE
Aloe somaliensis var. *marmorata*: #1 **II** LILIACEAE
Aloe somaliensis var. *somaliensis*: #1 **II** LILIACEAE
Aloe soutpansbergensis: #1 **II** LILIACEAE
Aloe speciosa: #1 **II** LILIACEAE
Aloe spectabilis = *Aloe marlothii* var. *marlothii*
Aloe spicata = *Aloe camperi*
Aloe spicata: #1 **II** LILIACEAE
Aloe splendens: #1 **II** LILIACEAE
Aloe squarrosa: #1 **II** LILIACEAE
Aloe steffanieana: #1 **II** LILIACEAE
Aloe stephaninii = *Aloe ruspoliana*
Aloe steudneri: #1 **II** LILIACEAE
Aloe striata: #1 **II** LILIACEAE
Aloe striata ssp. *karasbergensis*: #1 **II** LILIACEAE
Aloe striata ssp. *komaggasensis*: #1 **II** LILIACEAE
Aloe striata ssp. *striata*: #1 **II** LILIACEAE
Aloe striata var. *oligospila* = *Aloe striata* ssp. *striata*
Aloe striatula: #1 **II** LILIACEAE
Aloe striatula f. *conimbricensis* = *Aloe striatula* var. *caesia*
Aloe striatula f. *haworthi* = *Aloe striatula* var. *caesia*
Aloe striatula f. *typica* = *Aloe striatula* var. *caesia*
Aloe striatula var. *caesia*: #1 **II** LILIACEAE
Aloe striatula var. *striatula*: #1 **II** LILIACEAE
Aloe stuhlmannii = *Aloe volkensii* ssp. *volkensii*
Aloe suarezensis: #1 **II** LILIACEAE
Aloe subacutissima: #1 **II** LILIACEAE
Aloe suberecta = *Aloe humilis*
Aloe suberecta var. *acuminata* = *Aloe humilis*
Aloe subferox = *Aloe ferox*
Aloe subfulta = *Aloe suffulta*
Aloe subtuberculata = *Aloe humilis*
Aloe succotrina: #1 **II** LILIACEAE
Aloe succotrina var. *saxigena* = *Aloe succotrina*
Aloe suffulta: #1 **II** LILIACEAE
Aloe suprafoliata: #1 **II** LILIACEAE
Aloe suprafoliolata = *Aloe suprafoliata*
Aloe supralaevis = *Aloe ferox*
Aloe supralaevis var. *hanburyi* = *Aloe marlothii* var. *marlothii*
Aloe suzannae: **I** LILIACEAE

Aloe swynnertonii: #1 **II** LILIACEAE
Aloe tauri = *Aloe spicata*
Aloe tenuior: #1 **II** LILIACEAE
Aloe tenuior var. *decidua* = *Aloe tenuior*
Aloe tenuior var. *densiflora* = *Aloe tenuior*
Aloe tenuior var. *glaucescens* = *Aloe tenuior*
Aloe tenuior var. *rubriflora* = *Aloe tenuior*
Aloe termetophila = *Aloe greatheadii* var. *greatheadii*
Aloe tewoldei: #1 **II** LILIACEAE
Aloe thompsoniae: #1 **II** LILIACEAE
Aloe thorncroftii: **II** LILIACEAE
Aloe thraskii: #1 **II** LILIACEAE
Aloe tidmarshii = *Aloe ciliaris* var. *tidmarshii*
Aloe tomentosa: #1 **II** LILIACEAE
Aloe tomentosa f. *viridiflora* = *Aloe tomentosa*
Aloe tormentorii: #1 **II** LILIACEAE
Aloe tororoana: #1 **II** LILIACEAE
Aloe torrei: #1 **II** LILIACEAE
Aloe torrei var. *wildii* = *Aloe wildii*
Aloe trachyticola: #1 **II** LILIACEAE
Aloe transvaalensis = *Aloe zebrina*
Aloe transvaalensis var. *stenacantha* = *Aloe zebrina*
Aloe trichosantha: #1 **II** LILIACEAE
Aloe trichosantha ssp. *longiflora*: #1 **II** LILIACEAE
Aloe trichosantha ssp. *trichosantha*: #1 **II** LILIACEAE
Aloe trichosantha var. *menachensis* = *Aloe menachensis*
Aloe trigonantha: #1 **II** LILIACEAE
Aloe tripetala = *Aloe plicatilis*
Aloe trivialis = *Aloe schweinfurthii*
Aloe trothae = *Aloe bulbicaulis*
Aloe tuberculata = *Aloe humilis*
Aloe tugenensis: #1 **II** LILIACEAE
Aloe turkanensis: #1 **II** LILIACEAE
Aloe tweediae: #1 **II** LILIACEAE
Aloe ukambensis: #1 **II** LILIACEAE
Aloe umbellata = *Aloe maculata*
Aloe umfoloziensis: #1 **II** LILIACEAE
Aloe vacillans: #1 **II** LILIACEAE
Aloe vahontsohy = *Aloe divaricata* var. *divaricata*
Aloe vallaris: #1 **II** LILIACEAE
Aloe vanbalenii: #1 **II** LILIACEAE
Aloe vandermerwei: #1 **II** LILIACEAE
Aloe vaombe: #1 **II** LILIACEAE
Aloe vaombe var. *poissonii*: #1 **II** LILIACEAE
Aloe vaombe var. *vaombe*: #1 **II** LILIACEAE
Aloe vaotsanda: #1 **II** LILIACEAE
Aloe vaotsohy = *Aloe divaricata* var. *divaricata*
Aloe vaotsohy var. *rosea* = *Aloe divaricata* var. *rosea*
Aloe variegata = *Aloe pendens*
Aloe variegata: (E) Partridge-breasted aloe #1 **II** LILIACEAE
Aloe variegata var. *haworthii* = *Aloe variegata*
Aloe venusta = *Aloe bicomitum*
Aloe vera = *Aloe succotrina*
Aloe vera: **NC** LILIACEAE
Aloe vera var. *aethiopica* = *Aloe elegans*
Aloe vera var. *angustifolia* = *Aloe officinalis*
Aloe vera var. *officinalis* = *Aloe officinalis*
Aloe verdoorniae = *Aloe greatheadii* var. *davyana*
Aloe verecunda: #1 **II** LILIACEAE
Aloe versicolor: **I** LILIACEAE
Aloe veseyi: #1 **II** LILIACEAE
Aloe viguieri: #1 **II** LILIACEAE
Aloe viridiflora: #1 **II** LILIACEAE
Aloe vituensis: #1 **II** LILIACEAE
Aloe vogtsii: #1 **II** LILIACEAE
Aloe volkensii: #1 **II** LILIACEAE
Aloe volkensii ssp. *multicaulis*: #1 **II** LILIACEAE
Aloe volkensii ssp. *volkensii*: #1 **II** LILIACEAE
Aloe vossii: **I** LILIACEAE
Aloe vryheidensis: #1 **II** LILIACEAE
Aloe whitcombei: #1 **II** LILIACEAE
Aloe wickensii = *Aloe cryptopoda*
Aloe wickensii var. *lutea* = *Aloe cryptopoda*
Aloe wickensii var. *wickensii* = *Aloe cryptopoda*
Aloe wildii: #1 **II** LILIACEAE

Aloe wilsonii: #1 **II** LILIACEAE
Aloe wollastonii: #1 **II** LILIACEAE
Aloe woodii: #1 **II** LILIACEAE
Aloe woolliana = *Aloe chortolirioides* var. *woolliana*
Aloe wrefordii: #1 **II** LILIACEAE
Aloe xanthacantha = *Aloe mitriformis*
Aloe yavellana: #1 **II** LILIACEAE
Aloe yemenica: #1 **II** LILIACEAE
Aloe zanzibarica = *Aloe squarrosa*
Aloe zebrina: #1 **II** LILIACEAE
Aloe zombitsiensis: #1 **II** LILIACEAE
Aloes (E): *Aloe* spp.
Aloès (F): *Aloe* spp.
Aloewood (E): *Aquilaria malaccensis*
Alpargata (S): *Consolea macracantha*/ *Opuntia macracantha*
Alsophila abbottii = *Cyathea abbottii*
Alsophila brooksii = *Cyathea brooksii*
Alsophila cuspidata = *Cyathea cuspidata*
Alsophila engelii = *Cyathea elongata*
Alsophila firma = *Cyathea firma*
Alsophila manniana = *Cyathea manniana*
Alsophila minor = *Cyathea minor*
Alsophila polystichoides = *Cyathea polystichoides*
Alsophila spinulosa = *Cyathea spinulosa*
Alsophila urbanii = *Cyathea urbanii*
Altensteinia spp.: #7 **II** ORCHIDACEAE
Alverson's pincushion cactus (E): *Escobaria vivipara*
Alvisia = *Eria*
Amalia = *Laelia*
Amaryllis aetnensis = *Sternbergia colchiciflora*
Amaryllis citrina = *Sternbergia colchiciflora*
Amaryllis clusiana = *Sternbergia clusiana*
Amaryllis colchiciflora = *Sternbergia colchiciflora*
Amaryllis lutea = *Sternbergia fischeriana*
Amaryllis lutea = *Sternbergia lutea*
Amaryllis vernalis = *Sternbergia fischeriana*
Amblostoma = *Encyclia*
Amblyanthe = *Dendrobium*
Amblyglottis = *Calanthe*
Ambrella spp.: #7 **II** ORCHIDACEAE
American ginseng (E): *Panax quinquefolius*
American mahogany (E): *Swietenia mahagoni*
Amerorchis spp.: #7 **II** ORCHIDACEAE
Amesia = *Epipactis*
Amesiella spp.: #7 **II** ORCHIDACEAE
Amitostigma spp.: #7 **II** ORCHIDACEAE
Amparoa spp.: #7 **II** ORCHIDACEAE
Amphigena = *Disa*
Amphiglottis = *Epidendrum*
Amphorchis = *Cynorkis*
Anacampseros spp.: (E) purselanes (F) #1 **II** PORTULACACEAE
Anacampseros affinis = *Anacampseros lanceolata* ssp. *lanceolata*
Anacampseros albidiflora: #1 **II** PORTULACACEAE
Anacampseros albissima = *Avonia albissima*
Anacampseros alstonii = *Avonia quinaria* ssp. *alstonii*
Anacampseros alta = *Anacampseros filamentosa* ssp. *namaquensis*
Anacampseros angustifolia = *Anacampseros lanceolata*
Anacampseros arachnoides: #1 **II** PORTULACACEAE
Anacampseros arachnoides var. *grandiflora* = *Anacampseros rufescens*
Anacampseros baeseckei: #1 **II** PORTULACACEAE
Anacampseros bayeriana: #1 **II** PORTULACACEAE
Anacampseros buderiana = *Avonia recurvata*
Anacampseros comptonii: #1 **II** PORTULACACEAE
Anacampseros decipiens = *Avonia rhodesica*
Anacampseros densifolia = *Anacampseros filamentosa* ssp. *tomentosa*
Anacampseros depauperata = *Anacampseros arachnoides*
Anacampseros dielsiana: #1 **II** PORTULACACEAE
Anacampseros dinteri = *Avonia dinteri*
Anacampseros filamentosa: #1 **II** PORTULACACEAE
Anacampseros filamentosa ssp. *filamentosa*: #1 **II** PORTULACACEAE
Anacampseros filamentosa ssp. *namaquensis*: #1 **II** PORTULACACEAE

Anacampseros filamentosa ssp. *tomentosa*: #1 **II** PORTULACACEAE
Anacampseros fissa = *Avonia rhodesica*
Anacampseros gracilis = *Anacampseros arachnoides*
Anacampseros herreana = *Avonia herreana*
Anacampseros karasmontana = *Anacampseros dielsiana*
Anacampseros lanceolata: #1 **II** PORTULACACEAE
Anacampseros lanceolata ssp. *lanceolata*: #1 **II** PORTULACACEAE
Anacampseros lanceolata ssp. *nebrownii*: #1 **II** PORTULACACEAE
Anacampseros lanigera = *Anacampseros filamentosa*
Anacampseros lubbersii = *Anacampseros subnuda* ssp. *lubbersii*
Anacampseros margarethae = *Anacampseros filamentosa* ssp. *tomentosa*
Anacampseros marlothii: #1 **II** PORTULACACEAE
Anacampseros meyeri = *Avonia papyracea* ssp. *namaensis*
Anacampseros nebrownii = *Anacampseros lanceolata* ssp. *nebrownii*
Anacampseros nitida = *Anacampseros retusa*
Anacampseros ombonensis = *Avonia dinteri*
Anacampseros papyracea = *Avonia papyracea*
Anacampseros papyracea ssp. *namaensis* = *Avonia papyracea* ssp. *namaensis*
Anacampseros paradoxa = *Anacampseros filamentosa* ssp. *tomentosa*
Anacampseros parviflora = *Anacampseros baeseckei*
Anacampseros poellnitziana = *Anacampseros filamentosa* ssp. *namaquensis*
Anacampseros quinaria = *Avonia quinaria*
Anacampseros recurvata ssp. *buderiana* = *Avonia recurvata*
Anacampseros recurvata ssp. *minuta* = *Avonia recurvata* ssp. *minuta*
Anacampseros retusa: #1 **II** PORTULACACEAE
Anacampseros rhodesica = *Avonia rhodesica*
Anacampseros rubens = *Anacampseros arachnoides*
Anacampseros rubroviridis = *Anacampseros arachnoides*
Anacampseros rufescens: #1 **II** PORTULACACEAE
Anacampseros ruschii = *Avonia ruschii*
Anacampseros schoenlandii = *Anacampseros arachnoides*
Anacampseros scopata: #1 **II** PORTULACACEAE
Anacampseros starkiana = *Anacampseros subnuda*
Anacampseros subnuda: #1 **II** PORTULACACEAE
Anacampseros subnuda ssp. *lubbersii*: #1 **II** PORTULACACEAE
Anacampseros subnuda ssp. *subnuda*: #1 **II** PORTULACACEAE
Anacampseros telephiastrum: #1 **II** PORTULACACEAE
Anacampseros tomentosa = *Anacampseros filamentosa* ssp. *tomentosa*
Anacampseros trigona = *Anacampseros lanceolata*
Anacampseros truncata = *Anacampseros retusa*
Anacampseros ustulata = *Avonia ustulata*
Anacampseros variabilis = *Avonia papyracea* ssp. *namaensis*
Anacampseros varians = *Anacampseros telephiastrum*
Anacampseros wischkonii = *Avonia dinteri*
Anacamptis spp.: #7 **II** ORCHIDACEAE
Anacheilium = *Epidendrum*
Anathallis = *Pleurothallis*
Ancistrocactus brevihamatus = *Sclerocactus brevihamatus* ssp. *brevihamatus*
Ancistrocactus crassihamatus = *Sclerocactus uncinatus* ssp. *crassihamatus*
Ancistrocactus megarhizus = *Sclerocactus scheeri*
Ancistrocactus scheeri = *Sclerocactus scheeri*
Ancistrocactus tobuschii = *Sclerocactus brevihamatus* ssp. *tobuschii*
Ancistrocactus uncinatus = *Sclerocactus uncinatus* ssp. *uncinatus*
Ancistrochilus spp.: #7 **II** ORCHIDACEAE
Ancistrorhynchus spp.: #7 **II** ORCHIDACEAE
Andreettaea = *Pleurothallis*
Androchilus spp.: #7 **II** ORCHIDACEAE
Androcorys spp.: #7 **II** ORCHIDACEAE
Androgyne = *Panisea*
Anectochilus = *Anoectochilus*
Angorchis = *Angraecum*
Angorchis ellisii = *Aerangis ellisii*

Angraecopsis spp.: #7 **II** ORCHIDACEAE
Angraecum spp.: #7 **II** ORCHIDACEAE
Angraecum buyssonii = Aerangis ellisii
Angraecum dubuyssonii = Aerangis ellisii
Angraecum ellisii = Aerangis ellisii
Anguloa spp.: #7 **II** ORCHIDACEAE
Ania = Tainia
Anisopetalum = Bulbophyllum
Anisophyllum atoto = Euphorbia atoto
Anistylis = Liparis
Ankylocheilos = Taeniophyllum
Anneliesia spp.: #7 **II** ORCHIDACEAE
Anocheile = Epidendrum
Anochilus = Pterygodium
Anoectochilus spp.: #7 **II** ORCHIDACEAE
Anota = Rhynchostylis
Ansellia spp.: #7 **II** ORCHIDACEAE
Anteriorchis = Orchis
Anthacantha desmetiana = Euphorbia heptagona var. *heptagona*
Anthacantha mamillosa = Euphorbia squarrosa
Anthericlis = Tipularia
Anthogonium spp.: #7 **II** ORCHIDACEAE
Anthogyas = Bletia
Anthosiphon spp.: #7 **II** ORCHIDACEAE
Anticheirostylis = Genoplesium
Antillanorchis spp.: #7 **II** ORCHIDACEAE
Aopla = Herminium
Aorchis spp.: #7 **II** ORCHIDACEAE
Apation = Liparis
Apatostelis = Stelis
Apaturia = Pachystoma
Apetalon = Didymoplexis
Aphyllorchis spp.: #7 **II** ORCHIDACEAE
Apista = Podochilus
Aplectrum spp.: #7 **II** ORCHIDACEAE
Aporocactus conzattii = Disocactus martianus
Aporocactus flagelliformis = Disocactus flagelliformis
Aporocactus flagriformis = Disocactus flagelliformis
Aporocactus leptophis = Disocactus flagelliformis
Aporocactus martianus = Disocactus martianus
Aporostylis spp.: #7 **II** ORCHIDACEAE
Aporum = Dendrobium
Apostasia spp.: #7 **II** ORCHIDACEAE
Appendicula spp.: #7 **II** ORCHIDACEAE
Aquilaria agallocha = Aquilaria malaccensis
Aquilaria malaccensis: (E) Agarwood, Aloewood, Eaglewood, Malayan eaglewood tree, (S) Madera de Agar (F) Bois d'aigle de Malacca, #1 **II** THYMELAEACEAE
Aracamunia spp.: #7 **II** ORCHIDACEAE
Arachnanthe = Arachnis
Arachnis spp.: #7 **II** ORCHIDACEAE
Arachnites = Ophrys
Araucana (S): *Araucaria araucana*
Araucaria (F/S): *Araucaria araucana*
Araucaria araucana: (E) Chilean pine, monkey puzzle, (S) araucana, araucaria, araucaria de Neuquén, araucaria imbricada, gúillo, pino araucana, pino araucaria, pino chileno, pino de Chile, pino de Neuquén, pino hachado, pino piñonero, pino solo (F) araucaria, pin du Chili, **I** ARAUCARIACEAE
Araucaria columbaria = Araucaria araucana
Araucaria de Neuquén (S): *Araucaria araucana*
Araucaria dombeyi = Araucaria araucana
Araucaria imbricada (S): *Araucaria araucana*
Araucaria imbricata = Araucaria araucana
Arbol del barril (S): *Fouquieria fasciculata*
Arbre pieuvre (F): *Alluaudia procera*
Archineottia = Neottia
Arequipa australis = Oreocereus hempelianus
Arequipa myriacantha = Matucana haynei ssp. *myriacantha*
Arequipa weingartiana = Oreocereus hempelianus
Arethusa spp.: #7 **II** ORCHIDACEAE
Arethusantha = Cymbidium
Argyrorchis = Macodes
Arhynchium = Armodorum
Arietinum = Cypripedium

Ariocarpus agavoides: (E) Tamaulipas living-rock cactus **I** CACTACEAE
Ariocarpus aselliformis = Pelecyphora aselliformis
Ariocarpus bravoanus ssp. *bravoanus*: **I** CACTACEAE
Ariocarpus bravoanus ssp. *hintonii*: **I** CACTACEAE
Ariocarpus bravoanus: **I** CACTACEAE
Ariocarpus confusus = Ariocarpus retusus ssp. *retusus*
Ariocarpus elongatus = Ariocarpus retusus
Ariocarpus fissuratus: (E) Chautle-living Rock **I** CACTACEAE
Ariocarpus furfuraceus = Ariocarpus retusus ssp. *retusus*
Ariocarpus kotschoubeyanus: (S) Pezuña de venado **I** CACTACEAE
Ariocarpus kotschoubeyanus ssp. *albiflorus = Ariocarpus kotschoubeyanus*
Ariocarpus retusus: **I** CACTACEAE
Ariocarpus retusus ssp. *retusus*: **I** CACTACEAE
Ariocarpus retusus ssp. *scapharostroides = Ariocarpus retusus*
Ariocarpus retusus ssp. *trigonus*: **I** CACTACEAE
Ariocarpus scaphirostris: (E) Nuevo Leon living-rock cactus, (S) Orejas de conejo, Orejitas **I** CACTACEAE
Ariocarpus scapharostrus = Ariocarpus scaphirostris
Ariocarpus spp.: (E) living rock cacti, (S) roca viviente **I** CACTACEAE
Ariocarpus trigonus = Ariocarpus retusus ssp. *trigonus*
Arisanorchis = Cheirostylis
Aristolelea = Spiranthes
Arizona agave (E): *Agave arizonica*
Arizona hedgehog cactus (E): *Echinocereus coccineus*
Arizona rainbow cactus (E): *Echinocereus rigidissimus* ssp. *rigidissimus*
Armatocereus arboreus = Armatocereus matucanensis
Armatocereus arduus: #4 **II** CACTACEAE
Armatocereus balsasensis = Armatocereus rauhii ssp. *balsasensis*
Armatocereus brevispinus: #4 **II** CACTACEAE
Armatocereus cartwrightianus: #4 **II** CACTACEAE
Armatocereus churinensis = Armatocereus matucanensis
Armatocereus godingianus: #4 **II** CACTACEAE
Armatocereus humilis: #4 **II** CACTACEAE
Armatocereus laetus: #4 **II** CACTACEAE
Armatocereus mataranus: #4 **II** CACTACEAE
Armatocereus mataranus ssp. *ancashensis*: #4 **II** CACTACEAE
Armatocereus mataranus ssp. *mataranus*: #4 **II** CACTACEAE
Armatocereus matucanensis: #4 **II** CACTACEAE
Armatocereus oligogonus: #4 **II** CACTACEAE
Armatocereus procerus: #4 **II** CACTACEAE
Armatocereus rauhii: #4 **II** CACTACEAE
Armatocereus rauhii ssp. *balsasensis*: #4 **II** CACTACEAE
Armatocereus rauhii ssp. *rauhii*: #4 **II** CACTACEAE
Armatocereus riomajensis: #4 **II** CACTACEAE
Armatocereus rupicola: #4 **II** CACTACEAE
Armodorum spp.: #7 **II** ORCHIDACEAE
Arnedina = Arundina
Arnottia spp.: #7 **II** ORCHIDACEAE
Arpón (S): *Opuntia decumbens*
Arpophyllum spp.: #7 **II** ORCHIDACEAE
Arrojadoa aureispina = Arrojadoa rhodantha
Arrojadoa bahiensis: #4 **II** CACTACEAE
Arrojadoa beateae = Arrojadoa dinae ssp. *dinae*
Arrojadoa canudosensis = Arrojadoa rhodantha
Arrojadoa dinae: #4 **II** CACTACEAE
Arrojadoa dinae ssp. *dinae*: #4 **II** CACTACEAE
Arrojadoa dinae ssp. *eriocaulis*: #4 **II** CACTACEAE
Arrojadoa dinae ssp. *nana = Arrojadoa dinae* ssp. *dinae*
Arrojadoa eriocaulis = Arrojadoa dinae ssp. *eriocaulis*
Arrojadoa eriocaulis ssp. *albicoronata = Arrojadoa dinae* ssp. *eriocaulis*
Arrojadoa horstiana = Arrojadoa rhodantha
Arrojadoa multiflora = Arrojadoa dinae ssp. *dinae*
Arrojadoa penicillata: #4 **II** CACTACEAE
Arrojadoa polyantha = Micranthocereus polyanthus
Arrojadoa rhodantha: #4 **II** CACTACEAE
Arrojadoa rhodantha ssp. *aureispina = Arrojadoa rhodantha*
Arrojadoa rhodantha ssp. *canudosensis = Arrojadoa rhodantha*
Arrojadoa rhodantha ssp. *reflexa = Arrojadoa rhodantha*
Arrojadoa theunisseniana = Arrojadoa rhodantha

Checklist of flora/Lista de especies de flora/Liste des espèces végétales

Arthrocereus campos-portoi = Arthrocereus glaziovii
Arthrocereus damazioi = Arthocereus glaziovii
Arthrocereus glaziovii: #4 **II** CACTACEAE
Arthrocereus itabiriticola = Arthrocereus glaziovii
Arthrocereus melanurus: #4 **II** CACTACEAE
Arthrocereus melanurus ssp. *estevesii = Arthrocereus melanurus* ssp. *melanurus*
Arthrocereus melanurus ssp. *magnus*: #4 **II** CACTACEAE
Arthrocereus melanurus ssp. *melanurus*: #4 **II** CACTACEAE
Arthrocereus melanurus ssp. *mello-barretoi = Arthrocereus melanurus* ssp. *melanurus*
Arthrocereus melanurus ssp. *odorus*: #4 **II** CACTACEAE
Arthrocereus mello-barretoi = Arthrocereus melanurus ssp. *melanurus*
Arthrocereus odorus = Arthrocereus melanurus ssp. *odorus*
Arthrocereus rondonianus: #4 **II** CACTACEAE
Arthrocereus spinosissimus: #4 **II** CACTACEAE
Arthrochilium = Epipactis
Arthrochilus spp.: #7 **II** ORCHIDACEAE
Arthrothamnus brachiatus = Euphorbia brachiata
Arthrothamnus burmannii = Euphorbia burmannii
Arthrothamnus cassythoides = Euphorbia cassythoides
Arthrothamnus densiflorus = Euphorbia mundtii
Arthrothamnus schimperi = Euphorbia schimperi
Arthrothamnus scopiformis = Euphorbia arceuthobioides
Artichoke cactus (E): *Obregonia denegrii*
Artomeria = Eria
Artorima spp.: #7 **II** ORCHIDACEAE
Arundina spp.: #7 **II** ORCHIDACEAE
Asarca = Gavilea
Ascidieria spp.: #7 **II** ORCHIDACEAE
Ascocentrum spp.: #7 **II** ORCHIDACEAE
Ascochilopsis spp.: #7 **II** ORCHIDACEAE
Ascochilus spp.: #7 **II** ORCHIDACEAE
Ascoglossum spp.: #7 **II** ORCHIDACEAE
Ascolabium = Ascocentrum
Ascotainia = Tainia
Asian slipper orchids (E): *Paphiopedilum* spp.
Aspasia spp.: #7 **II** ORCHIDACEAE
Aspegrenia = Octomeria
Aspidogyne spp.: #7 **II** ORCHIDACEAE
Aspla = Herminium
Assamela (F): *Pericopsis elata*
Astroglossus = Stellilabium
Astrophytum asterias: (E) Star cactus, (S) Cacto estrella **I** CACTACEAE
Astrophytum capricorne: #4 **II** CACTACEAE
Astrophytum coahuilense = Astrophytum myriostigma
Astrophytum columnare = Astrophytum myriostigma
Astrophytum myriostigma: #4 **II** CACTACEAE
Astrophytum myriostigma ssp. *potosinum = Astrophytum myriostigma*
Astrophytum myriostigma ssp. *tulense = Astrophytum myriostigma*
Astrophytum ornatum: #4 **II** CACTACEAE
Astrophytum senile = Astrophytum capricorne
Astrophytum tulense = Astrophytum myriostigma
Ate = Habenaria
Atrapmoscas (S): *Dionaea muscipula*
Aulacophyllum lindeni = Zamia poeppigiana
Aulacophyllum montanum = Zamia montana
Aulacophyllum ortgiesi = Zamia chigua
Aulacophyllum roezli = Zamia roezlii
Aulacophyllum skinneri = Zamia skinneri
Auliza = Epidendrum
Aulosepalum spp.: #7 **II** ORCHIDACEAE
Aulostylis spp.: #7 **II** ORCHIDACEAE
Australorchis = Dendrobium
Austrocactus bertinii: #4 **II** CACTACEAE
Austrocactus coxii: #4 **II** CACTACEAE
Austrocactus dusenii = Austrocactus bertinii
Austrocactus gracilis = Austrocactus bertinii
Austrocactus hibernus = Austrocactus philippii
Austrocactus patagonicus: #4 **II** CACTACEAE
Austrocactus philippii: #4 **II** CACTACEAE
Austrocactus spiniflorus: #4 **II** CACTACEAE

Austrocephalocereus albicephalus = Micranthocereus albicephalus
Austrocephalocereus dolichospermaticus = Micranthocereus dolichospermaticus
Austrocephalocereus dybowskii = Espostoopsis dybowskii
Austrocephalocereus estevesii = Micranthocereus estevesii
Austrocephalocereus estevesii ssp. *grandiflorus = Micranthocereus estevesii*
Austrocephalocereus estevesii ssp. *insigniflorus = Micranthocereus estevesii*
Austrocephalocereus fluminensis = Coleocephalocereus fluminensis
Austrocephalocereus lehmannianus = Micranthocereus purpureus
Austrocephalocereus purpureus = Micranthocereus purpureus
Austrocylindropuntia clavarioides = Opuntia clavarioides
Austrocylindropuntia colubrina = Opuntia colubrina
Austrocylindropuntia cylindrica = Opuntia cylindrica
Austrocylindropuntia exaltata = Opuntia subulata
Austrocylindropuntia floccosa = Opuntia floccosa
Austrocylindropuntia humahuacana = Opuntia shaferi
Austrocylindropuntia inarmata = Opuntia verschaffeltii
Austrocylindropuntia intermedia = Opuntia cylindrica
Austrocylindropuntia ipatiana = Opuntia salmiana
Austrocylindropuntia lagopus = Opuntia lagopus
Austrocylindropuntia lauliacoana = Opuntia floccosa
Austrocylindropuntia machacana = Opuntia floccosa
Austrocylindropuntia malyana = Opuntia lagopus
Austrocylindropuntia miquelii = Opuntia miquelii
Austrocylindropuntia pachypus = Opuntia pachypus
Austrocylindropuntia salmiana = Opuntia salmiana
Austrocylindropuntia schickendantzii = Opuntia schickendantzii
Austrocylindropuntia shaferi = Opuntia shaferi
Austrocylindropuntia steiniana = Opuntia verschaffeltii
Austrocylindropuntia subulata = Opuntia subulata
Austrocylindropuntia tephrocactoides = Opuntia floccosa
Austrocylindropuntia weingartiana = Opuntia shaferi
Autumn lady's tresses orchid (E): *Vanda coerulea*
Auxopus spp.: #7 **II** ORCHIDACEAE
Aviceps = Satyrium
Avonia spp.: #1 **II** PORTULACACEAE
Avonia albissima: #1 **II** PORTULACACEAE
Avonia dinteri: #1 **II** PORTULACACEAE
Avonia herreana: #1 **II** PORTULACACEAE
Avonia mallei: #1 **II** PORTULACACEAE
Avonia papyracea: #1 **II** PORTULACACEAE
Avonia papyracea ssp. *namaensis*: #1 **II** PORTULACACEAE
Avonia papyracea ssp. *papyracea*: #1 **II** PORTULACACEAE
Avonia quinaria: #1 **II** PORTULACACEAE
Avonia quinaria ssp. *alstonii*: #1 **II** PORTULACACEAE
Avonia quinaria ssp. *quinaria*: #1 **II** PORTULACACEAE
Avonia recurvata: #1 **II** PORTULACACEAE
Avonia recurvata ssp. *minuta*: #1 **II** PORTULACACEAE
Avonia recurvata ssp. *recurvata*: #1 **II** PORTULACACEAE
Avonia rhodesica: #1 **II** PORTULACACEAE
Avonia ruschii: #1 **II** PORTULACACEAE
Avonia ustulata: #1 **II** PORTULACACEAE
Ayugue (E): *Alluaudia stormiae*
Ayuque (S): *Balmea stormiae*
Azadehdelia = Cribbia
Aztec cactus (E): *Aztekium ritteri*
Aztekium hintonii: #4 **II** CACTACEAE
Aztekium ritteri: (E) Aztec cactus, (S) Cacto azteca **I** CACTACEAE
Azureocereus deflexispinus = Echinopsis knuthiana
Azureocereus hertlingianus = Browningia hertlingiana
Azureocereus viridis = Browningia viridis
Backebergia militaris = Pachycereus militaris
Bahama dildo (E): *Pilosocereus robinii*
Bahia rosewood (E): *Dalbergia nigra*
Bakersfield beavertail cactus (E): *Opuntia treleasei*
Balanitum arborescens = Dicksonia arborescens
Balanitum auricomum = Dicksonia arborescens
Balanitum berteriana = Dicksonia berteriana
Balanitum blumei = Dicksonia blumei
Balanitum karstenianum = Dicksonia sellowiana
Balanitum squarrosa = Dicksonia squarrosa

Balanitum thyrsopteroides = *Dicksonia thyrsopteroides*
Balmea stormiae: (E) Ayugue, (S) Ayuque **I** RUBIACEAE
Baptistonia = *Oncidium*
Barbosella spp.: #7 **II** ORCHIDACEAE
Barbrodria spp.: #7 **II** ORCHIDACEAE
Barbwire apple-cactus (E): *Acanthocereus tetragonus*
Barkeria spp.: #7 **II** ORCHIDACEAE
Barlaea = *Cynorkis*
Barlia spp.: #7 **II** ORCHIDACEAE
Barombia spp.: #7 **II** ORCHIDACEAE
Bartholina spp.: #7 **II** ORCHIDACEAE
Bartschella schumannii = *Mammillaria schumannii*
Basigyne spp.: #7 **II** ORCHIDACEAE
Basiphyllaea spp.: #7 **II** ORCHIDACEAE
Baskervilla spp.: #7 **II** ORCHIDACEAE
Bastard quiver tree (E): *Aloe pillansii*
Batemannia spp.: #7 **II** ORCHIDACEAE
Bathiea = *Neobathiea*
Beadlea = *Cyclopogon*
Beccariophoenix madagascariensis: **II** PALMAE
Beclardia spp.: #7 **II** ORCHIDACEAE
Belonites bispinosa = *Pachypodium bispinosum*
Belonites succulenta = *Pachypodium succulentum*
Benthamia spp.: #7 **II** ORCHIDACEAE
Benzingia spp.: #7 **II** ORCHIDACEAE
Bergerocactus emoryi: (E) Golden-spine cereus #4 **II**
    CACTACEAE
Bicchia = *Habenaria*
Bicornella = *Cynorkis*
Bieneria = *Chloraea*
Biermannia spp.: #7 **II** ORCHIDACEAE
Bifolium = *Listera*
Big-leaf mahogany (E): *Swietenia macrophylla*
Big pine key prickly-pear (E): *Opuntia triacantha*
Big-nipple cory cactus (E): *Coryphantha macromeris* ssp. *runyonii*
Bilabrella = *Habenaria*
Binotia spp.: #7 **II** ORCHIDACEAE
Bipinnula spp.: #7 **II** ORCHIDACEAE
Birchea = *Luisia*
Black kangeroo paw (E): *Macropidia fuliginosa*
Black tree fern (E): *Cyathea medullaris*
Blaine's pincushion (E): *Sclerocactus blainei*
Blephariglottis = *Platanthera*
Bletia spp.: #7 **II** ORCHIDACEAE
Bletiana = *Bletia*
Bletilla spp.: #7 **II** ORCHIDACEAE
Blind prickly-pear (E): *Opuntia rufida*
Blossfeldia atroviridis = *Blossfeldia liliputana*
Blossfeldia campaniflora = *Blossfeldia liliputana*
Blossfeldia fechseri = *Blossfeldia liliputana*
Blossfeldia liliputana: #4 **II** CACTACEAE
Blossfeldia minima = *Blossfeldia liliputana*
Blossfeldia pedicellata = *Blossfeldia liliputana*
Blue vanda (E): *Vanda coerulea*
Bogoria spp.: #7 **II** ORCHIDACEAE
Bois d'aigle de Malacca (F): *Aquilaria malaccensis*
Bois d'Alerce (F): *Fitzroya cupressoides*
Bois de gaïac (F): *Guaiacum* spp.
Bois de vie (F): *Guaiacum* spp.
Bois saint (F): *Guaiacum* spp.
Bolbidium = *Dendrobium*
Bolborchis = *Coelogyne*
Bolivicereus brevicaulis = *Cleistocactus samaipatanus*
Bolivicereus croceus = *Cleistocactus samaipatanus*
Bolivicereus pisacensis = *Corryocactus erectus*
Bolivicereus rufus = *Cleistocactus samaipatanus*
Bolivicereus samaipatanus = *Cleistocactus samaipatanus*
Bolivicereus serpens = *Cleistocactus serpens*
Bolivicereus soukupii = *Corryocactus erectus*
Bolivicereus tenuiserpens = *Cleistocactus tenuiserpens*
Bollea spp.: #7 **II** ORCHIDACEAE
Bolusiella spp.: #7 **II** ORCHIDACEAE
Bonatea spp.: #7 **II** ORCHIDACEAE
Bonniera spp.: #7 **II** ORCHIDACEAE
Boojum tree (E): *Fouquieria columnaris*

Border prickly-pear (E): *Opuntia atrispina*
Borzicactus acanthurus = *Cleistocactus acanthurus* ssp.
    acanthurus
Borzicactus aequatorialis = *Cleistocactus sepium*
Borzicactus aurantiacus = *Matucana aurantiaca* ssp. *aurantiaca*
Borzicactus aurivillus = *Cleistocactus icosagonus*
Borzicactus cajamarcensis = *Cleistocactus fieldianus* ssp.
    fieldianus
Borzicactus calocephalus = *Matucana haynei* ssp. *myriacantha*
Borzicactus calvescens = *Matucana aurantiaca* ssp. *aurantiaca*
Borzicactus calviflorus = *Cleistocactus fieldianus* ssp. *fieldianus*
Borzicactus decumbens = *Haageocereus decumbens*
Borzicactus fieldianus = *Cleistocactus fieldianus* ssp. *fieldianus*
Borzicactus formosus = *Matucana formosa*
Borzicactus fruticosus = *Matucana fruticosa*
Borzicactus haynei = *Matucana haynei* ssp. *haynei*
Borzicactus huagalensis = *Matucana huagalensis*
Borzicactus icosagonus = *Cleistocactus icosagonus*
Borzicactus intertextus = *Matucana intertexta*
Borzicactus krahnii = *Matucana krahnii*
Borzicactus madisoniorum = *Matucana madisoniorum*
Borzicactus morleyanus = *Cleistocactus sepium*
Borzicactus myriacanthus = *Matucana haynei* ssp. *myriacantha*
Borzicactus neoroezlii = *Cleistocactus neoroezlii*
Borzicactus oreodoxus = *Matucana oreodoxa*
Borzicactus paucicostatus = *Matucana paucicostata*
Borzicactus pisacensis = *Corryocactus erectus*
Borzicactus plagiostoma = *Cleistocactus plagiostoma*
Borzicactus psuedothelegonus = *Cleistocactus serpens*
Borzicactus purpureus = *Cleistocactus plagiostoma*
Borzicactus ritteri = *Matucana ritteri*
Borzicactus samaipatanus = *Cleistocactus samaipatanus*
Borzicactus samnensis = *Cleistocactus fieldianus* ssp. *samnensis*
Borzicactus sepium = *Cleistocactus sepium*
Borzicactus serpens = *Cleistocactus serpens*
Borzicactus sextonianus = *Cleistocactus sextonianus*
Borzicactus soukupii = *Corryocactus erectus*
Borzicactus sulcifer = *Cleistocactus serpens*
Borzicactus tenuiserpens = *Cleistocactus tenuiserpens*
Borzicactus tuberculatus = *Matucana tuberculata*
Borzicactus variabilis = *Matucana haynei* ssp. *haynei*
Borzicactus ventimigliae = *Cleistocactus sepium*
Borzicactus weberbaueri = *Matucana weberbaueri*
Borzicactus websterianus = *Cleistocactus sepium*
Bothriochilus = *Coelia*
Bowenia spp.: (E) cycads #1 **II** STANGERIACEAE
Bowenia serrulata: #1 **II** STANGERIACEAE
Bowenia spectabilis: #1 **II** STANGERIACEAE
Bowenia spectabilis var. *serrata* = *Bowenia serrulata*
Bowenia spectabilis var. *serrulata* = *Bowenia serrulata*
Braasiella = *Oncidium*
Brachionidium spp.: #7 **II** ORCHIDACEAE
Brachtia spp.: #7 **II** ORCHIDACEAE
Brachycalycium tilcarense = *Gymnocalycium saglionis* ssp.
    tilcarense
Brachycereus nesioticus: #4 **II** CACTACEAE
Brachycorythis spp.: #7 **II** ORCHIDACEAE
Brachypeza spp.: #7 **II** ORCHIDACEAE
Brachystele spp.: #7 **II** ORCHIDACEAE
Brachystepis = *Oeonia*
Bracisepalum spp.: #7 **II** ORCHIDACEAE
Brady's pincushion cactus (E): *Pediocactus bradyi*
Braemia = *Houlletia*
Brasilicereus breviflorus = *Brasilicereus phaeacanthus*
Brasilicereus markgrafii: #4 **II** CACTACEAE
Brasilicereus phaeacanthus: #4 **II** CACTACEAE
Brasilicereus phaeacanthus ssp. *breviflorus* = *Brasilicereus*
    phaeacanthus
Brasiliopuntia bahiensis = *Opuntia brasiliensis*
Brasiliopuntia brasiliensis = *Opuntia brasiliensis*
Brasiliopuntia neoargentina = *Opuntia brasiliensis*
Brasiliopuntia schulzii = *Opuntia brasiliensis*
Brasiliopuntia subacarpa = *Opuntia brasiliensis*
Brassavola spp.: #7 **II** ORCHIDACEAE
Brassia spp.: #7 **II** ORCHIDACEAE

Brazilian mahogany (E): *Swietenia macrophylla*
Brazilian rosewood (E): *Dalbergia nigra*
Bread palms (E): *Encephalartos* spp.
Brenesia = Pleurothallis
Briegeria = Jacquiniella
Bromheadia spp.: #7 **II** ORCHIDACEAE
Broughtonia spp.: #7 **II** ORCHIDACEAE
Browningia albiceps: #4 **II** CACTACEAE
Browningia altissima: #4 **II** CACTACEAE
Browningia amstutziae: #4 **II** CACTACEAE
Browningia caineana: #4 **II** CACTACEAE
Browningia candelaris: #4 **II** CACTACEAE
Browningia chlorocarpa: #4 **II** CACTACEAE
Browningia columnaris: #4 **II** CACTACEAE
Browningia hertlingiana: #4 **II** CACTACEAE
Browningia icaensis = Browningia candelaris
Browningia microsperma: #4 **II** CACTACEAE
Browningia pilleifera: #4 **II** CACTACEAE
Browningia riosaniensis = Rauhocereus riosaniensis ssp.
   riosaniensis
Browningia viridis: #4 **II** CACTACEAE
Brownleea spp.: #7 **II** ORCHIDACEAE
Bryobium = Eria
Bucculina = Holothrix
Buchtienia spp.: #7 **II** ORCHIDACEAE
Buiningia aurea = Coleocephalocereus aureus
Buiningia brevicylindrica = Coleocephalocereus aureus
Buiningia purpurea = Coleocephalocereus purpureus
Bulbophyllaria = Bulbophyllum
Bulbophyllopsis = Bulbophyllum
Bulbophyllum spp.: #7 **II** ORCHIDACEAE
Bulleyia spp.: #7 **II** ORCHIDACEAE
Bunched cory cactus (E): *Coryphantha ramillosa*
Burlingtonia = Rodriguezia
Burnettia spp.: #7 **II** ORCHIDACEAE
Burnsbaloghia spp.: #7 **II** ORCHIDACEAE
Butterfly palm (E): *Chrysalidocarpus decipiens*
Button-cactus (E): *Epithelantha bokei*
Cachimbo (S): *Platymiscium pleiostachyum*
CACTACEAE spp.: (E/S/F) Cacti #4 **I/II**
Cacti (E/S/F): CACTACEAE spp.
Cacto alcachofa (S): *Obregonia denegrii*
Cacto azteca (S): *Aztekium ritteri*
Cacto de Lindsay (S): *Echinocereus ferreirianus* ssp. *lindsayi*
Cacto estrella (S): *Astrophytum asterias*
Cadetia spp.: #7 **II** ORCHIDACEAE
Caladenia spp.: #7 **II** ORCHIDACEAE
Calanthe spp.: #7 **II** ORCHIDACEAE
Calanthidum = Calanthe
Calcearia = Corybas
Calceolaria = Cypripedium
Calceolus = Cypripedium
Caleana spp.: #7 **II** ORCHIDACEAE
Caleya = Caleana
Calliphyllon = Epipactis
Callista = Dendrobium
Callithronum = Cephalanthera
Callostylis = Eria
Calochilus spp.: #7 **II** ORCHIDACEAE
Caloglossum = Cymbidiella
Calophyllum = Epipactis
Calopogon spp.: #7 **II** ORCHIDACEAE
Calorchis = Ponthieva
Caluera spp.: #7 **II** ORCHIDACEAE
Calymmanthera spp.: #7 **II** ORCHIDACEAE
Calymmanthium fertile = Calymmanthium substerile
Calymmanthium substerile: #4 **II** CACTACEAE
Calypso spp.: #7 **II** ORCHIDACEAE
Calypsodium = Calypso
Calyptrochilum spp.: #7 **II** ORCHIDACEAE
Camaridium = Maxillaria
Camarotis = Micropera
Camelostalix = Pholidota
Camilleugenia = Cynorkis
Campanas de Oconee (S): *Shortia galacifolia*

Campanillas de nieve (S): *Galanthus* spp.
Campanulorchis = Eria
Campylocentrum spp.: #7 **II** ORCHIDACEAE
Canacorchis = Bulbophyllum
Candelabra aloe (E): *Aloe arborescens*
Candelilla (E): *Euphorbia antisyphilitica*
Candle cholla (E): *Opuntia kleiniae*
Cane prickly-pear (E): *Opuntia spinosior*
Cántaro de India (S): *Nepenthes khasiana*
Cántaro tropical gigante (S): *Nepenthes rajah*
Cántaros (S): *Nepenthes* spp.
Cántaros (S): *Sarracenia* spp.
Caoba (S): *Swietenia macrophylla*
Caoba de Honduras (S): *Swietenia humilis*
Caoba de Pacífico (S): *Swietenia humilis*
Caoba española (S): *Swietenia mahagoni*
Capanemia spp.: #7 **II** ORCHIDACEAE
Cape aloe (E): *Aloe ferox*
Carbones (E): *Euphorbia* spp.
Cardiochilos spp.: #7 **II** ORCHIDACEAE
Cardiophyllum = Listera
Cardón (S): *Selenicereus grandiflorus*
Caribbean apple-cactus (E): *Harrisia eriophora*
Carnegiea euphorbioides = Neobuxbaumia euphorbioides
Carnegiea gigantea: #4 **II** CACTACEAE
Carnegiea laui = Neobuxbaumia laui
Carnegiea macrocephala = Neobuxbaumia macrocephala
Carnegiea mezcalaensis = Neobuxbaumia mezcalaensis
Carnegiea nova = Neobuxbaumia mezcalaensis
Carnegiea polylopha = Neobuxbaumia polylopha
Carnegiea scoparia = Neobuxbaumia scoparia
Carnegiea squamulosa = Neobuxbaumia squamulosa
Carnegiea tetetzo = Neobuxbaumia tetetzo
Carteretia = Cleisostoma
Caryocar costaricense: (E) Costus, (S) Ajillo, Ajo, Almendrillo,
   Almendrón, Manú, Plomillo, Swari #1 **II**
   CARYOCARACEAE
Cassyta = Rhipsalis
Castellanosia caineana = Browningia caineana
Catachaetum = Catasetum
Catakidozamia hopei = Lepidozamia hopei
Catasetum spp.: #7 **II** ORCHIDACEAE
Cathea = Calopogon
Cattleya spp.: #7 **II** ORCHIDACEAE
Cattleya trianaei: (E) Christmas orchid, Winter cattleya **I**
   ORCHIDACEAE
Cattleyopsis = Broughtonia
Caucaea spp.: #7 **II** ORCHIDACEAE
Caularthron spp.: #7 **II** ORCHIDACEAE
Cedar (E): *Cedrela odorata*
Cederwood (E): *Cedrela odorata*
Cedrat (F): *Cedrela odorata*
Cedrela (F): *Cedrela odorata*
Cedrela mexicana = Cedrela odorata
Cedrela odorata: (E) Cedar, cederwood, cigar-box cedar, cigar-box
   wood, red cedar, Spanish cedar, stinking mahogany, West
   Indian cedar, (S) Cedro rojo (F) Cedrat, Cedrela, #5 **III**
   MELIACEAE
Cedro (S): *Pilgerodendron uviferum*
Cedro rojo (S): *Cedrela odorata*
Centranthera = Pleurothallis
Centrochilus = Habenaria
Centrogenium = Stenorrhynchos
Centroglossa spp.: #7 **II** ORCHIDACEAE
Centropetalum = Fernandezia
Centrosia = Calanthe
Centrosis = Calanthe
Centrostigma spp.: #7 **II** ORCHIDACEAE
Cephalangraecum = Ancistrorhynchus
Cephalanthera spp.: #7 **II** ORCHIDACEAE
Cephalantheropsis spp.: #7 **II** ORCHIDACEAE
Cephalocereus alensis = Pilosocereus alensis
Cephalocereus apicicephalium: #4 **II** CACTACEAE
Cephalocereus barbadensis = Pilosocereus royenii
Cephalocereus chrysacanthus = Pilosocereus chrysacanthus

Cephalocereus collinsii = *Pilosocereus purpusii*
Cephalocereus columbianus = *Pilosocereus lanuginosus*
Cephalocereus columna-trajani: #4 **II** CACTACEAE
Cephalocereus cometes = *Pilosocereus leucocephalus*
Cephalocereus dybowskii = *Espostoopsis dybowskii*
Cephalocereus fluminensis = *Coleocephalocereus fluminensis*
Cephalocereus guentheri = *Espostoa guentheri*
Cephalocereus guerreronis = *Pilosocereus alensis*
Cephalocereus hoppenstedtii = *Cephalocereus columna-trajani*
Cephalocereus leucocephalus = *Pilosocereus leucocephalus*
Cephalocereus macrocephalus = *Neobuxbaumia macrocephala*
Cephalocereus millspaughii = *Pilosocereus royenii*
Cephalocereus nizandensis: #4 **II** CACTACEAE
Cephalocereus nobilis = *Pilosocereus royenii*
Cephalocereus palmeri = *Pilosocereus leucocephalus*
Cephalocereus palmeri var. *palmeri* = *Pilosocereus leucocephalus*
Cephalocereus palmeri var. *victoriensis* = *Pilosocereus leucocephalus*
Cephalocereus phaeacanthus = *Brasilicereus phaeacanthus*
Cephalocereus polygonus = *Pilosocereus polygonus*
Cephalocereus polylophus = *Neobuxbaumia polylopha*
Cephalocereus purpusii = *Pilosocereus purpusii*
Cephalocereus quadricentralis = *Pilosocereus quadricentralis*
Cephalocereus royenii = *Pilosocereus royenii*
Cephalocereus russelianus = *Cereus fricii*
Cephalocereus sartorianus = *Pilosocereus leucocephalus*
Cephalocereus scoparius = *Neobuxbaumia scoparia*
Cephalocereus senilis: #4 **II** CACTACEAE
Cephalocereus swartzii = *Pilosocereus royenii*
Cephalocereus totolapensis: #4 **II** CACTACEAE
Cephalocleistocactus chrysocephalus: #4 **II** CACTACEAE
Cephalocleistocactus pallidus = *Cleistocactus palhuayensis*
Cephalocleistocactus ritteri = *Cleistocactus ritteri*
Cephalocleistocactus schattatianus = *Cleistocactus varispinus*
Ceraia = *Dendrobium*
Ceratandra spp.: #7 **II** ORCHIDACEAE
Ceratandropsis = *Ceratandra*
Ceratium = *Eria*
Ceratocentron spp.: #7 **II** ORCHIDACEAE
Ceratochilus spp.: #7 **II** ORCHIDACEAE
Ceratopsis = *Epipogium*
Ceratostylis spp.: #7 **II** ORCHIDACEAE
Ceratozamia spp.: (E) cycads, horncones, (S) tapacapón **I** ZAMIACEAE
Ceratozamia alvarezii: **I** ZAMIACEAE
Ceratozamia boliviana = *Zamia boliviana*
Ceratozamia brevifrons = *Ceratozamia mexicana*
Ceratozamia euryphyllidia: **I** ZAMIACEAE
Ceratozamia hildae: **I** ZAMIACEAE
Ceratozamia kuesteriana: **I** ZAMIACEAE
Ceratozamia latifolia: **I** ZAMIACEAE
Ceratozamia longifolia = *Ceratozamia mexicana*
Ceratozamia matudae: **I** ZAMIACEAE
Ceratozamia mexicana: **I** ZAMIACEAE
Ceratozamia mexicana var. *latifolia* = *Ceratozamia latifolia*
Ceratozamia mexicana var. *longifolia* = *Ceratozamia mexicana*
Ceratozamia mexicana var. *tenuis* = *Ceratozamia mexicana*
Ceratozamia microstrobila: **I** ZAMIACEAE
Ceratozamia miqueliana: **I** ZAMIACEAE
Ceratozamia mixeorum: **I** ZAMIACEAE
Ceratozamia morettii: **I** ZAMIACEAE
Ceratozamia norstogii: **I** ZAMIACEAE
Ceratozamia robusta: **I** ZAMIACEAE
Ceratozamia sabatoi: **I** ZAMIACEAE
Ceratozamia whitelockiana: **I** ZAMIACEAE
Ceratozamia zaragozae: **I** ZAMIACEAE
Ceratozamia zoquensis: **I** ZAMIACEAE
Cereus adelmarii: #4 **II** CACTACEAE
Cereus aethiops: #4 **II** CACTACEAE
Cereus albicaulis: #4 **II** CACTACEAE
Cereus amazonicus = *Praecereus euchlorus* ssp. *amazonicus*
Cereus anisitsii = *Cereus spegazzinii*
Cereus argentinensis: #4 **II** CACTACEAE
Cereus atroviridis = *Cereus repandus*
Cereus azureus = *Cereus aethiops*

Cereus baumannii = *Cleistocactus baumannii* ssp. *baumannii*
Cereus bertinii = *Austrocactus bertinii*
Cereus bicolor: #4 **II** CACTACEAE
Cereus braunii: #4 **II** CACTACEAE
Cereus calcirupicola = *Cereus jamacaru* ssp. *calcirupicola*
Cereus calcirupicola ssp. *cabralensis* = *Cereus jamacaru* ssp. *calcirupicola*
Cereus calcirupicola ssp. *cipoensis* = *Cereus jamacaru* ssp. *calcirupicola*
Cereus chalybaeus = *Cereus aethiops*
Cereus cochabambensis: #4 **II** CACTACEAE
Cereus comarapanus: #4 **II** CACTACEAE
Cereus crassisepalus = *Cipocereus crassisepalus*
Cereus dayami = *Cereus stenogonus*
Cereus diffusus = *Praecereus euchlorus* ssp. *diffusus*
Cereus emoryi = *Bergerocactus emoryi*
Cereus eriophorus = *Harrisia eriophora*
Cereus euchlorus = *Praecereus euchlorus* ssp. *euchlorus*
Cereus extensus = *Hylocereus lemairei*
Cereus fernambucensis: #4 **II** CACTACEAE
Cereus fernambucensis ssp. *fernambucensis*: #4 **II** CACTACEAE
Cereus fernambucensis ssp. *sericifer*: #4 **II** CACTACEAE
Cereus forbesii = *Cereus validus*
Cereus fricii: #4 **II** CACTACEAE
Cereus giganteus = *Carnegiea gigantea*
Cereus goiasensis = *Cereus jamacaru* ssp. *goiasensis*
Cereus gracilis = *Harrisia gracilis*
Cereus grandiflorus = *Selenicereus grandiflorus*
Cereus greggii = *Peniocereus greggii*
Cereus grenadensis = *Cereus repandus*
Cereus haageanus: #4 **II** CACTACEAE
Cereus hankeanus: #4 **II** CACTACEAE
Cereus hexagonus: #4 **II** CACTACEAE
Cereus hildmannianus: #4 **II** CACTACEAE
Cereus hildmannianus ssp. *hildmannianus*: #4 **II** CACTACEAE
Cereus hildmannianus ssp. *uruguayanus*: #4 **II** CACTACEAE
Cereus hildmannianus ssp. *xanthocarpus* = *Cereus hildmannianus*
Cereus horrispinus: #4 **II** CACTACEAE
Cereus huilunchu: #4 **II** CACTACEAE
Cereus insularis: #4 **II** CACTACEAE
Cereus jamacaru: #4 **II** CACTACEAE
Cereus jamacaru ssp. *calcirupicola*: #4 **II** CACTACEAE
Cereus jamacaru ssp. *goiasensis*: #4 **II** CACTACEAE
Cereus jamacaru ssp. *jamacaru*: #4 **II** CACTACEAE
Cereus kroenleinii: #4 **II** CACTACEAE
Cereus lamprospermus: #4 **II** CACTACEAE
Cereus lamprospermus ssp. *colosseus* = *Cereus lamprospermus*
Cereus lanosus: #4 **II** CACTACEAE
Cereus lauterbachii = *Praecereus euchlorus* ssp. *euchlorus*
Cereus longiflorus = *Cereus hexagonus*
Cereus margaritensis = *Cereus repandus*
Cereus markgrafii = *Brasilicereus markgrafii*
Cereus martinii = *Harrisia martinii*
Cereus milesimus = *Cereus hildmannianus* ssp. *hildmannianus*
Cereus mirabella: #4 **II** CACTACEAE
Cereus mortensenii: #4 **II** CACTACEAE
Cereus neonesioticus = *Cereus hildmannianus*
Cereus neotetragonus = *Cereus fernambucensis* ssp. *fernambucensis*
Cereus nudiflorus = *Dendrocereus nudiflorus*
Cereus pachyrrhizus: #4 **II** CACTACEAE
Cereus pentagonus = *Acanthocereus tetragonus*
Cereus perlucens = *Cereus hexagonus*
Cereus pernambucensis = = *Cereus fernambucensis* ssp. *fernambucensis*
Cereus peruvianus = *Cereus repandus*
Cereus peruvianus = *Cereus hildmannianus*
Cereus phatnospermus: #4 **II** CACTACEAE
Cereus phatnospermus ssp. *adelmarii* = *Cereus adelmarii*
Cereus phatnospermus ssp. *kroenleinii* = *Cereus kroenleinii*
Cereus poselgeri = *Echinocereus poselgeri*
Cereus repandus: #4 **II** CACTACEAE
Cereus rhodoleucanthus = *Praecereus saxicola*
Cereus ridleii: #4 **II** CACTACEAE
Cereus robinii = *Pilosocereus polygonus*

Cereus roseiflorus: #4 **II** CACTACEAE
Cereus russelianus = Cereus fricii
Cereus saddianus: #4 **II** CACTACEAE
Cereus saxicola = Praecereus saxicola
Cereus sericifer = Cereus fernambucensis ssp. *sericifer*
Cereus smithianus = Praecereus euchlorus ssp. *smithianus*
Cereus spachianus = Echinopsis spachiana
Cereus spegazzinii: #4 **II** CACTACEAE
Cereus stenogonus: #4 **II** CACTACEAE
Cereus striatus = Peniocereus striatus
Cereus tacaquirensis = Echinopsis tacaquirensis
Cereus tacuaralensis: #4 **II** CACTACEAE
Cereus tetragonas = = Cereus fernambucensis ssp. *fernambucensis*
Cereus tortuosus = Harrisia tortuosa
Cereus trigonodendron: #4 **II** CACTACEAE
Cereus undatus = Hylocereus undatus
Cereus uruguayanus = Cereus hildmannianus ssp. *uruguayanus*
Cereus validus: #4 **II** CACTACEAE
Cereus vargasianus: #4 **II** CACTACEAE
Cereus variabilis = Acanthocereus tetragonus
Cereus xanthocarpus = Cereus hildmannianus
Cereus yunckeri = Stenocereus yunckeri
Cerochilus = Hetaeria
Cestichis = Liparis
Chaenanthe = Diadenium
Chaetocephala = Myoxanthus
Chamaeangis spp.: #7 **II** ORCHIDACEAE
Chamaeanthus spp.: #7 **II** ORCHIDACEAE
Chamaecereus silvestrii = Echinopsis chamaecereus
Chamaegastrodia spp.: #7 **II** ORCHIDACEAE
Chamaerepes = Herminium
Chamelophyton spp.: #7 **II** ORCHIDACEAE
Chamorchis spp.: #7 **II** ORCHIDACEAE
Changnienia spp.: #7 **II** ORCHIDACEAE
Chaparral prickly-pear (E): *Opuntia oricola*
Chaseella spp.: #7 **II** ORCHIDACEAE
Chaubardia spp.: #7 **II** ORCHIDACEAE
Chaubardiella spp.: #7 **II** ORCHIDACEAE
Chauliodon spp.: #7 **II** ORCHIDACEAE
Chautle-living rock (E): *Ariocarpus fissuratus*
Cheiradenia spp.: #7 **II** ORCHIDACEAE
Cheiropterocephalus = Malaxis
Cheirorchis = Cordiglottis
Cheirostylis spp.: #7 **II** ORCHIDACEAE
Chelonanthera = Pholidota
Chelonistele spp.: #7 **II** ORCHIDACEAE
Chianthemum elwesii = Galanthus elwesii
Chianthemum graecum = Galanthus elwesii
Chianthemum nivale = Galanthus nivalis
Chianthemum olgae = Galanthus reginae-olgae ssp. *reginae-olgae*
Chianthemum plicatum = Galanthus plicatus ssp. *plicatus*
Chiapasia nelsonii = Disocactus nelsonii
Chigua spp.: (E) cycads **I** ZAMIACEAE
Chigua bernalii: **I** ZAMIACEAE
Chigua restrepoi: **I** ZAMIACEAE
Chihuahuan Desert butterfly-cactus (E): *Neolloydia conoidea*
Chihuahuan fish-hook cactus (E): *Sclerocactus uncinatus*
Chihuahuan foxtail-cactus (E): *Coryphantha cornifera*
Chilean false larch (E): *Fitzroya cupressoides*
Chilean pine (E): *Araucaria araucana*
Chileorebutia duripulpa = Eriosyce napina ssp. *lembckei*
Chileorebutia esmeraldana = Eriosyce esmeraldana
Chileorebutia malleolata = Eriosyce krausii
Chiloglottis spp.: #7 **II** ORCHIDACEAE
Chilopogon = Appendicula
Chiloschista spp.: #7 **II** ORCHIDACEAE
Chitonanthera = Octarrhena
Chitonochilus = Agrostophyllum
Chloraea spp.: #7 **II** ORCHIDACEAE
Chlorosa = Cryptostylis
Choeradoplectron = Habenaria
Chondradenia = Orchis
Chondrorhyncha spp.: #7 **II** ORCHIDACEAE
Christensonia spp.: #7 **II** ORCHIDACEAE
Christmas orchid (E): *Cattleya trianaei*

Chroniochilus spp.: #7 **II** ORCHIDACEAE
Chrysalidocarpus decipiens: (E) Butterfly palm #1 **II** PALMAE
Chrysobaphus = Anoectochilus
Chrysocycnis spp.: #7 **II** ORCHIDACEAE
Chrysoglossum spp.: #7 **II** ORCHIDACEAE
Chusua spp.: #7 **II** ORCHIDACEAE
Chysis spp.: #7 **II** ORCHIDACEAE
Chytroglossa spp.: #7 **II** ORCHIDACEAE
Cibotium barometz: #1 **II** DICKSONIACEAE
Cícadas (S): CYCADACEAE spp/ ZAMIACEAE spp.
Ciclámenes (S): *Cyclamen* spp.
Cigar-box cedar (E): *Cedrela odorata*
Cigar-box wood (E): *Cedrela odorata*
Cintia knizei: #4 **II** CACTACEAE
Cionisaccus = Goodyera
Cipocereus bradei: #4 **II** CACTACEAE
Cipocereus crassisepalus: #4 **II** CACTACEAE
Cipocereus laniflorus: #4 **II** CACTACEAE
Cipocereus minensis ssp. *minensis*: #4 **II** CACTACEAE
Cipocereus minensis ssp. *pleurocarpus*: #4 **II** CACTACEAE
Cipocereus minensis: #4 **II** CACTACEAE
Cipocereus pleurocarpus = Cipocereus minensis ssp. *pleurocarpus*
Cipocereus pusilliflorus: #4 **II** CACTACEAE
Ciprès (F): *Pilgerodendron uviferum*
Ciprés chileno (S): *Pilgerodendron uviferum*
Ciprés de la Patagonia (S): *Fitzroya cupressoides*
Ciprés de las Guaitecas (S): *Pilgerodendron uviferum*
Ciprés de las Guayatecas (S): *Pilgerodendron uviferum*
Ciprés de las Islas Len (S): *Pilgerodendron uviferum*
Cirio (S): *Fouquieria columnaris*
Ciripedium = Cypripedium
Cirrhaea spp.: #7 **II** ORCHIDACEAE
Cirrhopetalum = Bulbophyllum
Cischweinfia spp.: #7 **II** ORCHIDACEAE
Cistanche deserticola: (E) Desert cistanche, Desert living cistanche #3 **II** SCROPHULARIACEAE
Cistella = Geodorum
Claderia spp.: #7 **II** ORCHIDACEAE
Cladobium = Scaphyglottis
Cladobium = Stenorrhynchos
Clanwilliam aloe (E): *Aloe comosa*
Clavel del aire (S): *Tillandsia* spp.
Cleisocentron spp.: #7 **II** ORCHIDACEAE
Cleisomeria spp.: #7 **II** ORCHIDACEAE
Cleisostoma spp.: #7 **II** ORCHIDACEAE
Cleisostomopsis spp.: #7 **II** ORCHIDACEAE
Cleistes spp.: #7 **II** ORCHIDACEAE
Cleistocactus acanthurus: #4 **II** CACTACEAE
Cleistocactus acanthurus ssp. *acanthurus*: #4 **II** CACTACEAE
Cleistocactus acanthurus ssp. *faustianus*: #4 **II** CACTACEAE
Cleistocactus acanthurus ssp. *pullatus*: #4 **II** CACTACEAE
Cleistocactus angosturensis = Cleistocactus buchtienii
Cleistocactus anguinus = Cleistocactus baumannii ssp. *anguinus*
Cleistocactus apurimacensis = Cleistocactus morawetzianus
Cleistocactus areolatus = Cleistocactus parviflorus
Cleistocactus aureispinus = Cleistocactus baumannii ssp. *baumannii*
Cleistocactus ayopayanus = Cleistocactus buchtienii
Cleistocactus azerensis = Cleistocactus parapetiensis
Cleistocactus baumannii: #4 **II** CACTACEAE
Cleistocactus baumannii ssp. *anguinus*: #4 **II** CACTACEAE
Cleistocactus baumannii ssp. *baumannii*: #4 **II** CACTACEAE
Cleistocactus baumannii ssp. *chacoanus*: #4 **II** CACTACEAE
Cleistocactus baumannii ssp. *croceiflorus*: #4 **II** CACTACEAE
Cleistocactus baumannii ssp. *horstii*: #4 **II** CACTACEAE
Cleistocactus baumannii ssp. *santacruzensis*: #4 **II** CACTACEAE
Cleistocactus brevispinus = Cleistocactus peculiaris
Cleistocactus brookeae: #4 **II** CACTACEAE
Cleistocactus bruneispinus = Cleistocactus baumannii ssp. *baumannii*
Cleistocactus buchtienii: #4 **II** CACTACEAE
Cleistocactus candelilla: #4 **II** CACTACEAE
Cleistocactus capadalensis = Cleistocactus tominensis
Cleistocactus chacoanus = Cleistocactus baumannii ssp. *chacoanus*

Cleistocactus chotaensis: #4 **II** CACTACEAE
Cleistocactus clavicaulis = *Cleistocactus tominensis*
Cleistocactus clavispinus: #4 **II** CACTACEAE
Cleistocactus compactus = *Cleistocactus tarijensis*
Cleistocactus crassicaulis = *Cleistocactus tominensis*
Cleistocactus croceiflorus = *Cleistocactus baumannii* ssp.
    croceiflorus
Cleistocactus dependens: #4 **II** CACTACEAE
Cleistocactus ferrarii: #4 **II** CACTACEAE
Cleistocactus fieldianus: #4 **II** CACTACEAE
Cleistocactus fieldianus ssp. *fieldianus*: #4 **II** CACTACEAE
Cleistocactus fieldianus ssp. *samnensis*: #4 **II** CACTACEAE
Cleistocactus fieldianus ssp. *tessellatus*: #4 **II** CACTACEAE
Cleistocactus flavispinus = *Cleistocactus baumannii* ssp.
    baumannii
Cleistocactus fusiflorus = *Cleistocactus parviflorus*
Cleistocactus glaucus = *Cleistocactus luribayensis*
Cleistocactus granjaensis = *Cleistocactus luribayensis*
Cleistocactus grossei: #4 **II** CACTACEAE
Cleistocactus herzogianus = *Cleistocactus parviflorus*
Cleistocactus hildegardiae: #4 **II** CACTACEAE
Cleistocactus horstii = *Cleistocactus baumannii* ssp. *horstii*
Cleistocactus humboldtii = *Cleistocactus icosagonus*
Cleistocactus hyalacanthus: #4 **II** CACTACEAE
Cleistocactus hystrix: #4 **II** CACTACEAE
Cleistocactus ianthinus = *Cleistocactus candelilla*
Cleistocactus icosagonus: #4 **II** CACTACEAE
Cleistocactus jujuyensis = *Cleistocactus hyalacanthus*
Cleistocactus laniceps: #4 **II** CACTACEAE
Cleistocactus leonensis = *Cleistocactus serpens*
Cleistocactus luminosus = *Cleistocactus morawetzianus*
Cleistocactus luribayensis: #4 **II** CACTACEAE
Cleistocactus mendozae = *Cleistocactus tominensis*
Cleistocactus micropetalus: #4 **II** CACTACEAE
Cleistocactus morawetzianus: #4 **II** CACTACEAE
Cleistocactus muyurinensis: #4 **II** CACTACEAE
Cleistocactus neoroezlii: #4 **II** CACTACEAE
Cleistocactus orthogonus: #4 **II** CACTACEAE
Cleistocactus pachycladus: #4 **II** CACTACEAE
Cleistocactus palhuayensis: #4 **II** CACTACEAE
Cleistocactus paraguariensis: #4 **II** CACTACEAE
Cleistocactus parapetiensis: #4 **II** CACTACEAE
Cleistocactus parviflorus: #4 **II** CACTACEAE
Cleistocactus peculiaris: #4 **II** CACTACEAE
Cleistocactus piraymirensis: #4 **II** CACTACEAE
Cleistocactus plagiostoma: #4 **II** CACTACEAE
Cleistocactus pojoensis = *Cleistocactus candelilla*
Cleistocactus pungens: #4 **II** CACTACEAE
Cleistocactus pycnacanthus = *Cleistocactus morawetzianus*
Cleistocactus reae: #4 **II** CACTACEAE
Cleistocactus ressinianus = *Cleistocactus buchtienii*
Cleistocactus ritteri: #4 **II** CACTACEAE
Cleistocactus roezlii: #4 **II** CACTACEAE
Cleistocactus samaipatanus: #4 **II** CACTACEAE
Cleistocactus santacruzensis = *Cleistocactus baumannii* ssp.
    santacruzensis
Cleistocactus sepium: #4 **II** CACTACEAE
Cleistocactus serpens: #4 **II** CACTACEAE
Cleistocactus sextonianus: #4 **II** CACTACEAE
Cleistocactus smaragdiflorus: #4 **II** CACTACEAE
Cleistocactus strausii: #4 **II** CACTACEAE
Cleistocactus sucrensis = *Cleistocactus buchtienii*
Cleistocactus tarijensis: #4 **II** CACTACEAE
Cleistocactus tenuiserpens: #4 **II** CACTACEAE
Cleistocactus tominensis: #4 **II** CACTACEAE
Cleistocactus tupizensis: #4 **II** CACTACEAE
Cleistocactus vallegrandensis = *Cleistocactus candelilla*
Cleistocactus varispinus: #4 **II** CACTACEAE
Cleistocactus villaazulensis = *Cleistocactus morawetzianus*
Cleistocactus viridialabastri = *Cleistocactus tominensis*
Cleistocactus viridiflorus = *Cleistocactus palhuayensis*
Cleistocactus vulpis-cauda: #4 **II** CACTACEAE
Cleistocactus wendlandiorum = *Cleistocactus brookeae*
Cleistocactus winteri: #4 **II** CACTACEAE
Cleistocactus xylorhizus: #4 **II** CACTACEAE

Clematepistephium spp.: #7 **II** ORCHIDACEAE
Cliff spurge (E): *Euphorbia misera*
Clistanthocereus calviflorus = *Cleistocactus fieldianus* ssp.
    fieldianus
Clistanthocereus fieldianus = *Cleistocactus fieldianus* ssp.
    fieldianus
Clistanthocereus samnensis = *Cleistocactus fieldianus* ssp.
    samnensis
Clistanthocereus tessellatus = *Cleistocactus fieldianus* ssp.
    tessellatus
Clowesia spp.: #7 **II** ORCHIDACEAE
Club cholla (E): *Opuntia clavata*
Club-shaped euphorb (E): *Euphorbia clava*
Cnemidaria apiculata = *Cyathea aristata*
Cnemidaria choricarpa = *Cyathea choricarpa*
Cnemidaria cruciata = *Cyathea leprieurii*
Cnemidaria decurrens = *Cyathea lucida*
Cnemidaria glandulosa = *Cyathea glandulosa*
Cnemidaria grandifolia var. *grandifolia* = *Cyathea grandifolia*
Cnemidaria horrida = *Cyathea horrida*
Cnemidaria quitensis = *Cyathea andicola*
Cnemidaria uleana = *Cyathea subarborescens*
Cnemidia = *Tropidia*
Coast Barrel cactus (E): *Ferocactus viridescens*
Coastal cholla (E): *Opuntia prolifera*
Coastal prickly-pear (E): *Opuntia littoralis*
Cobano (S): *Swietenia humilis*
Coccineorchis = *Stenorrhynchos*
Cochemiea halei = *Mammillaria halei*
Cochemiea maritima = *Mammillaria pondii* ssp. *maritima*
Cochemiea pondii = *Mammillaria pondii* ssp. *pondii*
Cochemiea poselgeri = *Mammillaria poselgeri*
Cochemiea setispina = *Mammillaria pondii* ssp. *setispina*
Cochineal cactus (E): *Opuntia cochenillifera*
Cochiseia robbinsorum = *Escobaria robbinsorum*
Cochleanthes spp.: #7 **II** ORCHIDACEAE
Cochlia = *Bulbophyllum*
Cochlioda spp.: #7 **II** ORCHIDACEAE
Codonorchis spp.: #7 **II** ORCHIDACEAE
Codonosiphon = *Bulbophyllum*
Coelandria = *Dendrobium*
Coelia spp.: #7 **II** ORCHIDACEAE
Coeliopsis spp.: #7 **II** ORCHIDACEAE
Coeloglossum spp.: #7 **II** ORCHIDACEAE
Coelogyne spp.: #7 **II** ORCHIDACEAE
Cogniauxiocharis = *Stenorrhynchos*
Cohnia = *Cohniella*
Cohniella spp.: #7 **II** ORCHIDACEAE
Coilochilus spp.: #7 **II** ORCHIDACEAE
Coilostylis = *Epidendrum*
Cola de mono (S): *Cyathea mexicana*
Colax = *Pabstia*
Coleocephalocereus albicephalus = *Micranthocereus albicephalus*
Coleocephalocereus aureus: #4 **II** CACTACEAE
Coleocephalocereus aureus ssp. *brevicylindricus* =
    Coleocephalocereus aureus
Coleocephalocereus aureus ssp. *elongatus* = *Coleocephalocereus*
    aureus
Coleocephalocereus aureus ssp. *longispinus* = *Coleocephalocereus*
    aureus
Coleocephalocereus braunii = *Coleocephalocereus buxbaumianus*
    ssp. *buxbaumianus*
Coleocephalocereus brevicylindricus = *Coleocephalocereus aureus*
Coleocephalocereus buxbaumianus: #4 **II** CACTACEAE
Coleocephalocereus buxbaumianus ssp. *buxbaumianus*: #4 **II**
    CACTACEAE
Coleocephalocereus buxbaumianus ssp. *flavisetus*: #4 **II**
    CACTACEAE
Coleocephalocereus decumbens = *Coleocephalocereus fluminensis*
    ssp. *decumbens*
Coleocephalocereus diersianus = *Coleocephalocereus fluminensis*
    ssp. *fluminensis*
Coleocephalocereus dybowskii = *Espostoopsis dybowskii*
Coleocephalocereus elongatus = *Coleocephalocereus aureus*

Coleocephalocereus estevesii = *Coleocephalocereus buxbaumianus* ssp. *flavisetus*
Coleocephalocereus flavisetus = *Coleocephalocereus buxbaumianus* ssp. *flavisetus*
Coleocephalocereus fluminensis: #4 **II** CACTACEAE
Coleocephalocereus fluminensis ssp. *braamhaarii* = *Coleocephalocereus fluminensis* ssp. *fluminensis*
Coleocephalocereus fluminensis ssp. *decumbens*: #4 **II** CACTACEAE
Coleocephalocereus fluminensis ssp. *fluminensis*: #4 **II** CACTACEAE
Coleocephalocereus fluminensis ssp. *paulensis* = *Coleocephalocereus fluminensis* ssp. *fluminensis*
Coleocephalocereus goebelianus: #4 **II** CACTACEAE
Coleocephalocereus lehmannianus = *Micranthocereus purpureus*
Coleocephalocereus pachystele = *Coleocephalocereus goebelianus*
Coleocephalocereus paulensis = *Coleocephalocereus fluminensis* ssp. *fluminensis*
Coleocephalocereus pluricostatus: #4 **II** CACTACEAE
Coleocephalocereus pluricostatus ssp. *uebelmanniorum* = *Coleocephalocereus pluricostatus*
Coleocephalocereus purpureus: #4 **II** CACTACEAE
Collabiopsis = *Collabium*
Collabium spp.: #7 **II** ORCHIDACEAE
Collea = *Pelexia*
Colombiana = *Pleurothallis*
Columbea imbricata = *Araucaria araucana*
Columbea quadrifaria = *Araucaria araucana*
Common snowdrop (E): *Galanthus nivalis*
Common sternbergia (E): *Sternbergia lutea*
Commoner lignum vitae (E): *Guaiacum officinale*
Comparettia spp.: #7 **II** ORCHIDACEAE
Comperia spp.: #7 **II** ORCHIDACEAE
Conchidium = *Eria*
Conchochilus = *Appendicula*
Condylago spp.: #7 **II** ORCHIDACEAE
Conelike Turk's-cap cactus (E): *Melocactus conoideus*
Conostalix = *Eria*
Consolea corallicola = *Opuntia spinosissima*
Consolea falcata = *Opuntia falcata*
Consolea macracantha = *Opuntia macracantha*
Consolea millspaughii = *Opuntia millspaughii*
Consolea moniliformis = *Opuntia moniliformis*
Consolea moniliformis ssp. *guantanamana* = *Opuntia moniliformis*
Consolea nashii = *Opuntia nashii*
Consolea nashii ssp. *gibarensis* = *Opuntia nashii*
Consolea rubescens = *Opuntia rubescens*
Consolea spinosissima = *Opuntia spinosissima*
Constantia spp.: #7 **II** ORCHIDACEAE
Copey oak (E): *Quercus copeyensis*
Copiapoa alticostata = *Copiapoa coquimbana*
Copiapoa applanata = *Copiapoa cinerascens*
Copiapoa atacamensis = *Copiapoa calderana* ssp. *calderana*
Copiapoa barquitensis = *Copiapoa hypogaeae*
Copiapoa boliviana = *Copiapoa calderana* ssp. *calderana*
Copiapoa bridgesii: #4 **II** CACTACEAE
Copiapoa brunnescens = *Copiapoa megarhiza*
Copiapoa calderana: #4 **II** CACTACEAE
Copiapoa calderana ssp. *calderana*: #4 **II** CACTACEAE
Copiapoa calderana ssp. *longistaminea*: #4 **II** CACTACEAE
Copiapoa carrizalensis = *Copiapoa malletiana*
Copiapoa castanea = *Copiapoa serpentisulcata*
Copiapoa chanaralensis: #4 **II** CACTACEAE
Copiapoa chaniaralensis = *Copiapoa chanaralensis*
Copiapoa cinerascens: #4 **II** CACTACEAE
Copiapoa cinerea: #4 **II** CACTACEAE
Copiapoa cinerea ssp. *cinerea*: #4 **II** CACTACEAE
Copiapoa cinerea ssp. *columna-alba* = *Copiapoa cinerea* ssp. *cinerea*
Copiapoa cinerea ssp. *dealbata* = *Copiapoa malletiana*
Copiapoa cinerea ssp. *gigantea* = *Copiapoa cinerea* ssp. *haseltoniana*
Copiapoa cinerea ssp. *haseltoniana*: #4 **II** CACTACEAE
Copiapoa cinerea ssp. *krainziana*: #4 **II** CACTACEAE

Copiapoa cinerea ssp. *longistaminea* = *Copiapoa calderana* ssp. *longistaminea*
Copiapoa conglomerata = *Copiapoa solaris*
Copiapoa copiapensis: #4 **II** CACTACEAE
Copiapoa coquimbana: #4 **II** CACTACEAE
Copiapoa cuprea = *Copiapoa echinoides*
Copiapoa cupreata = *Copiapoa echinoides*
Copiapoa dealbata = *Copiapoa malletiana*
Copiapoa desertorum: #4 **II** CACTACEAE
Copiapoa dura = *Copiapoa echinoides*
Copiapoa echinata = *Copiapoa fiedleriana*
Copiapoa echinoides: #4 **II** CACTACEAE
Copiapoa eremophila = *Copiapoa cinerea* ssp. *haseltoniana*
Copiapoa esmeraldana = *Copiapoa humilis*
Copiapoa ferox = *Copiapoa solaris*
Copiapoa fiedleriana: #4 **II** CACTACEAE
Copiapoa gigantea = *Copiapoa cinerea* ssp. *haseltoniana*
Copiapoa grandiflora = *Copiapoa montana* ssp. *grandiflora*
Copiapoa haseltoniana = *Copiapoa cinerea* ssp. *haseltoniana*
Copiapoa hornilloensis: #4 **II** CACTACEAE
Copiapoa humilis: #4 **II** CACTACEAE
Copiapoa hypogaea: #4 **II** CACTACEAE
Copiapoa intermedia = *Copiapoa fiedleriana*
Copiapoa krainziana = *Copiapoa cinerea* ssp. *krainziana*
Copiapoa laui: #4 **II** CACTACEAE
Copiapoa lembckei = *Copiapoa calderana* spp. *calderana*
Copiapoa longispina = *Copiapoa humilis*
Copiapoa longistaminea = *Copiapoa calderana* ssp. *longistaminea*
Copiapoa macracantha: #4 **II** CACTACEAE
Copiapoa malletiana: #4 **II** CACTACEAE
Copiapoa marginata: #4 **II** CACTACEAE
Copiapoa megarhiza: #4 **II** CACTACEAE
Copiapoa melanohystrix = *Copiapoa cinerea* ssp. *haseltoniana*
Copiapoa mollicula = *Copiapoa montana* ssp. *montana*
Copiapoa montana: #4 **II** CACTACEAE
Copiapoa montana ssp. *grandiflora*: #4 **II** CACTACEAE
Copiapoa montana ssp. *montana*: #4 **II** CACTACEAE
Copiapoa olivana = *Copiapoa montana* ssp. *montana*
Copiapoa paposoensis = *Copiapoa humilis*
Copiapoa pendulina = *Copiapoa coquimbana*
Copiapoa pepiniana = *Copiapoa coquimbana*
Copiapoa psuedocoquimbana = *Copiapoa fiedleriana*
Copiapoa rarissima = *Copiapoa montana* ssp. *montana*
Copiapoa rubriflora = *Copiapoa rupestris*
Copiapoa rupestris: #4 **II** CACTACEAE
Copiapoa serenana = *Copiapoa coquimbana*
Copiapoa serpentisulcata: #4 **II** CACTACEAE
Copiapoa solaris: #4 **II** CACTACEAE
Copiapoa streptocaulon = *Copiapoa marginata*
Copiapoa taltalensis = *Copiapoa humilis*
Copiapoa tenebrosa = *Copiapoa cinerea* ssp. *haseltoniana*
Copiapoa tenuissima: #4 **II** CACTACEAE
Copiapoa tocopillana: #4 **II** CACTACEAE
Copiapoa totoralensis = *Copiapoa fiedleriana*
Copiapoa vallenarensis = *Copiapoa coquimbana*
Copiapoa varispinata: #4 **II** CACTACEAE
Copiapoa wagenknechtii = *Copiapoa coquimbana*
Copos de nieve (S): *Galanthus* spp.
Corallorhiza = *Corallorrhiza*
Corallorrhiza spp.: #7 **II** ORCHIDACEAE
Cordanthera spp.: #7 **II** ORCHIDACEAE
Cordiglottis spp.: #7 **II** ORCHIDACEAE
Cordula = *Paphiopedilum*
Cordula amabilis = *Paphiopedilum bullenianum*
Cordula appletoniana = *Paphiopedilum appletonianum*
Cordula argus = *Paphiopedilum argus*
Cordula barbata = *Paphiopedilum barbatum*
Cordula bellatula = *Paphiopedilum bellatulum*
Cordula boxallii = *Paphiopedilum villosum* var. *boxallii*
Cordula bulleniana = *Paphiopedilum bullenianum*
Cordula callosa = *Paphiopedilum callosum*
Cordula charlesworthii = *Paphiopedilum charlesworthii*
Cordula ciliolaris = *Paphiopedilum ciliolare*
Cordula concolor = *Paphiopedilum concolor*
Cordula curtisii = *Paphiopedilum superbiens* var. *curtisii*

Checklist of flora/Lista de especies de flora/Liste des espèces végétales

Cordula dayana = Paphiopedilum dayanum
Cordula druryi = Paphiopedilum druryi
Cordula fairrieana = Paphiopedilum fairrieanum
Cordula glandulifera = Paphiopedilum glanduliferum
Cordula glaucophylla = Paphiopedilum glaucophyllum
Cordula godefroyae = Paphiopedilum godefroyae
Cordula haynaldiana = Paphiopedilum haynaldianum
Cordula hirsutissima = Paphiopedilum hirsutissimum
Cordula hookerae = Paphiopedilum hookerae
Cordula insignis = Paphiopedilum insigne
Cordula javanica = Paphiopedilum javanicum
Cordula lawrenceana = Paphiopedilum lawrenceanum
Cordula lowii = Paphiopedilum lowii
Cordula mastersiana = Paphiopedilum mastersianum
Cordula nigrita = Paphiopedilum barbatum
Cordula nivea = Paphiopedilum niveum
Cordula parishii = Paphiopedilum parishii
Cordula petri = Paphiopedilum dayanum
Cordula philippinensis = Paphiopedilum philippinense
Cordula purpurata = Paphiopedilum purpuratum
Cordula rothschildiana = Paphiopedilum rothschildianum
Cordula sanderiana = Paphiopedilum sanderianum
Cordula spiceriana = Paphiopedilum spicerianum
Cordula stonei = Paphiopedilum stonei
Cordula superbiens = Paphiopedilum superbiens
Cordula tonsa = Paphiopedilum tonsum
Cordula venusta = Paphiopedilum venustum
Cordula victoria-mariae = Paphiopedilum victoria-mariae
Cordula villosa = Paphiopedilum villosum
Cordula violascens = Paphiopedilum violascens
Cordyla = Nervilia
Cordylestylis = Goodyera
Correll's Green Pitaya (E): *Echinocereus viridiflorus* ssp. *correllii*
Corryocactus acervatus: #4 **II** CACTACEAE
Corryocactus apiciflorus: #4 **II** CACTACEAE
Corryocactus aureus: #4 **II** CACTACEAE
Corryocactus ayacuchoensis: #4 **II** CACTACEAE
Corryocactus ayopayanus: #4 **II** CACTACEAE
Corryocactus brachycladus: #4 **II** CACTACEAE
Corryocactus brachypetalus: #4 **II** CACTACEAE
Corryocactus brevispinus: #4 **II** CACTACEAE
Corryocactus brevistylus: #4 **II** CACTACEAE
Corryocactus brevistylus ssp. *brevistylus*: #4 **II** CACTACEAE
Corryocactus brevistylus ssp. *puquiensis*: #4 **II** CACTACEAE
Corryocactus chachapoyensis: #4 **II** CACTACEAE
Corryocactus charazanensis: #4 **II** CACTACEAE
Corryocactus chavinilloensis: #4 **II** CACTACEAE
Corryocactus cuajonesensis: #4 **II** CACTACEAE
Corryocactus erectus: #4 **II** CACTACEAE
Corryocactus gracilis: #4 **II** CACTACEAE
Corryocactus heteracanthus: #4 **II** CACTACEAE
Corryocactus huincoensis: #4 **II** CACTACEAE
Corryocactus krausii = Corryocactus brevistylus ssp. *brevistylus*
Corryocactus matucanensis = Corryocactus huincoensis
Corryocactus maximus = Corryocactus apiciflorus
Corryocactus megarhizus: #4 **II** CACTACEAE
Corryocactus melaleucus: #4 **II** CACTACEAE
Corryocactus melanotrichus: #4 **II** CACTACEAE
Corryocactus odoratus: #4 **II** CACTACEAE
Corryocactus otuyensis: #4 **II** CACTACEAE
Corryocactus pachycladus = Corryocactus pulquinensis
Corryocactus perezianus: #4 **II** CACTACEAE
Corryocactus pilispinus: #4 **II** CACTACEAE
Corryocactus prostratus: #4 **II** CACTACEAE
Corryocactus pulquinensis: #4 **II** CACTACEAE
Corryocactus puquiensis = Corryocactus brevistylus ssp. *puquiensis*
Corryocactus pyroporphyranthus: #4 **II** CACTACEAE
Corryocactus quadrangularis: #4 **II** CACTACEAE
Corryocactus quivillanus: #4 **II** CACTACEAE
Corryocactus serpens: #4 **II** CACTACEAE
Corryocactus solitarius: #4 **II** CACTACEAE
Corryocactus spiniflorus = Austrocactus spiniflorus
Corryocactus squarrosus: #4 **II** CACTACEAE
Corryocactus tarijensis: #4 **II** CACTACEAE

Corryocactus tenuiculus: #4 **II** CACTACEAE
Corunastylis = Genoplesium
Coryanthes spp.: #7 **II** ORCHIDACEAE
Corybas spp.: #7 **II** ORCHIDACEAE
Corycium spp.: #7 **II** ORCHIDACEAE
Corymbis = Corymborkis
Corymborchis = Corymborkis
Corymborkis spp.: #7 **II** ORCHIDACEAE
Corynopuntia agglomerata = Opuntia agglomerata
Corynopuntia bulbispina = Opuntia bulbispina
Corynopuntia clavata = Opuntia clavata
Corynopuntia dumetorum = Opuntia dumetorum
Corynopuntia grahamii = Opuntia grahamii
Corynopuntia moelleriana = Opuntia moelleri
Corynopuntia pulchella = Opuntia pulchella
Corynopuntia reflexispina = Opuntia reflexispina
Corynopuntia schottii = Opuntia schottii
Corynopuntia stanlyi = Opuntia emoryi
Coryphantha aggregata = Escobaria vivipara
Coryphantha albicolumnaria = Escobaria albicolumnaria
Coryphantha alversonii = Escobaria alversonii
Coryphantha andreae = Coryphantha pycnacantha
Coryphantha arizonica = Escobaria vivipara
Coryphantha asterias = Coryphantha ottonis
Coryphantha bergeriana = Coryphantha glanduligera
Coryphantha bernalensis = Coryphantha radians
Coryphantha borwigii = Coryphantha salinensis
Coryphantha bumamma = Coryphantha elephantidens
Coryphantha bussleri = Coryphantha ottonis
Coryphantha calipensis: #4 **II** CACTACEAE
Coryphantha calochlora: #4 **II** CACTACEAE
Coryphantha chlorantha = Escobaria deserti
Coryphantha clava = Coryphantha octacantha
Coryphantha clavata: #4 **II** CACTACEAE
Coryphantha columnaris = Escobaria vivipara
Coryphantha compacta: #4 **II** CACTACEAE
Coryphantha conimamma = Coryphantha sulcolanata
Coryphantha connivens = Coryphantha pycnacantha
Coryphantha cornifera: (E) Chihuahuan Foxtail-cactus #4 **II** CACTACEAE
Coryphantha cornuta: #4 **II** CACTACEAE
Coryphantha cubensis = Escobaria cubensis
Coryphantha cuencamensis = Coryphantha delaetiana
Coryphantha daimonoceras = Coryphantha radians
Coryphantha delaetiana: #4 **II** CACTACEAE
Coryphantha delicata = Coryphantha radians
Coryphantha densispina = Coryphantha werdermannii
Coryphantha deserti = Escobaria deserti
Coryphantha difficilis: #4 **II** CACTACEAE
Coryphantha duncanii = Escobaria duncanii
Coryphantha durangensis: #4 **II** CACTACEAE
Coryphantha echinoidea: #4 **II** CACTACEAE
Coryphantha echinus: #4 **II** CACTACEAE
Coryphantha elephantidens: #4 **II** CACTACEAE
Coryphantha erecta: #4 **II** CACTACEAE
Coryphantha exsudans = Coryphantha ottonis
Coryphantha garessii = Coryphantha elephantidens
Coryphantha georgii: #4 **II** CACTACEAE
Coryphantha gladiispina = Coryphantha delaetiana
Coryphantha glanduligera: #4 **II** CACTACEAE
Coryphantha gracilis: #4 **II** CACTACEAE
Coryphantha grandis = Coryphantha longicornis
Coryphantha grata: #4 **II** CACTACEAE
Coryphantha greenwoodii = Coryphantha elephantidens
Coryphantha guerkeana: #4 **II** CACTACEAE
Coryphantha henricksonii = Escobaria chihuahuensis ssp. *henricksonii*
Coryphantha indensis: #4 **II** CACTACEAE
Coryphantha jalpanensis: #4 **II** CACTACEAE
Coryphantha jaumavei: #4 **II** CACTACEAE
Coryphantha laredoi = Escobaria laredoi
Coryphantha laui = Coryphantha delaetiana
Coryphantha longicornis: #4 **II** CACTACEAE
Coryphantha macromeris: (E) Long Mamma Foxtail-cactus #4 **II** CACTACEAE

Coryphantha macromeris ssp. *macromeris*: #4 **II** CACTACEAE
Coryphantha macromeris ssp. *runyonii*: (E) Big-nipple Cory cactus #4 **II** CACTACEAE
Coryphantha maiz-tablasensis: #4 **II** CACTACEAE
Coryphantha maliterrarum: #4 **II** CACTACEAE
Coryphantha melleospina: #4 **II** CACTACEAE
Coryphantha minima = *Escobaria minima*
Coryphantha missouriensis = *Escobaria missouriensis* ssp. *missouriensis*
Coryphantha muehlenpfordtii = *Coryphantha robustispina* ssp. *scheeri*
Coryphantha muehlenpfordtii ssp. *robustispina* = *Coryphantha robustispina* ssp. *robustispina*
Coryphantha muehlenpfordtii ssp. *uncinata* = *Coryphantha robustispina* ssp. *uncinata*
Coryphantha neglecta: #4 **II** CACTACEAE
Coryphantha neoscheeri = *Coryphantha robustispina* ssp. *scheeri*
Coryphantha nickelsiae: #4 **II** CACTACEAE
Coryphantha obscura = *Coryphantha sulcata*
Coryphantha octacantha: #4 **II** CACTACEAE
Coryphantha odorata: #4 **II** CACTACEAE
Coryphantha orcuttii = *Escobaria orcuttii*
Coryphantha organensis = *Escobaria organensis*
Coryphantha ottonis: #4 **II** CACTACEAE
Coryphantha pallida: #4 **II** CACTACEAE
Coryphantha palmeri = *Coryphantha compacta*
Coryphantha palmeri = *Coryphantha jaumavei*
Coryphantha pectinata = *Coryphantha echinus*
Coryphantha pirtlei = *Coryphantha macromeris*
Coryphantha poselgeriana: #4 **II** CACTACEAE
Coryphantha potosiana: #4 **II** CACTACEAE
Coryphantha pseudoechinus: #4 **II** CACTACEAE
Coryphantha pseudonickelsiae = *Coryphantha delaetiana*
Coryphantha pseudoradians: #4 **II** CACTACEAE
Coryphantha pulleineana: #4 **II** CACTACEAE
Coryphantha pusilliflora: #4 **II** CACTACEAE
Coryphantha pycnacantha: #4 **II** CACTACEAE
Coryphantha radians: #4 **II** CACTACEAE
Coryphantha ramillosa: (E) Bunched Cory Cactus #4 **II** CACTACEAE
Coryphantha recurvata: (E) Recurved Corycactus #4 **II** CACTACEAE
Coryphantha recurvispina = *Coryphantha elephantidens*
Coryphantha reduncispina: #4 **II** CACTACEAE
Coryphantha retusa: #4 **II** CACTACEAE
Coryphantha robbinsorum = *Escobaria robbinsorum*
Coryphantha robustispina: #4 **II** CACTACEAE
Coryphantha robustispina ssp. *robustispina*: #4 **II** CACTACEAE
Coryphantha robustispina ssp. *scheeri*: #4 **II** CACTACEAE
Coryphantha robustispina ssp. *uncinata*: #4 **II** CACTACEAE
Coryphantha roederiana = *Coryphantha salinensis*
Coryphantha runyonii = *Coryphantha macromeris* ssp. *runyonii*
Coryphantha salinensis: #4 **II** CACTACEAE
Coryphantha salm-dyckiana = *Coryphantha delaetiana*
Coryphantha scheeri = *Coryphantha robustispina* ssp. *scheeri*
Coryphantha schwarziana = *Coryphantha echinoidea*
Coryphantha sneedii = *Escobaria sneedii*
Coryphantha speciosa = *Coryphantha sulcata*
Coryphantha sulcata: #4 **II** CACTACEAE
Coryphantha sulcolanata: #4 **II** CACTACEAE
Coryphantha tripugionacantha: #4 **II** CACTACEAE
Coryphantha unicornis: #4 **II** CACTACEAE
Coryphantha valida = *Coryphantha poselgeriana*
Coryphantha vaupeliana: #4 **II** CACTACEAE
Coryphantha villarensis = *Coryphantha georgii*
Coryphantha vivipara = *Escobaria vivipara*
Coryphantha vogtherriana: #4 **II** CACTACEAE
Coryphantha werdermannii: (E) Jabali pincushion cactus **I** CACTACEAE
Coryphantha wohlschlageri: #4 **II** CACTACEAE
Corysanthes = *Corybas*
Costaricaea = *Hexisea*
Costus (E): *Caryocar costaricense*
Costus root (E): *Saussurea costus*
Cottonia spp.: #7 **II** ORCHIDACEAE

Cotton-top cactus (E): *Echinocactus polycephalus*
Cotylolabium = *Stenorrhynchos*
Covill's barrel cactus (E): *Ferocactus emoryi*
Cranichis spp.: #7 **II** ORCHIDACEAE
Cremastra spp.: #7 **II** ORCHIDACEAE
Crepidium = *Malaxis*
Cribbia spp.: #7 **II** ORCHIDACEAE
Crimson pitcherplant (E): *Sarracenia leucophylla*
Crinonia = *Pholidota*
Criogenes = *Cypripedium*
Criosanthes = *Cypripedium*
Cristóbal (S): *Platymiscium pleiostachyum*
Crocodeilanthe = *Pleurothallis*
Crossangis = *Diaphananthe*
Crown of thorns (E): *Euphorbia milii* var. *milii*/ *Euphorbia milii* var. *splendens*
Crybe spp.: #7 **II** ORCHIDACEAE
Cryptanthemis = *Rhizanthella*
Cryptarrhena spp.: #7 **II** ORCHIDACEAE
Cryptocentrum spp.: #7 **II** ORCHIDACEAE
Cryptocereus anthonyanus = *Selenicereus anthonyanus*
Cryptochilus spp.: #7 **II** ORCHIDACEAE
Cryptoglottis = *Podochilus*
Cryptophoranthus = *Pleurothallis*
Cryptopus spp.: #7 **II** ORCHIDACEAE
Cryptopylos spp.: #7 **II** ORCHIDACEAE
Cryptosanus = *Leochilus*
Cryptostylis spp.: #7 **II** ORCHIDACEAE
Ctenitis gomezii = *Cyathea excelsa*
Ctenorchis = *Angraecum*
Cuban mahogany (E): *Swietenia mahagoni*
Cuculina = *Catasetum*
Cuitlauzina spp.: #7 **II** ORCHIDACEAE
Cumarinia odorata = *Coryphantha odorata*
Cumulopuntia berteri = *Opuntia sphaerica*
Cumulopuntia boliviana = *Opuntia chichensis*
Cumulopuntia crassicylindrica = *Opuntia crassicylindrica*
Cumulopuntia echinacea = *Opuntia boldinghii*
Cumulopuntia famatinenesis = *Opuntia boldinghii*
Cumulopuntia frigida = *Opuntia frigida*
Cumulopuntia galerasensis = *Opuntia galerasensis*
Cumulopuntia hystrix = *Opuntia sanctae-barbarae*
Cumulopuntia ignescens = *Opuntia ignescens*
Cumulopuntia ignota = *Opuntia corotilla*
Cumulopuntia kuehnrichiana = *Opuntia sphaerica*
Cumulopuntia multiareolata = *Opuntia sphaerica*
Cumulopuntia pampana = *Opuntia boldinghii*
Cumulopuntia pentlandii = *Opuntia pentlandii*
Cumulopuntia pyrrhacantha = *Opuntia pyrrhacantha*
Cumulopuntia rauppiana = *Opuntia sphaerica*
Cumulopuntia rossiana = *Opuntia rossiana*
Cumulopuntia subterranea = *Opuntiasubterranea*
Cumulopuntia ticnamarensis = *Opuntia ticnamarensis*
Cumulopuntia tortispina = *Opuntia guatinensis*
Cumulopuntia tubercularis = *Opuntia sphaerica*
Cumulopuntia tumida = *Opuntia tumida*
Cupresstellata patagonica = *Fitzroya cupressoides*
Cutsis = *Dichromanthus*
Cyanaeorchis spp.: #7 **II** ORCHIDACEAE
Cyanicula spp.: #7 **II** ORCHIDACEAE
Cyanorchis = *Phaius*
Cyathea spp.: (E) Tree ferns, (S) Helechos arborescentes **II** CYATHEACEAE
Cyathea abbottii: #1 **II** CYATHEACEAE
Cyathea abitaguensis: #1 **II** CYATHEACEAE
Cyathea acanthomelas: #1 **II** CYATHEACEAE
Cyathea acanthophora: #1 **II** CYATHEACEAE
Cyathea aciculosa: #1**II** CYATHEACEAE
Cyathea acrostichoides: #1 **II** CYATHEACEAE
Cyathea acuminata: #1 **II** CYATHEACEAE
Cyathea acutidens: #1 **II** CYATHEACEAE
Cyathea aeneifolia var. *aeneifolia*: #1 **II** CYATHEACEAE
Cyathea aeneifolia var. *macrophylla*: #1 **II** CYATHEACEAE
Cyathea aeneifolia var. *melanacantha*: #1 **II** CYATHEACEAE
Cyathea affinis: #1 **II** CYATHEACEAE

Cyathea agatheti: #1 **II** CYATHEACEAE
Cyathea akawaiorum::#1 **II** CYATHEACEAE
Cyathea alata: #1 **II** CYATHEACEAE
Cyathea alatissima: #1 **II** CYATHEACEAE
Cyathea albida: #1 **II** CYATHEACEAE
Cyathea albidosquamata: #1 **II** CYATHEACEAE
Cyathea albifrons: #1 **II** CYATHEACEAE
Cyathea albomarginata: #1 **II** CYATHEACEAE
Cyathea albosetacea: #1 **II** CYATHEACEAE
Cyathea alderwereltii: #1 **II** CYATHEACEAE
Cyathea alfonsiana: #1 **II** CYATHEACEAE
Cyathea alleniae: #1 **II** CYATHEACEAE
Cyathea alstonii: #1 **II** CYATHEACEAE
Cyathea alta: #1 **II** CYATHEACEAE
Cyathea alternans: #1 **II** CYATHEACEAE
Cyathea alticola: #1 **II** CYATHEACEAE
Cyathea amabilis: #1 **II** CYATHEACEAE
Cyathea amboinensis: #1 **II** CYATHEACEAE
Cyathea andersonii: #1 **II** CYATHEACEAE
Cyathea andicola: #1 **II** CYATHEACEAE
Cyathea andina: #1 **II** CYATHEACEAE
Cyathea aneitensis: #1 **II** CYATHEACEAE
Cyathea angiensis: #1 **II** CYATHEACEAE
Cyathea angustipinna: #1 **II** CYATHEACEAE
Cyathea annae: #1 **II** CYATHEACEAE
Cyathea apiculata: #1 **II** CYATHEACEAE
Cyathea apoensis: #1 **II** CYATHEACEAE
Cyathea appendiculata: #1 **II** CYATHEACEAE
Cyathea approximata var. *approximata*: #1 **II** CYATHEACEAE
Cyathea approximata var. *sorisquamata*: #1 **II** CYATHEACEAE
Cyathea aramaganensis: #1 **II** CYATHEACEAE
Cyathea arborea: #1 **II** CYATHEACEAE
Cyathea archboldii: #1 **II** CYATHEACEAE
Cyathea arfakensis: #1 **II** CYATHEACEAE
Cyathea aristata: #1 **II** CYATHEACEAE
Cyathea armata: #1 **II** CYATHEACEAE
Cyathea arthropoda: #1 **II** CYATHEACEAE
Cyathea ascendens: #1 **II** CYATHEACEAE
Cyathea aspera: #1 **II** CYATHEACEAE
Cyathea assimilis: #1 **II** CYATHEACEAE
Cyathea assurgens: #1 **II** CYATHEACEAE
Cyathea atahualpa: #1 **II** CYATHEACEAE
Cyathea aterima: #1 **II** CYATHEACEAE
Cyathea atropurpurea: #1 **II** CYATHEACEAE
Cyathea atrospinosa: #1 **II** CYATHEACEAE
Cyathea atrovirens: #1 **II** CYATHEACEAE
Cyathea atrox var. *atrox*: #1 **II** CYATHEACEAE
Cyathea atrox var. *inermis*: #1 **II** CYATHEACEAE
Cyathea auriculata: #1 **II** CYATHEACEAE
Cyathea auriculifera: #1 **II** CYATHEACEAE
Cyathea australis ssp. *australis*: #1 **II** CYATHEACEAE
Cyathea australis ssp. *norfolkensis*: #1 **II** CYATHEACEAE
Cyathea axillaris: #1 **II** CYATHEACEAE
Cyathea baileyana: (E) Wig tree fern #1 **II** CYATHEACEAE
Cyathea balakrishnanii: #1 **II** CYATHEACEAE
Cyathea balanocarpa: #1 **II** CYATHEACEAE
Cyathea ballardii: #1 **II** CYATHEACEAE
Cyathea barringtonii: #1 **II** CYATHEACEAE
Cyathea basilaris: #1 **II** CYATHEACEAE
Cyathea batjanensis: #1 **II** CYATHEACEAE
Cyathea bellisquamata var. *basilobata*: #1 **II** CYATHEACEAE
Cyathea bellisquamata var. *bellisquamata*: #1 **II** CYATHEACEAE
Cyathea bicrenata: (S) Palo de la vida, Pelma #1 **II** CYATHEACEAE
Cyathea biformis: #1 **II** CYATHEACEAE
Cyathea binuangensis: #1 **II** CYATHEACEAE
Cyathea bipinnata: #1 **II** CYATHEACEAE
Cyathea bipinnatifida = *Cyathea medullaris*
Cyathea boivini var. *boivini*: #1 **II** CYATHEACEAE
Cyathea boivini var. *concava*: #1 **II** CYATHEACEAE
Cyathea boivini var. *humblotii*: #1 **II** CYATHEACEAE
Cyathea boliviana: #1 **II** CYATHEACEAE
Cyathea borbonica var. *borbonica*: #1 **II** CYATHEACEAE
Cyathea borbonica var. *laevigata*: #1 **II** CYATHEACEAE
Cyathea borbonica var. *madagascariensis*: #1 **II** CYATHEACEAE

Cyathea borbonica var. *pesvilleana*: #1 **II** CYATHEACEAE
Cyathea borbonica var. *simulans*: #1 **II** CYATHEACEAE
Cyathea borinquena: #1 **II** CYATHEACEAE
Cyathea borneensis: #1 **II** CYATHEACEAE
Cyathea brachyphylla: #1 **II** CYATHEACEAE
Cyathea brackenridgei: #1 **II** CYATHEACEAE
Cyathea bradei: #1 **II** CYATHEACEAE
Cyathea brevipinna: #1 **II** CYATHEACEAE
Cyathea brevistipes: #1 **II** CYATHEACEAE
Cyathea brooksii: #1 **II** CYATHEACEAE
Cyathea brownii: #1 **II** CYATHEACEAE
Cyathea brunei: #1 **II** CYATHEACEAE
Cyathea brunnescens: #1 **II** CYATHEACEAE
Cyathea brunoniana = *Cyathea chinensis*
Cyathea bryophila: #1 **II** CYATHEACEAE
Cyathea bunnemeijerii: #1 **II** CYATHEACEAE
Cyathea callosa: #1 **II** CYATHEACEAE
Cyathea camerooniana: #1 **II** CYATHEACEAE
Cyathea camerooniana var. *aethiopica*: #1 **II** CYATHEACEAE
Cyathea camerooniana var. *camerooniana*: #1 **II** CYATHEACEAE
Cyathea camerooniana var. *congi*: #1 **II** CYATHEACEAE
Cyathea camerooniana var. *currorii*: #1 **II** CYATHEACEAE
Cyathea camerooniana var. *occidentalis*: #1 **II** CYATHEACEAE
Cyathea camerooniana var. *ugandensis*: #1 **II** CYATHEACEAE
Cyathea camerooniana var. *zenkeri*: #1 **II** CYATHEACEAE
Cyathea capensis: #1 **II** CYATHEACEAE
Cyathea capitata: #1 **II** CYATHEACEAE
Cyathea caracasana: #1 **II** CYATHEACEAE
Cyathea caracasana var. *boliviensis*: #1 **II** CYATHEACEAE
Cyathea caracasana var. *caracasana*: #1 **II** CYATHEACEAE
Cyathea caracasana var. *chimborazensis*: #1 **II** CYATHEACEAE
Cyathea caracasana var. *maxonii*: #1 **II** CYATHEACEAE
Cyathea caracasana var. *meridensis*: #1 **II** CYATHEACEAE
Cyathea carrii: #1 **II** CYATHEACEAE
Cyathea catillifera: #1 **II** CYATHEACEAE
Cyathea caudata: #1 **II** CYATHEACEAE
Cyathea celebica: #1 **II** CYATHEACEAE
Cyathea chinensis: #1 **II** CYATHEACEAE
Cyathea chocoensis: #1 **II** CYATHEACEAE
Cyathea choricarpa: #1 **II** CYATHEACEAE
Cyathea christii: #1 **II** CYATHEACEAE
Cyathea cicatricosa: #1 **II** CYATHEACEAE
Cyathea cincinnata: #1 **II** CYATHEACEAE
Cyathea cinerea: #1 **II** CYATHEACEAE
Cyathea coactilis: #1 **II** CYATHEACEAE
Cyathea cocleana: #1 **II** CYATHEACEAE
Cyathea colensoi: #1 **II** CYATHEACEAE
Cyathea concinna: #1 **II** CYATHEACEAE
Cyathea conformis: #1 **II** CYATHEACEAE
Cyathea conjugata: #1 **II** CYATHEACEAE
Cyathea consimilis: #1 **II** CYATHEACEAE
Cyathea contaminans: (E) Tree fern #1 **II** CYATHEACEAE
Cyathea cooperi: #1 **II** CYATHEACEAE
Cyathea corallifera: #1 **II** CYATHEACEAE
Cyathea corcovadensis: #1 **II** CYATHEACEAE
Cyathea costalisora: #1 **II** CYATHEACEAE
Cyathea costaricensis: (S) Palmita de terra fría #1 **II** CYATHEACEAE
Cyathea costularis: #1 **II** CYATHEACEAE
Cyathea costulisora: #1 **II** CYATHEACEAE
Cyathea crassa: #1 **II** CYATHEACEAE
Cyathea crenulata: #1 **II** CYATHEACEAE
Cyathea crinita: #1 **II** CYATHEACEAE
Cyathea croftii: #1 **II** CYATHEACEAE
Cyathea cuatrecasasii: #1 **II** CYATHEACEAE
Cyathea cucullifera: #1 **II** CYATHEACEAE
Cyathea cumingii = *Cyathea medullaris*
Cyathea cunninghamii: (E) Slender tree fern #1 **II** CYATHEACEAE
Cyathea curranii: #1 **II** CYATHEACEAE
Cyathea cuspidata: #1 **II** CYATHEACEAE
Cyathea cyatheoides: #1 **II** CYATHEACEAE
Cyathea cyclopodium: #1 **II** CYATHEACEAE
Cyathea darienensis: #1 **II** CYATHEACEAE

Cyathea dealbata: (E) Silver tree fern #1 **II** CYATHEACEAE
Cyathea decomposita: #1 **II** CYATHEACEAE
Cyathea decorata: #1 **II** CYATHEACEAE
Cyathea decrescens: #1 **II** CYATHEACEAE
Cyathea decrescens var. *decrescens*: #1 **II** CYATHEACEAE
Cyathea decrescens var. *hirsutifolia*: #1 **II** CYATHEACEAE
Cyathea decurrens: #1 **II** CYATHEACEAE
Cyathea decurrens var. *decurrens*: #1 **II** CYATHEACEAE
Cyathea decurrens var. *vaupelii*: #1 **II** CYATHEACEAE
Cyathea delgadii: #1 **II** CYATHEACEAE
Cyathea deminuens: #1 **II** CYATHEACEAE
Cyathea demissa: #1 **II** CYATHEACEAE
Cyathea demissa var. *demissa*: #1 **II** CYATHEACEAE
Cyathea demissa var. *thysanolepis*: #1 **II** CYATHEACEAE
Cyathea dichromatolepis: #1 **II** CYATHEACEAE
Cyathea dicksonioides: #1 **II** CYATHEACEAE
Cyathea dimorpha: #1 **II** CYATHEACEAE
Cyathea discophora: #1 **II** CYATHEACEAE
Cyathea dissimilis: #1 **II** CYATHEACEAE
Cyathea dissoluta: #1 **II** CYATHEACEAE
Cyathea divergens: #1 **II** CYATHEACEAE
Cyathea divergens var. *divergens*: #1 **II** CYATHEACEAE
Cyathea divergens var. *tuerckheimii*: #1 **II** CYATHEACEAE
Cyathea doctersii: #1 **II** CYATHEACEAE
Cyathea dombeyi: #1 **II** CYATHEACEAE
Cyathea dregei: **II/II** CYATHEACEAE
Cyathea dregei var. *burkei*: #1 **II** CYATHEACEAE
Cyathea dregei var. *dregei*: #1 **II** CYATHEACEAE
Cyathea dregei var. *polyphlebia*: #1 **II** CYATHEACEAE
Cyathea dregei var. *segregata*: #1 **II** CYATHEACEAE
Cyathea dryopteroides: (E) Elfin Tree Fern #1 **II** CYATHEACEAE
Cyathea dudleyi: #1 **II** CYATHEACEAE
Cyathea ebenina: #1 **II** CYATHEACEAE
Cyathea edanoi: #1 **II** CYATHEACEAE
Cyathea elmeri: #1 **II** CYATHEACEAE
Cyathea elongata: #1 **II** CYATHEACEAE
Cyathea epaleata: #1 **II** CYATHEACEAE
Cyathea eriophora: #1 **II** CYATHEACEAE
Cyathea estelae: #1 **II** CYATHEACEAE
Cyathea everta: #1 **II** CYATHEACEAE
Cyathea ewanii: #1 **II** CYATHEACEAE
Cyathea excavata: #1 **II** CYATHEACEAE
Cyathea excelsa: #1 **II** CYATHEACEAE
Cyathea exilis: #1 **II** CYATHEACEAE
Cyathea fadenii: #1 **II** CYATHEACEAE
Cyathea falcata: #1 **II** CYATHEACEAE
Cyathea feani: #1 **II** CYATHEACEAE
Cyathea felina: #1 **II** CYATHEACEAE
Cyathea felinum: #1 **II** CYATHEACEAE
Cyathea fenicis: #1 **II** CYATHEACEAE
Cyathea ferruginea: #1 **II** CYATHEACEAE
Cyathea firma: #1 **II** CYATHEACEAE
Cyathea foersteri: #1 **II** CYATHEACEAE
Cyathea frigida: #1 **II** CYATHEACEAE
Cyathea fugax: #1 **II** CYATHEACEAE
Cyathea fulgens: #1 **II** CYATHEACEAE
Cyathea fuliginosa: #1 **II** CYATHEACEAE
Cyathea fulva: #1 **II** CYATHEACEAE
Cyathea furfuracea: #1 **II** CYATHEACEAE
Cyathea fusca: #1 **II** CYATHEACEAE
Cyathea gardneri: #1 **II** CYATHEACEAE
Cyathea geluensis: #1 **II** CYATHEACEAE
Cyathea gibbosa: #1 **II** CYATHEACEAE
Cyathea gigantea: #1 **II** CYATHEACEAE
Cyathea glaberrima: #1 **II** CYATHEACEAE
Cyathea glabra: #1 **II** CYATHEACEAE
Cyathea glandulosa: #1 **II** CYATHEACEAE
Cyathea glauca: #1 **II** CYATHEACEAE
Cyathea gleichenioides: #1 **II** CYATHEACEAE
Cyathea gracilis: #1 **II** CYATHEACEAE
Cyathea grandifolia: #1 **II** CYATHEACEAE
Cyathea gregaria: #1 **II** CYATHEACEAE
Cyathea grevilleana: #1 **II** CYATHEACEAE
Cyathea hainanensis: #1 **II** CYATHEACEAE

Cyathea halconensis: #1 **II** CYATHEACEAE
Cyathea hancockii: #1 **II** CYATHEACEAE
Cyathea harrisii: #1 **II** CYATHEACEAE
Cyathea haughtii: #1 **II** CYATHEACEAE
Cyathea havilandii: #1 **II** CYATHEACEAE
Cyathea heliophila: #1 **II** CYATHEACEAE
Cyathea henryi: #1 **II** CYATHEACEAE
Cyathea heterochlamydea: #1 **II** CYATHEACEAE
Cyathea hildebrandtii: #1 **II** CYATHEACEAE
Cyathea hirsuta: #1 **II** CYATHEACEAE
Cyathea hodgeana: #1 **II** CYATHEACEAE
Cyathea hooglandii: #1 **II** CYATHEACEAE
Cyathea hookeri: #1 **II** CYATHEACEAE
Cyathea hornei: #1 **II** CYATHEACEAE
Cyathea horrida: #1 **II** CYATHEACEAE
Cyathea horridula: #1 **II** CYATHEACEAE
Cyathea hotteana: #1 **II** CYATHEACEAE
Cyathea howeana: #1 **II** CYATHEACEAE
Cyathea humbertiana: #1 **II** CYATHEACEAE
Cyathea humilis: #1 **II** CYATHEACEAE
Cyathea humilis var. *humilis*: #1 **II** CYATHEACEAE
Cyathea humilis var. *pycnophylla*: #1 **II** CYATHEACEAE
Cyathea hunsteiniana: #1 **II** CYATHEACEAE
Cyathea hymenodes: #1 **II** CYATHEACEAE
Cyathea imbricata: #1 **II** CYATHEACEAE
Cyathea impar: #1 **II** CYATHEACEAE
Cyathea imrayana: #1 **II** CYATHEACEAE
Cyathea imrayana var. *basilaris*: #1 **II** CYATHEACEAE
Cyathea imrayana var. *imrayana*: #1 **II** CYATHEACEAE
Cyathea inaequalis: #1 **II** CYATHEACEAE
Cyathea incana: #1 **II** CYATHEACEAE
Cyathea incisoserrata: #1 **II** CYATHEACEAE
Cyathea inheringii: #1 **II** CYATHEACEAE
Cyathea inquinans: #1 **II** CYATHEACEAE
Cyathea insignis: #1 **II** CYATHEACEAE
Cyathea insulana: #1 **II** CYATHEACEAE
Cyathea insularum: #1 **II** CYATHEACEAE
Cyathea integra: #1 **II** CYATHEACEAE
Cyathea intermedia: #1 **II** CYATHEACEAE
Cyathea intramarginalis: #1 **II** CYATHEACEAE
Cyathea isaloensis: #1 **II** CYATHEACEAE
Cyathea jacobsii: #1 **II** CYATHEACEAE
Cyathea javanica: #1 **II** CYATHEACEAE
Cyathea junghuhniana: #1 **II** CYATHEACEAE
Cyathea kalbreyeri: #1 **II** CYATHEACEAE
Cyathea kanehirae: #1 **II** CYATHEACEAE
Cyathea karsteniana: #1 **II** CYATHEACEAE
Cyathea kermadecensis: #1 **II** CYATHEACEAE
Cyathea khasyana: #1 **II** CYATHEACEAE
Cyathea kirkii: #1 **II** CYATHEACEAE
Cyathea klossii: #1 **II** CYATHEACEAE
Cyathea lasiosora: #1 **II** CYATHEACEAE
Cyathea lastii: #1 **II** CYATHEACEAE
Cyathea latebrosa: #1 **II** CYATHEACEAE
Cyathea latevagans: #1 **II** CYATHEACEAE
Cyathea latipinnula: #1 **II** CYATHEACEAE
Cyathea lechleri: #1 **II** CYATHEACEAE
Cyathea ledermannii: #1 **II** CYATHEACEAE
Cyathea leichardtiana: (E) Prickly tree fern #1 **II** CYATHEACEAE
Cyathea lepidoclada: #1 **II** CYATHEACEAE
Cyathea lepifera: #1 **II** CYATHEACEAE
Cyathea leprieurii: #1 **II** CYATHEACEAE
Cyathea leptochlamys: #1 **II** CYATHEACEAE
Cyathea leucolepis: #1 **II** CYATHEACEAE
Cyathea leucotricha: #1 **II** CYATHEACEAE
Cyathea ligulata: #1 **II** CYATHEACEAE
Cyathea lindseyana: #1 **II** CYATHEACEAE
Cyathea lockwoodiana: #1 **II** CYATHEACEAE
Cyathea loerzingii: #1 **II** CYATHEACEAE
Cyathea loheri: #1 **II** CYATHEACEAE
Cyathea longipes: #1 **II** CYATHEACEAE
Cyathea longipinnata: #1 **II** CYATHEACEAE
Cyathea lucida: #1 **II** CYATHEACEAE
Cyathea lunulata: #1 **II** CYATHEACEAE

Cyathea lurida: #1 **II** CYATHEACEAE
Cyathea macarthurii: #1 **II** CYATHEACEAE
Cyathea macgillivrayi: #1 **II** CYATHEACEAE
Cyathea macgregorii: #1 **II** CYATHEACEAE
Cyathea macrocarpa: #1 **II** CYATHEACEAE
Cyathea macrophylla: #1 **II** CYATHEACEAE
Cyathea macrophylla var. *macrophylla*: #1 **II** CYATHEACEAE
Cyathea macrophylla var. *quadripinnata*: #1 **II** CYATHEACEAE
Cyathea macropoda: #1 **II** CYATHEACEAE
Cyathea macrosora: #1 **II** CYATHEACEAE
Cyathea macrosora var. *macrosora*: #1 **II** CYATHEACEAE
Cyathea macrosora var. *reginae*: #1 **II** CYATHEACEAE
Cyathea macrosora var. *vaupensis*: #1 **II** CYATHEACEAE
Cyathea madagascarica: #1 **II** CYATHEACEAE
Cyathea magna: #1 **II** CYATHEACEAE
Cyathea magnifolia: #1 **II** CYATHEACEAE
Cyathea manniana: #1 **II** CYATHEACEAE
Cyathea marattioides: #1 **II** CYATHEACEAE
Cyathea marcescens: #1 **II** CYATHEACEAE
Cyathea marginalis: #1 **II** CYATHEACEAE
Cyathea marginata: #1 **II** CYATHEACEAE
Cyathea masapilidensis: #1 **II** CYATHEACEAE
Cyathea media: #1 **II** CYATHEACEAE
Cyathea medullaris: (E) Black tree fern #1 **II** CYATHEACEAE
Cyathea megalosora: #1 **II** CYATHEACEAE
Cyathea melanocaula: #1 **II** CYATHEACEAE
Cyathea melleri: #1 **II** CYATHEACEAE
Cyathea mertensiana: #1 **II** CYATHEACEAE
Cyathea mesosora: #1 **II** CYATHEACEAE
Cyathea metteniana: #1 **II** CYATHEACEAE
Cyathea mexiae: #1 **II** CYATHEACEAE
Cyathea mexicana: (S) Cola de mono #1 **II** CYATHEACEAE
Cyathea microchlamys: #1 **II** CYATHEACEAE
Cyathea microdonta: #1 **II** CYATHEACEAE
Cyathea microlepidota: #1 **II** CYATHEACEAE
Cyathea microphylla: #1 **II** CYATHEACEAE
Cyathea microphylloides: #1 **II** CYATHEACEAE
Cyathea mildbraedii: #1 **II** CYATHEACEAE
Cyathea milnei: #1 **II** CYATHEACEAE
Cyathea minor: #1 **II** CYATHEACEAE
Cyathea modesta: #1 **II** CYATHEACEAE
Cyathea moluccana: #1 **II** CYATHEACEAE
Cyathea moseleyi: #1 **II** CYATHEACEAE
Cyathea mossambicensis: #1 **II** CYATHEACEAE
Cyathea mucilagina: #1 **II** CYATHEACEAE
Cyathea muelleri: #1 **II** CYATHEACEAE
Cyathea multiflora: #1 **II** CYATHEACEAE
Cyathea multisegmenta: #1 **II** CYATHEACEAE
Cyathea muricata: #1 **II** CYATHEACEAE
Cyathea myosuroides: #1 **II** CYATHEACEAE
Cyathea nanna: #1 **II** CYATHEACEAE
Cyathea negrosiana: #1 **II** CYATHEACEAE
Cyathea nervosa: #1 **II** CYATHEACEAE
Cyathea nesiotica: #1 **II** CYATHEACEAE
Cyathea nicklesii: #1 **II** CYATHEACEAE
Cyathea nicobarica: #1 **II** CYATHEACEAE
Cyathea nigricans: #1 **II** CYATHEACEAE
Cyathea nigripes: #1 **II** CYATHEACEAE
Cyathea nigripes var. *brunnescens* = *Cyathea brunnescens*
Cyathea nigrolineata: #1 **II** CYATHEACEAE
Cyathea nigropaleata: #1 **II** CYATHEACEAE
Cyathea nilgirensis: #1 **II** CYATHEACEAE
Cyathea nockii: #1 **II** CYATHEACEAE
Cyathea nodulifera: #1 **II** CYATHEACEAE
Cyathea notabilis: #1 **II** CYATHEACEAE
Cyathea nothofagorum: #1 **II** CYATHEACEAE
Cyathea novae-caledoniae: #1 **II** CYATHEACEAE
Cyathea obliqua: #1 **II** CYATHEACEAE
Cyathea oblonga: #1 **II** CYATHEACEAE
Cyathea obscura: #1 **II** CYATHEACEAE
Cyathea obtusa: #1 **II** CYATHEACEAE
Cyathea obtusiloba: #1 **II** CYATHEACEAE
Cyathea ogurae: #1 **II** CYATHEACEAE
Cyathea oinops: #1 **II** CYATHEACEAE
Cyathea oosora: #1 **II** CYATHEACEAE

Cyathea orientalis: #1 **II** CYATHEACEAE
Cyathea orthogonalis: #1 **II** CYATHEACEAE
Cyathea pachyrrhachis: #1 **II** CYATHEACEAE
Cyathea pallescens: #1 **II** CYATHEACEAE
Cyathea pallidipaleata: #1 **II** CYATHEACEAE
Cyathea pansamalana: #1 **II** CYATHEACEAE
Cyathea papuana: #1 **II** CYATHEACEAE
Cyathea parianensis: #1 **II** CYATHEACEAE
Cyathea parksiae: #1 **II** CYATHEACEAE
Cyathea parva: #1 **II** CYATHEACEAE
Cyathea parvipinna: #1 **II** CYATHEACEAE
Cyathea parvula: #1 **II** CYATHEACEAE
Cyathea patellifera: #1 **II** CYATHEACEAE
Cyathea pauciflora: #1 **II** CYATHEACEAE
Cyathea paucifolia: #1 **II** CYATHEACEAE
Cyathea pectinata: #1 **II** CYATHEACEAE
Cyathea peladensis: #1 **II** CYATHEACEAE
Cyathea percrassa: #1 **II** CYATHEACEAE
Cyathea perpelvigera: #1 **II** CYATHEACEAE
Cyathea perpunctulata: #1 **II** CYATHEACEAE
Cyathea perrieriana: #1 **II** CYATHEACEAE
Cyathea persquamulifera: #1 **II** CYATHEACEAE
Cyathea petiolata: #1 **II** CYATHEACEAE
Cyathea petiolulata: #1 **II** CYATHEACEAE
Cyathea phalaenolepis: #1 **II** CYATHEACEAE
Cyathea phalerata: #1 **II** CYATHEACEAE
Cyathea phegopteroides: #1 **II** CYATHEACEAE
Cyathea philippinensis: #1 **II** CYATHEACEAE
Cyathea physolepidota: #1 **II** CYATHEACEAE
Cyathea pilosissima: #1 **II** CYATHEACEAE
Cyathea pilosula: #1 **II** CYATHEACEAE
Cyathea pilulifera: #1 **II** CYATHEACEAE
Cyathea pinnula: #1 **II** CYATHEACEAE
Cyathea plagiostegia: #1 **II** CYATHEACEAE
Cyathea platylepis: #1 **II** CYATHEACEAE
Cyathea podophylla: #1 **II** CYATHEACEAE
Cyathea poeppigii: #1 **II** CYATHEACEAE
Cyathea polypoda: #1 **II** CYATHEACEAE
Cyathea polystichoides: #1 **II** CYATHEACEAE
Cyathea ponapeana: #1 **II** CYATHEACEAE
Cyathea portoricensis: #1 **II** CYATHEACEAE
Cyathea praecincta: #1 **II** CYATHEACEAE
Cyathea procera: #1 **II** CYATHEACEAE
Cyathea propinqua: #1 **II** CYATHEACEAE
Cyathea pruinosa: #1 **II** CYATHEACEAE
Cyathea pseudogigantea: #1 **II** CYATHEACEAE
Cyathea pseudomuelleri: #1 **II** CYATHEACEAE
Cyathea pseudonanna: #1 **II** CYATHEACEAE
Cyathea pubens = *Cyathea bipinnatifida*
Cyathea pubescens: #1 **II** CYATHEACEAE
Cyathea pulcherrima: #1 **II** CYATHEACEAE
Cyathea punctulata: #1 **II** CYATHEACEAE
Cyathea pungens: #1 **II** CYATHEACEAE
Cyathea pycnoneura: #1 **II** CYATHEACEAE
Cyathea quadrata: #1 **II** CYATHEACEAE
Cyathea quadrata var. *ivohibensis*: #1 **II** CYATHEACEAE
Cyathea quadrata var. *quadrata*: #1 **II** CYATHEACEAE
Cyathea quindiuensis: #1 **II** CYATHEACEAE
Cyathea raciborskii: #1 **II** CYATHEACEAE
Cyathea ramispina: #1 **II** CYATHEACEAE
Cyathea rebeccae: #1 **II** CYATHEACEAE
Cyathea recommutata: #1 **II** CYATHEACEAE
Cyathea recurvata: #1 **II** CYATHEACEAE
Cyathea rigens: #1 **II** CYATHEACEAE
Cyathea robertsiana: #1 **II** CYATHEACEAE
Cyathea robinsonii: #1 **II** CYATHEACEAE
Cyathea robusta: #1 **II** CYATHEACEAE
Cyathea roraimensis: #1 **II** CYATHEACEAE
Cyathea roroka: #1 **II** CYATHEACEAE
Cyathea rosenstockii: #1 **II** CYATHEACEAE
Cyathea rubella: #1 **II** CYATHEACEAE
Cyathea rubiginosa: #1 **II** CYATHEACEAE
Cyathea rufa: #1 **II** CYATHEACEAE
Cyathea rufescens: #1 **II** CYATHEACEAE
Cyathea rufopannosa: #1 **II** CYATHEACEAE

Cyathea ruiziana: #1 **II** CYATHEACEAE
Cyathea runensis: #1 **II** CYATHEACEAE
Cyathea rupestris: #1 **II** CYATHEACEAE
Cyathea saccata: #1 **II** CYATHEACEAE
Cyathea sagittifolia: #1 **II** CYATHEACEAE
Cyathea salletii: #1 **II** CYATHEACEAE
Cyathea salvinii: #1 **II** CYATHEACEAE
Cyathea sangirensis: #1 **II** CYATHEACEAE
Cyathea sarasinorum: #1 **II** CYATHEACEAE
Cyathea scabriuscula: #1 **II** CYATHEACEAE
Cyathea scandens: #1 **II** CYATHEACEAE
Cyathea schiedeana: #1 **II** CYATHEACEAE
Cyathea schlechteri: #1 **II** CYATHEACEAE
Cyathea schliebenii: #1 **II** CYATHEACEAE
Cyathea schlimii: #1 **II** CYATHEACEAE
Cyathea sechellarum: #1 **II** CYATHEACEAE
Cyathea semiamplectens: #1 **II** CYATHEACEAE
Cyathea senex: #1 **II** CYATHEACEAE
Cyathea senilis: #1 **II** CYATHEACEAE
Cyathea serratifolia: #1 **II** CYATHEACEAE
Cyathea setifera: #1 **II** CYATHEACEAE
Cyathea setosa: #1 **II** CYATHEACEAE
Cyathea setulosa: #1 **II** CYATHEACEAE
Cyathea sibuyanensis: #1 **II** CYATHEACEAE
Cyathea similis: #1 **II** CYATHEACEAE
Cyathea simplex: #1 **II** CYATHEACEAE
Cyathea singularis: #1 **II** CYATHEACEAE
Cyathea sinuata: #1 **II** CYATHEACEAE
Cyathea sipapoensis: #1 **II** CYATHEACEAE
Cyathea smithii: (E) Soft tree fern #1 **II** CYATHEACEAE
Cyathea solomonensis: #1 **II** CYATHEACEAE
Cyathea speciosa: #1 **II** CYATHEACEAE
Cyathea spectabilis var. *colombiensis*: #1 **II** CYATHEACEAE
Cyathea spectabilis var. *spectabilis*: #1 **II** CYATHEACEAE
Cyathea spinulosa: #1 **II** CYATHEACEAE
Cyathea squamata: #1 **II** CYATHEACEAE
Cyathea squamulata: #1 **II** CYATHEACEAE
Cyathea squamulosa: #1 **II** CYATHEACEAE
Cyathea stelligera: #1 **II** CYATHEACEAE
Cyathea sternbergii: #1 **II** CYATHEACEAE
Cyathea steyermarkii: #1 **II** CYATHEACEAE
Cyathea stipitipinnula: #1 **II** CYATHEACEAE
Cyathea stipularis = *Cyathea bicrenata*
Cyathea stokesii: #1 **II** CYATHEACEAE
Cyathea stolzei: #1 **II** CYATHEACEAE
Cyathea straminea: #1 **II** CYATHEACEAE
Cyathea strigillosa: #1 **II** CYATHEACEAE
Cyathea strigosa: #1 **II** CYATHEACEAE
Cyathea subarborescens: #1 **II** CYATHEACEAE
Cyathea subdubia: #1 **II** CYATHEACEAE
Cyathea subincisa: #1 **II** CYATHEACEAE
Cyathea subsessilis: #1 **II** CYATHEACEAE
Cyathea subtripinnata: #1 **II** CYATHEACEAE
Cyathea subtropica: #1 **II** CYATHEACEAE
Cyathea suluensis: #1 **II** CYATHEACEAE
Cyathea sumatrana: #1 **II** CYATHEACEAE
Cyathea suprastrigosa: #1 **II** CYATHEACEAE
Cyathea surinamensis: #1 **II** CYATHEACEAE
Cyathea taiwanense: #1 **II** CYATHEACEAE
Cyathea tenera: #1 **II** CYATHEACEAE
Cyathea tenggerensis: #1 **II** CYATHEACEAE
Cyathea tenuicaulis: #1 **II** CYATHEACEAE
Cyathea ternatea: #1 **II** CYATHEACEAE
Cyathea teysmannii: #1 **II** CYATHEACEAE
Cyathea thomsonii: #1 **II** CYATHEACEAE
Cyathea thwaitesii: #1 **II** CYATHEACEAE
Cyathea tinganensis: #1 **II** CYATHEACEAE
Cyathea tomentosa: #1 **II** CYATHEACEAE
Cyathea tomentosissima: #1 **II** CYATHEACEAE
Cyathea tortuosa: #1 **II** CYATHEACEAE
Cyathea trachypoda: #1 **II** CYATHEACEAE
Cyathea trichiata = *Cyathea bicrenata*
Cyathea trichodesma: #1 **II** CYATHEACEAE
Cyathea trichophora: #1 **II** CYATHEACEAE
Cyathea tripinnata: #1 **II** CYATHEACEAE

Cyathea tripinnatifida: #1 **II** CYATHEACEAE
Cyathea truncata: #1 **II** CYATHEACEAE
Cyathea tryonorum: #1 **II** CYATHEACEAE
Cyathea tsangii: #1 **II** CYATHEACEAE
Cyathea tsaratananensis: #1 **II** CYATHEACEAE
Cyathea tsilotsilensis: #1 **II** CYATHEACEAE
Cyathea tussacii: #1 **II** CYATHEACEAE
Cyathea tuyamae: #1 **II** CYATHEACEAE
Cyathea urbanii: #1 **II** CYATHEACEAE
Cyathea ursina: #1 **II** CYATHEACEAE
Cyathea usambarensis: #1 **II** CYATHEACEAE
Cyathea valdecrenata: #1 **II** CYATHEACEAE
Cyathea vandeusenii: #1 **II** CYATHEACEAE
Cyathea vaupelii: #1 **II** CYATHEACEAE
Cyathea velaminosa: #1 **II** CYATHEACEAE
Cyathea venezuelensis: #1 **II** CYATHEACEAE
Cyathea verrucosa: #1 **II** CYATHEACEAE
Cyathea vieillardii: #1 **II** CYATHEACEAE
Cyathea viguieri: #1 **II** CYATHEACEAE
Cyathea vilhelmii: #1 **II** CYATHEACEAE
Cyathea villosa: #1 **II** CYATHEACEAE
Cyathea vittata: #1 **II** CYATHEACEAE
Cyathea walkerae: #1 **II** CYATHEACEAE
Cyathea walkerae var. *tripinnata*: #1 **II** CYATHEACEAE
Cyathea walkerae var. *walkerae*: #1 **II** CYATHEACEAE
Cyathea wallacei: #1 **II** CYATHEACEAE
Cyathea weatherbyana: #1 **II** CYATHEACEAE
Cyathea welwitschii: #1 **II** CYATHEACEAE
Cyathea wendlandii: #1 **II** CYATHEACEAE
Cyathea wengiensis: #1 **II** CYATHEACEAE
Cyathea werffii: #1 **II** CYATHEACEAE
Cyathea werneri: #1 **II** CYATHEACEAE
Cyathea whitmeei: #1 **II** CYATHEACEAE
Cyathea williamsii: #1 **II** CYATHEACEAE
Cyathea womersleyi: #1 **II** CYATHEACEAE
Cyathea woodwardioides: #1 **II** CYATHEACEAE
Cyathea woodwardioides var. *cubensis*: #1 **II** CYATHEACEAE
Cyathea woodwardioides var. *hieronymi*: #1 **II** CYATHEACEAE
Cyathea woodwardioides var. *woodwardioides*: #1 **II** CYATHEACEAE
Cyathea woollsiana: #1 **II** CYATHEACEAE
Cyathea zakamenensis: #1 **II** CYATHEACEAE
Cyathea zamboangana: #1 **II** CYATHEACEAE
Cyathoglottis = *Sobralia*
Cybebus spp.: #7 **II** ORCHIDACEAE
Cybelion = *Ionopsis*
Cycad (E): *Stangeria eriopus*
CYCADACEAE spp.: (E) cycads, (S) cícadas, (F) cycades #1 **I/II**
Cycades (F): CYCADACEAE spp./ ZAMIACEAE spp.
Cycads (E): *Bowenia* spp./ *Ceratozamia* spp./ *Chigua* spp./ CYCADACEAE spp./ ZAMIACEAE spp.
Cycas aculeata: #1 **II** CYCADACEAE
Cycas acuminatissima = *Cycas sexseminifera*
Cycas angulata: #1 **II** CYCADACEAE
Cycas apoa: #1 **II** CYCADACEAE
Cycas arenicola: #1 **II** CYCADACEAE
Cycas armstrongii: #1 **II** CYCADACEAE
Cycas arnhemica: #1 **II** CYCADACEAE
Cycas arnhemica ssp. *arnhemica*: #1 **II** CYCADACEAE
Cycas arnhemica ssp. *muninga*: #1 **II** CYCADACEAE
Cycas arnhemica ssp. *natja*: #1 **II** CYCADACEAE
Cycas aurea: #1 **II** CYCADACEAE
Cycas badensis: #1 **II** CYCADACEAE
Cycas baguanheensis = *Cycas panzhihuaensis*
Cycas balansae: #1 **II** CYCADACEAE
Cycas basaltica: #1 **II** CYCADACEAE
Cycas beddomei: **I** CYCADACEAE
Cycas bifida: #1 **II** CYCADACEAE
Cycas bougainvilleana: #1 **II** CYCADACEAE
Cycas brachycantha: #1 **II** CYCADACEAE
Cycas brevipinnata = *Cycas sexseminifera*
Cycas brunnea: #1 **II** CYCADACEAE
Cycas caffra = *Encephalartos caffer*
Cycas cairnsiana: #1 **II** CYCADACEAE
Cycas calcicola: #1 **II** CYCADACEAE

Cycas campestris: #1 **II** CYCADACEAE
Cycas canalis: #1 **II** CYCADACEAE
Cycas canalis ssp. *canalis*: #1 **II** CYCADACEAE
Cycas canalis ssp. *carinata*: #1 **II** CYCADACEAE
Cycas celebica = *Cycas rumphii*
Cycas chamaoensis: #1 **II** CYCADACEAE
Cycas chamberlainii = *Cycas riuminiana*
Cycas changjiangens: #1 **II** CYCADACEAE
Cycas chevalieri: #1 **II** CYCADACEAE
Cycas circinalis: (E) Sago-palm #1 **II** CYCADACEAE
Cycas circinalis f. *undulata* = *Cycas circinalis*
Cycas circinalis ssp. *madagascariensis* f. *trigonocarpoi* = *Cycas thouarsii*
Cycas circinalis ssp. *papuana* = *Cycas papuana*
Cycas circinalis ssp. *papuana* f. *scratchleyana* = *Cycas scratchleyana*
Cycas circinalis ssp. *riuminiana* f. *curranii* = *Cycas curranii*
Cycas circinalis ssp. *riuminiana* ssp. *curranii* f. *graminea* = *Cycas wadei*
Cycas circinalis ssp. *riuminiana* ssp. *curranii* f. *maritima* = *Cycas edentata*
Cycas circinalis ssp. *ruiminiana* = *Cycas riuminiana*
Cycas circinalis ssp. *ruiminiana* ssp. *curranii* f. *chamberlai* = *Cycas riuminiana*
Cycas circinalis ssp. *seemannii* = *Cycas seemannii*
Cycas circinalis ssp. *thouarsii* = *Cycas thouarsii*
Cycas circinalis ssp. *vera* f. *beddomei* = *Cycas beddomei*
Cycas circinalis ssp. *vera* f. *pectinata* = *Cycas pectinata*
Cycas circinalis var. *angustifolia* = *Cycas circinalis*
Cycas circinalis var. *circinalis*: #1 **II** CYCADACEAE
Cycas circinalis var. *javana* = *Cycas javana*
Cycas clivicola: #1 **II** CYCADACEAE
Cycas clivicola ssp. *clivicola*: #1 **II** CYCADACEAE
Cycas clivicola ssp. *lutea*: #1 **II** CYCADACEAE
Cycas collina: #1 **II** CYCADACEAE
Cycas comorensis = *Cycas thouarsii*
Cycas condaoensis: #1 **II** CYCADACEAE
Cycas conferta: #1 **II** CYCADACEAE
Cycas couttsiana: #1 **II** CYCADACEAE
Cycas curranii: #1 **II** CYCADACEAE
Cycas debaoensis: #1 **II** CYCADACEAE
Cycas desolata: #1 **II** CYCADACEAE
Cycas diannanensis: #1 **II** CYCADACEAE
Cycas dolichophylla: #1 **II** CYCADACEAE
Cycas edentata: #1 **II** CYCADACEAE
Cycas elephantipes: #1 **II** CYCADACEAE
Cycas elongata: #1 **II** CYCADACEAE
Cycas fairylakea: #1 **II** CYCADACEAE
Cycas falcata: #1 **II** CYCADACEAE
Cycas ferruginea: #1 **II** CYCADACEAE
Cycas fugax: #1 **II** CYCADACEAE
Cycas furfuracea: #1 **II** CYCADACEAE
Cycas gracilis = *Cycas media*
Cycas gracilis var. *glauca* = *Cycas media*
Cycas gracilis var. *viridis* = *Cycas media*
Cycas guizhouensis: #1 **II** CYCADACEAE
Cycas hainanensis: #1 **II** CYCADACEAE
Cycas hoabinhensis: #1 **II** CYCADACEAE
Cycas hongheensis: #1 **II** CYCADACEAE
Cycas immersa = *Cycas siamensis*
Cycas inermis: #1 **II** CYCADACEAE
Cycas javana: #1 **II** CYCADACEAE
Cycas jenkinsiana = *Cycas pectinata*
Cycas kennedyana = *Cycas media* ssp. *media*
Cycas lane-poolei: #1 **II** CYCADACEAE
Cycas lindstromii: #1 **II** CYCADACEAE
Cycas litoralis: #1 **II** CYCADACEAE
Cycas longiconifera = *Cycas segmentifida*
Cycas longipetiolula = *Cycas bifida*
Cycas longisporophylla = *Cycas sexseminifera*
Cycas longlinensis = *Cycas guizhouensis*
Cycas maconochii: #1 **II** CYCADACEAE
Cycas maconochii ssp. *lanata*: #1 **II** CYCADACEAE
Cycas maconochii ssp. *maconochii*: #1 **II** CYCADACEAE
Cycas maconochii ssp. *viridis*: #1 **II** CYCADACEAE

Cycas macrocarpa: #1 **II** CYCADACEAE
Cycas madagascariensis = *Cycas thouarsii*
Cycas media: #1 **II** CYCADACEAE
Cycas media ssp. *banksii*: #1 **II** CYCADACEAE
Cycas media ssp. *ensata*: #1 **II** CYCADACEAE
Cycas media ssp. *media*: #1 **II** CYCADACEAE
Cycas media var. *basaltica* = *Cycas basaltica*
Cycas media var. *furfuracea* = *Cycas furfuracea*
Cycas media var. *inermis* = *Cycas armstrongii*
Cycas media var. *lane-poolei* = *Cycas lane-poolei*
Cycas megacarpa: #1 **II** CYCADACEAE
Cycas micholitzii: #1 **II** CYCADACEAE
Cycas micholitzii var. *simplicipinna* = *Cycas simplicipinna*
Cycas micronesica: #1 **II** CYCADACEAE
Cycas miquelii = *Cycas revoluta*
Cycas multifida = *Cycas segmentifida*
Cycas multifrondis = *Cycas bifida*
Cycas multiovula = *Cycas guizhouensis*
Cycas multipinnata: #1 **II** CYCADACEAE
Cycas nathorstii: #1 **II** CYCADACEAE
Cycas nongnoochiae: #1 **II** CYCADACEAE
Cycas normanbyana = *Cycas media* ssp. *media*
Cycas ophiolitica: #1 **II** CYCADACEAE
Cycas orientis: #1 **II** CYCADACEAE
Cycas pachypoda: #1 **II** CYCADACEAE
Cycas palmatifida = *Cycas balansae*
Cycas panzhihuaensis: #1 **II** CYCADACEAE
Cycas papuana: #1 **II** CYCADACEAE
Cycas parvulus = *Cycas diannanensis*
Cycas pectinata: #1 **II** CYCADACEAE
Cycas pectinata var. *elongata* = *Cycas elongata*
Cycas pectinata var. *manhaoensis* = *Cycas diannanensis*
Cycas petraea: #1 **II** CYCADACEAE
Cycas platyphylla: #1 **II** CYCADACEAE
Cycas pranburiensis: #1 **II** CYCADACEAE
Cycas pruinosa: #1 **II** CYCADACEAE
Cycas revoluta: #1 **II** CYCADACEAE
Cycas revoluta var. *brevifrons* = *Cycas revoluta*
Cycas revoluta var. *planifolia* = *Cycas revoluta*
Cycas revoluta var. *prolifera* = *Cycas revoluta*
Cycas revoluta var. *robusta* = *Cycas revoluta*
Cycas revoluta var. *taiwaniana* = *Cycas taiwaniana*
Cycas riedlei = *Macrozamia riedlei*
Cycas riuminiana: #1 **II** CYCADACEAE
Cycas rumphii: (E) Malayan fern palm #1 **II** CYCADACEAE
Cycas rumphii f. *papuana* = *Cycas papuana*
Cycas rumphii f. *seemannii* = *Cycas seemannii*
Cycas rumphii f. *undulata* = *Cycas circinalis*
Cycas rumphii ssp. *normanbyana* = *Cycas media*
Cycas rumphii var. *bifida* = *Cycas bifida*
Cycas schumanniana: #1 **II** CYCADACEAE
Cycas scratchleyana: #1 **II** CYCADACEAE
Cycas seemannii: #1 **II** CYCADACEAE
Cycas segmentifida: #1 **II** CYCADACEAE
Cycas semota: #1 **II** CYCADACEAE
Cycas septemsperma = *Cycas sexseminifera*
Cycas sexseminifera: #1 **II** CYCADACEAE
Cycas shiwandashanica = *Cycas balansae*
Cycas siamensis: #1 **II** CYCADACEAE
Cycas siamensis ssp. *balansae* = *Cycas balansae*
Cycas siamensis ssp. *inermis* = *Cycas inermis*
Cycas silvestris: #1 **II** CYCADACEAE
Cycas simplicipinna: #1 **II** CYCADACEAE
Cycas spherica: #1 **II** CYCADACEAE
Cycas spiniformis = *Cycas sexseminifera*
Cycas szechuanensis: #1 **II** CYCADACEAE
Cycas taitungensis: #1 **II** CYCADACEAE
Cycas taiwaniana: #1 **II** CYCADACEAE
Cycas tanqingii: #1 **II** CYCADACEAE
Cycas tansachana: #1 **II** CYCADACEAE
Cycas thouarsii: #1 **II** CYCADACEAE
Cycas tropophylla: #1 **II** CYCADACEAE
Cycas tuckeri: #1 **II** CYCADACEAE
Cycas undulata = *Cycas circinalis*
Cycas wadei: #1 **II** CYCADACEAE

Cycas wallichii = *Cycas circinalis*
Cycas xilingensis = *Cycas segmentifida*
Cycas xipholepis: #1 **II** CYCADACEAE
Cycas yorkiana: #1 **II** CYCADACEAE
Cycas yunnanensis: #1 **II** CYCADACEAE
Cycas zeylanica: #1 **II** CYCADACEAE
Cyclamen spp.: (E) Cyclamen (S) Ciclámenes #1 **II**
    PRIMULACEAE
Cyclamen abchasicum = *Cyclamen coum* ssp. *caucasicum*
Cyclamen adzharicum = *Cyclamen coum* ssp. *caucasicum*
Cyclamen aedirhizum = *Cyclamen hederifolium* var. *hederifolium* f.
    hederifolium
Cyclamen aegineticum = *Cyclamen graecum* ssp. *Graecum* f.
    graecum
Cyclamen aestivum = *Cyclamen purpurascens f. purpurascens*
Cyclamen africanum: #1 **II** PRIMULACEAE
Cyclamen albidum = *Cyclamen persicum* var. *persicum* f. *albidum*
Cyclamen albiflorum = *Cyclamen hederifolium* var. *hederifolium* f.
    albiflorum
Cyclamen aleppicum = *Cyclamen persicum* var. *persicum* f.
    persicum
Cyclamen aleppicum ssp. *puniceum* = *Cyclamen persicum* var.
    persicum f. *puniceum*
Cyclamen algeriense = *Cyclamen africanum*
Cyclamen alpinum #1 **II** PRIMULACEAE
Cyclamen ambiguum = *Cyclamen africanum*
Cyclamen angulare = *Cyclamen hederifolium* var. *hederifolium* f.
    hederifolium
Cyclamen antilochium = *Cyclamen persicum* var. *persicum* f.
    persicum
Cyclamen apiculatum = *Cyclamen coum* ssp. *coum* f. *coum*
Cyclamen atkinsii = *Cyclamen coum* ssp. *caucasicum*
Cyclamen atkinsii = *Cyclamen coum* ssp. *coum* f. *coum*
Cyclamen baborense = *Cyclamen repandum* ssp. *repandum* var.
    baborense
Cyclamen balearicum: (S) pa porcí (F) cyclamen des baléares, #1
    II PRIMULACEAE
Cyclamen breviflorum = *Cyclamen purpurascens* f. *purpurascens*
Cyclamen brevifrons = *Cyclamen coum* ssp. *coum* f. *coum*
Cyclamen calcareum = *Cyclamen coum* ssp. *caucasicum*
Cyclamen caucasicum = *Cyclamen coum* ssp. *caucasicum*
Cyclamen cilicicum = *Cyclamen cilicium*
Cyclamen cilicium: #1 **II** PRIMULACEAE
Cyclamen cilicium f. *album*: #1 **II** PRIMULACEAE
Cyclamen cilicium f. *cilicium*: #1 **II** PRIMULACEAE
Cyclamen cilicium var. *alpinum* = *Cyclamen intaminatum*
Cyclamen cilicium var. *intaminatum* = *Cyclamen intaminatum*
Cyclamen cilicium var. [sic] = *Cyclamen intaminatum*
Cyclamen circassicum = *Cyclamen coum* ssp. *caucasicum*
Cyclamen clusii = *Cyclamen purpurascens* f. *purpurascens*
Cyclamen colchicum: #1 **II** PRIMULACEAE
Cyclamen commutatum = *Cyclamen africanum*
Cyclamen coum: #1 **II** PRIMULACEAE
Cyclamen coum ssp. *caucasicum* : #1 **II** PRIMULACEAE
Cyclamen coum ssp. *coum* f. *albissimum*: #1 **II** PRIMULACEAE
Cyclamen coum ssp. *coum* f. *coum*: #1 **II** PRIMULACEAE
Cyclamen coum ssp. *coum* f. *pallidum*: #1 **II** PRIMULACEAE
Cyclamen coum ssp. *coum*: #1 **II** PRIMULACEAE
Cyclamen coum ssp. *elegans*: #1 **II** PRIMULACEAE
Cyclamen coum ssp. *hiemale* = *Cyclamen coum* ssp. *coum* f. *coum*
Cyclamen coum var. *abchasicum* = *Cyclamen coum* ssp.
    caucasicum
Cyclamen coum var. *caucasicum* = *Cyclamen coum* ssp.
    caucasicum
Cyclamen coum var. *ibericum* = *Cyclamen coum* ssp. *caucasicum*
Cyclamen creticum: #1 **II** PRIMULACEAE
Cyclamen creticum f. *creticum*: #1 **II** PRIMULACEAE
Cyclamen creticum f. *pallide-roseum*: #1 **II** PRIMULACEAE
Cyclamen cyclaminus = *Cyclamen hederifolium* var. *hederifolium* f.
    hederifolium
Cyclamen cyclophyllum = *Cyclamen purpurascens* f. *purpurascens*
Cyclamen cyprium = *Cyclamen graecum* ssp. *anatolicum*
Cyclamen cyprium = *Cyclamen persicum* var. *persicum* f.
    persicum
Cyclamen cyprium: #1 **II** PRIMULACEAE

Cyclamen cypro-graecum = *Cyclamen graecum* ssp. *anatolicum*
Cyclamen deltoideum = *Cyclamen purpurascens* f. *purpurascens*
Cyclamen des baléares (F): *Cyclamen balearicum*
Cyclamen d'Europe (F): *Cyclamen purpurascens* f. *purpurascens*
Cyclamen durostoricum = *Cyclamen coum*
Cyclamen elegans = *Cyclamen coum* ssp. *elegans*
Cyclamen étalé (F): *Cyclamen repandum*
Cyclamen eucardium = *Cyclamen repandum* ssp. *peloponnesiacum*
    var. *vividum*
Cyclamen europaeum = *Cyclamen colchicum*
Cyclamen europaeum = *Cyclamen coum* ssp. *coum* f. *coum*
Cyclamen europaeum = *Cyclamen hederifolium* var. *hederifolium* f.
    hederifolium
Cyclamen europaeum = *Cyclamen purpurascens* f. *purpurascens*
Cyclamen europaeum = *Cyclamen repandum* var. *repandum* f.
    repandum
Cyclamen europaeum ssp. *orbiculatum* = *Cyclamen purpurascens*
    f. *purpurascens*
Cyclamen europaeum ssp. *orbiculatum* var. *immaculatum* =
    Cyclamen purpurascens f. *purpurascens*
Cyclamen europaeum ssp. *ponticum* = *Cyclamen colchicum*
Cyclamen europaeum var. *caucasicum* = *Cyclamen coum* ssp.
    caucasicum
Cyclamen europaeum var. *colchicum* = *Cyclamen colchicum*
Cyclamen europaeum var. *ponticum* = *Cyclamen colchicum*
Cyclamen europaeum var. *typicum* = *Cyclamen purpurascens* f.
    purpurascens
Cyclamen fatrense = *Cyclamen purpurascens* f. *purpurascens*
Cyclamen ficariifolium = *Cyclamen repandum* ssp. *repandum* var.
    repandum f. *repandum*
Cyclamen floridum = *Cyclamen purpurascens* f. *purpurascens*
Cyclamen gaidurowryssii = *Cyclamen graecum* ssp. *graecum* f.
    graecum
Cyclamen gaydurowryssii = *Cyclamen graecum* ssp. *graecum* f.
    graecum
Cyclamen gaydurowryssii: #1 **II** PRIMULACEAE
Cyclamen graecum: #1 **II** PRIMULACEAE
Cyclamen graecum ssp. *anatolicum*: #1 **II** PRIMULACEAE
Cyclamen graecum ssp. *candicum* = *Cyclamen graecum* ssp.
    mindleri
Cyclamen graecum ssp. *graecum* f. *album*: #1 **II** PRIMULACEAE
Cyclamen graecum ssp. *graecum* f. *graecum*: #1 **II**
    PRIMULACEAE
Cyclamen graecum ssp. *mindleri*: #1 **II** PRIMULACEAE
Cyclamen hastatum = *Cyclamen purpurascens* f. *purpurascens*
Cyclamen hederaceum = *Cyclamen persicum* var. *persicum* f.
    persicum
Cyclamen hederifolium = *Cyclamen hederifolium* var. *hederifolium*
    f. *hederifolium*
Cyclamen hederifolium = *Cyclamen persicum* var. *persicum* f.
    persicum
Cyclamen hederifolium = *Cyclamen repandum* ssp. *repandum* var.
    repandum f. *repandum*
Cyclamen hederifolium: (E) sowbread #1 **II** PRIMULACEAE
Cyclamen hederifolium ssp. *balearicum* = *Cyclamen balearicum*
Cyclamen hederifolium ssp. *creticum* = *Cyclamen creticum* f.
    creticum
Cyclamen hederifolium ssp. *romanum* = *Cyclamen hederifolium*
    var. *hederifolium* f. *hederifolium*
Cyclamen hederifolium var. *confusum*: #1 **II** PRIMULACEAE
Cyclamen hederifolium var. *hederifolium* f. *albiflorum*: #1 **II**
    PRIMULACEAE
Cyclamen hederifolium var. *hederifolium* f. *hederifolium*: #1 **II**
    PRIMULACEAE
Cyclamen hiemale = *Cyclamen coum* ssp. *coum* f. *coum*
Cyclamen holochlorum = *Cyclamen purpurascens* f. *purpurascens*
Cyclamen hyemale = *Cyclamen coum* ssp. *coum* f. *coum*
Cyclamen ibericum = *Cyclamen coum* ssp. *caucasicum*
Cyclamen ilicetorum = *Cyclamen repandum* ssp. *repandum* f.
    repandum
Cyclamen insulare = *Cyclamen hederifolium* var. *hederifolium* f.
    hederifolium
Cyclamen intaminatum: #1 **II** PRIMULACEAE
Cyclamen kusnetzovii = *Cyclamen coum* ssp. *coum* f. *coum*

270

Cyclamen latifolium = Cyclamen persicum var. *persicum* f. *persicum*

Cyclamen libanoticum.: #1 **II** PRIMULACEAE

Cyclamen libanoticum ssp. *pseudibericum = Cyclamen pseudibericum* f. *pseudibericum*

Cyclamen lilacinum = Cyclamen purpurascens f. *purpurascens*

Cyclamen linaerifolium = Cyclamen hederifolium var. *hederifolium* f. *hederifolium*

Cyclamen littorale = Cyclamen purpurascens f. *purpurascens*

Cyclamen lobospilum = Cyclamen repandum ssp. *repandum* var. *repandum* f. *repandum*

Cyclamen maritimum = Cyclamen graecum ssp. *anatolicum*

Cyclamen miliarakesii = Cyclamen graecum ssp. *graecum* f. *graecum*

Cyclamen mindleri = Cyclamen graecum ssp. *mindleri*

Cyclamen mirabile.: #1 **II** PRIMULACEAE

Cyclamen mirabile. f. *mirabile*: #1 **II** PRIMULACEAE

Cyclamen mirabile. f. *niveum*: #1 **II** PRIMULACEAE

Cyclamen neapolitanum = Cyclamen africanum

Cyclamen neapolitanum = Cyclamen cyprium

Cyclamen neapolitanum = Cyclamen hederifolium var. *hederifolium* f. *hederifolium*

Cyclamen numidicum = Cyclamen africanum

Cyclamen orbiculatum = Cyclamen coum ssp. *coum* f. *coum*

Cyclamen orbiculatum var. *alpinum = Cyclamen trochopteranthum* f. *trochopteranthum*

Cyclamen orbiculatum var. *coum = Cyclamen coum* ssp. *coum* f. *coum*

Cyclamen pachylobum = Cyclamen africanum

Cyclamen parviflorum: #1 **II** PRIMULACEAE

Cyclamen parviflorum var. *parviflorum*: #1 **II** PRIMULACEAE

Cyclamen parviflorum var. *subalpinum*: #1 **II** PRIMULACEAE

Cyclamen pentelici = Cyclamen graecum ssp. *graecum* f. *graecum*

Cyclamen persicum = Cyclamen graecum ssp. *graecum* f. *graecum*

Cyclamen persicum: **II** PRIMULACEAE

Cyclamen persicum ssp. *eupersicum = Cyclamen persicum* var. *persicum* f. *persicum*

Cyclamen persicum ssp. *mindleri = Cyclamen graecum* ssp. *mindleri*

Cyclamen persicum var. *autumnale*: #1 **II** PRIMULACEAE

Cyclamen persicum var. *persicum* f. *puniceum*: #1 **II** PRIMULACEAE

Cyclamen persicum var. *persicum* f. *albidum*: #1 **II** PRIMULACEAE

Cyclamen persicum var. *persicum* f. *persicum*: #1 **II** PRIMULACEAE

Cyclamen persicum var. *persicum* f. *roseum*: #1 **II** PRIMULACEAE

Cyclamen poli = Cyclamen hederifolium var. *hederifolium* f. *hederifolium*

Cyclamen ponticum = Cyclamen colchicum

Cyclamen pseudibericum: #1 **II** PRIMULACEAE

Cyclamen pseudibericum f. *pseudibericum*: #1 **II** PRIMULACEAE

Cyclamen pseudibericum f. *roseum*: #1 **II** PRIMULACEAE

Cyclamen pseudograecum = Cyclamen graecum ssp. *mindleri*

Cyclamen pseudomaritimum = Cyclamen graecum ssp. *anatolicum*

Cyclamen punicum = Cyclamen persicum var. *persicum* f. *persicum*

Cyclamen purpurascens: (F) cyclamen rouge pourpre #1 **II** PRIMULACEAE

Cyclamen purpurascens f. *album*: #1 **II** PRIMULACEAE

Cyclamen purpurascens f. *niveum*: #1 **II** PRIMULACEAE

Cyclamen purpurascens: (E) European cyclamen, (F) cyclamen d'Europe #1 **II** PRIMULACEAE

Cyclamen purpurascens ssp. *immaculatum = Cyclamen purpurascens* f. *purpurascens*

Cyclamen purpurascens ssp. *ponticum = Cyclamen colchicum*

Cyclamen pyrolifolium = Cyclamen persicum var. *persicum* f. *persicum*

Cyclamen rarinaevum = Cyclamen repandum ssp. *repandum* var. *repandum* f. *repandum*

Cyclamen repandum = Cyclamen balearicum

Cyclamen repandum: (F) Cyclamen étalé #1 **II** PRIMULACEAE

Cyclamen repandum ssp. *atlanticum = Cyclamen repandum* ssp. *repandum* var. *baborense*

Cyclamen repandum ssp. *balearicum = Cyclamen balearicum*

Cyclamen repandum ssp. *peloponnesiacum* f. *peloponnesiacu = Cyclamen repandum* ssp. *peloponnesiacum* f. *peloponnesiacum*

Cyclamen repandum ssp. *peloponnesiacum* f. *vividum = Cyclamen repandum* ssp. *peloponnesiacum* var. *vividum*

Cyclamen repandum ssp. *peloponnesiacum* var. *peloponnesiacum*: #1 **II** PRIMULACEAE

Cyclamen repandum ssp. *peloponnesiacum* var. *vividum*: #1 **II** PRIMULACEAE

Cyclamen repandum ssp. *repandum* var. *baborense*: #1 **II** PRIMULACEAE

Cyclamen repandum ssp. *repandum* var. *repandum* f. *repandum*: #1 **II** PRIMULACEAE

Cyclamen repandum ssp. *repandum* var. *repandum* f. *album*: #1 **II** PRIMULACEAE

Cyclamen repandum ssp. *rhodense*: #1 **II** PRIMULACEAE

Cyclamen repandum var. *creticum = Cyclamen creticum f. creticum*

Cyclamen repandum var. *rhodense = Cyclamen repandum* ssp. *rhodense*

Cyclamen repandum var. *stenopetalum = Cyclamen balearicum*

Cyclamen retroflexum = Cyclamen purpurascens f. *purpurascens*

Cyclamen rhodium = Cyclamen repandum ssp. *rhodense*

Cyclamen rohlfsianum: #1 **II** PRIMULACEAE

Cyclamen romanum = Cyclamen hederifolium var. *hederifolium* f. *hederifolium*

Cyclamen rouge pourpre (F): *Cyclamen purpurascens*

Cyclamen sabaudum = Cyclamen hederifolium var. *hederifolium* f. *hederifolium*

Cyclamen saldense = Cyclamen africanum

Cyclamen somalense: #1 **II** PRIMULACEAE

Cyclamen spectabile = Cyclamen repandum ssp. *peloponnesiacum* f. *vividum*

Cyclamen stenopetalum = Cyclamen repandum ssp. *peloponnesiacum* f. *vividum*

Cyclamen subhastatum = Cyclamen hederifolium var. *hederifolium* f. *hederifolium*

Cyclamen subtrotundum = Cyclamen africanum

Cyclamen trochopteranthum: #1 **II** PRIMULACEAE

Cyclamen trochopteranthum f. *leucanthum*: #1 **II** PRIMULACEAE

Cyclamen trochopteranthum f. *trochopteranthum*: #1 **II** PRIMULACEAE

Cyclamen tunetanum = Cyclamen persicum var. *persicum* f. *persicum*

Cyclamen umbratile = Cyclamen purpurascens f. *purpurascens*

Cyclamen utopicum = Cyclamen persicum var. *persicum* f. *persicum*

Cyclamen variegatum = Cyclamen purpurascens f. *purpurascens*

Cyclamen velutinum = Cyclamen graecum ssp. *graecum* f. *graecum*

Cyclamen venustum = Cyclamen africanum

Cyclamen vernale = Cyclamen coum ssp. *coum* f. *coum*

Cyclamen vernale = Cyclamen persicum var. *persicum* f. *persicum*

Cyclamen vernale = Cyclamen repandum ssp. *repandum* var. *repandum* f. *repandum*

Cyclamen vernum = Cyclamen balearicum

Cyclamen vernum = Cyclamen coum ssp. *caucasicum*

Cyclamen vernum = Cyclamen repandum ssp. *repandum* f. *repandum* f. *repandum*

Cyclamen vernum var. *caucasicum = Cyclamen coum* ssp. *caucasicum*

Cyclamen vernum var. *hiemale* f. *pseudocoum = Cyclamen coum* ssp. *coum* f. *coum*

Cyclamen zonale = Cyclamen coum ssp. *caucasicum*

Cyclaminos graeca = Cyclamen graecum ssp. *graecum* f. *graecum*

Cyclaminos miliarakesii = Cyclamen graecum ssp. *graecum* *graecum*

Cyclaminos mindleri = Cyclamen graecum ssp. *mindleri*

Cyclaminus coa = Cyclamen coum ssp. *coum* f. *coum*

Cyclaminus graeca = Cyclamen graecum ssp. *graecum* f. *graecum*

Cyclaminus neopolitana = Cyclamen hederifolium var. *hederifolium* f. *hederifolium*

Cyclaminus persica = Cyclamen persicum var. *persicum* f. *persicum*

271

Checklist of flora/Lista de especies de flora/Liste des espèces végétales

Cyclaminus repanda = *Cyclamen repandum* ssp. *repandum* f. *repandum*
Cyclopogon spp.: #7 **II** ORCHIDACEAE
Cycnoches spp.: #7 **II** ORCHIDACEAE
Cylindrolobus = *Eria*
Cylindropuntia abyssi = *Opuntia abyssi*
Cylindropuntia acanthocarpa = *Opuntia acanthocarpa*
Cylindropuntia alcahes = *Opuntia prolifera*
Cylindropuntia arbuscula = *Opuntia arbuscula*
Cylindropuntia bigelowii = *Opuntia bigelovii*
Cylindropuntia brevispina = *Opuntia alcahes*
Cylindropuntia brittonii = *Opuntia leptocaulis*
Cylindropuntia burrageana = *Opuntia burrageana*
Cylindropuntia californica = *Opuntia californica*
Cylindropuntia calmalliana = *Opuntia molesta*
Cylindropuntia caribaea = *Opuntia caribaea*
Cylindropuntia cholla = *Opuntia cholla*
Cylindropuntia ciribe = *Opuntia bigelovii*
Cylindropuntia clavellina = *Opuntia molesta*
Cylindropuntia davisii = *Opuntia davisii*
Cylindropuntia echinocarpa = *Opuntia echinocarpa*
Cylindropuntia fulgida = *Opuntia fulgida*
Cylindropuntia humahuacana = *Opuntia shaferi*
Cylindropuntia imbricata = *Opuntia imbricata*
Cylindropuntia intermedia = *Opuntia cylindrica*
Cylindropuntia kleiniae = *Opuntia kleiniae*
Cylindropuntia leptocaulis = *Opuntia leptocaulis*
Cylindropuntia lloydii = *Opuntia lloydii*
Cylindropuntia metuenda = *Opuntia caribaea*
Cylindropuntia molesta = *Opuntia molesta*
Cylindropuntia multigeniculata = *Opuntia multigeniculata*
Cylindropuntia munzii = *Opuntia munzii*
Cylindropuntia parryi = *Opuntia parryi*
Cylindropuntia prolifera = *Opuntia prolifera*
Cylindropuntia ramosissima = *Opuntia ramosissima*
Cylindropuntia recondita = *Opuntia kleiniae*
Cylindropuntia rosarica = *Opuntia rosarica*
Cylindropuntia rosea = *Opuntia rosea*
Cylindropuntia spinosior = *Opuntia spinosior*
Cylindropuntia vivipara = *Opuntia arbuscula*
Cylindropuntia weingartiana = *Opuntia shaferi*
Cymbidiella spp.: #7 **II** ORCHIDACEAE
Cymbidium spp.: #7 **II** ORCHIDACEAE
Cymbiglossum = *Lemboglossum*
Cymboglossum = *Eria*
Cynorchis = *Cynorkis*
Cynorkis spp.: #7 **II** ORCHIDACEAE
Cynosorchis = *Cynorkis*
Cyperochis = *Cymbidium*
Cyphochilus = *Appendicula*
Cypholoron spp.: #7 **II** ORCHIDACEAE
Cypripedium spp.: #7 **II** ORCHIDACEAE
Cypripedium appletonianum = *Paphiopedilum appletonianum*
Cypripedium argus = *Paphiopedilum argus*
Cypripedium barbatum var. *biflorum*= *Paphiopedilum barbatum*
Cypripedium barbatum var. *crossii*= *Paphiopedilum callosum*
Cypripedium barbatum var. *superbum*= *Paphiopedilum superbiens*
Cypripedium barbatum var. *veitchii*= *Paphiopedilum superbiens*
Cypripedium barbatum var. *warneri*= *Paphiopedilum callosum* var.*sublaeve*
Cypripedium barbatum var. *warnerianum*= *Paphiopedilum callosum* var. *sublaeve*
Cypripedium barbatum = *Paphiopedilum barbatum*
Cypripedium bellatulum = *Paphiopedilum bellatulum*
Cypripedium biflorum = *Paphiopedilum barbatum*
Cypripedium binoti = *Phragmipedium vittatum*
Cypripedium boxallii var. *atratum*= *Paphiopedilum villosum* var. *boxallii*
Cypripedium boxallii = *Paphiopedilum villosum* var. *boxallii*
Cypripedium bullenianum var. *appletonianum* = *Paphiopedilum appletonianum*
Cypripedium bullenianum = *Paphiopedilum bullenianum*
Cypripedium burbidgei = *Paphiopedilum dayanum*

Cypripedium callosum var. *sublaeve* = *Paphiopedilum callosum* var. *sublaeve*
Cypripedium callosum = *Paphiopedilum callosum*
Cypripedium cannartianum = *Paphiopedilum philippinense*
Cypripedium caricinum = *Phragmipedium pearcei*
Cypripedium caricinum = *Phragmipedium caricinum*
Cypripedium caudatum var. *lindenii* = *Phragmipedium lindenii*
Cypripedium caudatum var. *wallisii* = *Phragmipedium wallisii*
Cypripedium caudatum = *Phragmipedium caudatum*
Cypripedium chamberlainianum = *Paphiopedilum victoria-regina*
Cypripedium charlesworthii = *Paphiopedilum charlesworthii*
Cypripedium ciliolare var. *miteauanum* = *Paphiopedilum ciliolare*
Cypripedium ciliolare = *Paphiopedilum ciliolare*
Cypripedium concolor var. *godefroyae* = *Paphiopedilum godefroyae*
Cypripedium concolor = *Paphiopedilum concolor*
Cypripedium crossii = *Paphiopedilum callosum*
Cypripedium cruciforme = *Paphiopedilum lowii*
Cypripedium curtisii = *Paphiopedilum superbiens* var. *curtisii*
Cypripedium dayanum = *Paphiopedilum dayanum*
Cypripedium dayi = *Paphiopedilum dayanum*
Cypripedium delenatii = *Paphiopedilum delenatii*
Cypripedium dilectum = *Paphiopedilum villosum* var. *boxallii*
Cypripedium druryi = *Paphiopedilum druryi*
Cypripedium elliottianum = *Paphiopedilum rothschildianum*
Cypripedium ernestianum = *Paphiopedilum dayanum*
Cypripedium exul = *Paphiopedilum exul*
Cypripedium fairrieanum = *Paphiopedilum fairrieanum*
Cypripedium gardineri = *Paphiopedilum glanduliferum*
Cypripedium glanduliferum = *Paphiopedilum glanduliferum*
Cypripedium glaucophyllum = *Paphiopedilum glaucophyllum*
Cypripedium godefroyae var. *leucochilum* = *Paphiopedilum godefroyae* var. *leucochilum*
Cypripedium godefroyae = *Paphiopedilum godefroyae*
Cypripedium grandiflorum = *Phragmipedium boissierianum*
Cypripedium gratrixianum = *Paphiopedilum gratrixianum*
Cypripedium haynaldianum = *Paphiopedilum haynaldianum*
Cypripedium hincksianum = *Phragmipedium longifolium*
Cypripedium hirsutissimum = *Paphiopedilum hirsutissimum*
Cypripedium hookerae var. *amabile* = *Paphiopedilum bullenianum*
Cypripedium hookerae var. *bullenianum* = *Paphiopedilum bullenianum*
Cypripedium hookerae var. *volonteanum* = *Paphiopedilum hookerae* var. *volonteanum*
Cypripedium hookerae = *Paphiopedilum hookerae*
Cypripedium humboldtii = *Phragmipedium caudatum*
Cypripedium insigne var. *exul* = *Paphiopedilum exul*
Cypripedium insigne = *Paphiopedilum insigne*
Cypripedium javanicum var. *virens* = *Paphiopedilum javanicum* var. *virens*
Cypripedium javanicum = *Paphiopedilum javanicum*
Cypripedium klotzschianum = *Phragmipedium klotzschianum*
Cypripedium laevigatum = *Paphiopedilum philippinense*
Cypripedium lawrenceanum = *Paphiopedilum lawrenceanum*
Cypripedium lindenii = *Phragmipedium lindenii*
Cypripedium lindleyanum = *Phragmipedium lindleyanum*
Cypripedium longifolium = *Phragmipedium longifolium*
Cypripedium lowii = *Paphiopedilum lowii*
Cypripedium mastersianum = *Paphiopedilum mastersianum*
Cypripedium miteauanum = *Paphiopedilum ciliolare*
Cypripedium neo-guineense = *Paphiopedilum rothschildianum*
Cypripedium nigritum = *Paphiopedilum barbatum*
Cypripedium niveum = *Paphiopedilum niveum*
Cypripedium papuanum = *Paphiopedilum papuanum*
Cypripedium pardinum = *Paphiopedilum venustum*
Cypripedium parishii = *Paphiopedilum parishii*
Cypripedium paulistanum = *Phragmipedium vittatum*
Cypripedium peteri = *Paphiopedilum dayanum*
Cypripedium petri var. *burbidgei* = *Paphiopedilum dayanum*
Cypripedium petri = *Paphiopedilum dayanum*
Cypripedium philippinense var. *roebelenii* = *Paphiopedilum philippinense* var. *roebelenii*
Cypripedium philippinense = *Paphiopedilum philippinense*
Cypripedium pitcherianum = *Paphiopedilum argus*

Checklist of flora/Lista de especies de flora/Liste des espèces végétales

Cypripedium poyntzianum = *Paphiopedilum appletonianum*
Cypripedium praestans var. *kimballianum* = *Paphiopedilum glanduliferum*
Cypripedium praestans = *Paphiopedilum glanduliferum*
Cypripedium purpuratum = *Paphiopedilum purpuratum*
Cypripedium robinsonii = *Paphiopedilum bullenianum*
Cypripedium roebelenii var. *cannartianum* = *Paphiopedilum philippinense*
Cypripedium roebelenii = *Paphiopedilum philippinense* var. *roebelenii*
Cypripedium rothschildianum = *Paphiopedilum rothschildianum*
Cypripedium sanderianum = *Paphiopedilum sanderianum*
Cypripedium sargentianum = *Phragmipedium sargentianum*
Cypripedium schlimii = *Phragmipedium schlimii*
Cypripedium schmidtianum = *Paphiopedilum callosum*
Cypripedium schomburgkianum = *Phragmipedium klotzschianum*
Cypripedium sinicum = *Paphiopedilum purpuratum*
Cypripedium spectabile var. *dayanum* = *Paphiopedilum dayanum*
Cypripedium spicerianum = *Paphiopedilum spicerianum*
Cypripedium stonei = *Paphiopedilum stonei*
Cypripedium superbiens var. *dayanum* = *Paphiopedilum dayanum*
Cypripedium superbiens = *Paphiopedilum superbiens*
Cypripedium tonkinense = *Paphiopedilum concolor*
Cypripedium tonsum = *Paphiopedilum tonsum*
Cypripedium veitchianum = *Paphiopedilum superbiens*
Cypripedium venustum = *Paphiopedilum venustum*
Cypripedium venustum = *Paphiopedilum venustum*
Cypripedium victoria-mariae = *Paphiopedilum victoria-mariae*
Cypripedium victoria-regina = *Paphiopedilum victoria-regina*
Cypripedium villosum var. *boxallii* = *Paphiopedilum villosum* var. *boxallii*
Cypripedium villosum = *Paphiopedilum villosum*
Cypripedium virens = *Paphiopedilum javanicum* var. *virens*
Cypripedium vittatum = *Phragmipedium vittatum*
Cypripedium volonteanum = *Paphiopedilum hookerae* var. *volonteanum*
Cypripedium waltersianum = *Paphiopedilum appletonianum*
Cypripedium wardii = *Paphiopedilum wardii*
Cypripedium wolterianum = *Paphiopedilum appletonianum*
Cyrtidiorchis spp.: #7 **II** ORCHIDACEAE
Cyrtidium = *Cyrtidiorchis*
Cyrtochilum = *Oncidium*
Cyrtoglottis = *Podochilus*
Cyrtopera = *Eulophia*
Cyrtopodium spp.: #7 **II** ORCHIDACEAE
Cyrtorchis spp.: #7 **II** ORCHIDACEAE
Cyrtosia spp.: #7 **II** ORCHIDACEAE
Cyrtostylis spp.: #7 **II** ORCHIDACEAE
Cystochilum = *Cranichis*
Cystopus = *Pristiglottis*
Cystorchis spp.: #7 **II** ORCHIDACEAE
Cytherea = *Calypso*
Cytheris = *Calanthe*
Dactylanthes anacantha = *Euphorbia tridentata*
Dactylanthes globosa = *Euphorbia globosa*
Dactylanthes hamata = *Euphorbia hamata*
Dactylanthes patula = *Euphorbia tridentata*
Dactylanthes tuberculata = *Euphorbia tuberculata*
Dactylorchis = *Dactylorhiza*
Dactylorhiza spp.: #7 **II** ORCHIDACEAE
Dactylorhynchus = *Bulbophyllum*
Dactylostalix spp.: #7 **II** ORCHIDACEAE
Dactylostylis = *Zygostates*
Dahlia's apple-cactus (E): *Echinocereus poselgeri*
Dalbergia nigra: (E) Bahia rosewood, Brazilian rosewood, Rio rosewood, (S) Jacaranda de Bahía, Jacarandá de Brasil, Palisandro del Brasil (F) Palissandre du Brésil, **I** LEGUMINOSAE
Darwiniella = *Trichoceros*
Darwiniera spp.: #7 **II** ORCHIDACEAE
Davallia berteriana = *Dicksonia berteriana*
Davis' green pitaya (E): *Echinocereus viridiflorus* ssp. *davisii*
Decaisnea = *Prescottia*
Decaisnea = *Tropidia*
Decarya madagascariensis: #1 **II** DIDIEREACEAE

Deceptor spp.: #7 **II** ORCHIDACEAE
Degranvillea spp.: #7 **II** ORCHIDACEAE
Dehesa bear-grass (E): *Nolina interrata*
Deiregyne spp.: #7 **II** ORCHIDACEAE
Deiregynopsis = *Aulosepalum*
Delaetia woutersiana = *Erisyce taltalensis* spp. *paucicostata*
Dendrobium spp.: #7 **I/II** ORCHIDACEAE
Dendrobium cruentum: **I** ORCHIDACEAE
Dendrocereus nudiflorus: #4 **II** CACTACEAE
Dendrocereus undulosus: #4 **II** CACTACEAE
Dendrochilum spp.: #7 **II** ORCHIDACEAE
Dendrocoryne = *Dendrobium*
Dendrolirium = *Eria*
Dendrophylax spp.: #7 **II** ORCHIDACEAE
Dendrorkis = *Aerides*
Denmoza erythrocephala = *Denmoza rhodacantha*
Denmoza rhodacantha: #4 **II** CACTACEAE
Denslovia = *Habenaria*
Deppia = *Lycaste*
Deroemeria = *Holothrix*
Desert cistanche (E): *Cistanche deserticola*
Desert living cistanche (E): *Cistanche deserticola*
Desert Valley fishhook-cactus (E): *Sclerocactus spinosior*
Desmotrichum = *Flickingeria*
Devil's prickley-pear (E): *Opuntia emoryi*
Diacrium = *Caularthron*
Diadenium spp.: #7 **II** ORCHIDACEAE
Dialissa = *Stelis*
Diaphananthe spp.: #7 **II** ORCHIDACEAE
Diceratostele spp.: #7 **II** ORCHIDACEAE
Dicerostylis spp.: #7 **II** ORCHIDACEAE
Dichaea spp.: #7 **II** ORCHIDACEAE
Dichaeopsis = *Dichaea*
Dichopus = *Dendrobium*
Dichromanthus spp.: #7 **II** ORCHIDACEAE
Dickasonia spp.: #7 **II** ORCHIDACEAE
Dicksonia spp.: (E) tree ferns, (S) helechos arborescentes #1 **II**[1] DICKSONIACEAE
Dicksonia berteriana: #1 **II** DICKSONIACEAE
Dicksonia berteriana var. *virgata* = *Dicksonia externa*
Dicksonia chrysotricha = *Dicksonia blumei*
Dicksonia cicutaria var. *incisa* = *Dicksonia incisa*
Dicksonia deplanchei = *Dicksonia baudouini*
Dicksonia externa: #1 **II** DICKSONIACEAE
Dicksonia ghiesbreghtii = *Dicksonia sellowiana*
Dicksonia gigantea = *Dicksonia sellowiana*
Dicksonia gracilis = *Dicksonia squarrosa*
Dicksonia integra = *Dicksonia arborescens*
Dicksonia karsteniana = *Dicksonia sellowiana*
Dicksonia ledermannii = *Dicksonia grandis*
Dicksonia lobularia = *Dicksonia sellowiana*
Dicksonia lobulata = *Dicksonia sellowiana*
Dicksonia navarrensis = *Dicksonia sellowiana*
Dicksonia schlechteri = *Dicksonia grandis*
Dicksonia sellowiana: #1 **II** DICKSONIACEAE
Dicksonia sellowiana var. *arachneosa* = *Dicksonia sellowiana*
Dicksonia sellowiana var. *karsteniana* = *Dicksonia sellowiana*
Dicksonia stuebelii: #1 **II** DICKSONIACEAE
Dicranotaenia = *Microcoelia*
Dicrypta = *Maxillaria*
Dictyophyllaria spp.: #7 **II** ORCHIDACEAE
Didactyle = *Bulbophyllum*
Didiciea spp.: #7 **II** ORCHIDACEAE
Didierea ascendens: #1 **II** DIDIEREACEAE
Didierea comosa: #1 **II** DIDIEREACEAE
Didierea dumosa: #1 **II** DIDIEREACEAE
Didierea madagascariensis: #1 **II** DIDIEREACEAE
Didierea mirabilis: #1 **II** DIDIEREACEAE
Didierea procera: #1 **II** DIDIEREACEAE
Didierea trollii: #1 **II** DIDIEREACEAE

---

[1] Only the population of the Americas/Sólo la población de las Américas /Seulement la population d'Amérique

273

Checklist of flora/Lista de especies de flora/Liste des espèces végétales

DIDIEREACEAE spp.: (E) alluaudias, didiereas (S) didiereas (F) didiéréacées #1 **II**

Didiéréacées (F): DIDIEREACEAE spp.

Didiereas (E/S): DIDIEREACEAE spp.

Didothion = Epidendrum

Didymoplexiella spp.: #7 **II** ORCHIDACEAE

Didymoplexis spp.: #7 **II** ORCHIDACEAE

Dienia = Malaxis

Diglyphis = Diglyphosa

Diglyphosa spp.: #7 **II** ORCHIDACEAE

Dignathe = Leochilus

Digomphotis = Habenaria

Dikylikostigma = Discyphus

Dilochia spp.: #7 **II** ORCHIDACEAE

Dilochiopsis = Eria

Dilomilis spp.: #7 **II** ORCHIDACEAE

Dimerandra spp.: #7 **II** ORCHIDACEAE

Dimorphorchis spp.: #7 **II** ORCHIDACEAE

Dinema = Encyclia

Dinklagiella spp.: #7 **II** ORCHIDACEAE

Dionaea corymbosa = Dionaea muscipula

Dionaea muscicapa = Dionaea muscipula

Dionaea muscipula: (E) Venus flytrap, (S) Atrapmoscas (F) Dionée attrapemouches, #1 **II** DROSERACEAE

Dionaea muscipula f. *atrorubens = Dionaea muscipula*

Dionaea muscipula f. *erecta = Dionaea muscipula*

Dionaea muscipula f. *filiformis = Dionaea muscipula*

Dionaea muscipula f. *linearis = Dionaea muscipula*

Dionaea muscipula f. *prostrata = Dionaea muscipula*

Dionaea muscipula f. *viridis = Dionaea muscipula*

Dionaea sensitiva = Dionaea muscipula

Dionaea sessiliflora = Dionaea muscipula

Dionaea uniflora = Dionaea muscipula

Dionée attrapemouches (F): *Dionaea muscipula*

Dioon aculeatum = Dioon edule

Dioon angustifolium = Dioon edule

Dioon califanoi: #1 **II** ZAMIACEAE

Dioon caputoi: #1 **II** ZAMIACEAE

Dioon edule: #1 **II** ZAMIACEAE

Dioon edule f. *angustifolium = Dioon edule*

Dioon edule f. *imbricatum = Dioon edule*

Dioon edule ssp. *angustifolium = Dioon edule*

Dioon edule var. *edule*: #1 **II** ZAMIACEAE

Dioon edule var. *imbricatum = Dioon edule*

Dioon edule var. *sonorense = Dioon sonorense*

Dioon holmgrenii: #1 **II** ZAMIACEAE

Dioon imbricatum = Dioon edule

Dioon mejiae: #1 **II** ZAMIACEAE

Dioon merolae: #1 **II** ZAMIACEAE

Dioon purpusii: #1 **II** ZAMIACEAE

Dioon rzedowskii: #1 **II** ZAMIACEAE

Dioon sonorense: #1 **II** ZAMIACEAE

Dioon spinulosum: #1 **II** ZAMIACEAE

Dioon strobilaceum = Dioon edule

Dioon strobilosum = Dioon edule

Dioon tomasellii var. *sonorense = Dioon sonorense*

Dioon tomasellii var. *tomasellii*: #1 **II** ZAMIACEAE

Dioscorea (E): *Dioscorea deltoidea*

Dioscorea deltoidea: (E) Dioscorea, Elephant's foot, (S) Pie de elefante #1 **II** DIOSCOREACEAE

Diothonea = Epidendrum

Dipera = Disperis

Diphryllum = Listera

Diphyes = Bulbophyllum

Diphylax spp.: #7 **II** ORCHIDACEAE

Diplacorchis = Brachycorythis

Diplandrorchis = Neottia

Diplanthera = Platanthera

Diplectraden = Habenaria

Diplectrum = Satyrium

Diplocaulobium spp.: #7 **II** ORCHIDACEAE

Diplocentrum spp.: #7 **II** ORCHIDACEAE

Diplochilus = Diplomeris

Diploconchium = Agrostophyllum

Diplodium = Pterostylis

Diplolabellum spp.: #7 **II** ORCHIDACEAE

Diplomeris spp.: #7 **II** ORCHIDACEAE

Diploprora spp.: #7 **II** ORCHIDACEAE

Dipodium spp.: #7 **II** ORCHIDACEAE

Dipteranthus spp.: #7 **II** ORCHIDACEAE

Dipterostele = Stellilabium

Dipteryx panamensis: **III** LEGUMINOSAE

Disa spp.: #7 **II** ORCHIDACEAE

Disc cactus (E): *Strombocactus disciformis*

Discocacti (E): *Discocactus* spp.

Discocacto (S): *Discocactus* spp.

Discocactus spp.: (E) discocacti, (S) discocacto **I** CACTACEAE

Discocactus albispinus = Discocactus zehntneri ssp. *zehntneri*

Discocactus alteolens = Discocactus placentiformis

Discocactus araneispinus = Discocactus zehntneri ssp. *boomianus*

Discocactus bahiensis: **I** CACTACEAE

Discocactus bahiensis ssp. *subviridigriseus = Discocactus bahiensis*

Discocactus boliviensis = Discocactus heptacanthus ssp. *heptacanthus*

Discocactus boomianus = Discocactus zehntneri ssp. *boomianus*

Discocactus buenekeri = Discocactus zehntneri ssp. *boomianus*

Discocactus cangaensis = Discocactus heptacanthus ssp. *heptacanthus*

Discocactus catingicola = Discocactus heptacanthus ssp. *catingicola*

Discocactus catingicola ssp. *griseus = Discocactus heptacanthus* ssp. *heptacanthus*

Discocactus catingicola ssp. *rapirhizus = Discocactus heptacanthus* ssp. *heptacanthus*

Discocactus cephaliaciculosus = Discocactus heptacanthus ssp. *heptacanthus*

Discocactus cephaliaciculosus ssp. *nudicephalus = Discocactus heptacanthus* ssp. *heptacanthus*

Discocactus crassispinus = Discocactus heptacanthus ssp. *heptacanthus*

Discocactus crassispinus ssp. *araguaiensis = Discocactus heptacanthus* ssp. *heptacanthus*

Discocactus crystallophilus = Discocactus placentiformis

Discocactus diersianus = Discocactus heptacanthus ssp. *heptacanthus*

Discocactus diersianus ssp. *goianus = Discocactus heptacanthus* ssp. *heptacanthus*

Discocactus estevesii = Discocactus heptacanthus ssp. *heptacanthus*

Discocactus ferricola: **I** CACTACEAE

Discocactus flavispinus = Discocactus heptacanthus ssp. *heptacanthus*

Discocactus goianus = Discocactus heptacanthus ssp. *heptacanthus*

Discocactus griseus = Discocactus heptacanthus ssp. *heptacanthus*

Discocactus hartmannii = Discocactus heptacanthus ssp. *magnimammus*

Discocactus hartmannii ssp. *giganteus = Discocactus heptacanthus* ssp. *magnimammus*

Discocactus hartmannii ssp. *magnimammus = Discocactus heptacanthus* ssp. *magnimammus*

Discocactus hartmannii ssp. *patulifolius = Discocactus heptacanthus* ssp. *magnimammus*

Discocactus hartmannii ssp. *setosiflorus = Discocactus heptacanthus* ssp. *heptacanthus*

Discocactus heptacanthus: **I** CACTACEAE

Discocactus heptacanthus ssp. *catingicola*: **I** CACTACEAE

Discocactus heptacanthus ssp. *heptacanthus*: **I** CACTACEAE

Discocactus heptacanthus ssp. *magnimammus*: **I** CACTACEAE

Discocactus heptacanthus ssp. *melanochlorus = Discocactus heptacanthus* ssp. *heptacanthus*

Discocactus horstii: **I** CACTACEAE

Discocactus insignis = Discocactus placentiformis

Discocactus latispinus = Discocactus placentiformis

Discocactus latispinus ssp. *pseudolatispinus = Discocactus placentiformis*

Discocactus latispinus ssp. *pulvinicapitatus = Discocactus placentiformis*

Checklist of flora/Lista de especies de flora/Liste des espèces végétales

Discocactus lindaianus = *Discocactus heptacanthus* ssp. *heptacanthus*
Discocactus lindanus = *Discocactus heptacanthus* ssp. *heptacanthus*
Discocactus magnimammus = *Discocactus heptacanthus* ssp. *magnimammus*
Discocactus magnimammus ssp. *bonitoensis* = *Discocactus heptacanthus* ssp. *magnimammus*
Discocactus melanochlorus = *Discocactus heptacanthus* ssp. *heptacanthus*
Discocactus multicolorispinus = *Discocactus placentiformis*
Discocactus nigrisaetosus = *Discocactus heptacanthus* ssp. *catingicola*
Discocactus pachythele = *Discocactus heptacanthus* ssp. *magnimammus*
Discocactus paranaensis = *Discocactus heptacanthus*
Discocactus patulifolius = *Discocactus heptacanthus* ssp. *magnimammus*
Discocactus piauiensis = *Discocactus heptacanthus* ssp. *catingicola*
Discocactus placentiformis: **I** CACTACEAE
Discocactus placentiformis ssp. *alteolens* = *Discocactus placentiformis*
Discocactus placentiformis ssp. *multicolorispinus* = *Discocactus placentiformis*
Discocactus placentiformis ssp. *pugionacanthus* = *Discocactus placentiformis*
Discocactus prominentigibbus = *Discocactus heptacanthus* ssp. *heptacanthus*
Discocactus pseudoinsignis: **I** CACTACEAE
Discocactus pseudolatispinus = *Discocactus placentiformis*
Discocactus pugionacanthus = *Discocactus placentiformis*
Discocactus pulvinicapitatus = *Discocactus placentiformis*
Discocactus rapirhizus = *Discocactus heptacanthus* ssp. *heptacanthus*
Discocactus semicampaniflorus = *Discocactus heptacanthus* ssp. *heptacanthus*
Discocactus silicicola = *Discocactus heptacanthus* ssp. *heptacanthus*
Discocactus silvaticus = *Discocactus heptacanthus* ssp. *heptacanthus*
Discocactus spinosior = *Discocactus heptacanthus* ssp. *catingicola*
Discocactus squamibaccatus = *Discocactus heptacanthus* ssp. *heptacanthus*
Discocactus subterraneo-proliferans = *Discocactus heptacanthus* ssp. *heptacanthus*
Discocactus subviridigriseus = *Discocactus bahiensis*
Discocactus tricornis = *Discocactus placentiformis*
Discocactus woutersianus = *Discocactus horstii*
Discocactus zehntneri: **I** CACTACEAE
Discocactus zehntneri ssp. *albispinus* = *Discocactus zehntneri* ssp. *zehntneri*
Discocactus zehntneri ssp. *araneispinus* = *Discocactus zehntneri* ssp. *boomianus*
Discocactus zehntneri ssp. *boomianus*: **I** CACTACEAE
Discocactus zehntneri ssp. *buenekeri* = *Discocactus zehntneri* ssp. *boomianus*
Discocactus zehntneri ssp. *horstiorum* = *Discocactus zehntneri* ssp. *boomianus*
Discocactus zehntneri ssp. *zehntneri*: **I** CACTACEAE
Discyphus spp.: #7 **II** ORCHIDACEAE
Diseris = *Disperis*
Disocactus ackermannii: #4 **II** CACTACEAE
Disocactus alatus = *Pseudorhipsalis alata*
Disocactus amazonicus: #4 **II** CACTACEAE
Disocactus aurantiacus: #4 **II** CACTACEAE
Disocactus biformis: #4 **II** CACTACEAE
Disocactus cinnabarinus: #4 **II** CACTACEAE
Disocactus eichlamii: #4 **II** CACTACEAE
Disocactus flagelliformis: #4 **II** CACTACEAE
Disocactus kimnachii: #4 **II** CACTACEAE
Disocactus macdougallii: (E) McDougal's cactus #4 **II** CACTACEAE
Disocactus macranthus: #4 **II** CACTACEAE
Disocactus martianus: #4 **II** CACTACEAE

Disocactus nelsonii: #4 **II** CACTACEAE
Disocactus phyllanthoides: #4 **II** CACTACEAE
Disocactus quezaltecus: #4 **II** CACTACEAE
Disocactus schrankii: #4 **II** CACTACEAE
Disocactus speciosus: #4 **II** CACTACEAE
Disperis spp.: #7 **II** ORCHIDACEAE
Dissorhynchium = *Habenaria*
Distichis = *Liparis*
Distomaea = *Listera*
Distylodon spp.: #7 **II** ORCHIDACEAE
Diteilis = *Liparis*
Dithrix = *Habenaria*
Dithyridanthus = *Schiedeella*
Ditulima = *Dendrobium*
Diuris spp.: #7 **II** ORCHIDACEAE
Dockrillia = *Dendrobium*
Dodsonia spp.: #7 **II** ORCHIDACEAE
Dolichocentrum = *Dendrobium*
Dolichothele albescens = *Mammillaria decipiens* ssp. *albescens*
Dolichothele balsasoides = *Mammillaria beneckei*
Dolichothele baumii = *Mammillaria baumii*
Dolichothele beneckei = *Mammillaria beneckei*
Dolichothele camptotricha = *Mammillaria decipiens* ssp. *camptotricha*
Dolichothele decipiens = *Mammillaria decipiens* ssp. *decipiens*
Dolichothele longimamma = *Mammillaria longimamma*
Dolichothele longimamma ssp. *uberiformis* = *Mammillaria longimamma*
Dolichothele melaleuca = *Mammillaria melaleuca*
Dolichothele nelsonii = *Mammillaria beneckei*
Dolichothele sphaerica = *Mammillaria sphaerica*
Dolichothele surculosa = *Mammillaria surculosa*
Dolichothele uberiformis = *Mammillaria longimamma*
Dombeyana chilensis = *Araucaria araucana*
Domingoa spp.: #7 **II** ORCHIDACEAE
Doritis spp.: #7 **II** ORCHIDACEAE
Dorycheile = *Cephalanthera*
Dossinia spp.: #7 **II** ORCHIDACEAE
Dothilis = *Spiranthes*
Dothilophis = *Epidendrum*
Doxosma = *Epidendrum*
Dracula spp.: #7 **II** ORCHIDACEAE
Drakaea spp.: #7 **II** ORCHIDACEAE
Dresslerella spp.: #7 **II** ORCHIDACEAE
Dressleria spp.: #7 **II** ORCHIDACEAE
Dressleriella = *Jacquiniella*
Drury's slipper orchid (E): *Paphiopedilum druryi*
Dryadella spp.: #7 **II** ORCHIDACEAE
Dryadorchis spp.: #7 **II** ORCHIDACEAE
Drymoanthus spp.: #7 **II** ORCHIDACEAE
Drymoda spp.: #7 **II** ORCHIDACEAE
Dryopeia = *Disperis*
Dryorchis = *Disperis*
Duboisia = *Myoxanthus*
Dubois-reymondia = *Myoxanthus*
Duckeella spp.: #7 **II** ORCHIDACEAE
Dudleya stolonifera: (E) Laguna Beach Liveforever #4 **II** CRASSULACEAE
Dudleya traskiae: (E) Santa Barbara Island dudleya, Santa Barbara Island liveforever **II** CRASSULACEAE
Duncan's corycactus (E): *Escobaria duncanii*
Dunstervillea spp.: #7 **II** ORCHIDACEAE
Dyakia spp.: #7 **II** ORCHIDACEAE
Dyerocycas micholitzii = *Cycas micholitzii*
Dypsis decaryi = *Neodypsis decaryi*
Dypsis decipiens = *Chrysalidocarpus decipiens*
Eaglewood (E): *Aquilaria malaccensis*
Earina spp.: #7 **II** ORCHIDACEAE
Eburophyton = *Cephalanthera*
Eccremocactus bradei = *Weberocereus bradei*
Eccremocactus imitans = *Weberocereus imitans*
Echinocactus asterias = *Astrophytum asterias*
Echinocactus grandis = *Echinocactus platyacanthus*
Echinocactus grusonii: #4 **II** CACTACEAE

Checklist of flora/Lista de especies de flora/Liste des espèces végétales

Echinocactus horizonthalonius: (E) Turk's-head cactus #4 **II** CACTACEAE
Echinocactus ingens = *Echinocactus platyacanthus*
Echinocactus palmeri = *Echinocactus platyacanthus*
Echinocactus parryi: #4 **II** CACTACEAE
Echinocactus platyacanthus: #4 **II** CACTACEAE
Echinocactus polycephalus: (E) Cotton-top cactus #4 **II** CACTACEAE
Echinocactus polycephalus ssp. *polycephalus*: #4 **II** CACTACEAE
Echinocactus polycephalus ssp. *xeranthemoides*: #4 **II** CACTACEAE
Echinocactus texensis: (E) Horse Crippler #4 **II** CACTACEAE
Echinocactus visnaga = *Echinocactus platyacanthus*
Echinocereus abbeae = *Echinocereus fasciculatus*
Echinocereus acifer = *Echinocereus polyacanthus* ssp. *acifer*
Echinocereus acifer ssp. *huitcholensis* = *Echinocereus polyacanthus* ssp. *huitcholensis*
Echinocereus acifer ssp. *tubiflorus* = *Echinocereus polyacanthus* ssp. *acifer*
Echinocereus adustus: #4 **II** CACTACEAE
Echinocereus adustus ssp. *adustus*: #4 **II** CACTACEAE
Echinocereus adustus ssp. *bonatzii*: #4 **II** CACTACEAE
Echinocereus adustus ssp. *schwarzii*: #4 **II** CACTACEAE
Echinocereus albatus = *Echinocereus nivosus*
Echinocereus albispinus = *Echinocereus reichenbachii* ssp. *baileyi*
Echinocereus amoenus = *Echinocereus pulchellus* ssp. *pulchellus*
Echinocereus angusticeps = *Echinocereus papillosus*
Echinocereus apachensis: #4 **II** CACTACEAE
Echinocereus arizonicus = *Echinocereus coccineus* ssp. *coccineus*
Echinocereus arizonicus ssp. *matudae* = *Echinocereus coccineus* ssp. *coccineus*
Echinocereus arizonicus ssp. *nigrihorridispinus* = *Echinocereus coccineus* ssp. *coccineus*
Echinocereus armatus = *Echinocereus reichenbachii* ssp. *armatus*
Echinocereus baileyi = *Echinocereus reichenbachii* ssp. *baileyi*
Echinocereus barthelowanus: #4 **II** CACTACEAE
Echinocereus berlandieri: #4 **II** CACTACEAE
Echinocereus blanckii = *Echinocereus berlandieri*
Echinocereus bonatzii = *Echinocereus adustus* ssp. *bonatzii*
Echinocereus bonkerae: #4 **II** CACTACEAE
Echinocereus boyce-thompsonii: #4 **II** CACTACEAE
Echinocereus brandegeei: #4 **II** CACTACEAE
Echinocereus bristolii: #4 **II** CACTACEAE
Echinocereus bristolii ssp. *floresii* = *Echinocereus sciurus* ssp. *floresii*
Echinocereus caespitosus = *Echinocereus reichenbachii*
Echinocereus canyonensis = *Echinocereus coccineus* ssp. *coccineus*
Echinocereus carmenensis = *Echinocereus viridiflorus* ssp. *chloranthus*
Echinocereus chisoensis: (E) Chisos Hedgehog Cactus #4 **II** CACTACEAE
Echinocereus chloranthus = *Echinocereus viridiflorus* ssp. *chloranthus*
Echinocereus chloranthus ssp. *cylindricus* = *Echinocereus viridiflorus* ssp. *cylindricus*
Echinocereus chloranthus ssp. *neocapillus* = *Echinocereus viridiflorus* ssp. *chloranthus*
Echinocereus chloranthus ssp. *rhyolithensis* = *Echinocereus viridiflorus* ssp. *chloranthus*
Echinocereus chlorophthalmus = *Echinocereus cinerascens* ssp. *cinerascens*
Echinocereus cinerascens: #4 **II** CACTACEAE
Echinocereus cinerascens ssp. *cinerascens*: #4 **II** CACTACEAE
Echinocereus cinerascens ssp. *ehrenbergii* = *Echinocereus cinerascens* ssp. *cinerascens*
Echinocereus cinerascens ssp. *septentrionalis*: #4 **II** CACTACEAE
Echinocereus cinerascens ssp. *tulensis*: #4 **II** CACTACEAE
Echinocereus coccineus: (E) Arizona hedgehog cactus #4 **II** CACTACEAE
Echinocereus coccineus ssp. *aggregatus* = *Echinocereus coccineus* ssp. *coccineus*
Echinocereus coccineus ssp. *coccineus*: #4 **II** CACTACEAE

Echinocereus coccineus ssp. *mojavensis* = *Echinocereus mojavensis*
Echinocereus coccineus ssp. *paucispinus* = *Echinocereus coccineus* ssp. *coccineus*
Echinocereus coccineus ssp. *roemeri* = *Echinocereus coccineus* ssp. *coccineus*
Echinocereus coccineus ssp. *rosei* = *Echinocereus coccineus* ssp. *coccineus*
Echinocereus conglomeratus = *Echinocereus stramineus* ssp. *stramineus*
Echinocereus ctenoides = *Echinocereus dasyacanthus*
Echinocereus dasyacanthus: #4 **II** CACTACEAE
Echinocereus dasyacanthus ssp. *dasyacanthus*: #4 **II** CACTACEAE
Echinocereus dasyacanthus ssp. *rectispinus*: #4 **II** CACTACEAE
Echinocereus davisii = *Echinocereus viridiflorus* ssp. *davisii*
Echinocereus decumbens = *Echinocereus coccineus* ssp. *coccineus*
Echinocereus delaetii = *Echinocereus longisetus* ssp. *delaetii*
Echinocereus dubius = *Echinocereus enneacanthus* ssp. *enneacanthus*
Echinocereus durangensis = *Echinocereus polyacanthus* ssp. *polyacanthus*
Echinocereus ehrenbergii = *Echinocereus cinerascens* ssp. *cinerascens*
Echinocereus engelmannii: #4 **II** CACTACEAE
Echinocereus engelmannii ssp. *decumbens*: #4 **II** CACTACEAE
Echinocereus engelmannii ssp. *fasciculatus* = *Echinocereus fasciculatus*
Echinocereus enneacanthus: #4 **II** CACTACEAE
Echinocereus enneacanthus ssp. *brevispinus*: #4 **II** CACTACEAE
Echinocereus enneacanthus ssp. *enneacanthus*: #4 **II** CACTACEAE
Echinocereus fasciculatus: #4 **II** CACTACEAE
Echinocereus fasciculatus ssp. *bonkerae* = *Echinocereus bonkerae*
Echinocereus fasciculatus ssp. *boyce-thompsonii* = *Echinocereus boyce-thompsonii*
Echinocereus fendleri: #4 **II** CACTACEAE
Echinocereus fendleri ssp. *fendleri*: #4 **II** CACTACEAE
Echinocereus fendleri ssp. *hempelii*: #4 **II** CACTACEAE
Echinocereus fendleri ssp. *rectispinus*: #4 **II** CACTACEAE
Echinocereus ferreirianus: #4 **II** CACTACEAE
Echinocereus ferreirianus ssp. *ferreirianus*: #4 **II** CACTACEAE
Echinocereus ferreirianus ssp. *lindsayi*: (E) Lindsay's cactus, Lindsay's hedgehog cactus, (S) Cacto de Lindsay **I** CACTACEAE
Echinocereus fitchii = *Echinocereus reichenbachii* ssp. *fitchii*
Echinocereus fitchii ssp. *albertii* = *Echinocereus reichenbachii* ssp. *fitchii*
Echinocereus floresii = *Echinocereus sciurus* ssp. *floresii*
Echinocereus fobeanus = *Echinocereus chisoensis*
Echinocereus fobeanus ssp. *metornii* = *Echinocereus chisoensis*
Echinocereus freudenbergeri: #4 **II** CACTACEAE
Echinocereus gentryi = *Echinocereus scheeri* ssp. *gentryi*
Echinocereus glycimorphus = *Echinocereus cinerascens* ssp. *cinerascens*
Echinocereus gonacanthus = *Echinocereus triglochidiatus*
Echinocereus grandis: #4 **II** CACTACEAE
Echinocereus hancockii = *Echinocereus maritimus* ssp. *hancockii*
Echinocereus hempelii = *Echinocereus fendleri* ssp. *hempelii*
Echinocereus hexaedrus = *Echinocereus coccineus* ssp. *coccineus*
Echinocereus hildmannii = *Echinocereus dasyacanthus*
Echinocereus huitcholensis = *Echinocereus polyacanthus* ssp. *huitcholensis*
Echinocereus klapperi: #4 **II** CACTACEAE
Echinocereus knippelianus: #4 **II** CACTACEAE
Echinocereus knippelianus ssp. *kruegeri* = *Echinocereus knippelianus*
Echinocereus knippelianus ssp. *reyesii* = *Echinocereus knippelianus*
Echinocereus krausei = *Echinocereus coccineus* ssp. *coccineus*
Echinocereus kuenzleri = *Echinocereus fendleri* ssp. *fendleri*
Echinocereus kunzei = *Echinocereus coccineus* ssp. *coccineus*
Echinocereus laui: #4 **II** CACTACEAE
Echinocereus ledingii: #4 **II** CACTACEAE

Checklist of flora/Lista de especies de flora/Liste des espèces végétales

Echinocereus leeanus = *Echinocereus polyacanthus* ssp. *polyacanthus*

Echinocereus leeanus var. *leeanus* = *Echinocereus polyacanthus* ssp. *polyacanthus*

Echinocereus leeanus var. *multicostatus* = *Echinocereus polyacanthus* ssp. *polyacanthus*

Echinocereus leonensis = *Echinocereus pentalophus* ssp. *leonensis*

Echinocereus leptacanthus = *Echinocereus pentalophus* ssp. *pentalophus*

Echinocereus leucanthus: #4 **II** CACTACEAE

Echinocereus lindsayi = *Echinocereus ferreirianus* ssp. *lindsayi*

Echinocereus longisetus: #4 **II** CACTACEAE

Echinocereus longisetus ssp. *delaetii*: #4 **II** CACTACEAE

Echinocereus longisetus ssp. *freudenbergeri* = *Echinocereus freudenbergeri*

Echinocereus longisetus ssp. *longisetus*: #4 **II** CACTACEAE

Echinocereus luteus = *Echinocereus subinermis* ssp. *subinermis*

Echinocereus mamillatus = *Echinocereus brandegeei*

Echinocereus mapimiensis: #4 **II** CACTACEAE

Echinocereus mariae = *Echinocereus reichenbachii*

Echinocereus maritimus: #4 **II** CACTACEAE

Echinocereus maritimus ssp. *hancockii*: #4 **II** CACTACEAE

Echinocereus marksianus = *Echinocereus polyacanthus* ssp. *acifer*

Echinocereus matthesianus = *Echinocereus polyacanthus* ssp. *huitcholensis*

Echinocereus matudae = *Echinocereus coccineus* ssp. *coccineus*

Echinocereus melanocentrus = *Echinocereus reichenbachii* ssp. *fitchii*

Echinocereus merkeri = *Echinocereus enneacanthus* ssp. *enneacanthus*

Echinocereus metornii = *Echinocereus chisoensis*

Echinocereus mojavensis: #4 **II** CACTACEAE

Echinocereus mombergerianus = *Echinocereus polyacanthus* ssp. *pacificus*

Echinocereus morricalii = *Echinocereus viereckii* ssp. *morricalii*

Echinocereus munzii = *Echinocereus engelmannii*

Echinocereus neocapillus = *Echinocereus viridiflorus* ssp. *chloranthus*

Echinocereus neomexicanus = *Echinocereus coccineus* ssp. *coccineus*

Echinocereus nicholii: #4 **II** CACTACEAE

Echinocereus nicholii ssp. *llanuraensis*: #4 **II** CACTACEAE

Echinocereus nicholii ssp. *nicholii*: #4 **II** CACTACEAE

Echinocereus nivosus: #4 **II** CACTACEAE

Echinocereus ochoterenae = *Echinocereus subinermis* ssp. *ochoterenae*

Echinocereus ortegae ssp. *koehresianus* = *Echinocereus ortegae*

Echinocereus ortegae: #4 **II** CACTACEAE

Echinocereus pacificus = *Echinocereus polyacanthus* ssp. *pacificus*

Echinocereus pacificus ssp. *mombergerianus* = *Echinocereus polyacanthus* ssp. *pacificus*

Echinocereus palmeri: #4 **II** CACTACEAE

Echinocereus pamanesiorum: #4 **II** CACTACEAE

Echinocereus pamanesiorum ssp. *bonatzii* = *Echinocereus adustus* ssp. *bonatzii*

Echinocereus papillosus: #4 **II** CACTACEAE

Echinocereus parkeri: #4 **II** CACTACEAE

Echinocereus parkeri ssp. *arteagensis*: #4 **II** CACTACEAE

Echinocereus parkeri ssp. *gonzalezii*: #4 **II** CACTACEAE

Echinocereus parkeri ssp. *mazapilensis*: #4 **II** CACTACEAE

Echinocereus parkeri ssp. *parkeri*: #4 **II** CACTACEAE

Echinocereus pectinatus: #4 **II** CACTACEAE

Echinocereus pectinatus ssp. *ctenoides* = *Echinocereus dasyacanthus*

Echinocereus pectinatus ssp. *wenigeri*: #4 **II** CACTACEAE

Echinocereus pensilis: #4 **II** CACTACEAE

Echinocereus pentalophus: #4 **II** CACTACEAE

Echinocereus pentalophus ssp. *leonensis*: #4 **II** CACTACEAE

Echinocereus pentalophus ssp. *pentalophus*: (E) Lady-finger hedgehog cactus #4 **II** CACTACEAE

Echinocereus pentalophus ssp. *procumbens*: #4 **II** CACTACEAE

Echinocereus perbellus = *Echinocereus reichenbachii* ssp. *perbellus*

Echinocereus pleiogonus = *Echinocereus* sp.

Echinocereus polyacanthus: #4 **II** CACTACEAE

Echinocereus polyacanthus ssp. *acifer*: #4 **II** CACTACEAE

Echinocereus polyacanthus ssp. *huitcholensis*: #4 **II** CACTACEAE

Echinocereus polyacanthus ssp. *mombergerianus* = *Echinocereus polyacanthus* ssp. *pacificus*

Echinocereus polyacanthus ssp. *pacificus*: #4 **II** CACTACEAE

Echinocereus polyacanthus ssp. *polyacanthus*: #4 **II** CACTACEAE

Echinocereus poselgeri: (E) Dahlia's apple-cactus #4 **II** CACTACEAE

Echinocereus poselgeri ssp. *kroenleinii* = *Echinocereus poselgeri*

Echinocereus primolanatus: #4 **II** CACTACEAE

Echinocereus pseudopectinatus: #4 **II** CACTACEAE

Echinocereus pulchellus: #4 **II** CACTACEAE

Echinocereus pulchellus ssp. *acanthosetus*: #4 **II** CACTACEAE

Echinocereus pulchellus ssp. *pulchellus*: #4 **II** CACTACEAE

Echinocereus pulchellus ssp. *sharpii*: #4 **II** CACTACEAE

Echinocereus pulchellus ssp. *venustus* = *Echinocereus pulchellus* ssp. *weinbergii*

Echinocereus pulchellus ssp. *weinbergii*: #4 **II** CACTACEAE

Echinocereus pulchellus var. *amoenus* = *Echinocereus pulchellus* ssp. *pulchellus*

Echinocereus purpureus = *Echinocereus reichenbachii*

Echinocereus radians = *Echinocereus adustus* ssp. *adustus*

Echinocereus rayonesensis: #4 **II** CACTACEAE

Echinocereus rectispinus = *Echinocereus fendleri* ssp. *rectispinus*

Echinocereus reichenbachii: #4 **II** CACTACEAE

Echinocereus reichenbachii ssp. *armatus*: #4 **II** CACTACEAE

Echinocereus reichenbachii ssp. *baileyi*: #4 **II** CACTACEAE

Echinocereus reichenbachii ssp. *caespitosus* = *Echinocereus reichenbachii* ssp. *perbellus*

Echinocereus reichenbachii ssp. *fitchii*: (E) Fitch's hedgehog cactus #4 **II** CACTACEAE

Echinocereus reichenbachii ssp. *perbellus*: #4 **II** CACTACEAE

Echinocereus reichenbachii ssp. *reichenbachii*: #4 **II** CACTACEAE

Echinocereus reichenbachii var. *chisosensis* = *Echinocereus chisoensis* var. *chisoensis*

Echinocereus rigidissimus: #4 **II** CACTACEAE

Echinocereus rigidissimus ssp. *rigidissimus*: (E) Arizona rainbow cactus #4 **II** CACTACEAE

Echinocereus rigidissimus ssp. *rubispinus*: #4 **II** CACTACEAE

Echinocereus roemeri = *Echinocereus coccineus* ssp. *coccineus*

Echinocereus rosei = *Echinocereus coccineus* ssp. *coccineus*

Echinocereus rufispinus = *Echinocereus adustus* ssp. *adustus*

Echinocereus russanthus: (E) Rusty hedgehog cactus #4 **II** CACTACEAE

Echinocereus russanthus ssp. *fiehnii* = *Echinocereus russanthus*

Echinocereus russanthus ssp. *weedinii* = *Echinocereus russanthus*

Echinocereus salm-dyckianus = *Echinocereus scheeri* ssp. *scheeri*

Echinocereus salm-dyckianus ssp. *obscuriensis* = *Echinocereus scheeri* ssp. *scheeri*

Echinocereus salmianus = *Echinocereus scheeri* ssp. *scheeri*

Echinocereus sanpedroensis = *Echinocereus scheeri* ssp. *scheeri*

Echinocereus santaritensis = *Echinocereus polyacanthus* ssp. *polyacanthus*

Echinocereus sarissophorus = *Echinocereus enneacanthus* ssp. *enneacanthus*

Echinocereus scheeri: #4 **II** CACTACEAE

Echinocereus scheeri ssp. *gentryi*: #4 **II** CACTACEAE

Echinocereus scheeri ssp. *scheeri*: #4 **II** CACTACEAE

Echinocereus scheeri var. *koehresianus* = *Echinocereus ortegae*

Echinocereus schereri: #4 **II** CACTACEAE

Echinocereus schmollii: (E) Lamb's-tail cactus **I** CACTACEAE

Echinocereus schwarzii = *Echinocereus adustus* ssp. *schwarzii*

Echinocereus sciurus: #4 **II** CACTACEAE

Echinocereus sciurus ssp. *floresii*: #4 **II** CACTACEAE

Echinocereus sciurus ssp. *sciurus*: #4 **II** CACTACEAE

Echinocereus scopulorum: #4 **II** CACTACEAE

Echinocereus scopulorum ssp. *pseudopectinatus* = *Echinocereus pseudopectinatus*

Echinocereus spinigemmatus: #4 **II** CACTACEAE

Echinocereus standleyi = *Echinocereus viridiflorus* ssp. *viridiflorus*

Echinocereus steereae = *Echinocereus dasyacanthus*

Echinocereus stoloniferus: #4 **II** CACTACEAE

Echinocereus stoloniferus ssp. *stoloniferus*: #4 **II** CACTACEAE

Echinocereus stoloniferus ssp. *tayopensis*: #4 **II** CACTACEAE
Echinocereus stramineus: #4 **II** CACTACEAE
Echinocereus stramineus ssp. *occidentalis*: #4 **II** CACTACEAE
Echinocereus stramineus ssp. *stramineus*: #4 **II** CACTACEAE
Echinocereus subinermis: #4 **II** CACTACEAE
Echinocereus subinermis ssp. *ochoterenae*: #4 **II** CACTACEAE
Echinocereus subinermis ssp. *subinermis*: #4 **II** CACTACEAE
Echinocereus subterraneus = *Echinocereus sciurus*
Echinocereus tamaulipensis ssp. *deherdtii* = *Echinocereus poselgeri*
Echinocereus tamaulipensis ssp. *waldeisii* = *Echinocereus poselgeri*
Echinocereus tayopensis = *Echinocereus stoloniferus* ssp. *tayopensis*
Echinocereus toroweapensis = *Echinocereus coccineus* ssp. *coccineus*
Echinocereus triglochidiatus: #4 **II** CACTACEAE
Echinocereus triglochidiatus ssp. *mojavensis* = *Echinocereus mojavensis*
Echinocereus triglochidiatus var. *arizonicus*: #4 **II** CACTACEAE
Echinocereus tulensis = *Echinocereus cinerascens* ssp. *tulensis*
Echinocereus uspenskii = *Echinocereus enneacanthus* ssp. *enneacanthus*
Echinocereus viereckii: #4 **II** CACTACEAE
Echinocereus viereckii ssp. *huastecensis* = *Echinocereus viereckii* ssp. *morricalii*
Echinocereus viereckii ssp. *morricalii*: #4 **II** CACTACEAE
Echinocereus viereckii ssp. *viereckii*: #4 **II** CACTACEAE
Echinocereus viridiflorus: #4 **II** CACTACEAE
Echinocereus viridiflorus ssp. *chloranthus*: #4 **II** CACTACEAE
Echinocereus viridiflorus ssp. *correllii*: (E) Correll's Green Pitaya #4 **II** CACTACEAE
Echinocereus viridiflorus ssp. *cylindricus*: #4 **II** CACTACEAE
Echinocereus viridiflorus ssp. *davisii*: (E) Davis' Green Pitaya #4 **II** CACTACEAE
Echinocereus viridiflorus ssp. *viridiflorus*: #4 **II** CACTACEAE
Echinocereus waldeisii = *Echinocereus poselgeri*
Echinocereus websterianus: #4 **II** CACTACEAE
Echinocereus weinbergii = *Echinocereus pulchellus* ssp. *weinbergii*
Echinomastus acunensis = *Sclerocactus erectocentrus*
Echinomastus erectocentrus = *Sclerocactus erectocentrus*
Echinomastus erectocentrus var. *acunensis* = *Sclerocactus erectocentrus* var. *acunensis*
Echinomastus intertextus = *Sclerocactus intertextus*
Echinomastus krausei = *Sclerocactus erectocentrus*
Echinomastus mariposensis = *Sclerocactus mariposensis*
Echinomastus unguispinus = *Sclerocactus unguispinus*
Echinomastus unguispinus ssp. *laui* = *Sclerocactus unguispinus*
Echinopsis adolfofriedrichii: #4 **II** CACTACEAE
Echinopsis albispinosa = *Echinopsis tubiflora*
Echinopsis amblayensis = *Echinopsis haematantha*
Echinopsis ancistrophora: #4 **II** CACTACEAE
Echinopsis ancistrophora ssp. *ancistrophora*: #4 **II** CACTACEAE
Echinopsis ancistrophora ssp. *arachnacantha*: #4 **II** CACTACEAE
Echinopsis ancistrophora ssp. *cardenasiana*: #4 **II** CACTACEAE
Echinopsis ancistrophora ssp. *pojoensis*: #4 **II** CACTACEAE
Echinopsis angelesiae: #4 **II** CACTACEAE
Echinopsis antezanae: #4 **II** CACTACEAE
Echinopsis arachnacantha = *Echinopsis ancistrophora* ssp. *arachnacantha*
Echinopsis arboricola: #4 **II** CACTACEAE
Echinopsis arebaloi: #4 **II** CACTACEAE
Echinopsis atacamensis: #4 **II** CACTACEAE
Echinopsis atacamensis ssp. *atacamensis*: #4 **II** CACTACEAE
Echinopsis atacamensis ssp. *pasacana*: #4 **II** CACTACEAE
Echinopsis aurantiaca = *Echinopsis glaucina*
Echinopsis aurea: #4 **II** CACTACEAE
Echinopsis ayopayana = *Echinopsis comarapana*
Echinopsis backebergii: #4 **II** CACTACEAE
Echinopsis baldiana: #4 **II** CACTACEAE
Echinopsis bertramiana: #4 **II** CACTACEAE
Echinopsis boedekeriana = *Echinopsis backebergii*
Echinopsis boyuibensis: #4 **II** CACTACEAE
Echinopsis brasiliensis: #4 **II** CACTACEAE

Echinopsis brevispina = *Echinopsis thionantha*
Echinopsis bridgesii: #4 **II** CACTACEAE
Echinopsis bridgesii ssp. *bridgesii*: #4 **II** CACTACEAE
Echinopsis bridgesii ssp. *yungasensis*: #4 **II** CACTACEAE
Echinopsis bruchii: #4 **II** CACTACEAE
Echinopsis caineana: #4 **II** CACTACEAE
Echinopsis cajasensis: #4 **II** CACTACEAE
Echinopsis calliantholilacina: #4 **II** CACTACEAE
Echinopsis callichroma: #4 **II** CACTACEAE
Echinopsis calochlora: #4 **II** CACTACEAE
Echinopsis calochlora ssp. *calochlora*: #4 **II** CACTACEAE
Echinopsis calochlora ssp. *glaetzleana*: #4 **II** CACTACEAE
Echinopsis calorubra = *Echinopsis obrepanda* ssp. *calorubra*
Echinopsis camarguensis: #4 **II** CACTACEAE
Echinopsis candicans: #4 **II** CACTACEAE
Echinopsis cardenasiana = *Echinopsis ancistrophora* ssp. *cardenasiana*
Echinopsis carmineiflora = *Echinopsis obrepanda*
Echinopsis cephalomacrostibas: #4 **II** CACTACEAE
Echinopsis cerdana: #4 **II** CACTACEAE
Echinopsis chacoana = *Echinopsis rhodotricha* ssp. *chacoana*
Echinopsis chalaensis: #4 **II** CACTACEAE
Echinopsis chamaecereus: #4 **II** CACTACEAE
Echinopsis chiloensis: #4 **II** CACTACEAE
Echinopsis chrysantha: #4 **II** CACTACEAE
Echinopsis chrysochete: #4 **II** CACTACEAE
Echinopsis cinnabarina: #4 **II** CACTACEAE
Echinopsis clavatus: #4 **II** CACTACEAE
Echinopsis cochabambensis: #4 **II** CACTACEAE
Echinopsis comarapana: #4 **II** CACTACEAE
Echinopsis conaconensis: #4 **II** CACTACEAE
Echinopsis coquimbana: #4 **II** CACTACEAE
Echinopsis cordobensis = *Echinopsis leucantha*
Echinopsis coronata: #4 **II** CACTACEAE
Echinopsis cotacajesii: #4 **II** CACTACEAE
Echinopsis courantii = *Echinopsis candicans*
Echinopsis crassicaulis: #4 **II** CACTACEAE
Echinopsis cuzcoensis: #4 **II** CACTACEAE
Echinopsis cylindracea = *Echinopsis aurea*
Echinopsis densispina: #4 **II** CACTACEAE
Echinopsis derenbergii: #4 **II** CACTACEAE
Echinopsis deserticola: #4 **II** CACTACEAE
Echinopsis elongata = *Echinopsis haematantha*
Echinopsis escayachensis: #4 **II** CACTACEAE
Echinopsis eyriesii: #4 **II** CACTACEAE
Echinopsis fabrisii: #4 **II** CACTACEAE
Echinopsis fallax = *Echinopsis aurea*
Echinopsis famatinensis: #4 **II** CACTACEAE
Echinopsis ferox: #4 **II** CACTACEAE
Echinopsis fiebrigii = *Echinopsis obrepanda*
Echinopsis forbesii = *Echinopsis rhodotricha*
Echinopsis formosa: #4 **II** CACTACEAE
Echinopsis formosissima = *Echinopsis atacamensis* ssp. *pasacana*
Echinopsis fricii = *Echinopsis tiegeliana*
Echinopsis friedrichii: #4 **II** CACTACEAE
Echinopsis fulvilana = *Echinopsis deserticola*
Echinopsis glauca: #4 **II** CACTACEAE
Echinopsis glaucina: #4 **II** CACTACEAE
Echinopsis graciliflora: #4 **II** CACTACEAE
Echinopsis grandiflora = *Echinopsis calochlora*
Echinopsis grandis = *Echinopsis bruchii*
Echinopsis haematantha: #4 **II** CACTACEAE
Echinopsis hahniana: #4 **II** CACTACEAE
Echinopsis hamatacantha = *Echinopsis ancistrophora*
Echinopsis hammerschmidii: #4 **II** CACTACEAE
Echinopsis hardeniana = *Echinopsis pentlandii*
Echinopsis herbasii = *Echinopsis mamillosa*
Echinopsis hertrichiana: #4 **II** CACTACEAE
Echinopsis herzogiana = *Echinopsis tarijensis* ssp. *herzogianus*
Echinopsis hualfinensis = *Echinopsis haematantha*
Echinopsis huascha: #4 **II** CACTACEAE
Echinopsis huotii: #4 **II** CACTACEAE
Echinopsis huotii ssp. *huotii*: #4 **II** CACTACEAE
Echinopsis huotii ssp. *vallegrandensis*: #4 **II** CACTACEAE
Echinopsis hystrichoides: #4 **II** CACTACEAE

Checklist of flora/Lista de especies de flora/Liste des espèces végétales

Echinopsis ibicuatensis: #4 **II** CACTACEAE
Echinopsis ingens = *Echinopsis bruchii*
Echinopsis intricatissima = *Echinopsis leucantha*
Echinopsis kermesina = *Echinopsis mamillosa*
Echinopsis kladiwana: #4 **II** CACTACEAE
Echinopsis klingleriana: #4 **II** CACTACEAE
Echinopsis knuthiana: #4 **II** CACTACEAE
Echinopsis korethroides: #4 **II** CACTACEAE
Echinopsis kratochviliana = *Echinopsis ancistrophora* ssp. *arachnacantha*
Echinopsis kuehnrichii = *Echinopsis haematantha*
Echinopsis lageniformis: #4 **II** CACTACEAE
Echinopsis lamprochlora: #4 **II** CACTACEAE
Echinopsis lateritia: #4 **II** CACTACEAE
Echinopsis lecoriensis = *Echinopsis ferox*
Echinopsis leucantha: #4 **II** CACTACEAE
Echinopsis leucomalla = *Echinopsis aurea*
Echinopsis litoralis: #4 **II** CACTACEAE
Echinopsis longispina = *Echinopsis ferox*
Echinopsis macrogona: #4 **II** CACTACEAE
Echinopsis mamillosa: #4 **II** CACTACEAE
Echinopsis mamillosa ssp. *mamillosa*: #4 **II** CACTACEAE
Echinopsis mamillosa ssp. *silvatica*: #4 **II** CACTACEAE
Echinopsis manguinii = *Echinopsis schickendantzii*
Echinopsis marsoneri: #4 **II** CACTACEAE
Echinopsis mataranensis: #4 **II** CACTACEAE
Echinopsis maximiliana: #4 **II** CACTACEAE
Echinopsis melanopotamica = *Echinopsis leucantha*
Echinopsis meyeri: #4 **II** CACTACEAE
Echinopsis mieckleyi: #4 **II** CACTACEAE
Echinopsis minuana: #4 **II** CACTACEAE
Echinopsis mirabilis: #4 **II** CACTACEAE
Echinopsis molesta: #4 **II** CACTACEAE
Echinopsis multiplex = *Echinopsis oxygona*
Echinopsis narvaecensis = *Echinopsis tarijensis*
Echinopsis nealeana = *Echinopsis saltensis*
Echinopsis nigra: #4 **II** CACTACEAE
Echinopsis obrepanda: #4 **II** CACTACEAE
Echinopsis obrepanda ssp. *calorubra*: #4 **II** CACTACEAE
Echinopsis obrepanda ssp. *obrepanda*: #4 **II** CACTACEAE
Echinopsis obrepanda ssp. *tapecuana*: #4 **II** CACTACEAE
Echinopsis orurensis = *Echinopsis ferox*
Echinopsis oxygona: #4 **II** CACTACEAE
Echinopsis pachanoi: #4 **II** CACTACEAE
Echinopsis pampana: #4 **II** CACTACEAE
Echinopsis pamparuizii = *Echinopsis huotii*
Echinopsis paraguayensis = *Echinopsis oxygona*
Echinopsis pasacana = *Echinopsis atacamensis* ssp. *pasacana*
Echinopsis pecheretiana = *Echinopsis huascha*
Echinopsis peitscheriana = *Acanthocalycium klimpelianum*
Echinopsis pentlandii: #4 **II** CACTACEAE
Echinopsis pentlandii ssp. *hardeniana* = *Echinopsis pentlandii*
Echinopsis pentlandii ssp. *larae* = *Echinopsis pentlandii*
Echinopsis pereziensis = *Echinopsis comarapana*
Echinopsis peruviana: #4 **II** CACTACEAE
Echinopsis peruviana ssp. *peruviana*: #4 **II** CACTACEAE
Echinopsis peruviana ssp. *puquiensis*: #4 **II** CACTACEAE
Echinopsis poco = *Echinopsis tarijensis*
Echinopsis pojoensis: #4 **II** CACTACEAE
Echinopsis polyancistra = *Echinopsis ancistrophora*
Echinopsis potosina = *Echinopsis ferox*
Echinopsis pseudocachensis = *Echinopsis saltensis*
Echinopsis pseudocandicans = *Echinopsis candicans*
Echinopsis pseudomamillosa: #4 **II** CACTACEAE
Echinopsis pudantii = *Echinopsis eyriesii*
Echinopsis pugionacantha: #4 **II** CACTACEAE
Echinopsis pugionacantha ssp. *pugionacantha*: #4 **II** CACTACEAE
Echinopsis pugionacantha ssp. *rossii*: #4 **II** CACTACEAE
Echinopsis puquiensis = *Echinopsis peruviana* ssp. *puquiensis*
Echinopsis purpureopilosa = *Echinopsis lamprochlora*
Echinopsis quadratiumbonatus: #4 **II** CACTACEAE
Echinopsis quinesensis = *Echinopsis aurea*
Echinopsis randallii = *Echinopsis formosa*
Echinopsis rauschii = *Echinopsis obrepanda* ssp. *calorubra*

Echinopsis rebutioides = *Echinopsis densispina*
Echinopsis rhodotricha: #4 **II** CACTACEAE
Echinopsis rhodotricha ssp. *chacoana*: #4 **II** CACTACEAE
Echinopsis rhodotricha ssp. *rhodotricha*: #4 **II** CACTACEAE
Echinopsis ritteri = *Echinopsis mamillosa*
Echinopsis riviere-de-caraltii: #4 **II** CACTACEAE
Echinopsis rivierei = *Echinopsis atacamensis* ssp. *pasacana*
Echinopsis rojasii = *Echinopsis obrepanda*
Echinopsis roseolilacina = *Echinopsis mamillosa*
Echinopsis rowleyi = *Echinopsis huascha*
Echinopsis rubinghiana = *Echinopsis thelegonoides*
Echinopsis saltensis: #4 **II** CACTACEAE
Echinopsis sanguiniflora: #4 **II** CACTACEAE
Echinopsis santaensis: #4 **II** CACTACEAE
Echinopsis schickendantzii: #4 **II** CACTACEAE
Echinopsis schieliana: #4 **II** CACTACEAE
Echinopsis schoenii: #4 **II** CACTACEAE
Echinopsis schreiteri: #4 **II** CACTACEAE
Echinopsis schwantesii = *Echinopsis oxygona*
Echinopsis scopulicola: #4 **II** CACTACEAE
Echinopsis semidenudata = *Echinopsis huotii*
Echinopsis shaferi = *Echinopsis leucantha*
Echinopsis silvatica = *Echinopsis mamillosa* ssp. *silvatica*
Echinopsis silvestrii: #4 **II** CACTACEAE
Echinopsis skottsbergii: #4 **II** CACTACEAE
Echinopsis smrziana: #4 **II** CACTACEAE
Echinopsis spachiana: #4 **II** CACTACEAE
Echinopsis spegazziniana = *Echinopsis leucantha*
Echinopsis spinibarbis: #4 **II** CACTACEAE
Echinopsis spiniflora = *Acanthocalycium spiniflorum*
Echinopsis stollenwerkiana = *Echinopsis pugionacantha*
Echinopsis strigosa: #4 **II** CACTACEAE
Echinopsis subdenudata: #4 **II** CACTACEAE
Echinopsis sucrensis: #4 **II** CACTACEAE
Echinopsis tacaquirensis: #4 **II** CACTACEAE
Echinopsis tacaquirensis ssp. *tacaquirensis*: #4 **II** CACTACEAE
Echinopsis tacaquirensis ssp. *taquimbalensis*: #4 **II** CACTACEAE
Echinopsis tapecuana = *Echinopsis obrepanda* ssp. *tapecuana*
Echinopsis taquimbalensis = *Echinopsis tacaquirensis* ssp. *taquimbalensis*
Echinopsis taratensis: #4 **II** CACTACEAE
Echinopsis tarijensis: #4 **II** CACTACEAE
Echinopsis tarijensis ssp. *herzogianus*: #4 **II** CACTACEAE
Echinopsis tarijensis ssp. *tarijensis*: #4 **II** CACTACEAE
Echinopsis tarijensis ssp. *totorensis*: #4 **II** CACTACEAE
Echinopsis tarmaensis: #4 **II** CACTACEAE
Echinopsis tegeleriana: #4 **II** CACTACEAE
Echinopsis terscheckii: #4 **II** CACTACEAE
Echinopsis thelegona: #4 **II** CACTACEAE
Echinopsis thelegonoides: #4 **II** CACTACEAE
Echinopsis thionantha: #4 **II** CACTACEAE
Echinopsis tiegeliana: #4 **II** CACTACEAE
Echinopsis toralapana = *Echinopsis obrepanda*
Echinopsis torrecillasensis = *Echinopsis ancistrophora* ssp. *arachnacantha*
Echinopsis trichosa: #4 **II** CACTACEAE
Echinopsis tubiflora: #4 **II** CACTACEAE
Echinopsis tulhuayacensis: #4 **II** CACTACEAE
Echinopsis tunariensis: #4 **II** CACTACEAE
Echinopsis turbinata = *Echinopsis eyriesii*
Echinopsis uebelmanniana = *Echinopsis formosa*
Echinopsis uyupampensis: #4 **II** CACTACEAE
Echinopsis vallegrandensis = *Echinopsis huotii* ssp. *vallegrandensis*
Echinopsis vasquezii: #4 **II** CACTACEAE
Echinopsis vatteri: #4 **II** CACTACEAE
Echinopsis volliana: #4 **II** CACTACEAE
Echinopsis walteri: #4 **II** CACTACEAE
Echinopsis werdermanniana = *Echinopsis terscheckii*
Echinopsis werdermannii: #4 **II** CACTACEAE
Echinopsis yungasensis = *Echinopsis bridgesii* ssp. *yungasensis*
Echinopsis yuquina: #4 **II** CACTACEAE
Echioglossum = *Cleisostoma*
Echites bispinosa = *Pachypodium bispinosum*
Echites succulenta = *Pachypodium succulentum*

Eckartia = *Peristeria*
Eggelingia spp.: #7 **II** ORCHIDACEAE
Eleorchis spp.: #7 **II** ORCHIDACEAE
Elephant trunks (E): *Pachypodium* spp.
Elephant's foot (E): *Dioscorea deltoidea*
Elephant's trunk (E): *Pachypodium namaquanum*
Elfin tree fern (E): *Cyathea dryopteroides*
Elleanthus spp.: #7 **II** ORCHIDACEAE
Eloyella = *Phymatidium*
Eltroplectris = *Stenorrhynchos*
Elythranthera spp.: #7 **II** ORCHIDACEAE
Embreea spp.: #7 **II** ORCHIDACEAE
Emorycactus parryi = *Echinocactus parryi*
Emorycactus polycephalus = *Echinocactus polycephalus*
Emorycactus xeranthemoides = *Echinocactus polycephalus* ssp.
    xeranthemoides
Empusa = *Liparis*
Empusaria = *Liparis*
Encephalartos spp.: (E) bread palms, (S) palmas del pan **I**
    ZAMIACEAE
Encephalartos acanthus = *Encephalartos cycadifolius*
Encephalartos aemulans: **I** ZAMIACEAE
Encephalartos altensteinii: **I** ZAMIACEAE
Encephalartos altensteinii var. *angustifolia* = *Encephalartos*
    altensteinii
Encephalartos altensteinii var. *bispinna* = *Encephalartos woodii*
Encephalartos altensteinii var. *distans* = *Encephalartos altensteinii*
Encephalartos altensteinii var. *eriocephalus* = *Encephalartos*
    altensteinii
Encephalartos altensteinii var. *parvifolius* = *Encephalartos*
    altensteinii
Encephalartos altensteinii var. *paucidentatus* = *Encephalartos*
    paucidentatus
Encephalartos altensteinii var. *semidentatus* = *Encephalartos*
    altensteinii
Encephalartos altensteinii var. *spinosior* = *Encephalartos*
    altensteinii
Encephalartos aplanatus: **I** ZAMIACEAE
Encephalartos arenarius: **I** ZAMIACEAE
Encephalartos barteri: **I** ZAMIACEAE
Encephalartos barteri ssp. *allochrous*: **I** ZAMIACEAE
Encephalartos barteri ssp. *barteri*: **I** ZAMIACEAE
Encephalartos brachyphyllus = *Encephalartos caffer*
Encephalartos brevifoliolatus: **I** ZAMIACEAE
Encephalartos bubalinus: **I** ZAMIACEAE
Encephalartos caffer: **I** ZAMIACEAE
Encephalartos caffer var. *brachyphyllus* = *Encephalartos caffer*
Encephalartos caffer var. *integrifolius* = *Encephalartos caffer*
Encephalartos caffer var. *unidentatus* = *Encephalartos caffer*
Encephalartos cerinus: **I** ZAMIACEAE
Encephalartos chimanimaniensis: **I** ZAMIACEAE
Encephalartos concinnus: **I** ZAMIACEAE
Encephalartos cupidus: **I** ZAMIACEAE
Encephalartos cycadifolius: **I** ZAMIACEAE
Encephalartos cycadifolius var. *glaber* = *Encephalartos*
    cycadifolius
Encephalartos cycadis = *Encephalartos caffer*
Encephalartos delucanus: **I** ZAMIACEAE
Encephalartos denisonii = *Lepidozamia peroffskyana*
Encephalartos dolomiticus: **I** ZAMIACEAE
Encephalartos douglasii = *Macrozamia fraseri*
Encephalartos dyeri = *Macrozamia dyeri*
Encephalartos dyerianus: **I** ZAMIACEAE
Encephalartos elliptica = *Encephalartos caffer*
Encephalartos equatorialis: **I** ZAMIACEAE
Encephalartos eugene-maraisii: **I** ZAMIACEAE
Encephalartos eximius = *Encephalartos cycadifolius*
Encephalartos ferox: **I** ZAMIACEAE
Encephalartos fraseri = *Macrozamia fraseri*
Encephalartos friderici-guilielmi: **I** ZAMIACEAE
Encephalartos ghellinckii: **I** ZAMIACEAE
Encephalartos graniticolus = *Encephalartos dyerianus*
Encephalartos gratus: **I** ZAMIACEAE
Encephalartos gratus var. *manikensis* = *Encephalartos manikensis*

Encephalartos heenanii: **I** ZAMIACEAE
Encephalartos hildebrandtii: **I** ZAMIACEAE
Encephalartos hildebrandtii var. *dentatus*: **I** ZAMIACEAE
Encephalartos hildebrandtii var. *hildebrandtii*: **I** ZAMIACEAE
Encephalartos hirsutus: **I** ZAMIACEAE
Encephalartos horridus: **I** ZAMIACEAE
Encephalartos horridus var. *hallianus* = *Encephalartos horridus*
Encephalartos horridus var. *latifrons* = *Encephalartos latifrons*
Encephalartos horridus var. *nanus* = *Encephalartos horridus*
Encephalartos horridus var. *tridens* = *Encephalartos horridus*
Encephalartos horridus var. *trispinosus* = *Encephalartos*
    trispinosus
Encephalartos horridus var. *van hallii* = *Encephalartos horridus*
Encephalartos humilis: **I** ZAMIACEAE
Encephalartos imbricans = *Encephalartos equatorialis*
Encephalartos inopinus: **I** ZAMIACEAE
Encephalartos ituriensis: **I** ZAMIACEAE
Encephalartos kisambo: **I** ZAMIACEAE
Encephalartos kosiensis = *Encephalartos ferox*
Encephalartos laevifolius: **I** ZAMIACEAE
Encephalartos lanatus: **I** ZAMIACEAE
Encephalartos lanuginosus = *Encephalartos longifolius*
Encephalartos latifrons: **I** ZAMIACEAE
Encephalartos laurentianus: **I** ZAMIACEAE
Encephalartos lebomboensis: **I** ZAMIACEAE
Encephalartos lehmannii: **I** ZAMIACEAE
Encephalartos lehmannii f. *dentatus* = *Encephalartos lehmannii*
Encephalartos lehmannii f. *spinulosus* = *Encephalartos lehmannii*
Encephalartos lehmannii var. *spinulosus* = *Encephalartos*
    lehmannii
Encephalartos lemarinellianus = *Encephalartos poggei*
Encephalartos longifolius: **I** ZAMIACEAE
Encephalartos longifolius var. *angustifolius* = *Encephalartos*
    longifolius
Encephalartos longifolius var. *latifolius* = *Encephalartos*
    longifolius
Encephalartos longifolius var. *revolutus* = *Encephalartos*
    longifolius
Encephalartos macdonnellii = *Macrozamia macdonnellii*
Encephalartos macrostrobilus: **I** ZAMIACEAE
Encephalartos manikensis: **I** ZAMIACEAE
Encephalartos marumii = *Encephalartos altensteinii*
Encephalartos marunguensis: **I** ZAMIACEAE
Encephalartos mauritianus = *Encephalartos longifolius*
Encephalartos middelburgensis: **I** ZAMIACEAE
Encephalartos miquelii = *Macrozamia miquelii*
Encephalartos moorei = *Macrozamia moorei*
Encephalartos msinganus: **I** ZAMIACEAE
Encephalartos munchii: **I** ZAMIACEAE
Encephalartos nanus = *Encephalartos horridus*
Encephalartos natalensis: **I** ZAMIACEAE
Encephalartos ngoyanus: **I** ZAMIACEAE
Encephalartos nubimontanus: **I** ZAMIACEAE
Encephalartos oldfieldii = *Macrozamia fraseri*
Encephalartos paucidentatus: **I** ZAMIACEAE
Encephalartos pauli-guilielmi = *Macrozamia pauli-guilielmi*
Encephalartos poggei: **I** ZAMIACEAE
Encephalartos powysorum: **I** ZAMIACEAE
Encephalartos preissii = *Macrozamia fraseri*
Encephalartos princeps: **I** ZAMIACEAE
Encephalartos pterogonus: **I** ZAMIACEAE
Encephalartos pumilus = *Zamia pumila*
Encephalartos regalis = *Encephalartos altensteinii*
Encephalartos schaijesii: **I** ZAMIACEAE
Encephalartos schmitzii: **I** ZAMIACEAE
Encephalartos sclavoi: **I** ZAMIACEAE
Encephalartos senticosus: **I** ZAMIACEAE
Encephalartos septentrionalis: **I** ZAMIACEAE
Encephalartos spinulosus = *Encephalartos lehmannii*
Encephalartos spiralis = *Macrozamia spiralis*
Encephalartos spiralis var. *diplomera* = *Macrozamia diplomera*
Encephalartos spiralis var. *major* = *Macrozamia communis*
Encephalartos successibus = *Encephalartos whitelockii*
Encephalartos tegulaneus: **I** ZAMIACEAE
Encephalartos transvenosus: **I** ZAMIACEAE

Encephalartos trispinosus: **I** ZAMIACEAE
Encephalartos turneri: **I** ZAMIACEAE
Encephalartos umbeluziensis: **I** ZAMIACEAE
Encephalartos vanhallii = *Encephalartos horridus*
Encephalartos venetus = *Encephalartos nubimontanus*
Encephalartos verrucosus = *Encephalartos dolomiticus*
Encephalartos verschaffelti = *Encephalartos cycadifolius*
Encephalartos villosus: **I** ZAMIACEAE
Encephalartos villosus f. *hildebrandtii* = *Encephalartos hildebrandtii*
Encephalartos villosus f. *intermedia* = *Encephalartos villosus*
Encephalartos voiensis = *Encephalartos kisambo*
Encephalartos whitelockii: **I** ZAMIACEAE
Encephalartos woodii: **I** ZAMIACEAE
Encheiridion = *Microcoelia*
Encyclia spp.: #7 **II** ORCHIDACEAE
Endeisa = *Dendrobium*
Endresiella = *Trevoria*
Engelhardtia pterocarpa = *Oreomunnea pterocarpa*
Enothrea = *Octomeria*
Entaticus = *Habenaria*
Entomophobia spp.: #7 **II** ORCHIDACEAE
Eomatucana madisoniorum = *Matucana madisoniorum*
Eomatucana oreodoxa = *Matucana oreodoxa*
Eparmatostigma spp.: #7 **II** ORCHIDACEAE
Ephemerantha = *Flickingeria*
Ephippianthus spp.: #7 **II** ORCHIDACEAE
Ephippium = *Bulbophyllum*
Epiblastus spp.: #7 **II** ORCHIDACEAE
Epiblema spp.: #7 **II** ORCHIDACEAE
Epicladium = *Epidendrum*
Epicranthes = *Bulbophyllum*
Epicrianthus = *Bulbophyllum*
Epicycas elongata = *Cycas elongata*
Epicycas lindstromii = *Cycas lindstromii*
Epicycas micholitzii = *Cycas micholitzii*
Epicycas multipinnata = *Cycas multipinnata*
Epicycas siamensis = *Cycas siamensis*
Epidanthus = *Epidendrum*
Epidendropsis = *Epidendrum*
Epidendrum spp.: #7 **II** ORCHIDACEAE
Epigeneium spp.: #7 **II** ORCHIDACEAE
Epilyna = *Elleanthus*
Epipactis spp.: #7 **II** ORCHIDACEAE
Epiphora = *Polystachya*
Epiphyllopsis gaertneri = *Hatiora gaertneri*
Epiphyllum ackermannii = *Disocactus ackermannii*
Epiphyllum anguliger: #4 **II** CACTACEAE
Epiphyllum biforme = *Disocactus biformis*
Epiphyllum cartagense: #4 **II** CACTACEAE
Epiphyllum caudatum: #4 **II** CACTACEAE
Epiphyllum caulorhizum = *Epiphyllum crenatum*
Epiphyllum chrysocardium = *Selenicereus chrysocardium*
Epiphyllum columbiense: #4 **II** CACTACEAE
Epiphyllum costaricense: #4 **II** CACTACEAE
Epiphyllum crenatum: #4 **II** CACTACEAE
Epiphyllum darrahii = *Epiphyllum anguliger*
Epiphyllum eichlamii = *Disocactus eichlamii*
Epiphyllum floribundum: #4 **II** CACTACEAE
Epiphyllum gigas = *Epiphyllum grandilobum*
Epiphyllum grandilobum: #4 **II** CACTACEAE
Epiphyllum guatemalense: #4 **II** CACTACEAE
Epiphyllum hookeri: #4 **II** CACTACEAE
Epiphyllum laui: #4 **II** CACTACEAE
Epiphyllum lepidocarpum: #4 **II** CACTACEAE
Epiphyllum macrocarpum = *Epiphyllum costaricense*
Epiphyllum macropterum = *Epiphyllum* sp.
Epiphyllum nelsonii = *Disocactus nelsonii*
Epiphyllum oxypetalum: #4 **II** CACTACEAE
Epiphyllum phyllanthus: #4 **II** CACTACEAE
Epiphyllum pittieri: #4 **II** CACTACEAE
Epiphyllum pumilum: #4 **II** CACTACEAE
Epiphyllum quezaltecum = *Disocactus quezaltecus*
Epiphyllum rubrocoronatum: #4 **II** CACTACEAE
Epiphyllum stenopetalum = *Epiphyllum hookeri*

Epiphyllum strictum = *Epiphyllum hookeri*
Epiphyllum thomasianum: #4 **II** CACTACEAE
Epiphyllum thomasianum var. *costaricensis* = *Epiphyllum costaricense*
Epiphyllum trimetrale: #4 **II** CACTACEAE
Epipogium spp.: #7 **II** ORCHIDACEAE
Epipogon = *Epipogium*
Epistephium spp.: #7 **II** ORCHIDACEAE
Epithelantha bokei: (E) Button-cactus #4 **II** CACTACEAE
Epithelantha densispina = *Epithelantha micromeris* ssp. *greggii*
Epithelantha greggii = *Epithelantha micromeris* ssp. *greggii*
Epithelantha micromeris: #4 **II** CACTACEAE
Epithelantha micromeris ssp. *greggii*: #4 **II** CACTACEAE
Epithelantha micromeris ssp. *micromeris*: (E) Ping-pong ball button-cactus #4 **II** CACTACEAE
Epithelantha micromeris ssp. *pachyrhiza*: #4 **II** CACTACEAE
Epithelantha micromeris ssp. *polycephala*: #4 **II** CACTACEAE
Epithelantha micromeris ssp. *unguispina*: #4 **II** CACTACEAE
Epithelantha pachyrhiza = *Epithelantha micromeris* ssp. *pachyrhiza*
Epithelantha polycephala = *Epithelantha micromeris* ssp. *polycephala*
Epithelantha rufispina = *Epithelantha micromeris* ssp. *greggii*
Erdisia apiciflora = *Corryocactus apiciflorus*
Erdisia aureispina = *Corryocactus erectus*
Erdisia erecta = *Corryocactus erectus*
Erdisia fortalezensis = *Corryocactus tenuiculus*
Erdisia maxima = *Corryocactus apiciflorus*
Erdisia meyenii = *Corryocactus aureus*
Erdisia philippii = *Austrocactus philippii*
Erdisia quadrangularis = *Corryocactus quadrangularis*
Erdisia ruthae = *Corryocactus erectus*
Erdisia spiniflora = *Austrocactus spiniflorus*
Erdisia squarrosa = *Corryocactus squarrosus*
Erdisia tenuicula = *Corryocactus tenuiculus*
Eria spp.: #7 **II** ORCHIDACEAE
Eriaxis spp.: #7 **II** ORCHIDACEAE
Eriocereus adscendens = *Harrisia adscendens*
Eriocereus arendtii = *Harrisia tortuosa*
Eriocereus bonplandii = *Harrisia pomanensis*
Eriocereus guelichii = *Harrisia balansae*
Eriocereus martinii = *Harrisia martinii*
Eriocereus polyacanthus = *Harrisia pomanensis*
Eriocereus pomanensis = *Harrisia pomanensis*
Eriocereus regelii = *Harrisia pomanensis* ssp. *regelii*
Eriocereus spinosissimus = *Arthrocereus spinosissimus*
Eriocereus tarijensis = *Harrisia pomanensis*
Eriocereus tephracanthus = *Harrisia tetracantha*
Eriocereus tortuosus = *Harrisia tortuosa*
Eriochilum = *Eriochilus*
Eriochilus spp.: #7 **II** ORCHIDACEAE
Eriochylus = *Eriochilus*
Eriodes spp.: #7 **II** ORCHIDACEAE
Eriopexis = *Dendrobium*
Eriopsis spp.: #7 **II** ORCHIDACEAE
Eriosyce aerocarpa: #4 **II** CACTACEAE
Eriosyce algarrobensis = *Eriosyce aurata*
Eriosyce andreaeana: #4 **II** CACTACEAE
Eriosyce aspillagae: #4 **II** CACTACEAE
Eriosyce aurata: #4 **II** CACTACEAE
Eriosyce bulbocalyx: #4 **II** CACTACEAE
Eriosyce ceratistes = *Eriosyce aurata*
Eriosyce chilensis: #4 **II** CACTACEAE
Eriosyce confinis: #4 **II** CACTACEAE
Eriosyce crispa: #4 **II** CACTACEAE
Eriosyce crispa ssp. *atroviridis*: #4 **II** CACTACEAE
Eriosyce crispa ssp. *crispa*: #4 **II** CACTACEAE
Eriosyce curvispina: #4 **II** CACTACEAE
Eriosyce engleri: #4 **II** CACTACEAE
Eriosyce esmeraldana: #4 **II** CACTACEAE
Eriosyce garaventae: #4 **II** CACTACEAE
Eriosyce heinrichiana: #4 **II** CACTACEAE
Eriosyce heinrichiana ssp. *heinrichiana*: #4 **II** CACTACEAE
Eriosyce heinrichiana ssp. *intermedia*: #4 **II** CACTACEAE
Eriosyce heinrichiana ssp. *simulans*: #4 **II** CACTACEAE

Eriosyce ihotzkyanae = *Eriosyce aurata*
Eriosyce islayensis: #4 **II** CACTACEAE
Eriosyce krausii: #4 **II** CACTACEAE
Eriosyce kunzei: #4 **II** CACTACEAE
Eriosyce lapampaensis = *Eriosyce aurata*
Eriosyce laui: #4 **II** CACTACEAE
Eriosyce limariensis: #4 **II** CACTACEAE
Eriosyce marksiana: #4 **II** CACTACEAE
Eriosyce megacarpa = *Eriosyce rodentiophila*
Eriosyce napina: #4 **II** CACTACEAE
Eriosyce napina ssp. *lembckei*: #4 **II** CACTACEAE
Eriosyce napina ssp. *napina*: #4 **II** CACTACEAE
Eriosyce occulta: #4 **II** CACTACEAE
Eriosyce odieri: #4 **II** CACTACEAE
Eriosyce odieri ssp. *fulva*: #4 **II** CACTACEAE
Eriosyce odieri ssp. *glabrescens*: #4 **II** CACTACEAE
Eriosyce odieri ssp. *odieri*: #4 **II** CACTACEAE
Eriosyce omasensis: #4 **II** CACTACEAE
Eriosyce recondita: #4 **II** CACTACEAE
Eriosyce recondita ssp. *iquiquensis*: #4 **II** CACTACEAE
Eriosyce recondita ssp. *recondita*: #4 **II** CACTACEAE
Eriosyce rodentiophila: #4 **II** CACTACEAE
Eriosyce sandillon = *Eriosyce aurata*
Eriosyce senilis: #4 **II** CACTACEAE
Eriosyce senilis ssp. *coimasensis*: #4 **II** CACTACEAE
Eriosyce senilis ssp. *elquiensis*: #4 **II** CACTACEAE
Eriosyce senilis ssp. *senilis*: #4 **II** CACTACEAE
Eriosyce sociabilis: #4 **II** CACTACEAE
Eriosyce spinibarbis = *Eriosyce aurata*
Eriosyce strausiana: #4 **II** CACTACEAE
Eriosyce subgibbosa: #4 **II** CACTACEAE
Eriosyce subgibbosa ssp. *clavata*: #4 **II** CACTACEAE
Eriosyce subgibbosa ssp. *subgibbosa*: #4 **II** CACTACEAE
Eriosyce taltalensis: #4 **II** CACTACEAE
Eriosyce taltalensis ssp. *echinus*: #4 **II** CACTACEAE
Eriosyce taltalensis ssp. *paucicostata*: #4 **II** CACTACEAE
Eriosyce taltalensis ssp. *pilispina*: #4 **II** CACTACEAE
Eriosyce taltalensis ssp. *taltalensis*: #4 **II** CACTACEAE
Eriosyce tenebrica: #4 **II** CACTACEAE
Eriosyce umadeave: #4 **II** CACTACEAE
Eriosyce vertongenii: #4 **II** CACTACEAE
Eriosyce villicumensis: #4 **II** CACTACEAE
Eriosyce villosa: #4 **II** CACTACEAE
Erioxantha = *Eria*
Erycina spp.: #7 **II** ORCHIDACEAE
Erythrodes spp.: #7 **II** ORCHIDACEAE
Erythrorchis spp.: #7 **II** ORCHIDACEAE
Escobaria aguirreana: #4 **II** CACTACEAE
Escobaria albicolumnaria: (E) White column #4 **II** CACTACEAE
Escobaria alversonii: #4 **II** CACTACEAE
Escobaria asperispina = *Escobaria missouriensis* ssp. *asperispina*
Escobaria bella = *Escobaria emskoetteriana*
Escobaria bisbeeana = *Escobaria vivipara*
Escobaria chaffeyi = *Escobaria dasyacantha* ssp. *chaffeyi*
Escobaria chihuahuensis: #4 **II** CACTACEAE
Escobaria chihuahuensis ssp. *chihuahuensis*: #4 **II** CACTACEAE
Escobaria chihuahuensis ssp. *henricksonii*: #4 **II** CACTACEAE
Escobaria cubensis: #4 **II** CACTACEAE
Escobaria dasyacantha: #4 **II** CACTACEAE
Escobaria dasyacantha ssp. *chaffeyi*: #4 **II** CACTACEAE
Escobaria dasyacantha ssp. *dasyacantha*: #4 **II** CACTACEAE
Escobaria deserti: #4 **II** CACTACEAE
Escobaria duncanii: (E) Duncan's corycactus #4 **II** CACTACEAE
Escobaria emskoetteriana: #4 **II** CACTACEAE
Escobaria guadalupensis: #4 **II** CACTACEAE
Escobaria henricksonii = *Escobaria chihuahuensis* ssp. *henricksonii*
Escobaria hesteri: #4 **II** CACTACEAE
Escobaria laredoi: #4 **II** CACTACEAE
Escobaria leei = *Escobaria sneedii* ssp. *leei*
Escobaria lloydii: #4 **II** CACTACEAE
Escobaria minima: (E) Nelle' cactus, Nellie's cory cactus **I** CACTACEAE
Escobaria missouriensis: #4 **II** CACTACEAE
Escobaria missouriensis ssp. *asperispina*: #4 **II** CACTACEAE

Escobaria missouriensis ssp. *missouriensis*: #4 **II** CACTACEAE
Escobaria missouriensis ssp. *navajoensis* = *Escobaria missouriensis* ssp. *missouriensis*
Escobaria muehlbaueriana = *Escobaria emskoetteriana*
Escobaria nellieae = *Escobaria minima*
Escobaria neomexicana = *Escobaria vivipara*
Escobaria orcuttii: #4 **II** CACTACEAE
Escobaria organensis: (E) Organ mountain foxtail-cactus #4 **II** CACTACEAE
Escobaria radiosa = *Escobaria vivipara*
Escobaria rigida = *Escobaria laredoi*
Escobaria robbinsorum: #4 **II** CACTACEAE
Escobaria roseana: #4 **II** CACTACEAE
Escobaria roseana ssp. *galeanensis*: #4 **II** CACTACEAE
Escobaria roseana ssp. *roseana*: #4 **II** CACTACEAE
Escobaria runyonii = *Escobaria emskoetteriana*
Escobaria sandbergii: #4 **II** CACTACEAE
Escobaria sneedii: (E) Lee pincushion cactus, Sneed's cory cactus, Sneed's pincushion cactus **I** CACTACEAE
Escobaria sneedii ssp. *leei*: **I** CACTACEAE
Escobaria sneedii ssp. *sneedii*: **I** CACTACEAE
Escobaria strobiliformis = *Escobaria chihuahuensis*
Escobaria strobiliformis = *Escobaria tuberculosa*
Escobaria tuberculosa: #4 **II** CACTACEAE
Escobaria varicolor = *Escobaria tuberculosa*
Escobaria villardii: #4 **II** CACTACEAE
Escobaria vivipara: (E) Alverson's pincushion cactus #4 **II** CACTACEAE
Escobaria zilziana: #4 **II** CACTACEAE
Escontria chiotilla: #4 **II** CACTACEAE
Esmeralda spp.: #7 **II** ORCHIDACEAE
Espíritu Santu (S): *Peristeria elata*
Espostoa baumannii: #4 **II** CACTACEAE
Espostoa blossfeldiorum: #4 **II** CACTACEAE
Espostoa calva: #4 **II** CACTACEAE
Espostoa dautwitzii = *Espostoa lanata*
Espostoa frutescens: #4 **II** CACTACEAE
Espostoa guentheri: #4 **II** CACTACEAE
Espostoa haagei = *Espostoa melanostele*
Espostoa huanucoensis: #4 **II** CACTACEAE
Espostoa hylaea: #4 **II** CACTACEAE
Espostoa lanata: #4 **II** CACTACEAE
Espostoa lanianuligera: #4 **II** CACTACEAE
Espostoa laticornua = *Espostoa lanata*
Espostoa melanostele: #4 **II** CACTACEAE
Espostoa mirabilis: #4 **II** CACTACEAE
Espostoa nana: #4 **II** CACTACEAE
Espostoa procera = *Espostoa lanata*
Espostoa ritteri: #4 **II** CACTACEAE
Espostoa ruficeps: #4 **II** CACTACEAE
Espostoa senilis: #4 **II** CACTACEAE
Espostoa superba: #4 **II** CACTACEAE
Espostoopsis dybowskii: #4 **II** CACTACEAE
Esula dendroides = *Euphorbia dendroides*
Etaeria = *Hetaeria*
Euanthe = *Vanda*
Eucnemia = *Govenia*
Eucnemis = *Govenia*
Eucosia spp.: #7 **II** ORCHIDACEAE
Eudisanthema = *Brassavola*
Eulophia spp.: #7 **II** ORCHIDACEAE
Eulophidium = *Oeceoclades*
Eulophiella spp.: #7 **II** ORCHIDACEAE
Eulophiopsis = *Graphorkis*
Eulychnia acida: #4 **II** CACTACEAE
Eulychnia aricensis: #4 **II** CACTACEAE
Eulychnia barquitensis = *Eulychnia breviflora*
Eulychnia breviflora: #4 **II** CACTACEAE
Eulychnia castanea: #4 **II** CACTACEAE
Eulychnia iquiquensis: #4 **II** CACTACEAE
Eulychnia morromorenoensis = *Eulychnia iquiquensis*
Eulychnia procumbens: #4 **II** CACTACEAE
Eulychnia ritteri: #4 **II** CACTACEAE
Eulychnia saint-pieana = *Eulychnia breviflora*
Eulychnia spinibarbis = *Echinopsis spinibarbis*

Euothonaea = *Hexisea*
Euphlebium = *Dendrobium*
Euphorbia spp.: (E) carbones, euphorbias, spurges (S) lechetreznas #1 **I/II**[2] EUPHORBIACEAE
Euphorbia abdelkuri: #1 **II** EUPHORBIACEAE
Euphorbia abyssinica: #1 **II** EUPHORBIACEAE
Euphorbia abyssinica var. *mozambicensis* = *Euphorbia angularis*
Euphorbia abyssinica var. *tetragona* = *Euphorbia abyssinica*
Euphorbia acaulis = *Euphorbia fusiformis*
Euphorbia acrurensis = *Euphorbia abyssinica*
Euphorbia actinoclada: #1 **II** EUPHORBIACEAE
Euphorbia aculeata: #1 **II** EUPHORBIACEAE
Euphorbia adenensis = *Euphorbia balsamifera* ssp. *adenensis*
Euphorbia adenochila: #1 **II** EUPHORBIACEAE
Euphorbia adjurana: #1 **II** EUPHORBIACEAE
Euphorbia aequoris: #1 **II** EUPHORBIACEAE
Euphorbia aeruginosa: #1 **II** EUPHORBIACEAE
Euphorbia aethiopium = *Euphorbia abyssinica*
Euphorbia aggregata: #1 **II** EUPHORBIACEAE
Euphorbia aggregata var. *aggregata*: #1 **II** EUPHORBIACEAE
Euphorbia aggregata var. *alternicolor*: #1 **II** EUPHORBIACEAE
Euphorbia alata: #1 **II** EUPHORBIACEAE
Euphorbia albertensis: #1 **II** EUPHORBIACEAE
Euphorbia albipollinifera: #1 **II** EUPHORBIACEAE
Euphorbia albovillosa = *Euphorbia gueinzii* var. *albovillosa*
Euphorbia alcicornis: #1 **II** EUPHORBIACEAE
Euphorbia alfredii: #1 **II** EUPHORBIACEAE
Euphorbia alluaudii = *Euphorbia leucodendron*
Euphorbia alluaudii ssp. *alluaudii* = *Euphorbia leucodendron*
Euphorbia alluaudii ssp. *oncoclada* = *Euphorbia oncoclada*
Euphorbia alternicolor = *Euphorbia aggregata* var. *alternicolor*
Euphorbia amarifontana: #1 **II** EUPHORBIACEAE
Euphorbia ambacensis = *Euphorbia ingens*
Euphorbia ambatofinandranae = *Euphorbia stenoclada* ssp. *ambatofinandranae*
Euphorbia ambovombensis: **I** EUPHORBIACEAE
Euphorbia ambroseae: #1 **II** EUPHORBIACEAE
Euphorbia ambroseae var. *ambroseae*: #1 **II** EUPHORBIACEAE
Euphorbia ambroseae var. *spinosa*: #1 **II** EUPHORBIACEAE
Euphorbia ammak: #1 **II** EUPHORBIACEAE
Euphorbia ampliphylla: #1 **II** EUPHORBIACEAE
Euphorbia anacantha = *Euphorbia tridentata*
Euphorbia anachoreta = *Euphorbia despoliata*
Euphorbia analalavensis: #1 **II** EUPHORBIACEAE
Euphorbia angrae: #1 **II** EUPHORBIACEAE
Euphorbia angularis: #1 **II** EUPHORBIACEAE
Euphorbia angustiflora: #1 **II** EUPHORBIACEAE
Euphorbia ankarensis: #1 **II** EUPHORBIACEAE
Euphorbia annamarieae: #1 **II** EUPHORBIACEAE
Euphorbia anoplia: #1 **II** EUPHORBIACEAE
Euphorbia antankara = *Euphorbia pachypodioides*
Euphorbia antiquorum: #1 **II** EUPHORBIACEAE
Euphorbia antisyphilitica: (E) Candelilla #1 **II** EUPHORBIACEAE
Euphorbia antso: #1 **II** EUPHORBIACEAE
Euphorbia aphylla: #1 **II** EUPHORBIACEAE
Euphorbia appariciana: #1 **II** EUPHORBIACEAE
Euphorbia applanata: #1 **II** EUPHORBIACEAE
Euphorbia arahaka: #1 **II** EUPHORBIACEAE
Euphorbia arbuscula: #1 **II** EUPHORBIACEAE
Euphorbia arbuscula var. *arbuscula*: #1 **II** EUPHORBIACEAE
Euphorbia arbuscula var. *montana*: #1 **II** EUPHORBIACEAE
Euphorbia arceuthobioides: #1 **II** EUPHORBIACEAE
Euphorbia argillicola = *Euphorbia namibensis*
Euphorbia arida: #1 **II** EUPHORBIACEAE
Euphorbia armata = *Euphorbia loricata*
Euphorbia arrecta = *Euphorbia mixta*
Euphorbia aspericaulis: #1 **II** EUPHORBIACEAE
Euphorbia asthenacantha: #1 **II** EUPHORBIACEAE
Euphorbia astrispina = *Euphorbia stellispina* var. *astrispina*
Euphorbia astrophora: #1 **II** EUPHORBIACEAE

Euphorbia atoto: #1 **II** EUPHORBIACEAE
Euphorbia atrispina: #1 **II** EUPHORBIACEAE
Euphorbia atrispina var. *atrispina*: #1 **II** EUPHORBIACEAE
Euphorbia atrispina var. *viridis*: #1 **II** EUPHORBIACEAE
Euphorbia atrocarmesina: #1 **II** EUPHORBIACEAE
Euphorbia atrocarmesina ssp. *arborea*: #1 **II** EUPHORBIACEAE
Euphorbia atrocarmesina ssp. *atrocarmesina*: #1 **II** EUPHORBIACEAE
Euphorbia atroflora: #1 **II** EUPHORBIACEAE
Euphorbia atropurpurea: #1 **II** EUPHORBIACEAE
Euphorbia atropurpurea f. *lutea*: #1 **II** EUPHORBIACEAE
Euphorbia atropurpurea var. *atropurpurea*: #1 **II** EUPHORBIACEAE
Euphorbia atropurpurea var. *modesta*: #1 **II** EUPHORBIACEAE
Euphorbia atrox: #1 **II** EUPHORBIACEAE
Euphorbia attastoma: #1 **II** EUPHORBIACEAE
Euphorbia attastoma var. *attastoma*: #1 **II** EUPHORBIACEAE
Euphorbia attastoma var. *xanthochlora*: #1 **II** EUPHORBIACEAE
Euphorbia aureoviridiflora: #1 **II** EUPHORBIACEAE
Euphorbia avasmontana: #1 **II** EUPHORBIACEAE
Euphorbia avasmontana var. *avasmontana*: #1 **II** EUPHORBIACEAE
Euphorbia avasmontana var. *sagittaria*: #1 **II** EUPHORBIACEAE
Euphorbia awashensis: #1 **II** EUPHORBIACEAE
Euphorbia baga: #1 **II** EUPHORBIACEAE
Euphorbia baga var. *baga*: #1 **II** EUPHORBIACEAE
Euphorbia baga var. *parvifolia*: #1 **II** EUPHORBIACEAE
Euphorbia baioensis: #1 **II** EUPHORBIACEAE
Euphorbia baleensis: #1 **II** EUPHORBIACEAE
Euphorbia baliola: #1 **II** EUPHORBIACEAE
Euphorbia ballyana: #1 **II** EUPHORBIACEAE
Euphorbia ballyi: #1 **II** EUPHORBIACEAE
Euphorbia balsamea = *Euphorbia gariepina* ssp. *balsamea*
Euphorbia balsamifera: #1 **II** EUPHORBIACEAE
Euphorbia balsamifera ssp. *adenensis*: #1 **II** EUPHORBIACEAE
Euphorbia balsamifera ssp. *balsamifera*: #1 **II** EUPHORBIACEAE
Euphorbia balsamifera ssp. *eubalsamifera* = *Euphorbia balsamifera* ssp. *balsamifera*
Euphorbia balsamifera ssp. *rogeri* = *Euphorbia balsamifera*
Euphorbia balsamifera ssp. *sepium* = *Euphorbia balsamifera*
Euphorbia banae: #1 **II** EUPHORBIACEAE
Euphorbia baradii: #1 **II** EUPHORBIACEAE
Euphorbia barbicollis: #1 **II** EUPHORBIACEAE
Euphorbia bariensis: #1 **II** EUPHORBIACEAE
Euphorbia barnardii: #1 **II** EUPHORBIACEAE
Euphorbia barnhartii: #1 **II** EUPHORBIACEAE
Euphorbia barteri = *Euphorbia kamerunica*
Euphorbia basutica = *Euphorbia clavarioides* var. *clavarioides*
Euphorbia baumii = *Euphorbia monteiri* ssp. *monteiri*
Euphorbia bayeri: #1 **II** EUPHORBIACEAE
Euphorbia baylissii: #1 **II** EUPHORBIACEAE
Euphorbia beaumieriana = *Euphorbia officinarum*
Euphorbia beharensis: #1 **II** EUPHORBIACEAE
Euphorbia beillei: #1 **II** EUPHORBIACEAE
Euphorbia bellica = *Euphorbia virosa* ssp. *virosa*
Euphorbia benguelensis = *Euphorbia trichadenia*
Euphorbia bergeri: #1 **II** EUPHORBIACEAE
Euphorbia bergeriana = *Euphorbia gariepina* ssp. *balsamea*
Euphorbia bergii: #1 **II** EUPHORBIACEAE
Euphorbia berorohae: #1 **II** EUPHORBIACEAE
Euphorbia berotica: #1 **II** EUPHORBIACEAE
Euphorbia berthelotii: #1 **II** EUPHORBIACEAE
Euphorbia bevilaniensis = *Euphorbia milii* var. *bevilaniensis*
Euphorbia biaculeata: #1 **II** EUPHORBIACEAE
Euphorbia biglandulosa = *Euphorbia burmannii*
Euphorbia biharamulensis: #1 **II** EUPHORBIACEAE
Euphorbia bilocularis = *Euphorbia candelabrum* var. *bilocularis*
Euphorbia bitataensis: #1 **II** EUPHORBIACEAE
Euphorbia boinensis: #1 **II** EUPHORBIACEAE
Euphorbia boissieri: #1 **II** EUPHORBIACEAE
Euphorbia boiteaui: #1 **II** EUPHORBIACEAE
Euphorbia bojeri = *Euphorbia milii* var. *milii*
Euphorbia bolusii: #1 **II** EUPHORBIACEAE
Euphorbia bongolavensis: #1 **II** EUPHORBIACEAE

---

[2] Succulent species only/Sólo las especies suculentas /Seulement les espèces succulentes

Euphorbia boranensis: #1 **II** EUPHORBIACEAE
Euphorbia bosseri: #1 **II** EUPHORBIACEAE
Euphorbia bottae: #1 **II** EUPHORBIACEAE
Euphorbia bougheyi: #1 **II** EUPHORBIACEAE
Euphorbia bourgaeana: #1 **II** EUPHORBIACEAE
Euphorbia brachiata: #1 **II** EUPHORBIACEAE
Euphorbia brachyphylla: #1 **II** EUPHORBIACEAE
Euphorbia brakdamensis: #1 **II** EUPHORBIACEAE
Euphorbia brassii: #1 **II** EUPHORBIACEAE
Euphorbia braunsii: #1 **II** EUPHORBIACEAE
Euphorbia bravoana: #1 **II** EUPHORBIACEAE
Euphorbia breonii = Euphorbia milii var. *milii*
Euphorbia breviarticulata: #1 **II** EUPHORBIACEAE
Euphorbia breviarticulata var. *breviarticulata*: #1 **II**
 EUPHORBIACEAE
Euphorbia breviarticulata var. *trunciformis*: #1 **II**
 EUPHORBIACEAE
Euphorbia brevirama: #1 **II** EUPHORBIACEAE
Euphorbia brevis: #1 **II** EUPHORBIACEAE
Euphorbia brevitorta: #1 **II** EUPHORBIACEAE
Euphorbia broussonetii: #1 **II** EUPHORBIACEAE
Euphorbia brunellii: #1 **II** EUPHORBIACEAE
Euphorbia bruynsii: #1 **II** EUPHORBIACEAE
Euphorbia bubalina: #1 **II** EUPHORBIACEAE
Euphorbia bulbispina: #1 **II** EUPHORBIACEAE
Euphorbia bupleurifolia: #1 **II** EUPHORBIACEAE
Euphorbia burgeri: #1 **II** EUPHORBIACEAE
Euphorbia burmannii: #1 **II** EUPHORBIACEAE
Euphorbia burmannii var. *karroensis = Euphorbia karroensis*
Euphorbia buruana: #1 **II** EUPHORBIACEAE
Euphorbia bussei: #1 **II** EUPHORBIACEAE
Euphorbia bussei var. *bussei*: #1 **II** EUPHORBIACEAE
Euphorbia bussei var. *kibwezensis*: #1 **II** EUPHORBIACEAE
Euphorbia bwambensis: #1 **II** EUPHORBIACEAE
Euphorbia cactus: #1 **II** EUPHORBIACEAE
Euphorbia cactus var. *cactus*: #1 **II** EUPHORBIACEAE
Euphorbia cactus var. *tortirama*: #1 **II** EUPHORBIACEAE
Euphorbia caducifolia: #1 **II** EUPHORBIACEAE
Euphorbia caerulans: #1 **II** EUPHORBIACEAE
Euphorbia caerulescens: #1 **II** EUPHORBIACEAE
Euphorbia calamiformis: #1 **II** EUPHORBIACEAE
Euphorbia calderensis = Euphorbia copiapina
Euphorbia californica: #1 **II** EUPHORBIACEAE
Euphorbia californica var. *californica*: #1 **II** EUPHORBIACEAE
Euphorbia californica var. *hindsiana*: #1 **II** EUPHORBIACEAE
Euphorbia calycina = Euphorbia candelabrum var. *candelabrum*
Euphorbia cameronii: #1 **II** EUPHORBIACEAE
Euphorbia canaliculata = Euphorbia clava
Euphorbia canariensis: #1 **II** EUPHORBIACEAE
Euphorbia canariensis f. *viridis = Euphorbia canariensis*
Euphorbia canariensis var. *spiralis = Euphorbia canariensis*
Euphorbia candelabrum: #1 **II** EUPHORBIACEAE
Euphorbia candelabrum var. *bilocularis*: #1 **II**
 EUPHORBIACEAE
Euphorbia candelabrum var. *candelabrum*: #1 **II**
 EUPHORBIACEAE
Euphorbia candelabrum var. *erythraeae = Euphorbia abyssinica*
Euphorbia cannellii: #1 **II** EUPHORBIACEAE
Euphorbia capazzi = Euphorbia balsamifera ssp. *balsamifera*
Euphorbia capmanambatoensis: #1 **II** EUPHORBIACEAE
Euphorbia capsaintemariensis: **I** EUPHORBIACEAE
Euphorbia capsaintemariensis var. *tulearensis = Euphorbia*
 tulearensis
Euphorbia captiosa = Euphorbia ferox
Euphorbia capuronii: #1 **II** EUPHORBIACEAE
Euphorbia caput-aureum: #1 **II** EUPHORBIACEAE
Euphorbia caput-medusae: #1 **II** EUPHORBIACEAE
Euphorbia caput-medusae var. β = *Euphorbia tridentata*
Euphorbia caput-medusae var. δ = *Euphorbia pugniformis*
Euphorbia caput-medusae var. *geminata = Euphorbia caput-*
 medusae
Euphorbia caput-medusae var. *major = Euphorbia caput-medusae*
Euphorbia caput-medusae var. *minor = Euphorbia caput-medusae*
Euphorbia caput-medusae var. γ = *Euphorbia tridentata*
Euphorbia carteriana: #1 **II** EUPHORBIACEAE

Euphorbia carunculifera: #1 **II** EUPHORBIACEAE
Euphorbia carunculifera ssp. *carunculifera*: #1 **II**
 EUPHORBIACEAE
Euphorbia carunculifera ssp. *subfastigiata*: #1 **II**
 EUPHORBIACEAE
Euphorbia cassythoides: #1 **II** EUPHORBIACEAE
Euphorbia cataractarum: #1 **II** EUPHORBIACEAE
Euphorbia caterviflora: #1 **II** EUPHORBIACEAE
Euphorbia cattimandoo: #1 **II** EUPHORBIACEAE
Euphorbia cedrorum: #1 **II** EUPHORBIACEAE
Euphorbia celata: #1 **II** EUPHORBIACEAE
Euphorbia cereiformis: #1 **II** EUPHORBIACEAE
Euphorbia cereiformis var. *echinata = Euphorbia cereiformis*
Euphorbia cereiformis var. *submammillaris = Euphorbia*
 submammillaris
Euphorbia cerifera = Euphorbia antisyphilitica
Euphorbia cervicornis = Euphorbia hamata
Euphorbia chamaecormos = Euphorbia schizacantha
Euphorbia charleswilsoniana: #1 **II** EUPHORBIACEAE
Euphorbia chersina: #1 **II** EUPHORBIACEAE
Euphorbia cibdela: #1 **II** EUPHORBIACEAE
Euphorbia ciliolata = Euphorbia transvaalensis
Euphorbia cirsioides = Euphorbia stenoclada ssp. *stenoclada*
Euphorbia cirsioides f. *longispinosa = Euphorbia stenoclada* ssp.
 stenoclada
Euphorbia cirsioides f. *pterospinosa = Euphorbia stenoclada* ssp.
 stenoclada
Euphorbia clandestina: #1 **II** EUPHORBIACEAE
Euphorbia classenii: #1 **II** EUPHORBIACEAE
Euphorbia clava: (E) Club-shaped euphorb #1 **II**
 EUPHORBIACEAE
Euphorbia clavarioides: #1 **II** EUPHORBIACEAE
Euphorbia clavarioides var. *clavarioides*: #1 **II**
 EUPHORBIACEAE
Euphorbia clavarioides var. *truncata*: #1 **II** EUPHORBIACEAE
Euphorbia clavata = Euphorbia clava
Euphorbia clavigera: #1 **II** EUPHORBIACEAE
Euphorbia clivicola: #1 **II** EUPHORBIACEAE
Euphorbia coerulans = Euphorbia caerulans
Euphorbia coerulescens = Euphorbia caerulescens
Euphorbia colliculina: #1 **II** EUPHORBIACEAE
Euphorbia colubrina: #1 **II** EUPHORBIACEAE
Euphorbia columnaris: #1 **II** EUPHORBIACEAE
Euphorbia commelinii = Euphorbia caput-medusae
Euphorbia commersonii = Euphorbia thouarsiana
Euphorbia comosa: #1 **II** EUPHORBIACEAE
Euphorbia complexa: #1 **II** EUPHORBIACEAE
Euphorbia confertiflora = Euphorbia candelabrum var.
 candelabrum
Euphorbia confinalis: #1 **II** EUPHORBIACEAE
Euphorbia confinalis ssp. *confinalis*: #1 **II** EUPHORBIACEAE
Euphorbia confinalis ssp. *rhodesiaca*: #1 **II** EUPHORBIACEAE
Euphorbia confluens: #1 **II** EUPHORBIACEAE
Euphorbia conformis = Euphorbia negromontana
Euphorbia congestiflora: #1 **II** EUPHORBIACEAE
Euphorbia consobrina: #1 **II** EUPHORBIACEAE
Euphorbia conspicua: #1 **II** EUPHORBIACEAE
Euphorbia contorta: #1 **II** EUPHORBIACEAE
Euphorbia controversa = Euphorbia abyssinica
Euphorbia cooperi: #1 **II** EUPHORBIACEAE
Euphorbia cooperi var. *calidicola*: #1 **II** EUPHORBIACEAE
Euphorbia cooperi var. *cooperi*: #1 **II** EUPHORBIACEAE
Euphorbia cooperi var. *ussanguensis*: #1 **II** EUPHORBIACEAE
Euphorbia copiapina: #1 **II** EUPHORBIACEAE
Euphorbia corniculata: #1 **II** EUPHORBIACEAE
Euphorbia coronata = Euphorbia clava
Euphorbia corymbosa: #1 **II** EUPHORBIACEAE
Euphorbia corynoclada = Euphorbia plumerioides
Euphorbia crassipes: #1 **II** EUPHORBIACEAE
Euphorbia cremersii: **I** EUPHORBIACEAE
Euphorbia cremersii f. *viridifolia*: #1 **II** EUPHORBIACEAE
Euphorbia cremersii var. *cremersii*: #1 **II** EUPHORBIACEAE
Euphorbia cremersii var. *rakotozafyi*: #1 **II** EUPHORBIACEAE
Euphorbia crispa: #1 **II** EUPHORBIACEAE
Euphorbia crispata = Euphorbia lemaireana

Checklist of flora/Lista de especies de flora/Liste des espèces végétales

Euphorbia croizatii: #1 **II** EUPHORBIACEAE
Euphorbia cryptocaulis: #1 **II** EUPHORBIACEAE
Euphorbia cryptospinosa: #1 **II** EUPHORBIACEAE
Euphorbia cucumerina: #1 **II** EUPHORBIACEAE
Euphorbia cumulata: #1 **II** EUPHORBIACEAE
Euphorbia cuneata: #1 **II** EUPHORBIACEAE
Euphorbia cuneata var. *carpasus* = *Euphorbia cuneata*
Euphorbia cuneata var. *perrottetii* = *Euphorbia cuneata*
Euphorbia cuneneana: #1 **II** EUPHORBIACEAE
Euphorbia cuneneana ssp. *cuneneana*: #1 **II** EUPHORBIACEAE
Euphorbia cuneneana ssp. *rhizomatosa*: #1 **II** EUPHORBIACEAE
Euphorbia cuprispina: #1 **II** EUPHORBIACEAE
Euphorbia curocana: #1 **II** EUPHORBIACEAE
Euphorbia currorii = *Euphorbia matabelensis*
Euphorbia curvirama: #1 **II** EUPHORBIACEAE
Euphorbia cussonioides: #1 **II** EUPHORBIACEAE
Euphorbia cylindrica: #1 **II** EUPHORBIACEAE
Euphorbia cylindrifolia: **I** EUPHORBIACEAE
Euphorbia cylindrifolia ssp. *cylindrifolia*: **I** EUPHORBIACEAE
Euphorbia cylindrifolia ssp. *tuberifera*: **I** EUPHORBIACEAE
Euphorbia dalettiensis: #1 **II** EUPHORBIACEAE
Euphorbia damarana: #1 **II** EUPHORBIACEAE
Euphorbia darbandensis: #1 **II** EUPHORBIACEAE
Euphorbia dasyacantha: #1 **II** EUPHORBIACEAE
Euphorbia dauana: #1 **II** EUPHORBIACEAE
Euphorbia davyi: #1 **II** EUPHORBIACEAE
Euphorbia davyi ssp. *tlapanensis* = *Euphorbia davyi*
Euphorbia davyi var. *maleolens* = *Euphorbia maleolens*
Euphorbia dawei: #1 **II** EUPHORBIACEAE
Euphorbia debilispina: #1 **II** EUPHORBIACEAE
Euphorbia decariana = *Euphorbia hedyotoides*
Euphorbia decaryi: **I** EUPHORBIACEAE
Euphorbia decaryi var. *ampanihyensis*: **I** EUPHORBIACEAE
Euphorbia decaryi var. *capsaintemariensis* = *Euphorbia capsaintemariensis*
Euphorbia decaryi var. *decaryi*: **I** EUPHORBIACEAE
Euphorbia decaryi var. *robinsonii*: **I** EUPHORBIACEAE
Euphorbia decaryi var. *spirosticha*: **I** EUPHORBIACEAE
Euphorbia decepta: #1 **II** EUPHORBIACEAE
Euphorbia decidua: #1 **II** EUPHORBIACEAE
Euphorbia decliviticola: #1 **II** EUPHORBIACEAE
Euphorbia decorsei: #1 **II** EUPHORBIACEAE
Euphorbia decussata = *Euphorbia indecora*
Euphorbia dedzana: #1 **II** EUPHORBIACEAE
Euphorbia deightonii: #1 **II** EUPHORBIACEAE
Euphorbia dekindtii: #1 **II** EUPHORBIACEAE
Euphorbia delphinensis: #1 **II** EUPHORBIACEAE
Euphorbia demissa: #1 **II** EUPHORBIACEAE
Euphorbia dendroides: #1 **II** EUPHORBIACEAE
Euphorbia denisiana: #1 **II** EUPHORBIACEAE
Euphorbia desmondii: #1 **II** EUPHORBIACEAE
Euphorbia despoliata: #1 **II** EUPHORBIACEAE
Euphorbia dhofarensis: #1 **II** EUPHORBIACEAE
Euphorbia dichroa: #1 **II** EUPHORBIACEAE
Euphorbia didiereoides: #1 **II** EUPHORBIACEAE
Euphorbia dinteri = *Euphorbia virosa* ssp. *virosa*
Euphorbia dinteri = *Euphorbia venenata*
Euphorbia disclusa = *Euphorbia abyssinica*
Euphorbia discrepans: #1 **II** EUPHORBIACEAE
Euphorbia discreta = *Euphorbia woodii*
Euphorbia dispersa: #1 **II** EUPHORBIACEAE
Euphorbia dissitispina: #1 **II** EUPHORBIACEAE
Euphorbia distinctissima: #1 **II** EUPHORBIACEAE
Euphorbia divaricata = *Euphorbia dendroides*
Euphorbia dolichoceras: #1 **II** EUPHORBIACEAE
Euphorbia dregeana: #1 **II** EUPHORBIACEAE
Euphorbia dumeticola: #1 **II** EUPHORBIACEAE
Euphorbia duranii: #1 **II** EUPHORBIACEAE
Euphorbia duranii var. *ankaratrae*: #1 **II** EUPHORBIACEAE
Euphorbia duranii var. *duranii*: #1 **II** EUPHORBIACEAE
Euphorbia duseimata: #1 **II** EUPHORBIACEAE
Euphorbia echinus: #1 **II** EUPHORBIACEAE
Euphorbia echinus var. *brevispina* = *Euphorbia echinus*
Euphorbia echinus var. *chlorantha* = *Euphorbia echinus*
Euphorbia echinus var. *chlorosoma* = *Euphorbia echinus*

Euphorbia echinus var. *hernandez-pachecoi* = *Euphorbia echinus*
Euphorbia ecklonii: #1 **II** EUPHORBIACEAE
Euphorbia eduardoi: #1 **II** EUPHORBIACEAE
Euphorbia eendornensis = *Euphorbia fusca*
Euphorbia eilensis: #1 **II** EUPHORBIACEAE
Euphorbia elastica = *Euphorbia dregeana*
Euphorbia elegantissima: #1 **II** EUPHORBIACEAE
Euphorbia ellenbeckii: #1 **II** EUPHORBIACEAE
Euphorbia elliotii: #1 **II** EUPHORBIACEAE
Euphorbia elliptica = *Euphorbia silenifolia*
Euphorbia elliptica var. *undulata* = *Euphorbia crispa*
Euphorbia enopla: #1 **II** EUPHORBIACEAE
Euphorbia enopla var. *dentata* = *Euphorbia heptagona* var. *dentata*
Euphorbia enopla var. *enopla*: #1 **II** EUPHORBIACEAE
Euphorbia enopla var. *viridis*: #1 **II** EUPHORBIACEAE
Euphorbia enormis: #1 **II** EUPHORBIACEAE
Euphorbia enterophora: #1 **II** EUPHORBIACEAE
Euphorbia enterophora ssp. *crassa*: #1 **II** EUPHORBIACEAE
Euphorbia enterophora ssp. *enterophora*: #1 **II** EUPHORBIACEAE
Euphorbia ephedroides: #1 **II** EUPHORBIACEAE
Euphorbia ephedroides var. *debilis*: #1 **II** EUPHORBIACEAE
Euphorbia ephedroides var. *ephedroides*: #1 **II** EUPHORBIACEAE
Euphorbia ephedroides var. *imminuta*: #1 **II** EUPHORBIACEAE
Euphorbia epiphylloides: #1 **II** EUPHORBIACEAE
Euphorbia erigavensis: #1 **II** EUPHORBIACEAE
Euphorbia erlangeri: #1 **II** EUPHORBIACEAE
Euphorbia ernestii: #1 **II** EUPHORBIACEAE
Euphorbia erosa = *Euphorbia cereiformis*
Euphorbia erythraeae = *Euphorbia abyssinica*
Euphorbia esculenta: #1 **II** EUPHORBIACEAE
Euphorbia espinosa: #1 **II** EUPHORBIACEAE
Euphorbia etuberculosa: #1 **II** EUPHORBIACEAE
Euphorbia eustacei: #1 **II** EUPHORBIACEAE
Euphorbia evansii: #1 **II** EUPHORBIACEAE
Euphorbia excelsa: #1 **II** EUPHORBIACEAE
Euphorbia exilis: #1 **II** EUPHORBIACEAE
Euphorbia exilispina: #1 **II** EUPHORBIACEAE
Euphorbia eyassiana: #1 **II** EUPHORBIACEAE
Euphorbia falsa = *Euphorbia meloformis*
Euphorbia famatamboay: #1 **II** EUPHORBIACEAE
Euphorbia famatamboay ssp. *famatamboay*: #1 **II** EUPHORBIACEAE
Euphorbia famatamboay ssp. *itampolensis*: #1 **II** EUPHORBIACEAE
Euphorbia fanshawei: #1 **II** EUPHORBIACEAE
Euphorbia fascicaulis: #1 **II** EUPHORBIACEAE
Euphorbia fasciculata: #1 **II** EUPHORBIACEAE
Euphorbia faucicola: #1 **II** EUPHORBIACEAE
Euphorbia faurotii = *Euphorbia triaculeata*
Euphorbia ferox: #1 **II** EUPHORBIACEAE
Euphorbia fianarantsoae: #1 **II** EUPHORBIACEAE
Euphorbia fidjiana = *Euphorbia plumerioides*
Euphorbia fiherenensis: #1 **II** EUPHORBIACEAE
Euphorbia filiflora: #1 **II** EUPHORBIACEAE
Euphorbia fimbriata: #1 **II** EUPHORBIACEAE
Euphorbia fissispina: #1 **II** EUPHORBIACEAE
Euphorbia flanaganii: #1 **II** EUPHORBIACEAE
Euphorbia fleckii: #1 **II** EUPHORBIACEAE
Euphorbia fluminis: #1 **II** EUPHORBIACEAE
Euphorbia foliiflua = *Euphorbia heterodoxa*
Euphorbia forolensis: #1 **II** EUPHORBIACEAE
Euphorbia fortissima: #1 **II** EUPHORBIACEAE
Euphorbia fortuita: #1 **II** EUPHORBIACEAE
Euphorbia fournieri = *Euphorbia leuconeura*
Euphorbia fractiflexa: #1 **II** EUPHORBIACEAE
Euphorbia fragiliramulosa = *Euphorbia negromontana*
Euphorbia francescae = *Euphorbia quadrata*
Euphorbia franckiana: #1 **II** EUPHORBIACEAE
Euphorbia francoisii: **I** EUPHORBIACEAE
Euphorbia francoisii var. *crassicaulis*: **I** EUPHORBIACEAE
Euphorbia francoisii var. *francoisii*: **I** EUPHORBIACEAE
Euphorbia francoisii var. *rakotozafyi* = *Euphorbia cremersii* var. *rakotozafyi*

Euphorbia franksiae: #1 **II** EUPHORBIACEAE
Euphorbia franksiae var. *franksiae*: #1 **II** EUPHORBIACEAE
Euphorbia franksiae var. *zuluensis*: #1 **II** EUPHORBIACEAE
Euphorbia fraterna = *Euphorbia dekindtii*
Euphorbia frickiana = *Euphorbia pseudoglobosa*
Euphorbia friedrichiae: #1 **II** EUPHORBIACEAE
Euphorbia fructus-pini = *Euphorbia caput-medusae*
Euphorbia fructus-pini var. *geminata* = *Euphorbia caput-medusae*
Euphorbia fruticosa = *Euphorbia cuneata*
Euphorbia fruticosa: #1 **II** EUPHORBIACEAE
Euphorbia furcata: #1 **II** EUPHORBIACEAE
Euphorbia fusca: #1 **II** EUPHORBIACEAE
Euphorbia fusiformis: #1 **II** EUPHORBIACEAE
Euphorbia galgalana: #1 **II** EUPHORBIACEAE
Euphorbia galpinii = *Euphorbia transvaalensis*
Euphorbia gariepina: #1 **II** EUPHORBIACEAE
Euphorbia gariepina ssp. *balsamea*: #1 **II** EUPHORBIACEAE
Euphorbia gariepina ssp. *gariepina*: #1 **II** EUPHORBIACEAE
Euphorbia garuana = *Euphorbia kamerunica*
Euphorbia gatbergensis: #1 **II** EUPHORBIACEAE
Euphorbia geayi = *Euphorbia tirucalli*
Euphorbia geldorensis: #1 **II** EUPHORBIACEAE
Euphorbia gemmea: #1 **II** EUPHORBIACEAE
Euphorbia genoudiana: #1 **II** EUPHORBIACEAE
Euphorbia gentilis: #1 **II** EUPHORBIACEAE
Euphorbia gentilis ssp. *gentilis*: #1 **II** EUPHORBIACEAE
Euphorbia gentilis ssp. *tanquana*: #1 **II** EUPHORBIACEAE
Euphorbia geroldii: #1 **II** EUPHORBIACEAE
Euphorbia giessii: #1 **II** EUPHORBIACEAE
Euphorbia gilbertii = *Euphorbia micracantha*
Euphorbia gillettii: #1 **II** EUPHORBIACEAE
Euphorbia gillettii ssp. *gillettii*: #1 **II** EUPHORBIACEAE
Euphorbia gillettii ssp. *tenuior*: #1 **II** EUPHORBIACEAE
Euphorbia glandularis: #1 **II** EUPHORBIACEAE
Euphorbia globosa: #1 **II** EUPHORBIACEAE
Euphorbia globulicaulis: #1 **II** EUPHORBIACEAE
Euphorbia glochidiata: #1 **II** EUPHORBIACEAE
Euphorbia glomerata = *Euphorbia globosa*
Euphorbia goetzei: #1 **II** EUPHORBIACEAE
Euphorbia golisana = *Euphorbia phillipsiae*
Euphorbia gollmeriana = *Euphorbia lupulina*
Euphorbia gorgonis: #1 **II** EUPHORBIACEAE
Euphorbia gossweileri = *Euphorbia trichadenia*
Euphorbia gossypina: #1 **II** EUPHORBIACEAE
Euphorbia gossypina var. *coccinea*: #1 **II** EUPHORBIACEAE
Euphorbia gossypina var. *gossypina*: #1 **II** EUPHORBIACEAE
Euphorbia gottlebei: #1 **II** EUPHORBIACEAE
Euphorbia gracilicaulis: #1 **II** EUPHORBIACEAE
Euphorbia graciliramea: #1 **II** EUPHORBIACEAE
Euphorbia grandialata: #1 **II** EUPHORBIACEAE
Euphorbia grandicornis: #1 **II** EUPHORBIACEAE
Euphorbia grandicornis ssp. *grandicornis*: #1 **II** EUPHORBIACEAE
Euphorbia grandicornis ssp. *sejuncta*: #1 **II** EUPHORBIACEAE
Euphorbia grandidens: #1 **II** EUPHORBIACEAE
Euphorbia grandilobata = *Euphorbia breviarticulata* var. *breviarticulata*
Euphorbia grandis = *Euphorbia abyssinica*
Euphorbia graniticola: #1 **II** EUPHORBIACEAE
Euphorbia graveolens = *Euphorbia restituta*
Euphorbia greenwayi: #1 **II** EUPHORBIACEAE
Euphorbia greenwayi ssp. *breviaculeata*: #1 **II** EUPHORBIACEAE
Euphorbia greenwayi ssp. *greenwayi*: #1 **II** EUPHORBIACEAE
Euphorbia gregaria: #1 **II** EUPHORBIACEAE
Euphorbia griseola: #1 **II** EUPHORBIACEAE
Euphorbia griseola ssp. *griseola*: #1 **II** EUPHORBIACEAE
Euphorbia griseola ssp. *mashonica*: #1 **II** EUPHORBIACEAE
Euphorbia griseola ssp. *zambiensis*: #1 **II** EUPHORBIACEAE
Euphorbia griseola var. *robusta* = *Euphorbia griseola* ssp. *griseola*
Euphorbia groenewaldii: #1 **II** EUPHORBIACEAE
Euphorbia gueinzii: #1 **II** EUPHORBIACEAE
Euphorbia gueinzii var. *albovillosa*: #1 **II** EUPHORBIACEAE
Euphorbia gueinzii var. *gueinzii*: #1 **II** EUPHORBIACEAE
Euphorbia guerichiana: #1 **II** EUPHORBIACEAE

Euphorbia guillauminiana: #1 **II** EUPHORBIACEAE
Euphorbia guillemetii: #1 **II** EUPHORBIACEAE
Euphorbia gummifera: #1 **II** EUPHORBIACEAE
Euphorbia gymnocalycioides: #1 **II** EUPHORBIACEAE
Euphorbia gymnoclada: #1 **II** EUPHORBIACEAE
Euphorbia gynophora = *Euphorbia espinosa*
Euphorbia hadramautica: #1 **II** EUPHORBIACEAE
Euphorbia halipedicola: #1 **II** EUPHORBIACEAE
Euphorbia halleri = *Euphorbia gariepina* ssp. *balsamea*
Euphorbia hallii: #1 **II** EUPHORBIACEAE
Euphorbia hamata: #1 **II** EUPHORBIACEAE
Euphorbia handiensis: #1 **II** EUPHORBIACEAE
Euphorbia hararensis = *Euphorbia abyssinica*
Euphorbia hastisquama = *Euphorbia caterviflora*
Euphorbia hedyotoides: #1 **II** EUPHORBIACEAE
Euphorbia helicothele = *Euphorbia nivulia*
Euphorbia hepatica = *Euphorbia reclinata*
Euphorbia heptagona: #1 **II** EUPHORBIACEAE
Euphorbia heptagona var. *dentata*: #1 **II** EUPHORBIACEAE
Euphorbia heptagona var. *heptagona*: #1 **II** EUPHORBIACEAE
Euphorbia heptagona var. *ramosa*: #1 **II** EUPHORBIACEAE
Euphorbia heptagona var. *subsessilis*: #1 **II** EUPHORBIACEAE
Euphorbia heptagona var. *viridis*: #1 **II** EUPHORBIACEAE
Euphorbia herman-schwartzii: #1 **II** EUPHORBIACEAE
Euphorbia hermentiana = *Euphorbia trigona*
Euphorbia hernandez-pachecoi = *Euphorbia echinus*
Euphorbia herrei: #1 **II** EUPHORBIACEAE
Euphorbia heteracantha = *Euphorbia subsalsa* ssp. *subsalsa*
Euphorbia heterochroma: #1 **II** EUPHORBIACEAE
Euphorbia heterochroma ssp. *heterochroma*: #1 **II** EUPHORBIACEAE
Euphorbia heterochroma ssp. *tsavoensis*: #1 **II** EUPHORBIACEAE
Euphorbia heterochroma var. *mitis* = *Euphorbia heterochroma* ssp. *heterochroma*
Euphorbia heterodoxa: #1 **II** EUPHORBIACEAE
Euphorbia heterospina: #1 **II** EUPHORBIACEAE
Euphorbia heterospina ssp. *baringoensis*: #1 **II** EUPHORBIACEAE
Euphorbia heterospina ssp. *heterospina*: #1 **II** EUPHORBIACEAE
Euphorbia hislopii = *Euphorbia milii* var. *hislopii*
Euphorbia hofstaetteri: #1 **II** EUPHORBIACEAE
Euphorbia holmesiae: #1 **II** EUPHORBIACEAE
Euphorbia holmseae = *Euphorbia holmesiae*
Euphorbia holochlorina: #1 **II** EUPHORBIACEAE
Euphorbia hopetownensis: #1 **II** EUPHORBIACEAE
Euphorbia horombensis: #1 **II** EUPHORBIACEAE
Euphorbia horrida: #1 **II** EUPHORBIACEAE
Euphorbia horrida var. *horrida*: #1 **II** EUPHORBIACEAE
Euphorbia horrida var. *major*: #1 **II** EUPHORBIACEAE
Euphorbia horrida var. *noorsveldensis*: #1 **II** EUPHORBIACEAE
Euphorbia horrida var. *striata*: #1 **II** EUPHORBIACEAE
Euphorbia horwoodii: #1 **II** EUPHORBIACEAE
Euphorbia hottentota: #1 **II** EUPHORBIACEAE
Euphorbia hubertii: #1 **II** EUPHORBIACEAE
Euphorbia huttoniae = *Euphorbia inermis* var. *huttoniae*
Euphorbia hydnorae = *Euphorbia mauritanica* var. *mauritanica*
Euphorbia hypogaea: #1 **II** EUPHORBIACEAE
Euphorbia hystrix = *Euphorbia loricata*
Euphorbia iharanae: #1 **II** EUPHORBIACEAE
Euphorbia imerina: #1 **II** EUPHORBIACEAE
Euphorbia imitata: #1 **II** EUPHORBIACEAE
Euphorbia immersa: #1 **II** EUPHORBIACEAE
Euphorbia imparispina: #1 **II** EUPHORBIACEAE
Euphorbia impervia = *Euphorbia heterochroma* ssp. *heterochroma*
Euphorbia implexa = *Euphorbia gossypina* var. *gossypina*
Euphorbia inaequispina: #1 **II** EUPHORBIACEAE
Euphorbia inarticulata: #1 **II** EUPHORBIACEAE
Euphorbia inconstantia: #1 **II** EUPHORBIACEAE
Euphorbia inculta: #1 **II** EUPHORBIACEAE
Euphorbia indecora: #1 **II** EUPHORBIACEAE
Euphorbia indurescens: #1 **II** EUPHORBIACEAE
Euphorbia inelegans = *Euphorbia inornata*
Euphorbia inermis: #1 **II** EUPHORBIACEAE
Euphorbia inermis var. *huttoniae*: #1 **II** EUPHORBIACEAE

Euphorbia inermis var. *inermis*: #1 **II** EUPHORBIACEAE
Euphorbia inermis var. *laniglans* = *Euphorbia esculenta*
Euphorbia infesta = *Euphorbia triaculeata*
Euphorbia ingens: #1 **II** EUPHORBIACEAE
Euphorbia ingenticapsa: #1 **II** EUPHORBIACEAE
Euphorbia inornata: #1 **II** EUPHORBIACEAE
Euphorbia insulae-europae = *Euphorbia stenoclada* ssp.
   stenoclada
Euphorbia intercedens = *Euphorbia quinquecostata*
Euphorbia intisy: #1 **II** EUPHORBIACEAE
Euphorbia intisy var. *mainty* = *Euphorbia mainty*
Euphorbia inundaticola: #1 **II** EUPHORBIACEAE
Euphorbia invaginata: #1 **II** EUPHORBIACEAE
Euphorbia isacantha: #1 **II** EUPHORBIACEAE
Euphorbia isalensis = *Euphorbia milii* var. *splendens*
Euphorbia jaegeriana = *Euphorbia matabelensis*
Euphorbia jansenvillensis: #1 **II** EUPHORBIACEAE
Euphorbia johannis: #1 **II** EUPHORBIACEAE
Euphorbia johnsonii = *Euphorbia knuthii* ssp. *johnsonii*
Euphorbia jubata: #1 **II** EUPHORBIACEAE
Euphorbia juglans: #1 **II** EUPHORBIACEAE
Euphorbia juttae: #1 **II** EUPHORBIACEAE
Euphorbia kalaharica = *Euphorbia avasmontana* var. *avasmontana*
Euphorbia kalisana: #1 **II** EUPHORBIACEAE
Euphorbia kamerunica: #1 **II** EUPHORBIACEAE
Euphorbia kamerunica var. *barteri* = *Euphorbia kamerunica*
Euphorbia kamponii: #1 **II** EUPHORBIACEAE
Euphorbia kanalensis: #1 **II** EUPHORBIACEAE
Euphorbia kaokoensis: #1 **II** EUPHORBIACEAE
Euphorbia karroensis: #1 **II** EUPHORBIACEAE
Euphorbia keithii: #1 **II** EUPHORBIACEAE
Euphorbia khandallensis: #1 **II** EUPHORBIACEAE
Euphorbia kibwezensis = *Euphorbia bussei* var. *kibwezensis*
Euphorbia knobelii: #1 **II** EUPHORBIACEAE
Euphorbia knuthii: #1 **II** EUPHORBIACEAE
Euphorbia knuthii ssp. *johnsonii*: #1 **II** EUPHORBIACEAE
Euphorbia knuthii ssp. *knuthii*: #1 **II** EUPHORBIACEAE
Euphorbia kondoi: #1 **II** EUPHORBIACEAE
Euphorbia lacei: #1 **II** EUPHORBIACEAE
Euphorbia lactea: #1 **II** EUPHORBIACEAE
Euphorbia lactiflua: #1 **II** EUPHORBIACEAE
Euphorbia laeta = *Euphorbia dendroides*
Euphorbia lagunillarum = *Euphorbia lupulina*
Euphorbia laikipiensis: #1 **II** EUPHORBIACEAE
Euphorbia lamarckii: #1 **II** EUPHORBIACEAE
Euphorbia lamarckii f. *latibracteata* = *Euphorbia broussonetii*
Euphorbia lamarckii ssp. *regis-jubae* = *Euphorbia regis-jubae*
Euphorbia lamarckii var. *berthelotii* = *Euphorbia berthelotii*
Euphorbia lamarckii var. *despoliata* = *Euphorbia despoliata*
Euphorbia lamarckii var. *pseudodendroides* = *Euphorbia lamarckii*
Euphorbia lambii: (E) Gomeran spurge #1 **II** EUPHORBIACEAE
Euphorbia larica: #1 **II** EUPHORBIACEAE
Euphorbia laro = *Euphorbia tirucalli*
Euphorbia lateriflora: #1 **II** EUPHORBIACEAE
Euphorbia laurentii = *Euphorbia teke*
Euphorbia lavrani: #1 **II** EUPHORBIACEAE
Euphorbia laxiflora = *Euphorbia bubalina*
Euphorbia leandriana: #1 **II** EUPHORBIACEAE
Euphorbia ledienii: #1 **II** EUPHORBIACEAE
Euphorbia ledienii var. *dregei*: #1 **II** EUPHORBIACEAE
Euphorbia ledienii var. *ledienii*: #1 **II** EUPHORBIACEAE
Euphorbia lemaireana: #1 **II** EUPHORBIACEAE
Euphorbia leonensis: #1 **II** EUPHORBIACEAE
Euphorbia leontopoda: #1 **II** EUPHORBIACEAE
Euphorbia letestui: #1 **II** EUPHORBIACEAE
Euphorbia leucodendron: #1 **II** EUPHORBIACEAE
Euphorbia leuconeura: #1 **II** EUPHORBIACEAE
Euphorbia lignosa: #1 **II** EUPHORBIACEAE
Euphorbia ligularia = *Euphorbia neriifolia*
Euphorbia lividiflora: #1 **II** EUPHORBIACEAE
Euphorbia lombardensis = *Euphorbia micracantha*
Euphorbia longibracteata = *Euphorbia monteiri* ssp. *monteiri*
Euphorbia longifolia: #1 **II** EUPHORBIACEAE
Euphorbia longifolia var. *canariensis* = *Euphorbia longifolia*
Euphorbia longispina: #1 **II** EUPHORBIACEAE

Euphorbia longituberculosa: #1 **II** EUPHORBIACEAE
Euphorbia lophogona: #1 **II** EUPHORBIACEAE
Euphorbia lophogona var. *lophogona*: #1 **II** EUPHORBIACEAE
Euphorbia lophogona var. *tenuicaulis*: #1 **II** EUPHORBIACEAE
Euphorbia loricata: #1 **II** EUPHORBIACEAE
Euphorbia louwii: #1 **II** EUPHORBIACEAE
Euphorbia luapulana: #1 **II** EUPHORBIACEAE
Euphorbia lumbricalis: #1 **II** EUPHORBIACEAE
Euphorbia lupulina: #1 **II** EUPHORBIACEAE
Euphorbia lutzenbergeriana = *Euphorbia lupulina*
Euphorbia lydenburgensis: #1 **II** EUPHORBIACEAE
Euphorbia lyttoniana = *Euphorbia pseudocactus*
Euphorbia macella: #1 **II** EUPHORBIACEAE
Euphorbia macowanii = *Euphorbia tuberculata* var. *macowanii*
Euphorbia madagascariensis = *Euphorbia lophogona*
Euphorbia magnicapsula: #1 **II** EUPHORBIACEAE
Euphorbia magnicapsula var. *lacertosa*: #1 **II** EUPHORBIACEAE
Euphorbia magnicapsula var. *magnicapsula*: #1 **II**
   EUPHORBIACEAE
Euphorbia mahabobokensis: #1 **II** EUPHORBIACEAE
Euphorbia mahafalensis: #1 **II** EUPHORBIACEAE
Euphorbia mahafalensis var. *mahafalensis*: #1 **II**
   EUPHORBIACEAE
Euphorbia mahafalensis var. *xanthadenia*: #1 **II**
   EUPHORBIACEAE
Euphorbia mainiana = *Euphorbia milii* var. *splendens*
Euphorbia mainty: #1 **II** EUPHORBIACEAE
Euphorbia makallensis: #1 **II** EUPHORBIACEAE
Euphorbia maleolens: #1 **II** EUPHORBIACEAE
Euphorbia malevola: #1 **II** EUPHORBIACEAE
Euphorbia malevola ssp. *bechuanica*: #1 **II** EUPHORBIACEAE
Euphorbia malevola ssp. *malevola*: #1 **II** EUPHORBIACEAE
Euphorbia mamillosa = *Euphorbia squarrosa*
Euphorbia mammillaris: #1 **II** EUPHORBIACEAE
Euphorbia mammillaris var. *spinosior* = *Euphorbia fimbriata*
Euphorbia mangokyensis: #1 **II** EUPHORBIACEAE
Euphorbia margaretae: #1 **II** EUPHORBIACEAE
Euphorbia marlothiana: #1 **II** EUPHORBIACEAE
Euphorbia marlothii = *Euphorbia monteiri* ssp. *monteiri*
Euphorbia marsabitensis: #1 **II** EUPHORBIACEAE
Euphorbia masirahensis: #1 **II** EUPHORBIACEAE
Euphorbia matabelensis: #1 **II** EUPHORBIACEAE
Euphorbia mauritanica: #1 **II** EUPHORBIACEAE
Euphorbia mauritanica var. *corallothamnus*: #1 **II**
   EUPHORBIACEAE
Euphorbia mauritanica var. *foetens*: #1 **II** EUPHORBIACEAE
Euphorbia mauritanica var. *lignosa*: #1 **II** EUPHORBIACEAE
Euphorbia mauritanica var. *mauritanica*: #1 **II**
   EUPHORBIACEAE
Euphorbia mauritanica var. *minor*: #1 **II** EUPHORBIACEAE
Euphorbia mauritanica var. *namaquensis*: #1 **II**
   EUPHORBIACEAE
Euphorbia mayuranathanii: #1 **II** EUPHORBIACEAE
Euphorbia mbaluensis = *Euphorbia bussei* var. *bussei*
Euphorbia mcvaughii: #1 **II** EUPHORBIACEAE
Euphorbia media = *Euphorbia tirucalli*
Euphorbia media var. *bagshawei* = *Euphorbia tirucalli*
Euphorbia medusae = *Euphorbia caput-medusae*
Euphorbia melanacantha = *Euphorbia milii* var. *splendens*
Euphorbia melanohydrata: #1 **II** EUPHORBIACEAE
Euphorbia melanosticta = *Euphorbia mauritanica* var. *mauritanica*
Euphorbia mellifera = *Euphorbia longifolia*
Euphorbia mellifera var. *canariensis* = *Euphorbia longifolia*
Euphorbia meloformis: #1 **II** EUPHORBIACEAE
Euphorbia meloformis var. *pomiformis* = *Euphorbia meloformis*
Euphorbia meloformis var. *prolifera* = *Euphorbia meloformis*
Euphorbia meloniformis = *Euphorbia meloformis*
Euphorbia memoralis: #1 **II** EUPHORBIACEAE
Euphorbia menelikii = *Euphorbia ampliphylla*
Euphorbia meridionalis: #1 **II** EUPHORBIACEAE
Euphorbia merkeri = *Euphorbia gossypina* var. *gossypina*
Euphorbia meyeri = *Euphorbia filiflora*
Euphorbia micracantha: #1 **II** EUPHORBIACEAE
Euphorbia migiurtinorum: #1 **II** EUPHORBIACEAE
Euphorbia milii: #1 **II** EUPHORBIACEAE

Euphorbia milii f. *lutea* = *Euphorbia milii* var. *milii*
Euphorbia milii var. *betsileana* = *Euphorbia milii* var. *splendens*
Euphorbia milii var. *bevilaniensis*: #1 **II** EUPHORBIACEAE
Euphorbia milii var. *bojeri* = *Euphorbia milii* var. *milii*
Euphorbia milii var. *bosseri* = *Euphorbia neobosseri*
Euphorbia milii var. *breonii* = *Euphorbia milii* var. *hislopii*
Euphorbia milii var. *bulbispina* = *Euphorbia bulbispina*
Euphorbia milii var. *hislopii*: #1 **II** EUPHORBIACEAE
Euphorbia milii var. *imperatae*: #1 **II** EUPHORBIACEAE
Euphorbia milii var. *longifolia*: #1 **II** EUPHORBIACEAE
Euphorbia milii var. *mainiana* = *Euphorbia milii* var. *splendens*
Euphorbia milii var. *milii*: (E) Crown of thorns #1 **II** EUPHORBIACEAE
Euphorbia milii var. *roseana*: #1 **II** EUPHORBIACEAE
Euphorbia milii var. *splendens*: (E) Crown of thorns #1 **II** EUPHORBIACEAE
Euphorbia milii var. *tananarivae*: #1 **II** EUPHORBIACEAE
Euphorbia milii var. *tenuispina*: #1 **II** EUPHORBIACEAE
Euphorbia milii var. *tulearensis*: #1 **II** EUPHORBIACEAE
Euphorbia milii var. *vulcanii*: #1 **II** EUPHORBIACEAE
Euphorbia millotii: #1 **II** EUPHORBIACEAE
Euphorbia mira: #1 **II** EUPHORBIACEAE
Euphorbia miscella = *Euphorbia celata*
Euphorbia misera: (E) Cliff spurge #1 **II** EUPHORBIACEAE
Euphorbia mitis = *Euphorbia heterochroma* ssp. *heterochroma*
Euphorbia mitriformis: #1 **II** EUPHORBIACEAE
Euphorbia mixta: #1 **II** EUPHORBIACEAE
Euphorbia mlanjeana: #1 **II** EUPHORBIACEAE
Euphorbia monacantha: #1 **II** EUPHORBIACEAE
Euphorbia monadenioides: #1 **II** EUPHORBIACEAE
Euphorbia monteiri: #1 **II** EUPHORBIACEAE
Euphorbia monteiri ssp. *brandbergensis*: #1 **II** EUPHORBIACEAE
Euphorbia monteiri ssp. *monteiri*: #1 **II** EUPHORBIACEAE
Euphorbia monteiri ssp. *ramosa*: #1 **II** EUPHORBIACEAE
Euphorbia moratii: **I** EUPHORBIACEAE
Euphorbia moratii var. *antsingiensis*: **I** EUPHORBIACEAE
Euphorbia moratii var. *bemarahensis*: **I** EUPHORBIACEAE
Euphorbia moratii var. *moratii*: **I** EUPHORBIACEAE
Euphorbia moratii var. *multiflora*: **I** EUPHORBIACEAE
Euphorbia morinii = *Euphorbia heptagona* var. *heptagona*
Euphorbia mosaica: #1 **II** EUPHORBIACEAE
Euphorbia muirii: #1 **II** EUPHORBIACEAE
Euphorbia multiceps: #1 **II** EUPHORBIACEAE
Euphorbia multiclava: #1 **II** EUPHORBIACEAE
Euphorbia multifida: #1 **II** EUPHORBIACEAE
Euphorbia multifolia: #1 **II** EUPHORBIACEAE
Euphorbia multiramosa = *Euphorbia friedrichiae*
Euphorbia mundtii: #1 **II** EUPHORBIACEAE
Euphorbia muricata: #1 **II** EUPHORBIACEAE
Euphorbia murielii = *Euphorbia candelabrum* var. *candelabrum*
Euphorbia mwinilungensis: #1 **II** EUPHORBIACEAE
Euphorbia myrioclada: #1 **II** EUPHORBIACEAE
Euphorbia namaquensis = *Euphorbia friedrichiae*
Euphorbia namibensis: #1 **II** EUPHORBIACEAE
Euphorbia namuskluftensis: #1 **II** EUPHORBIACEAE
Euphorbia nana = *Euphorbia fusiformis*
Euphorbia napoides = *Euphorbia hadramautica*
Euphorbia natalensis = *Euphorbia ingens*
Euphorbia ndurumensis = *Euphorbia tenuispinosa* var. *tenuispinosa*
Euphorbia neglecta = *Euphorbia abyssinica*
Euphorbia negromontana: #1 **II** EUPHORBIACEAE
Euphorbia nelii = *Euphorbia filiflora*
Euphorbia neobosseri: #1 **II** EUPHORBIACEAE
Euphorbia neohumbertii: #1 **II** EUPHORBIACEAE
Euphorbia neohumbertii var. *aureoviridiflora* = *Euphorbia aureoviridiflora*
Euphorbia neovolkensii = *Euphorbia nyikae* var. *neovolkensii*
Euphorbia neriifolia: #1 **II** EUPHORBIACEAE
Euphorbia nesemannii: #1 **II** EUPHORBIACEAE
Euphorbia neumanii = *Euphorbia milii* var. *milii*
Euphorbia neutra = *Euphorbia abyssinica*
Euphorbia nigrispina: #1 **II** EUPHORBIACEAE
Euphorbia nigrispinoides: #1 **II** EUPHORBIACEAE

Euphorbia nivulia: #1 **II** EUPHORBIACEAE
Euphorbia nivulia var. *helicothele* = *Euphorbia nivulia*
Euphorbia nogalensis: #1 **II** EUPHORBIACEAE
Euphorbia norfolkiana: #1 **II** EUPHORBIACEAE
Euphorbia nubica: #1 **II** EUPHORBIACEAE
Euphorbia nubica var. *consobrina* = *Euphorbia consobrina*
Euphorbia nubigena: #1 **II** EUPHORBIACEAE
Euphorbia nubigena var. *nubigena*: #1 **II** EUPHORBIACEAE
Euphorbia nubigena var. *rutilans*: #1 **II** EUPHORBIACEAE
Euphorbia nyassae: #1 **II** EUPHORBIACEAE
Euphorbia nyassae ssp. *mentiens* = *Euphorbia perplexa* var. *perplexa*
Euphorbia nyikae: #1 **II** EUPHORBIACEAE
Euphorbia nyikae var. *neovolkensii*: #1 **II** EUPHORBIACEAE
Euphorbia nyikae var. *nyikae*: #1 **II** EUPHORBIACEAE
Euphorbia obesa: #1 **II** EUPHORBIACEAE
Euphorbia oblongicaulis = *Euphorbia hadramautica*
Euphorbia obovalifolia = *Euphorbia abyssinica*
Euphorbia obovalifolia = *Euphorbia ampliphylla*
Euphorbia obtusifolia = *Euphorbia lamarckii*
Euphorbia obtusifolia f. *latibracteata* = *Euphorbia broussonetii*
Euphorbia obtusifolia ssp. *regis-jubae* = *Euphorbia regis-jubae*
Euphorbia obtusifolia var. *despoliata* = *Euphorbia despoliata*
Euphorbia obtusifolia var. *pseudodendroides* = *Euphorbia lamarckii*
Euphorbia odontophora: #1 **II** EUPHORBIACEAE
Euphorbia odontophylla = *Euphorbia cereiformis*
Euphorbia officinarum: #1 **II** EUPHORBIACEAE
Euphorbia officinarum ssp. *beaumieriana* = *Euphorbia officinarum*
Euphorbia officinarum ssp. *echinus* = *Euphorbia echinus*
Euphorbia officinarum var. *arborea* = *Euphorbia ammak*
Euphorbia officinarum var. *hernandez-pachecoi* = *Euphorbia echinus*
Euphorbia officinarum var. *kolquall* = *Euphorbia abyssinica*
Euphorbia officinarum var. *officinarum* = *Euphorbia officinarum*
Euphorbia oligoclada: #1 **II** EUPHORBIACEAE
Euphorbia omariana: #1 **II** EUPHORBIACEAE
Euphorbia oncoclada: #1 **II** EUPHORBIACEAE
Euphorbia opuntioides: #1 **II** EUPHORBIACEAE
Euphorbia orbiculifolia: #1 **II** EUPHORBIACEAE
Euphorbia ornithopus: #1 **II** EUPHORBIACEAE
Euphorbia otjipembana: #1 **II** EUPHORBIACEAE
Euphorbia oxystegia: #1 **II** EUPHORBIACEAE
Euphorbia pachyclada: #1 **II** EUPHORBIACEAE
Euphorbia pachypodioides: #1 **II** EUPHORBIACEAE
Euphorbia paganorum: #1 **II** EUPHORBIACEAE
Euphorbia panchganiensis: #1 **II** EUPHORBIACEAE
Euphorbia papilionum: #1 **II** EUPHORBIACEAE
Euphorbia parciramulosa: #1 **II** EUPHORBIACEAE
Euphorbia parviceps: #1 **II** EUPHORBIACEAE
Euphorbia parvicyathophora: **I** EUPHORBIACEAE
Euphorbia passa = *Euphorbia woodii*
Euphorbia patula = *Euphorbia tridentata*
Euphorbia paulianii: #1 **II** EUPHORBIACEAE
Euphorbia paxiana = *Euphorbia mauritanica* var. *mauritanica*
Euphorbia pedemontana: #1 **II** EUPHORBIACEAE
Euphorbia pedilanthoides: #1 **II** EUPHORBIACEAE
Euphorbia peltigera = *Euphorbia hamata*
Euphorbia pentagona: #1 **II** EUPHORBIACEAE
Euphorbia pentops: #1 **II** EUPHORBIACEAE
Euphorbia perangusta: #1 **II** EUPHORBIACEAE
Euphorbia perarmata: #1 **II** EUPHORBIACEAE
Euphorbia perpera: #1 **II** EUPHORBIACEAE
Euphorbia perplexa: #1 **II** EUPHORBIACEAE
Euphorbia perplexa var. *kasamana*: #1 **II** EUPHORBIACEAE
Euphorbia perplexa var. *perplexa*: #1 **II** EUPHORBIACEAE
Euphorbia perrieri: #1 **II** EUPHORBIACEAE
Euphorbia perrieri var. *elongata*: #1 **II** EUPHORBIACEAE
Euphorbia perrieri var. *perrieri*: #1 **II** EUPHORBIACEAE
Euphorbia perrottetii = *Euphorbia cuneata*
Euphorbia persistens: #1 **II** EUPHORBIACEAE
Euphorbia persistentifolia: #1 **II** EUPHORBIACEAE
Euphorbia petraea: #1 **II** EUPHORBIACEAE
Euphorbia petricola: #1 **II** EUPHORBIACEAE
Euphorbia phillipsiae: #1 **II** EUPHORBIACEAE

Euphorbia phillipsioides: #1 **II** EUPHORBIACEAE
Euphorbia phosphorea: #1 **II** EUPHORBIACEAE
Euphorbia phymatoclada = *Euphorbia mauritanica* var. *mauritanica*
Euphorbia pillansii: #1 **II** EUPHORBIACEAE
Euphorbia pillansii var. *albovirens*: #1 **II** EUPHORBIACEAE
Euphorbia pillansii var. *pillansii*: #1 **II** EUPHORBIACEAE
Euphorbia pillansii var. *ramosissima*: #1 **II** EUPHORBIACEAE
Euphorbia pimeleodendron = *Euphorbia robecchii*
Euphorbia piscatoria: #1 **II** EUPHORBIACEAE
Euphorbia piscidermis: #1 **II** EUPHORBIACEAE
Euphorbia pistiifolia = *Euphorbia ecklonii*
Euphorbia plagiantha: #1 **II** EUPHORBIACEAE
Euphorbia planiceps: #1 **II** EUPHORBIACEAE
Euphorbia platyacantha = *Euphorbia milii* var. *splendens*
Euphorbia platyacantha = *Euphorbia dumeticola*
Euphorbia platycephala: #1 **II** EUPHORBIACEAE
Euphorbia platyclada: #1 **II** EUPHORBIACEAE
Euphorbia platyclada var. *hardyi*: #1 **II** EUPHORBIACEAE
Euphorbia platyclada var. *platyclada*: #1 **II** EUPHORBIACEAE
Euphorbia platymammillaris = *Euphorbia fimbriata*
Euphorbia platyrrhiza: #1 **II** EUPHORBIACEAE
Euphorbia plumerioides: #1 **II** EUPHORBIACEAE
Euphorbia plumerioides var. *acuminata* = *Euphorbia kanalensis*
Euphorbia plumerioides var. *macrocarpa* = *Euphorbia brassii*
Euphorbia plumerioides var. *microphylla* = *Euphorbia kanalensis*
Euphorbia plumerioides var. *plumerioides* = *Euphorbia plumerioides*
Euphorbia poissonii: #1 **II** EUPHORBIACEAE
Euphorbia polyacantha: #1 **II** EUPHORBIACEAE
Euphorbia polyacantha ssp. *rosenii* = *Euphorbia polyacantha*
Euphorbia polyacantha var. *subinarticulata* = *Euphorbia polyacantha*
Euphorbia polycephala: #1 **II** EUPHORBIACEAE
Euphorbia polygona: #1 **II** EUPHORBIACEAE
Euphorbia polygonata = *Euphorbia cereiformis*
Euphorbia pomiformis = *Euphorbia meloformis*
Euphorbia ponderosa: #1 **II** EUPHORBIACEAE
Euphorbia porphyrantha: #1 **II** EUPHORBIACEAE
Euphorbia primulifolia: **II/I** EUPHORBIACEAE
Euphorbia primulifolia var. *begardii*: #1 **II** EUPHORBIACEAE
Euphorbia primulifolia var. *primulifolia*: #1 **II** EUPHORBIACEAE
Euphorbia proballyana: #1 **II** EUPHORBIACEAE
Euphorbia procumbens = *Euphorbia stellata*
Euphorbia prona: #1 **II** EUPHORBIACEAE
Euphorbia proteifolia = *Euphorbia bupleurifolia*
Euphorbia psammophila: #1 **II** EUPHORBIACEAE
Euphorbia pseudobrachiata = *Euphorbia cibdela*
Euphorbia pseudoburuana: #1 **II** EUPHORBIACEAE
Euphorbia pseudocactus: #1 **II** EUPHORBIACEAE
Euphorbia pseudodendroides = *Euphorbia lamarckii*
Euphorbia pseudoduseimata: #1 **II** EUPHORBIACEAE
Euphorbia pseudoglobosa: #1 **II** EUPHORBIACEAE
Euphorbia pseudotuberosa: #1 **II** EUPHORBIACEAE
Euphorbia pteroclada: #1 **II** EUPHORBIACEAE
Euphorbia pteroneura: #1 **II** EUPHORBIACEAE
Euphorbia pubiglans: #1 **II** EUPHORBIACEAE
Euphorbia pugniformis: #1 **II** EUPHORBIACEAE
Euphorbia pulvinata: #1 **II** EUPHORBIACEAE
Euphorbia pyriformis = *Euphorbia meloformis*
Euphorbia qarad: #1 **II** EUPHORBIACEAE
Euphorbia quadrangularis: #1 **II** EUPHORBIACEAE
Euphorbia quadrata: #1 **II** EUPHORBIACEAE
Euphorbia quadrialata: #1 **II** EUPHORBIACEAE
Euphorbia quadrilatera: #1 **II** EUPHORBIACEAE
Euphorbia quadrispina: #1 **II** EUPHORBIACEAE
Euphorbia quaitensis: #1 **II** EUPHORBIACEAE
Euphorbia quartziticola: **I** EUPHORBIACEAE
Euphorbia quinquecostata: #1 **II** EUPHORBIACEAE
Euphorbia racemosa = *Euphorbia rhombifolia*
Euphorbia radians: #1 **II** EUPHORBIACEAE
Euphorbia radians var. *radians*: #1 **II** EUPHORBIACEAE
Euphorbia radians var. *stormiae*: #1 **II** EUPHORBIACEAE
Euphorbia radiata = *Euphorbia stellata*

Euphorbia radiata = *Euphorbia clava*
Euphorbia ramiglans: #1 **II** EUPHORBIACEAE
Euphorbia ramipressa = *Euphorbia epiphylloides*
Euphorbia ramulosa: #1 **II** EUPHORBIACEAE
Euphorbia rangeana = *Euphorbia rudis*
Euphorbia razafinjohanii: #1 **II** EUPHORBIACEAE
Euphorbia reclinata: #1 **II** EUPHORBIACEAE
Euphorbia rectirama: #1 **II** EUPHORBIACEAE
Euphorbia regis-jubae: #1 **II** EUPHORBIACEAE
Euphorbia regis-jubae ssp. *pseudodendroides* = *Euphorbia lamarckii*
Euphorbia reinhardtii = *Euphorbia candelabrum* var. *candelabrum*
Euphorbia reinhardtii var. *bilocularis* = *Euphorbia candelabrum* var. *bilocularis*
Euphorbia reptans: #1 **II** EUPHORBIACEAE
Euphorbia resinifera: #1 **II** EUPHORBIACEAE
Euphorbia restituta: #1 **II** EUPHORBIACEAE
Euphorbia restricta: #1 **II** EUPHORBIACEAE
Euphorbia rhabdodes: #1 **II** EUPHORBIACEAE
Euphorbia rhipsaloides = *Euphorbia tirucalli*
Euphorbia rhipsaloides = *Euphorbia phosphorea*
Euphorbia rhombifolia: #1 **II** EUPHORBIACEAE
Euphorbia rhombifolia var. *cymosa* = *Euphorbia rhombifolia*
Euphorbia rhombifolia var. *laxa* = *Euphorbia rhombifolia*
Euphorbia rhombifolia var. *triceps* = *Euphorbia rhombifolia*
Euphorbia richardiana = *Euphorbia abyssinica*
Euphorbia richardsiae: #1 **II** EUPHORBIACEAE
Euphorbia richardsiae ssp. *richardsiae*: #1 **II** EUPHORBIACEAE
Euphorbia richardsiae ssp. *robusta*: #1 **II** EUPHORBIACEAE
Euphorbia rivae: #1 **II** EUPHORBIACEAE
Euphorbia robecchii: #1 **II** EUPHORBIACEAE
Euphorbia robivelonae: #1 **II** EUPHORBIACEAE
Euphorbia rogeri = *Euphorbia balsamifera*
Euphorbia rossii: #1 **II** EUPHORBIACEAE
Euphorbia rossii f. *glabra* = *Euphorbia rossii*
Euphorbia rowlandii: #1 **II** EUPHORBIACEAE
Euphorbia royleana: #1 **II** EUPHORBIACEAE
Euphorbia rubella: #1 **II** EUPHORBIACEAE
Euphorbia rubella var. *brunellii* = *Euphorbia brunellii*
Euphorbia rubrimarginata: #1 **II** EUPHORBIACEAE
Euphorbia rubriseminalis: #1 **II** EUPHORBIACEAE
Euphorbia rubrispinosa: #1 **II** EUPHORBIACEAE
Euphorbia rubrostriata = *Euphorbia milii* var. *splendens*
Euphorbia rudis: #1 **II** EUPHORBIACEAE
Euphorbia rudolfii: #1 **II** EUPHORBIACEAE
Euphorbia rugosiflora: #1 **II** EUPHORBIACEAE
Euphorbia ruspolii = *Euphorbia robecchii*
Euphorbia sagittaria = *Euphorbia avasmontana* var. *sagittaria*
Euphorbia sakarahaensis: #1 **II** EUPHORBIACEAE
Euphorbia samburuensis: #1 **II** EUPHORBIACEAE
Euphorbia sancta = *Euphorbia ampliphylla*
Euphorbia santapaui: #1 **II** EUPHORBIACEAE
Euphorbia sapinii: #1 **II** EUPHORBIACEAE
Euphorbia sarcodes: #1 **II** EUPHORBIACEAE
Euphorbia sarcostemmatoides = *Euphorbia mauritanica* var. *mauritanica*
Euphorbia sarcostemmoides: #1 **II** EUPHORBIACEAE
Euphorbia saxorum: #1 **II** EUPHORBIACEAE
Euphorbia scarlatina: #1 **II** EUPHORBIACEAE
Euphorbia schaeferi = *Euphorbia gariepina* ssp. *gariepina*
Euphorbia schimperi: #1 **II** EUPHORBIACEAE
Euphorbia schinzii: #1 **II** EUPHORBIACEAE
Euphorbia schizacantha: #1 **II** EUPHORBIACEAE
Euphorbia schmitzii: #1 **II** EUPHORBIACEAE
Euphorbia schoenlandii: #1 **II** EUPHORBIACEAE
Euphorbia scitula: #1 **II** EUPHORBIACEAE
Euphorbia scolopendrea = *Euphorbia stellata*
Euphorbia scoparia = *Euphorbia tirucalli*
Euphorbia scopiformis = *Euphorbia arceuthobioides*
Euphorbia scopoliana = *Euphorbia fimbriata*
Euphorbia scyphadena: #1 **II** EUPHORBIACEAE
Euphorbia sebsebei: #1 **II** EUPHORBIACEAE
Euphorbia sekukuniensis: #1 **II** EUPHORBIACEAE
Euphorbia semperflorens: #1 **II** EUPHORBIACEAE
Euphorbia sepium = *Euphorbia balsamifera*

Euphorbia septemsulcata = *Euphorbia spiralis*
Euphorbia septentrionalis: #1 **II** EUPHORBIACEAE
Euphorbia septentrionalis ssp. *gamugofana*: #1 **II** EUPHORBIACEAE
Euphorbia septentrionalis ssp. *septentrionalis*: #1 **II** EUPHORBIACEAE
Euphorbia sepulta: #1 **II** EUPHORBIACEAE
Euphorbia serendipita: #1 **II** EUPHORBIACEAE
Euphorbia seretii: #1 **II** EUPHORBIACEAE
Euphorbia seretii ssp. *seretii*: #1 **II** EUPHORBIACEAE
Euphorbia seretii ssp. *variantissima*: #1 **II** EUPHORBIACEAE
Euphorbia sessiliflora: #1 **II** EUPHORBIACEAE
Euphorbia setispina: #1 **II** EUPHORBIACEAE
Euphorbia silenifolia: #1 **II** EUPHORBIACEAE
Euphorbia siliciicola = *Euphorbia juttae*
Euphorbia similiramea: #1 **II** EUPHORBIACEAE
Euphorbia similis = *Euphorbia ingens*
Euphorbia sipolisii: #1 **II** EUPHORBIACEAE
Euphorbia spartaria: #1 **II** EUPHORBIACEAE
Euphorbia spatulata = *Euphorbia thouarsiana*
Euphorbia speciosa: #1 **II** EUPHORBIACEAE
Euphorbia spicata: #1 **II** EUPHORBIACEAE
Euphorbia spinea: #1 **II** EUPHORBIACEAE
Euphorbia spiralis: #1 **II** EUPHORBIACEAE
Euphorbia splendens = *Euphorbia milii* var. *splendens*
Euphorbia splendens ssp. *bojeri* = *Euphorbia milii* var. *milii*
Euphorbia splendens var. *betsileana* = *Euphorbia milii* var. *splendens*
Euphorbia splendens var. *bevilaniensis* = *Euphorbia milii* var. *bevilaniensis*
Euphorbia splendens var. *bojeri* = *Euphorbia milii* var. *milii*
Euphorbia splendens var. *breonii* = *Euphorbia milii* var. *hislopii*
Euphorbia splendens var. *hislopii* = *Euphorbia milii* var. *hislopii*
Euphorbia splendens var. *imperatae* = *Euphorbia milii* var. *imperatae*
Euphorbia splendens var. *tananarivae* = *Euphorbia milii* var. *tananarivae*
Euphorbia splendens var. *typica* = *Euphorbia milii* var. *splendens*
Euphorbia splendens var. *vulcanii* = *Euphorbia milii* var. *vulcanii*
Euphorbia squarrosa: #1 **II** EUPHORBIACEAE
Euphorbia stapelioides: #1 **II** EUPHORBIACEAE
Euphorbia stapfii: #1 **II** EUPHORBIACEAE
Euphorbia stegmatica = *Euphorbia oxystegia*
Euphorbia stellaespina = *Euphorbia stellispina*
Euphorbia stellaespina var. *astrispina* = *Euphorbia stellispina* var. *astrispina*
Euphorbia stellaespina var. *stellaespina* = *Euphorbia stellispina* var. *stellispina*
Euphorbia stellata: #1 **II** EUPHORBIACEAE
Euphorbia stellispina: #1 **II** EUPHORBIACEAE
Euphorbia stellispina var. *astrispina*: #1 **II** EUPHORBIACEAE
Euphorbia stellispina var. *stellispina*: #1 **II** EUPHORBIACEAE
Euphorbia stenoclada: #1 **II** EUPHORBIACEAE
Euphorbia stenoclada f. *globulosa* = *Euphorbia stenoclada* ssp. *stenoclada*
Euphorbia stenoclada f. *laevigata* = *Euphorbia stenoclada* ssp. *stenoclada*
Euphorbia stenoclada f. *striata* = *Euphorbia stenoclada* ssp. *stenoclada*
Euphorbia stenoclada ssp. *ambatofinandranae*: #1 **II** EUPHORBIACEAE
Euphorbia stenoclada ssp. *stenoclada*: #1 **II** EUPHORBIACEAE
Euphorbia stolonifera: #1 **II** EUPHORBIACEAE
Euphorbia stormiae = *Euphorbia radians* var. *stormiae*
Euphorbia strangulata: #1 **II** EUPHORBIACEAE
Euphorbia strangulata ssp. *deminuens*: #1 **II** EUPHORBIACEAE
Euphorbia strangulata ssp. *strangulata*: #1 **II** EUPHORBIACEAE
Euphorbia strigosa: #1 **II** EUPHORBIACEAE
Euphorbia stuhlmannii = *Euphorbia heterochroma* ssp. *heterochroma*
Euphorbia stygiana: #1 **II** EUPHORBIACEAE
Euphorbia suareziana = *Euphorbia tirucalli*
Euphorbia subapoda = *Euphorbia primulifolia* var. *primulifolia*
Euphorbia subfalcata = *Euphorbia trichadenia*
Euphorbia submammillaris: #1 **II** EUPHORBIACEAE

Euphorbia subsalsa: #1 **II** EUPHORBIACEAE
Euphorbia subsalsa ssp. *fluvialis*: #1 **II** EUPHORBIACEAE
Euphorbia subsalsa ssp. *subsalsa*: #1 **II** EUPHORBIACEAE
Euphorbia subsalsa var. *kaokoensis* = *Euphorbia kaokoensis*
Euphorbia subscandens: #1 **II** EUPHORBIACEAE
Euphorbia subumbellata = *Euphorbia copiapina*
Euphorbia sudanica: #1 **II** EUPHORBIACEAE
Euphorbia suffulta: #1 **II** EUPHORBIACEAE
Euphorbia superans: #1 **II** EUPHORBIACEAE
Euphorbia susan-holmesiae: #1 **II** EUPHORBIACEAE
Euphorbia susannae: #1 **II** EUPHORBIACEAE
Euphorbia suzannae-marnierae: #1 **II** EUPHORBIACEAE
Euphorbia symmetrica: #1 **II** EUPHORBIACEAE
Euphorbia taboraensis: #1 **II** EUPHORBIACEAE
Euphorbia taitensis = *Euphorbia tenuispinosa* var. *tenuispinosa*
Euphorbia tanaensis: #1 **II** EUPHORBIACEAE
Euphorbia tardieuana: #1 **II** EUPHORBIACEAE
Euphorbia taruensis: #1 **II** EUPHORBIACEAE
Euphorbia teixeirae: #1 **II** EUPHORBIACEAE
Euphorbia teke: #1 **II** EUPHORBIACEAE
Euphorbia tellieri = *Euphorbia sudanica*
Euphorbia tenax: #1 **II** EUPHORBIACEAE
Euphorbia tenebrosa = *Euphorbia ingens*
Euphorbia tenuispinosa: #1 **II** EUPHORBIACEAE
Euphorbia tenuispinosa var. *robusta*: #1 **II** EUPHORBIACEAE
Euphorbia tenuispinosa var. *tenuispinosa*: #1 **II** EUPHORBIACEAE
Euphorbia tescorum: #1 **II** EUPHORBIACEAE
Euphorbia tetracantha: #1 **II** EUPHORBIACEAE
Euphorbia tetracanthoides: #1 **II** EUPHORBIACEAE
Euphorbia tetragona: #1 **II** EUPHORBIACEAE
Euphorbia thi = *Euphorbia polyacantha*
Euphorbia thi var. *subinarticulata* = *Euphorbia polyacantha*
Euphorbia thinophila: #1 **II** EUPHORBIACEAE
Euphorbia tholicola: #1 **II** EUPHORBIACEAE
Euphorbia thouarsiana: #1 **II** EUPHORBIACEAE
Euphorbia tirucalli: #1 **II** EUPHORBIACEAE
Euphorbia tirucalli var. *rhipsaloides* = *Euphorbia tirucalli*
Euphorbia tisserantii = *Euphorbia teke*
Euphorbia togoensis = *Euphorbia lateriflora*
Euphorbia torta: #1 **II** EUPHORBIACEAE
Euphorbia tortilis: #1 **II** EUPHORBIACEAE
Euphorbia tortirama: #1 **II** EUPHORBIACEAE
Euphorbia tortistyla: #1 **II** EUPHORBIACEAE
Euphorbia tozzii = *Euphorbia candelabrum* var. *candelabrum*
Euphorbia transvaalensis: #1 **II** EUPHORBIACEAE
Euphorbia trapaeifolia = *Euphorbia sudanica*
Euphorbia triacantha = *Euphorbia triaculeata*
Euphorbia triaculeata: #1 **II** EUPHORBIACEAE
Euphorbia triaculeata var. *triacantha* = *Euphorbia triaculeata*
Euphorbia triangularis: #1 **II** EUPHORBIACEAE
Euphorbia trichadenia: #1 **II** EUPHORBIACEAE
Euphorbia trichadenia var. *gibbsiae*: #1 **II** EUPHORBIACEAE
Euphorbia trichadenia var. *trichadenia*: #1 **II** EUPHORBIACEAE
Euphorbia tridentata: #1 **II** EUPHORBIACEAE
Euphorbia trigona: #1 **II**[3] EUPHORBIACEAE
Euphorbia truncata = *Euphorbia clavarioides* var. *truncata*
Euphorbia tsimbazazae: #1 **II** EUPHORBIACEAE
Euphorbia tuberculata: #1 **II** EUPHORBIACEAE
Euphorbia tuberculata var. *cristata* = *Euphorbia tuberculata* var. *tuberculata*
Euphorbia tuberculata var. *macowanii*: #1 **II** EUPHORBIACEAE
Euphorbia tuberculata var. *tuberculata*: #1 **II** EUPHORBIACEAE
Euphorbia tuberculatoides: #1 **II** EUPHORBIACEAE
Euphorbia tuberosa: #1 **II** EUPHORBIACEAE
Euphorbia tubiglans: #1 **II** EUPHORBIACEAE
Euphorbia tuckeyana: #1 **II** EUPHORBIACEAE

---

[3] Artificially propagated specimens or cultivars are not subject to the provisions of the Convention/los especímenes reproducidos artificialmente de cultivares no están sujetos a las disposiciones de la Convención/les spécimens reproduits artificiellement de cultivars ne sont pas soumis aux dispositions de la Convention

Euphorbia tuckeyana var. *mezereum*: #1 **II** EUPHORBIACEAE
Euphorbia tuckeyana var. *tuckeyana*: #1 **II** EUPHORBIACEAE
Euphorbia tugelensis: #1 **II** EUPHORBIACEAE
Euphorbia tulearensis: **I** EUPHORBIACEAE
Euphorbia turbiniformis: #1 **II** EUPHORBIACEAE
Euphorbia turkanensis: #1 **II** EUPHORBIACEAE
Euphorbia uhehensis = Euphorbia platycephala
Euphorbia uhligiana: #1 **II** EUPHORBIACEAE
Euphorbia umbonata: #1 **II** EUPHORBIACEAE
Euphorbia umfoloziensis: #1 **II** EUPHORBIACEAE
Euphorbia uncinata = Euphorbia stellata
Euphorbia undulatifolia: #1 **II** EUPHORBIACEAE
Euphorbia unicornis: #1 **II** EUPHORBIACEAE
Euphorbia unispina: #1 **II** EUPHORBIACEAE
Euphorbia ussanguensis = Euphorbia cooperi var. *ussanguensis*
Euphorbia uzmuk: #1 **II** EUPHORBIACEAE
Euphorbia vaalputsiana: #1 **II** EUPHORBIACEAE
Euphorbia vajravelui: #1 **II** EUPHORBIACEAE
Euphorbia valida: #1 **II** EUPHORBIACEAE
Euphorbia vallaris: #1 **II** EUPHORBIACEAE
Euphorbia vandermerwei: #1 **II** EUPHORBIACEAE
Euphorbia venenata: #1 **II** EUPHORBIACEAE
Euphorbia venenifica: #1 **II** EUPHORBIACEAE
Euphorbia verruculosa: #1 **II** EUPHORBIACEAE
Euphorbia versicolores: #1 **II** EUPHORBIACEAE
Euphorbia viduiflora: #1 **II** EUPHORBIACEAE
Euphorbia viguieri: #1 **II** EUPHORBIACEAE
Euphorbia viguieri var. *ankarafantsiensis*: #1 **II** EUPHORBIACEAE
Euphorbia viguieri var. *capuroniana*: #1 **II** EUPHORBIACEAE
Euphorbia viguieri var. *tsimbazazae*: #1 **II** EUPHORBIACEAE
Euphorbia viguieri var. *viguieri*: #1 **II** EUPHORBIACEAE
Euphorbia viguieri var. *vilanandrensis*: #1 **II** EUPHORBIACEAE
Euphorbia viminalis = Euphorbia burmannii
Euphorbia viperina = Euphorbia inermis var. *inermis*
Euphorbia virgata = Euphorbia lamarckii
Euphorbia virosa: #1 **II** EUPHORBIACEAE
Euphorbia virosa f. *caespitosa = Euphorbia virosa* ssp. *virosa*
Euphorbia virosa f. *striata = Euphorbia virosa* ssp. *virosa*
Euphorbia virosa ssp. *arenicola*: #1 **II** EUPHORBIACEAE
Euphorbia virosa ssp. *virosa*: #1 **II** EUPHORBIACEAE
Euphorbia virosa var. *caerulescens = Euphorbia caerulescens*
Euphorbia vittata: #1 **II** EUPHORBIACEAE
Euphorbia volkensii = Euphorbia nyikae var. *neovolkensii*
Euphorbia volkmanniae: #1 **II** EUPHORBIACEAE
Euphorbia vulcanorum: #1 **II** EUPHORBIACEAE
Euphorbia wakefieldii: #1 **II** EUPHORBIACEAE
Euphorbia waterbergensis: #1 **II** EUPHORBIACEAE
Euphorbia weberbaueri: #1 **II** EUPHORBIACEAE
Euphorbia whellanii: #1 **II** EUPHORBIACEAE
Euphorbia wildii: #1 **II** EUPHORBIACEAE
Euphorbia williamsonii: #1 **II** EUPHORBIACEAE
Euphorbia wilmaniae: #1 **II** EUPHORBIACEAE
Euphorbia winkleri = Euphorbia ampliphylla
Euphorbia woodii: #1 **II** EUPHORBIACEAE
Euphorbia xanthadenia = Euphorbia mahafalensis var. *xanthadenia*
Euphorbia xanti: #1 **II** EUPHORBIACEAE
Euphorbia xylacantha: #1 **II** EUPHORBIACEAE
Euphorbia zoutpansbergensis: #1 **II** EUPHORBIACEAE
Euphorbias (E): *Euphorbia* spp.
Euphorbion dendroides = Euphorbia dendroides
Euphroboscis = Thelasis
European cyclamen (E): *Cyclamen purpurascens* f. *purpurascens*
Eurycentrum spp.: #7 **II** ORCHIDACEAE
Eurychone spp.: #7 **II** ORCHIDACEAE
Eurystyles spp.: #7 **II** ORCHIDACEAE
Evelyna = Elleanthus
Evota = Ceratandra
Evotella spp.: #7 **II** ORCHIDACEAE
Evrardia = Evrardianthe
Evrardiana = Evrardianthe
Evrardianthe spp.: #7 **II** ORCHIDACEAE
Exeria = Eria
Exophya = Epidendrum

Facheiroa cephaliomelana: #4 **II** CACTACEAE
Facheiroa cephaliomelana ssp. *cephaliomelana*: #4 **II** CACTACEAE
Facheiroa cephaliomelana ssp. *estevesii*: #4 **II** CACTACEAE
Facheiroa chaetacantha = Facheiroa squamosa
Facheiroa estevesii = Facheiroa cephaliomelana ssp. *estevesii*
Facheiroa pilosa = Facheiroa cephaliomelana ssp. *cephaliomelana*
Facheiroa pubiflora = Facheiroa ulei
Facheiroa squamosa: #4 **II** CACTACEAE
Facheiroa squamosa ssp. *polygona = Facheiroa squamosa*
Facheiroa tenebrosa = Facheiroa cephaliomelana ssp. *cephaliomelana*
Facheiroa ulei: #4 **II** CACTACEAE
False alerce chileno (S): *Fitzroya cupressoides*
Feather palm (E): *Neodypsis decaryi*
Fernandezia spp.: #7 **II** ORCHIDACEAE
Ferocactus acanthodes = Ferocactus cylindraceus
Ferocactus alamosanus: #4 **II** CACTACEAE
Ferocactus alamosanus ssp. *alamosanus*: #4 **II** CACTACEAE
Ferocactus alamosanus ssp. *reppenhagenii*: #4 **II** CACTACEAE
Ferocactus bicolor = Thelocactus bicolor ssp. *bicolor*
Ferocactus bicolor var. *flavidispinus = Thelocactus bicolor* ssp. *flavidispinus*
Ferocactus bicolor var. *schwarzii = Thelocactus bicolor* ssp. *schwarzii*
Ferocactus chrysacanthus: #4 **II** CACTACEAE
Ferocactus chrysacanthus ssp. *chrysacanthus*: #4 **II** CACTACEAE
Ferocactus chrysacanthus ssp. *grandiflorus*: #4 **II** CACTACEAE
Ferocactus coloratus = Ferocactus gracilis ssp. *coloratus*
Ferocactus covillei = Ferocactus emoryi ssp. *emoryi*
Ferocactus cylindraceus: #4 **II** CACTACEAE
Ferocactus cylindraceus ssp. *cylindraceus*: #4 **II** CACTACEAE
Ferocactus cylindraceus ssp. *lecontei*: #4 **II** CACTACEAE
Ferocactus cylindraceus ssp. *tortulispinus*: #4 **II** CACTACEAE
Ferocactus diguetii: #4 **II** CACTACEAE
Ferocactus eastwoodiae: #4 **II** CACTACEAE
Ferocactus echidne: #4 **II** CACTACEAE
Ferocactus emoryi: (E) Covill's barrel cactus #4 **II** CACTACEAE
Ferocactus emoryi ssp. *emoryi*: #4 **II** CACTACEAE
Ferocactus emoryi ssp. *rectispinus*: #4 **II** CACTACEAE
Ferocactus flavovirens: #4 **II** CACTACEAE
Ferocactus fordii: #4 **II** CACTACEAE
Ferocactus gatesii = Ferocactus gracilis ssp. *gatesii*
Ferocactus glaucescens: #4 **II** CACTACEAE
Ferocactus glaucus = Sclerocactus glaucus
Ferocactus gracilis: #4 **II** CACTACEAE
Ferocactus gracilis ssp. *coloratus*: #4 **II** CACTACEAE
Ferocactus gracilis ssp. *gatesii*: #4 **II** CACTACEAE
Ferocactus gracilis ssp. *gracilis*: #4 **II** CACTACEAE
Ferocactus haematacanthus: #4 **II** CACTACEAE
Ferocactus hamatacanthus: #4 **II** CACTACEAE
Ferocactus hamatacanthus ssp. *hamatacanthus*: #4 **II** CACTACEAE
Ferocactus hamatacanthus ssp. *sinuatus*: #4 **II** CACTACEAE
Ferocactus hastifer = Thelocactus hastifer
Ferocactus herrerae: #4 **II** CACTACEAE
Ferocactus hertrichii = Ferocactus cylindraceus ssp. *lecontei*
Ferocactus heterochromus = Thelocactus heterochromus
Ferocactus histrix: #4 **II** CACTACEAE
Ferocactus horridus = Ferocactus peninsulae
Ferocactus johnstonianus: #4 **II** CACTACEAE
Ferocactus latispinus: #4 **II** CACTACEAE
Ferocactus latispinus ssp. *latispinus*: #4 **II** CACTACEAE
Ferocactus latispinus ssp. *spiralis*: #4 **II** CACTACEAE
Ferocactus lecontei = Ferocactus cylindraceus ssp. *lecontei*
Ferocactus leucacanthus = Thelocactus leucacanthus
Ferocactus lindsayi: #4 **II** CACTACEAE
Ferocactus macrodiscus: #4 **II** CACTACEAE
Ferocactus macrodiscus ssp. *macrodiscus*: #4 **II** CACTACEAE
Ferocactus macrodiscus ssp. *septentrionalis*: #4 **II** CACTACEAE
Ferocactus mathssonii = Sclerocactus uncinatus ssp. *crassihamatus*
Ferocactus melocactiformis = Ferocactus histrix
Ferocactus nobilis = Ferocactus latispinus
Ferocactus orcuttii = Ferocactus viridescens

Ferocactus peninsulae: #4 **II** CACTACEAE
Ferocactus peninsulae ssp. *santa-maria*: #4 **II** CACTACEAE
Ferocactus pfeifferi = *Ferocactus glaucescens*
Ferocactus piliferus = *Ferocactus pilosus*
Ferocactus pilosus: #4 **II** CACTACEAE
Ferocactus pottsii: #4 **II** CACTACEAE
Ferocactus pringlei = *Ferocactus pilosus*
Ferocactus rectispinus = *Ferocactus emoryi* ssp. *rectispinus*
Ferocactus recurvus = *Ferocactus latispinus*
Ferocactus reppenhagenii = *Ferocactus alamosanus* ssp.
    reppenhagenii
Ferocactus rhodanthus = *Ferocactus echidne*
Ferocactus robustus: #4 **II** CACTACEAE
Ferocactus rostii = *Ferocactus cylindraceus*
Ferocactus santa-maria: #4 **II** CACTACEAE
Ferocactus schwarzii: #4 **II** CACTACEAE
Ferocactus setispinus = *Thelocactus setispinus*
Ferocactus stainesii = *Ferocactus pilosus*
Ferocactus tiburonensis: #4 **II** CACTACEAE
Ferocactus tobuschii = *Sclerocactus brevihamatus* ssp. *tobuschii*
Ferocactus tortulispinus = *Ferocactus cylindraceus* ssp.
    tortulispinus
Ferocactus tortulospinus = *Ferocactus cylindraceus* ssp.
    tortulispinus
Ferocactus townsendianus: #4 **II** CACTACEAE
Ferocactus victoriensis = *Ferocactus echidne*
Ferocactus viridescens: (E) Coast Barrel Cactus, San Diego Barrel
    Cactus #4 **II** CACTACEAE
Ferocactus viscainensis = *Ferocactus gracilis* ssp. *coloratus*
Ferocactus wislizeni var. *tiburonensis* = *Ferocactus tiburonensis*
Few-spined Turk's-cap cactus (E): *Melocactus paucispinus*
Fickeisen hedgehog-cactus (E): *Pediocactus peeblesianus* var.
    fickeiseniae
Fieldia = *Vandopsis*
Fimbriella = *Platanthera*
Finetia = *Neofinetia*
Fissipes = *Cypripedium*
Fitch's hedgehog cactus (E): *Echinocereus reichenbachii* ssp. *fitchii*
Fitroia (F): *Fitzroya cupressoides*
Fitzgeraldia = *Lyperanthus*
Fitzroya cupressoides: (E) Chilean false larch, Patagonian cypress,
    (S) Alerce, Ciprés de la Patagonia, False alerce chileno, Lahual
    (F) Bois d'Alerce, Fitroia, **I** CUPRESSACEAE
Fitzroya patagonica = *Fitzroya cupressoides*
Flickingeria spp.: #7 **II** ORCHIDACEAE
Floribunda bahiensis = *Arrojadoa bahiensis*
Floribunda pusilliflora = *Cipocereus pusilliflorus*
Florida arrowroot (E): *Zamia integrifolia*
Florida coontie (E): *Zamia integrifolia*
Forbesina = *Eria*
Forficaria spp.: #7 **II** ORCHIDACEAE
Fouquieria columnaris: (E) Boojum tree, (S) Cirio #1 **II**
    FOUQUIERIACEAE
Fouquieria fasciculata: (S) Arbol del barril **I** FOUQUIERIACEAE
Fouquieria purpusii: **I** FOUQUIERIACEAE
Fractiunguis = *Reichenbachanthus*
Fragrant prickly-apple cactus (E): *Harrisia eriophora/ Harrisia*
    fragrans
Fragrant woolly cactus (E): *Harrisia eriophora/ Harrisia fragrans*
Frailea alacriportana = *Frailea gracillima* ssp. *gracillima*
Frailea albiareolata = *Frailea pumila*
Frailea albicolumnaris = *Frailea pygmaea* ssp. *albicolumnaris*
Frailea albifusca = *Frailea gracillima* ssp. *gracillima*
Frailea asperispina = *Frailea pygmaea* ssp. *pygmaea*
Frailea aureinitens = *Frailea pygmaea* ssp. *pygmaea*
Frailea aureispina = *Frailea pygmaea* ssp. *pygmaea*
Frailea buenekeri: #4 **II** CACTACEAE
Frailea buenekeri ssp. *densispina*: #4 **II** CACTACEAE
Frailea buiningiana: #4 **II** CACTACEAE
Frailea carminifilamentosa = *Frailea pumila*
Frailea castanea: #4 **II** CACTACEAE
Frailea castanea ssp. *harmoniana*: #4 **II** CACTACEAE
Frailea cataphracta: #4 **II** CACTACEAE
Frailea cataphracta ssp. *cataphracta*: #4 **II** CACTACEAE
Frailea cataphracta ssp. *duchii*: #4 **II** CACTACEAE

Frailea cataphracta ssp. *melitae* = *Frailea cataphracta* ssp. *duchii*
Frailea cataphracta ssp. *tuyensis* = *Frailea cataphracta* ssp.
    cataphracta
Frailea cataphractoides = *Frailea cataphracta* ssp. *duchii*
Frailea chiquitana: #4 **II** CACTACEAE
Frailea chrysacantha = *Frailea pumila*
Frailea colombiana = *Frailea pumila*
Frailea concepcionensis = *Frailea schilinzkyana*
Frailea curvispina: #4 **II** CACTACEAE
Frailea deminuta = *Frailea pumila* ssp. *deminuta*
Frailea friedrichii: #4 **II** CACTACEAE
Frailea fulviseta = *Frailea pygmaea* ssp. *fulviseta*
Frailea gracillima: #4 **II** CACTACEAE
Frailea gracillima ssp. *alacriportana* = *Frailea gracillima* ssp.
    gracillima
Frailea gracillima ssp. *albifusca* = *Frailea gracillima* ssp.
    gracillima
Frailea gracillima ssp. *gracillima*: #4 **II** CACTACEAE
Frailea gracillima ssp. *horstii*: #4 **II** CACTACEAE
Frailea grahliana: #4 **II** CACTACEAE
Frailea grahliana ssp. *concepcionensis* = *Frailea schilinzkyana*
Frailea grahliana ssp. *moseriana*: #4 **II** CACTACEAE
Frailea grahliana ssp. *ybatensis* = *Frailea schilinzkyana*
Frailea hlineckyana = *Frailea pumila*
Frailea horstii = *Frailea gracillima* ssp. *horstii*
Frailea horstii ssp. *fecotrigensis* = *Frailea gracillima* ssp. *horstii*
Frailea ignacionensis = *Frailea schilinzkyana*
Frailea jajoiana = *Frailea pumila*
Frailea knippeliana: #4 **II** CACTACEAE
Frailea larae = *Frailea chiquitana*
Frailea lepida = *Frailea gracillima* ssp. *gracillima*
Frailea magnifica = *Frailea mammifera*
Frailea mammifera: #4 **II** CACTACEAE
Frailea matoana = *Frailea cataphracta* ssp. *duchii*
Frailea melitae = *Frailea cataphracta* ssp. *duchii*
Frailea moseriana = *Frailea grahliana* ssp. *moseriana*
Frailea perbella = *Frailea phaeodisca*
Frailea perumbilicata: #4 **II** CACTACEAE
Frailea phaeodisca: #4 **II** CACTACEAE
Frailea pseudogracillima = *Frailea gracillima* ssp. *gracillima*
Frailea pseudopulcherrima: #4 **II** CACTACEAE
Frailea pulcherrima = *Frailea pygmaea*
Frailea pullispina = *Frailea chiquitana*
Frailea pumila: #4 **II** CACTACEAE
Frailea pumila ssp. *albiareolata* = *Frailea pumila*
Frailea pumila ssp. *colombiana* = *Frailea pumila*
Frailea pumila ssp. *deminuta*: #4 **II** CACTACEAE
Frailea pumila ssp. *hlineckyana* = *Frailea pumila*
Frailea pumila ssp. *jajoiana* = *Frailea pumila*
Frailea pumila ssp. *maior* = *Frailea pumila*
Frailea pygmaea: #4 **II** CACTACEAE
Frailea pygmaea ssp. *albicolumnaris*: #4 **II** CACTACEAE
Frailea pygmaea ssp. *altigibbera* = *Frailea pygmaea* ssp. *pygmaea*
Frailea pygmaea ssp. *asperispina* = *Frailea pygmaea* ssp. *pygmaea*
Frailea pygmaea ssp. *aureinitens* = *Frailea pygmaea* ssp. *pygmaea*
Frailea pygmaea ssp. *aureispina* = *Frailea pygmaea* ssp. *pygmaea*
Frailea pygmaea ssp. *fulviseta*: #4 **II** CACTACEAE
Frailea pygmaea ssp. *lilalunula* = *Frailea pygmaea* ssp. *pygmaea*
Frailea pygmaea ssp. *pygmaea*: #4 **II** CACTACEAE
Frailea schilinzkyana: #4 **II** CACTACEAE
Frailea schilinzkyana ssp. *concepcionensis* = *Frailea schilinzkyana*
Frailea uhligiana = *Frailea cataphracta* ssp. *duchii*
Frailea ybatensis = *Frailea schilinzkyana*
Fregea = *Sobralia*
Frondaria spp.: #7 **II** ORCHIDACEAE
Froscula = *Dendrobium*
Fuertesiella spp.: #7 **II** ORCHIDACEAE
Funkiella = *Schiedeella*
Gabertia = *Grammatophyllum*
Gaïac (F): *Guaiacum* spp.
Galanthus spp.: (E) snowdrops, (F) perceneige, (S) campanillas de
    nieve, copo de nieve #1 **II** AMARYLLIDACEAE
Galanthus alexandrii = *Galanthus nivalis*
Galanthus alpinus: #1 **II** AMARYLLIDACEAE
Galanthus alpinus var. *alpinus*: #1 **II** AMARYLLIDACEAE

Checklist of flora/Lista de especies de flora/Liste des espèces végétales

Galanthus alpinus var. *bortkewitschianus*: #1 **II**
    AMARYLLIDACEAE
Galanthus angustifolius: #1 **II** AMARYLLIDACEAE
Galanthus atkinsii = *Galanthus nivalis*
Galanthus bortkewitschianus = *Galanthus alpinus* var.
    bortkewitschianus
Galanthus bulgaricus = *Galanthus elwesii*
Galanthus byzantinus = *Galanthus plicatus* ssp. *byzantinus*
Galanthus byzantinus ssp. *brauneri* = *Galanthus plicatus* ssp.
    byzantinus
Galanthus byzantinus ssp. *saueri* = *Galanthus plicatus* ssp.
    byzantinus
Galanthus byzantinus ssp. *tughrulii* = *Galanthus plicatus* ssp.
    byzantinus
Galanthus cabardensis = *Galanthus lagodechianus*
Galanthus caspius = *Galanthus transcaucasicus*
Galanthus caucasicus = *Galanthus alpinus* var. *alpinus*
Galanthus caucasicus var. *hiemalis* = *Galanthus elwesii*
Galanthus cilicicus = *Galanthus rizehensis*
Galanthus cilicicus = *Galanthus peshmenii*
Galanthus cilicicus: #1 **II** AMARYLLIDACEAE
Galanthus cilicicus ssp. *caucasicus* = *Galanthus alpinus* var.
    alpinus
Galanthus clusii = *Galanthus plicatus* ssp. *plicatus*
Galanthus corcynensis (sic) = *Galanthus reginae-olgae* ssp.
    reginae-olgae
Galanthus corcyrensis = *Galanthus reginae-olgae* ssp. *reginae-*
    olgae
Galanthus corcyrensis (*praecox*) = *Galanthus reginae-olgae* ssp.
    reginae-olgae
Galanthus elsae = *Galanthus reginae-olgae* ssp. *reginae-olgae*
Galanthus elwesii: #1 **II** AMARYLLIDACEAE
Galanthus elwesii ssp. *akmanii* = *Galanthus elwesii*
Galanthus elwesii ssp. *baytopii* = *Galanthus elwesii*
Galanthus elwesii ssp. *melihae* = *Galanthus elwesii*
Galanthus elwesii ssp. *minor* = *Galanthus gracilis*
Galanthus elwesii ssp. *monostictus* = *Galanthus elwesii*
Galanthus elwesii ssp. *tuebitaki* = *Galanthus elwesii*
Galanthus elwesii ssp. *wagenitzii* = *Galanthus elwesii*
Galanthus elwesii ssp. *yayintaschii* = *Galanthus elwesii*
Galanthus elwesii var. *globosus* = *Galanthus elwesii*
Galanthus elwesii var. *maximus* = *Galanthus elwesii*
Galanthus elwesii var. *platyphyllus* = *Galanthus elwesii*
Galanthus elwesii var. *reflexus* = *Galanthus gracilis*
Galanthus elwesii var. *robustus* = *Galanthus elwesii*
Galanthus elwesii var. *stenophyllus* = *Galanthus gracilis*
Galanthus elwesii var. *whittallii* = *Galanthus elwesii*
Galanthus fosteri var. *antepensis* = *Galanthus fosteri*
Galanthus fosteri: #1 **II** AMARYLLIDACEAE
Galanthus glaucescens = *Galanthus rizehensis*
Galanthus globosus = *Galanthus elwesii*
Galanthus gracilis: #1 **II** AMARYLLIDACEAE
Galanthus gracilis ssp. *baytopii* = *Galanthus elwesii*
Galanthus graecus = *Galanthus elwesii*
Galanthus graecus = *Galanthus gracilis*
Galanthus graecus f. *gracilis* = *Galanthus gracilis*
Galanthus graecus f. *maximus* = *Galanthus elwesii*
Galanthus graecus var. *maximus* = *Galanthus elwesii*
Galanthus grandis = *Galanthus alpinus* var. *alpinus*
Galanthus ikariae = *Galanthus woronowii*
Galanthus ikariae: #1 **II** AMARYLLIDACEAE
Galanthus ikariae ssp. *latifolius* = *Galanthus platyphyllus*
Galanthus ikariae ssp. *latifolius* = *Galanthus woronowii*
Galanthus ikariae ssp. *snogerupii* = *Galanthus ikariae*
Galanthus imperati = *Galanthus nivalis*
Galanthus imperati f. *australis* = *Galanthus reginae-olgae* ssp.
    reginae-olgae
Galanthus kemulariae = *Galanthus lagodechianus*
Galanthus ketzhovelii = *Galanthus lagodechianus*
Galanthus koenenianus: #1 **II** AMARYLLIDACEAE
Galanthus krasnovii: #1 **II** AMARYLLIDACEAE
Galanthus krasnovii ssp. *maculatus* = *Galanthus krasnovii*
Galanthus lagodechianus: #1 **II** AMARYLLIDACEAE
Galanthus latifolius = *Galanthus platyphyllus*
Galanthus latifolius = *Galanthus plicatus* ssp. *plicatus*

Galanthus latifolius = *Galanthus woronowii*
Galanthus latifolius f. *fosteri* = *Galanthus fosteri*
Galanthus latifolius f. *typicus* = *Galanthus platyphyllus*
Galanthus latifolius var. *rizaensis* (sic) = *Galanthus rizehensis*
Galanthus latifolius var. *rizehensis* = *Galanthus rizehensis*
Galanthus maximus = *Galanthus elwesii*
Galanthus melihae = *Galanthus elwesii*
Galanthus montana = *Galanthus nivalis*
Galanthus nivalis = *Galanthus alpinus* var. *alpinus*
Galanthus nivalis: (E) Common snowdrop #1 **II**
    AMARYLLIDACEAE
Galanthus nivalis f. *octobrinus* = *Galanthus reginae-olgae* ssp.
    reginae-olgae
Galanthus nivalis f. *pictus* = *Galanthus nivalis*
Galanthus nivalis f. *pleniflorus* = *Galanthus nivalis* "flore pleno"
Galanthus nivalis ssp. *angustifolius* = *Galanthus angustifolius*
Galanthus nivalis ssp. *byzantinus* = *Galanthus plicatus* ssp.
    byzantinus
Galanthus nivalis ssp. *caucasicus* = *Galanthus alpinus* var. *alpinus*
Galanthus nivalis ssp. *cilicicus* = *Galanthus cilicicus*
Galanthus nivalis ssp. *cilicicus* = *Galanthus peshmenii*
Galanthus nivalis ssp. *elwesii* = *Galanthus elwesii*
Galanthus nivalis ssp. *graecus* = *Galanthus elwesii*
Galanthus nivalis ssp. *humboldtii* = *Galanthus nivalis*
Galanthus nivalis ssp. *imperati* = *Galanthus nivalis*
Galanthus nivalis ssp. *nivalis* = *Galanthus nivalis*
Galanthus nivalis ssp. *nivalis* ssp. *nivalis* = *Galanthus nivalis*
Galanthus nivalis ssp. *plicatus* = *Galanthus plicatus* ssp. *plicatus*
Galanthus nivalis ssp. *reginae-olgae* = *Galanthus reginae-olgae*
    ssp. *reginae-olgae*
Galanthus nivalis ssp. *subplicatus* = *Galanthus nivalis*
Galanthus nivalis var. *atkinsii* = *Galanthus nivalis*
Galanthus nivalis var. *carpaticus* = *Galanthus nivalis*
Galanthus nivalis var. *caspius* = *Galanthus transcaucasicus*
Galanthus nivalis var. *caucasicus* = *Galanthus alpinus* var. *alpinus*
Galanthus nivalis var. *corcyrensis* = *Galanthus reginae-olgae* ssp.
    reginae-olgae
Galanthus nivalis var. *elsae* = *Galanthus reginae-olgae* ssp.
    reginae-olgae
Galanthus nivalis var. *europaeus* ssp. *corcyrensis* = *Galanthus*
    reginae-olgae ssp. *reginae-olgae*
Galanthus nivalis var. *europaeus* ssp. *hololeucus* = *Galanthus*
    nivalis
Galanthus nivalis var. *europaeus* ssp. *hortensis* = *Galanthus nivalis*
Galanthus nivalis var. *europaeus* ssp. *olgae* = *Galanthus reginae-*
    olgae ssp. *reginae-olgae*
Galanthus nivalis var. *europaeus* ssp. *scharloki* (sic) = *Galanthus*
    nivalis
Galanthus nivalis var. *grandior* = *Galanthus nivalis*
Galanthus nivalis var. *hololeucus* = *Galanthus nivalis*
Galanthus nivalis var. *hortensis* = *Galanthus nivalis*
Galanthus nivalis var. *imperati* = *Galanthus nivalis*
Galanthus nivalis var. *major* = *Galanthus alpinus* var. *alpinus*
Galanthus nivalis var. *major* = *Galanthus nivalis*
Galanthus nivalis var. *majus* (sic) = *Galanthus nivalis*
Galanthus nivalis var. *maximus* = *Galanthus elwesii*
Galanthus nivalis var. *minus* = *Galanthus nivalis*
Galanthus nivalis var. *montanus* = *Galanthus nivalis*
Galanthus nivalis var. *octobrensis* = *Galanthus reginae-olgae* ssp.
    reginae-olgae
Galanthus nivalis var. *praecox* = *Galanthus reginae-olgae* ssp.
    reginae-olgae
Galanthus nivalis var. *rachelae* = *Galanthus reginae-olgae* ssp.
    reginae-olgae
Galanthus nivalis var. *redoutei* = *Galanthus alpinus* var. *alpinus*
Galanthus nivalis var. *reginae-olgae* = *Galanthus reginae-olgae*
    ssp. *reginae-olgae*
Galanthus nivalis var. *scharlockii* = *Galanthus nivalis*
Galanthus nivalis var. *shaylockii* (sic) = *Galanthus nivalis*
Galanthus nivalis var. *typicus* = *Galanthus nivalis*
Galanthus octobrensis = *Galanthus reginae-olgae* ssp. *reginae-*
    olgae
Galanthus olgae = *Galanthus reginae-olgae* ssp. *reginae-olgae*
Galanthus olgae reginae = *Galanthus reginae-olgae* ssp. *reginae-*
    olgae

Galanthus peshmenii: #1 **II** AMARYLLIDACEAE
Galanthus platyphyllus: #1 **II** AMARYLLIDACEAE
Galanthus plicatus = *Galanthus nivalis*
Galanthus plicatus = *Galanthus transcaucasicus*
Galanthus plicatus: #1 **II** AMARYLLIDACEAE
Galanthus plicatus ssp. *byzantinus*: #1 **II** AMARYLLIDACEAE
Galanthus plicatus ssp. *gueneri* = *Galanthus plicatus* ssp. *plicatus*
Galanthus plicatus ssp. *karamanoghluensis* = *Galanthus plicatus* ssp. *plicatus*
Galanthus plicatus ssp. *plicatus* ssp. *viridifolius* = *Galanthus plicatus* ssp. *plicatus*
Galanthus plicatus ssp. *plicatus*: (E) Plicate-leaved snowdrop #1 **II** AMARYLLIDACEAE
Galanthus plicatus ssp. *subplicatus* = *Galanthus nivalis*
Galanthus plicatus ssp. *vardarii* = *Galanthus plicatus* ssp. *plicatus*
Galanthus plicatus var. *byzantinus* = *Galanthus plicatus* ssp. *plicatus*
Galanthus plicatus var. *genuinus* ssp. *excelsior* = *Galanthus plicatus* ssp. *plicatus*
Galanthus plicatus var. *genuinus* ssp. *maximus* = *Galanthus plicatus* ssp. *plicatus*
Galanthus plicatus var. *genuinus* ssp. *typicus* = *Galanthus plicatus* ssp. *plicatus*
Galanthus praecox = *Galanthus reginae-olgae* ssp. *reginae-olgae*
Galanthus rachelae = *Galanthus reginae-olgae* ssp. *reginae-olgae*
Galanthus redoutei = *Galanthus alpinus* var. *alpinus*
Galanthus reflexus = *Galanthus gracilis*
Galanthus reflexus = *Galanthus nivalis*
Galanthus reginae-olgae: #1 **II** AMARYLLIDACEAE
Galanthus reginae-olgae = *Galanthus peshmenii*
Galanthus reginae-olgae ssp. *corcyrensis* = *Galanthus reginae-olgae* ssp. *reginae-olgae*
Galanthus reginae-olgae ssp. *reginae-olgae*: #1 **II** AMARYLLIDACEAE
Galanthus reginae-olgae ssp. *vernalis*: #1 **II** AMARYLLIDACEAE
Galanthus rizehensis: #1 **II** AMARYLLIDACEAE
Galanthus schaoricus = *Galanthus alpinus* var. *alpinus*
Galanthus sharlokii = *Galanthus nivalis*
Galanthus shaylockii (sic) = *Galanthus nivalis*
Galanthus transcaucasicus: #1 **II** AMARYLLIDACEAE
Galanthus valentinae = *Galanthus krasnovii*
Galanthus woronowii: #1 **II** AMARYLLIDACEAE
Galeandra spp.: #7 **II** ORCHIDACEAE
Galearis spp.: #7 **II** ORCHIDACEAE
Galeoglossum = *Prescottia*
Galeola spp.: #7 **II** ORCHIDACEAE
Galeorchis = *Orchis*
Galeottia spp.: #7 **II** ORCHIDACEAE
Galeottiella spp.: #7 **II** ORCHIDACEAE
Galera = *Epipogium*
Gamaria = *Disa*
Gamoplexis = *Gastrodia*
Gamosepalum = *Aulosepalum*
Garaya spp.: #7 **II** ORCHIDACEAE
Garayella = *Chamelophyton*
Gastorchis = *Phaius*
Gastrochilus spp.: #7 **II** ORCHIDACEAE
Gastrodia spp.: #7 **II** ORCHIDACEAE
Gastroglottis = *Liparis*
Gastrorchis = *Phaius*
Gaut's Butterfly (E): *Neolloydia gautii*
Gavilán (S): *Oreomunnea pterocarpa*
Gavilán blanco (S): *Oreomunnea pterocarpa*
Gavilea spp.: #7 **II** ORCHIDACEAE
Gayac(F): *Guaiacum* spp.
Geesinkorchis spp.: #7 **II** ORCHIDACEAE
Geissanthera = *Microtatorchis*
Gennaria spp.: #7 **II** ORCHIDACEAE
Genoplesium spp.: #7 **II** ORCHIDACEAE
Genyorchis spp.: #7 **II** ORCHIDACEAE
Geobina = *Goodyera*
Geoblasta spp.: #7 **II** ORCHIDACEAE
Geocalpa = *Pleurothallis*
Geodorum spp.: #7 **II** ORCHIDACEAE

Geohintonia mexicana: #4 **II** CACTACEAE
Georchis = *Goodyera*
Gerocephalus dybowskii = *Espostoopsis dybowskii*
Gersinia = *Bulbophyllum*
Ghiesbreghtia = *Calanthe*
Giant pitcher plant (E): *Nepenthes rajah*
Giant snowdrop (E): *Galanthus elwesii* ssp. *elwesii*
Giant tropical pitcher plant (E): *Nepenthes rajah*
Gigliolia = *Octomeria*
Ginger lily (E): *Hedychium philippinense*
Ginseng (E): *Panax ginseng*
Ginseng americano (S): *Panax quinquefolius*
Ginseng d'Amérique (F): *Panax quinquefolius*
Giulianettia = *Glossorhyncha*
Glomera spp.: #7 **II** ORCHIDACEAE
Glossapis = *Habenaria*
Glossodia spp.: #7 **II** ORCHIDACEAE
Glossorhyncha spp.: #7 **II** ORCHIDACEAE
Glossula = *Habenaria*
Gnetum montanum: #1 **III** GNETACEAE
Goadbyella = *Microtis*
Goldenseal (E): *Hydrastis canadensis*
Golden-spine cereus (E): *Bergerocactus emoryi*
Golden-spine hedgehog cactus (E): *Echinocereus chloranthus* ssp. *neocapillus*
Golden-spined Prickly-pear (E): *Opuntia aureispina*
Goldschmidtia = *Dendrobium*
Gomeran spurge (E): *Euphorbia lambii*
Gomesa spp.: #7 **II** ORCHIDACEAE
Gomphichis spp.: #7 **II** ORCHIDACEAE
Gonatostylis spp.: #7 **II** ORCHIDACEAE
Gongora spp.: #7 **II** ORCHIDACEAE
Goniochilus spp.: #7 **II** ORCHIDACEAE
Gonogona = *Goodyera*
Gonystylus spp.: (E) ramin #1 **III** THYMELAEACEAE
Gonystylus acuminatus: (E) #1 **III** THYMELAEACEAE
Gonystylus affinis: #1 **III** THYMELAEACEAE
Gonystylus affinis var. *elegans*: #1 **III** THYMELAEACEAE
Gonystylus areolatus: (E) #1 **III** THYMELAEACEAE
Gonystylus augescens: (E) #1 **III** THYMELAEACEAE
Gonystylus bancanus = *Gonystylus miquelianus*
Gonystylus bancanus: #1 **III** THYMELAEACEAE
Gonystylus beccarianus: #1 **III** THYMELAEACEAE
Gonystylus borneensis: (E) #1 **III** THYMELAEACEAE
Gonystylus brunnescens: #1 **III** THYMELAEACEAE
Gonystylus calophylloides: (E) #1 **III** THYMELAEACEAE
Gonystylus calophyllus: (E) #1 **III** THYMELAEACEAE
Gonystylus confusus: (E) #1 **III** THYMELAEACEAE
Gonystylus consanguineus: #1 **III** THYMELAEACEAE
Gonystylus costalis: (E) #1 **III** THYMELAEACEAE
Gonystylus decipiens: (E) #1 **III** THYMELAEACEAE
Gonystylus eximius: #1 **III** THYMELAEACEAE
Gonystylus forbesii: #1 **III** THYMELAEACEAE
Gonystylus glaucescens: (E) #1 **III** THYMELAEACEAE
Gonystylus hackenbergii: #1 **III** THYMELAEACEAE
Gonystylus keithii: #1 **III** THYMELAEACEAE
Gonystylus lucidulus: (E) #1 **III** THYMELAEACEAE
Gonystylus macrocarpus: #1 **III** THYMELAEACEAE
Gonystylus macrophyllus: #1 **III** THYMELAEACEAE
Gonystylus maingayi: #1 **III** THYMELAEACEAE
Gonystylus micranthus: (E) #1 **III** THYMELAEACEAE
Gonystylus miquelianus: #1 **III** THYMELAEACEAE
Gonystylus nervosus: (E) #1 **III** THYMELAEACEAE
Gonystylus nobilis: (E) #1 **III** THYMELAEACEAE
Gonystylus obovatus: #1 **III** THYMELAEACEAE
Gonystylus othmanii: #1 **III** THYMELAEACEAE
Gonystylus pendulus: (E) #1 **III** THYMELAEACEAE
Gonystylus philippinensis: #1 **III** THYMELAEACEAE
Gonystylus pluricornis: #1 **III** THYMELAEACEAE
Gonystylus punctatus: #1 **III** THYMELAEACEAE
Gonystylus reticulatus: #1 **III** THYMELAEACEAE
Gonystylus spectabilis: (E) #1 **III** THYMELAEACEAE
Gonystylus stenosepalus: (E) #1 **III** THYMELAEACEAE
Gonystylus sympetala: #1 **III** THYMELAEACEAE
Gonystylus velutinus: #1 **III** THYMELAEACEAE

Gonystylus warburgianus: #1 **III** THYMELAEACEAE
Gonystylus xylocarpus: (E) #1 **III** THYMELAEACEAE
Goodyera spp.: #7 **II** ORCHIDACEAE
Gorgoglossum = Sievekingia
Govenia spp.: #7 **II** ORCHIDACEAE
Govindooia = Tropidia
Grafia = Phalaenopsis
Graham's Nipple-cactus (E): *Mammillaria grahamii*
Grammangis spp.: #7 **II** ORCHIDACEAE
Grammatophyllum spp.: #7 **II** ORCHIDACEAE
Graphorkis spp.: #7 **II** ORCHIDACEAE
Grastidium = Dendrobium
Green pitcherplant (E): *Sarracenia oreophila*
Green-flower Nipple-cactus (E): *Mammillaria viridiflora*
Green-fruit Nipple-cactus (E): *Mammillaria longimamma*
Greenwoodia spp.: #7 **II** ORCHIDACEAE
Grenadier's cap (E): *Pachycereus militaris*
Grobya spp.: #7 **II** ORCHIDACEAE
Grosourdya spp.: #7 **II** ORCHIDACEAE
Ground-rose (E): *Protea odorata*
Grusonia bradtiana = Opuntia bradtiana
Grusonia bulbispina = Opuntia bulbispina
Grusonia hamiltonii = Opuntia rosarica
Grusonia santamaria = Opuntia santa-rita
Grusonia wrightiana = Opuntia kunzei
Guaiac tree (E): *Guaiacum officinale*
Guaiacum spp.: (E) Sonora guaiacum, lignum-vitae, pockwood, wood of life, tree of life, (S) guayacán, guajacum, leño de guayaco, palosanto, trimarindillo, (F) bois de gaïac, bois de vie, bois saint, gaïac, gayac #1 **II** ZYGOPHYLLACEAE
Guaiacum angustifolium: #2 **II** ZYGOPHYLLACEAE
Guaiacum bijugum = Guaiacum officinale
Guaiacum coulteri: #2 **II** ZYGOPHYLLACEAE
Guaiacum coulteri var. *palmeri*: #2 **II** ZYGOPHYLLACEAE
Guaiacum guatemalense: #2 **II** ZYGOPHYLLACEAE
Guaiacum multijugum = Guaiacum sanctum
Guaiacum officinale: (E) Commoner lignum vitae, Guaiac tree, (S) Guayacán negro, Palo de vida, Palo santo #1 **II** ZYGOPHYLLACEAE
Guaiacum palmeri = Guaiacum coulteri var. *palmeri*
Guaiacum parvifolium = Guaiacum coulteri
Guaiacum planchoni = Guaiacum coulteri
Guaiacum sanctum: (E) Holywood lignum vitae, (S) Guayacán blanco, Guayacán real, Guayacancillo #2 **II** ZYGOPHYLLACEAE
Guaiacum sloanei = Guaiacum sanctum
Guaiacum unijugum: #2 **II** ZYGOPHYLLACEAE
Guaiacum verticale = Guaiacum sanctum
Guajacum (S): *Guaiacum* spp.
Guatemala fir (E): *Abies guatemalensis*
Guayacán (S): *Guaiacum* spp.
Guayacán blanco (S): *Guaiacum sanctum*
Guayacán negro (S): *Guaiacum officinale*
Guayacán real (S): *Guaiacum sanctum*
Guayacancillo (S): *Guaiacum sanctum*
Gúillo (S): *Araucaria araucana*
Guirnalda de Filipinas (S): *Hedychium philippinense*
Gularia = Schiedeella
Gunnarella spp.: #7 **II** ORCHIDACEAE
Gunnarorchis = Dendrobium
Gunnia = Sarcochilus
Gussonea = Solenangis
Gyaladenia = Brachycorythis
Gyas = Bletia
Gymnadenia spp.: #7 **II** ORCHIDACEAE
Gymnadeniopsis = Platanthera
Gymnanthocereus macracanthus = Browningia pilleifera
Gymnanthocereus pilleifera = Browningia pilleifera
Gymnocactus aguirreanus = Escobaria aguirreana
Gymnocactus beguinii = Turbinicarpus beguinii
Gymnocactus gielsdorfianus = Turbinicarpus gielsdorfianus
Gymnocactus horripilus = Turbinicarpus horripilus
Gymnocactus knuthianus = Turbinicarpus knuthianus
Gymnocactus mandragora = Turbinicarpus mandragora
Gymnocactus roseanus = Escobaria roseana

Gymnocactus saueri = Turbinicarpus saueri
Gymnocactus subterraneus = Turbinicarpus subterraneus
Gymnocactus subterraneus var. *zaragosae = Turbinicarpus subterraneus* var. *zaragosae*
Gymnocactus viereckii = Turbinicarpus viereckii
Gymnocactus viereckii var. *major = Turbinicarpus viereckii*
Gymnocactus ysabelae = Turbinicarpus ysabelae
Gymnocalycium achirasense = Gymnocalycium monvillei ssp. *achirasense*
Gymnocalycium acorrugatum = Gymnocalycium castellanosii
Gymnocalycium albispinum = Gymnocalycium bruchii
Gymnocalycium ambatoense: #4 **II** CACTACEAE
Gymnocalycium amerhauseri: #4 **II** CACTACEAE
Gymnocalycium andreae: #4 **II** CACTACEAE
Gymnocalycium andreae ssp. *carolinense*: #4 **II** CACTACEAE
Gymnocalycium angelae: #4 **II** CACTACEAE
Gymnocalycium anisitsii: #4 **II** CACTACEAE
Gymnocalycium anisitsii ssp. *multiproliferum*: #4 **II** CACTACEAE
Gymnocalycium antherostele = Gymnocalycium schickendantzii
Gymnocalycium armatum = Gymnocalycium spegazzinii ssp. *cardenasianum*
Gymnocalycium artigas = Gymnocalycium uruguayense
Gymnocalycium asterium = Gymnocalycium stellatum
Gymnocalycium baldianum: #4 **II** CACTACEAE
Gymnocalycium bayrianum: #4 **II** CACTACEAE
Gymnocalycium berchtii: #4 **II** CACTACEAE
Gymnocalycium bicolor = Gymnocalycium mostii
Gymnocalycium bodenbenderianum: #4 **II** CACTACEAE
Gymnocalycium bodenbenderianum ssp. *intertextum*: #4 **II** CACTACEAE
Gymnocalycium borthii: #4 **II** CACTACEAE
Gymnocalycium bozsingianum = Gymnocalycium castellanosii
Gymnocalycium brachyanthum = Gymnocalycium monvillei ssp. *brachyanthum*
Gymnocalycium brachypetalum = Gymnocalycium gibbosum
Gymnocalycium brevistylum = Gymnocalycium marsoneri ssp. *matoense*
Gymnocalycium bruchii: #4 **II** CACTACEAE
Gymnocalycium buenekeri: #4 **II** CACTACEAE
Gymnocalycium calochlorum: #4 **II** CACTACEAE
Gymnocalycium capillaense: #4 **II** CACTACEAE
Gymnocalycium cardenasianum = Gymnocalycium spegazzinii ssp. *cardenasianum*
Gymnocalycium carminanthum: #4 **II** CACTACEAE
Gymnocalycium castellanosii: #4 **II** CACTACEAE
Gymnocalycium catamarcense: #4 **II** CACTACEAE
Gymnocalycium catamarcense ssp. *acinacispinum*: #4 **II** CACTACEAE
Gymnocalycium catamarcense ssp. *schmidianum*: #4 **II** CACTACEAE
Gymnocalycium chiquitanum: #4 **II** CACTACEAE
Gymnocalycium chubutense = Gymnocalycium gibbosum
Gymnocalycium chuquisacanum = Gymnocalycium pflanzii
Gymnocalycium comarapense = Gymnocalycium pflanzii
Gymnocalycium curvispinum = Gymnocalycium neuhuberi
Gymnocalycium damsii = Gymnocalycium anisitsii
Gymnocalycium deeszianum: #4 **II** CACTACEAE
Gymnocalycium delaetii: #4 **II** CACTACEAE
Gymnocalycium denudatum: #4 **II** CACTACEAE
Gymnocalycium erinaceum: #4 **II** CACTACEAE
Gymnocalycium eurypleurum: #4 **II** CACTACEAE
Gymnocalycium eytianum: #4 **II** CACTACEAE
Gymnocalycium ferox = Gymnocalycium castellanosii
Gymnocalycium ferrarii = Gymnocalycium mucidum
Gymnocalycium fleischerianum: #4 **II** CACTACEAE
Gymnocalycium fricianum = Gymnocalycium marsoneri
Gymnocalycium friedrichii = Gymnocalycium stenopleurum
Gymnocalycium gerardii = Gymnocalycium gibbosum
Gymnocalycium gibbosum: #4 **II** CACTACEAE
Gymnocalycium gibbosum ssp. *ferox*: #4 **II** CACTACEAE
Gymnocalycium glaucum = Gymnocalycium mucidum
Gymnocalycium grandiflorum = Gymnocalycium mostii
Gymnocalycium griseopallidum = Gymnocalycium anisitsii
Gymnocalycium guanchinense = Gymnocalycium hossei
Gymnocalycium guerkeanum = Gymnocalycium uruguayense

Gymnocalycium hamatum = *Gymnocalycium marsoneri*
Gymnocalycium hammerschmidii = *Gymnocalycium chiquitanum*
Gymnocalycium horizonthalonium = *Gymnocalycium spegazzinii*
Gymnocalycium horridispinum = *Gymnocalycium monvillei* ssp. *horridispinum*
Gymnocalycium horstii: #4 **II** CACTACEAE
Gymnocalycium hossei: #4 **II** CACTACEAE
Gymnocalycium hybopleurum: #4 **II** CACTACEAE
Gymnocalycium hyptiacanthum: #4 **II** CACTACEAE
Gymnocalycium immemoratum = *Gymnocalycium mostii*
Gymnocalycium intertextum = *Gymnocalycium bodenbenderianum* ssp. *intertextum*
Gymnocalycium izozogsii = *Gymnocalycium pflanzii*
Gymnocalycium joossensianum = *Gymnocalycium anisitsii*
Gymnocalycium kieslingii: #4 **II** CACTACEAE
Gymnocalycium kurtzianum = *Gymnocalycium mostii*
Gymnocalycium lagunillasense = *Gymnocalycium pflanzii*
Gymnocalycium leeanum: #4 **II** CACTACEAE
Gymnocalycium leptanthum: #4 **II** CACTACEAE
Gymnocalycium loricatum = *Gymnocalycium spegazzinii*
Gymnocalycium mackieanum: #4 **II** CACTACEAE
Gymnocalycium marquezii = *Gymnocalycium pflanzii*
Gymnocalycium marsoneri: #4 **II** CACTACEAE
Gymnocalycium marsoneri ssp. *matoense*: #4 **II** CACTACEAE
Gymnocalycium matoense = *Gymnocalycium marsoneri* ssp. *matoense*
Gymnocalycium mazanense = *Gymnocalycium hossei*
Gymnocalycium megalothelon = *Gymnocalycium monvillei*
Gymnocalycium megatae = *Gymnocalycium marsoneri* ssp. *matoense*
Gymnocalycium melanocarpum = *Gymnocalycium uruguayense*
Gymnocalycium mesopotamicum: #4 **II** CACTACEAE
Gymnocalycium michoga = *Gymnocalycium schickendantzii*
Gymnocalycium mihanovichii: #4 **II** CACTACEAE
Gymnocalycium millaresii = *Gymnocalycium pflanzii*
Gymnocalycium monvillei: #4 **II** CACTACEAE
Gymnocalycium monvillei ssp. *achirasense*: #4 **II** CACTACEAE
Gymnocalycium monvillei ssp. *brachyanthum*: #4 **II** CACTACEAE
Gymnocalycium monvillei ssp. *horridispinum*: #4 **II** CACTACEAE
Gymnocalycium moserianum = *Gymnocalycium bodenbenderianum* ssp. *intertextum*
Gymnocalycium mostii: #4 **II** CACTACEAE
Gymnocalycium mucidum: #4 **II** CACTACEAE
Gymnocalycium multiflorum = *Gymnocalycium monvillei*
Gymnocalycium netrelianum: #4 **II** CACTACEAE
Gymnocalycium neuhuberi: #4 **II** CACTACEAE
Gymnocalycium nidulans = *Gymnocalycium hossei*
Gymnocalycium nigriareolatum = *Gymnocalycium hybopleurum*
Gymnocalycium obductum: #4 **II** CACTACEAE
Gymnocalycium occultum = *Gymnocalycium stellatum* ssp. *occultum*
Gymnocalycium ochoterenae: #4 **II** CACTACEAE
Gymnocalycium ochoterenae ssp. *herbsthoferianum*: #4 **II** CACTACEAE
Gymnocalycium ochoterenae ssp. *ochoterenae*: #4 **II** CACTACEAE
Gymnocalycium ochoterenae ssp. *vatteri*: #4 **II** CACTACEAE
Gymnocalycium oenanthemum: #4 **II** CACTACEAE
Gymnocalycium onychacanthum = *Gymnocalycium marsoneri*
Gymnocalycium ourselianum = *Gymnocalycium monvillei*
Gymnocalycium paediophilum = *Gymnocalycium pediophilum*
Gymnocalycium paraguayense: #4 **II** CACTACEAE
Gymnocalycium parvulum: #4 **II** CACTACEAE
Gymnocalycium pediophilum: #4 **II** CACTACEAE
Gymnocalycium pflanzii: #4 **II** CACTACEAE
Gymnocalycium pflanzii ssp. *argentinense* = *Gymnocalycium pflanzii*
Gymnocalycium piltziorum = *Gymnocalycium riojense* ssp. *piltziorum*
Gymnocalycium platense: #4 **II** CACTACEAE
Gymnocalycium platygonum = *Gymnocalycium riojense*
Gymnocalycium proliferum = *Gymnocalycium calochlorum*
Gymnocalycium pseudomalacocarpus = *Gymnocalycium marsoneri* ssp. *matoense*
Gymnocalycium pugionacanthum: #4 **II** CACTACEAE

Gymnocalycium quehlianum: #4 **II** CACTACEAE
Gymnocalycium ragonesei: #4 **II** CACTACEAE
Gymnocalycium rauschii: #4 **II** CACTACEAE
Gymnocalycium reductum = *Gymnocalycium gibbosum*
Gymnocalycium rhodantherum = *Gymnocalycium hossei*
Gymnocalycium riograndense = *Gymnocalycium pflanzii*
Gymnocalycium riojense: #4 **II** CACTACEAE
Gymnocalycium riojense ssp. *kozelskyanum*: #4 **II** CACTACEAE
Gymnocalycium riojense ssp. *paucispinum*: #4 **II** CACTACEAE
Gymnocalycium riojense ssp. *piltziorum*: #4 **II** CACTACEAE
Gymnocalycium ritterianum: #4 **II** CACTACEAE
Gymnocalycium rosae: #4 **II** CACTACEAE
Gymnocalycium saglione = *Gymnocalycium saglionis*
Gymnocalycium saglionis: #4 **II** CACTACEAE
Gymnocalycium saglionis ssp. *tilcarense*: #4 **II** CACTACEAE
Gymnocalycium sanguiniflorum = *Gymnocalycium baldianum*
Gymnocalycium schatzlianum = *Gymnocalycium mackieanum*
Gymnocalycium schickendantzii: #4 **II** CACTACEAE
Gymnocalycium schroederianum: #4 **II** CACTACEAE
Gymnocalycium schroederianum ssp. *bayense*: #4 **II** CACTACEAE
Gymnocalycium schroederianum ssp. *paucicostatum*: #4 **II** CACTACEAE
Gymnocalycium schuetzianum = *Gymnocalycium monvillei*
Gymnocalycium sigelianum = *Gymnocalycium capillaense*
Gymnocalycium spegazzinii: #4 **II** CACTACEAE
Gymnocalycium spegazzinii ssp. *cardenasianum*: #4 **II** CACTACEAE
Gymnocalycium stellatum: #4 **II** CACTACEAE
Gymnocalycium stellatum ssp. *occultum*: #4 **II** CACTACEAE
Gymnocalycium stenopleurum: #4 **II** CACTACEAE
Gymnocalycium striglianum: #4 **II** CACTACEAE
Gymnocalycium stuckertii: #4 **II** CACTACEAE
Gymnocalycium sutterianum = *Gymnocalycium capillaense*
Gymnocalycium taningaense: #4 **II** CACTACEAE
Gymnocalycium terweemeanum: #4 **II** CACTACEAE
Gymnocalycium tilcarense = *Gymnocalycium saglionis* ssp. *tilcarense*
Gymnocalycium tillianum: #4 **II** CACTACEAE
Gymnocalycium tobuschianum = *Gymnocalycium mostii*
Gymnocalycium tortuga = *Gymnocalycium marsoneri* ssp. *matoense*
Gymnocalycium triacanthum = *Gymnocalycium riojense*
Gymnocalycium tudae = *Gymnocalycium marsoneri* ssp. *matoense*
Gymnocalycium uebelmannianum: #4 **II** CACTACEAE
Gymnocalycium uruguayense: #4 **II** CACTACEAE
Gymnocalycium valnicekianum = *Gymnocalycium mostii*
Gymnocalycium vatteri = *Gymnocalycium ochoterenae* ssp. *vatteri*
Gymnocalycium weissianum = *Gymnocalycium hossei*
Gymnocalycium zegarrae = *Gymnocalycium pflanzii*
Gymnocereus altissimus = *Browningia altissima*
Gymnocereus amstutziae = *Browningia amstutziae*
Gymnocereus microspermus = *Browningia microsperma*
Gymnochilus spp.: #7 **II** ORCHIDACEAE
Gymnosphaera nicklesii = *Cyathea nicklesii*
Gynizodon = *Oncidium*
Gynoglottis spp.: #7 **II** ORCHIDACEAE
Gyrostachis = *Spiranthes*
Gyrostachys = *Spiranthes*
Haageocereus acanthocladus = *Haageocereus pseudomelanostele*
Haageocereus achaetus = *Haageocereus acranthus* ssp. *acranthus*
Haageocereus acranthus: #4 **II** CACTACEAE
Haageocereus acranthus ssp. *acranthus*: #4 **II** CACTACEAE
Haageocereus acranthus ssp. *olowinskianus*: #4 **II** CACTACEAE
Haageocereus akersii = *Haageocereus pseudomelanostele*
Haageocereus albispinus: #4 **II** CACTACEAE
Haageocereus ambiguus = *Haageocereus decumbens*
Haageocereus aureispinus = *Haageocereus pseudomelanostele* ssp. *aureispinus*
Haageocereus australis: #4 **II** CACTACEAE
Haageocereus cephalomacrostibas = *Echinopsis cephalomacrostibas*
Haageocereus chalaensis: #4 **II** CACTACEAE
Haageocereus chosicensis = *Haageocereus pseudomelanostele*
Haageocereus chrysanthus = *Haageocereus pseudomelanostele*

Haageocereus chryseus: #4 **II** CACTACEAE
Haageocereus clavatus = *Haageocereus pseudomelanostele*
Haageocereus clavispinus = *Haageocereus acranthus* ssp. *acranthus*
Haageocereus crassiareolatus = *Haageocereus pseudomelanostele*
Haageocereus decumbens: #4 **II** CACTACEAE
Haageocereus deflexispinus = *Haageocereus acranthus* ssp. *acranthus*
Haageocereus dichromus = *Haageocereus pseudomelanostele*
Haageocereus divaricatispinus = *Haageocereus pseudomelanostele*
Haageocereus fascicularis: #4 **II** CACTACEAE
Haageocereus fulvus: #4 **II** CACTACEAE
Haageocereus horrens = *Haageocereus pacalaensis*
Haageocereus icensis: #4 **II** CACTACEAE
Haageocereus icosagonoides: #4 **II** CACTACEAE
Haageocereus lachayensis = *Haageocereus acranthus* ssp. *acranthus*
Haageocereus lanugispinus: #4 **II** CACTACEAE
Haageocereus laredensis = *Haageocereus pacalaensis*
Haageocereus limensis = *Haageocereus acranthus* ssp. *acranthus*
Haageocereus litoralis = *Haageocereus decumbens*
Haageocereus longiareolatus = *Haageocereus pseudomelanostele*
Haageocereus mamillatus = *Haageocereus decumbens*
Haageocereus multangularis = *Haageocereus pseudomelanostele*
Haageocereus multicolorispinus = *Haageocereus australis*
Haageocereus olowinskianus = *Haageocereus acranthus* ssp. *olowinskianus*
Haageocereus pacalaensis: #4 **II** CACTACEAE
Haageocereus pachystele = *Haageocereus pseudomelanostele*
Haageocereus paradoxus = *Cleistocactus acanthurus* ssp. *acanthurus*
Haageocereus peculiaris = *Cleistocactus peculiaris*
Haageocereus peniculatus = *Haageocereus albispinus*
Haageocereus piliger = *Haageocereus pseudomelanostele*
Haageocereus platinospinus: #4 **II** CACTACEAE
Haageocereus pluriflorus: #4 **II** CACTACEAE
Haageocereus pseudoacranthus = *Haageocereus acranthus* ssp. *acranthus*
Haageocereus pseudomelanostele: #4 **II** CACTACEAE
Haageocereus pseudomelanostele ssp. *aureispinus*: #4 **II** CACTACEAE
Haageocereus pseudomelanostele ssp. *carminiflorus*: #4 **II** CACTACEAE
Haageocereus pseudomelanostele ssp. *pseudomelanostele*: #4 **II** CACTACEAE
Haageocereus pseudomelanostele ssp. *turbidus*: #4 **II** CACTACEAE
Haageocereus pseudoversicolor: #4 **II** CACTACEAE
Haageocereus repens = *Haageocereus pacalaensis*
Haageocereus setosus = *Haageocereus pseudomelanostele*
Haageocereus subtilispinus: #4 **II** CACTACEAE
Haageocereus symmetros = *Haageocereus pseudomelanostele*
Haageocereus tenuis: #4 **II** CACTACEAE
Haageocereus tenuispinus = *Haageocereus pacalaensis*
Haageocereus turbidus = *Haageocereus pseudomelanostele* ssp. *turbidus*
Haageocereus versicolor: #4 **II** CACTACEAE
Haageocereus viridiflorus = *Haageocereus pseudomelanostele*
Haageocereus vulpes: #4 **II** CACTACEAE
Haageocereus zangalensis: #4 **II** CACTACEAE
Haageocereus zehnderi = *Haageocereus pseudomelanostele*
Haageocereus zonatus = *Haageocereus acranthus* ssp. *acranthus*
Habenaria spp.: #7 **II** ORCHIDACEAE
Habenella = *Habenaria*
Habenorkis = *Habenaria*
Haemaria = *Ludisia*
Haematorchis = *Galeola*
Hagsatera spp.: #7 **II** ORCHIDACEAE
Hakoneaste = *Ephippianthus*
Hamatocactus crassihamatus = *Sclerocactus uncinatus* ssp. *crassihamatus*
Hamatocactus hamatacanthus = *Ferocactus hamatacanthus* ssp. *hamatacanthus*
Hamatocactus sinuatus = *Ferocactus hamatacanthus* ssp. *sinuatus*
Hamatocactus uncinatus = *Sclerocactus uncinatus* ssp. *uncinatus*

Hammarbya = *Malaxis*
Hancockia spp.: #7 **II** ORCHIDACEAE
Hapalochilus = *Bulbophyllum*
Hapalorchis spp.: #7 **II** ORCHIDACEAE
Haplochilus = *Bulbophyllum*
Haplostellis = *Nervilia*
Haraella spp.: #7 **II** ORCHIDACEAE
Harris' tillandsia (E): *Tillandsia harrisii*
Harrisella spp.: #7 **II** ORCHIDACEAE
Harrisia aboriginum: (E) Aboriginal prickly-apple cactus #4 **II** CACTACEAE
Harrisia adscendens: #4 **II** CACTACEAE
Harrisia balansae: #4 **II** CACTACEAE
Harrisia bonplandii = *Harrisia pomanensis*
Harrisia brookii: #4 **II** CACTACEAE
Harrisia deeringii = *Harrisia simpsonii*
Harrisia divaricata: #4 **II** CACTACEAE
Harrisia donae-antoniae = *Harrisia gracilis*
Harrisia earlei: #4 **II** CACTACEAE
Harrisia eriophora: (E) Caribbean apple-cactus, Fragrant prickly-apple cactus, Fragrant woolly cactus #4 **II** CACTACEAE
Harrisia fernowii: #4 **II** CACTACEAE
Harrisia fragrans: (E) Fragrant prickly-apple cactus, Fragrant woolly cactus #4 **II** CACTACEAE
Harrisia gracilis: #4 **II** CACTACEAE
Harrisia guelichii = *Harrisia balansae*
Harrisia hahniana = *Echinopsis hahniana*
Harrisia hurstii: #4 **II** CACTACEAE
Harrisia martinii: #4 **II** CACTACEAE
Harrisia pomanensis: #4 **II** CACTACEAE
Harrisia pomanensis ssp. *bonplandii* = *Harrisia pomanensis*
Harrisia pomanensis ssp. *regelii*: #4 **II** CACTACEAE
Harrisia pomanensis ssp. *tarijensis* = *Harrisia pomanensis*
Harrisia portoricensis: #4 **II** CACTACEAE
Harrisia regelii = *Harrisia pomanensis* ssp. *regelii*
Harrisia serruliflora = *Harrisia divaricata*
Harrisia simpsonii: (E) Simpson's prickly-apple cactus #4 **II** CACTACEAE
Harrisia taetra: #4 **II** CACTACEAE
Harrisia taylori: #4 **II** CACTACEAE
Harrisia tetracantha: #4 **II** CACTACEAE
Harrisia tortuosa: #4 **II** CACTACEAE
Hartwegia = *Nageliella*
Haseltonia columna-trajani = *Cephalocereus columna-trajani*
Hatchet cacti (E): *Pelecyphora* spp.
Hatiora bambusoides = *Hatiora salicornioides*
Hatiora cylindrica = *Hatiora salicornioides*
Hatiora epiphylloides: #4 **II** CACTACEAE
Hatiora epiphylloides ssp. *bradei*: #4 **II** CACTACEAE
Hatiora epiphylloides ssp. *epiphylloides*: #4 **II** CACTACEAE
Hatiora gaertneri: #4 **II** CACTACEAE
Hatiora herminiae: #4 **II** CACTACEAE
Hatiora rosea: #4 **II** CACTACEAE
Hatiora salicornioides: #4 **II** CACTACEAE
Hecabe = *Phaius*
Hederorkis spp.: #7 **II** ORCHIDACEAE
Hedgehog cactus (E): *Echinocereus chloranthus*
Hedychium philippinense: (E) Ginger lily, Philippine garland flower, (S) Guirnalda de Filipinas #1 **II** ZINGIBERACEAE
Helcia spp.: #7 **II** ORCHIDACEAE
Helechos arborescentes (S): *Cyathea* spp./ *Dicksonia* spp.
Helianthocereus antezanae = *Echinopsis antezanae*
Helianthocereus atacamensis = *Echinopsis atacamensis*
Helianthocereus bertramianus = *Echinopsis bertramiana*
Helianthocereus conaconensis = *Echinopsis conaconensis*
Helianthocereus crassicaulis = *Echinopsis crassicaulis*
Helianthocereus escayachensis = *Echinopsis escayachensis*
Helianthocereus grandiflorus = *Echinopsis huascha*
Helianthocereus herzogianus = *Echinopsis tarijensis* ssp. *herzogianus*
Helianthocereus huascha = *Echinopsis huascha*
Helianthocereus hyalacanthus = *Echinopsis huascha*
Helianthocereus narvaecensis = *Echinopsis tarijensis*
Helianthocereus orurensis = *Echinopsis ferox*

Helianthocereus pasacana = *Echinopsis atacamensis* ssp.
  pasacana
Helianthocereus pecheretianus = *Echinopsis huascha*
Helianthocereus poco = *Echinopsis tarijensis*
Helianthocereus pseudocandicans = *Echinopsis candicans*
Helianthocereus randallii = *Echinopsis formosa*
Helianthocereus tarijensis = *Echinopsis tarijensis*
Helictonia = *Spiranthes*
Heliocereus aurantiacus = *Disocactus aurantiacus*
Heliocereus cinnabarinus = *Disocactus cinnabarinus*
Heliocereus elegantissimus = *Disocactus schrankii*
Heliocereus heterodoxus = *Disocactus cinnabarinus*
Heliocereus luzmariae = *Disocactus schrankii*
Heliocereus schrankii = *Disocactus schrankii*
Heliocereus speciosissimus = *Disocactus speciosus*
Heliocereus speciosus = *Disocactus speciosus*
Helleborine = *Calopogon*
Helleriella spp.: #7 **II** ORCHIDACEAE
Hellerorchis = *Rodrigueziella*
Helonoma spp.: #7 **II** ORCHIDACEAE
Helorchis = *Cynorkis*
Hemiperis = *Habenaria*
Hemipilia spp.: #7 **II** ORCHIDACEAE
Hemiscleria spp.: #7 **II** ORCHIDACEAE
Henosis = *Bulbophyllum*
Herminium spp.: #7 **II** ORCHIDACEAE
Herpetophytum = *Dendrobium*
Herpysma spp.: #7 **II** ORCHIDACEAE
Herschelia = *Forficaria*
Herschelianthe = *Forficaria*
Hetaeria spp.: #7 **II** ORCHIDACEAE
Heterotaxis = *Maxillaria*
Heterozeuxine = *Zeuxine*
Hexadesmia = *Scaphyglottis*
Hexalectris spp.: #7 **II** ORCHIDACEAE
Hexameria = *Podochilus*
Hexisea = *Scaphyglottis*
Hexopia = *Scaphyglottis*
Higo chumbo (S): *Opuntia ficus-indica*
Hildewintera aureispina = *Cleistocactus winteri*
Himalayan poppy (E): *Meconopsis regia*
Himalayan yew (E): *Taxus wallichiana*
Himantoglossum spp.: #7 **II** ORCHIDACEAE
Himilayan may-apple (E): *Podophyllum hexandrum*
Hintonella spp.: #7 **II** ORCHIDACEAE
Hippeophyllum spp.: #7 **II** ORCHIDACEAE
Hippoglossum = *Bulbophyllum*
Hippopodium = *Ceratandra*
Hipporkis = *Satyrium*
Hispaniella = *Oncidium*
Hoehneella spp.: #7 **II** ORCHIDACEAE
Hofmeistera = *Hofmeisterella*
Hofmeisterella spp.: #7 **II** ORCHIDACEAE
Holcoglossum spp.: #7 **II** ORCHIDACEAE
Holmesia = *Angraecopsis*
Hologyne = *Coelogyne*
Holopogon = *Neottia*
Holothrix spp.: #7 **II** ORCHIDACEAE
Holy Ghost orchid (E): *Peristeria elata*
Holywood lignum vitae (E): *Guaiacum sanctum*
Homalocephala texensis = *Echinocactus texensis*
Homalopetalum spp.: #7 **II** ORCHIDACEAE
Honduras mahogany (E): *Swietenia humilis/ Swietenia macrophylla*
Hong Kong slipper orchid (E): *Paphiopedilum purpuratum*
Hooded pitcher-plant (E): *Sarracenia minor*
Horichia spp.: #7 **II** ORCHIDACEAE
Hormidium = *Encyclia*
Horncones (E): *Ceratozamia* spp.
Horridocactus aconcaguensis = *Eriosyce curvispina*
Horridocactus andicola = *Eriosyce curvispina*
Horridocactus armatus = *Eriosyce curvispina*
Horridocactus atroviridis = *Eriosyce crispa* ssp. *atroviridis*
Horridocactus carrizalensis = *Eriosyce crispa* ssp. *atroviridis*
Horridocactus choapensis = *Eriosyce curvispina*
Horridocactus crispus = *Eriosyce crispa* ssp. *crispa*

Horridocactus curvispinus = *Eriosyce curvispina*
Horridocactus echinus = *Eriosyce taltalensis* ssp. *echinus*
Horridocactus engleri = *Eriosyce engleri*
Horridocactus froehlichianus = *Eriosyce curvispina*
Horridocactus garaventae = *Eriosyce garaventae*
Horridocactus geissei = *Eriosyce kunzei*
Horridocactus grandiflorus = *Eriosyce curvispina*
Horridocactus heinrichianus = *Eriosyce heinrichiana*
Horridocactus kesselringianus = *Eriosyce curvispina*
Horridocactus lissocarpus = *Eriosyce marksiana*
Horridocactus marksianus = *Eriosyce marksiana*
Horridocactus nigricans = *Eriosyce limariensis*
Horridocactus robustus = *Eriosyce curvispina*
Horridocactus tuberisulcatus = *Eriosyce curvispina*
Horridocactus vallenarensis = *Eriosyce kunzei*
Horse crippler (E): *Echinocactus texensis*
Horvatia spp.: #7 **II** ORCHIDACEAE
Hottentot's head (E): *Stangeria eriopus*
Houlletia spp.: #7 **II** ORCHIDACEAE
Houserock valley cactus (E): *Pediocactus paradinei*
Huebneria = *Orleanesia*
Huevo de buey (S): *Sclerocactus mariposensis*
Humboldtia = *Stelis*
Huntleya spp.: #7 **II** ORCHIDACEAE
Huntsman's cap (E): *Sarracenia purpurea* ssp. *purpurea*
Huntsman's horn (E): *Sarracenia purpurea* ssp. *purpurea*
Huttonaea spp.: #7 **II** ORCHIDACEAE
Hyacinthorchis = *Cremastra*
Hyalosema = *Bulbophyllum*
Hybochilus spp.: #7 **II** ORCHIDACEAE
Hydranthus = *Dipodium*
Hydrastis canadensis: (E) Goldenseal #3 **II** RANUNCULACEAE
Hygrochilus spp.: #7 **II** ORCHIDACEAE
Hylocereus antiguensis = *Hylocereus trigonus*
Hylocereus calcaratus: #4 **II** CACTACEAE
Hylocereus compressus = *Hylocereus triangularis*
Hylocereus costaricensis: #4 **II** CACTACEAE
Hylocereus cubensis = *Hylocereus triangularis*
Hylocereus escuintlensis: #4 **II** CACTACEAE
Hylocereus estebanensis: #4 **II** CACTACEAE
Hylocereus extensus = *Hylocereus lemairei*
Hylocereus guatemalensis: #4 **II** CACTACEAE
Hylocereus lemairei: #4 **II** CACTACEAE
Hylocereus microcladus: #4 **II** CACTACEAE
Hylocereus minutiflorus: #4 **II** CACTACEAE
Hylocereus monacanthus: #4 **II** CACTACEAE
Hylocereus napoleonis = *Hylocereus trigonus*
Hylocereus ocamponis: #4 **II** CACTACEAE
Hylocereus peruvianus: #4 **II** CACTACEAE
Hylocereus plumieri = *Hylocereus trigonus*
Hylocereus polyrhizus: #4 **II** CACTACEAE
Hylocereus purpusii: #4 **II** CACTACEAE
Hylocereus scandens: #4 **II** CACTACEAE
Hylocereus stenopterus: #4 **II** CACTACEAE
Hylocereus triangularis: #4 **II** CACTACEAE
Hylocereus trigonus: (E) Night-blooming cereus #4 **II** CACTACEAE
Hylocereus trinitatensis = *Hylocereus lemairei*
Hylocereus undatus: #4 **II** CACTACEAE
Hylocereus venezuelensis = *Hylocereus lemairei*
Hylophila spp.: #7 **II** ORCHIDACEAE
Hymanthoglossum = *Himantoglossum*
Hymenorchis spp.: #7 **II** ORCHIDACEAE
Hymenorebutia aurea = *Echinopsis aurea*
Hymenorebutia chlorogona = *Echinopsis densispina*
Hymenorebutia chrysantha = *Echinopsis chrysantha*
Hymenorebutia cintiensis = *Echinopsis lateritia*
Hymenorebutia drijveriana = *Echinopsis haematantha*
Hymenorebutia kuehnrichii = *Echinopsis haematantha*
Hymenorebutia pusilla = *Echinopsis tiegeliana*
Hymenorebutia quinesensis = *Echinopsis aurea*
Hymenorebutia tiegeliana = *Echinopsis tiegeliana*
Hymenorebutia torataensis = *Echinopsis lateritia*
Hymenorebutia torreana = *Echinopsis lateritia*
Hypodema = *Cypripedium*

Hypodematium = Eulophia
Hysteria = Corymborkis
Iantha = Ionopsis
Ibidium = Spiranthes
Iebine = Liparis
If de l'Himalaya (F): *Taxus wallichiana*
Imerinaea spp.: #7 **II** ORCHIDACEAE
Indian fig (E): *Opuntia ficus-indica*
Indian pitcher-plant (E): *Nepenthes khasiana*
Inobulbon = Dendrobium
Ione = Sunipia
Ionopsis spp.: #7 **II** ORCHIDACEAE
Ionorchis = Limodorum
Ipsea spp.: #7 **II** ORCHIDACEAE
Iridorchis = Cymbidium
Iridorkis = Oberonia
Isabelia spp.: #7 **II** ORCHIDACEAE
Ischnocentrum = Glossorhyncha
Ischnogyne spp.: #7 **II** ORCHIDACEAE
Islaya bicolor = Eriosyce islayensis
Islaya brevicylindrica = Eriosyce islayensis
Islaya copiapoides = Eriosyce islayensis
Islaya divaricatiflora = Eriosyce islayensis
Islaya flavida = Eriosyce islayensis
Islaya grandiflorens = Eriosyce islayensis
Islaya grandis = Eriosyce islayensis
Islaya islayensis = Eriosyce islayensis
Islaya krainziana = Eriosyce islayensis
Islaya maritima = Eriosyce islayensis
Islaya minor = Eriosyce islayensis
Islaya minuscula = Eriosyce islayensis
Islaya mollendensis = Eriosyce islayensis
Islaya omasensis = Eriosyce omasensis
Islaya paucispina = Eriosyce islayensis
Islaya paucispinosa = Eriosyce islayensis
Islaya unguispina = Eriosyce islayensis
Isochilus spp.: #7 **II** ORCHIDACEAE
Isotria spp.: #7 **II** ORCHIDACEAE
Itaculumia = Habenaria
Jabali pincushion cactus (E): *Coryphantha werdermannii*
Jacaranda de Bahía (S): *Dalbergia nigra*
Jacarandá de Brasil (S): *Dalbergia nigra*
Jacquiniella spp.: #7 **II** ORCHIDACEAE
Jamaiciella = Oncidium
Jansenia = Plectrophora
Jarras (S): *Sarracenia* spp.
Jasminocereus galapagensis = Jasminocereus thouarsii
Jasminocereus howellii = Jasminocereus thouarsii
Jasminocereus sclerocarpus = Jasminocereus thouarsii
Jasminocereus thouarsii: #4 **II** CACTACEAE
Jejosephia spp.: #7 **II** ORCHIDACEAE
Jenmania = Palmorchis
Jensoa = Cymbidium
Jimensia = Bletilla
Johnson butterfly (E): *Sclerocactus johnsonii*
Josephia = Sirhookera
Jumellea spp.: #7 **II** ORCHIDACEAE
Juniperus uvifera = Pilgerodendron uviferum
Kaibab pincushion cactus (E): *Pediocactus paradinei*
Kalimpongia = Dickasonia
Kalopternix = Epidendrum
Kamm's tillandsia (E): *Tillandsia kammii*
Kanda stick (E): *Prunus africana*
Katherinea = Epigeneium
Kautsky's tillandsia (E): *Tillandsia kautskyi*
Kefersteinia spp.: #7 **II** ORCHIDACEAE
Kegelia = Kegeliella
Kegeliella spp.: #7 **II** ORCHIDACEAE
Kerigomnia = Octarrhena
Key Tree-cactus (E): *Cephalocereus robinii*
Kinabalu pitcher plant (E): *Nepenthes rajah*
Kinetochilus = Dendrobium
Kingidium = Phalaenopsis
Kingiella = Phalaenopsis
Kingman's prickly-pear (E): *Opuntia superbospina*

Kionophyton = Stenorrhynchos
Kitigorchis = Oreorchis
Knowlton's cactus (E): *Pediocactus knowltonii*
Knowlton's miniature cactus (E): *Pediocactus knowltonii*
Knowlton's pincushion cactus (E): *Pediocactus knowltonii*
Kochiophyton = Aganisia
Koellensteinia spp.: #7 **II** ORCHIDACEAE
Konantzia spp.: #7 **II** ORCHIDACEAE
Kraenzlinella = Pleurothallis
Krainzia guelzowiana = Mammillaria guelzowiana
Krainzia longiflora = Mammillaria longiflora ssp. *longiflora*
Kreodanthus spp.: #7 **II** ORCHIDACEAE
Kryptostoma = Habenaria
Kuhlhasseltia spp.: #7 **II** ORCHIDACEAE
Lacaena spp.: #7 **II** ORCHIDACEAE
Lacanthis splendens = Euphorbia milii var. *splendens*
Lace-spine nipple-cactus (E): *Mammillaria lasiacantha*
Lady-finger hedgehog cactus (E): *Echinocereus pentalophus* ssp. *pentalophus*
Laelia jongheana: **I** ORCHIDACEAE
Laelia lobata: **I** ORCHIDACEAE
Laelia spp.: #7 **I/II** ORCHIDACEAE
Laeliopsis = Broughtonia
Laguna Beach liveforever (E): *Dudleya stolonifera*
Lahual (S): *Fitzroya cupressoides*
Lahuán (S): *Pilgerodendron uviferum*
Lamb's-tail cactus (E): *Echinocereus schmollii*
Lanium = Epidendrum
Lankesterella = Stenorrhynchos
Larnandra = Epidendrum
Lasiocereus fulvus: #4 **II** CACTACEAE
Lasiocereus rupicola: #4 **II** CACTACEAE
Lathrisia = Bartholina
Latourea = Dendrobium
Latourorchis = Dendrobium
Lead-pencil cholla (E): *Opuntia ramosissima*
Leaoa = Scaphyglottis
Lecanorchis spp.: #7 **II** ORCHIDACEAE
Lechetreznas (E): *Euphorbia* spp.
Lectandra = Poaephyllum
Ledgeria = Galeola
Lee pincushion cactus (E): *Escobaria leei*
Lemaireocereus aragonii = Stenocereus aragonii
Lemaireocereus cartwrightianus = Armatocereus cartwrightianus
Lemaireocereus godingianus = Armatocereus godingianus
Lemaireocereus humilis = Armatocereus humilis
Lemaireocereus laetus = Armatocereus laetus
Lemboglossum spp.: #7 **II** ORCHIDACEAE
Lemuranthe = Cynorkis
Lemurella spp.: #7 **II** ORCHIDACEAE
Lemurophoenix halleuxii: (E) Red-lemur palm **II** PALMAE
Lemurorchis spp.: #7 **II** ORCHIDACEAE
Lengua de vaca (S): *Opuntia decumbens*
Leño de guayaco(S): *Guaiacum* spp.
Leocereus bahiensis: #4 **II** CACTACEAE
Leocereus bahiensis ssp. *barreirensis = Leocereus bahiensis*
Leocereus bahiensis ssp. *exiguospinus = Leocereus bahiensis*
Leocereus bahiensis ssp. *robustispinus = Leocereus bahiensis*
Leocereus bahiensis ssp. *urandianus = Leocereus bahiensis*
Leocereus estevesii = Leocereus bahiensis
Leocereus glaziovii = Arthrocereus glaziovii
Leocereus melanurus = Arthrocereus melanurus
Leocereus paulensis = Coleocephalocereus fluminensis ssp. *fluminensis*
Leocereus urandianus = Leocereus bahiensis
Leochilus spp.: #7 **II** ORCHIDACEAE
Leopardanthus = Dipodium
Lepanthes spp.: #7 **II** ORCHIDACEAE
Lepanthopsis spp.: #7 **II** ORCHIDACEAE
Lepervenchea = Angraecum
Lepidocoryphantha macromeris = Coryphantha macromeris
Lepidocoryphantha runyonii = Coryphantha macromeris ssp. *runyonii*
Lepidogyne spp.: #7 **II** ORCHIDACEAE
Lepidozamia hopei: #1 **II** ZAMIACEAE

Lepidozamia peroffskyana: #1 **II** ZAMIACEAE
Lepismium aculeatum: #4 **II** CACTACEAE
Lepismium bolivianum: #4 **II** CACTACEAE
Lepismium brevispinum: #4 **II** CACTACEAE
Lepismium crenatum: #4 **II** CACTACEAE
Lepismium cruciforme: #4 **II** CACTACEAE
Lepismium erectum = Lepismium ianthothele
Lepismium houlletianum: #4 **II** CACTACEAE
Lepismium ianthothele: #4 **II** CACTACEAE
Lepismium incachacanum: #4 **II** CACTACEAE
Lepismium lineare = Lepismium warmingianum
Lepismium lorentzianum: #4 **II** CACTACEAE
Lepismium lumbricoides: #4 **II** CACTACEAE
Lepismium mataralense = Lepismium ianthothele
Lepismium micranthum: #4 **II** CACTACEAE
Lepismium miyagawae: #4 **II** CACTACEAE
Lepismium monacanthum: #4 **II** CACTACEAE
Lepismium paranganiense: #4 **II** CACTACEAE
Lepismium warmingianum: #4 **II** CACTACEAE
Leporella spp.: #7 **II** ORCHIDACEAE
Leptocentrum = Rangaeris
Leptoceras = Caladenia
Leptocereus arboreus: #4 **II** CACTACEAE
Leptocereus assurgens: #4 **II** CACTACEAE
Leptocereus carinatus: #4 **II** CACTACEAE
Leptocereus ekmanii: #4 **II** CACTACEAE
Leptocereus grantianus: (E) Puerto Rico Apple-cactus #4 **II**
    CACTACEAE
Leptocereus leonii: #4 **II** CACTACEAE
Leptocereus maxonii: #4 **II** CACTACEAE
Leptocereus paniculatus: #4 **II** CACTACEAE
Leptocereus prostratus: #4 **II** CACTACEAE
Leptocereus quadricostatus: #4 **II** CACTACEAE
Leptocereus santamarinae: #4 **II** CACTACEAE
Leptocereus scopulophilus: #4 **II** CACTACEAE
Leptocereus sylvestris: #4 **II** CACTACEAE
Leptocereus weingartianus: #4 **II** CACTACEAE
Leptocereus wrightii: (S) Pitahaya #4 **II** CACTACEAE
Leptocladodia microhelia = Mammillaria microhelia
Leptocladodia microheliopsis = Mammillaria microhelia
Leptorkis = Liparis
Leptotes spp.: #7 **II** ORCHIDACEAE
Lequeetia = Limodorum
Lesliea spp.: #7 **II** ORCHIDACEAE
Leuchtenbergia principis: (E) Agave cactus #4 **II** CACTACEAE
Leucohyle spp.: #7 **II** ORCHIDACEAE
Leucolaena = Didymoplexis
Leucorchis = Didymoplexis
Leucorchis = Pseudorchis
Leucostachys = Goodyera
Leucostele rivierei = Echinopsis atacamensis ssp. *pasacana*
Lewisia serrata: (E) Saw-toothed lewisia #1 **II**
    PORTULACACEAE
Liane-raquette (E): *Acanthocereus tetragonus*
Libocedrus cupressoides = Fitzroya cupressoides
Libocedrus tetragona = Pilgerodendron uviferum
Libocedrus uvifera = Pilgerodendron uviferum
Lichinora = Porpax
Ligeophila spp.: #7 **II** ORCHIDACEAE
Lignum-vitae (E): *Guaiacum* spp.
Limatodes = Calanthe
Limnorchis = Platanthera
Limodorum spp.: #7 **II** ORCHIDACEAE
Lindblomia = Coeloglossum
Lindleyella = Rudolfiella
Lindsayella spp.: #7 **II** ORCHIDACEAE
Lindsay's cactus (E): *Echinocereus ferreirianus* ssp. *lindsayi*
Lindsay's hedgehog cactus (E): *Echinocereus ferreirianus* ssp.
    lindsayi
Liparis spp.: #7 **II** ORCHIDACEAE
Lissochilus = Eulophia
Listera spp.: #7 **II** ORCHIDACEAE
Listrostachys spp.: #7 **II** ORCHIDACEAE
Little nipple-cactus (E): *Mammillaria heyderi*
Little prickly-pear (E): *Opuntia pusilla*

Living rock cacti (E): *Ariocarpus* spp.
Living rock cactus (E): *Ariocarpus trigonus*
Lloyd's mariposa cactus (E): *Sclerocactus mariposensis*
Lobeira macdougallii = Disocactus macdougallii
Lobivia acanthoplegma = Echinopsis cinnabarina
Lobivia aculeata = Echinopsis pentlandii
Lobivia adpressispina = Echinopsis pugionacantha
Lobivia aguilarii = Echinopsis obrepanda ssp. *calorubra*
Lobivia akersii = Echinopsis tegeleriana
Lobivia allegraiana = Echinopsis hertrichiana
Lobivia amblayensis = Echinopsis haematantha
Lobivia andalgalensis = Echinopsis huascha
Lobivia arachnacantha = Echinopsis ancistrophora ssp.
    arachnacantha
Lobivia argentea = Echinopsis pentlandii
Lobivia atrovirens = Rebutia pygmaea
Lobivia aurantiaca = Echinopsis pentlandii
Lobivia aurea = Echinopsis aurea
Lobivia aureolilacina = Echinopsis ferox
Lobivia aureosenilis = Echinopsis pampana
Lobivia backebergiana = Echinopsis ferox
Lobivia backebergii = Echinopsis backebergii
Lobivia backebergii ssp. *hertrichiana = Echinopsis hertrichiana*
Lobivia backebergii ssp. *schieliana = Echinopsis schieliana*
Lobivia backebergii ssp. *wrightiana = Echinopsis backebergii*
Lobivia backebergii ssp. *zecheri = Echinopsis backebergii*
Lobivia binghamiana = Echinopsis hertrichiana
Lobivia boliviensis = Echinopsis pentlandii
Lobivia breviflora = Echinopsis sanguiniflora
Lobivia bruchii = Echinopsis bruchii
Lobivia brunneo-rosea = Echinopsis pentlandii
Lobivia buiningiana = Echinopsis marsoneri
Lobivia cabradae = Echinopsis haematantha
Lobivia cachensis = Echinopsis saltensis
Lobivia caespitosa = Echinopsis maximiliana
Lobivia caineana = Echinopsis caineana
Lobivia calorubra = Echinopsis obrepanda ssp. *calorubra*
Lobivia camataquiensis = Echinopsis lateritia
Lobivia campicola = Echinopsis pugionacantha
Lobivia cardenasiana = Echinopsis ancistrophora ssp.
    cardenasiana
Lobivia cariquinensis = Echinopsis maximiliana
Lobivia carminantha = Echinopsis lateritia
Lobivia cerasiflora = Echinopsis haematantha
Lobivia charazanensis = Echinopsis maximiliana
Lobivia charcasina = Echinopsis cinnabarina
Lobivia chionantha = Echinopsis thionantha
Lobivia chorrillosensis = Echinopsis haematantha
Lobivia chrysantha = Echinopsis chrysantha
Lobivia chrysantha ssp. *jajoiana = Echinopsis marsoneri*
Lobivia chrysantha ssp. *marsoneri = Echinopsis marsoneri*
Lobivia chrysochete = Echinopsis chrysochete
Lobivia cinnabarina = Echinopsis cinnabarina
Lobivia cinnabarina ssp. *acanthoplegma = Echinopsis cinnabarina*
Lobivia cinnabarina ssp. *prestoana = Echinopsis cinnabarina*
Lobivia cinnabarina ssp. *taratensis = Echinopsis cinnabarina*
Lobivia cintiensis = Echinopsis lateritia
Lobivia claeysiana = Echinopsis ferox
Lobivia corbula = Echinopsis maximiliana
Lobivia coriquinensis = Echinopsis maximiliana
Lobivia cornuta = Echinopsis pugionacantha
Lobivia crassicaulis = Echinopsis crassicaulis
Lobivia cruciaureispina = Echinopsis maximiliana
Lobivia culpinensis = Echinopsis pugionacantha
Lobivia cylindracea = Echinopsis aurea
Lobivia cylindrica = Echinopsis aurea
Lobivia draxleriana = Echinopsis cinnabarina
Lobivia drijveriana = Echinopsis haematantha
Lobivia duursmainana = Echinopsis sanguiniflora
Lobivia echinata = Echinopsis hertrichiana
Lobivia elongata = Echinopsis haematantha
Lobivia emmae = Echinopsis saltensis
Lobivia fallax ssp. *aurea = Echinopsis aurea*
Lobivia famatimensis = Echinopsis famatinensis
Lobivia ferox = Echinopsis ferox

Lobivia formosa = *Echinopsis formosa*
Lobivia formosa ssp. *bruchii* = *Echinopsis bruchii*
Lobivia formosa ssp. *grandis* = *Echinopsis bruchii*
Lobivia formosa ssp. *tarijensis* = *Echinopsis tarijensis*
Lobivia fricii = *Echinopsis tiegeliana*
Lobivia glauca = *Echinopsis marsoneri*
Lobivia glaucescens = *Echinopsis pampana*
Lobivia grandiflora = *Echinopsis huascha*
Lobivia grandis = *Echinopsis bruchii*
Lobivia haageana = *Echinopsis marsoneri*
Lobivia haematantha = *Echinopsis haematantha*
Lobivia haematantha ssp. *chorrillosensis* = *Echinopsis haematantha*
Lobivia haematantha ssp. *densispina* = *Echinopsis densispina*
Lobivia haematantha ssp. *kuehnrichii* = *Echinopsis haematantha*
Lobivia hastifera = *Echinopsis ferox*
Lobivia hermanniana = *Echinopsis maximiliana*
Lobivia hertrichiana = *Echinopsis hertrichiana*
Lobivia higginsiana = *Echinopsis pentlandii*
Lobivia horrida = *Echinopsis ferox*
Lobivia hualfinensis = *Echinopsis haematantha*
Lobivia huascha = *Echinopsis huascha*
Lobivia huilcanota = *Echinopsis hertrichiana*
Lobivia hystrix = *Echinopsis chrysochete*
Lobivia incaica = *Echinopsis hertrichiana*
Lobivia incuiensis = *Echinopsis tegeleriana*
Lobivia intermedia = *Echinopsis maximiliana*
Lobivia iridescens = *Echinopsis marsoneri*
Lobivia jajoiana = *Echinopsis marsoneri*
Lobivia johnsoniana = *Echinopsis pentlandii*
Lobivia jujuiensis = *Echinopsis chrysantha*
Lobivia kieslingii = *Echinopsis formosa*
Lobivia kuehnrichii = *Echinopsis haematantha*
Lobivia kupperiana = *Echinopsis lateritia*
Lobivia larabei = *Echinopsis hertrichiana*
Lobivia larae = *Echinopsis pentlandii*
Lobivia lateritia = *Echinopsis lateritia*
Lobivia laui = *Echinopsis hertrichiana*
Lobivia lauramarca = *Echinopsis pentlandii*
Lobivia leptacantha = *Echinopsis schieliana*
Lobivia leucorhodon = *Echinopsis pentlandii*
Lobivia leucoviolacea = *Echinopsis pentlandii*
Lobivia longispina = *Echinopsis ferox*
Lobivia markusii = *Echinopsis chrysochete*
Lobivia marsoneri = *Echinopsis marsoneri*
Lobivia maximiliana = *Echinopsis maximiliana*
Lobivia maximiliana ssp. *caespitosa* = *Echinopsis maximiliana*
Lobivia maximiliana ssp. *quiabayensis* = *Echinopsis schieliana*
Lobivia maximiliana ssp. *westii* = *Echinopsis maximiliana*
Lobivia miniatiflora = *Echinopsis maximiliana*
Lobivia minuta = *Echinopsis hertrichiana*
Lobivia mirabunda = *Echinopsis haematantha*
Lobivia mistiensis = *Echinopsis pampana*
Lobivia mizquensis = *Echinopsis obrepanda* ssp. *calorubra*
Lobivia muhriae = *Echinopsis marsoneri*
Lobivia multicostata = *Echinopsis pentlandii*
Lobivia napina = *Echinopsis densispina*
Lobivia nealeana = *Echinopsis saltensis*
Lobivia neocinnabarina = *Echinopsis cinnabarina*
Lobivia nigrostoma = *Echinopsis marsoneri*
Lobivia oligotricha = *Echinopsis cinnabarina*
Lobivia omasuyana = *Echinopsis pentlandii*
Lobivia oxyalabastra = *Echinopsis backebergii*
Lobivia pachyacantha = *Echinopsis ferox*
Lobivia pampana = *Echinopsis pampana*
Lobivia peclardiana = *Echinopsis tiegeliana*
Lobivia pentlandii = *Echinopsis pentlandii*
Lobivia pictiflora = *Echinopsis ferox*
Lobivia planiceps = *Echinopsis hertrichiana*
Lobivia pojoensis = *Echinopsis ancistrophora* ssp. *pojoensis*
Lobivia polaskiana = *Echinopsis chrysantha*
Lobivia polycephala = *Echinopsis sanguiniflora*
Lobivia potosina = *Echinopsis ferox*
Lobivia prestoana = *Echinopsis cinnabarina*
Lobivia pseudocachensis = *Echinopsis saltensis*

Lobivia pseudocariquinensis = *Echinopsis maximiliana*
Lobivia pseudocinnabarina = *Echinopsis cinnabarina*
Lobivia pugionacantha = *Echinopsis pugionacantha*
Lobivia purpureominiata = *Echinopsis huascha*
Lobivia pusilla = *Echinopsis tiegeliana*
Lobivia quiabayensis = *Echinopsis schieliana*
Lobivia raphidacantha = *Echinopsis pentlandii*
Lobivia rauschii = *Echinopsis yuquina*
Lobivia rebutioides = *Echinopsis densispina*
Lobivia rosarioana = *Echinopsis formosa*
Lobivia rossii = *Echinopsis pugionacantha* ssp. *rossii*
Lobivia rubescens = *Echinopsis marsoneri*
Lobivia salitrensis = *Echinopsis pugionacantha*
Lobivia saltensis = *Echinopsis saltensis*
Lobivia sanguiniflora = *Echinopsis sanguiniflora*
Lobivia scheeri = *Echinopsis pentlandii*
Lobivia schieliana = *Echinopsis schieliana*
Lobivia schneideriana = *Echinopsis pentlandii*
Lobivia schreiteri = *Echinopsis schreiteri*
Lobivia scoparia = *Echinopsis densispina*
Lobivia scopulina = *Echinopsis lateritia*
Lobivia shaferi = *Echinopsis aurea*
Lobivia shaferi ssp. *fallax* = *Echinopsis aurea*
Lobivia shaferi ssp. *leucomalla* = *Echinopsis aurea*
Lobivia shaferi ssp. *rubriflora* = *Echinopsis aurea*
Lobivia sicuaniensis = *Echinopsis maximiliana*
Lobivia silvestrii = *Echinopsis chamaecereus*
Lobivia simplex = *Echinopsis hertrichiana*
Lobivia stilowiana = *Echinopsis schreiteri*
Lobivia taratensis = *Echinopsis cinnabarina*
Lobivia thionantha = *Echinopsis thionantha*
Lobivia tiegeliana = *Echinopsis tiegeliana*
Lobivia titicacensis = *Echinopsis pentlandii*
Lobivia tuberculosa = *Echinopsis marsoneri*
Lobivia uitewaaleana = *Echinopsis marsoneri*
Lobivia varians = *Echinopsis pentlandii*
Lobivia varispina = *Echinopsis ferox*
Lobivia versicolor = *Echinopsis pugionacantha*
Lobivia vilcabambae = *Echinopsis hertrichiana*
Lobivia walteri = *Echinopsis walteri*
Lobivia walterspielii = *Echinopsis cinnabarina*
Lobivia wegheiana = *Echinopsis pentlandii*
Lobivia westii = *Echinopsis maximiliana*
Lobivia wilkeae = *Echinopsis ferox*
Lobivia winteriana = *Echinopsis backebergii*
Lobivia wrightiana = *Echinopsis backebergii*
Lobivia zecheri = *Echinopsis backebergii*
Lobivia zudanensis = *Echinopsis cinnabarina*
Lobogyne = *Appendicula*
Lockhartia spp.: #7 **II** ORCHIDACEAE
Loefgrenianthus spp.: #7 **II** ORCHIDACEAE
Lomaria eriopus = *Stangeria eriopus*
Lomatophyllum lomatophylloides = *Aloe lomatophylloides*
Lomatophyllum tormentorii = *Aloe tormentorii*
Lonchitis = *Serapias*
Long Mamma foxtail-cactus (E): *Coryphantha macromeris*
Lophiaris = *Oncidium*
Lophocereus gatesii = *Pachycereus gatesii*
Lophocereus schottii = *Pachycereus schottii*
Lophocereus schottii var. *tenuis* = *Pachycereus schottii*
Lophoglottis = *Sophronitis*
Lophophora diffusa: (S) Peyote #4 **II** CACTACEAE
Lophophora diffusa ssp. *fricii* = *Lophophora williamsii*
Lophophora diffusa ssp. *viridescens* = *Lophophora williamsii*
Lophophora echinata = *Lophophora williamsii*
Lophophora fricii = *Lophophora williamsii*
Lophophora jourdaniana = *Lophophora williamsii*
Lophophora lutea = *Lophophora diffusa*
Lophophora williamsii: #4 **II** CACTACEAE
Loroglossum = *Aceras*
Lothiania = *Porroglossum*
Lothoniana = *Porroglossum*
Louvelia madagascariensis = *Ravenea louvelii*
Loxanthocereus acanthurus = *Cleistocactus acanthurus* ssp. *acanthurus*

Checklist of flora/Lista de especies de flora/Liste des espèces végétales

Loxanthocereus aticensis = Cleistocactus sextonianus
Loxanthocereus bicolor = Cleistocactus acanthurus ssp.
   acanthurus
Loxanthocereus brevispinus = Cleistocactus peculiaris
Loxanthocereus camanaensis = Cleistocactus sextonianus
Loxanthocereus canetensis = Cleistocactus acanthurus ssp.
   acanthurus
Loxanthocereus cantaensis = Cleistocactus peculiaris
Loxanthocereus convergens = Cleistocactus acanthurus ssp.
   acanthurus
Loxanthocereus cullmannianus = Cleistocactus acanthurus ssp.
   acanthurus
Loxanthocereus deserticola = Cleistocactus clavispinus
Loxanthocereus eremiticus = Cleistocactus acanthurus ssp.
   acanthurus
Loxanthocereus erigens = Cleistocactus acanthurus ssp.
   acanthurus
Loxanthocereus eriotrichus = Cleistocactus acanthurus ssp.
   acanthurus
Loxanthocereus eulalianus = Cleistocactus acanthurus ssp.
   acanthurus
Loxanthocereus faustianus = Cleistocactus acanthurus ssp.
   faustianus
Loxanthocereus ferrugineus = Cleistocactus clavispinus
Loxanthocereus formosus = Matucana formosa
Loxanthocereus gracilis = Cleistocactus sextonianus
Loxanthocereus gracilispinus = Cleistocactus acanthurus ssp.
   acanthurus
Loxanthocereus granditessellatus = Cleistocactus serpens
Loxanthocereus hystrix = Cleistocactus hystrix
Loxanthocereus jajoianus = Cleistocactus sepium
Loxanthocereus keller-badensis = Cleistocactus acanthurus ssp.
   acanthurus
Loxanthocereus madisoniorum = Matucana madisoniorum
Loxanthocereus montanus = Cleistocactus hystrix
Loxanthocereus multifloccosus = Cleistocactus acanthurus ssp.
   acanthurus
Loxanthocereus nanus = Cleistocactus sextonianus
Loxanthocereus neglectus = Cleistocactus acanthurus ssp.
   acanthurus
Loxanthocereus otuscensis = Cleistocactus serpens
Loxanthocereus pacaranensis = Cleistocactus acanthurus ssp.
   acanthurus
Loxanthocereus pachycladus = Cleistocactus pachycladus
Loxanthocereus parvitesselatus = Cleistocactus serpens
Loxanthocereus peculiaris = Cleistocactus peculiaris
Loxanthocereus piscoensis = Cleistocactus pachycladus
Loxanthocereus pullatus = Cleistocactus acanthurus ssp. *pullatus*
Loxanthocereus puquiensis = Cleistocactus sextonianus
Loxanthocereus riomajensis = Cleistocactus sextonianus
Loxanthocereus sextonianus = Cleistocactus sextonianus
Loxanthocereus splendens = Cleistocactus sextonianus
Loxanthocereus sulcifer = Cleistocactus serpens
Loxanthocereus trujilloensis = Cleistocactus chotaensis
Loxanthocereus variabilis = Cleistocactus sextonianus
Loxanthocereus xylorhisus = Cleistocactus xylorhizus
Loxanthocereus yauyosensis = Cleistocactus pachycladus
Loxomorchis = Smithsonia
Ludisia spp.: #7 **II** ORCHIDACEAE
Lueddemannia spp.: #7 **II** ORCHIDACEAE
Luerella = Masdevallia
Luisia spp.: #7 **II** ORCHIDACEAE
Lycaste spp.: #7 **II** ORCHIDACEAE
Lycomormium spp.: #7 **II** ORCHIDACEAE
Lymanbensonia micrantha = Lepismium micranthum
Lyperanthus spp.: #7 **II** ORCHIDACEAE
Lyraea = Bulbophyllum
Lyroglossa = Stenorrhynchos
Lysias = Platanthera
Lysiella = Platanthera
Lysimnia = Brassavola
Macacuaba (S): *Platymiscium pleiostachyum*
Macdonaldia = Thelymitra
Macodes spp.: #7 **II** ORCHIDACEAE
Macradenia spp.: #7 **II** ORCHIDACEAE

Macrocentrum = Habenaria
Macrochilus = Miltonia
Macroclinium = Notylia
Macrolepis = Bulbophyllum
Macroplectrum = Angraecum
Macropodanthus spp.: #7 **II** ORCHIDACEAE
Macrostomium = Dendrobium
Macrostylis = Corymborkis
Macrozamia cardiacensis: #1 **II** ZAMIACEAE
Macrozamia communis: #1 **II** ZAMIACEAE
Macrozamia concinna: #1 **II** ZAMIACEAE
Macrozamia conferta: #1 **II** ZAMIACEAE
Macrozamia corallipes = Macrozamia spiralis
Macrozamia cranei: #1 **II** ZAMIACEAE
Macrozamia crassifolia: #1 **II** ZAMIACEAE
Macrozamia denisonii = Lepidozamia peroffskyana
Macrozamia denisonii var. *hopei = Lepidozamia hopei*
Macrozamia diplomera: #1 **II** ZAMIACEAE
Macrozamia douglasii: #1 **II** ZAMIACEAE
Macrozamia dyeri: #1 **II** ZAMIACEAE
Macrozamia elegans: #1 **II** ZAMIACEAE
Macrozamia fawcettii: #1 **II** ZAMIACEAE
Macrozamia fearnsidei: #1 **II** ZAMIACEAE
Macrozamia flexuosa: #1 **II** ZAMIACEAE
Macrozamia fraseri: #1 **II** ZAMIACEAE
Macrozamia glaucophylla: #1 **II** ZAMIACEAE
Macrozamia heteromera: #1 **II** ZAMIACEAE
Macrozamia heteromera var. *dicranophylloides = Macrozamia*
   stenomera
Macrozamia heteromera var. *glauca = Macrozamia glaucophylla*
Macrozamia heteromera var. *tenuifolia = Macrozamia stenomera*
Macrozamia heteromera var. *tenuifoliaÂ²harmsii = Macrozamia*
   stenomera
Macrozamia hopei = Lepidozamia hopei
Macrozamia humilis: #1 **II** ZAMIACEAE
Macrozamia johnsonii: #1 **II** ZAMIACEAE
Macrozamia littoralis = Dioon edule
Macrozamia lomandroides: #1 **II** ZAMIACEAE
Macrozamia longispina: #1 **II** ZAMIACEAE
Macrozamia lucida: #1 **II** ZAMIACEAE
Macrozamia macdonnellii: #1 **II** ZAMIACEAE
Macrozamia machinii = Macrozamia plurinervia
Macrozamia mackenzii = Macrozamia miquelii
Macrozamia miquelii: #1 **II** ZAMIACEAE
Macrozamia montana: #1 **II** ZAMIACEAE
Macrozamia moorei: #1 **II** ZAMIACEAE
Macrozamia mountperriensis: #1 **II** ZAMIACEAE
Macrozamia occidua: #1 **II** ZAMIACEAE
Macrozamia oldfieldii = Macrozamia fraseri
Macrozamia parcifolia: #1 **II** ZAMIACEAE
Macrozamia pauli-guilielmi: #1 **II** ZAMIACEAE
Macrozamia pauli-guilielmi ssp. *flexuosa = Macrozamia flexuosa*
Macrozamia pauli-guilielmi ssp. *plurinervia = Macrozamia*
   plurinervia
Macrozamia pectinata = Dioon edule
Macrozamia platyrhachis: #1 **II** ZAMIACEAE
Macrozamia plumosa = Macrozamia pauli-guilielmi
Macrozamia plurinervia: #1 **II** ZAMIACEAE
Macrozamia polymorpha: #1 **II** ZAMIACEAE
Macrozamia preissii = Macrozamia fraseri
Macrozamia preissii ssp. *dyeri = Macrozamia dyeri*
Macrozamia reducta: #1 **II** ZAMIACEAE
Macrozamia riedlei: #1 **II** ZAMIACEAE
Macrozamia secunda: #1 **II** ZAMIACEAE
Macrozamia spiralis: #1 **II** ZAMIACEAE
Macrozamia spiralis var. *corallipes = Macrozamia spiralis*
Macrozamia spiralis var. *cylindracea = Macrozamia pauli-*
   guilielmi
Macrozamia spiralis var. *diplomera = Macrozamia diplomera*
Macrozamia spiralis var. *fawcettii = Macrozamia fawcettii*
Macrozamia spiralis var. *flexuosa = Macrozamia flexuosa*
Macrozamia spiralis var. *heteromera = Macrozamia heteromera*
Macrozamia spiralis var. *secunda = Macrozamia secunda*
Macrozamia stenomera: #1 **II** ZAMIACEAE

Checklist of flora/Lista de especies de flora/Liste des espèces végétales

Macrozamia tridentata ssp. *cylindrica* var. *corallipes* = *Macrozamia spiralis*

Macrozamia tridentata ssp. *cylindrica* var. corallipes f. *dielsii* = *Macrozamia reducta*

Macrozamia tridentata ssp. *cylindrica* var. corallipes f. *wallsend* = *Macrozamia reducta*

Macrozamia tridentata ssp. *cylindrica* var. *secunda* = *Macrozamia secunda*

Macrozamia tridentata ssp. *mountperriensis* = *Macrozamia mountperriensis*

Macrozamia tridentata ssp. *mountperriensis* var. *douglasii* = *Macrozamia douglasii*

Macrozamia tridentata ssp. *mountperriensis* var. *mackenzii* = *Macrozamia miquelii*

Macrozamia tridentata ssp. *mountperriensis* var. *miquelii* = *Macrozamia miquelii*

Macrozamia tridentata ssp. *mountperriensis* var. *miquelii* f. *diels* = *Macrozamia reducta*

Macrozamia tridentata ssp. *mountperriensis* var. *miquelii* f. milka = *Macrozamia miquelii*

Macrozamia viridis: #1 **II** ZAMIACEAE

Madera de Agar (S): *Aquilaria malaccensis*

Maelenia = *Cattleya*

Magnolia candollei var. *obovata* = *Magnolia liliifera* var. *obovata*

Magnolia hodgsonii = *Magnolia liliifera* var. *obovata*

Magnolia liliifera var. *obovata*: #1 **III** MAGNOLIACEAE

Mahogani à grands feuilles (F): *Swietenia macrophylla*

Mahogani à petites feuilles (F): *Swietenia mahagoni*

Mahogani de Saint-Dominique (F): *Swietenia mahagoni*

Maiden's quiver tree (E): *Aloe ramosissima*

Maihuenia albolanata = *Maihuenia patagonica*

Maihuenia brachydelphys = *Maihuenia patagonica*

Maihuenia cumulata = *Maihuenia patagonica*

Maihuenia latispina = *Maihuenia patagonica*

Maihuenia patagonica: #4 **II** CACTACEAE

Maihuenia philippii = *Maihuenia poeppigii*

Maihuenia poeppigii: #4 **II** CACTACEAE

Maihuenia valentinii = *Maihuenia patagonica*

Maihueniopsis albomarginata = *Opuntia darwinii*

Maihueniopsis archiconoidea = *Opuntia archiconoidea*

Maihueniopsis boliviana = *Opuntia boldinghii*

Maihueniopsis camachoi = *Opuntia camachoi*

Maihueniopsis colorea = *Opuntia colorea*

Maihueniopsis conoidea = *Opuntia conoidea*

Maihueniopsis crassispina = *Opuntia crassipina*

Maihueniopsis darwinii = *Opuntia darwinii*

Maihueniopsis domeykoensis = *Opuntia domeykoensis*

Maihueniopsis glomerata = *Opuntia glomerata*

Maihueniopsis grandiflora = *Opuntia llanos-de-huanta*

Maihueniopsis hypogaea = *Opuntia glomerata*

Maihueniopsis leoncito = *Opuntia glomerata*

Maihueniopsis leptoclada = *Opuntia glomerata*

Maihueniopsis mandragora = *Opuntia minuta*

Maihueniopsis minuta = *Opuntia minuta*

Maihueniopsis molfinoi = *Opuntia glomerata*

Maihueniopsis molinensis = *Opuntia molinensis*

Maihueniopsis neuquensis = *Opuntia darwinii*

Maihueniopsis nigrispina = *Opuntia nigrispina*

Maihueniopsis ochrocentra = *Opuntia crystalenia*

Maihueniopsis ovallei = *Opuntia glomerata*

Maihueniopsis ovata = *Opuntia ovata*

Maihueniopsis pentlandii = *Opuntia pentlandii*

Maihueniopsis rahmeri = *Opuntia rahmeri*

Maihueniopsis wagenknechtii = *Opuntia wagenknechtii*

Main's nipple-cactus (E): *Mammillaria mainiae*

Malachadenia = *Bulbophyllum*

Malaxis spp.: #7 **II** ORCHIDACEAE

Malayan eaglewood tree (E): *Aquilaria malaccensis*

Malayan fern palm (E): *Cycas rumphii*

Malleola spp.: #7 **II** ORCHIDACEAE

Mamillopsis diguetii = *Mammillaria senilis*

Mamillopsis senilis = *Mammillaria senilis*

Mammillaria acultzingensis = *Mammillaria haageana* ssp. *acultzingensis*

Mammillaria alamensis = *Mammillaria sheldonii*

Mammillaria albata = *Mammillaria geminispina* ssp. *leucocentra*

Mammillaria albescens = *Mammillaria decipiens* ssp. *albescens*

Mammillaria albiarmata = *Mammillaria coahuilensis* ssp. *albiarmata*

Mammillaria albicans: #4 **II** CACTACEAE

Mammillaria albicans ssp. *albicans*: #4 **II** CACTACEAE

Mammillaria albicans ssp. *fraileana*: #4 **II** CACTACEAE

Mammillaria albicoma: #4 **II** CACTACEAE

Mammillaria albidula = *Mammillaria haageana* ssp. *conspicua*

Mammillaria albiflora: #4 **II** CACTACEAE

Mammillaria albilanata: #4 **II** CACTACEAE

Mammillaria albilanata ssp. *albilanata*: #4 **II** CACTACEAE

Mammillaria albilanata ssp. *oaxacana*: #4 **II** CACTACEAE

Mammillaria albilanata ssp. *reppenhagenii*: #4 **II** CACTACEAE

Mammillaria albilanata ssp. *tegelbergiana*: #4 **II** CACTACEAE

Mammillaria albrechtiana = *Mammillaria rekoi*

Mammillaria amajacensis: #4 **II** CACTACEAE

Mammillaria angelensis = *Mammillaria dioica* ssp. *angelensis*

Mammillaria anniana: #4 **II** CACTACEAE

Mammillaria antesbergeriana = *Mammillaria wagneriana*

Mammillaria apamensis = *Mammillaria wiesingeri* ssp. *apamensis*

Mammillaria apozolensis = *Mammillaria petterssonii*

Mammillaria applanata = *Mammillaria heyderi* ssp. *hemisphaerica*

Mammillaria arida = *Mammillaria petrophila* ssp. *arida*

Mammillaria armatissima = *Mammillaria gigantea*

Mammillaria armillata: #4 **II** CACTACEAE

Mammillaria armillata ssp. *armillata*: #4 **II** CACTACEAE

Mammillaria armillata ssp. *cerralboa*: #4 **II** CACTACEAE

Mammillaria arroyensis = *Mammillaria formosa*

Mammillaria ascensionis = *Mammillaria glassii* ssp. *ascensionis*

Mammillaria atroflorens = *Mammillaria mystax*

Mammillaria aureiceps = *Mammillaria rhodantha* ssp. *aureiceps*

Mammillaria aureilanata: #4 **II** CACTACEAE

Mammillaria aureispina = *Mammillaria rekoi* ssp. *aureispina*

Mammillaria aureoviridis = *Mammillaria crinita* ssp. *leucantha*

Mammillaria auriareolis = *Mammillaria parkinsonii*

Mammillaria auricantha = *Mammillaria standleyi*

Mammillaria auricoma = *Mammillaria spinosissima* ssp. *tepoxtlana*

Mammillaria aurihamata = *Mammillaria crinita* ssp. *leucantha*

Mammillaria aurisaeta = *Mammillaria picta* ssp. *picta*

Mammillaria auritricha = *Mammillaria standleyi*

Mammillaria avila-camachoi = *Mammillaria perbella*

Mammillaria backebergiana: #4 **II** CACTACEAE

Mammillaria backebergiana ssp. *backebergiana*: #4 **II** CACTACEAE

Mammillaria backebergiana ssp. *ernestii*: #4 **II** CACTACEAE

Mammillaria balsasoides = *Mammillaria beneckei*

Mammillaria bambusiphila = *Mammillaria xaltianguensis* ssp. *bambusiphila*

Mammillaria barbata: #4 **II** CACTACEAE

Mammillaria barkeri = *Mammillaria beneckei*

Mammillaria baumii: #4 **II** CACTACEAE

Mammillaria baxteriana = *Mammillaria petrophila* ssp. *baxteriana*

Mammillaria beiselii = *Mammillaria karwinskiana* ssp. *beiselii*

Mammillaria bella = *Mammillaria nunezii* ssp. *bella*

Mammillaria bellacantha = *Mammillaria canelensis*

Mammillaria bellisiana = *Mammillaria sonorensis*

Mammillaria beneckei: #4 **II** CACTACEAE

Mammillaria berkiana: #4 **II** CACTACEAE

Mammillaria bernalensis = *Mammillaria compressa* ssp. *compressa*

Mammillaria blossfeldiana: #4 **II** CACTACEAE

Mammillaria bocasana: #4 **II** CACTACEAE

Mammillaria bocasana ssp. *bocasana*: #4 **II** CACTACEAE

Mammillaria bocasana ssp. *eschauzieri*: #4 **II** CACTACEAE

Mammillaria bocensis: #4 **II** CACTACEAE

Mammillaria boelderliana: #4 **II** CACTACEAE

Mammillaria bombycina: #4 **II** CACTACEAE

Mammillaria bombycina ssp. *bombycina*: #4 **II** CACTACEAE

Mammillaria bombycina ssp. *perezdelarosae*: #4 **II** CACTACEAE

Mammillaria bonavitii = *Mammillaria rhodantha*

Mammillaria boolii: #4 **II** CACTACEAE

Mammillaria brachytrichion = *Mammillaria mercadensis*

Mammillaria brandegeei: #4 **II** CACTACEAE

Mammillaria brandegeei ssp. *brandegeei*: #4 **II** CACTACEAE
Mammillaria brandegeei ssp. *gabbii*: #4 **II** CACTACEAE
Mammillaria brandegeei ssp. *glareosa*: #4 **II** CACTACEAE
Mammillaria brandegeei ssp. *lewisiana*: #4 **II** CACTACEAE
Mammillaria brauneana = *Mammillaria klissingiana*
Mammillaria bravoae = *Mammillaria hahniana* ssp. *bravoae*
Mammillaria brevicrinita = *Mammillaria crinita* ssp. *leucantha*
Mammillaria bucareliensis = *Mammillaria magnimamma*
Mammillaria buchenaui = *Mammillaria crucigera* ssp. *crucigera*
Mammillaria bullardiana = *Mammillaria hutchisoniana* ssp. *hutchisoniana*
Mammillaria buxbaumiana = *Mammillaria densispina*
Mammillaria cadereytana = *Mammillaria crinita* ssp. *crinita*
Mammillaria cadereytensis = *Mammillaria perbella*
Mammillaria caerulea = *Mammillaria formosa* ssp. *chionocephala*
Mammillaria calacantha = *Mammillaria rhodantha*
Mammillaria calleana = *Mammillaria crinita* ssp. *wildii*
Mammillaria camptotricha = *Mammillaria decipiens* ssp. *camptotricha*
Mammillaria candida = *Mammilloydia candida*
Mammillaria canelensis: #4 **II** CACTACEAE
Mammillaria capensis: #4 **II** CACTACEAE
Mammillaria carmenae: #4 **II** CACTACEAE
Mammillaria carnea: #4 **II** CACTACEAE
Mammillaria carretii: #4 **II** CACTACEAE
Mammillaria casoi = *Mammillaria mystax*
Mammillaria celsiana = *Mammillaria muehlenpfordtii*
Mammillaria centralifera = *Mammillaria compressa* ssp. *centralifera*
Mammillaria centraliplumosa = *Mammillaria spinosissima* ssp. *spinosissima*
Mammillaria centricirrha = *Mammillaria magnimamma*
Mammillaria cerralboa = *Mammillaria armillata* ssp. *cerralboa*
Mammillaria chavezei = *Mammillaria barbata*
Mammillaria chiapensis = *Mammillaria columbiana* ssp. *yucatanensis*
Mammillaria chica = *Mammillaria stella-de-tacubaya*
Mammillaria chionocephala = *Mammillaria formosa* ssp. *chionocephala*
Mammillaria claviformis = *Mammillaria duoformis*
Mammillaria coahuilensis: #4 **II** CACTACEAE
Mammillaria coahuilensis ssp. *albiarmata*: #4 **II** CACTACEAE
Mammillaria coahuilensis ssp. *coahuilensis*: #4 **II** CACTACEAE
Mammillaria collina = *Mammillaria haageana* ssp. *elegans*
Mammillaria collinsii = *Mammillaria karwinskiana* ssp. *collinsii*
Mammillaria colonensis = *Mammillaria beneckei*
Mammillaria columbiana: #4 **II** CACTACEAE
Mammillaria columbiana ssp. *columbiana*: #4 **II** CACTACEAE
Mammillaria columbiana ssp. *yucatanensis*: #4 **II** CACTACEAE
Mammillaria compacticaulis = *Mammillaria matudae*
Mammillaria compressa: #4 **II** CACTACEAE
Mammillaria compressa ssp. *centralifera*: #4 **II** CACTACEAE
Mammillaria compressa ssp. *compressa*: #4 **II** CACTACEAE
Mammillaria confusa = *Mammillaria karwinskiana* ssp. *karwinskiana*
Mammillaria conspicua = *Mammillaria haageana* ssp. *conspicua*
Mammillaria cowperae = *Mammillaria moelleriana*
Mammillaria craigii: #4 **II** CACTACEAE
Mammillaria crassa = *Mammillaria wagneriana*
Mammillaria crassimammillis = *Mammillaria winterae* ssp. *aramberri*
Mammillaria crassior = *Mammillaria spinosissima* ssp. *tepoxtlana*
Mammillaria criniformis = *Mammillaria crinita*
Mammillaria crinita: #4 **II** CACTACEAE
Mammillaria crinita ssp. *crinita*: #4 **II** CACTACEAE
Mammillaria crinita ssp. *leucantha*: #4 **II** CACTACEAE
Mammillaria crinita ssp. *scheinvariana* = *Mammillaria scheinvariana*
Mammillaria crinita ssp. *wildii*: #4 **II** CACTACEAE
Mammillaria crispiseta = *Mammillaria mystax*
Mammillaria crucigera: #4 **II** CACTACEAE
Mammillaria crucigera ssp. *crucigera*: #4 **II** CACTACEAE
Mammillaria crucigera ssp. *tlalocii*: #4 **II** CACTACEAE
Mammillaria dasyacantha = *Escobaria dasyacantha*
Mammillaria dasyacantha = *Mammillaria laui* ssp. *dasyacantha*

Mammillaria dawsonii = *Mammillaria brandegeei* ssp. *glareosa*
Mammillaria dealbata = *Mammillaria haageana*
Mammillaria decipiens: #4 **II** CACTACEAE
Mammillaria decipiens ssp. *albescens*: #4 **II** CACTACEAE
Mammillaria decipiens ssp. *camptotricha*: #4 **II** CACTACEAE
Mammillaria decipiens ssp. *decipiens*: #4 **II** CACTACEAE
Mammillaria deherdtiana: #4 **II** CACTACEAE
Mammillaria deherdtiana ssp. *deherdtiana*: #4 **II** CACTACEAE
Mammillaria deherdtiana ssp. *dodsonii*: #4 **II** CACTACEAE
Mammillaria densispina: #4 **II** CACTACEAE
Mammillaria denudata = *Mammillaria lasiacantha* ssp. *lasiacantha*
Mammillaria diguetii = *Mammillaria senilis*
Mammillaria dioica: (E) Strawberry cactus #4 **II** CACTACEAE
Mammillaria dioica ssp. *angelensis*: #4 **II** CACTACEAE
Mammillaria dioica ssp. *dioica*: #4 **II** CACTACEAE
Mammillaria dioica ssp. *estebanensis*: #4 **II** CACTACEAE
Mammillaria discolor: #4 **II** CACTACEAE
Mammillaria discolor ssp. *discolor*: #4 **II** CACTACEAE
Mammillaria discolor ssp. *esperanzaensis*: #4 **II** CACTACEAE
Mammillaria dixanthocentron: #4 **II** CACTACEAE
Mammillaria dodsonii = *Mammillaria deherdtiana* ssp. *dodsonii*
Mammillaria donatii = *Mammillaria haageana*
Mammillaria droegeana = *Mammillaria microhelia*
Mammillaria dumetorum = *Mammillaria schiedeana* ssp. *dumetorum*
Mammillaria duoformis: #4 **II** CACTACEAE
Mammillaria durangicola = *Mammillaria grusonii*
Mammillaria durispina = *Mammillaria polythele* ssp. *durispina*
Mammillaria duwei: #4 **II** CACTACEAE
Mammillaria dyckiana = *Mammillaria haageana*
Mammillaria ebenacantha = *Mammillaria karwinskiana*
Mammillaria echinaria = *Mammillaria elongata* ssp. *echinaria*
Mammillaria egregaria = *Mammillaria lasiacantha* ssp. *egregia*
Mammillaria eichlamii = *Mammillaria voburnensis* ssp. *eichlamii*
Mammillaria ekmanii: #4 **II** CACTACEAE
Mammillaria elegans = *Mammillaria geminispina*
Mammillaria elegans = *Mammillaria haageana* ssp. *elegans*
Mammillaria elongata: #4 **II** CACTACEAE
Mammillaria elongata ssp. *echinaria*: #4 **II** CACTACEAE
Mammillaria elongata ssp. *elongata*: #4 **II** CACTACEAE
Mammillaria erectacantha = *Mammillaria wiesingeri* ssp. *apamensis*
Mammillaria erectohamata = *Mammillaria crinita* ssp. *leucantha*
Mammillaria eriacantha: #4 **II** CACTACEAE
Mammillaria ernestii = *Mammillaria backebergiana* ssp. *ernestii*
Mammillaria erythra = *Mammillaria mystax*
Mammillaria erythrocalyx = *Mammillaria duoformis*
Mammillaria erythrosperma: #4 **II** CACTACEAE
Mammillaria eschauzieri = *Mammillaria bocasana* ssp. *eschauzieri*
Mammillaria esperanzaensis = *Mammillaria discolor* ssp. *esperanzaensis*
Mammillaria esseriana = *Mammillaria compressa*
Mammillaria estanzuelensis = *Mammilloydia candida*
Mammillaria estebanensis = *Mammillaria dioica* ssp. *estebanensis*
Mammillaria evermanniana: #4 **II** CACTACEAE
Mammillaria fasciculata = *Mammillaria thornberi* ssp. *thornberi*
Mammillaria felicis = *Mammillaria voburnensis* ssp. *voburnensis*
Mammillaria felipensis = *Mammillaria nana*
Mammillaria fera-rubra = *Mammillaria rhodantha* ssp. *fera-rubra*
Mammillaria fittkaui: #4 **II** CACTACEAE
Mammillaria fittkaui ssp. *fittkaui*: #4 **II** CACTACEAE
Mammillaria fittkaui ssp. *limonensis*: #4 **II** CACTACEAE
Mammillaria fittkaui ssp. *mathildae* = *Mammillaria mathildae*
Mammillaria flavescens = *Mammillaria nivosa*
Mammillaria flavicentra: #4 **II** CACTACEAE
Mammillaria flavihamata = *Mammillaria rettigiana*
Mammillaria floresii = *Mammillaria standleyi*
Mammillaria formosa: #4 **II** CACTACEAE
Mammillaria formosa ssp. *chionocephala*: #4 **II** CACTACEAE
Mammillaria formosa ssp. *formosa*: #4 **II** CACTACEAE
Mammillaria formosa ssp. *microthele*: #4 **II** CACTACEAE
Mammillaria formosa ssp. *pseudocrucigera*: #4 **II** CACTACEAE
Mammillaria fraileana = *Mammillaria albicans* ssp. *fraileana*
Mammillaria freudenbergeri = *Mammillaria winterae* ssp. *winterae*

Checklist of flora/Lista de especies de flora/Liste des espèces végétales

Mammillaria fuauxiana = Mammillaria albilanata ssp. *albilanata*
Mammillaria fuscohamata = Mammillaria jaliscana
Mammillaria gabbii = Mammillaria brandegeei ssp. *gabbii*
Mammillaria garessii = Mammillaria barbata
Mammillaria gasseriana = Mammillaria stella-de-tacubaya
Mammillaria gasterantha = Mammillaria spinosissima
Mammillaria gatesii = Mammillaria petrophila ssp. *petrophila*
Mammillaria gaumeri = Mammillaria heyderi ssp. *gaumeri*
Mammillaria geminispina: #4 **II** CACTACEAE
Mammillaria geminispina ssp. *geminispina*: #4 **II** CACTACEAE
Mammillaria geminispina ssp. *leucocentra*: #4 **II** CACTACEAE
Mammillaria gigantea: #4 **II** CACTACEAE
Mammillaria gilensis = Mammillaria rettigiana
Mammillaria giselae = Mammillaria schiedeana ssp. *giselae*
Mammillaria glareosa = Mammillaria brandegeei ssp. *glareosa*
Mammillaria glassii: #4 **II** CACTACEAE
Mammillaria glassii ssp. *ascensionis*: #4 **II** CACTACEAE
Mammillaria glassii ssp. *glassii*: #4 **II** CACTACEAE
Mammillaria glochidiata: #4 **II** CACTACEAE
Mammillaria glomerata = Mammillaria prolifera
Mammillaria goldii = Mammillaria saboae ssp. *goldii*
Mammillaria goodridgii: #4 **II** CACTACEAE
Mammillaria gracilis = Mammillaria vetula ssp. *gracilis*
Mammillaria grahamii: (E) Graham's Nipple-cactus #4 **II** CACTACEAE
Mammillaria grusonii: #4 **II** CACTACEAE
Mammillaria gueldemanniana = Mammillaria sheldonii
Mammillaria guelzowiana: #4 **II** CACTACEAE
Mammillaria guerreronis: #4 **II** CACTACEAE
Mammillaria guiengolensis = Mammillaria beneckei
Mammillaria guillauminiana: #4 **II** CACTACEAE
Mammillaria guirocobensis = Mammillaria sheldonii
Mammillaria gummifera = Mammillaria heyderi ssp. *gummifera*
Mammillaria haageana: #4 **II** CACTACEAE
Mammillaria haageana ssp. *acultzingensis*: #4 **II** CACTACEAE
Mammillaria haageana ssp. *conspicua*: #4 **II** CACTACEAE
Mammillaria haageana ssp. *elegans*: #4 **II** CACTACEAE
Mammillaria haageana ssp. *haageana*: #4 **II** CACTACEAE
Mammillaria haageana ssp. *san-angelensis*: #4 **II** CACTACEAE
Mammillaria haageana ssp. *schmollii*: #4 **II** CACTACEAE
Mammillaria haasii = Mammillaria spinosissima ssp. *spinosissima*
Mammillaria hahniana: #4 **II** CACTACEAE
Mammillaria hahniana ssp. *bravoae*: #4 **II** CACTACEAE
Mammillaria hahniana ssp. *hahniana*: #4 **II** CACTACEAE
Mammillaria hahniana ssp. *mendeliana*: #4 **II** CACTACEAE
Mammillaria hahniana ssp. *woodsii*: #4 **II** CACTACEAE
Mammillaria halbingeri: #4 **II** CACTACEAE
Mammillaria halei: #4 **II** CACTACEAE
Mammillaria hamata: #4 **II** CACTACEAE
Mammillaria hamiltonhoytea = Mammillaria gigantea
Mammillaria hastifera = Mammillaria gigantea
Mammillaria haudeana = Mammillaria saboae ssp. *haudeana*
Mammillaria heidiae: #4 **II** CACTACEAE
Mammillaria hemisphaerica = Mammillaria heyderi ssp. *hemisphaerica*
Mammillaria hennisii = Mammillaria columbiana ssp. *columbiana*
Mammillaria hernandezii: #4 **II** CACTACEAE
Mammillaria herrerae: #4 **II** CACTACEAE
Mammillaria hertrichiana: #4 **II** CACTACEAE
Mammillaria heyderi: (E) Little Nipple-cactus #4 **II** CACTACEAE
Mammillaria heyderi ssp. *coahuilensis = Mammillaria coahuilensis* ssp. *coahuilensis*
Mammillaria heyderi ssp. *gaumeri*: #4 **II** CACTACEAE
Mammillaria heyderi ssp. *gummifera*: #4 **II** CACTACEAE
Mammillaria heyderi ssp. *hemisphaerica*: #4 **II** CACTACEAE
Mammillaria heyderi ssp. *heyderi*: #4 **II** CACTACEAE
Mammillaria heyderi ssp. *macdougalii*: #4 **II** CACTACEAE
Mammillaria heyderi ssp. *meiacantha*: #4 **II** CACTACEAE
Mammillaria hidalgensis = Mammillaria polythele ssp. *polythele*
Mammillaria hirsuta = Mammillaria bocasana ssp. *eschauzieri*
Mammillaria hoffmanniana = Mammillaria polythele ssp. *polythele*
Mammillaria huajuapensis = Mammillaria mystax
Mammillaria hubertmulleri = Mammillaria nunezii ssp. *nunezii*
Mammillaria huiguerensis = Mammillaria petterssonii
Mammillaria huitzilopochtli: #4 **II** CACTACEAE

Mammillaria humboldtii: #4 **II** CACTACEAE
Mammillaria hutchisoniana: #4 **II** CACTACEAE
Mammillaria hutchisoniana ssp. *hutchisoniana*: #4 **II** CACTACEAE
Mammillaria hutchisoniana ssp. *louisae*: #4 **II** CACTACEAE
Mammillaria ignota = Mammillaria albilanata ssp. *oaxacana*
Mammillaria igualensis = Mammillaria albilanata ssp. *albilanata*
Mammillaria inae = Mammillaria sheldonii
Mammillaria infernillensis = Mammillaria perbella
Mammillaria ingens = Mammillaria polythele ssp. *obconella*
Mammillaria insularis: #4 **II** CACTACEAE
Mammillaria isotensis = Mammillaria backebergiana ssp. *ernestii*
Mammillaria jaliscana: #4 **II** CACTACEAE
Mammillaria jaliscana ssp. *jaliscana*: #4 **II** CACTACEAE
Mammillaria jaliscana ssp. *zacatecasensis*: #4 **II** CACTACEAE
Mammillaria johnstonii: #4 **II** CACTACEAE
Mammillaria jozef-bergeri = Mammillaria karwinskiana
Mammillaria karwinskiana: #4 **II** CACTACEAE
Mammillaria karwinskiana ssp. *beiselii*: #4 **II** CACTACEAE
Mammillaria karwinskiana ssp. *collinsii*: #4 **II** CACTACEAE
Mammillaria karwinskiana ssp. *karwinskiana*: #4 **II** CACTACEAE
Mammillaria karwinskiana ssp. *nejapensis*: #4 **II** CACTACEAE
Mammillaria kewensis = Mammillaria polythele ssp. *polythele*
Mammillaria kleiniorum = Mammillaria jaliscana
Mammillaria klissingiana: #4 **II** CACTACEAE
Mammillaria knebeliana = Mammillaria bocasana ssp. *eschauzieri*
Mammillaria knippeliana: #4 **II** CACTACEAE
Mammillaria kraehenbuehlii: #4 **II** CACTACEAE
Mammillaria krasuckae = Mammillaria rekoi
Mammillaria kuentziana = Mammillaria vetula ssp. *vetula*
Mammillaria kunthii = Mammillaria haageana
Mammillaria kunzeana = Mammillaria bocasana ssp. *eschauzieri*
Mammillaria lanata = Mammillaria supertexta
Mammillaria lanigera = Mammillaria albilanata ssp. *oaxacana*
Mammillaria lanisumma = Mammillaria standleyi
Mammillaria lasiacantha: (E) Lace-spine Nipple-cactus #4 **II** CACTACEAE
Mammillaria lasiacantha ssp. *egregia*: #4 **II** CACTACEAE
Mammillaria lasiacantha ssp. *hyalina*: #4 **II** CACTACEAE
Mammillaria lasiacantha ssp. *lasiacantha*: #4 **II** CACTACEAE
Mammillaria lasiacantha ssp. *magallanii*: #4 **II** CACTACEAE
Mammillaria laui: #4 **II** CACTACEAE
Mammillaria laui ssp. *dasyacantha*: #4 **II** CACTACEAE
Mammillaria laui ssp. *laui*: #4 **II** CACTACEAE
Mammillaria laui ssp. *subducta*: #4 **II** CACTACEAE
Mammillaria lengdobleriana = Mammillaria lasiacantha ssp. *magallanii*
Mammillaria lenta: #4 **II** CACTACEAE
Mammillaria leona = Mammillaria pottsii
Mammillaria leptacantha = Mammillaria rekoi ssp. *leptacantha*
Mammillaria leucantha = Mammillaria crinita ssp. *leucantha*
Mammillaria leucocentra = Mammillaria geminispina ssp. *leucocentra*
Mammillaria lewisiana = Mammillaria brandegeei ssp. *lewisiana*
Mammillaria limonensis = Mammillaria fittkaui ssp. *limonensis*
Mammillaria linaresensis = Mammillaria melanocentra ssp. *linaresensis*
Mammillaria lindsayi: #4 **II** CACTACEAE
Mammillaria lloydii: #4 **II** CACTACEAE
Mammillaria longicoma = Mammillaria bocasana ssp. *eschauzieri*
Mammillaria longiflora: #4 **II** CACTACEAE
Mammillaria longiflora ssp. *longiflora*: #4 **II** CACTACEAE
Mammillaria longiflora ssp. *stampferi*: #4 **II** CACTACEAE
Mammillaria longimamma: (E) Green-fruit Nipple-cactus #4 **II** CACTACEAE
Mammillaria louisiae = Mammillaria hutchisoniana ssp. *louisae*
Mammillaria luethyi: #4 **II** CACTACEAE
Mammillaria macdougalii = Mammillaria heyderi ssp. *macdougalii*
Mammillaria macracantha = Mammillaria magnimamma
Mammillaria magallanii = Mammillaria lasiacantha ssp. *magallanii*
Mammillaria magneticola = Mammillaria vetula ssp. *vetula*
Mammillaria magnifica: #4 **II** CACTACEAE
Mammillaria magnimamma: #4 **II** CACTACEAE

Mammillaria mainiae: (E) Main's nipple-cactus #4 **II** CACTACEAE

Mammillaria mammillaris: #4 **II** CACTACEAE

Mammillaria marcosii: #4 **II** CACTACEAE

Mammillaria maritima = Mammillaria pondii ssp. *maritima*

Mammillaria marksiana: #4 **II** CACTACEAE

Mammillaria marnieriana = Mammillaria sheldonii

Mammillaria marshalliana = Mammillaria petrophila ssp. *baxteriana*

Mammillaria martinezii = Mammillaria supertexta

Mammillaria mathildae: #4 **II** CACTACEAE

Mammillaria matudae: #4 **II** CACTACEAE

Mammillaria mayensis = Mammillaria standleyi

Mammillaria mazatlanensis: #4 **II** CACTACEAE

Mammillaria mazatlanensis ssp. *mazatlanensis*: #4 **II** CACTACEAE

Mammillaria mazatlanensis ssp. *patonii*: #4 **II** CACTACEAE

Mammillaria meiacantha = Mammillaria heyderi ssp. *meiacantha*

Mammillaria meissneri = Mammillaria haageana ssp. *schmollii*

Mammillaria melaleuca: #4 **II** CACTACEAE

Mammillaria melanocentra: #4 **II** CACTACEAE

Mammillaria melanocentra ssp. *linaresensis*: #4 **II** CACTACEAE

Mammillaria melanocentra ssp. *melanocentra*: #4 **II** CACTACEAE

Mammillaria melanocentra ssp. *rubrograndis*: #4 **II** CACTACEAE

Mammillaria mendeliana = Mammillaria hahniana ssp. *mendeliana*

Mammillaria mercadensis: #4 **II** CACTACEAE

Mammillaria meridiorosei = Mammillaria wrightii ssp. *wilcoxii*

Mammillaria meyranii: #4 **II** CACTACEAE

Mammillaria microcarpa = Mammillaria grahamii

Mammillaria microcarpa ssp. *grahamii = Mammillaria grahamii*

Mammillaria microhelia: #4 **II** CACTACEAE

Mammillaria microheliopsis = Mammillaria microhelia

Mammillaria microthele = Mammillaria formosa ssp. *microthele*

Mammillaria miegiana: #4 **II** CACTACEAE

Mammillaria mieheana: #4 **II** CACTACEAE

Mammillaria milleri = Mammillaria grahamii

Mammillaria mitlensis = Mammillaria rekoi

Mammillaria mixtecensis = Mammillaria mystax

Mammillaria moelleriana: #4 **II** CACTACEAE

Mammillaria moeller-valdeziana = Mammillaria crinita ssp. *leucantha*

Mammillaria mollendorffiana = Mammillaria rhodantha ssp. *mollendorffiana*

Mammillaria mollihamata = Mammillaria crinita ssp. *crinita*

Mammillaria monancistracantha = Mammillaria nana

Mammillaria montensis = Mammillaria standleyi

Mammillaria monticola = Mammillaria albilanata ssp. *oaxacana*

Mammillaria morganiana: #4 **II** CACTACEAE

Mammillaria morricalii = Mammillaria barbata

Mammillaria movensis = Mammillaria sonorensis

Mammillaria muehlenpfordtii: #4 **II** CACTACEAE

Mammillaria multiceps = Mammillaria prolifera ssp. *texana*

Mammillaria multidigitata: #4 **II** CACTACEAE

Mammillaria multiformis = Mammillaria erythrosperma

Mammillaria multihamata = Mammillaria marcosii

Mammillaria multiseta = Mammillaria karwinskiana

Mammillaria mundtii = Mammillaria wiesingeri ssp. *apamensis*

Mammillaria mystax: #4 **II** CACTACEAE

Mammillaria nagliana = Mammillaria karwinskiana ssp. *collinsii*

Mammillaria nana: #4 **II** CACTACEAE

Mammillaria napina: #4 **II** CACTACEAE

Mammillaria nazasensis = Mammillaria pennispinosa ssp. *nazasensis*

Mammillaria nejapensis = Mammillaria karwinskiana ssp. *nejapensis*

Mammillaria neobertrandiana = Mammillaria lasiacantha ssp. *magallanii*

Mammillaria neocrucigera = Mammillaria parkinsonii

Mammillaria neomystax = Mammillaria karwinskiana

Mammillaria neopalmeri: #4 **II** CACTACEAE

Mammillaria neophaeacantha = Mammillaria polythele ssp. *polythele*

Mammillaria neopotosina = Mammillaria muehlenpfordtii

Mammillaria neoschwarzeana = Mammillaria bocensis

Mammillaria nivosa: (E) Pope's head #4 **II** CACTACEAE

Mammillaria noureddineana = Mammillaria albilanata ssp. *oaxacana*

Mammillaria nunezii: #4 **II** CACTACEAE

Mammillaria nunezii ssp. *bella*: #4 **II** CACTACEAE

Mammillaria nunezii ssp. *nunezii*: #4 **II** CACTACEAE

Mammillaria obconella = Mammillaria polythele ssp. *obconella*

Mammillaria obscura = Mammillaria petterssonii

Mammillaria occidentalis = Mammillaria mazatlanensis ssp. *mazatlanensis*

Mammillaria ochoterenae = Mammillaria discolor

Mammillaria ocotillensis = Mammillaria gigantea

Mammillaria oliviae = Mammillaria grahamii

Mammillaria orcuttii = Mammillaria carnea

Mammillaria orestera = Mammillaria barbata

Mammillaria ortizrubiana = Mammilloydia candida

Mammillaria oteroi: #4 **II** CACTACEAE

Mammillaria pachycylindrica = Mammillaria grusonii

Mammillaria pachyrhiza = Mammillaria discolor

Mammillaria pacifica = Mammillaria petrophila ssp. *baxteriana*

Mammillaria painteri: #4 **II** CACTACEAE

Mammillaria papasquiarensis = Mammillaria grusonii

Mammillaria parensis = Mammillaria rhodantha ssp. *pringlei*

Mammillaria parkinsonii: #4 **II** CACTACEAE

Mammillaria parrasensis = Mammillaria heyderi

Mammillaria patonii = Mammillaria mazatlanensis ssp. *patonii*

Mammillaria pectinifera: **I** CACTACEAE

Mammillaria peninsularis: #4 **II** CACTACEAE

Mammillaria pennispinosa: #4 **II** CACTACEAE

Mammillaria pennispinosa ssp. *nazasensis*: #4 **II** CACTACEAE

Mammillaria pennispinosa ssp. *pennispinosa*: #4 **II** CACTACEAE

Mammillaria perbella: #4 **II** CACTACEAE

Mammillaria perezdelarosae = Mammillaria bombycina ssp. *perezdelarosae*

Mammillaria petrophila: #4 **II** CACTACEAE

Mammillaria petrophila ssp. *arida*: #4 **II** CACTACEAE

Mammillaria petrophila ssp. *baxteriana*: #4 **II** CACTACEAE

Mammillaria petrophila ssp. *petrophila*: #4 **II** CACTACEAE

Mammillaria petterssonii: #4 **II** CACTACEAE

Mammillaria phitauiana: #4 **II** CACTACEAE

Mammillaria picta: #4 **II** CACTACEAE

Mammillaria picta ssp. *picta*: #4 **II** CACTACEAE

Mammillaria picta ssp. *viereckii*: #4 **II** CACTACEAE

Mammillaria pilcayensis = Mammillaria spinosissima ssp. *pilcayensis*

Mammillaria pilensis = Mammillaria petterssonii

Mammillaria pilispina: #4 **II** CACTACEAE

Mammillaria pitcayensis = Mammillaria spinosissima ssp. *pilcayensis*

Mammillaria plumosa: #4 **II** CACTACEAE

Mammillaria polyedra: #4 **II** CACTACEAE

Mammillaria polythele: #4 **II** CACTACEAE

Mammillaria polythele ssp. *durispina*: #4 **II** CACTACEAE

Mammillaria polythele ssp. *obconella*: #4 **II** CACTACEAE

Mammillaria polythele ssp. *polythele*: #4 **II** CACTACEAE

Mammillaria pondii: #4 **II** CACTACEAE

Mammillaria pondii ssp. *maritima*: #4 **II** CACTACEAE

Mammillaria pondii ssp. *pondii*: #4 **II** CACTACEAE

Mammillaria pondii ssp. *setispina*: #4 **II** CACTACEAE

Mammillaria poselgeri: #4 **II** CACTACEAE

Mammillaria posseltiana = Mammillaria rettigiana

Mammillaria pottsii: (E) Potts' Nipple-cactus #4 **II** CACTACEAE

Mammillaria praelii = Mammillaria karwinskiana

Mammillaria priessnitzii = Mammillaria magnimamma

Mammillaria pringlei = Mammillaria rhodantha ssp. *pringlei*

Mammillaria prolifera: #4 **II** CACTACEAE

Mammillaria prolifera ssp. *arachnoidea*: #4 **II** CACTACEAE

Mammillaria prolifera ssp. *haitiensis*: #4 **II** CACTACEAE

Mammillaria prolifera ssp. *prolifera*: #4 **II** CACTACEAE

Mammillaria prolifera ssp. *texana*: (E) West Indian nipple-cactus #4 **II** CACTACEAE

Mammillaria prolifera ssp. *zublerae*: #4 **II** CACTACEAE

Mammillaria pseudocrucigera = Mammillaria formosa ssp. *pseudocrucigera*
Mammillaria pseudorekoi = Mammillaria rekoi
Mammillaria pseudoscrippsiana = Mammillaria scrippsiana
Mammillaria pseudosimplex = Mammillaria mammillaris
Mammillaria puberula = Mammillaria crinita ssp. *leucantha*
Mammillaria pubispina = Mammillaria crinita
Mammillaria pullihamata = Mammillaria rekoi
Mammillaria pygmaea = Mammillaria crinita ssp. *crinita*
Mammillaria queretarica = Mammillaria perbella
Mammillaria radiaissima = Mammillaria baumii
Mammillaria rayonensis = Mammillaria pilispina
Mammillaria rectispina = Mammillaria dioica
Mammillaria rekoi: #4 **II** CACTACEAE
Mammillaria rekoi ssp. *aureispina*: #4 **II** CACTACEAE
Mammillaria rekoi ssp. *leptacantha*: #4 **II** CACTACEAE
Mammillaria rekoi ssp. *rekoi*: #4 **II** CACTACEAE
Mammillaria rekoiana = Mammillaria rekoi ssp. *rekoi*
Mammillaria reppenhagenii = Mammillaria albilanata ssp. *reppenhagenii*
Mammillaria rettigiana: #4 **II** CACTACEAE
Mammillaria rhodantha: #4 **II** CACTACEAE
Mammillaria rhodantha ssp. *aureiceps*: #4 **II** CACTACEAE
Mammillaria rhodantha ssp. *fera-rubra*: #4 **II** CACTACEAE
Mammillaria rhodantha ssp. *mccartenii*: #4 **II** CACTACEAE
Mammillaria rhodantha ssp. *mollendorffiana*: #4 **II** CACTACEAE
Mammillaria rhodantha ssp. *pringlei*: #4 **II** CACTACEAE
Mammillaria rhodantha ssp. *rhodantha*: #4 **II** CACTACEAE
Mammillaria ritteriana = Mammillaria formosa ssp. *chionocephala*
Mammillaria rosensis = Mammillaria parkinsonii
Mammillaria roseoalba: #4 **II** CACTACEAE
Mammillaria rossiana = Mammillaria duoformis
Mammillaria rubida = Mammillaria bocensis
Mammillaria rubrograndis = Mammillaria melanocentra ssp. *rubrograndis*
Mammillaria ruestii = Mammillaria columbiana ssp. *yucatanensis*
Mammillaria saboae: #4 **II** CACTACEAE
Mammillaria saboae ssp. *goldii*: #4 **II** CACTACEAE
Mammillaria saboae ssp. *haudeana*: #4 **II** CACTACEAE
Mammillaria saboae ssp. *saboae*: #4 **II** CACTACEAE
Mammillaria saffordii = Mammillaria carretii
Mammillaria saint-pieana = Mammillaria gigantea
Mammillaria san-angelensis = Mammillaria haageana ssp. *san-angelensis*
Mammillaria sanchez-mejoradae: #4 **II** CACTACEAE
Mammillaria sanjuanensis = Mammillaria rekoi
Mammillaria sanluisensis = Mammillaria pilispina
Mammillaria santaclarensis = Mammillaria barbata
Mammillaria sartorii: #4 **II** CACTACEAE
Mammillaria saxicola = Mammillaria magnimamma
Mammillaria scheinvariana: #4 **II** CACTACEAE
Mammillaria schelhasii = Mammillaria crinita
Mammillaria schiedeana: #4 **II** CACTACEAE
Mammillaria schiedeana ssp. *dumetorum*: #4 **II** CACTACEAE
Mammillaria schiedeana ssp. *giselae*: #4 **II** CACTACEAE
Mammillaria schiedeana ssp. *schiedeana*: #4 **II** CACTACEAE
Mammillaria schieliana = Mammillaria picta ssp. *picta*
Mammillaria schmollii = Mammillaria discolor
Mammillaria schumannii: #4 **II** CACTACEAE
Mammillaria schwartzii = Mammillaria coahuilensis ssp. *coahuilensis*
Mammillaria scrippsiana: #4 **II** CACTACEAE
Mammillaria sempervivi: #4 **II** CACTACEAE
Mammillaria senilis: #4 **II** CACTACEAE
Mammillaria setispina = Mammillaria pondii ssp. *setispina*
Mammillaria sheldonii: #4 **II** CACTACEAE
Mammillaria shurliana = Mammillaria blossfeldiana
Mammillaria silvatica = Mammillaria nunezii
Mammillaria simplex = Mammillaria mammillaris
Mammillaria sinistrohamata: #4 **II** CACTACEAE
Mammillaria slevinii = Mammillaria albicans ssp. *albicans*
Mammillaria soehlemannii = Mammillaria columbiana ssp. *columbiana*
Mammillaria solisii = Mammillaria nunezii ssp. *nunezii*
Mammillaria solisioides: **I** CACTACEAE

Mammillaria sonorensis: #4 **II** CACTACEAE
Mammillaria sphacelata: #4 **II** CACTACEAE
Mammillaria sphacelata ssp. *sphacelata*: #4 **II** CACTACEAE
Mammillaria sphacelata ssp. *viperina*: #4 **II** CACTACEAE
Mammillaria sphaerica: #4 **II** CACTACEAE
Mammillaria spinosissima: #4 **II** CACTACEAE
Mammillaria spinosissima ssp. *pilcayensis*: #4 **II** CACTACEAE
Mammillaria spinosissima ssp. *spinosissima*: #4 **II** CACTACEAE
Mammillaria spinosissima ssp. *tepoxtlana*: #4 **II** CACTACEAE
Mammillaria stampferi = Mammillaria longiflora ssp. *stampferi*
Mammillaria standleyi: #4 **II** CACTACEAE
Mammillaria stella-de-tacubaya: #4 **II** CACTACEAE
Mammillaria strobilina = Mammillaria karwinskiana
Mammillaria subducta = Mammillaria laui ssp. *subducta*
Mammillaria subtilis = Mammillaria pilispina
Mammillaria supertexta: #4 **II** CACTACEAE
Mammillaria supraflumen = Mammillaria nunezii
Mammillaria surculosa: #4 **II** CACTACEAE
Mammillaria swinglei = Mammillaria sheldonii
Mammillaria tayloriorum: #4 **II** CACTACEAE
Mammillaria tegelbergiana = Mammillaria albilanata ssp. *tegelbergiana*
Mammillaria tenampensis = Mammillaria sartorii
Mammillaria tepexicensis: #4 **II** CACTACEAE
Mammillaria tesopacensis = Mammillaria sonorensis
Mammillaria tetracantha = Mammillaria polythele ssp. *polythele*
Mammillaria tetrancistra: #4 **II** CACTACEAE
Mammillaria tezontle = Mammillaria crinita ssp. *leucantha*
Mammillaria theresae: #4 **II** CACTACEAE
Mammillaria thornberi: (E) Thornber's Fishhook cactus #4 **II** CACTACEAE
Mammillaria thornberi ssp. *thornberi*: #4 **II** CACTACEAE
Mammillaria thornberi ssp. *yaquensis*: #4 **II** CACTACEAE
Mammillaria tlalocii = Mammillaria crucigera ssp. *tlalocii*
Mammillaria tolimensis = Mammillaria compressa ssp. *compressa*
Mammillaria tonalensis: #4 **II** CACTACEAE
Mammillaria tropica = Mammillaria karwinskiana ssp. *collinsii*
Mammillaria uberiformis = Mammillaria longimamma
Mammillaria uncinata: #4 **II** CACTACEAE
Mammillaria unihamata = Mammillaria weingartiana
Mammillaria vagaspina = Mammillaria magnimamma
Mammillaria vallensis = Mammillaria magnimamma
Mammillaria variabilis = Mammillaria fittkaui
Mammillaria varieaculeata: #4 **II** CACTACEAE
Mammillaria vaupelii = Mammillaria haageana
Mammillaria verhaertiana = Mammillaria phitauiana
Mammillaria verticealba = Mammillaria rhodantha ssp. *mccartenii*
Mammillaria vetula: #4 **II** CACTACEAE
Mammillaria vetula ssp. *gracilis*: #4 **II** CACTACEAE
Mammillaria vetula ssp. *vetula*: #4 **II** CACTACEAE
Mammillaria viereckii = Mammillaria picta ssp. *viereckii*
Mammillaria viescensis = Mammillaria stella-de-tacubaya
Mammillaria viperina = Mammillaria sphacelata ssp. *viperina*
Mammillaria virginis = Mammillaria spinosissima ssp. *spinosissima*
Mammillaria viridiflora = Mammillaria barbata
Mammillaria voburnensis = Mammillaria voburnensis
Mammillaria voburnensis ssp. *eichlamii*: #4 **II** CACTACEAE
Mammillaria voburnensis ssp. *voburnensis*: #4 **II** CACTACEAE
Mammillaria wagneriana: #4 **II** CACTACEAE
Mammillaria weingartiana: #4 **II** CACTACEAE
Mammillaria wiesingeri: #4 **II** CACTACEAE
Mammillaria wiesingeri ssp. *apamensis*: #4 **II** CACTACEAE
Mammillaria wiesingeri ssp. *wiesingeri*: #4 **II** CACTACEAE
Mammillaria wilcoxii = Mammillaria wrightii ssp. *wilcoxii*
Mammillaria wildii = Mammillaria crinita ssp. *wildii*
Mammillaria winterae: #4 **II** CACTACEAE
Mammillaria winterae ssp. *aramberri*: #4 **II** CACTACEAE
Mammillaria winterae ssp. *winterae*: #4 **II** CACTACEAE
Mammillaria woburnensis: #4 **II** CACTACEAE
Mammillaria wohlschlageri = Mammillaria lasiacantha ssp. *hyalina*
Mammillaria woodsii = Mammillaria hahniana ssp. *woodsii*
Mammillaria wrightii: (E) Wright's fishhook cactus #4 **II** CACTACEAE

Mammillaria wrightii ssp. *wilcoxii*: #4 **II** CACTACEAE
Mammillaria wrightii ssp. *wrightii*: #4 **II** CACTACEAE
Mammillaria wuthenauiana = *Mammillaria nunezii* ssp. *nunezii*
Mammillaria xaltianguensis: #4 **II** CACTACEAE
Mammillaria xaltianguensis ssp. *bambusiphila*: #4 **II** CACTACEAE
Mammillaria xaltianguensis ssp. *xaltianguensis*: #4 **II** CACTACEAE
Mammillaria xanthina = *Mammillaria standleyi*
Mammillaria xochipilli = *Mammillaria polythele* ssp. *polythele*
Mammillaria yaquensis = *Mammillaria thornberi* ssp. *yaquensis*
Mammillaria yucatanensis = *Mammillaria columbiana* ssp. *yucatanensis*
Mammillaria zacatecasensis = *Mammillaria jaliscana* ssp. *zacatecasensis*
Mammillaria zahniana = *Mammillaria winterae* ssp. *winterae*
Mammillaria zeilmanniana: #4 **II** CACTACEAE
Mammillaria zephyranthoides: #4 **II** CACTACEAE
Mammillaria zeyeriana = *Mammillaria grusonii*
Mammillaria zopilotensis = *Mammillaria guerreronis*
Mammillaria zublerae = *Mammillaria prolifera* ssp. *zublerae*
Mammillaria zuccariniana = *Mammillaria magnimamma*
Mammilloydia candida: #4 **II** CACTACEAE
Mammilloydia candida ssp. *ortizrubiana* = *Mammilloydia candida*
Manniella spp.: #7 **II** ORCHIDACEAE
Manú (S): *Caryocar costaricense*
Mara (S): *Swietenia macrophylla*
Marenopuntia marenae = *Opuntia marenae*
Margarita de otoño (S): *Sternbergia* spp.
Margbensonia neriifolia = *Podocarpus neriifolius*
Margelliantha spp.: #7 **II** ORCHIDACEAE
Mariarisqueta = *Cheirostylis*
Marojejya darianii: **II** PALMAE
Marsh rose (E): *Orothamnus zeyheri*
Marsupiaria = *Maxillaria*
Masdevallia spp.: #7 **II** ORCHIDACEAE
Matucana aurantiaca: #4 **II** CACTACEAE
Matucana aurantiaca ssp. *aurantiaca*: #4 **II** CACTACEAE
Matucana aurantiaca ssp. *currundayensis*: #4 **II** CACTACEAE
Matucana aureiflora: #4 **II** CACTACEAE
Matucana blancii = *Matucana haynei* ssp. *herzogiana*
Matucana breviflora = *Matucana haynei* ssp. *hystrix*
Matucana calliantha = *Matucana krahnii*
Matucana calocephala = *Matucana haynei* ssp. *myriacantha*
Matucana calvescens = *Matucana aurantiaca* ssp. *aurantiaca*
Matucana celendinensis = *Matucana aureiflora*
Matucana cereoides = *Matucana haynei* ssp. *haynei*
Matucana comacephala: #4 **II** CACTACEAE
Matucana crinifera = *Matucana haynei* ssp. *herzogiana*
Matucana currundayensis = *Matucana aurantiaca* ssp. *currundayensis*
Matucana elongata = *Matucana haynei* ssp. *haynei*
Matucana formosa: #4 **II** CACTACEAE
Matucana fruticosa: #4 **II** CACTACEAE
Matucana hastifera = *Matucana aurantiaca* ssp. *currundayensis*
Matucana haynei: #4 **II** CACTACEAE
Matucana haynei ssp. *haynei*: #4 **II** CACTACEAE
Matucana haynei ssp. *herzogiana*: #4 **II** CACTACEAE
Matucana haynei ssp. *hystrix*: #4 **II** CACTACEAE
Matucana haynei ssp. *myriacantha*: #4 **II** CACTACEAE
Matucana herzogiana = *Matucana haynei* ssp. *herzogiana*
Matucana huagalensis: #4 **II** CACTACEAE
Matucana humboldtii = *Cleistocactus icosagonus*
Matucana hystrix = *Matucana haynei* ssp. *hystrix*
Matucana intertexta: #4 **II** CACTACEAE
Matucana krahnii: #4 **II** CACTACEAE
Matucana madisoniorum: #4 **II** CACTACEAE
Matucana megalantha = *Matucana haynei* ssp. *herzogiana*
Matucana multicolor = *Matucana haynei* ssp. *hystrix*
Matucana myriacantha = *Matucana haynei* ssp. *myriacantha*
Matucana oreodoxa: #4 **II** CACTACEAE
Matucana pallarensis = *Matucana aurantiaca* ssp. *aurantiaca*
Matucana paucicostata: #4 **II** CACTACEAE
Matucana polzii: #4 **II** CACTACEAE
Matucana pujupatii: #4 **II** CACTACEAE

Matucana purpureoalba = *Matucana haynei* ssp. *myriacantha*
Matucana ritteri: #4 **II** CACTACEAE
Matucana supertexta = *Matucana haynei* ssp. *haynei*
Matucana tuberculata: #4 **II** CACTACEAE
Matucana tuberculosa = *Matucana tuberculata*
Matucana variabilis = *Matucana haynei* ssp. *haynei*
Matucana weberbaueri: #4 **II** CACTACEAE
Matucana winteri = *Matucana haynei* ssp. *myriacantha*
Matucana yanganucensis = *Matucana haynei* ssp. *herzogiana*
Maturna = *Gomesa*
Maury's tillandsia (E): *Tillandsia mauryana*
Maxillaria spp.: #7 **II** ORCHIDACEAE
McDougal's cactus (E): *Disocactus macdougallii*
Meciclis = *Coryanthes*
Meconopsis regia: (E) Himalayan poppy #1 **III** PAPAVERACEAE
Mecosa = *Platanthera*
Mediocactus hahnianus = *Echinopsis hahniana*
Mediocactus pomifer = *Hylocereus trigonus*
Mediocalcar spp.: #7 **II** ORCHIDACEAE
Mediolobivia hirsutissima = *Echinopsis tiegeliana*
Medusea fructus-pini = *Euphorbia caput-medusae*
Medusea globosa = *Euphorbia globosa*
Medusea hamata = *Euphorbia hamata*
Medusea major = *Euphorbia caput-medusae*
Medusea patula = *Euphorbia tridentata*
Medusea tessellata = *Euphorbia caput-medusae*
Medusea tridentata = *Euphorbia tridentata*
Medusea tuberculata = *Euphorbia tuberculata*
Megaclinium = *Bulbophyllum*
Megalorchis = *Galeottia*
Megalotus spp.: #7 **II** ORCHIDACEAE
Megastylis spp.: #7 **II** ORCHIDACEAE
Meiracyllium spp.: #7 **II** ORCHIDACEAE
Melocactus actinacanthus = *Melocactus matanzanus*
Melocactus acunae = *Melocactus harlowii*
Melocactus acunae ssp. *lagunaensis* = *Melocactus harlowii*
Melocactus acunae var. *acunae* = *Melocactus harlowii*
Melocactus acunae var. *flavispinus* = *Melocactus harlowii*
Melocactus amethystinus = *Melocactus bahiensis* ssp. *amethystinus*
Melocactus ammotrophus = *Melocactus bahiensis* ssp. *amethystinus*
Melocactus amoenus = *Melocactus curvispinus* ssp. *caesius*
Melocactus amstutziae = *Melocactus peruvianus*
Melocactus andinus: #4 **II** CACTACEAE
Melocactus arcuatispinus = *Melocactus zehntneri*
Melocactus axiniphorus = *Melocactus concinnus*
Melocactus azulensis = *Melocactus ernestii* ssp. *ernestii*
Melocactus azureus: #4 **II** CACTACEAE
Melocactus azureus ssp. *azureus*: #4 **II** CACTACEAE
Melocactus azureus ssp. *ferreophilus*: #4 **II** CACTACEAE
Melocactus bahiensis: #4 **II** CACTACEAE
Melocactus bahiensis ssp. *amethystinus*: #4 **II** CACTACEAE
Melocactus bahiensis ssp. *bahiensis*: #4 **II** CACTACEAE
Melocactus barbarae = *Melocactus macracanthos*
Melocactus bellavistensis: #4 **II** CACTACEAE
Melocactus bellavistensis ssp. *bellavistensis*: #4 **II** CACTACEAE
Melocactus bellavistensis ssp. *onychacanthus*: #4 **II** CACTACEAE
Melocactus borhidii = *Melocactus harlowii*
Melocactus bozsingianus = *Melocactus macracanthos*
Melocactus broadwayi: #4 **II** CACTACEAE
Melocactus caesius = *Melocactus curvispinus* ssp. *caesius*
Melocactus canescens = *Melocactus zehntneri*
Melocactus caroli-linnaei: #4 **II** CACTACEAE
Melocactus communis = *Melocactus intortus*
Melocactus concinnus: #4 **II** CACTACEAE
Melocactus conoideus: (E) Conelike Turl's-cap cactus **I** CACTACEAE
Melocactus cremnophilus = *Melocactus oreas* ssp. *cremnophilus*
Melocactus curvicornis = *Melocactus zehntneri*
Melocactus curvispinus: #4 **II** CACTACEAE
Melocactus curvispinus ssp. *caesius*: #4 **II** CACTACEAE
Melocactus curvispinus ssp. *curvispinus*: #4 **II** CACTACEAE
Melocactus curvispinus ssp. *dawsonii*: #4 **II** CACTACEAE
Melocactus dawsonii = *Melocactus curvispinus* ssp. *dawsonii*

Melocactus deinacanthus: (E) Wonderfully-bristled Turk's-cap cactus **I** CACTACEAE
Melocactus deinacanthus ssp. *florschuetzianus* = *Melocactus ernestii* ssp. *longicarpus*
Melocactus deinacanthus ssp. *longicarpus* = *Melocactus ernestii* ssp. *longicarpus*
Melocactus delessertianus = *Melocactus curvispinus* ssp. *curvispinus*
Melocactus depressus = *Melocactus violaceus* ssp. *violaceus*
Melocactus diersianus = *Melocactus levitestatus*
Melocactus douradaensis = *Melocactus zehntneri*
Melocactus ellemeetii = *Melocactus violaceus* ssp. *margaritaceus*
Melocactus ernestii: #4 **II** CACTACEAE
Melocactus ernestii ssp. *ernestii*: #4 **II** CACTACEAE
Melocactus ernestii ssp. *longicarpus*: #4 **II** CACTACEAE
Melocactus erythracanthus = *Melocactus ernestii* ssp. *ernestii*
Melocactus erythranthus = *Melocactus ernestii* ssp. *ernestii*
Melocactus estevesii: #4 **II** CACTACEAE
Melocactus evae = *Melocactus harlowii*
Melocactus ferreophilus = *Melocactus azureus* ssp. *ferreophilus*
Melocactus florschuetzianus = *Melocactus ernestii* ssp. *longicarpus*
Melocactus fortalezensis = *Melocactus peruvianus*
Melocactus giganteus = *Melocactus zehntneri*
Melocactus glaucescens: (E) Woolly waxy-stemmed Turk's-cap cactus **I** CACTACEAE
Melocactus glauxianus = *Melocactus bahiensis* ssp. *amethystinus*
Melocactus griseoloviridis = *Melocactus bahiensis* ssp. *amethystinus*
Melocactus guaricensis = *Melocactus neryi*
Melocactus guitartii = *Melocactus curvispinus*
Melocactus harlowii: #4 **II** CACTACEAE
Melocactus helvolilanatus = *Melocactus zehntneri*
Melocactus hispaniolicus = *Melocactus lemairei*
Melocactus holguinensis = *Melocactus curvispinus*
Melocactus huallancaensis = *Melocactus peruvianus*
Melocactus inclinatus = *Melocactus macracanthos*
Melocactus inconcinnus = *Melocactus salvadorensis*
Melocactus interpositus = *Melocactus ernestii* ssp. *ernestii*
Melocactus intortus: (E) Pope's head, Red-topped barrel cactus #4 **II** CACTACEAE
Melocactus intortus ssp. *dominguensis*: #4 **II** CACTACEAE
Melocactus intortus ssp. *intortus*: #4 **II** CACTACEAE
Melocactus jakusii = *Melocactus curvispinus*
Melocactus jansenianus = *Melocactus peruvianus*
Melocactus krainzianus = *Melocactus azureus* ssp. *azureus*
Melocactus lanssensianus: #4 **II** CACTACEAE
Melocactus laui = *Melocactus macracanthos*
Melocactus lemairei: #4 **II** CACTACEAE
Melocactus lensselinkianus = *Melocactus bahiensis* ssp. *amethystinus*
Melocactus levitestatus: #4 **II** CACTACEAE
Melocactus lobelii = *Melocactus curvispinus* ssp. *caesius*
Melocactus loboguerreroi = *Melocactus curvispinus* ssp. *curvispinus*
Melocactus longicarpus = *Melocactus ernestii* ssp. *longicarpus*
Melocactus longispinus = *Melocactus ernestii* ssp. *ernestii*
Melocactus macracanthos: #4 **II** CACTACEAE
Melocactus macrodsicus = *Melocactus zehntneri*
Melocactus margaritaceus = *Melocactus violaceus* ssp. *margaritaceus*
Melocactus matanzanus: #4 **II** CACTACEAE
Melocactus maxonii = *Melocactus curvispinus* ssp. *curvispinus*
Melocactus mazelianus: #4 **II** CACTACEAE
Melocactus melocactoides = *Melocactus violaceus*
Melocactus montanus = *Melocactus ernestii* ssp. *longicarpus*
Melocactus mulequensis = *Melocactus ernestii* ssp. *longicarpus*
Melocactus nagyi = *Melocactus harlowii*
Melocactus neomontanus = *Melocactus ernestii* ssp. *longicarpus*
Melocactus neryi: #4 **II** CACTACEAE
Melocactus nitidus = *Melocactus ernestii* ssp. *ernestii*
Melocactus oaxacensis = *Melocactus curvispinus* ssp. *curvispinus*
Melocactus obtusipetalus = *Melocactus curvispinus* ssp. *curvispinus*
Melocactus ocujalii = *Melocactus harlowii*

Melocactus onychacanthus = *Melocactus bellavistensis* ssp. *onychacanthus*
Melocactus oreas: #4 **II** CACTACEAE
Melocactus oreas ssp. *bahiensis* = *Melocactus oreas* ssp. *oreas*
Melocactus oreas ssp. *cremnophilus*: #4 **II** CACTACEAE
Melocactus oreas ssp. *ernestii* = *Melocactus ernestii* ssp. *ernestii*
Melocactus oreas ssp. *oreas*: #4 **II** CACTACEAE
Melocactus oreas ssp. *rubrisaetosus* = *Melocactus oreas* ssp. *oreas*
Melocactus pachyacanthus: #4 **II** CACTACEAE
Melocactus pachyacanthus ssp. *pachyacanthus*: #4 **II** CACTACEAE
Melocactus pachyacanthus ssp. *viridis*: #4 **II** CACTACEAE
Melocactus paucispinus: (E) Few-spined Turk's-cap cactus **I** CACTACEAE
Melocactus pedernalensis = *Melocactus intortus* ssp. *dominguensis*
Melocactus perezassoi: #4 **II** CACTACEAE
Melocactus peruvianus: #4 **II** CACTACEAE
Melocactus pruinosus = *Melocactus concinnus*
Melocactus radoczii = *Melocactus harlowii*
Melocactus robustispinus = *Melocactus concinnus*
Melocactus roraimensis = *Melocactus smithii*
Melocactus rubrisaetosus = *Melocactus oreas* ssp. *oreas*
Melocactus rubrispinus = *Melocactus levitestatus*
Melocactus ruestii = *Melocactus curvispinus* ssp. *curvispinus*
Melocactus ruestii ssp. *cintalapensis* = *Melocactus curvispinus* ssp. *curvispinus*
Melocactus ruestii ssp. *maxonii* = *Melocactus curvispinus* ssp. *curvispinus*
Melocactus ruestii ssp. *oaxacensis* = *Melocactus curvispinus* ssp. *curvispinus*
Melocactus ruestii ssp. *sanctae-rosae* = *Melocactus curvispinus* ssp. *curvispinus*
Melocactus salvador = *Melocactus curvispinus* ssp. *curvispinus*
Melocactus salvadorensis: #4 **II** CACTACEAE
Melocactus saxicola = *Melocactus zehntneri*
Melocactus schatzlii: #4 **II** CACTACEAE
Melocactus schulzianus = *Melocactus neryi*
Melocactus securituberculatus = *Melocactus levitestatus*
Melocactus smithii: #4 **II** CACTACEAE
Melocactus trujilloensis = *Melocactus peruvianus*
Melocactus uebelmannii = *Melocactus levitestatus*
Melocactus unguispinus = *Melocactus peruvianus*
Melocactus violaceus: #4 **II** CACTACEAE
Melocactus violaceus ssp. *margaritaceus*: #4 **II** CACTACEAE
Melocactus violaceus ssp. *natalensis* = *Melocactus violaceus* ssp. *violaceus*
Melocactus violaceus ssp. *ritteri*: #4 **II** CACTACEAE
Melocactus violaceus ssp. *violaceus*: #4 **II** CACTACEAE
Melocactus warasii = *Melocactus levitestatus*
Melocactus zehntneri: #4 **II** CACTACEAE
Melocactus zehntneri ssp. *canescens* = *Melocactus zehntneri*
Melocactus zehntneri ssp. *robustispinus* = *Melocactus concinnus*
Menadena = *Maxillaria*
Menadenium = *Zygosepalum*
Mendoncella = *Galeottia*
Menephora = *Paphiopedilum*
Mesadenella = *Stenorrhynchos*
Mesadenus = *Brachystele*
Mesa-Verde cactus (E): *Sclerocactus mesae-verdae*
Mesoclastes = *Luisia*
Mesodactylis = *Apostasia*
Mesoglossum spp.: #7 **II** ORCHIDACEAE
Mesoptera = *Liparis*
Mesospinidium spp.: #7 **II** ORCHIDACEAE
Metachilum = *Appendicula*
Mexican mahogany (E): *Swietenia humilis*
Mexicoa spp.: #7 **II** ORCHIDACEAE
Mexipedium spp.: #7 **II** ORCHIDACEAE
Mexipedium xerophyticum = *Phragmipedium xerophyticum*
Meyerocactus horizonthalonius = *Echinocactus horizonthalonius*
Micranthocereus albicephalus: #4 **II** CACTACEAE
Micranthocereus aureispinus = *Micranthocereus albicephalus*
Micranthocereus auriazureus: #4 **II** CACTACEAE
Micranthocereus densiflorus = *Micranthocereus flaviflorus*
Micranthocereus dolichospermaticus: #4 **II** CACTACEAE

Micranthocereus estevesii: #4 **II** CACTACEAE
Micranthocereus flaviflorus: #4 **II** CACTACEAE
Micranthocereus flaviflorus ssp. *densiflorus* = *Micranthocereus flaviflorus*
Micranthocereus haematocarpus = *Micranthocereus purpureus*
Micranthocereus lehmannianus = *Micranthocereus purpureus*
Micranthocereus monteazulensis = *Micranthocereus albicephalus*
Micranthocereus polyanthus: #4 **II** CACTACEAE
Micranthocereus purpureus: #4 **II** CACTACEAE
Micranthocereus ruficeps = *Micranthocereus purpureus*
Micranthocereus streckeri: #4 **II** CACTACEAE
Micranthocereus uilianus = *Micranthocereus flaviflorus*
Micranthocereus violaciflorus: #4 **II** CACTACEAE
Microchilus = *Erythrodes*
Microcoelia spp.: #7 **II** ORCHIDACEAE
Microcycas calocoma: (E) Palm corcho, (S) Palma corcho **I** ZAMIACEAE
Microepidendrum = *Epidendrum*
Microholmesia = *Angraecopsis*
Micropera spp.: #7 **II** ORCHIDACEAE
Microphytanthe = *Dendrobium*
Micropuntia barkleyana = *Opuntia pulchella*
Micropuntia brachyrhopalica = *Opuntia pulchella*
Micropuntia gracilicylindrica = *Opuntia pulchella*
Micropuntia pulchella = *Opuntia pulchella*
Micropuntia pygmaea = *Opuntia pulchella*
Micropuntia tuberculosirhopalica = *Opuntia pulchella*
Micropuntia weigandii = *Opuntia pulchella*
Microsaccus spp.: #7 **II** ORCHIDACEAE
Microstylis = *Malaxis*
Microtatorchis spp.: #7 **II** ORCHIDACEAE
Microterangis spp.: #7 **II** ORCHIDACEAE
Microtheca = *Cynorkis*
Microthelys = *Brachystele*
Microtis spp.: #7 **II** ORCHIDACEAE
Mila albisaetacens = *Mila pugionifera*
Mila alboareolata = *Mila nealeana*
Mila breviseta = *Mila nealeana*
Mila caespitosa: #4 **II** CACTACEAE
Mila caespitosa ssp. *nealana* = *Mila nealeana*
Mila cereoides = *Mila pugionifera*
Mila colorea: #4 **II** CACTACEAE
Mila densiseta = *Mila nealeana*
Mila fortalezensis = *Mila pugionifera*
Mila kubeana = *Mila nealeana*
Mila lurinensis = *Mila nealeana*
Mila nealeana: #4 **II** CACTACEAE
Mila pugionifera: #4 **II** CACTACEAE
Mila sublanata = *Mila pugionifera*
Miltonia spp.: #7 **II** ORCHIDACEAE
Miltonioides = *Oncidium*
Miltoniopsis spp.: #7 **II** ORCHIDACEAE
Miniature barrel cactus (E): *Thelocactus setispinus*
Minicolumna = *Epidendrum*
Miqueliopuntia miquelii = *Opuntia miquelii*
Mirabella albicaulis = *Cereus albicaulis*
Mirabella minensis = *Cereus mirabella*
Mischobulbon = *Mischobulbum*
Mischobulbum spp.: #7 **II** ORCHIDACEAE
Mistletoe cactus (E): *Rhipsalis baccifera*
Mitopetalum = *Tainia*
Mitostigma = *Amitostigma*
Mitrocereus fulviceps = *Pachycereus fulviceps*
Mitrocereus militaris = *Pachycereus militaris*
Mitrocereus ruficeps = *Neobuxbaumia macrocephala*
Mobilabium spp.: #7 **II** ORCHIDACEAE
Moerenhoutia spp.: #7 **II** ORCHIDACEAE
Mohave Fishhook cactus (E): *Sclerocactus polyancistrus*
Monachanthus = *Catasetum*
Monadenia spp.: #7 **II** ORCHIDACEAE
Monanthos = *Dendrobium*
Monixus = *Angraecum*
Monkey puzzle (E): *Araucaria araucana*
Monomeria spp.: #7 **II** ORCHIDACEAE
Monophyllorchis spp.: #7 **II** ORCHIDACEAE

Monorchis = *Herminium*
Monosepalum spp.: #7 **II** ORCHIDACEAE
Monotris = *Holothrix*
Montolivaea = *Habenaria*
Monustes = *Spiranthes*
Monvillea adelmarii = *Cereus adelmarii*
Monvillea albicaulis = *Cereus albicaulis*
Monvillea apoloensis = *Praecereus euchlorus* ssp. *amazonicus*
Monvillea ballivianii = *Praecereus euchlorus* ssp. *amazonicus*
Monvillea chacoana = *Praecereus saxicola*
Monvillea ebenacantha = *Cereus spegazzinii*
Monvillea haageana = *Cereus haageanus*
Monvillea insularis = *Cereus insularis*
Monvillea jaenensis = *Praecereus euchlorus* ssp. *jaenensis*
Monvillea kroenleinii = *Cereus kroenleinii*
Monvillea leucantha = *Praecereus euchlorus* ssp. *euchlorus*
Monvillea lindenzweigianus = *Cereus spegazzinii*
Monvillea minensis = *Cereus mirabella*
Monvillea parapetiensis = *Praecereus saxicola*
Monvillea phatnosperma = *Cereus phatnospermus*
Monvillea saddiana = *Cereus saddianus*
Monvillea spegazzini = *Cereus spegazzinii*
Moorea = *Neomoorea*
Morangaya pensilis = *Echinocereus pensilis*
Mormodes spp.: #7 **II** ORCHIDACEAE
Mormolyca spp.: #7 **II** ORCHIDACEAE
Mountain sweet pitcherplant (E): *Sarracenia rubra* ssp. *jonesii*
Muluorchis = *Tropidia*
Munz cholla (E): *Opuntia munzii*
Myanthus = *Catasetum*
Mycaranthes = *Eria*
Mycaridanthes = *Eria*
Myoda = *Ludisia*
Myodium = *Ophrys*
Myoxanthus spp.: #7 **II** ORCHIDACEAE
Myrmechis spp.: #7 **II** ORCHIDACEAE
Myrmecophila spp.: #7 **II** ORCHIDACEAE
Myrobroma = *Vanilla*
Myrosmodes spp.: #7 **II** ORCHIDACEAE
Myrtillocactus chiotilla = *Escontria chiotilla*
Myrtillocactus cochal: #4 **II** CACTACEAE
Myrtillocactus eichlamii: #4 **II** CACTACEAE
Myrtillocactus geometrizans: #4 **II** CACTACEAE
Myrtillocactus grandiareolatus = *Myrtillocactus geometrizans*
Myrtillocactus schenckii: #4 **II** CACTACEAE
Mystacidium spp.: #7 **II** ORCHIDACEAE
Nabaluia spp.: #7 **II** ORCHIDACEAE
Nageia angustifolia = *Podocarpus parlatorei*
Nageia discolor = *Podocarpus neriifolius*
Nageia endlicheriana = *Podocarpus neriifolius*
Nageia leptostachya = *Podocarpus neriifolius*
Nageia neglecta = *Podocarpus neriifolius*
Nageia neriifolia = *Podocarpus neriifolius*
Nageliella spp.: #7 **II** ORCHIDACEAE
Namaqua aloe (E): *Aloe khamiesensis*
Nambar (S): *Platymiscium pleiostachyum*
Ñambar (S): *Platymiscium pleiostachyum*
Nanodes = *Epidendrum*
Nardostachys grandiflora: #3 **II** VALERIANACEAE
Narica = *Sarcoglottis*
Narrow-lidded pitcher-plant (E): *Nepenthes ampullaria*
Nash's prickly-pear (E): *Opuntia nashii*
Nasonia = *Fernandezia*
Nauenia = *Lacaena*
Navajoa fickeisenii = *Pediocactus peeblesianus*
Navajoa peeblesianu ssp. *fickeisenii* = *Pediocactus peeblesianus*
Needle-spined pineapple cactus (E): *Sclerocactus erectocentrus* var. *erectocentrus*
Neippergia = *Acineta*
Nelle' cactus (E): *Escobaria minima*
Nellie's cory cactus (E): *Escobaria minima*
Nemaconia = *Ponera*
Nematoceras = *Corybas*
Nemuranthes = *Habenaria*
Neoabbottia grantiana = *Leptocereus grantianus*

Checklist of flora/Lista de especies de flora/Liste des espèces végétales

Neoabbottia paniculata = Leptocereus paniculatus
Neobartlettia spp.: #7 **II** ORCHIDACEAE
Neobathiea spp.: #7 **II** ORCHIDACEAE
Neobenthamia spp.: #7 **II** ORCHIDACEAE
Neobesseya asperispina = Escobaria missouriensis ssp.
    asperispina
Neobesseya missouriensis = Escobaria missouriensis ssp.
    missouriensis
Neobesseya notesteinii = Escobaria missouriensis ssp.
    missouriensis
Neobesseya rosiflora = Escobaria missouriensis ssp. missouriensis
Neobesseya similis = Escobaria missouriensis ssp. missouriensis
Neobesseya wissmannii = Escobaria missouriensis ssp.
    missouriensis
Neobolusia spp.: #7 **II** ORCHIDACEAE
Neobuxbaumia euphorbioides: #4 **II** CACTACEAE
Neobuxbaumia laui: #4 **II** CACTACEAE
Neobuxbaumia macrocephala: #4 **II** CACTACEAE
Neobuxbaumia mezcalaensis: #4 **II** CACTACEAE
Neobuxbaumia mezcalaensis var. multiareolata = Neobuxbaumia
    multiareolata
Neobuxbaumia multiareolata: #4 **II** CACTACEAE
Neobuxbaumia polylopha: #4 **II** CACTACEAE
Neobuxbaumia sanchezmejoradae = Neobuxbaumia laui
Neobuxbaumia scoparia: #4 **II** CACTACEAE
Neobuxbaumia squamulosa: #4 **II** CACTACEAE
Neobuxbaumia tetazo = Neobuxbaumia tetetzo
Neobuxbaumia tetetzo: #4 **II** CACTACEAE
Neocardenasia herzogiana = Neoraimondia herzogiana
Neochilenia aerocarpa = Eriosyce aerocarpa
Neochilenia andreaeana = Eriosyce andreaeana
Neochilenia aricensis = Eriosyce recondita ssp. iquiquensis
Neochilenia aspillagae = Eriosyce aspillagae
Neochilenia atra = Eriosyce odieri
Neochilenia calderana = Eriosyce taltalensis ssp. taltalensis
Neochilenia carneoflora = Eriosyce odieri ssp. glabrescens
Neochilenia chilensis = Eriosyce chilensis
Neochilenia chorosensis = Eriosyce heinrichiana
Neochilenia confinis = Eriosyce confinis
Neochilenia deherdtiana = Eriosyce heinrichiana
Neochilenia dimorpha = Eriosyce heinrichiana ssp. intermedia
Neochilenia duripulpa = Eriosyce napina ssp. lembckei
Neochilenia eriocephala = Eriosyce taltalensis ssp. echinus
Neochilenia eriosyzoides = Eriosyce kunzei
Neochilenia esmeraldana = Eriosyce esmeraldana
Neochilenia floccosa = Eriosyce taltalensis ssp. echinus
Neochilenia fobeana = Eriosyce taltalensis ssp. paucicostata
Neochilenia fusca = Eriosyce taltalensis ssp. paucicostata
Neochilenia glabrescens = Eriosyce odieri ssp. glabrescens
Neochilenia glaucescens = Eriosyce taltalensis ssp. echinus
Neochilenia gracilis = Eriosyce taltalensis ssp. taltalensis
Neochilenia hankeana = Eriosyce taltalensis ssp. paucicostata
Neochilenia huascensis = Eriosyce crispa ssp. atroviridis
Neochilenia imitans = Eriosyce napina ssp. lembckei
Neochilenia intermedia = Eriosyce taltalensis ssp. taltalensis
Neochilenia iquiquensis = Eriosyce recondita ssp. iquiquensis
Neochilenia jussieui = Eriosyce heinrichiana
Neochilenia krausii = Eriosyce krausii
Neochilenia kunzei = Eriosyce kunzei
Neochilenia lembckei = Eriosyce napina ssp. lembckei
Neochilenia malleolata = Eriosyce krausii
Neochilenia mitis = Eriosyce napina
Neochilenia monte-amargensis = Eriosyce odieri ssp. odieri
Neochilenia napina = Eriosyce napina
Neochilenia neofusca = Eriosyce taltalensis
Neochilenia neoreichei = Eriosyce napina ssp. lembckei
Neochilenia nigriscoparia = Eriosyce crispa ssp. crispa
Neochilenia occulta = Eriosyce heinrichiana
Neochilenia odieri = Eriosyce odieri ssp. odieri
Neochilenia odoriflora = Eriosyce curvispina
Neochilenia paucicostata = Eriosyce taltalensis ssp. paucicostata
Neochilenia pilispina = Eriosyce taltalensis ssp. pilispina
Neochilenia pseudoreichei = Eriosyce odieri
Neochilenia pulchella = Eriosyce taltalensis ssp. taltalensis
Neochilenia pygmaea = Eriosyce taltalensis ssp. taltalensis

Neochilenia recondita = Eriosyce recondita
Neochilenia reichei = Eriosyce odieri
Neochilenia residua = Eriosyce recondita ssp. iquiquensis
Neochilenia robusta = Eriosyce curvispina
Neochilenia rupicola = Eriosyce taltalensis ssp. taltalensis
Neochilenia scoparia = Eriosyce taltalensis ssp. taltalensis
Neochilenia setosiflora = Eriosyce heinrichiana ssp. intermedia
Neochilenia simulans = Eriosyce heinrichiana ssp. simulans
Neochilenia taltalensis = Eriosyce taltalensis
Neochilenia tenebrica = Eriosyce tenebrica
Neochilenia totoralensis = Eriosyce crispa ssp. atroviridis
Neochilenia transitensis = Eriosyce kunzei
Neochilenia trapichensis = Eriosyce heinrichiana
Neochilenia wagenknechtii = Eriosyce heinrichiana ssp. intermedia
Neoclemensia spp.: #7 **II** ORCHIDACEAE
Neocogniauxia spp.: #7 **II** ORCHIDACEAE
Neodawsonia apicicephalium = Cephalocereus nizandensis
Neodawsonia nizandensis = Cephalocereus nizandensis
Neodawsonia totolapensis = Cephalocereus totolapensis
Neodryas spp.: #7 **II** ORCHIDACEAE
Neodypsis decaryi: (E) Feather palm, Triangle palm #1 **II**
    PALMAE
Neoescobaria = Helcia
Neoevansia zopilotensis = Peniocereus zopilotensis
Neofinetia spp.: #7 **II** ORCHIDACEAE
Neogardneria spp.: #7 **II** ORCHIDACEAE
Neogomesia agavoides = Ariocarpus agavoides
Neogyna spp.: #7 **II** ORCHIDACEAE
Neogyne = Neogyna
Neokoehleria spp.: #7 **II** ORCHIDACEAE
Neolauchea = Isabelia
Neolehmannia = Epidendrum
Neolindleya = Platanthera
Neolloydia ceratites = Neolloydia conoidea
Neolloydia clavata = Coryphantha clavata
Neolloydia conoidea: (E) Chihuahuan Desert Butterfly-cactus #4 **II**
    CACTACEAE
Neolloydia erectocentra = Sclerocactus erectocentrus
Neolloydia erectocentra var. acunensis = Sclerocactus
    erectocentrus var. acunensis
Neolloydia erectocentra var. erectocentra = Sclerocactus
    erectocentrus var. erectocentrus
Neolloydia gautii = Sclerocactus warnockii
Neolloydia grandiflora = Neolloydia conoidea
Neolloydia intertexta = Sclerocactus intertextus
Neolloydia intertexta var. dasyacantha = Sclerocactus intertextus
Neolloydia johnsonii = Sclerocactus johnsonii
Neolloydia mariposensis = Sclerocactus mariposensis
Neolloydia matehualensis: #4 **II** CACTACEAE
Neolloydia odorata = Coryphantha odorata
Neolloydia pilispina = Mammillaria pilispina
Neolloydia pulleineana = Coryphantha pulleineana
Neolloydia texensis = Neolloydia conoidea
Neolloydia viereckii = Turbinicarpus viereckii
Neolloydia warnockii = Sclerocactus warnockii
Neolobivia echinata = Echinopsis hertrichiana
Neolobivia hertrichiana = Echinopsis hertrichiana
Neolobivia incaica = Echinopsis hertrichiana
Neolobivia minuta = Echinopsis hertrichiana
Neolobivia vilcabambae = Echinopsis hertrichiana
Neolobivia winteriana = Echinopsis backebergii
Neomoorea spp.: #7 **II** ORCHIDACEAE
Neoporteria andreaeana = Eriosyce andreaeana
Neoporteria aricensis = Eriosyce recondita ssp. iquiquensis
Neoporteria armata = Eriosyce curvispina
Neoporteria aspillagae = Eriosyce aspillagae
Neoporteria atrispinosa = Eriosyce villosa
Neoporteria atroviridis = Eriosyce crispa ssp. atroviridis
Neoporteria backebergii = Eriosyce strausiana
Neoporteria bicolor = Eriosyce islayensis
Neoporteria bulbocalyx = Eriosyce bulbocalyx
Neoporteria calderana = Eriosyce taltalensis ssp. taltalensis
Neoporteria carrizalensis = Eriosyce crispa ssp. atroviridis
Neoporteria castanea = Eriosyce subgibbosa ssp. subgibbosa
Neoporteria castaneoides = Eriosyce subgibbosa

Neoporteria cephalophora = *Eriosyce villosa*
Neoporteria chilensis = *Eriosyce chilensis*
Neoporteria choapensis = *Eriosyce curvispina*
Neoporteria chorosensis = *Eriosyce heinrichiana*
Neoporteria clavata = *Eriosyce subgibbosa* ssp. *clavata*
Neoporteria clavata var. *clavata* = *Eriosyce subgibbosa* ssp. *clavata*
Neoporteria clavata var. *nigrihorrida* = *Eriosyce subgibbosa* ssp. *clavata*
Neoporteria coimasensis = *Eriosyce senilis* ssp. *coimasensis*
Neoporteria confinis = *Eriosyce confinis*
Neoporteria crispa = *Eriosyce crispa* ssp. *crispa*
Neoporteria curvispina = *Eriosyce curvispina*
Neoporteria deherdtiana = *Eriosyce heinrichiana*
Neoporteria dimorpha = *Eriosyce heinrichiana* ssp. *intermedia*
Neoporteria dubia = *Eriosyce bulbocalyx*
Neoporteria echinus = *Eriosyce taltalensis* ssp. *echinus*
Neoporteria engleri = *Eriosyce engleri*
Neoporteria eriocephala = *Eriosyce taltalensis* ssp. *echinus*
Neoporteria eriosyzoides = *Eriosyce kunzei*
Neoporteria esmeraldana = *Eriosyce esmeraldana*
Neoporteria floccosa = *Eriosyce taltalensis* ssp. *echinus*
Neoporteria fusca = *Eriosyce taltalensis* ssp. *paucicostata*
Neoporteria garaventae = *Eriosyce garaventae*
Neoporteria gerocephala = *Eriosyce senilis* ssp. *senilis*
Neoporteria hankeana = *Eriosyce taltalensis* ssp. *paucicostata*
Neoporteria heinrichiana = *Eriosyce heinrichiana*
Neoporteria heteracantha = *Eriosyce subgibbosa* ssp. *subgibbosa*
Neoporteria horrida = *Eriosyce curvispina*
Neoporteria horrida var. *armata* = *Eriosyce curvispina*
Neoporteria horrida var. *aspillagae* = *Eriosyce curvispina*
Neoporteria huascensis = *Eriosyce crispa* ssp. *crispa*
Neoporteria intermedia = *Eriosyce taltalensis* ssp. *taltalensis*
Neoporteria iquiquensis = *Eriosyce recondita* ssp. *iquiquensis*
Neoporteria islayensis = *Eriosyce islayensis*
Neoporteria jussieui = *Eriosyce heinrichiana*
Neoporteria krainziana = *Eriosyce islayensis*
Neoporteria kunzei = *Eriosyce kunzei*
Neoporteria laniceps = *Eriosyce villosa*
Neoporteria limariensis = *Eriosyce limariensis*
Neoporteria litoralis = *Eriosyce subgibbosa* ssp. *subgibbosa*
Neoporteria marksiana = *Eriosyce marksiana*
Neoporteria megliolii = *Eriosyce bulbocalyx*
Neoporteria melanacantha = *Eriosyce villicumensis*
Neoporteria microsperma = *Eriosyce subgibbosa* ssp. *clavata*
Neoporteria monte-amargensis = *Eriosyce odieri* ssp. *odieri*
Neoporteria multicolor = *Eriosyce senilis* ssp. *senilis*
Neoporteria napina = *Eriosyce napina*
Neoporteria nidus = *Eriosyce kunzei*
Neoporteria nidus var. *gerocephala* = *Neoporteria kunzei* var. *kunzei*
Neoporteria nigricans = *Eriosyce limariensis*
Neoporteria nigrihorrida = *Eriosyce subgibbosa* ssp. *clavata*
Neoporteria occulta = *Eriosyce heinrichiana*
Neoporteria odieri = *Eriosyce odieri* ssp. *odieri*
Neoporteria omasensis = *Eriosyce omasensis*
Neoporteria paucicostata = *Eriosyce taltalensis* ssp. *paucicostata*
Neoporteria pilispina = *Eriosyce taltalensis* ssp. *pilispina*
Neoporteria polyraphis = *Eriosyce villosa*
Neoporteria pulchella = *Eriosyce taltalensis* ssp. *taltalensis*
Neoporteria recondita = *Eriosyce recondita*
Neoporteria reichii = *Eriosyce odieri*
Neoporteria residua = *Eriosyce recondita* ssp. *iquiquensis*
Neoporteria ritteri = *Eriosyce heinrichiana* ssp. *intermedia*
Neoporteria robusta = *Eriosyce senilis* ssp. *coimasensis*
Neoporteria rupicola = *Eriosyce taltalensis* ssp. *taltalensis*
Neoporteria sanjuanensis = *Eriosyce strausiana*
Neoporteria scoparia = *Eriosyce taltalensis* ssp. *taltalensis*
Neoporteria setiflora = *Eriosyce strausiana*
Neoporteria setosiflora = *Eriosyce heinrichiana* ssp. *intermedia*
Neoporteria simulans = *Eriosyce heinrichiana* ssp. *simulans*
Neoporteria sociabilis = *Eriosyce sociabilis*
Neoporteria strausiana = *Eriosyce strausiana*
Neoporteria subaiana = *Eriosyce garaventae*
Neoporteria subcylindrica = *Eriosyce subgibbosa* ssp. *subgibbosa*

Neoporteria subgibbosa = *Eriosyce subgibbosa*
Neoporteria taltalensis = *Eriosyce taltalensis*
Neoporteria totoralensis = *Eriosyce crispa* ssp. *atroviridis*
Neoporteria transiens = *Eriosyce taltalensis* ssp. *taltalensis*
Neoporteria transitensis = *Eriosyce kunzei*
Neoporteria tuberisulcata = *Eriosyce curvispina*
Neoporteria umadeave = *Eriosyce umadeave*
Neoporteria vallenarensis = *Eriosyce subgibbosa* ssp. *clavata*
Neoporteria vallenarensis = *Eriosyce kunzei*
Neoporteria villicumensis = *Eriosyce villicumensis*
Neoporteria villosa = *Eriosyce villosa*
Neoporteria volliana = *Eriosyce strausiana*
Neoporteria wagenknechtii = *Eriosyce subgibbosa* ssp. *clavata*
Neoporteria woutersiana = *Eriosyce taltalensis* ssp. *paucicostata*
Neoraimondia arequipensis: #4 **II** CACTACEAE
Neoraimondia aticensis = *Neoraimondia arequipensis*
Neoraimondia gigantea = *Neoraimondia arequipensis*
Neoraimondia herzogiana: #4 **II** CACTACEAE
Neoraimondia macrostibas = *Neoraimondia arequipensis*
Neoraimondia peruviana = *Neoraimondia arequipensis*
Neoraimondia roseiflora = *Neoraimondia arequipensis*
Neotainiopsis = *Eriodes*
Neotinea spp.: #7 **II** ORCHIDACEAE
Neottia spp.: #7 **II** ORCHIDACEAE
Neottianthe spp.: #7 **II** ORCHIDACEAE
Neottidium = *Neottia*
Neo-urbania = *Maxillaria*
Neowerdermannia chilensis: #4 **II** CACTACEAE
Neowerdermannia chilensis ssp. *chilensis*: #4 **II** CACTACEAE
Neowerdermannia chilensis ssp. *peruviana*: #4 **II** CACTACEAE
Neowerdermannia peruviana = *Neowerdermannia chilensis* ssp. *peruviana*
Neowerdermannia vorwerkii: #4 **II** CACTACEAE
Neowilliamsia = *Epidendrum*
Népenthès (F): *Nepenthes* spp.
Nepenthes spp.: (E) tropical pitcher plants, (F) népenthès, (S) cántaros #1 **I/II** NEPENTHACEAE
Nepenthes adnata: #1 **II** NEPENTHACEAE
Nepenthes alata = *Nepenthes eustachya*
Nepenthes alata: #1 **II** NEPENTHACEAE
Nepenthes alata f. *variegata* = *Nepenthes alata*
Nepenthes alata var. *biflora* = *Nepenthes alata*
Nepenthes alata var. *ecristata* = *Nepenthes alata*
Nepenthes alba = *Nepenthes gracillima*
Nepenthes albocinta = *Nepenthes albomarginata*
Nepenthes albocinta var. *rubra* = *Nepenthes albomarginata*
Nepenthes albolineata = *Nepenthes mirabilis*
Nepenthes albomarginata: #1 **II** NEPENTHACEAE
Nepenthes albomarginata f. *sanguinea* = *Nepenthes albomarginata*
Nepenthes albomarginata var. *rubra* = *Nepenthes albomarginata*
Nepenthes albomarginata var. *tomentella* = *Nepenthes albomarginata*
Nepenthes albomarginata var. *typica* = *Nepenthes albomarginata*
Nepenthes albomarginata var. *villosa* = *Nepenthes albomarginata*
Nepenthes alicae = *Nepenthes mirabilis*
Nepenthes ampullacea = *Nepenthes ampullaria*
Nepenthes ampullaria = *Nepenthes vieillardii*
Nepenthes ampullaria: (E) Narrow-lidded pitcher-plant #1 **II** NEPENTHACEAE
Nepenthes ampullaria var. *geelvinkiana* = *Nepenthes ampullaria*
Nepenthes ampullaria var. *guttata* = *Nepenthes ampullaria*
Nepenthes ampullaria var. *longicarpa* = *Nepenthes ampullaria*
Nepenthes ampullaria var. *microsepala* = *Nepenthes ampullaria*
Nepenthes ampullaria var. *racemosa* = *Nepenthes ampullaria*
Nepenthes ampullaria var. *vittata* = *Nepenthes ampullaria*
Nepenthes anamensis: #1 **II** NEPENTHACEAE
Nepenthes angasanensis: #1 **II** NEPENTHACEAE
Nepenthes angustifolia = *Nepenthes gracilis*
Nepenthes argentii: #1 **II** NEPENTHACEAE
Nepenthes aristolochioides: #1 **II** NEPENTHACEAE
Nepenthes armbrustae = *Nepenthes mirabilis*
Nepenthes beccariana: #1 **II** NEPENTHACEAE
Nepenthes bellii: #1 **II** NEPENTHACEAE
Nepenthes benstonei: #1 **II** NEPENTHACEAE
Nepenthes bernaysii = *Nepenthes mirabilis*

Nepenthes bicalcarata: #1 **II** NEPENTHACEAE
Nepenthes blancoi = *Nepenthes alata*
Nepenthes bongso = *Nepenthes dubia*
Nepenthes bongso = *Nepenthes inermis*
Nepenthes bongso = *Nepenthes talangensis*
Nepenthes bongso = *Nepenthes vieillardii*
Nepenthes bongso: #1 **II** NEPENTHACEAE
Nepenthes bongso x pectinata = *Nepenthes densiflora*
Nepenthes borneensis = *Nepenthes boschiana*
Nepenthes boschiana = *Nepenthes maxima*
Nepenthes boschiana = *Nepenthes stenophylla*
Nepenthes boschiana: #1 **II** NEPENTHACEAE
Nepenthes boschiana var. *lowii* = *Nepenthes stenophylla*
Nepenthes boschiniana = *Nepenthes sumatrana*
Nepenthes boschiniana var. *sumatrana* = *Nepenthes sumatrana*
Nepenthes brachycarpa = *Nepenthes philippinensis*
Nepenthes burbidgeae: #1 **II** NEPENTHACEAE
Nepenthes burbidgei = *Nepenthes burbidgeae*
Nepenthes burkei: #1 **II** NEPENTHACEAE
Nepenthes burkei var. *burkei*: #1 **II** NEPENTHACEAE
Nepenthes burkei var. *excellens* = *Nepenthes burkei*
Nepenthes burkei var. *prolifica*: #1 **II** NEPENTHACEAE
Nepenthes campanulata: #1 **II** NEPENTHACEAE
Nepenthes carunculata = *Nepenthes bongso*
Nepenthes carunculata var. *robusta* = *Nepenthes bongso*
Nepenthes celebica = *Nepenthes maxima*
Nepenthes chapmanii = *Nepenthes distillatoria*
Nepenthes cholmondeleyi = *Nepenthes mirabilis*
Nepenthes clipeata: #1 **II** NEPENTHACEAE
Nepenthes copelandii: #1 **II** NEPENTHACEAE
Nepenthes cristata = *Nepenthes alata*
Nepenthes cristata = *Nepenthes madagascariensis*
Nepenthes curtisii = *Nepenthes maxima*
Nepenthes curtisii var. *hybrida* = *Nepenthes maxima*
Nepenthes curtisii var. *superba* = *Nepenthes maxima*
Nepenthes danseri: #1 **II** NEPENTHACEAE
Nepenthes deaniana: #1 **II** NEPENTHACEAE
Nepenthes decurrens = *Nepenthes northiana*
Nepenthes densiflora: #1 **II** NEPENTHACEAE
Nepenthes dentata = *Nepenthes hamata*
Nepenthes destillatoria = *Nepenthes distillatoria*
Nepenthes diatas: #1 **II** NEPENTHACEAE
Nepenthes distillatoria = *Nepenthes gracilis*
Nepenthes distillatoria = *Nepenthes khasiana*
Nepenthes distillatoria = *Nepenthes madagascariensis*
Nepenthes distillatoria = *Nepenthes mirabilis*
Nepenthes distillatoria = *Nepenthes vieillardii*
Nepenthes distillatoria: #1 **II** NEPENTHACEAE
Nepenthes distillatoria var. *rubra* = *Nepenthes distillatoria*
Nepenthes dubia = *Nepenthes tenuis*
Nepenthes dubia: #1 **II** NEPENTHACEAE
Nepenthes dyak = *Nepenthes bicalcarata*
Nepenthes echinostoma = *Nepenthes mirabilis*
Nepenthes edgeworthii = *Nepenthes edwardsiana*
Nepenthes edwardsiana: #1 **II** NEPENTHACEAE
Nepenthes edwardsiana ssp. *macrophylla* = *Nepenthes macrophylla*
Nepenthes ephippiata: #1 **II** NEPENTHACEAE
Nepenthes eustachia = *Nepenthes eustachya*
Nepenthes eustachya: #1 **II** NEPENTHACEAE
Nepenthes eustachys = *Nepenthes eustachya*
Nepenthes eymae: #1 **II** NEPENTHACEAE
Nepenthes faizaliana: #1 **II** NEPENTHACEAE
Nepenthes fallax = *Nepenthes stenophylla*
Nepenthes fimbriata = *Nepenthes mirabilis*
Nepenthes fimbriata var. *leptostachya* = *Nepenthes mirabilis*
Nepenthes fusca: #1 **II** NEPENTHACEAE
Nepenthes garrawayae = *Nepenthes mirabilis*
Nepenthes geoffrayi = *Nepenthes anamensis*
Nepenthes glabrata: #1 **II** NEPENTHACEAE
Nepenthes globamphora = *Nepenthes bellii*
Nepenthes globamphora: #1 **II** NEPENTHACEAE
Nepenthes graciliflora = *Nepenthes alata*
Nepenthes gracilis: (E) Slender pitcher-plant #1 **II** NEPENTHACEAE

Nepenthes gracilis f. *angustifolia* = *Nepenthes gracilis*
Nepenthes gracilis var. *angustifolia* = *Nepenthes gracilis*
Nepenthes gracilis var. *arenaria* = *Nepenthes gracilis*
Nepenthes gracilis var. *elongata* = *Nepenthes gracilis*
Nepenthes gracilis var. *longinodis* = *Nepenthes gracilis*
Nepenthes gracilis var. *major* = *Nepenthes gracilis*
Nepenthes gracilis var. *teysmanniana* = *Nepenthes gracilis*
Nepenthes gracillima: #1 **II** NEPENTHACEAE
Nepenthes gracillima = *Nepenthes ramispina*
Nepenthes gracillima var. *major* = *Nepenthes ramispina*
Nepenthes gymnamphora: #1 **II** NEPENTHACEAE
Nepenthes gymnaphora var. *haematamphora* = *Nepenthes gymnamphora*
Nepenthes hainanensis = *Nepenthes mirabilis*
Nepenthes hamata: #1 **II** NEPENTHACEAE
Nepenthes hemsleyana = *Nepenthes rafflesiana*
Nepenthes hirsuta: #1 **II** NEPENTHACEAE
Nepenthes hirsuta var. *glabrata* = *Nepenthes hirsuta*
Nepenthes hirsuta var. *glabrescens* = *Nepenthes distillatoria*
Nepenthes hispida: #1 **II** NEPENTHACEAE
Nepenthes hookeriana = *Nepenthes rafflesiana*
Nepenthes humilis = *Nepenthes vieillardii*
Nepenthes inermis: #1 **II** NEPENTHACEAE
Nepenthes infundibuliformis = *Nepenthes eymae*
Nepenthes insignis: #1 **II** NEPENTHACEAE
Nepenthes jacquelineae: #1 **II** NEPENTHACEAE
Nepenthes jardinei = *Nepenthes mirabilis*
Nepenthes kampotiana = *Nepenthes anamensis*
Nepenthes kampotiana = *Nepenthes mirabilis*
Nepenthes kennedyana = *Nepenthes mirabilis*
Nepenthes kennedyi = *Nepenthes mirabilis*
Nepenthes khasiana: (E) Indian pitcher-plant, (S) Cántaro de India **I** NEPENTHACEAE
Nepenthes klossii: #1 **II** NEPENTHACEAE
Nepenthes kookeriana = *Nepenthes rafflesiana*
Nepenthes korthalsiana = *Nepenthes gracilis*
Nepenthes korthalsiana = *Nepenthes reinwardtiana*
Nepenthes laevis = *Nepenthes albomarginata*
Nepenthes laevis = *Nepenthes gracilis*
Nepenthes lamii: #1 **II** NEPENTHACEAE
Nepenthes lanata = *Nepenthes veitchii*
Nepenthes lavicola: #1 **II** NEPENTHACEAE
Nepenthes leptochila = *Nepenthes hirsuta*
Nepenthes leptochila: #1 **II** NEPENTHACEAE
Nepenthes leptoptera = *Nepenthes neoguineensis*
Nepenthes longifolia: #1 **II** NEPENTHACEAE
Nepenthes longinodis = *Nepenthes gracilis*
Nepenthes lowii: #1 **II** NEPENTHACEAE
Nepenthes macfarlanei: #1 **II** NEPENTHACEAE
Nepenthes macrophylla: #1 **II** NEPENTHACEAE
Nepenthes macrostachya = *Nepenthes mirabilis*
Nepenthes macrovulgaris: #1 **II** NEPENTHACEAE
Nepenthes madagascariensis: #1 **II** NEPENTHACEAE
Nepenthes madagascariensis var. *cylindrica* = *Nepenthes madagascariensis*
Nepenthes madagascariensis var. *macrocarpa* = *Nepenthes madagascariensis*
Nepenthes mapuluensis: #1 **II** NEPENTHACEAE
Nepenthes masaolensis: #1 **II** NEPENTHACEAE
Nepenthes maxima = *Nepenthes boschiana*
Nepenthes maxima = *Nepenthes fusca*
Nepenthes maxima = *Nepenthes stenophylla*
Nepenthes maxima = *Nepenthes sumatrana*
Nepenthes maxima: #1 **II** NEPENTHACEAE
Nepenthes maxima var. *lowii* = *Nepenthes stenophylla*
Nepenthes maxima var. *minor* = *Nepenthes maxima*
Nepenthes maxima var. *sumatrana* = *Nepenthes sumatrana*
Nepenthes maxima var. *superba* = *Nepenthes maxima*
Nepenthes megamphora = *Nepenthes truncata*
Nepenthes melamphora = *Nepenthes alata*
Nepenthes melamphora = *Nepenthes gymnamphora*
Nepenthes melamphora = *Nepenthes khasiana*
Nepenthes melamphora var. *haematamphora* = *Nepenthes gymnamphora*
Nepenthes melamphora var. *lucida* = *Nepenthes gymnamphora*

Nepenthes melamphora var. *pubescens* = *Nepenthes gymnamphora*
Nepenthes melamphora var. *tomentella* = *Nepenthes gymnamphora*
Nepenthes merrilliana: #1 **II** NEPENTHACEAE
Nepenthes merrillii = *Nepenthes merrilliana*
Nepenthes micholitzii = *Nepenthes anamensis*
Nepenthes mikei: #1 **II** NEPENTHACEAE
Nepenthes mindanaoensis: #1 **II** NEPENTHACEAE
Nepenthes mira: #1 **II** NEPENTHACEAE
Nepenthes mirabilis: #1 **II** NEPENTHACEAE
Nepenthes mirabilis f. *anamensis* = *Nepenthes mirabilis*
Nepenthes mirabilis f. *simensis* = *Nepenthes mirabilis*
Nepenthes mirabilis var. *biflora* = *Nepenthes mirabilis*
Nepenthes mirabilis var. *echinostoma* = *Nepenthes mirabilis*
Nepenthes mirabilis var. *smilesii* = *Nepenthes mirabilis*
Nepenthes mollis: #1 **II** NEPENTHACEAE
Nepenthes moluccensis = *Nepenthes mirabilis*
Nepenthes montrouzieri = *Nepenthes vieillardii*
Nepenthes moorei = *Nepenthes mirabilis*
Nepenthes muluensis: #1 **II** NEPENTHACEAE
Nepenthes murudensis: #1 **II** NEPENTHACEAE
Nepenthes neglecta = *Nepenthes hirsuta*
Nepenthes neglecta: #1 **II** NEPENTHACEAE
Nepenthes neocaledonica = *Nepenthes vieillardii*
Nepenthes neoguineensis = *Nepenthes papuana*
Nepenthes neoguineensis: #1 **II** NEPENTHACEAE
Nepenthes nigropurpurea = *Nepenthes rafflesiana*
Nepenthes nordtiana = *Nepenthes northiana*
Nepenthes northiana: #1 **II** NEPENTHACEAE
Nepenthes northiana var. *pulchra* = *Nepenthes northiana*
Nepenthes oblanceolata = *Nepenthes maxima*
Nepenthes obrieniana = *Nepenthes mirabilis*
Nepenthes ovata: #1 **II** NEPENTHACEAE
Nepenthes paniculata: #1 **II** NEPENTHACEAE
Nepenthes papuana: #1 **II** NEPENTHACEAE
Nepenthes pascoensis = *Nepenthes mirabilis*
Nepenthes pecinata = *Nepenthes gymnamphora*
Nepenthes pectinata = *Nepenthes ovata*
Nepenthes pectinata: #1 **II** NEPENTHACEAE
Nepenthes pervillei: #1 **II** NEPENTHACEAE
Nepenthes petiolata = *Nepenthes mindanaoensis*
Nepenthes petiolata: #1 **II** NEPENTHACEAE
Nepenthes philippinensis: #1 **II** NEPENTHACEAE
Nepenthes phyllamphora = *Nepenthes gymnamphora*
Nepenthes phyllamphora = *Nepenthes khasiana*
Nepenthes phyllamphora var. *macrantha* = *Nepenthes mirabilis*
Nepenthes phyllamphora var. *pediculata* = *Nepenthes mirabilis*
Nepenthes phyllamphora var. *platyphylla* = *Nepenthes mirabilis*
Nepenthes pilosa = *Nepenthes stenophylla*
Nepenthes pilosa: #1 **II** NEPENTHACEAE
Nepenthes pyriformis: #1 **II** NEPENTHACEAE
Nepenthes rafflesiana = *Nepenthes gymnamphora*
Nepenthes rafflesiana: (E) Raffles' pitcher-plant #1 **II** NEPENTHACEAE
Nepenthes rafflesiana var. *alata* = *Nepenthes rafflesiana*
Nepenthes rafflesiana var. *ambigua* = *Nepenthes rafflesiana*
Nepenthes rafflesiana var. *elongata* = *Nepenthes rafflesiana*
Nepenthes rafflesiana var. *glaberrima* = *Nepenthes rafflesiana*
Nepenthes rafflesiana var. *hookeriana* = *Nepenthes rafflesiana*
Nepenthes rafflesiana var. *insignis* = *Nepenthes rafflesiana*
Nepenthes rafflesiana var. *minor* = *Nepenthes rafflesiana*
Nepenthes rafflesiana var. *nigropurpurea* = *Nepenthes rafflesiana*
Nepenthes rafflesiana var. *nivea* = *Nepenthes rafflesiana*
Nepenthes raflesea = *Nepenthes rafflesiana*
Nepenthes rajah: (E) Giant pitcher plant, Giant tropical pitcher plant, Kinabalu pitcher plant, (S) Cántaro tropical gigante NEPENTHACEAE
Nepenthes ramispina: #1 **II** NEPENTHACEAE
Nepenthes reinwardtiana = *Nepenthes khasiana*
Nepenthes reinwardtiana: #1 **II** NEPENTHACEAE
Nepenthes reinwardtiana var. *samarindaensis* = *Nepenthes reinwardtiana*
Nepenthes reinwardtii = *Nepenthes reinwardtiana*
Nepenthes rhombicaulis = *Nepenthes gymnamphora*
Nepenthes rhombicaulis: #1 **II** NEPENTHACEAE
Nepenthes rosulata: #1 **II** NEPENTHACEAE

Nepenthes rowanae = *Nepenthes mirabilis*
Nepenthes rubra = *Nepenthes distillatoria*
Nepenthes rubra = *Nepenthes khasiana*
Nepenthes sandakanensis var. *egandulosa* = *Nepenthes stenophylla*
Nepenthes sandakanensis var. *ferruginea* = *Nepenthes stenophylla*
Nepenthes sanderiana = *Nepenthes rafflesiana*
Nepenthes sanguinea = *Nepenthes veitchii*
Nepenthes sanguinea: #1 **II** NEPENTHACEAE
Nepenthes sibuyanensis: #1 **II** NEPENTHACEAE
Nepenthes singalana = *Nepenthes bongso*
Nepenthes singalana = *Nepenthes densiflora*
Nepenthes singalana = *Nepenthes gracillima*
Nepenthes singalana = *Nepenthes gymnamphora*
Nepenthes singalana = *Nepenthes spathulata*
Nepenthes singalana: #1 **II** NEPENTHACEAE
Nepenthes smilesii = *Nepenthes mirabilis*
Nepenthes spathulata: #1 **II** NEPENTHACEAE
Nepenthes spectabilis: #1 **II** NEPENTHACEAE
Nepenthes spinosa: #1 **II** NEPENTHACEAE
Nepenthes stenophylla: #1 **II** NEPENTHACEAE
Nepenthes sumatrana = *Nepenthes longifolia*
Nepenthes sumatrana: #1 **II** NEPENTHACEAE
Nepenthes surigaoensis = *Nepenthes merrilliana*
Nepenthes talangensis: #1 **II** NEPENTHACEAE
Nepenthes tentaculata: #1 **II** NEPENTHACEAE
Nepenthes tentaculata var. *imberbis* = *Nepenthes tentaculata*
Nepenthes tentaculata var. *tomentosa* = *Nepenthes tentaculata*
Nepenthes tenuis: #1 **II** NEPENTHACEAE
Nepenthes teysmanniana = *Nepenthes albomarginata*
Nepenthes teysmanniana = *Nepenthes gracilis*
Nepenthes thorelii: #1 **II** NEPENTHACEAE
Nepenthes thorelii f. *rubra* = *Nepenthes thorelii*
Nepenthes tobaica: #1 **II** NEPENTHACEAE
Nepenthes tomentella = *Nepenthes albomarginata*
Nepenthes tomoriana: #1 **II** NEPENTHACEAE
Nepenthes treubiana = *Nepenthes sumatrana*
Nepenthes treubiana: #1 **II** NEPENTHACEAE
Nepenthes trichocarpa = *Nepenthes distillatoria*
Nepenthes truncata: #1 **II** NEPENTHACEAE
Nepenthes tubulosa = *Nepenthes mirabilis*
Nepenthes tupmanniana = *Nepenthes albomarginata*
Nepenthes veitchii = *Nepenthes fusca*
Nepenthes veitchii: #1 **II** NEPENTHACEAE
Nepenthes ventricosa: #1 **II** NEPENTHACEAE
Nepenthes vieillardii = *Nepenthes lamii*
Nepenthes vieillardii = *Nepenthes mirabilis*
Nepenthes vieillardii: #1 **II** NEPENTHACEAE
Nepenthes vieillardii var. *deplanchei* = *Nepenthes vieillardii*
Nepenthes vieillardii var. *humilis* = *Nepenthes vieillardii*
Nepenthes vieillardii var. *minima* = *Nepenthes vieillardii*
Nepenthes vieillardii var. *montrouzieri* = *Nepenthes vieillardii*
Nepenthes villosa = *Nepenthes edwardsiana*
Nepenthes villosa = *Nepenthes veitchii*
Nepenthes villosa: #1 **II** NEPENTHACEAE
Nepenthes wilkiei = *Nepenthes philippinensis*
Nepenthes xiphioides = *Nepenthes gymnamphora*
Nepenthes zeylanica = *Nepenthes distillatoria*
Nepenthes zeylanica var. *rubra* = *Nepenthes distillatoria*
Nephelaphyllum spp.: #7 **II** ORCHIDACEAE
Nephelea cuspidata = *Cyathea cuspidata*
Nephelea fulgens = *Cyathea fulgens*
Nephelea grevilleana = *Cyathea grevilleana*
Nephelea imrayana var. *basilaris* = *Cyathea basilaris*
Nephelea imrayana var. *imrayana* = *Cyathea imrayana* var. *imrayana*
Nephelea polystichoides = *Cyathea polystichoides*
Nephelea woodwardioides var. *cubensis* = *Cyathea woodwardioides* var. *cubensis*
Nephelea woodwardioides var. *hieronymi* = *Cyathea woodwardioides* var. *hieronymi*
Nephelea woodwardioides var. *woodwardioides* = *Cyathea woodwardioides* var. *woodwardioides*
Nephrangis spp.: #7 **II** ORCHIDACEAE
Nephranthera = *Renanthera*
Nerissa = *Ponthieva*

Nervilia spp.: #7 **II** ORCHIDACEAE
Neuwiedia spp.: #7 **II** ORCHIDACEAE
New River agave (E): *Agave arizonica*
Nidema spp.: #7 **II** ORCHIDACEAE
Nidus = Neottia
Niemeyera = Apostasia
Nienokuea = Polystachya
Night-blooming cereus (E): *Hylocereus trigonus/ Selenicereus grandiflorus*
Nigritella spp.: #7 **II** ORCHIDACEAE
Nipponorchis = Neofinetia
Nolina interrata: (E) Dehesa bear-grass, San Diego bear-grass **I** AGAVACEAE
Nopalea auberi = Opuntia auberi
Nopalea cochenillifera = Opuntia cochenillifera
Nopalea dejecta = Opuntia dejecta
Nopalea escuintlensis = Opuntia inaperta
Nopalea gaumeri = Opuntia inaperta
Nopalea guatemalensis = Opuntia lutea
Nopalea inaperta = Opuntia inaperta
Nopalea karwinskiana = Opuntia karwinskiana
Nopalea lutea = Opuntia lutea
Nopalea nuda = Opuntia nuda
Nopalxochia ackermannii = Disocactus ackermannii
Nopalxochia ackermannii var. *ackermannii = Disocactus ackermannii*
Nopalxochia ackermannii var. *conzattianum = Disocactus ackermannii*
Nopalxochia conzattiana = Disocactus ackermannii
Nopalxochia horichii = Disocactus kimnachii
Nopalxochia macdougallii = Disocactus macdougallii
Nopalxochia phyllanthoides = Disocactus phyllanthoides
Norna = Calypso
Nothodoritis spp.: #7 **II** ORCHIDACEAE
Nothostele spp.: #7 **II** ORCHIDACEAE
Notocactus arnostianus = Parodia arnostiana
Notocactus brederooianus = Parodia tabularis ssp. *bommeljei*
Notocactus campestrensis = Parodia oxycostata
Notocactus cristatoides = Parodia mammulosa
Notocactus curvispinus = Parodia curvispina
Notocactus erubescens = Parodia erubescens
Notocactus erythracanthus = Parodia mammulosa ssp. *erythracantha*
Notocactus eugeniae = Parodia mammulosa ssp. *eugeniae*
Notocactus ferrugineus = Parodia werdermanniana
Notocactus glomeratus = Parodia rudibuenekeri ssp. *glomerata*
Notocactus grandiensis = Parodia ottonis
Notocactus gutierrezii = Parodia mueller-melchersii ssp. *gutierrezii*
Notocactus incomptus = Parodia oxycostata
Notocactus leucocarpus = Parodia sellowii
Notocactus macambarensis = Parodia mammulosa
Notocactus macracanthus = Parodia sellowii
Notocactus macrogonus = Parodia sellowii
Notocactus maldonadensis = Parodia neoarechavaletae
Notocactus megalanthus = Parodia mammulosa
Notocactus memorialis = Parodia werdermanniana
Notocactus meonacanthus = Parodia meonacantha
Notocactus miniatispinus = Parodia oxycostata
Notocactus neoarechavaletae = Parodia neoarechavaletae
Notocactus olimarensis = Parodia concinna
Notocactus ottonis = Parodia ottonis ssp. *ottonis*
Notocactus paulus = Parodia mammulosa
Notocactus permutatus = Parodia permutata
Notocactus polyacanthus = Parodia langsdorfii
Notocactus pseudoherteri = Parodia herteri
Notocactus pulvinatus = Parodia langsdorfii
Notocactus rauschii = Parodia nothorauschii
Notocactus ritterianus = Parodia mammulosa
Notocactus roseiflorus = Parodia rutilans
Notocactus rubriflorus = Parodia herteri
Notocactus rubropedatus = Parodia curvispina
Notocactus rudibuenekeri = Parodia rudibuenekeri
Notocactus schaeferianus = Parodia turbinata
Notocactus schlosseri = Parodia erubescens

Notocactus soldtianus = Parodia scopa ssp. *scopa*
Notocactus spinibarbis = Parodia nothorauschii
Notocactus stegmannii = Parodia sellowii
Notocactus stockingeri = Parodia stockingeri
Notocactus submammulosus = Parodia mammulosa ssp. *submammulosa*
Notocactus veenianus = Parodia rutilans ssp. *veeniana*
Notocactus winkleri = Parodia mueller-melchersii ssp. *winkleri*
Notylia spp.: #7 **II** ORCHIDACEAE
Nuevo Leon living-rock cactus (E): *Ariocarpus scaphirostris*
Nyctocereus chontalensis = Selenicereus chontalensis
Nyctocereus guatemalensis = Peniocereus hirschtianus
Nyctocereus hirschtianus = Peniocereus hirschtianus
Nyctocereus neumannii = Peniocereus hirschtianus
Nyctocereus oaxacensis = Peniocereus oaxacensis
Nyctocereus serpentinus = Peniocereus serpentinus
Nyctocereus serpentinus var. *pietatus = Peniocereus serpentinus*
Nyctocereus serpentinus var. *serpentinus = Peniocereus serpentinus*
Nyctosma = Epidendrum
Oakes-amesia = Sphyrastylis
Oberonia spp.: #7 **II** ORCHIDACEAE
Obregonia denegrii: (E) Artichoke cactus, (S) Cacto alcachofa **I** CACTACEAE
Ocampoa = Cranichis
Oconee bells (E): *Shortia galacifolia*
Octadesmia = Dilomilis
Octandrorchis = Octomeria
Octarrhena spp.: #7 **II** ORCHIDACEAE
Octomeria spp.: #7 **II** ORCHIDACEAE
Octopus plant (E): *Aloe arborescens*
Odonectis = Isotria
Odontochilus = Anoectochilus
Odontoglossum spp.: #7 **II** ORCHIDACEAE
Odontorrhynchus spp.: #7 **II** ORCHIDACEAE
Odontostyles = Bulbophyllum
Oeceoclades spp.: #7 **II** ORCHIDACEAE
Oehmea beneckei = Mammillaria beneckei
Oenia spp.: #7 **II** ORCHIDACEAE
Oeoniella spp.: #7 **II** ORCHIDACEAE
Oerstedella spp.: #7 **II** ORCHIDACEAE
Oestlundorchis spp.: #7 **II** ORCHIDACEAE
Ojoche macho (S): *Batocarpus costaricensis*
Olgasis = Oncidium
Oligophyton spp.: #7 **II** ORCHIDACEAE
Oliveriana spp.: #7 **II** ORCHIDACEAE
Ommatodium = Pterygodium
Omoea spp.: #7 **II** ORCHIDACEAE
Oncidium spp.: #7 **II** ORCHIDACEAE
Oncodia = Brachtia
Onkeripus = Xylobium
Onychium = Dendrobium
Ophidion spp.: #7 **II** ORCHIDACEAE
Ophrys spp.: #7 **II** ORCHIDACEAE
Oporanthus colchicflorus = Sternbergia colchiciflora
Oporanthus fisherianus = Sternbergia fischeriana
Oporanthus luteus = Sternbergia lutea
Oporanthus luteus var. *angustifolia = Sternbergia lutea*
Oporanthus luteus var. *latifolia = Sternbergia lutea*
Opuntia abyssi: #4 **II** CACTACEAE
Opuntia acanthocarpa: #4 **II** CACTACEAE
Opuntia acanthocarpa ssp. *ganderi*: #4 **II** CACTACEAE
Opuntia acaulis: #4 **II** CACTACEAE
Opuntia aciculata: #4 **II** CACTACEAE
Opuntia aggeria: #4 **II** CACTACEAE
Opuntia agglomerata: #4 **II** CACTACEAE
Opuntia albisaetacens: #4 **II** CACTACEAE
Opuntia alcahes: #4 **II** CACTACEAE
Opuntia alcerrecensis: #4 **II** CACTACEAE
Opuntia alexanderi: #4 **II** CACTACEAE
Opuntia alko-tuna: #4 **II** CACTACEAE
Opuntia allairei = Opuntia humifusa
Opuntia ammophila: #4 **II** CACTACEAE
Opuntia amyclaea: #4 **II** CACTACEAE
Opuntia anacantha: #4 **II** CACTACEAE

Opuntia anahuacensis = *Opuntia dillenii*
Opuntia angustata = *Opuntia phaeacantha*
Opuntia anteojoensis: #4 **II** CACTACEAE
Opuntia antillana: #4 **II** CACTACEAE
Opuntia aoracantha: #4 **II** CACTACEAE
Opuntia apurimacensis: #4 **II** CACTACEAE
Opuntia arbuscula: (E) Pencil Cholla #4 **II** CACTACEAE
Opuntia arcei: #4 **II** CACTACEAE
Opuntia archiconoidea: #4 **II** CACTACEAE
Opuntia arechavaletae = *Opuntia monacantha*
Opuntia arenaria = *Opuntia polyacantha*
Opuntia argentina = *Opuntia brasiliensis*
Opuntia armata: #4 **II** CACTACEAE
Opuntia arrastradillo = *Opuntia stenopetala*
Opuntia articulata: #4 **II** CACTACEAE
Opuntia asplundii = *Opuntia boldinghii*
Opuntia assumptionis: #4 **II** CACTACEAE
Opuntia atacamensis: #4 **II** CACTACEAE
Opuntia atrispina: (E) Border Prickly-pear #4 **II** CACTACEAE
Opuntia atrocapensis = *Opuntia dillenii*
Opuntia atroglobosa = *Opuntia nigrispina*
Opuntia atropes: #4 **II** CACTACEAE
Opuntia atrovirens: #4 **II** CACTACEAE
Opuntia atroviridis = *Opuntia floccosa*
Opuntia auberi: #4 **II** CACTACEAE
Opuntia aurantiaca: #4 **II** CACTACEAE
Opuntia aurea: #4 **II** CACTACEAE
Opuntia aureispina: (E) Golden-spined Prickly-pear #4 **II** CACTACEAE
Opuntia austrina: #4 **II** CACTACEAE
Opuntia azurea: #4 **II** CACTACEAE
Opuntia backebergii: #4 **II** CACTACEAE
Opuntia bahamana = *Opuntia stricta*
Opuntia bahiensis = *Opuntia brasiliensis*
Opuntia ballii = *Opuntia macrorhiza*
Opuntia basilaris: #4 **II** CACTACEAE
Opuntia bella: #4 **II** CACTACEAE
Opuntia bensonii: #4 **II** CACTACEAE
Opuntia bergeriana = *Opuntia elatior*
Opuntia berteri = *Opuntia sphaerica*
Opuntia bigelovii: (E) Teddy-bear Cactus #4 **II** CACTACEAE
Opuntia bisetosa: #4 **II** CACTACEAE
Opuntia bispinosa = *Opuntia anacantha*
Opuntia blancii: #4 **II** CACTACEAE
Opuntia boldinghii: #4 **II** CACTACEAE
Opuntia boliviana: #4 **II** CACTACEAE
Opuntia boliviensis = *Opuntia soehrensis*
Opuntia bonaerensis = *Opuntia paraguayensis*
Opuntia bonplandii: #4 **II** CACTACEAE
Opuntia borinquensis: #4 **II** CACTACEAE
Opuntia brachyacantha = *Opuntia sulphurea* ssp. *brachyacantha*
Opuntia brachyarthra: #4 **II** CACTACEAE
Opuntia brachyclada: #4 **II** CACTACEAE
Opuntia bradleyi: #4 **II** CACTACEAE
Opuntia bradtiana: #4 **II** CACTACEAE
Opuntia brasiliensis: #4 **II** CACTACEAE
Opuntia brasiliensis ssp. *bahiensis* = *Opuntia brasiliensis*
Opuntia brasiliensis ssp. *subacarpa* = *Opuntia brasiliensis*
Opuntia bravoana: #4 **II** CACTACEAE
Opuntia brevispina = *Opuntia alcahes*
Opuntia bruchii = *Opuntia alexanderi*
Opuntia brunneogemmia = *Opuntia monacantha*
Opuntia brunnescens = *Opuntia sulphurea*
Opuntia bulbispina: #4 **II** CACTACEAE
Opuntia burrageana: #4 **II** CACTACEAE
Opuntia calcicola = *Opuntia humifusa*
Opuntia californica: #4 **II** CACTACEAE
Opuntia camachoi: #4 **II** CACTACEAE
Opuntia camanchica: #4 **II** CACTACEAE
Opuntia campestris = *Opuntia sphaerica*
Opuntia candelabriformis = *Opuntia spinulifera*
Opuntia canina = *Opuntia anacantha*
Opuntia cantabrigiensis = *Opuntia engelmannii*
Opuntia canterae: #4 **II** CACTACEAE
Opuntia caracassana: #4 **II** CACTACEAE

Opuntia cardenche: #4 **II** CACTACEAE
Opuntia cardiosperma: #4 **II** CACTACEAE
Opuntia caribaea: #4 **II** CACTACEAE
Opuntia cedergreniana = *Opuntia soehrensis*
Opuntia chaffeyi: #4 **II** CACTACEAE
Opuntia chakensis: #4 **II** CACTACEAE
Opuntia chavena: #4 **II** CACTACEAE
Opuntia chichensis: #4 **II** CACTACEAE
Opuntia chihuahuensis: #4 **II** CACTACEAE
Opuntia chisosensis: #4 **II** CACTACEAE
Opuntia chlorotica: #4 **II** CACTACEAE
Opuntia cholla: #4 **II** CACTACEAE
Opuntia cineracea: #4 **II** CACTACEAE
Opuntia ciribe = *Opuntia bigelovii*
Opuntia clavarioides: #4 **II** CACTACEAE
Opuntia clavata: (E) Club Cholla #4 **II** CACTACEAE
Opuntia cochabambensis: #4 **II** CACTACEAE
Opuntia cochenillifera: (E) Cochineal cactus, Roast pork, Smooth pear #4 **II** CACTACEAE
Opuntia cognata: #4 **II** CACTACEAE
Opuntia colorea: #4 **II** CACTACEAE
Opuntia colubrina: #4 **II** CACTACEAE
Opuntia compressa = *Opuntia humifusa*
Opuntia conjungens: #4 **II** CACTACEAE
Opuntia conoidea: #4 **II** CACTACEAE
Opuntia cordobensis = *Opuntia ficus-indica*
Opuntia corotilla: #4 **II** CACTACEAE
Opuntia corrugata: #4 **II** CACTACEAE
Opuntia crassa: #4 **II** CACTACEAE
Opuntia crassicylindrica: #4 **II** CACTACEAE
Opuntia crassipina: #4 **II** CACTACEAE
Opuntia cretochaeta = *Opuntia hyptiacantha*
Opuntia crispicrinita = *Opuntia floccosa*
Opuntia crystalenia: #4 **II** CACTACEAE
Opuntia cuija = *Opuntia engelmannii*
Opuntia cumulicola = *Opuntia humifusa*
Opuntia curassavica: (E) Pin-cushion, Suckers #4 **II** CACTACEAE
Opuntia cylindrarticulata = *Opuntia dactylifera*
Opuntia cylindrica: #4 **II** CACTACEAE
Opuntia cylindrolanata = *Opuntia floccosa*
Opuntia cymochila: #4 **II** CACTACEAE
Opuntia dactylifera: #4 **II** CACTACEAE
Opuntia darrahiana: #4 **II** CACTACEAE
Opuntia darwinii: #4 **II** CACTACEAE
Opuntia davisii: #4 **II** CACTACEAE
Opuntia deamii: #4 **II** CACTACEAE
Opuntia decumbens: (S) Arpón, Lengua de vaca #4 **II** CACTACEAE
Opuntia dejecta: #4 **II** CACTACEAE
Opuntia delaetiana: #4 **II** CACTACEAE
Opuntia delicata = *Opuntia macrorhiza*
Opuntia densispina: #4 **II** CACTACEAE
Opuntia depauperata: #4 **II** CACTACEAE
Opuntia depressa: #4 **II** CACTACEAE
Opuntia dillenii: #4 **II** CACTACEAE
Opuntia dimorpha = *Opuntia sphaerica*
Opuntia discata = *Opuntia engelmannii*
Opuntia discolor: #4 **II** CACTACEAE
Opuntia distans = *Opuntia quimilo*
Opuntia dobbieana = *Opuntia soederstromiana*
Opuntia domeykoensis: #4 **II** CACTACEAE
Opuntia domingensis = *Opuntia antillana*
Opuntia drummondii = *Opuntia pusilla*
Opuntia dumetorum: #4 **II** CACTACEAE
Opuntia durangensis: #4 **II** CACTACEAE
Opuntia echinacea = *Opuntia boldinghii*
Opuntia echinocarpa: #4 **II** CACTACEAE
Opuntia echios: #4 **II** CACTACEAE
Opuntia edwardsii: #4 **II** CACTACEAE
Opuntia eichlamii: #4 **II** CACTACEAE
Opuntia ekmanii: #4 **II** CACTACEAE
Opuntia elata: #4 **II** CACTACEAE
Opuntia elatior: #4 **II** CACTACEAE
Opuntia elizondoana: #4 **II** CACTACEAE

Opuntia emoryi: (E) Devil's prickley-pear #4 **II** CACTACEAE
Opuntia engelmannii: #4 **II** CACTACEAE
Opuntia erectoclada: #4 **II** CACTACEAE
Opuntia erinacea: #4 **II** CACTACEAE
Opuntia estevesii: #4 **II** CACTACEAE
Opuntia excelsa: #4 **II** CACTACEAE
Opuntia falcata: #4 **II** CACTACEAE
Opuntia feracantha: #4 **II** CACTACEAE
Opuntia ferocior = Opuntia chichensis
Opuntia ficus-indica: (E) Indian fig, (S) Higo chumbo, Tuna, Tuna
    de España, Tuna mansa #4 **II** CACTACEAE
Opuntia flexospina = Opuntia engelmannii
Opuntia flexuosa: #4 **II** CACTACEAE
Opuntia floccosa: #4 **II** CACTACEAE
Opuntia fragilis: #4 **II** CACTACEAE
Opuntia fragilis ssp. *brachyarthra = Opuntia brachyarthra*
Opuntia frigida: #4 **II** CACTACEAE
Opuntia fulgida: (E) Sonoran Jumping Cholla #4 **II** CACTACEAE
Opuntia fuliginosa: #4 **II** CACTACEAE
Opuntia fulvicoma: #4 **II** CACTACEAE
Opuntia fuscoatra = Opuntia humifusa
Opuntia galapageia: #4 **II** CACTACEAE
Opuntia galerasensis: #4 **II** CACTACEAE
Opuntia ganderi = Opuntia acanthocarpa ssp. *ganderi*
Opuntia geometrica = Opuntia alexanderi
Opuntia glaucescens = Opuntia stenopetala
Opuntia glomerata = Opuntia articulata
Opuntia glomerata: #4 **II** CACTACEAE
Opuntia gosseliniana: #4 **II** CACTACEAE
Opuntia grahamii: #4 **II** CACTACEAE
Opuntia grandis = Opuntia stenopetala
Opuntia grosseana: #4 **II** CACTACEAE
Opuntia guatemalensis: #4 **II** CACTACEAE
Opuntia guatinensis: #4 **II** CACTACEAE
Opuntia guerrana = Opuntia robusta
Opuntia guilanchi: #4 **II** CACTACEAE
Opuntia haitiensis = Opuntia moniliformis
Opuntia halophila: #4 **II** CACTACEAE
Opuntia hamiltonii = Opuntia rosarica
Opuntia heacockiae: #4 **II** CACTACEAE
Opuntia heliabravoana = Opuntia spinulifera
Opuntia heliae = Opuntia puberula
Opuntia helleri: #4 **II** CACTACEAE
Opuntia herrfeldtii = Opuntia rufida
Opuntia heteromorpha: #4 **II** CACTACEAE
Opuntia hickenii = Opuntia darwinii
Opuntia hirschii: #4 **II** CACTACEAE
Opuntia hitchcockii: #4 **II** CACTACEAE
Opuntia hoffmannii = Opuntia pubescens
Opuntia hondurensis: #4 **II** CACTACEAE
Opuntia howeyi: #4 **II** CACTACEAE
Opuntia huajuapensis: #4 **II** CACTACEAE
Opuntia humifusa: #4 **II** CACTACEAE
Opuntia hyptiacantha: #4 **II** CACTACEAE
Opuntia hystricina = Opuntia polyacantha
Opuntia ianthinantha: #4 **II** CACTACEAE
Opuntia ignescens: #4 **II** CACTACEAE
Opuntia ignota = Opuntia corotilla
Opuntia imbricata: #4 **II** CACTACEAE
Opuntia impedata = Opuntia humifusa
Opuntia inaequilateralis: #4 **II** CACTACEAE
Opuntia inamoena: #4 **II** CACTACEAE
Opuntia inaperta: #4 **II** CACTACEAE
Opuntia infesta: #4 **II** CACTACEAE
Opuntia insularis: #4 **II** CACTACEAE
Opuntia invicta: #4 **II** CACTACEAE
Opuntia italica = Opuntia humifusa
Opuntia jaliscana: #4 **II** CACTACEAE
Opuntia jamaicensis: #4 **II** CACTACEAE
Opuntia joconostle: #4 **II** CACTACEAE
Opuntia juniperina = Opuntia sphaerocarpa
Opuntia karwinskiana: #4 **II** CACTACEAE
Opuntia keyensis = Opuntia stricta
Opuntia kiska-loro = Opuntia anacantha
Opuntia kleiniae: (E) Candle Cholla #4 **II** CACTACEAE

Opuntia kuehnrichiana = Opuntia sphaerica
Opuntia kunzei: #4 **II** CACTACEAE
Opuntia laevis: #4 **II** CACTACEAE
Opuntia lagopus: #4 **II** CACTACEAE
Opuntia lagunae: #4 **II** CACTACEAE
Opuntia larreyi: #4 **II** CACTACEAE
Opuntia lasiacantha: #4 **II** CACTACEAE
Opuntia lata = Opuntia ammophila
Opuntia leoncito = Opuntia glomerata
Opuntia leptocaulis: #4 **II** CACTACEAE
Opuntia leucophaea: #4 **II** CACTACEAE
Opuntia leucotricha: #4 **II** CACTACEAE
Opuntia lilae: #4 **II** CACTACEAE
Opuntia limitata: #4 **II** CACTACEAE
Opuntia lindheimeri = Opuntia engelmannii
Opuntia lindsayi: #4 **II** CACTACEAE
Opuntia linguiformis: #4 **II** CACTACEAE
Opuntia littoralis: (E) Coastal Prickly-pear #4 **II** CACTACEAE
Opuntia llanos-de-huanta: #4 **II** CACTACEAE
Opuntia lloydii: #4 **II** CACTACEAE
Opuntia longiareolata: #4 **II** CACTACEAE
Opuntia longispina: #4 **II** CACTACEAE
Opuntia lubrica = Opuntia rufida
Opuntia lutea: #4 **II** CACTACEAE
Opuntia macateei = Opuntia pusilla
Opuntia macbridei = Opuntia quitensis
Opuntia mackensii = Opuntia cymochila
Opuntia macracantha: (S) Alpargata, Tuna de cruz #4 **II**
    CACTACEAE
Opuntia macrarthra = Opuntia stricta
Opuntia macrocalyx = Opuntia microdasys
Opuntia macrocentra: #4 **II** CACTACEAE
Opuntia macrorhiza: #4 **II** CACTACEAE
Opuntia magnifica = Opuntia stricta
Opuntia mamillata: #4 **II** CACTACEAE
Opuntia mandragora = Opuntia minuta
Opuntia marenae: #4 **II** CACTACEAE
Opuntia marnieriana = Opuntia stenopetala
Opuntia martiniana: #4 **II** CACTACEAE
Opuntia matudae = Opuntia hyptiacantha
Opuntia maxonii = Opuntia puberula
Opuntia megacantha: #4 **II** CACTACEAE
Opuntia megapotamica: #4 **II** CACTACEAE
Opuntia megarhiza: #4 **II** CACTACEAE
Opuntia megasperma: #4 **II** CACTACEAE
Opuntia melanosperma = Opuntia dillenii
Opuntia microcarpa = Opuntia engelmannii
Opuntia microdasys: #4 **II** CACTACEAE
Opuntia microdisca: #4 **II** CACTACEAE
Opuntia mieckleyi: #4 **II** CACTACEAE
Opuntia militaris = Opuntia triacantha
Opuntia millspaughii: #4 **II** CACTACEAE
Opuntia minuscula: #4 **II** CACTACEAE
Opuntia minuta: #4 **II** CACTACEAE
Opuntia miquelii: #4 **II** CACTACEAE
Opuntia mira = Opuntia sphaerica
Opuntia mistiensis: #4 **II** CACTACEAE
Opuntia moelleri: #4 **II** CACTACEAE
Opuntia mojavensis: #4 **II** CACTACEAE
Opuntia molesta: #4 **II** CACTACEAE
Opuntia molinensis: #4 **II** CACTACEAE
Opuntia monacantha: #4 **II** CACTACEAE
Opuntia monacantha ssp. *brunneogemmia = Opuntia monacantha*
Opuntia moniliformis: #4 **II** CACTACEAE
Opuntia montevideensis: #4 **II** CACTACEAE
Opuntia multiareolata = Opuntia soehrensii
Opuntia multigeniculata: #4 **II** CACTACEAE
Opuntia munzii: (E) Munz cholla #4 **II** CACTACEAE
Opuntia nashii: (E) Nash's prickly-pear #4 **II** CACTACEAE
Opuntia nejapensis: #4 **II** CACTACEAE
Opuntia nemoralis = Opuntia humifusa
Opuntia neoargentina = Opuntia brasiliensis
Opuntia neochrysacantha: #4 **II** CACTACEAE
Opuntia neuquensis = Opuntia darwinii
Opuntia nicholii = Opuntia polyacantha

Opuntia nigrispina: #4 **II** CACTACEAE
Opuntia nitens = *Opuntia dillenii*
Opuntia noodtiae = *Opuntia dactylifera*
Opuntia nuda: #4 **II** CACTACEAE
Opuntia obliqua = *Opuntia soehrensii*
Opuntia orbiculata: #4 **II** CACTACEAE
Opuntia oricola: (E) Chaparral Prickly-pear #4 **II** CACTACEAE
Opuntia orurensis: #4 **II** CACTACEAE
Opuntia ovata: #4 **II** CACTACEAE
Opuntia pachona: #4 **II** CACTACEAE
Opuntia pachypus: #4 **II** CACTACEAE
Opuntia paediophila = *Opuntia aoracantha*
Opuntia pailana: #4 **II** CACTACEAE
Opuntia pallida = *Opuntia rosea*
Opuntia palmadora: #4 **II** CACTACEAE
Opuntia palmeri = *Opuntia chlorotica*
Opuntia papyracantha = *Opuntia articulata*
Opuntia paraguayensis: #4 **II** CACTACEAE
Opuntia parishii: #4 **II** CACTACEAE
Opuntia parryi: #4 **II** CACTACEAE
Opuntia parviclada: #4 **II** CACTACEAE
Opuntia pascoensis = *Opuntia pubescens*
Opuntia patagonica = *Maihuenia patagonica*
Opuntia penicilligera: #4 **II** CACTACEAE
Opuntia pennellii: #4 **II** CACTACEAE
Opuntia pentlandii: #4 **II** CACTACEAE
Opuntia pes-corvi = *Opuntia pusilla*
Opuntia pestifer = *Opuntia pubescens*
Opuntia phaeacantha: #4 **II** CACTACEAE
Opuntia picardae = *Opuntia moniliformis*
Opuntia picardoi: #4 **II** CACTACEAE
Opuntia pilifera: #4 **II** CACTACEAE
Opuntia pittieri: #4 **II** CACTACEAE
Opuntia pituitosa: #4 **II** CACTACEAE
Opuntia platyacantha = *Opuntia darwinii*
Opuntia plumbea: #4 **II** CACTACEAE
Opuntia poecilacantha = *Opuntia microdisca*
Opuntia pollardii = *Opuntia austrina*
Opuntia polyacantha: (E) Sand prickly pear #4 **II** CACTACEAE
Opuntia polycarpa = *Opuntia austrina*
Opuntia pottsii = *Opuntia macrorhiza*
Opuntia prasina: #4 **II** CACTACEAE
Opuntia procumbens = *Opuntia engelmannii*
Opuntia prolifera: (E) Coastal Cholla #4 **II** CACTACEAE
Opuntia pseudo-udonis = *Opuntia floccosa*
Opuntia puberula: #4 **II** CACTACEAE
Opuntia pubescens: #4 **II** CACTACEAE
Opuntia puelchana = *Opuntia tunicata*
Opuntia pulchella: (E) Sand Cholla #4 **II** CACTACEAE
Opuntia pumila: #4 **II** CACTACEAE
Opuntia punta-caillan: #4 **II** CACTACEAE
Opuntia purpurea = *Opuntia nigrispina*
Opuntia pusilla: (E) Little Prickly-pear #4 **II** CACTACEAE
Opuntia pycnantha: #4 **II** CACTACEAE
Opuntia pyriformis: #4 **II** CACTACEAE
Opuntia pyrrhacantha: #4 **II** CACTACEAE
Opuntia pyrrhantha: #4 **II** CACTACEAE
Opuntia quimilo: #4 **II** CACTACEAE
Opuntia quitensis: #4 **II** CACTACEAE
Opuntia rafinesquei = *Opuntia humifusa*
Opuntia rahmeri: #4 **II** CACTACEAE
Opuntia ramosissima: (E) Lead-pencil Cholla #4 **II** CACTACEAE
Opuntia rastrera: #4 **II** CACTACEAE
Opuntia rauhii = *Opuntia floccosa*
Opuntia rauppiana = *Opuntia sphaerica*
Opuntia reflexispina: #4 **II** CACTACEAE
Opuntia reicheana = *Opuntia glomerata*
Opuntia repens: #4 **II** CACTACEAE
Opuntia retrorsa = *Opuntia anacantha*
Opuntia rhodantha = *Opuntia polyacantha*
Opuntia rileyi: #4 **II** CACTACEAE
Opuntia ritteri: #4 **II** CACTACEAE
Opuntia riviereana = *Opuntia stenopetala*
Opuntia robinsonii: #4 **II** CACTACEAE
Opuntia roborensis: #4 **II** CACTACEAE

Opuntia robusta: #4 **II** CACTACEAE
Opuntia rosarica: #4 **II** CACTACEAE
Opuntia rosea: #4 **II** CACTACEAE
Opuntia rossiana: #4 **II** CACTACEAE
Opuntia rubescens: (E) Tree cactus #4 **II** CACTACEAE
Opuntia rubiflora = *Opuntia humifusa*
Opuntia rufida: (E) Blind Prickly-pear #4 **II** CACTACEAE
Opuntia russellii = *Opuntia ovata*
Opuntia rutila: #4 **II** CACTACEAE
Opuntia rzedowskii = *Opuntia lasiacantha*
Opuntia salagria: #4 **II** CACTACEAE
Opuntia salmiana: #4 **II** CACTACEAE
Opuntia salvadorensis: #4 **II** CACTACEAE
Opuntia sanctae-barbarae: #4 **II** CACTACEAE
Opuntia sanguinea: #4 **II** CACTACEAE
Opuntia santamaria: #4 **II** CACTACEAE
Opuntia santa-rita: #4 **II** CACTACEAE
Opuntia saxatilis: #4 **II** CACTACEAE
Opuntia saxicola: #4 **II** CACTACEAE
Opuntia scheeri: #4 **II** CACTACEAE
Opuntia scheinvariana = *Opuntia puberula*
Opuntia schickendantzii: #4 **II** CACTACEAE
Opuntia schottii: (E) Schott's Prickly-pear #4 **II** CACTACEAE
Opuntia schulzii = *Opuntia brasiliensis*
Opuntia schumannii: #4 **II** CACTACEAE
Opuntia securigera: #4 **II** CACTACEAE
Opuntia serpentina = *Opuntia californica*
Opuntia setispina = *Opuntia macrorhiza*
Opuntia shaferi: #4 **II** CACTACEAE
Opuntia shreveana = *Opuntia santa-rita*
Opuntia silvestris: #4 **II** CACTACEAE
Opuntia soederstromiana: #4 **II** CACTACEAE
Opuntia soehrensii: #4 **II** CACTACEAE
Opuntia sphaerica: #4 **II** CACTACEAE
Opuntia sphaerocarpa: #4 **II** CACTACEAE
Opuntia spinosior: (E) Cane Prickly-pear #4 **II** CACTACEAE
Opuntia spinosissima: (E) Prickly pear tree, Semaphore Cactus #4 **II** CACTACEAE
Opuntia spinulifera: #4 **II** CACTACEAE
Opuntia spraguei: #4 **II** CACTACEAE
Opuntia stanlyi = *Opuntia emoryi*
Opuntia stenarthra: #4 **II** CACTACEAE
Opuntia stenopetala: #4 **II** CACTACEAE
Opuntia streptacantha: #4 **II** CACTACEAE
Opuntia stricta: #4 **II** CACTACEAE
Opuntia subarmata = *Opuntia engelmannii*
Opuntia subsphaerocarpa: #4 **II** CACTACEAE
Opuntia subterranea: #4 **II** CACTACEAE
Opuntia subulata: #4 **II** CACTACEAE
Opuntia sulphurea: #4 **II** CACTACEAE
Opuntia sulphurea ssp. *brachyacantha*: #4 **II** CACTACEAE
Opuntia sulphurea ssp. *spinibarbis*: #4 **II** CACTACEAE
Opuntia superbospina: (E) Kingman's Prickly-pear #4 **II** CACTACEAE
Opuntia tapona: #4 **II** CACTACEAE
Opuntia tarapacana: #4 **II** CACTACEAE
Opuntia tardospina = *Opuntia engelmannii*
Opuntia tayapayensis = *Opuntia pubescens*
Opuntia taylorii: #4 **II** CACTACEAE
Opuntia tehuacana: #4 **II** CACTACEAE
Opuntia tehuantepecana: #4 **II** CACTACEAE
Opuntia tenuiflora: #4 **II** CACTACEAE
Opuntia tenuispina = *Opuntia macrorhiza*
Opuntia tephrocactoides = *Opuntia floccosa*
Opuntia tesajo: #4 **II** CACTACEAE
Opuntia testudinis-crus = *Opuntia moniliformis*
Opuntia thornberi = *Opuntia acanthocarpa*
Opuntia thurberi: #4 **II** CACTACEAE
Opuntia ticnamarensis: #4 **II** CACTACEAE
Opuntia tilcarensis = *Opuntia soehrensii*
Opuntia tomentella: #4 **II** CACTACEAE
Opuntia tomentosa: #4 **II** CACTACEAE
Opuntia tracyi = *Opuntia pusilla*
Opuntia treleasei: (E) Bakersfield Beavertail Cactus #4 **II** CACTACEAE

Opuntia triacantha: (E) Big Pine Key Prickly-pear #4 **II**
    CACTACEAE
Opuntia trichophora: #4 **II** CACTACEAE
Opuntia tricolor = Opuntia engelmannii
Opuntia tumida: #4 **II** CACTACEAE
Opuntia tuna: #4 **II** CACTACEAE
Opuntia tuna-blanca = Opuntia ficus-indica
Opuntia tunicata: (E) Tuna Cholla #4 **II** CACTACEAE
Opuntia turbinata: #4 **II** CACTACEAE
Opuntia turgida = Opuntia ammophila
Opuntia udonis = Opuntia floccosa
Opuntia undulata: #4 **II** CACTACEAE
Opuntia unguispina: #4 **II** CACTACEAE
Opuntia urbaniana: #4 **II** CACTACEAE
Opuntia utkilio = Opuntia anacantha
Opuntia vaginata: #4 **II** CACTACEAE
Opuntia velutina: #4 **II** CACTACEAE
Opuntia verschaffeltii: #4 **II** CACTACEAE
Opuntia versicolor: (E) Stag-horn Cholla #4 **II** CACTACEAE
Opuntia verticosa = Opuntia floccosa
Opuntia vestita: #4 **II** CACTACEAE
Opuntia vilis: #4 **II** CACTACEAE
Opuntia violacea = Opuntia macrocentra
Opuntia viridirubra: #4 **II** CACTACEAE
Opuntia viridirubra ssp. *rubrogemmia*: #4 **II** CACTACEAE
Opuntia vitelliniflora: #4 **II** CACTACEAE
Opuntia vitelliniflora ssp. *interjecta*: #4 **II** CACTACEAE
Opuntia vulgaris = Opuntia monacantha
Opuntia vulpina = Opuntia sulphurea
Opuntia wagenknechtii: #4 **II** CACTACEAE
Opuntia weberi: #4 **II** CACTACEAE
Opuntia weingartiana = Opuntia shaferi
Opuntia wentiana = Opuntia caracassana
Opuntia werneri: #4 **II** CACTACEAE
Opuntia wetmorei: #4 **II** CACTACEAE
Opuntia whipplei: (E) Whipple's Cactus #4 **II** CACTACEAE
Opuntia whitneyana = Opuntia basilaris
Opuntia wigginsii: (E) Wiggins cholla #4 **II** CACTACEAE
Opuntia wilcoxii: #4 **II** CACTACEAE
Opuntia wolfei: #4 **II** CACTACEAE
Opuntia woodsii = Opuntia phaeacantha
Opuntia wootonii: #4 **II** CACTACEAE
Opuntia wrightiana = Opuntia kunzei
Opuntia yanganucensis: #4 **II** CACTACEAE
Opuntia zacana = Opuntia echios
Opuntia zebrina = Opuntia dillenii
Opuntia zehnderi: #4 **II** CACTACEAE
Orchiastrum = Spiranthes
ORCHIDACEAE spp.: (E) orchids, (S) orchidéas, (F) orquidées #8
    I/II
Orchidées (F): ORCHIDACEAE spp.
Orchidium = Calypso
Orchidofunckia = Cryptarrhena
Orchidotypus = Pachyphyllum
Orchids (E): ORCHIDACEAE spp.
Orchiodes = Goodyera
Orchipedum spp.: #7 **II** ORCHIDACEAE
Orchis spp.: #7 **II** ORCHIDACEAE
Orejas de conejo (S): *Ariocarpus scaphirostris*
Orejitas (S): *Ariocarpus scaphirostris*
Oreocereus australis = Oreocereus hempelianus
Oreocereus celsianus: #4 **II** CACTACEAE
Oreocereus doelzianus: #4 **II** CACTACEAE
Oreocereus hempelianus: #4 **II** CACTACEAE
Oreocereus leucotrichus: #4 **II** CACTACEAE
Oreocereus piscoensis = Cleistocactus pachycladus
Oreocereus pseudofossulatus: #4 **II** CACTACEAE
Oreocereus ritteri: #4 **II** CACTACEAE
Oreocereus tacnaensis: #4 **II** CACTACEAE
Oreocereus trollii: #4 **II** CACTACEAE
Oreocereus varicolor: #4 **II** CACTACEAE
Oreomunnea pterocarpa: (S) Gavilán, Gavilán blanco #1 **II**
    JUGLANDACEAE
Oreorchis spp.: #7 **II** ORCHIDACEAE
Orestias spp.: #7 **II** ORCHIDACEAE

Organ Mountain foxtail-cactus (E): *Escobaria organensis*
Orleanesia spp.: #7 **II** ORCHIDACEAE
Ormostema = Dendrobium
Ornitharium = Pteroceras
Ornithidium = Maxillaria
Ornithocephalus spp.: #7 **II** ORCHIDACEAE
Ornithochilus spp.: #7 **II** ORCHIDACEAE
Ornithophora = Sigmatostalix
Orothamnus zeyheri: (E) Marsh rose #1 **II** PROTEACEAE
Oroya baumannii = Oroya peruviana
Oroya borchersii: #4 **II** CACTACEAE
Oroya peruviana: #4 **II** CACTACEAE
Orquidéas (S): ORCHIDACEAE spp.
Orsidice = Thrixspermum
Ortegocactus macdougallii: #4 **II** CACTACEAE
Orthoceras spp.: #7 **II** ORCHIDACEAE
Orthochilus = Eulophia
Orthopenthea = Disa
Ortmannia = Geodorum
Orxera = Aerides
Osmoglossum spp.: #7 **II** ORCHIDACEAE
Ossiculum spp.: #7 **II** ORCHIDACEAE
Osyricera = Bulbophyllum
Otandra = Geodorum
Otochilus spp.: #7 **II** ORCHIDACEAE
Otoglossum spp.: #7 **II** ORCHIDACEAE
Otopetalum = Pleurothallis
Otostylis spp.: #7 **II** ORCHIDACEAE
Oxyanthera = Thelasis
Oxysepala = Bulbophyllum
Oxystophyllum = Dendrobium
Pa porcí (S): *Cyclamen balearicum*
Pabstia spp.: #7 **II** ORCHIDACEAE
Pabstiella = Pleurothallis
Pachites spp.: #7 **II** ORCHIDACEAE
Pachycereus chrysomallus = Pachycereus militaris
Pachycereus columna-trajani = Cephalocereus columna-trajani
Pachycereus fulviceps: #4 **II** CACTACEAE
Pachycereus gatesii: #4 **II** CACTACEAE
Pachycereus gaumeri: #4 **II** CACTACEAE
Pachycereus grandis: #4 **II** CACTACEAE
Pachycereus hollianus: #4 **II** CACTACEAE
Pachycereus lepidanthus: #4 **II** CACTACEAE
Pachycereus marginatus: #4 **II** CACTACEAE
Pachycereus militaris: (E) Grenadier's cap, Teddy-bear cactus **I**
    CACTACEAE
Pachycereus pecten-aboriginum: #4 **II** CACTACEAE
Pachycereus pringlei: #4 **II** CACTACEAE
Pachycereus ruficeps = Neobuxbaumia macrocephala
Pachycereus schottii: #4 **II** CACTACEAE
Pachycereus weberi: #4 **II** CACTACEAE
Pachychilus = Pachystoma
Pachyclada dendroides = Euphorbia dendroides
Pachyne = Phaius
Pachyphyllum spp.: #7 **II** ORCHIDACEAE
Pachyplectron spp.: #7 **II** ORCHIDACEAE
Pachypodium spp.: (E) elephant trunks, (S) trompa de elefante #1
    I/II APOCYNACEAE
Pachypodium ambongense: **I** APOCYNACEAE
Pachypodium baronii: **I** APOCYNACEAE
Pachypodium baronii var. *baronii*: **I** APOCYNACEAE
Pachypodium baronii var. *erythreum = Pachypodium baronii* var.
    baronii
Pachypodium baronii var. *typicum = Pachypodium baronii* var.
    baronii
Pachypodium baronii var. *windsorii*: **I** APOCYNACEAE
Pachypodium bicolor = Pachypodium rosulatum var. *rosulatum* f.
    bicolor
Pachypodium bispinosum: #1 **II** APOCYNACEAE
Pachypodium brevicalyx = Pachypodium densiflorum
Pachypodium brevicaule: #1 **II** APOCYNACEAE
Pachypodium cactipes = Pachypodium rosulatum
Pachypodium champenoisianum = Pachypodium lamerei
Pachypodium decaryi: **I** APOCYNACEAE
Pachypodium densiflorum: #1 **II** APOCYNACEAE

Pachypodium densiflorum var. *brevicalyx* = *Pachypodium densiflorum*
Pachypodium densiflorum var. *densiflorum*: #1 **II** APOCYNACEAE
Pachypodium drakei = *Pachypodium rosulatum*
Pachypodium eburneum = *Pachypodium rosulatum* var. *eburneum*
Pachypodium geayi: #1 **II** APOCYNACEAE
Pachypodium giganteum = *Pachypodium lealii*
Pachypodium glabrum = *Pachypodium bispinosum*
Pachypodium gracilius = *Pachypodium rosulatum* var. *gracilius*
Pachypodium griquense = *Pachypodium succulentum*
Pachypodium horombense: #1 **II** APOCYNACEAE
Pachypodium inopinatum = *Pachypodium rosulatum* var. *inopinatum*
Pachypodium jasminiflorum = *Pachypodium succulentum*
Pachypodium lamerei: #1 **II** APOCYNACEAE
Pachypodium lamerei var. *lamerei* = *Pachypodium lamerei*
Pachypodium lamerei var. *ramosum* = *Pachypodium lamerei*
Pachypodium lamerei var. *typicum* = *Pachypodium lamerei*
Pachypodium lealii: #1 **II** APOCYNACEAE
Pachypodium lealii ssp. *lealii*: #1 **II** APOCYNACEAE
Pachypodium lealii ssp. *saundersii*: #1 **II** APOCYNACEAE
Pachypodium menabeum = *Pachypodium lamerei*
Pachypodium meridionale = *Pachypodium rutenbergianum* var. *meridionale*
Pachypodium namaquanum: (E) Elephant's trunk #1 **II** APOCYNACEAE
Pachypodium ramosum = *Pachypodium lamerei*
Pachypodium rosulatum: #1 **II** APOCYNACEAE
Pachypodium rosulatum f. *bicolor*: #1 **II** APOCYNACEAE
Pachypodium rosulatum var. *delphinense* = *Pachypodium rosulatum* var. *rosulatum*
Pachypodium rosulatum var. *drakei* = *Pachypodium rosulatum* var. *rosulatum*
Pachypodium rosulatum var. *eburneum*: #1 **II** APOCYNACEAE
Pachypodium rosulatum var. *gracilius*: #1 **II** APOCYNACEAE
Pachypodium rosulatum var. *horombense* = *Pachypodium horombense*
Pachypodium rosulatum var. *inopinatum*: #1 **II** APOCYNACEAE
Pachypodium rosulatum var. *rosulatum*: #1 **II** APOCYNACEAE
Pachypodium rosulatum var. *rosulatum* f. *bicolor*: #1 **II** APOCYNACEAE
Pachypodium rosulatum var. *stenanthum* = *Pachypodium rosulatum* var. *rosulatum*
Pachypodium rosulatum var. *typicum* = *Pachypodium rosulatum* var. *rosulatum*
Pachypodium rutenbergianum: #1 **II** APOCYNACEAE
Pachypodium rutenbergianum f. *lamerei* = *Pachypodium lamerei*
Pachypodium rutenbergianum var. *meridionale*: #1 **II** APOCYNACEAE
Pachypodium rutenbergianum var. *perrieri* = *Pachypodium rutenbergianum* var. *sofiense*
Pachypodium rutenbergianum var. *rutenbergianum*: #1 **II** APOCYNACEAE
Pachypodium rutenbergianum var. *sofiense*: #1 **II** APOCYNACEAE
Pachypodium rutenbergianum var. *typicum* = *Pachypodium rutenbergianum* var. *rutenbergianum*
Pachypodium saundersii = *Pachypodium lealii* ssp. *saundersii*
Pachypodium sofiense = *Pachypodium rutenbergianum* var. *sofiense*
Pachypodium succulentum: #1 **II** APOCYNACEAE
Pachypodium tomentosum = *Pachypodium succulentum*
Pachypodium tuberosum = *Pachypodium succulentum*
Pachypodium tuberosum var. *loddigesii* = *Pachypodium bispinosum*
Pachypodium windsorii = *Pachypodium baronii* var. *windsorii*
Pachyrhizanthe = *Cymbidium*
Pachystele = *Scaphyglottis*
Pachystelis = *Pachystele*
Pachystoma spp.: #7 **II** ORCHIDACEAE
Pachystylis = *Pachystoma*
Pale pitcher-plant (E): *Sarracenia alata*
Paliris = *Liparis*
Palisandro del Brasil (S): *Dalbergia nigra*

Palissandre du Brésil (F): *Dalbergia nigra*
Palm corcho (E): *Microcycas calocoma*
Palma corcho (S): *Microcycas calocoma*
Palmas del pan (S): *Encephalartos* spp.
Palmita de terra fría (S): *Cyathea costaricensis*
Palmoglossum = *Pleurothallis*
Palmorchis spp.: #7 **II** ORCHIDACEAE
Palo de la vida (S): *Cyathea bicrenata*
Palo de vida (S): *Guaiacum officinale*
Palo santo (S): *Guaiacum officinale*
Palomón (S): *Peristeria elata*
Palosanto (S): *Guaiacum* spp.
Palumbina spp.: #7 **II** ORCHIDACEAE
Panax ginseng: (E) Ginseng, Red ginseng #3 **II**[4] ARALIACEAE
Panax quinquefolius: (E) American ginseng, (S) Ginseng americano (F) Ginseng d'Amérique, #3 **II** ARALIACEAE
Panisea spp.: #7 **II** ORCHIDACEAE
Panstrepis = *Coryanthes*
Pantlingia = *Stigmatodactylus*
Paper-spine pincushion cactus (E): *Sclerocactus papyracanthus*
Paphinia spp.: #7 **II** ORCHIDACEAE
Paphiopedilum spp.: (E) Asian slipper orchids, slipper orchids, (S) sandalia de Venus **I** ORCHIDACEAE
Paphiopedilum acmodontum: **I** ORCHIDACEAE
Paphiopedilum adductum: **I** ORCHIDACEAE
Paphiopedilum affine = *Paphiopedilum gratrixianum*
Paphiopedilum amabile = *Paphiopedilum bullenianum*
Paphiopedilum ambonensis = *Paphiopedilum bullenianum* var. *celebesense*
Paphiopedilum appletonianum: **I** ORCHIDACEAE
Paphiopedilum appletonianum var. *poyntziamum* = *Paphiopedilum appletonianum*
Paphiopedilum argus: **I** ORCHIDACEAE
Paphiopedilum argus var. *sriwaniae* = *Paphiopedilum argus*
Paphiopedilum armeniacum: **I** ORCHIDACEAE
Paphiopedilum bacanum = *Paphiopedilum schoseri*
Paphiopedilum barbatum: **I** ORCHIDACEAE
Paphiopedilum barbatum ssp. *lawrenceanum* = *Paphiopedilum lawrenceanum*
Paphiopedilum barbatum var. *argus* = *Paphiopedilum argus*
Paphiopedilum barbatum var. *nigritum* = *Paphiopedilum barbatum*
Paphiopedilum barbigerum: **I** ORCHIDACEAE
Paphiopedilum barbigerum f. *aureum*: **I** ORCHIDACEAE
Paphiopedilum bellatulum: **I** ORCHIDACEAE
Paphiopedilum birkii = *Paphiopedilum callosum* var. *sublaeve*
Paphiopedilum bodegomii = *Paphiopedilum glanduliferum* var. *wilhelminae*
Paphiopedilum boissierianum = *Phragmipedium boissierianum*
Paphiopedilum bougainvilleanum: **I** ORCHIDACEAE
Paphiopedilum boxallii = *Paphiopedilum villosum* var. *boxallii*
Paphiopedilum braemii = *Paphiopedilum tonsum* var. *braemii*
Paphiopedilum bullenianum: **I** ORCHIDACEAE
Paphiopedilum bullenianum var. *amabile*: **I** ORCHIDACEAE
Paphiopedilum bullenianum var. *celebesense*: **I** ORCHIDACEAE
Paphiopedilum burbidgei = *Paphiopedilum dayanum*
Paphiopedilum callosum: **I** ORCHIDACEAE
Paphiopedilum callosum f. *viridiflorum*: **I** ORCHIDACEAE
Paphiopedilum callosum ssp. *sublaeve* = *Paphiopedilum callosum* var. *sublaeve*
Paphiopedilum callosum var. *angustipetalum* = *Paphiopedilum callosum*
Paphiopedilum callosum var. *schmidtianum* = *Paphiopedilum callosum*
Paphiopedilum callosum var. *sublaeve*: **I** ORCHIDACEAE
Paphiopedilum caricinum = *Phragmipedium caricinum*
Paphiopedilum caudatum = *Phragmipedium caudatum*
Paphiopedilum caudatum var. *lindenii* = *Phragmipedium lindenii*
Paphiopedilum caudatum var. *wallisii* = *Phragmipedium wallisii*
Paphiopedilum celebesense = *Paphiopedilum bullenianum* var. *celebesense*

---

[4] Only the population of the Russian Federation/Sólo la población de la Federación de Rusia /Seulement la population de la Fédération de Russie

Paphiopedilum ceramensis = Paphiopedilum bullenianum var.
  celebesense
*Paphiopedilum chamberlainianum = Paphiopedilum victoria-
  regina*
Paphiopedilum chamberlainianum ssp. *liemianum =
  Paphiopedilum liemianum*
Paphiopedilum chamberlainianum var. *liemianum =
  Paphiopedilum liemianum*
Paphiopedilum chamberlainianum var. *primulinum =
  Paphiopedilum primulinum*
Paphiopedilum charlesworthii: **I** ORCHIDACEAE
Paphiopedilum charlesworthii f. *crawshawiae*: **I** ORCHIDACEAE
Paphiopedilum chiwuanum = Paphiopedilum hirsutissimum
Paphiopedilum ciliolare: **I** ORCHIDACEAE
Paphiopedilum ciliolare var. *miteauanum = Paphiopedilum
  ciliolare*
Paphiopedilum concolor: **I** ORCHIDACEAE
Paphiopedilum concolor var. *niveum = Paphiopedilum niveum*
Paphiopedilum curtisii = Paphiopedilum superbiens var. *curtisii*
Paphiopedilum dariense = Phragmipedium longifolium
Paphiopedilum dayanum: **I** ORCHIDACEAE
Paphiopedilum dayanum var. *petri = Paphiopedilum dayanum*
Paphiopedilum delenatii: **I** ORCHIDACEAE
Paphiopedilum dennisii = Paphiopedilum wentworthianum
Paphiopedilum devogelii = Paphiopedilum supardii
Paphiopedilum dianthum: **I** ORCHIDACEAE
Paphiopedilum dilectum = Paphiopedilum villosum var. *boxallii*
Paphiopedilum dollii = Paphiopedilum henryanum
Paphiopedilum druryi: (E) Drury's slipper orchid **I**
  ORCHIDACEAE
Paphiopedilum elliottianum = Paphiopedilum adductum
Paphiopedilum elliottianum = Paphiopedilum rothschildianum
Paphiopedilum emersonii: **I** ORCHIDACEAE
Paphiopedilum exul: **I** ORCHIDACEAE
Paphiopedilum fairrieanum: **I** ORCHIDACEAE
Paphiopedilum fowliei: **I** ORCHIDACEAE
Paphiopedilum fowliei f. *sangianum*: **I** ORCHIDACEAE
Paphiopedilum gardineri = Paphiopedilum glanduliferum
Paphiopedilum gardineri = Paphiopedilum glanduliferum var.
  wilhelminae
Paphiopedilum glanduliferum: **I** ORCHIDACEAE
Paphiopedilum glanduliferum var. *gardineri = Paphiopedilum
  glanduliferum*
Paphiopedilum glanduliferum var. *praestans = Paphiopedilum
  glanduliferum*
Paphiopedilum glanduliferum var. *wilhelminae*: **I**
  ORCHIDACEAE
Paphiopedilum glaucophyllum: **I** ORCHIDACEAE
Paphiopedilum glaucophyllum var. *moquetteanum*: **I**
  ORCHIDACEAE
Paphiopedilum godefroyae: **I** ORCHIDACEAE
Paphiopedilum godefroyae var. *leucochilum*: **I** ORCHIDACEAE
Paphiopedilum gratrixianum: **I** ORCHIDACEAE
Paphiopedilum hainanense = Paphiopedilum appletonianum
Paphiopedilum haynaldianum: **I** ORCHIDACEAE
Paphiopedilum hennisianum: **I** ORCHIDACEAE
Paphiopedilum hennisianum f. *christiansenii*: **I** ORCHIDACEAE
Paphiopedilum hennisianum var. *fowliei = Paphiopedilum fowliei*
Paphiopedilum henryanum: **I** ORCHIDACEAE
Paphiopedilum henryanum f. *christae*: **I** ORCHIDACEAE
Paphiopedilum hiepii = Paphiopedilum malipoense var. *hiepii*
Paphiopedilum hincksianum = Phragmipedium longifolium
Paphiopedilum hirsutissimum: **I** ORCHIDACEAE
Paphiopedilum hirsutissimum f. *viride*: **I** ORCHIDACEAE
Paphiopedilum hirsutissimum var. *chiwuanum = Paphiopedilum
  hirsutissimum*
Paphiopedilum hirsutissimum var. *chiwuanum = Paphiopedilum
  hirsutissimum*
Paphiopedilum hirsutissimum var. *esquirolei*: **I** ORCHIDACEAE
Paphiopedilum hookerae: **I** ORCHIDACEAE
Paphiopedilum hookerae f. *sandowiae*: **I** ORCHIDACEAE
Paphiopedilum hookerae var. *bullenianum = Paphiopedilum
  bullenianum*
Paphiopedilum hookerae var. *hookerae*: **I** ORCHIDACEAE
Paphiopedilum hookerae var. *volonteanum*: **I** ORCHIDACEAE

Paphiopedilum insigne: **I** ORCHIDACEAE
Paphiopedilum insigne f. *sanderae*: **I** ORCHIDACEAE
Paphiopedilum insigne f. *sanderianum*: **I** ORCHIDACEAE
Paphiopedilum insigne var. *barbigerum = Paphiopedilum
  barbigerum*
Paphiopedilum insigne var. *exul = Paphiopedilum exul*
Paphiopedilum javanicum: **I** ORCHIDACEAE
Paphiopedilum javanicum var. *virens*: **I** ORCHIDACEAE
Paphiopedilum johorense = Paphiopedilum bullenianum
Paphiopedilum klotzschianum = Phragmipedium klotzschianum
Paphiopedilum kolopakingii: **I** ORCHIDACEAE
Paphiopedilum laevigatum = Paphiopedilum philippinense
Paphiopedilum lawrenceanum: **I** ORCHIDACEAE
Paphiopedilum leucochilum = Paphiopedilum godefroyae var.
  leucochilum
Paphiopedilum liemianum: **I** ORCHIDACEAE
Paphiopedilum liemianum var. *primulinum = Paphiopedilum
  primulinum*
Paphiopedilum lindleyanum = Phragmipedium lindleyanum
Paphiopedilum linii = Paphiopedilum bullenianum
Paphiopedilum longifolium = Phragmipedium longifolium
Paphiopedilum lowii: **I** ORCHIDACEAE
Paphiopedilum lowii var. *richardianum*: **I** ORCHIDACEAE
Paphiopedilum malipoense: **I** ORCHIDACEAE
Paphiopedilum malipoense var. *hiepii*: **I** ORCHIDACEAE
Paphiopedilum markianum = Paphiopedilum tigrinum
Paphiopedilum mastersianum: **I** ORCHIDACEAE
Paphiopedilum micranthum: **I** ORCHIDACEAE
Paphiopedilum micranthum f. *glanzeanum*: **I** ORCHIDACEAE
Paphiopedilum mohrianum: **I** ORCHIDACEAE
Paphiopedilum moquetteanum = Paphiopedilum glaucophyllum
  var. *moquetteanum*
Paphiopedilum nicholsonianum = Paphiopedilum rothschildianum
Paphiopedilum nigritum = Paphiopedilum barbatum
Paphiopedilum niveum: **I** ORCHIDACEAE
Paphiopedilum niveum f. *album*: **I** ORCHIDACEAE
Paphiopedilum orbum = Paphiopedilum callosum
Paphiopedilum papuanum: **I** ORCHIDACEAE
Paphiopedilum pardinum = Paphiopedilum venustum
Paphiopedilum parishii: **I** ORCHIDACEAE
Paphiopedilum parishii var. *dianthum = Paphiopedilum dianthum*
Paphiopedilum petri = Paphiopedilum dayanum
Paphiopedilum philippinense: **I** ORCHIDACEAE
Paphiopedilum philippinense var. *cannartianum = Paphiopedilum
  philippinense*
Paphiopedilum philippinense var. *roebelenii*: **I** ORCHIDACEAE
Paphiopedilum praestans = Paphiopedilum glanduliferum
Paphiopedilum praestans ssp. *wilhelminae = Paphiopedilum
  glanduliferum* var. *wilhelminae*
Paphiopedilum praestans var. *kimballianum = Paphiopedilum
  glanduliferum*
Paphiopedilum primulinum: **I** ORCHIDACEAE
Paphiopedilum primulinum var. *purpurascens*: **I** ORCHIDACEAE
Paphiopedilum purpurascens = Paphiopedilum javanicum var.
  virens
Paphiopedilum purpuratum: (E) Hong Kong slipper orchid **I**
  ORCHIDACEAE
Paphiopedilum randsii: **I** ORCHIDACEAE
Paphiopedilum reflexum = Paphiopedilum callosum
Paphiopedilum regnieri = Paphiopedilum callosum
Paphiopedilum richardianum = Paphiopedilum lowii var.
  richardianum
Paphiopedilum robinsonii = Paphiopedilum bullenianum
Paphiopedilum roebelenii = Paphiopedilum philippinense var.
  roebelenii
Paphiopedilum rothschildianum: **I** ORCHIDACEAE
Paphiopedilum rothschildianum var. *elliottianum = Paphiopedilum
  rothschildianum*
Paphiopedilum sanderianum: **I** ORCHIDACEAE
Paphiopedilum sangii: **I** ORCHIDACEAE
Paphiopedilum schlimii = Phragmipedium schlimii
Paphiopedilum schoseri: **I** ORCHIDACEAE
Paphiopedilum sinicum = Paphiopedilum purpuratum
Paphiopedilum spicerianum: **I** ORCHIDACEAE
Paphiopedilum sriwaniae = Paphiopedilum argus

Paphiopedilum stonei: **I** ORCHIDACEAE
Paphiopedilum sublaeve = *Paphiopedilum callosum* var. *sublaeve*
Paphiopedilum sukhakulii: **I** ORCHIDACEAE
Paphiopedilum supardii: **I** ORCHIDACEAE
Paphiopedilum superbiens: **I** ORCHIDACEAE
Paphiopedilum superbiens ssp. *ciliolare* = *Paphiopedilum ciliolare*
Paphiopedilum superbiens var. *curtisii*: **I** ORCHIDACEAE
Paphiopedilum thailandense = *Paphiopedilum callosum* var. *sublaeve*
Paphiopedilum tigrinum: **I** ORCHIDACEAE
Paphiopedilum tonsum: **I** ORCHIDACEAE
Paphiopedilum tonsum var. *braemii*: **I** ORCHIDACEAE
Paphiopedilum topperi = *Paphiopedilum kolopakingii*
Paphiopedilum tortipetalum = *Paphiopedilum bullenianum*
Paphiopedilum urbanianum: **I** ORCHIDACEAE
Paphiopedilum venustum: **I** ORCHIDACEAE
Paphiopedilum venustum var. *pardinum* = *Paphiopedilum venustum*
Paphiopedilum 'victoria' = *Paphiopedilum supardii*
Paphiopedilum victoria-mariae: **I** ORCHIDACEAE
Paphiopedilum victoria-regina: **I** ORCHIDACEAE
Paphiopedilum victoria-regina ssp. *glaucophyllum* = *Paphiopedilum glaucophyllum* var. *moquetteanum*
Paphiopedilum victoria-reginae ssp. *glaucophyllum* = *Paphiopedilum glaucophyllum*
Paphiopedilum victoria-reginae ssp. *liemianum* = *Paphiopedilum liemianum*
Paphiopedilum victoria-reginae var. *primulinum* = *Paphiopedilum primulinum*
Paphiopedilum villosum: **I** ORCHIDACEAE
Paphiopedilum villosum var. *affine* = *Paphiopedilum gratrixianum*
Paphiopedilum villosum var. *annamense*: **I** ORCHIDACEAE
Paphiopedilum villosum var. *boxallii*: **I** ORCHIDACEAE
Paphiopedilum villosum var. *gratrixianum* = *Paphiopedilum gratrixianum*
Paphiopedilum violascens: **I** ORCHIDACEAE
Paphiopedilum violascens var. *gautierense* = *Paphiopedilum violascens*
Paphiopedilum virens = *Paphiopedilum javanicum* var. *virens*
Paphiopedilum vittatum = *Phragmipedium vittatum*
Paphiopedilum volonteanum = *Paphiopedilum hookerae* var. *volonteanum*
Paphiopedilum wardii: **I** ORCHIDACEAE
Paphiopedilum wentworthianum: **I** ORCHIDACEAE
Paphiopedilum wilhelminae = *Paphiopedilum glanduliferum* var. *wilhelminae*
Paphiopedilum wolterianum = *Paphiopedilum appletonianum*
Paphiopedilum zieckianum = *Paphiopedilum papuanum*
Papilionanthe spp.: #7 **II** ORCHIDACEAE
Papiliopsis = *Oncidium*
Papillilabium spp.: #7 **II** ORCHIDACEAE
Papperitzia spp.: #7 **II** ORCHIDACEAE
Papuaea spp.: #7 **II** ORCHIDACEAE
Paracalanthe = *Calanthe*
Paracaleana = *Caleana*
Paradisanthus spp.: #7 **II** ORCHIDACEAE
Paragnathis = *Diplomeris*
Parapactis = *Epipactis*
Paraphalaenopsis spp.: #7 **II** ORCHIDACEAE
Parapteroceras spp.: #7 **II** ORCHIDACEAE
Parasarcochilus = *Pteroceras*
Parhabenaria spp.: #7 **II** ORCHIDACEAE
Park Pincushion-cactus (E): *Pediocactus paradinei*
Parlatorea = *Sanderella*
Parlatore's podocarp (E): *Podocarpus parlatorei*
Parodia aconquijaensis = *Parodia microsperma*
Parodia alacriportana: #4 **II** CACTACEAE
Parodia alacriportana ssp. *alacriportana*: #4 **II** CACTACEAE
Parodia alacriportana ssp. *brevihamata*: #4 **II** CACTACEAE
Parodia alacriportana ssp. *buenekeri*: #4 **II** CACTACEAE
Parodia alacriportana ssp. *catarinensis*: #4 **II** CACTACEAE
Parodia allosiphon: #4 **II** CACTACEAE
Parodia arnostiana: #4 **II** CACTACEAE
Parodia aureicentra: #4 **II** CACTACEAE
Parodia ayopayana: #4 **II** CACTACEAE

Parodia backebergiana = *Parodia tuberculata*
Parodia bellavistana = *Parodia formosa*
Parodia belliata = *Parodia ritteri*
Parodia bermejoensis = *Parodia maassii*
Parodia bilbaoensis = *Parodia taratensis*
Parodia buiningii: #4 **II** CACTACEAE
Parodia buxbaumiana = *Parodia ayopayana*
Parodia caespitosa = *Parodia concinna*
Parodia camblayana = *Parodia ritteri*
Parodia carambeiensis: #4 **II** CACTACEAE
Parodia carrerana = *Parodia ritteri*
Parodia castanea = *Parodia ritteri*
Parodia chirimoyarana = *Parodia formosa*
Parodia chrysacanthion: #4 **II** CACTACEAE
Parodia claviceps = *Parodia schumanniana* ssp. *claviceps*
Parodia columnaris: #4 **II** CACTACEAE
Parodia comarapana: #4 **II** CACTACEAE
Parodia commutans: #4 **II** CACTACEAE
Parodia compressa = *Parodia ocampoi*
Parodia concinna: #4 **II** CACTACEAE
Parodia concinna ssp. *agnetae*: #4 **II** CACTACEAE
Parodia concinna ssp. *blauuwiana*: #4 **II** CACTACEAE
Parodia concinna ssp. *concinna*: #4 **II** CACTACEAE
Parodia cotacajensis = *Parodia ayopayana*
Parodia crassigibba: #4 **II** CACTACEAE
Parodia curvispina: #4 **II** CACTACEAE
Parodia elachisantha = *Parodia haselbergii* ssp. *graessneri*
Parodia elachista = *Parodia ocampoi*
Parodia elegans = *Parodia microsperma*
Parodia erinacea: #4 **II** CACTACEAE
Parodia erubescens: #4 **II** CACTACEAE
Parodia escayachensis = *Parodia maassii*
Parodia formosa: #4 **II** CACTACEAE
Parodia fusca: #4 **II** CACTACEAE
Parodia gibbulosa = *Parodia ocampoi*
Parodia glischrocarpa = *Parodia microsperma*
Parodia gracilis = *Parodia procera*
Parodia graessneri = *Parodia haselbergii* ssp. *graessneri*
Parodia gutekunstiana = *Parodia stuemeri*
Parodia haselbergii: #4 **II** CACTACEAE
Parodia haselbergii ssp. *graessneri*: #4 **II** CACTACEAE
Parodia haselbergii ssp. *haselbergii*: #4 **II** CACTACEAE
Parodia hausteiniana: #4 **II** CACTACEAE
Parodia herteri: #4 **II** CACTACEAE
Parodia herzogii = *Parodia microsperma* ssp. *microsperma*
Parodia horstii: #4 **II** CACTACEAE
Parodia ignorata = *Parodia tuberculata*
Parodia koehresiana = *Parodia maassii*
Parodia krahnii = *Parodia taratensis*
Parodia langsdorfii: #4 **II** CACTACEAE
Parodia laui = *Parodia hausteiniana*
Parodia leninghausii: #4 **II** CACTACEAE
Parodia liliputana = *Blossfeldia liliputana*
Parodia linkii: #4 **II** CACTACEAE
Parodia lychnosa = *Parodia procera*
Parodia maassii: #4 **II** CACTACEAE
Parodia magnifica: #4 **II** CACTACEAE
Parodia mairanana = *Parodia comarapana*
Parodia mammulosa: #4 **II** CACTACEAE
Parodia mammulosa ssp. *brasiliensis*: #4 **II** CACTACEAE
Parodia mammulosa ssp. *erythracantha*: #4 **II** CACTACEAE
Parodia mammulosa ssp. *eugeniae*: #4 **II** CACTACEAE
Parodia mammulosa ssp. *mammulosa*: #4 **II** CACTACEAE
Parodia mammulosa ssp. *submammulosa*: #4 **II** CACTACEAE
Parodia meonacantha: #4 **II** CACTACEAE
Parodia microsperma: #4 **II** CACTACEAE
Parodia microsperma ssp. *horrida*: #4 **II** CACTACEAE
Parodia microsperma ssp. *microsperma*: #4 **II** CACTACEAE
Parodia miguillensis = *Parodia ayopayana*
Parodia minuta = *Parodia ocampoi*
Parodia miranda = *Parodia subterrranea*
Parodia mueller-melchersii: #4 **II** CACTACEAE
Parodia mueller-melchersii ssp. *gutierrezii*: #4 **II** CACTACEAE
Parodia mueller-melchersii ssp. *mueller-merchersii*: #4 **II** CACTACEAE

Parodia mueller-melchersii ssp. *winkleri*: #4 **II** CACTACEAE
Parodia multicostata = *Parodia tuberculata*
Parodia muricata: #4 **II** CACTACEAE
Parodia nana = *Parodia microsperma*
Parodia neglecta = *Parodia comarapana*
Parodia neoarechavaletae: #4 **II** CACTACEAE
Parodia neohorstii: #4 **II** CACTACEAE
Parodia nigrispina: #4 **II** CACTACEAE
Parodia nivosa: #4 **II** CACTACEAE
Parodia nothominuscula: #4 **II** CACTACEAE
Parodia nothorauschii: #4 **II** CACTACEAE
Parodia ocampoi: #4 **II** CACTACEAE
Parodia occulta = *Parodia subterrranea*
Parodia otaviana = *Parodia maassii*
Parodia ottonis: #4 **II** CACTACEAE
Parodia ottonis ssp. *horstii*: #4 **II** CACTACEAE
Parodia ottonis ssp. *ottonis*: #4 **II** CACTACEAE
Parodia oxycostata: #4 **II** CACTACEAE
Parodia oxycostata ssp. *gracilis*: #4 **II** CACTACEAE
Parodia oxycostata ssp. *oxycostata*: #4 **II** CACTACEAE
Parodia paraguayensis = *Parodia ottonis*
Parodia penicillata: #4 **II** CACTACEAE
Parodia permutata: #4 **II** CACTACEAE
Parodia perplexa = *Parodia procera*
Parodia procera: #4 **II** CACTACEAE
Parodia pseudoayopayana = *Parodia ayopayana*
Parodia pseudosubterranea = *Parodia subterrranea*
Parodia punae = *Parodia ocampoi*
Parodia rechensis: #4 **II** CACTACEAE
Parodia rigidispina = *Parodia microsperma*
Parodia ritteri: #4 **II** CACTACEAE
Parodia rubrispina = *Parodia stuemeri*
Parodia rudibuenekeri: #4 **II** CACTACEAE
Parodia rudibuenekeri ssp. *glomerata*: #4 **II** CACTACEAE
Parodia rudibuenekeri ssp. *rudibuenekeri*: #4 **II** CACTACEAE
Parodia rutilans: #4 **II** CACTACEAE
Parodia rutilans ssp. *rutilans*: #4 **II** CACTACEAE
Parodia rutilans ssp. *veeniana*: #4 **II** CACTACEAE
Parodia saint-pieana: #4 **II** CACTACEAE
Parodia schumanniana: #4 **II** CACTACEAE
Parodia schumanniana ssp. *claviceps*: #4 **II** CACTACEAE
Parodia schumanniana ssp. *schumanniana*: #4 **II** CACTACEAE
Parodia schwebsiana: #4 **II** CACTACEAE
Parodia scopa: #4 **II** CACTACEAE
Parodia scopa ssp. *marchesii*: #4 **II** CACTACEAE
Parodia scopa ssp. *neobuenekeri*: #4 **II** CACTACEAE
Parodia scopa ssp. *scopa*: #4 **II** CACTACEAE
Parodia scopa ssp. *succinea*: #4 **II** CACTACEAE
Parodia sellowii: #4 **II** CACTACEAE
Parodia setifera = *Parodia microsperma*
Parodia sotomayorensis = *Parodia tuberculata*
Parodia splendens = *Parodia ritteri*
Parodia stockingeri: #4 **II** CACTACEAE
Parodia stuemeri: #4 **II** CACTACEAE
Parodia subterrranea: #4 **II** CACTACEAE
Parodia subtilihamata = *Parodia procera*
Parodia succinea = *Parodia scopa* ssp. *succinea*
Parodia sucrensis = *Parodia tuberculata*
Parodia tabularis: #4 **II** CACTACEAE
Parodia tabularis ssp. *bommeljei*: #4 **II** CACTACEAE
Parodia tabularis ssp. *tabularis*: #4 **II** CACTACEAE
Parodia taratensis: #4 **II** CACTACEAE
Parodia tenuicylindrica: #4 **II** CACTACEAE
Parodia tilcarensis: #4 **II** CACTACEAE
Parodia tillii = *Parodia formosa*
Parodia tojoensis = *Parodia ritteri*
Parodia tredecimcostata = *Parodia procera*
Parodia tuberculata: #4 **II** CACTACEAE
Parodia tucumanensis = *Parodia microsperma* ssp. *microsperma*
Parodia turbinata: #4 **II** CACTACEAE
Parodia turecekiana: #4 **II** CACTACEAE
Parodia warasii: #4 **II** CACTACEAE
Parodia werdermanniana: #4 **II** CACTACEAE
Parodia werneri: #4 **II** CACTACEAE
Parodia werneri ssp. *pleicephala*: #4 **II** CACTACEAE

Parodia werneri ssp. *werneri*: #4 **II** CACTACEAE
Parodia yamparaezi = *Parodia tuberculata*
Parodia zaletaewana = *Parodia subterrranea*
Parodia zecheri = *Parodia ocampoi*
Parrot pitcherplant (E): *Sarracenia psittacina*
Partridge-breasted aloe (E): *Aloe variegata*
Patagonian cypress (E): *Fitzroya cupressoides*
Pattonia = *Grammatophyllum*
Paxtonia = *Spathoglottis*
Pecteilis spp.: #7 **II** ORCHIDACEAE
Pectinaria = *Angraecum*
Pedilanthus lycioides = *Euphorbia pedilanthoides*
Pedilea = *Malaxis*
Pedilochilus spp.: #7 **II** ORCHIDACEAE
Pedilonum = *Dendrobium*
Pediocactus bradyi: (E) Brady's Pincushion Cactus **I** CACTACEAE
Pediocactus bradyi ssp. *despainii*: **I** CACTACEAE
Pediocactus bradyi ssp. *winkleri*: **I** CACTACEAE
Pediocactus brevihamatus ssp. *tobuschii* = *Sclerocactus brevihamatus* ssp. *tobuschii*
Pediocactus conoideus = *Neolloydia conoidea*
Pediocactus fickeisenii = *Pediocactus peeblesianus*
Pediocactus hermannii: #4 **II** CACTACEAE
Pediocactus knowltonii: (E) Knowlton's cactus, Knowlton's miniature cactus, Knowlton's pincushion cactus **I** CACTACEAE
Pediocactus mariposensis = *Sclerocactus mariposensis*
Pediocactus nigrispinus: #4 **II** CACTACEAE
Pediocactus nigrispinus ssp. *beastonii*: #4 **II** CACTACEAE
Pediocactus nigrispinus ssp. *puebloensis*: #4 **II** CACTACEAE
Pediocactus papyracanthus = *Sclerocactus papyracanthus*
Pediocactus paradinei: (E) Houserock valley cactus, Kaibab pincushion cactus, Park Pincushion-cactus **I** CACTACEAE
Pediocactus peeblesianus: (E) Peebles' Navajo cactus **I** CACTACEAE
Pediocactus peeblesianus var. *fickeiseniae*: (E) Fickeisen Hedgehog-cactus **I** CACTACEAE
Pediocactus peeblesianus var. *peeblesianus*: (E) Peebles' Hedgehog-cactus **I** CACTACEAE
Pediocactus robustior = *Pediocactus simpsonii* ssp. *robustior*
Pediocactus sileri: (E) Siler's Pincushion Cactus **I** CACTACEAE
Pediocactus simpsonii: #4 **II** CACTACEAE
Pediocactus simpsonii ssp. *bensonii*: #4 **II** CACTACEAE
Pediocactus simpsonii ssp. *idahoensis*: #4 **II** CACTACEAE
Pediocactus simpsonii ssp. *indranus*: #4 **II** CACTACEAE
Pediocactus simpsonii ssp. *robustior*: #4 **II** CACTACEAE
Peebles' hedgehog-cactus (E): *Pediocactus peeblesianus* var. *peeblesianus*
Peebles' Navajo cactus (E): *Pediocactus peeblesianus*
Pelatantheria spp.: #7 **II** ORCHIDACEAE
Pelecyphora spp.: (E) hatchet cacti, pine cane cacti, (S) peyotillo **I** CACTACEAE
Pelecyphora aselliformis: (E) Hatchet cactus, Woodlouse cactus **I** CACTACEAE
Pelecyphora pseudopectinata = *Turbinicarpus pseudopectinatus*
Pelecyphora pulcherrima = *Turbinicarpus pseudopectinatus*
Pelecyphora strobiliformis: (E) Pine cone cactus **I** CACTACEAE
Pelexia spp.: #7 **II** ORCHIDACEAE
Pelma (S): *Cyathea bicrenata*
Pelma = *Bulbophyllum*
Pencil cholla (E): *Opuntia arbuscula*
Peniocereus castellae: #4 **II** CACTACEAE
Peniocereus cuixmalensis: #4 **II** CACTACEAE
Peniocereus fosterianus: #4 **II** CACTACEAE
Peniocereus greggii: #4 **II** CACTACEAE
Peniocereus hirschtianus: #4 **II** CACTACEAE
Peniocereus johnstonii: #4 **II** CACTACEAE
Peniocereus lazaro-cardenasii: #4 **II** CACTACEAE
Peniocereus macdougallii: #4 **II** CACTACEAE
Peniocereus maculatus: #4 **II** CACTACEAE
Peniocereus marianus: #4 **II** CACTACEAE
Peniocereus oaxacensis: #4 **II** CACTACEAE
Peniocereus occidentalis: #4 **II** CACTACEAE
Peniocereus rosei: #4 **II** CACTACEAE

Peniocereus serpentinus: #4 **II** CACTACEAE
Peniocereus striatus: #4 **II** CACTACEAE
Peniocereus tepalcatepecanus: #4 **II** CACTACEAE
Peniocereus viperinus: #4 **II** CACTACEAE
Peniocereus zopilotensis: #4 **II** CACTACEAE
Pennilabium spp.: #7 **II** ORCHIDACEAE
Penthea = *Disa*
Pentulops = *Maxillaria*
Peramium = *Goodyera*
Perceneige (F): *Galanthus* spp.
Pereskia aculeata: #4 **II** CACTACEAE
Pereskia aureiflora: #4 **II** CACTACEAE
Pereskia bahiensis: #4 **II** CACTACEAE
Pereskia bleo: #4 **II** CACTACEAE
Pereskia colombiana = *Pereskia guamacho*
Pereskia cubensis = *Pereskia zinniiflora*
Pereskia diaz-romeroana: #4 **II** CACTACEAE
Pereskia grandifolia: #4 **II** CACTACEAE
Pereskia grandifolia ssp. *grandifolia*: #4 **II** CACTACEAE
Pereskia grandifolia ssp. *violacea*: #4 **II** CACTACEAE
Pereskia guamacho: #4 **II** CACTACEAE
Pereskia horrida: #4 **II** CACTACEAE
Pereskia horrida ssp. *horrida*: #4 **II** CACTACEAE
Pereskia horrida ssp. *rauhii*: #4 **II** CACTACEAE
Pereskia humboldtii = *Pereskia horrida* ssp. *horrida*
Pereskia lychnidiflora: #4 **II** CACTACEAE
Pereskia marcanoi: #4 **II** CACTACEAE
Pereskia nemorosa: #4 **II** CACTACEAE
Pereskia portulacifolia: #4 **II** CACTACEAE
Pereskia quisqueyana: #4 **II** CACTACEAE
Pereskia sacharosa: #4 **II** CACTACEAE
Pereskia stenantha: #4 **II** CACTACEAE
Pereskia weberiana: #4 **II** CACTACEAE
Pereskia zinniiflora: #4 **II** CACTACEAE
Pereskiopsis aquosa: #4 **II** CACTACEAE
Pereskiopsis blakeana: #4 **II** CACTACEAE
Pereskiopsis diguetii: #4 **II** CACTACEAE
Pereskiopsis gatesii = *Pereskiopsis porteri*
Pereskiopsis kellermanii: #4 **II** CACTACEAE
Pereskiopsis opuntiiflora = *Pereskia lychnidiflora*
Pereskiopsis porteri: #4 **II** CACTACEAE
Pereskiopsis rotundifolia: #4 **II** CACTACEAE
Pereskiopsis scandens = *Pereskiopsis kellermanii*
Pereskiopsis spathulata: #4 **II** CACTACEAE
Pergamena = *Dactylostalix*
Pericopsis elata: (E) African teak, (S) Afrormosia, Teca africana
    (F) Assamela, Teck d'Afrique, #5 **II** LEGUMINOSAE
Peristeranthus spp.: #7 **II** ORCHIDACEAE
Peristeria elata: (E) Holy Ghost orchid, (S) Espíritu Santu,
    Palomón **I** ORCHIDACEAE
Peristeria spp.: #7 **I/II** ORCHIDACEAE
Peristylus spp.: #7 **II** ORCHIDACEAE
Perrieriella spp.: #7 **II** ORCHIDACEAE
Perularia = *Platanthera*
Pescatoria spp.: #7 **II** ORCHIDACEAE
Pesomeria = *Phaius*
Petalocentrum = *Sigmatostalix*
Petalochilus = *Caladenia*
Peyote (S): *Lophophora diffusa*
Peyotillo (S): *Pelecyphora* spp.
Pezuña de venado (S): *Ariocarpus kotschoubeyanus*
Pfeiffera brevispina = *Lepismium brevispinum*
Pfeiffera crenata = *Lepismium crenatum*
Pfeiffera erecta = *Lepismium ianthothele*
Pfeiffera gracilis = *Lepismium ianthothele*
Pfeiffera ianthothele = *Lepismium ianthothele*
Pfeiffera incahuasina = *Lepismium monacanthum*
Pfeiffera mataralensis = *Lepismium ianthothele*
Pfeiffera micrantha = *Lepismium micranthum*
Pfeiffera miyagawae = *Lepismium miyagawae*
Pfeiffera monacantha = *Lepismium monacanthum*
Pfeiffera multigona = *Lepismium ianthothele*
Pfeiffera paranganiensis = *Lepismium paranganiense*
Phadrosanthus = *Epidendrum*
Phaius spp.: #7 **II** ORCHIDACEAE

Phalaenopsis spp.: #7 **II** ORCHIDACEAE
Phaniasia = *Habenaria*
Phellosperma tetrancistra = *Mammillaria tetrancistra*
Philippicereus castaneus = *Eulychnia castanea*
Philippinaea = *Orchipedum*
Philippine garland flower (E): *Hedychium philippinense*
Phloeophila = *Pleurothallis*
Pholidota spp.: #7 **II** ORCHIDACEAE
Phormangis = *Ancistrorhynchus*
Phragmipedilum = *Phragmipedium*
Phragmipedium spp.: (E) slipper orchids, South American slipper
    orchids **I** ORCHIDACEAE
Phragmipedium besseae: **I** ORCHIDACEAE
Phragmipedium besseae f. *flavum*: **I** ORCHIDACEAE
Phragmipedium boissierianum: **I** ORCHIDACEAE
Phragmipedium cajamarcae = *Phragmipedium boissierianum*
Phragmipedium caricinum: **I** ORCHIDACEAE
Phragmipedium caudatum: **I** ORCHIDACEAE
Phragmipedium caudatum var. *lindenii* = *Phragmipedium lindenii*
Phragmipedium czerwiakowianum = *Phragmipedium*
    boissierianum
Phragmipedium dariense = *Phragmipedium longifolium*
Phragmipedium ecuadorense = *Phragmipedium pearcei*
Phragmipedium exstaminodium: **I** ORCHIDACEAE
Phragmipedium hartwegii = *Phragmipedium longifolium*
Phragmipedium hincksianum = *Phragmipedium longifolium*
Phragmipedium hirtzii: **I** ORCHIDACEAE
Phragmipedium kaieteurum = *Phragmipedium lindleyanum* var.
    kaieteurum
Phragmipedium klotzschianum: **I** ORCHIDACEAE
Phragmipedium lindenii: **I** ORCHIDACEAE
Phragmipedium lindleyanum: **I** ORCHIDACEAE
Phragmipedium lindleyanum var. *kaieteurum*: **I** ORCHIDACEAE
Phragmipedium longifolium: **I** ORCHIDACEAE
Phragmipedium pearcei: **I** ORCHIDACEAE
Phragmipedium phalaenopsis: **I** ORCHIDACEAE
Phragmipedium portillae: **I** ORCHIDACEAE
Phragmipedium reticulatum = *Phragmipedium boissierianum*
Phragmipedium richteri: **I** ORCHIDACEAE
Phragmipedium roezlii = *Phragmipedium longifolium*
Phragmipedium sargentianum: **I** ORCHIDACEAE
Phragmipedium schlimii: **I** ORCHIDACEAE
Phragmipedium sedenii: **I** ORCHIDACEAE
Phragmipedium vittatum: **I** ORCHIDACEAE
Phragmipedium wallisii: **I** ORCHIDACEAE
Phragmipedium warszewiczianum = *Phragmipedium caudatum*
Phragmipedium xerophyticum: **I** ORCHIDACEAE
Phragmopedilum = *Phragmipedium*
Phragmorchis spp.: #7 **II** ORCHIDACEAE
Phreatia spp.: #7 **II** ORCHIDACEAE
Phyllomphax = *Brachycorythis*
Phyllorkis = *Bulbophyllum*
Phymatidium spp.: #7 **II** ORCHIDACEAE
Physinga = *Epidendrum*
Physoceras spp.: #7 **II** ORCHIDACEAE
Physogyne = *Schiedeella*
Physosiphon = *Pleurothallis*
Physothallis = *Pleurothallis*
Physurus = *Erythrodes*
Picrorhiza kurrooa: #3 **II** SCROPHULARIACEAE
Pie de elefante (S): *Dioscorea deltoidea*
Pierardia = *Dendrobium*
Pierrebraunia bahiensis = *Arrojadoa bahiensis*
Pilgerodendron uviferum: (S) Cedro, Ciprés chileno, Ciprés de las
    Guaitecas, Ciprés de las Guayatecas, Ciprés de las Islas Len,
    Lahuán (F) Ciprès, **I** CUPRESSACEAE
Pilocopiapoa solaris = *Copiapoa solaris*
Pilophyllum = *Chrysoglossum*
Pilosocereus albisummus: #4 **II** CACTACEAE
Pilosocereus alensis: #4 **II** CACTACEAE
Pilosocereus arrabidae: #4 **II** CACTACEAE
Pilosocereus aureispinus: #4 **II** CACTACEAE
Pilosocereus aurilanatus = *Pilosocereus aurisetus* ssp. *aurilanatus*
Pilosocereus aurisetus: #4 **II** CACTACEAE
Pilosocereus aurisetus ssp. *aurilanatus*: #4 **II** CACTACEAE

Pilosocereus aurisetus ssp. *aurisetus*: #4 **II** CACTACEAE
Pilosocereus azulensis: #4 **II** CACTACEAE
Pilosocereus azureus = *Pilosocereus pachycladus* ssp. *pachycladus*
Pilosocereus bahamensis = *Pilosocereus polygonus*
Pilosocereus bradei = *Cipocereus bradei*
Pilosocereus brasiliensis: #4 **II** CACTACEAE
Pilosocereus brasiliensis ssp. *brasiliensis*: #4 **II** CACTACEAE
Pilosocereus brasiliensis ssp. *ruschianus*: #4 **II** CACTACEAE
Pilosocereus braunii = *Pilosocereus gounellei* ssp. *zehntneri*
Pilosocereus catingicola: #4 **II** CACTACEAE
Pilosocereus catingicola ssp. *catingicola*: #4 **II** CACTACEAE
Pilosocereus catingicola ssp. *salvadorensis*: #4 **II** CACTACEAE
Pilosocereus chrysacanthus: #4 **II** CACTACEAE
Pilosocereus chrysostele: #4 **II** CACTACEAE
Pilosocereus coerulescens = *Pilosocereus aurisetus*
Pilosocereus collinsii = *Pilosocereus purpusii*
Pilosocereus cometes = *Pilosocereus leucocephalus*
Pilosocereus cristalinensis = *Pilosocereus machrisii*
Pilosocereus deeringii = *Pilosocereus polygonus*
Pilosocereus densiareolatus: #4 **II** CACTACEAE
Pilosocereus diersianus: #4 **II** CACTACEAE
Pilosocereus flavipulvinatus: #4 **II** CACTACEAE
Pilosocereus flexibilispinus: #4 **II** CACTACEAE
Pilosocereus floccosus: #4 **II** CACTACEAE
Pilosocereus floccosus ssp. *floccosus*: #4 **II** CACTACEAE
Pilosocereus floccosus ssp. *quadricostatus*: #4 **II** CACTACEAE
Pilosocereus fulvilanatus: #4 **II** CACTACEAE
Pilosocereus fulvilanatus ssp. *fulvilanatus*: #4 **II** CACTACEAE
Pilosocereus fulvilanatus ssp. *rosae*: #4 **II** CACTACEAE
Pilosocereus gaumeri = *Pilosocereus royenii*
Pilosocereus glaucochrous: #4 **II** CACTACEAE
Pilosocereus gounellei: #4 **II** CACTACEAE
Pilosocereus gounellei ssp. *gounellei*: #4 **II** CACTACEAE
Pilosocereus gounellei ssp. *zehntneri*: #4 **II** CACTACEAE
Pilosocereus gruberi = *Cereus mortensenii*
Pilosocereus guerreronis = *Pilosocereus alensis*
Pilosocereus juaruensis = *Pilosocereus machrisii*
Pilosocereus lanuginosus: #4 **II** CACTACEAE
Pilosocereus leucocephalus: #4 **II** CACTACEAE
Pilosocereus lindaianus = *Pilosocereus machrisii*
Pilosocereus machrisii: #4 **II** CACTACEAE
Pilosocereus magnificus: #4 **II** CACTACEAE
Pilosocereus minensis = *Cipocereus minensis* ssp. *minensis*
Pilosocereus monoclonos = *Pilosocereus royenii*
Pilosocereus moritzianus = *Pilosocereus lanuginosus*
Pilosocereus mortensenii = *Cereus mortensenii*
Pilosocereus multicostatus: #4 **II** CACTACEAE
Pilosocereus oligolepis: #4 **II** CACTACEAE
Pilosocereus pachycladus: #4 **II** CACTACEAE
Pilosocereus pachycladus ssp. *pachycladus*: #4 **II** CACTACEAE
Pilosocereus pachycladus ssp. *pernambucoensis*: #4 **II** CACTACEAE
Pilosocereus parvus = *Pilosocereus machrisii*
Pilosocereus pentaedrophorus: #4 **II** CACTACEAE
Pilosocereus pentaedrophorus ssp. *pentaedrophorus*: #4 **II** CACTACEAE
Pilosocereus pentaedrophorus ssp. *robustus*: #4 **II** CACTACEAE
Pilosocereus pernambucoensis = *Pilosocereus pachycladus* ssp. *pernambucoensis*
Pilosocereus piauhyensis: #4 **II** CACTACEAE
Pilosocereus pleurocarpus = *Cipocereus minensis* ssp. *pleurocarpus*
Pilosocereus polygonus: #4 **II** CACTACEAE
Pilosocereus purpusii: #4 **II** CACTACEAE
Pilosocereus pusillibaccatus = *Pilosocereus machrisii*
Pilosocereus pusilliflorus = *Cipocereus pusilliflorus*
Pilosocereus quadricentralis: #4 **II** CACTACEAE
Pilosocereus quadricostatus = *Pilosocereus floccosus* ssp. *quadricostatus*
Pilosocereus robinii = *Pilosocereus polygonus*
Pilosocereus rosae = *Pilosocereus fulvilanatus* ssp. *rosae*
Pilosocereus royenii: (E) Vine pear #4 **II** CACTACEAE
Pilosocereus rupicola = *Pilosocereus catingicola* ssp. *salvadorensis*

Pilosocereus ruschianus = *Pilosocereus brasiliensis* ssp. *ruschianus*
Pilosocereus salvadorensis = *Pilosocereus catingicola* ssp. *salvadorensis*
Pilosocereus sartorianus = *Pilosocereus leucocephalus*
Pilosocereus saudadensis = *Pilosocereus machrisii*
Pilosocereus sublanatus = *Pilosocereus brasiliensis*
Pilosocereus tehuacanus = *Pilosocereus leucocephalus*
Pilosocereus tuberculatus: #4 **II** CACTACEAE
Pilosocereus tuberculosus = *Pilosocereus lanuginosus*
Pilosocereus tweedyanus = *Pilosocereus lanuginosus*
Pilosocereus ulei: #4 **II** CACTACEAE
Pilosocereu urbanianus = *Pilosocereus royenii*
Pilosocereus vilaboensis: #4 **II** CACTACEAE
Pilosocereus zehntneri = *Pilosocereus gounellei* ssp. *zehntneri*
Pilumna = *Trichopilia*
Pima pineapple cactus (E): *Coryphantha scheeri* var. *robustispina*
Pin du Chili (F): *Araucaria araucana*
Pinabete (S): *Abies guatemalensis*
Pin-cushion (E): *Opuntia curassavica*
Pine-cone cactus (E): *Pelecyphora strobiliformis*
Pinelia spp.: #7 **II** ORCHIDACEAE
Pinelianthe = *Pinelia*
Ping-pong ball button-cactus (E): *Epithelantha micromeris* ssp. *micromeris*
Pino araucana (S): *Araucaria araucana*
Pino araucaria (S): *Araucaria araucana*
Pino chileno (S): *Araucaria araucana*
Pino de cerro (S): *Podocarpus parlatorei*
Pino de Chile (S): *Araucaria araucana*
Pino de Neuquén (S): *Araucaria araucana*
Pino hachado (S): *Araucaria araucana*
Pino piñonero (S): *Araucaria araucana*
Pino solo (S): *Araucaria araucana*
Pinus araucana = *Araucaria araucana*
Pinus cupressoides = *Fitzroya cupressoides*
Piperia spp.: #7 **II** ORCHIDACEAE
Piptanthocereus aethiops = *Cereus aethiops*
Piptanthocereus bageanus = *Cereus hildmannianus* ssp. *uruguayanus*
Piptanthocereus cabralensis = *Cereus jamacaru* ssp. *calcirupicola*
Piptanthocereus calcirupicola = *Cereus jamacaru* ssp. *calcirupicola*
Piptanthocereus cipoensis = *Cereus jamacaru* ssp. *calcirupicola*
Piptanthocereus colosseus = *Cereus lamprospermus*
Piptanthocereus comarapanus = *Cereus comarapanus*
Piptanthocereus crassisepalus = *Cipocereus crassisepalus*
Piptanthocereus dayamii = *Cereus stenogonus*
Piptanthocereus goiasensis = *Cereus jamacaru* ssp. *goiasensis*
Piptanthocereus huilunchu = *Cereus huilunchu*
Piptanthocereus lanosus = *Cereus lanosus*
Piptanthocereus lindenzweigianus = *Cereus spegazzinii*
Piptanthocereus neonesioticus = *Cereus hildmannianus*
Piptanthocereus pachyrhizus = *Cereus pachyrrhizus*
Piptanthocereus sericifer = *Cereus fernambucensis* ssp. *sericifer*
Piptanthocereus stenogonus = *Cereus stenogonus*
Piptanthocereus uruguayanus = *Cereus hildmannianus* ssp. *uruguayanus*
Piptanthocereus xanthocarpus = *Cereus hildmannianus*
Pitahaya (S): *Leptocereus wrightii*
Pittierella = *Cryptocentrum*
Pityphyllum spp.: #7 **II** ORCHIDACEAE
Placostigma = *Podochilus*
Platanthera spp.: #7 **II** ORCHIDACEAE
Platyclinis = *Dendrochilum*
Platycoryne spp.: #7 **II** ORCHIDACEAE
Platyglottis spp.: #7 **II** ORCHIDACEAE
Platylepis spp.: #7 **II** ORCHIDACEAE
Platymiscium pleiostachyum: (S) Cachimbo, Cristóbal, Macacuaba, Nambar, Ñambar, Roble colorado #1 **II** LEGUMINOSAE
Platyopuntia albisaetacens = *Opuntia albisaetacens*
Platyopuntia apurimacensis = *Opuntia apurimacensis*
Platyopuntia atroglobosa = *Opuntia nigrispina*

Platyopuntia brachyacantha = *Opuntia sulphurea* ssp. *brachyacantha*
Platyopuntia brunneogemmia = *Opuntia monacantha*
Platyopuntia cardiosperma = *Opuntia cardiosperma*
Platyopuntia chilensis = *Opuntia alcerrecensis*
Platyopuntia cognata = *Opuntia cognata*
Platyopuntia conjungens = *Opuntia conjungens*
Platyopuntia cordobensis = *Opuntia ficus-indica*
Platyopuntia corrugata = *Opuntia corrugata*
Platyopuntia discolor = *Opuntia discolor*
Platyopuntia dumetorum = *Opuntia dumetorum*
Platyopuntia ianthinantha = *Opuntia ianthinantha*
Platyopuntia inaequilateralis = *Opuntia inaequilateralis*
Platyopuntia inamoena = *Opuntia inamoena*
Platyopuntia infesta = *Opuntia infesta*
Platyopuntia interjecta = *Opuntia vitelliniflora* ssp. *interjecta*
Platyopuntia invicta = *Opuntia invicta*
Platyopuntia kiska-loro = *Opuntia anacantha*
Platyopuntia limitata = *Opuntia limitata*
Platyopuntia microdisca = *Opuntia microdisca*
Platyopuntia nana = *Opuntia pubescens*
Platyopuntia nigrispina = *Opuntia nigrispina*
Platyopuntia orurensis = *Opuntia orurensis*
Platyopuntia pituitosa = *Opuntia pituitosa*
Platyopuntia pyrrhantha = *Opuntia pyrrhantha*
Platyopuntia quimilo = *Opuntia quimilo*
Platyopuntia quitensis = *Opuntia quitensis*
Platyopuntia retrorsa = *Opuntia anacantha*
Platyopuntia salmiana = *Opuntia salmiana*
Platyopuntia saxatilis = *Opuntia saxatilis*
Platyopuntia soehrensii = *Opuntia soehrensii*
Platyopuntia spinibarbis = *Opuntia sulphurea* ssp. *spinibarbis*
Platyopuntia sulphurea = *Opuntia sulphurea*
Platyopuntia viridirubra = *Opuntia viridirubra*
Platyopuntia vitelliniflora = *Opuntia vitelliniflora*
Platyopuntia vulgaris = *Opuntia monacantha*
Platypus = *Eulophia*
Platyrhiza spp.: #7 **II** ORCHIDACEAE
Platysma = *Podochilus*
Platystele spp.: #7 **II** ORCHIDACEAE
Platystylis = *Liparis*
Platythelys spp.: #7 **II** ORCHIDACEAE
Platyzamia rigida = *Dioon edule*
Plectorrhiza spp.: #7 **II** ORCHIDACEAE
Plectrelminthus spp.: #7 **II** ORCHIDACEAE
Plectrophora spp.: #7 **II** ORCHIDACEAE
Plecturus = *Tipularia*
Pleione spp.: #7 **II** ORCHIDACEAE
Pleuranthium = *Epidendrum*
Pleurobotryum = *Pleurothallis*
Pleurothallis spp.: #7 **II** ORCHIDACEAE
Pleurothallopsis = *Octomeria*
Plexaure = *Phreatia*
Plicate-leaved snowdrop (E): *Galanthus plicatus* ssp. *plicatus*
Plocoglottis spp.: #7 **II** ORCHIDACEAE
Plomillo (S): *Caryocar costaricense*
Poaephyllum spp.: #7 **II** ORCHIDACEAE
Pockwood (E): *Guaiacum* spp.
Podangis spp.: #7 **II** ORCHIDACEAE
Podanthera = *Epipogium*
Podocarpo (S): *Podocarpus parlatorei*
Podocarpus angustifolius = *Podocarpus parlatorei*
Podocarpus decipiens = *Podocarpus neriifolius*
Podocarpus discolor = *Podocarpus neriifolius*
Podocarpus endlicherianus = *Podocarpus neriifolius*
Podocarpus junghuhnianus = *Podocarpus neriifolius*
Podocarpus leptostachys = *Podocarpus neriifolius*
Podocarpus macrophyllus var. *acuminatissima* = *Podocarpus neriifolius*
Podocarpus neglectus = *Podocarpus neriifolius*
Podocarpus neriifolius: #1 **III** PODOCARPACEAE
Podocarpus neriifolius var. *decipiens* = *Podocarpus neriifolius*
Podocarpus neriifolius var. *linearis* = *Podocarpus neriifolius*
Podocarpus neriifolius var. *membranaceus* = *Podocarpus neriifolius*

Podocarpus neriifolius var. *penibukanensis* = *Podocarpus neriifolius*
Podocarpus neriifolius var. *polyanthus* = *Podocarpus neriifolius*
Podocarpus neriifolius var. *staintonii* = *Podocarpus neriifolius*
Podocarpus parlatorei: (E) Parlatore's podocarp, (S) Pino de cerro, Podocarpo **I** PODOCARPACEAE
Podochilopsis = *Adenoncos*
Podochilus spp.: #7 **II** ORCHIDACEAE
Podofilo del Himalaya (S): *Podophyllum hexandrum*
Podophyllum emodi = *Podophyllum hexandrum*
Podophyllum hexandrum: (E) Himilayan may-apple, (S) Podofilo del Himalaya #2 **II** BERBERIDACEAE
Pogochilus = *Galeola*
Pogonia spp.: #7 **II** ORCHIDACEAE
Pogoniopsis spp.: #7 **II** ORCHIDACEAE
Poinsettia pedunculata = *Euphorbia strigosa*
Poinsettia radians = *Euphorbia radians*
Poinsettia strigosa = *Euphorbia strigosa*
Polaskia chende: #4 **II** CACTACEAE
Polaskia chichipe: #4 **II** CACTACEAE
Pollinirhiza = *Listera*
Polybactrum = *Pseudorchis*
Polychilos = *Phalaenopsis*
Polycycnis spp.: #7 **II** ORCHIDACEAE
Polyotidium spp.: #7 **II** ORCHIDACEAE
Polyradicion spp.: #7 **II** ORCHIDACEAE
Polyrrhiza = *Polyradicion*
Polystachya spp.: #7 **II** ORCHIDACEAE
Polystylus = *Phalaenopsis*
Polytoma = *Bletilla*
Pomatocalpa spp.: #7 **II** ORCHIDACEAE
Ponera spp.: #7 **II** ORCHIDACEAE
Ponerorchis = *Gymnadenia*
Ponthieva spp.: #7 **II** ORCHIDACEAE
Pope's head (E): *Mammillaria nivosa*/ *Melocactus intortus*
Porliera angustifolia = *Guaiacum sanctum*
Porolabium spp.: #7 **II** ORCHIDACEAE
Porpax spp.: #7 **II** ORCHIDACEAE
Porphyrodesme spp.: #7 **II** ORCHIDACEAE
Porphyroglottis spp.: #7 **II** ORCHIDACEAE
Porphyrostachys spp.: #7 **II** ORCHIDACEAE
Porroglossum spp.: #7 **II** ORCHIDACEAE
Porrorhachis spp.: #7 **II** ORCHIDACEAE
Potts' Nipple-cactus (E): *Mammillaria pottsii*
Praecereus euchlorus: #4 **II** CACTACEAE
Praecereus euchlorus ssp. *amazonicus*: #4 **II** CACTACEAE
Praecereus euchlorus ssp. *diffusus*: #4 **II** CACTACEAE
Praecereus euchlorus ssp. *euchlorus*: #4 **II** CACTACEAE
Praecereus euchlorus ssp. *jaenensis*: #4 **II** CACTACEAE
Praecereus euchlorus ssp. *smithianus*: #4 **II** CACTACEAE
Praecereus saxicola: #4 **II** CACTACEAE
Prasophyllum spp.: #7 **II** ORCHIDACEAE
Preptanthe = *Calanthe*
Prescottia spp.: #7 **II** ORCHIDACEAE
Prickly pear tree (E): *Opuntia spinosissima*
Prickly tree fern (E): *Cyathea leichardtiana*
Prickly-apple Cereus (E): *Cereus gracilis*
Pristiglottis spp.: #7 **II** ORCHIDACEAE
Promenaea spp.: #7 **II** ORCHIDACEAE
Prosthechea = *Epidendrum*
Protea odorata: (E) Ground-rose #1 **II** PROTEACEAE
Protoceras spp.: #7 **II** ORCHIDACEAE
Prunus africana: (E) African cherry, Kanda stick, Red stinkwood #1 **II** ROSACEAE
Pseudacoridium spp.: #7 **II** ORCHIDACEAE
Pseudelleanthus = *Elleanthus*
Pseudepidendrum = *Epidendrum*
Pseuderia spp.: #7 **II** ORCHIDACEAE
Pseuderiopsis = *Eriopsis*
Pseudoacanthocereus brasiliensis: #4 **II** CACTACEAE
Pseudoacanthocereus sicariguensis: #4 **II** CACTACEAE
Pseudocentrum spp.: #7 **II** ORCHIDACEAE
Pseudocranichis spp.: #7 **II** ORCHIDACEAE
Pseudoctomeria = *Pleurothallis*
Pseudodiphryllum = *Platanthera*

Pseudoeria = *Pseuderia*
Pseudoespostoa melanostele = *Espostoa melanostele*
Pseudoespostoa nana = *Espostoa nana*
Pseudoeurystyles = *Eurystyles*
Pseudogoodyera spp.: #7 **II** ORCHIDACEAE
Pseudohexadesmia = *Hexadesmia*
Pseudolaelia spp.: #7 **II** ORCHIDACEAE
Pseudoliparis = *Malaxis*
Pseudolobivia acanthoplegma = *Echinopsis cinnabarina*
Pseudolobivia ancistrophora = *Echinopsis ancistrophora*
Pseudolobivia aurea = *Echinopsis aurea*
Pseudolobivia boyuibensis = *Echinopsis boyuibensis*
Pseudolobivia callichroma = *Echinopsis callichroma*
Pseudolobivia calorubra = *Echinopsis obrepanda* ssp. *calorubra*
Pseudolobivia carmineoflora = *Echinopsis obrepanda*
Pseudolobivia ferox = *Echinopsis ferox*
Pseudolobivia hamatacantha = *Echinopsis ancistrophora*
Pseudolobivia kermesina = *Echinopsis mamillosa*
Pseudolobivia kratochviliana = *Echinopsis ancistrophora* ssp. *arachnacantha*
Pseudolobivia lecoriensis = *Echinopsis ferox*
Pseudolobivia leucorhodantha = *Echinopsis ancistrophora*
Pseudolobivia longispina = *Echinopsis ferox*
Pseudolobivia luteiflora = *Echinopsis aurea*
Pseudolobivia obrepanda = *Echinopsis obrepanda*
Pseudolobivia orozasana = *Echinopsis obrepanda*
Pseudolobivia pelecyrhachis = *Echinopsis ancistrophora*
Pseudolobivia polyancistra = *Echinopsis ancistrophora*
Pseudolobivia potosina = *Echinopsis ferox*
Pseudolobivia rojasii = *Echinopsis obrepanda*
Pseudolobivia toralapana = *Echinopsis obrepanda*
Pseudolobivia torrecillasensis = *Echinopsis ancistrophora* ssp. *arachnacantha*
Pseudolobivia wilkeae = *Echinopsis ferox*
Pseudomacodes = *Macodes*
Pseudomammillaria kraehenbuehlii = *Mammillaria kraehenbuehlii*
Pseudomaxillaria spp.: #7 **II** ORCHIDACEAE
Pseudonopalxochia conzattiana = *Disocactus ackermannii*
Pseudopilocereus bradei = *Cipocereus bradei*
Pseudoponera = *Ponera*
Pseudorchis spp.: #7 **II** ORCHIDACEAE
Pseudorhipsalis acuminata: #4 **II** CACTACEAE
Pseudorhipsalis alata: #4 **II** CACTACEAE
Pseudorhipsalis himantoclada: #4 **II** CACTACEAE
Pseudorhipsalis horichii: #4 **II** CACTACEAE
Pseudorhipsalis lankesteri: #4 **II** CACTACEAE
Pseudorhipsalis macrantha = *Disocactus macranthus*
Pseudorhipsalis ramulosa: #4 **II** CACTACEAE
Pseudorleanesia = *Orleanesia*
Pseudostelis = *Pleurothallis*
Pseudovanilla spp.: #7 **II** ORCHIDACEAE
Pseudozygocactus epiphylloides = *Hatiora epiphylloides*
Psilochilus spp.: #7 **II** ORCHIDACEAE
Psittacoglossum = *Maxillaria*
Psychechilos = *Zeuxine*
Psychilis spp.: #7 **II** ORCHIDACEAE
Psychopsiella spp.: #7 **II** ORCHIDACEAE
Psychopsis spp.: #7 **II** ORCHIDACEAE
Psygmorchis spp.: #7 **II** ORCHIDACEAE
Pterichis spp.: #7 **II** ORCHIDACEAE
Pterocactus araucanus: #4 **II** CACTACEAE
Pterocactus australis: #4 **II** CACTACEAE
Pterocactus fischeri: #4 **II** CACTACEAE
Pterocactus gonjianii: #4 **II** CACTACEAE
Pterocactus hickenii: #4 **II** CACTACEAE
Pterocactus kuntzei = *Pterocactus tuberosus*
Pterocactus megliolii: #4 **II** CACTACEAE
Pterocactus reticulatus: #4 **II** CACTACEAE
Pterocactus skottsbergii = *Pterocactus hickenii*
Pterocactus tuberosus: #4 **II** CACTACEAE
Pterocactus valentinii: #4 **II** CACTACEAE
Pterocarpus santalinus: (E) Red sandalwood, Saunderswood, (S) Sándalo rojo (F) Santal rouge, #6 **II** LEGUMINOSAE
Pteroceras spp.: #7 **II** ORCHIDACEAE
Pterocereus foetidus = *Pachycereus gaumeri*

Pterocereus gaumeri = *Pachycereus gaumeri*
Pterochilus = *Malaxis*
Pteroglossa spp.: #7 **II** ORCHIDACEAE
Pteroglossaspis spp.: #7 **II** ORCHIDACEAE
Pterostemma spp.: #7 **II** ORCHIDACEAE
Pterostylis spp.: #7 **II** ORCHIDACEAE
Pterygodium spp.: #7 **II** ORCHIDACEAE
Ptilocnema = *Pholidota*
Ptychogyne = *Coelogyne*
Puerto Rico Apple-cactus (E): *Cereus grantianus*/ *Leptocereus grantianus*
Puna bonnieae = *Opuntia subterranea*
Puna clavarioides = *Opuntia clavarioides*
Puna subterraneus = *Opuntia subterranea*
Puntia exaltata = *Opuntia subulata*
Purselanes (E): *Anacampseros* spp.
Pygeum africanum = *Prunus africana*
Pygmaeocereus bieblii: #4 **II** CACTACEAE
Pygmaeocereus bylesianus: #4 **II** CACTACEAE
Pygmaeocereus familiaris: #4 **II** CACTACEAE
Pygmaeorchis spp.: #7 **II** ORCHIDACEAE
Pyrrhocactus andicola = *Eriosyce curvispina*
Pyrrhocactus aricensis = *Eriosyce recondita* ssp. *iquiquensis*
Pyrrhocactus armatus = *Eriosyce curvispina*
Pyrrhocactus aspillagae = *Eriosyce aspillagae*
Pyrrhocactus atrospinosus = *Eriosyce strausiana*
Pyrrhocactus atroviridis = *Eriosyce crispa* ssp. *atroviridis*
Pyrrhocactus bulbocalyx = *Eriosyce bulbocalyx*
Pyrrhocactus calderanus = *Eriosyce taltalensis* ssp. *taltalensis*
Pyrrhocactus carrizalensis = *Eriosyce crispa* ssp. *atroviridis*
Pyrrhocactus chaniarensis = *Eriosyce heinrichiana*
Pyrrhocactus chilensis = *Eriosyce chilensis*
Pyrrhocactus choapensis = *Eriosyce curvispina*
Pyrrhocactus chorosensis = *Eriosyce heinrichiana*
Pyrrhocactus coliguayensis = *Eriosyce curvispina*
Pyrrhocactus confinis = *Eriosyce confinis*
Pyrrhocactus crispus = *Eriosyce crispa* ssp. *crispa*
Pyrrhocactus curvispinus = *Eriosyce curvispina*
Pyrrhocactus deherdtianus = *Eriosyce heinrichiana*
Pyrrhocactus dimorphus = *Eriosyce heinrichiana* ssp. *intermedia*
Pyrrhocactus dubius = *Eriosyce bulbocalyx*
Pyrrhocactus echinus = *Eriosyce taltalensis* ssp. *echinus*
Pyrrhocactus engleri = *Eriosyce engleri*
Pyrrhocactus eriosyzoides = *Eriosyce kunzei*
Pyrrhocactus floccosus = *Eriosyce taltalensis* ssp. *echinus*
Pyrrhocactus floribundus = *Eriosyce recondita* ssp. *iquiquensis*
Pyrrhocactus garaventae = *Eriosyce garaventae*
Pyrrhocactus glaucescens = *Eriosyce taltalensis* ssp. *echinus*
Pyrrhocactus gracilis = *Eriosyce taltalensis* ssp. *taltalensis*
Pyrrhocactus grandiflorus = *Eriosyce curvispina*
Pyrrhocactus horridus = *Eriosyce curvispina*
Pyrrhocactus huascensis = *Eriosyce crispa* ssp. *crispa*
Pyrrhocactus intermedius = *Eriosyce taltalensis* ssp. *taltalensis*
Pyrrhocactus iquiquensis = *Eriosyce recondita* ssp. *iquiquensis*
Pyrrhocactus jussieui = *Eriosyce heinrichiana*
Pyrrhocactus krausii = *Eriosyce chilensis*
Pyrrhocactus limariensis = *Eriosyce limariensis*
Pyrrhocactus lissocarpus = *Eriosyce marksiana*
Pyrrhocactus marayesensis = *Eriosyce bulbocalyx*
Pyrrhocactus marksianus = *Eriosyce marksiana*
Pyrrhocactus megliolii = *Eriosyce bulbocalyx*
Pyrrhocactus melanacanthus = *Eriosyce villicumensis*
Pyrrhocactus neohankeanus = *Eriosyce taltalensis* ssp. *paucicostata*
Pyrrhocactus occultus = *Eriosyce occulta*
Pyrrhocactus odoriflorus = *Eriosyce curvispina*
Pyrrhocactus pachacoensis = *Eriosyce strausiana*
Pyrrhocactus pamaensis = *Eriosyce curvispina*
Pyrrhocactus paucicostatus = *Eriosyce taltalensis* ssp. *paucicostata*
Pyrrhocactus pilispinus = *Eriosyce taltalensis* ssp. *pilispina*
Pyrrhocactus platyacanthus = *Eriosyce strausiana*
Pyrrhocactus pulchellus = *Eriosyce taltalensis* ssp. *taltalensis*
Pyrrhocactus pygmaeus = *Eriosyce taltalensis* ssp. *taltalensis*
Pyrrhocactus reconditus = *Eriosyce recondita*

Pyrrhocactus residuus = *Eriosyce recondita* ssp. *iquiquensis*
Pyrrhocactus rupicola = *Eriosyce taltalensis* ssp. *taltalensis*
Pyrrhocactus sanjuanensis = *Eriosyce strausiana*
Pyrrhocactus saxifragus = *Eriosyce recondita* ssp. *iquiquensis*
Pyrrhocactus scoparius = *Eriosyce taltalensis* ssp. *taltalensis*
Pyrrhocactus setiflorus = *Eriosyce strausiana*
Pyrrhocactus setosiflorus = *Eriosyce heinrichiana* ssp. *intermedia*
Pyrrhocactus simulans = *Eriosyce heinrichiana* ssp. *simulans*
Pyrrhocactus strausianus = *Eriosyce strausiana*
Pyrrhocactus subaianus = *Eriosyce garaventae*
Pyrrhocactus taltalensis = *Eriosyce taltalensis*
Pyrrhocactus tenuis = *Eriosyce taltalensis* ssp. *taltalensis*
Pyrrhocactus totoralensis = *Eriosyce crispa* ssp. *atroviridis*
Pyrrhocactus transiens = *Eriosyce taltalensis* ssp. *taltalensis*
Pyrrhocactus transitensis = *Eriosyce kunzei*
Pyrrhocactus trapichensis = *Eriosyce heinrichiana*
Pyrrhocactus truncatipetalus = *Eriosyce curvispina*
Pyrrhocactus umadeave = *Eriosyce umadeave*
Pyrrhocactus vallenarensis = *Eriosyce kunzei*
Pyrrhocactus vertongenii = *Eriosyce vertongenii*
Pyrrhocactus vexatus = *Eriosyce recondita* ssp. *recondita*
Pyrrhocactus villicumensis = *Eriosyce villicumensis*
Pyrrhocactus vollianus = *Eriosyce strausiana*
Pyrrhocactus wagenknechtii = *Eriosyce heinrichiana* ssp.
    intermedia
Queen agave (E): *Agave victoriae-reginae*
Queen of the night (E): *Selenicereus grandiflorus*
Queen Victoria agave (E): *Agave victoriae-reginae*
Quekettia spp.: #7 **II** ORCHIDACEAE
Queteletia = *Orchipedum*
Quiabentia verticillata: #4 **II** CACTACEAE
Quiabentia zehntneri: #4 **II** CACTACEAE
Quisqueya spp.: #7 **II** ORCHIDACEAE
Radinocion = *Aerangis*
Raffles' pitcher-plant (E): *Nepenthes rafflesiana*
Rainbow trumpet (E): *Sarracenia minor*
Ramin (E): *Gonystylus* spp.
Ramonia = *Scaphyglottis*
Ramphidia = *Myrmechis*
Rangaeris spp.: #7 **II** ORCHIDACEAE
Rat aloe (E): *Aloe ballyi*
Rathbunia sonorensis = *Stenocereus alamosensis*
Rauhiella spp.: #7 **II** ORCHIDACEAE
Rauhocereus riosaniensis: #4 **II** CACTACEAE
Rauhocereus riosaniensis ssp. *jaenensis*: #4 **II** CACTACEAE
Rauhocereus riosaniensis ssp. *riosaniensis*: #4 **II** CACTACEAE
Rauvolfia serpentina: (E) Snake-root devil-pepper #2 **II**
    APOCYNACEAE
Ravenea louvelii: **II** PALMAE
Ravenea rivularis: **II** PALMAE
Raycadenco spp.: #7 **II** ORCHIDACEAE
Rebutia albiflora: #4 **II** CACTACEAE
Rebutia albopectinata: #4 **II** CACTACEAE
Rebutia arenacea: #4 **II** CACTACEAE
Rebutia aureiflora: #4 **II** CACTACEAE
Rebutia brunescens: #4 **II** CACTACEAE
Rebutia caineana: #4 **II** CACTACEAE
Rebutia canigueralii: #4 **II** CACTACEAE
Rebutia canigueralii ssp. *crispata*: #4 **II** CACTACEAE
Rebutia canigueralii ssp. *pulchra*: #4 **II** CACTACEAE
Rebutia cardenasiana: #4 **II** CACTACEAE
Rebutia cylindrica: #4 **II** CACTACEAE
Rebutia deminuta: #4 **II** CACTACEAE
Rebutia einsteinii: #4 **II** CACTACEAE
Rebutia fabrisii: #4 **II** CACTACEAE
Rebutia famatinensis = *Echinopsis famatinensis*
Rebutia fidaiana: #4 **II** CACTACEAE
Rebutia fidaiana ssp. *cintiensis*: #4 **II** CACTACEAE
Rebutia fidaiana ssp. *fidaiana*: #4 **II** CACTACEAE
Rebutia fiebrigii: #4 **II** CACTACEAE
Rebutia flavistyla: #4 **II** CACTACEAE
Rebutia fulviseta: #4 **II** CACTACEAE
Rebutia gonjianii: #4 **II** CACTACEAE
Rebutia heliosa: #4 **II** CACTACEAE
Rebutia huasiensis: #4 **II** CACTACEAE

Rebutia jujuyana = *Rebutia fiebrigii*
Rebutia kieslingii = *Rebutia fiebrigii*
Rebutia leucanthema: #4 **II** CACTACEAE
Rebutia margarethae = *Rebutia padcayensis*
Rebutia marsoneri: #4 **II** CACTACEAE
Rebutia mentosa: #4 **II** CACTACEAE
Rebutia mentosa ssp. *mentosa*: #4 **II** CACTACEAE
Rebutia mentosa ssp. *purpurea*: #4 **II** CACTACEAE
Rebutia minuscula: #4 **II** CACTACEAE
Rebutia muscula = *Rebutia fiebrigii*
Rebutia narvaecensis: #4 **II** CACTACEAE
Rebutia neocumingii: #4 **II** CACTACEAE
Rebutia neocumingii ssp. *neocumingii*: #4 **II** CACTACEAE
Rebutia neocumingii ssp. *pilcomayensis*: #4 **II** CACTACEAE
Rebutia neocumingii ssp. *riograndensis*: #4 **II** CACTACEAE
Rebutia neocumingii ssp. *saipinensis*: #4 **II** CACTACEAE
Rebutia neocumingii ssp. *trollii*: #4 **II** CACTACEAE
Rebutia neumanniana: #4 **II** CACTACEAE
Rebutia nigricans: #4 **II** CACTACEAE
Rebutia oligacantha: #4 **II** CACTACEAE
Rebutia padcayensis: #4 **II** CACTACEAE
Rebutia perplexa: #4 **II** CACTACEAE
Rebutia pseudodeminuta: #4 **II** CACTACEAE
Rebutia pulvinosa: #4 **II** CACTACEAE
Rebutia pygmaea: #4 **II** CACTACEAE
Rebutia ritteri: #4 **II** CACTACEAE
Rebutia simoniana: #4 **II** CACTACEAE
Rebutia spegazziniana: #4 **II** CACTACEAE
Rebutia spinosissima: #4 **II** CACTACEAE
Rebutia steinbachii: #4 **II** CACTACEAE
Rebutia steinbachii ssp. *kruegeri*: #4 **II** CACTACEAE
Rebutia steinbachii ssp. *steinbachii*: #4 **II** CACTACEAE
Rebutia steinbachii ssp. *tiraquensis*: #4 **II** CACTACEAE
Rebutia steinbachii ssp. *verticillacantha*: #4 **II** CACTACEAE
Rebutia steinmannii: #4 **II** CACTACEAE
Rebutia walteri = *Rebutia spinosissima*
Rebutia wessneriana: #4 **II** CACTACEAE
Rebutia xanthocarpa: #4 **II** CACTACEAE
Recurved corycactus (E): *Coryphantha recurvata*
Red cedar (E): *Cedrela odorata*
Red ginseng (E): *Panax ginseng*
Red sandalwood (E): *Pterocarpus santalinus*
Red stinkwood (E): *Prunus africana*
Red vanda orchid (E): *Renanthera imschootiana*
Red-flowered sweet pitcherplant (E): *Sarracenia rubra* ssp. *rubra*
Red-lemur palm (E): *Lemurophoenix halleuxii*
Red-topped barrel cactus (E): *Melocactus intortus*
Regnellia = *Bletia*
Reichenbachanthus spp.: #7 **II** ORCHIDACEAE
Reicheocactus floribundus = *Eriosyce recondita* ssp. *iquiquensis*
Reicheocactus neoreichei = *Eriosyce napina* ssp. *lembckei*
Reicheocactus pseudoreicheanus = *Echinopsis famatinensis*
Reina de la noche (S): *Selenicereus grandiflorus*
Renanthera imschootiana: (E) Red vanda orchid, (S) Vanda roja **I**
    ORCHIDACEAE
Renanthera spp.: #7 **I/II** ORCHIDACEAE
Renantherella spp.: #7 **II** ORCHIDACEAE
Renata = *Pseudolaelia*
Restrepia spp.: #7 **II** ORCHIDACEAE
Restrepiella spp.: #7 **II** ORCHIDACEAE
Restrepiopsis spp.: #7 **II** ORCHIDACEAE
Reymondia = *Myoxanthus*
Rhaesteria spp.: #7 **II** ORCHIDACEAE
Rhamphidia = *Hetaeria*
Rhamphorhynchus spp.: #7 **II** ORCHIDACEAE
Rhaphidorhynchus = *Microcoelia*
Rhinerrhiza spp.: #7 **II** ORCHIDACEAE
Rhipidoglossum = *Diaphananthe*
Rhipsalidopsis gaertneri = *Hatiora gaertneri*
Rhipsalidopsis rosea = *Hatiora rosea*
Rhipsalis aculeata = *Lepismium aculeatum*
Rhipsalis asperula = *Lepismium micranthum*
Rhipsalis baccifera: (E) Mistletoe cactus **II** CACTACEAE
Rhipsalis baccifera ssp. *baccifera*: #4 **II** CACTACEAE
Rhipsalis baccifera ssp. *erythrocarpa*: #4 **II** CACTACEAE

Rhipsalis baccifera ssp. *hileiabaiana*: #4 **II** CACTACEAE
Rhipsalis baccifera ssp. *horrida*: #4 **II** CACTACEAE
Rhipsalis baccifera ssp. *mauritiana*: #4 **II** CACTACEAE
Rhipsalis baccifera ssp. *shaferi*: #4 **II** CACTACEAE
Rhipsalis boliviana = *Lepismium bolivianum*
Rhipsalis brevispina = *Lepismium brevispinum*
Rhipsalis brevispina = *Lepismium brevispinum*
Rhipsalis burchellii: #4 **II** CACTACEAE
Rhipsalis campos-portoana: **II** CACTACEAE
Rhipsalis cassutha = *Rhipsalis baccifera*
Rhipsalis cereoides: #4 **II** CACTACEAE
Rhipsalis cereuscula: #4 **II** CACTACEAE
Rhipsalis chloroptera = *Rhipsalis elliptica*
Rhipsalis chrysantha = *Rhipsalis dissimilis*
Rhipsalis chrysocarpa = *Rhipsalis puniceodiscus*
Rhipsalis clavata: #4 **II** CACTACEAE
Rhipsalis crenata = *Lepismium crenatum*
Rhipsalis crispata: #4 **II** CACTACEAE
Rhipsalis cuneata: #4 **II** CACTACEAE
Rhipsalis dissimilis: #4 **II** CACTACEAE
Rhipsalis dusenii = *Rhipsalis pachyptera*
Rhipsalis elliptica: #4 **II** CACTACEAE
Rhipsalis ewaldiana: #4 **II** CACTACEAE
Rhipsalis fasciculata = *Rhipsalis baccifera*
Rhipsalis floccosa: #4 **II** CACTACEAE
Rhipsalis floccosa ssp. *floccosa*: #4 **II** CACTACEAE
Rhipsalis floccosa ssp. *hohenauensis*: #4 **II** CACTACEAE
Rhipsalis floccosa ssp. *oreophila*: #4 **II** CACTACEAE
Rhipsalis floccosa ssp. *pittieri*: #4 **II** CACTACEAE
Rhipsalis floccosa ssp. *pulvinigera*: #4 **II** CACTACEAE
Rhipsalis floccosa ssp. *tucumanensis*: #4 **II** CACTACEAE
Rhipsalis goebeliana: #4 **II** CACTACEAE
Rhipsalis gonocarpa = *Lepismium warmingianum*
Rhipsalis grandiflora: #4 **II** CACTACEAE
Rhipsalis hadrosoma = *Rhipsalis grandiflora*
Rhipsalis herminiae = *Hatiora herminiae*
Rhipsalis hoelleri: #4 **II** CACTACEAE
Rhipsalis horrida = *Rhipsalis baccifera* ssp. *horrida*
Rhipsalis houlletiana = *Lepismium houlletianum*
Rhipsalis hylaea = *Rhipsalis baccifera*
Rhipsalis incachacana = *Lepismium incachacanum*
Rhipsalis juengeri: #4 **II** CACTACEAE
Rhipsalis kirbergii = *Rhipsalis micrantha*
Rhipsalis leucoraphis = *Lepismium lumbricoides*
Rhipsalis lindbergiana: #4 **II** CACTACEAE
Rhipsalis linearis = *Lepismium warmingianum*
Rhipsalis loefgrenii = *Lepismium lumbricoides*
Rhipsalis lorentziana = *Lepismium lorentzianum*
Rhipsalis lumbricoides = *Lepismium lumbricoides*
Rhipsalis mesembryanthemoides: #4 **II** CACTACEAE
Rhipsalis micrantha: #4 **II** CACTACEAE
Rhipsalis miyagawae = *Lepismium miyagawae*
Rhipsalis myosurus = *Lepismium cruciforme*
Rhipsalis neves-armondii: #4 **II** CACTACEAE
Rhipsalis oblonga: #4 **II** CACTACEAE
Rhipsalis occidentalis: #4 **II** CACTACEAE
Rhipsalis olivifera: #4 **II** CACTACEAE
Rhipsalis ormindoi: #4 **II** CACTACEAE
Rhipsalis pacheco-leonis: #4 **II** CACTACEAE
Rhipsalis pacheco-leonis ssp. *catenulata*: #4 **II** CACTACEAE
Rhipsalis pacheo-leonis ssp. *pacheo-leonis*: #4 **II** CACTACEAE
Rhipsalis pachyptera: #4 **II** CACTACEAE
Rhipsalis paradoxa: #4 **II** CACTACEAE
Rhipsalis paradoxa ssp. *paradoxa*: #4 **II** CACTACEAE
Rhipsalis paradoxa ssp. *septentrionalis*: #4 **II** CACTACEAE
Rhipsalis paranganiensis = *Lepismium paranganiense*
Rhipsalis pentaptera: #4 **II** CACTACEAE
Rhipsalis pilocarpa: #4 **II** CACTACEAE
Rhipsalis pulchra: #4 **II** CACTACEAE
Rhipsalis pulvinigera = *Rhipsalis floccosa* ssp. *pulvinigera*
Rhipsalis puniceodiscus: #4 **II** CACTACEAE
Rhipsalis rigida = *Rhipsalis dissimilis*
Rhipsalis russellii: #4 **II** CACTACEAE
Rhipsalis squamulosa = *Lepismium cruciforme*
Rhipsalis sulcata: #4 **II** CACTACEAE

Rhipsalis teres: #4 **II** CACTACEAE
Rhipsalis trigona: #4 **II** CACTACEAE
Rhipsalis warmingiana = *Lepismium warmingianum*
Rhizanthella spp.: #7 **II** ORCHIDACEAE
Rhomboda = *Hetaeria*
Rhynchadenia = *Macradenia*
Rhynchandra = *Corymborkis*
Rhynchanthera = *Corymborkis*
Rhynchogyna spp.: #7 **II** ORCHIDACEAE
Rhyncholaelia spp.: #7 **II** ORCHIDACEAE
Rhynchopera = *Pleurothallis*
Rhynchophreatia spp.: #7 **II** ORCHIDACEAE
Rhynchostele = *Leochilus*
Rhynchostylis spp.: #7 **II** ORCHIDACEAE
Ridleya = *Thrixspermum*
Ridleyella spp.: #7 **II** ORCHIDACEAE
Rimacola spp.: #7 **II** ORCHIDACEAE
Rio rosewood (E): *Dalbergia nigra*
Risleya spp.: #7 **II** ORCHIDACEAE
Ritaia = *Ceratostylis*
Ritterocereus fimbriatus = *Stenocereus fimbriatus*
Roast pork (E): *Opuntia cochenillifera*
Robin tree-cactus (E): *Pilosocereus robinii*
Robiquetia spp.: #7 **II** ORCHIDACEAE
Roble colorado (S): *Platymiscium pleiostachyum*
Roca viviente (S): *Ariocarpus* spp.
Rodentiophila atacamensis = *Erisyce rodentiophila*
Rodentiophila megacarpa = *Eriosyce rodentiophila*
Rodrigoa = *Masdevallia*
Rodriguezia spp.: #7 **II** ORCHIDACEAE
Rodrigueziella spp.: #7 **II** ORCHIDACEAE
Rodrigueziopsis spp.: #7 **II** ORCHIDACEAE
Roeperocharis spp.: #7 **II** ORCHIDACEAE
Roezliella = *Sigmatostalix*
Rolfea = *Palmorchis*
Rolfeella = *Benthamia*
Rooksbya euphorbioides = *Neobuxbaumia euphorbioides*
Rophostemon = *Nervilia*
Roptrostemon = *Nervilia*
Roseocactus fissuratus = *Ariocarpus fissuratus*
Roseocactus intermedius = *Ariocarpus fissuratus*
Roseocactus kotschoubeyanus = *Ariocarpus kotschoubeyanus*
Roseocactus kotschoubeyanus ssp. *macdowellii* = *Ariocarpus kotschoubeyanus*
Roseocactus lloydii = *Ariocarpus fissuratus*
Roseocereus tephracanthus = *Harrisia tetracantha*
Rossioglossum spp.: #7 **II** ORCHIDACEAE
Rudolfiella spp.: #7 **II** ORCHIDACEAE
Rusbyella spp.: #7 **II** ORCHIDACEAE
Rusty hedgehog cactus (E): *Echinocereus russanthus*
Saccidium = *Holothrix*
Saccochilus = *Thrixspermum*
Saccoglossum spp.: #7 **II** ORCHIDACEAE
Saccolabiopsis spp.: #7 **II** ORCHIDACEAE
Saccolabium spp.: #7 **II** ORCHIDACEAE
Sacodon = *Cypripedium*
Sacoila spp.: #7 **II** ORCHIDACEAE
Sago-palm (E): *Cycas circinalis*
Salacistis = *Goodyera*
Salpistele spp.: #7 **II** ORCHIDACEAE
Samaipaticereus corroanus: #4 **II** CACTACEAE
Samaipaticereus inquisivensis = *Yungasocereus inquisivensis*
San Diego barrel cactus (E): *Ferocactus viridescens*
San Diego bear-grass (E): *Nolina interrata*
San Rafael cactus (E): *Pediocactus despainii*
Sand cholla (E): *Opuntia pulchella*
Sand prickly pear (E): *Opuntia polyacantha*
Sandalia de Venus (S): *Paphiopedilum* spp.
Sándalo rojo (S): *Pterocarpus santalinus*
Sanderella spp.: #7 **II** ORCHIDACEAE
Santa Barbara Island dudleya (E): *Dudleya traskiae*
Santa Barbara Island liveforever (E): *Dudleya traskiae*
Santa Cruz striped agave (E): *Agave parviflora*
Santal rouge (F): *Pterocarpus santalinus*
Sarcanthopsis spp.: #7 **II** ORCHIDACEAE

Sarcanthus = Cleisostoma
Sarcobodium = Bulbophyllum
Sarcochilus spp.: #7 **II** ORCHIDACEAE
Sarcoglossum = Cirrhaea
Sarcoglottis spp.: #7 **II** ORCHIDACEAE
Sarcoglyphis spp.: #7 **II** ORCHIDACEAE
Sarcophyton spp.: #7 **II** ORCHIDACEAE
Sarcopodium = Epigeneium
Sarcorhynchus = Diaphananthe
Sarcostoma spp.: #7 **II** ORCHIDACEAE
Sardinian gooseberry (E): *Ribes sardoum*
Sarothrochilus = Staurochilus
Sarracenella = Pleurothallis
Sarracenia spp.: (S) cántaros, jarras #1 **I/II** SARRACENIACEAE
Sarracenia acuta = Sarracenia rubra ssp. *rubra*
Sarracenia adunca = Sarracenia minor
Sarracenia alabamensis = Sarracenia rubra ssp. *alabamensis*
Sarracenia alabamensis ssp. *alabamensis = Sarracenia rubra* ssp. *alabamensis*
Sarracenia alabamensis ssp. *wherryi = Sarracenia rubra* ssp. *wherryi*
Sarracenia alata: (E) Pale pitcher-plant, Winged pitcher-plant, Yellow pitcher-plant #1 **II** SARRACENIACEAE
Sarracenia alba = Sarracenia leucophylla
Sarracenia atropurpurea = Sarracenia flava var. *atropurpurea*
Sarracenia atrosanguinea = Sarracenia flava var. *atropurpurea*
Sarracenia aurea = Sarracenia purpurea f. *heterophylla*
Sarracenia calceolata = Sarracenia psittacina
Sarracenia catesbaei = Sarracenia alata
Sarracenia catesbaei = Sarracenia oreophila
Sarracenia crispata = Sarracenia alata
Sarracenia drummondii = Sarracenia leucophylla
Sarracenia drummondii var. *alba = Sarracenia leucophylla*
Sarracenia drummondii var. *albiflora = Sarracenia leucophylla*
Sarracenia drummondii var. *atropurpurea = Sarracenia leucophylla*
Sarracenia drummondii var. *major = Sarracenia leucophylla*
Sarracenia drummondii var. *rubra = Sarracenia leucophylla*
Sarracenia drummondii var. *undulata = Sarracenia leucophylla*
Sarracenia erythropus = Sarracenia flava var. *rugelii*
Sarracenia fildesii = Sarracenia flava var. *flava*
Sarracenia flava = Sarracenia alata
Sarracenia flava = Sarracenia oreophila
Sarracenia flava: (E) Yellow pitcher-plant #1 **II** SARRACENIACEAE
Sarracenia flava f. *rugelii = Sarracenia flava* var. *rugelii*
Sarracenia flava var. *atropurpurea*: #1 **II** SARRACENIACEAE
Sarracenia flava var. *atrosanguinea = Sarracenia flava* var. *atropurpurea*
Sarracenia flava var. *catesbaei = Sarracenia alata*
Sarracenia flava var. *catesbaei = Sarracenia oreophila*
Sarracenia flava var. *crispata = Sarracenia alata*
Sarracenia flava var. *cuprea*: #1 **II** SARRACENIACEAE
Sarracenia flava var. *erythropus = Sarracenia flava* var. *rugelii*
Sarracenia flava var. *flava*: #1 **II** SARRACENIACEAE
Sarracenia flava var. *gigantea = Sarracenia flava* var. *rugelii*
Sarracenia flava var. *limbata = Sarracenia flava* var. *rugelii*
Sarracenia flava var. *major = Sarracenia flava* var. *rugelii*
Sarracenia flava var. *media = Sarracenia flava* var. *flava*
Sarracenia flava var. *minima = Sarracenia flava* var. *flava*
Sarracenia flava var. *oreophila = Sarracenia oreophila*
Sarracenia flava var. *ornata*: #1 **II** SARRACENIACEAE
Sarracenia flava var. *picta = Sarracenia alata*
Sarracenia flava var. *rubra = Sarracenia flava* var. *atropurpurea*
Sarracenia flava var. *rubricorpora*: #1 **II** SARRACENIACEAE
Sarracenia flava var. *rugelii*: #1 **II** SARRACENIACEAE
Sarracenia gronovii var. *alata = Sarracenia alata*
Sarracenia gronovii var. *drummondii = Sarracenia leucophylla*
Sarracenia gronovii var. *flava = Sarracenia flava* var. *flava*
Sarracenia gronovii var. *rubra = Sarracenia rubra* ssp. *rubra*
Sarracenia heterophylla = Sarracenia purpurea f. *heterophylla*
Sarracenia intermedia = Sarracenia alata
Sarracenia jonesii = Sarracenia rubra ssp. *jonesii*
Sarracenia jonesii = Sarracenia rubra ssp. *wherryi*
Sarracenia laciniata = Sarracenia leucophylla

Sarracenia lacunosa = Sarracenia leucophylla
Sarracenia leucophylla: (E) Crimson pitcherplant, White-topped pitcherplant #1 **II** SARRACENIACEAE
Sarracenia media = Sarracenia rubra ssp. *rubra*
Sarracenia mexicana = Sarracenia leucophylla
Sarracenia minor = Sarracenia rubra ssp. *rubra*
Sarracenia minor: (E) Hooded pitcher-plant, Rainbow trumpet #1 **II** SARRACENIACEAE
Sarracenia nigra = Sarracenia rubra ssp. *rubra*
Sarracenia oreophila: (E) Green pitcherplant **I** SARRACENIACEAE
Sarracenia parviflora = Sarracenia purpurea ssp. *venosa*
Sarracenia psittacina: (E) Parrot pitcherplant #1 **II** SARRACENIACEAE
Sarracenia psittacina var. *minor = Sarracenia psittacina*
Sarracenia pulchella = Sarracenia psittacina
Sarracenia purpurea: #1 **II** SARRACENIACEAE
Sarracenia purpurea f. *heterophylla*: #1 **II** SARRACENIACEAE
Sarracenia purpurea f. *incisa = Sarracenia purpurea* ssp. *purpurea*
Sarracenia purpurea f. *luteola*: #1 **II** SARRACENIACEAE
Sarracenia purpurea f. *plena = Sarracenia purpurea* ssp. *purpurea*
Sarracenia purpurea ssp. *purpurea*: (E) Huntsman's cap, Huntsman's horn, Side-saddle plant #1 **II** SARRACENIACEAE
Sarracenia purpurea ssp. *purpurea*Â²*heterophylla = Sarracenia purpurea* f. *heterophylla*
Sarracenia purpurea ssp. *venosa* var. *burkii = Sarracenia purpurea* var. *burkii*
Sarracenia purpurea ssp. *venosa* var. *burkii* f. *luteola = Sarracenia purpurea* var. *burkii*
Sarracenia purpurea ssp. *venosa* var. *montana = Sarracenia purpurea* var. *montana*
Sarracenia purpurea ssp. *venosa*: #1 **II** SARRACENIACEAE
Sarracenia purpurea var. *alata = Sarracenia alata*
Sarracenia purpurea var. *burkii*: #1 **II** SARRACENIACEAE
Sarracenia purpurea var. *heterophylla = Sarracenia purpurea* f. *heterophylla*
Sarracenia purpurea var. *montana*: #1 **II** SARRACENIACEAE
Sarracenia purpurea var. *ripicola = Sarracenia purpurea* ssp. *purpurea*
Sarracenia purpurea var. *stolonifera = Sarracenia purpurea* ssp. *purpurea*
Sarracenia purpurea var. *terrae-novae = Sarracenia purpurea* ssp. *purpurea*
Sarracenia purpurea var. *terrae-novae* f. *heterophylla = Sarracenia purpurea* f. *heterophylla*
Sarracenia purpurea var. *venosa = Sarracenia purpurea* ssp. *venosa*
Sarracenia rosea = Sarracenia purpurea var. *burkii*
Sarracenia rosea f. *luteola = Sarracenia purpurea* f. *luteola*
Sarracenia rubra = Sarracenia psittacina
Sarracenia rubra: #1 **II** SARRACENIACEAE
Sarracenia rubra f. *jonesii = Sarracenia rubra* ssp. *jonesii*
Sarracenia rubra ssp. *alabamensis*: **I** SARRACENIACEAE
Sarracenia rubra ssp. *gulfensis*: #1 **II** SARRACENIACEAE
Sarracenia rubra ssp. *jonesii*: (E) Mountain sweet pitcherplant, Sweet pitcherplant **I** SARRACENIACEAE
Sarracenia rubra ssp. *rubra*: (E) Red-flowered sweet pitcherplant #1 **II** SARRACENIACEAE
Sarracenia rubra ssp. *wherryi*: (E) Wherry's pitcherplant #1 **II** SARRACENIACEAE
Sarracenia rubra var. *acuminata = Sarracenia rubra* ssp. *rubra*
Sarracenia rugelii = Sarracenia flava var. *rugelii*
Sarracenia sledgei = Sarracenia alata
Sarracenia sweetii = Sarracenia rubra ssp. *rubra*
Sarracenia terrae-novae = Sarracenia purpurea ssp. *purpurea*
Sarracenia undulata = Sarracenia leucophylla
Sarracenia undulata var. *alba = Sarracenia leucophylla*
Sarracenia variolaris = Sarracenia minor
Sarracenia venosa = Sarracenia purpurea ssp. *venosa*
Sarracenia viridis = Sarracenia purpurea ssp. *purpurea*
Satorkis = Coeloglossum
Satranala decussilvae: **II** PALMAE
Satyridium spp.: #7 **II** ORCHIDACEAE
Satyrium spp.: #7 **II** ORCHIDACEAE

Saundersia spp.: #7 **II** ORCHIDACEAE
Saunderswood (E): *Pterocarpus santalinus*
Sauroglossum spp.: #7 **II** ORCHIDACEAE
Saussurea costus: (E) Costus root **I** COMPOSITAE
Saussurea lappa = Saussurea costus
Saw-toothed lewisia (E): *Lewisia serrata*
Sayeria = Dendrobium
Scaphosepalum spp.: #7 **II** ORCHIDACEAE
Scaphyglottis spp.: #7 **II** ORCHIDACEAE
Scaredederis = Dendrobium
Scelochiloides spp.: #7 **II** ORCHIDACEAE
Scelochilus spp.: #7 **II** ORCHIDACEAE
Schaenomorphus = Tropidia
Scheer's cory cactus (E): *Coryphantha scheeri*
Scheer's fish hook-cactus (E): *Sclerocactus scheeri*
Scheer's strong-spined cory cactus (E): *Coryphantha robustispina*
    var. *scheeri*
Schiedeella spp.: #7 **II** ORCHIDACEAE
Schismoceras = Dendrobium
Schistotylus spp.: #7 **II** ORCHIDACEAE
Schizochilus spp.: #7 **II** ORCHIDACEAE
Schizodium spp.: #7 **II** ORCHIDACEAE
Schizopedium = Cypripedium
Schlechterella = Rudolfiella
Schlesser's Pincushion (E): *Sclerocactus schlesseri*
Schlimmia spp.: #7 **II** ORCHIDACEAE
Schlumbergera gaertneri = Hatiora gaertneri
Schlumbergera kautskyi: #4 **II** CACTACEAE
Schlumbergera microsphaerica: #4 **II** CACTACEAE
Schlumbergera microsphaerica ssp. *candida*: #4 **II** CACTACEAE
Schlumbergera obtusangula = Schlumbergera microsphaerica
Schlumbergera opuntioides: #4 **II** CACTACEAE
Schlumbergera orssichiana: #4 **II** CACTACEAE
Schlumbergera russelliana: #4 **II** CACTACEAE
Schlumbergera truncata: #4 **II** CACTACEAE
Schoenleinia = Ponthieva
Schoenorchis spp.: #7 **II** ORCHIDACEAE
Schomburgkia spp.: #7 **II** ORCHIDACEAE
Schott's Prickly-pear (E): *Opuntia schottii*
Schwartzkopffia = Brachycorythis
Sclerocactus blainei = Sclerocactus spinosior ssp. *blainei*
Sclerocactus brevihamatus: (E) Tobusch fishhook cactus **I/II**
    CACTACEAE
Sclerocactus brevihamatus ssp. *brevihamatus*: #4 **II** CACTACEAE
Sclerocactus brevihamatus ssp. *tobuschii*: **I** CACTACEAE
Sclerocactus brevispinus = Sclerocactus glaucus
Sclerocactus contortus = Sclerocactus parviflorus ssp. *parviflorus*
Sclerocactus erectocentrus: **I** CACTACEAE
Sclerocactus erectocentrus var. *acunensis*: (E) Acuña cactus **I**
    CACTACEAE
Sclerocactus erectocentrus var. *erectocentrus*: (E) Needle-spined
    pineapple cactus **I** CACTACEAE
Sclerocactus glaucus: (E) Vinta Basin hookless cactus **I**
    CACTACEAE
Sclerocactus intermedius = Sclerocactus parviflorus ssp.
    intermedius
Sclerocactus intertextus: (E) White butterfly-cactus #4 **II**
    CACTACEAE
Sclerocactus johnsonii: (E) Johnson Butterfly #4 **II** CACTACEAE
Sclerocactus mariposensis: (E) Lloyd's mariposa cactus, (S) Huevo
    de buey **I** CACTACEAE
Sclerocactus mesae-verdae: (E) Mesa-Verde cactus **I**
    CACTACEAE
Sclerocactus nyensis: (E) Tonopah fishhook cactus **I**
    CACTACEAE
Sclerocactus papyracanthus: (E) Paper-spine pincushion cactus **I**
    CACTACEAE
Sclerocactus parviflorus: #4 **II** CACTACEAE
Sclerocactus parviflorus ssp. *havasupaiensis*: #4 **II** CACTACEAE
Sclerocactus parviflorus ssp. *intermedius*: #4 **II** CACTACEAE
Sclerocactus parviflorus ssp. *parviflorus*: #4 **II** CACTACEAE
Sclerocactus parviflorus ssp. *terrae-canyonae*: #4 **II**
    CACTACEAE
Sclerocactus polyancistrus: (E) Mohave Fishhook Cactus #4 **II**
    CACTACEAE

Sclerocactus pubispinus: **I** CACTACEAE
Sclerocactus pubispinus var. *pubispinus*: **I** CACTACEAE
Sclerocactus pubispinus var. *spinosior*: **I** CACTACEAE
Sclerocactus scheeri: (E) Scheer's fishook-cactus #4 **II**
    CACTACEAE
Sclerocactus schlesseri = Sclerocactus spinosior ssp. *blainei*
Sclerocactus sileri: #4 **II** CACTACEAE
Sclerocactus spinosior: (E) Desert Valley Fishhook-cactus #4 **II**
    CACTACEAE
Sclerocactus spinosior ssp. *blainei*: #4 **II** CACTACEAE
Sclerocactus terrae-canyonae = Sclerocactus parviflorus ssp.
    terrae-canyonae
Sclerocactus uncinatus: (E) Chihuahuan fish-hook cactus #4 **II**
    CACTACEAE
Sclerocactus uncinatus ssp. *crassihamatus*: #4 **II** CACTACEAE
Sclerocactus uncinatus ssp. *uncinatus*: #4 **II** CACTACEAE
Sclerocactus uncinatus ssp. *wrightii*: #4 **II** CACTACEAE
Sclerocactus unguispinus: #4 **II** CACTACEAE
Sclerocactus warnockii: #4 **II** CACTACEAE
Sclerocactus wetlandicus = Sclerocactus glaucus
Sclerocactus wetlandicus ssp. *ilseae = Sclerocactus glaucus*
Sclerocactus whipplei: #4 **II** CACTACEAE
Sclerocactus whipplei ssp. *busekii*: #4 **II** CACTACEAE
Sclerocactus wrightiae: (E) Wright's fishhook cactus **I**
    CACTACEAE
Scleropterys = Cirrhaea
Scoliochilus = Appendicula
Scopularia = Holothrix
Scuticaria spp.: #7 **II** ORCHIDACEAE
Sedirea spp.: #7 **II** ORCHIDACEAE
Seidenfadenia spp.: #7 **II** ORCHIDACEAE
Selenicereus anthonyanus: #4 **II** CACTACEAE
Selenicereus atropilosus: #4 **II** CACTACEAE
Selenicereus boeckmannii: #4 **II** CACTACEAE
Selenicereus brevispinus: #4 **II** CACTACEAE
Selenicereus chontalensis: #4 **II** CACTACEAE
Selenicereus chrysocardium: #4 **II** CACTACEAE
Selenicereus coniflorus: #4 **II** CACTACEAE
Selenicereus donkelaarii: #4 **II** CACTACEAE
Selenicereus grandiflorus: (E) Night-blooming cereus, Queen of
    the night, (S) Cardón, Reina de la noche #4 **II** CACTACEAE
Selenicereus hamatus: #4 **II** CACTACEAE
Selenicereus hondurensis: #4 **II** CACTACEAE
Selenicereus inermis: #4 **II** CACTACEAE
Selenicereus innesii: #4 **II** CACTACEAE
Selenicereus kunthianus = Selenicereus grandiflorus
Selenicereus macdonaldiae: #4 **II** CACTACEAE
Selenicereus maxonii = Selenicereus urbanianus
Selenicereus megalanthus: #4 **II** CACTACEAE
Selenicereus murrillii: #4 **II** CACTACEAE
Selenicereus nelsonii: #4 **II** CACTACEAE
Selenicereus pteranthus: #4 **II** CACTACEAE
Selenicereus rothii = Selenicereus macdonaldiae
Selenicereus setaceus: #4 **II** CACTACEAE
Selenicereus spinulosus: #4 **II** CACTACEAE
Selenicereus testudo: #4 **II** CACTACEAE
Selenicereus tricae: #4 **II** CACTACEAE
Selenicereus urbanianus: #4 **II** CACTACEAE
Selenicereus vagans: #4 **II** CACTACEAE
Selenicereus validus: #4 **II** CACTACEAE
Selenicereus vaupelii = Selenicereus boeckmannii
Selenicereus wercklei: #4 **II** CACTACEAE
Selenicereus wittii: #4 **II** CACTACEAE
Selenipedium spp.: #7 **II** ORCHIDACEAE
Selenipedium boissierianum = Phragmipedium boissierianum
Selenipedium caricinum = Phragmipedium caricinum
Selenipedium caudatum var. lindenii = Phragmipedium lindenii
Selenipedium caudatum var. uropedium = Phragmipedium lindenii
Selenipedium caudatum var. wallisii = Phragmipedium wallisii
Selenipedium caudatum = Phragmipedium caudatum
Selenipedium dariense = Phragmipedium longifolium
Selenipedium duboisii = Phragmipedium boissierianum
Selenipedium duboissierianum = Phragmipedium boissierianum
Selenipedium elliottianum = Paphiopedilum rothschildianum

331

Selenipedium kaieteurum = *Phragmipedium lindleyanum* var. *kaieteurum*
Selenipedium klotzschianum = *Phragmipedium klotzschianum*
Selenipedium laevigatum = *Paphiopedilum philippinense*
Selenipedium lindenii = *Phragmipedium lindenii*
Selenipedium lindleyanum var. *kaieteurum* = *Phragmipedium lindleyanum* var. *kaieteurum*
Selenipedium lindleyanum = *Phragmipedium lindleyanum*
Selenipedium longifolium = *Phragmipedium longifolium*
Selenipedium parishii = *Paphiopedilum parishii*
Selenipedium paulistanum = *Phragmipedium vittatum*
Selenipedium pearcei = *Phragmipedium pearcei*
Selenipedium reichenbachii = *Phragmipedium longifolium*
Selenipedium sargentianum = *Phragmipedium sargentianum*
Selenipedium schlimii = *Phragmipedium schlimii*
Selenipedium schomburgkianum = *Phragmipedium klotzschianum*
Selenipedium vittatum = *Phragmipedium vittatum*
Selenipedium wallisii = *Phragmipedium wallisii*
Sello de oro (S): *Adonis vernalis*
Semaphore cactus (E): *Opuntia spinosissima*
Semiphajus = *Eulophia*
Sepalosaccus = *Maxillaria*
Sepalosiphon = *Glossorhyncha*
Seraphyta = *Epidendrum*
Serapias spp.: #7 **II** ORCHIDACEAE
Serapiastrum = *Serapias*
Serrastylis = *Macradenia*
Sertifera = *Elleanthus*
Sessilibulbum = *Scaphyglottis*
Sestochilos = *Bulbophyllum*
Seticereus chlorocarpus = *Browningia chlorocarpa*
Seticereus humboldtii = *Cleistocactus icosagonus*
Seticereus icosagonus = *Cleistocactus icosagonus*
Seticereus roezlii = *Cleistocactus roezlii*
Seticleistocactus dependens = *Cleistocactus dependens*
Seticleistocactus piraymirensis = *Cleistocactus piraymirensis*
Setiechinopsis mirabilis = *Echinopsis mirabilis*
Shortia galacifolia: (E) Oconee bells, (S) Campanas de Oconee #1 **II** DIAPENSIACEAE
Siagonanthus = *Maxillaria*
Siccobaccatus dolichospermaticus = *Micranthocereus dolichospermaticus*
Siccobaccatus estevesii = *Micranthocereus estevesii*
Siccobaccatus estevesii ssp. *grandiflorus* = *Micranthocereus estevesii*
Siccobaccatus estevesii ssp. *insigniflorus* = *Micranthocereus estevesii*
Sicilian fir (E): *Abies nebrodensis*
Side-saddle plant (E): *Sarracenia purpurea* ssp. *purpurea*
Sieberia = *Platanthera*
Sievekingia spp.: #7 **II** ORCHIDACEAE
Sigmatochilus = *Chelonistele*
Sigmatogyne = *Panisea*
Sigmatostalix spp.: #7 **II** ORCHIDACEAE
Siler's Pincushion cactus (E): *Pediocactus sileri*
Silver tree fern (E): *Cyathea dealbata*
Silvorchis spp.: #7 **II** ORCHIDACEAE
Simpson's prickly-apple cactus (E): *Harrisia simpsonii*
Sinopodophyllum hexandrum = *Podophyllum hexandrum*
Sinorchis = *Cephalanthera*
Sirhookera spp.: #7 **II** ORCHIDACEAE
Skeptrostachys spp.: #7 **II** ORCHIDACEAE
Slender pitcher-plant (E): *Nepenthes gracilis*
Slender sternbergia (E): *Sternbergia colchiciflora*
Slender tree fern (E): *Cyathea cunninghamii*
Slipper orchids (E): *Paphiopedilum* spp./ *Phragmipedium* spp.
Smallia = *Pteroglossaspis*
Smithorchis spp.: #7 **II** ORCHIDACEAE
Smithsonia spp.: #7 **II** ORCHIDACEAE
Smitinandia spp.: #7 **II** ORCHIDACEAE
Smooth pear (E): *Opuntia cochenillifera*
Snake-root devil-pepper (E): *Rauvolfia serpentina*
Sneed's cory cactus (E): *Escobaria sneedii*
Sneed's pincushion cactus (E): *Escobaria sneedii*
Snowdrops (E): *Galanthus* spp.

Sobennikoffia spp.: #7 **II** ORCHIDACEAE
Sobralia spp.: #7 **II** ORCHIDACEAE
Sodiroella = *Stellilabium*
Soehrensia bruchii = *Echinopsis bruchii*
Soehrensia formosa = *Echinopsis formosa*
Soehrensia grandis = *Echinopsis bruchii*
Soehrensia ingens = *Echinopsis bruchii*
Soehrensia korethroides = *Echinopsis korethroides*
Soehrensia oreopepon = *Echinopsis formosa*
Soehrensia smrziana = *Echinopsis smrziana*
Soehrensia uebelmanniana = *Echinopsis formosa*
Soft tree fern (E): *Cyathea smithii*
Solenangis spp.: #7 **II** ORCHIDACEAE
Solenidiopsis spp.: #7 **II** ORCHIDACEAE
Solenidium spp.: #7 **II** ORCHIDACEAE
Solenocentrum spp.: #7 **II** ORCHIDACEAE
Solisia pectinata = *Mammillaria pectinifera*
Sonora guaiacum (E): *Guaiacum* spp.
Sonoran Jumping cholla (E): *Opuntia fulgida*
Sophronia = *Sophronitis*
Sophronitella = *Isabelia*
Sophronitis spp.: #7 **II** ORCHIDACEAE
Soterosanthus spp.: #7 **II** ORCHIDACEAE
South American slipper orchids (E): *Phragmipedium* spp.
Sowbread (E): *Cyclamen hederifolium*
Spanish cedar (E): *Cedrela odorata*
Spathiger = *Epidendrum*
Spathoglottis spp.: #7 **II** ORCHIDACEAE
Specklinia = *Pleurothallis*
Sphaeropteris albosetacea = *Cyathea albosetacea*
Sphaeropteris crinita = *Cyathea crinita*
Sphaeropteris elongata = *Cyathea poeppigii*
Sphaeropteris insignis = *Cyathea insignis*
Sphaeropteris lepifera = *Cyathea lepifera*
Sphyrarhynchus spp.: #7 **II** ORCHIDACEAE
Sphyrastylis spp.: #7 **II** ORCHIDACEAE
Spiculaea spp.: #7 **II** ORCHIDACEAE
Spiral aloe (E): *Aloe polyphylla*
Spiranthes spp.: #7 **II** ORCHIDACEAE
Spongiola spp.: #7 **II** ORCHIDACEAE
Sprengei's tillandsia (E): *Tillandsia sprengeliana*
Sprenge's tillandsia (E): *Tillandsia sprengeliana*
Spring adonis (E): *Adonis vernalis*
Spring pheasant's-eye (E): *Adonis vernalis*
Spurges (E): *Euphorbia* spp.
Stachyanthus = *Bulbophyllum*
Stag-horn cholla (E): *Opuntia versicolor*
Stalkya spp.: #7 **II** ORCHIDACEAE
Stangeria eriopus: (E) Cycad, Hottentot's head **I** STANGERIACEAE
Stangeria paradoxa = *Stangeria eriopus*
Stanhopea spp.: #7 **II** ORCHIDACEAE
Stanhopeastrum = *Stanhopea*
Star cactus (E): *Astrophytum asterias*
Staurites = *Phalaenopsis*
Staurochilus spp.: #7 **II** ORCHIDACEAE
Stauroglottis = *Phalaenopsis*
Stauropsis = *Trichoglottis*
Steliopsis = *Stelis*
Stelis spp.: #7 **II** ORCHIDACEAE
Stellilabium spp.: #7 **II** ORCHIDACEAE
Stellorchis = *Nervilia*
Stellorkis = *Nervilia*
Stenia spp.: #7 **II** ORCHIDACEAE
Stenocactus arrigens = *Stenocactus crispatus*
Stenocactus boedekerianus = *Stenocactus* sp.
Stenocactus bustamantei = *Stenocactus ochoterenanus*
Stenocactus coptonogonus: #4 **II** CACTACEAE
Stenocactus crispatus: #4 **II** CACTACEAE
Stenocactus hastatus: #4 **II** CACTACEAE
Stenocactus heteracanthus = *Stenocactus ochoterenanus*
Stenocactus kellerianus = *Stenocactus crispatus*
Stenocactus lamellosus = *Stenocactus crispatus*
Stenocactus lloydii = *Stenocactus multicostatus*
Stenocactus multicostatus: #4 **II** CACTACEAE

Stenocactus obvallatus: #4 **II** CACTACEAE
Stenocactus ochoterenanus: #4 **II** CACTACEAE
Stenocactus phyllacanthus: #4 **II** CACTACEAE
Stenocactus rectispinus: #4 **II** CACTACEAE
Stenocactus sulphureus: #4 **II** CACTACEAE
Stenocactus vaupelianus: #4 **II** CACTACEAE
Stenocactus zacatecasensis = *Stenocactus multicostatus*
Stenocereus alamosensis: #4 **II** CACTACEAE
Stenocereus aragonii: #4 **II** CACTACEAE
Stenocereus beneckei: #4 **II** CACTACEAE
Stenocereus chacalapensis: #4 **II** CACTACEAE
Stenocereus chrysocarpus: #4 **II** CACTACEAE
Stenocereus dumortieri: #4 **II** CACTACEAE
Stenocereus eichlamii: #4 **II** CACTACEAE
Stenocereus eruca: #4 **II** CACTACEAE
Stenocereus fimbriatus: #4 **II** CACTACEAE
Stenocereus fricii: #4 **II** CACTACEAE
Stenocereus griseus: #4 **II** CACTACEAE
Stenocereus gummosus: #4 **II** CACTACEAE
Stenocereus hystrix = *Stenocereus fimbriatus*
Stenocereus kerberi: #4 **II** CACTACEAE
Stenocereus laevigatus: #4 **II** CACTACEAE
Stenocereus martinezii: #4 **II** CACTACEAE
Stenocereus montanus: #4 **II** CACTACEAE
Stenocereus pruinosus: #4 **II** CACTACEAE
Stenocereus queretaroensis: #4 **II** CACTACEAE
Stenocereus quevedonis: #4 **II** CACTACEAE
Stenocereus standleyi: #4 **II** CACTACEAE
Stenocereus stellatus: #4 **II** CACTACEAE
Stenocereus thurberi: #4 **II** CACTACEAE
Stenocereus thurberi ssp. *littoralis*: #4 **II** CACTACEAE
Stenocereus thurberi ssp. *thurberi*: #4 **II** CACTACEAE
Stenocereus treleasei: #4 **II** CACTACEAE
Stenocereus yunckeri: #4 **II** CACTACEAE
Stenocoryne = *Bifrenaria*
Stenoglossum = *Epidendrum*
Stenoglottis spp.: #7 **II** ORCHIDACEAE
Stenopolen = *Stenia*
Stenoptera spp.: #7 **II** ORCHIDACEAE
Stenorrhynchos spp.: #7 **II** ORCHIDACEAE
Stenorrhynchus = *Stenorrhynchos*
Stephanocereus leucostele: #4 **II** CACTACEAE
Stephanocereus luetzelburgii: #4 **II** CACTACEAE
Stephanothelys spp.: #7 **II** ORCHIDACEAE
Stereochilus spp.: #7 **II** ORCHIDACEAE
Stereosandra spp.: #7 **II** ORCHIDACEAE
Sterigmanthe bojeri = *Euphorbia milii* var. *milii*
Sterigmanthe splendens = *Euphorbia milii* var. *splendens*
Sternbergia spp.: (E) sternbergias, (S) margarita de otoño #1 **II** AMARYLLIDACEAE
Sternbergia aetnensis = *Sternbergia colchiciflora*
Sternbergia alexandrae = *Sternbergia colchiciflora*
Sternbergia aurantiaca = *Sternbergia lutea*
Sternbergia candida: #1 **II** AMARYLLIDACEAE
Sternbergia citrina = *Sternbergia colchiciflora*
Sternbergia clusiana: #1 **II** AMARYLLIDACEAE
Sternbergia colchiciflora: (E) Slender sternbergia, (F) Sternbergie à fleurs de colchique #1 **II** AMARYLLIDACEAE
Sternbergia colchiciflora var. *aetnensis* = *Sternbergia colchiciflora*
Sternbergia colchiciflora var. *alexandrae* = *Sternbergia colchiciflora*
Sternbergia colchiciflora var. *dalmatica* = *Sternbergia colchiciflora*
Sternbergia dalmatica = *Sternbergia colchiciflora*
Sternbergia exscapa = *Sternbergia colchiciflora*
Sternbergia fischeriana: #1 **II** AMARYLLIDACEAE
Sternbergia fischeriana f. *hissarica* = *Sternbergia fischeriana*
Sternbergia fischeriana ssp. *hissarica* = *Sternbergia fischeriana*
Sternbergia grandiflora = *Sternbergia clusiana*
Sternbergia greuteriana: #1 **II** AMARYLLIDACEAE
Sternbergia latifolia = *Sternbergia clusiana*
Sternbergia lutea = *Sternbergia colchiciflora*
Sternbergia lutea: (E) Common sternbergia #1 **II** AMARYLLIDACEAE
Sternbergia lutea ssp. *sicula* = *Sternbergia sicula*

Sternbergia lutea var. *graeca* = *Sternbergia sicula*
Sternbergia lutea var. *sicula* = *Sternbergia sicula*
Sternbergia macrantha = *Sternbergia clusiana*
Sternbergia pulchella: #1 **II** AMARYLLIDACEAE
Sternbergia schubertii: #1 **II** AMARYLLIDACEAE
Sternbergia sicula: #1 **II** AMARYLLIDACEAE
Sternbergia spaffordiana = *Sternbergia clusiana*
Sternbergia stipitata = *Sternbergia clusiana*
Sternbergia vernalis = *Sternbergia fischeriana*
Sternbergie à fleurs de colchique (F): *Sternbergia colchiciflora*
Stetsonia coryne: #4 **II** CACTACEAE
Steveniella spp.: #7 **II** ORCHIDACEAE
Stevenorchis = *Steveniella*
Stichorkis = *Liparis*
Stictophyllorchis spp.: #7 **II** ORCHIDACEAE
Stictophyllum = *Stictophyllorchis*
Stigmatodactylus = *Pantlingia*
Stigmatosema spp.: #7 **II** ORCHIDACEAE
Stimegas = *Cypripedium*
Stimegas venustum = *Paphiopedilum venustum*
Stinking mahogany (E): *Cedrela odorata*
Stolzia spp.: #7 **II** ORCHIDACEAE
Strateuma = *Orchis*
Strateuma = *Zeuxine*
Straw Spine cactus (E): *Thelocactus bicolor* ssp. *flavidispinus*
Strawberry cactus (E): *Mammillaria dioica*
Striped Apple-cactus (E): *Cereus striatus*
Strombocactus spp.: **I** CACTACEAE
Strombocactus denegrii = *Obregonia denegrii*
Strombocactus disciformis: (E) Disc cactus **I** CACTACEAE
Strombocactus disciformis ssp. *disciformis*: **I** CACTACEAE
Strombocactus disciformis ssp. *esperanzae*: **I** CACTACEAE
Strombocactus jarmilae = *Strombocactus disciformis*
Strombocactus laui = *Turbinicarpus laui*
Strombocactus polaskii = *Turbinicarpus schmiedickeanus* ssp. *schwarzii*
Strombocactus pulcherrimus = *Strombocactus disciformis* ssp. *esperanzae*
Strombocactus roseiflorus = *Turbinicarpus roseiflorus*
Sturmia = *Liparis*
Styloglossum = *Calanthe*
Suarezia spp.: #7 **II** ORCHIDACEAE
Submatucana aurantiaca = *Matucana aurantiaca* ssp. *aurantiaca*
Submatucana aureiflora = *Matucana aureiflora*
Submatucana calvescens = *Matucana aurantiaca* ssp. *aurantiaca*
Submatucana currundayensis = *Matucana aurantiaca* ssp. *currundayensis*
Submatucana formosa = *Matucana formosa*
Submatucana formosa var. *minor* = *Matucana formosa*
Submatucana intertexta = *Matucana intertexta*
Submatucana madisoniorum = *Matucana madisoniorum*
Submatucana myriacantha = *Matucana haynei* ssp. *myriacantha*
Submatucana paucicostata = *Matucana paucicostata*
Submatucana ritteri = *Matucana ritteri*
Subpilocereus atroviridis = *Cereus repandus*
Subpilocereus grenadensis = *Cereus repandus*
Subpilocereus horrispinus = *Cereus horrispinus*
Subpilocereus mortensenii = *Cereus mortensenii*
Subpilocereus ottonis = *Cereus horrispinus*
Subpilocereus remolinensis = *Cereus repandus*
Subpilocereus repandus = *Cereus repandus*
Subpilocereus repandus ssp. *micracanthus* = *Cereus repandus*
Subpilocereus repandus var. *repandus* = *Cereus repandus*
Subpilocereus repandus var. *weberi* = *Cereus repandus*
Subpilocereus russelianus = *Cereus fricii*
Suckers (E): *Opuntia curassavica*
Sucre tillandsia (E): *Tillandsia sucrei*
Sulcorebutia cardenasiana = *Rebutia cardenasiana*
Sulcorebutia chilensis = *Neowerdermannia chilensis* ssp. *chilensis*
Sulcorebutia vorwerkii = *Neowerdermannia vorwerkii*
Sulpitia = *Encyclia*
Summerhayesia spp.: #7 **II** ORCHIDACEAE
Sunipia spp.: #7 **II** ORCHIDACEAE
Sutrina spp.: #7 **II** ORCHIDACEAE
Svenkoeltzia = *Funkiella*

Checklist of flora/Lista de especies de flora/Liste des espèces végétales

Swari (S): *Caryocar costaricense*
Sweet pitcherplant (E): *Sarracenia rubra* ssp. *jonesii*
Swietenia humilis: (E) Honduras mahogany, Mexican mahogany, (S) Caoba de Honduras, Caoba de Pacífico, Cobano #1 **II** MELIACEAE
Swietenia macrophylla: (E) big-leaf mahogany, Brazilian mahogany, Honduras mahogany, (S) aguano, ahuano, caoba, mara (F) acajou d'Amérique, acajou des Antilles, mahogani à grands feuilles, swiéténie (#5 **III** until 15/11/2003), (#6 **II** from 15/11/2003)⁵ MELIACEAE
Swietenia mahagoni: (E) American mahogany, Cuban mahogany, West Indian Mahogany, (S) Caoba española (F) Mahogani de Saint-Dominique, Mahogani à petites feuilles, #5 **II** MELIACEAE
Swiéténie (S): *Swietenia macrophylla*
Sylvalismis = Calanthe
Symphyglossum spp.: #7 **II** ORCHIDACEAE
Symphyosepalum spp.: #7 **II** ORCHIDACEAE
Synadena = Phalaenopsis
Synanthes = Eurystyles
Synassa = Sauroglossum
Synoplectris = Sarcoglottis
Synptera = Trichoglottis
Systeloglossum spp.: #7 **II** ORCHIDACEAE
Tacinga braunii: #4 **II** CACTACEAE
Tacinga funalis: #4 **II** CACTACEAE
Taeniophyllum spp.: #7 **II** ORCHIDACEAE
Taeniorrhiza spp.: #7 **II** ORCHIDACEAE
Tainia spp.: #7 **II** ORCHIDACEAE
Tainiopsis = Eriodes
Talauma hodgsonii = Magnolia liliifera var. *obovata*
Talpinaria = Pleurothallis
Tamaulipas living-rock cactus (E): *Ariocarpus agavoides*
Tangtsinia = Cephalanthera
Tankervillia = Phaius
Tapacapón (S): *Ceratozamia* spp.
Tapeinoglossum = Bulbophyllum
Taprobanea spp.: #7 **II** ORCHIDACEAE
Taurostalix = Bulbophyllum
Taxus baccata ssp. *wallichiana = Taxus wallichiana*
Taxus wallichiana: (E) Himalayan yew, (S) Tejo del Himalaya (F) If de l'Himalaya, #2 **II** TAXACEAE
Teagueia spp.: #7 **II** ORCHIDACEAE
Teca africana (S): *Pericopsis elata*
Teck d'Afrique (F): *Pericopsis elata*
Teddy-bear cactus (E): *Opuntia bigelovii/ Pachycereus militaris*
Tejo del Himalaya (S): *Taxus wallichiana*
Telipogon spp.: #7 **II** ORCHIDACEAE
Tephrocactus albiscoparius = Opuntia boldinghii
Tephrocactus alexanderi = Opuntia alexanderi
Tephrocactus articulatus = Opuntia articulata
Tephrocactus asplundii = Opuntia boldinghii
Tephrocactus atacamensis = Opuntia atacamensis
Tephrocactus atroglobosus = Opuntia nigrispina
Tephrocactus atroviridis = Opuntia floccosa
Tephrocactus blancii = Opuntia blancii
Tephrocactus bolivianus = Opuntia boldinghii
Tephrocactus camachoi = Opuntia camachoi
Tephrocactus chichensis = Opuntia chichensis
Tephrocactus coloreus = Opuntia colorea
Tephrocactus conoideus = Opuntia conoidea
Tephrocactus corotilla = Opuntia corotilla
Tephrocactus crassicylindricus = Opuntia crassicylindrica
Tephrocactus crispicrinitus = Opuntia floccosa
Tephrocactus cylindrarticulatus = Opuntia dactylifera
Tephrocactus cylindrolanatus = Opuntia floccosa
Tephrocactus dactylifer = Opuntia dactylifera
Tephrocactus darwinii = Opuntia darwinii
Tephrocactus dimorphus = Opuntia sphaerica
Tephrocactus echinaceus = Opuntia boldinghii
Tephrocactus ferocior = Opuntia chichensis
Tephrocactus flexosus = Opuntia flexuosa

Tephrocactus floccosus = Opuntia floccosa
Tephrocactus fulvicomus = Opuntia fulvicoma
Tephrocactus geometricus = Opuntia alexanderi
Tephrocactus glomeratus = Opuntia glomerata
Tephrocactus heteromorphus = Opuntia heteromorpha
Tephrocactus hickenii = Opuntia darwinii
Tephrocactus hirschii = Opuntia hirschii
Tephrocactus ignescens = Opuntia ignescens
Tephrocactus kuehnrichianus = Opuntia sphaerica
Tephrocactus lagopus = Opuntia lagopus
Tephrocactus malyanus = Opuntia lagopus
Tephrocactus mandragora = Opuntia minuta
Tephrocactus melanacanthus = Opuntia boldinghii
Tephrocactus microclados = Opuntia rossiana
Tephrocactus microsphaericus = Opuntia alexanderi
Tephrocactus minor = Opuntia backebergii
Tephrocactus minusculus = Opuntia minuscula
Tephrocactus minutus = Opuntia minuta
Tephrocactus mirus = Opuntia sphaerica
Tephrocactus mistiensis = Opuntia mistiensis
Tephrocactus molinensis = Opuntia molinensis
Tephrocactus muellerianus = Opuntia sphaerica
Tephrocactus multiareolatus = Opuntia sphaerica
Tephrocactus neuquensis = Opuntia darwinii
Tephrocactus nigrispinus = Opuntia nigrispina
Tephrocactus noodtiae = Opuntia dactylifera
Tephrocactus ovallei = Opuntia glomerata
Tephrocactus ovatus = Opuntia aoracantha
Tephrocactus ovatus = Opuntia ovata
Tephrocactus paediophilus = Opuntia aoracantha
Tephrocactus pentlandii = Opuntia pentlandii
Tephrocactus platyacanthus = Opuntia darwinii
Tephrocactus pseudo-udonis = Opuntia floccosa
Tephrocactus punta-caillan = Opuntia punta-caillan
Tephrocactus pyrrhacanthus = Opuntia pyrrhacantha
Tephrocactus rarissimus = Opuntia pentlandii
Tephrocactus rauhii = Opuntia floccosa
Tephrocactus reicheanus = Opuntia glomerata
Tephrocactus russellii = Opuntia ovata
Tephrocactus silvestris = Opuntia silvestris
Tephrocactus sphaericus = Opuntia sphaerica
Tephrocactus subinermus = Opuntia pentlandii
Tephrocactus subterraneus = Opuntia subterranea
Tephrocactus tarapacanus = Opuntia tarapacana
Tephrocactus udonis = Opuntia floccosa
Tephrocactus variflorus = Opuntia subterranea
Tephrocactus verticosus = Opuntia floccosa
Tephrocactus wilkeanus = Opuntia pentlandii
Tephrocactus yanganucensis = Opuntia yanganucensis
Tetracentron sinense: #1 **III** TETRACENTRACEAE
Tetragamestus = Scaphyglottis
Tetramicra spp.: #7 **II** ORCHIDACEAE
Tetrapeltis = Otochilus
Teuscheria spp.: #7 **II** ORCHIDACEAE
Thaia spp.: #7 **II** ORCHIDACEAE
Thecopus spp.: #7 **II** ORCHIDACEAE
Thecostele spp.: #7 **II** ORCHIDACEAE
Thelasis spp.: #7 **II** ORCHIDACEAE
Thelocactus aguirreanus = Escobaria aguirreana
Thelocactus bicolor: #4 **II** CACTACEAE
Thelocactus bicolor ssp. *bicolor*: #4 **II** CACTACEAE
Thelocactus bicolor ssp. *flavidispinus*: (E) Straw Spine cactus #4 **II** CACTACEAE
Thelocactus bicolor ssp. *schwarzii*: #4 **II** CACTACEAE
Thelocactus buekii = Thelocactus tulensis ssp. *buekii*
Thelocactus conothelos: #4 **II** CACTACEAE
Thelocactus conothelos ssp. *argenteus*: #4 **II** CACTACEAE
Thelocactus conothelos ssp. *aurantiacus*: #4 **II** CACTACEAE
Thelocactus conothelos ssp. *conothelos*: #4 **II** CACTACEAE
Thelocactus flavidispinus = Thelocactus bicolor ssp. *flavidispinus*
Thelocactus garciae: #4 **II** CACTACEAE
Thelocactus hastifer: #4 **II** CACTACEAE
Thelocactus heterochromus: #4 **II** CACTACEAE
Thelocactus hexaedrophorus: #4 **II** CACTACEAE

---

⁵ Populations of the Neotropics/Las poblaciones de los neotrópicos/Populations néotropicales.

Thelocactus hexaedrophorus ssp. *hexaedrophorus*: #4 **II**
    CACTACEAE
Thelocactus hexaedrophorus ssp. *lloydii*: #4 **II** CACTACEAE
Thelocactus krainzianus = Thelocactus tulensis
Thelocactus lausseri: #4 **II** CACTACEAE
Thelocactus leucacanthus: #4 **II** CACTACEAE
Thelocactus macdowellii: #4 **II** CACTACEAE
Thelocactus matudae = Thelocactus tulensis ssp. *matudae*
Thelocactus rinconensis: #4 **II** CACTACEAE
Thelocactus rinconensis ssp. *hintonii*: #4 **II** CACTACEAE
Thelocactus rinconensis ssp. *nidulans = Thelocactus rinconensis*
Thelocactus rinconensis ssp. *phymatothelos = Thelocactus*
    rinconensis
Thelocactus rinconensis ssp. *rinconensis*: #4 **II** CACTACEAE
Thelocactus roseanus = Escobaria roseana
Thelocactus schwarzii = Thelocactus bicolor ssp. *schwarzii*
Thelocactus setispinus: (E) Miniature barrel cactus #4 **II**
    CACTACEAE
Thelocactus tulensis: #4 **II** CACTACEAE
Thelocactus tulensis ssp. *buekii*: #4 **II** CACTACEAE
Thelocactus tulensis ssp. *matudae*: #4 **II** CACTACEAE
Thelocactus tulensis ssp. *tulensis*: #4 **II** CACTACEAE
Thelocephala aerocarpa = Eriosyce aerocarpa
Thelocephala duripulpa = Eriosyce napina ssp. *lembckei*
Thelocephala esmeraldana = Eriosyce esmeraldana
Thelocephala fankhauseri = Eriosyce tenebrica
Thelocephala fulva = Eriosyce odieri ssp. *fulva*
Thelocephala glabrescens = Eriosyce odieri ssp. *glabrescens*
Thelocephala krausii = Eriosyce krausii
Thelocephala lembckei = Eriosyce napina ssp. *lembckei*
Thelocephala longirapa = Eriosyce krausii
Thelocephala malleolata = Eriosyce krausii
Thelocephala napina = Eriosyce napina
Thelocephala nuda = Eriosyce aerocarpa
Thelocephala odieri = Eriosyce odieri ssp. *odieri*
Thelocephala reichei = Eriosyce odieri
Thelocephala tenebrica = Eriosyce tenebrica
Thelychiton = Dendrobium
Thelymitra spp.: #7 **II** ORCHIDACEAE
Thelyschista spp.: #7 **II** ORCHIDACEAE
Theodorea = Rodrigueziella
Thicuania = Dendrobium
Thiebautia = Bletia
Thornber's Fishhook cactus (E): *Mammillaria thornberi*
Thorvaldsenia = Chysis
Thrixanthocereus blossfeldiorum = Espostoa blossfeldiorum
Thrixanthocereus cullmannianus = Espostoa senilis
Thrixanthocereus longispinus = Espostoa senilis
Thrixanthocereus senilis = Espostoa senilis
Thrixspermum spp.: #7 **II** ORCHIDACEAE
Thuja tetragona = Pilgerodendron uviferum
Thulinia spp.: #7 **II** ORCHIDACEAE
Thunia spp.: #7 **II** ORCHIDACEAE
Thylacis = Thrixspermum
Thysanochilus = Eulophia
Thysanoglossa spp.: #7 **II** ORCHIDACEAE
Ticoglossum spp.: #7 **II** ORCHIDACEAE
Tillandsia harrisii: (E) Harris' tillandsia, (S) Clavel del aire #1 **II**
    BROMELIACEAE
Tillandsia kammii: (E) Kamm's tillandsia, (S) Clavel del aire #1 **II**
    BROMELIACEAE
Tillandsia kautskyi: (E) Kautsky's tillandsia, (S) Clavel del aire #1
    II BROMELIACEAE
Tillandsia mauryana: (E) Maury's tillandsia, (S) Clavel del aire #1
    II BROMELIACEAE
Tillandsia sprengeliana: (E) Sprengei's tillandsia, Sprenge's
    tillandsia, (S) Clavel del aire #1 **II** BROMELIACEAE
Tillandsia sucrei: (E) Sucre tillandsia, (S) Clavel del aire #1 **II**
    BROMELIACEAE
Tillandsia xerographica: (E) Xerographic tillandsia, (S) Clavel del
    aire #1 **II** BROMELIACEAE
Tinea = Neotinea
Tipularia spp.: #7 **II** ORCHIDACEAE
Tirucallia aequoris = Euphorbia aequoris
Tirucallia alata = Euphorbia alata

Tirucallia alluaudii = Euphorbia leucodendron
Tirucallia alluaudii ssp. *oncoclada = Euphorbia oncoclada*
Tirucallia amarifontana = Euphorbia amarifontana
Tirucallia angrae = Euphorbia angrae
Tirucallia antisyphilitica = Euphorbia antisyphilitica
Tirucallia aphylla = Euphorbia aphylla
Tirucallia arceuthobioides = Euphorbia arceuthobioides
Tirucallia aspericaulis = Euphorbia aspericaulis
Tirucallia berotica = Euphorbia berotica
Tirucallia bottae = Euphorbia bottae
Tirucallia brachiata = Euphorbia brachiata
Tirucallia burmannii = Euphorbia burmannii
Tirucallia calamiformis = Euphorbia calamiformis
Tirucallia cameronii = Euphorbia cameronii
Tirucallia carunculifera = Euphorbia carunculifera
Tirucallia carunculifera var. *fasciata = Euphorbia carunculifera*
    ssp. *subfastigiata*
Tirucallia cassythoides = Euphorbia cassythoides
Tirucallia caterviflora = Euphorbia caterviflora
Tirucallia chersina = Euphorbia chersina
Tirucallia cibdela = Euphorbia cibdela
Tirucallia congestiflora = Euphorbia congestiflora
Tirucallia corymbosa = Euphorbia corymbosa
Tirucallia cuneata = Euphorbia cuneata
Tirucallia curocana = Euphorbia curocana
Tirucallia damarana = Euphorbia damarana
Tirucallia densiflora = Euphorbia mundtii
Tirucallia dregeana = Euphorbia dregeana
Tirucallia enterophora = Euphorbia enterophora
Tirucallia epehedroides var. *imminuta = Euphorbia ephedroides*
    var. *imminuta*
Tirucallia ephedroides = Euphorbia ephedroides
Tirucallia ephedroides var. *debilis = Euphorbia ephedroides* var.
    debilis
Tirucallia fiherensis = Euphorbia fiherenensis
Tirucallia gentilis = Euphorbia gentilis
Tirucallia giessii = Euphorbia giessii
Tirucallia goetzei = Euphorbia goetzei
Tirucallia gossypina = Euphorbia gossypina
Tirucallia gossypina var. *coccinea = Euphorbia gossypina* var.
    coccinea
Tirucallia gregaria = Euphorbia gregaria
Tirucallia gummifera = Euphorbia gummifera
Tirucallia herrei = Euphorbia herrei
Tirucallia indecora = Euphorbia indecora
Tirucallia indurescens = Euphorbia indurescens
Tirucallia intisy = Euphorbia intisy
Tirucallia juttae = Euphorbia juttae
Tirucallia karroensis = Euphorbia karroensis
Tirucallia lactiflua = Euphorbia lactiflua
Tirucallia larica = Euphorbia larica
Tirucallia lateriflora = Euphorbia lateriflora
Tirucallia lignosa = Euphorbia lignosa
Tirucallia macella = Euphorbia macella
Tirucallia mainty = Euphorbia mainty
Tirucallia mauritanica = Euphorbia mauritanica
Tirucallia mixta = Euphorbia mixta
Tirucallia muricata = Euphorbia muricata
Tirucallia negromontana = Euphorbia negromontana
Tirucallia nubica = Euphorbia nubica
Tirucallia paxiana = Euphorbia mauritanica var. *mauritanica*
Tirucallia perpera = Euphorbia perpera
Tirucallia plagiantha = Euphorbia plagiantha
Tirucallia platyclada = Euphorbia platyclada
Tirucallia platyclada var. *hardyi = Euphorbia platyclada* var.
    hardyi
Tirucallia rectirama = Euphorbia rectirama
Tirucallia rhombifolia = Euphorbia rhombifolia
Tirucallia rudolfii = Euphorbia rudolfii
Tirucallia sarcostemmatoides = Euphorbia mauritanica var.
    mauritanica
Tirucallia schimperi = Euphorbia schimperi
Tirucallia spartaria = Euphorbia spartaria
Tirucallia spicata = Euphorbia spicata
Tirucallia spinea = Euphorbia spinea

Checklist of flora/Lista de especies de flora/Liste des espèces végétales

Tirucallia stapelioides = Euphorbia stapelioides
Tirucallia stenoclada = Euphorbia stenoclada
Tirucallia stolonifera = Euphorbia stolonifera
Tirucallia tenax = Euphorbia tenax
Tirucallia tirucalli = Euphorbia tirucalli
Tirucallia transvaalensis = Euphorbia transvaalensis
Tirucallia verruculosa = Euphorbia verruculosa
Tirucallia virgata = Euphorbia lamarckii
Tirucallia virgata var. *berthelotii = Euphorbia berthelotii*
Tirucallia virgata var. *despoliata = Euphorbia despoliata*
Tirucallia virgata var. *latibracteata = Euphorbia broussonetii*
Tirucallia virgata var. *pseudodendroides = Euphorbia lamarckii*
Tirucallia virgata var. *regis-jubae = Euphorbia regis-jubae*
Titania = Oberonia
Tithymalus aphyllus = Euphorbia aphylla
Tithymalus attenuatus = Euphorbia silenifolia
Tithymalus bergii = Euphorbia silenifolia
Tithymalus brachypus = Euphorbia mauritanica var. *mauritanica*
Tithymalus braunii = Euphorbia longituberculosa
Tithymalus bupleurifolius = Euphorbia bupleurifolia
Tithymalus crispus = Euphorbia crispa
Tithymalus dendroides = Euphorbia dendroides
Tithymalus ecklonii = Euphorbia ecklonii
Tithymalus ellipticus = Euphorbia silenifolia
Tithymalus laetus = Euphorbia dendroides
Tithymalus longipetiolatus = Euphorbia silenifolia
Tithymalus mauritanicus = Euphorbia mauritanica
Tithymalus piscatorius = Euphorbia piscatoria
Tithymalus silenifolius = Euphorbia silenifolia
Tithymalus tirucalli = Euphorbia tirucalli
Tithymalus tuberosus = Euphorbia tuberosa
Tithymalus zeyheri = Euphorbia mauritanica var. *mauritanica*
Tobusch fishhook cactus (E): *Sclerocactus brevihamatus*
Todaroa = Campylocentrum
Tomotris = Corymborkis
Tonopah fishhook cactus (E): *Sclerocactus nyensis*
Torch plant (E): *Aloe arborescens*
Townsonia spp.: #7 **II** ORCHIDACEAE
Trachelosiphon = Eurystyles
Trachoma = Tuberolabium
Trachyrhizum = Dendrobium
Traunsteinera spp.: #7 **II** ORCHIDACEAE
Tree cactus (E): *Opuntia rubescens*
Tree ferns (E): *Cyathea* spp./ *Dicksonia* spp.
Tree of life (S): *Guaiacum* spp.
Treisia clava = Euphorbia clava
Treisia erosa = Euphorbia cereiformis
Treisia hystrix = Euphorbia loricata
Treisia tuberculata = Euphorbia pubiglans
Trevoria spp.: #7 **II** ORCHIDACEAE
Triangle palm (E): *Neodypsis decaryi*
Triaristella = Trisetella
Triaristellina = Trisetella
Trias spp.: #7 **II** ORCHIDACEAE
Tribrachia = Bulbophyllum
Triceratorhynchus spp.: #7 **II** ORCHIDACEAE
Trichipteris costaricensis = Cyathea costaricensis
Trichipteris leucolepis = Cyathea axillaris
Trichipteris mexicana = Cyathea valdecrenata
Trichipteris microdonta = Cyathea microdonta
Trichipteris microphylla = Cyathea squamata
Trichipteris nigra = Cyathea lasiosora
Trichipteris nigripes var. *brunnescens = Cyathea brunnescens*
Trichipteris nigripes var. *nigripes = Cyathea nigripes*
Trichipteris pubescens = Cyathea bipinnatifida
Trichipteris schiedeana = Cyathea schiedeana
Trichipteris ursina = Cyathea ursina
Trichocentrum spp.: #7 **II** ORCHIDACEAE
Trichocereus angelesii = Echinopsis angelesiae
Trichocereus antezanae = Echinopsis antezanae
Trichocereus arboricola = Echinopsis arboricola
Trichocereus bertramianus = Echinopsis bertramiana
Trichocereus bridgesii = Echinopsis lageniformis
Trichocereus bruchii = Echinopsis bruchii
Trichocereus camarguensis = Echinopsis camarguensis

Trichocereus candicans = Echinopsis candicans
Trichocereus catamarcensis = Echinopsis huascha
Trichocereus cephalomacrostibas = Echinopsis cephalomacrostibas
Trichocereus chalaensis = Echinopsis chalaensis
Trichocereus chiloensis = Echinopsis chiloensis
Trichocereus clavatus = Echinopsis clavatus
Trichocereus conaconensis = Echinopsis conaconensis
Trichocereus coquimbanus = Echinopsis coquimbana
Trichocereus courantii = Echinopsis candicans
Trichocereus cuzcoensis = Echinopsis cuzcoensis
Trichocereus deserticola = Echinopsis deserticola
Trichocereus eremophilus = Echinopsis atacamensis ssp. *pasacana*
Trichocereus escayachensis = Echinopsis escayachensis
Trichocereus fabrisii = Echinopsis fabrisii
Trichocereus formosus = Echinopsis formosa
Trichocereus fulvilanus = Echinopsis deserticola
Trichocereus glaucus = Echinopsis glauca
Trichocereus grandiflorus = Echinopsis huascha
Trichocereus grandis = Echinopsis bruchii
Trichocereus herzogianus = Echinopsis tarijensis ssp. *herzogianus*
Trichocereus huascha = Echinopsis huascha
Trichocereus ingens = Echinopsis bruchii
Trichocereus knuthianus = Echinopsis knuthiana
Trichocereus korethroides = Echinopsis korethroides
Trichocereus lamprochlorus = Echinopsis lamprochlora
Trichocereus litoralis = Echinopsis litoralis
Trichocereus lobivioides = Echinopsis huascha
Trichocereus macrogonus = Echinopsis macrogona
Trichocereus manguinii = Echinopsis schickendantzii
Trichocereus narvaecensis = Echinopsis tarijensis
Trichocereus neolamprochlorus = Echinopsis candicans
Trichocereus orurensis = Echinopsis ferox
Trichocereus pachanoi = Echinopsis pachanoi
Trichocereus pasacana = Echinopsis atacamensis ssp. *pasacana*
Trichocereus peruvianus = Echinopsis peruviana ssp. *peruviana*
Trichocereus poco = Echinopsis tarijensis
Trichocereus pseudocandicans = Echinopsis candicans
Trichocereus puquiensis = Echinopsis peruviana ssp. *puquiensis*
Trichocereus quadratiumbonatus = Echinopsis quadratiumbonatus
Trichocereus randallii = Echinopsis formosa
Trichocereus rivierei = Echinopsis atacamensis ssp. *pasacana*
Trichocereus rowleyi = Echinopsis huascha
Trichocereus rubinghianus = Echinopsis thelegonoides
Trichocereus santaensis = Echinopsis santaensis
Trichocereus santiaguensis = Echinopsis spachiana
Trichocereus schickendantzii = Echinopsis schickendantzii
Trichocereus schoenii = Echinopsis schoenii
Trichocereus scopulicola = Echinopsis scopulicola
Trichocereus serenanus = Echinopsis coquimbana
Trichocereus shaferi = Echinopsis schickendantzii
Trichocereus skottsbergii = Echinopsis skottsbergii
Trichocereus smrzianus = Echinopsis smrziana
Trichocereus spachianus = Echinopsis spachiana
Trichocereus spinibarbis = Echinopsis spinibarbis
Trichocereus strigosus = Echinopsis strigosa
Trichocereus tacaquirensis = Echinopsis tacaquirensis
Trichocereus tacnaensis = Echinopsis peruviana ssp. *peruviana*
Trichocereus taquimbalensis = Echinopsis tacaquirensis ssp. *taquimbalensis*
Trichocereus taratensis = Echinopsis taratensis
Trichocereus tarijensis = Echinopsis tarijensis
Trichocereus tarmaensis = Echinopsis tarmaensis
Trichocereus tenuispinus = Echinopsis bridgesii
Trichocereus terscheckii = Echinopsis terscheckii
Trichocereus thelegonoides = Echinopsis thelegonoides
Trichocereus thelegonus = Echinopsis thelegona
Trichocereus torataensis = Echinopsis peruviana ssp. *peruviana*
Trichocereus totorensis = Echinopsis tarijensis ssp. *totorensis*
Trichocereus trichosus = Echinopsis trichosa
Trichocereus tulhuayacensis = Echinopsis tulhuayacensis
Trichocereus tunariensis = Echinopsis tunariensis
Trichocereus uyupampensis = Echinopsis uyupampensis
Trichocereus validus = Echinopsis uyupampensis
Trichocereus vasquezii = Echinopsis vasquezii

Checklist of flora/Lista de especies de flora/Liste des espèces végétales

Trichocereus vatteri = Echinopsis vatteri
Trichocereus volcanensis = Echinopsis schickendantzii
Trichocereus vollianus = Echinopsis volliana
Trichocereus walteri = Echinopsis walteri
Trichocereus werdermannianus = Echinopsis terscheckii
Trichoceros spp.: #7 **II** ORCHIDACEAE
Trichoglottis spp.: #7 **II** ORCHIDACEAE
Trichomanes squarrosa = Dicksonia squarrosa
Trichopilia spp.: #7 **II** ORCHIDACEAE
Trichosalpinx spp.: #7 **II** ORCHIDACEAE
Trichosia = Eria
Trichosma = Eria
Trichosterigma antisyphiliticum = Euphorbia antisyphilitica
Trichosterigma miserum = Euphorbia misera
Trichotosia spp.: #7 **II** ORCHIDACEAE
Tricochilus = Dipodium
Tridactyle spp.: #7 **II** ORCHIDACEAE
Trigonanthe = Dryadella
Trigonidium spp.: #7 **II** ORCHIDACEAE
Trimarindillo (S): *Guaiacum* spp.
Triorchis = Spiranthes
Triorchos = Pteroglossaspis
Triphora spp.: #7 **II** ORCHIDACEAE
Tripleura = Zeuxine
Triplorhiza = Pseudorchis
Trisetella spp.: #7 **II** ORCHIDACEAE
Tritelandra = Epidendrum
Trizeuxis spp.: #7 **II** ORCHIDACEAE
Trompa de elefante (S): *Pachypodium* spp.
Trophianthus = Aspasia
Tropical pitcher plants (E): *Nepenthes* spp.
Tropidia spp.: #7 **II** ORCHIDACEAE
Tropilis = Dendrobium
Trudelia spp.: #7 **II** ORCHIDACEAE
Tryphia = Holothrix
Tsaiorchis spp.: #7 **II** ORCHIDACEAE
Tuberolabium spp.: #7 **II** ORCHIDACEAE
Tubilabium spp.: #7 **II** ORCHIDACEAE
Tulexis = Brassavola
Tulotis = Platanthera
Tumalis bojeri = Euphorbia milii var. *milii*
Tuna (S): *Opuntia ficus-indica*
Tuna cholla (E): *Opuntia tunicata*
Tuna de cruz (S): *Consolea macracantha/ Opuntia macracantha*
Tuna de España (S): *Opuntia ficus-indica*
Tuna mansa (S): *Opuntia ficus-indica*
Turbinicacto (S): *Turbinicarpus* spp.
Turbinicarps (E): *Turbinicarpus* spp.
Turbinicarpus spp.: (E) turbinicarps, (F) (S) turbinicacto **I** CACTACEAE
Turbinicarpus alonsoi: **I** CACTACEAE
Turbinicarpus beguinii: **I** CACTACEAE
Turbinicarpus bonatzii: **I** CACTACEAE
Turbinicarpus booleanus: **I** CACTACEAE
Turbinicarpus dickisoniae = Turbinicarpus schmiedickeanus ssp. *dicksoniae*
Turbinicarpus flaviflorus = Turbinicarpus schmiedickeanus ssp. *flaviflorus*
Turbinicarpus gautii = Sclerocactus warnockii
Turbinicarpus gielsdorfianus: **I** CACTACEAE
Turbinicarpus gracilis = Turbinicarpus schmiedickeanus ssp. *gracilis*
Turbinicarpus hoferi: **I** CACTACEAE
Turbinicarpus horripilus: **I** CACTACEAE
Turbinicarpus jauernigii: **I** CACTACEAE
Turbinicarpus klinkerianus = Turbinicarpus schmiedickeanus ssp. *klinkerianus*
Turbinicarpus knuthianus: **I** CACTACEAE
Turbinicarpus krainzianus = Turbinicarpus pseudomacrochele
Turbinicarpus laui: **I** CACTACEAE
Turbinicarpus lophophoroides: **I** CACTACEAE
Turbinicarpus lophophoroides ssp. *jauernigii = Turbinicarpus jauernigii*
Turbinicarpus macrochele = Turbinicarpus schmiedickeanus ssp. *macrochele*

Turbinicarpus mandragora: **I** CACTACEAE
Turbinicarpus polaskii = Turbinicarpus schmiedickeanus ssp. *schwarzii*
Turbinicarpus pseudomacrochele: **I** CACTACEAE
Turbinicarpus pseudomacrochele ssp. *krainzianus = Turbinicarpus pseudomacrochele*
Turbinicarpus pseudomacrochele ssp. *lausseri*: **I** CACTACEAE
Turbinicarpus pseudomacrochele ssp. *pseudomacrochele*: **I** CACTACEAE
Turbinicarpus pseudopectinatus: **I** CACTACEAE
Turbinicarpus rioverdensis: **I** CACTACEAE
Turbinicarpus roseiflorus: **I** CACTACEAE
Turbinicarpus saueri: **I** CACTACEAE
Turbinicarpus schmiedickeanus: **I** CACTACEAE
Turbinicarpus schmiedickeanus ssp. *dicksoniae*: **I** CACTACEAE
Turbinicarpus schmiedickeanus ssp. *flaviflorus*: **I** CACTACEAE
Turbinicarpus schmiedickeanus ssp. *gracilis*: **I** CACTACEAE
Turbinicarpus schmiedickeanus ssp. *klinkerianus*: **I** CACTACEAE
Turbinicarpus schmiedickeanus ssp. *macrochele*: **I** CACTACEAE
Turbinicarpus schmiedickeanus ssp. *schmiedickeanus*: **I** CACTACEAE
Turbinicarpus schmiedickeanus ssp. *schwarzii*: **I** CACTACEAE
Turbinicarpus schwarzii = Turbinicarpus schmiedickeanus ssp. *schwarzii*
Turbinicarpus subterraneus: **I** CACTACEAE
Turbinicarpus swobodae: **I** CACTACEAE
Turbinicarpus valdezianus: **I** CACTACEAE
Turbinicarpus viereckii: **I** CACTACEAE
Turbinicarpus viereckii ssp. *major*: **I** CACTACEAE
Turbinicarpus ysabelae: **I** CACTACEAE
Turbinicarpus zaragozae: **I** CACTACEAE
Turk's cap (E): *Melocactus communis*
Turk's head (E): *Melocactus communis*
Turk's-head cactus (E): *Echinocactus horizonthalonius*
Tussaca = Goodyera
Tylochilus = Cyrtopodium
Tylostigma spp.: #7 **II** ORCHIDACEAE
Tylostylis = Eria
Uebelmannia spp.: **I** CACTACEAE
Uebelmannia buiningii: **I** CACTACEAE
Uebelmannia flavispina = Uebelmannia pectinifera ssp. *flavispina*
Uebelmannia gummifera: **I** CACTACEAE
Uebelmannia gummifera ssp. *meninensis = Uebelmannia gummifera*
Uebelmannia meninensis = Uebelmannia gummifera
Uebelmannia pectinifera: **I** CACTACEAE
Uebelmannia pectinifera ssp. *flavispina*: **I** CACTACEAE
Uebelmannia pectinifera ssp. *horrida*: **I** CACTACEAE
Uebelmannia pectinifera ssp. *pectinifera*: **I** CACTACEAE
Ulantha = Chloraea
Uleiorchis spp.: #7 **II** ORCHIDACEAE
Uncifera spp.: #7 **II** ORCHIDACEAE
Uropedium = Phragmipedium
Uropedium lindenii = Phragmipedium lindenii
Urostachya = Eria
Vanda azul (S): *Vanda coerulea*
Vanda coerulea: (E) Autumn lady's tresses orchid, Blue vanda, (S) Vanda azul **I** ORCHIDACEAE
Vanda roja (S): *Renanthera imschootiana*
Vanda spp.: #7 **I/II** ORCHIDACEAE
Vandopsis spp.: #7 **II** ORCHIDACEAE
Vanilla spp.: #7 **II** ORCHIDACEAE
Vargasiella spp.: #7 **II** ORCHIDACEAE
Vasqueziella spp.: #7 **II** ORCHIDACEAE
Vatricania guentheri = Espostoa guentheri
Ventricularia spp.: #7 **II** ORCHIDACEAE
Venus flytrap (E): *Dionaea muscipula*
Vermeulenia = Orchis
Vesicisepalum = Bulbophyllum
Vexillabium spp.: #7 **II** ORCHIDACEAE
Vieillardorchis = Goodyera
Vine pear (E): *Pilosocereus royenii*
Vinta Basin hookless cactus (E): *Sclerocactus glaucus*
Voanioala gerardii: **II** PALMAE
Vonroemeria = Octarrhena

337

Checklist of flora/Lista de especies de flora/Liste des espèces végétales

Vrydagzynea spp.: #7 **II** ORCHIDACEAE
Wailesia = Dipodium
Waluewa = Leochilus
Warczewitzia = Catasetum
Warmingia spp.: #7 **II** ORCHIDACEAE
Warrea spp.: #7 **II** ORCHIDACEAE
Warreella spp.: #7 **II** ORCHIDACEAE
Warreopsis spp.: #7 **II** ORCHIDACEAE
Warscewiczella = Chondrorhyncha
Weberbauerocereus cephalomacrostibas = Echinopsis cephalomacrostibas
Weberbauerocereus churinensis: #4 **II** CACTACEAE
Weberbauerocereus cuzcoensis: #4 **II** CACTACEAE
Weberbauerocereus johnsonii: #4 **II** CACTACEAE
Weberbauerocereus longicomus: #4 **II** CACTACEAE
Weberbauerocereus rauhii: #4 **II** CACTACEAE
Weberbauerocereus torataensis: #4 **II** CACTACEAE
Weberbauerocereus weberbaueri: #4 **II** CACTACEAE
Weberbauerocereus winterianus: #4 **II** CACTACEAE
Weberocereus biolleyi: #4 **II** CACTACEAE
Weberocereus bradei: #4 **II** CACTACEAE
Weberocereus glaber: #4 **II** CACTACEAE
Weberocereus imitans: #4 **II** CACTACEAE
Weberocereus panamensis: #4 **II** CACTACEAE
Weberocereus rosei: #4 **II** CACTACEAE
Weberocereus tonduzii: #4 **II** CACTACEAE
Weberocereus trichophorus: #4 **II** CACTACEAE
Weberocereus tunilla: #4 **II** CACTACEAE
Weingartia attenuata = Rebutia neocumingii
Weingartia chilensis = Neowerdermannia chilensis ssp. *chilensis*
Weingartia columnaris = Rebutia neocumingii
Weingartia kargliana = Rebutia neumanniana
Weingartia miranda = Rebutia neocumingii
Weingartia neglecta = Rebutia neocumingii
Weingartia neumanniana = Rebutia neumanniana
Weingartia oligacantha = Rebutia oligacantha
Weingartia vorwerkii = Neowerdermannia vorwerkii
Welwitschia baines = Welwitschia mirabilis
Welwitschia mirabilis: #1 **II** WELWITSCHIACEAE
Werckleocereus glaber = Weberocereus glaber
Werckleocereus imitans = Weberocereus imitans
Werckleocereus tonduzii = Weberocereus tonduzii
West Indian cedar (E): *Cedrela odorata*
West Indian Mahogany (E): *Swietenia mahagoni*
West Indian nipple-cactus (E): *Mammillaria prolifera* ssp. *texana*
Wherry's pitcherplant (E): *Sarracenia rubra* ssp. *wherryi*
Whipple's cactus (E): *Opuntia whipplei*
White butterfly-cactus (E): *Sclerocactus intertextus*
White column (E): *Escobaria albicolumnaria*
White-topped pitcherplant (E): *Sarracenia leucophylla*
Wig tree fern (E): *Cyathea baileyana*
Wiggins' cholla (E): *Opuntia wigginsii*
Wilcoxia albiflora = Echinocereus leucanthus
Wilcoxia kroenleinii = Echinocereus poselgeri
Wilcoxia nerispina = Echinocereus schmollii
Wilcoxia papillosa = Peniocereus viperinus
Wilcoxia poselgeri = Echinocereus poselgeri
Wilcoxia schmollii = Echinocereus schmollii
Wilcoxia tamaulipensis = Echinocereus poselgeri
Wilcoxia tuberosa = Echinocereus poselgeri
Wilcoxia viperina = Peniocereus viperinus
Wilmattea minutiflora = Hylocereus minutiflorus
Wilmattea venezuelensis = Hylocereus lemairei
Winged pitcher-plant (E): *Sarracenia alata*
Winkler's Pincushion-cactus (E): *Pediocactus winkleri*
Winter cattleya (E): *Cattleya trianaei*
Wittia amazonica = Disocactus amazonicus
Wittia panamensis = Disocactus amazonicus
Wittiocactus amazonicus = Disocactus amazonicus
Wittiocactus panamensis = Disocactus amazonicus
Wonderfully-bristled Turk's-cap cactus (E): *Melocactus deinacanthus*
Wood of life (E): *Guaiacum* spp.
Woodlouse cactus (E): *Pelecyphora aselliformis*

Woolly waxy-stemmed Turk's-cap cactus (E): *Melocactus glaucescens*
Wright's fishhook cactus (E): *Mammillaria wrightii*
Wright's fishhook cactus (E): *Sclerocactus wrightiae*
Wullschlaegelia spp.: #7 **II** ORCHIDACEAE
Xaritonia = Oncidium
Xeilyathum = Oncidium
Xenikophyton spp.: #7 **II** ORCHIDACEAE
Xerographic tillandsia (E): *Tillandsia xerographica*
Xerorchis spp.: #7 **II** ORCHIDACEAE
Xiphizusa = Bulbophyllum
Xiphophyllum = Cephalanthera
Xiphosium = Eria
Xylobium spp.: #7 **II** ORCHIDACEAE
Yellow adonis (E): *Adonis vernalis*
Yellow pitcher-plant (E): *Sarracenia alata/ Sarracenia flava*
Yerba de Adonis (S): *Adonis vernalis*
Yoania spp.: #7 **II** ORCHIDACEAE
Yolanda = Brachionidium
Ypsilopus spp.: #7 **II** ORCHIDACEAE
Yungasocereus inquisivensis: #4 **II** CACTACEAE
Zamia allison-armourii = Zamia pumila
Zamia altensteinii = Encephalartos altensteinii
Zamia amazonum: #1 **II** ZAMIACEAE
Zamia amblyphyllidia: #1 **II** ZAMIACEAE
Zamia amplifolia: #1 **II** ZAMIACEAE
Zamia angustifolia: #1 **II** ZAMIACEAE
Zamia angustifolia var. *angustissima = Zamia angustifolia*
Zamia angustifolia var. *floridana = Zamia integrifolia*
Zamia angustifolia var. *stricta = Zamia angustifolia*
Zamia angustifolia var. *yatesii = Zamia angustifolia*
Zamia angustissima = Zamia angustifolia
Zamia atropurpurea: #1 **II** ZAMIACEAE
Zamia aurea = Encephalartos horridus
Zamia baraquiniana = Zamia poeppigiana
Zamia biserrulata: #1 **II** ZAMIACEAE
Zamia boliviana: #1 **II** ZAMIACEAE
Zamia brongniartii = Zamia boliviana
Zamia caffra = Encephalartos caffer
Zamia calocoma = Microcycas calocoma
Zamia chamberlanii = Zamia pygmaea
Zamia chigua: #1 **II** ZAMIACEAE
Zamia crassifolia = Encephalartos caffer
Zamia cremnophila: #1 **II** ZAMIACEAE
Zamia cunaria: #1 **II** ZAMIACEAE
Zamia cupatiensis = Zamia ulei
Zamia cycadifolia = Macrozamia fraseri
Zamia cycadifolia = Zamia loddigesii
Zamia cycadifolius = Encephalartos cycadifolius
Zamia debilis = Zamia pumila
Zamia dentata = Zamia integrifolia
Zamia disodon: #1 **II** ZAMIACEAE
Zamia dressleri: #1 **II** ZAMIACEAE
Zamia elegantissima: #1 **II** ZAMIACEAE
Zamia encephalartoides: #1 **II** ZAMIACEAE
Zamia erosa = Zamia integrifolia
Zamia fairchildiana: #1 **II** ZAMIACEAE
Zamia fischeri: #1 **II** ZAMIACEAE
Zamia floridana = Zamia integrifolia
Zamia floridana var. *purshiana = Zamia integrifolia*
Zamia floridana var. *purshiana* f. *silvicola = Zamia integrifolia*
Zamia friderici-guilielmi = Encephalartos friderici-guilielmi
Zamia furfuracea: #1 **II** ZAMIACEAE
Zamia furfuracea var. *trewii = Zamia furfuracea*
Zamia galeotti = Zamia loddigesii
Zamia gentryi: #1 **II** ZAMIACEAE
Zamia guggenheimiana = Zamia angustifolia
Zamia gutierrezi = Zamia muricata
Zamia herrerae: #1 **II** ZAMIACEAE
Zamia heyderi = Zamia integrifolia
Zamia hildebrandtii = Encephalartos hildebrandtii
Zamia horrida = Encephalartos horridus
Zamia humilis = Zamia pumila
Zamia hymenophyllidia: #1 **II** ZAMIACEAE
Zamia inermis: #1 **II** ZAMIACEAE

Checklist of flora/Lista de especies de flora/Liste des espèces végétales

Zamia integrifolia: (E) Florida arrowroot, Florida coontie #1 **II** ZAMIACEAE
Zamia ipetiensis: #1 **II** ZAMIACEAE
Zamia jirijirimensis = *Zamia lecointei*
Zamia kickxii = *Zamia pygmaea*
Zamia lacandona: #1 **II** ZAMIACEAE
Zamia lanuginosa = *Encephalartos longifolius*
Zamia latifoliolata = *Zamia pumila*
Zamia lawsoniana = *Zamia loddigesii*
Zamia lecointei: #1 **II** ZAMIACEAE
Zamia leiboldii = *Zamia loddigesii*
Zamia leiboldii var. *angustifolia* = *Zamia loddigesii*
Zamia leiboldii var. *latifolia* = *Zamia loddigesii*
Zamia lindeni = *Zamia poeppigiana*
Zamia loddigesii: #1 **II** ZAMIACEAE
Zamia loddigesii var. *angustifolia* = *Zamia loddigesii*
Zamia loddigesii var. *cycadifolia* = *Zamia loddigesii*
Zamia loddigesii var. *longifolia* = *Zamia loddigesii*
Zamia loddigesii var. *obtusifolia* = *Zamia loddigesii*
Zamia loddigesii var. *spartea* = *Zamia spartea*
Zamia longifolia = *Encephalartos longifolius*
Zamia lucayana = *Zamia integrifolia*
Zamia mackenii = *Macrozamia pauli-guilielmi*
Zamia madida = *Zamia manicata*
Zamia maeleni = *Dioon edule*
Zamia manicata: #1 **II** ZAMIACEAE
Zamia media = *Zamia integrifolia*
Zamia media var. *commeniliana* = *Zamia integrifolia*
Zamia media var. *gutierrezii* = *Zamia muricata*
Zamia media var. *gutierrezii* f. *calcicola* = *Zamia integrifolia*
Zamia media var. *jacquiniana* = *Zamia integrifolia*
Zamia media var. *jacquiniana* f. *brevipinnata* = *Zamia integrifolia*
Zamia media var. *tenuis* = *Zamia integrifolia*
Zamia melanorrhachis: #1 **II** ZAMIACEAE
Zamia mexicana = *Zamia loddigesii*
Zamia montana: #1 **II** ZAMIACEAE
Zamia monticola: #1 **II** ZAMIACEAE
Zamia multifoliolata = *Zamia angustifolia*
Zamia muricata: #1 **II** ZAMIACEAE
Zamia muricata var. *angustifolia* = *Zamia muricata*
Zamia muricata var. *obtusifolia* = *Zamia muricata*
Zamia neurophyllidia: #1 **II** ZAMIACEAE
Zamia obidensis = *Zamia lecointei*
Zamia obliqua: #1 **II** ZAMIACEAE
Zamia ottonis = *Zamia pygmaea*
Zamia paucijuga: #1 **II** ZAMIACEAE
Zamia picta: #1 **II** ZAMIACEAE
Zamia poeppigiana: #1 **II** ZAMIACEAE
Zamia polymorpha: #1 **II** ZAMIACEAE
Zamia portoricensis: #1 **II** ZAMIACEAE
Zamia prasina: #1 **II** ZAMIACEAE
Zamia pseudomonticola: #1 **II** ZAMIACEAE
Zamia pseudoparasitica: #1 **II** ZAMIACEAE
Zamia pseudoparasitica var. *latifolia* = *Zamia pseudoparasitica*
Zamia pumila: #1 **II** ZAMIACEAE
Zamia pumila ssp. *pygmaea* = *Zamia pygmaea*
Zamia purpurea: #1 **II** ZAMIACEAE
Zamia pygmaea: #1 **II** ZAMIACEAE
Zamia pygmaea var. *kickxii* = *Zamia pygmaea*
Zamia pygmaea var. *ottonis* = *Zamia pygmaea*
Zamia pygmaea var. *wrightii* = *Zamia pygmaea*
Zamia roezlii: #1 **II** ZAMIACEAE
Zamia silicea = *Zamia pygmaea*
Zamia silvicola = *Zamia integrifolia*
Zamia skinneri: #1 **II** ZAMIACEAE
Zamia soconuscensis: #1 **II** ZAMIACEAE
Zamia spartea: #1 **II** ZAMIACEAE
Zamia spiralis = *Macrozamia spiralis*
Zamia splendens: #1 **II** ZAMIACEAE
Zamia standleyi: #1 **II** ZAMIACEAE
Zamia stricta = *Zamia angustifolia*
Zamia sylvatica = *Zamia loddigesii*
Zamia tenuis = *Zamia integrifolia*
Zamia tricuspidata = *Encephalartos horridus*
Zamia tuerckheimii: #1 **II** ZAMIACEAE

Zamia ulei: #1 **II** ZAMIACEAE
Zamia ulei ssp. *lecointei* = *Zamia lecointei*
Zamia umbrosa = *Zamia integrifolia*
Zamia urep: #1 **II** ZAMIACEAE
Zamia variegata: #1 **II** ZAMIACEAE
Zamia vasquezii: #1 **II** ZAMIACEAE
Zamia verschaffeltii: #1 **II** ZAMIACEAE
Zamia villosa = *Encephalartos cycadifolius*
Zamia vroomi = *Encephalartos altensteinii*
Zamia wallisii: #1 **II** ZAMIACEAE
Zamia weilandii = *Zamia poeppigiana*
Zamia yatesii = *Zamia angustifolia*
ZAMIACEAE spp.: (E) cycads, (S) cícadas, (F) cycades #1 **I/II**
Zehntnerella chaetacantha = *Facheiroa squamosa*
Zehntnerella polygona = *Facheiroa squamosa*
Zehntnerella squamulosa = *Facheiroa squamosa*
Zetagyne spp.: #7 **II** ORCHIDACEAE
Zeuxine spp.: #7 **II** ORCHIDACEAE
Zoophora = *Orchis*
Zootrophion = *Pleurothallis*
Zosterostylis = *Cryptostylis*
Zygoglossum = *Bulbophyllum*
Zygopetalum spp.: #7 **II** ORCHIDACEAE
Zygosepalum spp.: #7 **II** ORCHIDACEAE
Zygostates spp.: #7 **II** ORCHIDACEAE

E.03.III.D.63